BILLBOARD'S
HOTTEST
HOT 100
HITS

UPDATED & EXPANDED 4TH EDITION

FRED BRONSON

BILLBOARD'S HOTTEST HOT 100 HITS

UPDATED & EXPANDED 4TH EDITION

FRED BRONSON

BILLBOARD BOOKS
An imprint of Watson-Guptill Publications/New York

Executive Editor: Robert Nirkind
Editor: Sylvia Warren
Production manager: Sal Destro
Designer: Bob Fillie, Graphiti Design, Inc.
Text set in Helvetica Neue

ISBN 13: 978-0-8230-1556-6
ISBN 10: 0-8230-1556-4

First published in 2007 by Watson-Guptill Publications,
Nielsen Business Media,
A division of the Nielsen Company
770 Broadway, New York, N.Y. 10003
www.watsonguptill.com

Library of Congress Control Number: 2007929166

Manufactured in the United States of America

First printing, 2007

1 2 3 4 5 6 7/10 09 08 07

For my aunt

BEATRICE GOLDMAN

For a lifetime of constant love and support.

ACKNOWLEDGMENTS

THIS BOOK was born on a flight from London to Los Angeles in January 1984. I had just spent 15 months living in London, and on my way home, speculated about what I wanted to do with the rest of my life. Before this U.K. sabbatical, I had spent 12 years working as a publicist at NBC. Did I want to return to that life, or commit myself to what I knew I always wanted to do—write full time?

I spent most of the flight writing down notes in my brand-new FiloFax. I still have those notes—they form the idea for this book. I had not written a book before, nor did I know anyone at Billboard Books. Strangely, before I could find out whom to call about my idea, I received a phone call from an editor at Billboard Books. She wanted to know if I was interested in writing something called *The Billboard Book of Number One Hits*. I said yes. Five years later, the notes written down on that flight home became my second book.

Over the last 18 years, many people have contributed time and energy to the ongoing project that is *Billboard's Hottest Hot 100 Hits*. Many of the people who have lent support are still in my life, while I have lost touch with others. But I appreciate the many contributions and haven't forgotten any of them.

The first person I want to thank is my good friend and chief research assistant, Brian Carroll. A former writer for both Dick Clark and Casey Kasem, Brian has given unselfishly of his time and expertise over many years. He has conducted countless interviews, proofread untold pages, and has lent excellent counsel. I appreciate all of his outstanding work.

It's rare that a neighbor turns into a good friend, and I am blessed to live next door to Robert Dilley. I can navigate my way around a computer if someone else sets everything up and rescues me when things happen that I don't understand. Robert has offered that technical support, and I don't know how I would have completed this third edition without him.

Many people assisted with the gigantic task of ranking the top hits of the rock era. Len Brugnano and Mark Sherwin added up most of the numbers. Ted Cordes and Bill Derby hosted a marathon to track calculations. Joining them were Matt DeTroia, Russell Doe, Jimmy Donato, Mark Cadoury, John Glueckert, Ernie Koneck, Frank Mason, Mike Resnick, and John Zook.

Thanks to everyone at *Billboard*, past and present. I'm very fortunate to work with the people who toil at our New York headquarters as well as bureaus all over the world, including my home base in Los Angeles. It would be folly to try and list everyone at *Billboard* who has meant so much to me, and I would be sure to unintentionally leave out a name or two, so I won't even try to name them all. I do want to single out (no pun intended) the chart department under the guidance of Geoff Mayfield, and his assistant, Keith Caulfield.

I also owe a debt of thanks for the special support of Dan Allen, Brett Atwood, Brady L. Benton, Bill Buster, Dennis Clark, Michael Ellis, Mark Hahn, Ron Hamill, Ronnie Hertzman, Alan Jones, Mike King, Roland Lyons, Simon Lythgoe, Mark Milett, Peo Nylen, Dan Olmstead, Jose Promis, Jim Richliano, Marcia Rovins, Todd Russ, Susan Sackett, Ayhan Sahin, Ronny Schiff, Lou Simon, Josh Skinner, Andrew Skurow, Christopher Snell, Horst Stipp, Phil Swern, Chuck Taylor, Adam White, Merrick Wolfe, and Guy Zapoleon, as well as some friends no longer with us—Sherman Cohen, Louie Dorado, and Louis Iacueo.

Many thanks to the many people I've worked with at Dick Clark Productions through the years, especially Dick and Kari, and the totally unique (in the best way possible) Larry Klein.

I've been fortunate enough to work with editors who have patience, understanding, and a love for music. I'd like to thank executive editor of Billboard Books, Bob Nirkind, for having all of those qualities many times over. I also want to acknowledge Sylvia Warren for her passion and devotion to editing this edition and Paul Lukas, Joy Aquilino, Tad Lathrop, and Fred Weiler for their work on previous editions.

Finally, my family has always been the center of my life and a constant source of love and support. My parents, Irving and Mildred Bronson, always believed in me and encouraged my talents at an early age. They provided so much, tangible and intangible, and I miss them both. My aunt, Beatrice Goldman, has been as close as any parent and has provided the same love and support, and I'm grateful for everything she has done for me.

CONTENTS

INTRODUCTION

October 12, 1959

December 27, 1969

I BECAME FASCINATED with record charts just after turning 14. Every Friday afternoon, I made sure I was home from school by 3 P.M. to write down the KRLA Top 30 Tune-Dex. Soon, I found out those surveys were available at my local record store, and a few months later, I discovered that a weekly trade paper called *Billboard* published a national singles chart, the Hot 100.

As much as I enjoyed following the charts, I was frustrated when some of my favorite singles barely made it into the top 30, and other songs that I thought were dreadful sailed into the top 10. So I found a way to make sure that the songs I liked would become hits—I started keeping my own chart. Every Friday, I sat down at my typewriter and produced my own survey, deciding which songs would bullet up and which songs would tumble down. I kept abreast of new releases, and the ones I thought would be hits were "picked to click." The highlight of the year, of course, came in December, when I could take all of the charts from the preceding 12 months and figure out my own year-end survey. The accepted method was to assign points in descending order to each song on the chart. For a top 40, the No. 1 song of the week would receive 40 points, the No. 2 song would receive 39, and so on down the chart. When the points were added up, all of the songs that had made the chart that year could be ranked in order. Not surprisingly, I discovered that other chart fanatics also performed this annual ritual.

Some time later, I wondered what it would be like to apply this same process to the *Billboard* charts—all of the pop singles charts, dating back to the beginning of the rock era. One could then produce a master list of the biggest hits of all time, ranked in order.

It took more than a cumulative six years to complete the research for the four editions of this book, beginning with the process of compiling the top 5000 songs of the rock era. The method I used was very similar to my teenage practice of computing the biggest hits of the year. First, I assembled all of the *Billboard* pop singles charts dating back to July 9, 1955, the date that "(We're Gonna) Rock Around The Clock" by Bill Haley & His Comets went to No. 1.

The Hot 100, the definitive pop singles chart of the music industry, was first published on August 4, 1958. Prior to that date, *Billboard* published several different charts each week. The chart data in this book is based on the Best Sellers in Stores chart from July 1955 to July 1958, and the Hot 100 from that time forward through the week of February 3, 2007.

It's important to realize that all of the charts in this book, including the top 5000, are based on *chart performance*. They are not ranked in the order of how many copies each title has sold, how critically acclaimed they are, or how much I like them personally. It is a totally objective ranking, based on the highest position reached and length of stay on the Hot 100.

Many songs earned the same number of points, so there were multiple ties. These ties were broken by first determining the song's highest position on the chart and how many weeks it remained there. Remaining ties were broken according to how many weeks a title was in the top 10, the top 40, and the entire Hot 100. If a tie persisted, the song that debuted in the highest position on the Hot 100 was listed first. After all of these tie-breaking conditions were applied, there were no remaining ties.

A few singles have had more than one chart life, such as "Unchained Melody" by the Righteous Brothers. A hit in 1965, the original version re-entered the Hot 100 after it appeared in the 1990 movie *Ghost*. The song continued to accumulate points, and its ranking in the top 5000 includes its entire chart life from 1965 and 1990. When an artist recorded a new version of his or her own previous hit, the points were not added together. Neil Sedaka, for example, recorded a new version of his 1962 hit "Breaking Up Is Hard To Do" in 1975. Because they are different recordings, they are listed separately.

Methods of compiling the Hot 100 have varied over the years, although the chart has always been an amalgam of sales and airplay—that was the reason the chart was created in 1958, to have one singles chart that was based on how many copies of a single were sold in a given week combined with how many times the single was played on the radio. For years that information was tracked manually, but as of November 30, 1990, the Hot 100 has been compiled using new technologies. Sales are tracked by Nielsen SoundScan, via bar code scanning at the point of purchase. Airplay is tracked by Nielsen Broadcast Data Systems via electronic monitoring of radio stations, 24 hours a day, seven days a week.

Until December 1998, a commercial single had to be available for sale in order for a title to appear on the Hot 100. Because an increasing number of songs were not released as commercial singles, but became popular strictly through radio airplay, the commercial availability rule was dropped beginning with the 1999 chart year. Thus, album tracks appear in this book alongside actual singles. Think of it as a ranking of songs, not singles, and it all makes sense.

The major change in the charts since the previous edition of this book is the rising popularity of paid digital downloads. Before the digital age began, sales of physical singles had dropped to such a low level that airplay had a huge influence on the chart. With digital sales creating a new singles market, the balance between sales and airplay has been restored.

March 18, 1978

May 4, 1985

April 2, 1994

June 29, 2002

September 30, 2006

Digital sales have become so important that a bonus section has been added at the end of this book—a chart reflecting the most popular titles on the Hot Digital Songs chart since that tally was introduced to the pages of *Billboard* in the issue dated February 12, 2005.

Over the years, the average number of weeks that a song stays on the chart has fluctuated. In 1956, for example, it was not unusual for a song to move up and down the Best Sellers chart very slowly. But in 1965, the Beatles' "Yesterday" zipped up and down in no time at all. Since SoundScan and BDS information have helped produce a more accurate chart, songs have had longer chart lives. As a result, songs that were popular in the mid-'60s may be ranked lower than hits from 1956 or 1993. That could have been modified by artificially weighting songs from different years, but that wouldn't have produced an accurate listing of how every song from the rock era has performed on the *Billboard* chart. I decided to forego any weighting system in favor of creating a clearer picture of *Billboard*'s biggest hits.

This book covers the entire rock era, which now spans more than 50 years. It includes artists as diverse as Gogi Grant and the Pussycat Dolls, the Beatles and Madonna, and Conway Twitty and Kanye West. There's probably no radio station in America today that would play all six of those artists, or all 5000 of *Billboard*'s Hottest Hot 100 Hits. Compiling the data for this book helped me focus on the big picture of rock and roll that includes all of the artists, writers, producers, and others involved in this business of music. If you're a Janet Jackson fan, you may not be familiar with the music of Perry Como. Conversely, if you stopped listening to music after "The Shifting, Whispering Sands" was a hit, you may not know "Fall Out Boy" from Alicia Keyes. As you read this book, you may also get a sense of that big picture, and join me in thanking all of the people whose musical contributions have enriched our lives.

Fred Bronson
July 2007

The ARTISTS

THE FIRST section of this book looks at the top songs of some of the leading artists of the rock era. The Top 100 Songs of the Beatles includes singles by the group as well as the four individual members when they went out on their own (or formed other bands). The Top 50 Songs of Diana Ross & the Supremes includes singles by the original trio as well as recordings by the "new" Supremes featuring Jean Terrell; the list also features solo and duet performances by Diana Ross. Similarly, The Top 50 Songs of the Jacksons includes group recordings by the Jackson 5 and the Jacksons, as well as titles by siblings Michael, Janet, and Jermaine. The balance of the artists in this section are treated in similar fashion. Peter Cetera's solo recordings are included with Chicago's top hits; Aretha Franklin's duets with George Michael and Elton John are included in her top 30. All members of Genesis and their spin-offs are included in the top 30 songs by that group. The top 20 songs of Crosby, Stills, Nash & Young also include efforts by the other groups they were in, such as the Byrds, Buffalo Springfield, and the Hollies.

It seems fitting to have the artists be up front in the book, because they always *are* up front. Supporting them behind the scenes are the writers, the producers, and the labels listed in subsequent sections.

The Top 100 Songs of
THE BEATLES

N O GROUP or individual has dominated The Billboard Hot 100 the way the Beatles did between the years 1964–70. Although their chart span as a foursome is brief compared to someone like Ray Charles (with a chart span of 33 years, from 1957 to 1990), the Beatles set records that may never be toppled by anyone.

The Beatles made their first appearance on the British chart on October 11, 1962, when "Love Me Do" debuted. It would take them one year, three months, and one week to have their first American chart entry: "I Want To Hold Your Hand" entered the Hot 100 on January 18, 1964. During that interval, they did have singles issued in America, but Capitol Records declined to release their early material. "Love Me Do," "Please Please Me," and "From Me To You" were issued by the Chicago-based Vee Jay label and "She Loves You" came out on a Philadelphia label, Swan. Their highest chart ranking during this time was No. 116 on *Billboard*'s Bubbling Under chart with "From Me To You."

In November 1963, Beatles manager Brian Epstein flew to New York with a demo of "I Want To Hold Your Hand." Brown Meggs, director of Eastern operations for Capitol, decided this song deserved to be on the label, and set a release date of January 13, 1964. But when Carroll Baker, a DJ at WWDC in Washington, D.C., played a copy he had received from a British flight attendant, other radio stations picked up on the record, and the date was advanced to December 26.

Beatlemania did not take long to catch on in America. Jack Paar showed a film clip of the Fab Four on his Friday night NBC series on January 3. Two weeks later, "I Want To Hold Your Hand" debuted on the *Billboard* chart at No. 45. The next week, it moved to No. 3, and "She Loves You" debuted at No. 69. The following week, "I Want To Hold Your Hand" was No. 1; "She Loves You" had moved to No. 21; and "Please Please Me" debuted at No. 68. On March 14, those three songs held the top three positions on the chart. On March 28, "Twist And Shout" had joined them in the top four, and a week later, "Can't Buy Me Love" moved from No. 27 to the top of the Hot 100—giving the Beatles an unprecedented hammerlock on the top five. One week later, the Beatles occupied 14 positions out of 100, another all-time record.

The top 100 Beatles songs include 15 songs from 1964 alone. The pace had settled down somewhat by 1965, although they did have 10 chart entries that year. Every new Beatles single went to No. 1, until "Nowhere Man" in early 1966—it stalled at No. 3. Later that year, "Yellow Submarine" stopped at No. 2, held back by the Supremes' "You Can't Hurry Love." But then the Beatles had three more chart-toppers, interrupted again by "Lady Madonna," which went to No. 4 in 1968.

In the summer of that year, they released their first single on the Apple label. "Hey Jude" became the first single in the history of the Hot 100 to enter the chart in the top 10. On September 14, 1968, it debuted at No. 10. The next week, it moved to No. 3, and the following week, to No. 1. "Hey Jude" stayed at the top for nine weeks—the longest of any Beatles single.

There would be only five more Beatles singles released in America while the group was still together. "Get Back" was next, and it matched "Hey Jude" by also debuting at No. 10. "The Ballad Of John And Yoko" debuted when "Get Back" was in its fourth week at the top, "Come Together" and "Something" were back-to-back on the Beatles' final No. 1 single of the '60s, and "Let It Be" was their first of the '70s. It entered the Hot 100 at No. 6, the highest debut of all time to that point. The final original Beatles single was "The Long And Winding Road," their 20th No. 1 hit.

The release of solo Beatles singles had started as early as 1969, when John Lennon's "Give Peace A Chance" was issued on Apple under the moniker "Plastic Ono Band." It was recorded live in John and Yoko's hotel room in Montreal, where six months later they would hold a bed-in for peace. George Harrison was the first Beatle to have a solo No. 1. "My Sweet Lord," ranked eighth on the top 100 Beatles songs, was inspired by the Edwin Hawkins Singers' "Oh Happy Day," according to Harrison—although a judge would one day rule that it was unconsciously copied from Ronnie Mack's "He's So Fine," a chart-topper for the Chiffons in 1963.

Ringo Starr also charted as a solo act in 1970 with the countrified "Beaucoups Of Blues" (not one of his biggest hits). The following year, he made the top 10 with "It Don't Come Easy"; "Back Off Boogaloo" did the same in 1972. In 1973–74, he had two successive No. 1 singles: "Photograph" (written by Ringo and George) and a cover of Johnny Burnette's "You're Sixteen." The latter is Ringo's most successful *Billboard* single, ranked 28th on the list of top 100 Beatles songs.

Paul McCartney's first solo Hot 100 entry was "Another Day" backed with "Oh Woman Oh Why," No. 5 in 1971. That was followed by his first post-Beatles No. 1 hit, "Uncle Albert/Admiral Halsey." His next single was the first to credit Wings, but "Give Ireland Back To The Irish" was not a major hit, stalling at No. 21. Paul hit a creative peak with "Band On The Run," No. 1 in 1974, and a commercial peak with "Silly Love Songs," No. 1 for five weeks in 1976. His most successful solo effort released under the name Paul McCartney remains a live single, "Coming Up," recorded in Glasgow. His two most successful post-Beatles singles are superstar duets recorded with Michael Jackson and Stevie Wonder. Although they are considered to be among Paul's lighter material, "Say, Say, Say" and "Ebony And Ivory" proved to be the most popular with his fans.

Following "Give Peace A Chance" and "Cold Turkey," the first solo record to bear John Lennon's name was "Instant Karma (We All Shine On)," which was on the chart at the same time as "Let It Be." Lennon's singles were not as commercial as the other Beatles, and songs like "Mother" and "Woman Is The Nigger Of The World" found it tough going at top 40 radio. "Imagine" was an exception; it played for weeks as an album track before its release as a single. Its late release resulted in an exceptionally short chart run of only nine weeks.

Lennon was the last of the Beatles to have a No. 1 of his own. "Whatever Gets You Thru The Night," with Elton John on backing vocals, spent a week in pole position in 1974. His next No. 1 would come posthumously. After a five-year hiatus to raise his son Sean, John returned to the studio to record the *Double Fantasy* album with Yoko (he was one of the first artists signed to the Geffen label in 1980). The first single, "(Just Like) Starting Over," was climbing the chart when Lennon was murdered on December 8, 1980. Three weeks later, the single was an ironic No. 1.

The most recent titles on the top 100 Beatles hits are "Free As A Bird" and "Real Love," both from 1996. Both were demos recorded by Lennon, with his version of "Real Love" appearing on the *Imagine* soundtrack. The surviving Beatles went into the studio and added their vocals to the songs. "Free As A Bird" appeared on the *Anthology 1* album, while "Real Love" was included on *Anthology 2*.

68 HELEN WHEELS
Wings *Apple* 74

69 HI, HI, HI
Wings *Apple* 73

70 DAY TRIPPER
The Beatles *Capitol* 66

71 THE BEATLES MOVIE MEDLEY
The Beatles *Capitol* 82

72 STRAWBERRY FIELDS FOREVER
The Beatles *Capitol* 67

73 #9 DREAM
John Lennon *Apple* 75

74 WHAT IS LIFE
George Harrison *Apple* 71

75 MIND GAMES
John Lennon *Apple* 73

76 AND I LOVE HER
The Beatles *Capitol* 64

77 GIVE PEACE A CHANCE
Plastic Ono Band *Apple* 69

78 BLOW AWAY
George Harrison *Dark Horse* 79

79 P.S. I LOVE YOU
The Beatles *Tollie* 64

80 POWER TO THE PEOPLE
John Lennon/Plastic Ono Band *Apple* 71

81 ELEANOR RIGBY
The Beatles *Capitol* 66

82 I SAW HER STANDING THERE
The Beatles *Capitol* 64

83 CRACKERBOX PALACE
George Harrison *Dark Horse* 77

84 AIN'T SHE SWEET
The Beatles *Atco* 64

85 SO BAD
Paul McCartney *Columbia* 84

86 VENUS AND MARS ROCK SHOW
Wings *Capitol* 75

87 DARK HORSE
George Harrison *Apple* 75

88 MATCHBOX
The Beatles *Capitol* 64

89 GETTING CLOSER
Wings *Columbia* 79

90 YOU
George Harrison *Apple* 75

91 STAND BY ME
John Lennon *Apple* 75

92 GIVE IRELAND BACK TO THE IRISH
Wings *Apple* 72

93 PRESS
Paul McCartney *Capitol* 86

94 RAIN
The Beatles *Capitol* 66

95 THIS SONG
George Harrison *Dark Horse* 77

96 I'VE HAD ENOUGH
Wings *Capitol* 78

97 FREE AS A BIRD
The Beatles *Apple* 96

98 BACK OFF BOOGALOO
Ringo Starr *Apple* 72

99 REAL LOVE
The Beatles *Apple* 96

100 BANGLA-DESH
George Harrison *Apple* 71

The Top 50 Songs of ELVIS PRESLEY

ELVIS PRESLEY has had more song titles chart on The Billboard Hot 100 than any other artist. By the time of his death in 1977, he had amassed 146 chart entries, with four more posthumous ones to follow. His total of No. 1 hits (17) is second only to the Beatles (20), although he spent more weeks at the top of the chart—79 compared to the Beatles' 59. He was the first artist in the rock era to have two consecutive No. 1 songs. Only the Beatles, with three chart-toppers in a row, have bested that achievement.

Sun Records employee Marion Keisker could hardly have guessed what a phenomenon Elvis was going to become when she observed his first recording session in July 1953. Working as a truck driver for Crown Electric in Memphis, Elvis took his lunch hour to record two songs on acetate as a birthday present for his mother. Keisker liked his voice, and quickly turned on a tape recorder so she could play "My Happiness" and "That's When Your Heartaches Begin" for the owner of the Memphis Recording Service (and Sun Records), Sam Phillips.

He didn't agree with Keisker and was unimpressed with Elvis—even when the teenager returned on January 4, 1954, to record two more songs, "Casual Love Affair" and "I'll Never Stand In Your Way." Presley and Phillips didn't connect again until a few months later, when the studio owner needed a vocalist to record a song called "Without You." Keisker suggested Presley, and Sam couldn't find anyone else. The session didn't go well until Elvis ran through his repertoire of R&B, country, gospel, and Dean Martin favorites. That led to a recording session on July 5, 1954, where Elvis started a jam session on "That's All Right Mama." Suddenly,

01 DON'T BE CRUEL / HOUND DOG
Elvis Presley *RCA* 56

02 LOVE ME TENDER
Elvis Presley *RCA* 56

03 HEARTBREAK HOTEL
Elvis Presley *RCA* 56

04 JAILHOUSE ROCK / TREAT ME NICE
Elvis Presley *RCA* 57

05 ALL SHOOK UP
Elvis Presley *RCA* 57

06 (LET ME BE YOUR) TEDDY BEAR / LOVING YOU
Elvis Presley *RCA* 57

07 ARE YOU LONESOME TONIGHT?
Elvis Presley *RCA* 60

08 IT'S NOW OR NEVER
Elvis Presley *RCA* 60

09 DON'T / I BEG OF YOU
Elvis Presley *RCA* 58

10 STUCK ON YOU
Elvis Presley *RCA* 60

11 TOO MUCH
Elvis Presley *RCA* 57

12 RETURN TO SENDER
Elvis Presley *RCA* 62

13 I WANT YOU, I NEED YOU, I LOVE YOU
Elvis Presley *RCA* 56

14 SURRENDER
Elvis Presley *RCA* 61

15 GOOD LUCK CHARM
Elvis Presley *RCA* 62

16 HARD HEADED WOMAN
Elvis Presley *RCA* 58

17 WEAR MY RING AROUND YOUR NECK
Elvis Presley *RCA* 58

Phillips realized he had the kind of singer he'd been looking for—a white kid who sounded black.

After five singles released on Sun, Elvis' new manager, Col. Tom Parker, let it be known that Presley's contract was for sale. Decca was willing to pay $5,000, but was quickly outbid by Dot with an offer of $7,500. Mercury was willing to sign Elvis for $10,000, and Parker used that information to get a bid from Mitch Miller at Columbia for $15,000. The Colonel told Mitch that RCA was going to offer $20,000. Atlantic upped that to $25,000, but RCA got Elvis for an unprecedented $35,000 plus a $5,000 bonus to Elvis for song royalties.

Elvis went into a Nashville studio on January 10, 1956, to record his first RCA single. Producer Steve Sholes brought in Sun musicians Scotty Moore on guitar, Bill Black on bass, and D.J. Fontana on drums. Five songs were recorded in two days, including "Heartbreak Hotel." It was released on January 27, and by April 21, "Heartbreak Hotel" was No. 1.

Elvis' most successful single was his third 45 on RCA, "Don't Be Cruel" backed with "Hound Dog." Together, both sides spent 11 weeks at the top of the chart, the longest run for a No. 1 single until 1992, when "End Of The Road" by Boyz II Men reigned for 13 weeks.

Otis Blackwell, the composer of "Don't Be Cruel," was sitting in his publisher's office looking for inspiration when Al Stanton, one of the company's owners, walked in shaking a bottle of Pepsi. Two days later, Blackwell had written "All Shook Up," which would spend nine weeks at No. 1.

Seven of Elvis' top 10 singles are from the '50s, and 18 of his top 50 are from that decade. He remained strong on the charts through 1963, but from 1964–68 he had only one top 10 single, "Crying In The Chapel." His career was revived by a one-hour NBC-TV special directed by Steve Binder. The show closed with "If I Can Dream," written by Earl Brown specifically for the final segment. Released as a single, "If I Can Dream" reached No. 12—the highest-charting Elvis single in almost four years. By the end of the decade, Elvis had topped the Hot 100 for the final time with "Suspicious Minds." Of Elvis' top 50 singles, 22 are from the '60s.

Ten songs on his top 50 are from the '70s. His highest-charting single of the decade was "Burning Love," which reached No. 2 in 1972. "Way Down" had already peaked at No. 31 when news of Elvis' death shocked the world. On September 3, 1977, "Way Down" started moving back up the Hot 100—finally stopping at No. 18 on September 24.

The Top 50 Songs of
DIANA ROSS & THE SUPREMES

THE SUPREMES dominated the Hot 100 during the '60s in a way that no American group had done before. They had 12 No. 1 songs in just over five years, and established the Motown sound as "The Sound of Young America."

While they are one of the most successful trios of the rock era, the Supremes actually began as a quartet. Milton Jenkins, manager of a male group known as the Primes, needed a female counterpart for the Primes for personal appearances. Florence Ballard wanted to be a nurse, but her desire to sing was even stronger, so she accepted Jenkins' offer to form a group. She recruited Mary Wilson, and the two of them chose Betty Travis to be the third member. Paul Williams of the Primes found a young girl from the Brewster Projects (a Detroit public-housing project) to complete the quartet. Diane Ross, who would be known professionally as Diana Ross, was rehearsing with the other Primes when Betty Travis was pulled out of the group by her mother; she was replaced by Barbara Martin.

Diane's former neighbor, Smokey Robinson, introduced the girls to Motown founder Berry Gordy, Jr., but they were still in high school and he told them they weren't ready to record. They auditioned for another Detroit label, Lu-Pine, and were signed. After a couple of singles, they returned to Motown—Gordy still wasn't ready to sign them, but he let them hang around. Soon they were singing backing vocals for Marvin Gaye.

When Gordy did offer them a Motown contract, he asked the Primettes to change their name. The Primes had also signed with Motown and were known as the Temptations. Florence picked the name "Supremes" because it was the only one suggested that didn't end in "ette." Diana and Mary hated it.

01 **ENDLESS LOVE**
Diana Ross & Lionel Richie *Motown* 81
02 **UPSIDE DOWN**
Diana Ross *Motown* 80
03 **LOVE CHILD**
Diana Ross & the Supremes *Motown* 68
04 **WHERE DID OUR LOVE GO**
The Supremes *Motown* 64
05 **AIN'T NO MOUNTAIN HIGH ENOUGH**
Diana Ross *Motown* 70
06 **BABY LOVE**
The Supremes *Motown* 64
07 **COME SEE ABOUT ME**
The Supremes *Motown* 64
08 **STOP! IN THE NAME OF LOVE**
The Supremes *Motown* 65
09 **SOMEDAY WE'LL BE TOGETHER**
Diana Ross & the Supremes *Motown* 69
10 **YOU CAN'T HURRY LOVE**
The Supremes *Motown* 66
11 **LOVE HANGOVER**
Diana Ross *Motown* 76
12 **I HEAR A SYMPHONY**
The Supremes *Motown* 65
13 **TOUCH ME IN THE MORNING**
Diana Ross *Motown* 73
14 **THEME FROM "MAHOGANY" (DO YOU KNOW WHERE YOU'RE GOING TO)**
Diana Ross *Motown* 76
15 **LOVE IS HERE AND NOW YOU'RE GONE**
The Supremes *Motown* 67
16 **YOU KEEP ME HANGIN' ON**
The Supremes *Motown* 66
17 **I'M GONNA MAKE YOU LOVE ME**
Diana Ross & the Supremes and the Temptations *Motown* 69

Barbara Martin exited from the group, leaving them a trio. Berry released their first single on the Tamla label, but "I Want A Guy" failed to make the chart, as did their second single, "Buttered Popcorn," featuring Ballard on lead. Through their next five singles, issued on the Motown label, they earned the title "no-hit Supremes." That changed with their eighth release, a tune written and produced by Brian Holland, Lamont Dozier, and Eddie Holland. The Marvelettes had turned down "Where Did Our Love Go," but the Supremes didn't have that kind of clout.

In a dramatic reversal of fortune, the Supremes scored five consecutive No. 1 singles. They continued to work with Holland, Dozier, and Holland, garnering four more No. 1 songs. In 1967, Florence Ballard was asked to leave the group and was replaced by Cindy Birdsong of Patti LaBelle and the Blue Belles. When Holland-Dozier-Holland left Motown, other producers vied to work with the group, now billed as Diana Ross & the Supremes. Nick Ashford and Valerie Simpson were given the first opportunity and helmed "Some Things You Never Get Used To."

The Supremes had two more No. 1 singles: "Love Child" and "Someday We'll Be Together." In 1970, after a final performance at the Frontier Hotel in Las Vegas, Diana officially was off on a solo career, so Jean Terrell took over lead vocal duties. Surprisingly, the first Supremes' single bested Diana's first solo 45: "Up The Ladder To The Roof" peaked at No. 10, while Diana's "Reach Out And Touch (Somebody's Hand)" stopped at No. 20. The Supremes continued to have hits, going as high as No. 7 with "Stoned Love." But it was Diana who proved she was in it for the long run with six more No. 1 singles—including "Ain't No Mountain High Enough," the Nile Rodgers–Bernard Edwards–produced "Upside Down," and a duet with Lionel Richie, "Endless Love."

Jean Terrell remained with the Supremes through the single "Bad Weather" in 1973. Cindy Birdsong left the group and was replaced by Lynda Laurence, but when Scherrie Payne stepped in as lead singer, Birdsong returned briefly. The one constant member of the Supremes was Mary Wilson.

In 1981, Diana signed with RCA for North America and EMI for the rest of the world. By the end of the decade, she was back on Motown. In the summer of 2000, a Diana Ross & the Supremes reunion tour fizzled when Ross and Wilson couldn't reach a business agreement. Diana went out on the road with Laurence and Payne, two Supremes she had never worked with, and halfway through the tour, the plug was pulled.

ALL NINE of Joe and Katharine Jackson's children have been represented on The Billboard Hot 100. Michael, Jermaine, Tito, Jackie,
Marlon, Randy, Janet, LaToya, and Rebbie, in that order, have had
singles enter the chart.

First there was the Jackson 5, featuring the lead vocals of 11-year-old
Michael supported by his four eldest brothers. The group began as a trio
with Sigmund Esco (Jackie), Toriano Adaryll (Tito), and Jermaine LaJaune.
Marlon David and Michael Joe joined later. Michael was only five when the
brothers—named the Jackson 5 by a neighbor in Gary, Indiana—made
their professional debut in a local nightclub. They became well known to
some of Motown's biggest acts by supporting them in local shows, and
eventually Gladys Knight and Bobby Taylor put a word in Berry Gordy's ear
about the talented brothers.

After a couple of singles on the Gary-based Steeltown label, the group
was signed to Motown and moved to Los Angeles for a year of rehearsals.
They opened for Diana Ross & the Supremes at the Forum in Inglewood,
California, and in the fall of 1969, Motown released their first single, "I Want
You Back." It was the first of four consecutive No. 1 songs, including
"ABC," "The Love You Save," and "I'll Be There." The latter is the most suc-
cessful Hot 100 single by the five brothers.

In May 1975, four of the Jacksons departed Motown for a new home
at Epic Records; Jermaine, married to Berry Gordy's daughter Hazel,
stayed behind. Motown claimed the rights to the name "Jackson 5," so
with youngest brother Randy now on board, the brothers called themselves
the Jacksons.

Michael had already been recording as a solo artist for Motown; the title song from the movie *Ben* had been a No. 1 hit for him. While filming *The Wiz,* he approached Quincy Jones about producing his first solo LP for Epic. *Off the Wall* featured two No. 1 hits, "Don't Stop 'Til You Get Enough" and "Rock With You." The first single from Michael's next album, *Thriller,* was "The Girl Is Mine," a duet with Paul McCartney. Michael returned the favor by guest-starring on McCartney's "Say, Say, Say," the most successful *Billboard* song for Michael. *Thriller,* with seven top 10 singles, became the best-selling record of all time, and *Bad* was the first album to yield five No. 1 hits.

Jermaine's first solo chart single was "That's How Love Goes" in the fall of 1972, just one year after the release of Michael's "Got To Be There." His next Hot 100 single was a remake of Shep & the Limelites' 1961 recording, "Daddy's Home." Jermaine's version peaked at No. 9 on the Hot 100. Jermaine's most successful solo effort was "Let's Get Serious," a song written by Stevie Wonder and Lee Garrett for Wonder to record. Jermaine's father-in-law heard the song and decided that Jermaine should record it instead. Jermaine's final chart single on Motown was "Let Me Tickle Your Fancy," a collaboration with Devo released in 1982. With Berry's blessing, Jermaine left Motown and signed with Clive Davis at Arista in 1984. That same year, Jermaine rejoined his brothers for the Jacksons' *Victory* album and tour. The LP included "State Of Shock," with Michael duetting with Mick Jagger. It is No. 38 on the Jacksons' top 50.

Janet Jackson was only seven when she appeared with her brothers onstage at the MGM Grand Hotel in Las Vegas. She signed with A&M Records in November 1982. Her first two albums failed to produce any top 40 hits, but that became irrelevant when her third LP, *Control,* hit the streets. Produced by Jimmy Jam and Terry Lewis, the album rapidly yielded five top five hits: "What Have You Done For Me Lately" (No. 4), "Nasty" (No. 3), "When I Think Of You" (No. 1), "Control" (No. 5), and "Let's Wait Awhile" (No. 2). Janet kept up the barrage of hits with the *Rhythm Nation 1814* album. She then signed a $32 million, three-album deal with Virgin in March 1991, the largest contract for any artist to that date. Her 1993 single, "That's The Way Love Goes," is the most successful Jackson family single in *Billboard* history.

LaToya Jackson had recorded for Polydor before moving to the Private I label, where she charted on the Hot 100 with "Heart Don't Lie" (No. 56 in 1984). The eldest Jackson sibling, Rebbie (née Maureen), went to No. 24 in 1984 with "Centipede," a song written and produced by her brother Michael.

MADONNA LOUISE Veronica Ciccone was named after her mother, who died when she was six. With her five brothers and two sisters, she was raised in Michigan by her father, an engineer with Chrysler. Madonna studied piano and ballet and acted in plays in Catholic school. After a year at the University of Michigan on a dance scholarship, she moved to New York City, where she held a number of jobs, including working in a Times Square doughnut shop. She also did some modeling.

Madonna won another scholarship, this one to study at Alvin Ailey's dance studio, and a brief detour took her to Paris, where she sang backing vocals for Patrick Hernandez, who had already scored an international hit with "Born To Be Alive." She returned to Manhattan and formed a band, the Breakfast Club, with her boyfriend, Dan Gilroy.

In 1980, Madonna left that group and formed Emmenon, later shortened to Emmy. Her big break came in 1982 when Mark Kamins, a DJ at the Danceteria, heard a tape she made with Stephen Bray, a friend from her college days in Michigan. Kamins introduced Madonna to Michael Rosenblatt of Sire Records, who liked her demo enough to play it for label founder Seymour Stein.

Recovering from endocarditis, Stein heard Madonna's cassette while in the hospital. After listening to the song "Everybody," Stein told

Rosenblatt he wanted to sign Madonna immediately. He had a new robe brought from home and asked Madonna to come to his hospital room to seal the deal.

Her first two Sire singles, "Everybody" and "Physical Attraction," were dance hits but failed to reach the Hot 100. "Holiday" remedied that, debuting the week of October 29, 1983, and peaking at No. 16. Her second chart entry, "Borderline," climbed to No. 10 and initiated a string of 17 consecutive top 10 hits that stretched to "Cherish" in 1989.

The first No. 1 single was "Like A Virgin," which began a six-week reign in December 1984. The song had been written by Billy Steinberg and Tom Kelly for a male singer, and producer Nile Rodgers didn't want Madonna to record it because his initial reaction was that the song didn't have a great hook. But after four days he couldn't get it out of his head; realizing he had been wrong, he apologized to Madonna and said they should record it after all.

Madonna was back on top of the Hot 100 in May 1985 with a song from the film *Vision Quest*. Songwriters John Bettis and Jon Lind were shocked when they found out who was going to sing their composition on the soundtrack. At the time, they only knew her dance song, "Borderline," and their reaction was, "Can she sing a song like this?"

As Madonna continued her chart conquest, it was obvious that she had a talent for reinventing herself with each new album, never repeating what she had done in the past. At the same time, she built a parallel career in films, with roles in *Desperately Seeking Susan, Shanghai Surprise*, and *Who's That Girl*. Her marriage to Sean Penn in 1985 gave the tabloids plenty to write about, as did their divorce in 1989.

Her film roles continued in the new decade with the 1990 release *Dick Tracy*, in which she played opposite Warren Beatty and sang tunes composed for the movie by Stephen Sondheim, including the Academy Award–winning Best Song, "Sooner Or Later." Her ultimate film role would hit screens in 1997, when she starred in the cinematic adaptation of the stage musical *Evita*. For the second time, she sang vocals on an Oscar-winning song, as the new composition "You Must Love Me" captured the Academy Award.

In 1995, Madonna scored the longest-running No. 1 of her career when she collaborated with Babyface on "Take A Bow." He had already written the music but didn't know what to do with it. "I played it for Madonna and she immediately heard something in it," he recalls. "She clearly gave the song direction. We both wrote lyrics but she was the driving force." Babyface and Madonna agreed that the first line of the lyrics should be the title, even though the words "take a bow" are never repeated. The single spent seven weeks in pole position.

In 2000, Madonna collected her 12th No. 1 single with "Music," which she co-wrote and co-produced with a Swiss-born musician from France, Mirwais Ahmadzai. The first two days of recording proved frustrating, as Mirwais spoke little English and Madonna little French. She says it was so difficult to communicate that she wanted to tear her hair out, but tensions eased as the two got to know each other. "I was intent on making it work," Madonna said in *Billboard*, "because I truly believe that man's a genius."

32 **DIE ANOTHER DAY**
Madonna *Warner Bros.* 02

33 **THE POWER OF GOOD-BYE**
Madonna *Maverick* 98

34 **DRESS YOU UP**
Madonna *Sire* 85

35 **KEEP IT TOGETHER**
Madonna *Sire* 90

36 **RAY OF LIGHT**
Madonna *Maverick* 98

37 **BEAUTIFUL STRANGER**
Madonna *Maverick* 99

38 **DON'T CRY FOR ME ARGENTINA**
Madonna *Warner Bros.* 97

39 **RESCUE ME**
Madonna *Sire* 91

40 **HOLIDAY**
Madonna *Sire* 84

41 **OH FATHER**
Madonna *Sire* 90

42 **HANKY PANKY**
Madonna *Sire* 90

43 **WHAT IT FEELS LIKE FOR A GIRL**
Madonna *Maverick* 01

44 **AMERICAN PIE**
Madonna *Maverick* 00

45 **HUMAN NATURE**
Madonna *Maverick* 95

46 **ME AGAINST THE MUSIC**
Britney Spears f/Madonna *Jive* 03

47 **BAD GIRL**
Madonna *Maverick* 93

48 **AMERICAN LIFE**
Madonna *Maverick* 03

49 **BEDTIME STORY**
Madonna *Maverick* 95

50 **SORRY**
Madonna *Warner Bros.* 06

THE BEACH BOYS surprised everyone—perhaps even themselves—when "Kokomo," a single culled from the soundtrack of the Tom Cruise film *Cocktail,* surged to the top of the Hot 100 in November, 1988—24 years and four months after their first No. 1 song, "I Get Around." That gave the Beach Boys the longest span of rock-era No. 1 singles to that date.

Brothers Brian, Dennis, and Carl Wilson grew up in Hawthorne, California. In 1961, they formed the Beach Boys with cousin Mike Love and friend Al Jardine, and recorded "Surfin'"—their own composition—on the Candix label. "Surfin'" was a hit in Los Angeles, struggling to No. 75 on The Billboard Hot 100. The next year, the group signed a contract with Capitol Records; before long, the Beach Boys were scoring top 10 records like "Surfin' U.S.A." (No. 3), "Surfer Girl" (No. 7), "Be True To Your School" (No. 6), and "Fun, Fun, Fun" (No. 5).

The group's seventh Capitol single, "I Get Around," became their first No. 1 hit, and remains their most successful single to date. "Good Vibrations," their second-biggest hit, was the most expensive, most elaborate single ever produced when it was released in October 1966. According to Brian, it cost over $16,000 to record this one track, an amount unheard of in those days. The song was recorded in 17 sessions over a period of six months, at four different studios. Brian explained that each studio had its own unique sound, and each one contributed something different to the final version.

The Top 30 Songs of
BEYONCÉ / DESTINY'S CHILD

EYONCÉ KNOWLES, Kelly Rowland, LaTavia Roberson, and LeToya Luckett were friends growing up in Houston. When they were 9 and 10 years old, the girls sang for customers at the Headliners Hair Salon, owned by Beyoncé's mother, Tina. Her husband Matthew had enough faith in the girls to quit his job and become their manager. Calling themselves Girls' Tyme, they competed on *Star Search*, but didn't win. It was a painful loss for the group at the time, but turned out to be only a minor setback.

A few name changes later, Destiny's Child was signed to Elektra Records, but after an unproductive period the group was dropped. A new chapter began in 1997 when they were added to the roster of the Columbia label. Before their first album was released, a track by the quartet appeared on the *Men In Black* soundtrack. In November 1997, Destiny's Child appeared on the Hot 100 for the first time. The debut single "No, No, No Part 2" peaked at No. 3.

The group's second album yielded two No. 1 hits, "Bills, Bills, Bills" and "Say My Name." That album was the swan song for Roberson and Luckett, who saw the video premiere of "Say My Name" on BET and were surprised to find two new members lip-syncing their parts. Michelle Williams and Farrah Franklin were the replacements; Franklin departed five months later, leaving Destiny's Child a trio.

The line-up of Beyoncé, Kelly, and Michelle remained intact until the group amiably dissolved in 2005. Beyoncé had already scored with solo recordings by this time, including the No. 1 hits "Crazy In Love" and "Baby Boy." Kelly had guest starred on Nelly's "Dilemma," a 2002 hit that ruled the Hot 100 for 10 weeks.

In 2006, Beyoncé matched that 10-week total with her No. 1 hit "Irreplaceable" and starred in the film version of the Broadway musical *Dreamgirls*.

The Top 30 Songs of JAMES BROWN

WHEN JAMES BROWN died on Christmas Day 2006, it was as if royalty or a world-renowned statesman had shuffled off his mortal coil. Thousands of people passed by his gold casket as the Godfather of Soul lay in state at the Apollo Theater in Harlem. It was an appropriate goodbye to the man who had single-handedly changed the direction of R&B music and was the founder of funk. Brown was also a civil rights activist who stood up for his community in word and deed and in songs like "Say It Loud—I'm Black And I'm Proud."

Brown was born in Barnwell, South Carolina, and grew up in abject poverty. He learned to play the guitar and the harmonica and thought he could become a performer after watching '40s musician Louis Jordan in the movie *Caldonia*.

A seventh-grade dropout, Brown was jailed for stealing. He put together a gospel group while in a Georgia prison and met a local musician, Bobby Byrd, who became a mentor. They formed a group, the Avons, which became the Flames and then the Famous Flames. Their demo of "Please, Please, Please" was picked up by King Records and released on the Federal imprint. The single, billed to James Brown and the Famous Flames, peaked at No. 6 on the R&B Best Sellers in Stores chart in 1956. Brown made his Hot 100 debut in December 1958 with "Try Me," but didn't reach the top 10 until 1965, when "Papa's Got A Brand New Bag Part I" checked in at No. 8. The follow-up, "I Got You (I Feel Good)," peaked at No. 3 and is Brown's highest-charting title.

Brown last appeared on the Hot 100 in 1986, with "Living In America," a No. 4 hit that is his second-highest charting single, and "Gravity." Brown's 94 chart entries represent the second highest total of all time, second only to Elvis Presley.

MARIAH CAREY'S mother Patricia was a vocal coach, jazz vocalist, and singer with the New York City Opera. She named her second daughter after a song in the Broadway musical *Paint Your Wagon*—"They Call The Wind Mariah." Carey grew up listening to her older siblings' 45s by Aretha Franklin, Stevie Wonder, and Gladys Knight. By age four Mariah was singing, and two years later she was writing poetry.

Carey was 16 when her brother financed a studio session so she could record some demos. Ben Margulies was hired as keyboardist and became Mariah's writing partner. After graduation Mariah worked as a waitress and coat-checker, then heard from a friend who played drums for Brenda K. Starr that she needed a backing singer.

Mariah got the job and through Starr was invited to a CBS Records party, in 1990. Mariah brought her demo tape and Starr kindly handed it to Tommy Mottola, then president of the Columbia Records Group. Mottola was on his way home when he popped the cassette into his car player. He liked it so much he went back to the party to find the multi-octave vocalist but she had gone home and there was no phone number on her tape.

Mottola found Carey a few days later, and signed her to Columbia (they were married a few years later). Carey's first five singles for Columbia all went to No. 1, an unprecedented debut streak. By the time her marriage ended and she split from Columbia, she had earned 15 No. 1 singles.

She had a brief run on Virgin, then signed with Island and had two more No. 1 hits ("We Belong Together" and "Don't Forget About Us"), bringing her total to 17. That tied her with Elvis Presley for the second highest total of No. 1 hits in the rock era, surpassed only by the Beatles with 20.

The Top 30 Songs of RAY CHARLES

RAY CHARLES ROBINSON was born in Albany, Georgia, and raised in Greenville, Florida. It was a difficult childhood. His father, Bailey, was a handyman and his mother, Aretha, took in washing. Ray was four when his younger brother George fell into a wash basin in the front yard and drowned. A year later, Ray began to have trouble with his vision, which slipped away in increments, his family too poor to afford an eye specialist. By age seven, Ray was completely blind.

Ray was 10 when his father died. He was sent away to a school for the deaf and blind in Orlando, and when he was 15 received the news that his mother had passed away. Soon after being orphaned, Ray left school and moved to Jacksonville, where he played in a hillbilly band called the Honeydippers. After three years, he wanted to get away from the South. He asked a friend to look at a map and find the city the farthest away from Florida that would still be in the United States. Ray arrived in Seattle with $600 in his pocket.

He found work in a nightclub but soon grew tired of people telling him he sounded like Nat King Cole. He signed with a Los Angeles–based label, Swingtime, in 1949 and three years later his contract was purchased by Atlantic Records. A series of R&B hits was followed by some crossover success, but his real breakthrough on the Hot 100 didn't happen until 1959, when "What'd I Say" peaked at No. 6.

In the wake of his new popularity, he received an offer from the ABC-Paramount label that was too generous to turn down. He asked Atlantic execs if they could match the deal, but they couldn't and they let Charles go with their blessings.

The Top 30 Songs of CHICAGO

FIRST THEY were the Missing Links, then the Big Thing—until the band changed its name to Chicago Transit Authority. Mayor Richard Daley was not amused, especially since the group's first album for Columbia interspersed dramatic sounds from the 1968 Democratic Convention. A lawsuit was threatened, and the group shortened its name to Chicago.

Chicago achieved top 10 status with its second single, "Make Me Smile." By 1976, the group had amassed nine more top 10 singles. In October of that year, Chicago had its first No. 1 with "If You Leave Me Now." There would be only one more top 10 single in the decade—"Baby, What A Big Surprise" in 1977.

The band was badly shaken by the accidental shooting death of lead guitarist Terry Kath on January 23, 1978. Their albums suffered, and there was a further setback in 1981 when Columbia unceremoniously dropped the group from its roster. Manager Irving Azoff then signed them to his Full Moon label through Warner Bros.

They were redeemed by their very first single for their new company, "Hard To Say I'm Sorry," from the soundtrack to the film *Summer Lovers.* The song fared much better than the movie—the single advanced to the top of the *Billboard* chart, giving Chicago its second No. 1 single and the group's biggest hit of all time. Moving over to Warner Bros.' Reprise label, the group scored its third No. 1 song with Diane Warren's "Look Away."

Five of the songs in Chicago's top 30 are by former lead singer Peter Cetera, who left the group in 1985.

The Top 30 Songs of FATS DOMINO

ANTOINE DOMINO, JR. was born in New Orleans, Louisiana. He lived in the Ninth Ward with his parents and eight older siblings and was inspired by his brother-in-law, Harrison Verret, a Dixieland musician who played guitar and banjo. There was a piano in the Domino home and Verret taught Antoine how to play.

As a teenager, Domino held down day jobs but also found work in nightclubs. In 1946 he started playing at the Hideaway, in a band headed by Billy Diamond, the man who nicknamed him "Fats." One Friday night in 1949, Imperial Records founder Lew Chudd walked into the Hideaway with his new A&R man Dave Bartholomew to see the boogie-woogie piano player everyone was talking about. Chudd offered Domino a contract, and on December 10, 1949, Fats recorded his first eight songs for Imperial, including "The Fat Man," which became a million-seller and is considered to be one of the first rock and roll recordings.

"The Fat Man" was followed by 12 more R&B hits, but it wasn't until 1955 that Domino finally cracked the pop chart with "Ain't It A Shame," covered by Pat Boone as "Ain't That A Shame." Domino's version went to No. 1 on the R&B chart and No. 16 on the Best Sellers in Stores chart. It was the first of 66 entries on the pop charts, including hits like "I'm In Love Again," "Blueberry Hill," and "I'm Walkin'." Domino personified New Orleans R&B, and the Beatles paid tribute to his unique sound in their 1968 single "Lady Madonna." Six months after the Beatles' version entered the Hot 100, Domino's remake debuted. That single, which peaked at No. 100, was Domino's final entry on that chart.

When Hurricane Katrina struck New Orleans in 2005, Domino was among the missing, and it was feared that he was dead. A few days later, his daughter identified him from a photo on CNN. Fats had been rescued by the Coast Guard. He was alive, but his home in the lower Ninth Ward was gone.

The Top 30 Songs of THE EAGLES

GLENN FREY and Don Henley were on the road for two months with Linda Ronstadt when they decided to put their own group together. Frey wanted to blend the best qualities of two country-rock groups that frequented the Troubadour in Los Angeles: Poco and the Flying Burrito Brothers. He recruited one member from each: bassist Randy Meisner from Poco and guitarist Bernie Leadon from the Burrito Brothers. In August 1971, Asylum Records founder David Geffen paid a visit to the home of one of his artists, Jackson Browne, where he met Frey and the other Eagles and was impressed enough to sign them to his label.

The Eagles expanded to a quintet in 1974 with the addition of guitarist Don Felder. Leadon departed in 1975, and was replaced by Joe Walsh. When Meisner left two years later, another member of Poco, Timothy B. Schmit, took his place.

With each album release, the Eagles soared to new heights, becoming the best-selling American rock band of the '70s. By the early '80s, rumors were rife that the group was breaking up. Manager Irving Azoff said he knew the Eagles had come to the end of the road when Frey and Henley realized they could make great solo albums and didn't need the Eagles. Relations between Glenn and Don were so acrimonious that an Eagles reunion seemed out of the question. In December 1993, the Eagles finally got together to appear in Travis Tritt's video of their song "Take It Easy." That led to a "Hell Freezes Over" tour and a pact with Geffen Records, which released a live album and a new single, "Get Over It."

MICK FLEETWOOD, John McVie, and Peter Green were members of John Mayall's Bluesbreakers in 1967 when they were given some extra studio time to record on their own. Fleetwood and Green, along with guitarist Jeremy Spencer, were the nucleus of the first incarnation of Fleetwood Mac, originally formed as a blues band. A month after the group made its first public appearance at the Windsor Jazz & Blues Festival in August 1967, McVie became a member. Danny Kirwan joined a year later, and McVie's girlfriend, Christine Perfect of the group Chicken Shack, guest-starred on the U.K. single "Mr. Wonderful" in September 1968.

Fleetwood Mac was on tour in America when "Albatross" became its only No. 1 single at home in Britain. Green announced his departure in April 1970, and four months later the former Christine Perfect—now married to John McVie—became a permanent addition. The musical chairs continued in February 1971, when during a Los Angeles stopover, Spencer went out to buy a book and never returned.

Fleetwood Mac took in its first American member, Bob Welch, in April 1971. Kirwan was fired a year later, and Welch departed in December 1974. That same month, Mick Fleetwood was checking out Sound City Studios in Van Nuys, California, where producer Keith Olsen used the album *Buckingham Nicks* as a demonstration of the studio's capabilities. Lindsey Buckingham was in the studio at the time and met Fleetwood, and soon after accepted his invitation to join Fleetwood Mac, along with his girlfriend, Stevie Nicks. That cemented the line-up of Fleetwood Mac that would bring the band its greatest success, beginning with *Fleetwood Mac* and *Rumours*.

LEVI STUBBS, Abdul "Duke" Fakir, Lawrence Payton, and Renaldo "Obie" Benson, all born in Detroit, were friends who played ball together, even though they sang with different groups. One night in 1954, a woman they knew asked them to sing at a party. Stubbs handled lead and the others backed him up. The combination sounded so good they met the next day and decided to form a quartet called the Four Aims because they were "aiming" for the top.

The name was too close to the Ames Brothers, so, in 1956, they became the Four Tops and signed with Chess Records. When "Kiss Me Baby" failed to make a dent in the charts, they pacted with Red Top Records. Then they met with Berry Gordy about joining his new company, but chose instead to make a deal with the long-established Columbia label. After one release, "Ain't That Love," the Tops parted company with CBS and returned to Gordy to sign a deal. They recorded a jazz-oriented album for Motown's little-known Workshop label and backing vocals for other Motown groups. One night in 1964, Brian Holland asked them to come to the studio after a gig. At 2:00 A.M., Eddie Holland sang "Baby I Need Your Loving" for them, and they recorded the Holland-Dozier-Holland tune that night. It was the first in a long string of Motown hits that continued until 1972, when the Tops signed with Dunhill Records. Teamed with the writing and producing team of Dennis Lambert and Brian Potter, they had their first top 10 hits in five years with "Keeper Of The Castle" and "Ain't No Woman (Like The One I've Got)." They later recorded for Casablanca, returned to Motown briefly, and then signed with Arista.

01 **MY HEART HAS A MIND OF ITS OWN**
Connie Francis *MGM* 60

02 **EVERYBODY'S SOMEBODY'S FOOL**
Connie Francis *MGM* 60

03 **DON'T BREAK THE HEART THAT LOVES YOU** Connie Francis *MGM* 62

04 **MY HAPPINESS**
Connie Francis *MGM* 59

05 **WHERE THE BOYS ARE**
Connie Francis *MGM* 61

06 **WHO'S SORRY NOW**
Connie Francis *MGM* 58

07 **LIPSTICK ON YOUR COLLAR**
Connie Francis *MGM* 59

08 **FRANKIE**
Connie Francis *MGM* 59

09 **MANY TEARS AGO**
Connie Francis *MGM* 60

10 **AMONG MY SOUVENIRS**
Connie Francis *MGM* 59

11 **TOGETHER**
Connie Francis *MGM* 61

12 **BREAKIN' IN A BRAND NEW BROKEN HEART**
Connie Francis *MGM* 61

13 **MAMA**
Connie Francis *MGM* 60

14 **WHEN THE BOY IN YOUR ARMS IS THE BOY IN YOUR HEART**
Connie Francis *MGM* 62

15 **STUPID CUPID**
Connie Francis *MGM* 58

16 **JEALOUS OF YOU**
Connie Francis *MGM* 60

17 **SECOND HAND LOVE**
Connie Francis *MGM* 62

18 **FOLLOW THE BOYS**
Connie Francis *MGM* 63

19 **TEDDY**
Connie Francis *MGM* 60

20 **VACATION**
Connie Francis *MGM* 62

21 **(HE'S MY) DREAMBOAT**
Connie Francis *MGM* 61

22 **BLUE WINTER**
Connie Francis *MGM* 64

23 **I'M GONNA BE WARM THIS WINTER**
Connie Francis *MGM* 63

24 **IF MY PILLOW COULD TALK**
Connie Francis *MGM* 63

25 **I WAS SUCH A FOOL (TO FALL IN LOVE WITH YOU)**
Connie Francis *MGM* 62

26 **BE ANYTHING (BUT BE MINE)**
Connie Francis *MGM* 64

27 **YOUR OTHER LOVE**
Connie Francis *MGM* 63

28 **BABY'S FIRST CHRISTMAS**
Connie Francis *MGM* 61

29 **YOU'RE GONNA MISS ME**
Connie Francis *MGM* 50

30 **NO ONE**
Connie Francis *MGM* 61

CONCETTA ROSA MARIA FRANCONERO was born in Newark, New Jersey. Her father, George, was a roofing contractor who played the concertina for a hobby. His daughter was three years old when he gave her an accordion and soon she was singing at church benefits and family gatherings. She appeared on *Arthur Godfrey's Talent Scouts* and Godfrey suggested she change her name to Connie Francis.

Connie was 11 when her father asked George Scheck, producer of the TV series *Startime*, to feature his daughter as a singer. Scheck said he couldn't use any more singers. "That's when the accordion saved my life," says Francis. She was a regular on *Startime* for four years.

Scheck became her manager and eventually told her to lose the accordion, as did Godfrey and Ted Mack. Connie's singing career was launched by recording demos for songwriters, but she had to sound like Patti Page or Kay Starr or Jo Stafford. Finally, when she was 16, music publisher Lou Levy funded her first session on her own. Every record company turned down Connie's demos including Columbia, where Mitch Miller said, "This girl's got nothing."

The one label executive who said yes was Harry Myerson at *MGM*. The company released 10 singles and none of them were hits. The label was losing interest in Francis but she had one recording session left. Her father suggested a song Connie thought was too old-fashioned, a 1923 song titled "Who's Sorry Now." Released in 1958, the single became Connie's first hit, reaching the top five. More top 10 hits followed, including "My Happiness," "Lipstick On Your Collar," and "Among My Souvenirs."

In 1960, Francis asked Howard Greenfield to write a country song for her. He brought her a bluesy ballad he had composed with Jack Keller, and with an uptempo country arrangement, "Everybody's Somebody's Fool" became Connie's first No. 1 on the Hot 100, followed by "My Heart Has A Mind Of Its Own" and "Don't Break The Heart That Loves You."

ARETHA FRANKLIN was born in Memphis and raised in Detroit, the daughter of the Rev. C.L. Franklin. He was the pastor of the New Bethel Baptist Church, and Aretha grew up listening to artists like Mahalia Jackson and Clara Ward sing in her father's church.

In 1956, Aretha made her first recordings of gospel songs for the Checker label. Four years later, with encouragement from Sam Cooke, she moved to New York to perform more secular material. John Hammond heard one of her demo tracks, "Today I Sing The Blues," and signed her to Columbia Records, where she found herself stifled into recording show tunes and other standards with lush arrangements. Eight of her Columbia singles charted on the Hot 100, but in September 1966, she decided not to renew her Columbia contract. She signed instead with Atlantic Records after Jerry Wexler encouraged Ahmet Ertegun to outbid CBS.

In January 1967, Wexler brought Franklin to the Fame studios in Muscle Shoals, Alabama, using the same rhythm section that had worked with Wilson Pickett. The idea was to record material for an album, but after one day, an argument between Aretha's husband and a horn player led to Aretha's departure. Only one song had been completed, "I Never Loved A Man (The Way I Love You)." Aretha later recorded the flip side in New York and the single was released. Aretha's Atlantic debut soared to No. 9 on the *Billboard* chart; her follow-up, a version of Otis Redding's "Respect," spent two weeks in pole position.

Aretha remained prolific, with four top 10 singles released in 1968 alone. Her 27th Atlantic chart single became her last top 10 hit for the label. "Until You Come Back To Me (That's What I'm Gonna Do)" had actually been written and recorded by Stevie Wonder in 1967 but was not released until after Aretha's version was a hit.

A series of routine recordings and lackluster performances led to a slump in the late '70s. It wasn't until 1980, when she gave a rousing performance as a waitress in *The Blues Brothers* movie, that the public "rediscovered" her. Working with producer Narada Michael Walden in 1985, she recorded her sixth biggest *Billboard* hit, "Freeway Of Love." The follow-up, "Who's Zoomin' Who," gave her two consecutive top 10 hits for the first time since 1971.

In 1987 Aretha was back on top of the Hot 100 for the second time with "I Knew You Were Waiting (For Me)," a duet with George Michael.

01 **RESPECT**
Aretha Franklin *Atlantic* 67

02 **I KNEW YOU WERE WAITING (FOR ME)**
Aretha Franklin & George Michael *Arista* 87

03 **CHAIN OF FOOLS**
Aretha Franklin *Atlantic* 68

04 **SPANISH HARLEM**
Aretha Franklin *Atlantic* 71

05 **UNTIL YOU COME BACK TO ME (THAT'S WHAT I'M GONNA DO)**
Aretha Franklin *Atlantic* 74

06 **FREEWAY OF LOVE**
Aretha Franklin *Arista* 85

07 **(SWEET SWEET BABY) SINCE YOU'VE BEEN GONE**
Aretha Franklin *Atlantic* 68

08 **BRIDGE OVER TROUBLED WATER**
Aretha Franklin *Atlantic* 71

09 **BABY I LOVE YOU**
Aretha Franklin *Atlantic* 67

10 **WHO'S ZOOMIN' WHO**
Aretha Franklin *Arista* 85

11 **DAY DREAMING**
Aretha Franklin *Atlantic* 72

12 **THINK**
Aretha Franklin *Atlantic* 68

13 **I SAY A LITTLE PRAYER**
Aretha Franklin *Atlantic* 68

14 **I NEVER LOVED A MAN (THE WAY I LOVE YOU)**
Aretha Franklin *Atlantic* 67

15 **THE HOUSE THAT JACK BUILT**
Aretha Franklin *Atlantic* 68

16 **DON'T PLAY THAT SONG**
Aretha Franklin *Atlantic* 70

17 **CALL ME**
Aretha Franklin *Atlantic* 70

18 **ANGEL**
Aretha Franklin *Atlantic* 73

19 **ROCK STEADY**
Aretha Franklin *Atlantic* 71

20 **A NATURAL WOMAN (YOU MAKE ME FEEL LIKE)**
Aretha Franklin *Atlantic* 67

21 **SEE SAW**
Aretha Franklin *Atlantic* 68

22 **THROUGH THE STORM**
Aretha Franklin & Elton John *Arista* 89

23 **SHARE YOUR LOVE WITH ME**
Aretha Franklin *Atlantic* 69

24 **I'M IN LOVE**
Aretha Franklin *Atlantic* 74

25 **YOU'RE ALL I NEED TO GET BY**
Aretha Franklin *Atlantic* 71

26 **JUMP TO IT**
Aretha Franklin *Arista* 82

27 **THE WEIGHT**
Aretha Franklin *Atlantic* 69

28 **ELEANOR RIGBY**
Aretha Franklin *Atlantic* 69

29 **SISTERS ARE DOIN' IT FOR THEMSELVES**
Eurythmics & Aretha Franklin *RCA* 85

30 **JUMPIN' JACK FLASH**
Aretha Franklin *Arista* 86

The Top 30 Songs of MARVIN GAYE

SEXY. SOULFUL. Stubborn. All accurately describe Motown's premier male vocalist, Marvin Gaye. His sex appeal oozed between the grooves of hits like "Let's Get It On" and his post-Motown "Sexual Healing." His soul shone through early hits like "Can I Get A Witness," as well as on later work like "Inner City Blues." And according to Berry Gordy, Gaye was obstinate enough to serve as the inspiration for his first Tamla chart entry, "Stubborn Kind Of Fellow."

He was born Marvin Pentz Gay, Jr., on April 2, 1939, in Washington, D.C. His father, the Rev. Marvin Gay, was an apostolic preacher, and Marvin started singing in his church at age three. In 1957 he joined a group, the Marquees, and recorded a couple of tracks for the Okeh label.

Harvey Fuqua of the Moonglows caught the group's act and thought they sounded a lot like his own. When the Moonglows broke up, Fuqua recruited the Marquees to become the new Moonglows. In 1960, Fuqua relocated to Detroit, where he started the Tri-Phi and Harvey labels and signed as an artist to Gwen Gordy's label, Anna. Gaye also moved to Detroit and played drums on some sessions for Anna. He fell in love with the real Anna, another Gordy sibling, and they were later married.

Gaye did session work at Motown—he was just 22 when he played drums on the Marvelettes' "Please Mr. Postman"—but he recorded on his own as well. During his tenure at Motown, he gave the label some of its biggest hits, including the seven-weeks-at-No. 1 "I Heard It Through The Grapevine."

THE GENESIS of Genesis began in 1966 at the Charterhouse School, with Peter Gabriel, Mike Rutherford, Tony Banks, and Anthony Phillips. After numerous shifts in personnel, the group was signed to Charisma Records in March 1970. Five months later, when they needed a new drummer, they advertised anonymously in *Melody Maker*. Of the 14 people who auditioned, they chose a 19-year-old former child actor named Phil Collins.

Gabriel, who had sung a majority of the lead vocals, departed in August 1975. When the search for a new lead singer proved unsuccessful, Collins stepped into the position. Hackett left in June 1977, reducing Genesis to a trio. Less than a year later, they had their first top 30 hit in America, "Follow You Follow Me."

In 1981, inspired by his divorce, Collins poured his feelings into his first solo album, *Face Value.* "I Missed Again" and "In The Air Tonight" both peaked at No. 19. His second album, *Hello I Must Be Going,* provided him with a No. 10 single, a faithful remake of the Supremes' "You Can't Hurry Love." In 1984, producer Taylor Hackford convinced Collins to sing the title song for his film *Against All Odds;* the song went to No. 1. Collins' own movie *Buster* gave him two chart-toppers: a remake of the Mindbenders' "Groovy Kind Of Love" and a song written with Lamont Dozier, "Two Hearts."

Rutherford also scored a No. 1 single with his own band, Mike + the Mechanics—"The Living Years." In 1996, Collins confirmed his departure from Genesis. He was replaced by Ray Wilson from the band Stiltskin.

Another Genesis alumnus, guitarist Steve Hackett, formed the rock quintet GTR with Steve Howe from Yes and Asia in 1986. The "supergroup" only recorded one album, which yielded the No. 14 single, "When The Heart Rules The Mind."

The Top 30 Songs of JAY-Z

RAISED IN a Brooklyn housing project in Bedford-Stuyvesant, high school dropout Shawn Corey Carter was nicknamed "Jazzy," which led to the name he's known by all over the world, Jay-Z. Rapper, songwriter, producer, label founder, actor, clothing line owner all belong on his resume—not that he needs one.

He earned a reputation in rap circles but found it hard to secure a record deal, so with Damon Dash and Kareem Burke, he started his own label. Roc-A-Fella was distributed by Priority when Jay-Z's first album, *Reasonable Doubt*, was issued. By the time his second album *(In My Lifetime, Vol. 1)* was issued, Roc-A-Fella was under the umbrella of Def Jam Records, which purchased a half-interest in Jay-Z's label. It was his third CD, *Vol. 2 . . . Hard Knock Life*, that took Jay-Z to the top of the album chart for the first time. Selling five times platinum, the album contained his first two top 20 hits as a lead artist, "Can I Get A. . ." and "Hard Knock Life (Ghetto Anthem)," a rap song based, improbably, on a song from the Broadway musical *Annie*.

As a featured artist, Jay-Z hit No. 1 on the Hot 100 when he partnered with Mariah Carey on "Heartbreaker" in 1999. As lead artist, he had his first top five hit in 2002 when he teamed with romantic partner Beyoncé Knowles on "'03 Bonnie & Clyde."

A year later, a charity concert at Madison Square Garden served as Jay-Z's retirement party as a performer. It wasn't a complete retirement, as he continued to produce other artists, run his label, and even perform from time to time. So it wasn't a big surprise when the hip-hop entrepreneur announced his return in 2006. The single "Show Me What You Got" showed up in October 2006, followed one month later by the album *Kingdom Come*.

The Top 30 Songs of BILLY JOEL

FOUR-YEAR-OLD Billy Joel enjoyed banging on the family's Lester upright piano until his mother dragged him to his first piano lesson. He soon decided he didn't mind, and kept up the lessons until he was 11, when he yearned to be more creative than his teacher would allow.

At 14, Billy was inspired by the Beatles' appearances on *The Ed Sullivan Show* to join a band called the Echoes. His schoolwork suffered, as he frequently played gigs in all-night bars. The young piano man also became an amateur boxer, winning 22 of his 28 fights but breaking his nose in the process. Fortunately, his hands survived, and in 1967 he became the keyboardist for a Long Island group, the Hassles. After two unsuccessful albums on United Artists, the group split, and with drummer Jon Small, Joel formed a duo called Attila. One Columbia album later, Attila was history.

In 1971, Joel signed with Artie Ripp's Family Productions, and recorded *Cold Spring Harbor,* released through Paramount's record label. The following year Joel moved to Los Angeles and played piano for six months at the Executive Room on Wilshire Boulevard, an experience that led him to compose "Piano Man." Clive Davis, then with Columbia Records, caught Joel at the Executive Room and signed him to the label in 1973. Two decades later, Joel had given the label 12 top 10 hits, including three No. 1 singles. His most successful, "It's Still Rock And Roll To Me," was a self-described spoof, a reaction to the Rolling Stones' "It's Only Rock 'N Roll (But I Like It)."

The Top 30 Songs of ELTON JOHN

E LTON JOHN was born Reginald Kenneth Dwight in Pinner, Middlesex, England. A child prodigy in music, he took piano lessons at age four, and later won a scholarship to study part-time at the Royal Academy of Music in London. He resented studying, but absorbed knowledge about classical music, and also became a fan of R&B. In 1961, he helped found Bluesology, a small outfit playing soul music that backed American R&B stars like Major Lance, Patti LaBelle, and Billy Stewart on their British tours.

When Long John Baldry became front man for the group, Elton became disillusioned with playing in cabarets and split. He met Bernie Taupin at the office of music publisher Dick James; their first collaboration was a song called "Scarecrow." Reginald Dwight was now officially Elton John, a name culled from Elton Dean of Bluesology and Long John Baldry. Signed to MCA's Uni label for America, Elton went top 10 with his second single, "Your Song"—two years later, he had the first of his eight No. 1 hits, "Crocodile Rock."

Elton remained with MCA through 1980. On December 21 of that year, he jumped ship, becoming one of the first artists signed to Geffen. Unhappy with the label, Elton returned to MCA in 1987 with a live recording of "Candle In The Wind." In 1994, he collaborated with Tim Rice on the soundtrack of Walt Disney's *The Lion King*. Three years later, his funeral tribute to Princess Diana was a revised version of "Candle In The Wind." A world in mourning helped make that 1997 release the biggest-selling single of all time.

01 **CANDLE IN THE WIND 1997 / SOMETHING ABOUT THE WAY YOU LOOK TONIGHT**
Elton John *Rocket* 97
02 **PHILADELPHIA FREEDOM**
The Elton John Band *MCA* 75
03 **CROCODILE ROCK**
Elton John *MCA* 73
04 **BENNIE AND THE JETS**
Elton John *MCA* 74
05 **DON'T GO BREAKING MY HEART**
Elton John & Kiki Dee *Rocket* 76
06 **ISLAND GIRL**
Elton John *MCA* 75
07 **DON'T LET THE SUN GO DOWN ON ME**
George Michael/Elton John *Columbia* 92
08 **LITTLE JEANNIE**
Elton John *MCA* 80
09 **GOODBYE YELLOW BRICK ROAD**
Elton John *MCA* 73
10 **LUCY IN THE SKY WITH DIAMONDS**
Elton John *MCA* 75
11 **CAN YOU FEEL THE LOVE TONIGHT**
Elton John *Hollywood* 94
12 **DANIEL**
Elton John *MCA* 73
13 **DON'T LET THE SUN GO DOWN ON ME**
Elton John *MCA* 74
14 **I DON'T WANNA GO ON WITH YOU LIKE THAT**
Elton John *MCA* 88
15 **THE ONE**
Elton John *MCA* 92
16 **I GUESS THAT'S WHY THEY CALL IT THE BLUES**
Elton John *Geffen* 84
17 **BELIEVE**
Elton John *Rocket* 95
18 **MAMA CAN'T BUY YOU LOVE**
Elton John *MCA* 79
19 **SAD SONGS (SAY SO MUCH)**
Elton John *Geffen* 84
20 **CANDLE IN THE WIND**
Elton John *MCA* 88
21 **SOMEONE SAVED MY LIFE TONIGHT**
Elton John *MCA* 75
22 **THE BITCH IS BACK**
Elton John *MCA* 74
23 **SORRY SEEMS TO BE THE HARDEST WORD**
Elton John *MCA/Rocket* 76
24 **YOUR SONG**
Elton John *Uni* 71
25 **I'M STILL STANDING**
Elton John *Geffen* 83
26 **ROCKET MAN**
Elton John *Uni* 72
27 **NIKITA**
Elton John *Geffen* 86
28 **BLUE EYES**
Elton John *Geffen* 82
29 **EMPTY GARDEN (HEY HEY JOHNNY)**
Elton John *Geffen* 82
30 **SATURDAY NIGHT'S ALRIGHT FOR FIGHTING**
Elton John *MCA* 73

The Top 30 Songs of R. KELLY

THEATRICAL PRODUCER and artist manager Barry Hankerson was searching for talent for a new musical when a playwright told him about a singer from Chicago named Robert Kelly. At the audition, Kelly was the standout, but Hankerson didn't cast him in the musical. Instead, he told the vocalist they were going to record an album.

Hankerson had a longtime working relationship with Jive Records founder Clive Calder. Kelly was signed to Jive but was marketed as a group: R. Kelly and Public Announcement. Under that configuration, Kelly earned his first four chart singles on the Hot 100 in 1992–93, but none went higher than No. 31.

That all changed with the release of the first single credited to Kelly as a solo artist. "Sex Me" peaked at No. 20 at the end of 1993. The follow-up was a song inspired by a relationship that didn't work out. "Bump N' Grind" spent four weeks at the top of the Hot 100, and 12 weeks at No. 1 on the R&B tally.

In September 1995, Kelly returned to pole position on the Hot 100, but this time as a songwriter. When first contacted by Michael Jackson, Kelly thought he was kidding about wanting a song. "But it was serious," Kelly says. Jackson flew to Chicago to work with Kelly on "You Are Not Alone."

Right after Jackson had that No. 1 hit, Kelly's chart fortunes took an upward turn. "You Remind Me Of Something" began a streak of six consecutive top 10 hits that included "I Believe I Can Fly" and another No. 1 single, "I'm Your Angel," a duet with Celine Dion.

Kelly also became the go-to guy for collaborations. He has appeared on the charts paired with Puff Daddy, Jay-Z, Nas, Fat Joe, Ronald Isley, Nick Cannon, and Cassidy.

His biggest hit is a single that didn't reach the top. In 2003, "Ignition" spent five weeks in the runner-up spot.

THE NELSONS are a musical family, no matter which generation you're talking about. From 1930 to 1940, years before he put his family in a radio show or television sitcom, Ozzie Nelson had an active recording career, signed to the Brunswick label and later Bluebird. A year after he married Harriet Hilliard in 1935, she sang on his recording of "But Where Are You?" from the film *Follow The Fleet,* in which she starred with Fred Astaire and Ginger Rogers.

One of Ozzie and Harriet's sons, Ricky, became a recording artist only after a girlfriend raved about Elvis Presley. A defensive Ricky told her he would be making a record, too, and she laughed. That's when he became determined to record something, even if only to make one copy and hand it to her. Ricky asked his father if he could use the series' TV orchestra to cut a demo. He covered Fats Domino's "I'm Walking," but the flip side, "A Teenager's Romance," was the bigger hit, peaking at No. 2 in 1957. After two singles on the Verve label, he had a long string of hits on Imperial. A major bidding war erupted as that contract was ending, and in 1963 Nelson signed a 20-year pact with Decca for one million dollars.

By the time the '60s ended, Nelson had only scored one top 10 hit on Decca, "For You." But in 1972, he matched that single's No. 6 peak with "Garden Party," a song inspired by a performance at Madison Square Garden where his diehard fans were more interested in his older songs than his new material with the Stone Canyon Band.

Nelson's twin sons, Matthew and Gunnar, grew up in the family's Laurel Canyon home in Southern California hearing the Stone Canyon Band rehearse. Their neighbor, for a time, was George Harrison. At age 7, Gunnar received a drum set and Matthew a bass guitar. Three years later, they wrote their first song, "Feelings Of Love." As a birthday present, their parents arranged a recording session at a studio so they could produce the composition.

When their parents divorced, the twins' musical gear went to their father's house and they went to live with their mother. But at age 18, they moved back in with Ricky. Three months later, he was killed in a New Year's Eve plane crash.

After a period they describe as self-destructive, the twins were signed to the Geffen label under the name Nelson. David Geffen reminded them that when they were two years old he had visited their dad and joked that someday he would be publishing the twins' songs.

The Top 30 Songs of KENNY ROGERS/FIRST EDITION

H E'S AN AUTHOR, an actor, and owner of a restaurant chain, but Kenny Rogers is primarily known for singing, with a chart career that stretches across five decades. He made his Hot 100 debut as lead singer of the First Edition when "Just Dropped In (To See What Condition My Condition Was In)" went to No. 5 in 1968. But there had been a number of recordings and label deals before then.

Kenneth Rogers was born in Houston and was attending Jefferson Davis High School when his doo-wop group, the Scholars, recorded for a local label, Cue, and then Imperial. As a solo artist, he cut more sides for the Carlton label and Ken-Lee, an imprint he owned with his brother. As a member of the Bobby Doyle Trio he recorded for Columbia and then issued another solo effort on Mercury. In 1966, Rogers joined the New Christy Minstrels; he made one album with them and gained a new manager, Ken Kragen.

In 1967, Rogers organized the First Edition with Mickey Jones and Christy Minstrels alumni Thelma Camacho, Mike Settle, and Terry Williams. Signed to Reprise, the group placed 10 singles on the Hot 100 between 1968 and 1972. In 1969 the billing was changed to Kenny Rogers & the First Edition, beginning with the No. 6 hit "Ruby, Don't Take Your Love To Town." The group disbanded in 1974, and the following year Rogers, a solo act once more, signed with United Artists.

His first UA single, "Love Lifted Me," stalled at No. 97 in 1976, but one year later his second UA chart entry, "Lucille," raced to No. 5. In 1979 "The Gambler" only went to No. 16 but more importantly led to a series of telefilms for CBS.

Rogers had the biggest hit of his career in 1980 when the Lionel Richie–composed "Lady" spent six weeks at No. 1. He returned to pole position in 1983 when he teamed with Dolly Parton on a Barry, Robin, and Maurice Gibb song, "Islands In The Stream."

01 **LADY**
Kenny Rogers *Liberty* 80

02 **ISLANDS IN THE STREAM**
Kenny Rogers & Dolly Parton *RCA* 83

03 **COWARD OF THE COUNTY**
Kenny Rogers *UA* 80

04 **I DON'T NEED YOU**
Kenny Rogers *Liberty* 81

05 **DON'T FALL IN LOVE WITH A DREAMER**
Kenny Rogers w/Kim Carnes *UA* 80

06 **WE'VE GOT TONIGHT**
Kenny Rogers & Sheena Easton *Liberty* 83

07 **SHE BELIEVES IN ME**
Kenny Rogers *UA* 79

08 **LUCILLE** Kenny Rogers *UA* 77

09 **YOU DECORATED MY LIFE**
Kenny Rogers *UA* 79

10 **LOVE WILL TURN YOU AROUND**
Kenny Rogers *Liberty* 82

11 **SOMETHING'S BURNING**
Kenny Rogers & the First Edition *Reprise* 70

12 **THROUGH THE YEARS**
Kenny Rogers *Liberty* 82

13 **THE GAMBLER**
Kenny Rogers *UA* 79

14 **RUBY, DON'T TAKE YOUR LOVE TO TOWN**
Kenny Rogers & the First Edition *Reprise* 69

15 **SHARE YOUR LOVE WITH ME**
Kenny Rogers *Liberty* 81

16 **JUST DROPPED IN (TO SEE WHAT CONDITION MY CONDITION WAS IN)**
The First Edition *Reprise* 68

17 **LOVE THE WORLD AWAY**
Kenny Rogers *UA* 80

18 **WHAT ABOUT ME?**
Kenny Rogers w/Kim Carnes & James Ingram *RCA* 84

19 **TELL IT ALL BROTHER**
Kenny Rogers & the First Edition *Reprise* 70

20 **BUT YOU KNOW I LOVE YOU**
The First Edition *Reprise* 69

21 **THIS WOMAN**
Kenny Rogers *RCA* 84

22 **RUBEN JAMES**
Kenny Rogers & the First Edition *Reprise* 69

23 **DAYTIME FRIENDS**
Kenny Rogers *UA* 77

24 **BUY ME A ROSE**
Kenny Rogers w/Alison Krauss & Billy Dean *DreamCatcher* 00

25 **HEED THE CALL**
Kenny Rogers & the First Edition *Reprise* 70

26 **LOVE OR SOMETHING LIKE IT**
Kenny Rogers *UA* 78

27 **ALL MY LIFE**
Kenny Rogers *Liberty* 83

28 **A LOVE SONG**
Kenny Rogers *Liberty* 82

29 **SWEET MUSIC MAN**
Kenny Rogers *UA* 78

30 **SOMEONE WHO CARES**
Kenny Rogers & the First Edition *Reprise* 71

The Top 30 Songs of THE ROLLING STONES

O N JULY 12, 1962, a group consisting of Mick Jagger, Keith Richards, Brian Jones, and Derek Taylor appeared at the Marquee in London as the Rollin' Stones, named after a Muddy Waters song. Bill Wyman replaced Derek Taylor on bass in December of that year, and Charlie Watts became the band's drummer in January 1963.

Their early demo tapes having been rejected by record companies, the Rollin' Stones took a regular Sunday job as the house band at the Crawdaddy Club in Richmond, Surrey. Andrew Loog Oldham, a 19-year-old former publicist for the Beatles, saw the group there at the end of April and signed on as their manager.

Adding a "g" to make them the Rolling Stones, Oldham secured a record deal with Dick Rowe of Decca in May. The Rolling Stones' first British single, a cover of Chuck Berry's "Come On," peaked at No. 21 in the U.K. in September. Through Oldham's contact with his former clients, the Stones were given a John Lennon–Paul McCartney song to record. "I Wanna Be Your Man" went to No. 12 in the U.K. in December.

The Stones made their U.S. chart debut in May 1964, with a cover of Buddy Holly's "Not Fade Away"; their first American top 10 single was "Time Is On My Side." But the record that established their reputation and reinforced their image as the bad boys of rock and roll was "(I Can't Get No) Satisfaction." It spent four weeks at No. 1 in 1965, and is the Stones' second most successful chart single.

Their biggest American hit is "Honky Tonk Women," released one day after the funeral of Brian Jones. Like "Satisfaction," it spent four weeks at No. 1, but was on the Hot 100 for 15 weeks, one frame beyond the run of "Satisfaction."

01 HONKY TONK WOMEN
The Rolling Stones *London* 69

02 (I CAN'T GET NO) SATISFACTION
The Rolling Stones *London* 65

03 MISS YOU
The Rolling Stones *Rolling Stones* 78

04 START ME UP
The Rolling Stones *Rolling Stones* 81

05 BROWN SUGAR
The Rolling Stones *Rolling Stones* 71

06 PAINT IT, BLACK
The Rolling Stones *London* 66

07 ANGIE
The Rolling Stones *Rolling Stones* 73

08 GET OFF OF MY CLOUD
The Rolling Stones *London* 65

09 RUBY TUESDAY
The Rolling Stones *London* 67

10 19TH NERVOUS BREAKDOWN
The Rolling Stones *London* 66

11 EMOTIONAL RESCUE
The Rolling Stones *Rolling Stones* 80

12 JUMPIN' JACK FLASH
The Rolling Stones *London* 68

13 WAITING ON A FRIEND
The Rolling Stones *Rolling Stones* 82

14 TIME IS ON MY SIDE
The Rolling Stones *London* 64

15 HARLEM SHUFFLE
The Rolling Stones *Rolling Stones* 86

16 UNDERCOVER OF THE NIGHT
The Rolling Stones *Rolling Stones* 83

17 TUMBLING DICE
The Rolling Stones *Rolling Stones* 72

18 DANCING IN THE STREET
Mick Jagger/David Bowie *EMI America* 85

19 JUST ANOTHER NIGHT
Mick Jagger *Columbia* 85

20 MIXED EMOTIONS
The Rolling Stones *Columbia* 89

21 FOOL TO CRY
The Rolling Stones *Rolling Stones* 76

22 BEAST OF BURDEN
The Rolling Stones *Rolling Stones* 78

23 MOTHERS LITTLE HELPER
The Rolling Stones *London* 66

24 AS TEARS GO BY
The Rolling Stones *London* 66

25 THE LAST TIME
The Rolling Stones *London* 65

26 IT'S ONLY ROCK 'N ROLL (BUT I LIKE IT)
The Rolling Stones *Rolling Stones* 74

27 HAVE YOU SEEN YOUR MOTHER, BABY, STANDING IN THE SHADOW?
The Rolling Stones *London* 66

28 DOO DOO DOO DOO DOO (HEARTBREAKER)
The Rolling Stones *Rolling Stones* 74

29 DANDELION
The Rolling Stones *London* 67

30 HEART OF STONE
The Rolling Stones *London* 65

The Top 30 Songs of ROD STEWART

ROD STEWART'S top three solo singles, chart toppers all, spent a total of 16 weeks at No. 1. That's the same number of weeks that the Supremes spent at the summit with their first eight No. 1 songs.

Roderick David Stewart was born January 10, 1945, in the Highgate section of London. Inspired by the success of Bob Dylan, he hitchhiked around Europe in his teens playing guitar until he was kicked out of Spain for vagrancy. Back in England, he worked as a gravedigger, and after stints with blues singer Long John Baldry, Rod found himself in the Shotgun Express with Mick Fleetwood and Peter Green. One single later, Rod moved on again, to sing vocals for ex-Yardbird Jeff Beck. In 1968, Rod signed a solo contract with Phonogram that allowed him to continue with the Jeff Beck Group. But that unit broke up, and Rod joined the Small Faces, who later became just plain Faces.

Rod's first two solo albums, released on Mercury in America, were well received, but didn't produce any hit singles. His first chart entry came from *Every Picture Tells A Story*. The original A-side was a remake of Tim Hardin's "Reason To Believe"; it wasn't until its fifth week on the Hot 100 that "Maggie May" was even listed, and then only as the B-side. The following week, "Maggie May" had taken over the lead position. Nobody liked it, Rod said in his liner notes for his *Storyteller* collection, and "if it wasn't for a diligent DJ in Cleveland who flipped it over, I would've still been digging graves."

The Faces officially split at the end of 1975. Rod's solo career continued to shine, with the 1976 single "Tonight's The Night (Gonna Be Alright)" becoming his most successful American solo single.

The Top 30 Songs of THE TEMPTATIONS

THEY COULD be called the turbulent Temptations. New members have joined, old members have left. Four of them have died. Some of them have sued. But they could also be called the tenacious Temptations, for they persevered, albeit with only one original member, Otis Williams, surviving into the group's fifth decade.

They were to become one of Motown's mainstays, but they probably didn't foresee that in 1960, when the Temptations were formed by a merger of two groups, the Primes and the Distants: Eddie Kendricks, Paul Williams, and Cal Osborne were in the Primes; Otis Williams and Melvin Franklin were part of the Distants. Manager Milton Jenkins combined them into a new unit called the Elgins, and they were drafted by Berry Gordy for his new label, Miracle. Before their first single, "Oh Mother Of Mine," was released, Otis Williams and Bill Mitchell of Motown came up with a new name: the Temptations.

David Ruffin joined the group in time for 1964's "The Way You Do The Things You Do," the quintet's first hit. With the release of "My Girl" in 1965, Ruffin took on lead vocals. While the line-up remained intact for most of the decade, Ruffin left for a solo career in 1968 and was replaced by former Contour Dennis Edwards, whose first lead vocal was "Cloud Nine." Kendricks also moved on to a solo career in 1971. Paul Williams departed that year too, and died in 1973. Ruffin died of an apparent overdose in June 1991; Kendricks died of lung cancer in October 1992; and Melvin Franklin died of heart failure in February 1995. Except for a brief visit with Atlantic, the Temptations have remained with Motown during their 40-plus years.

The Top 30 Songs of
FRANKIE VALLI & THE FOUR SEASONS

FRANCIS CASTELLUCIO released his first single in 1953. "My Mothers Eyes" featured his distinctive falsetto voice and the name Frank Valley on the label—the first of many names he would use before settling on Frankie Valli.

By 1956, Frankie was singing with a group called the Four Lovers. Their songwriter and producer, Bob Crewe, had them doing background vocals for people like Bobby Darin, Freddy Cannon, and Danny & the Juniors. The first release to feature their new name, inspired by a New Jersey bowling alley, was "Bermuda" by the Four Seasons. It failed to chart.

The group recorded five songs, including "Sherry." Crewe took the masters to a record convention in Miami, and word got around fast. Several different labels bid for them, but the winner was Chicago-based Vee Jay Records.

After "Sherry" spent five weeks at No. 1, Vee Jay released another of the five masters, "Big Girls Don't Cry"; it also spent five weeks at No. 1. A Christmas release of "Santa Claus Is Coming To Town" followed; the Four Seasons then had a third No. 1 single: "Walk Like A Man."

By the end of 1963, the Four Seasons left Vee Jay because of royalty disputes, signing with Philips and releasing "Dawn (Go Away)." After their final top 30 hit on Philips in 1968, the Seasons experienced several years of chart obscurity. The success of Valli's "My Eyes Adored You" in 1975 led to a new Four Seasons line-up. The group was signed to Warner/Curb, and "Who Loves You" put them back in the top 10 for the first time since 1967. The follow-up—"December, 1963 (Oh, What a Night)," originally written about Prohibition in the year 1933—was the Four Seasons' first No. 1 record since "Rag Doll" in 1964.

S TEVIE WONDER'S initial hit was the first live single to go to No. 1 on the Hot 100. There was already a studio version of "Fingertips" when producer Clarence Paul cut a version during a show at the Regal Theater in Chicago. Paul was escorting Wonder offstage when the youngster broke away and resumed singing "Fingertips." The bass player had already left the stage, so Mary Wells' bassist jumped in but had to ask, "What key, what key?"

"We're not sure why the record was such a big hit, but leaving that mistake in didn't hurt," Motown founder Berry Gordy wrote in his autobiography *To Be Loved.* "There are certain kinds of mistakes I love."

Stevie was dubbed "the 12-year-old genius" early in his career and, while he may have grown older, the term "genius" is as applicable today as ever. Steveland Morris was born blind on May 13, 1950, in Saginaw, Michigan. Later, he used his father's last name, Judkins. The family moved to Detroit, where Stevie grew up listening to the city's most popular radio stations. His first instrument was a six-hole harmonica, followed by drums and piano. At nine, he formed a duo with best friend John Glover, who had a cousin named Ronnie White, newly signed to Tamla as one of the Miracles. White introduced Stevie to producer Brian Holland, who interrupted Gordy's dinner to urge him to sign the little wonder.

Wonder renegotiated his contract at 21, and shortly after began producing a series of more mature albums, including *Talking Book, Innervisions,* and *Songs In The Key Of Life.* His most successful solo chart single, "I Just Called To Say I Love You," is an Oscar-winner from the soundtrack of *The Woman In Red.*

The Top 20 Songs of ABBA

KNOWING IT was the only way to move beyond the borders of their own country, Abba entered the Eurovision Song Contest in 1974. By winning with "Waterloo," they made the world pay attention to Swedish pop music for the first time. But fame seemed like it might be fleeting for the group, which was heavily influenced by the Beach Boys, Phil Spector, the Kingston Trio, and skiffle music. The immediate follow-ups to "Waterloo" didn't perform that well, and it wasn't until "S.O.S." that the group's incredible hit streak began, at least, in Europe; it was more difficult to make an impact in the U.S. Although the quartet had nine No. 1 singles in the U.K., in America only "Dancing Queen" managed to reach the top. "We were at the office together that day and suddenly we heard a scream, 'Abba is No. 1 this week in the States!'" Agnetha Fältskog recalls. "That was a big moment. We celebrated with a bottle of champagne."

The final new Abba single was "Under Attack" in 1982. With Agnetha's marriage to Björn Ulvaeus over, and with the split of Frida Lyngstad and Benny Andersson, Abba's dissolution was perhaps inevitable. But the group never planned to stop—it just happened. Benny and Björn concentrated on writing the musical *Chess* with Tim Rice, and Frida and Agnetha recorded solo albums.

In 1992, a new wave of interest in Abba was sparked by *Abba-esque*, an EP of the group's songs by Erasure. With acts like U2 praising the Swedish outfit, Abba finally found the respect they had never earned during their active years. Awareness of the group continued to build, thanks to tribute bands like Björn Again, who toured all over the world. A greatest-hits collection, *Abba Gold*, was released in 1992, and by the end of the decade had gone platinum 15 times over. Benny and Björn wrote a second musical, *Kristina Från Duvemåla*, which was performed in Sweden in Swedish. A third musical, *Mamma Mia!*, opened in London's West End on April 6, 1999, 25 years to the day after Abba won Eurovision.

But despite all this new activity, there was no Abba revival tour. Even an offer of one billion dollars didn't entice the members to reunite. "We've had ridiculous offers for just one televison show," says Ulvaeus. "We just say no. If we were to come back—which is not going to happen—the motivation has to be something completely different from money. It has to be the feeling that we have something to give."

01 DANCING QUEEN
Abba *Atlantic* 77
02 TAKE A CHANCE ON ME
Abba *Atlantic* 78
03 THE WINNER TAKES IT ALL
Abba *Atlantic* 81
04 WATERLOO
Abba *Atlantic* 74
05 FERNANDO
Abba *Atlantic* 76
06 I KNOW THERE'S SOMETHING GOING ON
Frida *Atlantic* 83
07 DOES YOUR MOTHER KNOW
Abba *Atlantic* 79
08 KNOWING ME, KNOWING YOU
Abba *Atlantic* 77
09 THE NAME OF THE GAME
Abba *Atlantic* 78
10 S.O.S.
Abba *Atlantic* 75
11 I DO, I DO, I DO, I DO, I DO
Abba *Atlantic* 76
12 WHEN ALL IS SAID AND DONE
Abba *Atlantic* 82
13 HONEY, HONEY
Abba *Atlantic* 74
14 CHIQUITITA
Abba *Atlantic* 80
15 CAN'T SHAKE LOOSE
Agnetha Fältskog *Polydor* 83
16 MAMMA MIA
Abba *Atlantic* 76
17 SUPER TROUPER
Abba *Atlantic* 81
18 MONEY, MONEY, MONEY
Abba *Atlantic* 77
19 THE VISITORS
Abba *Atlantic* 82
20 ANGELEYES
Abba *Atlantic* 79

The Top 20 Songs of BRYAN ADAMS

ALTHOUGH HE was born in Kingston, Ontario, Canada, Bryan Adams moved around quite a bit as a child, thanks to his father, who worked for the British and Canadian military and then the United Nations. After living in Israel, Portugal, and Austria, Adams moved back to Canada, ready to rock and roll. He was 17 when he met Jim Vallance at a music store. Formerly in the band Prism, Vallance was looking for a singer to record a demo. They formed a songwriting partnership, and Adams thought he and Vallance would work as a duo. But the older, more conservative musician was happier working behind the scenes. They sent out a raft of demo tapes until they heard back from A&M executives, who wanted Adams to cut four songs.

Adams' first single for the label was "Let Me Take You Dancing," conceived as a pop song. But it was remixed in New York, the beats were jacked up, and the track was converted to a dance hit, sounding like nothing else Adams would release in the future.

His pop breakthrough came in 1983 with "Straight From The Heart," which sailed to No. 10 on the Hot 100. Two years later, Adams was top of the pops with "Heaven." Ironically, it was a two-year-old song from the soundtrack to a Christopher Atkins flick, *A Night In Heaven*. The film had flopped, but Guy Zapoleon, then program director of KZZP in Phoenix, believed the song could be No. 1. A&M was working singles from Adams' second album, *Reckless,* when the growing demand for "Heaven" grew so loud that the label had to release it.

Adams' most successful single is also from a soundtrack. Many other artists, including Kate Bush, Annie Lennox, Peter Cetera, and Lisa Stansfield were candidates to record the main theme from *Robin Hood: Prince of Thieves,* a Kevin Costner film. Composer Michael Kamen was happy with the choice of Adams to co-write and record "(Everything I Do) I Do It For You," although there were disagreements about instrumentation. Kamen and the producers wanted to use period instruments, but Adams didn't think lutes and mandolins would suit his pop song. Adams won, but the song was buried at the end of the film, halfway through the credits. That didn't stop it from ruling the Hot 100 for seven weeks. The song performed even better in the U.K., where it had a 16-week reign, the longest consecutive run at the top in British chart history.

01 **(EVERYTHING I DO) I DO IT FOR YOU**
Bryan Adams *A&M* 91

02 **HAVE YOU EVER REALLY LOVED A WOMAN?**
Bryan Adams *A&M* 95

03 **ALL FOR LOVE**
Bryan Adams/Rod Stewart/Sting *A&M* 94

04 **HEAVEN**
Bryan Adams *A&M* 85

05 **CAN'T STOP THIS THING WE STARTED**
Bryan Adams *A&M* 91

06 **PLEASE FORGIVE ME**
Bryan Adams *A&M* 93

07 **I FINALLY FOUND SOMEONE**
Barbra Streisand & Bryan Adams *Columbia* 96

08 **RUN TO YOU**
Bryan Adams *A&M* 85

09 **DO I HAVE TO SAY THE WORDS?**
Bryan Adams *A&M* 92

10 **THOUGHT I'D DIED AND GONE TO HEAVEN**
Bryan Adams *A&M* 92

11 **SUMMER OF '69**
Bryan Adams *A&M* 85

12 **HEAT OF THE NIGHT**
Bryan Adams *A&M* 87

13 **LET'S MAKE A NIGHT TO REMEMBER**
Bryan Adams *A&M* 96

14 **STRAIGHT FROM THE HEART**
Bryan Adams *A&M* 83

15 **SOMEBODY**
Bryan Adams *A&M* 92

16 **ONE NIGHT LOVE AFFAIR**
Bryan Adams *A&M* 85

17 **IT'S ONLY LOVE**
Bryan Adams/Tina Turner *A&M* 86

18 **CUTS LIKE A KNIFE**
Bryan Adams *A&M* 83

19 **THIS TIME**
Bryan Adams *A&M* 83

20 **HEARTS ON FIRE**
Bryan Adams *A&M* 87

The Top 20 Songs of PAUL ANKA

I N HIS pre-teen years in Ottawa, Ontario, Canada, Paul Anka imagined he would become a lawyer or a journalist. Then he discovered music. At 13, he spent the summer in Los Angeles. Before returning to school in the fall, he had to complete a book report on *Prestor John* by John Buchan, and he composed a song about an African town in the novel, "Blau Wildebeeste Fontaine." Anka hung out at Wallich's Music City, a large record store at the corner of Sunset and Vine in Hollywood, where he took advantage of the customer listening booths to keep up with the latest hits. One of the 45s he played was "Stranded In The Jungle" by the Cadets on the Modern label. Anka noticed the address was in nearby Culver City, and went to see A&R director Ernie Freeman, who loved "Blau Wildebeeste Fontaine" enough to record it, with the Cadets singing background. The single flopped, and Anka returned home to Ottawa.

The next summer was more productive. Anka collected enough labels to win a train trip to Manhattan in a Campbell's Soup contest. He liked New York City so much, he returned later that summer with four songs he had written. His first appointment was with Don Costa at ABC-Paramount Records. Costa was impressed with a love song Anka had written about his younger siblings' babysitter. She was three years older than Paul and, despite his crush on her, showed no interest. Costa told Anka to have his parents come to New York so they could sign contracts and the label could release "Diana."

After "Diana" spent a week at No. 1 in September 1957, Anka had a string of hits, including "You Are My Destiny" and "Crazy Love." In July 1959, he had an even bigger hit when "Lonely Boy" had a four-week run in pole position. Anka remained with ABC-Paramount until November 1961, when he signed a worldwide pact with RCA. His biggest hit for that label was "Love Me Warm And Tender," No. 12 in 1962.

Twelve years later, Anka had a chart renaissance, thanks to the controversial No. 1 hit, "(You're) Having My Baby." The National Organization of Women "honored" the singer with one of their "Keep Her In Her Place" awards. Nevertheless, the duet with singer Odia Coates was the first of five top 20 hits, Anka's best chart placing in years.

Anka also had great success as a songwriter, composing hits like "My Way" (Frank Sinatra) and "She's A Lady" (Tom Jones). One of his most successful copyrights was the theme for NBC-TV's *The Tonight Show Starring Johnny Carson.*

The Top 20 Songs of PAT BOONE

CHARLES EUGENE BOONE, the great-great-great-great grandson of frontiersman Daniel Boone, was born in Jacksonville, Florida. Later, the family moved to Nashville, where his mother taught him and younger brother Nick to sing harmony on songs like "Sentimental Journey." The brothers sang at family gatherings, church, and school.

Pat won the semifinal round on Ted Mack's *The Original Amateur Hour*, but before the final round he appeared on *Arthur Godfrey's Talent Scouts* and won. That made him a "professional" and disqualified him from competing as an amateur on Mack's show. He lost the opportunity to win a $6,000 scholarship from Mack after winning $600 from Godfrey.

After appearing on those two shows in new York, Boone was on his way home to his wife in Denton, Texas, when he stopped to visit his parents in Nashville. Local DJ Hugh Cherry at WMAK introduced him to Randy Wood, owner of Dot Records. Wood had seen Boone on the Godfrey and Mack shows and told him he should be making records. Six months later, Wood asked Boone to come to Chicago and record a pop version of an R&B song by Otis Williams & the Charms, "Two Hearts, Two Kisses." Boone's version peaked at No. 16 in April 1955. Boone continued to record pop versions of R&B hits like Fats Domino's "Ain't That A Shame," the El Dorados' "At My Front Door (Crazy Little Mama)," and Little Richard's "Tutti Frutti" and "Long Tall Sally," usually scoring the bigger hit.

With his movie star looks, Boone received the inevitable call from Hollywood. A screen test for 20th Century Fox secured him a seven-year contract with the studio. He was cast as the male lead in *Bernadine*, opposite Terry Moore. The movie wasn't a musical but the producers realized audiences would be expecting to hear Boone sing. Two numbers were added: a title tune written by Johnny Mercer and a song Pat had already recorded, "Love Letters In The Sand."

Boone was not the first artist to record the song. There were earlier versions by Rudy Vallee and Bing Crosby. Dot's founder knew the song because he also owned Randy's Record Shop in Gallatin, Tennessee, and had been selling the earlier recordings over a 10-year period. Boone's version had been sitting on the shelf until the song was used in the film; it became the biggest hit of his career, spending five weeks at No. 1 in 1957.

Boone's second chart-topper was also from a film, Sammy Fain and Paul Francis Webster's title song for *April Love*. After Boone recorded the song, he didn't think it was commercial enough to be a hit. During the session, he goosed it up by writing 10 new notes to open the song. Years later Boone bought a Ferrari in Italy and had the horn play the opening notes of "April Love." Boone says, "I liked the horn better than I liked the car."

The Top 20 Songs of THE CARPENTERS

GROWING UP in New Haven, Connecticut, Richard Carpenter became fascinated with his father's record collection. Richard studied classical piano, but loved playing pop tunes, and with two older friends played live at a local pizza joint. His interest in music continued after the family moved to Downey, California, where he joined the high school marching band as an alternative to gym. When his younger sister Karen entered the same high school, she also selected the band over P.E. Her chosen instrument was the drum, and when the band director said it wasn't "normal" for a girl to play drums, that cemented her decision.

At California State University, Long Beach, Richard became friends with music major Wes Jacobs, who joined the siblings in a jazz trio. They competed in a battle of the bands at the Hollywood Bowl in 1966, where an A&R staffer from RCA Records offered them a contract.

They cut four songs for RCA that were never released. The Carpenter Trio was dropped from the label, and Jacobs headed east to Juilliard. Richard put together another group, Spectrum, with Karen taking on lead vocal duties in addition to the drums. A demo tape circulated, and among the labels turning them down was A&M. But co-founder Herb Alpert liked Karen's voice, and after Spectrum dissolved, later signed the Carpenters.

Their first hit was a song that had been previously recorded by Dionne Warwick and Richard Chamberlain. Alpert himself had rejected it when Burt Bacharach offered it to him, but suggested that the duo consider it. "(They Long To Be) Close To You" launched the Carpenters' career with a No. 1 single, and remains their most successful Hot 100 entry.

The Carpenters mined many different sources for their singles. "We've Only Just Begun" was originally heard in a bank commercial. "Superstar" was a Leon Russell–Bonnie Bramlett tune that had been recorded several different times. "For All We Know" came from the film *Lovers And Other Strangers;* "Sing" was from *Sesame Street;* "Please Mr. Postman" was an early Marvelettes hit; and "Hurting Each Other" was originally recorded by Ruby & the Romantics.

The duo's final top 20 hit was "Touch Me When We're Dancing" in August 1981. Less than two years later, the world was shocked by the sudden death of Karen at age 32. She had suffered from a disorder marked by compulsive dieting. The official cause of death was "heartbeat irregularities brought on by chemical imbalances associated with anorexia nervosa."

The Top 20 Songs of CHUBBY CHECKER

I N DECEMBER 1958, Dick Clark was looking for an original way to send Christmas greetings to his friends. He asked the staff at Cameo-Parkway Records in Philadelphia if someone could record an audio holiday "card." The label suggested a new artist, Ernest Evans, who had a remarkable talent for imitating some of the well-known singers of the day, including Fats Domino and Elvis Presley.

Evans was born in South Carolina and raised in Philadelphia. By the age of five he had made up his mind to become a famous singer. His mother was strongly religious and discouraged that notion, but when he was only eight years old, he formed his own singing group. During his high school years he worked as a chicken plucker in a poultry market and often sang for the customers. The market owner, Henry Colt, was so impressed he brought Evans to Kal Mann and Dave Appell, producers at Cameo-Parkway.

For Clark's holiday card, Evans recorded a song called "The Class." He had already been nicknamed "Chubby" by a friend, and Clark's first wife, Bobbie, suggested he call himself "Chubby Checker," as a humorous take on the name Fats Domino.

"The Class" was such a hit with Clark's friends that Cameo-Parkway released it as a commercial single in the spring of 1959. The novelty hit became Checker's first entry on the Hot 100, peaking at No. 38.

Dick Clark was also responsible for Checker's second chart single. In 1958, the Detroit group Hank Ballard and the Midnighters recorded a song called "Teardrops On Your Letter." The B-side was a song Ballard wrote after seeing some teenagers in Tampa, Florida, doing a new dance. The song was named after the dance: "The Twist." When the dance became popular on *American Bandstand*, Clark told the group Danny and the Juniors they should record a cover version of the Ballard song. When that didn't work out, Clark called staffers at Cameo-Parkway and suggested Checker record "The Twist."

Backed by a vocal group known as the Dreamlovers, Checker recorded three takes in 35 minutes. He guest starred on *Bandstand*, giving Twist lessons and promoting his single. "The Twist" entered the Hot 100 on August 1, 1960, and seven weeks later it was No. 1. As other dances like the mashed potato and the fly became popular, the twist became passé for teens, but adults took up twisting until it became a worldwide sensation, embraced by society's elite. Because of its newfound popularity, Chubby was invited to perform the song on *The Ed Sullivan Show* on October 22, 1961, prompting Cameo-Parkway to re-release the single. Adults bought enough of the 45s to send the song back to No. 1 on the Hot 100 in January 1962, an unprecedented chart feat.

ERIC PATRICK CLAPP was 14 when his grandparents gave him his first guitar. He learned to play by listening to blues artists like Blind Lemon Jefferson and Son House. He studied stained glass window design at Kingston Art College, but was more interested in listening to his Chuck Berry and Muddy Waters records. He earned money for food by bussing and sometimes filled in for the lead singer of Blues, Incorporated, Mick Jagger, at London's Ealing Club.

In 1963, the Yardbirds needed a replacement for lead guitarist Tony "Top" Topham and recruited Clapton. Believing that the group was giving up its hardcore blues foundation to move in a pop direction, Clapton departed, yielding his spot to Jeff Beck. After a few months of construction work with his grandfather, Clapton signed on with John Mayall's Bluesbreakers. Over 14 months, he established himself as Britain's top guitarist, inspiring his fans to scrawl the graffiti "Clapton Is God" across London walls in 1965.

Near the end of Clapton's Bluesbreakers' stint, drummer Ginger Baker sat in on a session and suggested to the guitarist that they form a group. Clapton brought up the name of ex-Bluesbreakers bassist Jack Bruce as the third member and the trio began rehearsing in secret.

Dismissed from the Bluesbreakers by Mayall, Clapton's next gig was already secured. Robert Stigwood had signed the Clapton-Baker-Bruce supergroup, Cream, to his label in the United Kingdom. The group had its American singles breakthrough with "Sunshine Of My Love" in 1968, followed by the mid-charter "Anyone For Tennis" and a second top 10 hit, "White Room."

Cream dissolved, and Clapton and Baker moved on to another supergroup, with Steve Winwood and Rick Grech. Blind Faith only released one album and no singles. During its lone tour of the United States, Clapton found new compatriots in the opening band, Delaney and Bonnie and Friends. With three of the Friends, Clapton formed Derek and the Dominos. The single "Layla" went only to No. 51 when first released in 1971, but a year later the song returned to the Hot 100 and peaked at No. 10.

After struggling with drug addiction and recovery, Clapton returned to form in 1974 with a new album, *461 Ocean Boulevard*. The first single, a laid-back version of Bob Marley's reggae classic, "I Shot The Sheriff," brought Clapton to pole position on the Hot 100 for the first and only time.

He continued to have top 10 success, with "Lay Down Sally" in 1978, "Promises" in 1979, and "I Can't Stand It" in 1981. Then there was an 11-year wait until "Tears In Heaven" from the film *Rush* had a four-week run at No. 2. Four years later, "Change The World," from the movie *Phenomenon*, peaked at No. 5.

The Top 20 Songs of
CROSBY, STILLS, NASH & YOUNG

AVID CROSBY, Stephen Stills, and Graham Nash found themselves spending a summer afternoon together in a Laurel Canyon home. The year was 1968, some time after Crosby had experienced success with the Byrds, Stills had found fame with Buffalo Springfield, and Nash had helped form the Hollies.

A jam session developed in the living room, and with all three of them enjoying the spontaneous musical combustion, they decided it would be great to record together. Unfortunately, they were all signed to different labels. Fortunately, 26-year-old David Geffen was willing to work his way through the legal morass and sign the trio to Atlantic Records.

Crosby, Stills and Nash was released in June 1969. The initial single, a Nash song that the Hollies had attempted to record, was "Marrakesh Express." It peaked at No. 28 and was followed by Stills' ode to Judy Collins, "Suite: Judy Blue Eyes," which reached No. 21.

Looking for musicians to support them on tour, they accepted the suggestion of Atlantic Records chief Ahmet Ertegun, who thought Neil Young would complement the trio. He agreed to be lead guitarist as long as he could continue recording with his own backup band, Crazy Horse, for Reprise—a label that shared corporate affiliation with Atlantic under the Warner-Elektra-Atlantic banner.

In March of 1970, the first Crosby, Stills, Nash and Young single was released: "Woodstock," written by Joni Mitchell. It went to No. 11 on The Billboard Hot 100. The group's second album—and the first to feature Young—was *Deja Vu,* which included the hits "Teach Your Children" (No. 16) and "Our House" (No. 30). Between those two singles, the quartet released a non-LP song, "Ohio." Young wrote the song after watching a TV report about the killing of four students at Kent State University by the National Guard earlier that day. "Ohio" ascended the chart at the same time as "Teach Your Children" and peaked at No. 14.

The four musicians worked in different combinations during the '70s, recording solo material as well. Crosby, Stills, and Nash continued to come together whenever the feeling struck them. The album *CSN,* released in 1977, contained their first top 10 single, "Just A Song Before I Go" (No. 7). Their next LP didn't come out until 1982, but their fans were ready. "Wasted On The Way" peaked at No. 9 and is their most successful *Billboard* chart hit as a group. Six years later, Young joined them for the first time since January 1975. The result was the album *American Dream,* which yielded "Got It Made" (No. 69).

D ION DIMUCCI was born in the Bronx, in New York City. As a child, he enjoyed listening to his father's Al Jolson records. He also fell in love with the music of Hank Williams, which he heard when he accidentally tuned into a country station on the radio. At the age of eight, his parents gave him a Gibson guitar.

As a Valentine's Day present to his mother, Dion recorded four songs in a local studio. His mother played them for her friends, one of whom knew the owner of Mohawk Records. Dion was invited to record a song for the label. "The Chosen Few" was backed by a vocal group, the Timberlanes. Dion thought they weren't the real deal and said he would bring his own backing singers next time.

Searching the pool halls, candy stores, and streets of his Bronx neighborhood, Dion found three singers: Angelo D'Aleo, Freddie Milano, and Carlo Mastrangelo. The three teenagers named themselves the Belmonts, after Belmont Avenue.

Dion and the Belmonts recorded two more songs for Mohawk, including "Tag Along," written by Gene Schwartz, who started his own label, Laurie. He signed Dion and the Belmonts, and their first single, "I Wonder Why," went to No. 24. A year later, they made the top 10 for the first time when the Doc Pomus–Mort Shuman song "A Teenager In Love" peaked at No. 5. In early 1960, they had an even bigger hit with a Rodgers and Hammerstein song. "Where Or When" soared to No. 3.

By mid-1960, after nine chart singles, Dion and the Belmonts became two separate acts. Dion remained with Laurie, and the Belmonts' recordings were issued on Sabrina, later renamed Sabina. The Belmonts went to No. 18 with "Tell Me Why," while Dion's first solo effort, "Lonely Teenager," peaked at No. 12.

Then, after a couple of singles that failed to make the top 40, Laurie issued Dion's "Runaround Sue," which spent the last two weeks of October 1961 at No. 1. Written by Dion and Ernie Maresca, "The song was put together in a school yard," Dion recalls. "We used to hang out and just bang on cardboard boxes and get these riffs going. . . .That was one of those things that worked and I put some words to it."

After the next four Laurie singles all made the top 10, Dion signed with Columbia Records in 1963. Under the influence of ace A&R staffer John Hammond, Dion turned to country, folk, and blues material. His first Columbia single, a remake of the Drifters' "Ruby Baby," continued his top 10 streak, spending three weeks at No. 2. The official follow-up, "This Little Girl," had to compete with a single Laurie released at the same time, "Sandy." Both peaked at No. 21.

Dion returned to Laurie briefly and had a No. 4 hit with "Abraham, Martin and John." He later signed with Warner Bros., recorded a number of Christian albums, made one album with producer Phil Spector, and released a 1989 album on Arista.

The Top 20 Songs of ELECTRIC LIGHT ORCHESTRA

FIRST, THERE WAS THE MOVE. The quintet from Birmingham, England, was made up of alumni from earlier Birmingham-based beat groups. The creative force behind the Move was singer and guitarist Roy Wood, formerly of Mike Sheridan and the Nightriders. Successful in its homeland, the Move had a small cult following in the United States. Despite having albums issued on A&M and United Artists in America, the band failed to make a chart impact. The only single that made it to the Hot 100 was "Do Ya," No. 93 in late 1972.

In the United Kingdom, the Move had 10 chart singles, including the No. 1 hit "Blackberry Way." Another single, "Flowers In The Rain," earned its place in the history books by being the first song played on BBC Radio 1 when that station first went on the air, on September 30, 1967.

Another Birmingham band, the Idle Race, never achieved the celebrity status of the Move—it didn't appear on a U.K. singles or albums chart—but it did boast a talented leader in Jeff Lynne. Wood and Lynne were friends, and in 1969 the former asked the latter to join the Move. Lynne declined, hoping the Idle Race was still going to make it. A year later, when Move lead vocalist Carl Wayne split, Wood went back to Lynne and this time the Idle Race man said yes. But it was only because he was more interested in a side project Wood was planning to launch that would combine rock and classical music. Wood planned to keep the Move together while also leading the Electric Light Orchestra.

The initial line-up of ELO also included Bev Bevan from the Move. The new band made its live debut on April 16, 1972, in Croydon. In mid-July, Wood made a surprise announcement: he was pulling out of the newly-formed ELO to start his own band, Wizzard. Two weeks later, the first ELO single, "10538 Overture," debuted on the U.K. chart and went on to peak at No. 9. Wizzard started off with a bang, sending two singles to No. 1 in 1973, the Spector-ish "See My Baby Jive" and "Angel Fingers." But Wizzard was only together for a couple of years, while ELO under Lynne's stewardship had a long run of hits that included 28 U.K. chart entries through 1986.

The group's American chart run began in 1973 with a rousing remake of Chuck Berry's "Roll Over Beethoven," but the breakthrough came in 1975 with "Can't Get It Out Of My Head," which went to No. 9, and continued with hits like "Evil Woman," "Livin' Thing," and a remake of the Move's "Do Ya."

Lynne's last album with ELO was released in 1986. The band continued without him under the name Electric Light Orchestra II while Lynne recorded a solo album, produced George Harrison's *Cloud Nine*, supervised the release of the Beatles' *Anthology* CDs, and was a founding member of the Traveling Wilburys with Harrison and Tom Petty, Bob Dylan, and Roy Orbison.

01 **DON'T BRING ME DOWN**
   Electric Light Orchestra *Jet* 79
02 **TELEPHONE LINE**
   Electric Light Orchestra *UA* 77
03 **EVIL WOMAN**
   Electric Light Orchestra *UA* 76
04 **SHINE A LITTLE LOVE**
   Electric Light Orchestra *Jet* 79
05 **HOLD ON TIGHT**
   Electric Light Orchestra *Jet* 81
06 **LIVIN' THING**
   Electric Light Orchestra *UA* 77
07 **SWEET TALKIN' WOMAN**
   Electric Light Orchestra *Jet* 78
08 **XANADU**
   Olivia Newton-John/ELO *MCA* 80
09 **CAN'T GET IT OUT OF MY HEAD**
   Electric Light Orchestra *UA* 75
10 **ALL OVER THE WORLD**
   Electric Light Orchestra *MCA* 80
11 **STRANGE MAGIC**
   Electric Light Orchestra *UA* 76
12 **TURN TO STONE**
   Electric Light Orchestra *Jet* 78
13 **ROCK 'N' ROLL IS KING**
   Electric Light Orchestra *Jet* 83
14 **I'M ALIVE**
   Electric Light Orchestra *MCA* 80
15 **CALLING AMERICA**
   Electric Light Orchestra *CBS Associated* 86
16 **DO YA**
   Electric Light Orchestra *UA* 77
17 **ROLL OVER BEETHOVEN**
   Electric Light Orchestra *UA* 73
18 **SHOWDOWN**
   Electric Light Orchestra *UA* 74
19 **MR. BLUE SKY**
   Electric Light Orchestra *Jet* 78
20 **LAST TRAIN TO LONDON**
   Electric Light Orchestra *Jet* 80

The Top 20 Songs of GLORIA ESTEFAN

MIAMI, 1973. Cuban-born Emilio Estefan works for the marketing division of Bacardi. For fun, he plays accordion in local restaurants for tips. A friend at work asks him to put together a band to play at a private party. The host is so impressed he names them the Miami Latin Boys and suggests they keep working together. Within the year they are playing at a wedding when Estefan recognizes a singer he once advised. He invites her to join them for a couple of songs. She later turns down his request to join the band permanently in favor of attending the University of Miami, but then changes her mind. By 1977, she is dating Emilio, and in 1978 they are married. A year later, the renamed Miami Sound Machine, featuring Gloria Estefan on lead vocals, records their first album, which eventually is released by Columbia Records for the Latin market.

It isn't until 1984 that the band has its first international hit. "Dr. Beat" is a No. 6 hit in the U.K. In February 1986 the band finally has a pop hit in America, with "Conga." The infectious dance hit peaked at No. 10. After four hits, the band's name changed to Gloria Estefan and the Miami Sound Machine; five hits later, Estefan became a solo artist with a No. 1 hit, "Don't Wanna Lose You." Emilio explained that he was tired of hearing her referred to as "that girl from the Miami Sound Machine." He also wanted her to be eligible to win a Grammy as a solo artist.

Estefan was having a great year in 1990. She hosted the American Music Awards in January, and soon after received a crystal globe from Sony Music signifying sales of five million albums outside of the U.S. In March, along with Emilio and 10-year-old son Nayib, she met President George Bush at the White House. The next afternoon the Estefans were aboard their tour bus, on their way to a performance in Syracuse, New York. In a snowstorm, their stopped bus was rammed from behind by a speeding semi. Gloria was thrown violently to the floor. She had broken vertebrae, and it wasn't until after surgery she knew she would not be permanently paralyzed. Gloria recovered at home and worked her way back, making a dramatic public reappearance on the January 1991 American Music Awards to sing her emotional "Coming Out Of The Dark."

In 1999, Estefan received good notices for her acting in the Meryl Streep film, *Music Of The Heart*. Teamed with boy band 'N Sync, Estefan had her first top 10 hit in over eight years with "Music Of My Heart."

01 **ANYTHING FOR YOU**
Gloria Estefan & Miami Sound Machine *Epic* 83

02 **COMING OUT OF THE DARK**
Gloria Estefan *Epic* 91

03 **DON'T WANNA LOSE YOU**
Gloria Estefan *Epic* 89

04 **TURN THE BEAT AROUND**
Gloria Estefan *Crescent Moon* 94

05 **1-2-3**
Gloria Estefan & Miami Sound Machine *Epic* 88

06 **CONGA**
Miami Sound Machine *Epic* 86

07 **MUSIC OF MY HEART**
'N Sync & Gloria Estefan *Miramax* 99

08 **RHYTHM IS GONNA GET YOU**
Gloria Estefan & Miami Sound Machine *Epic* 87

09 **WORDS GET IN THE WAY**
Miami Sound Machine *Epic* 86

10 **BAD BOY**
Miami Sound Machine *Epic* 86

11 **LIVE FOR LOVING YOU**
Gloria Estefan *Epic* 91

12 **HERE WE ARE**
Gloria Estefan *Epic* 90

13 **CAN'T STAY AWAY FROM YOU**
Gloria Estefan & Miami Sound Machine *Epic* 88

14 **GET ON YOUR FEET**
Gloria Estefan *Epic* 89

15 **FALLING IN LOVE (UH-OH)**
Miami Sound Machine *Epic* 87

16 **HEAVEN'S WHAT I FEEL**
Gloria Estefan *Epic* 98

17 **EVERLASTING LOVE**
Gloria Estefan *Epic* 95

18 **REACH**
Gloria Estefan *Epic* 97

19 **I'M NOT GIVING YOU UP**
Gloria Estefan *Epic* 97

20 **I SEE YOUR SMILE**
Gloria Estefan *Epic* 93

The Top 20 Songs of THE EVERLY BROTHERS

IKE EVERLY was a coal miner until he became tired of the dangers of working underground. He quit his job and moved to Chicago with his two brothers to sing. Thus, there was an Everly Brothers team long before Ike's sons Don and Phil became world famous.

Ike and his wife Margaret were living in Shenadoah when they asked their young boys if they would like to sing on the family's half-hour radio show on KMA. The show aired at 6 A.M., before Don and Phil went to school. By the time he was seven, Don had his own 15-minute program on Saturday mornings, "The Little Donnie Show." After six years in Shenadoah and a short run on a Knoxville station, live radio work dried up and the family act came to an end.

Ike segued into the construction business and Margaret became a beautician. Don had already sold his first song, "Thou Shalt Not Steal" (to Kitty Wells), so he and Phil moved to Nashville and hung around the Grand Ole Opry, hoping to sell more songs. They recorded an audition tape for Archie Bleyer, owner of Cadence Records. Bleyer turned down the demos, as did almost every label in Nashville. In November 1955, Columbia Records offered a deal for four songs. The first single was "The Sun Keeps Shining."

Ike asked his friend Chet Atkins to introduce the boys to music publisher Wesley Rose, who signed the brothers. When Columbia didn't pick up the Everlys' option, Rose asked Bleyer to reconsider. Cadence was a New York–based label, but now Bleyer was looking for a country act, and he added the Everly Brothers to his roster.

Archie had a song from the Acuff-Rose publishing house that he wanted Don and Phil to record, even though 30 other artists had turned it down. The Everlys liked the idea of being paid $64 each to record the song, so they agreed. Cadence released "Bye Bye Love," and Don and Phil toured Mississippi, Alabama, and Florida. By the time they returned home, the single was moving up the pop singles chart, where it ultimately peaked at No. 2.

Rose became their manager and worked closely with Bleyer. The brothers' next single, "Wake Up Little Susie," was considered too suggestive, as it sounded like Susie and her boyfriend did more than sleep at the drive-in. Some radio stations banned it, but it became the Everlys' first No. 1 hit.

Less than a year later, the Everly Brothers were No. 1 again, with "All I Have To Do Is Dream." Their third chart-topper, "Cathy's Clown," was their first single on the Warner Bros. label. After nine consecutive hits on Cadence, Don and Phil signed a 10-year, $10 million contract with the brand-new WB imprint.

01 ALL I HAVE TO DO IS DREAM
Everly Brothers *Cadence* 58

02 WAKE UP LITTLE SUSIE
Everly Brothers *Cadence* 57

03 CATHY'S CLOWN
Everly Brothers *Warner Bros.* 60

04 BYE BYE LOVE
Everly Brothers *Cadence* 57

05 BIRD DOG
Everly Brothers *Cadence* 58

06 PROBLEMS
Everly Brothers *Cadence* 58

07 (TIL) I KISSED YOU
Everly Brothers *Cadence* 59

08 LET IT BE ME
Everly Brothers *Cadence* 60

09 DEVOTED TO YOU
Everly Brothers *Cadence* 58

10 CRYING IN THE RAIN
Everly Brothers *Warner Bros.* 62

11 SO SAD (TO WATCH GOOD LOVE GO BAD)
Everly Brothers *Warner Bros.* 60

12 WALK RIGHT BACK
Everly Brothers *Warner Bros.* 61

13 EBONY EYES
Everly Brothers *Warner Bros.* 61

14 WHEN WILL I BE LOVED
Everly Brothers *Cadence* 60

15 TAKE A MESSAGE TO MARY
Everly Brothers *Cadence* 59

16 THAT'S OLD-FASHIONED (THAT'S THE WAY LOVE SHOULD BE)
Everly Brothers *Warner Bros.* 62

17 DON'T BLAME ME
Everly Brothers *Warner Bros.* 61

18 POOR JENNY
Everly Brothers *Cadence* 59

19 LUCILLE
Everly Brothers *Warner Bros.* 60

20 LIKE STRANGERS
Everly Brothers *Cadence* 60

The Top 20 Songs of THE 5TH DIMENSION

AMONTE MCLEMORE was photographing the Miss Bronze California beauty contest in 1963. The winner, Florence LaRue, was crowned by the previous year's title-holder, Marilyn McCoo. Lamont and Marilyn both wanted to sing, and they teamed up with three other vocalists to form a group, the Hi-Fi's. After touring with Ray Charles, the quintet drifted apart. But then Lamont received a phone call from Billy Davis, Jr., a friend who was about to sign with Motown as a solo artist. Lamont and Billy got together, and the talk turned to forming another vocal group with Marilyn and an opera-trained singer, Ron Townson. They wanted two female singers, so Lamonte called Florence, who was teaching elementary school in Hollywood. The five members came together as the Versatiles.

They signed with Johnny Rivers' label, Soul City, but Rivers thought their name was old-fashioned. He asked them to come up with something more modern sounding. Ron and his wife Bobette suggested the 5th Dimension, which won instant approval.

Their first chart single was a cover of the Mamas and the Papas' "Go Where You Wanna Go," followed by "Another Day, Another Heartache." It was their third single of 1967, Jimmy Webb's "Up–Up And Away," that brought them to the top 10 for the first time. In 1968, the group had success with covers of two Laura Nyro songs, "Stoned Soul Picnic" and "Sweet Blindness." Their biggest success was to come in 1969, when they had two No. 1 hits.

It was still 1968 when the 5th Dimension headlined at the Americana Hotel in New York City. One afternoon, Davis went shopping and left his wallet in a cab. The next passenger found it and called Billy with the good news. That passenger was one of the producers of the Broadway musical *Hair*, and a grateful Davis invited him to see the 5th Dimension at the Americana. In return, the producer invited the group to see *Hair*.

All five loved Ronnie Dyson's performance of the opening song, "Aquarius," so much that before they left the theater they agreed they had to record it. Back in California, producer Bones Howe was not impressed. He said it was only "half a song" and needed something else. Howe flew to New York to see *Hair* and realized the last three bars of "The Flesh Failures," a song subtitled "Let The Sunshine In," would be perfect.

The medley of "Aquarius/Let The Sunshine In" spent six weeks at No. 1 in the spring of 1969. In the fall, the group spent three more weeks on top with a remake of another Laura Nyro song, "Wedding Bell Blues."

With the new decade came a new label. The group moved from Soul City to Bell Records. They never returned to pole position, but they enjoyed a series of top 10 hits, including "One Less Bell To Answer" and "If I Could Reach You."

The Top 20 Songs of
DARYL HALL and JOHN OATES

THE SOUND of Philadelphia was a strong influence on Daryl Franklin Hohl, who grew up in Pottstown, Pennsylvania, 40 miles west of the City of Brotherly Love. Daryl sang with street-corner groups, and at 17, played keyboards for local bands. A year later, he was recording with the Romeos, a group that included future producer Kenny Gamble.

Hall and Tim Moore made one album together as Gulliver before Hall split to form a duo with John Oates. The first meeting between the two took place under strange circumstances. Both had ducked into a service elevator trying to avoid a fight between rival gangs at a record hop at the Adelphia Ballroom. Daryl had been performing that night with his band, the Temptones, and John had been on stage with his group, the Masters. Both were students at Temple University, but it would be another two years before they officially began to work together. Three more years would pass before the release of their first album for Atlantic Records, *Whole Oates*.

Their second set for Atlantic, *Abandoned Luncheonette,* established them as blue-eyed soul singers. The album was produced by Arif Mardin and included their song "She's Gone," which had already been recorded by Lou Rawls and Tavares. Producer Todd Rundgren brought more of a pop influence to their next album, *War Babies,* their final LP for Atlantic.

In 1975, the pair switched to RCA. The album *Daryl Hall & John Oates* contained their first top 10 single, "Sara Smile," a No. 4 hit on the Hot 100 in June 1976. Their first of six No. 1 singles was "Rich Girl" in 1977. Three years later, they began to produce their own albums, unleashing a flood of hit 45s.

Their most successful Hot 100 single, "Maneater," sounded so much like the Supremes' "You Can't Hurry Love" that songwriter Lamont Dozier thought it was a cover of that hit the first time he heard the opening notes.

Hall and Oates' final chart single on RCA was a 1985 remake of the Temptations' "The Way You Do The Things You Do" with that Motown quintet's former members David Ruffin and Eddie Kendricks guest starring. A year later, Hall had his first solo hit with "Dreamtime," a No. 5 hit. In 1988, the pair moved over to Clive Davis' Arista label. "Everything Your Heart Desires" peaked at No. 3, giving the duo its biggest hit in four years.

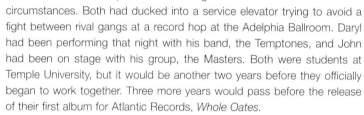

01 **MANEATER**
Daryl Hall and John Oates *RCA* 82
02 **I CAN'T GO FOR THAT (NO CAN DO)**
Daryl Hall and John Oates *RCA* 82
03 **OUT OF TOUCH**
Daryl Hall and John Oates *RCA* 84
04 **PRIVATE EYES**
Daryl Hall and John Oates *RCA* 81
05 **SAY IT ISN'T SO**
Daryl Hall and John Oates *RCA* 83
06 **KISS ON MY LIST**
Daryl Hall and John Oates *RCA* 81
07 **RICH GIRL**
Daryl Hall and John Oates *RCA* 77
08 **SARA SMILE**
Daryl Hall and John Oates *RCA* 76
09 **EVERYTHING YOUR HEART DESIRES**
Daryl Hall and John Oates *Arista* 88
10 **YOU'VE LOST THAT LOVIN' FEELING**
Daryl Hall and John Oates *RCA* 80
11 **ONE ON ONE**
Daryl Hall and John Oates *RCA* 83
12 **SHE'S GONE**
Daryl Hall and John Oates *Atlantic* 76
13 **YOU MAKE MY DREAMS**
Daryl Hall and John Oates *RCA* 81
14 **DID IT IN A MINUTE**
Daryl Hall and John Oates *RCA* 82
15 **ADULT EDUCATION**
Daryl Hall and John Oates *RCA* 84
16 **FAMILY MAN**
Daryl Hall and John Oates *RCA* 83
17 **METHOD OF MODERN LOVE**
Daryl Hall and John Oates *RCA* 85
18 **DREAMTIME**
Daryl Hall *RCA* 86
19 **WAIT FOR ME**
Daryl Hall and John Oates *RCA* 80
20 **SO CLOSE**
Daryl Hall and John Oates *Arista* 90

The Top 20 Songs of WHITNEY HOUSTON

WHITNEY HOUSTON'S career might have started in 1979 if her mother, Cissy Houston, had given her permission. The younger Houston was only 15 when she added vocals to the Michael Zager Band's "Life's A Party" single, issued on Private Stock. Zager wanted to sign Houston to a recording contract, but mama said no. And Cissy knew enough about the music business to make an informed decision, having joined her family's gospel singing group, the Drinkard Sisters, when she was six, and then organizing the R&B quartet the Sweet Inspirations.

Two years after the Zager project, Whitney signed with a manager. A host of labels wanted her, including Epic, Elektra, and Arista, but manager Gene Harvey turned them all down. He wanted Whitney to mature a little bit before committing to a label deal.

Houston tried acting and modeling and sang backing vocals for her mother's live appearances. In 1983, she auditioned for Arista label head Clive Davis. He said thank you and left, but the next day he made a generous offer. A year before her Arista debut, Whitney guest-starred on a Teddy Pendergrass single for Asylum, "Hold Me." Her solo debut on the Hot 100 was a song written by LaLa and originally intended for Roberta Flack. "You Give Good Love" went to No. 1 on the R&B chart, but only reached No. 3 on the Hot 100. Whitney's next seven chart singles, from "Saving All My Love For You" (originally recorded by Marilyn McCoo and Billy Davis, Jr.) to "Where Do Broken Hearts Go," all went to No. 1, an unprecedented feat. Included in those seven were "How Will I Know," a song written by George Merrill and Shannon Rubicam for Janet Jackson, and "Greatest Love Of All," a song Whitney had been performing when she had a solo spotlight during her mother's live performances.

Whitney's ninth biggest single, "I'm Your Baby Tonight," was written by L.A. Reid and Babyface after Clive Davis asked the red-hot production team to work on Houston's third album. The song returned her to the top of the Hot 100.

Houston's top two titles are both from soundtracks. "I Will Always Love You," a David Foster–produced cover of the Dolly Parton song that established a new record by remaining No. 1 for 14 weeks, was the main musical attraction of *The Bodyguard,* the film Houston starred in with Kevin Costner. The Babyface-helmed "Exhale (Shoop Shoop)" is from *Waiting To Exhale,* the film adaptation of the Terry McMillan novel.

01 I WILL ALWAYS LOVE YOU
Whitney Houston *Arista* 92

02 EXHALE (SHOOP SHOOP)
Whitney Houston *Arista* 95

03 HEARTBREAK HOTEL
Whitney Houston f/Faith Evans
& Kelly Price *Arista* 99

**04 I WANNA DANCE WITH SOMEBODY
(WHO LOVES ME)**
Whitney Houston *Arista* 87

05 GREATEST LOVE OF ALL
Whitney Houston *Arista* 86

06 SO EMOTIONAL
Whitney Houston *Arista* 88

07 ALL THE MAN THAT I NEED
Whitney Houston *Arista* 91

08 HOW WILL I KNOW
Whitney Houston *Arista* 86

09 I'M YOUR BABY TONIGHT
Whitney Houston *Arista* 90

10 DIDN'T WE ALMOST HAVE IT ALL
Whitney Houston *Arista* 87

11 MY LOVE IS YOUR LOVE
Whitney Houston *Arista* 00

12 WHERE DO BROKEN HEARTS GO
Whitney Houston *Arista* 88

13 SAVING ALL MY LOVE FOR YOU
Whitney Houston *Arista* 85

14 I HAVE NOTHING
Whitney Houston *Arista* 93

15 I'M EVERY WOMAN
Whitney Houston *Arista* 93

16 YOU GIVE GOOD LOVE
Whitney Houston *Arista* 85

17 I BELIEVE IN YOU AND ME
Whitney Houston *Arista* 97

18 IT'S NOT RIGHT BUT IT'S OKAY
Whitney Houston *Arista* 99

19 COUNT ON ME
Whitney Houston and Cece Winans *Arista* 96

20 ONE MOMENT IN TIME
Whitney Houston *Arista* 88

The Top 20 Songs of JEFFERSON AIRPLANE/ JEFFERSON STARSHIP/STARSHIP

JEFFERSON AIRPLANE was organized as a folk-rock group in 1965, the same year that found Bob Dylan and the Byrds charging up the Hot 100. By the time the band achieved its first top 10 success in 1967, it was the summer of love and Jefferson Airplane was forging a new path in psychedelic rock.

The idea to put Jefferson Airplane together started with Marty Balin, born in Cincinnati, Ohio, and raised in San Francisco. He was 23 when he turned a Fillmore Street pizza parlor into a club called the Matrix. The first musician he recruited for the house band was singer and rhythm guitarist Paul Kantner. Kantner brought in Jorma Kaukonen, also a singer and a lead guitarist. Bob Harvey was added as the bass player and Jerry Peloquin got the job of drummer. Balin wanted a female singer in the group and hired Signe Toly. Kaukonen came up with the group's name, inspired by a friend who jokingly called him Blind Thomas Jefferson Airplane, a play on the name of blues singer Blind Lemon Jefferson.

Jefferson Airplane built a reputation at the Matrix and attracted the attention of several record labels. In November 1965, RCA signed the band, with Skip Spence now on drums and Jack Casady on bass. Two singles were released ("It's No Secret" and "Come Up The Years"), but neither appeared on the Hot 100. The debut album *Jefferson Airplane Takes Off* never quite did, stopping at No. 128.

There were more personnel changes, as Spencer Dryden took over the drummer's position and Signe left to take care of her first child, replaced by the lead singer of another Bay Area band, the Great Society— a woman named Grace Slick. On the group's second album, *Surrealistic Pillow*, Slick brought two songs previously recorded by the Great Society. "Somebody To Love" marked the Airplane's debut on the Hot 100, peaking at No. 5. The follow-up, "White Rabbit," went to No. 8. Jefferson Airplane never returned to the top 10 of the singles chart.

The group remained intact while some members took up side projects. Kaukonen and Casady were the creative core of Hot Tuna, a rock group that included violinist Papa John Creach. Kantner recorded a concept album, the science-fiction themed *Blows Against The Empire*. Although it was a solo work, it did feature members of the Airplane, and the album was credited to Kantner and the Jefferson Starship, even though there was no real band with that name.

That changed in 1974 when Kantner and Slick, now married, reorganized Jefferson Airplane into Jefferson Starship. Balin, who left in 1971, returned in 1975 and composed "Miracles," which became the biggest hit for any incarnation of the group to that date, peaking at No. 3. Balin left again in 1978 and was eventually replaced by singer Mickey Thomas.

Kantner departed in 1984 and legally won the right to the name Jefferson Starship. The rest of the group, who continued as Starship, achieved the highest level of chart success yet, with three No. 1 singles on the Hot 100: "We Built This City," "Sara," and "Nothing's Gonna Stop Us Now."

The Top 20 Songs of GLADYS KNIGHT & THE PIPS

GLADYS KNIGHT & the Pips' top 20 hits are almost evenly divided between two major labels: the Soul imprint, their home during their stay with Motown; and Buddah, the label that signed the group when they left Berry Gordy's company. Gladys and the Pips' most successful chart single is "Midnight Train To Georgia," a song that began life as a country tune featuring a different mode of transportation, headed to a different destination (composer Jim Weatherly recorded his own "Midnight Plane To Houston" on the Amos label). When Whitney Houston's mother, Cissy, recorded the first R&B version, it was changed to "Midnight Train To Georgia." Weatherly's publisher forwarded the song to Gladys Knight & the Pips, but kept the revised title.

The group's second most successful chart single was also a cover version, although it didn't appear that way when Gladys' version of "I Heard It Through The Grapevine" was the first to be released. The Miracles, the Isley Brothers, and Marvin Gaye had all tackled the Norman Whitfield–Barrett Strong composition first, although all three remained on the shelf while Gladys' was released on Soul.

Gladys was born May 28, 1944, in Atlanta, where her parents Merald and Elizabeth were part of the Wings Over Jordan Gospel Choir. At seven, she sang "Too Young" on *Ted Mack's Original Amateur Hour* and won first prize.

Unlike other Motown acts, such as The Temptations, Martha & the Vandellas, and Stevie Wonder, Gladys Knight & the Pips were already established when they joined Gordy's company (on a three-to-one democratic vote, with Gladys voting "no"). The group was born at a birthday party for Merald Knight, when siblings Gladys, Merald, and Brenda sang a song with their cousins William and Elenor Guest. Another cousin, James Wood, thought they were good enough to become professional; they took his nickname, Pip, for the group name. Edward Patten and Langston George joined the group as Brenda and Elenor departed, but George left in 1962, creating the quartet that would remain intact for years to come. After a brief stint with Brunswick in 1957, the group recorded "Every Beat Of My Heart" for the Huntom label, which leased the master to Vee Jay. Signed to the Fury label, Gladys and the Pips recorded a new version of "Every Beat Of My Heart," and followed it with "Letter Full Of Tears." In 1964, after a two-year respite in which Gladys married and started her family, the group signed with another independent label, Maxx, before receiving the offer to join Motown.

IN 1964, 14-year-old bass player Robert "Kool" Bell put together his first group, the Jazziacs, made up of fellow students from Lincoln High in Jersey City, New Jersey. The roster included future Kool and the Gang players Robert "Spike" Mickens on trumpet, Dennis "D.T." Thomas on alto sax, George Brown on drums, Charles Smith on lead guitar, and Robert's brother, Ronald Bell, on tenor sax.

The band played jam sessions at a Jersey City club called St. John's, frequented by jazz musicians like Pharaoh Sanders and Leon Thomas. But they weren't earning enough money as a jazz outfit, so they continued to play jazz for fun while turning to R&B to make a living. As the Soul Town Band, they gathered a huge following by laying a heavy R&B/funk beat over their jazz roots. They changed names a few times and were known as the New Dimensions and the New Flames, and in local clubs they were billed as Kool and the New Flames. That was too close to James Brown's Famous Flames, so they finalized their moniker and became Kool and the Gang.

In New York, the band met Gene Redd, a writer/producer who was starting his own label, De-Lite. He signed the group in 1969 and the first single, an instrumental simply titled "Kool And The Gang," peaked at No. 59 on the Hot 100. It would take four years to earn their first top 30 single; "Funky Stuff" from the *Wild And Peaceful* LP found its way to No. 29 in October 1973. The next two singles from that album both reached the top 10. "Jungle Boogie" went to No. 4 and "Hollywood Swinging" swung to No. 6.

The success streak didn't continue. With disco growing in popularity, the band faced a rough period, and Kool knew the group needed a new sound if they were going to continue. A search for a new lead vocalist led them to James "J.T." Taylor, who had just lost his teaching job. He was in a band that had just broken up, so he was ready for something new. While working at the House of Music studio in New Jersey, the group met Brazilian producer Eumir Deodato, whose jazz albums had been charting in America since 1973. The band asked Deodato to helm its next album. The result was their first platinum-certified set, *Ladies Night*, which yielded two more top 10 singles, both in 1980: "Ladies Night" (No. 8) and "Too Hot" (No. 5), followed by Kool and the Gang's first and only No. 1 hit, "Celebration."

After a series of top 10 singles in the '80s, including "Joanna," "Fresh," and "Cherish," Taylor split in 1988. He returned in 1995, and while the group never regained a foothold on the singles chart, they continued to have success as a touring act.

01 CELEBRATION
Kool & the Gang *De-Lite* 81
02 CHERISH
Kool & the Gang *De-Lite* 85
03 JOANNA
Kool & the Gang *De-Lite* 84
04 TOO HOT
Kool & the Gang *De-Lite* 80
05 LADIES NIGHT
Kool & the Gang *Mercury* 80
06 VICTORY
Kool & the Gang *De-Lite* 87
07 FRESH
Kool & the Gang *De-Lite* 85
08 TAKE MY HEART
Kool & the Gang *De-Lite* 81
09 GET DOWN ON IT
Kool & the Gang *De-Lite* 82
10 MISLED Kool & the Gang *De-Lite* 85
11 TONIGHT
Kool & the Gang *De-Lite* 84
12 STONE LOVE
Kool & the Gang *Mercury* 87
13 EMERGENCY
Kool & the Gang *De-Lite* 85
14 BIG FUN
Kool & the Gang *De-Lite* 82
15 LET'S GO DANCIN' (OOH LA, LA, LA)
Kool & the Gang *De-Lite* 83
16 FUNKY STUFF
Kool & the Gang *De-Lite* 73
17 SPIRIT OF THE BOOGIE /
SUMMER MADNESS
Kool & the Gang *De-Lite* 75
18 JONES VS. JONES
Kool & the Gang *De-Lite* 81
19 HIGHER PLANE
Kool & the Gang *De-Lite* 74
20 OPEN SESAME - PART 1
Kool & the Gang *De-Lite* 77

The Top 20 Songs of BRENDA LEE

I N A 1966 *Billboard* interview, Brenda Lee's mother revealed that her daughter loved music ever since she was a baby, when she started listening to the radio at eight months old. As a three-year-old, Brenda could hear a song twice and sing part of it back. By five, she was memorizing complete songs. That's when she performed "Take Me Out To The Ball Game" at a talent and beauty contest for her school district. Finishing first in talent and second in beauty, she was invited to sing on an Atlanta weekly radio show, *Starmakers Revue*. A year later the young singer auditioned for a local TV program, *TV Ranch*, and was the first child singer hired to be a regular.

At 10, Brenda was signed to a TV series hosted by Augusta DJ Peanut Faircloth. Singer Red Foley heard her sing on the show and signed her to his ABC-TV series, *Ozark Jubilee*. Hearst columnist Jack O'Brien wrote a column praising her talent, which led to a booking on Perry Como's network variety program. Brenda followed that with guest appearances on Ed Sullivan and Steve Allen's shows, all before she had a recording contract.

In 1956, Foley's manager, Dub Albritton, signed Brenda to the same label that Foley recorded for, Decca Records. At her first session on July 30, she recorded "Jambalaya" and "BIgelow 6-200." *Billboard* reviewed the single, saying she "has the projection, voice, and sincerity that can skyrocket her to great heights, not only in the country field but in the pop field as well."

Brenda didn't appear on the pop singles chart until 1957, with "One Step At A Time." It wasn't a major hit, and Albritton decided to showcase Lee in Paris, hoping that would create interest at home. A date at the Olympia Music Hall in March 1959 was almost cancelled when the producer found out Brenda was a child. Albritton saved the day by planting a story in the Paris newspapers that his client was a 32-year-old little person. Then he denied the stories, creating so much demand to see her that the producer was forced to go on with the show. Brenda was held over for five weeks at the Olympia and then toured Germany, Italy, and England. She returned home an international star, and a subsequent tour of South America made her world-acclaimed. The result: her first hit single in America with "Sweet Nothin's," No. 4 in 1960.

The follow-up was a song cut at the tail end of a session, with just five minutes of recording time left. Producer Owen Bradley told *Billboard* it was one of the first Nashville sessions to use strings. Decca executives were concerned that at 15, Brenda was too young to sing about unrequited love and buried "I'm Sorry" on the B-side of the uptempo "That's All You Gotta Do." Both sides reached the top 10 on the Hot 100, but "I'm Sorry" was the side that went to No. 1.

The Top 20 Songs of LL COOL J

BORN IN QUEENS, New York, James Todd Smith was raised by his maternal grandparents after his mother and father divorced when he was four. Music ran in the family: his mother, Ondrea Smith, played the accordion and wrote poetry. His father, James Nunya, ran a trucking company but he also recorded songs in the style of Barry White and Marvin Gaye. One day James came home from school and discovered a gift from his grandfather—two turntables and a mixer.

James was nine when he discovered underground rappers like Cold Crush 4, Double Trouble, and the Fantastic Romantic 5. He was 11 when "Rapper's Delight" by the Sugarhill Gang became the first successful commercial rap single. And two years later, Smith was making his own demo tapes in his basement and sending them to labels that specialized in the genre.

Adapting the name LL Cool J, for Ladies Love Cool James, Smith was 16 when he sent a demo to Def Jam co-owner Rick Rubin and then called every day to see if Rubin had received the demo. Finally, Rubin called back and left a message with LL's grandmother. LL was signed to Def Jam and the label released his "I Need a Beat" as its first 12-inch single.

A year later, Def Jam signed with Columbia for distribution and the first album released was LL's *Radio*. The single "I Can't Live Without My Radio" marked his first appearance on the R&B singles chart, in 1986. In July 1987, LL made his Hot 100 debut with "I'm Bad." That first single stalled at No. 84, but the follow-up, "I Need Love," climbed to No. 14. That song was written in a half-hour in his grandmother's basement. His friends told him it was a terrible song and that no one wanted to hear a rap ballad. In September 1987, the song topped the R&B chart.

In 1995 "Hey Lover" peaked at No. 3 on the Hot 100, making it the highest-ranking LL Cool J title to that date. The next year, "Loungin" also went to No. 3. In February 2003, LL had his first No. 1 hit when he was featured on the Jennifer Lopez song "All I Have."

But LL Cool J's career isn't just about the music. He has also proven himself as an actor. After cameos in the motion pictures *Krush Groove* (1985) and *Wildcats* (1986), his first real acting role was playing Robin Williams' cousin in *Toys* (1992). His other film credits include *Out-of-Sync* (1995), *Deep Blue Sea* (1999), *Any Given Sunday* (1999), *Charlie's Angels* (2000), and *Rollerball* (2002). From 1995–1999, he starred in five seasons of the TV series *In The House*.

01 ALL I HAVE
Jennifer Lopez f/LL Cool J *Epic* 03

02 HEY LOVER
LL Cool J *Def Jam* 95

03 LOUNGIN
LL Cool J *Def Jam* 96

04 LUV U BETTER
LL Cool J *Def Jam* 02

05 THIS IS FOR THE LOVER IN YOU
Babyface f/LL Cool J, Howard Hewett, Jody Watley & Jeffrey Daniels *Epic* 96

06 DOIN IT
LL Cool J *Def Jam* 96

07 AROUND THE WAY GIRL
LL Cool J *Def Jam* 91

08 HEADSPRUNG
LL Cool J *Def Jam* 04

09 HUSH
LL Cool J f/7 Aurelius *Def Jam* 04

10 FATHER
LL Cool J *Def Jam* 98

11 I NEED LOVE
LL Cool J *Def Jam* 87

12 I'M THAT TYPE OF GUY
LL Cool J *Def Jam* 89

13 MAMA SAID KNOCK YOU OUT
LL Cool J f/Jennifer Lopez *Def Jam* 91

14 CONTROL MYSELF
LL Cool J *Def Jam* 06

15 GOING BACK TO CALI
LL Cool J *Def Jam* 88

16 PARADISE
LL Cool J f/Amerie *Def Jam* 03

17 BACK SEAT (OF MY JEEP)
LL Cool J *Def Jam* 93

18 THE BOOMIN' SYSTEM
LL Cool J *Def Jam* 90

19 AIN'T NOBODY
LL Cool J *Def Jam* 97

20 PHENOMENON
LL Cool J *Def Jam* 97

The Top 20 Songs of LUDACRIS

BEFORE HE WAS LUDACRIS, he was Chris Bridges—actually, Christopher Brian Bridges, born in Champaign, Illinois. He was seven years old when his father bought him a vinyl copy of UTFO's "Roxanne, Roxanne," one of the earliest rap singles, and the young boy fell in love with the music. By nine he was rapping at school, and was so good at it that the other fourth-graders expected him to come up with new rhymes all the time.

When he was 12, the family moved to Atlanta. That's where Bridges eventually became a DJ on Hot 97.5, and gained notoriety rhyming on the station's promos. Through his work at the station he met Timbaland and Jermaine Dupri. Both offered him record deals, but Ludacris recorded his first album for an independent label. Based on that debut, Ludacris was signed to Def Jam, and his albums were released under the Def Jam South logo. He was given his own imprint, Disturbing tha Peace.

The first album under Def Jam auspices, *Back for the First Time*, was a re-working of his indie debut. His first chart single on the Hot 100, "What's Your Fantasy," was included on both versions. Recorded with female rapper Shawnna, the daughter of blues singer Buddy Guy, "What's Your Fantasy" peaked at No. 21. Eight more singles followed (including titles on which Ludacris was the featured artist) before he claimed his first top 10 hit. "Move B***h," recorded with Mystikal and Infamous 2.0, peaked at No. 10 in October 2002.

The following year, Ludacris had his first No. 1 single, with "Stand Up," also recorded with Shawnna. He returned to pole position for a lengthy 12-week stay when he guest-starred with Lil Jon on Usher's biggest hit, "Yeah!" in 2004. Ludacris racked up two more No. 1 hits, in 2006 ("Money Maker," featuring Pharrell) and in 2007 ("Glamorous," a Fergie track that featured Ludacris).

Shortly after making his *Billboard* chart debut, Ludacris made his film debut, with a small role in *The Wash*, the 2001 release that starred Dr. Dre and Snoop Dogg. Two years later, Ludacris appeared in *2 Fast 2 Furious*. But his acting chops were perfected in two critically acclaimed movies, *Crash* and *Hustle & Flow*. He played numerous roles on TV series such as *Eve* and *Law and Order: Special Victims Unit,* and received praise for being a truly humorous host on *Saturday Night Live* in November 2006.

Already comfortable being in front of the camera from all of his music videos and television appearances (over 70 between 2002 and 2006), Ludacris was a natural on the silver screen, perfecting his craft by listening to the advice of more experienced actors on the sets, like *Crash* co-stars Don Cheadle and Terrence Howard.

01 **YEAH!**
Usher f/Lil Jon & Ludacris *LaFace* 04

02 **STAND UP**
Ludacris f/Shawnna *DTP/Def Jam South* 03

03 **MONEY MAKER**
Ludacris f/Pharrell *DTP/Def Jam* 06

04 **OH** Ciara f/Ludacris *Sho'Nuff/MusicLine/ LaFace* 05

05 **LOVERS & FRIENDS** Lil Jon & the East Side Boyz f/Usher & Ludacris *BME* 05

06 **HOLIDAE INN**
Chingy f/Ludacris & Snoop Dogg *DTP* 03

07 **SPLASH WATERFALLS**
Ludacris *DTP/Def Jam South* 04

08 **GET BACK** Ludacris *DTP/Def Jam South* 05

09 **MOVE B***H** Ludacris f/Mystikal & Infamous 2.0 *DTP/ Def Jam South* 02

10 **UNPREDICTABLE**
Jamie Foxx f/Ludacris *J* 06

11 **GOSSIP FOLKS**
Missy "Misdemeanor" Elliott f/Ludacris *The Gold Mind* 03

12 **SUGAR (GIMME SOME)**
Trick Daddy f/Ludacris, Lil Kim & Cee-Lo *Slip-N-Slide* 05

13 **PIMPIN' ALL OVER THE WORLD**
Ludacris f/Bobby Valentino *DTP/ Def Jam South* 05

14 **ROLL OUT (MY BUSINESS)**
Ludacris *DTP/Def Jam South* 02

15 **WHAT'S YOUR FANTASY**
Ludacris f/Shawnna *DTP/Def Jam South* 00

16 **SOUTHERN HOSPITALITY**
Ludacris *DTP/Def Jam South* 01

17 **RUNAWAY LOVE**
Ludacris f/Mary J. Blige *DTP/Def Jam* 07

18 **NUMBER ONE SPOT**
Ludacris *DTP/Def Jam South* 05

19 **SATURDAY (OOOH! OOOOH!)**
Ludacris f/Sleepy Brown *DTP/ Def Jam South* 02

20 **AREA CODES**
Ludacris f/Nate Dogg *DTP/Def Jam* 01

EDNA MANILOW says she saw the talent in her son Barry when, still a two-year-old in diapers, he would dance to the music on the radio. He was seven when she gave him an accordion, which he played until she bought him a piano. While she encouraged his musical passion, she wasn't schooled in contemporary music. It was her second husband, Willie Murphy, who expanded Barry's musical horizons, introducing him to jazz and show tunes. Barry's friends were into Elvis Presley, but the teenager searched his stepfather's record collection and discovered June Christy, Chris Connor, and Stan Kenton as well as Broadway cast albums like *The King And I* and *Carousel*.

Barry was voted "Best Musician" at Eastern District High School in Brooklyn, New York. He enrolled at City College of New York, thinking he would go into television advertising but decided he wanted to pursue music as a career and switched to the New York College of Music, then was accepted at Juilliard. To support himself, he had a series of jobs, including working at CBS—first in the mailroom and then as an editor.

In the '60s, Manilow was asked to write the score for an off-Broadway musical, *The Drunkard*, and was hired as musical director for WCBS-TV's *Callback!* series. As the 1970s started, Barry had a nightclub act with Jeanne Lucas. He played piano and was the arranger and she was the vocalist until a club in Richmond, Virginia, booked them as a vocal duo and Barry quickly learned to sing "Georgy Girl" and "Somethin' Stupid."

Jeanne and Barry played Manhattan's Upstairs at the Downstairs for two years, as the opening act for Joan Rivers. Then, Manilow was hired as the Saturday night pianist at the Continental Baths. In the spring of 1972 a red-headed singer named Bette Midler was booked to sing at the Baths. She asked Barry to be her musical director, arranger, and pianist. When she signed to Atlantic Records, Barry co-produced and arranged her first two albums.

Barry also had become successful at singing (and writing) commercial jingles. That's how he met singer Ron Dante, who was the voice of the Archies on "Sugar, Sugar" and a jingle singer himself. They decided to record a demo tape, and Barry provided the vocals. Bell Records, run by Larry Uttal, offered Barry a contract if he would agree to tour. At the same time, Midler asked him to be the musical director of her first national tour and he said yes, as long as he could sing three songs. She agreed that he would open act two.

Bell Records found a new leader in Clive Davis, who renamed the label Arista and kept three acts, including Barry Manilow. While recording his second album, Manilow accepted Clive's suggestion to record a song written by Scott English and Richard Kerr. "Brandy" was changed to "Mandy" and flew to No. 1 in January 1975.

01 **I WRITE THE SONGS**
Barry Manilow *Arista* 76
02 **CAN'T SMILE WITHOUT YOU**
Barry Manilow *Arista* 78
03 **LOOKS LIKE WE MADE IT**
Barry Manilow *Arista* 77
04 **MANDY**
Barry Manilow *Bell* 75
05 **COULD IT BE MAGIC**
Barry Manilow *Arista* 75
06 **SHIPS**
Barry Manilow *Arista* 79
07 **I MADE IT THROUGH THE RAIN**
Barry Manilow *Arista* 81
08 **COPACABANA (AT THE COPA)**
Barry Manilow *Arista* 78
09 **TRYIN' TO GET THE FEELING AGAIN**
Barry Manilow *Arista* 76
10 **READ 'EM AND WEEP**
Barry Manilow *Arista* 84
11 **READY TO TAKE A CHANCE AGAIN**
Barry Manilow *Arista* 78
12 **WEEKEND IN NEW ENGLAND**
Barry Manilow *Arista* 77
13 **SOMEWHERE IN THE NIGHT**
Barry Manilow *Arista* 79
14 **IT'S A MIRACLE**
Barry Manilow *Arista* 75
15 **THE OLD SONGS**
Barry Manilow *Arista* 81
16 **WHEN I WANTED YOU**
Barry Manilow *Arista* 80
17 **EVEN NOW**
Barry Manilow *Arista* 78
18 **SOMEWHERE DOWN THE ROAD**
Barry Manilow *Arista* 82
19 **DAYBREAK**
Barry Manilow *Arista* 77
20 **SOME KIND OF FRIEND**
Barry Manilow *Arista* 83

The Top 20 Songs of GEORGE MICHAEL

GEORGIOS PANAYIOTOU was 12 years old when he met Andrew Ridgely at the school in Bushey, England, where they were both students. As teenagers, they formed a band called the Executives, then signed with a small British label, Vision, as a duo called Wham!

After a few singles that did well in the U.K. but not in America, Wham! released their breakthrough hit, "Wake Me Up Before You Go-Go." It went to No. 1 in the U.S. as well as the U.K. "Careless Whisper" was released as a solo single by George at home, but in America, the label credit read "Wham! featuring George Michael." Written while he was riding on a bus at age 16, "Careless Whisper" is Michael's second most successful Hot 100 single.

The pair split in the fall of 1985, and Michael went to work on his first solo effort. It was his opportunity to mature beyond the bubblegum parameters set by Wham! A hint of what was to come was revealed in 1987, when Michael teamed with the first lady of soul, Aretha Franklin, on an '80s-style Marvin Gaye & Tammi Terrell–type duet, "I Knew You Were Waiting (For Me)." Six weeks after that single ruled the Hot 100, Michael's solo "I Want Your Sex" debuted. The controversial song was banned by the BBC, the video re-edited three times by MTV, and refused airplay by many U.S. radio stations. The diminished airplay kept the song from reaching pole position; it stalled at No. 2.

But "I Want Your Sex" served its purpose, transforming Michael's image. And if anyone doubted he was a serious musician, they just had to listen to the album that followed. It was titled *Faith,* after the next single, which spent four weeks at No. 1 at the end of 1987. And from that same album, Michael earned three more chart-toppers: "Father Figure," "One More Try," and "Monkey."

Michael would record only one more album for Columbia, *Listen Without Prejudice.* A lengthy lawsuit with parent company Sony followed, and George eventually signed with DreamWorks in the U.S. and Virgin outside of North America. The *Older* album yielded several hits internationally, but in America only two titles were significant hits: "Jesus To A Child" and "Fastlove."

On April 7, 1998, Michael was arrested in Beverly Hills for an alleged lewd sex act in a public bathroom. Four days later, he acknowledged being gay in a CNN interview. In October of that year, he released "Outside," inspired by his arrest.

01 **FAITH**
George Michael *Columbia* 87

02 **CARELESS WHISPER**
Wham! f/George Michael *Columbia* 85

03 **ONE MORE TRY**
George Michael *Columbia* 88

04 **WAKE ME UP BEFORE YOU GO-GO**
Wham! *Columbia* 84

05 **FATHER FIGURE**
George Michael *Columbia* 88

06 **EVERYTHING SHE WANTS**
Wham! *Columbia* 85

07 **DON'T LET THE SUN GO DOWN ON ME**
George Michael/Elton John *Columbia* 92

08 **MONKEY**
George Michael *Columbia* 88

09 **I KNEW YOU WERE WAITING (FOR ME)**
Aretha Franklin & George Michael *Arista* 87

10 **PRAYING FOR TIME**
George Michael *Columbia* 90

11 **I WANT YOUR SEX**
George Michael *Columbia* 87

12 **I'M YOUR MAN**
Wham! *Columbia* 86

13 **FREEDOM**
Wham! *Columbia* 85

14 **TOO FUNKY**
George Michael *Columbia* 92

15 **FASTLOVE**
George Michael *DreamWorks* 96

16 **FREEDOM**
George Michael *Columbia* 90

17 **A DIFFERENT CORNER**
George Michael *Columbia* 86

18 **KISSING A FOOL**
George Michael *Columbia* 88

19 **THE EDGE OF HEAVEN**
Wham! *Columbia* 86

20 **JESUS TO A CHILD**
George Michael *DreamWorks* 96

The Top 20 Songs of NEW EDITION

WHILE NEW EDITION performed well on the pop and R&B charts, the six talented members of the group achieved even greater success by going out on their own or by forming a spin-off trio. The most successful New Edition alumnus is Bobby Brown, but Ralph Tresvant and Johnny Gill have done well as solo artists, and Michael Bivins, Ricky Bell, and Ronnie DeVoe earned their stripes as Bell Biv DeVoe.

The original nucleus of New Edition was Brown, Bivins, Bell, and Tresvant. Choreographer Brook Payne contributed not only dazzling dance steps to the group, but also his nephew, DeVoe. While competing in a Boston talent show in the early '80s, the group placed second and caught the eye of the competition's sponsor, Maurice Starr. He signed them to Streetwise, a small New York label, and with his brother, Michael Jonzun, produced their first hit, "Candy Girl." In 1984, the quintet broke away from Starr and signed with MCA. Two years later, Brown departed for a solo career and was subsequently replaced by Gill. Brown began with a misstep; the *King Of Stage* album was not to his liking. "It was really a solo New Edition album," he protests. "The voice was there, the voice they remember from 'Candy Girl.' It didn't work out for me. We had to regroup and find out what my identity was as a singer." Seeking a new direction, Brown teamed up with producers L.A. Reid and Babyface, and for the first time blended rap and R&B in the commercially successful "Don't Be Cruel."

Gill and Tresvant were already planning their post–New Edition solo efforts during the group's *Heart Break* tour. At the final show, producers Jimmy Jam and Terry Lewis gathered backstage with the quintet. "[We were] talking to everybody about what they were going to do in the future," says Jimmy Jam. "We had already been lined up to do the Johnny Gill album and some things on Ralph, and we asked the other three guys, 'What are you going to do?'" Bivins was thinking about becoming a manager (and did, with Boyz II Men), and Bell thought he might do a solo album or take some time off. "They didn't really have a clear cut idea of what it was they wanted to do," says Jimmy, who suggested that Bell, Bivins, and DeVoe record an album with Ricky singing and Michael and Ronald rapping. "Coming from New Edition, no one thought we were able to do anything, because we were in the background for the most part . . . so we kind of snuck up out of nowhere," says DeVoe. The trio had two No. 3 hits in 1990, "Poison" and "Do Me!"

In 1997, all six former New Edition members reunited for an album, *Home Again.*

01 **MY PREROGATIVE**
Bobby Brown *MCA* 89

02 **HUMPIN' AROUND**
Bobby Brown *MCA* 92

03 **POISON**
Bell Biv DeVoe *MCA* 90

04 **ON OUR OWN**
Bobby Brown *MCA* 89

05 **DO ME!**
Bell Biv DeVoe *MCA* 90

06 **RUB YOU THE RIGHT WAY**
Johnny Gill *Motown* 90

07 **I'M STILL IN LOVE WITH YOU**
New Edition *MCA* 97

08 **GOOD ENOUGH**
Bobby Brown *MCA* 92

09 **SENSITIVITY**
Ralph Tresvant *MCA* 91

10 **EVERY LITTLE STEP**
Bobby Brown *MCA* 89

11 **THE BEST THINGS IN LIFE ARE FREE**
Luther Vandross & Janet Jackson w/BBD
& Ralph Tresvant *Perspective* 92

12 **COOL IT NOW**
New Edition *MCA* 85

13 **RONI**
Bobby Brown *MCA* 89

14 **IF IT ISN'T LOVE**
New Edition *MCA* 88

15 **DON'T BE CRUEL**
Bobby Brown *MCA* 88

16 **ROCK WIT'CHA**
Bobby Brown *MCA* 89

17 **HIT ME OFF**
New Edition *MCA* 96

18 **MY, MY, MY**
Johnny Gill *Motown* 90

19 **GET AWAY** Bobby Brown *MCA* 93

20 **MR. TELEPHONE MAN**
New Edition *MCA* 85

The Top 20 Songs of THE OSMONDS

"THE [MORMON] church encourages talent, beginning with such things as singing, sports, and speeches, when the children are small. That's how the four boys got started singing together," Olive Osmond is quoted in Irwin Stambler's *The Encyclopedia of Pop, Rock and Soul.*

In 1959, four Osmond brothers—Alan, Wayne, Merrill, and Jay—sang in church and rehearsed barbershop quartet songs at home. On a visit to Disneyland, the boys gave an impromptu performance with the park's barbershop quartet, the Dapper Dans, and landed a gig with the *Disneyland After Dark* show. The Osmonds made their first network television appearance on Andy Williams' NBC variety show on December 20, 1962; one year later, on his sixth birthday, younger brother Donny made the Osmonds a quintet.

The brothers remained with Williams until his final broadcast in May 1967. They were signed to Williams' Barnaby label, and then moved to MCA's Uni label, but without any chart hits. That changed in 1971, when they signed with MGM Records and Mike Curb set out to duplicate the success of another set of five brothers—the Jackson 5.

Curb sent the Osmonds to Rick Hall, owner of the Fame studios in Muscle Shoals, Alabama. One of his staff writers, George Jones, had already penned "One Bad Apple." The Osmonds' recording of it went to No. 1 and stayed there for five weeks.

While "One Bad Apple" was still in the top 10, Donny's solo recording of an old Roy Orbison song debuted on the Hot 100. "Sweet And Innocent" peaked at No. 7. Donny's next single, a remake of "Go Away Little Girl," went to No. 1. Donny continued to record new versions of old songs, including Paul Anka's "Puppy Love," Johnny Mathis' "The Twelfth Of Never," and Freddie Scott's "Hey Girl." His sister Marie followed the same pattern when she began releasing singles in 1973. Donny and Marie also did a series of duets together, again specializing in remakes.

The Osmonds' chart attack ended in 1978. Without Donny, the four elder brothers reunited and became a country act in 1982, recording for Elektra, Warner Bros., and EMI America. Marie also became a country singer, racking up three No. 1 hits and moving from Elektra to RCA to Capitol. Donny dropped out of recording until 1988, when he signed with Virgin Records in the U.K. Unmarked copies of his single "Soldier Of Love" started getting airplay in the States, and listeners were surprised to find out they were enjoying Donny Osmond.

01 **ONE BAD APPLE**
The Osmonds *MGM* 71
02 **GO AWAY LITTLE GIRL**
Donny Osmond *MGM* 71
03 **YO-YO**
The Osmonds *MGM* 71
04 **SOLDIER OF LOVE**
Donny Osmond *Capitol* 89
05 **PUPPY LOVE**
Donny Osmond *MGM* 72
06 **DOWN BY THE LAZY RIVER**
The Osmonds *MGM* 72
07 **PAPER ROSES**
Marie Osmond *MGM* 73
08 **SWEET AND INNOCENT**
Donny Osmond *MGM* 71
09 **I'M LEAVING IT (ALL) UP TO YOU**
Donny and Marie Osmond *MGM* 74
10 **DEEP PURPLE**
Donny and Marie Osmond *MGM* 76
11 **THE TWELFTH OF NEVER**
Donny Osmond *MGM* 73
12 **HEY GIRL / I KNEW YOU WHEN**
Donny Osmond *MGM* 72
13 **MORNING SIDE OF THE MOUNTAIN**
Donny and Marie Osmond *MGM* 75
14 **WHY / LONELY BOY**
Donny Osmond *MGM* 72
15 **SACRED EMOTION**
Donny Osmond *Capitol* 89
16 **TOO YOUNG**
Donny Osmond *MGM* 72
17 **DOUBLE LOVIN'**
The Osmonds *MGM* 71
18 **LOVE ME FOR A REASON**
The Osmonds *MGM* 74
19 **CRAZY HORSES**
The Osmonds *MGM* 72
20 **HOLD HER TIGHT**
The Osmonds *MGM* 72

The Top 20 Songs of
PUFF DADDY/P. DIDDY/DIDDY

WHEN SEAN "PUFFY" COMBS was a student at Howard University in Washington, he wanted to be a singer but realized that singing was not a talent he was blessed with. He considered being a rapper but didn't have the patience to write rhymes. He considered a dance career, but after a turn in a Fine Young Cannibals video, he concluded that wasn't his calling either. So he decided the business side of the record industry was for him.

Through his friend Heavy D, he obtained an unpaid internship at Andre Harrell's Uptown Records in New York. He went to the office two days a week, after hiding in the bathroom of the Amtrak commuter train because he couldn't afford to buy a ticket. He was 18 when he was given a paid position in the label's A&R department and worked his way up to vice-president. He was supervising the careers of Mary J. Blige and Jodeci when he clashed with Harrell over the hiring of a general manager for Uptown. That led to Combs' dismissal.

He was depressed about his future until producer and label owner L.A. Reid introduced him to Clive Davis. Other companies bid for Combs' Bad Boy Entertainment, but he signed a partnership deal with Davis' Arista Records. A year after starting up, the company had an enviable artists' roster that included Faith Evans, 112, Craig Mack, Total, and the Notorious B.I.G.

But the artist who gave Bad Boy its first No. 1 on the Hot 100 was the company's founder. "Can't Nobody Hold Me Down," based on the pop hit "Break My Stride" by Matthew Wilder and sampling the hook from Grandmaster Flash and the Furious Five's seminal rap hit "The Message," topped the chart in March 1997. Rapping on the song was provided by a new Bad Boy artist, 19-year-old Mase.

Combs dominated the Hot 100 in 1997. "Can't Nobody Hold Me Down" was succeeded by the Notorious B.I.G.'s posthumous single "Hypnotize." In June, "I'll Be Missing You" by Puff Daddy and Faith Evans featuring 112, a tribute to the late B.I.G., began an 11-week reign and was replaced by "Mo Money Mo Problems" by B.I.G., Puffy, and Mase. That in turn was followed by Mariah Carey's "Honey," co-written and co-produced by Combs, giving him 26 non-consecutive weeks at No. 1 in 1997.

Changing his name from Puff Daddy to P. Diddy to Diddy, Combs expanded into other businesses, as he started his own clothing line, opened restaurants, and produced the second and third seasons of *Making The Band* for MTV, giving birth to the groups Da Band and Danity Kane. He also became a serious actor, with roles in films (*Monster's Ball*) and Broadway (*A Raisin In The Sun*).

01 I'LL BE MISSING YOU
Puff Daddy & Faith Evans f/112 *Bad Boy* 97
02 MO MONEY MO PROBLEMS
The Notorious B.I.G. f/Puff Daddy & Mase
Bad Boy 97
03 CAN'T NOBODY HOLD ME DOWN
Puff Daddy f/Mase *Bad Boy* 97
04 SHAKE YA TAILFEATHER
Nelly, P. Diddy & Murphy Lee *Bad Boy* 03
05 I DON'T WANNA KNOW
Mario Winans f/Enya & P. Diddy *Bad Boy* 04
06 I NEED A GIRL (PART ONE)
P. Diddy f/Usher & Loon *Bad Boy* 02
07 BUMP, BUMP, BUMP
B2K & P. Diddy *T.U.G.* 03
08 I NEED A GIRL (PART TWO)
P. Diddy & Ginuwine f/Loon, Mario Winans &
Tammy Ruggeri *Bad Boy* 02
09 SATISFY YOU
Puff Daddy f/R. Kelly *Bad Boy* 99
10 BEEN AROUND THE WORLD
Puff Daddy & the Family f/
the Notorious B.I.G. & Mase *Bad Boy* 98
11 COME WITH ME
Puff Daddy f/Jimmy Page *Bad Boy* 98
12 LOOKIN' AT ME
Mase f/Puff Daddy *Bad Boy* 98
13 PASS THE COURVOISIER PART II
Busta Rhymes f/P. Diddy & Pharrell
Bad Boy 02
14 NO TIME
Lil' Kim f/Puff Daddy *Undeas/Big Beat* 97
15 COME TO ME
Diddy f/Nicole Scherzinger *Bad Boy* 06
16 ALL NIGHT LONG
Faith Evans f/Puff Daddy *Bad Boy* 99
17 SOMEONE
SWV f/Puff Daddy *RCA* 97
18 VICTORY Puff Daddy & the Family f/the
Notorious B.I.G. & Busta Rhymes *Bad Boy* 98
19 TRADE IT ALL
Fabolous f/P. Diddy & Jagged Edge *Epic* 02
20 BREATHE, STRETCH, SHAKE
Mase f/Puff Daddy *Bad Boy* 04

The Top 20 Songs of
MARTHA REEVES & THE VANDELLAS

WHEN MARTHA Reeves was very young, she was encouraged to sing by her mother Ruby and her elementary school teacher Emily Wagstaff. When her high school music teacher, Abraham Silver, asked her to sing lead soprano at a recital, she saw her name in print in the program, and her interest in singing as a career was sparked.

Martha formed a group called the Fascinations, and when that didn't work out, she joined the Del-Phis, a group that included future Vandellas Rosalind Ashford, Annette Beard, and lead singer Gloria Williamson. When they went their separate ways, Martha continued to perform. She won a talent contest in Detroit and was given three nights' work at the popular 20 Grand club. Mickey Stevenson, head of Motown's A&R department, caught her performance during Happy Hour and asked her to come to Motown. Martha was so excited she quit her job at Citywide Cleaners and reported to Motown the following morning. She then discovered her error—Stevenson had only intended for her to call and arrange an audition. In a fateful moment, the executive asked if she would answer the phone while he stepped out. An hour later, Martha had reorganized Mickey's office and was hired as a secretary.

Her singing ambitions were not forgotten. When Mary Wells missed a session, Martha was quickly recruited to step up to the microphone, as union reps were checking to make sure the company was following the rule that a vocalist would always be at the microphone when session musicians were playing. Soon after, Martha hired Rosalind, Annette, and Gloria to join her on backing vocals for a Marvin Gaye session. The women were then allowed to record on their own as the Vells, with Gloria singing lead. When Gloria decided to keep her job with the city, Berry Gordy wanted to find out who was staying and who was leaving and what they were going to call themselves. Martha combined the name of singer "Della Reese" with the name of a street in her neighborhood, Van Dyke, to come up with "the Vandellas."

The trio's first single, "I'll Have To Let Him Go," missed the mark, but then they were teamed up with Brian Holland, Lamont Dozier, and Eddie Holland. Martha & the Vandellas recorded one of their first songs, "Come And Get These Memories," and made it onto the Hot 100 at last.

Martha's best-performing chart single, "Dancing In The Street," was first offered to Kim Weston, who turned it down. Martha was asked to record a demo, and while she shared Kim's feelings about the song initially, writer/producer Mickey Stevenson knew immediately that the song belonged to Martha Reeves.

The Top 20 Songs of LINDA RONSTADT

L INDA MARIA RONSTADT was born in Tucson, Arizona, where her father Gilbert, who loved to play guitar for his three children, owned a hardware store. Along with brother Mike and sister Suzi, Linda formed a group, the Three Ronstadts, and sang at local functions. In her freshman year at the University of Arizona, Linda took off for California, where she organized an acoustic folk-rock band with friends Bob Kimmel and Ken Edwards. They called themselves the Stone Poneys and won fans through their gigs at the Troubadour in Los Angeles. They were signed to Capitol by staff producer Nick Venet. In November 1967, their recording of Michael Nesmith's "Different Drum" became their first chart entry on the Hot 100, where it peaked at No. 13.

The Stone Poneys disbanded, but they still owed their label another album. Ronstast fulfilled the commitment with a solo effort released under the group's name. Then she began her real solo career with the album *Hand Sown, Home Grown*. Her second solo LP, *Silk Purse*, contained her first hit single under her own name, "Long Long Time." On her third album, her band included Don Henley, Glenn Frey, Bernie Leadon, and Randy Meisner, who went on to form the Eagles.

In May 1973, Peter Asher of the British pop duo Peter and Gordon became Ronstadt's manager and took over the producer's role on her *Don't Cry Now* album, her first for the Asylum label. Ronstadt still owed Capitol one more album, and the label wisely decided to release her next effort, *Heart Like A Wheel*. The LP contained Ronstadt's only No. 1 single on the Hot 100, a remake of the Betty Everett hit from 1964, "You're No Good."

That kicked off a series of remakes, including cover versions of the Everly Brothers' "When Will I Be Loved," Martha and the Vandellas' "Heat Wave," Roy Orbison's "Blue Bayou," Buddy Holly's "It's So Easy" and "That'll Be The Day," the Miracles' "Ooh Baby Baby" and "The Tracks Of My Tears," and Little Anthony and the Imperials' "Hurt So Bad."

But Ronstadt didn't limit herself to covering other artists. She tried new wave ("How Do I Make You") and sentimental ballads ("Somewhere Out There"). She recorded three albums of standards with Nelson Riddle. She starred as Mabel in the New York Shakespeare Festival production of Gilbert and Sullivan's *The Pirates Of Penzance.* She recorded country albums with Dolly Parton and Emmylou Harris. She tapped her Mexican American heritage to record albums of Latin favorites.

"She's about the best girl singer in the world in my prejudiced view," says Asher. "She can sing anything and does so incredibly well."

01 **DON'T KNOW MUCH**
Linda Ronstadt f/Aaron Neville *Elektra* 89

02 **BLUE BAYOU**
Linda Ronstadt *Asylum* 77

03 **WHEN WILL I BE LOVED**
Linda Ronstadt *Capitol* 75

04 **YOU'RE NO GOOD**
Linda Ronstadt *Capitol* 75

05 **SOMEWHERE OUT THERE**
Linda Ronstadt and James Ingram *MCA* 87

06 **IT'S SO EASY**
Linda Ronstadt *Asylum* 77

07 **HURT SO BAD**
Linda Ronstadt *Asylum* 80

08 **OOH BABY BABY**
Linda Ronstadt *Asylum* 79

09 **HOW DO I MAKE YOU**
Linda Ronstadt *Asylum* 80

10 **DIFFERENT DRUM**
Stone Poneys f/Linda Ronstadt *Capitol* 68

11 **HEAT WAVE / LOVE IS A ROSE**
Linda Ronstadt *Asylum* 75

12 **THAT'LL BE THE DAY**
Linda Ronstadt *Asylum* 76

13 **BACK IN THE U.S.A.**
Linda Ronstadt *Asylum* 78

14 **ALL MY LIFE**
Linda Ronstadt f/Aaron Neville *Elektra* 90

15 **LONG LONG TIME**
Linda Ronstadt *Capitol* 70

16 **TRACKS OF MY TEARS**
Linda Ronstadt *Asylum* 76

17 **GET CLOSER**
Linda Ronstadt *Asylum* 82

18 **I CAN'T LET GO**
Linda Ronstadt *Asylum* 80

19 **I KNEW YOU WHEN**
Linda Ronstadt *Asylum* 83

20 **SOMEONE TO LAY DOWN BESIDE ME**
Linda Ronstadt *Asylum* 77

The Top 20 Songs of BOB SEGER

ROBERT CLARK SEGER was born in Dearborn, Michigan, and was raised in Ann Arbor, where his father Stewart was a medic for the Ford Motor Company and a part-time bandleader. After his father left the family, young Seger and his brother George moved from their middle-class neighborhood with their mother Charlotte to the poor side of town. Late at night, when he was supposed to be asleep, Seger tuned his transistor radio to 50,000-watt WLAC, which came beaming in from Nashville. That's when Seger listened to the music of James Brown and Garnet Mimms and the Enchanters ("Cry Baby").

In 1961, Seger and his band the Decibels recorded a demo and convinced a DJ at WPAG in Ann Arbor to give it some airplay. "The Lonely One" had been recorded in Max Crook's basement—the same man who co-wrote Del Shannon's 1961 hit, "Runaway."

Next, Seger joined a band called the Mushrooms with a pre-Eagles Glenn Frey. In 1965, Cameo-Parkway Records in Philadelphia released Seger's "East Side Story." Three years later he signed with Capitol and made his Hot 100 debut with "Ramblin' Gamblin' Man," a No. 17 hit credited to the Bob Seger System. There were three more chart entries, but none rose above No. 80, and by 1972 Seger had left Capitol for Palladium, a Warner/Reprise imprint. Seger had two chart entries on that subsidiary, but neither could rise higher than No. 75. Seger recorded an album called *Beautiful Loser* for the label, but it was rejected and he took the project to Capitol, who re-signed the Michigan rocker in 1975.

Fortunately, Capitol had patience because the first few singles on the label weren't chart-burners. It wasn't until late 1976, when "Night Moves" debuted on the Hot 100 and peaked at No. 4 in early 1977, that Seger established himself as a hit-maker. He went to No. 4 again in 1978 with "Still The Same." He followed his second top 10 hit with top 20 titles "Hollywood Nights" and "We've Got Tonite" and the top 30 single "Old Time Rock & Roll" before returning to the top 10 with "Fire Lake" and the follow-up, "Against The Wind."

In 1983 Seger had his biggest hit to date when "Shame on the Moon" spent four weeks at No. 2. A little over four years later, he finally reached the No. 1 spot with "Shakedown," from the *Beverly Hills Cop II* soundtrack. Glenn Frey was meant to record the song but came down with laryngitis. He called MCA Records president Irv Azoff to give him the bad news, and Azoff called Seger and asked him to fill in. Seger received the track on a Friday, wrote new verses and kept the chorus, and sang the revised song for Azoff on Monday. A week later, it was recorded and mixed and ready for release.

P AUL SIMON and Art Garfunkel first met in 1953 during a sixth-grade production of *Alice In Wonderland*—Simon was the White Rabbit, Garfunkel was the Cheshire Cat. Two years later, they wrote their first song together, "The Girl For Me."

In 1957, their first record was released—"Hey, Schoolgirl" by Tom and Jerry, on the Big Top label. It went as high as No. 49 on the Hot 100 and earned them an appearance on *American Bandstand*. Subsequent Tom and Jerry singles failed to chart, and Simon and Garfunkel went separate ways after high school. Paul attended Queens College as an English major, and Art studied mathematics and architecture at Columbia University. Both continued their recording careers under a variety of assumed names. Simon made two more appearances on the Hot 100—as the leader of Tico & the Triumphs, with "Motorcycle," and as Jerry Landis, with "The Lone Teen Ranger." Art had two singles released as Artie Garr.

They remained friends and worked together in 1964, performing in Greenwich Village coffeehouses. A demo tape impressed Tom Wilson at Columbia Records, who signed the duo to the label. Paul moved to England, but came back to record *Wednesday Morning, 3 AM*. When a Boston radio station played one of the tracks, "The Sounds Of Silence," Wilson was encouraged to remix the acoustic cut with electric guitar, bass, and drums. Paul received a phone call one day telling him the single had gone to No. 1 on the *Billboard* chart.

Simon & Garfunkel's most successful Hot 100 single was released in 1970. Paul wrote "Bridge Over Troubled Water" during the summer of '69; the song was inspired by his love of gospel quartets, particularly the Swan Silvertones.

While it was their biggest hit yet, it also marked the end of Simon and Garfunkel working together. Disagreements and tension during the recording of the album *Bridge Over Troubled Water* had built to a point where both felt it was best to pursue individual careers. The two came back together in 1975 for a reunion single, "My Little Town." Six years later, Simon and Garfunkel reunited again to give a free concert in Central Park, which led to a tour of Europe and then the United States. A single from the Central Park concert, a revival of "Wake Up Little Susie," made the top 30 in 1982.

Garfunkel hit No. 1 twice in Britain, with "I Only Have Eyes For You" and "Bright Eyes." Simon has won critical raves for albums like *Graceland* and *Rhythm Of The Saints,* but singles from those lauded albums did not perform well on the Hot 100.

01 BRIDGE OVER TROUBLED WATER
Simon and Garfunkel *Columbia* 70

02 MRS. ROBINSON
Simon and Garfunkel *Columbia* 70

03 50 WAYS TO LEAVE YOUR LOVER
Paul Simon *Columbia* 76

04 THE SOUNDS OF SILENCE
Simon and Garfunkel *Columbia* 66

05 LOVES ME LIKE A ROCK
Paul Simon *Columbia* 73

06 KODACHROME
Paul Simon *Columbia* 73

07 I AM A ROCK
Simon and Garfunkel *Columbia* 66

08 SLIP SLIDIN' AWAY
Paul Simon *Columbia* 78

09 LATE IN THE EVENING
Paul Simon *Warner Bros.* 80

10 CECELIA
Simon and Garfunkel *Columbia* 70

11 MOTHER AND CHILD REUNION
Paul Simon *Columbia* 72

12 THE BOXER
Simon and Garfunkel *Columbia* 69

13 ALL I KNOW
Art Garfunkel *Columbia* 73

14 MY LITTLE TOWN
Simon and Garfunkel *Columbia* 75

15 HOMEWARD BOUND
Simon and Garfunkel *Columbia* 66

16 I ONLY HAVE EYES FOR YOU
Art Garfunkel *Columbia* 75

17 SCARBOROUGH FAIR/CANTICLE
Simon and Garfunkel *Columbia* 68

18 ME AND JULIO DOWN BY THE SCHOOLYARD
Paul Simon *Columbia* 72

19 A HAZY SHADE OF WINTER
Simon and Garfunkel *Columbia* 66

20 (WHAT A) WONDERFUL WORLD
Art Garfunkel w/James Taylor & Paul Simon *Columbia* 78

The Top 20 Songs of SONNY and CHER

SONNY BONO first made his mark in the record business as a songwriter, penning songs like "Needles And Pins" for Jackie DeShannon and the Searchers, and "Koko Joe" for the Righteous Brothers. When he met Cherilyn Sarkisian LaPierre at a Hollywood coffee shop, he was working for producer Phil Spector. "I was his West Coast promotion man, I sang background, and I hired the musicians and background singers," Sonny explained. He hired Cher to sing backing vocals on Spector tracks like the Crystals' "Da Doo Ron Ron" and the Ronettes' "Be My Baby."

At Sonny's request, Spector even produced a track for Cher, "Ringo, I Love You" (released under the name Bonnie Jo Mason). Then Sonny borrowed enough money to produce his own session for Cher. She was too nervous to sing by herself and asked Sonny to duet with her on "Baby Don't Go." Vault Records released a song by the duo, "The Letter," under the names Caesar and Cleo, and Cher was signed as a solo artist to Imperial.

Ahmet Ertegun signed the duo to Atco; their first single as Sonny and Cher was "Just You." They were all over the Hot 100 in 1965, starting with "I Got You Babe." Cher's version of Bob Dylan's "All I Really Want To Do" bested the Byrds' recording of the same song, and Sonny's recording of "Laugh At Me"—inspired by being thrown out of Martoni's restaurant in Hollywood—was a top 10 entry.

It was a heady three years, but the top 10 hits stopped coming in 1967. Between 1968 and 1970, neither Sonny nor Cher appeared on The Billboard Hot 100. Their return was spearheaded by Snuff Garrett, who was asked by Johnny Musso of Kapp Records to produce the couple's first efforts for their new label. (Garrett had known Sonny and Cher for some time—he was at Liberty Records when Cher recorded for the Imperial subsidiary, and he was their neighbor in the affluent community of Bel Air.) Garrett gave Sonny and Cher their biggest hits outside of "I Got You Babe": "All I Ever Need Is You," a remake of a song Garrett heard on a Ray Charles album, and "A Cowboy's Work Is Never Done" returned the husband and wife to the top 10.

In 1975, Sonny and Cher's divorce was finalized. Sonny went into the restaurant business in 1983 and then into politics. In 1988, he was elected mayor of Palm Springs, and after a failed try for the U.S. Senate, was elected to the House of Representatives. He was killed on January 5, 1998, in a skiing accident. Cher concentrated on her film career during the '80s, and won an Oscar for her performance in *Moonstruck*. Thirty-four years after her chart debut, she had the biggest hit of her career in 1999 with "Believe."

The Top 20 Songs of RICK SPRINGFIELD

RICHARD LEWIS SPRINGTHORPE was born in Sydney, Australia. His father was in the military, which meant the family lived in many different places down under and in Great Britain before settling in Melbourne. The time in England made a great impression on nine-year-old Rick. The other kids made fun of his accent, which made him even more shy than he already was. At the same time, he was a fan of the British rock scene, which was influencing his musical tastes.

He received a guitar on his 13th birthday and was soon spending more time as front man for the Jordy Boys than on his homework. In 1967, he dropped out of high school to join a band called Rock House. Next came Wickedy Wak and then Zoot, a group that became popular in Australia as the '60s came to a close.

The next step was a solo career, and as Rick Springfield he scored a hit at home with "Speak To The Sky," which caught the attention of Capitol Records in America. Springfield knew he had to try for a career in the United States and signed with the Hollywood-based label. "Speak To The Sky" was his Hot 100 debut, peaking at No. 14 in 1972. But Rick was unhappy that Capitol was promoting him as a teen idol. He moved to Columbia and recorded an album called *Comic Book Heroes*. There were no hit singles and this time it was the label that was disappointed, as they expected Springfield to be the next David Cassidy.

Legal tangles with his manager and hassles with U.S. Immigration led to three inactive years in the recording industry. To fill the time, Springfield enrolled in acting school. When he was able to record again, he signed with Chelsea Records. His Chelsea album was released, and a short time later, while Rick was on the road promoting the album, the label closed its doors. But the acting lessons paid off as Universal signed him to a contract and he was cast as a guest star in episodic television shows like *Wonder Woman* and *The Rockford Files*.

A recurring role on *The Young And The Restless* was next, as was a deal with RCA Records. Two months after signing with the label, he was cast as Dr. Noah Drake on ABC-TV's *General Hospital*. The role made him a star, so he was a well-known quantity when RCA issued the single "Jessie's Girl." In August 1981, that single moved into the penthouse on the Hot 100 and stayed there for two weeks.

In 1984, Springfield starred in the film *Hard To Hold*. The soundtrack yielded the No. 5 hit, "Love Somebody." His most recent turn in the top 30 of the Hot 100 was in 1988.

Springfield returned to the role of Dr. Noah Drake on *General Hospital* in December 2005.

01 **JESSIE'S GIRL**
Rick Springfield *RCA* 81

02 **DON'T TALK TO STRANGERS**
Rick Springfield *RCA* 82

03 **AFFAIR OF THE HEART**
Rick Springfield *RCA* 83

04 **LOVE SOMEBODY**
Rick Springfield *RCA* 84

05 **I'VE DONE EVERYTHING FOR YOU**
Rick Springfield *RCA* 81

06 **HUMAN TOUCH**
Rick Springfield *RCA* 83

07 **SPEAK TO THE SKY**
Rick Springfield *Capitol* 72

08 **WHAT KIND OF FOOL AM I**
Rick Springfield *RCA* 82

09 **LOVE IS ALRIGHT TONITE**
Rick Springfield *RCA* 82

10 **BOP 'TIL YOU DROP**
Rick Springfield *RCA* 84

11 **STATE OF THE HEART**
Rick Springfield *RCA* 85

12 **ROCK OF LIFE**
Rick Springfield *RCA* 88

13 **SOULS**
Rick Springfield *RCA* 83

14 **DON'T WALK AWAY**
Rick Springfield *RCA* 84

15 **CELEBRATE YOUTH**
Rick Springfield *RCA* 85

16 **BRUCE**
Rick Springfield *RCA* 85

17 **I GET EXCITED**
Rick Springfield *RCA* 82

18 **TAKE A HAND**
Rick Springfield *Chelsea* 76

19 **TAXI DANCING**
Rick Springfield w/Randy Crawford *RCA* 84

20 **WHAT WOULD THE CHILDREN THINK**
Rick Springfield *Capitol* 72

The Top 20 Songs of STING/THE POLICE

GORDON SUMNER—nicknamed Sting because of the yellow and black jersey he liked to wear—was lucky enough to have diverse musical influences as a child. His father, a milkman, loved Sinatra, the soundtrack to *Singin' In The Rain,* and the works of Rodgers and Hammerstein. His mother was a piano player with a passion for tango music, but she also loved rock and roll. She brought Elvis Presley's "All Shook Up" and Jerry Lee Lewis' "Great Balls Of Fire" into the house, and young Gordon soaked it all in.

Growing up, he was a ditch digger, teacher, and civil servant before joining Lost Exit, a jazz band from Newcastle, England. Then he met an American drummer named Stewart Copeland, who was the son of a CIA agent and had been raised in the Middle East. Copeland was a member of Curved Air, a group that broke up in 1976. A year later, Sting and Copeland formed the Police with guitarist Henri Padovani. Their first single, "Fall Out," was issued on the Illegal label, owned by Stewart and his brother, Miles Copeland.

Soon after, Andy Summers joined as a second guitarist, but the group became a trio again with the departure of Padovani. In early 1978, A&M signed the band and made a deal to distribute the Copeland's label, now renamed I.R.S. In Britain, the first big hit was "Can't Stand Losing You," which peaked at No. 2 in the summer of 1979. In the U.S., real success didn't come until January 1981, when "De Do Do Do, De Da Da Da" went to No. 10.

Two-and-a-half years later, the Police captured the biggest hit of their career; "Every Breath You Take," from the *Synchronicity* album, featured a light reggae beat and lyrics about surveillance, ownership, and jealousy. The single ruled the Hot 100 for eight weeks. Despite including their biggest hit, *Synchronicity* turned out to be the band's final studio album. Rehearsals for a new album began in the summer of 1986, but Sting was more interested in acting and recording on his own. His first solo album, *Dream Of The Blue Turtles,* had a six-week run at No. 2 in 1985.

In January 1994 Sting reached the top of the Hot 100 for the first time without the Police, but still in the company of two mates. He had been recruited by Bryan Adams to join him and Rod Stewart on "All For Love," from the soundtrack to *The Three Musketeers.* What started as a solo project for Adams expanded when composer Michael Kamen suggested, "Why don't we make the song with two other guys, and the three of you are the 'three musketeers?'"

01 **EVERY BREATH YOU TAKE**
The Police *A&M* 83

02 **ALL FOR LOVE**
Bryan Adams/Rod Stewart/Sting *A&M* 94

03 **IF YOU LOVE SOMEBODY SET THEM FREE**
Sting *A&M* 85

04 **EVERY LITTLE THING SHE DOES IS MAGIC**
The Police *A&M* 81

05 **KING OF PAIN**
The Police *A&M* 83

06 **DESERT ROSE**
Sting f/Cheb Mami *A&M* 00

07 **DE DO DO DO, DE DA DA DA**
The Police *A&M* 81

08 **FORTRESS AROUND YOUR HEART**
Sting *A&M* 85

09 **WE'LL BE TOGETHER**
Sting *A&M* 87

10 **DON'T STAND SO CLOSE TO ME**
The Police *A&M* 81

11 **WRAPPED AROUND YOUR FINGER**
The Police *A&M* 84

12 **ALL THIS TIME**
Sting *A&M* 91

13 **SPIRITS IN THE MATERIAL WORLD**
The Police *A&M* 82

14 **SYNCHRONICITY II**
The Police *A&M* 83

15 **IF I EVER LOSE MY FAITH IN YOU**
Sting *A&M* 93

16 **BE STILL MY BEATING HEART**
The Police *A&M* 88

17 **LOVE IS THE SEVENTH WAVE**
Sting *A&M* 85

18 **RUSSIANS**
Sting *A&M* 86

19 **FIELDS OF GOLD**
The Police *A&M* 93

20 **WHEN WE DANCE**
Sting *A&M* 94

The Top 20 Songs of DONNA SUMMER

MUSIC GAVE Donna Adrian Gaines a way of carving out her own identity in a family of six sisters and one brother. As a child, Donna was a devout fan of Mahalia Jackson, and at age 10 she was singing with gospel groups in churches around her native Boston.

At 18, she moved to New York and auditioned to be Melba Moore's replacement in the Broadway cast of *Hair.* Instead, she was offered a road-company version—in Munich. She stayed a year, then transferred to the Vienna cast. She joined the Vienna Folk Opera for *Porgy And Bess* and *Show Boat,* and while living in Austria met and married an actor named Helmut Sommer. After their divorce, she retained an Anglicized spelling of his last name for her professional moniker.

After returning to Germany, Donna continued her stage work, but was also popular as a session vocalist, recording demos and backing vocals in English. It was at a demo session that she met producers Giorgio Moroder and Pete Bellotte, who signed her to their Oasis label and released a single, "The Hostage." It was a hit across Europe, but success failed to translate to England or America. Her transatlantic crossing took place when she collaborated with Moroder and Bellotte on a 16-minute, 50-second erotic dance track, "Love To Love You Baby." Neil Bogart of the American label Casablanca was captivated by the track and found himself with a huge hit in dance clubs as well as a No. 2 single on the Hot 100.

Donna's most successful chart single, "Hot Stuff," introduced a new ingredient to her dance hits—rock and roll. "We thought it was time to incorporate some other elements into the music," says Donna. "It was getting a little bit boring, with the strings. . . . I've always liked rock and roll music, so I wanted to give it a little bit of an edge." When Bogart first heard "Bad Girls," the follow-up to "Hot Stuff" and Summer's second-biggest hit, he thought it was too rock and roll for the disco diva and suggested she give the song to Casablanca labelmate Cher. "I really got upset with that!" Donna remembers. "It had nothing to do with Cher. I felt that it could be a hit record for me and I wasn't giving it to anybody. So I took it and put it away." It remained on the shelf for two years before it was rediscovered and recorded anew.

After Moroder and Bellotte, Donna worked with producers Quincy Jones, Michael Omartian, and the British trio of Mike Stock, Matt Aitken, and Pete Waterman, who brought her back to the top 10 in 1989 with "This Time I Know It's For Real."

01 HOT STUFF
Donna Summer *Casablanca* 79
02 BAD GIRLS
Donna Summer *Casablanca* 79
03 MACARTHUR PARK
Donna Summer *Casablanca* 78
04 NO MORE TEARS (ENOUGH IS ENOUGH)
Barbra Streisand and Donna Summer
Columbia 79
05 LOVE TO LOVE YOU BABY
Donna Summer *Oasis* 76
06 DIM ALL THE LIGHTS
Donna Summer *Casablanca* 79
07 SHE WORKS HARD FOR THE MONEY
Donna Summer *Mercury* 83
08 LAST DANCE
Donna Summer *Casablanca* 78
09 THE WANDERER
Donna Summer *Geffen* 80
10 HEAVEN KNOWS
Donna Summer w/Brooklyn Dreams
Casablanca 79
11 I FEEL LOVE
Donna Summer *Casablanca* 77
12 ON THE RADIO
Donna Summer *Casablanca* 80
13 LOVE IS IN CONTROL
(FINGER ON THE TRIGGER)
Donna Summer *Geffen* 82
14 THIS TIME I KNOW IT'S FOR REAL
Donna Summer *Atlantic* 89
15 THERE GOES MY BABY
Donna Summer *Geffen* 84
16 THE WOMAN IN ME
Donna Summer *Geffen* 83
17 COLD LOVE
Donna Summer *Geffen* 81
18 WALK AWAY
Donna Summer *Casablanca* 80
19 I LOVE YOU
Donna Summer *Casablanca* 78
20 STATE OF INDEPENDENCE
Donna Summer *Geffen* 82

The Top 20 Songs of THREE DOG NIGHT

T HERE WERE THREE VOCALISTS in Three Dog Night, but despite its moniker, the group was a septet of singers and musicians who had all worked together professionally before coming together as a band. Irish-born Danny Hutton worked for Walt Disney Studios before moving over to the Hanna-Barbera animation production house, where he did voice-overs. When Bill Hanna and Joseph Barbera formed a record company, HBR, Hutton was signed as an artist. He released "Roses And Rainbows" in 1965 and later moved to MGM, where he recorded "Funny How Love Can Be."

Buffalo, New York, native Cory Wells was lead vocalist for the Los Angeles–based group the Enemies, the house band at the Whisky-A-Go-Go on the Sunset Strip. Wanting to move on, Wells asked Hutton if he'd like to team up as an act, but Hutton wanted to concentrate on his solo career and declined. About 18 months later, Hutton was driving by the Ambassador Hotel on Wilshire Boulevard and noticed a display of classic cars on the front lawn. Hutton observed that each car was an integral part of the overall display and thought the same concept could be applied to a musical group. He called Wells, and they made a plan to invite their friend Chuck Negron over, supposedly to sit around the piano and sing some songs. But their secret plan was to enroll him in their new group.

Bronx-born Negron had a high tenor voice that blended well with Cory's soulful sound and Hutton's pop vocals. The three singers recruited four musicians to complete the band: lead guitarist Mike Allsup, organist Jim Greenspoon, bassist Joe Schermie, and drummer Floyd Sneed. The group name came from an expression used in the Australian outback. On a cold night, you sleep with one dog to keep you warm. If it's very cold, you need two dogs. And when the mercury plunges so low that your blood turns to icewater, that's a three dog night.

The debut single by the seven-man band, a remake of Kim Weston's "Nobody," failed to chart. In February 1969, Three Dog Night found itself on the Hot 100 with "Try A Little Tenderness," a hit in 1933 for Ted Lewis, but better known to the '70s band as an Otis Redding single from the '60s. The next batch of Three Dog Night singles highlighted the band's ability to hone in on outstanding songwriters. Before 1969 was over, the group charted with covers of Nilsson's "One" and Laura Nyro's "Eli's Coming" as well as a song from the Broadway musical *Hair*, "Easy To Be Hard."

In July 1970 Three Dog Night gave Randy Newman his only No. 1 song on the Hot 100 with a remake of his "Mama Told Me (Not To Come)." Wells was familiar with Newman's original and a cover by Eric Burdon and tried to get the group to record it when they first got together. He met with some resistance, but the other six members finally agreed to cut it for their third album.

The Top 20 Songs of IKE & TINA TURNER

TINA TURNER was born in Nutbush, Tennessee, and given the name Annie Mae Bullock by her family's Baptist minister. Annie's father was a caretaker on a plantation, and she grew up picking cotton. When her parents divorced, the teen-aged Annie Mae moved to St. Louis with her mother. The hottest band in the city played at an after-hours place called Club Manhattan. Annie Mae's sister was dating the drummer, and one night he came to the table and teased his girl with the microphone. Annie Mae grabbed the mic and started singing, and that's how she met the leader of the band, Ike Turner.

Married to Ike and renamed Tina (because "Ike and Tina Turner" sounded better, she has said), her career was launched. The husband-and-wife duo first appeared on the Hot 100 the week of August 29, 1960, with "A Fool In Love," which peaked at No. 27. A series of chart entries on the Sue label followed.

In early 1966, Ike and Tina appeared in a filmed rock concert, *The TNT Show*, under the musical direction of Phil Spector. He was so impressed with Tina that he signed the couple to his Philles label. Their first single together is considered a Spector masterpiece, even though "River Deep–Mountain High" only managed to reach No. 88 on the Hot 100.

In 1969, Ike and Tina signed with Blue Thumb and recorded a couple of albums. But top 10 success on the singles chart didn't arrive until 1971, when Liberty Records issued their take on Creedence Clearwater Revival's "Proud Mary." An autobiographical 1973 single, "Nutbush City Limits," outlined Tina's life and a year later Tina recorded some solo material. In 1975, director Ken Russell cast her as the Acid Queen in the filmed version of the Who's rock opera *Tommy*.

By this time, the Turner marriage was crumbling. As Tina would detail later, there was "one last bit of real violence" and she left. She had 36 cents in her pocket, a gasoline charge card, and the clothes she was wearing. She went to a Ramada Inn in Dallas, where the hotel manager gave her his best suite. Tina paid him back two years later.

She called Ann-Margret, a friend from the cast of *Tommy*, and asked if she would pay for an airline ticket to Los Angeles. Tina spent six months with Ann-Margret while Ike searched for her frantically. The couple was divorced in 1976.

For the next eight years, Tina toured 9 months out of every 12 to pay off her debts. She signed to Capitol in 1982 and released a cover of Al Green's "Let's Stay Together." Her second single for the label was composed by U.K. songwriters Terry Britten and Graham Lyle. She didn't care for their demo, but they promised they would change it to suit her style. In September 1984, Turner reached No. 1 for the first time with Britten and Lyle's "What's Love Got To Do With It."

L ARRY MULLEN was a 14-year-old student at Mount Temple Comprehensive School in Dublin when he posted a notice on the bulletin board announcing his intention to form a rock band and asking fellow students who were interested to contact him. Less than a week after the notice went up, a group of students gathered at his parents' home to play some Rolling Stones' songs.

Mullen knew right away that David Evans could play the guitar and that bass player Adam Clayton, with his bushy hair and long caftan coat, looked the part. Another student, Paul Hewson, wanted to play guitar, but he wasn't very good, so Hewson tried singing instead. "He couldn't do that either," Mullen told *Time* years later. "But he was such a charismatic character that he was in the band anyway, as soon as he arrived." Hewson got his nickname from a sign advertising a hearing aid store. It read, "Bono Vox of O'Connell Street." Bono in turn gave Evans his nickname, the Edge (which he described as "the border between something and nothing").

The four members considered different names, including Feedback and the Hype, but a local musician suggested U2, for the high-altitude spy plane, like the one U.S. pilot Francis Gary Powers was flying over the Soviet Union when it was shot down.

U2 spent a lot of time opening for other Irish bands. They won a talent competition for rock groups that led to a deal with CBS Records for Ireland only. After one EP of three songs, CBS declined to sign U2 for the rest of the world. That led Bono to distribute tapes of the band's live performances to friendly music journalists. The British rock weeklies like *Sounds* and *New Musical Express* wrote kind words about the band, but that didn't result in a new label deal.

Showcases in London didn't arouse any interest either, so U2 returned home and toured Ireland, concluding with a concert at a 2,000-seat stadium in Dublin. Bill Stewart from Island Records saw that show and, in 1980, signed U2 to the label.

Of the first six U2 albums to chart in America, none went higher than No. 12. In 1987, the group released an album named after the gnarled trees that grow in the desert areas of the southwestern United States. *The Joshua Tree* spent nine weeks at No. 1 and yielded two chart-topping singles, "With Or Without You" and "I Still Haven't Found What I'm Looking For."

Bono has become as well-known for his social activism as for his music. Among the causes he supports are relief of debt in developing countries and the eradication of AIDS in Africa.

01 **WITH OR WITHOUT YOU**
U2 *Island* 87

02 **I STILL HAVEN'T FOUND WHAT I'M LOOKING FOR**
U2 *Island* 87

03 **DESIRE**
U2 *Island* 88

04 **ONE**
U2 *Island* 92

05 **MYSTERIOUS WAYS**
U2 *Island* 92

06 **BEAUTIFUL DAY**
U2 *Island* 01

07 **THEME FROM MISSION: IMPOSSIBLE**
Adam Clayton & Larry Mullen *Mother* 96

08 **HOLD ME, THRILL ME, KISS ME, KILL ME**
U2 *Island* 95

09 **WHERE THE STREETS HAVE NO NAME**
U2 *Island* 87

10 **ANGEL OF HARLEM**
U2 *Island* 89

11 **STARING AT THE SUN**
U2 *Island* 97

12 **DISCOTHEQUE**
U2 *Island* 97

13 **VERTIGO**
U2 *Interscope* 04

14 **EVEN BETTER THAN THE REAL THING**
U2 *Island* 92

15 **WHO'S GONNA RIDE YOUR WILD HORSES**
U2 *Island* 92

16 **STUCK IN A MOMENT YOU CAN'T GET OUT OF** U2 *Interscope* 01

17 **PRIDE (IN THE NAME OF LOVE)**
U2 *Island* 84

18 **IN GOD'S COUNTRY**
U2 *Island* 88

19 **STAY (FARAWAY, SO CLOSE)**
U2 *Island* 94

20 **SWEETEST THING**
U2 *Island* 98

The Top 20 Songs of VAN HALEN/ DAVID LEE ROTH/SAMMY HAGAR

BORN IN HOLLAND, Eddie Van Halen and his older brother Alex relocated with their family to Pasadena, California, in 1968. As children they had studied classical music but once in Southern California they quickly got into the rock and roll scene. At first Eddie played the drums and Alex took up guitar but they switched instruments and formed a band at Pasadena High School called Mammoth.

Michael Anthony, a student at nearby Arcadia High School, led a rival group before joining the Van Halens. David Lee Roth, who attended Muir High in Pasadena, sang for another arch-rival band before joining forces with the Van Halen brothers. "I wanted to be in a real band, make records, travel, and do all that stuff," Roth explained to Robert Hilburn in *The Los Angeles Times*.

The Van Halens rocked the staid city of Pasadena and brought their hard-edged energy to clubs in Van Nuys, Glendora, and Redondo Beach. Gene Simmons from Kiss became a mentor, helping them record a demo tape and passing the word about them to staffers at various record labels in Los Angeles—all of which passed on signing the quartet. In 1977, producer Ted Templeman from the Warner Bros. label caught Van Halen at the Starwood club in West Hollywood and convinced company chairman Mo Ostin to sign the band.

From its chart debut in 1978, Van Halen was an album act, with five of its first six LPs hitting the top 10. On the Hot 100, the group missed the top 10 with its first seven entries. But in February 1984, Van Halen began a five-week reign with what would be the biggest single of the band's career, "Jump."

Exactly a year after "Jump" debuted on the Hot 100, Roth was on the chart with singles from a solo project. A remake of the Beach Boys' "California Girls" matched the original's peak position by reaching No. 3. A disciple of Al Jolson, Roth next turned to a couple of songs from the '20s and '30s, copying Louis Prima's arrangement of "Just A Gigolo/I Ain't Got Nobody," which went to No. 12.

In the middle of this solo success, Roth quit Van Halen and was replaced by rocker Sammy Hagar, who began his chart career as lead singer for the San Francisco band Montrose. That group charted four albums between 1974 and 1976, then broke up in 1977. Hagar made his solo debut that year and continued to record his own solo albums during his Van Halen tenure, which lasted until 1996. He was succeeded by Gary Cherone from Extreme for one album, though Roth returned briefly in 1997.

01 **JUMP**
Van Halen *Warner Bros.* 84

02 **WHY CAN'T THIS BE LOVE**
Van Halen *Warner Bros.* 86

03 **CALIFORNIA GIRLS**
David Lee Roth *Warner Bros.* 85

04 **WHEN IT'S LOVE**
Van Halen *Warner Bros.* 88

05 **JUST LIKE PARADISE**
David Lee Roth *Warner Bros.* 88

06 **YOUR LOVE IS DRIVING ME CRAZY**
Sammy Hagar *Geffen* 83

07 **(OH) PRETTY WOMAN**
Van Halen *Warner Bros.* 82

08 **FINISH WHAT YA STARTED**
Van Halen *Warner Bros.* 88

09 **JUST A GIGOLO/I AIN'T GOT NOBODY**
David Lee Roth *Warner Bros.* 85

10 **I'LL WAIT**
Van Halen *Warner Bros.* 84

11 **PANAMA**
Van Halen *Warner Bros.* 84

12 **DANCE THE NIGHT AWAY**
Van Halen *Warner Bros.* 79

13 **YANKEE ROSE**
David Lee Roth *Warner Bros.* 86

14 **LOVE WALKS IN**
Van Halen *Warner Bros.* 86

15 **DREAMS**
Van Halen *Warner Bros.* 86

16 **GIVE TO LIVE**
Sammy Hagar *Geffen* 87

17 **I CAN'T DRIVE 55**
Sammy Hagar *Geffen* 84

18 **TOP OF THE WORLD**
Van Halen *Warner Bros.* 91

19 **CAN'T STOP LOVIN' YOU**
Van Halen *Warner Bros.* 05

20 **FEELS SO GOOD**
Van Halen *Warner Bros.* 62

The Top 20 Songs of DIONNE WARWICK

MARIE DIONNE Warwick was born in East Orange, New Jersey, to a musical family—her father did gospel promotion for Chess Records, and her mother managed a church choir group. Forming a trio called the Gospelaires with her sister Dee Dee and cousin Cissy Houston, she did backing vocals for artists like Bobby Darin and the Drifters. One Drifters session found the girls singing background on "Mexican Divorce," written by Burt Bacharach and Bob Hilliard. Dionne asked to record some demos, so Florence Greenberg at Scepter Records suggested that Bacharach produce some sessions with Dionne. That resulted in a demo of "Don't Make Me Over."

Dionne charted with 38 different titles on Scepter between December 1962 and August 1971. All but five were written by Bacharach and Hal David. Her most successful Scepter single was one of those five, "(Theme From) *Valley Of The Dolls*," written by Dory and André Previn. Originally, that song was released as the B-side of Warwick's second-most-successful Scepter single, Bacharach-David's "I Say A Little Prayer."

Following her stint with Scepter, Dionne moved to Warner Bros. Records—without the services of her two main songwriters. Bacharach and David had ended their partnership, and despite working with writer/producers like Brian Holland and Lamont Dozier, Dionne had no chart success on Warner Bros. Her only hit between 1971 and 1978 was "Then Came You," produced by Thom Bell for Atlantic. Recorded with the Spinners, it was Dionne's first No. 1 hit.

Dionne's most successful single came about after the rift with Bacharach was repaired. When Bacharach and his wife Carole Bayer Sager were preparing material for Dionne to record in 1985, Carole remembered a song they had written three years earlier for the film *Night Shift*. Rod Stewart had recorded "That's What Friends Are For" for the closing credits, but Burt and Carole weren't happy with his rendition and it wasn't considered for single release.

Dionne thought the song would make a good duet with Stevie Wonder. When the two of them recorded the tune, Neil Simon and Elizabeth Taylor visited the studio. Knowing of Taylor's work to fight AIDS, Sager suggested that the proceeds from the song could be donated to the American Foundation for AIDS Research. Warwick, Wonder, and Taylor were all enthusiastic about the idea. Then a third vocalist was added to the track—Gladys Knight. Clive Davis then suggested that Elton John add his voice, and agreed to also donate Arista's profits.

The Top 20 Songs of THE WHO

WHEN YOU THINK of the Who, there are a number of things that might come immediately to mind, like smashing guitars and destroying hotel rooms, or the rock opera *Tommy*, or one of the most famous lines in rock music history, "Hope I die before I get old."

Two members of the Who did die before they got old. Drummer Keith Moon was 32 when he died on September 8, 1978, of an overdose of pills prescribed to prevent his abuse of alcohol. Bassist John Entwistle was 57 when he died of a heart attack on June 27, 2002. Singer Roger Daltrey and guitarist Pete Townshend continue to record and tour, with the *Endless Wire* album charting in 2006. Who songs can be heard on television every day of the week, in commercials and as the theme tunes to the three *CSI* series.

The story of the Who began in West London. Townshend and Entwistle, both born in Chiswick, formed their first group, the Confederates, while attending grammar school in Acton in 1959. Three years later, Daltrey started a group called the Detours, with Entwistle, who brought in Townshend. In 1964 they changed their name to the Who and became part of the London "mod" scene. They were playing a gig at the Oldfield pub and as they were without a drummer at the time, asked if anyone in the audience wanted to fill in. A drunk Keith Moon accepted the challenge, and the Who asked him to take the position permanently.

With a change of name to the High Numbers, the band was signed to the Brunswick label in the Unitd Kingdom. In February 1965, the quartet (known once again as the Who) made its U.K. singles chart debut with "I Can't Explain," which went to No. 8. One month later, the same song, issued on the Decca label in the United States, entered the Hot 100 but could only muster its way to No. 93. Two and a half years would pass before the Who earned its only top 10 single in America, "I Can See For Miles," which peaked at No. 9.

In May 1969, the Who's *Tommy* was released. The rock opera about a deaf, dumb, and blind boy reverberated on both sides of the Atlantic. "Pinball Wizard" was a single in the United Kingdom but not the United States, where "See Me, Feel Me" went to No. 12 and became the Who's second highest-charting single in America.

The Who released another rock opera, *Quadrophenia*, in 1973. It didn't match the success of *Tommy*, which lived on in adaptations directed by Ken Russell for the silver screen in 1975 and directed by Des McAnuff for the Broadway stage in 1993.

01 LET MY LOVE OPEN THE DOOR
Pete Townshend *Atco* 80

02 I CAN SEE FOR MILES
The Who *Decca* 67

03 WHO ARE YOU
The Who *MCA* 78

04 SQUEEZE BOX
The Who *MCA* 76

05 WON'T GET FOOLED AGAIN
The Who *Decca* 71

06 YOU BETTER YOU BET
The Who *Warner Bros.* 81

07 SEE ME, FEEL ME
The Who *Decca* 70

08 JOIN TOGETHER
The Who *Decca* 72

09 WITHOUT YOUR LOVE
Roger Daltrey *Polydor* 80

10 PINBALL WIZARD
The Who *Decca* 69

11 MAGIC BUS
The Who *Decca* 68

12 FACE THE FACE
Pete Townshend *Atco* 86

13 ATHENA
The Who *Warner Bros.* 82

14 SUMMERTIME BLUES
The Who *Decca* 70

15 HAPPY JACK
The Who *Decca* 67

16 BEHIND BLUE EYES
The Who *Decca* 71

17 AFTER THE FIRE
Roger Daltrey *Atlantic* 85

18 CALL ME LIGHTNING
The Who *Decca* 68

19 THE RELAY
The Who *Track* 73

20 I'M FREE
The Who *Decca* 69

The Top 20 Songs of JACKIE WILSON

BORN IN DETROIT and raised in Highland Park, Michigan, Jackie Wilson sang gospel music in church and was a member of the Ever Ready Gospel Singers before turning professional by recording for the Dee Gee label, owned by Dizzy Gillespie. He also did some boxing as Sonny Wilson, the same name that appeared on his Dee Gee recordings.

In 1953, Wilson heard that Clyde McPhatter, lead singer of Billy Ward and the Dominoes, was moving on and auditioned to take his spot. When McPhatter split to join the Drifters, Wilson stepped in and remained with Ward's group for three years. Jackie sang lead on "St. Therese of the Roses," which peaked at No. 20 on the pop singles chart for the Dominoes in 1956.

The next step was for Wilson to become a solo artist. He signed with Brunswick Records and was teamed with new songwriters Berry Gordy, Jr. and Roquel "Billy" Davis, a.k.a. Tyran Carlo. They came up with Jackie's first Brunswick hit, "Reet Petite (The Finest Girl You Ever Want To Meet)." Although the single only went to No. 62 in 1957, it was redeemed in 1987 in the United Kingdom when it was reissued and shot to No. 1.

Gordy and Davis continued to write hits for Wilson. The dramatic "To Be Loved" peaked at No. 22 in 1958 and by the end of the year, "Lonely Teardrops" was climbing the chart, ultimately peaking at No. 7 to become Wilson's biggest hit to that date. By the end of 1959, Gordy and Davis were no longer writing for Wilson after a disagreement with Brunswick's Nat Tarnapol over their wish to write both the A and B sides of Wilson's singles. To gain more control over his career, Gordy decided to start his own record company, and Davis joined the A&R staff of Chicago-based Chess Records.

That didn't stop Wilson from continuing his chart conquest. "Night" soared to No. 4 in 1960 to become the highest-ranking single of his career. After 11 songs in a row failed to reach the top 30 of the Hot 100, "Baby Workout" brought Wilson back to the top 10 when it peaked at No. 5 in 1963.

There were many more releases but only two more big hits. "Whispers (Gettin' Louder)" reached No. 11 in 1966 and "(Your Love Keeps Lifting Me) Higher And Higher" made its mark at No. 6 in 1967.

Wilson wasn't just a recording artist. On stage he was a force of energy, earning him the nickname "Mr. Excitement." Even when the hits stopped coming, he continued to be a live attraction. On September 29, 1975, he was singing "Lonely Teardrops" as part of Dick Clark's "Good Ol' Rock 'n' Roll" show at the Latin Casino in Cherry Hill, New Jersey, when he had a heart attack. He collapsed and hit his head on the stage, and remained in a coma for four months. Suffering brain damage, he never fully recovered, and his motor functions remained impaired until his death on January 21, 1984.

01 LONELY TEARDROPS
Jackie Wilson *Brunswick* 59

02 NIGHT
Jackie Wilson *Brunswick* 60

03 (YOUR LOVE KEEPS LIFTING ME) HIGHER AND HIGHER
Jackie Wilson *Brunswick* 67

04 ALONE AT LAST
Jackie Wilson *Brunswick* 60

05 BABY WORKOUT
Jackie Wilson *Brunswick* 63

06 THAT'S WHY (I LOVE YOU SO)
Jackie Wilson *Brunswick* 59

07 (YOU WERE MADE FOR) ALL MY LOVING
Jackie Wilson *Brunswick* 60

08 DOGGIN' AROUND
Jackie Wilson *Brunswick* 60

09 WHISPERS (GETTIN' LOUDER)
Jackie Wilson *Brunswick* 66

10 MY EMPTY ARMS
Jackie Wilson *Brunswick* 61

11 A WOMAN, A LOVER, A FRIEND
Jackie Wilson *Brunswick* 60

12 PLEASE TELL ME WHY
Jackie Wilson *Brunswick* 61

13 I'LL BE SATISFIED
Jackie Wilson *Brunswick* 59

14 TO BE LOVED
Jackie Wilson *Brunswick* 58

15 I'M COMIN' ON BACK TO YOU
Jackie Wilson *Brunswick* 61

16 TALK THAT TALK
Jackie Wilson *Brunswick* 60

17 THE GREATEST HURT
Jackie Wilson *Brunswick* 62

18 AM I THE MAN
Jackie Wilson *Brunswick* 60

19 YOU BETTER KNOW IT
Jackie Wilson *Brunswick* 59

20 I GET THE SWEETEST FEELING
Jackie Wilson *Brunswick* 68

The Top 10 Songs of PAULA ABDUL

SIX NO. 1 SONGS on the *Billboard* charts would be enough to cement anyone's place in music history, but Paula Abdul has also earned everlasting fame as a judge on the hit TV series *American Idol.*

Paula grew up in North Hollywood, California. Her father, Harry, sold livestock, and her mother, Lorraine, was an assistant to film director Billy Wilder. She started performing at seven, inspired by Gene Kelly's performance in the movie *Singin' in the Rain.* At Van Nuys High School, Paula was a cheerleader and senior class president. She enrolled at Cal State Northridge, and was planning to be a TV sportscaster until a friend begged her to try out with her for a cheerleading position with the Los Angeles Lakers. The friend didn't make the cut, but Paula became a Laker Girl and was soon named the troupe's choreographer. After one of the games, some of the Jackson brothers asked her to choreograph one of their videos.

She was also hired to choreograph dance routines for Janet Jackson, and was named choreographer for Fox-TV's *The Tracey Ullman Show.* While working on a ZZ Top video, Paula mentioned to the label's Jeff Ayeroff that she would like to record an album. When Ayeroff was named co-president of Virgin Records in America, one of the first artists he signed was Abdul.

01 **RUSH RUSH**
Paula Abdul *Captive* 91
02 **STRAIGHT UP**
Paula Abdul *Virgin* 89
03 **OPPOSITES ATTRACT**
Paula Abdul w/the Wild Pair *Virgin* 90
04 **COLD HEARTED**
Paula Abdul *Virgin* 89
05 **FOREVER YOUR GIRL**
Paula Abdul *Virgin* 89
06 **THE PROMISE OF A NEW DAY**
Paula Abdul *Captive* 91
07 **BLOWING KISSES IN THE WIND**
Paula Abdul *Captive* 91
08 **(IT'S JUST) THE WAY THAT YOU LOVE ME**
Paula Abdul *Virgin* 89
09 **VIBEOLOGY**
Paula Abdul *Captive* 92
10 **WILL YOU MARRY ME?**
Paula Abdul *Captive* 92

The Top 10 Songs of AEROSMITH

CLIVE DAVIS saw Steven Tyler, Joe Perry, Brad Whitford, Tom Hamilton, and Joey Kramer perform at Max's Kansas City in New York in 1972 and signed them to Columbia Records. Just over a year later, Aerosmith recorded their debut album and released a single, "Dream On," which sputtered out at No. 59. It wasn't until January 1976 that the re-released "Dream On" re-entered the Hot 100 and went to No. 6.

Aerosmith began to unravel when Perry left in December 1979 for a solo career. Whitford departed too, and Tyler was derailed by a motorcycle accident. Perry and Whitford saw Aerosmith perform on Valentine's Day 1984 at the Orpheum in Boston. A backstage visit led to meetings that in turn led to re-forming the original band. After their Columbia contract expired in 1985, Aerosmith signed with Geffen and had even greater success on the Hot 100. But Aerosmith earned its most successful single after returning to Columbia. With Tyler's daughter Liv starring in *Armageddon,* it was natural for the band to record the movie's main song, "I Don't Want To Miss A Thing."

01 **I DON'T WANT TO MISS A THING**
Aerosmith *Columbia* 98
02 **ANGEL**
Aerosmith *Geffen* 88
03 **JADED**
Aerosmith *Columbia* 01
04 **CRYIN'**
Aerosmith *Geffen* 93
05 **JANIE'S GOT A GUN**
Aerosmith *Geffen* 90
06 **CRAZY**
Aerosmith *Geffen* 94
07 **DREAM ON**
Aerosmith *Columbia* 76
08 **AMAZING**
Aerosmith *Geffen* 94
09 **LOVE IN AN ELEVATOR**
Aerosmith *Geffen* 89
10 **LIVIN' ON THE EDGE**
Aerosmith *Geffen* 93

CHRISTINA Maria Aguilera's parents were living on Staten Island, New York, when their daughter was born. Fausto Aguilera, a native of Ecuador, was a sergeant in the U.S. Army. Shelly Fidler, of German, Dutch, Welsh, and Irish stock, taught Spanish.

Christina's musical talent was evident early. At nine, she competed on *Star Search*, although she didn't win. When she was 12, she joined the cast of *The New Mickey Mouse Club* with other stars in the making, including Britney Spears and Justin Timberlake.

Aguilera was 14 when she had her first hit, but the single was only released in Japan. "All I Wanna Do" was a duet with Keizo Nakanishi. Her big break in America came when Walt Disney Studios asked her to sing "Reflection" on the soundtrack to *Mulan*. The song didn't chart on the Hot 100, but it did lead to a contract with RCA.

Her eponymous debut album contained three No. 1 songs: "Genie In A Bottle," "What A Girl Wants," and "Come On Over Baby (All I Want Is You)." After a Spanish-language set and a holiday CD, she transformed from teen pop star to sultry vixen on her next album, which yielded the No. 2 hit, "Beautiful."

The Top 10 Songs of AIR SUPPLY

AIR SUPPLY is an Anglo-Australian duo that was formed by two members of a Melbourne production of *Jesus Christ Superstar.* Graham Russell was born in Sherwood, Nottingham, England. His father and new stepmother announced they were moving to Australia when he was 13, but Russell didn't want to go and ran away from home. After living with an uncle for three years, he finally joined his family in Melbourne.

Russell Hitchcock grew up in an industrial neighborhood of that same city. He moved to Sydney and wanted to audition for a production of *Superstar* but missed the chance, so he flew home to Melbourne to audition there. He won a part and met chorus member Russell. They recorded a single together and had a top three hit with "Love And Other Bruises."

That success led them to leave the cast of the musical and go on the road. Russell took a six-month break and wrote material for the duo, including "Lost In Love" and "All Out Of Love." A bout of food poisoning left him ill and depressed, until he picked up a trade paper and discovered that Arista had decided to release "Lost In Love" in the United States.

01 **ALL OUT OF LOVE**
Air Supply *Arista* 80

02 **THE ONE THAT YOU LOVE**
Air Supply *Arista* 81

03 **MAKING LOVE OUT OF NOTHING AT ALL**
Air Supply *Arista* 83

04 **LOST IN LOVE**
Air Supply *Arista* 80

05 **EVERY WOMAN IN THE WORLD**
Air Supply *Arista* 81

06 **SWEET DREAMS**
Air Supply *Arista* 82

07 **HERE I AM (JUST WHEN I THOUGHT I WAS OVER YOU)**
Air Supply *Arista* 81

08 **EVEN THE NIGHTS ARE BETTER**
Air Supply *Arista* 82

09 **JUST AS I AM**
Air Supply *Arista* 85

10 **TWO LESS LONELY PEOPLE IN THE WORLD**
Air Supply *Arista* 83

The Top 10 Songs of
HERB ALPERT & THE TIJUANA BRASS

EVERYONE IN the Alpert family was musical. Herb's father played the mandolin, his mother the violin, his sister the piano, and his brother the drums. At Fairfax High School in Los Angeles, Herb thought he would be a jazz musician. His plans were interrupted by two years in the army, where he played the trumpet and bugle. After his military service, he became a session musician who worked on a lot of soundtracks. His trumpet can be heard in *The Ten Commandments.*

He met Lou Adler in 1957 and they wrote songs together, including "Wonderful World" for Sam Cooke. They produced hits for Jan and Dean, and in 1962 Alpert teamed up with Jerry Moss to form Carnival Records, which was quickly renamed A&M.

One of the label's first singles was Alpert's instrumental recording of "The Lonely Bull." Moss suggested it be credited to "Herb Alpert and the Tijuana Brass," even though there was no such group. By 1968, Alpert and the Brass had racked up 17 chart singles. That year, Alpert had a No. 1 hit with a vocal of Burt Bacharach and Hal David's "This Guy's In Love With You." In 1979, Alpert secured his first instrumental No. 1 with "Rise."

01 **THIS GUY'S IN LOVE WITH YOU**
Herb Alpert *A&M* 68

02 **RISE**
Herb Alpert *A&M* 79

03 **A TASTE OF HONEY**
Herb Alpert & the Tijuana Brass *A&M* 65

04 **THE LONELY BULL**
The Tijuana Brass f/Herb Alpert *A&M* 62

05 **DIAMONDS**
Herb Alpert *A&M* 87

06 **ZORBA THE GREEK**
Herb Alpert & the Tijuana Brass *A&M* 66

07 **THE WORK SONG**
Herb Alpert & the Tijuana Brass *A&M* 66

08 **MAME**
Herb Alpert & the Tijuana Brass *A&M* 66

09 **CASINO ROYALE**
Herb Alpert & the Tijuana Brass *A&M* 67

10 **ROTATION**
Herb Alpert *A&M* 80

The Top 10 Songs of AMERICA

THEY CALLED THEMSELVES America, even though Gerry Beckley, Dewey Bunnell, and Dan Peek met at Central High School in Bushey Park, London. The name makes more sense when you understand that the three students were all sons of American military personnel based in England and their school was primarily for children of military families.

Beckley, Bunnell, and Peek were part of a quintet called the Daze until the other two members left. The three remaining friends decided to form an acoustic trio and were booked to open for headliners at a popular London club, the Roundhouse. The idea for their new name came from an Americana brand jukebox at a local pub, but the connection to their homeland gave the moniker deeper meaning.

Ian Samwell, a staff producer at the London office of Warner Bros., beat offers from the Atlantic and DJM labels and signed the group. A debut album was recorded and it was unclear what the first single should be. The leading candidate was Beckley's song "I Need You," until America went back into the studio to record one more track. Written by Bunnell, it was inspired by a feeling of homesickness and memories of the desert countryside in Southern California. The song was "A Horse With No Name."

The Top 10 Songs of BACKSTREET BOYS

IN 1992, Orlando, Florida, was home not only to Disney World and Universal Studios, but a management company owned by Lou Pearlman. He held auditions to form a boy band in the mold of New Kids on the Block and found high school students Howie Dorough and AJ McLean and a junior high student named Nick Carter. They formed a trio that expanded with the addition of Kevin Richardson and his cousin from Kentucky, Brian Littrell.

Backstreet Boys became local favorites, playing venues like Sea World and the gym at an Orlando high school. They were signed to the Jive label and began recording in 1995. They failed to catch on in the United States but became stars in Europe, especially the United Kingdom, where boy bands like Take That and Boyzone were already doing well. Their fame spread to Germany and Canada before finally reaching the top 10 in America with "Quit Playing Games (With My Heart)" in 1997.

The quintet racked up five more top 10 hits between 1998 and 2000, then took a break from 2002 to 2004 while members worked on individual projects. In June 2005, the group returned to the Hot 100 with "Incomplete," which peaked at No. 13.

PATRICIA ANDRZEJEWSKI was born in Lindenhurst on Long Island in New York. She studied classical voice and opera and attended the Juilliard School of Music. She married her high school sweetheart, Dennis Benatar, and the couple moved to Richmond, Virginia, where Pat worked as a bank teller and a waitress.

In 1975 she was cast in the off-Broadway musical *The Zinger.* Then she performed at New York's popular Catch A Rising Star, and club owner Rick Newman suggested he manage her career. Divorced from her husband but retaining his last name, Benatar developed a hard-rock style and was turned down by a number of labels until Terry Ellis, co-founder of Chrysalis, offered her a deal.

Benatar first saw chart ink the week of October 20, 1979, when her album *In The Heat Of The Night* debuted on The Billboard 200. The first single, "Heartbreaker," entered the Hot 100 the week of December 22 and peaked at No. 23. Benatar's fourth single, "Hit Me With Your Best Shot," was her first top 10 hit, reaching No. 9 in 1980. In 1983, "Love Is A Battlefield" became her highest-ranking title when it went to No. 5. The follow-up, "We Belong," also peaked at No. 5.

01 **LOVE IS A BATTLEFIELD**
Pat Benatar *Chrysalis* 83

02 **HIT ME WITH YOUR BEST SHOT**
Pat Benatar *Chrysalis* 80

03 **WE BELONG**
Pat Benatar *Chrysalis* 85

04 **INVINCIBLE**
Pat Benatar *Chrysalis* 85

05 **SHADOWS OF THE NIGHT**
Pat Benatar *Chrysalis* 82

06 **TREAT ME RIGHT**
Pat Benatar *Chrysalis* 81

07 **FIRE AND ICE**
Pat Benatar *Chrysalis* 81

08 **HEARTBREAKER**
Pat Benatar *Chrysalis* 80

09 **ALL FIRED UP**
Pat Benatar *Chrysalis* 88

10 **LITTLE TOO LATE**
Pat Benatar *Chrysalis* 83

The Top 10 Songs of BROOK BENTON

BENJAMIN FRANKLIN PEAY, born in Camden, South Carolina, was the given name of Brook Benton. In his early years he sang gospel, and as an adult he moved to New York City where he pushed clothing racks around the garment district to pay the bills. He got a break in 1953 when he was signed to the Columbia-owned OKeh imprint. There was a brief stint with RCA's Vik label in 1957, but the real action began when he signed with Mercury and released the ballad, "It's Just A Matter Of Time." That 1959 single peaked at No. 3 on the Hot 100.

Benton found his way to Mercury by meeting music publisher Clyde Otis. When Otis joined the label in an executive capacity, one of the first artists he signed was Benton, even though Atlantic Records was in hot pursuit.

Benton followed "It's Just A Matter Of Time" with hits like "Endlessly" and "So Many Ways," and then Otis teamed him with another Mercury artist, the great Dinah Washington, for two stunning duets. After "Hotel Happiness" hit No. 3 in 1963, Benton's chart fortunes faded. He made a comeback in 1970, signing to Atlantic's Cotillion imprint. "Rainy Night In Georgia" peaked at No. 4.

Benton died of spinal meningitis on April 9, 1988.

01 **THE BOLL WEEVIL SONG**
Brook Benton *Mercury* 61

02 **IT'S JUST A MATTER OF TIME**
Brook Benton *Mercury* 59

03 **HOTEL HAPPINESS**
Brook Benton *Mercury* 63

04 **RAINY NIGHT IN GEORGIA**
Brook Benton *Cotillion* 70

05 **KIDDIO**
Brook Benton *Mercury* 60

06 **SO MANY WAYS**
Brook Benton *Mercury* 59

07 **BABY (YOU'VE GOT WHAT IT TAKES)**
Dinah Washington & Brook Benton
Mercury 60

08 **A ROCKIN' GOOD WAY (TO MESS AROUND AND FALL IN LOVE)**
Dinah Washington & Brook Benton
Mercury 80

09 **THINK TWICE**
Brook Benton *Mercury* 61

10 **ENDLESSLY**
Brook Benton *Mercury* 59

The Top 10 Songs of CHUCK BERRY

HE INSPIRED the Beach Boys, the Beatles, and the Rolling Stones, and is a founding father of rock and roll, but life didn't begin so well for Charles Edward Anderson Berry. As a teenager, he was sent to reform school for three years on a burglary charge. After his release, he worked at General Motors and studied hairdressing before he formed a trio that became popular in St. Louis.

In 1955, Berry heard Muddy Waters play in Chicago and asked to sit in. Waters was impressed and suggested that Berry audition for Leonard Chess. Berry played two songs at the audition, including "Ida Red." Chess suggested changing the lyrics, and "Ida Red" became the name of a cow in a children's story, "Maybellene." Released as a single, it was a top five hit on the pop chart.

Over the next three years, Berry had top 10 hits with "School Day," "Rock And Roll Music," "Sweet Little Sixteen," and "Johnny B. Goode." In 1963, Brian Wilson converted "Sweet Little Sixteen" into "Surfin' U.S.A." The Beatles recorded Berry's "Roll Over Beethoven" and "Rock And Roll Music," and the first Rolling Stones single in the United Kingdom was a cover of Berry's "Come On."

In 1972, Berry scored his first No. 1 single with the ribald "My Ding-a-Ling."

01 **SWEET LITTLE SIXTEEN**
Chuck Berry *Chess* 58

02 **MY DING-A-LING**
Chuck Berry *Chess* 72

03 **SCHOOL DAY**
Chuck Berry *Chess* 57

04 **ROCK AND ROLL MUSIC**
Chuck Berry *Chess* 57

05 **JOHNNY B. GOODE**
Chuck Berry *Chess* 58

06 **MAYBELLENE**
Chuck Berry *Chess* 55

07 **NO PARTICULAR PLACE TO GO**
Chuck Berry *Chess* 64

08 **YOU NEVER CAN TELL**
Chuck Berry *Chess* 64

09 **NADINE**
Chuck Berry *Chess* 64

10 **REELIN' AND ROCKIN'**
Chuck Berry *Chess* 73

MARY J. BLIGE grew up in the projects in Yonkers, New York, where she listened to the music that her mother loved, including songs by Sam Cooke, the Isley Brothers, and the O'Jays. When she was a child, she used her hairbrush as a microphone to belt out songs in her living room. Her career began when she stepped into a karaoke-like studio in a shopping mall to make a recording of Anita Baker's "Caught Up In The Rapture."

It took four years to land a recording contract. In her early work, Blige shared her darker emotions, moving listeners through her own depression and confusion. By the time she recorded the *No More Drama* album, Blige was ready to share feelings of joy. The biggest hit from the CD was a song with a strong anti-hate message, "Family Affair." The track was originally intended for a male rapper named Rakim until Blige heard it and wrote lyrics with her brother Bruce Miller. The result? Blige topped the Hot 100 for the first time, a reign that lasted six weeks.

In 2006, Blige topped the airplay chart and went to No. 3 on the Hot 100 with the first single from her album *The Breakthrough*. "Be Without You" also set a new record on Hot R&B/Hip-Hop Songs, where It reigned for 15 weeks.

01 FAMILY AFFAIR
Mary J. Blige *MCA* 01

02 BE WITHOUT YOU
Mary J. Blige *Geffen* 06

03 NOT GON' CRY
Mary J. Blige *Arista* 96

04 REAL LOVE
Mary J. Blige *Uptown* 92

**05 I'LL BE THERE FOR YOU/
YOU'RE ALL I NEED TO GET BY**
Method Man f/Mary J. Blige *Def Jam* 95

06 RAINY DAYZ
Mary J. Blige f/Ja Rule *MCA* 02

07 NO MORE DRAMA
Mary J. Blige *MCA* 02

08 EVERYTHING
Mary J. Blige *MCA* 97

09 SWEET THING
Mary J. Blige *Uptown* 93

10 RUNAWAY LOVE
Ludacris f/Mary J. Blige *DTP/Def Jam* 07

The Top 10 Songs of BON JOVI

GROWING UP in Sayreville, New Jersey, John Bongiovi had a good reason for taking guitar lessons: he wanted to meet "chicks." After high school, John moved to New York, where his cousin Tony Bongiovi ran the Power Station recording studio. For two years, John earned $50 a week as a gofer and was able to record his own songs when the studio wasn't busy. He soon had over 50 completed tracks, including "Runaway," which was chosen for a compilation album released by New York radio station WAPP.

The song received enough airplay to encourage John to form his own band. He asked his friend David Bryan to play keyboards, recruited Alec John Such to play bass and Tico Torres to play the drums, and asked Such's bandmate in a group called the Message to be lead guitarist. His name was Richie Sambora.

Derek Shulman of PolyGram signed the band to the Mercury label. The five members agreed to Anglicize Jon's last name and call themselves Bon Jovi. After two albums, they turned to Bruce Fairbairn to produce their next effort. They wanted to collaborate with a songwriter from outside the group and chose Desmond Child. The results: "You Give Love A Bad Name" and "Livin' On A Prayer," the band's first two No. 1 hits.

01 **LIVIN' ON A PRAYER**
Bon Jovi *Mercury* 87
02 **ALWAYS**
Bon Jovi *Mercury* 94
03 **BLAZE OF GLORY**
Jon Bon Jovi *Mercury* 90
04 **I'LL BE THERE FOR YOU**
Bon Jovi *Mercury* 89
05 **YOU GIVE LOVE A BAD NAME**
Bon Jovi *Mercury* 86
06 **BAD MEDICINE**
Bon Jovi *Mercury* 88
07 **BORN TO BE MY BABY**
Bon Jovi *Mercury* 89
08 **BED OF ROSES**
Bon Jovi *Jambco* 93
09 **WANTED DEAD OR ALIVE**
Bon Jovi *Mercury* 87
10 **LAY YOUR HANDS ON ME**
Bon Jovi *Mercury* 89

The Top 10 Songs of DAVID BOWIE

DAVID ROBERT JONES was born on Elvis Presley's 12th birthday. By the time he was 12, David was already interested in music and was studying the saxophone. He joined a series of bands, including the King Bees, the Mannish Boys, and David Jones and the Lower Third. To avoid being confused with Davy Jones of the Monkees, he named himself after the Bowie knife.

He studied with Lindsay Kemp's mime troupe and developed an interest in combining music with theater. Seven weeks after Neil Armstrong became the first man to walk on the moon, Bowie had his first chart single in the United Kingdom with "Space Oddity." He continually morphed into different characters, like "Ziggy Stardust." In 1975, Bowie turned into a born-again soul man, recording at Sigma Sound Studios in Philadelphia. The first single, "Young Americans," just broke into the top 30 of the Hot 100. The follow-up, "Fame," became Bowie's first No. 1 in the United States and led to an invitation to guest star on *Soul Train*.

After a successful run on RCA, Bowie signed with EMI in 1983. His debut album for the label found him teamed with producers Nile Rodgers and Bernard Edwards. The title track, "Let's Dance," gave Bowie his second American No. 1.

01 **LET'S DANCE**
David Bowie *EMI America* 83
02 **FAME**
David Bowie *RCA* 75
03 **GOLDEN YEARS**
David Bowie *RCA* 76
04 **CHINA GIRL**
David Bowie *EMI America* 83
05 **DANCING IN THE STREET**
Mick Jagger/David Bowie *EMI America* 85
06 **BLUE JEAN**
David Bowie *EMI America* 84
07 **MODERN LOVE**
David Bowie *EMI America* 83
08 **SPACE ODDITY**
David Bowie *RCA* 73
09 **UNDER PRESSURE**
Queen & David Bowie *Elektra* 82
10 **DAY-IN DAY-OUT**
David Bowie *EMI America* 87

The Top 10 Songs of BOYZ II MEN

MOTOWN'S HOTTEST ACT in the '90s was Boyz II Men, a vocal quartet that took its name from a New Edition song, "Boys To Men." Shawn Stockman, Wanya Morris, Nathan Morris, and Michael McCary were students at the High School for Creative and Performing Arts in South Philadelphia, where they performed in a talent show. In March 1989 they crashed an invitation-only concert where New Edition spinoff Bell Biv DeVoe was performing. The four students managed to meet Michael Bivins as he was leaving the stage and auditioned for him with a New Edition song, "Can You Stand The Rain." Bivins was impressed enough to give Nathan his phone number. Later, at a meeting in New York he agreed to manage the group and then signed them to Motown.

The first single, "Motownphilly," spoke to their love of Motown music as well as the Philly sound they grew up with. Then came "It's So Hard To Say Goodbye To Yesterday," an *a cappella* remake of a G.C. Cameron song from the soundtrack to *Cooley High*. "End Of The Road" started a chain of No. 1 songs that reigned for 13 weeks or more, including "I'll Make Love To You" (14 weeks) and "One Sweet Day" (16 weeks).

01 ONE SWEET DAY
Mariah Carey & Boyz II Men *Columbia* 95
02 I'LL MAKE LOVE TO YOU
Boyz II Men *Motown* 94
03 END OF THE ROAD
Boyz II Men *Biv 10* 92
04 ON BENDED KNEE
Boyz II Men *Motown* 94
05 IT'S SO HARD TO SAY GOODBYE TO YESTERDAY
Boyz II Men *Motown* 91
06 4 SEASONS OF LONELINESS
Boyz II Men *Motown* 97
07 WATER RUNS DRY
Boyz II Men *Motown* 95
08 IN THE STILL OF THE NITE
Boyz II Men *Motown* 93
09 MOTOWNPHILLY
Boyz II Men *Motown* 91
10 A SONG FOR MAMA
Boyz II Men *Motown* 98

The Top 10 Songs of BREAD

GROWING UP in Tulsa, Oklahoma, David Gates formed a band with his girlfriend's brother, Leon Russell. After Russell moved to Los Angeles and found work with artists like Ricky Nelson, Gates followed. After six hungry months, he found steady work as a session musician, recording demos for Jackie DeShannon and Randy Newman. Johnny Burnette recorded one of Gates' songs, and although it wasn't a hit, he was encouraged to keep writing. He turned out pop tunes for the Murmaids ("Popsicles And Icicles"), the Girlfriends ("My One And Only Jimmy Boy"), and Shelley Fabares ("Football Seasons Over").

In 1968, Russell suggested that Gates produce an album for James Griffin and Robb Royer, who had formed a band called Pleasure Faire. Gates joined the group, and the trio Pleasure Faire evolved into Bread. Signed to Elektra, the group released an album that didn't chart. Mike Botts joined the group to make it a quartet, and the first single from a follow-up album, "Make It With You," topped the Hot 100.

Although a couple of uptempo singles were released, Bread was best known for its soft-rock output, including "It Don't Matter To Me," "Baby I'm-A Want You," and "Everything I Own."

01 MAKE IT WITH YOU
Bread *Elektra* 70
02 BABY I'M-A WANT YOU
Bread *Elektra* 71
03 LOST WITHOUT YOUR LOVE
Bread *Elektra* 77
04 IF
Bread *Elektra* 71
05 EVERYTHING I OWN
Bread *Elektra* 72
06 GOODBYE GIRL
David Gates *Elektra* 78
07 THE GUITAR MAN
Bread *Elektra* 72
08 IT DON'T MATTER TO ME
Bread *Elektra* 70
09 DIARY
Bread *Elektra* 72
10 SWEET SURRENDER
Bread *Elektra* 72

The Top 10 Songs of JERRY BUTLER

TODAY, Jerry Butler is a commissioner in Cook County, Illinois. But he will always be known by fans as the legendary R&B singer "The Ice Man," a nickname bestowed on him by Philadelphia DJ Georgie Woods.

Butler was born in Sunflower, Mississippi, and was just three years old when his family moved to Chicago. He sang with the Northern Jubilee Gospel Singers, where he met Curtis Mayfield. They joined forces with a group from Tennessee known as the Roosters and evolved into the Impressions. Signed to Ewart Abner's record label, a Vee Jay subsidiary, the first chart single "For Your Precious Love" went to No. 11, but Abner billed it to "Jerry Butler and the Impressions," causing tension that led to Butler's departure. The Impressions eventually regrouped, but Butler kept going on his own, signed to Vee Jay. "He Will Break Your Heart," written with Mayfield, peaked at No. 7 in 1960, and in 1961 Butler's version of "Moon River" was released before the Henry Mancini original, sailing to No. 11.

Butler's last major hit on Vee Jay was a duet with label mate Betty Everett on "Let It Be Me" in 1964. Butler didn't return to the top 10 until the end of the decade, when he signed with Mercury and teamed up with writer/producers Kenny Gamble and Leon Huff.

01 HE WILL BREAK YOUR HEART
Jerry Butler *Vee Jay* 60
02 ONLY THE STRONG SURVIVE
Jerry Butler *Mercury* 69
03 LET IT BE ME
Jerry Butler & Betty Everett *Vee Jay* 64
04 MOON RIVER
Jerry Butler *Vee Jay* 61
05 HEY, WESTERN UNION MAN
Jerry Butler *Mercury* 68
06 FOR YOUR PRECIOUS LOVE
Jerry Butler *Abner/Falcon* 58
07 AIN'T UNDERSTANDING MELLOW
Jerry Butler & Brenda Lee Eager *Mercury* 72
08 NEVER GIVE YOU UP
Jerry Butler *Mercury* 68
09 MOODY WOMAN
Jerry Butler *Mercury* 69
10 WHAT'S THE USE OF BREAKING UP
Jerry Butler *Mercury* 69

The Top 10 Songs of ERIC CARMEN/RASPBERRIES

THE DIRECTION OF Eric Carmen's life was set when, at the age of three, he became the youngest student in history to enroll at the Cleveland Institute of Music. At six, he was taking violin lessons from his aunt, a member of the Cleveland Symphony Orchestra.

He might have become a classical musician if he had never heard the Beatles and the Rolling Stones. Under their influence, he formed a pop group, Cyrus Erie. With members of that group and musicians from another local act, the Choir, Carmen founded the power-pop outfit the Raspberries in 1971. Signed to Capitol, the quartet scored with its second entry on the Hot 100: "Go All The Way" went to No. 5.

By 1975, Carmen was a solo artist on the Arista roster. His first two singles were based on Rachmaninov melodies. "All By Myself" spent three weeks at No. 2 and "Never Gonna Fall In Love Again" stopped at No. 11. Twelve years passed before Carmen was back in the top 10. "Hungry Eyes," from the *Dirty Dancing* soundtrack, waltzed to No. 5 in 1988 and the follow-up, "Make Me Lose Control," peaked at No. 3.

01 ALL BY MYSELF
Eric Carmen *Arista* 76
02 MAKE ME LOSE CONTROL
Eric Carmen *Arista* 88
03 HUNGRY EYES
Eric Carmen *RCA* 88
04 GO ALL THE WAY
Raspberries *Capitol* 72
05 NEVER GONNA FALL IN LOVE AGAIN
Eric Carmen *Arista* 76
06 I WANNA BE WITH YOU
Raspberries *Capitol* 73
07 CHANGE OF HEART
Eric Carmen *Arista* 78
08 SHE DID IT
Eric Carmen *Arista* 77
09 OVERNIGHT SENSATION (HIT RECORD)
Raspberries *Capitol* 74
10 LET'S PRETEND
Raspberries *Capitol* 73

The Top 10 Songs of CREEDENCE CLEARWATER REVIVAL/JOHN FOGERTY

JOHN FOGERTY was in junior high school when he bought his first electric guitar. He formed a band, the Blue Velvets, with two other students, Doug Clifford (drums) and Stu Cook (piano). One of John's older brothers, Tom, had been singing with various local bands and writing his own songs. He recruited the Blue Velvets for his backup band for some demo sessions. By the time John and his friends were in high school, a San Francisco label, Orchestra Records, released the first single by Tom Fogerty and the Blue Velvets.

A TV documentary that featured jazz musician Vince Guaraldi inspired them to contact Guaraldi's label, Fantasy Records. They were signed to the label and wanted to call themselves the Visions, but label execs preferred the Golliwogs. Tom Fogerty was the vocalist on the band's first few singles, but in 1965 the band agreed that John should be the lead singer. By the summer of love, the name Golliwogs seemed hopelessly out of tune with the times, and a TV commercial for a beer brewed in "clear water" inspired the band's new name.

A number of singles failed to chart until the Bay Area band's bayou-inspired take on Dale Hawkins' "Suzie Q" brought them to the Hot 100 for the first time.

01 **PROUD MARY**
Creedence Clearwater Revival *Fantasy* 69
02 **BAD MOON RISING**
Creedence Clearwater Revival *Fantasy* 69
03 **GREEN RIVER**
Creedence Clearwater Revival *Fantasy* 69
04 **LOOKIN' OUT MY BACK DOOR / LONG AS I CAN SEE THE LIGHT**
Creedence Clearwater Revival *Fantasy* 70
05 **TRAVELIN' BAND / WHO'LL STOP THE RAIN**
Creedence Clearwater Revival *Fantasy* 70
06 **DOWN ON THE CORNER / FORTUNATE SON**
Creedence Clearwater Revival *Fantasy* 69
07 **UP AROUND THE BEND / RUN THROUGH THE JUNGLE**
Creedence Clearwater Revival *Fantasy* 70
08 **HAVE YOU EVER SEEN THE RAIN / HEY TONIGHT**
Creedence Clearwater Revival *Fantasy* 71
09 **THE OLD MAN DOWN THE ROAD**
John Fogerty *Warner Bros.* 85
10 **SUZIE Q. (PART ONE)**
Creedence Clearwater Revival *Fantasy* 68

The Top 10 Songs of JOHN DENVER

HENRY JOHN Deutschendorf, Jr., was born in Roswell, New Mexico, but as an Air Force brat, he moved all over the Southwest. He was eight when his grandmother in Oklahoma gave him a guitar. He took one year of basic lessons and joined a rock band when he was in high school. At Texas Tech his major was architecture, but he spent most of his time playing music. Midway through his junior year he relocated to Los Angeles to play folk clubs and renamed himself after his favorite city.

John Denver was selected from 250 candidates to replace Chad Mitchell in the trio bearing his name. During his three years with the group he began writing songs, some of which ended up on his first RCA solo album, *Rhymes And Reasons*. That LP included his own "Leaving On A Jet Plane," a No. 1 hit for Peter, Paul & Mary.

His ninth single to chart on the Hot 100, "Sunshine On My Shoulders," was the first of four chart-toppers. The others were "Annie's Song," "Thank God I'm A Country Boy," and "I'm Sorry" / "Calypso."

On October 12, 1997, Denver was piloting an experimental plane that crashed into Monterey Bay in California. Denver was 53 when he died.

01 **I'M SORRY / CALYPSO**
John Denver *RCA* 75
02 **ANNIE'S SONG**
John Denver *RCA* 74
03 **SUNSHINE ON MY SHOULDERS**
John Denver *RCA* 74
04 **TAKE ME HOME, COUNTRY ROADS**
John Denver *RCA* 71
05 **THANK GOD I'M A COUNTRY BOY**
John Denver *RCA* 75
06 **ROCKY MOUNTAIN HIGH**
John Denver *RCA* 73
07 **BACK HOME AGAIN**
John Denver *RCA* 74
08 **FLY AWAY**
John Denver *RCA* 76
09 **SWEET SURRENDER**
John Denver *RCA* 75
10 **LOOKING FOR SPACE**
John Denver *RCA* 76

The Top 10 Songs of CELINE DION

CELINE DION was born on March 30, 1968, in a small village in Quebec, the youngest of 14 children. She was 12 years old when one of her brothers sent her demo tape to manager and future husband René Angelil. He signed the young singer and she was well known in her own country by the time she sang for Switzerland in the 1988 Eurovision Song Contest. In one of the closest votes in that competition's history, Dion had to wait for the very last country to cast its final vote before she realized she had won the contest with her song "Ne Partez Pas Sans Moi." The following year, at the Palais de Beaulieu in Lausanne, Dion opened the show by reprising her winning song and performing her first single in English, "Where Does My Heart Beat Now." It took another two years for that song to become her first hit in the U.S.

"The Power Of Love" was her first U.S. No. 1, but her biggest hit is "Because You Loved Me," the Diane Warren–penned theme from the film *Up Close And Personal.*

01 **BECAUSE YOU LOVED ME**
Celine Dion *550 Music* 96
02 **THE POWER OF LOVE**
Celine Dion *550 Music* 94
03 **IT'S ALL COMING BACK TO ME NOW**
Celine Dion *550 Music* 96
04 **I'M YOUR ANGEL**
R. Kelly & Celine Dion *Jive* 98
05 **MY HEART WILL GO ON**
Celine Dion *550 Music* 98
06 **THAT'S THE WAY IT IS**
Celine Dion *550 Music* 00
07 **IF YOU ASKED ME TO**
Celine Dion *Epic* 92
08 **WHERE DOES MY HEART BEAT NOW**
Celine Dion *Epic* 91
09 **BEAUTY AND THE BEAST**
Celine Dion & Peabo Bryson *Epic* 92
10 **ALL BY MYSELF**
Celine Dion *550 Music* 97

The Top 10 Songs of EARTH, WIND & FIRE

EARTH, WIND & FIRE was a brassy, jazz-like band when it recorded its first album for Warner Bros. When the label dropped the group in 1971, founder Maurice White reworked the concept. Signed to Columbia in 1973, Earth, Wind & Fire reinvented itself as an exuberant dance band with life-affirming, metaphysical lyrics wrapped around a pulsating rhythm. The revamped approach didn't catch on at first; of the first five singles, only one made the top 30. But then came "Shining Star," the outfit's first No. 1 hit. White says the song speaks to each person's potential to become a star in his or her own way.

Over the next six years, six more top 10 hits followed. When the Columbia string of chart entries stopped, the band returned to the Warner Bros. family by signing with sister label Reprise.

Even when the run of hit singles ended, Earth, Wind & Fire remained a hot touring act. The band's induction into the Rock and Roll Hall of Fame in 2000 helped cement its legendary status, and the group remains active in the first decade of the 21st century.

01 **LET'S GROOVE**
Earth, Wind & Fire *ARC* 81
02 **EASY LOVER**
Philip Bailey w/Phil Collins *Columbia* 85
03 **AFTER THE LOVE HAS GONE**
Earth, Wind & Fire *ARC* 79
04 **SHINING STAR**
Earth, Wind & Fire *Columbia* 75
05 **BOOGIE WONDERLAND**
Earth, Wind & Fire w/the Emotions *Columbia* 79
06 **SING A SONG**
Earth, Wind & Fire *Columbia* 76
07 **SERPENTINE FIRE**
Earth, Wind & Fire *Columbia* 78
08 **SEPTEMBER**
Earth, Wind & Fire *ARC* 79
09 **THAT'S THE WAY OF THE WORLD**
Earth, Wind & Fire *Columbia* 75
10 **GETAWAY**
Earth, Wind & Fire *Columbia* 76

TWENTY-TWO YEARS before *American Idol* started creating recording stars, a British TV series called *The Big Time* launched the career of a Scottish singer named Sheena Easton.

Easton's big break came when the producers of the BBC documentary agreed to film her quest for a career. An audition with EMI was arranged with no guarantees: If the label passed, the production team would look for another singer to spotlight. EMI's head of A&R, Brian Shepherd, was impressed with her vocal talent and surprised everyone—including himself—by signing her.

The documentary was filmed over a period of 12 months, during which Easton was paired with producer Christopher Neil. She recorded the songs "Modern Girl" and "9 to 5." After the series aired in the summer of 1980, "Modern Girl" surged to No. 1 and "9 to 5" peaked at No. 3. Retitled "Morning Train (Nine to Five)" for America, the single went to No. 1 on the Hot 100. It was the first of five consecutive top 30 singles. After a couple of mid-charters, Easton returned to the top 10 with a remake of Bob Seger's "We've Got Tonight," recorded as a duet with Kenny Rogers.

01 **MORNING TRAIN**
Sheena Easton *EMI America* 81
02 **FOR YOUR EYES ONLY**
Sheena Easton *Liberty* 81
03 **THE LOVER IN ME**
Sheena Easton *MCA* 89
04 **WE'VE GOT TONIGHT**
Kenny Rogers & Sheena Easton *Liberty* 83
05 **STRUT**
Sheena Easton *EMI America* 84
06 **TELEFONE (LONG DISTANCE LOVE AFFAIR)**
Sheena Easton *EMI America* 83
07 **YOU COULD HAVE BEEN WITH ME**
Sheena Easton *EMI America* 82
08 **MODERN GIRL**
Sheena Easton *EMI America* 81
09 **SUGAR WALLS**
Sheena Easton *EMI America* 85
10 **WHAT COMES NATURALLY**
Sheena Easton *MCA* 91

The Top 10 Songs of MISSY ELLIOTT

MELISSA ELLIOTT, born in Portsmouth, Virginia, was lead singer and prime songwriter for Sista, an R&B singing group in the '80s produced by Elliott's friend, Timothy Mosley. DeVante Swing of Jodeci liked their sound and signed them to his Swing Mob label (and came up with Mosley's nickname, Timbaland). An album was recorded but never released. Undaunted, Elliott and Timbaland continued to write and produce for other artists, including SWV, 702, and Aaliyah.

Elliott's work was noticed by more than one label but she signed with Elektra in 1996 and was given her own imprint, The Gold Mind. Her first five albums all went platinum, making her the best-selling female rapper of the day. Her first top 10 single as lead artist was "Hot Boyz" in 1999. "Get Ur Freak On" also reached the top 10, in 2001, but her career-making single turned out to be "Work It," which held down the No. 2 spot for 10 weeks in 2002, equaling the record set by Foreigner's "Waiting For A Girl Like You" for the longest-running No. 2 song in Hot 100 history.

01 **WORK IT** Missy "Misdemeanor" Elliott *The Gold Mind* 02
02 **1, 2 STEP** Ciara f/Missy Elliott *Sho'Nuff/LaFace* 05
03 **LOSE CONTROL** Missy Elliott f/Ciara & Fat Man Scoop *The Gold Mind* 05
04 **HOT BOYZ** Missy "Misdemeanor" Elliott f/Nas, Eve & Q-Tip *The Gold Mind* 00
05 **GET UR FREAK ON** Missy "Misdemeanor" Elliott *The Gold Mind* 01
06 **MAKE IT HOT** Nicole f/Missy "Misdemeanor" Elliott & Mocha *The Gold Mind* 98
07 **TRIPPIN'** Total (f/Missy Elliott) *Bad Boy* 98
08 **NOT TONIGHT** Lil' Kim f/Da Brat, Left Eye, Missy "Misdemeanor" Elliott & Angie Martinez *Undeas/Big Beat* 97
09 **GOSSIP FOLKS** Missy Elliott f/Ludacris *The Gold Mind* 03
10 **SOCK IT 2 ME** Missy "Misdemeanor" Elliott f/Da Brat *EastWest* 97

The Top 10 Songs of
EURYTHMICS/ANNIE LENNOX

LIVING IN THE TOWN of Sutherland in the north of England, Dave Stewart was obsessed with sports. When he was 12, he broke his knee in a football match and was hospitalized for months. "I got so fidgety with nothing to do that someone brought me a guitar, which of course was fatal."

At 15 he saw his first rock concert, and was so fascinated with the act, Amazing Blondel, that he stowed away in their van. It was the beginning of his new life as a roadie and then a rock musician. His first band, Longdancer, was signed to Elton John's Rocket Records.

Life changed again when his waitress at a London restaurant turned out to be an unemployed singer named Annie Lennox. From that night, they were inseparable. They moved in together and formed a band called the Tourists.

The romantic connection between Dave and Annie ended—as did the Tourists—but the group almost immediately morphed into Eurythmics. Their first album, *In The Garden*, didn't produce any hit singles, but Eurythmics, undaunted, recorded new material that included their first U.S. chart entry and their only No. 1 song, "Sweet Dreams (Are Made Of This)."

01 **SWEET DREAMS (ARE MADE OF THIS)** Eurythmics *RCA* 83
02 **HERE COMES THE RAIN AGAIN** Eurythmics *RCA* 84
03 **WALKING ON BROKEN GLASS** Annie Lennox *Arista* 92
04 **WOULD I LIE TO YOU?** Eurythmics *RCA* 85
05 **PUT A LITTLE LOVE IN YOUR HEART** Annie Lennox & Al Green *A&M* 89
06 **MISSIONARY MAN** Eurythmics *RCA* 86
07 **NO MORE "I LOVE YOU'S"** Annie Lennox *Arista* 95
08 **WHO'S THAT GIRL?** Eurythmics *RCA* 84
09 **SISTERS ARE DOIN' IT FOR THEMSELVES** Eurythmics & Aretha Franklin *RCA* 85
10 **LOVE IS A STRANGER** Eurythmics *RCA* 83

The Top 10 Songs of AL GREEN

AL GREEN was raised in church and on gospel music. He was nine when his parents moved to Grand Rapids, Michigan. With siblings Robert, Walter, and William, he sang gospel songs as a member of the Greene Brothers. In 1964, during his high school years, Green formed a pop group, the Creations. Two of the members started their own record label, Hot Line, and released Green's first chart single, "Back Up Train" (No. 41 in 1968).

There was no proper follow-up and the label folded. A year later, Green was playing a gig at a club in Midland, Texas, with Willie Mitchell, who had just become head of A&R for Memphis-based Hi Records. Mitchell asked Green if he'd like to record for Hi, but Green said he didn't care for Memphis. Mitchell didn't give up, and two weeks later he persuaded Green to come to Memphis for a recording session.

Mitchell gave himself 18 months to make Green a star. He trimmed the singer's Afro and put him in a business suit. But Green didn't like how his voice sounded on "Let's Stay Together" and argued it shouldn't be released. Fortunately, Mitchell prevailed and Green had a No. 1 hit.

1. **LET'S STAY TOGETHER**
Al Green *Hi* 72
2. **YOU OUGHT TO BE WITH ME**
Al Green *Hi* 72
3. **I'M STILL IN LOVE WITH YOU**
Al Green *Hi* 72
4. **TIRED OF BEING ALONE**
Al Green *Hi* 71
5. **LOOK WHAT YOU DONE FOR ME**
Al Green *Hi* 72
6. **SHA-LA-LA (MAKE ME HAPPY)**
Al Green *Hi* 74
7. **HERE I AM (COME AND TAKE ME)**
Al Green *Hi* 73
8. **CALL ME (COME BACK HOME)**
Al Green *Hi* 73
9. **PUT A LITTLE LOVE IN YOUR HEART**
Annie Lennox & Al Green *A&M* 89
10. **L-O-V-E (LOVE)**
Al Green *Hi* 75

The Top 10 Songs of HERMAN'S HERMITS

PETER NOONE was born in Liverpool but raised in Manchester, where he was a child star, with running roles in TV series like *Knight Errant* and *Coronation Street*. He attended the Manchester School of Music and formed a band called the Cyclones, later renamed the Heartbeats.

When record producer Mickie Most saw Noone on *Coronation Street* he thought he resembled a young John F. Kennedy. The other Heartbeats thought he resembled Sherman, the human companion to the dog named Mr. Peabody on *The Bullwinkle Show*. So when Most approached the band about recording, they changed their name to Herman and the Hermits and then simply Herman's Hermits.

The first single produced by Most was "I'm Into Something Good," a Carole King/Gerry Goffin song originally recorded by Earl-Jean of the Cookies. It was Herman's Hermits' only No. 1 in the United Kingdom. In the United States, "Mrs. Brown You've Got A Lovely Daughter" entered the Hot 100 at No. 12, the highest debut in history at the time. One of seven songs by the Hermits to enter the Hot 100 in 1965, "Mrs. Brown" was the first American No. 1 for the group.

01. **MRS. BROWN YOU'VE GOT A LOVELY DAUGHTER**
Herman's Hermits *MGM* 65
02. **I'M HENRY VIII, I AM**
Herman's Hermits *MGM* 65
03. **CAN'T YOU HEAR MY HEARTBEAT**
Herman's Hermits *MGM* 65
04. **THERE'S A KIND OF HUSH**
Herman's Hermits *MGM* 67
05. **LISTEN PEOPLE**
Herman's Hermits *MGM* 66
06. **WONDERFUL WORLD**
Herman's Hermits *MGM* 65
07. **SILHOUETTES**
Herman's Hermits *MGM* 65
08. **I'M INTO SOMETHING GOOD**
Herman's Hermits *MGM* 64
09. **DANDY**
Herman's Hermits *MGM* 66
10. **A MUST TO AVOID**
Herman's Hermits *MGM* 66

The Top 10 Songs of THE ISLEY BROTHERS

THE ISLEY BROTHERS have been a force on the charts over six different decades, from their debut on the Hot 100 with "Shout—Part 1" in 1959 to the top 20 single "Contagious" in 2001. O'Kelly, Rudolph, Ronald, and Vernon grew up in Cincinnati, Ohio. When Vernon was killed in 1954, the other three brothers didn't want to continue singing. With their parents' encouragement they soldiered on, heading to New York in 1956. After a stint with George Goldner's various labels, RCA's Howard Bloom signed them and producers Hugo & Luigi recorded "Shout."

The brothers made enough money to buy houses in New Jersey. They changed labels, moving to Atlantic and then Wand. In 1962 they recorded a song that had flopped a year earlier for the Top Notes: "Twist And Shout." Next they signed with United Artists and then formed their own label, T-Neck, after Teaneck, New Jersey. After just one single they returned to Atlantic briefly, then in December 1965 signed with Motown and earned their biggest hit to date, "This Old Heart Of Mine (Is Weak For You)." In 1969 they reactivated T-Neck and recorded the highest-charting single of their career, "It's Your Thing."

01 **IT'S YOUR THING**
   Isley Brothers *T-Neck* 69
02 **DOWN LOW (NOBODY HAS TO KNOW)**
   R. Kelly f/Ronald Isley *Jive* 96
03 **FIGHT THE POWER (PART 1)**
   Isley Brothers *T-Neck* 75
04 **THAT LADY (PART 1)**
   Isley Brothers *T-Neck* 73
05 **THIS OLD HEART OF MINE**
   Rod Stewart w/Ronald Isley *Warner Bros.* 90
06 **TWIST AND SHOUT**
   Isley Brothers *Wand* 62
07 **THIS OLD HEART OF MINE
   (IS WEAK FOR YOU)**
   Isley Brothers *Tamla* 66
08 **CONTAGIOUS**
   Isley Brothers f/Ronald Isley aka Mr. Biggs
   DreamWorks 01
09 **LOVE THE ONE YOU'RE WITH**
   Isley Brothers *T-Neck* 71
10 **FOR THE LOVE OF YOU (PART 1 & 2)**
   Isley Brothers *T-Neck* 75

The Top 10 Songs of
STEVE LAWRENCE & EYDIE GORME

ONE OF HOLLYWOOD'S most enduring and endearing couples, Steve Lawrence and Eydie Gorme met at a drugstore near the Brill Building in New York City. Lawrence became a regular on Steve Allen's late-night TV show in July 1952 and soon after, Gorme became the show's "girl singer." They were married in Las Vegas on December 29, 1957.

Lawrence was born Sidney Leibowitz in Brooklyn, the son of a cantor. He was eight when he started singing in his father's synagogue. An appearance on *Arthur Godfrey's Talent Scouts* led to a contract with King Records. He then recorded for Coral, ABC-Paramount, and United Artists before signing with Columbia.

Gorme was born in the Bronx and sang in her high school's musicals and local bands. She also signed with Coral and recorded duets with Lawrence. After a stint on ABC-Paramount she moved to Columbia with her husband. Teamed with New York–based writers such as Carole King and Barry Mann, the couple soared up the Hot 100 with hits like "Go Away Little Girl" (Lawrence) and "Blame It On The Bossa Nova" (Gorme) as well as the duet "I Want To Stay Here."

01 **GO AWAY LITTLE GIRL**
   Steve Lawrence *Columbia* 63
02 **PRETTY BLUE EYES**
   Steve Lawrence *ABC-Paramount* 60
03 **PARTY DOLL**
   Steve Lawrence *Coral* 57
04 **BLAME IT ON THE BOSSA NOVA**
   Eydie Gorme *Columbia* 63
05 **PORTRAIT OF MY LOVE**
   Steve Lawrence *UA* 61
06 **FOOTSTEPS**
   Steve Lawrence *ABC-Paramount* 60
07 **WALKING PROUD**
   Steve Lawrence *Columbia* 63
08 **DON'T BE AFRAID, LITTLE DARLIN'**
   Steve Lawrence *Columbia* 63
09 **I WANT TO STAY HERE**
   Steve Lawrence & Eydie Gorme *Columbia* 63
10 **POOR LITTLE RICH GIRL**
   Steve Lawrence *Columbia* 63

The Top 10 Songs of
KENNY LOGGINS/LOGGINS & MESSINA

KENNY LOGGINS was a student at Pasadena City College in Southern California when he decided to pursue a career in music. He played in a band called Second Helping and held down a day job at a music publisher. He toured with the Electric Prunes and started writing songs. His first hit was "House at Pooh Corner," a Nitty Gritty Dirt Band single in 1971.

In September of that year, Loggins signed with Columbia as a solo artist. His first album featured a former member of Buffalo Springfield and was titled *Kenny Loggins With Jim Messina: Sittin' In.* Following that album's success, Loggins and Messina remained professional partners until 1975 and had 10 chart entries on the Hot 100. Their biggest hit together was "Your Mama Don't Dance," No. 4 in 1973.

After going their separate ways, Loggins began a successful solo career but still teamed up with other artists, among them an uncredited Stevie Nicks on "Whenever I Call You 'Friend'" and Steve Perry on "Don't Fight It."

Loggins' two biggest hits are both from soundtracks: "Footloose" from the movie of the same name and "Danger Zone" from *Top Gun*.

01 FOOTLOOSE
Kenny Loggins *Columbia* 84
02 DANGER ZONE
Kenny Loggins *Columbia* 86
03 YOUR MAMA DON'T DANCE
Kenny Loggins & Jim Messina *Columbia* 73
04 THIS IS IT
Kenny Loggins *Columbia* 80
05 WHENEVER I CALL YOU "FRIEND"
Kenny Loggins *Columbia* 78
06 HEART TO HEART
Kenny Loggins *Columbia* 83
07 I'M ALRIGHT
Kenny Loggins *Columbia* 80
08 NOBODY'S FOOL
Kenny Loggins *Columbia* 88
09 MEET ME HALF WAY
Kenny Loggins *Columbia* 87
10 MY MUSIC
Loggins & Messina *Columbia* 73

The Top 10 Songs of THE LOVIN' SPOONFUL

WHEN THE BEATLES appeared on *The Ed Sullivan Show* on February 9, 1964, it wasn't the only pivotal moment in rock and roll taking place. That same night, John Sebastian met Zal Yanovsky at the home of Cass Elliott. After watching the Fab Four on TV, they jammed for a couple of hours before retreating to their separate corners. Elliott played matchmaker, telling each one they should team up professionally. Along with Denny Doherty, they all ended up in a band called the Mugwumps.

Sebastian was fired from the group, and when the Mugwumps subsequently fell apart, Sebastian and Yanovsky met Steve Boone and Joe Butler in Greenwich Village. They organized as the Lovin' Spoonful', the name inspired by a Mississippi John Hurt lyric, "I love my baby by the lovin' spoonful."

"Do You Believe In Magic" was recorded as a demo, and many labels passed before the band was signed to Kama Sutra. After a run of hit singles, Sebastian left for a solo career. He had one chart entry on his own, "She's A Lady" in 1969, then didn't return to the Hot 100 until seven years later, when he recorded "Welcome Back" from the TV series *Welcome Back, Kotter.*

01 SUMMER IN THE CITY
The Lovin' Spoonful *Kama Sutra* 66
02 WELCOME BACK
John Sebastian *Reprise* 76
03 DAYDREAM
The Lovin' Spoonful *Kama Sutra* 66
04 DID YOU EVER HAVE TO MAKE UP YOUR MIND?
The Lovin' Spoonful *Kama Sutra* 66
05 DO YOU BELIEVE IN MAGIC
The Lovin' Spoonful *Kama Sutra* 65
06 YOU DIDN'T HAVE TO BE SO NICE
The Lovin' Spoonful *Kama Sutra* 66
07 NASHVILLE CATS
The Lovin' Spoonful *Kama Sutra* 67
08 RAIN ON THE ROOF
The Lovin' Spoonful *Kama Sutra* 66
09 DARLING BE HOME SOON
The Lovin' Spoonful *Kama Sutra* 67
10 SIX O'CLOCK
The Lovin' Spoonful *Kama Sutra* 67

The Top 10 Songs of
THE MAMAS AND THE PAPAS

JOHN PHILLIPS was in a folk trio called the Journeymen. While on tour, they had an opening act called the Halifax Three, which included Denny Doherty. Ellen Naomi Cohen, nicknamed Cassandra by her father, took the stage name Cass Elliot while recording with another trio, the Big Three. When the Halifax Three and the Big Three broke up, Doherty and Elliott teamed with future Lovin' Spoonful members John Sebastian and Zal Yanovsky to form the Mugwumps.

In 1964, the Journeymen and the Mugwumps both disbanded. Phillips, now married to Holly Michelle Gilliam, formed the New Journeymen with Denny to fulfill contract obligations. They spent time living in the Virgin Islands but ended up in California. With Elliott, they shared living quarters with singer Barry McGuire. Newly signed to Dunhill Records, McGuire introduced his friends to his producer, Lou Adler, who asked the foursome to sing backing vocals on McGuire's first album.

One of the tracks on McGuire's LP was a song written by John, "California Dreamin'." Later, McGuire's vocals were wiped off and replaced by the voices of his four roommates. They called themselves the Magic Circle, but a line of dialogue in a documentary about the Hell's Angels inspired John to change the name to the Mamas and the Papas.

01 MONDAY, MONDAY
The Mamas and the Papas *Dunhill* 66
02 DEDICATED TO THE ONE I LOVE
The Mamas and the Papas *Dunhill* 67
03 CALIFORNIA DREAMIN'
The Mamas and the Papas *Dunhill* 66
04 WORDS OF LOVE
The Mamas and the Papas *Dunhill* 67
05 I SAW HER AGAIN
The Mamas and the Papas *Dunhill* 66
06 DREAM A LITTLE DREAM OF ME
Mama Cass *Dunhill* 68
07 CREEQUE ALLEY
The Mamas and the Papas *Dunhill* 67
08 TWELVE THIRTY (YOUNG GIRLS ARE COMING TO THE CANYON)
The Mamas and the Papas *Dunhill* 67
09 LOOK THROUGH MY WINDOW
The Mamas and the Papas *Dunhill* 66
10 GLAD TO BE UNHAPPY
The Mamas and the Papas *Dunhill* 67

The Top 10 Songs of DEAN MARTIN

DINO CROCETTI'S FATHER, a barber, wanted his son to follow in his footsteps. Instead, Dino became a boxer, but he quit the ring after someone punched him in the nose too hard. He got a job singing with Sammy Watkins' band in Cleveland, then went out on his own with a new name and a nose job.

By 1946, Dean Martin was a headliner at the 500 Club in Atlantic City. The owner of the club suggested that Martin team up with a 20-year-old comedian who lip-synced to records. The first night with Jerry Lewis was a disaster, so they threw out the script and ad-libbed the second night. Soon, they were the hottest comedy team in America.

Martin signed with Capitol in 1948 and had a string of pre-rock era hits that included "That's Amore" and "Sway." In 1956, his single "Memories Are Made Of This" topped the pop charts for five weeks. Later that year, Martin and Lewis made headlines by breaking up the act.

In 1962, Martin left Capitol for Reprise, a label owned by his friend Frank Sinatra. For an album of low-key, moody songs, he recorded 11 tracks and needed one more when he settled on a tune Sinatra had recorded in 1950, "Everybody Loves Somebody."

01 MEMORIES ARE MADE OF THIS
Dean Martin *Capitol* 56
02 EVERYBODY LOVES SOMEBODY
Dean Martin *Reprise* 64
03 RETURN TO ME
Dean Martin *Capitol* 58
04 THE DOOR IS STILL OPEN TO MY HEART
Dean Martin *Reprise* 64
05 I WILL
Dean Martin *Reprise* 65
06 VOLARE (NEL BLU DIPINTO DI BLU)
Dean Martin *Capitol* 58
07 SEND ME THE PILLOW YOU DREAM ON
Dean Martin *Reprise* 65
08 HOUSTON
Dean Martin *Reprise* 65
09 YOU'RE NOBODY TILL SOMEBODY LOVES YOU
Dean Martin *Reprise* 65
10 IN THE CHAPEL IN THE MOONLIGHT
Dean Martin *Reprise* 67

The Top 10 Songs of RICHARD MARX

RICHARD MARX'S FATHER was a jazz pianist who wrote and produced 30-second commercial jingles on which his mother sang the vocals. "I did it too when I was a little kid," he says. He wasn't yet in his teens when he started playing guitar, but he soon switched over to keyboards. At 15 he started writing songs to impress girls in high school (he says it didn't work).

He sent his demos to record companies, and one tape ended up in the hands of Lionel Richie, who offered Marx a job singing backing vocals. He moved from his native Chicago to Los Angeles to accept the offer, and can be heard on Richie hits like "All Night Long (All Night)" and "Running With The Night."

Marx found more work as a session singer, and co-wrote "What About Me?" with David Foster and Kenny Rogers. The song peaked at No. 15 for Rogers. But Marx found it difficult to persuade record labels to sign him as an artist. When Foster told him he would never be an artist, he was devastated.

But it was through Foster that Marx met A&R veteran Bobby Colomby, who arranged an audition for Manhattan Records chief Bruce Lundvall, the man who signed Marx to the EMI-owned label.

01 **RIGHT HERE WAITING**
Richard Marx *EMI* 89
02 **HOLD ON TO THE NIGHTS**
Richard Marx *EMI-Manhattan* 88
03 **ENDLESS SUMMER NIGHTS**
Richard Marx *EMI-Manhattan* 88
04 **SATISFIED**
Richard Marx *EMI* 89
05 **NOW AND FOREVER**
Richard Marx *Capitol* 94
06 **SHOULD'VE KNOWN BETTER**
Richard Marx *Manhattan* 87
07 **DON'T MEAN NOTHING**
Richard Marx *Manhattan* 62
08 **ANGELIA**
Richard Marx *EMI* 89
09 **HAZARD**
Richard Marx *Capitol* 92
10 **KEEP COMING BACK**
Richard Marx *Capitol* 91

The Top 10 Songs of JOHNNY MATHIS

BEFORE HE BECAME the most popular romantic singer in America, Johnny Mathis was a high school student in San Francisco who lettered in sports. In college, he had to choose between high jumping at the 1956 Olympics in Melbourne or signing with Columbia Records. He decided to compete in Australia, but a spinal injury ended those plans and he traveled to New York to begin his recording career.

Mathis' first jazz-oriented album for the label went unnoticed and he was concerned he would be dropped. Instead, Columbia's A&R chief, Mitch Miller, looked for more appropriate songs and found "It's Not For Me To Say," "Chances Are," "The Twelfth Of Never," and "Wonderful! Wonderful!"

Mathis returned to the top 10 in 1962–63 with a pair of hits, "Gina" and "What Will Mary Say," then left for a brief stint with Mercury, returning to Columbia in 1967. Six years later he had a creative renaissance when he teamed with Thom Bell and Linda Creed for an album. In 1978, he topped the Hot 100 for the first time when he recorded "Too Much, Too Little, Too Late" with Deniece Williams.

01 **TOO MUCH, TOO LITTLE, TOO LATE**
Johnny Mathis & Deniece Williams
Columbia 78
02 **CHANCES ARE / THE TWELFTH OF NEVER**
Johnny Mathis *Columbia* 57
03 **IT'S NOT FOR ME TO SAY**
Johnny Mathis *Columbia* 57
04 **WONDERFUL! WONDERFUL!**
Johnny Mathis *Columbia* 57
05 **MISTY**
Johnny Mathis *Columbia* 59
06 **WHAT WILL MARY SAY**
Johnny Mathis *Columbia* 63
07 **GINA**
Johnny Mathis *Columbia* 62
08 **CALL ME**
Johnny Mathis *Columbia* 58
09 **SMALL WORLD**
Johnny Mathis *Columbia* 59
10 **ALL THE TIME / TEACHER, TEACHER**
Johnny Mathis *Columbia* 58

The Top 10 Songs of
JOHN COUGAR MELLENCAMP

JOHN MELLENCAMP had a rough start, growing up in working-class Seymour, Indiana. He was short and overweight, and he hated authority figures. He got into fights and was kicked off the high school football team for smoking. He was 18 when he married his pregnant 23-year-old girlfriend. They lived with her folks until they threw him out.

In 1975, David Bowie's manager, Tony DeFries, heard Mellencamp's demo tape and signed him to MCA. When the record came out, he was shocked to see his name on the label: Johnny Cougar. He thought the name was ridiculous and hated that he was stuck with it. The album failed and the label dropped him. He found a new manager, Billy Gaff, who had his own label, Riva. On the new imprint, he hit the Hot 100 for the first time with "I Need a Lover," a No. 28 hit in 1979.

In 1982, the *American Fool* album made him a star. The first single, "Hurts So Good," peaked at No. 3. The follow-up, "Jack and Diane," spent four weeks at No. 1. A year later, he insisted on adding his real last name, and by the time the 1991 album *Whenever We Wanted*, was released, "Cougar" had disappeared, leaving the heartland rocker to be known simply as John Mellencamp.

01 **JACK AND DIANE**
John Cougar *Riva* 82
02 **HURTS SO GOOD**
John Cougar *Riva* 82
03 **WILD NIGHT**
John Mellencamp & Me'Shell Ndegéocello *Mercury* 94
04 **R.O.C.K. IN THE U.S.A.**
John Cougar Mellencamp *Riva* 86
05 **KEY WEST INTERMEZZO (I SAW YOU FIRST)**
John Mellencamp *Mercury* 96
06 **SMALL TOWN**
John Cougar Mellencamp *Riva* 85
07 **LONELY OL' NIGHT**
John Cougar Mellencamp *Riva* 85
08 **CRUMBLIN' DOWN**
John Cougar Mellencamp *Riva* 83
09 **PINK HOUSES**
John Cougar Mellencamp *Riva* 84
10 **CHERRY BOMB**
John Cougar Mellencamp *Mercury* 88

The Top 10 Songs of THE MOODY BLUES

THE BRITISH BAND MB Five, named for the brewery (Mitchell & Butler) that financed the club where they had a residency, turned the "M" into Moody and the "B" into Blues. Based in Birmingham and founded by Denny Laine, the group caught America's attention in 1965 with a remake of a U.S. R&B song from 1964, Bessie Banks' "Go Now!" The Moody Blues' version peaked at No. 10 on the Hot 100.

In October 1966, Laine split for a solo career and the group decided not to continue. One month later, vocalist Ray Thomas and drummer Graeme Edge reconsidered. With keyboardist Mike Piner back in the fold and the addition of new members Justin Hayward on guitar and vocals and John Lodge on bass and vocals, the Moody Blues were still a group, though headed in an entirely new direction.

That became obvious with the 1968 release of the concept album *Days Of Future Passed*. The single "Nights In White Satin" missed the U.S. chart the first time around, but became the group's biggest American hit when it belatedly spent two weeks at No. 2 in 1972.

The Moody Blues continued to chart into the '80s and had its second highest-charting single in 1986, when "Your Wildest Dreams" climbed to No. 9.

01 **NIGHTS IN WHITE SATIN**
The Moody Blues *Deram* 72
02 **YOUR WILDEST DREAMS**
The Moody Blues *Threshold* 86
03 **GEMINI DREAM**
The Moody Blues *Threshold* 81
04 **I'M JUST A SINGER (IN A ROCK AND ROLL BAND)**
The Moody Blues *Threshold* 73
05 **THE VOICE**
The Moody Blues *Threshold* 81
06 **GO NOW!**
The Moody Blues *London* 65
07 **QUESTION**
The Moody Blues *Threshold* 70
08 **TUESDAY AFTERNOON (FOREVER AFTERNOON)**
The Moody Blues *Deram* 68
09 **THE STORY IN YOUR EYES**
The Moody Blues *Threshold* 71
10 **SITTING AT THE WHEEL**
The Moody Blues *Threshold* 83

The Top 10 Songs of NELLY

CORNELL HAYNES, JR., was born in Texas and lived in Spain with his mother and Air Force father until they settled in St. Louis. He excelled in sports in high school, and a pro career in baseball seemed a possibility until he formed a rap crew with a group of friends. "St. Louis didn't have a hip-hop scene," he says. "We borrowed it from everybody else's."

"Gimme What Ya Got" by the St. Lunatics made some local noise and when the group was asked to guest-star on an album by an artist named Kardan, they suggested that Nelly do it on his own. That led to a deal with Universal and a debut album, *Country Grammar*. It included the hit "Ride Wit Me" and went multi-platinum, but its success was eclipsed by the next album, *Nellyville*. The first single arrived on radio just as summer was about to begin, the right time to be singing "Hot in Herre." The Neptunes-produced track ruled the Hot 100 for seven weeks.

"Hot in Herre" was knocked off its perch by the next Nelly single, "Dilemma," which featured Kelly Rowland of Destiny's Child. This second release was an even bigger hit, dominating the Hot 100 for 10 weeks.

01 **DILEMMA**
Nelly f/Kelly Rowland *Fo' Reel* 02
02 **HOT IN HERRE**
Nelly *Fo' Reel* 02
03 **SHAKE YA TAILFEATHER**
Nelly, P. Diddy & Murphy Lee *Bad Boy* 03
04 **GRILLZ**
Nelly f/Paul Wall, Ali & Gipp
Derrty/Fo' Reel 06
05 **WHERE THE PARTY AT**
Nelly *So So Def* 01
06 **OVER AND OVER**
Nelly f/Tim McGraw *Derrty/Fo' Reel/Curb* 04
07 **RIDE WIT ME**
Nelly f/City Spud *Fo' Reel* 01
08 **AIR FORCE ONES**
Nelly f/Kyjuan, Ali & Murphy Lee *Fo' Reel* 03
09 **MY PLACE**
Nelly f/Jaheim *Derrty/Fo' Reel* 04
10 **(HOT S**T) COUNTRY GRAMMAR**
Nelly *Fo' Reel* 00

The Top 10 Songs of
'N SYNC/JUSTIN TIMBERLAKE

AFTER EXPERIENCING SUCCESS with the Backstreet Boys, music Svengali Lou Pearlman wanted to find another boy band. In Orlando, where Pearlman's Trans Continental management firm was based, Chris Kirkpatrick was looking for singers to join his group. First, he found a 14-year old former cast member of *The Mickey Mouse Club*, Justin Timberlake, who had been writing songs with another former Mouseketeer, JC Chasez. Kirkpatrick then recruited a friend he knew from performing at Universal Studios, Joey Fatone. They needed a bass singer to complete the quintet, and through their vocal coach from their *Mickey Mouse Club* days they found Lance Bass.

Pearlman signed 'N Sync and got them a deal with German-owned RCA Records. Like the Backstreet Boys, 'N Sync first found chart success in Germany, then made a U.S. debut in March 1998 with "I Want You Back."

In 2002, the Memphis-born Timberlake released his first solo album, *Justified*, which included the hit singles "Like I Love You," "Cry Me A River," and "Rock Your Body." Four years later, the album *FutureSex/LoveSounds* yielded three No. 1 hits: "SexyBack," "My Love," and "What Goes Around . . . Comes Around."

01 **SEXYBACK**
Justin Timberlake *Jive* 06
02 **MY LOVE**
Justin Timberlake f/T.I. *Jive* 06
03 **IT'S GONNA BE ME**
'N Sync *Jive* 00
04 **BYE BYE BYE**
'N Sync *Jive* 00
05 **THIS I PROMISE YOU**
'N Sync *Jive* 00
06 **CRY ME A RIVER**
Justin Timberlake *Jive* 03
07 **I WANT YOU BACK**
'N Sync *RCA* 98
08 **GONE**
'N Sync *Jive* 01
09 **ROCK YOUR BODY**
Justin Timberlake *Jive* 03
10 **GIRLFRIEND**
'N Sync f/Nelly *Jive* 02

The Top 10 Songs of ROY ORBISON

IT SEEMS LIKE Sam Phillips only signed legends to his Memphis-based Sun Records. The elite roster included Elvis Presley, Jerry Lee Lewis, Johnny Cash, Carl Perkins, and Roy Orbison. The artist from Vernon, Texas, might have remained with Sun if he had acceded to Phillips's request to record more rock and roll, but Orbison preferred ballads. Through his association with the Everly Brothers, Roy was signed to the RCA label, but publisher Wesley Rose eventually steered him to Fred Foster's Monument Records. His first two sessions for the label weren't very productive; it was the third session that yielded "Only The Lonely," the first of Orbison's nine top 10 singles for the label. The string ended with Orbison's biggest hit, "Oh, Pretty Woman." A year later, he was wooed to the MGM label, but couldn't even achieve a top 20 hit on that imprint. In 1987, Orbison signed with Virgin Records, but died of a heart attack in December 1988. Four months later, he returned to the top 10 of the Hot 100 with the posthumous hit, "You Got It."

01 OH, PRETTY WOMAN
Roy Orbison *Monument* 64

02 RUNNING SCARED
Roy Orbison *Monument* 61

03 ONLY THE LONELY (KNOW HOW I FEEL)
Roy Orbison *Monument* 60

04 CRYING
Roy Orbison *Monument* 61

05 IN DREAMS
Roy Orbison *Monument* 63

06 DREAM BABY (HOW LONG MUST I DREAM)
Roy Orbison *Monument* 62

07 MEAN WOMAN BLUES
Roy Orbison *Monument* 63

08 IT'S OVER
Roy Orbison *Monument* 64

09 YOU GOT IT
Roy Orbison *Virgin* 89

10 BLUE ANGEL
Roy Orbison *Monument* 60

The Top 10 Songs of TONY ORLANDO & DAWN

IN 1961, Epic Records had two hits by a teen idol named Tony Orlando. "Halfway to Paradise" and "Bless You" made him a household name, but his success did not continue into 1962. As the next decade began, Orlando was working for Clive Davis as a music publisher and reluctantly agreed to secretly moonlight as lead vocalist on a song he was certain would slip into obscurity. He was wrong. "Candida," released under the group name Dawn, went to No. 3 on the Hot 100 and Orlando was asked to record the follow-up, "Knock Three Times."

When that song achieved pole position, Bell Records wanted a real-live act to tour and promote the singles. Orlando hadn't even met backing singers Telma Hopkins and Joyce Vincent yet, but he asked if they'd be interested in becoming Dawn for real.

They went on the road, but the next few Dawn singles weren't huge hits and the three members were ready to go their separate ways after one final recording session. Fortunately, that was the session where they recorded "Tie A Yellow Ribbon Round The Ole Oak Tree," a corny yet irresistible pop hit that spent four weeks at No. 1 and became the trio's signature song, both on the road and on their prime-time TV variety series.

01 KNOCK THREE TIMES
Dawn *Bell* 71

02 TIE A YELLOW RIBBON ROUND THE OLE OAK TREE
Dawn *Bell* 73

03 HE DON'T LOVE YOU (LIKE I LOVE YOU)
Tony Orlando & Dawn *Elektra* 75

04 CANDIDA
Dawn *Bell* 70

05 SAY, HAS ANYBODY SEEN MY SWEET GYPSY ROSE
Dawn f/Tony Orlando *Bell* 73

06 STEPPIN' OUT (GONNA BOOGIE TONIGHT)
Tony Orlando & Dawn *Bell* 74

07 LOOK IN MY EYES PRETTY WOMAN
Tony Orlando & Dawn *Bell* 75

08 MORNIN' BEAUTIFUL
Tony Orlando & Dawn *Elektra* 75

09 BLESS YOU
Tony Orlando *Epic* 61

10 I PLAY AND SING
Dawn *Bell* 71

The Top 10 Songs of GENE PITNEY

BEFORE CONNECTICUT-BORN Gene Pitney signed with the Musicor label, he recorded some duets for Decca with Ginny Mazarro as Jamie & Jane. He was also sending demos of his songs to New York publishers, and Pitney's "Today's Teardrops" found its way to Roy Orbison. Another demo, "(I Wanna) Love My Life Away," impressed Musicor founder Aaron Schroeder enough to sign Pitney to his label.

Pitney's distinctive voice, teamed with songwriters Carole King and Gerry Goffin and producer Phil Spector, resulted in a top 50 hit with "Every Breath I Take," followed by the title song for the film *Town Without Pity*, which landed Pitney in the top 20 for the first time.

Pitney never made it to No. 1 on the Hot 100 as an artist. Ironically, his recording of Burt Bacharach and Hal David's "Only Love Can Break A Heart" stalled at No. 2, kept out of the top spot only by Pitney's composition "He's A Rebel," recorded by the Crystals.

01 **ONLY LOVE CAN BREAK A HEART**
Gene Pitney *Musicor* 62
02 **IT HURTS TO BE IN LOVE**
Gene Pitney *Musicor* 64
03 **(THE MAN WHO SHOT) LIBERTY VALANCE**
Gene Pitney *Musicor* 62
04 **I'M GONNA BE STRONG**
Gene Pitney *Musicor* 64
05 **HALF HEAVEN—HALF HEARTACHE**
Gene Pitney *Musicor* 63
06 **TOWN WITHOUT PITY**
Gene Pitney *Musicor* 62
07 **MECCA**
Gene Pitney *Musicor* 63
08 **LAST CHANCE TO TURN AROUND**
Gene Pitney *Musicor* 65
09 **SHE'S A HEARTBREAKER**
Gene Pitney *Musicor* 68
10 **TRUE LOVE NEVER RUNS SMOOTH**
Gene Pitney *Musicor* 63

The Top 10 Songs of THE PLATTERS

THE FOUR MALE MEMBERS of the Platters were already a group when they signed a management contract with producer Buck Ram in 1953. Ram wanted a female in the mix, and recruited 15-year-old Zola Taylor from Shirley Gunter and the Queens. Federal Records signed the Platters and released a single, "Only You (And You Alone)," but it didn't fare well.

When Mercury executives approached Ram about signing his other group, the Penguins, the manager agreed with one condition: The label also had to sign the Platters. The group's first single for Mercury was a new recording of "Only You." Lead singer Tony Williams' wife was secretary to influential Los Angeles disc jockey Hunter Hancock. He played the song on his show and it was heard by a Seattle jock who went home and gave it airplay, creating a national hit.

The Platters had three No. 1 singles ("My Prayer," "Twilight Time," and "Smoke Gets In Your Eyes"). The roster of singers continued to change over the years, so it was a slightly altered line-up that signed to Musicor in 1966 and scored a comeback single, "With This Ring."

Ram owned the copyrighted name of the group, and during his lifetime filed almost 50 lawsuits against ersatz Platters all over the world.

01 **MY PRAYER**
The Platters *Mercury* 56
02 **SMOKE GETS IN YOUR EYES**
The Platters *Mercury* 59
03 **THE GREAT PRETENDER**
The Platters *Mercury* 56
04 **TWILIGHT TIME**
The Platters *Mercury* 58
05 **ONLY YOU (AND YOU ALONE)**
The Platters *Mercury* 55
06 **(YOU'VE GOT) THE MAGIC TOUCH**
The Platters *Mercury* 56
07 **HARBOR LIGHTS**
The Platters *Mercury* 60
08 **I'M SORRY / HE'S MINE**
The Platters *Mercury* 57
09 **YOU'LL NEVER NEVER KNOW / IT ISN'T RIGHT**
The Platters *Mercury* 56
10 **ENCHANTED**
The Platters *Mercury* 59

ELTON AND SARAH POINTER were ministers at the Church of God in West Oakland, California, and did not permit their four daughters to listen to secular music. When Ruth, Anita, Bonnie, and June were alone in the house, they defied their parents, hoping their grandfather wouldn't tell on them.

Bonnie and June formed a singing duo, which expanded as first Anita and then Ruth joined. They hooked up with producer David Rubinson and were signed to Atlantic, but Rubinson was furious when the label turned the sisters into a generic R&B group. He took them to Blue Thumb, and their '40s-style look and sound clicked; they charted with "Yes We Can Can," "Wang Dang Doodle," and the country-tinged "Fairytale."

In 1976 Bonnie signed with Motown as a solo act. Her sisters began a long association with producer Richard Perry and recorded a series of hits for his label, Planet. Between 1978 and 1985 the Pointer Sisters scored seven top 10 hits, including "Fire" and "Slow Hand," which both peaked at No. 2.

Baby sister June eventually left the group, which continued under the guidance of Ruth and Anita. June died on April 11, 2006, of lung cancer.

The Top 10 Songs of QUEEN

BEFORE THERE WAS Queen there was Smile, a group formed in 1967 by guitarist Brian May and drummer Roger Taylor. In 1970, that duo teamed up with the singer of a heavy metal band known as Wreckage. His name was Freddie Mercury. With the addition of bassist John Deacon, Queen was a complete unit. They avoided the club circuit in England, playing for invited guests at private gigs, and only later became regulars at the Marquee Club. They struggled for two years, until producers Roy Thomas Baker and John Anthony heard a demo tape. Many labels were approached, but nothing happened until EMI offered a contract.

Queen dented the U.K. singles chart with "Seven Seas of Rhye," but it wasn't until the release of "Killer Queen" that the quartet made an impression in America. In Great Britain, the group had its biggest hit with the 1975 epic, "Bohemian Rhapsody." The single ruled the charts for nine weeks in its original chart run (and would add another five weeks to that total after Mercury's death in 1991). In the United States, "Bohemian Rhapsody" also had two chart runs, peaking at No. 9 in 1975 and No. 2 in 1992, thanks to its inclusion in the film *Wayne's World*. Queen scored two No. 1 hits on the Hot 100: "Crazy Little Thing Called Love" and "Another One Bites The Dust," both in 1980.

01 **ANOTHER ONE BITES THE DUST**
Queen *Elektra* 80
02 **CRAZY LITTLE THING CALLED LOVE**
Queen *Elektra* 80
03 **BOHEMIAN RHAPSODY**
Queen *Elektra* 76
04 **WE ARE THE CHAMPIONS /**
WE WILL ROCK YOU
Queen *Elektra* 78
05 **SOMEBODY TO LOVE**
Queen *Elektra* 77
06 **YOU'RE MY BEST FRIEND**
Queen *Elektra* 76
07 **KILLER QUEEN**
Queen *Elektra* 75
08 **BODY LANGUAGE**
Queen *Elektra* 82
09 **RADIO GA-GA**
Queen *Elektra* 84
10 **UNDER PRESSURE**
Queen & David Bowie *Elektra* 82

The Top 10 Songs of THE RASCALS

FELIX CAVALIERE, Eddie Brigati, and Gene Cornish were members of Joey Dee's backing band the Starliters when Dee left the Peppermint Lounge to open his own club. After they felt like they had played "Peppermint Twist" one too many times, they formed their own group with Dino Danelli. The Rascals made their debut in 1965 at the Choo Choo Club in Garfield, New Jersey. At a gig at the Barge in Long Island, they met promoter Sid Bernstein, who became their manager and signed them to Atlantic Records.

Before their first single was released, the quartet discovered their name conflicted with a group called the Harmonica Rascals. Without their knowledge, the name "Young Rascals" was chosen for them. Cavaliere would have preferred almost any other adjective, to avoid confusion with the Little Rascals.

With a heavy R&B influence, the Young Rascals became known as a blue-eyed soul group, especially after covering the Olympics' "Good Lovin'." After that No. 1 hit, the foursome focused on writing their own songs. It was starting to look like a bad move, until Cavaliere fell in love and was inspired to write "Groovin'" with Brigati. The single spent four weeks at No. 1.

01 **PEOPLE GOT TO BE FREE**
The Rascals *Atlantic* 68
02 **GROOVIN'**
The Young Rascals *Atlantic* 67
03 **GOOD LOVIN'**
The Young Rascals *Atlantic* 66
04 **A BEAUTIFUL MORNING**
The Rascals *Atlantic* 68
05 **HOW CAN I BE SURE**
The Young Rascals *Atlantic* 67
06 **I'VE BEEN LONELY TOO LONG**
The Young Rascals *Atlantic* 67
07 **A GIRL LIKE YOU**
The Young Rascals *Atlantic* 67
08 **SEE**
The Rascals *Atlantic* 69
09 **YOU BETTER RUN**
The Young Rascals *Atlantic* 66
10 **IT'S WONDERFUL**
The Young Rascals *Atlantic* 68

The Top 10 Songs of JOHNNY RIVERS

JOHN RAMISTELLA was born in New York City and moved to Baton Rouge, Louisiana, when he was three. On a return visit to Manhattan when he was 15, Johnny introduced himself to well-known DJ Alan Freed at radio station WINS. Freed liked the youngster's songs and arranged for him to be signed to George Goldner's Gone/End Records. It was Freed who suggested that Johnny find a shorter last name, and inspired by his bayou upbringing near the Mississippi River, he chose Rivers.

He did release a single with Goldner, but was uncomfortable recording in New York and returned to Louisiana. One of his songs was recorded by Ricky Nelson, and in 1958 Johnny flew to Los Angeles to meet Nelson. Rivers fell in love with Southern California and moved there in 1961. He found studio work and built a small following by playing at a club called Gazzarri's. Then he was asked to headline a new club on the Sunset Strip, the Whisky-a-Go-Go. At the same time, a meeting with producer Lou Adler led to a contract with Imperial Records.

A live album recorded at the Whisky spawned Rivers' first two chart singles, cover versions of Chuck Berry's "Memphis" and "Maybelline."

01 **POOR SIDE OF TOWN**
Johnny Rivers *Imperial* 66
02 **MEMPHIS**
Johnny Rivers *Imperial* 64
03 **BABY I NEED YOUR LOVIN'**
Johnny Rivers *Imperial* 67
04 **SWAYIN' TO THE MUSIC (SLOW DANCIN')**
Johnny Rivers *Big Tree* 77
05 **SECRET AGENT MAN**
Johnny Rivers *Imperial* 66
06 **ROCKIN' PNEUMONIA—BOOGIE WOOGIE FLU**
Johnny Rivers *UA* 73
07 **SEVENTH SON**
Johnny Rivers *Imperial* 65
08 **MOUNTAIN OF LOVE**
Johnny Rivers *Imperial* 64
09 **THE TRACKS OF MY TEARS**
Johnny Rivers *Imperial* 67
10 **MAYBELLINE**
Johnny Rivers *Imperial* 64

The Top 10 Songs of SANTANA

CARLOS SANTANA was born in Autlan, Mexico, the son of a mariachi violinist. The family moved to Tijuana and then to San Francisco. Carlos' father wanted him to take up the violin, but the youngster was more interested in the blues. After graduating from Mission High School, he formed the Santana Blues Band. Clive Davis signed the group to Columbia, and the name was shortened to Santana.

On August 16, 1969, Santana drew national attention by performing at Woodstock. One month later, the band's first LP debuted on the *Billboard* album chart, ultimately peaking at No. 4. In 1970, two Santana singles entered the Hot 100. "Evil Ways" and "Black Magic Woman" were both top 10 hits.

After a long stint with Columbia, Santana signed with Polydor in 1992, and then Carlos formed his own label through Island. While touring with Jeff Beck, Santana received a phone call from Clive Davis, who offered to sign him to Arista when his current contract was up. In 1999, Santana and Davis were reunited and as a result Santana had its biggest hit, a collaboration with Rob Thomas titled "Smooth." The single spent 12 weeks at No. 1 and the follow-up, "Maria Marla," had a 10 week reign.

01 **SMOOTH**
Santana f/Rob Thomas *Arista* 99
02 **MARIA MARIA**
Santana f/the Product G&B *Arista* 00
03 **THE GAME OF LOVE**
Santana f/Michelle Branch *Arista* 02
04 **BLACK MAGIC WOMAN**
Santana *Columbia* 71
05 **EVIL WAYS**
Santana *Columbia* 70
06 **HOLD ON**
Santana *Columbia* 82
07 **EVERYBODY'S EVERYTHING**
Santana *Columbia* 71
08 **OYE COMO VA**
Santana *Columbia* 71
09 **WINNING**
Santana *Columbia* 81
10 **WHY DON'T YOU AND I**
Santana f/Alex Brand or Chad Kroeger *Arista* 03

The Top 10 Songs of THE SHIRELLES

SHIRLEY OWENS and Addie "Micki" Harris were friends in elementary school in Passaic, New Jersey. In junior high they met Doris Kenner and Beverly Lee. Shirley and Beverly had the idea to start a singing group and asked their friends Micki and Doris to complete the quartet. A classmate, Mary Jane Greenberg, asked them to audition for her mother Florence, who owned a small label called Tiara. The four girls said no, and Mary Jane was so persistent they took to hiding when they saw her approaching. After winning a school talent contest with a song they composed, "I Met Him On A Sunday," they finally agreed to see Florence. She loved them and signed them immediately, with their parents' permission.

Unhappy with their group name, the Poquellos, they had only one day to find a new name before the labels for their first single were printed. They unanimously chose the Shirelles. Florence felt she didn't have the muscle to promote the single "I Met Him On A Sunday" nationally, so she leased it to Decca. When two follow-ups flopped, she brought the girls back to her own label, now renamed Scepter. In January 1961, the Shirelles became the first girl group in the rock era to have a No. 1 single when "Will You Love Me Tomorrow" hit pole position.

01 **SOLDIER BOY**
The Shirelles *Scepter* 62
02 **WILL YOU LOVE ME TOMORROW**
The Shirelles *Scepter* 61
03 **DEDICATED TO THE ONE I LOVE**
The Shirelles *Scepter* 61
04 **MAMA SAID**
The Shirelles *Scepter* 61
05 **FOOLISH LITTLE GIRL**
The Shirelles *Scepter* 63
06 **BABY IT'S YOU**
The Shirelles *Scepter* 62
07 **EVERYBODY LOVES A LOVER**
The Shirelles *Scepter* 63
08 **BIG JOHN**
The Shirelles *Scepter* 61
09 **WELCOME HOME BABY**
The Shirelles *Scepter* 62
10 **DON'T SAY GOODNIGHT AND MEAN GOODBYE**
The Shirelles *Scepter* 63

The Top 10 Songs of CARLY SIMON

CARLY SIMON'S first solo chart entry on the Hot 100, "That's The Way I've Always Heard It Should Be," addressed her childhood and family relationships. She was born in New York City to Richard and Andrea Simon. Her father was the co-founder of the Simon & Schuster publishing company; her mother was a voice student who impressed upon her children the importance of music.

The Simon children listened to their mother well. The eldest daughter, Joanna, became a mezzo-soprano opera singer. While a student at Sarah Lawrence, Carly and her sister Lucy formed a duo, the Simon Sisters, and signed with Kapp Records. Their single, "Winkin', Blinkin' And Nod" peaked at No. 74 on the Hot 100 in 1964.

Albert Grossman wanted to record Carly as the female Bob Dylan but the project was abandoned. Signed to Elektra, Carly's first album earned critical acclaim just as the singer/songwriter era was underway. In 1973, she spent three weeks at No. 1 with the lyrical mystery, "You're So Vain." Despite endless speculation, Simon has kept the song's inspiration a closely guarded secret.

She has said the song is not about James Taylor, her husband from 1972 to 1983. During their marriage, they released two duet singles, remakes of "Mockingbird" and "Devoted To You."

01 **YOU'RE SO VAIN**
Carly Simon *Elektra* 73
02 **NOBODY DOES IT BETTER**
Carly Simon *Elektra* 77
03 **MOCKINGBIRD**
Carly Simon & James Taylor *Elektra* 74
04 **YOU BELONG TO ME**
Carly Simon *Elektra* 78
05 **JESSE**
Carly Simon *Warner Bros.* 80
06 **ANTICIPATION**
Carly Simon *Elektra* 72
07 **THAT'S THE WAY I'VE ALWAYS HEARD IT SHOULD BE**
Carly Simon *Elektra* 71
08 **THE RIGHT THING TO DO**
Carly Simon *Elektra* 73
09 **COMING AROUND AGAIN**
Carly Simon *Arista* 87
10 **HAVEN'T GOT TIME FOR THE PAIN**
Carly Simon *Elektra* 74

The Top 10 Songs of THE SINATRAS

FRANCIS ALBERT Sinatra was born on December 12, 1915, in Hoboken, New Jersey. He wanted to be a professional singer, but at his mother's insistence went to work for a newspaper, moving up from copy boy to sportswriter. He pursued a singing career at the same time, and recorded his first demo in February 1939. In December of that year, Tommy Dorsey offered him a job singing with his band for $100 per week. With Dorsey's band, Sinatra sang "I'll Never Smile Again" in the film *Las Vegas Nights*. Released as a single, it topped the first *Billboard* chart, published on July 20, 1940. Sinatra's career spanned the war years and the rock era, as he graduated from teen idol to become the ultimate singing star of the century.

When he formed his own label, Reprise, in 1961, one of the first artists signed was daughter Nancy. But she wouldn't make an impact on the Hot 100 until five years later, when she teamed up with producer Lee Hazlewood to sing his composition "These Boots Are Made For Walkin'."

The Top 10 Songs of BARBRA STREISAND

BARBRA STREISAND burst on the scene in 1962 as a supporting player in Broadway's *I Can Get It For You Wholesale*. Two years later she was the star of another Broadway musical, *Funny Girl*. And while her appeal at first was mainly to adults, with albums like *Color Me Barbra* and *Je M'appelle Barbra,* she became the ultimate female pop icon of the last half of the 20th century.

She was born Barbra Joan Streisand in Brooklyn on April 24, 1942. At 14, she saw *The Diary Of Anne Frank* on Broadway and knew what she wanted to do with the rest of her life, even though her mother suggested she sharpen her secretarial skills. That wasn't necessary for the multi-dimensional star, who sings, acts, and directs. She even toured during the last half of the '90s, and in 2000 gave her final live performances. Her fields of conquest include the Hot 100, where she has scored five No. 1 hits and 12 top 10 singles. Her most successful is "Woman In Love," from the *Guilty* album, written and produced by the Bee Gees' Barry Gibb.

JAMES TAYLOR was the most prominent member of a musical dynasty that included his sister Kate and brothers Alex and Livingston. Their father, Isaac, was dean of a medical school and their mother, Trudy, was a lyric soprano. The family spent their summers at Martha's Vineyard, and that's where 15-year-old James met Danny Kortchmar. With James on guitar and Danny on harmonica, they won a local hootenanny contest. Back at boarding school in North Carolina, brothers James and Alex formed a group, the Fabulous Corsairs.

At 17, James was severely depressed and spent 10 months in a psychiatric hospital. While he was a patient, he began to write songs. After being discharged, he went to New York and joined Kortchmar's group, the Flying Machine. They broke up over Taylor's drug habit, and James moved to London to clean up his act. Kortchmar suggested he look up Peter Asher, who was heading up A&R for the Beatles' new Apple label. Asher liked the tape and Taylor was the first artist he signed. Paul McCartney and George Harrison sat in on the sessions.

Still grappling with his drug demons, Taylor returned to the United States. Asher left Apple for Warner Bros., and again signed Taylor. The single "Fire And Rain" broke from his first album for the label; his version of Carole King's "You've Got A Friend" gave him a No. 1 hit.

The Top 10 Songs of TLC

THE THREE MEMBERS of Atlanta's TLC soared to the heights of the Hot 100 but sunk to the depths in their personal lives, having to deal with arson charges, bankruptcy, and death in a foreign country.

Tionne "T-Boz" Watkins, Lisa "Left Eye" Lopes, and Rozonda "Chilli" Thomas were managed by R&B singer Pebbles, who was married at the time to writer/producer/record label owner L.A. Reid. Reid and his partner Babyface signed TLC to their LaFace imprint and the three women scored with their first chart single, "Ain't 2 Proud 2 Beg," followed by another hit, "Baby-Baby-Baby," and another, "What About Your Friends," all in 1992. Two years later, Lopes was charged with burning down the house of boyfriend Andre Rison, an NFL wide receiver. She received five years' probation. Despite that setback, TLC's second album yielded four big hits: "Creep," "Red Light Special," "Waterfalls," and "Diggin' On You."

The three women filed for bankruptcy in 1995 and their next album wasn't released until 1999. Their fans still loved them, and TLC scored two more No. 1 hits, "No Scrubs" and "Unpretty."

In April 2002, Lopes was on vacation in Honduras when she lost control of the SUV she was driving. She suffered severe head trauma and died, just 30 years old, effectively bringing TLC's story to a sad ending.

01 **CREEP**
TLC *LaFace* 95
02 **WATERFALLS**
TLC *LaFace* 95
03 **NO SCRUBS**
TLC *LaFace* 99
04 **BABY-BABY-BABY**
TLC *LaFace* 92
05 **UNPRETTY**
TLC *LaFace* 99
06 **RED LIGHT SPECIAL**
TLC *LaFace* 95
07 **WHAT ABOUT YOUR FRIENDS**
TLC *LaFace* 92
08 **DIGGIN' ON YOU**
TLC *LaFace* 95
09 **AIN'T 2 PROUD 2 BEG**
TLC *LaFace* 92
10 **NOT TONIGHT**
Lil' Kim f/Da Brat, Left Eye, Missy Elliott & Angie Martinez *Undeas/Big Beat* 97

The Top 10 Songs of USHER

USHER RAYMOND grew up in the '80s but was exposed to music from several decades through his grandmother, who loved Donny Hathaway, Stevie Wonder, Marvin Gaye, Miles Davis, and Fats Domino.

Born in Chattanooga, Tennessee, Usher relocated to Atlanta when he was 12. He entered the Atlanta Talent Search and met L.A. Reid, cofounder of the LaFace label. Reid asked Usher if he wanted to be a star and if he wanted to work for it. The young singer said yes. He was 15 when LaFace released his first album. There were no pop hits, although one song made the top 10 of the R&B chart.

Usher was teamed with different producers for his second album, including Jermaine Dupri. For the first time, Usher tried his hand at writing songs, including "You Make Me Wanna. . ." which peaked at No. 2 and "Nice & Slow," his first No. 1 hit.

Usher returned to pole position in July 2001 with "U Remind Me," quickly followed by another chart-topper, "U Got It Bad." His best year on the charts to date is 2004, when he had four consecutive No. 1 singles, starting with "Yeah!" which occupied the penthouse for 12 weeks.

01 **YEAH!**
Usher f/Lil Jon & Ludacris *LaFace* 04
02 **U GOT IT BAD**
Usher *Arista* 01
03 **BURN**
Usher *LaFace* 04
04 **MY BOO**
Usher & Alicia Keys *LaFace* 04
05 **YOU MAKE ME WANNA...**
Usher *LaFace* 97
06 **NICE & SLOW**
Usher *LaFace* 98
07 **CONFESSIONS PART II**
Usher *LaFace* 04
08 **MY WAY**
Usher *LaFace* 98
09 **U REMIND ME**
Usher *Arista* 01
10 **I NEED A GIRL (PART ONE)**
P. Diddy f/Usher & Loon *Bad Boy* 02

The Top 10 Songs of LUTHER VANDROSS

A S A CHILD, Luther Vandross was inspired by the divas he heard on the radio—Aretha Franklin, Diana Ross, and Dionne Warwick. As an adult he wrote and produced for all three.

After two semesters of college, the Bronx-born Vandross got a break when he ran into David Bowie at a recording studio and was hired to sing backing vocals on the *Young Americans* album. That led to similar work with Carly Simon, Donna Summer, Bette Midler, and Barbra Streisand. Working with writer/producer Marcus Miller on a Roberta Flack album inspired the formation of Luther, a group signed to Atlantic's Cottillion label in 1976.

Larkin Arnold signed Vandross to Epic as a solo artist. In 1981, Vandross had his first Hot 100 entry with "Never Too Much." He continued to chart on Epic through 1997, then switched to Virgin. None of his Virgin songs made the Hot 100, but in 2001 he signed with J Records and made a comeback with "Take You Out."

Vandross suffered a stroke on April 16, 2003. He never fully recovered and died on July 1, 2005. The soul maestro was 54.

The Top 10 Songs of MARY WELLS

W HEN BERRY GORDY launched his record company, he had one label: Tamla. In 1961 he added the Motown imprint, and the first artist to chart under that logo was Mary Wells.

Born in Detroit on May 13, 1943, Mary Esther Wells sang in church at age three and excelled in her junior high choir. In high school, she was the choir's featured vocalist, and she also sang with doo-wop groups in her neighborhood. She idolized Jackie Wilson, and when she tried her hand at songwriting, she decided to come up with a tune for Wilson.

At 17, she arranged an introduction to Wilson's producer—Gordy. She didn't want to become an artist, just get her song to Jackie. But Gordy said she should record "Bye Bye Baby" herself and signed her on the spot. After "Bye Bye Baby" was a hit, Wells was teamed with songwriter/producer Smokey Robinson, who gave her hits like "The One Who Really Loves You" and "You Beat Me To The Punch." In 1964, Robinson's song "My Guy" became the first No. 1 hit on the Motown label.

Wells left Motown shortly after and signed with 20th Century Fox Records. Later she recorded for Atco, Jubilee, Reprise, and Epic, but she never duplicated her Motown success. She died on July 26, 1992, a victim of throat cancer.

The Top 10 Songs of BARRY WHITE

BARRY WHITE was born in Galveston, Texas, but was raised by his mother in Los Angeles. As a teenager, he was sentenced to a couple of months in Juvenile Hall after stealing tires, and he vowed never to get in trouble again. At 16 he was singing bass with a local group, the Upfronts.

Right out of high school, White started learning about the record business. He was 17 when he was hired as an arranger at Rampart Records. He had success with Bob & Earl's "Harlem Shuffle" in 1964 and Jackie Lee's "The Duck" in 1966. Three years later he met the three women who would become Love Unlimited, and wrote and produced their recording of "Walkin' In The Rain With The One I Love."

He was too busy writing, producing, and arranging hits for others to record himself, but that changed when Russ Regan was named head of 20th Century Records. He signed White as an artist. Lush strings and a slow disco beat added to White's baritone voice proved a winning formula, sending "I'm Gonna Love You Just A Little More Baby" to No. 3 in 1973.

White had a stroke in May 2003 and died on July 4 from kidney failure caused by high blood pressure.

01 **LOVE'S THEME**
Love Unlimited Orchestra *20th Century* 74
02 **YOU'RE THE FIRST, THE LAST, MY EVERYTHING**
Barry White *20th Century* 73
03 **I'M GONNA LOVE YOU JUST A LITTLE MORE BABY**
Barry White *20th Century* 73
04 **IT'S ECSTASY WHEN YOU LAY DOWN NEXT TO ME**
Barry White *20th Century* 77
05 **CAN'T GET ENOUGH OF YOUR LOVE, BABE**
Barry White *20th Century* 74
06 **NEVER, NEVER GONNA GIVE YA UP**
Barry White *20th Century* 74
07 **PRACTICE WHAT YOU PREACH**
Barry White *A&M* 94
08 **WHAT AM I GONNA DO WITH YOU**
Barry White *20th Century* 75
09 **SATIN SOUL**
Love Unlimited Orchestra *20th Century* 75
10 **OH WHAT A NIGHT FOR DANCING**
Barry White *20th Century* 78

The Top 10 Songs of STEVE WINWOOD

WHEN STEVE WINWOOD earned his first No. 1 hit the week of August 30, 1986, more than 20 years had elapsed since he made his chart debut. He was 17 when the Spencer Davis Group first appeared on the Hot 100 with "Keep On Running."

Winwood's father, an iron foundry manager, played a variety of instruments in his own band. There was a piano in the family parlor, and Winwood started playing it when he was five. At 14, he joined his brother's group, the Muff Woody Jazz Band, and less than a year later they joined forces with university lecturer Spencer Davis and drummer Pete York. In 1967 the Spencer Davis Band had its biggest hits, with "Gimme Some Lovin'" and "I'm A Man." That didn't stop Winwood from exiting the group. His reason? He said he didn't want to play derivative American R&B. With Jim Capaldi, Dave Mason, and Chris Wood, he formed a psychedelic pop outfit, Traffic.

After three Traffic albums, Winwood teamed with Eric Clapton and Ginger Baker to form one of the first supergroups, Blind Faith. The group made only one album together, and then a planned Winwood solo album turned into a Traffic reunion that kept the band together until 1974. Winwood's first true solo LP was released in 1977, and he has continued on a solo course ever since.

01 **ROLL WITH IT**
Steve Winwood *Virgin* 88
02 **HIGHER LOVE**
Steve Winwood *Island* 86
03 **WHILE YOU SEE A CHANCE**
Steve Winwood *Island* 81
04 **THE FINER THINGS**
Steve Winwood *Island* 87
05 **DON'T YOU KNOW WHAT THE NIGHT CAN DO?**
Steve Winwood *Virgin* 88
06 **VALERIE**
Steve Winwood *Island* 87
07 **HOLDING ON**
Steve Winwood *Virgin* 89
08 **GIMME SOME LOVIN'**
Spencer Davis Group *UA* 67
09 **BACK IN THE HIGH LIFE AGAIN**
Steve Winwood *Island* 87
10 **ONE AND ONLY MAN**
Steve Winwood *Virgin* 90

The Top 10 Songs of BOBBY DARIN

AFTER BOBBY Darin and Don Kirshner, both former students at the Bronx High School of Science, teamed up to write some songs, they brought their compositions to George Scheck, Connie Francis' manager. Scheck arranged for Darin to sign with Decca as an artist, and the label issued four singles that flopped. Darin was dropped from Decca and Kirshner introduced him to Ahmet Ertegun at Atlantic Records. Darin was signed to the new Atco subsidiary, but still had no luck—just three failed singles. Darin was in danger of being let go from his second label when he recorded "Splish Splash."

It was a great start, but Darin knew the best way to build a long-lasting career was to sing more than rock and roll. Inspired by Louis Armstrong's recording of a song from *The Threepenny Opera*, Darin recorded the same song for his album *That's All*. Going against Darin's wishes, Atco released it and not only did "Mack The Knife" spend nine weeks at No. 1, but it became Darin's signature song.

Darin, who said he wanted to be a legend by the time he was 25, had a lifelong history of heart problems, and died at age 37 of congestive heart failure.

01 **MACK THE KNIFE**
Bobby Darin *Atco* 59
02 **DREAM LOVER**
Bobby Darin *Atco* 59
03 **SPLISH SPLASH**
Bobby Darin *Atco* 58
04 **YOU'RE THE REASON I'M LIVING**
Bobby Darin *Capitol* 63
05 **QUEEN OF THE HOP**
Bobby Darin *Atco* 58
06 **THINGS**
Bobby Darin *Atco* 62
07 **BEYOND THE SEA**
Bobby Darin *Atco* 60
08 **IF I WERE A CARPENTER**
Bobby Darin *Atlantic* 66
09 **YOU MUST HAVE BEEN A BEAUTIFUL BABY**
Bobby Darin *Atco* 61
10 **18 YELLOW ROSES**
Bobby Darin *Capitol* 63

The Top 10 Songs of BOBBY RYDELL

IMMORTALIZED BY having the high school in *Grease* named after him, Bobby Rydell was a member of the Philadelphia cadre of artists who received frequent exposure on *American Bandstand*. Like Frankie Avalon, Rydell was a member of the band Rocco & His Saints before going solo. After being turned down by labels like Capitol, RCA, and Decca, the teenager was signed to Kal Mann and Bernie Lowe's Cameo Records, and those label founders penned some of his biggest hits, including "We Got Love," "Wild One," and "Swingin' School." Rydell also covered more adult material, including "Volare" and "Sway," for the teen market.

In 1963, Rydell moved into a new arena by starring with Ann-Margret in the film version of *Bye Bye Birdie*. In a prescient move, Mann and Lowe also had Rydell record in England, where the song "Forget Him" was written and produced by Tony Hatch more than a year before his "Downtown" would become a hit for Petula Clark. But recording in the U.K. was not enough to sustain Rydell on the charts during the British Invasion, and his chart fortunes faded even after signing to Capitol, then RCA, and later, Reprise.

01 **WILD ONE**
Bobby Rydell *Cameo* 60
02 **FORGET HIM**
Bobby Rydell *Cameo* 64
03 **WE GOT LOVE**
Bobby Rydell *Cameo* 59
04 **VOLARE**
Bobby Rydell *Cameo* 60
05 **THE CHA-CHA-CHA**
Bobby Rydell *Cameo* 62
06 **SWAY**
Bobby Rydell *Cameo* 60
07 **SWINGIN' SCHOOL**
Bobby Rydell *Cameo* 60
08 **GOOD TIME BABY**
Bobby Rydell *Cameo* 61
09 **KISSIN' TIME**
Bobby Rydell *Cameo* 59
10 **LITTLE BITTY GIRL**
Bobby Rydell *Cameo* 60

The Top 10 Songs of BOBBY VEE

O N FEBRUARY 3, 1959, 15-year-old Robert Velline was looking forward to his first-ever rock concert. Just two weeks earlier, he had formed his own band with his older brother and a friend. On this fateful day, he came home from school for lunch and learned that the plane carrying Buddy Holly, Ritchie Valens, and the Big Bopper to Fargo, North Dakota, had crashed, and all the passengers were dead. Local top 40 station KFGO was broadcasting a plea for any local act to perform that night. Bobby's group volunteered. Second on the bill that night, the Shadows were a hit and a promoter started getting them gigs.

Four months later, Bobby wrote a Holly-inspired song, "Suzy Baby," and it became a hit in Minneapolis and San Diego. Bobby Vee and the Shadows were signed to Liberty Records under the direction of producer Snuff Garrett.

Vee's first national hit was a cover of the Clovers' "Devil Or Angel." His only No. 1 hit was the Carole King–Gerry Goffin song, "Take Good Care Of My Baby." Dion DiMucci had recorded it first as an album track, but never released it as a single.

01 **TAKE GOOD CARE OF MY BABY**
Bobby Vee *Liberty* 61
02 **RUN TO HIM**
Bobby Vee *Liberty* 61
03 **COME BACK WHEN YOU GROW UP**
Bobby Vee *Liberty* 67
04 **THE NIGHT HAS A THOUSAND EYES**
Bobby Vee *Liberty* 63
05 **DEVIL OR ANGEL**
Bobby Vee *Liberty* 60
06 **RUBBER BALL**
Bobby Vee *Liberty* 61
07 **CHARMS**
Bobby Vee *Liberty* 63
08 **SHARING YOU**
Bobby Vee *Liberty* 62
09 **PLEASE DON'T ASK ABOUT BARBARA**
Bobby Vee *Liberty* 62
10 **PUNISH HER**
Bobby Vee *Liberty* 62

The Top 10 Songs of BOBBY VINTON

B OBBY VINTON was signed to Epic Records as a big-band leader, but after two albums failed to sell, he was about to be dropped by the label. During a break in a meeting with Epic's lawyers, Vinton was looking through a pile of singles labeled "rejects" and found a song called "Roses Are Red (My Love)." When the meeting resumed, he insisted he could turn the song into a hit. Legally, the company owed Vinton another session, so it was agreed he could cut two more songs. He recorded "Roses Are Red" as an R&B song and it sounded terrible. "I'm not really a country singer, but I said we should do it country, and on the strength of the song I got a second shot," says the artist.

Vinton's recording spent four weeks at No. 1 and sold a million copies. He went on to remake vintage songs like "Blue Velvet" and "There! I've Said It Again," and became one of the few American solo artists to remain a force on the Hot 100 during the height of Beatlemania.

01 **ROSES ARE RED (MY LOVE)**
Bobby Vinton *Epic* 62
02 **BLUE VELVET**
Bobby Vinton *Epic* 63
03 **THERE! I'VE SAID IT AGAIN**
Bobby Vinton *Epic* 64
04 **MR. LONELY**
Bobby Vinton *Epic* 64
05 **MY MELODY OF LOVE**
Bobby Vinton *ABC* 74
06 **BLUE ON BLUE**
Bobby Vinton *Epic* 63
07 **I LOVE HOW YOU LOVE ME**
Bobby Vinton *Epic* 68
08 **PLEASE LOVE ME FOREVER**
Bobby Vinton *Epic* 67
09 **MY HEART BELONGS TO ONLY YOU**
Bobby Vinton *Epic* 64
10 **SEALED WITH A KISS**
Bobby Vinton *Epic* 72

The WRITERS

LONG BEFORE the rock era began, America exalted its songwriters. Composers like Irving Berlin, George and Ira Gershwin, Cole Porter, Richard Rodgers, and Lorenz Hart were as popular and as well-known as any performers of their day.

In the early days of rock and roll, astute record collectors who read the fine print on their 45s noticed some of the same names appearing underneath the titles of their favorite songs. Jerry Leiber and Mike Stoller, Doc Pomus and Mort Shuman, and Felice and Boudleaux Bryant were three teams who built up impressive repertoires during the 1950s.

Many of the top chart hits in the first part of the 1960s were written in or near the Brill Building, a latter-day Tin Pan Alley. Songsmiths pounded away on pianos in small cubicles, always within earshot of other writers working on similar tunes. Aldon Music, located at 1650 Broadway (across the street from the Brill Building), was a hotbed of activity. Al Nevins and Don Kirshner's publishing company was home to Gerry Goffin and Carole King, Barry Mann and Cynthia Weil, Neil Sedaka and Howard Greenfield, and Neil Diamond. In 1963 alone, the names "Goffin and King" appeared in parentheses under the titles of hits by the Cookies, the Drifters, Freddie Scott, the Chiffons, Little Eva, Lesley Gore, Skeeter Davis, Steve Lawrence, and Dion.

The songs that Aldon's staff of composers were writing proved to have longer life spans than the 10 or 12 weeks they spent on the Hot 100. It's unlikely that a single day has passed since 1965 that some radio station in the world hasn't played one of the many versions of the Barry Mann, Cynthia Weil, and Phil Spector composition, "You've Lost That Lovin' Feelin'." Goffin and King's "The Loco-Motion" was a No. 1 song in the 1960s and 1970s, and a top three hit in the 1980s.

It will be up to future historians to decide if Bacharach and the Beatles belong in the same category as Bach and Beethoven. But we already know that the Lennon-McCartney songbook is still active three decades after the Beatles stopped recording as a group—and that the Holland-Dozier-Hollabd catalog is as attractive to recording artists in the 21st century as it was when the Marvelettes, the Supremes, the Four Tops, and Martha & the Vandellas first recorded those songs in the 1960s.

The Top 100 Songs Written by
JOHN LENNON
and PAUL McCARTNEY

"WE WANTED to be the Goffin and King of England," is how John Lennon and Paul McCartney once described their goal as song writers. Lennon and McCartney began writing songs the same time Gerry Goffin and Carole King did, in the late 1950s. They were prolific, and while the songs were freshman efforts, they often wrote at the top of their lyric sheets: "Another Lennon-McCartney Original."

Their talents as composers were not always recognized. When they recorded 15 songs for an audition tape for Decca Records, manager Brian Epstein suggested they stay away from original songs. Twelve of the tracks were versions of songs that ranged from Bobby Vee's "Take Good Care Of My Baby" to Guy Lombardo's 1937 hit "September In The Rain." The three Lennon-McCartney songs recorded for that audition tape were never released by the Beatles: "Love Of The Loved" (later given to Cilla Black), "Hello Little Girl" (recorded by the Fourmost), and "Like Dreamers Do" (a hit for the Applejacks from Birmingham).

Decca Records signed Brian Poole and the Tremeloes instead of the Beatles. Music publisher Syd Coleman suggested that Epstein contact George Martin, head of EMI's relatively small Parlophone label. Martin produced the Beatles' first session at Abbey Road studios on September 11, 1962; two of the songs recorded that day were "Love Me Do" and "P.S. I Love You." "I was convinced that I had a hit group on my hands if only I could get hold of the right songs," Martin said. When he couldn't find anything he considered better than "Love Me Do" and "P.S. I Love You," he reluctantly agreed to release them back-to-back on the first single.

Martin, however, wasn't too keen on John and Paul's songwriting. He thought Mitch Murray's "How Do You Do It?" would be a better follow-up than Lennon and McCartney's "Please Please Me." The Beatles agreed to record "How Do You Do It?" but it was never officially released. They prevailed, and "Please Please Me" was issued instead; it peaked at No. 2. "How Do You Do It?" was subsequently recorded by another Mersey group, Gerry and the Pacemakers. It was their first single, and it went to No. 1.

While the Beatles recorded a mix of original songs and remakes like "Twist And Shout" and "Money," their own songs were soon in demand by other artists. Another of Brian Epstein's groups, Billy J. Kramer and the Dakotas, were given Lennon-McCartney songs for their first three releases: "Do You Want To Know A Secret" (also recorded by the Beatles), "Bad To Me" (recorded by the Beatles but never officially released by them), and "I'll Keep You Satisfied," all charted in 1963.

"Do You Want To Know A Secret" had a U.S. release by Kramer on Liberty but failed to chart. No one in America recognized the writers' names yet, although both the Vee Jay and Swan labels released Beatles singles in the U.S. in 1963.

The first artist to take a Lennon-McCartney song into The Billboard Hot 100 was Del Shannon. When "From Me To You" was popular in Britain, Shannon was coming off a hit single, "Little Town Flirt." Appearing at the Royal Albert Hall on a bill that featured the Beatles, Shannon told Lennon he was going to record "From Me To You" for America. John's first response was, "That'll be fine." But as he turned to go on stage, John had second thoughts, and shouted to Del, "Don't do that!"

Lennon had apparently realized the consequences of having one of his tunes covered by an American artist for America—the Beatles were having enough trouble being accepted in the States.

Despite Lennon's plea, Shannon recorded the song. It entered the Hot 100 on June 29, 1963. It had a brief four-week run on the chart and only reached No. 77—but that was better than the original version, which debuted on *Billboard*'s Bubbling Under chart on August 3 and peaked at No. 116.

Back in England, the Beatles continued to give songs away. Some did not fare well—like Tommy Quickly's "Tip Of My Tongue" and Mike Shannon's "One And One Is Two." But in 1964, Peter and Gordon had a No. 1 hit in the U.K. and the U.S. with "A World Without Love," a song given to them by Peter's friend, Paul McCartney. It helped that Paul was dating Peter's sister, actress Jane Asher. Peter and Gordon's next two singles—"Nobody I Know" and "I Don't Want To See You Again"—were also listed as Lennon-McCartney songs, although they were penned only by Paul (the two Beatles had an agreement that both their names would go on all of their songs, no matter who wrote them). For those who might have griped that Peter and Gordon had an advantage dipping into the Lennon-McCartney songbook, Paul McCartney wrote the song "Woman" and listed the composer as "Bernard Webb." The song went to No. 14 in 1966.

As early as 1964, other artists included Lennon-McCartney songs in their repertoires. Bobby Vee cut "She Loves You" and "From Me To You" on his album *Bobby Vee Sings The New Sound From England.* Later that year, the Supremes recorded "I Want To Hold Your Hand," "Can't Buy Me Love," "You Can't Do That," and "A Hard Day's Night" on *A Little Bit Of Liverpool.*

Some Lennon-McCartney covers were songs that the Beatles did not release as singles. In Britain, Marianne Faithfull released a 45 of "Yesterday" when the Beatles did not. "Michelle" was covered by the Overlanders, who took it to No. 1 in the U.K., and David and Jonathan, whose version peaked at No. 18 in America.

Of the top 100 Lennon-McCartney songs, 39 were recorded by the Beatles. Another 38 were recorded by either Paul or John away from the Beatles. Thirteen are remakes of Beatle songs, and another 10 were either never recorded or never released by the Beatles.

The most successful Lennon-McCartney song is "Hey Jude," No. 1 for nine weeks in 1968. It was the quartet's first single on their own Apple imprint, and was backed with a sped-up version of "Revolution." The original, slower version of that song was eventually released on *The Beatles,* a.k.a. the White Album. The idea for "Hey Jude" came to Paul as he was driving John's son Julian home one day. Some of the lyrics were meant as temporary, dummy lyrics ("the movement you need is on your shoulder"), but John liked them so much, he insisted they stay.

The second most popular Lennon-McCartney song is Paul's duet with Michael Jackson, "Say, Say, Say," followed by the Beatles' first chart entry in the U.S., "I Want To Hold Your Hand."

The most successful remake of a Lennon-McCartney song is actually a remake of eight songs—the medley by Stars on 45 that begins with the introduction of Shocking Blue's "Venus." Oddly, the four Beatles' songs in the medley that made the Hot 100 ("Do You Want To Know A Secret," "We Can Work It Out," "I Should Have Known Better," and "Nowhere Man") were all more successful in the Stars on 45 version than they had been when originally released.

The second most successful remake of a Beatles' song is Elton John's "Lucy In The Sky With Diamonds," followed by Anne Murray's "You Won't See Me," and Sergio Mendes and Brasil '66's "The Fool On The Hill." The Beatles released none of those three songs as singles.

Although it's been four decades since the first Lennon-McCartney song appeared on the Hot 100, there is no ebb to the release of new versions of their compositions. In the 21st century, the *I Am Sam* soundtrack included Sheryl Crow's "Mother Nature's Son," Eddie Vedder's "You've Got To Hide Your Love Away," and the Vines' "I'm Only Sleeping," among many others, and U.K. *Pop Idol* contestants Will Young and Gareth Gates had a British No. 1 with "The Long and Winding Road."

68 **GOT TO GET YOU INTO MY LIFE**
Earth, Wind & Fire *Columbia* 78

69 **THE BEATLES MOVIE MEDLEY**
The Beatles *Capitol* 82

70 **STRAWBERRY FIELDS FOREVER**
The Beatles *Capitol* 67

71 **#9 DREAM**
John Lennon *Apple* 75

72 **BAD TO ME**
Billy J. Kramer & the Dakotas *Imperial* 64

73 **GOODBYE**
Mary Hopkin *Apple* 69

74 **MIND GAMES**
John Lennon *Apple* 73

75 **NOBODY I KNOW**
Peter and Gordon *Capitol* 64

76 **AND I LOVE HER**
The Beatles *Capitol* 64

77 **WE CAN WORK IT OUT**
Stevie Wonder *Tamla* 71

78 **GIVE PEACE A CHANCE**
Plastic Ono Band *Apple* 69

79 **P.S. I LOVE YOU**
The Beatles *Tollie* 64

80 **POWER TO THE PEOPLE**
John Lennon/Plastic Ono Band *Apple* 71

81 **ELEANOR RIGBY**
The Beatles *Capitol* 66

82 **YOU'VE GOT TO HIDE YOUR LOVE AWAY**
The Silkie *Fontana* 65

83 **OH! DARLING**
Robin Gibb *RSO* 78

84 **I SAW HER STANDING THERE**
The Beatles *Capitol* 64

85 **I DON'T WANT TO SEE YOU AGAIN**
Peter and Gordon *Capitol* 64

86 **VERONICA**
Elvis Costello *Warner Bros.* 89

87 **SO BAD**
Paul McCartney *Columbia* 84

88 **HEY JUDE**
Wilson Pickett *Atlantic* 69

89 **VENUS AND MARS ROCK SHOW**
Wings *Capitol* 75

90 **GETTING CLOSER**
Wings *Columbia* 79

91 **ELEANOR RIGBY**
Aretha Franklin *Atlantic* 69

92 **MICHELLE**
David and Jonathan *Capitol* 66

93 **GIVE IRELAND BACK TO THE IRISH**
Wings *Apple* 72

94 **PRESS**
Paul McCartney *Capitol* 86

95 **RAIN**
The Beatles *Capitol* 66

96 **COME TOGETHER**
Aerosmith *Columbia* 78

97 **FROM A WINDOW**
Billy J. Kramer & the Dakotas *Imperial* 64

98 **I'VE HAD ENOUGH**
Wings *Capitol* 78

99 **FREE AS A BIRD**
The Beatles *Apple* 96

100 **REAL LOVE**
The Beatles *Apple* 96

The Top 50 Songs Written by CAROLE KING

BROOKLYN-BORN Carol Klein was only four when she learned to play the piano, and she started writing songs even then. The inspiration for her vocation came from going to see disc jockey Alan Freed's rock and roll shows when she was 13. She specifically remembers being inspired by Chuck Berry, Jerry Lee Lewis, and the Everly Brothers. "I wanted to be around these people, and get to know them personally, and have them like and respect me," she explains. "I thought the best way to do that would be to write songs for them."

In high school, Carol formed a quartet called the Co-Sines and wrote songs for the group. In 1958, she met Gerry Goffin when they were both students at Queens College. Gerry had been writing songs on his own since he was eight years old. They dated and began to collaborate on songs. His ambition was to write for the Broadway stage; she wanted to write rock and roll. They made a pact—Gerry would help Carol (who took the stage name Carole King) write lyrics for her rock songs, and she would help him write music for the Broadway show he had conceived.

Carole calls her early recordings "some of the worst songs you'd ever want to hear," including her first single, "Baby Sittin'," released on ABC-Paramount in March 1959. That same year, she released "Short Mort" on RCA and "Oh! Neil"—a response to Neil Sedaka's "Oh! Carol"—on Alpine.

Those early singles were surpassed in 1960 when Gerry and Carole went to work for Don Kirshner and Al Nevins' Aldon Music at 1650 Broadway in Manhattan. Married and the parents of a young daughter, Louise, Goffin and King earned $50 a week as staff writers, working alongside other Aldon songwriting teams like Barry Mann and Cynthia Weil, and Neil Sedaka and Howard Greenfield.

In 1960, Gerry and Carole wrote a four-and-a-half-minute country and western song. Kirshner asked them to shorten it, and offered the song to Johnny Mathis. After Johnny passed on it, the song went to producer Luther Dixon, who owed Goffin and King a favor. Dixon played it for the Shirelles, who thought that "Will You Love Me Tomorrow" was terrible. But as Dixon worked on the arrangement, with Carole playing kettle drums herself, the girls changed their minds. It became the first No. 1 hit for the Shirelles, as well as for Goffin and King.

"Will You Love Me Tomorrow" gave Gerry and Carole their first taste of economic freedom. They were soon in demand as songwriters, turning out hits for the Drifters ("Some Kind Of Wonderful"), Bobby Rydell ("I've Got Bonnie"), and Gene Pitney ("Every Breath I Take").

In 1962, Kirshner decided to transform his demo singers—the Cookies, Little Eva, and Carole—into recording artists. The first release on the new Dimension label was Carole's demo of "It Might As Well Rain Until September," written for Bobby Vee.

The years 1962–63 were very productive for Goffin and King, and they specialized in turning out follow-up hits like "Her Royal Majesty" for James Darren, "One Fine Day" for the Chiffons, and "I Can't Stay Mad At You" for Skeeter Davis.

Lou Adler, who headed Dimension's publishing division, formed the Ode label in 1967. A year later, Carole and Gerry moved to Los Angeles—but separately. The marriage was over. With Danny Kortchmar and Charles Larkey (who would become Carole's second husband), Carole formed a trio known as the City and signed with Adler's label. One album later, the City disbanded. Carole recorded her first solo album, *Writer: Carole King* in 1970. But it was her second album for Ode that brought her worldwide fame. *Tapestry* was meant to be a way for other artists to hear Carole's songs—"I don't want to be a star," she said just before the album was released. When the album sold more than 15 million copies, she had little choice.

The only new Goffin-King song on *Tapestry* was "Smackwater Jack." While Carole had collaborated with others in the past—she wrote the Everly Brothers' "Crying In The Rain" with Howard Greenfield—she was now working regularly with writers like Toni Stern and Dave Palmer. Songs written with Goffin ("Ferguson Road," "High Out Of Time," and "Speeding Time") have turned up on Carole's albums through the years; two Goffin-King compositions appeared on 1989's *City Streets*.

GERRY GOFFIN and Carole King sometimes wrote songs with other partners during their early days. Goffin often worked with Jack Keller, with whom he wrote Bobby Vee's "Run To Him." Nine months after that song entered the Hot 100, Goffin had a top 10 hit with "Who Put The Bomp (In The Bomp, Bomp, Bomp)," a collaboration with the song's artist, Barry Mann.

Just as Goffin and King created hits for the Monkees in 1966–67, Goffin teamed up with Partridge Family producer Wes Farrell to write "I'll Meet You Halfway," a No. 9 hit in 1971.

Goffin collaborated with Barry Goldberg to write "I've Got To Use My Imagination," covered by Gladys Knight & the Pips in 1974. But Goffin's regular partner during the '70s and '80s was Michael Masser. Together, they wrote Diana Ross' "Theme From *Mahogany* (Do You Know Where You're Going To)" and Whitney Houston's "Saving All My Love For You."

01 **SAVING ALL MY LOVE FOR YOU**
Whitney Houston *Arista* 85

02 **THEME FROM "MAHOGANY" (DO YOU KNOW WHERE YOU'RE GOING TO)**
Diana Ross *Motown* 76

03 **RUN TO HIM**
Bobby Vee *Liberty* 61

04 **I'VE GOT TO USE MY IMAGINATION**
Gladys Knight & the Pips *Buddah* 74

05 **MISS YOU LIKE CRAZY**
Natalie Cole *EMI* 89

06 **TONIGHT, I CELEBRATE MY LOVE**
Peabo Bryson/Roberta Flack *Capitol* 83

07 **NOTHING'S GONNA CHANGE MY LOVE FOR YOU**
Glenn Medeiros *Amherst* 87

08 **I'LL MEET YOU HALFWAY**
The Partridge Family *Bell* 71

09 **WHO PUT THE BOMP (IN THE BOMP, BOMP, BOMP)**
Barry Mann *ABC-Paramount* 61

10 **SOMEONE THAT I USED TO LOVE**
Natalie Cole *Capitol* 80

The Top 50 Songs Written by
BARRY MANN and CYNTHIA WEIL

AS A 12-YEAR-OLD growing up in Brooklyn, Barry Mann was inspired by a friend to take lessons from his piano teacher. A year later, he had written his first song, an ode to an "Evil Horde" that he can still recite today.

He gave up the idea of being an architect to concentrate on songwriting. The first Barry Mann song ever recorded was "A Little Less Talk And A Little More Action," written with Joe Shapiro, whose hits included "Round And Round" for Perry Como. The first Mann hit was the 1959 Diamonds' song, "She Say (Oom Dooby Doom)." Barry's friend Jack Keller went to work for Don Kirshner and Al Nevins' publishing company, Aldon Music, and suggested that the publishers also sign Mann.

Barry had been with Aldon for about a year when he and Howard Greenfield played a song for vocalist Teddy Randazzo. "I walked in and saw this cute girl," Barry recalls. "She asked Teddy who I was and found out I worked for Aldon." Soon Cynthia Weil came up to the Aldon office to play her songs. "We became romantically involved before we started writing together," Barry says.

They were married in 1961, the same year their first song was recorded. "Painting The Town With Teardrops" didn't make it. Their second composition became their first hit — "Bless You," written for the Drifters but recorded by a teenaged Tony Orlando. At the same time, Barry was moving up the Hot 100 with his own recording of "Who Put The Bomp (In The

Bomp, Bomp, Bomp)," written with Gerry Goffin. It would be his only recording to make the upper half of the chart, although he would release singles on Red Bird, Scepter, United Artists, Warner Bros., Arista, Casablanca, and Atlantic.

On his Casablanca album, Barry introduced the song "Don't Know Much." Bill Medley released it as a single in 1981, and it peaked at No. 88. Two years later, Bette Midler recorded it as "All I Need To Know," and it fared a little better, climbing to No. 77. It wasn't until Linda Ronstadt asked Aaron Neville to record it with her that the song became a smash, reaching No. 2 in 1989.

The No. 1 song on the Mann-Weil list is "You've Lost That Lovin' Feelin'," originally recorded by the Righteous Brothers. It was specifically written for Bill Medley and Bobby Hatfield at the request of their producer, Phil Spector. It was the first Mann-Weil song to top the *Billboard* singles chart. The song appears on the Mann-Weil top 50 three times: Dionne Warwick's version from 1969 is No. 37, and Daryl Hall and John Oates' recording from 1980 is No. 11. One of Barry and Cynthia's favorite versions was recorded by Long John Baldry and Kathi MacDonald; it peaked at No. 89 in 1979. The fifth version to chart on the Hot 100 was by Roberta Flack and Donny Hathaway, No. 71 in 1971.

Mann and Weil's sixth most successful chart single is "Never Gonna Let You Go." "I spent three weeks on that melody," explains Barry. "I was going to write something for Maurice White. He asked me to come up with something for Earth, Wind and Fire." James Ingram sang the demo and Dionne Warwick first recorded it in 1982. Robby Buchanan passed the song to Sergio Mendes who liked it enough to record it, with Joe Pizzulo and Leza Miller on vocals.

Ingram also sang "Just Once," Cynthia's favorite song of all their compositions. It's Barry's second favorite, runner-up to "You've Lost That Lovin' Feelin'." They didn't write "Just Once" for anyone in particular, according to Cynthia. Barry had been recording many of their demos, but they thought it might be better to find an outstanding male R&B singer instead. Linda Perry at ATV Music suggested Ingram. When Barry and Cynthia heard him sing, "we looked at each other and became weak," Cynthia recalls. Barry adds: "I stopped him and said, 'You are the greatest singer I've heard in 20 years.'"

Their least favorite version of one of their songs is the Animals' "We Gotta Get Out Of This Place." Written for the Righteous Brothers, the song was passed to British producer Mickie Most by Allen Klein. "When I heard the Animals' record, I went berserk because they left out half the lyric," says Cynthia. "They changed it radically. I called Kirshner and begged him to stop the song from coming out. He said, 'It's No. 2 in England, what do you want me to do?'"

17 **I LOVE HOW YOU LOVE ME**
Paris Sisters *Gregmark* 61

18 **ON BROADWAY**
George Benson *Warner Bros.* 78

19 **MY DAD**
Paul Petersen *Colpix* 63

20 **LOVE WILL CONQUER ALL**
Lionel Richie *Motown* 86

21 **I JUST CAN'T HELP BELIEVING**
B.J. Thomas *Scepter* 70

22 **HOW MUCH LOVE**
Leo Sayer *Warner Bros.* 77

23 **FOOTSTEPS**
Steve Lawrence *ABC-Paramount* 60

24 **JUST ONCE**
Quincy Jones f/James Ingram *A&M* 81

25 **I'M GONNA BE STRONG**
Gene Pitney *Musicor* 64

26 **HUNGRY**
Paul Revere & the Raiders *Columbia* 66

27 **WHO PUT THE BOMP (IN THE BOMP, BOMP, BOMP)**
Barry Mann *ABC-Paramount* 61

28 **UPTOWN**
The Crystals *Philles* 62

29 **ROCK AND ROLL LULLABY**
B.J. Thomas *Scepter* 72

30 **SHE SAY (OOM DOOBY DOOM)**
The Diamonds *Mercury* 59

31 **ON BROADWAY**
The Drifters *Atlantic* 63

32 **HE'S SURE THE BOY I LOVE**
The Crystals *Philles* 62

33 **WE GOTTA GET OUT OF THIS PLACE**
The Animals *MGM* 65

34 **I'LL NEVER DANCE AGAIN**
Bobby Rydell *Cameo* 62

35 **ALL OF YOU**
Julio Iglesias & Diana Ross *Columbia* 84

36 **SATURDAY NIGHT AT THE MOVIES**
The Drifters *Atlantic* 64

37 **YOU'VE LOST THAT LOVIN' FEELIN'**
Dionne Warwick *Scepter* 69

38 **BLESS YOU**
Tony Orlando *Epic* 61

39 **COME BACK SILLY GIRL**
The Lettermen *Capitol* 62

40 **WALKIN' IN THE RAIN**
Jay & the Americans *UA* 70

41 **JUST FOR TONIGHT**
Vanessa Williams *Wing* 92

42 **THE GRASS IS GREENER**
Brenda Lee *Decca* 63

43 **JOHNNY LOVES ME**
Shelley Fabares *Colpix* 62

44 **HOME OF THE BRAVE**
Jody Miller *Capitol* 65

45 **MAGIC TOWN**
The Vogues *Co & Ce* 66

46 **WALKING IN THE RAIN**
The Ronettes *Philles* 64

47 **DON'T BE AFRAID, LITTLE DARLIN'**
Steve Lawrence *Columbia* 63

48 **I'LL TAKE YOU HOME**
The Drifters *Atlantic* 63

49 **ONLY IN AMERICA**
Jay & the Americans *UA* 63

50 **LOOKING THROUGH THE EYES OF LOVE**
Gene Pitney *Musicor* 65

The Top 50 Songs Written by
JEFF BARRY and ELLIE GREENWICH

ELLIE GREENWICH was born in Brooklyn and grew up in Levittown, Long Island. As she loved music, her parents encouraged her to study the accordion, until she finally persuaded them to buy a piano. Through a local record store owner, she made contact with RCA Victor Records, and the label issued a single under the name Ellie Gaye. She met Jeff Barry at a Thanksgiving dinner hosted by her aunt. Jeff had already written a song called "Tell Laura I Love Her," and he told Ellie that Ray Peterson had recorded it and that it was going to be a big hit. He was right.

Ellie was attending Hofstra University, and after classes she would head into Manhattan to record demos of Jeff's songs and was paid $15 per session. Following graduation, Ellie accepted a position as a high school teacher. Three-and-a-half weeks into the job, she quit to pursue a career in music.

Ellie had an appointment in the Brill Building with songwriter John Gluck, Jr., and was playing the piano in his office when a man walked in and mistakenly took her for Carole King. Ellie corrected him and played him some of her songs. Jerry Leiber said he liked her material and introduced her to his partner, Mike Stoller; Ellie was signed to their Trio Music publishing company for $75 a week. With Tony Powers, she wrote "He's Got The Power," the follow-up to the Exciters' "Tell Him."

Phil Spector liked a Greenwich-Powers song, "(Today I Met) The Boy I'm Gonna Marry," and asked to meet the writers. Meanwhile, Jeff and Ellie were married, and made a decision to only write with each other, much to Tony Powers' disappointment.

Barry and Greenwich's early collaborations included a number of Phil Spector productions: "Da Doo Ron Ron (When He Walked Me Home)" for the Crystals, "Wait Til' My Bobby Gets Home" for Darlene Love, and "Be My Baby" for the Ronettes (all hits in 1963). That same year, Jeff and Ellie's demo of "What A Guy," a song they had written for the Sensations ("Let Me In"), was released under the name "the Raindrops" on Jubilee Records. The follow-up, "The Kind Of Boy You Can't Forget," was a top 20 hit.

The Raindrops also recorded "Do Wah Diddy Diddy," originally cut by the Exciters. "Jeff and I really believed in that song," Ellie explains. "We got a call from Leiber and Stoller at the studio saying, 'You ought to forget about it. It was just shipped by Manfred Mann.' We had finished recording it, but we never mixed it."

Another Raindrops track—written in 20 minutes so they could have a B-side for one of their singles—was a No. 1 hit for Tommy James & the Shondells. "Hanky Panky" was a local hit in the tri-state area of Michigan, Indiana, and Illinois two years before Roulette released it nationally.

Many other Barry-Greenwich hits were more successful when recorded the second time around. "Chapel Of Love" was written for the Ronettes, but when it wasn't released as a single, Jeff and Ellie produced a version for the Dixie Cups. It was the first hit on Leiber and Stoller's Red Bird label. "Da Doo Ron Ron" was a bigger hit for Shaun Cassidy when he remade the Crystals' song in 1977. "River Deep-Mountain High," considered a classic when Spector produced it for Ike & Tina Turner in 1966, didn't crack the top 30 until the Supremes and the Four Tops released a version in 1971. The Ronettes' "Baby, I Love You" was a bigger hit when Barry produced it on his Steed label for Andy Kim. Kim also recorded "Be My Baby," a song that was heard again in 1986 when Eddie Money incorporated it (with vocals by Ronnie Spector) into his song "Take Me Home Tonight."

Through Don Kirshner, Jeff produced some of the early Monkees' hits, including "I'm A Believer." Barry also started producing Andy Kim in 1968. The following year, they teamed up to write the biggest hit of Barry's career—"Sugar, Sugar," for the fictional Archies.

Barry continued to write with other collaborators, including Bobby Bloom ("Montego Bay" and "Heavy Makes You Happy") and Peter Allen ("I Honestly Love You"). Ellie was approached by Alan Pepper, one of the owners of Manhattan's Bottom Line, to put together a show based on her songs. After a successful off-Broadway run, *Leader Of The Pack* moved to the Great White Way in March 1985. The cast included Darlene Love and Ellie herself.

18 **CHIP CHIP**
Gene McDaniels *Liberty* 62
19 **LAY A LITTLE LOVIN' ON ME**
Robin McNamara *Steed* 70
20 **RIVER DEEP-MOUNTAIN HIGH**
The Supremes & Four Tops *Motown* 71
21 **BANG SHANG-A-LANG**
The Archies *Calendar* 68
22 **BE MY BABY**
Andy Kim *Steed* 70
23 **HOW'D WE EVER GET THIS WAY**
Andy Kim *Steed* 68
24 **PEOPLE SAY**
The Dixie Cups *Red Bird* 64
25 **MAYBE I KNOW**
Lesley Gore *Mercury* 64
26 **THE KIND OF BOY YOU CAN'T FORGET**
The Raindrops *Jubilee* 63
27 **SUGAR, SUGAR**
Wilson Pickett *Atlantic* 70
28 **BABY, I LOVE YOU**
The Ronettes *Philles* 64
29 **HEAVY MAKES YOU HAPPY
(SHA-NA-BOOM BOOM)**
The Staple Singers *Stax* 71
30 **WAIT TIL' MY BOBBY GETS HOME**
Darlene Love *Philles* 63
31 **LOOK OF LOVE**
Lesley Gore *Mercury* 65
32 **I CAN HEAR MUSIC**
The Beach Boys *Capitol* 69
33 **GIVE US YOUR BLESSINGS**
The Shangri-Las *Red Bird* 65
34 **THE LAST TIME I MADE LOVE**
Joyce Kennedy & Jeffrey Osborne *A&M* 84
35 **WHY DO LOVERS BREAK EACH
OTHER'S HEART?**
Bob B. Soxx & the Blue Jeans *Philles* 63
36 **WHAT A GUY**
The Raindrops *Jubilee* 63
37 **LEADER OF THE PACK**
Twisted Sister *Atlantic* 86
38 **WHO'S YOUR BABY?**
The Archies *Kirshner* 70
39 **(TODAY I MET) THE BOY I'M
GONNA MARRY**
Darlene Love *Philles* 63
40 **FEELIN' SO GOOD (SKOOBY-DOO)**
The Archies *Calendar* 69
41 **HE'S GOT THE POWER**
The Exciters *UA* 63
42 **SISTER JAMES**
Nino Tempo & Fifth Ave. Sax *A&M* 73
43 **BABY BE MINE**
The Jelly Beans *Red Bird* 64
44 **SUNSHINE** The Archies *Kirshner* 70
45 **I'LL TAKE YOU WHERE THE
MUSIC'S PLAYING**
The Drifters *Atlantic* 65
46 **GOOD NIGHT BABY**
The Butterflys *Red Bird* 64
47 **THAT BOY JOHN**
The Raindrops *Jubilee* 64
48 **RIVER DEEP-MOUNTAIN HIGH**
Deep Purple *Tetragrammaton* 69
49 **OUT IN THE STREETS**
The Shangri-Las *Red Bird* 65
50 **NOT TOO YOUNG TO GET MARRIED**
Bob B. Soxx & the Blue Jeans *Philles* 63

WHILE ATTENDING the Juilliard School, Neil Sedaka would often neglect his study of classical music in favor of writing songs with Howard Greenfield. The two would peddle their songs to Manhattan music publishers, and one trip to the city found them in the office building at 1650 Broadway. They knocked on the door of Aldon Music, and the next day, Don Kirshner and Al Nevins signed them to an exclusive contract.

Kirshner arranged for the two young songwriters to meet his friend Connie Francis, who had just scored her first hit, "Who's Sorry Now." Neil played her "Stupid Cupid"; Connie loved it, and invited Neil to play piano on the session. It was the first Sedaka-Greenfield hit, peaking at No. 14 on the Hot 100.

As an artist, Neil scored 12 top 30 hits between 1958 and 1963. Connie Francis continued to record his songs, but with the coming of the Beatles, Sedaka's chart fortunes sank. It wasn't until the 5th Dimension remade "Workin' On A Groovy Thing" (originally recorded by Patti Drew) in 1969 that Sedaka and Greenfield had another hit song. In 1970, the duo parted ways, and Sedaka's agent suggested he try for a comeback by performing in England. He recorded two albums in the U.K.

Collaborating with lyricist Phil Cody, Neil had a British hit with "Laughter In The Rain," which sailed up to No. 15 on the U.K. singles chart. Elton John signed Sedaka to his new label, Rocket Records, and a compilation LP with the title *Sedaka's Back* was released in the U.S. Neil and Elton agreed that "Laughter In The Rain" should be the first single—and it re-established Sedaka as an artist in his home country.

The Top 30 Songs Written by
JERRY LEIBER and MIKE STOLLER

A MUTUAL FRIEND who knew that Jerry Leiber wanted to write blues songs and that Mike Stoller played the piano suggested the two 16-year-olds meet. Stoller was reluctant, but Leiber was persuasive and showed up at his house with a notebook full of lyrics. A writing partnership was born.

A few months later, Lester Sill of Modern Records wandered into the Los Angeles record store where Stoller was working. The teenager was bold enough to sing some of his material for Sill. He was impressed, and introduced the young songwriters to people in the music business. Two years later, the Robins recorded Leiber and Stoller's first song—"That's What The Good Book Says."

During the following year, Leiber-Stoller songs were recorded by Johnny Otis, Little Esther, and Little Willie Littlefield, whose "K.C. Loving" later became "Kansas City," a No. 1 single for Wilbert Harrison. Otis asked the two writers to come up with some material for one of the singers in his revue, Willie Mae "Big Mama" Thornton. They wrote "Hound Dog" for her in 15 minutes.

Four years after Big Mama's record topped the R&B chart, Elvis Presley heard "Hound Dog" performed by Freddie Bell and the Bellboys in the lounge at the Frontier Hotel in Las Vegas. Elvis' recording of "Hound Dog" is Leiber and Stoller's most successful chart song. In second place is the title song from *Jailhouse Rock* and its flip, "Treat Me Nice." (Leiber and Stoller were sent scripts from Elvis' films with places marked where the producers wanted songs.) In all, seven of Leiber and Stoller's top 30 songs were recorded by Elvis, including the title track from the film *Loving You* and "Love Me"—a song originally recorded by the duo of Willy and Ruth on Leiber and Stoller's Spark label in 1954.

Five of Leiber and Stoller's greatest hits were recorded by the group that evolved from the Robins—the Coasters. The two-sided hit "Searchin'"/"Young Blood" established the group; it was their third single. "Searchin'" and "Young Blood" rank fifth on the list of the songwriting team's most successful chart singles.

Leiber and Stoller wrote and produced for the Drifters, and when Ben E. King left the group, they continued to work with him. "Stand By Me" is one of their most recorded songs, charting on the Hot 100 by King, Earl Grant, Spyder Turner, David and Jimmy Ruffin, John Lennon, Mickey Gilley, and Maurice White.

In 1969, Leiber and Stoller returned to the Hot 100 with Peggy Lee's "Is That All There Is." The most recent Leiber-Stoller song on their top 30 is "I Keep Forgettin' (Every Time You're Near)" by Michael McDonald.

01 **HOUND DOG**
Elvis Presley *RCA* 56

02 **JAILHOUSE ROCK / TREAT ME NICE**
Elvis Presley *RCA* 57

03 **LOVING YOU**
Elvis Presley *RCA* 57

04 **DON'T**
Elvis Presley *RCA* 58

05 **SEARCHIN' / YOUNG BLOOD**
The Coasters *Atco* 57

06 **KANSAS CITY**
Wilbert Harrison *Fury* 59

07 **CHARLIE BROWN**
The Coasters *Atco* 59

08 **YAKETY YAK**
The Coasters *Atco* 58

09 **RUBY BABY**
Dion *Columbia* 63

10 **STAND BY ME**
Ben E. King *Atco* 61

11 **SPANISH HARLEM**
Aretha Franklin *Atlantic* 71

12 **LOVE POTION NUMBER NINE**
The Searchers *Kapp* 65

13 **I KEEP FORGETTIN' (EVERY TIME YOU'RE NEAR)**
Michael McDonald *Warner Bros.* 82

14 **LOVE ME**
Elvis Presley *RCA* 57

15 **BLACK DENIM TROUSERS**
The Cheers *Capitol* 55

16 **POISON IVY**
The Coasters *Atco* 59

17 **ON BROADWAY**
George Benson *Warner Bros.* 78

18 **SPANISH HARLEM**
Ben E. King *Atco* 61

19 **SLEEP**
Little Willie John *Geffen* 89

20 **SHE'S NOT YOU**
Elvis Presley *RCA* 62

21 **DRIP DROP**
Dion *Columbia* 63

22 **ALONG CAME JONES**
The Coasters *Atco* 59

23 **STAND BY ME**
Spyder Turner *MGM* 67

24 **IS THAT ALL THERE IS**
Peggy Lee *Capitol* 69

25 **I'M A WOMAN**
Maria Muldaur *Reprise* 75

26 **ON BROADWAY**
The Drifters *Atlantic* 63

27 **BOSSA NOVA BABY**
Elvis Presley *RCA* 63

28 **I (WHO HAVE NOTHING)**
Tom Jones *Parrot* 70

29 **STAND BY ME**
Mickey Gilley *Full Moon* 80

30 **YOUNG AND IN LOVE**
Dick and Deedee *Warner Bros.* 63

The Top 30 Songs Written by NEIL DIAMOND

BROOKLYN-BORN Neil Diamond was inspired to write songs after meeting folksinger Pete Seeger at summer camp. "I took to writing songs to satisfy my need for expression, to gain acceptance and recognition," Diamond said in 1971. "I was pretty much an outsider most of the time. I was never accepted. That's why I took to songwriting."

Diamond's first successful song was "Sunday And Me," recorded by Jay & the Americans in 1965. "Neil Diamond came to me with that one," Jay Black told Steve Kolanjian. "He sang it for us with his guitar, then we recorded it. We did that before he did 'Solitary Man.' Somebody told me that they had heard him say in a radio interview that the biggest thrill of his life was coming home from the hospital after his daughter was born and hearing Jay & the Americans sing 'Sunday And Me.'"

Diamond's career went into high gear when he met Ellie Greenwich, who was hired to record one of his demos. She and husband Jeff Barry were impressed with Diamond, and helped him get a contract with Bang Records. They produced his first efforts for the label, including "Solitary Man," "Cherry, Cherry," and "I Got The Feelin' (Oh No No)."

Barry was also responsible for Diamond's most successful chart song. Producer Don Kirshner felt the Monkees hadn't reached their full sales potential with their debut single, "Last Train To Clarksville," even though it went to No. 1. He asked Barry to help find a follow-up song that would sell millions of copies, and Barry suggested Diamond's song "I'm A Believer." It spent seven weeks at No. 1.

After a long string of hits with MCA's Uni label, Neil signed a $4-million deal with Columbia in 1973. His first two Columbia singles failed to crack the top 30—but both were from the soundtrack of *Jonathan Livingston Seagull,* and the LP sold well. Then came "Longfellow Serenade," which peaked at No. 5 in November 1974. Diamond would not return to the top 10 until Bob Gaudio brought him into the studio to record a duet with Barbra Streisand. Their version of "You Don't Bring Me Flowers" is Diamond's second most successful chart song.

In third place is "Love On The Rocks," one of three singles from the soundtrack of *The Jazz Singer*. "Hello Again" and "America" are the other two songs from the film that made the list.

In a 1988 *Rolling Stone* interview, Diamond told David Wild that his favorite cover of one of his songs is Frank Sinatra's take on "Sweet Caroline." "And I loved UB40's 'Red Red Wine,' which came out of the blue."

The Top 50 Songs Written by
HOLLAND-DOZIER-HOLLAND

BRIAN HOLLAND, Lamont Dozier, and Eddie Holland were three of the main architects of the Motown sound. Best known for producing No. 1 hits for the Supremes and the Four Tops, they also worked with most of the artists on the Motown roster, including Marvin Gaye, the Temptations, the Miracles, Mary Wells, and the Marvelettes.

Brian Holland was a teenager when he first met Berry Gordy. He was a recording engineer before he started to write and produce. Eddie recorded for Mercury and United Artists, also doing demos for Jackie Wilson, and was initially signed to Motown as an artist. Dozier first met Gordy in 1957 after forming the Romeos. They had one local hit in Detroit, "Fine Fine Baby," released on Fox Records and picked up nationally by Atlantic's main subsidiary, Atco.

After the Romeos broke up, Dozier signed with Anna Records, the label owned by Berry's sister Gwen. He recorded "Popeye The Sailor Man" as Lamont Anthony. King Features didn't appreciate the copyright infringement, so the song was re-released as "Benny The Skinny Man." When Anna folded, Dozier signed with Berry's new company and had a single— "Dearest One"—released on the Melody label.

"As a producer, I had a budget that allowed me to record songs with other artists," Dozier explains. "At the end of the budget, if there weren't any songs worth releasing, I would be out on my can. I was down to my last two hundred dollars and had to come up with something fast. I figured it would help my chances if I would team up with some of the heavy-weights. Brian Holland was doing fine with 'Please Mr. Postman' by the Marvelettes. His writing partner, Robert Bateman, was disenchanted and wanted to leave." Bateman and Dozier were neighbors, and Bateman offered to introduce Dozier to Brian Holland. "Brian and I got together on some songs I had already written, like 'Locking Up My Heart.' Since the Marvelettes were his, I said this was the way to save myself. We cut 'Locking Up My Heart' on the Marvelettes and my career was saved."

Eddie Holland joined the team. "Brian and I started turning out these hits. Eddie didn't want to be a singer anymore. We needed a third writer . . . Eddie came in as a lyricist." In 1963, H-D-H scored with "Heat Wave" for Martha & the Vandellas, "Can I Get A Witness" for Marvin Gaye, "Mickey's Monkey" for the Miracles, and "You Lost The Sweetest Boy" for Mary Wells.

That same year, H-D-H wrote and produced "When The Lovelight Starts Shining Through His Eyes" for a group that had climbed no higher than No. 75 on the Hot 100. "Lovelight" peaked at No. 23 for the Supremes. When the Marvelettes turned down H-D-H's "Where Did Our Love Go," it was given to the Supremes—who weren't too fond of it, either.

After "Where Did Our Love Go" went to No. 1, Gordy told H-D-H to come up with an album for the trio. "We put our nose to the grindstone," says Dozier. "Brian came up with the melody for 'Baby Love' and I came up with 'Come See About Me.'" Both songs were recorded the same week, and are among the top four most successful H-D-H songs on the *Billboard* chart.

H-D-H also had their first taste of a cover version when Scepter/Wand released "Come See About Me" by Nella Dodds while "Baby Love" was still on the chart. "We hadn't thought anyone would have the nerve to cover any of the songs," laughs Dozier. "We had to rush out 'Come See About Me,' which cut 'Baby Love's' life short."

Artists have been covering H-D-H songs ever since. Twelve of their top 50 are remakes; the most successful is Kim Wilde's "You Keep Me Hangin' On." Dozier lists as his favorites "You Keep Me Hangin' On" by Vanilla Fudge and "Take Me In Your Arms (Rock Me)" by the Doobie Brothers.

Holland, Dozier, and Holland left Motown in 1968 and started two labels of their own, Invictus and Hot Wax. Legal problems prevented them from taking songwriting credits on Freda Payne's "Band Of Gold" and the Chairmen of the Board's "Give Me Just A Little More Time."

The trio eventually split up to pursue separate projects, reuniting years later as freelance producers for Motown.

WILLIAM ROBINSON, nicknamed Smokey Joe by an uncle, used to carry around a notebook when he was 16 years old so he could write down songs about his friends, his teachers, and the ghetto in his hometown of Detroit. He had been composing since he was six years old, including some numbers for a school play in which he played the part of Uncle Remus.

Smokey was scheduled to begin college in September 1957, to study dentistry. But before the semester began, he and friends Ronnie White, Pete Moore, Bobby Rogers, and Claudette Rogers auditioned for Jackie Wilson's manager. Five of the songs they performed were written by Smokey. The manager was unimpressed with the group but suggested that Smokey and Claudette form a duo along the lines of Mickey and Sylvia ("Love Is Strange").

One of Jackie Wilson's songwriters was at the audition. Berry Gordy, Jr. asked Smokey if he had written any more songs. Robinson took out his notebook and showed him over 100 compositions. Gordy only liked one— "My Mama Done Told Me," which eventually became the flip side of the Miracles' first record, "Get A Job."

Smokey's songwriting wasn't confined to the Miracles. After Mary Wells' self-penned debut single, "Bye Bye Baby," Smokey was assigned to write for her, producing hits like "The One Who Really Loves You," "You Beat Me To The Punch," and "My Guy." The Temptations were also early beneficiaries of Smokey's talent. Their first Hot 100 single, "The Way You Do The Things You Do," would become one of Smokey's most enduring copyrights, charting for Rita Coolidge, Daryl Hall and John Oates (with former Temptations David Ruffin and Eddie Kendrick), and UB40. Smokey also gave the Temptations their first No. 1 single, although the song was intended for the Miracles. After the Temptations heard it, they pleaded with Smokey to give them "My Girl."

Before Holland-Dozier-Holland started a streak of No. 1 hits for the Supremes, Smokey wrote one of their first singles, "Your Heart Belongs To Me." He would have another chance to write a Supremes hit after Holland-Dozier-Holland left the company: "The Composer" was the Supremes' penultimate single with Diana Ross as lead vocalist. And in 1966, after a long period without any top 10 hits, Smokey breathed new life into the Marvelettes with "Don't Mess With Bill" and "The Hunter Gets Captured By The Game."

Many non-Motown artists have turned to the Smokey Robinson songbook for hit singles. Linda Ronstadt scored with "Ooh Baby Baby" and "The Tracks Of My Tears"; the latter was also a hit for Johnny Rivers. The third most successful non-Motown cover of a Smokey song is "More Love" by Kim Carnes. Written in a baseball park, "More Love" became a hit for the Miracles soon after they changed their billing to "Smokey Robinson & the Miracles" in 1967.

That same year, Smokey and company released an album called *Make It Happen.* The final track on that LP was "The Tears Of A Clown." When John Marshall of Motown's London office was looking for a follow-up to a re-release of "The Tracks Of My Tears" in 1970, he discovered that the Miracles had another "tears" song. "The Tears Of A Clown" became the Miracles' first and only No. 1 song in Great Britain. A month after it topped the U.K. chart, Berry Gordy suggested an American release for "The Tears Of A Clown." It became their first No. 1 single in America.

In 1971, Smokey told his fellow Miracles that he was going out on his own. Billy Griffin took over lead vocals and surprisingly, the Miracles fared better on the Hot 100 than Smokey. While he failed to make the top 20 with his first 11 solo efforts, the Miracles went to No. 1 with "Love Machine." But that was the last Miracles single to chart, and Smokey rallied in 1980 with a No. 4 hit, "Cruisin'," originally written as "Easy Rider" for a girl group. It is Smokey's fifth-biggest chart single.

His most successful song came a year later. After Kim Carnes' good fortune with "More Love," Smokey sent additional material to her producer, George Tobin. But Tobin said he was no longer working with Carnes, and indicated that he would like to produce the songs with Smokey on vocals. "Being With You" soared to No. 2—held out of the top spot, ironically enough, by Carnes' "Bette Davis Eyes."

The Top 30 Songs Written by BERRY GORDY

MOST PEOPLE think of Berry Gordy as the founder of Motown and the man who helmed the company for 30 years. They might also think of him as a producer of some of Motown's greatest hits. But Gordy had such strong songwriters working for him—people like Smokey Robinson, Norman Whitfield, Nick Ashford and Valerie Simpson, and the team of Eddie Holland, Lamont Dozier, and Brian Holland—that it's often forgotten that he is also a songwriter of note, and that many Jobete copyrights bear his name.

Gordy was a songwriter even before he opened the doors of Hitsville USA in Detroit. His first chart success came in 1957 when Jackie Wilson recorded "Reet Petite," a song Gordy had written with Roquel Billy Davis. "I thought that was the end of the world," says Gordy. "I had made a hit record. I would be rich forever." He soon learned how wrong he was—but he continued to write smash hits for Wilson like "Lonely Teardrops," "That's Why (I Love You So)," and "I'll Be Satisfied."

Gordy wrote some of Motown's earliest hits, including the Miracles' "Shop Around" with Smokey Robinson and Barrett Strong's "Money (That's What I Want)." In 1968, after Eddie Holland, Lamont Dozier, and Brian Holland split from the company, Gordy gathered a group of writers, dubbed them the Clan, and worked with them to write "Love Child" for Diana Ross & the Supremes. In 1970, he put together another group of writers, called them the Corporation, and with them composed "I Want You Back," "ABC," and "The Love You Save" for his new signings, the Jackson 5. Gordy also co-wrote their fourth No. 1 in a row, "I'll Be There."

NORMAN WHITFIELD, born in New York City, made his professional musical debut playing tambourine for Popcorn & the Mohawks. He was more interested in writing and producing, though, so after working with some independent labels, he signed with Motown as a writer/producer. His first assignment: Marvin Gaye. In 1963, Whitfield, Gaye, and Mickey Stevenson wrote "Pride And Joy," Gaye's first top 10 single.

Whitfield's next assignment was to work with the Temptations. For their debut album he wrote "The Further You Look, The Less You See" with the group's primary writer/producer, Smokey Robinson. Eventually, Smokey bowed out of the picture, convinced—especially after "Ain't Too Proud To Beg"—that the group was in good hands with Norman.

Whitfield's main collaborator on many of the Temptations' hits in 1966–67 was Eddie Holland. Holland was succeeded, in turn, by Barrett Strong, who had charted with one hit single in 1960, "Money (That's What I Want)." "Norman was always the producer," Strong said in Sharon Davis' *Motown: The History.* "I'd come in with my ideas and he would translate them."

In 1968, Temptations lead singer David Ruffin went solo and was replaced by Dennis Edwards of the Contours. At the same time, Whitfield took the Temptations in an entirely new direction with a socially conscious song, "Cloud Nine." He used all five of the Temptations' voices—an approach that worked especially well on their second most successful chart single, "I Can't Get Next To You."

Whitfield's biggest chart song is "I Heard It Through The Grapevine," originally recorded by a group Whitfield usually did not work with—Smokey Robinson and the Miracles. The Isley Brothers recorded it next, then Marvin Gaye. But the first group to actually release the song was Gladys Knight & the Pips. Their recording peaked at No. 2; a year later, Marvin's version was No. 1 for seven weeks, Motown's biggest single to that date.

Similarly, the Temptations cut "Too Busy Thinking About My Baby" before Marvin Gaye did; "War" was recorded by the Temptations but released on 45 by Edwin Starr; "Papa Was A Rollin' Stone" was first recorded by the Undisputed Truth before it was passed to the Temptations.

The writer/producer left Motown to start his own label, Whitfield, which he originally intended to be distributed by Motown. When the two parties couldn't come to terms, Whitfield Records went to Warner Bros. instead. Five singles from the label made the Hot 100: two by the Undisputed Truth, and three by Rose Royce.

01 **I HEARD IT THROUGH THE GRAPEVINE**
Marvin Gaye *Tamla* 68

02 **WAR**
Edwin Starr *Gordy* 70

03 **JUST MY IMAGINATION (RUNNING AWAY WITH ME)**
The Temptations *Gordy* 71

04 **CAR WASH**
Rose Royce *MCA* 77

05 **I CAN'T GET NEXT TO YOU**
The Temptations *Gordy* 69

06 **I HEARD IT THROUGH THE GRAPEVINE**
Gladys Knight & the Pips *Soul* 67

07 **BALL OF CONFUSION (THAT'S WHAT THE WORLD IS TODAY)**
The Temptations *Gordy* 70

08 **PAPA WAS A ROLLIN' STONE**
The Temptations *Gordy* 72

09 **SMILING FACES SOMETIMES**
The Undisputed Truth *Gordy* 71

10 **I WISH IT WOULD RAIN**
The Temptations *Gordy* 68

11 **TOO BUSY THINKING ABOUT MY BABY**
Marvin Gaye *Tamla* 69

12 **BEAUTY IS ONLY SKIN DEEP**
The Temptations *Gordy* 66

13 **RUN AWAY CHILD, RUNNING WILD**
The Temptations *Gordy* 69

14 **CLOUD NINE**
The Temptations *Gordy* 69

15 **PSYCHEDELIC SHACK**
The Temptations *Gordy* 70

16 **MASTERPIECE**
The Temptations *Gordy* 73

17 **YOU'RE MY EVERYTHING**
The Temptations *Gordy* 67

18 **I WANNA GET NEXT TO YOU**
Rose Royce *MCA* 77

19 **(I KNOW) I'M LOSING YOU**
Rare Earth *Rare Earth* 70

20 **THAT'S THE WAY LOVE IS**
Marvin Gaye *Tamla* 69

21 **TRY IT BABY**
Marvin Gaye *Tamla* 64

22 **YOU GOT WHAT IT TAKES**
Dave Clark Five *Epic* 67

23 **SUGAR DADDY**
Jackson 5 *Motown* 72

24 **DO YOU LOVE ME**
Dave Clark Five *Epic* 64

25 **MONEY (THAT'S WHAT I WANT)**
Barrett Strong *Anna/Tamla* 60

26 **MAYBE TOMORROW**
Jackson 5 *Motown* 71

27 **I'LL BE SATISFIED**
Jackie Wilson *Brunswick* 59

28 **(YOU'VE GOT TO) MOVE TWO MOUNTAINS**
Marv Johnson *UA* 60

29 **GET IT TOGETHER**
Jackson 5 *Motown* 77

30 **COME TO ME**
Marv Johnson *UA/Tamla* 59

The Top 30 Songs Written by LIONEL RICHIE

T HE COMMODORES were signed to Motown in 1972, although they didn't have their first chart single until 1974, when the instrumental "Machine Gun" entered the Hot 100. In the meantime, Lionel Richie hung out with key Motown writer/producers like Norman Whitfield and Hal Davis, anxious to learn how to write songs. He would hum his musical ideas into a tape recorder, and approach his fellow Commodores with these snippets.

In December 1974, the Temptations' "Happy People" entered the Hot 100. The songwriting credits listed Jeffrey Bowen, Donald Baldwin, and a relative unknown—Lionel Richie. Lionel soon became known for writing ballads, giving a softer edge to the Commodores' funky sound. Their fourth chart single, "Sweet Love," propelled the group and songwriter Richie into the top five. After hits like "Just To Be Close To You" and "Easy," Richie's reputation as a songwriter was firmly established with the group's first No. 1 single, "Three Times Λ Lady."

In 1980, Lionel met with Kenny Rogers in Las Vegas, and played him demos of "Lady" and "Goin' Back To Alabama." Both songs were recorded the same night; "Lady" topped the Hot 100 for six weeks, becoming Richie's second most successful chart song.

Richie's biggest chart single, "Endless Love," was originally a *Love Story*–type instrumental theme that producer Jon Peters and director Franco Zeffirelli asked Lionel to write for their *Endless Love* movie. The success of "Lady" and "Endless Love" (a duet with Diana Ross) hastened Lionel's departure from the Commodores for a solo career.

01 ENDLESS LOVE
Diana Ross & Lionel Richie *Motown* 81
02 LADY
Kenny Rogers *Liberty* 80
03 ALL NIGHT LONG (ALL NIGHT)
Lionel Richie *Motown* 83
04 THREE TIMES A LADY
Commodores *Motown* 78
05 SAY YOU, SAY ME
Lionel Richie *Motown* 85
06 HELLO
Lionel Richie *Motown* 84
07 WE ARE THE WORLD
USA for Africa *Columbia* 85
08 STILL
Commodores *Motown* 79
09 TRULY
Lionel Richie *Motown* 82
10 ENDLESS LOVE
Luther Vandross & Mariah Carey
Columbia 94
11 DANCING ON THE CEILING
Lionel Richie *Motown* 86
12 STUCK ON YOU
Lionel Richie *Motown* 84
13 YOU ARE
Lionel Richie *Motown* 83
14 OH NO
Commodores *Motown* 81
15 SAIL ON
Commodores *Motown* 79
16 EASY
Commodores *Motown* 77
17 PENNY LOVER
Lionel Richie *Motown* 84
18 BRICK HOUSE
Commodores *Motown* 77
19 SWEET LOVE
Lionel Richie *Motown* 76
20 MY LOVE
Lionel Richie *Motown* 83
21 LOVE WILL CONQUER ALL
Lionel Richie *Motown* 86
22 JUST TO BE CLOSE TO YOU
Commodores *Motown* 76
23 BALLERINA GIRL
Lionel Richie *Motown* 87
24 MISSING YOU
Diana Ross *RCA* 85
25 DO IT TO ME
Lionel Richie *Motown* 92
26 SE LA
Lionel Richie *Motown* 87
27 TOO HOT TA TROT
Commodores *Motown* 78
28 HAPPY PEOPLE
The Temptations *Motown* 75
29 FLYING HIGH
Commodores *Motown* 78
30 FANCY DANCER
Commodores *Motown* 77

The Top 10 Songs Written by
NICK ASHFORD and VALERIE SIMPSON

NICK ASHFORD moved from his home state of Michigan to New York City, with hopes of becoming a singer or a dancer. He was 21 years old when he first saw 17-year-old Valerie Simpson at the White Rock Baptist Church in Harlem. Destitute, he was there for a free meal; she was there to sing during the service. The two started writing songs together—first gospel, then R&B. They recorded three singles for Glover Records before joining the Scepter label.

Ashford and Simpson had their first top 40 hit when Ray Charles recorded "Let's Go Get Stoned." Then the songwriting duo signed with Motown, and was assigned to write duets for Marvin Gaye and Tammi Terrell. They later wrote and produced Diana Ross' first post-Supremes album.

They left Motown in 1973 and signed as recording artists with Warner Bros. A long string of singles failed to break the top 30 until Ashford and Simpson moved to Capitol in the early '80s. At the beginning of 1985, they went to No. 12 with "Solid."

01 **AIN'T NO MOUNTAIN HIGH ENOUGH**
Diana Ross *Motown* 70
02 **I'M EVERY WOMAN**
Whitney Houston *Arista* 93
03 **I'LL BE THERE FOR YOU/YOU'RE ALL I NEED TO GET BY**
Method Man f/Mary J. Blige *Def Jam* 95
04 **AIN'T NOTHING LIKE THE REAL THING**
Marvin Gaye & Tammi Terrell *Tamla* 68
05 **YOUR PRECIOUS LOVE**
Marvin Gaye & Tammi Terrell *Tamla* 67
06 **YOU'RE ALL I NEED TO GET BY**
Marvin Gaye & Tammi Terrell *Tamla* 68
07 **SOLID**
Ashford & Simpson *Capitol* 85
08 **AIN'T NO MOUNTAIN HIGH ENOUGH**
Marvin Gaye & Tammi Terrell *Tamla* 67
09 **REMEMBER ME**
Diana Ross *Motown* 71
10 **THE BOSS**
Diana Ross *Motown* 79

The Top 30 Songs Written by
KENNY GAMBLE and LEON HUFF

KENNY GAMBLE and Leon Huff both had their first records chart in 1964. Huff co-wrote "Mixed-Up, Shook-Up, Girl" for Patty & the Emblems, which debuted on the Hot 100 in June. Gamble co-wrote Candy and the Kisses' "The 81," which debuted in November. The former peaked at No. 37, the latter at No. 51.

A year later, Gamble and Huff were writing together. Their first effort to be recorded was "Gee I'm Sorry Baby," released on the flip side of the Sapphires' "Gotta Have Your Love." With financial backing from a clothing manufacturer, Gamble and Huff started their own label, Excel, and signed their first act, the Intruders. After one release, they were legally challenged on the label name and changed it to Gamble.

While the Intruders were making inroads on the Hot 100, Philadelphia's Crimson label asked Gamble and Huff to write and produce for a group of young white kids, the Soul Survivors. "Expressway To Your Heart" peaked at No. 4 in 1967. Six months later, the Intruders went to No. 6 with "Cowboys To Girls." That established Gamble and Huff's Philadelphia sound, and soon they were being asked to write and produce for artists at major labels—like Jerry Butler at Mercury, and Wilson Pickett, Archie Bell & the Drells, and Dusty Springfield at Atlantic.

Their own Gamble label remained small, though, and the two writer/producers wanted to affiliate with a larger company. They made a deal with Leonard Chess to form Neptune Records, and their first signing was the O'Jays. Billy Paul signed with the label, too. But a few months later, Chess died and his label was sold, effectively closing down Neptune.

Luckily, Columbia Records was looking to gain a stronger toehold in the R&B market, so the head of the label, Clive Davis, arranged to distribute Gamble and Huff's Philadelphia International Records. By the end of 1972, PIR had three smash records. "Back Stabbers" (the first pop hit for the label) was a No. 3 hit for the O'Jays; "Me And Mrs. Jones," Gamble and Huff's biggest chart single as a team, was No. 1 for Billy Paul; and "If You Don't Know Me By Now" was No. 3 for Harold Melvin & the Blue Notes, with lead vocals by Teddy Pendergrass. Seventeen years later, "If You Don't Know Me By Now" would be a No. 1 hit for the British band Simply Red.

The Gamble-Huff catalog has been richly mined by other artists. The duo's second most successful chart song is "Don't Leave Me This Way" by Thelma Houston. It was first recorded by Harold Melvin & the Blue Notes, but that single failed to make the Hot 100.

The top song on the Gamble-Huff list is "Dilemma" by Nelly featuring Kelly Rowland, thanks to a sample of a 1984 song recorded by Patti LaBelle, "Love, Need And Want You," written by Gamble with Bunny Sigler.

01 **DILEMMA**
Nelly f/Kelly Rowland *Fo' Reel* 02

02 **ME AND MRS. JONES**
Billy Paul *PIR* 72

03 **DON'T LEAVE ME THIS WAY**
Thelma Houston *Tamla* 77

04 **TSOP (THE SOUND OF PHILADELPHIA)**
MFSB f/the Three Degrees *PIR* 74

05 **I'M GONNA MAKE YOU LOVE ME**
Diana Ross & the Supremes and the Temptations *Motown* 69

06 **YOU'LL NEVER FIND ANOTHER LOVE LIKE MINE** Lou Rawls *PIR* 76

07 **IF YOU DON'T KNOW ME BY NOW**
Simply Red *Elektra* 89

08 **LOVE TRAIN**
The O'Jays *PIR* 73

09 **WHEN WILL I SEE YOU AGAIN**
The Three Degrees *PIR* 74

10 **BACK STABBERS**
The O'Jays *PIR* 72

11 **IF YOU DON'T KNOW ME BY NOW**
Harold Melvin & the Blue Notes *PIR* 72

12 **USE TA BE MY GIRL**
The O'Jays *PIR* 78

13 **EXPRESSWAY TO YOUR HEART**
Soul Survivors *Crimson* 67

14 **I LOVE MUSIC (PART 1)**
The O'Jays *PIR* 76

15 **NOW THAT WE FOUND LOVE**
Heavy D. & the Boyz *Uptown* 91

16 **ENJOY YOURSELF**
The Jacksons *Epic* 77

17 **ONLY THE STRONG SURVIVE**
Jerry Butler *Mercury* 69

18 **COWBOYS TO GIRLS**
The Intruders *Gamble* 68

19 **TOGETHER**
Tierra *Boardwalk* 81

20 **THE LOVE I LOST (PART 1)**
Harold Melvin & the Blue Notes *PIR* 73

21 **BREAK UP TO MAKE UP**
The Stylistics *Avco* 73

22 **FOR THE LOVE OF MONEY**
The O'Jays *PIR* 74

23 **PUT YOUR HANDS TOGETHER**
The O'Jays *PIR* 74

24 **DROWNING IN THE SEA OF LOVE**
Joe Simon *Spring* 72

25 **DO IT ANY WAY YOU WANNA**
People's Choice *TSOP* 75

26 **ENGINE NUMBER 9**
Wilson Pickett *Atlantic* 70

27 **HEY, WESTERN UNION MAN**
Jerry Butler *Mercury* 68

28 **I CAN'T STOP DANCING**
Archie Bell & the Drells *Atlantic* 68

29 **NEVER GIVE YOU UP**
Jerry Butler *Mercury* 68

30 **MOODY WOMAN**
Jerry Butler *Mercury* 69

The Top 30 Songs Written by CURTIS MAYFIELD

CURTIS MAYFIELD was a nine-year-old member of a church choir in Chicago when he struck up a friendship with 12-year-old Jerry Butler. Six years later, Butler asked Mayfield to join him, Fred Cash, and Sam Gooden in a group called the Roosters. With brothers Arthur and Richard Brooks on board, the group changed its name to the Impressions and signed with Abner Records. When the label issued "For Your Precious Love" with the credit "Jerry Butler & the Impressions," the friction tore the group apart.

Butler had a major solo hit in 1960 with a song composed by Mayfield, "He Will Break Your Heart." Meanwhile, Mayfield re-formed the Impressions with Cash and Gooden. The success of "Gypsy Woman" in 1961 encouraged the trio to continue.

Mayfield began writing songs when he was 10. His early work reflected his interest in gospel; even some of his later socially conscious tunes, like "Keep On Pushing," were written as gospel songs, but he gave the lyrics a secular slant.

The Impressions continued as a trio with a new lead singer on Mayfield's Curtom label, while Curtis embarked on a solo career in 1970. Among his most successful songs were soundtrack hits from *Superfly* and *Sparkle,* a pre–*Dream Girls* look at the rise of a Supremes-like group. Aretha Franklin recorded the songs from *Sparkle* in 1976; En Vogue remade "Giving Him Something He Can Feel" in 1992.

In 1990, Mayfield was paralyzed by a blow from a falling lighting rig at an outdoor concert in Brooklyn. Three years later, artists like Bruce Springsteen, Aretha Franklin, and Elton John took part in the recording of a benefit album, *People Get Ready: A Tribute To Curtis Mayfield,* with proceeds going directly to Mayfield. The composer/artist died on December 26, 1999, at the age of 57.

01 HE DON'T LOVE YOU
(LIKE I LOVE YOU)
Tony Orlando & Dawn *Elektra* 75
02 LET'S DO IT AGAIN
The Staple Singers *Curtom* 75
03 WHAT YOU WANT
Mase f/Total *Bad Boy* 98
04 GYPSY WOMAN
Brian Hyland *Uni* 70
05 GIVING HIM SOMETHING HE CAN FEEL
En Vogue *Atco EastWest* 92
06 FREDDIE'S DEAD
Curtis Mayfield *Curtom* 72
07 HE WILL BREAK YOUR HEART
Jerry Butler *Vee Jay* 60
08 IT'S ALL RIGHT
The Impressions *ABC-Paramount* 63
09 SUPERFLY
Curtis Mayfield *Curtom* 73
10 ON AND ON
Gladys Knight & the Pips *Buddah* 74
11 UM, UM, UM, UM, UM, UM
Major Lance *Okeh* 64
12 THE MONKEY TIME
Major Lance *Okeh* 63
13 KEEP ON PUSHING
The Impressions *ABC-Paramount* 64
14 AMEN
The Impressions *ABC-Paramount* 65
15 MAMA DIDN'T LIE
Jan Bradley *Chess* 63
16 TALKING ABOUT MY BABY
The Impressions *ABC-Paramount* 64
17 YOU MUST BELIEVE ME
The Impressions *ABC-Paramount* 64
18 FOR YOUR PRECIOUS LOVE
Jerry Butler & the Impressions
Abner/Falcon 58
19 WE'RE A WINNER
The Impressions *ABC* 68
20 I'M SO PROUD
The Impressions *ABC-Paramount* 64
21 HEY LITTLE GIRL
Major Lance *Okeh* 63
22 GYPSY WOMAN
The Impressions *ABC-Paramount* 61
23 CHOICE OF COLORS
The Impressions *Curtom* 69
24 FOOL FOR YOU
The Impressions *Curtom* 68
25 JUST BE TRUE
Gene Chandler *Constellation* 64
26 PEOPLE GET READY
The Impressions
ABC-Paramount 65
27 NOTHING CAN STOP ME
Gene Chandler *Constellation* 65
28 THIS IS MY COUNTRY
The Impressions *Curtom* 69
29 I'M A-TELLING YOU
Jerry Butler *Vee Jay* 61
30 RHYTHM
Major Lance *Okeh* 64

BERT AND Irma Bacharach expected their first child to be a girl, and when he wasn't, Bert wanted to name his son after himself. His wife disagreed, so they compromised and named him Burt. "We never anticipated any future problems over the different spellings of the same name because, quite truthfully, we never expected that either Big Bert (who was a clothing buyer for a department store at the time) or Little Burt would become known outside the neighborhood," the senior Bacharach wrote in the *Saturday Evening Post*.

Burt wanted to play high school football, but was too short. He studied piano, and after graduation, he played on USO tours. His first published song, "The Night Plane To Heaven," vanished into obscurity. He accompanied artists like Vic Damone and the Ames Brothers, all the while writing songs on the side. One day in 1957, he met songwriter Hal David in the offices of Paramount Music. David had written "Four Winds And Seven Seas" for Sammy Kaye, "Bell Bottom Blues" for Teresa Brewer, and "My Heart Is An Open Book," later recorded by Carl Dobkins, Jr.

In 1958, Burt Bacharach and Hal David became the first writers to have consecutive No. 1 singles in Britain. "The Story Of My Life" by Michael Holliday and "Magic Moments" by Perry Como had a combined 10-week run at the top of the U.K. chart. In America, Marty Robbins had the original version of "The Story Of My Life," and "Magic Moments" was the flip of Como's two-sided hit, "Catch A Falling Star." Those two songs established Bacharach's musical credentials and David's sensitive lyrics.

01 **RAINDROPS KEEP FALLIN' ON MY HEAD**
B.J. Thomas *Scepter* 70
02 **(THEY LONG TO BE) CLOSE TO YOU**
Carpenters *A&M* 70
03 **SLOW JAMZ**
Twista f/Kanye West & Jamie Foxx *Atlantic* 04
04 **THAT'S WHAT FRIENDS ARE FOR**
Dionne and Friends *Arista* 86
05 **THIS GUY'S IN LOVE WITH YOU**
Herb Alpert *A&M* 68
06 **ARTHUR'S THEME**
(BEST THAT YOU CAN DO)
Christopher Cross *Warner Bros.* 81
07 **ON MY OWN**
Patti LaBelle & Michael McDonald *MCA* 86
08 **ONE LESS BELL TO ANSWER**
5th Dimension *Bell* 70
09 **MAGIC MOMENTS**
Perry Como *RCA* 58
10 **WARNING**
The Notorious B.I.G. *Bad Boy* 95
11 **ONLY LOVE CAN BREAK A HEART**
Gene Pitney *Musicor* 62
12 **WHAT'S NEW, PUSSYCAT?**
Tom Jones *Parrot* 65
13 **BLUE ON BLUE**
Bobby Vinton *Epic* 63
14 **THE LOOK OF LOVE**
Sergio Mendes & Brasil '66 *A&M* 68
15 **I SAY A LITTLE PRAYER**
Dionne Warwick *Scepter* 67
16 **BABY IT'S YOU**
Smith *Dunhill* 69

In 1961, Bacharach had two more significant hits: Gene McDaniels' "Tower Of Strength" and the Drifters' "Please Stay," both written with Bob Hilliard. It was during the recording of "Mexican Divorce" by the Drifters that Bacharach met a background singer named Dionne Warwick. By the end of 1962, Warwick had signed to Scepter and released her first Bacharach-David single, "Don't Make Me Over."

Their partnership flourished in the '60s, as Dionne had hits with Bacharach-David songs like "Anyone Who Had A Heart," "Walk On By," "I Say A Little Prayer," and "Do You Know The Way To San Jose."

In 1964, Bacharach's wife-to-be, actress Angie Dickinson, suggested to director Charles Feldman that her boyfriend score Feldman's next film, *What's New Pussycat?* The title track by Tom Jones went to No. 3. That led to other Bacharach film scores, including *Alfie* (with the title song released by Cilla Black, Cher, and Dionne Warwick) and *Casino Royale* (featuring the title track by Herb Alpert & the Tijuana Brass and "The Look Of Love" by Dusty Springfield).

By the end of the decade, Bacharach and David had scored the film that would win them two Oscars: *Butch Cassidy And The Sundance Kid.* The hit song from the film, B.J. Thomas' recording of "Raindrops Keep Fallin' On My Head," is the most successful Bacharach song on The Billboard Hot 100.

In fourth place is another song originally written for a movie. Rod Stewart sang "That's What Friends Are For" over the end credits of the 1982 release *Night Shift.* Bacharach and second wife Carole Bayer Sager were not happy with Stewart's rendition. A year later, Bacharach had a reunion with Warwick after not speaking with her for 10 years. Dionne had sued Bacharach and David after they split in 1971, for not fulfilling a contractual obligation.

Scheduled to produce new material for Dionne in 1985, Sager remembered "That's What Friends Are For." Dionne thought it would make a good duet with Stevie Wonder, and when friends Elizabeth Taylor and Neil Simon attended the recording session, Carole suggested that the proceeds from the song be donated to the American Foundation for AIDS Research. Gladys Knight and Elton John added their vocals to the recording later. It was No. 1 for four weeks.

In sixth place is another movie song, "Arthur's Theme (Best That You Can Do)" from *Arthur.* "I basically wrote it in one or two nights with Carole and Christopher [Cross]," Burt recalls. One line came from an old Peter Allen song that had never been recorded. "Carole just asked Peter the next day if it was okay if she used this line." The song won an Oscar for all four composers.

Both 21st-century titles on the Bacharach top 50 sample songs originally recorded by female artists in the '60s and later covered by male R&B singers. At No. 3, "Slow Jamz" samples "A House Is Not A Home" by Luther Vandross and at No. 18, "Rain On Me" includes a sample of "The Look Of Love" by Isaac Hayes.

BARRY GIBB is the only songwriter in the rock era to have four consecutive No. 1 singles. "Stayin' Alive," "(Love Is) Thicker Than Water," "Night Fever," and "If I Can't Have You" had a 15-week lock on *Billboard*'s top spot from January 29 to May 13, 1978.

Barry was nine and his twin brothers Robin and Maurice were seven when they first performed together professionally as the Rattlesnakes. They also called themselves Johnny Hays and the Bluecats, the Brothers Gibb, and the B.G.'s before they decided on the Bee Gees. After emigrating to Brisbane, Australia, in 1958, the brothers signed with the Festival label and had a succession of hit singles. Nine years later, they sailed home to England and signed a five-year contract with manager Robert Stigwood. A month later, they were in the back stairway in the Polydor Records office building when they wrote "New York Mining Disaster 1941 (Have You Seen My Wife, Mr. Jones)." A song about the Aberfan mining disaster in Wales that killed over 100 children, it became their first chart hit in America, peaking at No. 14 in July 1967.

Just three weeks before their ultimate hit, "Stayin' Alive," went to No. 1, the songwriting team of Barry, Robin, and Maurice Gibb were on top with "How Deep Is Your Love." "It's probably the nicest ballad we've ever written, apart from 'Words,' which will always be my favorite," says Barry.

"How Deep Is Your Love" was one of five songs written by the Gibbs for the film *Saturday Night Fever*. The movie was based on "Tribal Rites of the New Saturday Night," a *New York* magazine article by Nik Cohn. The Bee Gees were working on a studio album to follow *Children Of The World* when producer Robert Stigwood called them at the Chateau d'Herouville studio in France. Barry recalls: "He said, 'Do you have any ideas either for

01 **STAYIN' ALIVE**
Bee Gees *RSO* 78

02 **NIGHT FEVER**
Bee Gees *RSO* 78

03 **SHADOW DANCING**
Andy Gibb *RSO* 78

04 **I JUST WANT TO BE YOUR EVERYTHING**
Andy Gibb *RSO* 77

05 **HOW DEEP IS YOUR LOVE**
Bee Gees *RSO* 77

06 **WOMAN IN LOVE**
Barbra Streisand *Columbia* 80

07 **TOO MUCH HEAVEN**
Bee Gees *RSO* 79

08 **HOW CAN YOU MEND A BROKEN HEART**
Bee Gees *Atco* 71

09 **ISLANDS IN THE STREAM**
Kenny Rogers & Dolly Parton *RCA* 83

10 **(LOVE IS) THICKER THAN WATER**
Andy Gibb *RSO* 78

11 **GREASE**
Frankie Valli *RSO* 78

12 **TRAGEDY**
Bee Gees *RSO* 79

13 **IF I CAN'T HAVE YOU**
Yvonne Elliman *RSO* 78

14 **YOU SHOULD BE DANCING**
Bee Gees *RSO* 76

15 **JIVE TALKIN'**
Bee Gees *RSO* 75

16 **LOVE SO RIGHT**
Bee Gees *RSO* 76

17 **EMOTION**
Samantha Sang *Private Stock* 78

18 **LOVE YOU INSIDE OUT**
Bee Gees *RSO* 79

the title of the film or a title song?'. . . I scribbled down some titles within the next hour and called him back the same evening. 'Stayin' Alive' was one of them. 'More Than A Woman' was another. I said, 'What about something like "Night Fever,"' and he said it sounded pornographic. . . . That was the last conversation about the title, and the next thing I knew the film was called *Saturday Night Fever.*"

After three No. 1 singles from the soundtrack, radio stations played the Bee Gees' version of "More Than A Woman," but it was never released as a single. "Robert wanted us to go to No. 1 for the fourth time or not at all," Barry explains. Another version from the soundtrack, by Tavares, was released instead.

The Gibbs have never kept all their songs for themselves. Their first No. 1 single, "How Can You Mend A Broken Heart," was meant for Andy Williams, who passed on it. "How Deep Is Your Love" was written for Yvonne Elliman; instead she was given another song the Bee Gees had recorded but not yet released, "If I Can't Have You."

Other artists have approached the Gibbs for songs. Barbra Streisand asked Barry to produce an album for her. "Woman In Love," written by Barry and Robin, ranks sixth on the list of top 50 Gibb songs. When Kenny Rogers signed with RCA, he wanted Barry to produce his first album. Barry, Robin, and Maurice penned "Islands In The Stream," recorded as a duet with Dolly Parton. It ranks ninth on the Gibb top 50.

The Gibbs had similar luck with Australian singer Samantha Sang ("Emotion") and Dionne Warwick ("Heartbreaker"). Despite the success of these songs for other artists, Barry says he has never regretted giving some of his better material to others. "I've never pulled back a song once I've written it for somebody else. I don't believe you should take a song back; if it's written for that person it should go to that person. So I never turn around and say, 'Whoops, this song turned out to be too strong.'"

Eight of the singles on the Gibb top 50 were recorded by the fourth Gibb brother, Andy. He was 18 when Stigwood signed him to RSO Records. He and Barry wrote four songs in two days, including Andy's first two singles: "I Just Want To Be Your Everything" (penned by Barry) and "(Love Is) Thicker Than Water" (by Barry and Andy). All four brothers teamed to write "Shadow Dancing," the third most successful Gibb song.

19 **GUILTY**
Barbra Streisand & Barry Gibb *Columbia* 81
20 **DESIRE**
Andy Gibb *RSO* 80
21 **LONELY DAYS**
Bee Gees *Atco* 71
22 **GHETTO SUPASTAR**
(THAT IS WHAT YOU ARE)
Pras Michel f/Ol' Dirty Bastard
& i/Mya *Interscope* 98
23 **AN EVERLASTING LOVE**
Andy Gibb *RSO* 78
24 **TO LOVE SOMEBODY**
Michael Bolton *Columbia* 92
25 **(OUR LOVE) DON'T THROW IT ALL AWAY**
Andy Gibb *RSO* 78
26 **I'VE GOTTA GET A MESSAGE TO YOU**
Bee Gees *Atco* 68
27 **NIGHTS ON BROADWAY**
Bee Gees *RSO* 75
28 **HEARTBREAKER**
Dionne Warwick *Arista* 83
29 **EMOTION**
Destiny's Child *Columbia* 01
30 **LOVE ME**
Yvonne Elliman *RSO* 76
31 **FANNY (BE TENDER WITH MY LOVE)**
Bee Gees *RSO* 76
32 **WHAT KIND OF FOOL**
Barbra Streisand & Barry Gibb *Columbia* 81
33 **BOOGIE CHILD**
Bee Gees *RSO* 77
34 **ONE**
Bee Gees *Warner Bros.* 89
35 **I STARTED A JOKE**
Bee Gees *Atco* 69
36 **HOLD ON TO MY LOVE**
Jimmy Ruffin *RSO* 80
37 **I CAN'T HELP IT**
Andy Gibb & Olivia Newton-John *RSO* 80
38 **TIME IS TIME**
Andy Gibb *RSO* 81
39 **RUN TO ME**
Bee Gees *Atco* 72
40 **(THE LIGHTS WENT OUT IN)**
MASSACHUSETTS
Bee Gees *Atco* 67
41 **WORDS**
Bee Gees *Atco* 68
42 **MY WORLD**
Bee Gees *Atco* 72
43 **TO LOVE SOMEBODY**
Bee Gees *Atco* 67
44 **THE WOMAN IN YOU**
Bee Gees *RSO* 83
45 **NEW YORK MINING DISASTER 1941**
(HAVE YOU SEEN MY WIFE, MR. JONES)
Bee Gees *Atco* 67
46 **HOLIDAY**
Bee Gees *Atco* 67
47 **THIS WOMAN**
Kenny Rogers *RCA* 84
48 **ALONE**
Bee Gees *Polydor* 97
49 **COME ON OVER**
Olivia Newton-John *MCA* 76
50 **EDGE OF THE UNIVERSE**
Bee Gees *RSO* 77

The Top 30 Songs Written by BOB DYLAN

ROBERT ALLEN ZIMMERMAN grew up in Hibbing, a mining town in Minnesota near the Canadian border. It was during a six-month tenure as a student at the University of Minnesota that he became Bob Dylan, performing at a coffeehouse on campus. At the end of 1960, he took off for New York City, where he visited the hospital bedside of his idol, Woody Guthrie (who was then dying of Huntington's disease).

Dylan went to the Manhattan office of music publisher Hill & Range seeking a $50-a-week staff writing job, but was turned down. Shortly after, he played harmonica on a recording session for folksinger Carolyn Hester. The producer of that session, Columbia Records executive John Hammond, was impressed enough to set up a recording session. *Bob Dylan* was released in March 1962.

The Freewheelin' Bob Dylan was his second album. He sang the opening track, "Blowin' In The Wind," at the 1963 Newport Folk Festival, accompanied by Peter, Paul and Mary. The folk trio's versions of "Blowin' In The Wind" plus another track from *The Freewheelin' Bob Dylan,* "Don't Think Twice, It's All Right," marked Dylan's first appearances in the top 10. "Blowin' In The Wind" peaked at No. 2, and "Don't Think Twice" went to No. 9.

In 1965, Dylan had his very own pop hit—"Like A Rolling Stone." He would only have two more top 10 singles of his own: "Rainy Day Women #12 & 35" and "Lay Lady Lay."

The Top 30 Songs Written by PRINCE

"**M**Y SONGS are more about love than they are about sex," Prince once said. "I don't consider myself a great poet, or interpreter à la Moses. I just know I'm here to say what's on my mind, and I'm in a position where I can do that. It would be foolish for me to make up stories about going to Paris, knocking off the Queen, and things of that nature."

Prince's first Hot 100 single, "Soft And Wet," peaked at No. 92. A full year later, his second single went gold and climbed to No. 11. "I Wanna Be Your Lover" established the young recording artist from Minneapolis, but he had already signed a three-album deal with Warner Bros. that allowed him to produce his own material.

The track that first put Prince Rogers Nelson in the top 10 was "Little Red Corvette." Then his previous single, "1999," was reissued and went to No. 12. That was followed by another top 10 hit, "Delirious." His real break-through, though, came with the release of his autobiographical film, *Purple Rain.* The soundtrack yielded five Hot 100 hits, including "When Doves Cry."

There was no official soundtrack to Prince's next film, *Under The Cherry Moon,* but the *Parade* album did feature songs from the movie. "Kiss" was the first single released from the album; it is Prince's fourth most successful song.

On June 7, 1993—his 35th birthday—Prince changed his name to ♀. The unpronounceable symbol caused many journalists to refer to him as "the artist formerly known as Prince." In May 2000, he became the artist formerly known as the Artist Formerly Known as Prince, when he reverted to being called "Prince."

The Top 30 Songs Written by DIANE WARREN

SONGWRITING WAS a form of expression before it was a craft for Diane Warren, who was 12 when her parents gave her a small Mexican guitar. She picked out melodies that popped into her head and discovered an all-consuming passion that would take over her life.

Her songs are now as sought-after as those written by the great songwriters she idolized when she was growing up, like Holland-Dozier-Holland, Barry Mann and Cynthia Weil, and Jimmy Webb. It's a rare Hot 100 that doesn't feature at least one Diane Warren song bulleting up the chart.

Her initial success came from writing English lyrics to a French song that Americans came to know as "Solitaire" by Laura Branigan. Then Suzanne Coston, music supervisor for the film *The Last Dragon,* asked Diane to contribute a song to the soundtrack. Warren wrote the upbeat "Rhythm Of The Night," her next top 10 success, for DeBarge.

Mutual friends introduced her to songwriter Albert Hammond, and in one day they wrote "Nothing's Gonna Stop Us Now," a No. 1 hit for Starship. Hammond is also the co-writer on a track originally written for Tina Turner. Luther Ingram, Aswad, and Neil Diamond also recorded "Don't Turn Around" before Sweden's Ace of Base had a top 10 hit with it.

Warren says that "Un-Break My Heart," her most successful song, just "flew" into her head. "Everything's been said, but if you can twist it around slightly and come up with a new slant on it, and if you write a great melody, you'll probably have a great song."

The Top 10 Songs Written by
FELICE & BOUDLEAUX BRYANT

BOUDLEAUX BRYANT, born in Shellman, Georgia, played violin for the Atlanta Philharmonic Orchestra and radio station WSB. Felice Scaduto grew up in Milwaukee, and was working at the Sherwood Hotel when she met Boudleaux—he was playing there with his jazz band. The two married in September 1945, and began writing songs together just for fun—he wrote the music, she wrote the lyrics. They sent "Country Boy" to a publisher in Nashville, and in 1949 it was a No. 7 country hit for "Little" Jimmy Dickens. A year later, the Bryants decided to move to Nashville to be closer to the music scene.

In 1957, publisher Wesley Rose introduced them to an act he had signed with Archie Bleyer's New York–based label, Cadence. The Everly Brothers recorded the Bryants' "Bye Bye Love," and had their first chart entry, a No. 2 hit. Phil and Don's follow-up was also written by the Bryants. Although Bleyer thought the song was too suggestive, "Wake Up Little Susie" went to No. 1, and ranks second on the list of the Bryants' greatest hits.

01 ALL I HAVE TO DO IS DREAM
Everly Brothers *Cadence* 58

02 WAKE UP LITTLE SUSIE
Everly Brothers *Cadence* 57

03 BYE BYE LOVE
Everly Brothers *Cadence* 57

04 BIRD DOG
Everly Brothers *Cadence* 58

05 PROBLEMS
Everly Brothers *Cadence* 58

06 LOVE HURTS
Nazareth *A&M* 76

07 DEVOTED TO YOU
Everly Brothers *Cadence* 58

08 MEXICO
Bob Moore *Monument* 61

09 LET'S THINK ABOUT LIVING
Everly Brothers *Warner Bros.* 60

10 TAKE A MESSAGE TO MARY
Everly Brothers *Cadence* 59

The Top 10 Songs Written by
ALBERT HAMMOND

MOST PEOPLE associate the name Albert Hammond with the 1972 top five hit "It Never Rains In Southern California," a song he co-wrote with Mike Hazelwood for a Broadway musical that was never produced. But those who study the fine print know much more about the London-born songwriter, who has lived in Southern California for more than 30 years.

Before his solo hit, he wrote "Gimme Dat Ding" for the Pipkins and "Shame, Shame" for the Magic Lanterns. Later, he collaborated with Hal David. Their first song was "99 Miles From L.A."; the second was "To All The Girls I've Loved Before."

After seeing Paul McCartney play at Madison Square Garden, Hammond felt he had seen the best and was going to hang it all up. A reassuring phone call from his wife inspired "When I Need You," later a No. 1 hit for Leo Sayer, on which he collaborated with Carole Bayer Sager.

A mutual friend at Arista introduced him to Diane Warren, his collaborator on "Nothing's Gonna Stop Us Now," "Don't Turn Around," and "Through The Storm."

01 NOTHING'S GONNA STOP US NOW
Starship *Grunt* 87

02 DON'T TURN AROUND
Ace of Base *Arista* 94

03 WHEN I NEED YOU
Leo Sayer *Warner Bros.* 77

04 I DON'T WANNA LIVE WITHOUT YOUR LOVE
Chicago *Reprise* 88

05 IT NEVER RAINS IN SOUTHERN CALIFORNIA
Albert Hammond *Mums* 72

06 TO ALL THE GIRLS I'VE LOVED BEFORE
Julio Iglesias & Willie Nelson *Columbia* 84

07 THE AIR THAT I BREATHE
The Hollies *Epic* 74

08 ONE MOMENT IN TIME
Whitney Houston *Arista* 88

09 GIMME DAT DING
The Pipkins *Capitol* 70

10 THROUGH THE STORM
Aretha Franklin & Elton John *Arista* 89

The Top 10 Songs Written by
GEORGE HARRISON

GEORGE HARRISON was given little chance to shine as a song-writing Beatle, with only one or two songs allocated to him per album. Aside from the instrumental "Cry For A Shadow," his first song was "Don't Bother Me" on *With The Beatles*.

"'Something' was written on the piano while we were making the white album," Harrison wrote in *I Me Mine*. "I had a break while Paul was doing some overdubbing, so I went into an empty studio and began to write. That's really all there is to it. . . . It didn't go on the white album because we'd already finished all the tracks. I gave it to Joe Cocker a year before I did it."

Harrison produced "My Sweet Lord" for Billy Preston before recording his own version. According to George, the song was inspired by the Edwin Hawkins Singers' "Oh Happy Day." Unfortunately, U.S. District Court Judge Richard Owen ruled that Harrison was guilty of copyright infringement of Ronnie Mack's "He's So Fine," recorded by the Chiffons. Owen conceded that George did not deliberately plagiarize the song.

On November 30, 2001, Harrison died of complications from lung cancer.

01 **MY SWEET LORD / ISN'T IT A PITY**
George Harrison *Apple* 70
02 **SOMETHING**
The Beatles *Apple* 69
03 **FOR YOU BLUE**
The Beatles *Apple* 71
04 **PHOTOGRAPH**
Ringo Starr *Apple* 73
05 **ALL THOSE YEARS AGO**
George Harrison *Dark Horse* 81
06 **GIVE ME LOVE (GIVE ME PEACE ON EARTH)**
George Harrison *Apple* 73
07 **WHAT IS LIFE**
George Harrison *Apple* 71
08 **HERE COMES THE SUN**
Richie Havens *Stormy Forest* 71
09 **BLOW AWAY**
George Harrison *Dark Horse* 79
10 **CRACKERBOX PALACE**
George Harrison *Dark Horse* 77

The Top 10 Songs Written by
JOHN D. LOUDERMILK

JOHN D. LOUDERMILK, born in Durham, North Carolina, sang his own composition, "A Rose And A Baby Ruth," on local television in 1956. George Hamilton IV, a freshman at the University of North Carolina, saw the show and recorded the song for himself.

A year later, Loudermilk recorded "Sittin' In The Balcony." Sy Waronker wanted to buy it for Liberty, but was outbid by ABC-Paramount. In retaliation, he had one of his own artists, Eddie Cochran, record a cover version. Both versions of "Sittin' In The Balcony" charted but Cochran fared best, peaking at No. 22.

Loudermilk's biggest hit was a song he recorded in 1963. Five years later, the lead singer of the British group the Sorrows covered it. Don Maughn's manager changed his client's last name to Fardon and had him record "Indian Reservation." It peaked at No. 20. It didn't become a hit in Britain until two years later, when it peaked at No. 3. That's when Jack Gold at Columbia Records suggested to Mark Lindsay that Paul Revere & the Raiders cover the song.

01 **INDIAN RESERVATION (THE LAMENT OF THE CHEROKEE RESERVATION INDIAN)**
The Raiders *Columbia* 71
02 **NORMAN**
Sue Thompson *Hickory* 62
03 **WATERLOO**
Stonewall Jackson *Columbia* 59
04 **A ROSE AND A BABY RUTH**
George Hamilton IV *ABC-Paramount* 56
05 **THEN YOU CAN TELL ME GOODBYE**
The Casinos *Fraternity* 67
06 **SAD MOVIES (MAKE ME CRY)**
Sue Thompson *Hickory* 61
07 **TALK BACK TREMBLING LIPS**
Johnny Tillotson *MGM* 64
08 **INDIAN OUTLAW**
Tim McGraw *Curb* 94
09 **EBONY EYES**
Everly Brothers *Warner Bros.* 61
10 **TOBACCO ROAD**
Nashville Teens *London* 04

The Top 10 Songs Written by
MICHAEL MASSER

B Y THE time Michael Masser was in his twenties, he knew he wanted to write songs for a living, but instead he married, and soon had two children. With a background in law, he became a stockbroker, all the while yearning to become a professional songwriter. As he drove to the Pan Am building each morning, he had a strong desire to take a left turn and head for Juilliard. Encouraged by Johnny Mercer, he made the transition to songwriting at age 31.

Michael took two songs to producer Bones Howe and was told to leave his tape. Bones liked what he heard, and suggested Michael work with lyricist Gerry Goffin. Their composition "Turn Around To Me," recorded by the 5th Dimension, became Masser's first recorded work.

Then Masser met Motown executive Suzanne de Passe. "They were looking for a song for Diana Ross," he recalls. "Suzanne said, 'Why not start at the top?' 'Touch Me In The Morning' was my first time in the studio." It became his first No. 1 song.

01 **GREATEST LOVE OF ALL**
Whitney Houston *Arista* 86
02 **DIDN'T WE ALMOST HAVE IT ALL**
Whitney Houston *Arista* 87
03 **TOUCH ME IN THE MORNING**
Diana Ross *Motown* 73
04 **SAVING ALL MY LOVE FOR YOU**
Whitney Houston *Arista* 85
05 **THEME FROM "MAHOGANY" (DO YOU KNOW WHERE YOU'RE GOING TO)**
Diana Ross *Motown* 76
06 **IT'S MY TURN**
Diana Ross *Motown* 81
07 **MISS YOU LIKE CRAZY**
Natalie Cole *EMI* 89
08 **IF EVER YOU'RE IN MY ARMS AGAIN**
Peabo Bryson *Elektra* 84
09 **TONIGHT, I CELEBRATE MY LOVE**
Peabo Bryson/Roberta Flack *Capitol* 83
10 **NOTHING'S GONNA CHANGE MY LOVE FOR YOU**
Glenn Medeiros *Amherst* 87

The Top 10 Songs Written by LAURA NYRO

A FTER ATTENDING the High School of Music and Art in Manhattan, Laura Nyro moved to San Francisco and was booked for two months at the famous hungry i nightclub. Her first album, *More Than A New Discovery,* was released by Verve/Folkways in 1966. The next year, she appeared at the Monterey Pop Festival, but Jimi Hendrix and Janis Joplin fans didn't appreciate her quiet, thoughtful music.

In New York, Nyro hooked up with a young manager, David Geffen. He arranged for Laura to record *Eli And The 13th Confession,* her first album for Columbia. Geffen gave a demo of the album to producer Bones Howe, suggesting that "Stoned Soul Picnic" would be perfect for the 5th Dimension.

Howe continued to mine the Nyro catalog for the 5th Dimension. When he suggested they record "Wedding Bell Blues," Marilyn McCoo readily agreed. She was engaged to Billy Davis, Jr., of the group, and Laura's song began, "Bill, I love you so, I always will. . . ."

On April 8, 1997, Nyro died of cancer. She was 49.

01 **WEDDING BELL BLUES**
5th Dimension *Soul City* 69
02 **STONED SOUL PICNIC**
5th Dimension *Soul City* 68
03 **AND WHEN I DIE**
Blood, Sweat & Tears *Columbia* 69
04 **ELI'S COMING**
Three Dog Night *Dunhill* 69
05 **STONEY END**
Barbra Streisand *Columbia* 71
06 **SWEET BLINDNESS**
5th Dimension *Soul City* 68
07 **BLOWING AWAY**
5th Dimension *Soul City* 70
08 **SAVE THE COUNTRY**
5th Dimension *Bell* 70
09 **TIME AND LOVE**
Barbra Streisand *Columbia* 71
10 **FLIM FLAM MAN**
Barbra Streisand *Columbia* 71

The Top 10 Songs Written by
DOC POMUS and MORT SHUMAN

MORT SHUMAN was a friend of the Pomus family, and liked going to New York nightclubs with Jerome "Doc" Pomus. Doc had already penned "Boogie Woogie Country Girl," a Joe Turner B-side, and helped Leiber and Stoller with the Coasters' "Young Blood." When the two started writing together, Pomus did most of the work, and claimed 90 percent of the song publishing. After their first year of collaborating, though, the songwriters changed the split to 50-50.

At the suggestion of Otis Blackwell, who wrote many Elvis Presley hits (including "Don't Be Cruel"), Paul Case at Hill & Range Publishers signed Pomus and Shuman in 1959. That same year, they scored with "A Teenager In Love," the first top 10 single for Dion & the Belmonts.

Leiber and Stoller were producing the Drifters, and looked to other songwriters to supply material. Pomus and Shuman contributed "Save The Last Dance For Me," which went to No. 1 the week of October 17, 1960.

01 SAVE THE LAST DANCE FOR ME
The Drifters *Atlantic* 60
02 SURRENDER
Elvis Presley *RCA* 61
03 YOUNG BLOOD
The Coasters *Atco* 57
04 CAN'T GET USED TO LOSING YOU
Andy Williams *Columbia* 63
05 SUSPICION
Terry Stafford *Crusader* 64
06 LITTLE CHILDREN
Billy J. Kramer & the Dakotas *Imperial* 64
07 A TEENAGER IN LOVE
Dion & the Belmonts *Laurie* 59
08 TURN ME LOOSE
Fabian *Chancellor* 59
09 GO, JIMMY, GO
Jimmy Clanton *Ace* 60
10 THIS MAGIC MOMENT
Jay & the Americans *UA* 69

The Top 10 Songs Written by
BRUCE SPRINGSTEEN

BRUCE SPRINGSTEEN'S first chart single, "Born To Run," was his only top 30 hit until "Hungry Heart" peaked at No. 5 in 1980. Meanwhile, other artists were having better luck with his material. Manfred Mann's Earth Band covered "Spirit In The Night" (1975) and "Blinded By The Light" (1976); "Fire," originally recorded in 1977 by Robert Gordon, was the first top 10 single for the Pointer Sisters in 1979.

"Dancing In The Dark," Springsteen's most successful chart song, came about when Bruce's manager/producer, Jon Landau, insisted that *Born In The U.S.A.* needed a strong track for the first single. Springsteen said he didn't have a song like that, finally exploding, "Look, I've written 70 songs. You want another one, *you* write it," according to Dave Marsh in his book *Glory Days.* Alone in a hotel suite that night, Springsteen wrote "Dancing In The Dark." "It was just like my heart spoke straight through my mouth, without even having to pass through my brain. The chorus just poured out of me."

01 DANCING IN THE DARK
Bruce Springsteen *Columbia* 84
02 FIRE
Pointer Sisters *Planet* 79
03 BLINDED BY THE LIGHT
Manfred Mann's Earth Band *Warner Bros.* 77
04 BECAUSE THE NIGHT
10,000 Maniacs *Elektra* 94
05 HUNGRY HEART
Bruce Springsteen *Columbia* 80
06 STREETS OF PHILADELPHIA
Bruce Springsteen *Columbia* 94
07 GLORY DAYS
Bruce Springsteen *Columbia* 85
08 COVER ME
Bruce Springsteen *Columbia* 84
09 THIS LITTLE GIRL
Gary U.S. Bonds *EMI America* 81
10 PINK CADILLAC
Natalie Cole *EMI Manhattan* 88

The Top 10 Songs Written by
BILLY STEINBERG and TOM KELLY

TOM KELLY and Billy Steinberg both had songs on side one of Pat Benatar's *Precious Time* album. Tom had the hit single "Fire And Ice," and Billy had the title tune. As a result, both of them were invited to producer Keith Olsen's housewarming party, where they met for the first time. Kelly discovered that Steinberg, once a member of the band Billy Thermal, had written one of his favorite songs—Linda Ronstadt's "How Do I Make You."

Their first collaboration was "Just One Kiss," recorded by Rick Springfield. They then signed to Epic Records, under the name i-Ten. One of the songs from their LP, "Alone," became a hit—but not until it was recorded by Heart.

Steinberg and Kelly's most successful chart song, "Like A Virgin," was originally written for a man to sing. In fact, at the time, they didn't even know who Madonna was. Michael Ostin of Warner Bros. heard the song and played it for Madonna. "She went crazy," he says, "and knew instantly it was a song for her and that she could make a great record out of it."

01 LIKE A VIRGIN
Madonna *Sire* 84
02 ALONE
Heart *Capitol* 87
03 SO EMOTIONAL
Whitney Houston *Arista* 88
04 TRUE COLORS
Cyndi Lauper *Portrait* 86
05 ETERNAL FLAME
Bangles *Columbia* 89
06 I'LL STAND BY YOU
The Pretenders *Sire* 94
07 I TOUCH MYSELF
Divinyls *Virgin* 91
08 HOW DO I MAKE YOU
Linda Ronstadt *Asylum* 80
09 IN YOUR ROOM
Bangles *Columbia* 89
10 I DROVE ALL NIGHT
Cyndi Lauper *Epic* 89

The Top 10 Songs Written by JIMMY WEBB

JIMMY WEBB played the piano and organ in his father's church and was writing songs by the time he was 13. When his family moved to California, Webb enrolled in San Bernardino Valley College as a music major. Although he quit school during his second semester, Jimmy made an important contact—a DJ at local radio station KMEN heard his demo tapes and suggested they collaborate on a documentary film about ballooning. The film was never produced, but Webb composed a song for it: "Up-Up And Away." Another Webb song was written after he broke up with a girl he was dating in college: "By The Time I Get To Phoenix."

Webb's most successful chart song, "MacArthur Park," was inspired by lunchtime walks with his girlfriend around the lake in Los Angeles' MacArthur Park. The song has been recorded by actor Richard Harris, Waylon Jennings, and the Four Tops. In 1978, Donna Summer gave the song a disco treatment. Edited down from more than eight minutes to under four minutes for a single release, her recording is Webb's only No. 1 song.

01 MACARTHUR PARK
Donna Summer *Casablanca* 78
02 WICHITA LINEMAN
Glen Campbell *Capitol* 69
03 MACARTHUR PARK
Richard Harris *Dunhill* 68
04 WORST THAT COULD HAPPEN
Brooklyn Bridge *Buddah* 69
05 GALVESTON
Glen Campbell *Capitol* 69
06 UP-UP AND AWAY
5th Dimension *Soul City* 67
07 ALL I KNOW
Art Garfunkel *Columbia* 73
08 HONEY COME BACK
Glen Campbell *Capitol* 70
09 BY THE TIME I GET TO PHOENIX
Glen Campbell *Capitol* 67
10 WHERE'S THE PLAYGROUND SUSIE
Glen Campbell *Capitol* 69

The PRODUCERS

"**I** LOVE PRODUCING,**"** says Nile Rodgers, who has produced hit records for artists like Diana Ross, David Bowie, Madonna, and his own group, Chic. "I really like making records, I think more than just about anything in the world. It's a great thing to start a project and then analyze the project in the middle and then finish it. It's the one thing that I really get emotional about. I love to make records."

Producers haven't always been acknowledged—or even paid—for their work. Phil Spector, architect of the famed "Wall of Sound," was one of the first producers to receive label credit. When Jerry Leiber and Mike Stoller asked Jerry Wexler at Atlantic Records for a printed credit, he exploded, according to Dorothy Wade and Justine Picardie in their book *Music Man.* "What the hell do you want your name on the label for?" he asked them. "Your name is on the label as writers. How many times do you want your names on the record? We tell everybody that you made the record, they all know." After Leiber and Stoller were given label credit, they also wanted a producer's royalty. Miriam Abramson, business manager for Atlantic, was outraged, according to *Music Man.* "At that time there weren't many producers—especially ones getting royalties," she explained. "As a principal in the company, I just didn't want to pay it."

Today, producers are not only acknowledged and paid, but sought after. Jimmy Jam and Terry Lewis are as responsible for the success of *Control* as Janet Jackson. Clive Davis turned to L.A. Reid and Babyface to give Whitney Houston a rougher edge and re-establish her popularity on R&B radio. They came up with "I'm Your Baby Tonight," Houston's most successful chart single to that date.

Producers also are known by their sound. Mike Stock, Matt Aitken, and Pete Waterman are sometimes more identifiable than their artists. Kylie Minogue, Samantha Fox, Sonia, and Sinitta could have recorded each other's vocals and the records would still be similar; take away their producers, and the songs would sound very different.

Not every producer becomes as well-known as Phil Spector or Quincy Jones, but Tom Dowd, Arif Mardin, Narada Michael Walden, Giorgio Moroder and the other producers listed in this section have created their own distinctive styles and reputations over the years. They are as respected and appreciated for their talent as any artist they have produced.

QUINCY DELIGHT Jones, Jr., was born in Chicago. He was 10 years old when his father got a job with the Bremerton Shipyards in Seattle. Quincy made his professional debut at four, playing trumpet at a YMCA dance—he was paid seven dollars.

"My arranging career really got started when I was around 14," Quincy told Nelson George in *Billboard*. "I met Count Basie and Lionel Hampton around the same time." He also met 16-year-old Ray Charles at that point, and the two formed a band, learning from each other.

A scholarship took him to the Berklee School of Music in Boston, after which Quincy moved to New York and worked with Dizzy Gillespie. At 19, he began a three-year stint playing in Lionel Hampton's band. By the end of the '50s, he was living in Paris as musical director for the Barclay label. Back in the States, he was hired by Mercury Records president Irving Green to be head of A&R for the Chicago-based label.

One day at a staff meeting, Quincy heard a voice he liked: the singer was 16-year-old Lesley Gore. "She was the first young artist that I heard sing in tune in a long time," Quincy told George. In February 1963, Quincy showed up at Lesley's door with more than 250 demos so she could listen to them and select songs for her debut Mercury album. The first song they listened to was "It's My Party," written by John Gluck, Jr., Wally Gold, and Herb Wiener. "It's My Party" was rush-released after Quincy ran into Phil Spector in front of Carnegie Hall and found out that Spector had just produced the same song with the Crystals. Four weeks after her record entered the Hot 100, Lesley was No. 1.

01 BILLIE JEAN
Michael Jackson *Epic* 83

02 ROCK WITH YOU
Michael Jackson *Epic* 80

03 BEAT IT
Michael Jackson *Epic* 83

04 WE ARE THE WORLD
USA for Africa *Columbia* 85

05 IT'S MY PARTY
Lesley Gore *Mercury* 63

06 BABY, COME TO ME
Patti Austin w/James Ingram *Qwest* 83

07 THE GIRL IS MINE
Michael Jackson & Paul McCartney *Epic* 83

08 MAN IN THE MIRROR
Michael Jackson *Epic* 88

09 DON'T STOP 'TIL YOU GET ENOUGH
Michael Jackson *Epic* 79

10 I JUST CAN'T STOP LOVING YOU
Michael Jackson & Siedah Garrett *Epic* 87

11 YOU DON'T OWN ME
Lesley Gore *Mercury* 64

12 BAD
Michael Jackson *Epic* 87

13 THE WAY YOU MAKE ME FEEL
Michael Jackson *Epic* 88

14 DIRTY DIANA
Michael Jackson *Epic* 88

15 I'LL BE GOOD TO YOU
Brothers Johnson *A&M* 76

16 GIVE ME THE NIGHT
George Benson *Warner Bros.* 80

17 STOMP!
Brothers Johnson *A&M* 80

Quincy continued to work with Gore through 1965—ten of his top 50 songs are by the teenager from Tenafly, New Jersey. In 1965, Quincy also composed his first of more than 40 film scores, for *The Pawnbroker*. Four years later, he signed to A&M Records as an artist and released *Walking In Space*. His 1975 album *Mellow Madness* featured vocals by the Brothers Johnson; between 1976 and 1980, Quincy produced three top 10 singles for the Los Angeles duo.

It was another film project that led Quincy to produce *Thriller*, the best-selling album of all time. "I didn't want to do *The Wiz*," Quincy told Joe Smith in *Off The Record*. "Except for a couple of songs, I didn't like the music. But [director] Sidney Lumet, who I've done six movies with, said, 'You've got to do it,' and so I did it."

Jones had met Michael Jackson at Sammy Davis, Jr.'s house—when Michael was 12. But Quincy didn't get to know Michael until they worked on *The Wiz* together. "We talked and I started to see what a beautiful human being he was, how disciplined and talented," Quincy said in *Billboard*. "Really genius talent. Then I started to feel there was something inside of him that I had never heard before on his records. He kept asking me about [a] producer, so I said, 'You got a producer. I'll produce it.' So we went and did *Off The Wall* after that."

Michael had four top 10 singles from *Off The Wall*, including two No. 1 hits. "And then came *Thriller*, which was mind-boggling," according to Quincy. *Thriller* yielded seven top 10 singles, including two more No. 1 hits. The album sold more than 40 million copies, making it the best-selling record of all time.

Michael and Quincy did it again with *Bad*. This time, the first five singles from the album went to No. 1. In all, Michael has 18 songs on Quincy's top 50.

Michael co-wrote another Quincy Jones production: "We Are The World," recorded with an all-star supporting cast to raise money for the starving people of Africa and the United States. "The motivation behind involving me was, I believe, a song called 'State Of Independence' I'd done with Donna Summer three years before," Quincy told George. "Basically we have a third of 'We Are The World' on it: Stevie [Wonder], Michael, Lionel [Richie], Dionne Warwick, James Ingram. . . . I would not have taken on that job if I hadn't done that three years before . . . when you can collectively get together and put all that energy together and make your voice felt in a whole sea of voices that have the same concern, they can really do something. It's not just the money. . . . If you sacrifice compassion, you're going to die as a human being."

18 **THRILLER**
Michael Jackson *Epic* 84

19 **WANNA BE STARTIN' SOMETHIN'**
Michael Jackson *Epic* 83

20 **SHE'S A FOOL**
Lesley Gore *Mercury* 63

21 **STRAWBERRY LETTER 23**
Brothers Johnson *A&M* 77

22 **LOVE IS IN CONTROL (FINGER ON THE TRIGGER)**
Donna Summer *Geffen* 82

23 **HUMAN NATURE**
Michael Jackson *Epic* 83

24 **SHE'S OUT OF MY LIFE**
Michael Jackson *Epic* 80

25 **OFF THE WALL**
Michael Jackson *Epic* 80

26 **JUDY'S TURN TO CRY**
Lesley Gore *Mercury* 63

27 **SMOOTH CRIMINAL**
Michael Jackson *Epic* 89

28 **JUST ONCE**
Quincy Jones f/James Ingram *A&M* 81

29 **ANGEL**
Aretha Franklin *Atlantic* 73

30 **P.Y.T. (PRETTY YOUNG THING)**
Michael Jackson *Epic* 83

31 **ANOTHER PART OF ME**
Michael Jackson *Epic* 88

32 **YAH MO B THERE**
James Ingram w/Michael McDonald *Qwest* 84

33 **ONE HUNDRED WAYS**
Quincy Jones f/James Ingram *A&M* 82

34 **I'LL BE GOOD TO YOU**
Quincy Jones f/Ray Charles & Chaka Khan *Qwest* 90

35 **THAT'S THE WAY BOYS ARE**
Lesley Gore *Mercury* 64

36 **MAYBE I KNOW**
Lesley Gore *Mercury* 64

37 **SUNSHINE, LOLLIPOPS & RAINBOWS**
Lesley Gore *Mercury* 65

38 **STUFF LIKE THAT**
Quincy Jones *A&M* 78

39 **LOOK OF LOVE**
Lesley Gore *Mercury* 65

40 **AI NO CORRIDA**
Quincy Jones *A&M* 81

41 **THE WOMAN IN ME**
Donna Summer *Geffen* 83

42 **GET THE FUNK OUT MA FACE**
Brothers Johnson *A&M* 76

43 **HOW DO YOU KEEP THE MUSIC PLAYING**
James Ingram & Patti Austin *Qwest* 83

44 **DO YOU LOVE WHAT YOU FEEL**
Rufus and Chaka Khan *MCA* 80

45 **THE SECRET GARDEN**
Quincy Jones f/El DeBarge, James Ingram, Barry White and Al B. Sure! *Qwest* 90

46 **MASTER OF EYES**
Aretha Franklin *Atlantic* 73

47 **MY TOWN, MY GUY AND ME**
Lesley Gore *Mercury* 65

48 **STATE OF INDEPENDENCE**
Donna Summer *Geffen* 82

49 **EASE ON DOWN THE ROAD**
Diana Ross & Michael Jackson *MCA* 78

50 **I DON'T WANNA BE A LOSER**
Lesley Gore *Mercury* 64

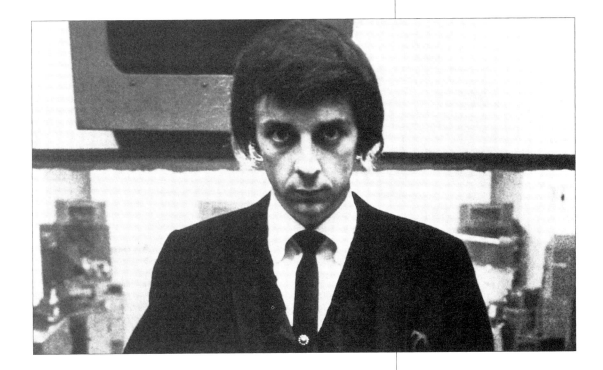

PHIL SPECTOR, creator of the "Wall of Sound," was born on December 26, 1940, in the Bronx. His father died in 1949, and four years later, his family moved to Los Angeles. He was 16 when he performed Lonnie Donegan's "Rock Island Line" at a talent show at Fairfax High School.

In the spring of 1958, Phil raised enough money to secure two hours of recording time at Gold Star Studios. Contributing to the fund were Marshall Leib, Harvey Goldstein, and Annette Kleinbard, and they joined Spector to record "Don't You Worry My Little Pet." That recording helped the group garner a deal with Era Records. At their next session, they recorded a song inspired by a photograph of the epitaph on the tombstone of Phil's father. "To Know Him Is To Love Him," recorded without Goldstein, became the Teddy Bears' first release on Era's Dore subsidiary.

Spector took the Teddy Bears to Imperial Records, but their next single failed to go higher than No. 90 on the Hot 100, and after several more recordings, the trio went their separate ways. While recording *The Teddy Bears Sing!* album, Spector had met Lester Sill, a former promotion man who was a mentor to Jerry Leiber and Mike Stoller. After the demise of the Teddy Bears, Spector signed a contract with Sill to produce and record.

Sill arranged for Spector to apprentice with Leiber and Stoller in New York. He worked with the Coasters, the Drifters, and Ben E. King; with

01 **MY SWEET LORD / ISN'T IT A PITY**
George Harrison *Apple* 70
02 **TO KNOW HIM IS TO LOVE HIM**
The Teddy Bears *Dore* 58
03 **YOU'VE LOST THAT LOVIN' FEELIN'**
Righteous Brothers *Philles* 65
04 **HE'S A REBEL** The Crystals *Philles* 62
05 **BE MY BABY** The Ronettes *Philles* 63
06 **INSTANT KARMA (WE ALL SHINE ON)**
John Ono Lennon *Apple* 70
07 **THE LONG AND WINDING ROAD /
FOR YOU BLUE**
The Beatles *Apple* 70
08 **UNCHAINED MELODY**
Righteous Brothers *Philles* 65
09 **IMAGINE**
John Lennon/Plastic Ono Band *Apple* 71
10 **DA DOO RON RON
(WHEN HE WALKED ME HOME)**
The Crystals *Philles* 63
11 **I LOVE HOW YOU LOVE ME**
The Paris Sisters *Gregmark* 61
12 **CORINNA, CORINNA**
Ray Peterson *Dunes* 61
13 **THEN HE KISSED ME**
The Crystals *Philles* 63
14 **JUST ONCE IN MY LIFE**
Righteous Brothers *Philles* 65
15 **ZIP-A-DEE DOO-DAH**
Bob B. Soxx & the Blue Jeans *Philles* 63

Leiber, he wrote "Spanish Harlem" for King. Spector also produced records by Ray Peterson ("Corinna, Corinna") and Curtis Lee ("Pretty Little Angel Eyes").

Back in Hollywood, Spector agreed to produce one of Sill's acts. When Liberty and Capitol turned down the master, Sill formed a new label with Lee Hazlewood and released "Be My Boy" by the Paris Sisters on Gregmark. It faltered at No. 58, but the follow-up, "I Love How You Love Me," peaked at No. 5.

Sill and Hazlewood split their business arrangement shortly after, and Phil suggested to Lester that they form a partnership. The result was Philles Records, named after both of them. Through Hill & Range Publishers, Spector found three groups he wanted to produce—the Ducanes, the Creations, and the Crystals. The first two were shuffled off to other companies, and Phil signed the five black teenage girls from Brooklyn known as the Crystals to his new label.

By the time "He's A Rebel" went to No. 1, Sill was out of the company, so Spector had the label all to himself. He created a new act called Bob B. Soxx & the Blue Jeans, featuring Darlene Love—who had actually sung the vocals on the Crystals' "He's A Rebel." Spector also released solo material by Darlene in 1963, the same year he released "Be My Baby" by the Ronettes. He was already in love with lead singer Veronica Bennett, and they married in 1967.

The Ronettes appeared at the Cow Palace in San Francisco during 1964; also on the bill were the Righteous Brothers. Spector was conducting the band for all the acts, and was so impressed with Bill Medley and Bobby Hatfield that he bought their contract from Moonglow Records and signed them to Philles. Spector asked Barry Mann and Cynthia Weil to write something for the duo, and "You've Lost That Lovin' Feelin'" was Philles' second No. 1 single.

Spector's final signing to Philles was the husband-and-wife team of Ike and Tina Turner. But when "River Deep-Mountain High" failed to rise higher than No. 88, Spector lost interest in his label and the recording industry.

He made a brief return in 1969 with a production deal for A&M Records. A Ronettes single flopped, but Spector was back on the Hot 100 with Sonny Charles and the Checkmates, Ltd. The A&M deal was short-lived, and Spector would have been out of the business again were it not for Allen Klein, who was managing the Beatles at the time. Through Klein, Spector was asked to work on the *Let It Be* tapes. He also produced "Instant Karma" for John Lennon. That, in turn, led to producing George Harrison's triple solo album, *All Things Must Pass*. In 1971, Spector was named director of A&R for Apple Records. He only held the post for a year, but he produced Lennon's classic "Imagine," Harrison's "Bangla-Desh," and Ronnie Spector's "Try Some, Buy Some."

16 **BLACK PEARL**
Sonny Charles & the Checkmates *A&M* 69

17 **EBB TIDE** Righteous Brothers *Philles* 66

18 **PRETTY LITTLE ANGEL EYES**
Curtis Lee *Dunes* 61

19 **THE BEATLES MOVIE MEDLEY**
The Beatles *Capitol* 82

20 **WHAT IS LIFE** George Harrison *Apple* 71

21 **UPTOWN** The Crystals *Philles* 62

22 **SECOND HAND LOVE**
Connie Francis *MGM* 62

23 **HE'S SURE THE BOY I LOVE**
The Crystals *Philles* 63

24 **POWER TO THE PEOPLE**
John Lennon/Plastic Ono Band *Apple* 71

25 **THERE'S NO OTHER (LIKE MY BABY)**
The Crystals *Philles* 62

26 **BABY, I LOVE YOU**
The Ronettes *Philles* 64

27 **BANGLA-DESH** George Harrison *Apple* 71

28 **WALKING IN THE RAIN**
The Ronettes *Philles* 64

29 **WAIT TIL' MY BOBBY GETS HOME**
Darlene Love *Philles* 63

30 **WHY DO LOVERS BREAK EACH OTHER'S HEART?**
Bob B. Soxx & the Blue Jeans *Philles* 63

31 **HE KNOWS I LOVE HIM TOO MUCH**
The Paris Sisters *Gregmark* 62

32 **DO I LOVE YOU?** The Ronettes *Philles* 64

33 **(THE BEST PART OF) BREAKIN' UP**
The Ronettes *Philles* 64

34 **(TODAY I MET) THE BOY I'M GONNA MARRY**
Darlene Love *Philles* 63

35 **PUDDIN' N' TAIN** The Alley Cats *Philles* 63

36 **EVERY BREATH I TAKE**
Gene Pitney *Musicor* 61

37 **MOTHER**
John Lennon/Plastic Ono Band *Apple* 71

38 **HUNG ON YOU**
Righteous Brothers *Philles* 65

39 **UNDER THE MOON OF LOVE**
Curtis Lee *Dunes* 61

40 **BORN TO BE TOGETHER**
The Ronettes *Philles* 65

41 **A FINE FINE BOY** Darlene Love *Philles* 63

42 **I COULD HAVE LOVED YOU SO WELL**
Ray Peterson *Dunes* 62

43 **LOVE IS ALL I HAVE TO GIVE**
Sonny Charles & the Checkmates, Ltd.
A&M 69

44 **WOMAN IS THE NIGGER OF THE WORLD**
John Lennon/Plastic Ono Band w/Elephant's Memory *Apple* 72

45 **BE MY BOY**
The Paris Sisters *Gregmark* 61

46 **NOT TOO YOUNG TO GET MARRIED**
Bob B. Soxx & the Blue Jeans *Philles* 63

47 **PROUD MARY**
The Checkmates, Ltd. f/Sonny Charles
A&M 69

48 **IS THIS WHAT I GET FOR LOVING YOU?**
The Ronettes *Philles* 65

49 **TRY SOME, BUY SOME**
Ronnie Spector *Apple* 71

50 **JEALOUS GUY**
John Lennon & the Plastic Ono Band
Capitol 88

G EORGE MARTIN has not only produced more No. 1 hits on the Hot 100 than any other producer—23 in all—he also has the longest span of No. 1 hits of any producer, stretching 33 years and 11 months, from the Beatles' "I Want To Hold Your Hand" to Elton John's "Candle In The Wind 1997."

Martin was born on January 3, 1926, in Holloway, located in North London. He grew up during the Depression in a family that did not have a lot of money. His older sister had taken piano lessons, and George wanted them too, but they were no longer affordable. So the youngster taught himself to play piano by ear. By the time he was 15, he had his own dance band. With the world embroiled in war, he went into the military and rose to the rank of lieutenant. He was decommissioned in 1947, and attended the Guildhall School of Music, where he received classical training.

He secured his first job in the music business in 1950, as an assistant to the head of EMI's Parlophone label. He worked not only in classical music, but produced jazz recordings, and then made his mark as the producer of comedy records by performers such as Bernard Cribbins, Peter Ustinov, Charlie Drake, Peter Cook and Dudley Moore, and the Goons, a troupe that included Peter Sellers and Spike Milligan. In 1955, when he was just 29, Martin was named head of Parlophone.

Jealous of fellow producer Norrie Paramour's success with Cliff Richard on EMI's sister label, Columbia, Martin was actively looking for pop acts when manager Brian Epstein approached him with four young lads from Liverpool. The Beatles had already been turned down by parent label EMI as well as by Decca, Pye, and Phillips, when EMI Publishing head Sid Coleman suggested Epstein take the demo tapes to Martin.

It was an instant match. Martin knew he liked the group personally after George Harrison insulted his tie, and the Beatles were impressed to be working with the man who had produced the classic recordings of their favorites, the Goons.

Martin made several key decisions that led to early success for the Beatles. He suggested they replace drummer Pete Best, which the other Beatles had been thinking about anyway. He speeded up a Roy Orbison–inspired "Please Please Me," turning the song into a rock and roll hit and the Beatles' first No. 1. His classical and comedy background also served the Beatles well, as Martin came up with the idea of a string quartet for "Yesterday," and was able to produce the layered, intricate sound of tracks like "I Am The Walrus" and "Tomorrow Never Knows."

Martin's initial success with the Beatles led to producing Epstein's other artists, including Cilla Black, Gerry & the Pacemakers, and Billy J. Kramer & the Dakotas. In 1963, recordings helmed by Martin held the No. 1 spot in the U.K. for 37 weeks, and Martin found himself practically living at the EMI-owned Abbey Road studios to keep up with his workload.

By 1965, Martin was unhappy with his financial arrangement at EMI, believing he should be collecting royalties to reward him for his success instead of a straight salary. He opted to leave the label and form his own company, Associated Independent Recordings. As he was no longer associated with EMI, the label could have assigned another producer to the Beatles, but wisely kept the partnership going. Not that the Beatles wanted to make a change—they had no desire to lose Martin's services. The producer moved from being a mentor to a wise uncle, then to a peer and friend.

There were some speed bumps along the way. Martin was hurt and disappointed when Paul McCartney asked Mike Leander to score "She's Leaving Home," and was unhappy when the Beatles asked Phil Spector to rework the production on the *Let It Be* album. But Martin worked with the Beatles on their final album, *Abbey Road,* and continued to helm recordings by Paul McCartney.

By 1998, Martin was looking at retirement—at least, from producing chores. With his hearing diminished, Martin closed his career with a final No. 1 single. Elton John asked Martin to produce his tribute to the late Princess Diana, "Candle In The Wind 1997." Born from tragedy, the recording became the best-selling single in history and is Martin's most successful chart entry, besting all of his work with the Beatles.

The Top 50 Songs Produced by
L.A. REID and BABYFACE

ANTONIO "L.A." REID and Kenny "Babyface" Edmonds first met at the Zodiac nightclub in Indianapolis, where Reid was playing with his band, the Deele. Edmonds recalls, "After they finished their set, L.A. came down to my table and introduced himself." Both thought the other to be arrogant. "It was a band I would have liked to been in," Babyface admits. But he moved to Michigan and played in a top 40 cover band called the Crowd Pleasers. He then wrote "Slow Jam" for Midnight Star and was asked to attend the recording session.

Reid, meanwhile, had hooked up with Midnight Star and signed a production deal with them. Babyface was reunited with the Deele at the session. "It was a different kind of meeting," he says, "like, we should be working together." After he wrote some songs for the Deele and worked on their demos, L.A. invited him to join the group. They first appeared on the Hot 100 in 1984 with "Body Talk," but their first real success came in May 1988, with a top 10 single, "Two Occasions." By this time Reid and Babyface already had a songwriting and producing credit with another top 10 single, "Rock Steady" by the Whispers.

Reid and Babyface became a hitmaking machine, producing records for Bobby Brown, Karyn White, Pebbles (who married Reid), and After 7, a trio that included two of Babyface's brothers and L.A.'s cousin. In 1990, the two producers were asked by Clive Davis, president of Arista Records, to work with his star act, Whitney Houston. The perception was that Davis wanted to restore Houston's credibility with her R&B audience. "We wanted to come up with something that was different than anything Whitney had sung," explains Reid. "We wanted to give her a new direction, and pick

01 I'LL MAKE LOVE TO YOU
Boyz II Men *Motown* 94

02 END OF THE ROAD
Boyz II Men *Biv 10* 92

03 TAKE A BOW
Madonna *Maverick* 95

04 YOU'RE MAKIN' ME HIGH / LET IT FLOW
Toni Braxton *LaFace* 96

05 EXHALE (SHOOP SHOOP)
Whitney Houston *Arista* 95

06 BABY-BABY-BABY
TLC *LaFace* 92

07 BREATHE AGAIN
Toni Braxton *LaFace* 94

08 SITTIN' UP IN MY ROOM
Brandy *Arista* 96

09 WATER RUNS DRY
Boyz II Men *Motown* 95

10 RED LIGHT SPECIAL
TLC *LaFace* 95

11 NOT GON' CRY
Mary J. Blige *Arista* 96

12 CHANGE THE WORLD
Eric Clapton *Reprise* 96

13 WHEN CAN I SEE YOU
Babyface *Epic* 94

14 I'M YOUR BABY TONIGHT
Whitney Houston *Arista* 90

15 HARD TO SAY I'M SORRY
Az Yet f/Peter Cetera *LaFace* 97

16 HUMPIN' AROUND
Bobby Brown *MCA* 92

17 YOU MEAN THE WORLD TO ME
Toni Braxton *LaFace* 94

up where we felt she was lacking. We felt she needed more of a black base." The result was "I'm Your Baby Tonight," which gave L.A. and Babyface their first No. 1 single on the Hot 100.

Next, Reid and Edmonds turned their attention to their own label, LaFace, based in Atlanta. They signed a female teen hip-hop group from that city, and a sophisticated female vocalist. TLC and Toni Braxton were soon giving the label a string of hits.

L.A. and Babyface continued to work with artists at other labels. They wanted to write and produce for Motown's Boyz II Men, so they called the quartet's manager, Michael Bivins. Their first project for the group was a song for the soundtrack to the Eddie Murphy film *Boomerang*.

"When I was close to finishing the song, L.A. and Daryl [Simmons] came in and helped me finish the lyrics," recalls Babyface, who liked "End Of The Road" so much he thought about recording it himself. "But then I thought Boyz II Men would take it further. That was probably one of the better feelings I've had in terms of handing a song over to somebody and watching them work it."

Boyz II Men were on tour and only had three hours on their schedule to record the song. They were rewarded with their first No. 1 hit, and a song that broke Elvis Presley's 36-year record for having the longest-running chart-topper of the rock era with "Don't Be Cruel" / "Hound Dog," which was No. 1 for 11 weeks. "End Of The Road" remained on top for 13 weeks. "As a writer, I always wanted to have one record that would be considered a classic," says Babyface. "Not to sound vain, but I think that's my first classic. That's the first record I know will be played for a long time because of how those guys sing it."

But Babyface wasn't through writing classics. When Boyz II Men began work on their second album, they turned to a number of producers, including Babyface. "He's not just a producer," says the group's Nathan Morris. "He's a vocalist as well, so he understands where you're trying to take the song." Looking for something to follow "End Of The Road" but not be exactly the same, Babyface came up with "I'll Make Love To You." The single went to No. 1 and stayed there for 14 weeks, tying the rock-era record at that date held by Whitney Houston's "I Will Always Love You."

JERMAINE DUPRI MAULDIN was born in Asheville, North Carolina. His 19-year-old father, Michael, was already working in the music business as a road manager, concert promoter, and artists' manager. Later, he would be named president of Columbia Records' black music division.

Jermaine was just 10 years old when his father promoted a 1982 Diana Ross concert in Atlanta. At one point in her show, Diana invited kids in the audience to come up on stage and dance. Jermaine commandeered the center of the stage with his break dancing and Diana jokingly accused him of stealing the show.

That might count as Jermaine's first day in the music industry, but he didn't really make up his mind to enter the business until he was 12. Impressed with the work of producer Teddy Riley, Jermaine wanted to follow in his footsteps. So it was no surprise that five years later, Dupri could relate to 12-year-old Chris Smith and 13-year-old Chris Kelly when he discovered them in an Atlanta mall. Dupri had written his first song when he was 14 for female rappers Silk Tymes Leather and was shopping with them when Smith and Kelly approached, asking for autographs. Dupri thought the youngsters were stars themselves. They weren't, but he turned them into Kris Kross, and his father Michael agreed to manage them. Dupri produced a demo tape and was turned down by several labels before Joe Nicolo, head of Columbia's Ruffhouse imprint, took a chance in the spring of 1991. That track that sealed the deal was "Lil' Boys In The Hood," which dealt with adult themes like gang violence and drug problems instead of what was happening on the school playground.

Dupri wrote and produced the song "Jump" for Kris Kross. The idea came to the producer while he was at a concert. "I watched the crowd," he explains. "I watched how people were just into jumping. Rappers had been doing it and I said we should make a record like this. I went home and wrote the song in an hour."

At a Kris Kross concert in Chicago, Dupri discovered teen female rapper Da Brat and turned her into his next star attraction. Having two hot artists on his roster led to a deal with Sony for Dupri's own label, So So Def, in 1993.

That didn't stop Dupri from producing artists for other labels, including Usher and Monica. It was Dupri's first hit, "Jump," that inspired Mariah Carey to seek out the man from College Park, Georgia, for her *Daydream* album. "He's got a very distinct style," Carey says of Dupri. The first result of their collaboration, "Always Be My Baby," hit No. 1 in May 1996. Carey and Dupri would make chart magic again in 2005 when Carey's comeback single, "We Belong Together," ruled the Hot 100 for 14 weeks. Dupri also produced two follow-ups, "Shake It Off" (No. 2) and "Don't Forget About Us" (No. 1).

When he was asked by LaFace execs to work on Usher's second album, Dupri began by hanging out with the artist for a couple of weeks. "I was just seeing where he was at, whether he was still a young man in his mind or whether he was older, how he dealt with girls—just a lot of stuff that was going to be good for writing songs for an R&B artist," says Dupri. As a result, he co-wrote and produced "Nice & Slow," which became Usher's first No. 1 on the Hot 100 in February 1998.

The Dupri-Usher team continued to turn out hits. In 2001, "U Got It Bad" was No. 1 for six weeks, Usher revealed the secret of making hit records with Dupri: "He's a party animal. If you work with him, you have to stay up. . . . But in all the conversations we have about relationships, he gets a chance to hear where I'm at and I get a chance to be familiar with him and loosen up. So by two o'clock in the morning we come back to the studio and it comes right out."

Five-and-a-half years after making his debut as a producer on the Hot 100, Dupri finally made his first appearance as an artist, guest starring as "JD" on his production of "The Way That You Talk" by Jagged Edge. Dupri's own first chart single as a lead artist, "The Party Continues," peaked at No. 29 in March 1998.

18 **LET ME HOLD YOU**
Bow Wow f/Omarion *Columbia* 05
19 **FUNKDAFIED**
Da Brat *So So Def* 94
20 **SHORTIE LIKE MINE**
Bow Wow f/Chris Brown & Johnta Austin *Columbia* 06
21 **LET'S GET MARRIED**
Jagged Edge *So So Def* 00
22 **UNDERSTANDING**
Xscape *So So Def* 94
23 **PULLIN' ME BACK**
Chingy f/Tyrese *Slot-a-Lot* 06
24 **PROMISE**
Jagged Edge *So So Def* 01
25 **WHO CAN I RUN TO?**
Xscape *So So Def* 95
26 **TONITE'S THA NIGHT**
Kris Kross *Ruffhouse* 96
27 **IT'S LIKE THAT**
Mariah Carey *Island* 05
28 **WARM IT UP**
Kris Kross *Ruffhouse* 92
29 **WAT DA HOOK GON BE**
Murphy Lee f/Jermaine Dupri *Fo' Reel* 03
30 **U SHOULD'VE KNOWN BETTER**
Monica *J* 04
31 **KEEP ON, KEEPIN' ON**
MC Lyte f/Xscape *Flavor Unit* 96
32 **BOUNCE WITH ME**
Lil Bow Wow f/Xscape *So So Def* 00
33 **MY LITTLE SECRET**
Xscape *So So Def* 98
34 **ALRIGHT**
Kris Kross f/Supercat *Ruffhouse* 93
35 **CONTROL MYSELF**
LL Cool J f/Jennifer Lopez *Def Jam* 06
36 **GIVE IT 2 YOU**
Da Brat *So So Def* 95
37 **THE PARTY CONTINUES**
JD f/Da Brat *So So Def* 98
38 **GHETTO LOVE**
Da Brat f/T-Boz *So So Def* 97
39 **BOW WOW (THAT'S MY NAME)**
Lil Bow Wow *So So Def* 01
40 **GOTTA BE**
Jagged Edge *So So Def* 98
41 **FRESH AZIMIZ**
Bow Wow f/J-Kwon & Jermaine Dupri *Columbia* 06
42 **WHAT'CHU LIKE**
Da Brat f/Tyrese *So So Def* 00
43 **WHAT'S GOING ON**
All Star Tribute *Columbia* 01
44 **SITTIN' ON TOP OF THE WORLD**
Da Brat *So So Def* 96
45 **CALL ON ME**
Janet & Nelly *Virgin* 06
46 **WELCOME TO ATLANTA**
Jermaine Dupri & Ludacris *So So Def* 02
47 **IMAGINATION**
Tamia *Qwest* 98
48 **FEELS SO GOOD**
Xscape *So So Def* 95
49 **FA ALL Y'ALL**
Da Brat *So So Def* 94
50 **DO YOU WANT TO / CAN'T HANG**
Xscape f/MC Lyte *So So Def* 96

The Top 30 Songs Produced by
WALTER AFANASIEFF

W ALTER AFANASIEFF'S first chance to produce on his own came unexpectedly. The opportunity arrived via a phone call from Tommy Mottola at Sony Music. He told Afanasieff that Mariah Carey's first album was complete, but she and songwriter Ben Margulies had written a new song, and Mottola wanted it on the album. "You only have a couple of days," Mottola told Afanasieff. "Are you ready to cut it?" The track, "Love Takes Time," made the debut album and was Carey's second No. 1, following "Vision Of Love."

Born Vladamir Nikitich to Russian parents in São Paulo, Brazil, in 1958, Afanasieff was five when his family moved to San Francisco. It was there that he was playing in a band called the Warriors when he met producer Narada Michael Walden in 1981. Afanasieff had been a touring musician, on the road with artists such as Gladys Knight, Kenny G, and James Brown. Afanasieff and Walden first worked together on Aretha Franklin's *Who's Zoomin' Who* album. When Mariah Carey flew to the Bay Area to work with Walden, Mottola and fellow Sony Music exec Don Ienner were impressed with Afanasieff, leading them to offer him a position as executive staff producer with the company.

That explains why the majority of titles among Afanasieff's top 30 *Billboard* hits are for artists on the various Sony labels—Columbia, Epic, 550 Music, and C2. Leading the list is the longest-running No. 1 hit of the rock era, "One Sweet Day" by Mariah Carey and Boyz II Men.

The Top 30 Songs Produced by
PETER ASHER

P ETER ASHER admits, "I never liked performing very much. I liked singing, but I can still sing with friends on stage or on a record. But the responsibility and nerve-wracking obligation of entertaining an audience never particularly appealed to me."

In 1964, Peter Asher was part of the British invasion that swept through America. Partnered with Gordon Waller, he vaulted to the No. 1 position his very first time out with a John Lennon–Paul McCartney song, "A World Without Love." Peter and Gordon had hits with a string of Lennon-McCartney tunes, including "Nobody I Know" and "I Don't Want To See You Again." The duo went their separate ways in 1967, and Peter produced a couple of records for former Manfred Mann lead singer Paul Jones. Paul McCartney was impressed with the results, and asked Asher to be head of A&R for Apple Records.

"James [Taylor] called me up one day," Peter recalls. "He'd been in a band with Danny Kortchmar called the Flying Machine in New York. Danny had been in a band called the Kingbees who had backed Peter and Gordon on a couple of American tours. Danny and I had become good friends. When the Flying Machine broke up, Kootch gave James my phone number in London." Peter listened to James' demo tape and promptly signed him up.

Taylor recorded one album for Apple. Asher left the label when Allen Klein started running the company, and eventually signed Taylor to Warner Bros. The initial single from Taylor's first Warner album was "Fire And Rain"; nine months later, Taylor had his biggest success on the Hot 100 with a cover version of Carole King's "You've Got A Friend."

Twenty-seven of Asher's top 30 songs have been recorded either by Taylor or Linda Ronstadt. "I first met her on one of my early trips to New York," Peter says. He saw her perform at the Bitter End, and met her after the show through friends. Later, while changing managers, she asked Asher if he would like to be her new manager.

"The first thing we had to do was find a producer to finish the album she was working on then, *Don't Cry Now*. I ended up helping her finish some of that record and we liked working together, so we decided to do the next one together and that was *Heart Like A Wheel*." The initial single from that LP gave Linda her only No. 1 hit, "You're No Good." It was a remake, like most of Ronstadt's hits—and most of Asher's. Of his top 30 productions, 18 of them are cover versions of older songs. His most successful chart single, "Don't Know Much," by Ronstadt and Aaron Neville, was originally recorded by songwriter Barry Mann.

01 **DON'T KNOW MUCH**
Linda Ronstadt f/Aaron Neville *Elektra* 89
02 **YOU'VE GOT A FRIEND**
James Taylor *Warner Bros.* 71
03 **BLUE BAYOU**
Linda Ronstadt *Asylum* 77
04 **WHEN WILL I BE LOVED**
Linda Ronstadt *Capitol* 75
05 **FIRE AND RAIN**
James Taylor *Warner Bros.* 70
06 **YOU'RE NO GOOD**
Linda Ronstadt *Capitol* 75
07 **SOMEWHERE OUT THERE**
Linda Ronstadt & James Ingram *MCA* 87
08 **HANDY MAN**
James Taylor *Columbia* 77
09 **IT'S SO EASY**
Linda Ronstadt *Asylum* 77
10 **LONELY BOY**
Andrew Gold *Asylum* 77
11 **HURT SO BAD**
Linda Ronstadt *Asylum* 80
12 **OOH BABY BABY**
Linda Ronstadt *Asylum* 79
13 **HOW DO I MAKE YOU**
Linda Ronstadt *Asylum* 80
14 **HEAT WAVE / LOVE IS A ROSE**
Linda Ronstadt *Asylum* 75
15 **AFTER ALL**
Cher & Peter Cetera *Geffen* 89
16 **THAT'LL BE THE DAY**
Linda Ronstadt *Asylum* 76
17 **HER TOWN TOO**
James Taylor & J.D. Souther *Columbia* 81
18 **BACK IN THE U.S.A.**
Linda Ronstadt *Asylum* 78
19 **DON'T LET ME BE LONELY TONIGHT**
James Taylor *Warner Bros.* 73
20 **ALL MY LIFE**
Linda Ronstadt f/Aaron Neville *Elektra* 90
21 **YOUR SMILING FACE**
James Taylor *Columbia* 77
22 **THE TRACKS OF MY TEARS**
Linda Ronstadt *Asylum* 76
23 **HEART OF STONE**
Cher *Geffen* 90
24 **UP ON THE ROOF**
James Taylor *Columbia* 79
25 **I CAN'T LET GO**
Linda Ronstadt *Asylum* 80
26 **GET CLOSER**
Linda Ronstadt *Asylum* 82
27 **I KNEW YOU WHEN**
Linda Ronstadt *Asylum* 83
28 **SOMEONE TO LAY DOWN BESIDE ME**
Linda Ronstadt *Asylum* 77
29 **WHAT'S NEW**
Linda Ronstadt *Asylum* 83
30 **LONG AGO AND FAR AWAY**
James Taylor *Warner Bros.* 71

The Top 30 Songs Produced by TOM DOWD

TOM DOWD, a native of Manhattan, did some early engineering work for Atlantic Records, the label he would become associated with in the '50s. Dowd was involved in recording many of the artists on the Atlantic roster, including LaVern Baker, the Coasters, the Drifters, and Ray Charles. Although credited as an engineer, he would work directly with the artists, arrangers, and songwriters, often functioning more like a producer.

In the '60s, Dowd engineered recordings for Wilson Pickett and Otis Redding. He was the engineer on Redding's "Respect," as well as on the hit cover version by Aretha Franklin. Working with Jerry Wexler and Arif Mardin, he was credited as a producer on Aretha Franklin songs like "The Weight," "Share Your Love With Me," and "Eleanor Rigby."

With Mardin, he produced "Good Lovin'" for the Young Rascals, and then worked with Cream—back in the engineer's seat while Felix Pappalardi of Mountain produced the trio of Eric Clapton, Ginger Baker, and Jack Bruce. As the decade closed, Dowd went to Memphis to produce another British artist—Dusty Springfield.

Through manager Phil Walden, Dowd produced the Allman Brothers' second album, *Idlewild South.* While working with Duane Allman, Dowd was asked by Robert Stigwood at RSO Records if he would like to work with Clapton again. Dowd brought Clapton to an Allman Brothers concert, where he met Duane for the first time. "That's how the whole *Layla* thing got to be," Dowd explains. "They just sat in the studio and traded instruments and licks for the next five days, and that made an album."

DAVID FOSTER'S musical talent was apparent even at age five, when he started taking piano lessons in his native Vancouver. At 13 he was enrolled in classes at the University of Washington, and three years later he made his first professional appearances, backing Chuck Berry for local gigs.

In 1971, Foster moved to Los Angeles. Two years later he was in the top 10 of the Hot 100 as a member of Skylark, a one-hit-wonder group that scored with "Wildflower." For the rest of the decade, he established solid credentials as a session keyboard player, working with Barbra Streisand, Rod Stewart, John Lennon, and George Harrison. He began to write and produce, and won a Grammy for co-writing Earth, Wind & Fire's "After The Love Has Gone." His next Grammy was for producing the *Dreamgirls* cast album.

Foster's most successful chart single as a producer is Toni Braxton's "Un-Break My Heart." Clive Davis told Diane Warren her song was perfect for Braxton, and Foster paid her a visit on the set of a video shoot, demo tucked under his arm. LaFace co-founder Kenny "Babyface" Edmonds was there, and Foster told him and Braxton that the demo was in a low key, but he would raise it to accommodate Toni's voice. Babyface protested, insisting that Braxton sing in the same key as the demo. Foster said that was almost a man's key, but Babyface said it would be very sexy. "He couldn't have been more right," says the producer.

Foster and Warren also teamed up for Celine Dion's "Because You Loved Me," from the soundtrack to *Up Close And Personal*. Warren thought the finished product was better than how she heard the song in her head. "When Celine sings your song, or David produces it, it's going to be better than you envisioned it."

The Top 30 Songs Produced by SNUFF GARRETT

TOMMY GARRETT quit school in Dallas, Texas, and went to California with a couple of DJ friends. He slept at night in Hollywood's Plummer Park. He searched for day work doing record promotion and looked up Al Bennett at Dot Records. Garrett had done some work for a record distributor in Dallas and had met Bennett; he was immediately hired as his assistant. But homesickness set in, and Garrett headed back to Texas.

While working as a DJ in Lubbock, Texas, Garrett—nicknamed "Snuff" after the well-known tobacco Garrett Snuff—met a local singer there, and they became best friends. The singer's name was Buddy Holly. Later, when Holly was successful and living in New York, he had plans to start a production company named Taupe, the color of his Cadillac. "He was going to hire three of us to come to New York and be with him," Snuff explains. "Bob Montgomery, a successful publisher and producer in Nashville; Waylon Jennings, and myself. When Buddy died, a lot of our futures died with him. It was the only real link we had in those early days with the music business."

Hired by the Liberty label to do promotion, Snuff insisted on also being allowed to produce records. He had success with singles by Johnny Burnette ("Dreamin'," "You're Sixteen") and Bobby Vee ("Devil Or Angel," "Rubber Ball"), and was soon the head of A&R for Liberty. He produced singles for Gene McDaniels and actor Walter Brennan, but lost one he thought was going to be a hit. He had hired a young man named Phil Spector to work in Liberty's New York office. After cutting "He's A Rebel" for Vikki Carr, Garrett was shocked to learn that Spector had taken Gene Pitney's demo of the song and raced to Los Angeles to cut it with Darlene Love of the Blossoms on lead vocals. Spector released "He's A Rebel" as a Crystals single, and it went to No. 1.

In the mid-'60s, Garrett produced a string of hits for the son of his neighbor, Jerry Lewis. Gary Lewis & the Playboys started at the top by recording a song Bobby Vee had turned down, "This Diamond Ring."

Snuff was back on top of the Hot 100 in 1971 with Cher's "Gypsys, Tramps & Thieves" (which was originally titled "Gypsys and White Trash"). One of his most successful *Billboard* singles is a song turned down by Liza Minnelli and Cher. "Sonny told me it was a piece of junk and she would never record it," Snuff maintains. "Liza didn't like the song." So Snuff told songwriter Bobby Russell that his wife Vicki Lawrence should record "The Night The Lights Went Out In Georgia." Snuff recalls: "We did two or three sides in no more than two-and-a-half hours."

The Top 30 Songs Produced by
JIMMY JAM and TERRY LEWIS

I N JANUARY 1981, Terry Lewis asked Jimmy Jam to join his band, Flyte Tyme. The other members included Alexander O'Neal, Jesse Johnson, and Morris Day. When Prince offered Day a recording contract, he brought along the other members, who shortened their name to the Time.

Jam and Lewis moonlighted as producers, against Prince's wishes. When they were stranded by a snowstorm in Atlanta while producing "Just Be Good To Me" for the S.O.S. Band, they missed a concert in San Antonio. Prince fined each of them a month's pay and then fired them from the Time.

That gave them the opportunity to become serious about producing. Their early hits included "Tender Love" for the Force M.D.'s and "Saturday Love" for Alexander O'Neal and Cherrelle. Then John McClain of A&M Records asked them to produce Janet Jackson's third album. *Control* yielded six hit singles, including a No. 1 hit, "When I Think Of You." Janet surpassed that feat with *Rhythm Nation 1814,* which contained four chart-toppers. When Jackson signed a $32 million pact with Virgin Records, Jam and Lewis produced the first album for her new label. Three of the producers' top 10 singles can be found on that Virgin debut, *janet.*

The producers' initial success with Janet resulted in a barrage of requests from artists who wanted to work with Jam and Lewis. The duo turned down most of these invitations, although they did consent to work with the Human League and Herb Alpert. They also remixed George Michael's "Monkey" and were given producers' credit on the single.

The Top 30 Songs Produced by
ROBERT JOHN "MUTT" LANGE

H E MAY be best known as the husband and producer of country superstar Shania Twain, but before he met the Canadian singer, Lange was more associated with headbanger music, producing albums for AC/DC and Def Leppard, and working with rock groups like the Cars and Foreigner. Still, he was always interested in country music, and as a high school student was a big fan of Slim Whitman. He also admired Tammy Wynette, and was partial to the steel guitar.

Lange, who remains reclusive when it comes to doing interviews, grew up in Zambia, then known as Rhodesia, and as a teenager moved to South Africa. Later, he relocated to Belfast. His earliest production to reach the Hot 100 was "5.7.0.5." by City Boy in 1978.

Next came his association with the original bad boys of metal, AC/DC. Formed in Sydney, the band had three albums that languished in the bottom half of the *Billboard* album chart before Lange took charge. The *Highway To Hell* LP peaked at No. 17 in 1979 and the follow-up, *Back In Black,* soared to No. 4. While AC/DC never made significant inroads on the Hot 100, that wasn't a problem for the fivesome from Sheffield, England. Def Leppard's Lange-produced *Pyromania* spent two weeks at No. 2 on The Billboard 200 in 1983 and yielded the hit single "Photograph," which reached No. 12. The follow-up album, *Hysteria,* spent six weeks at No. 1 in 1988, and gave up the singles "Love Bites," "Pour Some Sugar On Me," and "Armageddon It," the top three Def Leppard songs on Lange's top 30.

After working with heavy metal and rock bands in the '80s, Lange connected with Canadian rocker Bryan Adams in the early '90s, producing No. 1 hits like "(Everything I Do) I Do It For You" and "Have You Ever Really Loved A Woman?"

Lange was a fan of Twain's debut album and contacted the artist by telephone. For several weeks, they wrote songs without meeting in person. They first came face-to-face at Nashville's Fan Fair in 1993. Six months later, on December 29, they were married. Their collaboration on Twain's *Come On Over* resulted in the biggest-selling album by a female country artist, and Lange's most successful Hot 100 single, "You're Still The One."

01 YOU'RE STILL THE ONE
Shania Twain *Mercury* 98

02 WAITING FOR A GIRL LIKE YOU
Foreigner *Atlantic* 81

03 (EVERYTHING I DO) I DO IT FOR YOU
Bryan Adams *A&M* 91

04 HAVE YOU EVER REALLY LOVED A WOMAN?
Bryan Adams *A&M* 95

05 GET OUTTA MY DREAMS, GET INTO MY CAR
Billy Ocean *Jive* 88

06 LOVE BITES
Def Leppard *Mercury* 88

07 CAN'T STOP THIS THING WE STARTED
Bryan Adams *A&M* 91

08 PLEASE FORGIVE ME
Bryan Adams *A&M* 93

09 POUR SOME SUGAR ON ME
Def Leppard *Mercury* 88

10 DRIVE
The Cars *Elektra* 84

11 URGENT
Foreigner *Atlantic* 81

12 LOVERBOY
Billy Ocean *Jive* 85

13 SAID I LOVED YOU...BUT I LIED
Michael Bolton *Columbia* 94

14 ARMAGEDDON IT
Def Leppard *Mercury* 89

15 THAT DON'T IMPRESS ME MUCH
Shania Twain *Mercury* 99

16 FROM THIS MOMENT ON
Shania Twain *Mercury* 98

17 DO I HAVE TO SAY THE WORDS?
Bryan Adams *A&M* 92

18 THOUGHT I'D DIED AND GONE TO HEAVEN
Bryan Adams *A&M* 92

19 YOU MIGHT THINK
The Cars *Elektra* 84

20 MAGIC
The Cars *Elektra* 84

21 LET'S MAKE A NIGHT TO REMEMBER
Bryan Adams *A&M* 96

22 HYSTERIA
Def Leppard *Mercury* 88

23 PHOTOGRAPH
Def Leppard *Mercury* 83

24 FOREVER AND FOR ALWAYS
Shania Twain *Mercury* 03

25 ROCK OF AGES
Def Leppard *Mercury* 83

26 HELLO AGAIN
The Cars *Elektra* 85

27 ROCKET
Def Leppard *Mercury* 89

28 ANIMAL
Def Leppard *Mercury* 87

29 CAN I TOUCH YOU...THERE?
Michael Bolton *Columbia* 95

30 BREAK IT UP
Foreigner *Atlantic* 82

The Top 30 Songs Produced by ARIF MARDIN

ARIF MARDIN'S credits as a producer include artists with many different visions, from Judy Collins to Culture Club, from Bette Midler to the Rascals. Mardin was born in Istanbul, Turkey, and was a jazz fan by the time he was 10. He came to the United States in 1958 as the recipient of a Quincy Jones music scholarship at Boston's Berklee College of Music. Mardin met Nesuhi Ertegun of Atlantic Records, and was asked to join the label. "I started at the bottom and then I was given a production job with the Rascals in 1965. Tom Dowd and I were co-producing—it was the first time I was bitten by the pop bug." Mardin cites the Beatles, Motown, and Stax as major influences.

Mardin worked with Dowd and Jerry Wexler on projects by Atlantic artists like Aretha Franklin and Dusty Springfield, and went solo on Brook Benton's "Rainy Night In Georgia." In the mid-'70s, he produced *Main Course,* the album that gave the Bee Gees a resurgence with "Jive Talkin'" and "Nights On Broadway." Mardin suggested the Gibbs listen to current R&B records before recording the album. The producer recalls, "The rapport between the brothers and myself was fabulous. When we were in the studio together, one creative idea led to another." The Bee Gees wanted to continue working with Mardin, but when Robert Stigwood moved his RSO label from Atlantic to Polydor, Mardin's services were no longer available.

Two of Mardin's top 10 singles are by Bette Midler. "'Wind Beneath My Wings' was chosen for the film *Beaches* before I joined the project," he explains. Director Garry Marshall used a rough mix during the filming. From the emotional reaction of the crew, Mardin knew the track was a hit.

Mardin came up with the idea of using Melle Mel's rap as an introduction to Chaka Khan's "I Feel For You." He recalls, "I thought Chaka's name was a great source for percussive singing. The hybrid really worked, combining the hip hop technology of the day."

Two of Mardin's top three chart singles are movie songs by Phil Collins. "Phil asked me to do some string arrangements on his first Atlantic solo album—we got along famously." Collins requested that Mardin produce "Against All Odds (Take A Look At Me Now)." The producer took a few days off from working with British trio Scritti Politti to record Phil's vocals in Los Angeles. The song "Separate Lives," from *White Nights,* was crying out for a duet, according to Doug Morris, then president of Atlantic Records. "We overdubbed vocals by Marilyn Martin with great results," says Mardin.

Mardin was senior vice president of Atlantic when he retired in 2001. But that wasn't the end of his career. He joined EMI's reactivated Manhattan label as senior vice president and general manager, and produced tracks for Norah Jones' first two albums. After suffering from pancreatic cancer for a year, Mardin died on June 25, 2006. There was a funeral in Istanbul and a memorial service in Manhattan.

01 **PEOPLE GOT TO BE FREE**
The Rascals *Atlantic* 68
02 **AGAINST ALL ODDS
(TAKE A LOOK AT ME NOW)**
Phil Collins *Atlantic* 84
03 **SEPARATE LIVES**
Phil Collins & Marilyn Martin *Atlantic* 85
04 **FROM A DISTANCE**
Bette Midler *Atlantic* 90
05 **GOOD LOVIN'**
The Young Rascals *Atlantic* 66
06 **JIVE TALKIN'**
Bee Gees *RSO* 75
07 **I FEEL FOR YOU**
Chaka Khan *Warner Bros.* 84
08 **WIND BENEATH MY WINGS**
Bette Midler *Atlantic* 89
09 **PICK UP THE PIECES**
Average White Band *Atlantic* 75
10 **SPANISH HARLEM**
Aretha Franklin *Atlantic* 71
11 **UNTIL YOU COME BACK TO ME
(THAT'S WHAT I'M GONNA DO)**
Aretha Franklin *Atlantic* 74
12 **YOU SHOULD HEAR HOW
SHE TALKS ABOUT YOU**
Melissa Manchester *Arista* 82
13 **WAITING FOR A STAR TO FALL**
Boy Meets Girl *RCA* 88
14 **RAINY NIGHT IN GEORGIA**
Brook Benton *Cotillion* 70
15 **SHE'S GONE**
Daryl Hall and John Oates *Atlantic* 76
16 **NIGHTS ON BROADWAY**
Bee Gees *RSO* 75
17 **SET THE NIGHT TO MUSIC**
Roberta Flack w/Maxi Priest *Atlantic* 91
18 **BRIDGE OVER TROUBLED WATER**
Aretha Franklin *Atlantic* 71
19 **YOU BELONG TO ME**
Carly Simon *Elektra* 78
20 **CUT THE CAKE**
Average White Band *Atlantic* 75
21 **FANNY (BE TENDER WITH MY LOVE)**
Bee Gees *RSO* 76
22 **DAY DREAMING**
Aretha Franklin *Atlantic* 72
23 **WHERE IS THE LOVE**
Roberta Flack and Donny Hathaway
Atlantic 72
24 **SON-OF-A PREACHER MAN**
Dusty Springfield *Atlantic* 69
25 **DON'T PLAY THAT SONG**
Aretha Franklin *Atlantic* 70
26 **GOOD TIME CHARLIE'S GOT THE BLUES**
Danny O'Keefe *Signpost* 72
27 **CALL ME**
Aretha Franklin *Atlantic* 70
28 **YOU KNOW I LOVE YOU...DON'T YOU?**
Howard Jones *Elektra* 86
29 **ROCK STEADY**
Aretha Franklin *Atlantic* 71
30 **MOVE AWAY** Culture Club *Epic/Virgin* 86

The Top 30 Songs Produced by THE NEPTUNES

PHARRELL WILLIAMS and Chad Hugo were both 14 when they met at a summer school music class in Virginia Beach, Virginia. Williams was a drummer who wrote lyrics and rapped while Hugo played saxophone and keyboards. They performed together at a high school talent show in 1992 and connected with producer Teddy Riley, whose credits included working with Bobby Brown, Keith Sweat, and Al B. Sure!

Williams and Hugo learned a lot about production from Riley and were given the chance to work with artists like SWV and BLACKstreet. That led to meeting Sean "Puffy" Combs, who employed the duo to produce two of his acts, Mase and Total. Adopting the name Neptunes, after the Roman god of the sea, Williams and Hugo cemented their reputation in the hip-hop world in 1998 when they produced "Superthug" for rapper Noreaga.

As their fame grew, so did the list of artists who wanted to be produced by the Neptunes. Williams and Hugo have fashioned tracks for Britney Spears, Justin Timberlake, Gwen Stefani, Usher, Kelis, and LL Cool J. They've also come up with hits for Pharrell as an artist, who has been featured on hits by Snoop Dogg and Ludacris, and was lead artist with a featured Jay-Z on the 2003 single "Frontin'."

While helming hits for so many varied artists, Williams and Hugo kept crossing paths with Nelly's people and all agreed the Neptunes should work with the St. Louis rappper one day. That day finally arrived in 2002 when the Neptunes produced the summer smash "Hot In Herre." The track was based on a No. 1 R&B hit from 1979, "Bustin' Loose" by Chuck Brown & the Soul Searchers. "We like being inspired by old grooves," says Hugo, who explains that Nelly's voice "was the instrument added on top of the simple groove. It was minimal but it was perfect."

ICHARD PERRY grew up in Brooklyn. His doo-wop group, the Escorts, signed with Coral Records, and had a local hit in Detroit with "Somewhere" from *West Side Story.*

After the Escorts, Perry wrote some songs with Kenny Vance of Jay & the Americans. Then he went to work in the West Coast A&R department of Kama Sutra Records, where he received his first production assignment: working with Captain Beefheart on the *Safe As Milk* album.

Next, Perry moved to Warner Bros. as a staff producer. He worked with Ella Fitzgerald, Fats Domino, and Theodore Bikel, providing all three with a contemporary mix of songs that included a lot of Lennon-McCartney material. His first Hot 100 hit came not with any of those artists, but with the eccentric Herbert Khaury—better known as Tiny Tim.

Perry left Warner Bros. to become a freelance producer, and was selected by Clive Davis at Columbia Records to produce Barbra Streisand. He gave Streisand her first top 10 hit since 1964's "People" with Laura Nyro's "Stoney End."

Perry's next hit album was *Nilsson Schmilsson.* He had first met Harry Nilsson at a party Phil Spector threw for Tiny Tim in 1968. The first single from the album, a remake of Badfinger's "Without You," spent four weeks at No. 1. Perry had another chart-topper with Carly Simon's "You're So Vain"; more No. 1 hits followed for Ringo Starr and Leo Sayer. The Pointer Sisters' version of Bruce Springsteen's "Fire" peaked at No. 2.

The Top 30 Songs Produced by NILE RODGERS and BERNARD EDWARDS

I N 1973, Nile Rodgers and Bernard Edwards were backing up a Thom Bell group, New York City. When that outfit broke up, Rodgers and Edwards decided to continue working together. They tried to get a record deal. Record companies liked their tapes but nobody wanted to sign them. "We had been writing songs all along, but they were all rock 'n' roll songs," says Nile. "Power chords and the whole bit." Then Rodgers and Edwards formed a quartet with two female vocalists and became Chic. "As soon as we did 'Dance, Dance, Dance,' our first disco song, we got a record deal."

"Le Freak," the third single by Chic, became Atlantic's most successful single of all time to that date. While Chic was popular, Rodgers and Edwards toured and started to produce for other artists.

After "Good Times" hit No. 1 in 1979, Chic never made the top 40 of the Hot 100 again. In 1980, Nile and Bernard were asked to produce an album for Diana Ross. "We had never worked with stars before," Rodgers admitted. "We didn't realize what producers did." The "Upside Down" single from *diana* is Rodgers and Edwards' second biggest hit on the *Billboard* chart.

By 1983, Chic had dissolved, and Rodgers was in a downswing. A chance meeting at an after-hours club with one of his long-time heroes, David Bowie, resulted in Nile producing Bowie's *Let's Dance* album; the title track became Bowie's most successful Hot 100 song, revitalizing his career. Nile went on to produce albums for Madonna as well as Duran Duran.

Bernard Edwards also worked with Duran Duran, as well as Robert Palmer, ABC, Jody Watley, and Rod Stewart. Edwards was 43 when he died on April 18, 1996, of pneumonia.

The Top 30 Songs Produced by TIMBALAND

H E'S KNOWN around the world as Timbaland, but earlier in life he worked as "DJ Timmy Tim" and he was born Timothy Z. Mosley in Norfolk, Virginia. Long before he became one of the most sought-after producers in the business, Mosley was friends with a female rapper named Missy Elliott and a man named Melvin Barcliff, who would become known professionally as Magoo. Mosley started out creating tracks on an electronic keyboard. Elliott liked what she heard, and they began working together, with Barcliff as the third member of their team. All three joined the Swing Mob label owned by DeVante Swing of Jodeci, and it was Swing who gave Mosley his nickname of Timbaland.

In 1996, Timbaland produced the first album by R&B singer Ginuwine. That CD included "Pony," a song that peaked at No. 6 on the Hot 100, giving Timbaland his first top 10 hit. While he was in the studio with Ginuwine, Timbaland was also working with Aaliyah on her second album, *One In A Million*. That CD beat Ginwuine's debut to the charts, and the single "If Your Girl Only Knew" peaked at No. 11.

In 1997, Timbaland made his debut on the Hot 100 as an artist. "Up Jumps Da Boogie," billed to Magoo and Timbaland, peaked at No. 12. By the end of the decade, Timbaland had produced hits for Total and Nicole, and in 2000 he secured his first No. 1 single on the Hot 100, Aaliyah's "Try Again." But his legend would grow even larger after the turn of the century.

Timbaland remained close friends with Missy Elliott, producing hits like "Hot Boyz" and "Get Ur Freak On." In 2002, he gave Elliott the biggest hit of her career with "Work It," which stayed at No. 2 for 10 weeks, the longest run in history of a song that peaked in the runner-up spot, tied with Foreigner's "Waiting For A Girl Like You."

Timbaland reached new heights in 2006–07 when he produced two No. 1 hits for Nelly Furtado and three for Justin Timberlake.

01 **PROMISCUOUS**
Nelly Furtado f/Timbaland *Mosley* 06
02 **SEXYBACK**
Justin Timberlake *Jive* 06
03 **WORK IT**
Missy "Misdemeanor" Elliott *The Gold Mind* 02
04 **TRY AGAIN** Aaliyah *Blackground* 00
05 **MY LOVE**
Justin Timberlake f/T.I. *Jive* 06
06 **DIRT OFF YOUR SHOULDER**
Jay-Z *Roc-A-Fella/Def Jam* 04
07 **CRY ME A RIVER**
Justin Timberlake *Jive* 03
08 **HOT BOYZ**
Missy "Misdemeanor" Elliott f/Nas, Eve & Q-Tip
The Gold Mind 00
09 **PONY**
Ginuwine *550* 96
10 **GET UR FREAK ON**
Missy "Misdemeanor" Elliott *The Gold Mind* 01
11 **WHAT ABOUT US**
Total *LaFace* 97
12 **MAKE IT HOT**
Nicole f/Missy "Misdemeanor" Elliott & Mocha
The Gold Mind 98
13 **OOPS (OH MY)**
Tweet *The Gold Mind* 02
14 **SAY IT RIGHT**
Nelly Furtado *Mosley* 07
15 **GOSSIP FOLKS**
Missy "Misdemeanor" Elliott f/Ludacris
The Gold Mind 03
16 **SOCK IT 2 ME**
Missy "Misdemeanor" Elliott f/Da Brat
EastWest 97
17 **ONE MINUTE MAN**
Missy "Misdemeanor" Elliott *The Gold Mind* 01
18 **BIG PIMPIN'**
Jay-Z f/UGK *Roc-A-Fella/Def Jam* 00
19 **IF YOUR GIRL ONLY KNEW**
Aaliyah *Blackground* 96
20 **UP JUMPS DA BOOGIE**
Magoo & Timbaland *Blackground* 97
21 **HEADSPRUNG**
LL Cool J *Def Jam* 04
22 **I CARE 4 U**
Aaliyah *Blackground* 02
23 **SO ANXIOUS**
Ginuwine *550* 99
24 **ROLL OUT (MY BUSINESS)**
Ludacris *DTP/Def Jam South* 02
25 **MORE THAN A WOMAN**
Aaliyah *Blackground* 02
26 **UGLY**
Bubba Sparxxx *Beat Club* 01
27 **MANEATER**
Nelly Furtado *Mosley* 06
28 **WHAT GOES AROUND...COMES AROUND**
Justin Timberlake *Jive* 07
29 **ARE YOU THAT SOMEBODY?**
Aaliyah *Blackground* 98
30 **PASS THAT DUTCH**
Missy "Misdemeanor" Elliott *The Gold Mind* 03

The Top 10 Songs Produced by DALLAS AUSTIN

GROWING UP in Columbus, Georgia, Dallas Austin dreamed that one day his name would appear on an album, just like the names he was so familiar with, like Jimmy Jam and Terry Lewis and L.A. Reid and Babyface.

Relocating to Atlanta in 1986, Austin amazed his friends by flying off to California to work with artists like Joyce Irby (formerly of Klymaxx) and Troop. His Hot 100 breakthrough came with Motown's Another Bad Creation, which led to producing eight tracks for Boyz II Men's *Cooleyhighharmony*. He had attended high school with Tionne "T-Boz" Watkins and Rozonda "Chilli" Thomas, so when Reid and Babyface asked him to work with TLC, Austin already knew the women. "Before they had a concept of how they would look, I did five songs and I painted a picture of what these girls were all about."

Austin's first label was Rowdy, which started as a "street" division of LaFace before Austin found his most successful artist, Monica. In February 1997, Rowdy's deal with Arista was dissolved, and six months later, Austin started up his new Freeworld label.

01	**THE BOY IS MINE** Brandy & Monica *Atlantic* 98
02	**CREEP** TLC *LaFace* 95
03	**DON'T TAKE IT PERSONAL (JUST ONE OF DEM DAYS)** Monica *Rowdy* 95
04	**UNPRETTY** TLC *LaFace* 99
05	**IT'S SO HARD TO SAY GOODBYE TO YESTERDAY** Boyz II Men *Motown* 91
06	**SECRET** Madonna *Maverick* 94
07	**BEFORE YOU WALK OUT OF MY LIFE / LIKE THIS AND LIKE THAT** Monica *Rowdy* 95
08	**WHAT ABOUT YOUR FRIENDS** TLC *LaFace* 92
09	**AIN'T 2 PROUD 2 BEG** TLC *LaFace* 92
10	**DON'T LET ME GET ME** Pink *Arista* 02

The Top 10 Songs Produced by THOM BELL

THOM BELL teamed up with one of his sister Barbara's schoolmates, Kenny Gamble, to cut a song called "Someday," released on Jerry Ross's Heritage label. Later, with Gamble, he formed the Romeos, a group that became the house band at Cameo-Parkway Records in 1964. Two years later, Bell was the musical director for Chubby Checker's British tour.

After a brief stint with the Philly Groove label, where he produced the Delfonics' song "La La—Means I Love You," Bell worked with Gamble and his partner, Leon Huff. He arranged several Jerry Butler hits for them, and worked on a Dusty Springfield album recorded in Philadelphia. At the same time, Bell teamed up with Linda Creed to write songs.

Hugo Peretti and Luigi Creatore at Avco Records hired Bell to produce the Stylistics, who had immediate success with Bell-Creed songs like "You Are Everything," "Betcha By Golly, Wow," and "You Make Me Feel Brand New." Bell's later projects include the Spinners and Elton John.

01	**THE RUBBERBAND MAN** Spinners *Atlantic* 76
02	**THEN CAME YOU** Dionne Warwick & the Spinners *Atlantic* 74
03	**YOU MAKE ME FEEL BRAND NEW** The Stylistics *Avco* 74
04	**I DON'T HAVE THE HEART** James Ingram *Warner Bros.* 90
05	**BETCHA BY GOLLY, WOW** The Stylistics *Avco* 72
06	**I'LL BE AROUND** Spinners *Atlantic* 72
07	**COULD IT BE I'M FALLING IN LOVE** Spinners *Atlantic* 73
08	**YOU ARE EVERYTHING** The Stylistics *Avco* 72
09	**MAMA CAN'T BUY YOU LOVE** Elton John *MCA* 79
10	**LA LA—MEANS I LOVE YOU** The Delfonics *Philly Groove* 68

The Top 10 Songs Produced by MIKE CHAPMAN

MIKE CHAPMAN was working as a waiter in London in 1970 when he met Nicky Chinn. They decided to write songs together, and in less than a year they had their first top 20 hit in the U.K., "Funny Funny," the initial chart single by Sweet. They continued to turn out hits for the group.

Chapman's first real American triumph came in 1978, when he had two consecutive No. 1 singles. After working with Exile for two years, he and Chinn wrote "Kiss You All Over" for the band. Mike also produced Nick Gilder's "Hot Child In The City" for Chrysalis, then worked with Blondie. Debbie Harry and Chris Stein were initially reluctant to have him produce, but Chapman won them over with a new arrangement for their song "Heart Of Glass."

Chapman's most successful chart song in America is the first single by the Knack. "They approached me to produce them and the first song they played me was 'My Sharona,'" he recalls. "How could I not go into the studio with that song?"

01 **MY SHARONA**
The Knack *Capitol* 79

02 **KISS YOU ALL OVER**
Exile *Warner/Curb* 78

03 **HOT CHILD IN THE CITY**
Nick Gilder *Chrysalis* 78

04 **THE TIDE IS HIGH**
Blondie *Chrysalis* 81

05 **RAPTURE**
Blondie *Chrysalis* 81

06 **HEART OF GLASS**
Blondie *Chrysalis* 79

07 **STUMBLIN' IN**
Suzi Quatro & Chris Norman *RSO* 79

08 **THE WARRIOR**
Scandal f/Patty Smyth *Columbia* 84

09 **LOVE TOUCH**
Rod Stewart *Warner Bros.* 86

10 **CLOSE MY EYES (FOREVER)**
Lita Ford w/Ozzy Osbourne *RCA* 89

The Top 10 Songs Produced by
RODNEY JERKINS

RODNEY JERKINS' two dreams were to win a Grammy and to have his own label by the time he was 21. He made both dreams come true.

It helped that he started young. At 12 he was mixing tracks for his own enjoyment, and at 14, inspired by the "new jack swing" of Teddy Riley, he decided to drive to Riley's studio in Virginia and meet the producer in person. Impressed, Riley spread the word about Jerkins, and at age 15 he was given a production deal at Mercury. The result: Jerkins' first appearance on the Hot 100, as producer of Gina Thompson's "The Things That You Do." While remixing an Aaliyah track, Jerkins was introduced to the artist working in the next studio—Mary J. Blige. The teenager contributed five songs to her 1997 album, *Share My World*. He also worked with Joe, but helming Brandy's *Never Say Never* album gave Jerkins his biggest hit to date, the duet with Monica on "The Boy Is Mine."

In February 1999, Sony signed a worldwide deal with Jerkins for his own imprint, Darkchild Records.

01 **THE BOY IS MINE**
Brandy & Monica *Atlantic* 98

02 **IF YOU HAD MY LOVE**
Jennifer Lopez *Work* 99

03 **ANGEL OF MINE**
Monica *Arista* 99

04 **SAY MY NAME**
Destiny's Child *Columbia* 00

05 **HE WASN'T MAN ENOUGH**
Toni Braxton *LaFace* 00

06 **DAYDREAMIN'**
Tatyana Ali *MJJ* 98

07 **IT'S NOT RIGHT BUT IT'S OKAY**
Whitney Houston *Arista* 99

08 **WHAT ABOUT US?**
Brandy *Atlantic* 02

09 **DON'T WANNA BE A PLAYER**
Joe *Jive* 97

10 **YOU ROCK MY WORLD**
Michael Jackson *Epic* 01

The Top 10 Songs Produced by
DENNIS LAMBERT

ENNIS LAMBERT was not yet 18 when Quincy Jones signed him and songwriting partner Lou Courtney to Mercury as staff producers. Their first two hits for the company were "Do The Freddie" for Freddie & the Dreamers and "I Dig You Baby" for Lorraine Ellison. They also worked with Jerry Lee Lewis before Lambert moved to Los Angeles. There he began an 11-year collaboration with Brian Potter, a British songwriter he had met in the U.K. in 1965. They were courted by Jay Lasker and Steve Barri to join ABC/Dunhill, where they worked with Hamilton, Joe Frank & Reynolds; the Grass Roots; the Four Tops; and Gayle McCormick.

In 1974 Lambert and Potter started their own imprint, Haven, distributed at first by Capitol. For that company, they produced Glen Campbell. When label head Al Coury suggested Campbell record "Rhinestone Cowboy," Lambert already knew the tune from songwriter Larry Weiss' album on the 20th Century label, *Rhinestone Cowboy*.

01 **RHINESTONE COWBOY**
Glen Campbell *Capitol* 75
02 **BABY COME BACK**
Player *RSO* 78
03 **WE BUILT THIS CITY**
Starship *Grunt* 85
04 **SARA**
Starship *Grunt* 85
05 **NIGHTSHIFT**
Commodores *Motown* 85
06 **ROCK AND ROLL HEAVEN**
Righteous Brothers *Haven* 74
07 **AIN'T NO WOMAN
(LIKE THE ONE I'VE GOT)**
Four Tops *Dunhill* 73
08 **PINK CADILLAC**
Natalie Cole *EMI Manhattan* 88
09 **NOBODY'S FOOL**
Kenny Loggins *Columbia* 88
10 **COUNTRY BOY (YOU GOT YOUR
FEET IN L.A.)**
Glen Campbell *Capitol* 76

The Top 10 Songs Produced by
GIORGIO MORODER

IORGIO MORODER grew up in Italy, quitting school at 19 to become a professional musician. In 1972, his song *"Nachts Schient Die Sonne"*—translated into "Son Of My Father"—became a No. 1 hit in the U.K. for Chicory Tip. In America, it was released on Dunhill by Giorgio himself, and charted at No. 46.

After a three-year stay in Berlin, Moroder settled in Munich, where Donna Summer was also living. Summer recorded some early material with Moroder and his lyricist, Pete Bellotte. When they finally had a hit in France, Moroder sent a copy to Neil Bogart in the States and "Love To Love You Baby" introduced Donna in America. Giorgio's innovative use of synthesizers on Summer's "I Feel Love" started a wave of electronic pop hits. Seven of his top 10 chart singles are by Summer.

Giorgio won an Oscar with his first film score, for *Midnight Express*, and another one for composing the title song for *Flashdance*.

01 **FLASHDANCE...WHAT A FEELING**
Irene Cara *Casablanca* 83
02 **CALL ME**
Blondie *Chrysalis* 80
03 **HOT STUFF**
Donna Summer *Casablanca* 79
04 **BAD GIRLS**
Donna Summer *Casablanca* 79
05 **MACARTHUR PARK**
Donna Summer *Casablanca* 78
06 **NO MORE TEARS (ENOUGH IS ENOUGH)**
Barbra Streisand & Donna Summer
Columbia 79
07 **DIM ALL THE LIGHTS**
Donna Summer *Casablanca* 79
08 **TAKE MY BREATH AWAY**
Berlin *Columbia* 86
09 **LAST DANCE**
Donna Summer *Casablanca* 78
10 **THE WANDERER**
Donna Summer *Geffen* 80

The Top 10 Songs Produced by
MICHAEL OMARTIAN

MICHAEL OMARTIAN was encouraged by his parents to take piano lessons at age four and drum lessons at age six. He left Chicago in 1965 to move west and pursue a songwriting career, but found more success as a session keyboard player. He became an arranger before producing his first album, a project for Jay Gruska on ABC/Dunhill.

Omartian achieved success early in his producing career, coming up with "Rock Me Gently," a No. 1 single for Andy Kim in 1974. He worked as a staff producer for ABC, then for Warner Bros. Christopher Cross had submitted a tape to Warner Bros., and asked Omartian to produce his album—mainly, according to Michael, "because I played a lot of keyboards on Steely Dan albums."

Michael's most successful production is "Arthur's Theme (Best That You Can Do)" by Cross (co-written with Peter Allen, Burt Bacharach, and Carole Bayer Sager). He recalls: "There was no demo . . . we went in the studio and it took two days."

01 **ARTHUR'S THEME (BEST THAT YOU CAN DO)**
Christopher Cross *Warner Bros.* 81

02 **RIDE LIKE THE WIND**
Christopher Cross *Warner Bros.* 80

03 **HOW AM I SUPPOSED TO LIVE WITHOUT YOU**
Michael Bolton *Columbia* 90

04 **SAILING**
Christopher Cross *Warner Bros.* 80

05 **UNDERCOVER ANGEL**
Alan O'Day *Pacific* 77

06 **GLORY OF LOVE**
Peter Cetera *Warner Bros.* 86

07 **SHE WORKS HARD FOR THE MONEY**
Donna Summer *Mercury* 83

08 **THEME FROM "S.W.A.T."**
Rhythm Heritage *ABC* 76

09 **THE NEXT TIME I FALL**
Peter Cetera & Amy Grant *Full Moon* 86

10 **INFATUATION**
Rod Stewart *Warner Bros.* 84

The Top 10 Songs Produced by TEDDY RILEY

MARRYING HIP-HOP beats with old-school R&B, Teddy Riley became the father of a whole new musical movement, new jack swing, as exemplified in hits like Keith Sweat's "I Want Her" and Bobby Brown's "My Prerogative." A perfectionist in the studio, the Harlem-born Riley was more interested in producing hits and remaining an anonymous face than being a star in his own right. That explains why he had little interest in being Teddy Riley, artist. Instead, he formed groups like Guy and BLACKstreet. "I feel like the power is in the team more than in one person," he explains. "I'm a little afraid of getting out onstage by myself. I'm the shy one in the group," he said when BLACKstreet went to No. 1 on the Hot 100 with "No Diggity," Riley's most successful chart single.

Riley has also helmed separate hits for siblings Michael and Janet Jackson, as well as Wreck-N-Effect, a rap trio that included his brother, Markell Riley.

01 **NO DIGGITY**
BLACKstreet f/Dr. Dre *Interscope* 96

02 **STUTTER**
Joe f/Mystikal *Jive* 01

03 **RUMP SHAKER**
Wreckx-N-Effect *MCA* 92

04 **REMEMBER THE TIME**
Michael Jackson *Epic* 92

05 **I LIKE THE WAY (THE KISSING GAME)**
Hi-Five *Jive* 91

06 **BEFORE I LET YOU GO**
BLACKstreet *Interscope* 95

07 **I GET LONELY**
Janet Jackson f/BLACKstreet *Virgin* 98

08 **NOW THAT WE FOUND LOVE**
Heavy D. & the Boyz *Uptown* 91

09 **IN THE CLOSET**
Michael Jackson *Epic* 92

10 **TAKE ME THERE**
BLACKstreet & Mya f/Mase & Blinky Blink *Interscope* 99

The Top 10 Songs Produced by JIM STEINMAN

JIM STEINMAN was a college student when he wrote and starred in a play, *The Dream Engine.* Joseph Papp bought the rights, but New York City officials said it was too sexually explicit and violent to stage in Central Park. Papp commissioned Steinman to write a musical, and it was at the auditions for *More Than You Deserve* that the playwright met a hopeful actor named Meat Loaf.

That meeting led to the 1977 album *Bat Out of Hell,* which has sold over 25 million copies worldwide. Todd Rundgren produced, but the Phil-Spector-meets-Richard-Wagner-at-a-heavy-metal-concert songs were written and arranged by Steinman. He moved into the producer's chair to work with Bonnie Tyler, Air Supply, Barry Manilow, and even Barbra Streisand in 1983–84.

They hadn't seen each other in eight years when Meat Loaf paid a visit to Steinman at his home in 1989. That reconciliation led to *Bat Out Of Hell II.* The lead single, "I'd Do Anything For Love (But I Won't Do That)," spent five weeks at No. 1 in America and was the best-selling single of 1993 in the U.K.

01 **I'D DO ANYTHING FOR LOVE (BUT I WON'T DO THAT)**
Meat Loaf *MCA* 93

02 **TOTAL ECLIPSE OF THE HEART**
Bonnie Tyler *Columbia* 83

03 **MAKING LOVE OUT OF NOTHING AT ALL**
Air Supply *Arista* 83

04 **ROCK AND ROLL DREAMS COME THROUGH**
Meat Loaf *MCA* 94

05 **READ 'EM AND WEEP**
Barry Manilow *Arista* 84

06 **ROCK ME TONITE**
Billy Squier *Capitol* 84

07 **ROCK AND ROLL DREAMS COME THROUGH**
Jim Steinman *Epic* 81

08 **HOLDING OUT FOR A HERO**
Bonnie Tyler *Columbia* 84

09 **OBJECTS IN THE REAR VIEW MIRROR MAY APPEAR CLOSER THAN THEY ARE**
Meat Loaf *MCA* 94

10 **LEFT IN THE DARK**
Barbra Streisand *Columbia* 84

The Top 10 Songs Produced by
STOCK-AITKEN-WATERMAN

MIKE STOCK, Matt Aitken, and Pete Waterman have registered a few hits in America, but in their native Britain they have sold more than 10 million singles since 1984. By 1990, they had collected their 100th chart entry, "Use It Up And Wear It Out" by Pat & Mick.

The trio's first collaboration was "The Upstroke," which Stock and Aitken recorded under the name Agents Aren't Aeroplanes. Their subsequent work with Hazell Dean impressed Pete Burns from Dead or Alive. Stock, Aitken, and Waterman produced the group's "You Spin Me Round (Like A Record)," the first U.K. No. 1 and the first U.S. chart hit for the producers. The trio's biggest U.S. successes include Rick Astley, Nicki French, Bananarama, and Donna Summer. Their most consistent artists in the U.K. were Kylie Minogue and Jason Donovan.

In 1991, Aitken split from the trio. Three years later, Stock left Waterman's PWL company and opened his own studio in South London, resuming his working relationship with Aitken.

01 **NEVER GONNA GIVE YOU UP**
Rick Astley *RCA* 88

02 **TOTAL ECLIPSE OF THE HEART**
Nicki French *Critique* 95

03 **VENUS**
Bananarama *London* 86

04 **TOGETHER FOREVER**
Rick Astley *RCA* 88

05 **THE LOCO-MOTION**
Kylie Minogue *Geffen* 88

06 **I HEARD A RUMOUR**
Bananarama *London* 87

07 **THAT'S WHAT LOVE CAN DO**
Boy Krazy *Next Plateau* 93

08 **THIS TIME I KNOW IT'S FOR REAL**
Donna Summer *Atlantic* 89

09 **IT WOULD TAKE A STRONG STRONG MAN**
Rick Astley *RCA* 88

10 **YOU SPIN ME ROUND (LIKE A RECORD)**
Dead or Alive *Epic* 85

The Top 10 Songs Produced by SCOTT STORCH

BORN IN HALIFAX, Nova Scotia, Canada, Scott Storch grew up in Cherry Hill, New Jersey, and later lived in Ft. Lauderdale and Philadelphia. He dropped out of school in the ninth grade to follow his dream of working as a musician and got his first break playing piano on sessions for Ruffhouse Records. Storch credits label founders Joe Nicolo and Chris Schwartz for giving him his earliest opportunities.

Storch played keyboards for the Philly-based hip-hop outfit the Roots but left the group to find work as a producer. The group continued to become more popular and Storch produced tracks for their 1999 release *Things Fall Apart*. He also worked with rappers Noreaga and Busta Rhymes. Another rapper, Eve, introduced Storch to Dr. Dre, who employed Storch as keyboardist on his comeback single "Still D.R.E." Through Dre, the up-and-coming producer was given the job of producing tracks for rappers Xzibit and Snoop Dogg.

Now based in Miami, Storch has become a prolific hit-maker, producing No. 1 songs for Mario, Beyoncé, 50 Cent, and Terror Squad. He has also helmed tracks for Christina Aguilera, Pink, and Fat Joe.

1 **LET ME LOVE YOU**
   Mario *3rd Street/J* 05
2 **BABY BOY**
   Beyoncé f/Sean Paul *Columbia* 03
3 **RUN IT!**
   Chris Brown *Jive* 05
4 **CANDY SHOP**
   50 Cent f/Olivia *Shady/Aftermath* 05
5 **LEAN BACK**
   Terror Squad *SRC/Universal* 04
6 **LET ME BLOW YA MIND**
   Eve f/Gwen Stefani *Ruff Ryders* 01
7 **NAUGHTY GIRL**
   Beyoncé *Columbia* 04
8 **JUST A LIL BIT**
   50 Cent *Shady/Aftermath* 05
9 **ME, MYSELF AND I**
   Beyoncé *Columbia* 04
10 **GET IT POPPIN'**
   Fat Joe f/Nelly *Terror Squad* 05

The Top 10 Songs Produced by
NARADA MICHAEL WALDEN

MICHAEL WALDEN was 19 when he joined Deacon Williams and the Soul Revival Troupe. After hearing John McLaughlin's Mahavishnu Orchestra, he became interested in jazz fusion, and at 21, he replaced drummer Billy Cobham in that outfit. Walden also became interested in the teachings of McLaughlin's guru, Sri Chinmoy, who gave him the new first name of Narada ("supreme musician").

Walden worked with Jeff Beck and Weather Report, then recorded solo albums. His first experience as a producer was with jazz trumpeter Don Cherry; next he worked with pop artist Stacy Lattisaw. For Arista, he produced albums for Angela Bofill and Phyllis Hyman before taking on Aretha Franklin's *Who's Zoomin' Who?* He was planning to record "Freeway Of Love" for himself, but gave it to Aretha instead.

After working with Whitney Houston, Narada was called in by Tommy Mottola of Columbia Records to produce Mariah Carey. "Vision Of Love" started her career with a No. 1 hit.

01 **VISION OF LOVE**
   Mariah Carey *Columbia* 90
02 **I LOVE YOUR SMILE**
   Shanice *Motown* 92
03 **I WANNA DANCE WITH SOMEBODY (WHO LOVES ME)**
   Whitney Houston *Arista* 87
04 **NOTHING'S GONNA STOP US NOW**
   Starship *Grunt* 87
05 **SO EMOTIONAL**
   Whitney Houston *Arista* 88
06 **ALL THE MAN THAT I NEED**
   Whitney Houston *Arista* 91
07 **HOW WILL I KNOW**
   Whitney Houston *Arista* 86
08 **WHERE DO BROKEN HEARTS GO**
   Whitney Houston *Arista* 88
09 **I DON'T WANNA CRY**
   Mariah Carey *Columbia* 91
10 **I KNEW YOU WERE WAITING (FOR ME)**
   Aretha Franklin & George Michael *Arista* 87

The Top 10 Songs Produced by DON WAS

"EVERYTHING YOU need to know is in *Pet Sounds*," producer Don Was said in a special *Billboard* tribute section dedicated to the producer. "When I get stumped, I'll play a Brian Wilson record and I'll find the way out of a problem I might have."

The Beach Boys were just one influence on the Detroit-raised musician born Donald Fagenson. With fellow musician David Weiss, he used a two-track recorder to produce songs born out of frustration at their inability to pick up girls while cruising the Motor City's Woodward Avenue. They both adopted the last name "Was" and became the creative core of Was (Not Was), a funk ensemble whose first album became more successful in the U.K. than at home. That led to production work with British acts like Brother Beyond and Helen Terry. After "Spy In The House Of Love" was a U.S. top 20 hit for Was (Not Was) in 1988, Don Was produced hits for American acts like the B-52's and Bonnie Raitt. The success of the latter's *Nick Of Time* album elevated his status to superstar level.

01 LOVE SHACK
The B-52's *Reprise* 89
02 PINCH ME
Barenaked Ladies *Reprise* 00
03 SOMETHING TO TALK ABOUT
Bonnie Raitt *Capitol* 91
04 WALK THE DINOSAUR
Was (Not Was) *Chrysalis* 89
05 LOST IN YOU
Garth Brooks as Chris Gaines *Capitol* 99
06 LOVE SNEAKIN' UP ON YOU
Bonnie Raitt *Capitol* 94
07 I CAN'T MAKE YOU LOVE ME
Bonnie Raitt *Capitol* 92
08 GOOD STUFF
The B-52's *Reprise* 92
09 THE REAL LOVE
Bob Seger & the Silver Bullet Band *Capitol* 91
10 CANDY
Iggy Pop w/Kate Pierson *Virgin* 91

The Top 10 Songs Produced by FRANK WILSON

WHEN DIANA ROSS left the Supremes for a solo career, the man entrusted to produce the reformatted trio with Jean Terrell taking over lead vocal duties was Houston-born, Baton Rouge–raised Frank Wilson. He had amassed plenty of credits at Motown, working with Brenda Holloway, the Miracles, and Marvin Gaye. He had also helmed two Diana Ross & the Supremes hits, "Love Child" and "I'm Livin' In Shame," as part of "the Clan."

"The pressure was making sure that what the Supremes represented was not diminished," says Wilson. Impressed with the work of New York songwriter Vince DiMirco, Wilson collaborated with him on a song fashioned for Terrell's voice, "Up The Ladder To The Roof." It was a top 10 hit, as was the synth-laden masterpiece "Stoned Love," which peaked at No. 7.

After three albums with the Supremes, Wilson turned his attention to Eddie Kendricks following his departure from the Temptations. Wilson brought Kendricks a scratchy seven-minute demo of "Keep On Truckin," and the singer knew immediately it would be a hit. In November 1973 the song became Kendricks' one and only solo No. 1 single

01 LOVE CHILD
Diana Ross & the Supremes *Motown* 68
02 KEEP ON TRUCKIN' (PART 1)
Eddie Kendricks *Tamla* 73
03 I'M GONNA MAKE YOU LOVE ME
Diana Ross & the Supremes and the Temptations *Motown* 69
04 BOOGIE DOWN
Eddie Kendricks *Tamla* 74
05 STONED LOVE
The Supremes *Motown* 70
06 UP THE LADDER TO THE ROOF
The Supremes *Motown* 70
07 STILL WATER (LOVE)
Four Tops *Motown* 70
08 ALL I NEED
The Temptations *Gordy* 67
09 I'M LIVIN' IN SHAME
Diana Ross & the Supremes *Motown* 69
10 NATHAN JONES
The Supremes *Motown* 71

The LABELS

RECORD LABELS have their own distinct identities. Imagine "Baby Love" by the Supremes on Chrysalis or "That's Life" by Frank Sinatra on Island—they just wouldn't be the same.

Even though the concept of bonding a colorfully designed piece of paper to the center portion of a disc died when vinyl records passed away, record companies will still be referred to as "labels" well into the future. But one should feel sorry for today's 21st-century teens, who will never know the joy of searching the singles wall at their local record store for the latest release featuring Motown's map of Detroit, Apple Records' green Granny Smith, or the Elektra caterpillar that transformed into a butterfly on album labels. Part of the fun of collecting 45s was enjoying the graphic designs of the artists employed by the various labels, noticing when colors were altered or whole new logos were introduced. The plastic-coated aluminum surface of a CD allows artists to use their imaginations to some extent, but the design options are limited. And paid digital downloads? Well, they've made those artistic visions totally irrelevant.

This section lists the most successful chart singles of 46 different labels. These companies vary in age, size, and style. Columbia Records can trace its origins back to 1881; the company was pressing discs as early as 1901. Elektra Records marked its 40th anniversary in 1990 with the *Rubaiyat* collection of artists performing songs by former label artists. Arista celebrated its 15th birthday in 1990 with a concert to benefit the Gay Men's Health Crisis and its 25th anniversary in 2000 with an NBC-TV special. Labels that are even younger are included, like the American arm of Virgin, established in 1987, and Clive Davis' J Records, doing business since 2000. Labels that were owned or distributed by the same parent company are grouped together. Liberty—which bought Imperial, merged with United Artists, then was swallowed up by EMI—appears with all these labels in the same section as Capitol, the American label owned by Thorn-EMI of Great Britain. Decca and Uni were consolidated into MCA, so those three labels are grouped together.

Columbia and Epic, both owned by Sony, each have their own top 100 lists, as do most labels regardless of their affiliations. Exceptions were made for Motown, Stax, and EMI. All Motown labels were included in that company's top 100. Similarly, Stax, Volt, Enterprise, and KoKo singles are all included in the Stax list and EMI, EMI America, EMI Manhattan, and Manhattan singles are grouped together under EMI.

Sadly, many of the label names featured in this section have gone to that great cut-out bin in the sky. The MGM logo was retired when it was brought into the PolyGram corporate structure. ABC and Dot were purchased by MCA and laid to rest; Cameo-Parkway is dormant under the ownership of Allen Klein and his ABCKO Industries.

Of course, it's hard to keep a good label down. Warner Bros. reactivated its Reprise label in 1987, Atlantic once gave new priority to Atco before putting it to rest again and then revived the logo in 2007 for an Art Garfunkel album, and EMI brought back Liberty twice.

The Top 100 Songs on A&M

Styx

T HE A&M RECORD LABEL can trace its origin to an obscure single called "Hooray For The Big Slow Train" by the Diddley Oohs. The "group" was made up of Herb Alpert and Jerry Moss, and while their ode to the Seattle World's Fair of 1962 might have been a bomb, their partnership would create one of the most successful independent labels of the rock era.

Louis and Tillie Alpert came home from a weekend trip and found their eight-year-old son Herb with a rented trumpet from school. Louis played the mandolin and Tillie had studied the violin, so they happily encouraged their boy to practice. By the time he was 15, Herb was playing local dates as part of the Colonial Trio. At about the same age, he heard Ray Anthony's "Young Man With A Horn" on the radio, and became an avid record buyer.

Discharged from the army in 1956, Alpert met an insurance agent who wanted to be a lyricist. Herb agreed to collaborate with Lou Adler; their first sale was "Circle Rock," recorded by the Salmas Brothers on Keen. They were hired as staff writers for the label, where they worked with Sam Cooke and wrote "Wonderful World" with him. After Cooke signed with RCA, Alpert and Adler produced singles for Jan and Dean.

Jerry Moss grew up in the West Bronx, one of 11 children of Irving and Rose Moss. He worked as a page for ABC Television on the weekends while studying English at Brooklyn College. At a friend's wedding reception, a man named Marvin Cane suggested he would make a great promotion man, and in August 1958 Moss went to work for Cane promoting "Sixteen

Candles" by the Crests. Early in 1960, he headed for Los Angeles.

Alpert and Moss kept crossing paths in Los Angeles music circles. One day they agreed to form a partnership, and they both put up $100 to form Carnival Records. Their first release was Herb's vocal rendition of his song "Tell It To The Birds," released under the name Dore Alpert. Herb wanted to record an instrumental called "Twinkle Star," and a visit to a bullfight in Tijuana inspired him to add a mariachi beat and the sound of cheering spectators. Retitled "The Lonely Bull," the single was readied for release on Carnival, but someone else laid claim to the label name and the company had to be rechristened. The simplest thing to do was take their initials, A&M. Jerry decided the solo recording should be released under the name "The Tijuana Brass featuring Herb Alpert."

A&M moved offices from Herb's garage to the Sunset Strip. The Tijuana Brass recorded more albums, and promo man Gil Friesen joined the label. He suggested that Alpert create a real Tijuana Brass to play live dates: The TJB'S popularity soared, and the band had five albums in the top 20 of Billboard's album chart, including *Whipped Cream And Other Delights.*

The label also achieved early hits by the We Five ("You Were On My Mind"), Chris Montez, the Sandpipers, and Sergio Mendes and Brasil '66. With a need for more office space, A&M moved to the former Charlie Chaplin movie studio at the corner of LaBrea and Sunset on November 6, 1966.

"At that moment," Moss told Timothy White, "I think our image was a sort of semi-hip, jazz, Latin-sounding label using MOR stations to sell albums. At Monterey Pop in '67, the so-called underground emerged, and as successful as Herb was at that time, this new force was looked on as a different kind of medium. The movement was definitely toward rock 'n' roll."

Moss was depressed that A&M didn't have any artists at the Monterey Pop Festival. Shortly after, he traveled to England and signed Procol Harum and the Move for America. He made an agreement with Chris Blackwell of Island Records to license Jimmy Cliff, Cat Stevens, Spooky Tooth, Fairport Convention, and Free for the U.S. Other British deals brought the Strawbs and Humble Pie to the label. American artists were added to the roster, including Phil Ochs, Lee Michaels, and the Flying Burrito Brothers. When the Woodstock Music and Arts Festival took place in 1969, A&M had an artist on the bill: Joe Cocker.

As the new decade began, A&M was at the top of the Hot 100 with a brother-sister duo, the Carpenters. To many people, they were just another middle-of-the-road group. "The idea of a girl drummer who sang was shrugged off as too peculiar," Alpert told White, "but I heard something in Karen and Richard's music, a seductive delicacy. To go from early critical dismissal to selling 75 million records and holding an enormously loyal following was a very profound experience."

A&M fared well on the Hot 100 during the first half of the '70s with Billy Preston, the British duo Stealers Wheel (which included Gerry Rafferty), as well as Cat Stevens and Lee Michaels. In mid-decade, the label had its biggest hit to date with the Captain & Tennille's cover of Nell Sedaka's "Love Will Keep Us Together."

Humble Pie member Peter Frampton ventured out on his own as a solo artist and did well with his fourth LP, *Frampton*, in 1975. "After his 1975 album, we wanted Peter to do a live record," Moss said, "because his performances on the road in 1974–75 were so electric, and we weren't selling as many records as we thought we should be from the studio work. I asked him for a concert record, and later, at Electric Lady Studios in New York, heard the tapes. I thought it was fantastic." "Show Me The Way," released previously as a studio cut, became a hit when a live version was released from *Frampton Comes Alive.*

A&M closed the '70s with hits from Styx, Rita Coolidge (who had been on Joe Cocker's Mad Dogs And Englishmen tour), Chuck Mangione, and Supertramp. Alpert returned to the top of the Hot 100 with an instrumental, "Rise." "I know disco's not the rage anymore," Alpert said in *Rolling Stone* at the time, "but I also know that lots of people still dance. I wanted to plug into that—not to make another routine disco record, but to take some of those elements and come up with something I'd have fun playing."

A&M had more success in the '80s with British artists like Joe Jackson, the Human League, and Simple Minds. Moss had returned to London in 1977, and met with Miles Copeland of the International Records Syndicate. "Miles had a group he was out to prove had something special," Moss said to White. "Derek Green, our managing director at A&M in England, obliged by signing them. I remember hearing the Police for the first time over the speakers in a New York club and I was gone—it totally nailed me. The record was called 'Roxanne.'"

The ultimate success story for A&M in the last half of the '80s was Janet Jackson, signed to the company when she was just 16. Her first two albums, *Janet Jackson* and *Dream Street*, contained some juvenile pop songs, but *Control*, produced by Jimmy Jam and Terry Lewis, was her commercial breakthrough. *Rhythm Nation 1814* was another multi-platinum success for Janet, who has 12 singles on A&M's top 100. At the end of her A&M contract, Janet signed with Virgin, but the label still had a mega-star in Canadian artist Bryan Adams, who has six titles on the A&M top 100 and three in the top 10, including "Please Forgive Me" and "(Everything I Do) I Do It For You."

In 2000, Alpert and Moss settled a lawsuit against PolyGram, which purchased A&M in 1990. The suit claimed that the consolidation of Universal and PolyGram's music interests violated a provision of the A&M purchase agreement. A&M was brought into the Interscope music group and Ron Fair was named president of the label.

Under his direction, A&M prospered, with most of the label's 21st century chart action generated by the Black Eyed Peas and its lone female member, Fergie, as well as the Pussycat Dolls.

The Top 100 Songs on ARISTA

Carrie Underwood

WHEN ALAN Hirschfield, president of Columbia Pictures, wanted to strengthen the company's Bell Records subsidiary, he approached Clive Davis about heading up the label and offered him 20 percent of Bell's stock.

Davis, a lawyer educated at Harvard, had joined Columbia Records in 1960 as an attorney. Five years later, label president Goddard Lieberson asked the 33-year-old Davis to take the new position of administrative vice president. A year later, Clive was upped to vice president and general manager; in 1967, he was named president of Columbia Records. That was the year that the Monterey Pop Festival was taking place in California, and Davis thought it would be fun to go and mingle with people like Lou Adler, entertainment attorney Abe Somer, the Byrds, and Simon and Garfunkel. Davis didn't expect to find any new talent there, but he saw Janis Joplin perform with Big Brother & the Holding Company and signed her away from the small Mainstream label.

Davis helped usher Columbia into the rock and roll era, signing Blood, Sweat and Tears; Santana; Chicago; Laura Nyro; Boz Scaggs; Johnny Winter; and Loggins & Messina. When A&R executive John Hammond brought him Bruce Springsteen, Clive signed him, too.

In 1973, Davis was suddenly dismissed from the company, accused of misusing his expense account. He was indicted in 1975 on six counts of tax evasion in connection with those expenses, and then in May 1976, five of those counts were dismissed.

From mid-1973 to the spring of 1974, Davis took time out to write an autobiography, *Clive: Inside The Music Business*. He declined offers to work for Chris Blackwell of Island Records and Robert Stigwood, then accepted the Columbia Pictures offer in 1974.

Taking over Bell Records, Clive pared down the artist roster and concentrated on three acts: Barry Manilow, Melissa Manchester, and the Bay City Rollers. Manilow had been signed to Bell by the company's former head, Larry Uttal.

In his book *Sweet Life,* Manilow said that Uttal's departure made him nervous about his future at the company, especially when Clive started dropping artists. "He would have gladly dropped me too, because he didn't like my first album. But two things stopped him: I was in the middle of making my second album and had already spent money on it; and everyone in the company believed in me."

Clive made a point to see Barry perform at a concert in Central Park and went backstage to meet him. He reassured Manilow that he was a part of the Bell family. Later, when Clive heard Barry's proposed second album, he told him he still needed some hit songs for it. He telephoned to suggest a song written by Scott English and Richard Kerr called "Brandy."

"It was a strange phone call and I didn't know exactly how to respond because I was supposed to be the songwriter," Manilow wrote. "Yet here was the president of my record company, whose support I needed, saying I should sing another songwriter's song."

To keep Clive as an ally, Manilow and producer Ron Dante agreed to record the song. They copied the tempo of the version recorded by English. When Davis showed up at the recording session, he hated the result. So Barry slowed it down, and Clive loved the song as a ballad. With a title change so as not to confuse the song with the Looking Glass tune "Brandy (You're A Fine Girl)," "Mandy" was released and went to No. 1. It was the last chart-topper to be issued on Bell. Davis changed the name of the label to Arista, after the honor society he belonged to when he attended public school in Manhattan.

In its first two years of operation, Arista also had hits from the other artists Davis had retained from the Bell roster: Melissa Manchester ("Midnight Blue") and the Bay City Rollers ("Saturday Night"). Davis expanded the label's horizons, with modern artists like Patti Smith, Lou Reed, and Graham Parker; R&B singers like Ray Parker, Jr.; and British groups like the Kinks and the Alan Parsons Project.

In 1979, Clive signed Dionne Warwick after her long dry spell on Warner Bros. "I was flattered and touched that Dionne would sign with Arista for no guarantee beyond production costs, on the condition that I be involved," Davis said in *Rolling Stone.* Clive and Dionne debated who should produce her Arista debut, then Clive arranged for her to meet with Manilow. "Barry talked solidly for two hours," Warwick recalled to Stephen Holden in *Rolling Stone.* "He said, 'Honey, I've got to do this; nobody else can do it.' And at the end, I was totally convinced that this guy could do anything he wanted to."

The initial single—written by Will Jennings and "Mandy" co-writer Richard Kerr—was "I'll Never Love This Way Again," Dionne's first solo top 10 single in almost a decade. "I can see now that while I was at Warners everything was wrong but me. Now, once again, everything is being done absolutely for *me.* There's no overshadowing, I'm sitting on top of everything, which is the way it should be," Warwick told Holden.

The same year Dionne had her first success with Arista, Hirschfield was fired from his post as CEO of Columbia Pictures. The studio's board of directors decided to sell Arista. "[Hirschfield] believed in me and really was the main reason why Columbia Pictures financed the beginning of Arista," Davis said in Ted Fox's *In the Groove.* "I did feel a certain sense of alienation from the board of Columbia Pictures, and I motivated . . . the sale. . . . I came up with a purchaser of the stock of Arista, and recommended very highly to the board of Columbia Pictures that we both sell our interest in Arista to Bertelsmann [the German owners of Ariola Records]."

Arista moved into the '80s with a string of top 10 singles from the Australian duo Air Supply. Aretha Franklin signed with the label after a long run on Atlantic. And in 1983, Davis signed the artist who would assure the label of chart prominence through the rest of the decade and beyond. Her name was Whitney Houston.

Clive first saw her at the New York supper club Sweetwaters at the invitation of Gerry Griffith, then director of R&B music in Arista's A&R department. "From the moment he went down to Sweetwaters and heard her, he was relentless," Whitney's lawyer Paul Marshall said in Fredric Dannen's *Hit Men.* But there was competition for Whitney. CBS had expressed some interest, and Bruce Lundvall at Elektra wanted her. "Interestingly, [Clive] did not make the high bid," Marshall revealed. "Elektra kept upping their offer. And I finally recommended that she sign with Clive for less money." Whitney did sign with Arista, but included a key-man clause, stipulating that if Clive ever left the label, she would be free of her contract.

While that seemed unlikely, given the success rate at Arista, rumors started to float in November 1999 that the label's corporate owner, BMG, wanted a succession plan worked out, and that L.A. Reid, co-founder with Babyface of the LaFace imprint, would step into the presidency of the label when Davis' contract ended in June 2000. The industry rallied for Davis, who had just revived Santana's career with a multi-platinum album. But come June 2000, Davis did step down and was succeeded by Reid. BMG Entertainment President/CEO Strauss Zelnick left soon after. Davis formed a new label, J, financed by BMG, and scored immediate success with Alicia Keys, O-Town, and Luther Vandross. Despite her key-man clause, Houston re-signed with Arista, as did Carlos Santana, while Davis took acts like Next and Deborah Cox to his new imprint.

Ruben Studdard

A FTER LEADING Arista Records for 25 years, reports surfaced in *Billboard* in late 1999 that president Clive Davis was being forced out over his resistance to name a successor. BMG Entertainment CEO Strauss Zelnick claimed it was his responsibility to do "what's right for the company." The music industry rallied behind Davis, but BMG forces remained adamant. Davis said the company was treating him with "gross disrespect." One of Arista's most successful artists, Barry Manilow, said, "The blatant attempt to remove Clive from his position at Arista Records is offensive and alarming."

BMG named L.A. Reid as Davis' successor on May 2, 2000, and by the fall BMG had announced a new joint-venture label with Davis, named after his middle initial. J Records boasted a roster that included Monica, Luther Vandross, a newcomer named Alicia Keys, and O-Town from the TV series *Making The Band.*

Just two months after the first announcement of the formation of J Records, BMG asked for Zelnick's resignation. Davis turned J into a new crown jewel, just as he had done with Arista. In November 2002, BMG bought the half of J it didn't already own and named Davis as chairman of the RCA Music Group, which included the RCA and J labels. Under Davis' leadership, both logos thrived, with no small thanks to the *American Idol* franchise, which yielded No. 1 singles for RCA acts Kelly Clarkson and Clay Aiken, J artists Ruben Studdard and Fantasia, and Arista signings Carrie Underwood and Taylor Hicks.

In February 2004, Davis was promoted again, to chairman and CEO of BMG North America, placing him in charge of all BMG-owned labels: RCA, J, Arista, and Jive. The J label continued to prosper, earning its most successful single on the Hot 100 at the beginning of 2005 when Mario held down the No. 1 position for nine weeks with "Let Me Love You."

The Top 30 Songs on BELL

The Partridge Family

L ARRY UTTAL worked in his family's retail business. When the business was sold, he bought into a music publishing firm. After that, he worked for small record companies, like Madison. Then he received a call from Al Massler, a record-pressing-plant owner who had started his own record labels — Amy, Mala, and Bell. Massler wanted Uttal to head up the labels. Uttal acquired half-ownership of the company and spent a lot of time in southern cities looking for material. One of the people he met down South was Chips Moman, who produced "Angel Of The Morning" by Merrilee Rush & the Turnabouts.

In 1969, Uttal sold the record company to Columbia Pictures. In 1970, producer Hank Medress brought Uttal a demo he had produced on a song called "Candida." Uttal recalled, "We both agreed the record was pretty bad." They decided to hold onto the track and find another artist to sing lead vocals. Two months later, Medress played a new version for Uttal but wouldn't tell him who was singing. At Uttal's insistence, Medress revealed that the singer was Tony Orlando. He was running CBS' April-Blackwood Music and didn't want to lose his job. "We had a hit record and nobody knew who the voice was," said Uttal. The billing continued to be "Dawn" through Bell's most successful chart single, "Tie A Yellow Ribbon Round The Ole Oak Tree."

By 1974, Uttal had signed Barry Manilow and Melissa Manchester to the label, and had released some early singles from a group that had signed to Bell in the U.K., the Bay City Rollers. Those three artists were the ones Clive Davis decided to concentrate on when he was named the new head of Bell. Most other artists were dropped, and Davis changed the name of the label to Arista. Uttal departed to create his own company, Private Stock.

The Top 100 Songs on ATLANTIC

Foreigner

AHMET AND Nesuhi Ertegun's father, Munir, was named Turkey's ambassador to the United States in 1934. Ahmet, just 10 years old, had become fascinated with jazz music while his father was in his previous post as Ambassador to Britain. In Washington, Ahmet was befriended by Cleo Payne, a janitor at the Turkish embassy, who introduced the youngster to American R&B music. At 14, he accompanied the head of the Turkish air force on a trip to New York and managed to slip away long enough to visit nightclubs in Harlem.

When their father died in 1944, Ahmet and Nesuhi elected to stay in America while their mother and sister returned home to Turkey. With a $10,000 investment from his dentist, Dr. Vahdi Sabit, Ahmet partnered with Herb Abramson of National Records to start a new record company. When they launched their new venture in October 1947, they called it Atlantic Records.

The label concentrated on jazz at first. In 1949, the first national hit on Atlantic was an R&B song, "Drinking Wine, Spo-Dee-O-Dee, Drinking Wine" by Stick McGhee. Atlantic expanded its R&B base by signing artists like Ruth Brown, Joe Turner, and the Clovers. In 1952, Ahmet and Herb paid the Swingtime label $2,000 for Ray Charles, and a year later, Ahmet signed Clyde McPhatter, who became lead singer for the Drifters before recording on his own.

Abramson was drafted in 1953. His place at Atlantic was filled by Jerry Wexler, a former *Billboard* reporter who was working for a music publisher when the label called. With chief engineer Tom Dowd promoted to producer, Ertegun and Wexler turned out R&B hits like "Shake, Rattle And Roll" for Joe Turner and "Tweedlee Dee" for LaVern Baker, but many of their songs were covered by white artists who outsold the originals.

When Abramson returned to the company in 1955, Wexler was an integral part of Atlantic and wasn't willing to give up his desk next to Ertegun. Abramson was given his own company to run, a subsidiary called Atco.

Nesuhi officially joined the company in 1956 to supervise jazz recordings, and produced artists like John Coltrane, Ornette Coleman, Charles Mingus, Eddie Harris, and the Modern Jazz Quartet.

In 1959, Atlantic and Atco were experiencing new heights of success, thanks mostly to Ray Charles and Bobby Darin. Then Charles left for ABC-Paramount, and later, Darin was wooed away by Capitol.

Atlantic survived. Jerry Leiber and Mike Stoller had joined the company as staff producers in 1956. After a series of hits with the Coasters on Atco, Leiber and Stoller turned their attention to the Drifters. They put strings on a song called "There Goes My Baby"; Wexler hated it, but the record went to No. 2. Just over a year later, the Drifters gave Atlantic a No. 1 single with "Save The Last Dance For Me."

Atlantic prospered with a number of R&B artists like Wilson Pickett and Solomon Burke, and benefited from its association with Stax Records in Memphis. In November 1966, Wexler persuaded Ertegun to sign a woman who had been recording on Columbia for six years with little success. Wexler, Dowd, and Arif Mardin brought Aretha Franklin to Rick Hall's Fame studios in Muscle Shoals, Alabama, for her first Atlantic session.

She recorded "I Never Loved A Man (The Way I Love You)" and it was a triumph. But when she tried to record a second track, "Do Right Woman—Do Right Man," it didn't work. An argument between Aretha's husband Ted White and Hall ensued, and Aretha left town without completing anything but the first song. Wexler brought some of the Muscle Shoals musicians to New York and finished the session. Aretha's second single, "Respect," brought her to the top of The Billboard Hot 100 in June 1967.

In October of that year, Atlantic was sold to Warner Bros.–Seven Arts for $17.5 million. Wexler said it was half the amount the company was worth. When Ertegun tried to buy Atlantic back a year later for $40 million, he was turned down. But after another year, Ertegun forced a renegotiation by threatening a mass exit of Atlantic's top executives. He still wasn't thrilled with Elliot Hyman, head of Warner Bros.-Seven Arts, but then the company was sold to Kinney National Services, chaired by Steve Ross. "The only reason I'm here," Ertegun told Dorothy Wade and Justine Picardie in *Music Man,* "is because of Steve Ross, because I would have been long gone with the previous group. But Steve Ross has lived up to everything he ever said, and has given me total autonomy."

The company that had built its reputation with R&B artists built a pop base in the '60s. Buffalo Springfield was signed to Atco, and out of that group came Stephen Stills and Neil Young, who joined with David Crosby of the Byrds and Graham Nash of the Hollies to form Crosby, Stills, Nash and Young. At a party held in Wilson Pickett's honor in England, Ahmet first met Eric Clapton. Soon after, Clapton joined forces with Ginger Baker and Jack Bruce to form Cream; the trio was signed to Atco. Atlantic also had the British group, Yes, and in 1968 Wexler took Dusty Springfield's suggestion and signed Led Zeppelin.

The label had a diverse artist roster in the '70s. When the Spinners left Motown, they were courted by Stax and Avco, but Aretha Franklin suggested they sign with Atlantic. Similarly, Atlantic jazz maestro Les McCann was so touched by seeing Roberta Flack perform at a benefit, that he called Ertegun and staff producer Joel Dorn to arrange an audition for the high school teacher. She arrived with 600 songs under her arm, played 42 of them in three hours, and was awarded a contract. By the end of the '70s, Atlantic's hottest group was Chic. Their third chart single, "Le Freak," became Atlantic's most successful to that time.

After long negotiations with the Rolling Stones, Ertegun brought them to Atlantic on their own custom label, Rolling Stones Records. A deal with Stig Anderson's Polar Music of Sweden brought Abba to Atlantic for North America. The Anglo-American group, Foreigner, joined the company, as did pop diva Bette Midler.

In 1973, Atlantic president Jerry Greenberg closed the deal that brought Genesis to the label. With so many important British acts on the roster, Greenberg made several trips each year to the U.K. to look for new talent. "Genesis was the most intellectual band of its time and their songs weren't just rhymes or moon and June," Ertegun said in *Music Man*. After Peter Gabriel left the band, Ertegun worked closely with Genesis on the . . . *And Then There Were Three* album. He developed a mutual admiration society with Gabriel's replacement on lead vocals, Phil Collins.

Ertegun listened to a demo tape of some material Collins had recorded on his own. "I realized Phil could make a different sort of record than Genesis," Ahmet told Wade and Picardie. "I told him he should record those songs. There was something very magical about the original tape, so we used that. He produced it, and I helped a little bit at the end." Collins even took Ertegun's suggestion of adding extra drums to "In The Air Tonight" to give it a backbeat so it would be commercial enough for radio.

Eighteen of Atlantic's top 100 singles are by members of Genesis. Nine of those belong to Collins, eight to Genesis, and one to Mike + the Mechanics, an extracurricular band formed by Mike Rutherford.

The diversity of Atlantic Records was well demonstrated in 1987 at the marathon Madison Square Garden concert that celebrated the label's 40th anniversary. The all-day, all-night gala featured everyone from Ruth Brown and LaVern Baker to the Manhattan Transfer and the Rascals, from the label's youngest artist (Debbie Gibson) to Genesis, Foreigner, and Led Zeppelin.

The Top 50 Songs on ATCO

The Coasters

THE ATCO label was created in 1955 as a subsidiary of Atlantic Records, as a company for Herb Abramson to run when he returned home after two years of military service. Abramson, Ahmet Ertegun's original partner in the founding of Atlantic in 1947, was drafted in 1953. His place was taken by Jerry Wexler, a former *Billboard* staff reporter who loved jazz. Wexler loved the record business and he loved working with Ertegun. By the time Abramson was discharged, Wexler was occupying the desk next to Ahmet and there was no room—literally or figuratively—for Abramson. The tension was relieved when Ertegun created Atco for Herb to run. "Having gone away as the top executive—and being the president of the company even when I was away—when I came back I expected to carry on as usual," Abramson told Dorothy Wade and Justine Picardie in *Music Man*. "But I was surprised to see that there was not too much desire to work with me. They had a hot team going, and they wanted to keep it."

One of the first releases on Atco was "Smokey Joe's Cafe" by the Robins, originally issued on Spark, a label owned by writer-producers Jerry Leiber and Mike Stoller. When some of the Robins left the group, remaining members Carl Gardner and Bobby Nunn recruited Billy Guy and Leon Hughes to form the original line-up of the Coasters. Their second chart entry was a two-sided hit, "Searchin'" and "Young Blood." It ranks as the seventh most successful Atco single.

Atco's top-ranked chart single is "Mack The Knife" by Bobby Darin. Connie Francis' manager, George Scheck, helped Darin sign with Decca

01 MACK THE KNIFE
Bobby Darin *Atco* 59
02 HOW CAN YOU MEND A BROKEN HEART
Bee Gees *Atco* 71
03 OWNER OF A LONELY HEART
Yes *Atco* 84
04 STRANGER ON THE SHORE
Mr. Acker Bilk *Atco* 62
05 MY LOVIN' (YOU'RE NEVER GONNA GET IT)
En Vogue *Atco EastWest* 92
06 DREAM LOVER
Bobby Darin *Atco* 59
07 SEARCHIN'/ YOUNG BLOOD
The Coasters *Atco* 57
08 CHARLIE BROWN
The Coasters *Atco* 59
09 DEEP PURPLE
Nino Tempo and April Stevens *Atco* 63
10 I GOT YOU BABE
Sonny and Cher *Atco* 65
11 YAKETY YAK
The Coasters *Atco* 58
12 IF WISHES CAME TRUE
Sweet Sensation *Atco* 90
13 SWEET SOUL MUSIC
Arthur Conley *Atco* 67
14 STAND BY ME
Ben E. King *Atco* 61
15 APACHE
Jurgen Ingmann & His Guitar *Atco* 61
16 TAKE A LETTER MARIA
R.B. Greaves *Atco* 69

Records, but after four flop singles, he was dropped from the label. Darin had been writing songs with Don Kirshner, who told his friend Ahmet Ertegun about this hot new talent. Ertegun signed Darin to Atco.

"He started off really being a would-be R&B artist," Ertegun said in *Music Man.* "I thought he was a fantastic artist, and just needed to be recorded properly." Abramson disagreed, and wanted to drop Bobby from the label. Ertegun decided to produce Darin himself, and used Atlantic's new eight-track machine to record "Splish Splash." Doubting it would be a hit and assuming his contract would not be renewed, Darin went ahead and recorded "Early In The Morning" for Brunswick Records. When "Splish Splash" became a hit, Brunswick released their Darin recording under the name "the Rinky Dinks." Atco demanded that Brunswick recall their single; they complied and released the song by Buddy Holly instead.

At that point, the Erteguns bought out Abramson for $300,000, and he left the company. "Herb insisted on being bought out. He didn't have to go," Ahmet commented in *Music Man.*

Foreshadowing the company's future success with British artists, Atco had a No. 1 hit in 1962 with Mr. Acker Bilk's "Stranger On The Shore." It was the first chart-topping single by a British artist in America. The brother-and-sister act of Nino Tempo and April Stevens gave Atco another chart-topper in 1963 with "Deep Purple." Two years later, Sonny and Cher put the label back on top of the Hot 100 with "I Got You Babe."

Ertegun was impressed with the virtuoso guitar playing of Eric Clapton at a party for Wilson Pickett in England. When Clapton formed Cream with Jack Bruce and Ginger Baker, Ertegun suggested that Robert Stigwood manage them. Through Stigwood, Atco also signed the Bee Gees for North America.

During the latter half of the '70s, the Atco logo was practically dormant. Gary Numan brought the label back to the top 10 in 1980 with "Cars," and a re-formed Yes had a No. 1 song on Atco with "Owner Of A Lonely Heart" in 1984. But the momentum wasn't sustained, and the label had a low profile until Derek Shulman was named president in 1988. The former lead singer of Gentle Giant had been senior vice president of A&R at PolyGram before his Atco appointment. Shulman told Steve Gett in *Billboard* why he accepted the job: "Ahmet Ertegun, who built Atlantic and Atco Records, is probably one of my all-time heroes in this business. He is a music man, first and foremost."

In 1992, Atco was merged briefly with another Atlantic label, EastWest, but then the Atco name was retired, until it was reactivated one more time by Rhino Records in 2006. This latest incarnation of Atco issued an Art Garfunkel album in 2007, and has scheduled a release for actress Scarlett Johansson.

17 **SPLISH SPLASH**
Bobby Darin *Atco* 58

18 **LONELY DAYS**
Bee Gees *Atco* 71

19 **GIVING HIM SOMETHING HE CAN FEEL**
En Vogue *Atco EastWest* 92

20 **CARS**
Gary Numan *Atco* 80

21 **SIDESHOW**
Blue Magic *Atco* 74

22 **QUEEN OF THE HOP**
Bobby Darin *Atco* 58

23 **RIDE CAPTAIN RIDE**
Blues Image *Atco* 70

24 **FREE YOUR MIND**
En Vogue *Atco EastWest* 92

25 **I'VE GOTTA GET A MESSAGE TO YOU**
Bee Gees *Atco* 68

26 **THINGS**
Bobby Darin *Atco* 62

27 **POISON IVY**
The Coasters *Atco* 59

28 **SUNSHINE OF YOUR LOVE**
Cream *Atco* 68

29 **BEYOND THE SEA**
Bobby Darin *Atco* 60

30 **RIGHT PLACE WRONG TIME**
Dr. John *Atco* 73

31 **FOR WHAT IT'S WORTH
(STOP, HEY WHAT'S THAT SOUND)**
Buffalo Springfield *Atco* 67

32 **ALLEY CAT**
Bent Fabric & His Piano *Atco* 62

33 **BOTTLE OF WINE**
Fireballs *Atco* 68

34 **WHITE ROOM**
Cream *Atco* 68

35 **YOU KEEP ME HANGIN' ON**
Vanilla Fudge *Atco* 68

36 **LET MY LOVE OPEN THE DOOR**
Pete Townshend *Atco* 80

37 **NEVER ENDING SONG OF LOVE**
Delaney and Bonnie & Friends *Atco* 71

38 **SPANISH HARLEM**
Ben E. King *Atco* 61

39 **LAYLA**
Derek & the Dominos *Atco* 72

40 **LOVE CHILD**
Sweet Sensation *Atco* 90

41 **GIVE IT UP, TURN IT LOOSE**
En Vogue *Atco EastWest* 93

42 **YOU MUST HAVE BEEN A BEAUTIFUL BABY**
Bobby Darin *Atco* 61

43 **I STARTED A JOKE**
Bee Gees *Atco* 69

44 **ALONG CAME JONES**
The Coasters *Atco* 59

45 **LAUGH AT ME**
Sonny *Atco* 65

46 **SINCERELY YOURS**
Sweet Sensation w/Romeo J.D. *Atco* 89

47 **THIN LINE BETWEEN LOVE AND HATE**
The Persuaders *Atco* 71

48 **THE BEAT GOES ON**
Sonny and Cher *Atco* 67

49 **WHISPERING**
Nino Tempo and April Stevens *Atco* 64

50 **RUN TO ME**
Boe Gees *Atco* 72

The Top 100 Songs on CAPITOL

Nat King Cole

CAPITOL RECORDS, the first major label to be located in Los Angeles, was founded in 1942 by composer Johnny Mercer, record-store owner Glenn Wallichs, and movie producer B.G. "Buddy" DeSylva.

Capitol's initial batch of releases included the label's first hit, "Cow Cow Boogie" by Freddie Slack, with vocals by Ella Mae Morse. The label was innovative; Capitol was the first company to give free records to disc jockeys, record their masters on tape and, later, issue recordings in all three playing speeds.

Capitol expanded its roster in 1943, releasing material from Stan Kenton, Peggy Lee, Jo Stafford, Margaret Whiting, and an artist who would account for one-quarter of the label's sales by 1950—Nat King Cole. A country and western division was set up in 1948. The roster included many best-selling C&W artists, such as Tex Ritter, Tennessee Ernie Ford, Faron Young, Hank Thompson, Merle Travis, and Jean Sheppard, many of whom worked with staff producer Ken Nelson. In 1953, Capitol signed another important artist. After 10 years of recording on Columbia, Frank Sinatra moved over to the label and had a top 10 hit with his first Capitol single, "I'm Walking Behind You." Dean Martin, Les Paul and Mary Ford, and Stan Freberg also had major hits on Capitol during the first half of the '50s.

Flush with success, the owners sold Capitol to EMI of Great Britain in 1955. On April 6, 1956, the famed Capitol Tower building had its grand opening in Hollywood. Billed as the world's first round office building, the Tower included recording studios, with echo chambers buried beneath the structure's parking lot.

Capitol took a tentative step into rock and roll in 1956 when Ken Nelson signed a 21-year-old rocker from Norfolk, Virginia. Gene Vincent wrote his early songs while recovering in a hospital from a motorcycle accident. One song was inspired by the comic strip Little Lulu—Vincent called it "Be-Bop-A-Lula." He acquired a manager, Bill "Sheriff Tex" Davis, who met Nelson at a DJ convention and told him about his new star. Capitol wanted their own white rock singer to compete with RCA's Elvis Presley, and signed Vincent to the label. His first recording session took place in Nashville on May 4, 1956. Nelson chose "Woman Love" as the first single, but DJs preferred "Be-Bop-A-Lula" on the "B" side.

Despite Vincent's immediate success, Capitol wasn't ready to make a full commitment to rock and roll. Most of the label's hits in the early years of the rock era belonged to artists like Sinatra, Cole, Martin, and Ford, as well as instrumentalists Les Baxter and Nelson Riddle, whose "Lisbon Antigua" ranks as Capitol's third most successful chart single of the rock era.

The Kingston Trio signed with the label in January 1958, after Bob Hope's agent saw them perform at the hungry i in San Francisco and told Voyle Gilmore of Capitol's A&R staff about them. Capitol also signed the Four Freshmen, the Four Preps, and the Lettermen.

In the spring of 1962, Murry Wilson brought a demo tape of his sons' band, the Beach Boys, to Nick Venet at Capitol. The group had already released their debut single, "Surfin'," on Herb Newman's Candix label. Newman wasn't enthusiastic about the Beach Boys' other songs, including an early version of "Surfer Girl," and declined to release a follow-up. Venet played the tape for his boss, Gilmore, and within the hour Capitol agreed to sign the group.

Three months after the Beach Boys' first Capitol single entered the Hot 100, the first EMI single by the Beatles, released on the Parlophone label, started moving up the U.K. chart. But Capitol wasn't interested in releasing "Love Me Do," or any of the three singles that followed. "We don't think the Beatles will do anything in this market" is what one label executive told manager Brian Epstein. So the Beatles appeared on Vee Jay and Swan in the U. S., but they didn't chart. On October 19, 1963, the Beatles recorded "I Want To Hold Your Hand." Epstein took a demo copy with him when he flew to New York on Nov. 5 so he could play it for Brown Meggs, director of eastern operations for Capitol. Meggs felt this record was right for America, and scheduled a release date of January 13, 1964. But when Carroll Baker, a DJ at WWDC in Washington, D.C., started playing an import copy, the demand caused Capitol to advance the release date to December 26 and increase the press run from 200,000 copies to one million. All of the earlier Beatles singles were re-released and charted. The official follow-up to "I Want To Hold Your Hand" was "Can't Buy Me Love," which had an advance order of 2,100,000 copies.

Capitol's most consistent artists of the '70s included Grand Funk, Steve Miller, Helen Reddy, Dr. Hook, Anne Murray, Bob Seger, and Paul McCartney's second band, Wings. The label's biggest *Billboard* hit of the

'70s is "My Sharona" by the Knack, a Los Angeles quartet that suffered for its comparisons to the Beatles.

Like the Knack, Grand Funk Railroad was never popular with the rock press, but they managed to sell millions of records anyway. The band's origins can be traced to the Flint, Michigan, band called Terry Knight & the Pack. After a series of singles on Cameo-Parkway's Lucky Eleven label, the Pack signed with Capitol in April 1968. They returned to Lucky Eleven as the Fabulous Pack before breaking up. Mark Farner and Don Brewer then formed a new band, taking their name from Michigan's Grand Trunk Railroad. Knight became their manager and got them a deal with Capitol. Grand Funk's most successful chart single is their remake of Little Eva's "The Locomotion," produced by Todd Rundgren.

Capitol's biggest *Billboard* hit of the '80s is "Abracadabra," a track from Steve Miller's 12th album for the label. Miller formed his first band, the Marksmen Combo, back in 1955, when he was only 12. That ensemble featured future Steve Miller Band member Boz Scaggs. As the Ardells, they played Motown songs and other R&B covers, and while attending the University of Wisconsin, Miller and Scaggs fronted a group called the Fabulous Night Trains. After college, Miller teamed with Barry Goldberg in the Goldberg-Miller Blues Band, based in Chicago. Within four days of moving to San Francisco in 1966, Miller started a new outfit called the Steve Miller Blues Band. Their performance at the Monterey Pop Festival led to a contract with Capitol promising a $50,000 advance (astronomical at the time) and complete artistic freedom. Their first two albums were produced in Britain by Glyn Johns. Miller's eighth album yielded his first No. 1 single, "The Joker"; the 1976 album *Fly Like An Eagle* contained his next No. 1 hit, "Rock'n Me." Six years later, Miller had his third No. 1 song, "Abracadabra."

Another important signing in the '80s was Tina Turner. After recording a searing version of the Temptations' "Ball Of Confusion" with Martyn Ware and Ian Craig Marsh of the British Electric Foundation (a spin-off of Heaven 17), Tina was signed to a worldwide deal by EMI. Her single, "What's Love Got To Do With It," became the biggest hit of her career.

Capitol entered the '90s with hits from the Seattle-based Heart featuring sisters Ann and Nancy Wilson, Oakland rapper M.C. Hammer, a revitalized Duran Duran, and singer/songwriter Richard Marx, who moved over from sister label EMI.

The J. Geils Band

N AMERICA, EMI had a short history. But in the United Kingdom, the name dates back to the 1931 merger of Columbia and the Gramophone Company, resulting in Electrical and Musical Industries, one of the world's major record companies. EMI's purchase of Capitol Records in 1955 gave it a strong presence in America, and at home, it operated three important labels: HMV, Parlophone, and Columbia. In 1973, Gerry Oord from Holland set up an EMI label in Britain. One of the company's strongest artists, Cliff Richard, was shifted to the new division from Columbia, and in 1974 Queen had their debut single issued on EMI.

That same year, the EMI logo also appeared in America for the first time. The Swedish band Blue Swede gave the label a chart-topping hit with a remake of "Hooked On A Feeling." In 1975, the Scottish quartet Pilot had an American hit with "Magic," produced by Alan Parsons. But the EMI label was shuttered soon after, not to appear in the U.S. again until 1978, when the EMI America label was created.

Set up as a separate division from EMI's other American label, Capitol, EMI America issued singles from both British and American artists. From the U.K. came Cliff Richard, Sheena Easton, and Naked Eyes. From the U.S. came Kim Carnes, the J. Geils Band, Robert John, the Stray Cats, Gary U.S. Bonds, and Rocky Burnette.

In 1979, Robert John, who had recorded for Columbia, A&M, Atlantic, and Ariola, gave the new label its first No. 1 single on the Hot

100, "Sad Eyes." The following year, EMI had top 10 hits from Richard, Burnette, and Carnes.

Cliff Richard had been a consistent hitmaker in the U.K. since 1958, when his debut single, "Move It," went to No. 2. Labels like ABC-Paramount, Epic, and Uni had failed to break him in the States. It took Elton John and his Rocket label to finally land Cliff a top 10 hit in America with "Devil Woman" in 1976. But then he slipped back into obscurity until "We Don't Talk Anymore" went to No. 7 in January 1980.

Rocky Burnette—the son of Johnny and nephew of '60s rocker Dorsey Burnette—made the British chart first with "Tired Of Toein' The Line." It was a minor hit in the U.K., but in America it went to No. 8 in July 1980.

Kim Carnes was the first artist signed to EMI America by label president Jim Mazza. She went to No. 10 with a remake of Smokey Robinson's "More Love" in August 1980, but the song she will be remembered for is a remake of Jackie DeShannon and Donna Weiss' "Bette Davis Eyes," EMI's most successful chart single in America. Carnes credits Bill Cuomo, who played synthesizer on the track, for coming up with the arrangement that kept the single at No. 1 for nine weeks.

The label's British roots were helpful during the '80s, as David Bowie was signed to EMI worldwide after a long stint with RCA. In March 1985, EMI in Britain signed the Pet Shop Boys. An earlier version of their "West End Girls" had been released on Epic; a newly recorded version topped the charts in Britain and America.

A new EMI label was set up under Bruce Lundvall. The name Manhattan had previously been used for a United Artists–distributed label run by Charles Koppelman. EMI's Manhattan label signed Glass Tiger, Robbie Nevil, and, most importantly, Richard Marx (who has seven titles on EMI's top 50).

The EMI America and Manhattan labels were eventually merged, creating EMI Manhattan. But some artists, particularly the Pet Shop Boys, objected to having their records released on a label different from the one that had signed them. "Manhattan" was dropped, once again giving America an "EMI" label. One of the more unique releases on EMI Manhattan was "Don't Worry Be Happy," featuring the multi-tracked vocals of Bobby McFerrin, a San Francisco–based jazz singer. The song went to No. 1 in 1988.

The company had a new success story in 1989 with the Swedish duo Roxette, which quickly racked up four No. 1 songs: "The Look," "Listen To Your Heart," "It Must Have Been Love," and "Joyride."

16 **C'EST LA VIE**
Robbie Nevil *Manhattan* 87

17 **HOLD ON TO THE NIGHTS**
Richard Marx *EMI Manhattan* 88

18 **SIMPLY IRRESISTIBLE**
Robert Palmer *EMI Manhattan* 88

19 **DANGEROUS**
Roxette *EMI* 90

20 **STRAY CAT STRUT**
Stray Cats *EMI America* 83

21 **ENDLESS SUMMER NIGHTS**
Richard Marx *EMI Manhattan* 88

22 **SATISFIED**
Richard Marx *EMI* 89

23 **I BELIEVE**
Blessid Union of Souls *EMI* 95

24 **MORE THAN WORDS CAN SAY**
Alias *EMI* 90

25 **WHAT HAVE I DONE TO DESERVE THIS?**
Pet Shop Boys w/Dusty Springfield
EMI America 88

26 **NEVER SURRENDER**
Corey Hart *EMI America* 85

27 **FADING LIKE A FLOWER (EVERY TIME YOU LEAVE)**
Roxette *EMI* 91

28 **SHOULD'VE KNOWN BETTER**
Richard Marx *Manhattan* 87

29 **FREEZE-FRAME**
J. Geils Band *EMI America* 82

30 **DON'T FORGET ME (WHEN I'M GONE)**
Glass Tiger *Manhattan* 86

31 **DON'T MEAN NOTHING**
Richard Marx *Manhattan* 87

32 **HEARTS**
Marty Balin *EMI America* 81

33 **ANGELIA** Richard Marx *EMI* 89

34 **MORE LOVE**
Kim Carnes *EMI America* 80

35 **SUNGLASSES AT NIGHT**
Corey Hart *EMI America* 84

36 **ALWAYS ON MY MIND**
Pet Shop Boys *EMI Manhattan* 88

37 **WE DON'T TALK ANYMORE**
Cliff Richard *EMI America* 80

38 **TOO SHY**
Kajagoogoo *EMI America* 83

39 **STRUT** Sheena Easton *EMI America* 84

40 **TELEFONE (LONG DISTANCE LOVE AFFAIR)**
Sheena Easton *EMI America* 83

41 **MISS YOU LIKE CRAZY**
Natalie Cole *EMI* 8

42 **THIS LITTLE GIRL**
Gary U.S. Bonds *EMI America* 81

43 **SOMEDAY**
Glass Tiger *Manhattan* 87

44 **(SHE'S) SEXY + 17**
Stray Cats *EMI America* 83

45 **PINK CADILLAC**
Natalie Cole *EMI Manhattan* 88

46 **ROCK THIS TOWN**
Stray Cats *EMI America* 82

47 **MAGIC** Pilot *EMI* 75

48 **DREAMING**
Cliff Richard *EMI America* 80

49 **LADY** D'Angelo *EMI* 96

50 **SILENT LUCIDITY**
Queensrÿche *EMI* 91

Badfinger

THE BEATLES opened their own boutique on December 7, 1967, at 94 Baker Street in London. Paul McCartney described it as "a beautiful place where you could buy beautiful things." Inspired by a Magritte painting, Paul came up with the name of the new shop: Apple.

The exterior walls were painted in bright, psychedelic colors, shocking the neighbors. The goods flew out the door—sometimes in the hands of paying customers, but often fleeced by shoplifters. Business continued until July 30, 1968, when the Beatles decided to close up shop and give away all the remaining merchandise. By day's end, everything was gone.

Apple had other divisions, however. There was Apple Films, the production company that produced *Magical Mystery Tour*. There was the Apple Foundation for the Arts, designed to give grants to deserving artists. There was Apple Corps, which oversaw all of the Beatles' business interests. And there was Apple Records, headed by Ron Kass with Peter Asher in charge of A&R and Derek Taylor supervising publicity.

The record label and all of the other Apple businesses were housed in an elegant five-story Georgian building at 3 Savile Row. On August 11, 1968, the first four Apple singles were released. The new label sported a green Granny Smith on the A-side and a halved apple on the B-side. The Beatles' "Hey Jude," "Those Were The Days" by Mary Hopkin, "Sour Milk Sea" by Jackie Lomax, and "Thingummybob" by the Black Dyke Mills brass band were hand-delivered in gift presentation boxes to Queen Elizabeth, Princess Margaret, the Queen Mother, and Prime Minister Harold Wilson.

No word on what the Queen thought of "Thingummybob," but "Hey

Jude" debuted at No. 10 in America and held on to the No. 1 spot for nine weeks, becoming Apple's most successful chart single. During "Hey Jude"'s sixth week at the top, "Those Were The Days" began a three-week stint at No. 2, giving the brand-new label the top two positions on the *Billboard* chart. In the U.K., "Those Were The Days" succeeded "Hey Jude" at No. 1.

Mary Hopkin had caught the attention of Twiggy after winning a talent contest on the TV series *Opportunity Knocks*. The famed British model called Paul McCartney to tell him about the blonde singer from Wales. McCartney selected "Those Were The Days" for her to record.

The only other non-Beatle act to have more than one hit on Apple was a Welsh band, the Iveys. Their first single, "Maybe Tomorrow," flopped, and the group changed their name to Badfinger. Their next single was McCartney's "Come And Get It," from the film *The Magic Christian* starring Ringo Starr. It peaked at No. 7, and was followed by two more top 10 singles.

Asher signed James Taylor to Apple, but the Boston-born singer didn't have a hit until he moved over to Warner Bros. Billy Preston was also on the Apple roster, but aside from guest-starring on the Beatles' "Get Back," he didn't have chart success until he signed with A&M.

Apple had a short-lived subsidiary, Zapple, but it was shut down when Allen Klein took charge of the Beatles' business ventures. With Klein as the new head of Apple Corps, Kass and Asher were out, as were many other Apple executives and employees.

Apple Records continued to exist after the breakup of the Beatles, as all four members recorded their solo efforts for the label. But in 1975 their individual solo contracts with EMI came to an end, and so did Apple. "Junior's Farm" was McCartney's last single on Apple. He remained with EMI, appearing on Capitol in the U.S. until he signed with Columbia in 1979; he returned to Capitol in 1985. "You" was George Harrison's last Apple single. His next release was on his own label, Dark Horse, distributed first through A&M, then through Warner Bros. Ringo's swan song on Apple was "It's All Down To Goodnight Vienna." He subsequently recorded for Atlantic, Portrait, Boardwalk, and Rykodisc. After his last Apple chart single, "Stand By Me," Lennon began a five-year hiatus from recording. He returned in 1980 with the *Double Fantasy* album on Geffen. After his death, unreleased material appeared on Polydor and Capitol. The Apple logo continued to exist for Beatles compilations released through Capitol, including the No. 1 album of 2001, *1*.

17 **IMAGINE**
John Lennon/Plastic Ono Band 71

18 **NO NO SONG / SNOOKEROO**
Ringo Starr 75

19 **JUNIOR'S FARM**
Wings 75

20 **IT DON'T COME EASY**
Ringo Starr 71

21 **DAY AFTER DAY**
Badfinger 72

22 **REVOLUTION**
The Beatles 68

23 **ANOTHER DAY / OH WOMAN OH WHY**
Paul McCartney 71

24 **COME AND GET IT**
Badfinger 70

25 **OH MY MY**
Ringo Starr 74

26 **JET**
Wings 74

27 **THE BALLAD OF JOHN AND YOKO**
The Beatles 69

28 **ONLY YOU**
Ringo Starr 75

29 **NO MATTER WHAT**
Badfinger 70

30 **HELEN WHEELS**
Wings 74

31 **HI, HI, HI**
Wings 73

32 **#9 DREAM**
John Lennon 75

33 **WHAT IS LIFE**
George Harrison 71

34 **GOODBYE**
Mary Hopkin 69

35 **MIND GAMES**
John Lennon 73

36 **BABY BLUE**
Badfinger 72

37 **GIVE PEACE A CHANCE**
Plastic Ono Band 71

38 **POWER TO THE PEOPLE**
John Lennon/Plastic Ono Band 71

39 **DARK HORSE**
George Harrison 75

40 **YOU**
George Harrison 75

41 **STAND BY ME**
John Lennon 75

42 **GIVE IRELAND BACK TO THE IRISH**
Wings 72

43 **FREE AS A BIRD**
The Beatles 96

44 **BACK OFF BOOGALOO**
Ringo Starr 72

45 **REAL LOVE**
The Beatles 96

46 **BANGLA-DESH**
George Harrison 71

47 **MARY HAD A LITTLE LAMB / LITTLE WOMAN LOVE**
Wings 72

48 **COLD TURKEY**
Plastic Ono Band 70

49 **TEMMA HARBOUR**
Mary Hopkin 70

50 **WE'RE ON OUR WAY**
Chris Hodge 72

David Seville

SIMON (SY) WARONKER and Jack Ames founded Liberty as a West Coast label in 1955. At first, the focus was on easy listening, jazz, and pop. One of the label's earliest hits was "Cry Me A River" by Julie London, in December 1955.

It didn't take long for Liberty to find its first rock and roll artist. Manager Jerry Capehart brought demos of his client Eddie Cochran to Waronker and Alvin (Al) Bennett, head of A&R and later an owner of the company. After meeting Cochran, they signed him to the label. Another Liberty artist, Lionel Newman, needed some performers for a film he was working on as musical director. He asked Waronker for suggestions, and the label head recommended Cochran. Eddie sang "Twenty Flight Rock" in *The Girl Can't Help It,* and Waronker planned to release it as his first single. At the same time, Waronker wanted to lease a song called "Sittin' In The Balcony," recorded by songwriter John D. Loudermilk as Johnny Dee on the Colonial label. When he couldn't buy the master, Waronker had Cochran cut a cover version and released it in March 1957 as Eddie's debut single; it peaked at No. 18. Just over a year later, Cochran had his biggest hit with "Summertime Blues," which went to No. 8. Cochran never had another top

30 hit, and on April 17, 1960, he was killed in an automobile accident near Chippenham, England.

Liberty also had hits in the '50s with Patience and Prudence, two young sisters from Los Angeles; Billy Ward & His Dominoes, an R&B group that had recorded for Federal, King, Jubilee, and Decca before moving to Liberty in 1957; Martin Denny, a composer/arranger who moved to Hawaii in the '50s; and Ross Bagdasarian, better known as David Seville.

Bagdasarian declined to join his family's grape-growing business in Fresno, California, and moved to New York to be an actor and work with his cousin, author William Saroyan. They collaborated on the song "Come On-A My House," later recorded by Rosemary Clooney. In 1956, Bagdasarian signed with Liberty and was persuaded to use a different name professionally. He had been stationed near Seville, Spain, while serving in the Air Force, so he created the alter ego of David Seville. Ross had a No. 1 single in 1958 that was inspired by a book in his library, *Duel With The Witch Doctor.* The novelty song "Witch Doctor" was followed eight months later by "The Chipmunk Song."

Snuff Garrett was asked by Al Bennett to join Liberty's promotion department; he agreed to do so if he could also produce records. His first two artists were Johnny Burnette and Bobby Vee, and both artists helped to establish Liberty's credentials in the early '60s. Garrett was named head of A&R for the label, and continued to produce hits for artists like Gene McDaniels and actor Walter Brennan. Garrett also brought Gary Lewis & the Playboys to Liberty in 1965. The label's other major act of the mid-'60s was Jan and Dean, signed to Liberty in 1961 after having hits on Dore and Challenge.

Through its history, Liberty expanded by buying other labels. In 1957, it absorbed the Pacific Jazz label, changing the name to World Pacific. Six years later, the Imperial label was purchased, and three years after that, Blue Note came into the fold. Liberty also bought the Seattle-based Dolton label, which it had been distributing. In 1967, Liberty was purchased by the conglomerate TransAmerica, which also owned the United Artists label. Eventually the Liberty logo was dropped, and all of the artists were moved over to United Artists.

In 1979, the British company EMI bought United Artists. EMI had launched the EMI America label in the U.S. in January 1978, and in 1980, EMI reactivated the Liberty label. UA artists like Kenny Rogers and Dottie West were shifted to Liberty. Rogers' first single on Liberty was Lionel Richie's composition "Lady," the label's most successful chart single. Liberty also released the soundtrack to *For Your Eyes Only,* as all previous James Bond soundtracks had been issued on United Artists. Sheena Easton, who recorded for EMI America, had her title song from the film released on Liberty as well.

After a short second life, Liberty's artists were transferred to EMI America. The Liberty name was revived again in 1991 as a country label. Its most successful artist was Garth Brooks. While dormant in the U.S., EMI continues to use the Liberty logo in the U.K. for middle-of-the-road pop.

Billy J. Kramer & the Dakotas

F IVE DIFFERENT labels have been named Imperial in the 20th century; the first one dates back to 1905. The Crystalate Gramophone Manufacturing Company Ltd. had an Imperial label in the U.K. from 1920–34. Domestic EMI labels in Brazil and Holland were also called Imperial, but the Imperial that had the greatest impact on rock and roll was the one created by Lew Chudd in Los Angeles back in 1947.

Chudd, a businessman who enjoyed electronics as a hobby, signed some jump blues bands to the label in its early days, but his real breakthrough came one evening in 1949 when he walked into the Bronze Peacock Club in Houston. He was heading home after traveling in Mexico to promote some Spanish records. Interested in signing some R&B artists, he stopped in at the club to check out Dave Bartholomew's band. They met later in New Orleans, where Chudd hired Bartholomew to produce records for Imperial.

Searching for talent, the two men found a 20-year-old boogie-woogie blues singer at the Hideaway Club in New Orleans. Antoine "Fats" Domino had been playing in local clubs since the age of 10. "Fats Domino was doing one of the things that the original, old guys used to sing," Bartholomew told Steve Kolanjian. "We used to call them jailhouse-type blues. At that time there wasn't anyone doing that type of thing. I was amazed at it. Being my first venture, I wanted it to be good. We changed the whole thing around and we called it 'The Fat Man.' That's the very first record we made." The single entered the *Billboard* R&B chart in February

1950, and peaked at No. 6 on the Best Sellers chart. Domino's next 10 singles all made the R&B top 10.

Domino crossed over to the top 20 of the pop chart in 1955 with "Ain't It A Shame," covered by Pat Boone as "Ain't That A Shame." A year later, he went to No. 4 with "I'm In Love Again." Later in 1956, he recorded what would become his biggest hit, as well as Imperial's second most successful chart single—"Blueberry Hill." Originally recorded by Glenn Miller, and sung in a film by Gene Autry, the song was recorded by Fats at Bunny Robine's studio during a trip to Los Angeles. Fats came up with the idea of recording the song but couldn't remember the bridge. His brother-in-law recalled the words. "Fats could hardly get through it," Bartholomew told Kolanjian. "So Bunny took a scissors to the tape and put it together. It's a common practice now but *that* was a long time ago."

Ricky Nelson sang a Domino tune, "I'm Walkin'," on the April 10, 1957, installment of *The Adventures Of Ozzie And Harriet.* Along with his older brother David, Ricky starred with his parents on their radio show and the weekly TV series.

His recording career began when 16-year-old Ricky was on a date with his girlfriend Arline. He was driving her home when an Elvis Presley song came on the radio. Arline said how much she loved Elvis, and a jealous Ricky boasted that he was going to have his own record released in a few weeks. Arline laughed, and although Ricky didn't have a recording contract with anyone, he became even more determined to make a record. Ricky asked his dad if he could use the TV series orchestra and picked the Fats Domino song because he knew the two chords. Ozzie helped him sign with Verve Records; after "I'm Walking" hit the charts, the flip side, "A Teenager's Romance," proved to be an even bigger hit, peaking at No. 2.

Ozzie suspected Verve wasn't paying Ricky all of the royalties he earned and shopped around for a new label. Chudd was anxious to sign young Nelson—at least he wouldn't be able to cover any more of Domino's material—and sent Ricky into the studio on August 18, 1957. That day, Ricky cut his first recordings for Imperial: "Be-Bop Baby" and "Have I Told You Lately That I Love You?"

In 1963, Chudd sold his company to Liberty Records, and Ricky moved on to Decca Records. Imperial remained a strong pop label with Jackie DeShannon, Cher, Mel Carter, Johnny Rivers, the Classics IV, and a handful of British groups, including Billy J. Kramer & the Dakotas and the Hollies. After TransAmerica purchased Liberty and merged it with United Artists, the Imperial logo was laid to rest. The last singles to appear on the label were released in 1970.

17 **RAUNCHY**
Ernie Freeman 57

18 **BLUE MONDAY**
Fats Domino 57

19 **WHOLE LOTTA LOVING**
Fats Domino 59

20 **LITTLE CHILDREN**
Billy J. Kramer & the Dakotas 64

21 **I GOT A FEELING**
Ricky Nelson 58

22 **LET THERE BE DRUMS**
Sandy Nelson 61

23 **PUT A LITTLE LOVE IN YOUR HEART**
Jackie DeShannon 69

24 **BELIEVE WHAT YOU SAY /
   MY BUCKET'S GOT A HOLE IN IT**
Ricky Nelson 58

25 **STORMY**
Classics IV f/Dennis Yost 68

26 **NEVER BE ANYONE ELSE BUT YOU**
Ricky Nelson 59

27 **VALLEY OF TEARS / IT'S YOU I LOVE**
Fats Domino 57

28 **WALKING TO NEW ORLEANS**
Fats Domino 60

29 **I WANT TO WALK YOU HOME**
Fats Domino 595

30 **HOLD ME, THRILL ME, KISS ME**
Mel Carter 65

31 **BE MY GUEST**
Fats Domino 59

32 **YOUNG WORLD**
Rick Nelson 62

33 **SEVENTH SON**
Johnny Rivers 65

34 **BUS STOP**
The Hollies 66

35 **WHAT THE WORLD NEEDS NOW IS LOVE**
Jackie DeShannon 65

36 **MY GIRL, JOSEPHINE**
Fats Domino 60

37 **YOU BETTER SIT DOWN KIDS**
Cher 67

38 **ON A CAROUSEL**
The Hollies 67

39 **IT'S UP TO YOU**
Rick Nelson 63

40 **IT'S LATE**
Ricky Nelson 59

41 **YOUNG EMOTIONS**
Ricky Nelson 60

42 **SWEETER THAN YOU**
Ricky Nelson 59

43 **AIN'T IT A SHAME**
Fats Domino 55

44 **TEEN AGE IDOL**
Rick Nelson 62

45 **MOUNTAIN OF LOVE**
Johnny Rivers 64

46 **JUST A LITTLE TOO MUCH**
Ricky Nelson 59

47 **BAD TO ME**
Billy J. Kramer & the Dakotas 64

48 **A WONDER LIKE YOU**
Rick Nelson 61

49 **WHEN MY DREAMBOAT
   COMES HOME/SO-LONG**
Fats Domino 56

50 **STOP STOP STOP**
The Hollies 66

War

IKE OTHER major film studios, United Artists wanted to have its own record label primarily to release the company's motion picture soundtracks. Max Youngstein, a vice president of United Artists, started the record label in late 1957 with David Picker. UA did have soundtrack success with films like *The Apartment, The Great Escape, Irma La Douce, Mondo Cane, Tom Jones, A Man And A Woman,* and the James Bond movies, beginning with *Dr. No* in 1963. But the label also built a roster of easy listening, rock, and R&B artists and had its first No. 1 single in 1961 with "Michael" by the Highwaymen.

UA's biggest hits from the early '60s were from Arthur Ferrante and Louis Teicher, pianists who first met when they were students at the Juilliard School of Music in Manhattan. After graduating, they did some concert work, then returned to the school to teach. In 1947, they gave up their faculty positions to perform full-time as a duo, appearing as regulars on ABC's *Piano Playhouse* and recording for Columbia, ABC-Paramount, and MGM. In 1960, Ferrante and Teicher signed to United Artists and specialized in recording themes from films. Their two biggest hits were their twin-piano renditions of "Exodus" and "Theme From *The Apartment.*" They also had a hit single with the theme from *Midnight Cowboy.*

In 1963, UA had pop and R&B success with the Exciters ("Tell Him") and Garnett Mimms & the Enchanters ("Cry Baby"). The Exciters were produced by Jerry Leiber and Mike Stoller, as were United Artists' most successful group of the '60s, Jay & the Americans. Leiber and Stoller signed the group to the label and were responsible for producing hits like "She Cried" and "Only In America." The latter was one of many songs by the group that made them sound like a white version of the Drifters—in fact, "Only In America" had been written for and originally recorded by the Drifters. One of Jay & the Americans' biggest hits was a remake of the Drifters' "This Magic Moment."

Bobby Goldsboro signed with UA after one minor hit on Laurie called "Molly." His biggest hit for the label was a song written by Bobby Russell, "Honey." Released in 1968, it is UA's second most successful Hot 100 single. That same year, TransAmerica purchased United Artists—including the film company, the publishing company, and the record company. TransAmerica then bought the Liberty label and merged the two companies into Liberty-UA. Mike Stewart, who had been running UA on the East Coast, headed up the new label with Al Bennett, who had been in charge of Liberty on the West Coast. Eventually, Liberty was phased out, and its artists were moved over to the UA label.

In 1971, UA purchased the small Mediarts label, whose primary artist was a relatively unknown singer named Don McLean. His first album, *Tapestry,* was released on Mediarts in 1970, but only after 34 other labels had turned it down. McLean's second album included the title song "American Pie," which became the most successful chart single on United Artists.

During the '70s, UA flourished in different areas. Larry Butler ran the Nashville office and built up the country division with artists like Kenny Rogers and Crystal Gayle. The label also had an active office in the U.K., which provided the American company British artists like Maxine Nightingale and Gerry Rafferty. From Jet Records in the U.K. came the Electric Light Orchestra, and from Magnet Records came Chris Rea with "Fool (If You Think It's Over)."

Another major signing for UA in the '70s was Paul Anka, who hadn't had a top 10 single since 1961. His first UA single was "(You're) Having My Baby," which spent three weeks at No. 1 and was the label's fourth chart-topping single. Anka followed that with two more top 10 hits, both duets with Odia Coates. Anka left UA in 1978 and went to one of his former labels, RCA.

In May 1978, UA President Artie Mogull and his partner Jerry Rubinstein bought the company from TransAmerica for $30 million in a deal financed by EMI. Ten months later, Mogull and Rubinstein sold the company to EMI, and Jim Mazza was brought in to run UA. A year after that, the United Artists label disappeared after having chart hits with Kenny Rogers and the Dirt Band, who were shifted to the reactivated Liberty label.

The Top 100 Songs on COLUMBIA

Johnny Mathis

COLUMBIA RECORDS has been in business for more than a century, and the company's history parallels the history of the record business itself. The origins of the label can be traced back to 1881, when British inventors Chichester A. Bell and Charles Sumner Tainter received financial assistance from Bell's cousin, Alexander Graham Bell, to set up a laboratory in Washington, D.C. They were looking to improve upon Thomas A. Edison's 1878 patent for the phonograph machine.

Edison had recorded on tinfoil, but Bell and Tainter came up with the idea of recording on cardboard-coated wax. They received a patent on May 4, 1886, for such a disc, but chose to produce sounds on a cylinder. In early 1889, they demonstrated their Graphophone, a predecessor of the dictaphone recording device. Jesse Lippincott, a millionaire businessman from Pittsburgh, bought the rights to the machine as well as to Edison's patent and formed the North American Phonograph Company. Lippincott set up 33 franchises around the country, but only one survived: the Columbia Phonograph Company of Maryland, Delaware, and the District of Columbia.

Doing business from Bridgeport, Connecticut, the company had a catalog of 200 cylinders of recorded music for sale by 1891. At the turn of the century, they were also manufacturing discs, which went on sale in 1901. A year later, Columbia and its chief rival, the Victor Talking Machine Company, agreed to standardize their product and release 7-inch and 10-inch single-sided discs. Double-sided discs were introduced in 1904.

Columbia flourished by releasing discs of military bands, love ballads, patriotic songs, comedy recordings, and classical recordings leased from Europe. In 1912, cylinders fell by the wayside, and all music was released in disc form.

At the end of World War I, with the country facing a recession, Columbia was not in good financial shape. The British arm of Columbia was sold to its manager, Louis Sterling, in December 1922. Two years later, Sterling paid $2.5 million for the American company, and in 1925, Columbia released the first electrically recorded disc.

There were more financial woes during the Depression of the '30s. Columbia merged with another British company, HMV, to form Electrical and Musical Industries, Ltd. Because of antitrust laws in the United States, EMI had to sell the American company. Columbia's new owners were Grigsby-Grunow, a refrigerator manufacturer. When that company went bankrupt in 1933, Columbia was purchased by the American Record Corporation, whose parent company was a button manufacturer. ARC had also purchased the Brunswick label, and in 1938 William S. Paley, the president of CBS, bought the controlling interest in ARC. CBS sold the Brunswick label to the American Decca company and would continue to run Columbia Records until January 5, 1988—the day the label was sold to the Sony Corporation of Japan.

The company prospered in the '40s, thanks in large part to a perceptive talent scout named John Hammond. He signed a number of big bands to the label as well as big band singers. In 1940, Columbia Records had the first-ever No. 1 song on the *Billboard* pop singles chart, "I'll Never Smile Again" by the Tommy Dorsey Orchestra, featuring the vocals of Frank Sinatra.

The man in charge of Columbia Records, Edward Wallerstein, had been at RCA Victor when that company tried to develop the long-playing record in 1931. Under Wallerstein's direction, CBS engineers, working with Dr. Peter Goldmark, came up with a $33\frac{1}{3}$ RPM disc in 1948. The LP was born.

The new configuration helped usher in an age of Broadway musicals, overseen for CBS by Goddard Lieberson, who headed up the label in the 1950s.

One area Columbia did not rush into was rock and roll. While RCA Victor had the industry's hottest star in Elvis Presley, CBS avoided the trend (although they did bid for Presley). With Mitch Miller in charge of A&R, the company's stars of the '50s included Johnny Mathis, Doris Day, the Four Lads, Johnnie Ray, and Guy Mitchell.

Hammond moved the label in a new direction by signing Bob Dylan in 1962. Barbra Streisand also joined the company that year, and other rock or folk-rock acts were added to the roster, like Simon and Garfunkel, the Byrds, and Paul Revere & the Raiders.

Clive Davis became head of the label in 1966. He attended the

35 **A WHOLE NEW WORLD**
Peabo Bryson & Regina Belle 93

36 **EL PASO**
Marty Robbins 60

37 **LOVE THEME FROM "A STAR IS BORN" (EVERGREEN)**
Barbra Streisand 77

38 **WALK LIKE AN EGYPTIAN**
Bangles 86

39 **MOMENTS TO REMEMBER**
The Four Lads 55

40 **ROSANNA**
Toto 82

41 **JUMPIN', JUMPIN'**
Destiny's Child 00

42 **IT'S STILL ROCK AND ROLL TO ME**
Billy Joel 80

43 **FAITH**
George Michael 87

44 **FOOTLOOSE**
Kenny Loggins 84

45 **BUTTERFLY**
Crazy Town 01

46 **INDIAN RESERVATION (THE LAMENT OF THE CHEROKEE RESERVATION INDIAN)**
The Raiders 71

47 **CARELESS WHISPER**
Wham! f/George Michael 85

48 **I'LL BE THERE**
Mariah Carey 92

49 **OPEN ARMS**
Journey 82

50 **LOVE TAKES TIME**
Mariah Carey 90

51 **VISION OF LOVE**
Mariah Carey 90

52 **WHATEVER WILL BE, WILL BE (QUE SERA, SERA)**
Doris Day 56

53 **I NEED TO KNOW**
Marc Anthony 99

54 **MY ALL**
Mariah Carey 98

55 **LET'S HEAR IT FOR THE BOY**
Deniece Williams 84

56 **WITHOUT YOU / NEVER FORGET YOU**
Mariah Carey 94

57 **MRS. ROBINSON**
Simon and Garfunkel 68

58 **GONNA MAKE YOU SWEAT**
C + C Music Factory f/Freedom Williams 91

59 **YOU DON'T BRING ME FLOWERS**
Barbra Streisand & Neil Diamond 78

60 **LOSE MY BREATH**
Destiny's Child 04

61 **TURN! TURN! TURN!**
The Byrds 65

62 **ONE MORE TRY**
George Michael 88

63 **EMOTIONS**
Mariah Carey 91

64 **HEARTBREAKER**
Mariah Carey f/Jay-Z 99

65 **WAKE ME UP BEFORE YOU GO-GO**
Wham! 84

66 **DISCO LADY**
Johnnie Taylor 76

67 **DANCING IN THE DARK**
Bruce Springsteen 84

Monterey Pop Festival in 1967 and started to diversify the roster, signing acts like Big Brother & the Holding Company; Blood, Sweat & Tears; and Santana.

Davis resigned in 1975 and became the top executive at Arista. Lieberson returned briefly, but then the stewardship of the label was handed over to Walter Yetnikoff, who would remain at the top through the takeover by Sony.

Columbia's top 100 singles include recordings that span the rock era, from Mitch Miller to Train. Seven of the label's top 100 singles are from 1955–59, starting with "Singing The Blues" by Guy Mitchell at No. 4. There are nine titles from the '60s, including CBS' top single of the decade, Percy Faith's "Theme From 'A Summer Place'" at No. 12. Also representing the '60s are Jimmy Dean, Marty Robbins, Simon and Garfunkel, the Byrds, the Brothers Four, Steve Lawrence, and Gary Puckett & the Union Gap.

There are 13 songs from the '70s included in Columbia's top 100. The label's most successful single of the decade is "Best Of My Love" by the Emotions. Barbra Streisand has four singles from the '70s on the list: themes from the movies *A Star Is Born* and *The Way We Were* and duets with Neil Diamond ("You Don't Bring Me Flowers") and Donna Summer ("No More Tears (Enough Is Enough)").

The '80s are well-represented, with 27 songs. Columbia signed Paul McCartney for North America and he stayed with the label for six years before returning to Capitol. He gave Columbia its top song of the '80s with "Say, Say, Say," a duet with Michael Jackson. McCartney is also in the CBS top 100 with "Ebony And Ivory" and "Coming Up (Live At Glasgow)."

Columbia had a surfeit of hits in the '90s, with 32 titles from that decade in the top 100. An amazing 15 are by Mariah Carey, making her the artist with the most singles on Columbia's top 100. She's at the head of the list with "One Sweet Day," a collaboration with Boyz II Men that had the longest run at No. 1 in the rock era at 16 weeks. Four of Carey's singles are in Columbia's top 10.

There are eight Columbia titles from the '00s in the top 100. The highest-ranked is "Independent Women Part I," the track recorded by Destiny's Child for the *Charlie's Angels* soundtrack. Destiny's Child has seven songs included in Columbia's top 100, and charter member Beyoncé Knowles has five more. The other acts from the '00s are all male: Savage Garden, Crazy Town, Marc Anthony, and Train. Crazy Town's "Butterfly," No. 41 on Columbia's top 100, was originally released in 1999 on the *Gift Of Game album*, even though it didn't reach the top of the Hot 100 until March 2001.

The Top 100 Songs on EPIC

Michael Jackson

COLUMBIA RECORDS announced the formation of a new subsidiary label in June 1953. A story in *Billboard* promised that the Epic label would be "a full-fledged classical line." The story also cited the possibility of some of the pop artists on the Okeh label being transferred over to Epic.

The Okeh label was founded in September 1918 by Otto Heinemann, who incorporated his initials as well as an American Indian word meaning "it is so" into the Okeh name. Heinemann remained president of the label after Columbia Records absorbed Okeh in 1926. Okeh was inactive from 1935 to 1940, when CBS renamed its Vocalion label Okeh.

More details on Epic were forthcoming in the September 19, 1953, issue of *Billboard*. An article headlined "Columbia's Epic to Bow With Classic, Pop Line" announced that the label's initial release would consist of classical LPs featuring the music of composers like Dvorak, Beethoven, Tchaikovsky, Schubert, and Mozart. An EP of tunes from the British cast of *Call Me Madam* was also scheduled, as were EPs of older material from Al Jolson and Artie Shaw. The Epic pop roster was listed, including names like Helene Dixon, Dolores Hawkins, Sandy Stewart, and June Anthony. Dixon and Stewart had already charted on Okeh. Another Okeh artist who joined the label was Roy Hamilton, who gave Epic a No. 21 hit in February 1954, with "You'll Never Walk Alone."

Some executives at Epic felt the label was considered second-class at Columbia Records. "Even here at CBS, we were treated as country cousins," former general manager Al Shulman said in *Billboard* on Epic's 25th anniversary. One problem was that Columbia had its own in-house distribution network, while Epic was handled by independent distributors. "It was tough," Shulman recalled. "We had to deal with indies, versus Columbia's powerhouse sales force."

Shulman helped turn Epic into the major label it became in the '60s. "Just before I left, I wrote a critique of the label, indicating what I thought should be done to make it a viable record making organization. We needed a larger A&R budget . . . and we had to be competitive to bid for talent. We needed a unified sales force. In short, Epic needed to be treated like a company."

In the '50s, Epic made the *Billboard* chart with hits from Somethin' Smith & the Redheads and Sal Mineo. But the label's first artist with staying power was Bobby Vinton, who has five singles included in Epic's top 100. Bobby first recorded in 1960 when Pittsburgh DJ Dick Lawrence told him that End Records was interested in him. He recorded Bobby singing "I Love You The Way You Are," but then took the track to CBS Records. Not wishing to offend an important disc jockey, the label signed Bobby to Epic. "They weren't really interested in my songs or me," Vinton admits. "They just signed me and Lawrence held on to the tape." Vinton's ambition was to be a big-band leader, and he recorded two albums of big-band music that were flops.

At a meeting with Epic executives, Bobby was told he was being dropped from the label. He protested, claiming his contract called for two more recordings. The executives excused themselves to discuss the situation. "They were figuring out how to get rid of me. I saw a pile of records that said, 'reject pile,' and they still weren't back. I noticed the record player was turning so I started to listen to some of the records they were throwing out and all of a sudden I heard, 'Roses are red, my love, violets are blue.' When they came back, they said the band just wasn't making it. I said, 'I can sing a little, and there's a song you're throwing away that really sounds like something I would hear on the radio.'" They agreed to let Bobby record "Roses Are Red (My Love)." He cut it as an R&B song and hated it. He asked to record it again as a country song, and Epic agreed. The single became Epic's first No. 1 hit.

Epic also did well in the '60s with artists from the U.K. Lulu, Donovan, Georgie Fame, and the Hollies all had hits in America on the label. By the end of the decade, Epic's star attraction was Sly & the Family Stone, the San Francisco group that specialized in "psychedelic soul."

Sly & the Family Stone and the Hollies continued to have hits in the '70s as Epic's diverse roster grew to include LaBelle, Cheap Trick, Charlie Rich, Boston, Engelbert Humperdinck, and a former Motown group, the Jacksons.

Michael Jackson outlined his brothers' difficulties with Motown in his *Moonwalker* autobiography: "Our problems with Motown began around 1974, when we told them in no uncertain terms that we wanted to write and produce our own songs. Basically, we didn't like the way our music sounded at the time. We had a strong competitive urge and we felt we were in danger of being eclipsed by other groups who were creating a more contemporary sound." Motown wanted the group to continue using staff writers and producers, which led Michael to tell Berry Gordy that the Jackson Five were moving on.

Ron Alexenburg signed the group to Epic. Jermaine, who had become Berry's son-in-law, stayed behind and was replaced by the youngest Jackson brother, Randy. Motown laid claim to the name Jackson Five, so they called themselves the Jacksons. But Epic didn't give them carte blanche at first; Kenny Gamble and Leon Huff were named to write and produce their first album for their new label. The first track to be issued as a single was "Enjoy Yourself," which went to No. 6. But their next three singles failed to make the top 20. After their second album for the label, Michael and his father, Joe, met with Alexenburg and asked for the creative freedom they had wanted all along. They produced their third Epic album, *Destiny*, which included the top 10 hit "Shake Your Body (Down To The Ground)."

Meanwhile, Michael auditioned for the role of the Scarecrow in the film version of *The Wiz* and won the part. During production, he renewed his acquaintance with Quincy Jones, which led to Quincy producing Michael's first solo LP for Epic, *Off The Wall*. The set yielded two No. 1 singles, "Don't Stop 'Til You Get Enough" and "Rock With You."

Off The Wall sold over 8 million copies, but that was miniscule compared to the sales figures of the follow-up album. With over 40 million copies sold worldwide, *Thriller* remains the best-selling record in history. The first single released was a duet with Paul McCartney, "The Girl Is Mine." It was followed by the longest-running No. 1 single to that date for Epic, "Billie Jean," which remained on top of the Hot 100 for seven weeks.

Almost five years passed before Michael released his next solo album. "We worked on *Bad* for a long time. Years," Michael stated in *Moonwalker*. "There was a lot of tension because we felt we were competing with ourselves. It's very hard to create something when you feel like you're in competition with yourself because no matter how you look at it, people are always going to compare *Bad* to *Thriller*."

Michael racked up five No. 1 singles from *Bad*, beginning with "I Just Can't Stop Loving You." *Dangerous* yielded one chart-topper, "Black Or White." Michael has 13 titles in Epic's top 100, plus three more with the Jacksons.

The artist with the top two Epic songs is actress Jennifer Lopez, who got her big break when she was cast as a "Fly Girl" on the TV series *In Living Color*. In 1993 she won a role in the film *My Family, Mi Familia*, which led to starring in *U-Turn*, *Selena*, and *Out Of Sight*. Even with her success as a film actress, Lopez wanted a singing career. After screening *Selena*, Sony Music chairman Tommy Mottola set up meetings with a number of top record producers for Lopez. Her first No. 1 hit was "If You Had My Love" in 1999. Two years later she recorded her most successful single, "I'm Real," with Ja Rule. They teamed up again for the 2002 single "Ain't It Funny," Lopez' second most successful hit.

The Top 100 Songs on MCA

Olivia Newton-John

M CA RECORDS was created in 1972 to consolidate all of the labels owned by MCA, Inc., into one company. Legendary names like Decca, Brunswick, Coral, and Kapp disappeared, as did the company's youngest label, Uni. MCA Records inherited artists from its family of labels, and the very first single issued with the new logo was "Crocodile Rock" by Elton John, with the catalog number MCA 40000, followed by Ricky Nelson's "Palace Guard," MCA 40001.

The origin of MCA Records can be traced back to August 4, 1934, the day Decca Records was chartered as an American label. The founders were Jack Kapp, E.E. Stevens, Jr., and Milton R. Rackmil from America, and E.R. (Ted) Lewis from England. Lewis, a stockbroker, had formed Decca Records in the U.K. in 1929 by purchasing Barnett Samuel & Son Ltd., a company that manufactured portable gramophones under the name Decca.

Kapp had worked for Columbia Records from 1918–25, then was hired by Brunswick Records, where he became recording manager in 1930. Stevens and Rackmil also worked for Brunswick. On a trip to London, Kapp met with Lewis, who wanted to find an outlet for his product in America. When Columbia Records was up for sale in 1933, Lewis planned to buy it and have Kapp, Stevens, and Rackmil run it. But the deal fell through, and Lewis suggested forming a brand-new company. He wanted to sell records for 35 cents, cheaper than the 75-cent product sold by other companies. It was an excellent idea during the Depression, and helped bring the record industry out of the doldrums.

Now Kapp needed artists. He had worked closely with Bing Crosby at Brunswick, and Crosby had a clause in his contract that allowed him to leave if Kapp did. Bing joined the new company, and the first record issued, Decca 100, was his recording of "I Love You Truly" backed with "Just A-Wearyin' For You." Other Brunswick acts followed, including Guy Lombardo, the Mills Brothers, the Dorsey Brothers Orchestra, and the Boswell Sisters. The roster expanded with the Andrews Sisters, Al Jolson, Judy Garland, and Woody Herman. In 1939, Decca released the soundtrack to *The Wizard Of Oz*.

During the '40s, Ella Fitzgerald, Louis Armstrong, Louis Jordan, and the Ink Spots joined the company. The Coral label was created in November 1948 to sign new artists and compete with independent labels, and the Brunswick name was purchased from Warner Bros. and reactivated as a label. But tragedy struck at the end of the decade—on March 25, 1949, Kapp died of a heart attack at age 47.

Rackmil succeeded him as president and in the summer of 1951 oversaw the purchase of 26 percent of the outstanding stock of Universal Pictures Company, Inc. Universal had been founded in 1912 by Carl Laemmle as an amalgamation of several corporations. On March 15, 1915, the gates to Universal City Studios were opened in the San Fernando Valley. By 1954, Decca owned 72.5 percent of the stock. Rackmil became president of Universal, and the marriage of the two companies had immediate benefits: Decca released the soundtrack of Universal's *The Glenn Miller Story*.

Under Rackmil, Universal gradually stopped making "B" pictures and placed an emphasis on making fewer but better films. In 1962, Universal became a subsidiary of the Music Corporation of America, a talent-booking agency founded by Jules Stein before World War II.

Jack Kapp's brother, Dave, continued managing A&R for the company after his brother's death, but later left to head A&R for RCA. In 1955, he formed his own label. Kapp Records had a No. 1 single in its first year of operation with Roger Williams' "Autumn Leaves," the label's most successful chart single. The rest of Kapp's top 10: "Gypsys, Tramps & Thieves" by Cher; "Hello, Dolly!" by Louis Armstrong; "Our Day Will Come" by Ruby & the Romantics; "Midnight In Moscow" by Kenny Ball & His Jazzmen; "Love Potion Number Nine" by the Searchers; "Fascination" by Jane Morgan; "Rainbow" by Russ Hamilton; "Sailor (Your Home Is The Sea)" by Lolita; and "Born Free" by Roger Williams. Kapp also had chart hits from Jack Jones, the Critters, Jerry Keller, and Joe Harnell. Kapp sold his label to MCA in 1967; the only Kapp artist who continued to have hits on MCA was Cher.

In the '50s, the Coral and Brunswick labels were headed by Bob Thiele (who later married one of Coral's leading artists, Teresa Brewer). When Decca Records allowed its contract with an unknown singer named Buddy Holly to lapse, Thiele signed him and his band, the Crickets. "That'll Be The Day," originally recorded but unreleased by Decca, was a No. 1 single on Brunswick. Coral's most successful chart single is "Tammy" by Debbie Reynolds.

Olivia Newton-John and Elton John, two artists inherited from Uni, are responsible for more than 25 percent of MCA's top 100. Olivia has 11 singles on the list, and Elton has 16. Olivia left MCA and recorded an album of lullabies and children's songs for Geffen, then returned via the label's Nashville office. Elton also left for Geffen, but it proved to be a hiatus—he returned to MCA in 1987.

MCA bought ABC Records in 1979, bringing the Dot and Dunhill catalogs to Universal City. Steely Dan and Jimmy Buffett, clients of Irving Azoff signed to ABC, were transferred to MCA. In 1983, Azoff himself moved to the label by becoming its new president. It was a dramatic shot in the arm for the record company. By 1985, MCA's gross revenues had more than tripled over the 1982 figures.

Azoff started by trimming the roster—from 46 acts down to five, according to Fredric Dannen in *Hit Men.* On July 8, 1989, MCA and the I.R.S. label, which it distributed, had the No. 1 single on the Hot 100 ("Good Thing" by the Fine Young Cannibals), as well as the top three albums on *Billboard*'s LP chart.

Azoff built MCA back up by giving it a strong R&B base. Patti LaBelle joined the company and had a No. 1 duet with Michael McDonald. Jody Watley, formerly of Shalamar, had solo success on MCA. Ready for the World, a sextet from Flint, Michigan, was signed to MCA by Jheryl Busby and went to No. 1 with "Oh Sheila." And the members of New Edition proved to be a real bonanza. All teenagers when they signed with the label in 1983, the group itself only had two top 10 singles in the '80s, "Cool It Now" and "If It Isn't Love." Lead singer Bobby Brown left the group in 1986 for a solo career and scored with a succession of top 10 singles; he has eight titles in MCA's top 100. Ricky Bell, Michael Bivins, and Ronald DeVoe of the group formed an extracurricular trio, Bell Biv DeVoe. Their first two singles ("Poison" and "Do Me!") are in MCA's top 40. Two other group members, Johnny Gill and Ralph Tresvant, also developed successful solo careers.

Azoff, who became president of the MCA Music Entertainment Group, also brought Motown under MCA's distribution wing. In June 1988, MCA and an outside investment group, Boston Ventures, purchased Motown for $61 million.

In August 1988, Azoff brought in Al Teller, former president of CBS Records, to be president of the MCA label. Azoff left the company on September 5, 1989, to head up Giant Records, a new label financed by Warner Bros.

In December 1990, the Matsushita Electric Industrial Co. of Japan agreed to buy MCA Inc. for $6.13 billion, the largest purchase by a Japanese company in the United States. The Canadian liquor distributor Seagram became the new owner in 1995, paying a sum of $5.7 billion and changing the corporate name to Universal. In 2000, Seagram sold Universal to the French company, Vivendi, for $34 billion.

Patsy Cline

DECCA FIELDED a strong artist roster in the first half of the '50s, dominating the country chart with Red Foley, Webb Pierce, and Kitty Wells, also remaining strong on the pop chart with Kitty Kallen, the Mills Brothers, and the Four Aces. The label's presence on the R&B chart diminished after the death of founder Jack Kapp in 1949, but in the '40s, Decca had performed well with Louis Jordan, Buddy Johnson, and Lionel Hampton.

Milt Gabler, the man in charge of finding new talent for Decca, had been brought into the company in 1941 by Kapp. Gabler had been running his own label, Commodore, with an artist roster that included Billie Holiday and Jelly Roll Morton. At Decca, he was in charge of producing records for Jordan as well as the Ink Spots, Louis Armstrong, Ella Fitzgerald, Burl Ives, the Weavers, and Guy Lombardo, among others.

Gabler knew that rock and roll was the next big thing, so he gladly made an appointment with songwriter/music publisher Jim Myers to meet Bill Haley, who had been recording for the Essex label in Philadelphia. Myers and Max Freedman had written a song for Haley to record at Essex, but label owner Dave Miller disliked Myers and refused to let Haley record "(We're Gonna) Rock Around The Clock."

Gabler signed Haley instantly and took him into Decca's Pythian Temple recording studio in New York City on April 12, 1954. Two songs were recorded that day, "Thirteen Women" and "Rock Around The Clock." Released as a single, the latter title entered the *Billboard* chart on May 29 and peaked at No. 23. It sold well enough for Gabler to pick up Haley's option and record a follow-up. Haley selected "Shake, Rattle And Roll," an R&B hit by Joe Turner. It sold a million copies and went to No. 7.

With the Comets, Haley had two more hits: "Dim, Dim The Lights" and "Mambo Rock." But Myers hadn't given up on "Rock Around The Clock." He sent copies to everyone he could think of in Hollywood. When the producers of *Blackboard Jungle* used the song to open their film, there were riots in movie theaters. Decca re-serviced the single and it went to No. 1 on July 9, 1955. Historians mark that date as the beginning of the rock era.

Decca continued to have chart hits in the latter half of the '50s with their pop artists. The Four Aces recorded the title song from the film *Love Is A Many Splendored Thing*. The Tommy Dorsey Orchestra, Victor Young, Elmer Bernstein, and Sammy Davis, Jr., all had hits on the label.

In 1956 Decca signed an 11-year-old singer from Atlanta, Georgia. Brenda Lee was appearing on Peanut Faircloth's TV show in Augusta when Decca recording artist Red Foley and his manager, Dub Albritton, passed through town. Faircloth insisted they come and listen to Brenda sing. Foley and Albritton were impressed enough to have her open for Foley and appear on his ABC-TV series, *Ozark Jubilee*.

Albritton brought Brenda to Decca. On July 30, 1956, she recorded two sides for her first single, "Jambalaya" and "Bigelow 6-200." By 1959 she still hadn't reached the upper portion of the Hot 100, so Albritton took her to Europe and then South America. Rave notices and international acclaim finally paid off at home: in April 1960, Brenda had her first top 10 hit, "Sweet Nothin's." The follow-up was "I'm Sorry," but Decca was reluctant to let a 15-year-old sing about unrequited love. The ballad sat on a shelf for several months until it was released and became her first No. 1 single. By the middle of 1963, Brenda had racked up 12 top 10 hits. Decca rewarded her in July of that year with a 20-year contract guaranteeing her $35,000 per year and a two-picture deal with Universal.

During the British invasion, Decca had one major U.K. group, the Who. Originally signed with Brunswick in Great Britain, the Who remained with Decca in America despite litigation with Brunswick and a shift to Robert Stigwood's Reaction label.

The last single to be a hit on Decca was Dobie Gray's "Drift Away" in May 1973. Then Gray and Decca artists like Rick Nelson and the Who were moved to MCA, which replaced all of the company's labels, including Coral, Brunswick, and Uni. The Decca logo, dating back to 1934, disappeared for 21 years until MCA revived it as a Nashville-based country imprint in 1994.

The Top 20 Songs on UNI

UNI RECORDS was a subsidiary of MCA, the parent company of Universal. MCA was already operating its Decca and Brunswick subsidiaries when it started a newer, hipper imprint with psychedelic colors on the label. Russ Regan was national promotion director, and after the label's first seven months of operations, he was named general manager.

The first record Regan bought was the Strawberry Alarm Clock's "Incense And Peppermints," which turned out to be Uni's third-most-successful chart hit. "I bought it for $2,500 in August—by November 18, it was a No. 1 record," Regan recalls.

Regan traded the U.K. rights to "Incense And Peppermints" to Pye Records in Britain in exchange for the American rights to "Baby, Now That I've Found You" by the Foundations. Their third U.S. single, "Build Me Up Buttercup," is Uni's fourth biggest record.

Under Regan's administration, Uni signed three major artists: Neil Diamond, Elton John, and Olivia Newton-John.

Diamond had been signed to Bang Records with a "main man" clause; when the head of the label, Bert Berns, passed away, Diamond was a free agent. "We went after him and got him," Regan reports. "We were very fortunate. He's one of the great talents. I was very honest with him; we had a great working relationship. I played devil's advocate and he trusted my ears. If I felt something wasn't up to snuff, I would tell him."

Regan was also responsible for signing Elton John to Uni. "I was at the Continental Hyatt House [on the Sunset Strip] in those days. A friend of mine named Lenny Hodes walked in; he was working for Dick James at the time."

James was a music publisher who started the Page One and DJM labels in the United Kingdom. Elton was signed to DJM. Hodes told Regan that five companies had already turned Elton down for the States, but he was a great talent, and Hodes wanted Regan to listen to *Empty Sky.* "I said if five companies have turned him down, he can't be much." Regan listened to the album that afternoon, and ended up signing Elton John to Uni.

Olivia Newton-John had her first two singles released on Uni; neither was a big hit. Her first top 10 single was "Let Me Be There," released on MCA.

Uni was reactivated briefly in 1988. The Scottish quartet Wet Wet Wet went to No. 58 on the Hot 100 with "Wishing I Was Lucky." The label had two more chart singles—"Tell That Girl To Shut Up" by Transvision Vamp and "Love Train" by Holly Johnson—before the logo was quietly retired for a second time.

Neil Diamond

01 **SONG SUNG BLUE**
Neil Diamond 72
02 **CRACKLIN' ROSIE**
Neil Diamond 70
03 **INCENSE AND PEPPERMINTS**
Strawberry Alarm Clock 67
04 **BUILD ME UP BUTTERCUP**
The Foundations 69
05 **GRAZING IN THE GRASS**
Hugh Masekela 68
06 **GYPSY WOMAN**
Brian Hyland 70
07 **SWEET CAROLINE (GOOD TIMES NEVER SEEMED SO GOOD)**
Neil Diamond 69
08 **HOLLY HOLY**
Neil Diamond 69
09 **YOUR SONG**
Elton John 71
10 **I AM...I SAID**
Neil Diamond 71
11 **ROCKET MAN**
Elton John 72
12 **BABY, NOW THAT I'VE FOUND YOU**
The Foundations 68
13 **ISRAELITES**
Desmond Dekker & the Aces 69
14 **WALK ON WATER**
Neil Diamond 72
15 **PLAY ME**
Neil Diamond 72
16 **HONKY CAT**
Elton John 72
17 **WALKIN' IN THE RAIN WITH THE ONE I LOVE**
Love Unlimited 72
18 **STONES**
Neil Diamond 71
19 **HE AIN'T HEAVY, HE'S MY BROTHER**
Neil Diamond 70
20 **BROTHER LOVE'S TRAVELLING SALVATION SHOW**
Neil Diamond 69

The Top 100 Songs on MERCURY

The Platters

MERCURY RECORDS was established in Chicago in 1946. The independent company had hits in 1947 with Frankie Laine's "That's My Desire," which peaked at No. 4, and Vic Damone's "I Have But One Heart," which went to No. 7. A year later, the label added another star to its roster—Patti Page.

Mitch Miller headed up pop A&R from 1948 to 1950 before moving to Columbia. Eventually Laine, Damone, and Page would all follow him to CBS. Mercury's initial success in the rock era came from having white singers cover songs originally recorded by black artists. The Crew-Cuts had a No. 1 record in 1954 by covering the Chords' "Sh-Boom," and the practice continued with Georgia Gibbs, who had pop hits with LaVern Baker's "Tweedle Dee" and Etta James' "The Wallflower" (which became "Dance With Me Henry"). The Diamonds spent eight weeks at No. 2 with a cover of the Gladiolas' "Little Darlin'," Mercury's fourth most successful chart single of the rock era.

In the early part of 1955, the Penguins, a Los Angeles doo-wop group, had a top 10 single with "Earth Angel (Will You Be Mine)." Mercury wanted to sign them away from the DooTone label, and their manager Buck Ram agreed on one condition: Mercury also had to sign his other group, the Platters. John Sippel, a West Coast executive for Mercury, urged his superiors in Chicago to take both groups. The Penguins never had a chart single on Mercury and left in 1956 for Atlantic, but the Platters hit instantly and became the most popular vocal group of their day.

The Platters' first Mercury single was a reworking of an earlier release on Federal, "Only You (And You Alone)." It was issued on a purple Mercury label, indicating it was an R&B song. Ram insisted that the Platters were a pop group, so the single was reissued on the standard black Mercury label. "Only You" peaked at No. 5 and was followed by "The Great Pretender," which went to No. 2 on the Best Sellers chart. The Platters have 10 singles on Mercury's top 100; three of them are in the top 10.

In 1959, Brook Benton had his first hit on Mercury, "It's Just A Matter Of Time." Benton had recorded for Okeh, Epic, and Vik before a fateful appointment at Meridian Music introduced him to Clyde Otis. Benton and Otis wrote "Looking Back," a No. 5 song for Nat King Cole in 1958, and "A Lover's Question," a No. 7 hit for Clyde McPhatter at the beginning of 1957. The following year, Mercury A&R executive Art Talmadge went to New York and asked Otis to head the creative department of Mercury's office there. "Up to that time, no black had enjoyed both administrative and creative responsibilities—only creative," Otis told Colin Escott. "I said I wanted both. Art wasn't prepared to offer that and went back to Chicago. Finally, the president of Mercury, Irving Green, offered me both." Atlantic Records wanted to sign Benton, but Otis grabbed him for Mercury. The association lasted through 1965.

Shelby Singleton headed up A&R in the South and brought artists like Johnny Preston and the Big Bopper to the label, giving Mercury hits like "Running Bear" and "Chantilly Lace." In 1959, Mercury created a subsidiary label, Smash, and Singleton was responsible for signing the artists that gave Smash its first two No. 1 singles—Joe Dowell ("Wooden Heart") and Bruce Channel ("Hey! Baby").

In 1962, Mercury Records was sold to the Dutch multinational company Philips and became part of PolyGram, which had been formed by a merger of Philips' Phonogram Records division and the German company Polydor/Deutsche Grammophon. The Philips label was introduced in the U.S., followed later by the Fontana subsidiary. Green remained head of the company in Chicago, and one of his most important moves was bringing in Quincy Jones to head up the A&R department. In the first half of the '60s, Jones gave the label a run of hits by producing Lesley Gore.

In the latter half of the '60s, Mercury had chart singles by the Blues Magoos, Manfred Mann, and Keith. Jerry Butler began a run of hits in 1967, but the label's overall chart share was relatively insignificant. Gene Chandler and Daniel Boone had hits in the early '70s, and Rod Stewart gave the label its first No. 1 single in eight years with "Maggie May" and its flip side, "Reason To Believe." In the last half of the '70s, Mercury had a chart presence again with Bachman-Turner Overdrive, 10cc, and the Ohio Players.

Mercury's revitalization in the '80s was due to a combination of British and heavy-metal artists. Dexys Midnight Runners were signed to Phonogram in the U.K., and their "Come On Eileen" went to No. 1 in Britain as well as America. The British duo Tears For Fears, who signed with Mercury in the U.K. in 1982, had two No. 1 hits in the U.S. in 1985: "Everybody Wants To Rule The World" and "Shout." Martin Fry's ABC appeared on their own Neutron label at home in Britain; their American hits on Mercury included "The Look Of Love (Part One)," "Be Near Me," and "When Smokey Sings."

Mercury's most successful British heavy-metal band signed with Phonogram in the U.K. in 1979. Def Leppard formed in Sheffield in 1977 and had their first album released on the Vertigo subsidiary in November of 1979. Their real breakthrough came with the 1983 album *Pyromania,* which gave them a No. 12 single in the U.S., "Photograph." An automobile accident in which drummer Rick Allen lost his left arm resulted in a four-year delay between albums. When *Hysteria* was released in 1987, the group was poised for megastardom—"Pour Some Sugar On Me" went to No. 2 on the Hot 100, followed by the chart-topping "Love Bites." The title track and "Armageddon It" were also hits. In all, there are seven Def Leppard tracks on Mercury's top 100.

Mercury's other heavy-metal band proved even more successful. Bon Jovi and lead singer Jon Bon Jovi have 12 singles on Mercury's top 100. John Bongiovi formed his first band, Atlantic City Expressway, when he was in high school. His cousin Tony ran the Power Station recording studio in New York, home to Aerosmith, the Ramones, and the Talking Heads. Jon (he dropped the "h") worked there for two years as a gofer, and was allowed to record in the studio during off-hours. His song "Runaway" was included on radio station WAPP's *Homegrown* album and received some airplay around the country. He put together a band, and Derek Shulman signed them to Mercury. So that people would connect them with the "Runaway'" track, they anglicized Jon's last name as the group name.

Bon Jovi's first two albums were mildly successful. But it wasn't until their third release, *Slippery When Wet,* that the band achieved multi-platinum status. The first single from *Slippery When Wet,* "You Give Love A Bad Name," went to No. 1 in November 1986. Three months later, the follow-up single, "Livin' On A Prayer," also went to No. 1. Bon Jovi's next album, *New Jersey,* produced a bumper crop of hit singles: "Bad Medicine" and "I'll Be There For You" both went to No. 1, and three other songs made the top 10.

A&R executive Steve Greenberg signed the three Hanson brothers to the label. Their 1997 hit "MMMBop" would have been the label's top single of the '90s, if it hadn't been for the overwhelming crossover success of Shania Twain's "You're Still The One," Mercury's top-ranked title.

The Top 30 Songs on PHILIPS

N.V. PHILIPS GLOEILAMPENFABRIEKEN is the complete name of the Dutch manufacturer of audio equipment. Philips was also well known as a classical record label, part of the company's Phonogram record division. In 1962, the Dutch company merged with Polydor/Deutsche Grammophon, a Germany company that dated back to 1898. The merger of Phonogram and Polydor resulted in a new corporate name, PolyGram.

The Philips logo was seen in the U.K. on hits by the Springfields, the folk trio that included Dusty Springfield and her brother Tom. PolyGram purchased the Chicago-based Mercury Records in 1962, and that year, the Philips label appeared in America as a subsidiary of Mercury. The Springfields had a top 20 hit in 1962 with "Silver Threads And Golden Needles." The following year, Philips had two No. 1 hits in the U.S. First came "Hey Paula" by Paul and Paula, produced by Major Bill Smith. He had produced "Hey! Baby" by Bruce Channel, a No. 1 hit on Mercury's Smash imprint 11 months earlier. Smith issued "Hey Paula" on his own LeCam label, and it sold so well in Atlanta that Shelby Singleton of Mercury Records picked it up for the new Philips label. In December of '63, Philips had its second No. 1 in America with a song that was recorded under the auspices of the label's Brussels office. Sister Luc-Gabrielle and a friend had approached Philips about making a non-commercial recording of compositions they sang at their evening retreats at Fichermont Monastery. The result was so commercial that Philips released an album by *Soeur Sourire* throughout Europe. In America, the album was released under the name "The Singing Nun," but sales were sluggish until "Dominique" was released as a single.

While Philips also had a run of hits with Dusty Springfield, the label's primary source of record sales came from the Four Seasons. The New Jersey quartet signed with the label after a year of hits on Vee Jay. Unhappy with that label's accounting practices, the group looked for a better deal and found it with Philips. Sixteen of the label's top 30 songs are by the group or lead singer Frankie Valli.

Philips' most successful chart single is the instrumental "Love Is Blue," recorded in France by Paul Mauriat. It was just one of many cover versions included in his *Blooming Hits* album, alongside "Penny Lane," "This Is My Song," and "Somethin' Stupid." Written as "L'amour Est Bleu," the song was Luxembourg's entry in the 1967 Eurovision Song Contest. Vicky Leandros sang it in competition, and it only placed fourth. She recorded the song in 19 languages—but it took Mauriat's instrumental version to make "Love Is Blue" a worldwide hit.

01 **LOVE IS BLUE**
Paul Mauriat 68

02 **DOMINIQUE**
The Singing Nun 63

03 **HEY PAULA**
Paul and Paula 63

04 **RAG DOLL**
The Four Seasons 64

05 **CAN'T TAKE MY EYES OFF YOU**
Frankie Valli 67

06 **DAWN (GO AWAY)**
The Four Seasons 64

07 **LET'S HANG ON**
The Four Seasons 65

08 **SUNNY**
Bobby Hebb 66

09 **YOU DON'T HAVE TO SAY YOU LOVE ME**
Dusty Springfield 66

10 **WISHIN' AND HOPIN'**
Dusty Springfield 64

11 **HOW DO YOU DO?**
Mouth And Macneal 72

12 **DON'T LET THE RAIN COME DOWN (CROOKED LITTLE MAN)**
The Serendipity Singers 64

13 **RONNIE**
The Four Seasons 64

14 **YOUNG LOVERS**
Paul and Paula 63

15 **I'VE GOT YOU UNDER MY SKIN**
The Four Seasons 66

16 **SUMMERTIME BLUES**
Blue Cheer 68

17 **I ONLY WANT TO BE WITH YOU**
Dusty Springfield 64

18 **C'MON MARIANNE**
The Four Seasons 67

19 **TELL IT TO THE RAIN**
The Four Seasons 67

20 **WORKING MY WAY BACK TO YOU**
The Four Seasons 66

21 **DON'T THINK TWICE**
The Wonder Who? 65

22 **BEGGIN'**
The Four Seasons 67

23 **OPUS 17 (DON'T YOU WORRY 'BOUT ME)**
The Four Seasons 66

24 **SAVE IT FOR ME**
The Four Seasons 64

25 **BYE, BYE, BABY (BABY, GOODBYE)**
The Four Seasons 65

26 **BIG MAN IN TOWN**
The Four Seasons 64

27 **THE JOKER WENT WILD**
Brian Hyland 66

28 **WILL YOU LOVE ME TOMORROW**
The Four Seasons 68

29 **I MAKE A FOOL OF MYSELF**
Frankie Valli 67

30 **THE BOY NEXT DOOR**
The Secrets 63

The Top 100 Songs on MGM

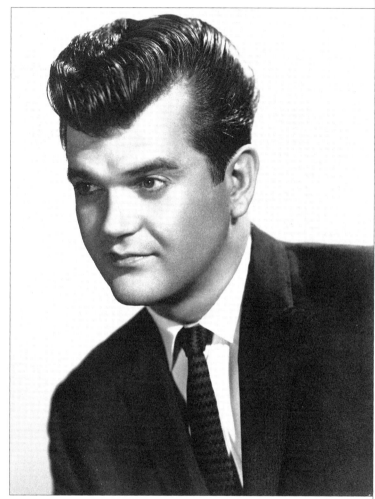

Conway Twitty

A LABEL CALLED Metro-Goldwyn-Mayer existed in 1928. The lion logo and *ars gratia artis* inscription were part of the label design, but the records were pressed by Columbia. MGM Records was founded in 1946 by the motion picture company, primarily to issue film soundtracks of MGM musicals and other theatrical releases. In 1947, the label made its mark on the country charts with one of the most influential artists of all time, Hank Williams. His first massive hit was "Lovesick Blues," which topped the country Best Sellers chart for 16 weeks. MGM Records also made an impact on the R&B chart with Billy Eckstine (11 titles between 1948 and 1952) and Ivory Joe Hunter (four titles in 1950). Tommy Edwards first made the pop chart in 1951, the same year Debbie Reynolds and

Carleton Carpenter had a top three hit with "Aba Daba Honeymoon" from the soundtrack of the film *Two Weeks In Love.*

While MGM had some success in the early years of the rock era with hits like Joni James' "You Are My Love" and Dick Hyman's "Moritat (A Theme From *The Three Penny Opera*)," the real breakthrough came in 1958 with a hat trick of No. 1 singles from Tommy Edwards, Conway Twitty, and Sheb Wooley, plus the chart debut of Connie Francis.

Tommy Edwards' first recording of "It's All In The Game" peaked at No. 18 in 1951. Seven years later, as Tommy was about to be dropped from the MGM artist roster, label executive Morty Craft asked him to re-record the song in stereo. The original arrangement was abandoned in favor of a rock and roll ballad; the single spent six weeks at No. 1, and became the most successful MGM chart single of the rock era. "It's All In The Game" was knocked off the top of the chart by Conway Twitty's "It's Only Make Believe," the label's fourth most successful chart single.

Connie Francis was 16 years old when she began recording demos for music publishers. One of them put up $5,000 for her to have her own recording session. She was turned down by a number of labels, including Columbia, before Harry Myerson signed her to MGM. According to Francis, Myerson was interested because she had recorded a "dippy" song titled "Freddy," which happened to be the name of Myerson's son. "He thought it would be a cute birthday present," she explains. MGM released 10 singles on Connie without having any hits. The label lost interest in her and she was working on her final recording session when her father suggested she record a standard from 1923, "Who's Sorry Now." Francis has 20 singles on the MGM top 100, including the label's fifth most successful title of the rock era, "My Heart Has A Mind Of Its Own."

While artists like Connie Francis saw their chart fortunes diminish during the British invasion, MGM performed strongly on the Hot 100 with two groups from the U.K.—Herman's Hermits and the Animals, both managed by Mickie Most. The Hermits, fronted by Peter Noone, were signed to EMI's Columbia label in the U.K. Their initial success in the States came with their first MGM single, a cover version of Earl-Jean's "I'm Into Something Good," written by Gerry Goffin and Carole King. The group formed in Manchester, England, as the Cyclones, and changed their name to the Heartbeats. Peter Noone joined the band in 1963 as lead vocalist. Bassist Karl Green pointed out Noone's resemblance to the cartoon character Sherman in the "Mr. Peabody" segments of TV's *The Bullwinkle Show,* so the group was renamed Herman and the Hermits, later altered to Herman's Hermits.

Eric Burdon joined the Newcastle-based Alan Price Combo in 1962, forming the group that would change their name to the Animals a year later. Producer Most recorded a four-track EP with the group and got them a gig as the opening act for Chuck Berry on his U.K. tour. To provide some contrast to Berry's music, they included the bluesy "House Of The Rising Sun" in their act. After Most signed the Animals to EMI's Columbia label, they traveled to London via British Rail and recorded the song in two takes. It ran over four minutes, and Columbia was reluctant to release it as a single, but Most convinced the label it would be a hit.

In 1969, MGM Records was revitalized by a new president. Studio head Jim Aubrey asked Mike Curb to merge his Curb Records with the MGM label and take charge of the new MGM Records. A week before he joined the company, Curb saw Burdon perform with the R&B band War. "When I got to MGM I found out there was no contract and they had new management, so I signed them," Curb recalls. A single was released. "The B-side was 'Spill The Wine,'" Curb confesses. "We flipped it after radio told us. I'm embarrassed to say I didn't know it was on there. I felt the other track was a hit."

Curb had already signed the Osmonds to Curb when the labels merged. "They hadn't hit yet. Right after we made the arrangement with MGM, our second single was 'One Bad Apple,' which was recorded in Muscle Shoals, Alabama. The idea was to use the Jackson 5 sound. We changed the name Osmond Brothers to the Osmonds. Everyone thought they were a black group—before that, everyone thought they were a barbershop quartet."

Curb recorded Donny Osmond as a solo artist. His first hit was a remake of an obscure Roy Orbison song, "Sweet And Innocent." The follow-up was a remake of Steve Lawrence's "Go Away Little Girl," Curb's second most successful chart single from his MGM tenure. He explains: "Most of the remakes were things I did. I've been a student of trivia . . . most of the things we brought back were songs that weren't closely identified with the artist." Curb followed that trend with the next Osmond to record solo: sister Marie. "Sonny James came up with the idea of recording 'Paper Roses,'" according to Curb. "I called Sonny and said I'd like to break Marie country and Sonny said she should do 'Paper Roses.'" The song, a No. 5 hit for Anita Bryant in 1960, also went to No. 5 for Marie. Counting all of the singles recorded by different members of the Osmond family, they are responsible for 20 of the top 100 MGM titles, the same number as Connie Francis.

The third biggest single of the Curb administration was "The Candy Man" by Sammy Davis, Jr. "We had a hit record with the Mike Curb Congregation's 'Burning Bridges' from the picture *Kelly's Heroes*," the former president remembers. "I recorded 'The Candy Man' to be a follow-up to that and released it on MGM and it wasn't breaking. So I asked Sammy to overdub his voice over the track of the Mike Curb Congregation and he gave me one of those looks that only Sammy can give you, but I convinced him to do it on the basis that we would try to make it like Frank Sinatra's 'High Hopes,' which had featured Sinatra with kids." Davis recorded the song in one take and was mixed in with the voices of the Mike Curb Congregation. His single spent three weeks at No. 1.

During the years Curb headed MGM, he also signed Jim Stafford and Gloria Gaynor. But the label's identity disappeared after it was purchased by PolyGram. The artists on the roster were moved over to the Polydor label and the lion logo was reserved for an occasional soundtrack before finally being put to rest. Curb, who would be elected lieutenant governor of California in 1978, took his label affiliation to Warner Bros. and had hits on Warner/Curb with Debby Boone, among others.

The Top 100 Songs on MOTOWN

Lionel Richie

BERRY GORDY had no interest in working in either of his father's businesses, printing or construction. He loved to listen to the radio and won first prize in a Detroit talent show by writing a song, "Berry's Boogie." He also had a passion for boxing, and after 15 amateur fights, dropped out of high school to turn pro. During his amateur career, he met a Golden Gloves champ named Jackie Wilson.

After a two-year army stint, Berry married and went to work in both of his father's businesses. In the summer of 1953, with a $700 loan from his father and his discharge pay from the army, he opened the 3-D Record Mart, a store specializing in jazz. He was bankrupt in two years and went to work in a Ford assembly plant.

Two of his sisters, Anna and Gwen, were employed at the Flame Show Bar, where one night in 1957, Berry found out that talent manager Al Greene was looking for songs for an old acquaintance of Berry's—Jackie Wilson. With Gwen's friend Billy Davis (who used the name Tyran Carlo), Gordy wrote "Reet Petite," Wilson's first Hot 100 single. Over a two-year period, Wilson recorded several songs written by Gordy and Davis, including "To Be Loved," "Lonely Teardrops," and "That's Why (I Love You So)."

In 1958, Anna and Gwen Gordy, along with Billy Davis, formed their own record company, distributed by Chess. Among the artists signed to Anna were David Ruffin, Johnny Bristol, Lamont Dozier, and Marvin Gaye (who worked as a session musician but never released anything on the label). Meanwhile, Smokey Robinson shared Berry Gordy's frustration in the agonizingly slow way they received royalties from other companies, and urged him to start his own business like Anna and Gwen had. With an $800 loan from his family, Berry took Smokey's advice and formed not only his own record company, but also a publishing firm (Jobete) and a talent agency to manage his artists. The Motown Record Corporation's first label was named Tammy after the Debbie Reynolds movie, but was changed for legal reasons to Tamla.

The company's first single was released in January 1959. "Come To Me" by Marv Johnson was issued locally in Detroit as Tamla 101, but for national distribution, Gordy leased the track to United Artists. Another single, "Money" by Barrett Strong, was also issued locally on Tamla but leased to Anna.

Then Berry decided to stop leasing his masters to other companies. Beginning with a Miracles single, "The Feeling Is So Fine," Tamla became a national label. That single was quickly withdrawn, however, in favor of "Way Over There," released in July 1960. Three months later, Berry took a song Smokey had written for Barrett Strong and recorded it with the Miracles. "Shop Around" became the company's first major hit.

With employees settled in at the Hitsville offices, located at 2648 West Grand Boulevard in Detroit, the roster of artists, producers, writers, and session players grew at a rapid rate. In September 1961, a second label was added: Motown's first release was "My Beloved" by the Satintones. The Temptations, who had recorded for the short-lived Miracle subsidiary in July 1961, were the first artists released on the Gordy label when "Dream Come True" was issued in March 1962. The Soul label was initiated in March 1964, with Shorty Long's "Devil With The Blue Dress." Motown had a number of other labels over the years, including V.I.P., Mowest, Prodigal, Chisa (for jazz), Melodyland and Hitsville (for country), and Rare Earth (for rock).

The company earned its first No. 1 single on the Hot 100 in December 1961, with "Please Mr. Postman" by the Marvelettes, five young girls from the suburb of Inkster, Michigan.

The drummer on "Please Mr. Postman" was 22-year-old Marvin Gaye. As a member of the Marquees, he was invited to join Harvey Fuqua in a revamped version of the Moonglows. When Fuqua went to work for Anna Records, he brought Gaye with him. Gordy first heard Gaye sing at a party in a Detroit nightclub. In May 1961, Gaye's first single, "Let Your Conscience Be Your Guide," was released; Marvin later referred to it as one of Gordy's rare "lemons."

Mary Wells originally wanted to meet Berry Gordy because she had written a song she thought Jackie Wilson should record. Gordy said she should cut "Bye Bye Baby" herself and signed her. Wells was thrilled to be in the same company as the Miracles and the Marvelettes, but was disappointed to find out her records would not be issued on the famous Tamla label—instead, she was relegated to Berry's new label, Motown. Teamed up with writer/producer Smokey Robinson, she had a series of top 10 singles, topped by the first No. 1 single on the Motown label itself, "My Guy."

The Temptations were created by a merger of two groups, the Primes and the Distants. They were to be called the Elgins until Motown employee Bill Mitchell came up with the name Temptations. Their initial success

33 **STOP! IN THE NAME OF LOVE**
The Supremes *Motown* 65

34 **THE LOVE YOU SAVE**
Jackson 5 *Motown* 70

35 **SOMEDAY WE'LL BE TOGETHER**
Diana Ross & the Supremes *Motown* 69

36 **WATER RUNS DRY**
Boyz II Men *Motown* 95

37 **STILL**
Commodores *Motown* 79

38 **KEEP ON TRUCKIN' (PART 1)**
Eddie Kendricks *Tamla* 73

39 **SIR DUKE**
Stevie Wonder *Tamla* 77

40 **TRULY**
Lionel Richie *Motown* 82

41 **MY GUY**
Mary Wells *Motown* 64

42 **DON'T LEAVE ME THIS WAY**
Thelma Houston *Tamla* 77

43 **IN THE STILL OF THE NITE (I'LL REMEMBER)**
Boyz II Men *Motown* 93

44 **YOU CAN'T HURRY LOVE**
The Supremes *Motown* 66

45 **GOT TO GIVE IT UP (PT. 1)**
Marvin Gaye *Tamla* 77

46 **REACH OUT I'LL BE THERE**
Four Tops *Motown* 66

47 **LOVE HANGOVER**
Diana Ross *Motown* 76

48 **I CAN'T GET NEXT TO YOU**
The Temptations *Motown* 69

49 **SUPERSTITION**
Stevie Wonder *Tamla* 73

50 **SOMEBODY'S WATCHING ME**
Rockwell *Motown* 84

51 **NEVER CAN SAY GOODBYE**
Jackson 5 *Motown* 71

52 **PART-TIME LOVER**
Stevie Wonder *Tamla* 85

53 **PLEASE MR. POSTMAN**
The Marvelettes *Tamla* 61

54 **I HEAR A SYMPHONY**
The Supremes *Motown* 65

55 **I WISH** Stevie Wonder *Tamla* 77

56 **LOVE MACHINE (PART 1)**
The Miracles *Tamla* 76

57 **DANCING MACHINE**
Jackson 5 *Motown* 74

58 **TOUCH ME IN THE MORNING**
Diana Ross *Motown* 73

59 **I HEARD IT THROUGH THE GRAPEVINE**
Gladys Knight & the Pips *Soul* 67

60 **FOR ONCE IN MY LIFE**
Stevie Wonder *Tamla* 68

61 **DO YOU LOVE ME**
The Contours *Gordy* 62

62 **YOU HAVEN'T DONE NOTHIN'**
Stevie Wonder *Tamla* 74

63 **WHAT'S GOING ON**
Marvin Gaye *Tamla* 71

64 **THEME FROM "MAHOGANY" (DO YOU KNOW WHERE YOU'RE GOING TO)**
Diana Ross *Motown* 76

65 **MY GIRL**
The Temptations *Gordy* 65

66 **LOVE IS HERE AND NOW YOU'RE GONE**
The Supremes *Motown* 67

also came with a Smokey Robinson song, "The Way You Do The Things You Do" in 1964. A year later, they went to No. 1 with Smokey's "My Girl."

The Primes' sister group, the Primettes, also had a change of name. Diana Ross and Mary Wilson were shocked to find out Florence Ballard had picked "The Supremes" from a list of possibilities because they thought it sounded too masculine. The group's first two singles, "I Want A Guy" and "Buttered Popcorn," were issued on Tamla. They moved over to Motown with "Your Heart Belongs To Me," but they didn't become household names until they recorded "Where Did Our Love Go" in 1964 and began their run of five No. 1 singles, all written and produced by Holland, Dozier, and Holland.

Stevie Wonder came to the company through Ronnie White of the Miracles, who introduced him to Brian Holland. Berry Gordy was in the middle of a steak dinner when Holland called and told him he had to sign the 11-year-old genius. "Fingertips—Pt 2" was Tamla's second chart-topping single.

The Four Aims became the Four Tops and recorded for Chess and Columbia before signing to a relatively unknown Motown subsidiary, Workshop. In 1964, they recorded Holland-Dozier-Holland's "Baby I Need Your Loving," the first of a series of hits released on the Motown label. Motown secretary Martha Reeves had her first recording session when Mary Wells missed an appointment in the studio. "Come And Get These Memories" was the first Martha & the Vandellas hit in 1963.

Motown's first No. 1 single of the '70s was "I Want You Back" by the Jackson 5. By the end of the decade, the label's leading attraction was the group that had opened for the Jackson 5 on their 1971 tour—the Commodores.

In June 1988, Berry Gordy sold Motown to MCA and an outside investment group, Boston Ventures, for $61 million. Jheryl Busby, who had been the president of black music at MCA, was named the new president of Motown. Under his administration, the Michael Bivins–managed group Boyz II Men were signed to the label. They blended their Philly roots with the Motown sound and gave the label its most successful chart single, "I'll Make Love To You." In 1993 Motown was sold again, to PolyGram. When Universal purchased PolyGram in 1998, Motown and MCA were once again under the same corporate roof.

The Top 100 Songs on RCA

Kelly Clarkson

MILE BERLINER built a gramophone machine in 1887 and invented the flat, laterally recorded disc, as opposed to the cylinder phonograph of Thomas Edison. Eldridge R. Johnson designed the first spring-driven gramophone, and in 1901—with Berliner's blessing—incorporated the Victor Talking Machine Company of Camden, New Jersey.

Berliner sold the European rights to his invention to a group of English investors, who formed the Gramophone Company in 1898. While visiting London, Berliner saw a painting by Francis Barraud titled *His Master's Voice*. It depicted Barraud's dog Nipper listening to a phonograph machine. The Gramophone Company had bought the painting and its copyright for £100, and Berliner asked permission to use the painting as a trademark in the U.S.

The Victor company had the first million-selling record, "Vesti La Giubba" from *Pagliacci* by Italian tenor Enrico Caruso, released in 1904. The company's Red Seal label specialized in classical music. Victor also recorded every U.S. President, from Theodore Roosevelt to Warren G. Harding. Billy Murray and Ada Jones, two of the most popular vocalists of the first quarter of the 20th century, recorded for Victor. The label also issued recordings of Broadway musicals, dance bands, marching bands, and jazz.

Eldridge Johnson sold his company to a banking firm on December 7, 1926. On January 4, 1929, the bankers resold Victor to the Radio Corporation of America, the company founded by David Sarnoff. Record sales dropped dramatically after the Wall Street crash in October of that year, and the factory in Camden was converted to manufacture radios. "It looked like records were going out of style altogether—the 1930 catalog was a tiny little thing," explains Chic Crumpacker, a music historian who joined RCA in 1953. "The Depression made people return to records because they couldn't afford to go to movies or plays or shows. They could buy a 35- or 50-cent record. And by the mid- to late '30s, the catalog was back up to snuff." Helping RCA Victor survive the Depression were artists like Benny Goodman, Glenn Miller, Tommy Dorsey, and Fats Waller.

By the end of World War II, the popularity of big bands began to fade in favor of crooners like Frank Sinatra and Dinah Shore, who were signed to Columbia. By the time Crumpacker became the manager of country and western promotion for RCA, the label had a strong roster of artists that included Eddy Arnold, Hank Snow, and Chet Atkins.

RCA was doing well in the pop department, too, with Perry Como being the standard-bearer for that section of the label. Como signed with RCA on June 17, 1943. His first single was "Goodbye, Sue." He had eight No. 1 singles between 1945 and 1954, and another, "Round And Round," in 1957. "Joe Carlton, head of the pop A&R department, favored Como with the very best songs that came in," says Crumpacker.

RCA was an early entrant in the rhythm and blues field. Arthur "Big Boy" Crudup appeared on the R&B charts with singles issued on the Bluebird subsidiary in 1945. He later wrote "That's Alright Mama" and was cited by Elvis Presley as being a major influence. Another subsidiary label, Groove, specialized in R&B, and in 1951, RCA cut some sides on Little Richard. They were in a big-band R&B style, and were more blues-oriented than Little Richard's later Specialty singles.

In 1955, Crumpacker was directly involved in the signing of the artist who would insure RCA's fortunes for years to come. "I was the first New York home office person to see and meet Elvis. I brought some of the Sun records back to Steve Sholes, who was head of C&W Artists and Repertoires. He had heard through field reports about this guy. But he had been in the business for a long time and wasn't falling for anything that might be transient, a 'flash in the pan.' But a lot of people, including myself, said we didn't think this was the case. The guy was simply dynamite in front of an audience. And his records were very mesmerizing—the Sun records." Crumpacker suggested Sholes make an offer to buy Elvis' contract.

"Which he did—to his credit. He offered Sam Phillips $25,000 for Presley's contract. That was, I think, a record for RCA at the time in the country field. The bad news was that Mercury Records came in with a higher offer, and suddenly it looked like we'd lost the ball game. But Sholes persevered—he went back to Phillips and said, '$40,000, but that's it.' And the deal was made. When I met Elvis at the annual Disc Jockey Convention in Nashville in November he said, 'Hey, it looks like I'm going to be with you guys.' In another few days, he was."

According to Crumpacker, there was resistance from the pop side of the label to push Elvis' career. "[A&R chief Jack] Carlton detested rock music. When he left in '57 and Sholes took his place, he founded his own label, Carlton, which had nothing but the most old-line pop recordings. Anita Bryant was one of his artists. That was indicative of the way he felt about rock. So everybody felt Elvis would last 15 minutes."

The list of RCA's most successful chart singles is dominated by Elvis. He occupies six places in the top 10, all with singles from the years 1956–57. He has 23 titles listed in the top 100. But Elvis wasn't RCA's only success story. The label's pop division continued to flourish in the opening years of the rock era with Kay Starr (signed from Capitol), the Ames Brothers, Harry Belafonte, the Browns, Eddie Fisher, and a young song-writer from Brooklyn who joined the label in 1958—Neil Sedaka.

RCA sat out the British invasion of 1964. The label's artist roster was all-American—Henry Mancini, Skeeter Davis, Little Peggy March, Jim Reeves, Floyd Cramer, the Tokens—and the arrival of the Fab Four didn't change that. One of RCA's most successful post-Beatles single of the '60s is as American as one could get: "The Ballad Of The Green Berets" by S/Sgt. Barry Sadler.

RCA's most popular artist on the *Billboard* singles chart during the '70s was John Denver, who has five singles listed on the label's top 100. He originally recorded for Mercury during his three-year tenure with the Chad Mitchell Trio. His first album for RCA as a solo artist, *Rhymes And Reasons,* included his song "Leaving On A Jet Plane," which was covered by Peter, Paul and Mary. In 1974, Denver had the first of four No. 1 singles, "Sunshine On My Shoulders."

Next to Elvis Presley, the act with the most titles on RCA's top 100 is Daryl Hall and John Oates. Originally signed to Atlantic, they failed to chart with their first album, *Whole Oats.* Their next two LPs were released in 1974. *Abandoned Luncheonette* peaked at No. 33, but manager Tommy Mottola felt the album was full of hit songs and should have been more successful. *War Babies,* more experimental than the duo's earlier work, ran out of steam at No. 86. Atlantic wasn't too pleased with the album, giving Mottola a chance to shop the duo to another label. RCA signed up Hall and Oates and released a top five single in 1976, "Sara Smile." The following year, they hit No. 1 with "Rich Girl."

The RCA record label was just one subsidiary of its parent company, which also included the NBC Television Network and a giant electronics manufacturing division. The entire company was purchased by General Electric in December 1985. That marked the beginning of the end for RCA as a corporate entity. GE was not interested in running a record company. Thorn-EMI of Great Britain bid for the label, but the Bertelsmann Music Group of Germany already had an interest in RCA, and purchased the rest.

The Top 100 Songs on
WARNER BROS.

Red Hot Chili Peppers

WARNER BROS.' first attempt at running a record label took place in April 1930, when the film studio purchased the American branch of Brunswick Records. Many of the stars under contract to the movie company recorded for Brunswick, including Gloria Swanson, Noah Beery, Harry Richman, and Al Jolson. During this period, Brunswick also signed Bing Crosby, the Mills Brothers, and the Boswell Sisters. But the Depression affected record sales, and the financial burden was too much to bear. In December 1931, Warner Bros. sold Brunswick to the American Record Corporation, and eventually the label came under the jurisdiction of Decca and MCA.

In 1958, Jack Warner once again wanted the studio to have its own record company. He was tired of seeing some of Warner's best motion picture soundtracks sell well for other labels, like MGM and 20th Century Fox. He hired Jim Conkling away from Columbia Records, and with a $3-million investment, Warner Bros. Records opened offices above the studio's machine shop on March 19, 1958. The label began with a middle-of-the-road slant and a release of 12 albums, all in stereo.

But there were no hits. It took just over a year to have initial success on the Hot 100. The first Warner Bros. single to make the top 10 was "Kookie, Kookie (Lend Me Your Comb)" by Edd Byrnes (listed as Edward on the label) and Connie Stevens. Byrnes played Kookie on the studio's popular television series *77 Sunset Strip,* and sang his hit in the first episode of the second season. Stevens starred as Cricket Blake in another Warner Bros. TV series, *Hawaiian Eye*; during that show's first season, Stevens had a No. 3 single of her own, "Sixteen Reasons," the label's second top 10 hit.

Despite the success of Byrnes' single, the label was $3 million in debt by December 1959. Two months later, the staff had been trimmed and the label completely reorganized. On February 17, 1960, Warner Bros. made a major investment by signing the Everly Brothers away from Cadence Records. The 10-year contract was worth $1 million to Don and Phil, who were then under pressure from the label to come up with a hit single. They didn't like the first eight songs they wrote, and finally recorded "Cathy's Clown," Warner Bros.' first No. 1 single.

Mike Maitland from Capitol Records was appointed the new president of Warner Bros. Records in 1961. He brought in a KFWB disc jockey and part-time promotion man to supervise the label's promotion department. Joe Smith turned down the job at first, but was eventually persuaded by Maitland to join the company.

The February 3, 1962, issue of *Billboard* announced that folk trio Peter, Paul & Mary had signed with Warner Bros. In 1963, the threesome had two consecutive singles peak at No. 2 on the Hot 100: "Puff The Magic Dragon" and "Blowin' In The Wind." In 1965, the label had another No. 1 single with a track leased from Pye Records in Britain—Petula Clark's "Downtown." Warner Bros. bought the Valiant label, bringing the Association to the company and netting another No. 1 song, "Windy." The next year, Warner Bros. acquired the Autumn label in San Francisco, and three new acts joined the roster: the Beau Brummels, the Mojo Men, and the Tikis. The Tikis changed their name to Harpers Bizarre. Lenny Waronker, who went on to become the chairman of Warner Bros. Records, produced their single "The 59th Street Bridge Song (Feelin' Groovy)"; group member Ted Templeman joined the company as a staff producer.

Jack Warner sold Warner Bros. to Seven Arts, a production and distribution company owned by Elliot Hyman, in 1967. The deal included the motion picture arm and the record label, and the company was renamed Warner Bros.-Seven Arts. Under this new banner, Warner Bros. purchased Atlantic Records. By 1969, the roster of artists included Van Morrison, Alice Cooper, the Grateful Dead, and—from Apple Records—James Taylor. Seven Arts became debt-laden and was in turn acquired by Kinney National Services. Kinney was run by Steve Ross, who had built a family business in funeral parlors into a company that owned car-rental agencies, parking lots, and the Ashley Famous Talent Agency. In 1971, the Kinney name was dropped from the parent company in favor of Warner Communications. Maitland left the company in 1970. Mo Ostin, who had headed the Reprise subsidiary, was named chairman of the board, and Joe Smith became president of Warner Bros. Records. At the same time, the

Warner-Elektra-Atlantic distribution system was set up, bringing the three companies together on the wholesale level.

In the first half of the '70s, Warner Bros. had consistent hitmakers in Seals and Crofts, America, and the Doobie Brothers.

Dewey Bunnell, Gerry Beckley, and Dan Peek were all sons of American servicemen stationed in the U.K. They formed a quintet called Daze and when the other two members left, they stayed together as an acoustic trio called America. Promoter Jeff Dexter introduced them to Ian Samwell, a staff producer at the London office of Warner Bros. Samwell outbid Atlantic and DJM to sign up America, whose biggest hit was "A Horse With No Name" in 1972.

The Doobie Brothers formed in San Jose, California, in March 1970, as a group called Pud. They signed with Warner Bros. the following year, and their first album was produced by Waronker and Templeman. The Doobie Brothers' biggest hit was "What A Fool Believes," featuring Michael McDonald on lead vocals.

Debby Boone was signed by Mike Curb and appeared on the Warner/Curb label, as did Exile, Shaun Cassidy, and the Four Seasons. "You Light Up My Life" was No. 1 for 10 weeks, but was Boone's only single to make the upper portion of the Hot 100. Rod Stewart, signed away from Mercury Records in December 1974, turned out to be a consistent hitmaker for the Warner Bros. label. Rod has had 11 top 10 singles on Warner Bros., the most successful being "Tonight's The Night (Gonna Be Alright)."

Prince has the sixth most successful chart single on Warner Bros. with the first 45 from *Purple Rain,* "When Doves Cry." The label signed the musician from Minneapolis when he was just 18, agreeing that he could produce his own albums. For several years he had his own custom label, the Warner-distributed Paisley Park, with a roster that included Sheila E. and the Family. However, he did return briefly to Warner Bros. in 1989 to release the singles from his *Batman* soundtrack.

The 12th most successful Warner Bros. single is by a band known for performing sans clothing, save for strategically placed socks over their genitalia. The Southern California–based Red Hot Chili Peppers were signed to EMI for eight years, but their 1991 Warner album debut, *Blood Sugar Sex Magik,* brought them new critical praise and their first platinum award from the RIAA, selling more than three million copies. The single "Under The Bridge" was written by lead vocalist Anthony Kiedis near the end of his heroin addiction. "Deep inside, it expresses the same sense of loneliness that everyone feels at one time or another," he told Bruce Britt of the Los Angeles *Daily News.* "When you're desperate, there's a desire to get to something warm and comfortable. I think the song gives off that type of energy."

The Kinks

FRANK SINATRA quit his job as a sports writer for the *New Jersey Observer* after attending a Bing Crosby concert. Signed to Tommy Dorsey's orchestra, he had the top song ("I'll Never Smile Again") on the first singles chart ever published by *Billboard.*

By the end of the 1950s, though, Sinatra was unhappy at Capitol Records and wanted to leave. Not just for another company—he wanted to create his own record label, having also recorded for RCA Victor (with the Tommy Dorsey Orchestra) and Columbia. His contract with Capitol ran through 1962, but the label agreed to let him go if he would record four more albums for them. Sinatra asked a former controller at Verve Records, Mo Ostin, to run his new company as executive vice president. One day, while walking past the Capitol tower on Vine Street in Hollywood, Sinatra said to Ostin, "I helped build that. Now I'm going to build one of my own."

Offices were opened on Melrose Avenue, above a carpet warehouse. At first the roster consisted of Sinatra's friends—Sammy Davis, Jr., Dean Martin, and Rosemary Clooney. But despite a top 20 single for Sammy ("What Kind Of Fool Am I") and a top three hit by Lou Monte ("Pepino The Italian Mouse"), the label did not get off to a good start. By the end of 1962, the company was $2 million in debt. In June 1963, Sinatra's attorney, Mickey Rudin, approached Jack Warner about buying Reprise. Warner wanted Sinatra to make films for the studio, and a deal was struck. Warner Bros. would buy two-thirds interest in Reprise for $10 million; Sinatra would retain one-third interest and make three movies.

Ostin relocated Reprise to the Burbank offices of Warner Bros. and the merged company became known as Warner-Reprise. The same deal that brought Petula Clark to Warner Bros. from Britain's Pye label gave Reprise access to the Kinks, who debuted in America in 1964 with "You Really Got Me." That same year, Dean Martin gave the label its biggest hit to date with a song previously recorded by Sinatra, "Everybody Loves Somebody." Sinatra continued to record for the label and achieved his own No. 1 hit, "Strangers In The Night," in 1966. His daughter Nancy was also signed to Reprise.

"I wasn't really interested in a career," Nancy told Todd Everett. "I was a happily married young woman, who wanted to be a good wife and raise a family. But when I told my father that I thought I could make a hit record, he said, 'Try it.'" Nancy approached Disney's musical director, Tutti Camarata, and told him she wanted to cut the kind of material that Annette Funicello was recording. "Like I Do" was a hit in other countries but not at home. More singles were produced by Camarata, Don Costa, and Jimmy Bowen. "By the end of my first contract, my records weren't selling as well. . . . I reminded Jimmy [Bowen], who was head of A&R at Reprise, that if my next single wasn't something very important, the label was going to drop me." Producer Lee Hazlewood asked Ostin and Bowen to give Nancy another chance and recorded three tracks, including "So Long Babe." That was Nancy's first chart single in America.

Nancy wanted to follow up "So Long Babe" with a song she heard that had been written for a man to sing, but Hazlewood argued against it. Her father agreed that the song about the boots would be a hit. A year after "These Boots Are Made For Walkin'" was No. 1, Nancy recorded a duet with Frank. "We cut 'Somethin' Stupid' at the end of a session that Dad was cutting with Antonio Carlos Jobim," Nancy told Everett. "We moved those musicians out, and mine in. We recorded the song in two takes." Ostin was in the studio and bet Sinatra two dollars that the song would not make the top 10. The check arrived already framed.

In 1976, the Reprise label was deactivated and most of the artists on the roster, like Fleetwood Mac and Gordon Lightfoot, were moved over to Warner Bros. The name was kept alive by Neil Young, who continued to have his albums released on Reprise. The label was brought back to life in 1987, as new artists were signed and some Warner Bros. artists were reassigned to Reprise; among them were Roger (Troutman) and Chicago. The most successful Reprise single is Eric Clapton's "Tears In Heaven" from the *Rush* soundtrack. The quiet, emotional ballad was written by Clapton and lyricist Will Jennings after Clapton's four-year-old son Conor fell to his death in New York City.

The highest-ranked song on the list of the top 50 Reprise hits is by a band that released its first album on the label in 1994 but didn't appear on the Hot 100 until 10 years later. Green Day's songs performed well on the Modern Rock Tracks chart but weren't released as commercial singles, so were not eligible for the Hot 100. The advent of the digital download age changed the rules, and "Boulevard Of Broken Dreams" spent five weeks at No. 2.

The Top 30 Songs on SIRE

Madonna

AT THE age of 13, Seymour Stein paid a visit to Tommy Noonan, then head of the *Billboard* charts and research department, and asked permission to copy down in longhand the pop, R&B, and country singles charts every week back to the year he was born. Two years later, the project was completed, and when he was 16, the boy with encyclopedic knowledge of the record industry was hired by Noonan to work in the chart department.

Stein left *Billboard* to work for Syd Nathan at King Records, then moved on to Red Bird, where his duties included chaperoning the Shangri-Las. After a stint as an independent promotion man, he formed Sire Productions with record producer Richard Gottehrer (of the Strangeloves) in 1966. Sire signed a distribution deal with Warner Bros. in 1976. In 1978, Stein sold half of his company to Warner Bros.; two years later, he sold the other half.

Sire's top 30 chart hits include songs by the Pretenders, Soft Cell, the Climax Blues Band, the Talking Heads, Tommy Page, and the woman who kept the Sire imprint at the top of the chart—Madonna.

Stein first heard a demo tape from Madonna when he was recovering from endocarditis in the hospital. He listened to the song "Everybody" and told his assistant, Michael Rosenblatt, that he wanted to sign Madonna—right then and there. Stein asked for a new robe to be brought from home while Madonna was on her way to the hospital. "The minute she walked in the room, I knew," Stein said in *Rolling Stone*. "I just sensed that there was something there. I just wanted to rush right in and do a deal."

Queen

J AC HOLZMAN was a student at St. John's College in Annapolis, Maryland, when he started Elektra Records in October 1950, with $600 from his bar mitzvah money and $600 borrowed from a friend.

Holzman was equally fascinated with audio engineering and music, and in December 1950, he approached composer John Gruen and soprano Georgiana Bannister about recording their campus recital. The result was catalog number Elektra 101; although a few hundred copies were pressed, Holzman couldn't sell any of them.

The second Elektra release was an album of Appalachian mountain ballads. For its first five years of existence the label released about 30 albums, none of which cost more than $45 to produce. Holzman paid the bills by doing hi-fi installations. The turning point came in 1955 when Holzman signed Josh White and Theodore Bikel. The label concentrated on folk music for the rest of the decade. "I expected the folk revival," Holzman told Lenny Kaye. "You could see it begin to happen in the festivals; it was easy music to make, friendly, collegiate."

The artist roster grew with the addition of Tom Paxton, Phil Ochs, Tom Rush, and Judy Collins, whose contemporary folk rendition of Joni Mitchell's "Both Sides Now" was a top 10 hit in December 1968.

It was a small step from folk to folk-rock, but Holzman was cautious and a subsidiary label, Bounty, was created to house acts like the Beefeaters—who would later sign to Columbia Records as the Byrds. Paul Butterfield, who participated in the *What's Shakin'* electric-guitar anthology

01 **ANOTHER ONE BITES THE DUST**
   Queen 80
02 **TWISTED**
   Keith Sweat 96
03 **CRAZY LITTLE THING CALLED LOVE**
   Queen 80
04 **GIVE ME ONE REASON**
   Tracy Chapman 96
05 **YOU'RE SO VAIN**
   Carly Simon 73
06 **LIGHT MY FIRE**
   The Doors 67
07 **NOBODY**
   Keith Sweat 96
08 **I LOVE A RAINY NIGHT**
   Eddie Rabbitt 81
09 **SEMI-CHARMED LIFE**
   Third Eye Blind 97
10 **MAKE IT WITH YOU**
   Bread 70
11 **BOHEMIAN RHAPSODY**
   Queen 76
12 **THEME FROM "GREATEST AMERICAN HERO" (BELIEVE IT OR NOT)**
   Joey Scarbury 81
13 **JUST THE TWO OF US**
   Grover Washington, Jr. w/Bill Withers 81
14 **HELLO, I LOVE YOU**
   The Doors 68
15 **IT'S BEEN AWHILE**
   Staind 01
16 **NOBODY DOES IT BETTER**
   Carly Simon 77

album, was the first electric artist signed to the acoustic label. Elektra immersed itself in rock and roll after Holzman met Arthur Lee at the Bito Lito club in Los Angeles. His group, Love, was signed to the label, and so was another Los Angeles club group—the Doors. Paul Rothchild, who joined the label in 1963, saw the Doors at the Whisky A Go-Go on the Sunset Strip and wanted to produce an album that would serve as an "aural commentary" on their live act. "Light My Fire" became Elektra's first No. 1 single.

In July 1970, Holzman sold his independent company to the Kinney National Services Corporation, then the parent company of Warner Bros. The label continued to flourish with Bread, Carly Simon, and Harry Chapin, but Holzman felt like he was repeating himself and took an extended sabbatical in Hawaii.

David Geffen, founder of Asylum Records, was hired to run the company in 1973. He brought Asylum with him from Atlantic, another label under the Kinney banner, to form Elektra-Asylum. Two years later, he was named vice chairman of Warner Bros. Pictures and Joe Smith took the label's helm. Under Smith's leadership, Elektra was well represented on the Hot 100 with the Cars, Eddie Rabbitt, and Queen.

The Cars were formed by Ric Ocasek and Ben Orr. They met in Columbus, Ohio, and had three earlier bands together before the Cars. Along with Greg Hawkes, Elliot Easton, and drummer David Robinson, Ocasek and Orr made their first appearance as the Cars at Pease Air Force Base in New Hampshire on New Year's Eve, 1976. Two Boston radio stations popularized their demo tape of "Just What I Needed," which landed them a contract with Elektra.

Eddie Rabbitt, raised in East Orange, New Jersey, wrote his first published song while soaking in a bath in a Nashville hotel. "Working My Way Up To The Bottom" was recorded by Roy Drusky. Elvis Presley cut his "Kentucky Rain" in 1970, which led artists like Ronnie Milsap, Tom Jones, and Dr. Hook to cover Rabbitt's material. Elektra signed him in 1974.

The label's top single is by Queen. Originally formed in 1971 in Middlesex, England, the band had its first American chart single with "Killer Queen" in 1975. "Crazy Little Thing Called Love" was a No. 2 hit in Britain before it was released in the States. "We all felt it was a hit, except Elektra, who didn't want to release it," the late Freddie Mercury once explained. Radio stations started playing import copies, which "forced the single," according to Mercury. The follow-up, "Play The Game," peaked at No. 42. Michael Jackson urged Freddie to have "Another One Bites The Dust" released as the next single. It remains Elektra's best-performing chart entry.

The Top 30 Songs on ASYLUM

The Eagles

A FTER WORKING as an usher at CBS and as a receptionist for a TV production company, 20-year-old David Geffen was hired to work in the mailroom of the William Morris agency in New York. He worked for William Morris until he was 23, then moved to the Ashley Famous agency. After hearing a tape of Laura Nyro he took her on as a client and made a deal with Clive Davis to sign her to Columbia. Then Geffen opened his own agency with Elliott Roberts, and in 1969 sold Nyro's publishing company to Columbia for $4.5 million worth of CBS stock, splitting the proceeds with her 50-50. That same year, he engineered the deal that put Crosby, Stills and Nash on Atlantic.

Geffen's next two clients were Joni Mitchell and Jackson Browne. Mitchell was recording for Reprise and Browne needed a record deal. Geffen approached Ahmet Ertegun at Atlantic, but he wasn't interested. Geffen was inspired to start his own label. He convinced Atlantic to finance Asylum Records for three years in return for a share of the profits. In the second year of the deal he released product by Linda Ronstadt, Jackson Browne, the Eagles, and Joni Mitchell.

Two years into the Atlantic deal, Warner Communications chairman Steve Ross told Geffen to name a price for his label. Within 24 hours, Geffen sold Asylum for $5 million in Warner stock and $2 million cash. Elektra Records' Jac Holzman stepped down in 1973, and Warner was willing to merge Elektra and Asylum with Geffen overseeing both labels.

In 1975, Geffen was given another promotion: he was named vice chairman of Warner Bros. Pictures.

Whitesnake

AFTER A year as vice chairman of Warner Bros. Pictures, David Geffen left the job. "I had to deal with bureaucracy and politics," he said in *Time.* "It just didn't work." Soon after leaving the post, he was diagnosed with cancer of the bladder. He spent the next four years collecting art and teaching at UCLA and Yale. Then he was told the original diagnosis had been incorrect. The tumor thought to be malignant had actually been benign, and there was no cancer. He took a trip to Barbados with Paul Simon and television producer Lorne Michaels and was advised to begin again in a field he already knew well: the record industry. Two days later, Warner Communications CEO Steve Ross agreed to finance a new record company headed by Geffen.

The label had no name when Geffen announced its creation in the May 15, 1980, issue of *Rolling Stone.* "I'm going to have a specialized, small record company," Geffen said in an article. "I think we'll be attractive both to established artists and new ones. . . . I think that I have a long history of being involved with the most creative, intelligent, and productive artists, and I believe people will be attracted to what that's all about."

In mid-June, Geffen announced his first signing for his new label, which still didn't have a name. He paid $1.5 million for Donna Summer, who was suing her former company, Casablanca. Geffen said in an August 7, 1980, *Rolling Stone* news story, "Before I had announced the label, Donna called up and said, 'I hear you're starting a record company. Would you be interested in me?' And you know, of course, I thought it was a fake." The same article mentioned rumors of Geffen signing Jackson Browne,

Elton John, Joni Mitchell, and Neil Young. With the exception of Browne, he signed them all.

Elton was the second artist signed to the label, finally named after its founder. Then Yoko Ono called and Geffen had his third artist: John Lennon was ready to come out of retirement. "(Just Like) Starting Over" became a posthumous No. 1 song and Geffen's most successful chart single.

Geffen stepped back from the day-to-day duties of running a record company. "I started to feel I was getting too old to go to clubs and hang out with teenagers and find music for their generation—I was no longer of their generation," Geffen said in *Forbes*. He relied on label president Ed Rosenblatt to helm the company and John Kalodner, Gary Gersh, and Tom Zutaut to run the A&R department. Kalodner signed Aerosmith and thought Cher was ready to return to the charts; Zutaut brought in Guns N' Roses. Geffen wasn't completely removed from the process, however. He managed to sign Peter Gabriel and Ric Ocasek of the Cars.

The company also made major investments in Broadway musicals, including *Dreamgirls, Cats,* and *Miss Saigon,* and did the same with motion pictures like *Risky Business, After Hours,* and *Beetlejuice.*

In 1989, Time-Life and Warner merged into one company. *Forbes* reported that in addition to Steve Ross making $100 million in the deal, people like Steven Spielberg, Clint Eastwood, and Barbra Streisand received generous stock options. "One of the things that really offended me was when I found out he had given these friends of his these stock options," Geffen said in *Forbes*. "Steve always told me that when the company got sold, he would buy my record company and I would be there for the ride. . . . But in the end no one thought that I should be included in the benefits from the success of the company." With his distribution agreement with Time Warner set to expire at the end of 1990, Geffen sold his record company in March of that same year. He spurned bids from Time Warner and Thorn EMI in favor of a deal with MCA that paid him $545 million in stock and gave him a 12 percent stake in MCA.

The deal became even sweeter eight months later when MCA was sold to Matsushita Electric Industrial Co. of Japan for $6.6 billion—Geffen netted $710 million from the deal. "It was smart to sell to MCA, but it was lucky that the Japanese bought it eight months later," Geffen said in *Vanity Fair*. "I had nothing whatever to do with it. The focus is only on me because I was the major beneficiary financially."

Danny and the Juniors

B ACK IN the early days of broadcasting, all three of America's television networks were affiliated with record labels. Columbia Records was owned by the Columbia Broadcasting System; RCA was a subsidiary of the Radio Corporation of America, as was NBC; and ABC-Paramount Records shared the same parent company as ABC-TV, American Broadcasting-Paramount Theaters, Inc.

The impending creation of the ABC-Paramount label was first announced in the February 5, 1955, issue of *Billboard*. Datelined Hollywood, the story reported the parent company was planning a division expected to enter the record market.

By November, the label was a reality. Sam Clark was the president and Don Costa was director of A&R. *Billboard* reported that the label's initial single was a "dramatic rush affair." Eydie Gorme recorded a cover of Bubber Johnson's R&B song "Come Home" on October 20, and it was in the hands of disc jockeys four days later. ABC wanted the pop hit on Johnson's song, but they needn't have hurried—it didn't chart, although Gorme did have a run of chart singles on the label. Husband Steve

Lawrence had top 10 hits on ABC with "Pretty Blue Eyes" and "Footsteps."

ABC-Paramount's first No. 1 hit was by a 15-year-old boy from Ottawa in Ontario, Canada. Paul Anka had spent the summer in Los Angeles when he was 13 and dropped by the offices of Modern Records in Culver City. He recorded a single for them, but it didn't make it, and he returned home to Ottawa. The following summer, he won a Campbell's Soup contest; the prize was a train trip to Manhattan. He loved the city, and later borrowed $100 from his father to return with four new songs. The first person he went to see was Costa, who was so impressed with "Diana" that he told Paul to have his parents come to New York immediately so they could sign contracts. Anka, who has seven singles listed in ABC's top 50, left the label in 1962 for RCA.

Four months after "Diana" was No. 1, ABC-Paramount was back on top of the *Billboard* chart with the first chart entry from a Philadelphia quartet, Danny & the Juniors. Their song was originally written as "Do The Bop," but Dick Clark told the group that bop was passé, and suggested changing it to "At The Hop." It was good advice: the song is the label's most successful chart single.

In 1959, ABC-Paramount scored a coup by signing Ray Charles away from Atlantic Records. The artist told Ahmet Ertegun about ABC's generous offer, but Atlantic couldn't match it. Working with Sid Feller of ABC's A&R department, Charles first recorded for the label on December 29, 1959. There are five Ray Charles singles on the ABC top 50, including the label's second most successful chart song, "I Can't Stop Loving You."

Feller also worked with Lloyd Price, who had a No. 1 hit with "Stagger Lee." Other artists who recorded for ABC-Paramount included the Impressions, George Hamilton IV, Tommy Roe, and Brian Hyland.

The label's name was shortened to ABC in 1966. In its final decade, the label had a roster that included Jim Croce, B.J. Thomas, Bo Donaldson & the Heywoods, and two acts managed by Irving Azoff—Steely Dan and Jimmy Buffett. The label also purchased the masters of Dot Records from Gulf + Western, and issued recordings by Freddy Fender and Donna Fargo on ABC/Dot.

The demise of ABC Records came suddenly on March 5, 1979, when all 300 employees were dismissed. A month before, MCA had purchased the company for a reported price of $20 million. *Rolling Stone* reported that ABC staffers had been told up to the "very last minute" that the ABC label would remain autonomous from MCA. Instead, the roster was pared down, and those acts invited to remain were shifted to the MCA label. Regarding the future of his two ABC acts, Azoff was quoted, "We'll have to wait and see, but anything's better than ABC." John Hartmann, manager of Poco, said he had been dealing "with a lack of corporate commitment." He reported that ABC refused to give Poco a $17,000 advance to support a tour. Bob Siner, president of MCA Records at the time, advanced the amount by 10 A.M. on March 5, the day Poco became an MCA act.

31 ON AND ON
Stephen Bishop *ABC* 77
32 MARGARITAVILLE
Jimmy Buffett *ABC* 77
33 IT'S TIME TO CRY
Paul Anka *ABC-Paramount* 59
34 IT'S ALL RIGHT
The Impressions *ABC-Paramount* 63
35 SWEET THING
Rufus f/Chaka Khan *ABC* 76
36 BORN TOO LATE
The Poni-Tails *ABC-Paramount* 58
37 WASTED DAYS AND WASTED NIGHTS
Freddy Fender *ABC/Dot* 75
38 GIRL WATCHER
The O'Kaysions *ABC* 68
39 RIKKI DON'T LOSE THAT NUMBER
Steely Dan *ABC* 74
40 REELING IN THE YEARS
Steely Dan *ABC* 73
41 I GOT A NAME
Jim Croce *ABC* 73
42 YOU DON'T KNOW ME
Ray Charles *ABC-Paramount* 62
43 DO IT AGAIN
Steely Dan *ABC* 73
44 WHY DON'T THEY UNDERSTAND
George Hamilton IV *ABC-Paramount* 58
45 HOORAY FOR HAZEL
Tommy Roe *ABC* 66
46 YOU GOT THE LOVE
Rufus f/Chaka Khan *ABC* 74
47 I'LL HAVE TO SAY I LOVE YOU IN A SONG
Jim Croce *ABC* 74
48 CRAZY LOVE / LET THE BELLS KEEP RINGING
Paul Anka *ABC-Paramount* 58
49 (ALL OF A SUDDEN) MY HEART SINGS
Paul Anka *ABC-Paramount* 59
50 SWEET PEA
Tommy Roe *ABC-Paramount* 66

Chubby Checker

ONGWRITERS Kal Mann and Bernie Lowe formed the Cameo label in Philadelphia at the end of 1956. Their first signing was a 20-year-old local singer who had starred in a 13-week TV series on a Pittsburgh station. Charlie Gracie sounded enough like Elvis to record Mann and Lowe's Presley-styled "Butterfly." Andy Williams released a cover version on Cadence, but Gracie had the bigger chart hit.

The company made the top 40 with comedian Timmie Rogers' "Back To School Again," but the imprint's next major hit was licensed from another label. The Rays had already recorded for Chess when they signed with Frank Slay's XYZ Records. Cameo licensed the doo-wop classic "Silhouettes," the Rays' only top 40 single.

In 1958, Cameo scored with singles by John Zacherle and Dave Appell's Applejacks. Zacherle, known as the "Cool Ghoul," hosted horror movies on WCAU-TV in Philadelphia. Appell was one of the label's most important signings, as he went on to write hits for the artists who would form the Cameo label's foundation in the early '60s.

Lowe and Mann expanded the company in 1959 by adding a second label, Parkway. Two important artists had their first chart entries that year — Robert Ridarelli and Ernest Evans. Ridarelli was in a band called Rocco & the Saints with Frankie Avalon. His first two singles—"Please Don't Be Mad" and "All I Want Is You"—failed to chart, but by the time "Kissin' Time" entered the Hot 100 in June, everyone knew the name Bobby Rydell. Ernest Evans was a chicken plucker working in a poultry market who was introduced to Kal Mann by his boss. Evans' first single, "The Class," featured him impersonating Elvis Presley, Fats Domino, and Ricky Nelson. His next two singles—"Whole Lotta Laughin'" and "Dancing Dinosaur"—disappeared without a trace, but he followed them with the most successful single of his career. Renamed Chubby Checker by Dick Clark's then-wife Bobbie, he recorded a cover version of Hank Ballard's "The Twist" at Clark's suggestion. That led to a series of other twist songs, like "Let's Twist Again" and "Slow Twistin'," as well as a rash of dance tunes like "Limbo Rock," "Pony Time," "The Fly," "Popeye The Hitchhiker," and "The Hucklebuck." Checker has 13 songs in Cameo-Parkway's top 50, tied with Bobby Rydell for the most hits by one artist on the label.

"Slow Twistin'" helped launch another successful career on Cameo. Dee Dee Sharp, signed to the company when she was 16, had been singing background vocals until she was brought to the front to duet with Checker on "Slow Twistin'." That song was recorded at four o'clock in the afternoon. After a dinner break, Dee Dee returned to the studio without Chubby and recorded a dance hit of her own, "Mashed Potato Time." The single spent two weeks at No. 2 and the follow-up was icing on the cake: "Gravy (For My Mashed Potatoes)" peaked at No. 9. Sharp's next two releases also made the top 10: "Ride!" and "Do The Bird."

Cameo-Parkway added two groups in 1960. Dave Appell, placed in charge of A&R for the label, signed the Cashmeres. They were renamed the Dovells and hit with yet another dance song, "Bristol Stomp." It was No. 2 for two weeks. Len Barry, lead singer of the Dovells, recommended a group called the Orlons, and they had their first hit with their third release, "The Wah-Watusi." It spent two weeks at No. 2. The Orlons' next two singles, "Don't Hang Up" and "South Street," both made the top five.

The Tymes gave the company a No. 1 single with "So Much In Love" in 1963. But with the onslaught of the Beatles and other British groups in 1964, the Cameo-Parkway star waned. Mann and Lowe sold the label that year to Texas financier William Bowen. The company relocated to New York, and a number of British masters were leased, although only one is listed in the label's top 50: "Cast Your Fate To The Wind" by Sounds Orchestral. Thom Bell and Kenny Gamble were writing and producing at the label, but their talents would blossom elsewhere. Neil Bogart signed artists like Bobby Sherman, Bob Seger, Evie Sands, and the Ohio Express, as well as a Michigan group that gave the company its final No. 1 hit: "96 Tears" by ? (Question Mark) & the Mysterians. In the summer of '67, Cameo-Parkway was sold to Allen Klein and was absorbed into his ABKCO Industries.

Huey Lewis & the News

CHRIS WRIGHT was booking college dates for bands and running a blues club in Manchester when he found a band called the Jaybirds, a group that made demos for a music publisher and backed the British pop band Ivy League. "They knew I did bookings on the weekends, and they persuaded me to book them," Wright told Joe Smith in *Off The Record*. "Then they persuaded me to manage them when they got to Manchester." The band was renamed Ten Years After and signed with Decca's Deram label in the U.K.

In December 1967, Jethro Tull signed on with the agency run by Wright and his partner Terry Ellis. Gary Wright of Spooky Tooth told Chris Blackwell at Island Records about Tull; Blackwell was intrigued. "I found out they were a new band managed by Terry Ellis, who at the time had a partnership with Chris Wright called the Ellis-Wright Agency," Blackwell told Ted Fox in *In The Groove*. "So I tracked him down. I made a deal with Terry Ellis. He wanted to start his own label. I told him that was great, I could really show him how to do it and guide him. He wanted to start it right away with Jethro Tull and I said, 'No, that doesn't make any sense, Island is really hot right now and our name is strong. It will help Jethro Tull to be on Island. What you do is this: when you have five chart entries—records in the top 40—on Jethro Tull or any other acts you bring through on the same deal, we'll start the Chrysalis label. All the acts will then go on Chrysalis.' Needless to say, Terry signed some other acts and worked them really hard and got five chart entries within a matter of a year. Then

01	**CALL ME**	
	Blondie 80	
02	**MICKEY**	
	Toni Basil 82	
03	**HOT CHILD IN THE CITY**	
	Nick Gilder 78	
04	**THE POWER OF LOVE**	
	Huey Lewis & the News 85	
05	**THE TIDE IS HIGH**	
	Blondie 81	
06	**RAPTURE**	
	Blondie 81	
07	**STUCK WITH YOU**	
	Huey Lewis & the News 86	
08	**HEART OF GLASS**	
	Blondie 79	
09	**MONY MONY**	
	Billy Idol 87	
10	**JACOB'S LADDER**	
	Huey Lewis & the News 87	
11	**CRADLE OF LOVE**	
	Billy Idol 90	
12	**I'M GONNA BE (500 MILES)**	
	The Proclaimers 93	
13	**MR. WENDAL**	
	Arrested Development 93	
14	**TRUE**	
	Spandau Ballet 83	
15	**HIP TO BE SQUARE**	
	Huey Lewis & the News 86	
16	**PERFECT WORLD**	
	Huey Lewis & the News 88	

Chrysalis started and it was with us for about 10 years. Now they are one of our main competitors."

Jethro Tull's first five albums were released in America on Reprise. The first LP on Chrysalis in the States was *Living In The Past* in 1972. The title track is the earliest song on the Chrysalis top 50.

The most successful chart single for Chrysalis is "Call Me" by Blondie, from the film *American Gigolo.* Debbie Harry and Chris Stein first worked together in the Stilettos, a band that had been parodying girl group songs of the '60s. That group gave way to Angel and the Snakes before they renamed themselves after Chic Young's comic book heroine, Blondie. They became popular at the New York punk club CBGB, and recorded an album with producer Richard Gottehrer that was released on Private Stock.

In August 1977, Chrysalis bought Blondie's contract from Private Stock for $500,000. Two months later, the label released the *Plastic Letters* album. The single "Denis"—an updating of Randy & the Rainbows' "Denise"—was a European hit, but failed to crack the Hot 100. Blondie's first chart single in the U.S. was the Mike Chapman–produced "Heart Of Glass," which went to No. 1. "Call Me," produced by Giorgio Moroder, spent six weeks at No. 1, and was followed by two more chart-toppers: "The Tide Is High" and "Rapture."

The group with the highest number of singles (13) on the Chrysalis top 50 is Huey Lewis & the News. Lewis joined the bar band Clover in Northern California in 1972. Manager Jake Riviera signed them to Phonogram's Vertigo label in the U.K. in 1976, where they released one album and backed Elvis Costello on *My Aim Is True.* They split in 1979, and Lewis returned to Marin County. Along with some pals who jammed at a club called Uncle Charlie's in Corte Medera, Huey recorded a demo tape as "Huey Lewis and American Express." Manager Bob Brown hated their cover of the Supremes' "Stop! In The Name Of Love," but liked the band well enough to sign them. Only there was no band—just Huey and his friends, who agreed to become "the News." In 1980, they were signed to Chrysalis. With their breakthrough album, *Sports,* and its follow-up, *Fore!,* the News had chart success with singles like "I Want A New Drug," "The Power Of Love," "Stuck With You," and "Jacob's Ladder," the latter three reaching No. 1 on the Hot 100.

Eight of Chrysalis' top 50 songs were recorded by Pat Benatar, an opera-trained singing waitress from Long Island, New York. She was appearing at Catch A Rising Star when club owner Rick Newman suggested he manage her career. Benatar developed a hard-rock vocal style and was signed to Chrysalis in 1978.

17 **EYES WITHOUT A FACE**
Billy Idol 84

18 **TENNESSEE**
Arrested Development 92

19 **PEOPLE EVERYDAY**
Arrested Development 92

20 **LOVE IS A BATTLEFIELD**
Pat Benatar 83

21 **HIT ME WITH YOUR BEST SHOT**
Pat Benatar 80

22 **THE HEART OF ROCK & ROLL**
Huey Lewis & the News 84

23 **WE BELONG**
Pat Benatar 85

24 **THE ONE AND ONLY**
Chesney Hawkes 91

25 **I WANT A NEW DRUG**
Huey Lewis & the News 84

26 **IF THIS IS IT**
Huey Lewis & the News 84

27 **TO BE A LOVER**
Billy Idol 86

28 **DO YOU BELIEVE IN LOVE**
Huey Lewis & the News 82

29 **ELECTRIC BLUE**
Icehouse 88

30 **HEART AND SOUL**
Huey Lewis & the News 83

31 **YOUR WOMAN**
White Town 97

32 **JEANS ON**
David Dundas 77

33 **DOING IT ALL FOR MY BABY**
Huey Lewis & the News 87

34 **DON'T SHED A TEAR**
Paul Carrack 88

35 **INVINCIBLE**
Pat Benatar 85

36 **SHADOWS OF THE NIGHT**
Pat Benatar 82

37 **ISN'T IT TIME**
The Babys 87

38 **LIVING IN THE PAST**
Jethro Tull 73

39 **CRAZY**
Icehouse 88

40 **TREAT ME RIGHT**
Pat Benatar 81

41 **WALK THE DINOSAUR**
Was (Not Was) 89

42 **I KNOW WHAT I LIKE**
Huey Lewis & the News 87

43 **19**
Paul Hardcastle 85

44 **WALKING ON A THIN LINE**
Huey Lewis & the News 84

45 **BUNGLE IN THE JUNGLE**
Jethro Tull 75

46 **EVERY TIME I THINK OF YOU**
The Babys 79

47 **SPY IN THE HOUSE OF LOVE**
Was (Not Was) 88

48 **FIRE AND ICE**
Pat Benatar 81

49 **HEARTBREAKER**
Pat Benatar 80

50 **DON'T SHUT ME OUT**
Kevin Paige 89

Rihanna

B Y THE TIME they met at the Danceteria in New York City in 1984, Russell Simmons and Rick Rubin both had impressive beginnings in the music industry. Simmons had been booking acts for rush parties at black fraternities at City College of New York, managing acts like Kurtis Blow and Whodini, and producing records. His younger brother Joe was Run in Run-D.M.C. Rubin, a film student at New York University, was 21 that year and had produced "It's Yours" by rappers T. LaRock and Jazzy Jay.

It was Rubin who suggested to Simmons that they start a record label. With an $8,000 investment they were in business with their independent company, Def Jam. Their earliest artists were LL Cool J and the Beastie Boys. The first Def Jam single was "I Need a Beat" by LL. Based on the output of seven singles that first year, Columbia Records brought Def Jam into its corporate fold. The first Def Jam album released by Columbia was

LL Cool J's *Radio*. The first hit single was "The Rain" by Oran "Juice" Jones. It shot to No. 9 on the Hot 100 and topped the R&B chart for two weeks in September 1986.

The first No. 1 single on Def Jam ended with a rap, but it was a last-minute addition. Three weeks before the single was due to be released, Jones listened to the competed track and felt something was missing. "So I wrote this little monologue. . . . I spent my own money and booked the time," says Jones. "That's what actually sold the record."

In 1987, the label topped the R&B chart again, with LL Cool J's "I Need Love." Born James Todd Smith, he was just 16 when he sent a demo to Rubin. "I Need Love" was the first rap ballad to be a hit, but it wasn't meant to be a breakthrough. "It was spontaneous," says LL Cool J. "No one sat down and said, 'We need a ballad' because there were no rap ballads. . . . It wasn't contrived. I didn't have all that industry know-how."

That same year, Def Jam released a soundtrack, *Less Than Zero*, and had a top 10 hit with the Bangles' cover of Simon & Garfunkel's "A Hazy Shade Of Winter," a single that peaked at No. 2 in 1988. That same year, disagreements over how to manage Def Jam led to a split in the Simmons-Rubin partnership. Rubin headed west to create the Def American imprint, which later metamorphosed into American Recordings. Lyor Cohen, an earlier believer that white teens would love rap music, was named the new president of Def Jam.

With the rise of rap on the radio, Def Jam grew in strength. Staten Island rapper Clifford Smith, better known as Method Man of the Wu Tang Clan, joined the roster as a solo artist in 1994. A year later, he went to No. 3 on the Hot 100 with a medley of two songs written by Nick Ashford and Valerie Simpson, "I'll Be There For You/You're All I Need To Get By," recorded with Mary J. Blige. By this time, the deal with Columbia had ended and Def Jam was part of the PolyGram family. In this new corpororate environment, Def Jam had a series of platinum singles that included the Method Man hit and "Regulate" by Warren G and "This Is How We Do It" by Montell Jordan.

In 1997, Def Jam struck a distribution deal with Roc-A-Fella Records, an independent label formed by Damon Dash, Kareem "Biggs" Burke, and Shawn Carter, better known as Jay-Z. When the Universal Music Group purchased and merged with PolyGram in 1998, the company purchased the remaining portion of Def Jam it didn't own and formed the Island Def Jam Music Group, with the Island and Def Jam imprints running under separate management.

In 1999, a spin-off label from Def Jam named Def Soul was created, with a roster that included Dru Hill, Musiq, and, later, Patti LaBelle. The Def Jam umbrella expanded to take in other imprints, including Disturbing Tha Peace, Murder Inc., and Slip-N-Slide.

Retiring as an artist, Jay-Z became president and CEO of Def Jam Records. He ended his retirement in 2006 and returned to recording.

In February 2004, less than a month after being forced out of the top spot at Arista, Antonio L.A. Reid was named chairman of the Island Def Jam Music Group, replacing Lyor Cohen, who had risen to the post from his Def Jam presidency and had moved on to the Warner Music Group.

14 **LET'S RIDE**
Montell Jordan f/Master P & Silkk the Shocker 98

15 **SOUL SURVIVOR**
Young Jeezy f/Akon 05

16 **'03 BONNIE & CLYDE**
Jay-Z f/Beyoncé Knowles 02

17 **HOW DEEP IS YOUR LOVE**
Dru Hill f/Redman 98

18 **LOUNGIN**
LL Cool J 96

19 **HEY MA**
Cam'ron f/Juelz Santana, Freekey Zekey & Toya 02

20 **DIRT OFF YOUR SHOULDER**
Jay-Z 04

21 **LIVIN' IT UP** Ja Rule f/Case 01

22 **PUT IT ON ME**
Ja Rule f/Lil' Mo & Vita 01

23 **LUV U BETTER**
LL Cool J 02

24 **HAZY SHADE OF WINTER**
Bangles 88

25 **OH BOY**
Cam'ron f/Juelz Santana 02

26 **THERE IT GO! (THE WHISTLE SONG)**
Juelz Santana 06

27 **UNFAITHFUL**
Rihanna 06

28 **I'LL BE THERE FOR YOU/ YOU'RE ALL I NEED TO GET BY**
Method Man f/Mary J. Blige 95

29 **JESUS WALKS**
Kanye West 04

30 **I JUST WANNA LOVE U (GIVE IT 2 ME)**
Jay-Z 00

31 **SPLASH WATERFALLS**
Ludacris 04

32 **HE'S MINE** MoKenStef 95

33 **NOTHIN'** N.O.R.E. 02

34 **SEXY LOVE** Ne-Yo 06

35 **WONDERFUL**
Ja Rule f/R. Kelly & Ashanti 04

36 **SLAM** Onyx 93

37 **GET BACK** Ludacris 05

38 **IZZO (H.O.V.A.)** Jay-Z 01

39 **MOVE B***H**
Ludacris f/Mystikal & Infamous 2.0 02

40 **OYE MI CANTO**
N.O.R.E. f/Daddy Yankee, Nina Sky, Gem Star & Big Mato 04

41 **DOWN 4 U**
Irv Gotti p/the Inc. f/Ja Rule, Ashanti, Charli Baltimore & Vita 02

42 **ALL FALLS DOWN**
Kanye West f/Syleena Johnson 04

43 **HAPPY** Ashanti 02

44 **BETWEEN ME AND YOU**
Ja Rule f/Christina Milian 00

45 **THIS D.J.** Warren G 94

46 **PIMPIN' ALL OVER THE WORLD**
Ludacris f/Bobby Valentino 05

47 **SLOW DOWN** Bobby Valentino 05

48 **GETTO JAM**
Domino 94

49 **EXCUSE ME MISS**
Jay-Z 03

50 **CAN I GET A. . .**
Jay-Z f/Amil of Major Coinz & Ja 99

Pat Boone

AFTER RANDY Wood left the U.S. Air Force in 1945, he opened up an appliance shop in Gallatin, Tennessee. As a service to his customers, he stocked a few records in the store. Eventually, he was selling so many that he decided to open "Randy's Record Store," and by 1950 he had a huge mail-order following.

Wood bought a small local radio station and advertised his mail-order business. Soon he was spending his time after office hours producing sessions in the station's studio. He released recordings on his own label, Dot, and signed artists like Johnny Maddox, the Griffin Brothers, Margie Day, and Mac Wiseman.

In 1952, Dot had its first top 10 single in *Billboard* with "Trying" by the Hilltoppers, a quartet from Western Kentucky College that included future Dot artist Billy Vaughn. In 1954, the Fontane Sisters switched from RCA to Dot and had a top 20 hit, "Happy Days And Lonely Nights." The Fontane Sisters' next chart single was a No. 1 hit, "Hearts Of Stone." In 1955, Dot had top 10 hits with the star of TV's *My Little Margie,* Gale Storm, as well as Billy Vaughn and a clean-cut young man originally from Jacksonville, Florida: Pat Boone.

Pat was born Charles Eugene Boone on June 1, 1934, to a family that could trace its lineage back to frontiersman Daniel Boone. He advanced to the final round on Ted Mack's *Original Amateur Hour*, but made the mistake of appearing professionally on *Arthur Godfrey's Talent Scouts*. His $600 fee from that show disqualified him from winning Mack's amateur talent contest, so Boone lost out on a $6,000 college scholarship.

On his way home from appearing on those shows in New York, Pat stopped in Nashville to visit his parents. His friend Hugh Cherry, a disc jockey at WMAK, introduced him to Randy Wood. Dot's owner had seen Boone on both talent shows, and remarked that he should be making records.

"He called me up in Denton, Texas, in March, 1955, and said, 'I've got a song I want you to record,'" Boone told Jeff Tamarkin in *Goldmine*. "This was eight months after we'd agreed to record and I thought he'd forgotten all about me. He said he had a song he thought was a hit and wanted me to meet him in Chicago. I asked him what the song was and he said it was called 'Two Hearts' by Otis Williams and the Charms."

Boone assumed the R&B song was a ballad. "I get to Chicago and find it's a real rhythm 'n' blues jumper. . . . I tried my best to do it vocally, not having been very familiar with R&B. I tried my best to capture their flavor and feeling, and did." Like other white pop singers, Boone continued to cover material by black R&B artists. His version of Fats Domino's 'Ain't That A Shame" went to No. 2 on the Best Sellers chart.

"Ninety percent of radio stations in America wouldn't play R&B hits no matter how big they were," says Boone. "To get them on radio, other artists had to do them. I talked to Fats and Little Richard—there was a definite ceiling on how far they could go. When a white artist came along and sang their songs, they were introduced to audiences they couldn't reach themselves."

Wood moved Boone into a broader pop arena with ballads like "Love Letters In The Sand," "April Love," and "Friendly Persuasion." Wood suggested "Love Letters In The Sand" for Boone because so many people requested the song at his record store (Bing Crosby and Rudy Vallee had done earlier versions).

"It's always been a mystery to me why 'Love Letters' had universal appeal," Boone confesses. "There's nothing exciting about the arrangement or the way I sang it." Despite his opinion, the single is Dot's most successful release.

The second most successful chart single on Dot is "The Green Door" by Jim Lowe, who was working in New York as a disc jockey when he wrote "Gambler's Guitar," a million-seller for Rusty Draper in 1953. Three years later, Lowe recorded the song written by Marvin Moore and Bob Davies.

Dot moved from Gallatin to Hollywood in 1956, and many of the label's biggest hits were leased from other labels, including "Come Go With Me" by the Dell-Vikings, "The Fool" by Sanford Clark, "You Cheated" by the Shields, "Susie Darlin'" by Robin Luke, "Pipeline" by the Chantays, and "Wipe Out" by the Surfaris.

Wood sold his company to Gulf + Western, owners of Paramount Pictures Corporation, in 1965. Later, the label was sold to ABC Records, which had hits with Donna Fargo and Freddy Fender under the ABC/Dot logo in the '70s. When ABC was sold to MCA, the Dot masters were included in the deal.

Melissa Etheridge

W HEN CHRIS BLACKWELL was inducted into the Rock and Roll Hall of Fame in 2001, he was called the person most responsible for turning the rest of the world on to reggae music. It was an accurate description of Blackwell, who was steeped in Jamaican culture.

He was born on June 22, 1937, in London, but raised in Jamaica, the homeland of his maternal family. They were involved in selling rum, sugar, coconut, and cattle. At the age of 10, Blackwell was sent home to England to complete his schooling.

Eight years later, Blackwell returned to Jamaica. To earn a living, he sold real estate, rented motor scooters, and worked as an aide to the governor. But his life changed the night he went to the Half Moon Hotel in Montego Bay and heard a blind jazz pianist, Lance Hayward. With an investment of $1,000, Blackwell started his own record label, Island, named after the Alec Waugh novel *Island in the Sun*, and signed Hayward as his first artist. Island built a roster that focused on native singers, including Laurel Aitken, Wilfred Edwards, and Owen Gray. Aitken's "Little Sheila" topped the charts in Jamaica. Three years later, Blackwell had released two albums and 26 singles. Many of those records sold so well in Britain that in May 1962, Blackwell returned to England and opened a London office, which became the new headquarters for Island Records

The music of Jamaica was still the mainstay of the label's success. Blackwell relied on some of the leading reggae producers (like Duke Reid, Leslie Kong, and Clement "Sir Coxsone" Dodd) from the Caribbean nation to come up with hit singles.

Island's first international success was "My Boy Lollipop" by Millie Small, a 15-year-old singer from Jamaica. Blackwell thought the single was going to be such a big hit that Island wouldn't be able to handle it, so he licensed the track to Philips (the single was released on the Smash subsidiary in the United States). Blackwell was right—Millie's single sold seven million copies worldwide.

Blackwell accompanied Millie to Birmingham for an appearance on BBC's *Top of the Pops*, and after the broadcast went to a club to see a group called Carl Wayne and the Vikings. Blackwell was more taken with the supporting act, the Spencer Davis Group, featuring vocals by 15-year-old Stevie Winwood. Blackwell signed them on the spot. As he had with Millie Small, he licensed the band to Philips. Their first chart single in America was "Keep On Running," issued on Atco and composed by the Jamaican songwriter Jackie Edwards. Blackwell then licensed the group's records to the United Artists label in the States and they had a top 10 hit with "Gimme Some Lovin'." When the Spencer Davis Group broke up in 1967, Winwood and his new group, Traffic, remained with Island, giving the label its first act geared toward the radio format then known as Album Oriented Rock.

Blackwell added Cat Stevens, King Crimson, Jethro Tull, and Emerson, Lake and Palmer to Island's roster in Britain, and continued to license them to other labels in America. In 1971, Blackwell signed Bob Marley, and two years later, he opened Island Records in the United States.

Marley had previously recorded for labels in Jamaica. Signing with Blackwell turned him into an international superstar and the leading proponent of reggae music. While the Island roster now contained acts from different musical genres, Blackwell continued to sign reggae bands, including Toots and the Maytals, Third World, Black Uhuru, Burning Spear, and Sly & Robbie.

Island continued to be strong in the '80s with chart hits by Robert Palmer and U2. Signed to Island in 1985, Melissa Etheridge released three albums with little success. She had a breakthrough in the '90s with her fourth album, *Yes I Am*. Blackwell thinks it no coincidence that Etheridge achieved her greatest success after coming out as a lesbian.

Blackwell sold Island to Polygram in 1989. He remained with the company until November 1997. In 1998 he started Palm Pictures to produce DVDs and merged the company with the Rykodisc label.

In the post-Blackwell years, Island was joined with Def Jam under the Universal Music Enterprises umbrella, becoming the powerful Island Def Jam Music Group. Both labels continued to operate under their own names, and in 2005, Island had its biggest hit to date with Mariah Carey's "We Belong Together," which ruled the Hot 100 for 14 weeks.

The Top 50 Songs on JIVE

Britney Spears

C LIVE CALDER'S goal was to create "the Motown of Willesden," the area of London where he opened the offices of Jive Records in 1975. Before starting his own record label, the native of South Africa was a musician (he played bass for local groups like Birds of a Feather, who became known as Calder's Collection) and a record producer, as well as a *Billboard* correspondent based in Johannesburg.

Kindred soul Clive Davis wanted Calder to head up Arista's A&R department in Los Angeles in the '70s, but Calder had a different idea. He told Davis of his plan for the Jive label, and Davis agreed to distribute the new imprint. The Arista chief was hoping the Jive label would improve Arista's rock roster, especially since producer Robert John "Mutt" Lange was part of the Jive team, and Calder was the manager of City Boy. Instead, some of the earliest Jive singles were from pop acts like Tight Fit

("The Lion Sleeps Tonight," "Fantasy Island") and Samantha Fox ("Touch Me (I Want Your Body)," "I Wanna Have Some Fun"). Jive's first three No. 1 hits were from an artist Calder signed away from CBS, Trinidad-born Billy Ocean. Other hits came from the U.K.'s A Flock of Seagulls and the New York rap group Whodini. With Kool Moe Dee and A Tribe Named Quest also on the roster, Jive earned a solid reputation as a rap label.

The distribution deal with Arista ended in 1987, but Davis told his BMG corporate bosses they should keep Calder's company in the fold. Jive switched over to another BMG imprint, RCA.

At BMG's annual international conference held in Malaysia in 1995, Jive showcased a new American group. The Backstreet Boys couldn't get arrested in the U.S., but they hurtled up the German charts and their popularity spread through Europe. The Orlando, Florida, quintet had one minor single hit on the Hot 100 in the fall of 1995 with "We've Got It Goin' On." They had to wait two more years before breaking through in their own country. Their single "Quit Playing Games (With My Heart)" entered the Hot 100 the week of June 28, 1997, ultimately peaking at No. 2 and spending 43 weeks on the chart. By the end of the decade, they were the biggest boy band in the world, and had scored top 10 hits in the U.S. with "Everybody (Backstreet's Back)," "All I Have To Give," and "I Want It That Way."

In 2000 Jive added the world's other biggest boy band to its roster when it signed 'N Sync away from RCA. The internal BMG political battle made headlines and caused much strife in the company, but when the dust settled 'N Sync was a Jive act.

Just having the Backstreet Boys and 'N Sync would make Jive the hottest teen-oriented label, but a 16-year-old former Mouseketeer joined the label in 1998 and made Jive the ultimate Radio Disney imprint. Britney Spears had a No. 1 hit her first time out with ". . .Baby One More Time," thanks to her being teamed with Swedish producer Max Martin, who also wrote her first hit single.

As big as Jive is, it's just part of Calder's Zomba Group, a company that also includes music publishing, software distribution and export, film and television studios, recording studios, and equipment rental.

The Top 50 Songs on RSO

Andy Gibb

ROBERT STIGWOOD arrived in London from Adelaide, Australia, with less than six pounds in his pocket. He was a door-to-door vacuum cleaner salesman in Notting Hill Gate before finding work in the theater. Then he opened a model agency. One of his clients was an actor who could also sing. John Leyton's cover of "Tell Laura I Love Her" missed the charts, but "Johnny Remember Me" went to No. 1 in the U.K. in 1961.

Stigwood expanded into other areas: he opened a television studio, published magazines, and represented Motown in Britain. The companies prospered and then crashed. People who believed in him refinanced him, and through them, Stigwood met Brian Epstein, manager of the Beatles. Epstein's company, NEMS, bought the Robert Stigwood Organization with the provision that Stigwood could gain controlling interest. But when Epstein died, the deal fell apart and RSO went its separate way. Stigwood had financial backing from PolyGram and had already signed the Bee Gees to a five-year contract.

Hugh Gibb, father of the Gibb brothers, had sent a copy of an Australian album by his sons to the NEMS office in London. Stigwood liked their sound, and within 24 hours of the Gibbs' arrival from Sydney, he arranged an audition for them at London's Savile Theatre.

In addition to the Bee Gees, Stigwood had Cream, perhaps the original "supergroup." Stigwood had represented the Graham Bond Organization, with Jack Bruce on bass and Ginger Baker on drums. Eric Clapton left John Mayall's Bluesbreakers to form Cream with Bruce and

Baker, and they were signed to Stigwood's Reaction label in the U.K.

Stigwood also had a financial interest in the Tim Rice and Andrew Lloyd Webber musical *Jesus Christ Superstar.* He produced the movie version of the Who's *Tommy* and sold the TV series *Beacon Hill* to CBS. And his initials graced a new American label, RSO, distributed in the U.S. by Atlantic. Artists like the Bee Gees, whose records had been released on Atlantic's Atco subsidiary, were transferred to the RSO label, and in 1976, RSO shifted to PolyGram.

RSO's golden period began in 1977, first with a No. 1 single from Andy Gibb, and then with the first single from the soundtrack of *Saturday Night Fever,* the Bee Gees' "How Deep Is Your Love."

In 1978, RSO had a year that most record companies can only dream about. *Saturday Night Fever* produced four No. 1 singles and became the best-selling album to that date. RSO had an unprecedented six consecutive No. 1 singles on the *Billboard* chart, for 21 uninterrupted weeks at the top. There were three more No. 1 songs that year. One was from Andy Gibb, and the other two were from the soundtrack of *Grease.* Parent company PolyGram did $1.2 billion in record sales that year, a new high for any record company.

Al Coury, president of the label in America, ran the day-to-day operations for Stigwood. "We're a small, tightknit, young group of people, mostly street-oriented," he told *Rolling Stone* in 1978. "We all come from the practical end of the record business: we either sold, promoted, or marketed. So when we do our thinking, we sit around here and put together some thoughts and ideas for a campaign; we think about it from a very practical level. We do things that instinctively feel good to us."

The top seven singles on RSO are all from the Gibb family. The Bee Gees are No. 1 and No. 2 with "Stayin' Alive" and "Night Fever," respectively. Younger brother Andy is No. 3 with "Shadow Dancing" and No. 4 with "I Just Want To Be Your Everything." The Bee Gees are No. 5 with "How Deep Is Your Love" and No. 6 with "Too Much Heaven," while Andy is No. 7 with "(Love Is) Thicker Than Water."

Ranked No. 9 is "Disco Duck (Part 1)" by Rick Dees & His Cast of Idiots. Dees was handling the morning-drive shift at WMPS in Memphis when he recorded the song for Fretone, a local label owned by Stax Records co-founder Estelle Axton. When the song became popular in the South, Dees flew to Hollywood to land a deal with a major record label. Everyone passed on the song except Al Coury, who played it for his kids. When they liked it, he leased "Disco Duck" for $3,500.

17 **LOVE SO RIGHT**
Bee Gees 76

18 **I SHOT THE SHERIFF**
Eric Clapton 74

19 **LOVE YOU INSIDE OUT**
Bee Gees 79

20 **HOPELESSLY DEVOTED TO YOU**
Olivia Newton-John 78

21 **STUMBLIN' IN**
Suzi Quatro & Chris Norman 79

22 **DESIRE**
Andy Gibb 80

23 **FAME**
Irene Cara 80

24 **MAKIN' IT**
David Naughton 79

25 **HEAVEN ON THE SEVENTH FLOOR**
Paul Nicholas 77

26 **AN EVERLASTING LOVE**
Andy Gibb 78

27 **GOLD**
John Stewart 79

28 **(OUR LOVE) DON'T THROW IT ALL AWAY**
Andy Gibb 78

29 **NIGHTS ON BROADWAY**
Bee Gees 75

30 **I CAN'T STAND IT**
Eric Clapton 81

31 **SUMMER NIGHTS**
John Travolta & Olivia Newton-John 78

32 **LOVE ME**
Yvonne Elliman 76

33 **FANNY (BE TENDER WITH MY LOVE)**
Bee Gees 76

34 **FAR FROM OVER**
Frank Stallone 83

35 **THIS TIME I'M IN IT FOR LOVE**
Player 78

36 **PROMISES**
Eric Clapton 79

37 **BOOGIE CHILD**
Bee Gees 77

38 **HOLD ON TO MY LOVE**
Jimmy Ruffin 80

39 **I CAN'T HELP IT**
Andy Gibb & Olivia Newton-John 80

40 **HELLO STRANGER**
Yvonne Elliman 77

41 **TIME IS TIME**
Andy Gibb 81

42 **EMPIRE STRIKES BACK**
Meco 80

43 **OUT HERE ON MY OWN**
Irene Cara 80

44 **OH! DARLING**
Robin Gibb 78

45 **WONDERFUL TONIGHT**
Eric Clapton 78

46 **THE WOMAN IN YOU**
Bee Gees 83

47 **LIVING NEXT DOOR TO ALICE**
Smokie 77

48 **HELLO OLD FRIEND**
Eric Clapton 76

49 **EDGE OF THE UNIVERSE**
Bee Gees 77

50 **STREET SINGIN'**
Lady Flash 76

The Top 50 Songs on VIRGIN

Janet Jackson

RICHARD BRANSON was born July 18, 1950, in Surrey, England. He was dyslexic, and so didn't do well in school. By age 15 he had become an entrepreneur, growing Christmas trees and raising parakeets known as "budgies," but neither of those ventures succeeded. He dropped out of high school and relocated to London, where he formed a new business, publishing a magazine called *Student* when he was 16. A year later he founded his first charity, the Student Advisory Centre. Then Branson started a new company, selling cut-out albums. A woman who worked for him suggested the name Virgin, since they were new to the music business. The mail-order company led to the opening of the first Virgin retail store, on Oxford Street in London.

Branson launched the Virgin label in May 1973 with business partner Nik Powell. One of the young company's first projects was providing financial backing for a 50-minute musical composition by Mike Oldfield that had already been turned down by several U.K. labels. Virgin's first albums were Oldfield's *Tubular Bells*, released a full year before it was heard on *The Exorcist* soundtrack, and *Manor Live*, a live jam session with various musicians.

The young company leased most of its recordings to other American labels, including Epic, Atlantic, and A&M. As the Virgin empire grew to include an airline, so the roster grew to include Culture Club, Heaven 17, UB40, and Simple Minds. In 1977 Virgin signed one of the U.K.'s most controversial bands, the Sex Pistols, following the group's short-lived, chaotic tenures at EMI and A&M.

As early as 1984, Branson had started talking to Jordan Harris of A&M Records about heading up the Virgin label in America. In 1986, Harris approached a former A&M colleague, Jeff Ayeroff of Warner Bros., about running the company with him. The next year, they scored Virgin's first No. 1 single on the Hot 100—Cutting Crew's "(I Just) Died In Your Arms."

Harris and Ayeroff outbid Island Records and signed Steve Winwood to a reported $13 million contract in February 1987. When Janet Jackson's A&M deal expired, Virgin signed her for $32 million in March 1991. The buzz on the street said Virgin was enriching its roster prior to being sold; in May 1992, the Virgin Music Group was acquired by Britain's Thorn-EMI for $961 million. The following year turned out to be Virgin's most successful to date, with two of the year's biggest hits: "Can't Help Falling In Love" by UB40 and "That's The Way Love Goes" by Janet Jackson. The former was No. 1 on the Hot 100 for seven weeks and the latter for eight weeks. In August of that year, Ayeroff and Harris resigned their positions as co-chairmen and were succeeded by label president Phil Quartararo. When he departed for Warner Bros. in 1997, Virgin Music Group chairman Ken Berry brought in the British duo of Ray Cooper and Ashley Newton to run the U.S. company.

In 2006, the Capitol and Virgin labels were merged worldwide into the Capitol Music Group. Jason Flom, who had worked in Atlantic's A&R department before forming the Lava label in 1995, was named the chairman of the blended company.

Four years after selling Virgin, Branson started another record label, V2. The company's most noted artists were Moby, Better Than Ezra, and the White Stripes. Branson sold the North American wing of V2 in 2006, and the label was effectively shut down in 2007 when all of the artists were released from their contracts.

Although Branson is no longer connected with the label that he founded, he remains one of the world's most prominent businessmen. His many ventures have included Virgin Mobile (sold in 2006), Virgin Cola, Virgin Vodka, Virgin Trains, Virgin Comics, and Virgin Animation. While Virgin Airways has added more routes, Branson has also established airline carriers Virgin Express, Virgin Nigeria, and Virgin America.

Branson's latest company is truly a 21st-century effort. Virgin Galactic has already signed up hundreds of civilians who have paid $200,000 each to travel into space on suborbital flights using the technology of aeronautical engineer Burt Rutan, who designed the award-winning Spaceship One.

Outside of the business world, Branson has also established a reputation as an adventurer. In 1985, he set out from New York in the Virgin Atlantic *Challenger*, hoping to break the record for a trans-Atlantic crossing, but the boat capsized. The next year, Virgin Atlantic's *Challenger II* succeeded in setting a new record. Branson later crossed the Atlantic in a hot air balloon, the *Virgin Atlantic Flyer.*

32 **BECAUSE OF LOVE**
Janet Jackson 94

33 **I GET LONELY**
Janet Jackson f/BLACKstreet 98

34 **HEART AND SOUL**
T'Pau 87

35 **I DON'T WANNA FIGHT**
Tina Turner 93

36 **THE WAY YOU DO THE THINGS YOU DO**
UB40 90

37 **I TOUCH MYSELF**
Divinyls 91

38 **(IT'S JUST) THE WAY THAT YOU LOVE ME**
Paula Abdul 89

39 **CAN'T STOP**
After 7 90

40 **FLY AWAY**
Lenny Kravitz 99

41 **(KEEP FEELING) FASCINATION**
Human League 83

42 **CATCH ME (I'M FALLING)**
Pretty Poison 87

43 **MISS ME BLIND**
Culture Club 84

44 **LOVERBOY**
Mariah Carey 01

45 **SPICE UP YOUR LIFE**
Spice Girls 97

46 **READY OR NOT**
After 7 90

47 **CHURCH OF THE POISON MIND**
Culture Club 83

48 **I'LL TUMBLE 4 YA**
Culture Club 83

49 **THE PROMISE**
When in Rome 88

50 **DON'T YOU KNOW WHAT THE NIGHT CAN DO?**
Steve Winwood 88

The Top 30 Songs on BUDDAH

Gladys Knight & the Pips

N EIL BOGART (née Bogatz) was born and raised in Brooklyn. He was just 19 when he had his first and only chart record, "Bobby," recorded under the name Neil Scott. He joined the promotion department of MGM Records, then moved to Cameo-Parkway as vice president and sales manager. After Allen Klein took over that company, Bogart left for a new label, Buddah.

Buddah had been founded by Art Kass and his partner at Kama Sutra Records, Artie Ripp, as well as two other partners. Kass, who had worked at MGM with Bogart, convinced the others to hire the 24-year-old as the label's general manager.

All of Buddah's earliest hits were bubblegum music, exemplified by the inane lyrics of songs like "Yummy Yummy Yummy" and "Chewy Chewy" by the Ohio Express, and "1, 2, 3, Red Light" and "Indian Giver" by the 1910 Fruitgum Co. The Lemon Pipers didn't want to be a bubblegum group, but they were told to record "Green Tambourine" or be dropped from the label.

As the bubblegum fad faded, Buddah expanded its roster to include other musical styles. Buddah began the '70s with hits from Melanie and the group that Bogart brought from Cameo, the Five Stairsteps. But the label's most important signing happened in January 1973, when Gladys Knight & the Pips moved over from Motown.

Bogart left Buddah in September 1973, to move to California and start a new label, Casablanca. Kass remained, and in 1976, the label's parent company, Viewlex, went bankrupt. Kass bought the label back, but eventually found himself $10 million in debt, so Buddah was shut down for good. With a slightly different spelling, the name was revived in the '90s as an archive label for BMG product.

The Top 30 Songs on CADENCE

Andy Williams

ARCHIE BLEYER was the on-camera bandleader for CBS' variety series *Arthur Godfrey and His Friends* from the program's debut on January 12, 1949, through his dismissal in 1954. Bleyer had been leading his own dance band for 17 years when he started Cadence in 1952. A month later, the label had its first hit, "Anywhere I Wander" / "This Is Heaven" by Julius LaRosa. Cadence had several pre-rock era hits, including "The Ballad Of Davy Crockett" by Bill Hayes, "Mr. Sandman" by the Chordettes, and Bleyer's own recording of "Hernando's Hideaway."

The Chordettes have four songs included in Cadence's top 30 chart hits; Bleyer produced them all.

In 1956, Bleyer signed Andy Williams, who covered Charlie Gracie's "Butterfly." After that one rock and roll outing, Williams turned to softer sounds for his subsequent releases.

Bleyer's most successful act was signed to Cadence in 1957. The Everly Brothers have four songs in the Cadence top 30, including the top four.

The Everly Brothers left Cadence in February 1960, and signed a million-dollar contract with Warner Bros. Later that year, Johnny Tillotson, a singer from Jacksonville, Florida, had his first top 10 single on Cadence with "Poetry In Motion." Tillotson continued to have hits on Cadence until the label's demise in 1963. Bleyer sold the label's masters to Andy Williams, who released them on his Barnaby label.

01 **ALL I HAVE TO DO IS DREAM**
   Everly Brothers 58
02 **WAKE UP LITTLE SUSIE**
   Everly Brothers 57
03 **BYE BYE LOVE**
   Everly Brothers 57
04 **BIRD DOG**
   Everly Brothers 58
05 **POETRY IN MOTION**
   Johnny Tillotson 60
06 **LOLLIPOP**
   The Chordettes 58
07 **PROBLEMS**
   Everly Brothers 58
08 **('TIL) I KISSED YOU**
   Everly Brothers 59
09 **IT KEEPS RIGHT ON A-HURTIN'**
   Johnny Tillotson 62
10 **SINCE I FELL FOR YOU**
   Lenny Welch 63
11 **BUTTERFLY**
   Andy Williams 57
12 **THE HAWAIIAN WEDDING SONG**
   Andy Williams 59
13 **BORN TO BE WITH YOU**
   The Chordettes 56
14 **CANADIAN SUNSET**
   Andy Williams 56
15 **LONELY STREET**
   Andy Williams 59
16 **ARE YOU SINCERE**
   Andy Williams 58
17 **LET IT BE ME**
   Everly Brothers 60
18 **DEVOTED TO YOU**
   Everly Brothers 58
19 **THE VILLAGE OF ST. BERNADETTE**
   Andy Williams 60
20 **I LIKE YOUR KIND OF LOVE**
   Andy Williams [and Peggy Powers] 57
21 **WITHOUT YOU**
   Johnny Tillotson 61
22 **WHEN WILL I BE LOVED**
   Everly Brothers 60
23 **NEVER ON SUNDAY**
   The Chordettes 61
24 **DOMANI**
   Julius LaRosa 55
25 **(GIRLS, GIRLS, GIRLS)**
   MADE TO LOVE
   Eddie Hodges 62
26 **JUST BETWEEN YOU AND ME**
   The Chordettes 57
27 **RUMBLE**
   Link Wray & His Ray Men 58
28 **TAKE A MESSAGE TO MARY**
   Everly Brothers 59
29 **I'M GONNA KNOCK ON YOUR DOOR**
   Eddie Hodges 61
30 **YOU CAN NEVER STOP**
   ME LOVING YOU
   Johnny Tillotson 63

Donna Summer

IN 1973, Mo Ostin of Warner Bros. agreed to finance a new label to be run by Neil Bogart of Buddah Records.

The Casablanca label's first important signing was a rock quartet from New York City—Kiss. But Bogart didn't believe that Warner Bros. supported the group, and in September 1974 Bogart ended the label's affiliation with Warner Bros.

The label's salvation came with a single from German producer Giorgio Moroder. Donna Summer's erotic "Love To Love You Baby" was released on Moroder's Oasis label through Casablanca. "Love To Love You Baby" helped establish a new genre of music—disco.

In 1977, Polygram gave the company a major cash infusion by buying half-interest in the label for $10 million.

Casablanca continued to pump out disco hits, particularly from Summer and a sextet formed by French producer Jacques Morali, the Village People.

Things began to fall apart in 1980. First, Summer sued for $10 million. Then Polygram bought the other 50 percent of Casablanca and, unhappy with diminishing profits, dismissed Bogart. Casablanca continued under the stewardship of Bruce Bird for the first 10 months after Bogart's departure, and was eventually folded into the Polygram group as another subsidiary. The label's biggest hit came in 1983 with Irene Cara's title song from the movie *Flashdance*.

Chuck Berry

BROTHERS LEONARD and Phil Chess, two Jewish immigrants from Poland, settled in Chicago in 1928. In 1947, the Chess brothers started a record company, Aristocrat, specializing in blues, jazz, and pop. A blues pianist named Sunnyland Smith showed up for a recording date with a singer from Mississippi, Muddy Waters, who was given some recording time of his own; "I Can't Be Satisfied" was released as a single, and became a hit.

In 1950, the label name was changed to Chess, and material was released by Howlin' Wolf, Elmore James, Rosco Gordon, and Willie Dixon.

In 1955, the Chess label signed Sonny Boy Williamson and Chuck Berry. Muddy Waters brought Berry to Phil Chess, who was impressed with Chuck's demo of "Ida Red." Leonard Chess suggested changing the name "Ida Red" to that of a cow in a children's story—Maybellene. "Maybellene" became Chess' first crossover hit, peaking at No. 5 on the pop chart. That began a streak of hits for Berry, including such seminal songs as "Roll Over Beethoven," "School Day," "Rock & Roll Music," "Sweet Little Sixteen," and "Johnny B. Goode."

Leonard Chess died in 1969, and Chess was sold to tape manufacturer GRT. Phil left to manage the family-owned radio station, WVON, and Leonard's son Marshall headed up the Rolling Stones' record label. The Chess masters are now owned by MCA.

01 SWEET LITTLE SIXTEEN
Chuck Berry *Chess* 58

02 MY DING-A-LING
Chuck Berry *Chess* 72

03 SCHOOL DAY
Chuck Berry *Chess* 57

04 LET ME IN
The Sensations *Argo* 62

05 THE "IN" CROWD
The Ramsey Lewis Trio *Argo* 65

06 BOOK OF LOVE
The Monotones *Argo* 58

07 ROCK & ROLL MUSIC
Chuck Berry *Chess* 57

08 HAPPY, HAPPY BIRTHDAY BABY
The Tune Weavers *Checker* 57

09 JOHNNY B. GOODE
Chuck Berry *Chess* 58

10 OVER THE MOUNTAIN, ACROSS THE SEA
Johnnie & Joe *Chess* 57

11 BUT I DO
Clarence "Frogman" Henry *Argo* 61

12 MAYBELLENE
Chuck Berry *Chess* 55

13 RESCUE ME
Fontella Bass *Checker* 65

14 STAY IN MY CORNER
The Dells *Cadet* 68

15 OH, WHAT A NIGHT
The Dells *Cadet* 69

16 THE WALK
Jimmy McCracklin *Checker* 58

17 PICTURES OF MATCHSTICK MEN
Status Quo *Cadet Concept* 68

18 MAMA DIDN'T LIE
Jan Bradley *Chess* 58

19 RINKY DINK
Dave "Baby" Cortez *Chess* 62

20 NO PARTICULAR PLACE TO GO
Chuck Berry *Chess* 64

21 YOU ALWAYS HURT THE ONE YOU LOVE
Clarence "Frogman" Henry *Argo* 61

22 HANG ON SLOOPY
The Ramsey Lewis Trio *Cadet* 65

23 HI-HEEL SNEAKERS
Tommy Tucker *Checker* 64

24 THIS SHOULD GO ON FOREVER
Rod Bernard *Argo* 59

25 SAY MAN
Bo Diddley *Checker* 59

26 TEAR DROPS
Lee Andrews & the Hearts *Chess* 57

27 SELFISH ONE
Jackie Ross *Chess* 64

28 SUMMERTIME
Billy Stewart *Chess* 66

29 YOU NEVER CAN TELL
Chuck Berry *Chess* 64

30 THERE IS
The Dells *Cadet* 68

Johnnie Taylor

JIM STEWART, a Memphis bank teller who also played the fiddle, wanted to be a record producer. In 1958, he and his sister, Estelle Axton, bought some recording equipment and started Satellite Records in a storeroom 25 miles out of town.

"Someday" by the Veltones was Satellite's first release, but it was an inauspicious start for the label. Stewart moved his office back to the city in 1960, occupying a vacant theater on McLemore Street.

Stewart's house musicians, the Mar-Keys, gave Satellite its first—and last—national hit with the instrumental "Last Night." Another company claimed the Satellite name, so Jim and Estelle took the first two letters from their last names to form Stax.

The Mar-Keys recorded a couple of impromptu tracks that Stewart liked. He released them under the name Booker T. & the MG's (which stood for "Booker T. Jones and the Memphis Group"), and "Green Onions" peaked at No. 3. The MG's included Steve Cropper and Donald "Duck" Dunn.

Otis Redding was signed to Stax's new Volt subsidiary in 1962. He was on the brink of stardom when he died in a plane crash on December 10, 1967. Released posthumously, "(Sittin' On) The Dock Of The Bay" became Stax's most successful chart song.

Stax had multiple successes in the early '70s, but by 1974, financial problems did the label in, and the masters were sold to California-based Fantasy Records.

James Darren

JONIE TAPS, an executive with Columbia Pictures, suggested to studio head Harry Cohn that the company start a record label so that they could issue their own soundtracks, instead of leasing them to other companies. Offices were opened in the Columbia Pictures building in New York, and Colpix Records was born.

Stu Phillips was hired as head of A&R for the label, and one of his first assignments was to produce a hit for the Skyliners. But when the Marcels unexpectedly showed up from Pittsburgh, Phillips snuck them into the studio late at night. With a few minutes of time left and one more song to record, Phillips produced Colpix's first No. 1 single: a doo-wop version of Rodgers and Hart's "Blue Moon." He later produced hit singles for the teen-aged stars of *The Donna Reed Show,* Shelley Fabares ("Johnny Angel") and Paul Petersen ("My Dad").

The name Colpix vanished and was replaced in 1966 by Columbia Pictures' new record label, Colgems.

01 **JOHNNY ANGEL**
Shelley Fabares 62
02 **BLUE MOON**
The Marcels 61
03 **GOODBYE CRUEL WORLD**
James Darren 61
04 **MY DAD**
Paul Petersen 63
05 **HER ROYAL MAJESTY**
James Darren 62
06 **HEY, GIRL**
Freddie Scott 63
07 **HEARTACHES**
The Marcels 61
08 **CONSCIENCE**
James Darren 62
09 **SHE CAN'T FIND HER KEYS**
Paul Petersen 62
10 **JOHNNY LOVES ME**
Shelley Fabares 62

The Top 10 Songs on SUN

IN 1950, former engineer and disc jockey Sam Phillips founded the Memphis Recording Service, the first permanent studio in the city. Many local black artists used the studio, including Bobby Bland, Howlin' Wolf, and Jackie Brenston (who recorded what many consider to be the first rock and roll record—"Rocket 88"—in Phillips' studio). In 1952, Phillips started his own label, Sun Records, releasing singles by Rufus Thomas, Little Milton, Junior Parker, and the Prisonaires. The first hit was Rufus Thomas' "Bear Cat," an answer song to Big Mama Thornton's recording of "Hound Dog."

Phillips' future was assured one summer day in July 1953, when Elvis Presley stopped in on his lunch hour to record a couple of songs for his mother. Sun released five singles by Elvis between July 1954 and November 1955 before selling Presley's contract to RCA. Phillips used the income to invest in the Holiday Inn chain, as well as in other up-and-coming artists: Carl Perkins, Jerry Lee Lewis, Johnny Cash, and Roy Orbison.

01 BLUE SUEDE SHOES
Carl Perkins 56
02 GREAT BALLS OF FIRE
Jerry Lee Lewis 58
03 WHOLE LOT OF SHAKIN' GOING ON
Jerry Lee Lewis 57
04 BREATHLESS
Jerry Lee Lewis 58
05 GUESS THINGS HAPPEN THAT WAY
Johnny Cash 58
06 BALLAD OF A TEENAGE QUEEN
Johnny Cash 58
07 HIGH SCHOOL CONFIDENTIAL
Jerry Lee Lewis 58
08 I WALK THE LINE
Johnny Cash 56
09 THE WAYS OF A WOMAN IN LOVE
Johnny Cash 58
10 WHAT'D I SAY
Jerry Lee Lewis 61

The Top 10 Songs on 20TH CENTURY

IN THE late '50s, 20th Century Fox followed the practice of other movie studios and started its own record label. Before it was shut down, two of its biggest hits were "Navy Blue" by Diane Renay and "The Little Drummer Boy" by the Harry Simeone Chorale. In 1972, Fox president Gordon Stulberg launched the 20th Century label, and hired Russ Regan away from MCA's Uni label to run the company. Regan had released a Love Unlimited album on Uni; he brought the female trio to 20th Century and signed their mentor, Barry White. He also licensed Carl Douglas' "Kung Fu Fighting" for U.S. release. The single is the label's most successful chart hit.

In 1974, Regan issued an album by the Eleventh Hour, the brainchild of Bob Crewe and Kenny Nolan. Nolan went on to record as a solo artist, giving the label a No. 3 hit in 1977 with "I Like Dreamin'."

20th Century went out of business when Marvin Davis bought the film studio and decided he didn't want to be in the record business. He sold the company's assets to Polygram.

01 KUNG FU FIGHTING
Carl Douglas 74
02 LOVE'S THEME
Love Unlimited Orchestra 74
03 THE MORNING AFTER
Maureen McGovern 73
04 YOU'RE THE FIRST, THE LAST, MY EVERYTHING
Barry White 75
05 BIGGEST PART OF ME
Ambrosia 80
06 I LIKE DREAMIN'
Kenny Nolan 77
07 SOMETIMES WHEN WE TOUCH
Dan Hill 78
08 HEARTBEAT—IT'S A LOVEBEAT
DeFranco Family f/Tony DeFranco 73
09 I'M GONNA LOVE YOU JUST A LITTLE MORE BABY
Barry White 73
10 DO YOU WANNA MAKE LOVE
Peter McCann 77

Gene Chandler

IN 1953, Vivian Carter and her husband Jimmy Bracken formed the Vee Jay label to produce gospel recordings. They signed Maceo Smith, the Staple Singers, and the Swan Silvertones, and converted their garage into a rehearsal studio. The label had its first hit in 1954 with the Spaniels' "Goodnite Sweetheart, Goodnite," a song covered for the pop chart by the McGuire Sisters. More success came with the Impressions and Dee Clark, whose earliest hits were on Vee Jay's Falcon subsidiary.

Vee Jay first went to No. 1 on the Hot 100 with "Duke Of Earl" by Gene Chandler in 1962.

Vee Jay's biggest success came from signing the Four Seasons in August 1962. But in December 1963, the Seasons left Vee Jay because of legal disputes over royalty payments, and moved to Philips. Vee Jay won the right to release Beatles songs in America when Capitol passed on some early hits, but only had the rights to a few tracks before Capitol exercised its option with "I Want To Hold Your Hand." Vee Jay never recovered from the loss of the Four Seasons and the Beatles, and finally had to shut its doors.

01 BIG GIRLS DON'T CRY
The Four Seasons 62
02 SHERRY
The Four Seasons 62
03 DUKE OF EARL
Gene Chandler 62
04 WALK LIKE A MAN
The Four Seasons 62
05 RAINDROPS
Dee Clark 61
06 PLEASE PLEASE ME
The Beatles 64
07 DO YOU WANT TO KNOW A SECRET
The Beatles 64
08 CANDY GIRL
The Four Seasons 63
09 HE WILL BREAK YOUR HEART
Jerry Butler 60
10 EVERY BEAT OF MY HEART
The Pips 61

The CHARTS AND CONFIGURATIONS

THERE MAY BE an infinite number of ways to look at the charts, but this section narrows down that view to a finite selection, based on chart criteria and different configurations.

First up is a look at the top 100 one-hit wonders, a popular topic among record enthusiasts. Wayne Jancik related many fascinating stories about them in *The Billboard Book Of One-Hit Wonders.* Most artists don't plan to be one-hit wonders, but the curse strikes anyway. Being on the list of the top 100 one-hit wonders is a mixed blessing; it says you were the best at having the shortest career.

It's a rare Hot 100 that doesn't include at least one remake of a previous hit. The next four charts focus on the most successful remakes of songs that were originally recorded after the rock era began in 1955, the biggest remakes of songs first recorded before the rock era began, and the top remakes of Motown and Beatles songs.

Motion pictures were a source of hit songs before the rock era began. One look at the top 100 soundtrack tunes proves that music and movies have been compatible in the rock era. The theater has traditionally been another valuable source of hit songs, but the synergy between rock and the Broadway stage hasn't been as successful as the marriage of movies and music.

Gender, musical style, and place of origin are some of the factors used to determine the next set of charts. Solo performances by men and women are ranked, as are songs by girl groups and instrumentals. The next set of charts in this section are based on birthplace and feature artists native to the United Kingdom, Canada, Australia, Ireland, Sweden, Germany, and the Netherlands.

Finally, there is a new list of the top 30 songs by contestants from the TV series *American Idol.* When the last edition of this book was published (in 2003), *American Idol* had existed only since June 2002. By the opening weeks of 2007, 26 contestants from the show had appeared on a *Billboard* chart and the franchise had racked up 108 No. 1s across the wide field of charts compiled by the Billboard Information Group.

The Top 100 Songs by
ONE-HIT WONDERS

The Elegants

A "ONE-HIT WONDER" is a recording by an artist who had one lone single solitary hit on the *Billboard* chart and nothing more. To determine the top 100 one-hit wonders of the rock era, a series of rules was established. First, the artist could only make one appearance on the Hot 100. This disqualified artists like Debby Boone, who spent 10 weeks at No. 1 with "You Light Up My Life" and then had two more chart entries, albeit none higher than the No. 50 peak of "California."

Second, an artist could only have one appearance on the Hot 100 in any form. So if someone had hits with a group and also had a lone appearance as a solo artist, that solo performance would not count. That disqualified people like Frida, who had one hit on her own ("I Know There's Something Going On"), but 20 previous chart appearances with Abba.

Third, all chart appearances were considered, even if the artist used different names. While "Alley-Oop" by the Hollywood Argyles is generally considered to be a one-hit wonder, it was actually a solo effort by Gary Paxton, who had previously charted as the latter half of Skip and Flip ("It Was I," "Cherry Pie").

Fourth, an artist's entire career was considered, so someone who had registered on the *Billboard* chart before the rock era began, and then had only one hit after July 9, 1955, was not considered to be a one-hit wonder. This eliminated a singer like Jane Powell, who had charted with Fred Astaire in 1951 before having a solitary rock era hit with a version of "True Love."

Finally, a cut-off date was established. The eligibility period was July 9, 1955, to December 31, 2004. This seemed only fair to artists who may have charted once between 2005 and 2006 and haven't had a second hit yet, but who could conceivably chart again. It's always possible that some of the artists who have been tabbed one-hit wonders will return to the Hot 100 one day; when they do, they'll be removed from this list.

Most artists who intend to have recording careers do not intentionally set out to be one-hit wonders. After experiencing success with an initial chart entry, it's reasonable to expect more. The reasons why some artists never experience a follow-up hit are diverse enough that there is no sure-fire way to prevent future one-hit wonders.

Nine records are the ultimate one-hit wonders of the rock era. They went to No. 1, and then the artist never charted again. The first of these is "Little Star" by the Elegants. The founders of the group were from Staten Island, New York. Vito Picone, lead singer, and Carman Romano, baritone, were in a short-lived group called the Crescents. When they broke up in 1957, Vito and Carman recruited Artie Venosa to sing first tenor, Frankie Fardogno to sing second tenor, and Jimmy Moschella to sing bass. They took their name from a billboard advertising Schenley's whiskey as the "liquor of elegance." Vito and Artie adapted Mozart's "Twinkle, Twinkle, Little Star" into a rock and roll song, "Little Star." When the record hit, the group toured the continental United States and Hawaii, and didn't have time to go back in the studio. By the time they released "Goodnight" 18 months later, the Elegants had lost their momentum and never had another entry on the Hot 100.

There is a one-hit wonder with a short chart life as well as the shortest name in the business. "Pop Muzik" was M's only chart appearance. "M" was actually British musician Robin Scott, who took his stage name from the large letter "M" that identified metro stations in Paris. Scott had three more pop hits in the U.K. and released a 10th anniversary edition of "Pop Muzik" in 1989 that also charted. In the U.S., he never returned to the Hot 100 either as M or as Robin Scott.

The second most popular one-hit wonder is "Dominique" by the Singing Nun. Sister Luc-Gabrielle composed songs for the sisters at Fichermont Monastery in Belgium to sing at their evening retreats. The convent asked executives at Philips Records if they could press a couple hundred copies of the songs to be given away as gifts, and the company agreed to a brief, non-commercial recording session. The company was so impressed with the result that they released the album *Soeur Sourire* (Sister Smile) in Europe. The American office of Philips changed the title to *The Singing Nun* for the U.S., but there was little reaction until "Dominique," a song eulogizing the founder of the Dominican order, was released as a single. Sister Luc-Gabrielle ended up singing on *The Ed Sullivan Show* and having Debbie Reynolds portray her in a film biography. After the movie was released, she left the convent and returned to private life as Jeanine Deckers. She recorded for Philips again, but songs like "Glory Be To God For The Golden Pill," an ode to birth control, didn't achieve commercial success.

The third most successful one-hit wonder is "We Are The World" by USA for Africa. The 45 artists who gathered at A&M Studios in Hollywood

34 **PLAYGROUND IN MY MIND**
Clint Holmes *Epic* 73

35 **AXEL F**
Harold Faltermeyer *MCA* 85

36 **SEX AND CANDY**
Marcy Playground *Capitol* 98

37 **IT FEELS SO GOOD**
Sonique *Farm Club.com* 00

38 **I DON'T EVER WANT TO SEE YOU AGAIN**
Uncle Sam *Stonecreek* 98

39 **STEAL MY SUNSHINE**
Len *Work* 99

40 **SHE'S LIKE THE WIND**
Patrick Swayze f/Wendy Fraser *RCA* 88

41 **THE ENTERTAINER**
Marvin Hamlisch *MCA* 74

42 **FLOAT ON**
The Floaters *ABC* 77

43 **CRAZY FOR THIS GIRL**
Evan & Jaron *Columbia* 01

44 **NO LETTING GO**
Wayne Wonder *Greensleeves* 03

45 **SUNNY CAME HOME**
Shawn Colvin *Columbia* 97

46 **SALLY, GO 'ROUND THE ROSES**
The Jaynetts *Tuff* 63

47 **POPSICLES AND ICICLES**
The Murmaids *Chattahoochee* 64

48 **RAINBOW**
Russ Hamilton *Kapp* 57

49 **SUNSHINE**
Jonathan Edwards *Capricorn* 72

50 **I GOT 5 ON IT**
Luniz *Noo Trybe* 95

51 **HE'S MINE**
MoKenStef *OutBurst* 95

52 **DAYDREAMIN'**
Tatyana Ali *MJJ* 98

53 **WASTING MY TIME**
Default *TVT* 02

54 **PUTTIN' ON THE RITZ**
Taco *RCA* 83

55 **INTO THE NIGHT**
Benny Mardones *Polydor* 80

56 **DÉJÀ VU (UPTOWN BABY)**
Lord Tariq & Peter Gunz *Columbia* 98

57 **IN THE SUMMERTIME**
Mungo Jerry *Janus* 70

58 **DO YOU WANNA MAKE LOVE**
Peter McCann *20th Century* 77

59 **HEART AND SOUL**
T'Pau *Virgin* 87

60 **SUSIE DARLIN'**
Robin Luke *Dot* 58

61 **CINDY, OH CINDY**
Vince Martin w/the Tarriers *Glory* 56

62 **HEAVEN**
DJ Sammy & Yanou f/Do *Robbins* 02

63 **ONE THING**
Finger Eleven *Wind-up* 04

64 **MAKIN' IT**
David Naughton *RSO* 79

65 **CARS**
Gary Numan *Atco* 80

66 **PIPELINE**
The Chantays *Dot* 63

67 **THE HAPPY WHISTLER**
Don Robertson *Capitol* 56

following the American Music Awards in 1985 only intended to record one song. They were there at the invitation of personal manager Ken Kragen, who had been approached by Harry Belafonte about raising money to feed the hungry people of Africa. Kragen asked his client Lionel Richie to get involved and approached Quincy Jones to produce. Lionel collaborated with Michael Jackson to write "We Are The World," and while ironically none of the performers who made up USA for Africa are one-hit wonders themselves, collectively they are classified as such.

It's difficult to blame the Heights for being one-hit wonders. Less than a week after "How Do You Talk To An Angel" fell from pole position on the Hot 100, the Fox series was canceled. No TV series, no more recordings, despite the success of the single that toppled Boyz II Men's "End Of The Road" after 13 weeks. Lead singer Jamie Walters found more work when he was cast in Aaron Spelling's *Beverly Hills 90210*. He also was signed to Atlantic Records. In April 1995 his single "Hold On" peaked at No. 16 on the Hot 100. He hasn't charted since, technically making him a one-hit wonder twice, if that's possible.

The other four No. 1 hits that are also one-hit wonders are "In The Year 2525 (Exordium & Terminus)" by Zager and Evans, "Miami Vice Theme" by Jan Hammer, "When I'm With You" by Sheriff, and "Butterfly" by Crazy Town. Zager and Evans did release a follow-up single, but Denny Zager says he had already decided to quit the duo before "2525" fell off the chart. Hammer, a former keyboardist for the Mahavishnu Orchestra, composed his first film score for the 1983 movie *A Night In Heaven*. Producer Michael Mann asked him to score the pilot of *Miami Vice*, which led to composing about 20 minutes of original music for every episode. When MCA released a soundtrack from the TV series, Hammer's title theme was released as a single. Sheriff's "When I'm With You" went to No. 1 in their native Canada but sputtered out at No. 63 in America in 1983. The group split, with two of the members becoming Frozen Ghost and two others forming the group Alias. "When I'm With You" was revived by radio in 1988, and even though there was no more Sheriff, the song topped the chart. Crazy Town co-founder Seth Binzer was inspired by his girlfriend's love of butterflies to write his band's only hit. The group was in Germany when the song reached pole position, and the band members went online to Billboard.com to see the chart for themselves.

Some artists are only one-hit wonders in America. British singer Russ Hamilton had two pop hits in his home country, although neither one of them was "Rainbow." "Cars" was Gary Numan's only American hit, but he had 25 chart entries in England. Soft Cell's only U.S. hit was "Tainted Love." In the U.K., the duo had nine different songs make the chart. Mungo Jerry, David Dundas, Argent, and Mike Oldfield are other U.K. artists who had more than one hit at home.

68 **TAINTED LOVE**
Soft Cell *Sire* 82

69 **SHE'S SO HIGH**
Tal Bachman *Columbia* 99

70 **BOOK OF LOVE**
Monotones *Argo* 58

71 **THE ONE AND ONLY**
Chesney Hawkes *Chrysalis* 91

72 **MULE SKINNER BLUES**
The Fendermen *Soma* 60

73 **HAPPY, HAPPY BIRTHDAY BABY**
The Tune Weavers *Checker* 57

74 **BLACK DENIM TROUSERS**
The Cheers *Capitol* 55

75 **KISS THE RAIN**
Billie Myers *Universal* 98

76 **LOVE YOU SO**
Ron Holden *Donna* 60

77 **HOOKED ON CLASSICS**
Royal Philharmonic Orchestra *RCA* 82

78 **WILDFLOWER**
Skylark *Capitol* 73

79 **CRIMINAL**
Fiona Apple *Clean Slate* 97

80 **MANHATTAN SPIRITUAL**
Reg Owen *Palette* 59

81 **NEVER HAD A DREAM COME TRUE**
S Club 7 *A&M* 01

82 **F**K IT (I DON'T WANT YOU BACK)**
Eamon *Jive* 04

83 **THE JERK**
The Larks *Money* 65

84 **ROMEO AND JULIET**
Sylk-E. Fine f/Chill *RCA* 98

85 **CHICK-A-BOOM (DON'T YA JES' LOVE IT)**
Daddy Dewdrop *Sunflower* 71

86 **RUMORS**
Timex Social Club *Jay* 86

87 **SILENT LUCIDITY**
Queensrÿche *EMI* 91

88 **WESTSIDE**
TQ *ClockWork* 98

89 **SWING MY WAY**
K.P. & Envyi *EastWest* 98

90 **BABY LOVE**
Regina *Atlantic* 86

91 **MY BABY DADDY**
B-Rock & the Bizz *Tony Mercedes* 97

92 **YOUR WOMAN**
White Town *Chrysalis* 97

93 **GARDEN OF EDEN**
Joe Valino *Vik* 56

94 **DON'T CLOSE YOUR EYES**
Kix *Atlantic* 89

95 **I WISH**
Skee-Lo *Sunshine* 95

96 **THE LORD'S PRAYER**
Sister Janet Mead *A&M* 74

97 **AMERICANS**
Byron MacGregor *Westbound* 74

98 **THE BATTLE HYMN OF THE REPUBLIC**
Mormon Tabernacle Choir *Columbia* 59

99 **THE MAN IN THE RAINCOAT**
Priscilla Wright *Unique* 55

100 **BABY FACE**
Wing & A Prayer Fife & Drum Corps *Wing & A Prayer* 76

The Top 100
ROCK-ERA REMAKES

Tab Hunter

SOME SONGS are so closely connected with the artists who record-
ed them, that to think of one automatically brings the other to mind.
Chubby Checker and "The Twist" are inexorably linked, as are Debby
Boone with "You Light Up My Life" and Kim Carnes with "Bette Davis Eyes."
But like thousands of other songs, those three hits were all originally record-
ed by someone else.

The practice of covering a song at the time of its release or remaking
it years later is an old one. Music publishers earn royalties when the songs
they own are recorded, and the more versions that are available, the more
royalties they earn. Artists appreciate good material, which is why a song
like "Cupid" can be a hit for Sam Cooke in 1961 and then chart again for
Johnny Rivers in 1965, Johnny Nash in 1975, Dawn in 1976, and the
Spinners (who used it in a medley) in 1980. Their version went to No. 4 on
the Hot 100—the song's fifth and most successful chart run so far.

In the '50s, it was common practice for white pop singers to cover songs written by black R&B artists. Radio stations that played rock and roll frequently would not give airplay to black artists, but would willingly play their songs if they were recorded by white singers. The highest-ranked example on the top 100 remakes of the rock era is Pat Boone's "Ain't That A Shame." The original recording by Fats Domino entered the R&B chart on May 14, 1955, and spent 11 weeks at No. 1. Dot Records owner Randy Wood had Pat Boone cover it, and his version entered the Best Sellers chart on July 9, 1955—literally the beginning of the rock era. Boone's record went to No. 2, while Domino's entered the Best Sellers chart the following week and peaked at No. 16.

Similarly, Teresa Brewer had a bigger pop hit with "Bo Weevil" than Fats Domino. Cathy Carr had a pop hit with "Ivory Tower," first recorded by Otis Williams & His Charms, and Gale Storm had the pop hit with Smiley Lewis' "I Hear You Knocking." The Gladiolas, the group that became Maurice Williams & the Zodiacs ("Stay"), lost out when the Diamonds—a vocal quartet from Ontario, Canada—took their "Little Darlin'" to No. 2 for eight weeks.

Not all of the songs remade in the '50s were new versions of R&B songs. Ric Cartey recorded a song he wrote with Carole Joyner, "Young Love," for RCA. When it failed to chart, Cartey played it for Sonny James, who liked it enough to record it on Capitol. At Dot, Wood thought James would have the country hit, and so he called actor Tab Hunter and asked him if he could carry a tune. Tab's version of "Young Love" went to No. 1 on the Best Sellers chart, while James' single peaked at No. 2. Guy Mitchell had two No. 1 hits by cutting pop versions of country recordings—first with Marty Robbins' "Singing The Blues" and then with Ray Price's "Heartaches By The Number."

The third most successful cover version of the rock era is Chubby Checker's recording of '"The Twist." Hank Ballard wrote the song after seeing teenagers in Tampa, Florida, dancing the Twist. He recorded it with his band, the Midnighters, and it was released on the flip side of their first pop hit, "Teardrops On Your Letter." When the dance became popular on *American Bandstand,* Dick Clark suggested to Danny & the Juniors that they record a cover version of the song. When nothing materialized, Clark approached Philadelphia-based Cameo-Parkway Records and proposed that Checker record it. Chubby's version of "The Twist" was such a close copy that when Ballard first heard it, he thought he was listening to his own recording.

Motion picture soundtracks and Broadway scores have long been a source of recording material, and there have been many successful cover versions of screen and stage songs. The most successful is Debby Boone's recording of the title song from *You Light Up My Life,* a film that starred Didi Conn as a young singer seeking fame. In the movie, Conn's vocals were provided by commercial jingle singer Kacey Cisyk. Mike Curb attended a screening of the film and thought the song would be perfect for Boone, so he borrowed the instrumental track from writer/producer Joe Brooks, dubbing Debby's vocal over it. Cisyk's version was also released, but the Arista single didn't even list her name: the label credit read "Original Cast."

33 **LOVE WILL KEEP US TOGETHER**
Captain & Tennille *[Neil Sedaka]*

34 **IT'S SO HARD TO SAY GOODBYE TO YESTERDAY** Boyz II Men *[G.C. Camoron]*

35 **INDIAN RESERVATION (THE LAMENT OF THE CHEROKEE RESERVATION INDIAN)**
The Raiders *[John D. Loudermilk]*

36 **I'LL BE THERE**
Mariah Carey *[Jackson 5]*

37 **SOMETHIN' STUPID**
Nancy Sinatra & Frank Sinatra
[Carson & Gaile]

38 **RHINESTONE COWBOY**
Glen Campbell *[Larry Weiss]*

39 **WITHOUT YOU** Nilsson *[Badfinger]*

40 **LOUIE LOUIE**
The Kingsmen *[Richard Berry]*

41 **WAR** Edwin Starr *[The Temptations]*

42 **CALCUTTA** Lawrence Welk *[Heino Gaze]*

43 **WITHOUT YOU** Mariah Carey *[Badfinger]*

44 **AIN'T NO MOUNTAIN HIGH ENOUGH**
Diana Ross *[Marvin Gaye & Tammi Terrell]*

45 **I WILL FOLLOW HIM**
Little Peggy March *[Petula Clark]*

46 **GO AWAY LITTLE GIRL**
Donny Osmond *[Bobby Vee]*

47 **ALONE** Heart *[I-Ten]*

48 **I WRITE THE SONGS**
Barry Manilow *[Captain & Tennille]*

49 **MAMA TOLD ME (NOT TO COME)**
Three Dog Night *[Randy Newman]*

50 **SHAME ON THE MOON**
Bob Seger & the Silver Bullet Band
[Rodney Crowell]

51 **MRS. BROWN YOU'VE GOT A LOVELY DAUGHTER**
Herman's Hermits *[Tom Courtenay]*

52 **LEAVING ON A JET PLANE**
Peter, Paul & Mary *[John Denver]*

53 **WILD NIGHT**
John Mellencamp & Me'Shell NdegéOcello
[Van Morrison]

54 **YOU DON'T BRING ME FLOWERS**
Barbra Streisand & Neil Diamond
[Neil Diamond]

55 **JOHNNY ANGEL**
Shelley Fabares *[unknown]*

56 **GLORIA**
Laura Branigan *[Umberto Tozzi]*

57 **DO WAH DIDDY DIDDY**
Manfred Mann *[The Exciters]*

58 **WEDDING BELL BLUES**
5th Dimension *[Laura Nyro]*

59 **SOMEDAY WE'LL BE TOGETHER**
Diana Ross & the Supremes
[Johnny & Jackie]

60 **THE CANDY MAN**
Sammy Davis, Jr. *[Aubrey Woods]*

61 **MICKEY** Toni Basil *[Smile]*

62 **HEARTACHES BY THE NUMBER**
Guy Mitchell *[Ray Price]*

63 **GREATEST LOVE OF ALL**
Whitney Houston *[George Benson]*

64 **ME AND BOBBY MCGEE**
Janis Joplin *[Roger Miller]*

65 **BROTHER LOUIE**
Stories *[Hot Chocolate]*

66 **MIDNIGHT TRAIN TO GEORGIA**
Gladys Knight & the Pips *[Jim Weatherly]*

Percy Faith had the No. 1 single of 1960 by recording Max Steiner's theme music from *A Summer Place.* Arthur Ferrante and Louis Teicher, who met as children when they were both studying at the Juilliard School of Music in the '20s, had several chart hits by playing movie themes on their twin Steinway pianos. The most successful was their 1961 recording of Ernest Gold's theme from *Exodus.* Aubrey Woods sang Anthony Newley and Leslie Bricusse's "The Candy Man" in *Willie Wonka And The Chocolate Factory,* and although Newley was certain the song would not be a hit, Mike Curb, then president of MGM Records, came up with the idea of having Sammy Davis, Jr. record it.

The 5th Dimension had the biggest hit of their career when they recorded a medley of "Aquarius" and "Let The Sunshine In" from the Broadway musical *Hair.* The Cowsills also had their biggest hit by recording a version of the title song from that musical. Louis Armstrong made the title song of *Hello, Dolly!* his own, even though he wasn't in the stage musical. The Four Lads went to No. 3 with "Standing On The Corner," originally heard in *The Most Happy Fella.*

Some original versions of songs remain obscure. Jackie DeShannon recorded "Bette Davis Eyes," which she wrote with Donna Weiss, on a Columbia album from 1975, *New Arrangement.* "Gloria" was originally an Italian song, recorded by its composer, Umberto Tozzi, before Laura Branigan released it. The Arrows were an Anglo-American band recording for the Rak label in the U.K., and one of their "B" sides was a song written by group members Jake Hooker and Alan Merrill to counter the Rolling Stones' "It's Only Rock 'N Roll (But I Like It)." Joan Jett wanted to record "I Love Rock 'N Roll" when she was in the Runaways, but the other members declined. Her version with the Blackhearts was No. 1 for seven weeks. "Whole Lot Of Shakin' Going On" was co-written by Roy Hall under the name Sunny David; his version was released on Decca in late 1955, but was preceded by a few months by an R&B version from Big Maybelle on the Okeh label. Jerry Lee Lewis made "Whole Lot Of Shakin' Going On" his own in 1957.

Steve Lawrence had the first hit with "Go Away Little Girl" and Donny Osmond remade it eight years later, but it originally appeared on an album by Bobby Vee. Fargo, North Dakota native Vee had a chart single with "More Than I Can Say" 19 years before Leo Sayer took it to No. 2 (the earliest version was by the Crickets). All of the Supremes' singles, from "I Want A Guy" to "No Matter What Sign You Are," were originals, so most people didn't realize that their final single with Diana Ross singing lead—"Someday We'll Be Together"—had actually been recorded nine years earlier by two of the song's composers, Jackie Beavers and Johnny Bristol, on the Tri-Phi label. David Martin, one of the writers of "Can't Smile Without You," recorded it in England before the Carpenters put it on one of their American albums; both versions preceded Barry Manilow's. Bill Medley and Bette Midler each made the Hot 100 with earlier versions of Linda Ronstadt and Aaron Neville's hit "Don't Know Much," but the song first appeared on a 1980 Casablanca album by songwriter Barry Mann.

67 **MORE THAN I CAN SAY**
Leo Sayer *[The Crickets]*

68 **RESPECT**
Aretha Franklin *[Otis Redding]*

69 **QUARTER TO THREE**
Gary U.S. Bonds *[The Church Street Five]*

70 **GO AWAY LITTLE GIRL**
Steve Lawrence *[Bobby Vee]*

71 **LOVE THEME FROM "ROMEO AND JULIET"**
Henry Mancini *[Nino Rota]*

72 **YOUNG LOVE** Sonny James *[Ric Cartey]*

73 **ALL THE MAN THAT I NEED**
Whitney Houston *[Linda Clifford]*

74 **DON'T LEAVE ME THIS WAY**
Thelma Houston *[Harold Melvin & the Blue Notes]*

75 **MEDLEY: INTRO VENUS...**
Stars on 45 *[Shocking Blue, The Archies, The Beatles]*

76 **WHEN A MAN LOVES A WOMAN**
Michael Bolton *[Percy Sledge]*

77 **IF I CAN'T HAVE YOU**
Yvonne Elliman *[Bee Gees]*

78 **THE TIDE IS HIGH** Blondie *[The Paragons]*

79 **IN THE STILL OF THE NITE (I'LL REMEMBER)**
Boyz II Men *[The Five Satins]*

80 **HOW AM I SUPPOSED TO LIVE WITHOUT YOU** Michael Bolton *[Laura Branigan]*

81 **DON'T TURN AROUND**
Ace of Base *[Tina Turner]*

82 **FANTASTIC VOYAGE** Coolio *[Lakeside]*

83 **TWIST AND SHOUT**
The Beatles *[The Top Notes]*

84 **WHEN I NEED YOU**
Leo Sayer *[Albert Hammond]*

85 **LAST KISS**
Pearl Jam *[J. Frank Wilson & the Cavaliers]*

86 **TOTAL ECLIPSE OF THE HEART**
Nicki French *[Bonnie Tyler]*

87 **SOUTHERN NIGHTS**
Glen Campbell *[Allen Toussaint]*

88 **LEAN ON ME** Club Nouveau *[Bill Withers]*

89 **I'M LEAVING IT UP TO YOU**
Dale and Grace *[Don and Dewey]*

90 **EVERYTIME YOU GO AWAY**
Paul Young *[Daryl Hall and John Oates]*

91 **IN THE SUMMERTIME**
Shaggy *[Mungo Jerry]*

92 **FROM A DISTANCE**
Bette Midler *[Nanci Griffith]*

93 **HE DON'T LOVE YOU (LIKE I LOVE YOU)**
Tony Orlando & Dawn *[Jerry Butler]*

94 **I HEAR YOU KNOCKING**
Gale Storm *[Smiley Lewis]*

95 **HOOKED ON A FEELING**
Blue Swede *[B.J. Thomas]*

96 **BILLY, DON'T BE A HERO**
Bo Donaldson & the Heywoods *[Paper Lace]*

97 **DON'T LET THE SUN GO DOWN ON ME**
George Michael/Elton John *[Elton John]*

98 **ENDLESS LOVE**
Luther Vandross & Mariah Carey *[Diana Ross & Lionel Richie]*

99 **HARD TO SAY I'M SORRY**
Az Yet f/Peter Cetera *[Chicago]*

100 **GROOVY KIND OF LOVE**
Phil Collins *[The Mindbenders]*

PRE-ROCK-ERA REMAKES

Bobby Darin

Many SONGS that have been popular in the rock era originated long before Bill Haley and His Comets ascended to number one with "(We're Gonna) Rock Around The Clock" on July 9, 1955. Even that rock classic had been recorded previously. Haley's recording first entered the *Billboard* chart on May 29, 1954, but it was preceded by an R&B recording of the song by Sonny Dae & the Knights.

The most successful remake of a pre-rock era song is "Hound Dog" by Elvis Presley. Jerry Leiber and Mike Stoller wrote it in 1952 when Johnny Otis asked them to come up with tunes for the singers in his band, Little Esther and Big Mama Thornton. Leiber and Stoller watched Thornton rehearse, then went home and wrote "Hound Dog" for her as a country blues song. They produced the song with Otis, and it entered the *Billboard* R&B Best Sellers chart on March 28, 1953. It spent six weeks at No. 1. Elvis heard the song while making his ill-fated debut in Las Vegas in April 1956. The middle-aged audience that came to see the show didn't appreciate the future king, and the two-week engagement was canceled at the end of the first week. One night during his run, Elvis walked into the lounge and saw Freddie Bell & the Bellboys perform a comedic version of "Hound

Dog." Elvis liked how they did the song and performed it in June on Milton Berle's TV show. He reluctantly recorded it in New York on July 2, at producer Steve Sholes' insistence. Along with "Don't Be Cruel," "Hound Dog" became Elvis' biggest hit of all time.

A number of rock era hits were first recorded in the early half of the '50s. Five inmates from Tennessee State Penitentiary, including songwriter Johnny Bragg, arrived at Sam Phillips' recording studio in Memphis on June 1, 1953, to rehearse some material they wanted to record. One of the songs they cut was an *a cappella* rendition of a song Bragg had written with Robert S. Riley, "Just Walking In The Rain." They returned to their prison cells, and six weeks later, Sun Records released the song on red vinyl with black stripes. Three years after that, Johnnie Ray recorded it, and it went to No. 3 on the Best Sellers chart.

In 1954, "The Poor People Of Paris" was a hit for Edith Piaf in France under its original title, *"La Goulante Du Pauvre Jean."* That should have translated as "The Ballad Of Poor John," but Capitol Records' Parisian representative substituted *gens* (meaning "people") for *Jean* when cabling the information to Hollywood.

Eight different artists have made the *Billboard* chart with "Unchained Melody," beginning with Les Baxter and Al Hibbler in 1955. The biggest hit version was by the Righteous Brothers, who enjoyed chart runs with the song in 1965 and 1990. The original version was sung by Todd Duncan in the film *Unchained.*

Ivory Joe Hunter took "I Almost Lost My Mind" to No. 1 on the R&B Best Sellers chart in 1950, six years before Pat Boone made it a pop hit. Archibald, a New Orleans singer whose real name was Leon T. Gross, had an R&B top 10 hit with "Stack-A-Lee" in 1950, and Lloyd Price turned it into "Stagger Lee" for a No. 1 hit on the Hot 100 in 1959. Tony Bennett peaked at No. 16 with "Blue Velvet" in 1951, 12 years before Bobby Vinton made it a No. 1 song. "Kansas City" was a Leiber-Stoller song first recorded as "K. C. Lovin'" by Little Willie Littlefield on Federal in 1952; Wilbert Harrison had a No. 1 pop hit with the song in 1959. Elvis Presley recorded "Crying In The Chapel" in 1960, although it wasn't released until 1965. There were seven different versions of the song on the chart in 1953, including recordings by June Valli, Rex Allen, and the Orioles. But the original was by 16-year-old Darrell Glenn from Waco, Texas; his father, Artie Glenn, wrote the song.

A lot of hits from the rock era originated in the '40s. "Autumn Leaves" was called *"Les Feuilles Mortes"* when Joseph Kosma wrote it in 1947, eight years before pianist Roger Williams had a No. 1 hit with it. Merle Travis wrote and recorded "Sixteen Tons" in 1947 for an album titled *Folk Songs Of The Hills.* Capitol wanted some mining songs on it, but Travis couldn't find any, so he wrote some. In 1955, Tennessee Ernie Ford took time out from his busy TV schedule to record Travis' song. Gene Autry sang "Blueberry Hill" in a 1940 movie; it was a No. 1 song for Glenn Miller that same year, preceding Fats Domino's version by 17 years.

Twenty-four of the top 100 remakes of pre-rock era songs originated In the '30s. "Love Letters In The Sand" was recorded by Pat Boone because Dot Records founder Randy Wood had requests for the song over

36 **BLUEBERRY HILL**
Fats Domino [Glenn Miller/Gene Autry, 1940]
37 **BLUE MOON**
The Marcels [1934]
38 **TWILIGHT TIME**
The Platters [Three Suns, 1944]
39 **WALK RIGHT IN**
The Rooftop Singers
[Gus Cannon & the Jugstompers, 1930]
40 **MAMBO NO. 5 (A LITTLE BIT OF...)**
Lou Bega [Perez Prado, 1950]
41 **THOSE WERE THE DAYS**
Mary Hopkin [Alexander Wertinsky, circa 1920]
42 **KANSAS CITY**
Wilbert Harrison [Little Willie Littlefield, 1952]
43 **DEEP PURPLE**
Nino Tempo & April Stevens [1934]
44 **THE BOLL WEEVIL SONG**
Brook Benton [Traditional]
45 **DON'T YOU KNOW**
Della Reese [Giacomo Puccini, 1896]
46 **I'M HENRY VIII, I AM**
Herman's Hermits [Harry Champion, 1911]
47 **TOPSY II**
Cozy Cole [1939]
48 **A LOVER'S CONCERTO**
The Toys [Bach, 1725]
49 **MY DING-A-LING**
Chuck Berry [Dave Bartholomew, 1952]
50 **HE'S GOT THE WHOLE WORLD (IN HIS HANDS)**
Laurie London [Traditional]
51 **WOODEN HEART (MUSS I DENN)**
Joe Dowell [Traditional German folk song]
52 **A WONDERFUL TIME UP THERE /
IT'S TOO SOON TO KNOW**
Pat Boone
[Lee Roy Abernathy, 1947/The Orioles, 1948]
53 **MY HAPPINESS**
Connie Francis [1933]
54 **UNCHAINED MELODY**
Righteous Brothers [Todd Duncan, 1955]
55 **HELLO MUDDUH, HELLO FADDUH!
(A LETTER FROM CAMP)**
Allan Sherman [Ponchielli, 1876]
56 **HAVE I TOLD YOU LATELY THAT I LOVE YOU?**
Ricky Nelson
[Bing Crosby & the Andrews Sisters, 1950]
57 **CAN'T HELP FALLING IN LOVE**
Elvis Presley [Giovanni Martini, 18th century]
58 **THE LION SLEEPS TONIGHT**
Robert John [Miriam Makeba, 1951]
59 **SAIL ALONG SILVERY MOON**
Billy Vaughn [1937]
60 **MY BLUE HEAVEN**
Fats Domino
[Paul Whiteman & His Orchestra, 1927]
61 **THE ENTERTAINER**
Marvin Hamlisch [Scott Joplin, 1902]
62 **ALSO SPRACH ZARATHUSTRA**
Deodato [Richard Strauss, 1896]
63 **TONIGHT YOU BELONG TO ME**
Patience and Prudence [Irving Kaufman, 1926]
64 **FASCINATION**
Jane Morgan [1904]
65 **LAVENDER-BLUE**
Sammy Turner [Traditional, 1750]
66 **GEORGIA ON MY MIND**
Ray Charles
[Frankie Trumbauer & His Orchestra, 1931]
67 **MOONGLOW AND THEME FROM "PICNIC"**
George Cates [OC/Blackbirds of 1934, 1934]
68 **I GOT RHYTHM**
The Happenings [OC/Girl Crazy, 1930]

a 10-year period at the record store he owned in Gallatin, Tennessee. Bing Crosby and Rudy Vallee had recorded it, but it was first a hit for Ted Black & His Orchestra in the fall of 1931. Jimmy Dorsey had a hit with "So Rare" in 1957, 20 years after Guy Lombardo recorded it. Nelson Riddle's recording of "Lisbon Antigua" was an updating of a song written by three Portuguese writers in 1937 as *"Lisboa Antigua,"* meaning "In Old Lisbon."

"Mack The Knife" was how Marc Blitzstein translated the song "Moritat" from *The Threepenny Opera* by Kurt Weill and Berthold Brecht. The show opened in Berlin in 1928. "Are You Lonesome Tonight?" was also from that decade; Roy Turk and Lou Handman wrote it in 1926. "My Blue Heaven," popularized by Fats Domino in 1956, was a hit for Paul Whiteman & His Orchestra in 1927.

"It's All In The Game" was first recorded by Tommy Edwards in 1951, the same year it was cut by Sammy Kaye, Carmen Cavallaro, and Dinah Shore. Edwards recorded a new, pop version in stereo in 1958, and it went to No. 1. But the song's origins can be traced back to 1912, when Charles Gates Dawes—who would later be Vice President under Calvin Coolidge—wrote a tune called "Melody In A Major" (Carl Sigman added lyrics in 1951). Elvis Presley's recording of "It's Now Or Never" was a No. 1 hit in 1960; the song is based on the Italian song *"O Sole Mio,"* written in 1901.

Some rock and roll hits can be traced back to the 19th century. "The Yellow Rose Of Texas," No. 1 for Mitch Miller in 1955, is an 1853 marching song written for traveling minstrel shows, and became popular during the Civil War. Elvis' "Love Me Tender" was based on "Aura Lee," a folk ballad from 1861. "The Battle Of New Orleans," a No. 1 hit for Johnny Horton in 1959, descended from a folk song called "The Eighth Of January," the date Andrew Jackson's forces defeated the British at New Orleans in the final battle of the War of 1812. The song was written in 1815.

A number of rock era hits are based on pieces of classical music. Perry Como's "Hot Diggity (Dog Ziggity Boom)" was adapted from the first theme of Chabrier's *"Espana Rhapsody,"* written in the 19th century. Walter Murphy gave Ludwig Van the disco treatment with the 1976 hit "A Fifth Of Beethoven." Della Reese' 1959 hit "Don't You Know" was based on Giacomo Puccini's "Musetta's Waltz," composed in 1896. Eric Carmen based his 1975 hit "All By Myself" on music from Rachmaninoff's "Second Concerto." Deodato's *"Also Sprach Zarathustra"* was a jazzy version of the dramatic theme heard in Stanley Kubrick's *2001: A Space Odyssey;* it was written by Richard Strauss in 1896. And Chopin's Prelude In C Minor provided the inspiration for Barry Manilow's third chart single, "Could It Be Magic."

69 **GOTTA TRAVEL ON**
Billy Grammer [Traditional, 19th century]

70 **CRYING IN THE CHAPEL**
Elvis Presley [Darrell Glenn, 1953]

71 **(NOW AND THEN THERE'S) A FOOL SUCH AS I**
Elvis Presley [Hank Snow, 1953]

72 **PUTTIN' ON THE RITZ**
Taco [Harry Richman, 1930]

73 **THE YELLOW ROSE OF TEXAS**
Johnny Desmond [Traditional, Civil War]

74 **IN THE MOOD**
Ernie Fields [Glenn Miller & His Orchestra, 1939]

75 **RELEASE ME (AND LET ME LOVE AGAIN)**
Engelbert Humperdinck [Jimmy Heap, 1954]

76 **I'VE TOLD EVERY LITTLE STAR**
Linda Scott [OC/Music In The Air, 1932]

77 **WHERE OR WHEN**
Dion & the Belmonts [OC/Babes In Arms, 1937]

78 **I'M GONNA SIT RIGHT DOWN
AND WRITE MYSELF A LETTER**
Billy Williams [Fats Waller, 1935]

79 **QUIET VILLAGE**
The Exotic Sounds of Martin Denny
[Les Baxter, 1952]

80 **THEME FROM "THE APARTMENT"**
Ferrante and Teicher [1949]

81 **SINCE I FELL FOR YOU**
Lenny Welch [Annie Laurie & Paul Gayten, 1947]

82 **LOVE ME** Elvis Presley [Willie & Ruth, 1954]

83 **WAY DOWN YONDER IN NEW ORLEANS**
Freddy Cannon [Peerless Quartet, 1922]

84 **MORITAT (A THEME FROM
"THE THREE PENNY OPERA")**
Dick Hyman [OC/The Threepenny Opera, 1928]

85 **ROCK-A-BYE YOUR BABY
WITH A DIXIE MELODY**
Jerry Lewis [Al Jolson, 1918]

86 **THE HAWAIIAN WEDDING SONG**
Andy Williams [1926]

87 **IT'S A SIN TO TELL A LIE**
Somethin' Smith & the Redheads
[Victor Young & His Orchestra, 1936]

88 **WHO'S SORRY NOW**
Connie Francis [Irving Kaufman, 1923]

89 **KISSES SWEETER THAN WINE**
Jimmie Rodgers [The Weavers, 1951]

90 **RED RIVER ROCK**
Johnny & the Hurricanes [Traditional]

91 **TEA FOR TWO CHA CHA**
Tommy Dorsey & the Orchestra
[OC/No, No, Nanette, 1924]

92 **SLOOP JOHN B**
The Beach Boys
[Traditional West Indies folk song, 1927]

93 **THE HOUSE OF BLUE LIGHTS**
Chuck Miller [Freddie Slack & His Orchestra, 1946]

94 **WHAT A DIFF'RENCE A DAY MAKES**
Dinah Washington
[Dorsey Brothers Orchestra, 1934]

95 **YOU DON'T HAVE TO BE A BABY TO CRY**
The Caravelles [Ernest Tubb, 1950]

96 **STARDUST**
Billy Ward & His Dominoes
[Irving Mills & His Hotsy Totsy Band, 1930]

97 **CARA, MIA**
Jay & the Americans [David Whitfield, 1954]

98 **MULE SKINNER BLUES**
The Fendermen [Jimmie Rodgers, 1931]

99 **BLUE MONDAY**
Fats Domino [Smiley Lewis, 1953]

100 **HOOKED ON CLASSICS**
Royal Philharmonic Orchestra [Various,
including Tchaikovsky, Mozart, and Grieg]

The Top 50 MOTOWN REMAKES

The Temptations

BERRY GORDY established his own song publishing company in 1958. He named it Jobete, for his daughters Hazel Joy, Betty, and Terry. The first song published by the new company was "I Need You," written by Gordy and recorded by Herman Griffin on the HOB label. Jobete would one day have one of the richest song catalogs in the world, in every sense of the word.

The earliest cover versions of Motown songs that were hits were released in 1964. The Kingsmen followed "Louie Louie" with a rendition of "Money," a song that went to No. 23 in 1960 for Barrett Strong. The original version had been released on Anna, a label run by Berry's sister Gwen, although it also appeared later on Tamla. The single by the Kingsmen fared even better than Strong's record, peaking at No. 16. Two months later, the Dave Clark Five released a remake of the Contours' 1962 hit "Do You Love Me," and the Beatles recorded three Motown songs—"Money," "Please Mr. Postman," and "You've Really Got A Hold On Me."

Later in the year, the Kingsmen's label, Wand, tried to cover a Holland-Dozier-Holland song. The Supremes were enjoying their second consecutive No. 1 single with "Baby Love" when Wand released "Come See About Me" by Nella Dodds. Motown was planning to issue that track as the third single from the Supremes' *Where Did Our Love Go* album, and had to rush it out to prevent the cover version from becoming a hit.

The next Motown song to be successfully covered was "Devil With A Blue Dress On," originally called "Devil With The Blue Dress" when Shorty Long released it as the first single on the Soul label. Mitch Ryder combined it with Little Richard's "Good Golly Miss Molly" in a medley that peaked at No. 4.

01 **GANGSTA'S PARADISE**
   Coolio f/L.V. [Stevie Wonder]
02 **I HEARD IT THROUGH THE GRAPEVINE**
   Marvin Gaye
   [Smokey Robinson & the Miracles]
03 **IT'S SO HARD TO SAY**
   GOODBYE TO YESTERDAY
   Boyz II Men [G.C. Cameron]
04 **I'LL BE THERE**
   Mariah Carey [Jackson 5]
05 **WAR**
   Edwin Starr [The Temptations]
06 **AIN'T NO MOUNTAIN HIGH ENOUGH**
   Diana Ross [Marvin Gaye & Tammi Terrell]
07 **ENDLESS LOVE**
   Luther Vandross & Mariah Carey
   [Diana Ross & Lionel Richie]
08 **I HEARD IT THROUGH THE GRAPEVINE**
   Gladys Knight & the Pips
   [Smokey Robinson & the Miracles]
09 **YOU KEEP ME HANGIN' ON**
   Kim Wilde [The Supremes]
10 **YOU'VE MADE ME SO VERY HAPPY**
   Blood, Sweat & Tears [Brenda Holloway]
11 **LATELY**
   Jodeci [Stevie Wonder]
12 **PAPA WAS A ROLLIN' STONE**
   The Temptations [The Undisputed Truth]
13 **DEVIL WITH A BLUE DRESS ON &**
   GOOD GOLLY MISS MOLLY
   Mitch Ryder & the Detroit Wheels
   [Shorty Long]
14 **PLEASE MR. POSTMAN**
   Carpenters [The Marvelettes]
15 **UNTIL YOU COME BACK TO ME**
   (THAT'S WHAT I'M GONNA DO)
   Aretha Franklin [Stevie Wonder]
16 **I'LL BE THERE FOR YOU/**
   YOU'RE ALL I NEED TO GET BY
   Method Man f/Mary J. Blige
   [Marvin Gaye & Tammi Terrell]
17 **GET READY**
   Rare Earth [The Temptations]
18 **BABY I NEED YOUR LOVIN'**
   Johnny Rivers [Four Tops]
19 **YOU CAN'T HURRY LOVE**
   Phil Collins [The Supremes]
20 **TOO BUSY THINKING ABOUT MY BABY**
   Marvin Gaye [The Temptations]
21 **THE WAY YOU DO THE THINGS YOU DO**
   UB40 [The Temptations]
22 **HEAVEN MUST HAVE SENT YOU**
   Bonnie Pointer [The Elgins]
23 **SHOP AROUND**
   Captain & Tennille [The Miracles]
24 **MORE LOVE**
   Kim Carnes
   [Smokey Robinson & the Miracles]
25 **OOH BABY BABY**
   Linda Ronstadt [The Miracles]

In 1967, Johnny Rivers remade the Four Tops' "Baby I Need Your Loving" and bested their version by peaking at No. 3 (the Tops went to No. 11). That same year, Bill Cosby put a new spin on Stevie Wonder's "Uptight" in a song called "Little Ole Man." Stevie had peaked at No. 3 and Cosby went to No. 4.

Motown did a great job of covering itself during the '60s and the first half of the '70s. In fact, five of the top 10 Motown remakes were recorded by Motown artists. It wasn't unusual for Motown producers to record one song with several different artists. The second most successful Motown remake, "I Heard It Through The Grapevine," was originally recorded by Smokey Robinson & the Miracles, but not released until the 1968 album *Special Occasion.* The Isley Brothers recorded it next; their version was never released. Then Marvin Gaye cut it, but it was held back in favor of a version by Gladys Knight & the Pips. It was Gladys' first big hit for Motown, spending three weeks at No. 2 at the end of 1967. In the fall of 1968, Gaye's version showed up on his *In The Groove* album, but it wasn't the first single released. Finally issued, it went to No. 1 for seven weeks.

Other Jobete songs covered by Motown artists include "It's So Hard To Say Goodbye To Yesterday," a G.C. Cameron track on the *Cooley High* soundtrack before Boyz II Men attempted it; "War," an album track for the Temptations before it was a single for Edwin Starr; "Ain't No Mountain High Enough," a top 20 single for Marvin Gaye and Tammi Terrell three years before it was rearranged for Diana Ross; "Until You Come Back To Me (That's What I'm Gonna Do)," recorded by Stevie Wonder in 1967 but unreleased until after Aretha Franklin had a hit with it in 1974; "Get Ready," done in a rock version by Rare Earth four years after it was a hit for the Temptations; "Heaven Must Have Sent You," a bigger hit for Bonnie Pointer than for the Elgins; "Too Busy Thinking About My Baby," recorded by the Temptations on the *Gettin' Ready* album three years before it was a single for Marvin Gaye; and "Papa Was A Rollin' Stone," an album track for the Undisputed Truth before the Temptations took it to No. 1.

Many of the songs written by Motown's stable of writers have proved timeless, as Kim Wilde took "You Keep Me Hangin' On" to No. 1 some 21 years after the Supremes did; Rod Stewart had a top 10 hit with '"This Old Heart Of Mine" 24 years after the Isley Brothers; UB40 had the most successful chart version of "The Way You Do The Things You Do" 26 years after it was recorded by the Temptations; and Jodeci updated the little-known ballad "Lately" 12 years after it charted for Stevie Wonder.

26 **HOW SWEET IT IS (TO BE LOVED BY YOU)**
James Taylor [Marvin Gaye]

27 **HEAT WAVE**
Linda Ronstadt [Martha & the Vandellas]

28 **YOU KEEP ME HANGIN' ON**
Vanilla Fudge [The Supremes]

29 **NEVER CAN SAY GOODBYE**
Gloria Gaynor [Jackson 5]

30 **DANCING IN THE STREET**
Mick Jagger/David Bowie
[Martha & the Vandellas]

31 **(I KNOW) I'M LOSING YOU**
Rare Earth [The Temptations]

32 **THAT'S THE WAY LOVE IS**
Marvin Gaye [Gladys Knight & the Pips]

33 **THIS OLD HEART OF MINE**
Rod Stewart & Ronald Isley [Isley Brothers]

34 **LOVE CHILD**
Sweet Sensation
[Diana Ross & the Supremes]

35 **LITTLE OLE MAN (UPTIGHT-EVERYTHING'S ALRIGHT)**
Bill Cosby [Stevie Wonder]

36 **MONEY**
The Kingsmen [Barrett Strong]

37 **MERCY MERCY ME (THE ECOLOGY)/ I WANT YOU**
Robert Palmer [Marvin Gaye]

38 **SIGNED, SEALED, DELIVERED (I'M YOURS)**
Peter Frampton [Stevie Wonder]

39 **WAR**
Bruce Springsteen & the E Street Band
[The Temptations]

40 **WHAT'S GOING ON**
Cyndi Lauper [Marvin Gaye]

41 **TAKE ME IN YOUR ARMS (ROCK ME)**
Doobie Brothers [Kim Weston]

42 **WHERE DID OUR LOVE GO**
Donnie Elbert [The Supremes]

43 **DO YOU LOVE ME**
Dave Clark Five [The Contours]

44 **THE TRACKS OF MY TEARS**
Johnny Rivers [The Miracles]

45 **HOW SWEET IT IS (TO BE LOVED BY YOU)**
Jr. Walker & the All Stars [Marvin Gaye]

46 **MY GIRL**
Suave' [The Temptations]

47 **YOU'RE ALL I NEED TO GET BY**
Aretha Franklin [Marvin Gaye & Tammi Terrell]

48 **WHAT BECOMES OF THE BROKENHEARTED**
Paul Young [Jimmy Ruffin]

49 **GOING TO A GO-GO**
The Rolling Stones [The Miracles]

50 **COME SEE ABOUT ME**
Jr. Walker & the All Stars [The Supremes]

The Top 10 BEATLES REMAKES

Earth, Wind & Fire

THE MOST successful remake of a Beatles song—or in this case, songs—on the Hot 100 is the medley recorded by producer Jaap Eggermont with studio musicians and singers collectively called Stars on 45. Recorded to prevent a similar bootleg medley from selling in Holland, it included pieces of "No Reply," "I'll Be Back," "Drive My Car," "Do You Want To Know A Secret," "We Can Work It Out," "I Should Have Known Better," "Nowhere Man," and "You're Going To Lose That Girl."

Of the nine other top 10 Beatle remakes, six were never released as singles by the Beatles. "Lucy In The Sky With Diamonds" (Elton John, with John Lennon guesting) came from the *Sgt. Pepper's Lonely Hearts Club Band* album; "You Won't See Me" (Anne Murray), from *Rubber Soul;* "The Fool On The Hill" (Sergio Mendes and Brasil '66), from *Magical Mystery Tour;* "Here Comes The Sun" (Richie Havens) and "Oh! Darling" (Robin Gibb), from *Abbey Road;* and "You've Got To Hide Your Love Away" (The Silkie), from *Help!*

The Top 100 Songs from
MOTION PICTURES

Tammy and the Bachelor

IT WAS OBVIOUS that rock and roll and the movies were meant for each other from the moment the curtain went up on *The Blackboard Jungle* in 1955 and Bill Haley's voice came thundering out of the giant theater speakers: "One, two, three o'clock, four o'clock rock. . ." Clare Booth Luce denounced the film as degenerate, causing it to be pulled from a film festival in Venice. And Haley's recording of "(We're Gonna) Rock Around The Clock," released in 1954 to a mediocre response, was re-released and shot to No. 1.

"Rock Around The Clock" wasn't written specifically for *The Blackboard Jungle*, so it's not included in the list of the top 100 songs from motion pictures. To qualify, a song had to be written or recorded specifically for a film. That eliminated cover versions of movie songs, like Debby Boone's "You Light Up My Life" and Meco's "Star Wars/Cantina Band." However, songs that weren't written for films were included if a version was recorded for a particular movie. "Wind Beneath My Wings," a top 10 country single for Gary Morris in 1983, qualifies because Bette Midler recorded it specifically for *Beaches*. The same holds true for Los Lobos' version of "La Bamba" from the Ritchie Valens film biography, and UB40's "Can't Help Falling In Love" from *Sliver*.

The cinema welcomed rock and roll right from the beginning. Elvis Presley flew to Hollywood for a screen test with Hal Wallis at Paramount Pictures even before "Heartbreak Hotel" became his first No. 1 hit. On April 1, 1956, Walls signed Elvis to a three-picture deal. He was supposed to make his debut in *The Rainmaker* with Burt Lancaster and Katharine Hepburn, but that was too serious a role by Col. Tom Parker's standards. He wanted Elvis to star in more lightweight fare, and he got his wish for 33 consecutive films.

Production on Elvis' first film started at 20th Century Fox on Aug. 22, 1956. Originally titled *The Reno Brothers*, it was later renamed after one of the four songs included in the soundtrack, "Love Me Tender." Ken Darby, musical director of the film, wrote the tune based on a folk ballad from 1861, "Aura Lee," although the songwriting credits went to Darby's wife, Vera Watson, and Elvis. Presley sang "Love Me Tender" when he made his first appearance on Ed Sullivan's show, on Sept. 9—more than two months before the movie was released. That caused such a demand for the single that RCA was forced to issue it during the first week of October, and it went to No. 1 13 days before the opening of the movie.

Elvis' second film was *Loving You* for Paramount. Kal Mann and Bernie Lowe wrote "(Let Me Be Your) Teddy Bear" for the movie, and it went to No. 1 the day before the picture opened. The big production number in Elvis' third film gave him his second most successful soundtrack single, "Jailhouse Rock." Jerry Leiber and Mike Stoller wrote the tune based on the script they received, which was marked where the songs were to be placed.

The most successful soundtrack single from the '50s is "Tammy," sung by Debbie Reynolds in the movie she starred in with Leslie Nielsen, *Tammy And The Bachelor.* Coral Records head Bob Thiele didn't expect the song to do very well, and the label released the unembellished version from the movie. Debbie's single went to No. 1 and a version by the Ames Brothers, heard over the closing credits, went to No. 5

There are only six songs from the '60s included in the top 100 soundtrack singles. The highest-rated is the title song from *To Sir With Love.* Lulu was given a part in the film after director James Clavell saw her perform on the bill of a Beach Boys concert in London. The producers came up with several songs that could be used in the movie and Lulu hated them all. She asked her friend Mark London to write something and he came up with the music in five minutes. The next day, lyricist Don Black added the words. "I was over the moon, I just knew it was going to be a great song," says Lulu.

The Beatles were quickly recruited into the movies. Production on *A Hard Day's Night* began March 2, 1964, at Paddington Station in London. John Lennon and Paul McCartney started working on the songs while in Paris two months earlier and the title song was recorded on April 16. Almost a year later, the Beatles recorded the title song for their second film, *Help!*

The best-selling soundtrack album of all time was released in the '70s. Four of the songs from *Saturday Night Fever* went to No. 1, and all are included in the top 100 songs from motion pictures. Robert Stigwood, who produced the films Tommy and Jesus Christ, Superstar, bought the rights to Nik Cohn's article in *New York* magazine, "Tribal Rites Of The New Saturday Night." The Bee Gees never saw the script for the film, but Stigwood verbally outlined the plot for them. Armed with that information and the fact that John Travolta was the lead, the Gibb brothers spent two-

34 DOESN'T REALLY MATTER
Janet Jackson *[The Nutty Professor II: The Klumps]*

35 LONELY BOY
Paul Anka *[Girl's Town]*

36 I DON'T WANT TO MISS A THING
Aerosmith *[Armageddon]*

37 SAY YOU, SAY ME
Lionel Richie *[White Nights]*

38 AGAINST ALL ODDS (TAKE A LOOK AT ME NOW) Phil Collins *[Against All Odds]*

39 MAGIC Olivia Newton-John *[Xanadu]*

40 TEARS IN HEAVEN
Eric Clapton *[Rush]*

41 THE WAY WE WERE
Barbra Streisand *[The Way We Were]*

42 GHOSTBUSTERS
Ray Parker Jr. *[Ghostbusters]*

43 I JUST CALLED TO SAY I LOVE YOU
Stevie Wonder *[The Woman In Red]*

44 A WHOLE NEW WORLD
Peabo Bryson & Regina Belle *[Aladdin]*

45 LOVE THEME FROM "A STAR IS BORN" (EVERGREEN)
Barbra Streisand *[A Star Is Born]*

46 ARTHUR'S THEME (BEST THAT YOU CAN DO)
Christopher Cross *[Arthur]*

47 I'LL REMEMBER
Madonna *[With Honors]*

48 9 TO 5
Dolly Parton *[9 To 5]*

49 FOOTLOOSE
Kenny Loggins *[Footloose]*

50 HARD TO SAY I'M SORRY
Chicago *[Summer Lovers]*

51 WHATEVER WILL BE, WILL BE (QUE SERA, SERA)
Doris Day *[The Man Who Knew Too Much]*

52 SITTIN' UP IN MY ROOM
Brandy *[Waiting To Exhale]*

53 LET'S HEAR IT FOR THE BOY
Deniece Williams *[Footloose]*

54 APRIL LOVE
Pat Boone *[April Love]*

55 MRS. ROBINSON
Simon and Garfunkel *[The Graduate]*

56 CRAZY FOR YOU
Madonna *[Vision Quest]*

57 THEME FROM "SHAFT"
Isaac Hayes *[Shaft]*

58 RETURN TO SENDER
Elvis Presley *[Girls! Girls! Girls!]*

59 I WANNA SEX YOU UP
Color Me Badd *[New Jack City]*

60 REGULATE
Warren G. & Nate Dogg *[Above The Rim]*

61 BAILAMOS
Enrique Iglesias *[Wild Wild West]*

62 CHARIOTS OF FIRE
Vangelis *[Chariots Of Fire]*

63 I'D DIE WITHOUT YOU
P.M. Dawn *[Boomerang]*

64 LA BAMBA Los Lobos *[La Bamba]*

65 GREASE Frankie Valli *[Grease]*

66 MANIAC Michael Sembello *[Flashdance]*

67 HELP! The Beatles *[Help!]*

68 IT MUST HAVE BEEN LOVE
Roxette *[Pretty Woman]*

and-a-half weeks coming up with "Stayin' Alive" and "Night Fever."

The second best-selling soundtrack album of the '70s was *Grease*. Most of the songs were from the theatrical version, including "Summer Nights," but the three biggest songs from the film were original. Travolta and Newton-John duetted on "You're The One That I Want," Olivia soloed on "Hopelessly Devoted To You," and Frankie Valli was asked to sing Barry Gibb's title song.

One movie song from the '70s served triple duty. Barry DeVorzon and Perry Botldn, Jr. composed the music for Bless *The Beasts And The Children*. An instrumental composition from the film *Cotton's Dream* was appropriated as the theme music for CBS' daytime soap, *The Young And The Restless*. After Romanian gymnast Nadia Comaneci used it as her theme music in the 1976 Olympics, it became a hit single under the title "Nadia's Theme (The Young And The Restless)."

The nature of soundtracks changed in the '80s. Record companies learned from the successes of *Saturday Night Fever* and *Grease* and became more interested in putting together collections of rock songs as soundtracks than issuing original instrumental background music. Sometimes the songs were integral to the plot, as in *Footloose*, and sometimes they were just used as incidental music, heard as filtered fragments when a character in the film happened to be listening to the radio or playing a CD.

Music was employed well in films like *Dirty Dancing*, which produced the hit singles "(I've Had) The Time Of My Life" by Bill Medley and Jennifer Warnes and "Hungry Eyes" by Eric Carmen, and *Flashdance*, which yielded two chart-topping singles. Prince triumphed with the critics in *Purple Rain* and had three hit singles in the top 100 from the soundtrack. Other films will be remembered for their music long after their place in cinematic history is reduced to a footnote. Eddie Rabbitt's "Drivin' My Life Away" will still be played on the radio long after *Roadie* is forgotten, and Madonna's "Live To Tell" will survive *At Close Range*.

The two most successful soundtrack singles of the '90s are also the two most successful movie hits of the rock era. Both set new records when they went to No. 1 on the Hot 100. "End Of The Road," Boyz II Men's contribution to the *Boomerang* soundtrack, stayed on top for 13 weeks, breaking Elvis Presley's 36-year-old record of 11 weeks for "Don't Be Cruel" and "Hound Dog." But Boyz II Men were quickly challenged by Whitney Houston. Her remake of Dolly Parton's "I Will Always Love You" from *The Bodyguard* reigned for 14 weeks.

As the calendar rolled over to 2000, Destiny's Child had the first major soundtrack hit with "Independent Women Part I" from *Charlie's Angels*. The song served as a marketing tool for the movie, with customized lyrics like, "Charlie, how do your Angels get down like that?" and an intro that had shout-outs to the actresses starring in the film. Two years later, Eminem starred in the movie *8 Mile* and won the Academy Award for Best Original Song with "Lose Yourself." The single ruled the Hot 100 for 12 weeks.

69 **A HARD DAY'S NIGHT**
The Beatles *[A Hard Day's Night]*

70 **NOTHING'S GONNA STOP US NOW**
Starship *[Mannequin]*

71 **MY HEART WILL GO ON**
Celine Dion *[Titanic]*

72 **LOVE ON THE ROCKS**
Neil Diamond *[The Jazz Singer]*

73 **FOR YOU I WILL**
Monica *[Space Jam]*

74 **THIS USED TO BE MY PLAYGROUND**
Madonna *[A League Of Their Own]*

75 **YOU'RE THE ONE THAT I WANT**
John Travolta & Olivia Newton-John *[Grease]*

76 **NOT GON' CRY**
Mary J. Blige *[Waiting To Exhale]*

77 **LET'S GO CRAZY**
Prince & the Revolution *[Purple Rain]*

78 **UP WHERE WE BELONG**
Joe Cocker & Jennifer Warnes
[An Officer And A Gentleman]

79 **KISS**
Prince & the Revolution
[Under The Cherry Moon]

80 **THE POWER OF LOVE**
Huey Lewis & the News
[Back To The Future]

81 **SHAKEDOWN**
Bob Seger *[Beverly Hills Cop II]*

82 **I AM WOMAN**
Helen Reddy *[Stand Up And Be Counted]*

83 **ST. ELMO'S FIRE (MAN IN MOTION)**
John Parr *[St. Elmo's Fire]*

84 **IF I CAN'T HAVE YOU**
Yvonne Elliman *[Saturday Night Fever]*

85 **BREAKAWAY**
Kelly Clarkson *[The Princess Diaries 2]*

86 **SEPARATE LIVES**
Phil Collins & Marilyn Martin *[White Nights]*

87 **BLAZE OF GLORY**
Jon Bon Jovi *[Young Guns II]*

88 **CAR WASH**
Rose Royce *[Car Wash]*

89 **CHANGE THE WORLD**
Eric Clapton *[Phenomenon]*

90 **A VIEW TO A KILL**
Duran Duran *[A View To A Kill]*

91 **(I'VE HAD) THE TIME OF MY LIFE**
Bill Medley & Jennifer Warnes *[Dirty Dancing]*

92 **LIVE TO TELL**
Madonna *[At Close Range]*

93 **HARD HEADED WOMAN**
Elvis Presley *[King Creole]*

94 **TWO HEARTS**
Phil Collins *[Buster]*

95 **NOBODY DOES IT BETTER**
Carly Simon *[The Spy Who Loved Me]*

96 **HEAVEN**
Bryan Adams *[A Night In Heaven]*

97 **(THEME FROM) VALLEY OF THE DOLLS**
Dionne Warwick *[Valley Of The Dolls]*

98 **DON'T YOU (FORGET ABOUT ME)**
Simple Minds *[The Breakfast Club]*

99 **GONNA FLY NOW (THEME FROM "ROCKY")**
Bill Conti *[Rocky]*

100 **TIL I HEAR IT FROM YOU**
Gin Blossoms *[Empire State]*

The Top 30 Songs from MUSICAL THEATER

WHEN *The Black Crook* opened in New York City on September 12, 1866, it ushered in a new era of American musical theater. At the start of the 20th century, that form was nurtured by Victor Herbert and George M. Cohan, who were followed by Jerome Kern, George and Ira Gershwin, Oscar Hammerstein II, Rodgers and Hart, and Cole Porter. By the middle of the century, Broadway audiences were enjoying musicals like *Pal Joey* and *Oklahoma!* But while Hollywood embraced rock and roll in 1955, Broadway theater resisted the new music. Twelve days after Elvis Presley made his first appearance on the *Billboard* singles chart, *My Fair Lady* opened on Broadway.

Pop artists had some success covering songs from Broadway shows in the '50s. *The Most Happy Fella* opened on Broadway on May 3, 1956, and the Four Lads recorded one of Frank Loesser's tunes from the show, "Standing On The Corner." Vic Damone had a top 10 single with "On The Street Where You Live" from *My Fair Lady*. In 1959, Bobby Darin recorded the most successful chart single to originate in a stage production. The song "Moritat" was from the 1928 German musical *The Threepenny Opera,* written by Kurt Weill and Bertholt Brecht. The show had a brief run in New York in 1933, and was revived off-Broadway on March 10, 1954 with a new translation by Marc Blitzstein—who turned "Moritat" into "Mack The Knife." With three songs in the top 30 stage songs list, *The Threepenny Opera* has proven to have more successful songs than any other show, with the exception of *Hair*.

One of the first new musicals of the new decade, *Bye, Bye Birdie,* took a good poke at rock and roll. But rock music and Broadway didn't successfully merge until *Hair* moved from off-Broadway to the Great White Way on April 29, 1968. Four songs from *Hair* are included in the top 30 songs from the stage: a medley of "Aquarius/Let The Sunshine In" by the 5th Dimension, "Hair" by the Cowsills, "Easy To Be Hard" by Three Dog Night, and "Good Morning Starshine" by Oliver. No other Broadway show has had such an impact on the Hot 100.

In 1970, Andrew Lloyd Webber and Tim Rice oversaw production of an album version of *Jesus Christ, Superstar* a year before it opened at the Hellinger Theater in New York. Murray Head's "Superstar" was from the album, and Helen Reddy covered Yvonne Elliman's "I Don't Know How To Love Him." Fourteen years later, Rice repeated the formula with *Chess,* written with Benny Andersson and Björn Ulvaeus of Abba. Head had his second American hit with "One Night In Bangkok" before the show actually opened in London.

01 **MACK THE KNIFE**
Bobby Darin *[The Threepenny Opera]*

02 **AQUARIUS/LET THE SUNSHINE IN**
5th Dimension *[Hair]*

03 **SMOKE GETS IN YOUR EYES**
The Platters *[Roberta]*

04 **HELLO, DOLLY!**
Louis Armstrong *[Hello, Dolly!]*

05 **HAIR** The Cowsills *[Hair]*

06 **STANDING ON THE CORNER**
The Four Lads *[The Most Happy Fella]*

07 **GOOD MORNING STARSHINE**
Oliver *[Hair]*

08 **RICH GIRL**
Gwen Stefani f/Eve *[Fiddler on the Roof]*

09 **I GOT RHYTHM**
The Happenings *[Girl Crazy]*

10 **I'VE TOLD EVERY LITTLE STAR**
Linda Scott *[Music In The Air]*

11 **EASY TO BE HARD**
Three Dog Night *[Hair]*

12 **ONE NIGHT IN BANGKOK**
Murray Head *[Chess]*

13 **MORITAT (A THEME FROM "THE THREE PENNY OPERA")**
Dick Hyman Trio *[The Threepenny Opera]*

14 **ON THE STREET WHERE YOU LIVE**
Vic Damone *[My Fair Lady]*

15 **PEOPLE** Barbra Streisand *[Funny Girl]*

16 **SUMMER NIGHTS**
John Travolta & Olivia Newton-John *[Grease]*

17 **THE WAY WE WERE/TRY TO REMEMBER**
Gladys Knight & the Pips *[The Fantasticks]*

18 **I'LL NEVER FALL IN LOVE AGAIN**
Dionne Warwick *[Promises, Promises]*

19 **IF YOU LET ME MAKE LOVE TO YOU (THEN WHY CAN'T I TOUCH YOU)**
Ronnie Dyson *[Salvation]*

20 **I'VE GOTTA BE ME**
Sammy Davis, Jr. *[Golden Rainbow]*

21 **MY CUP RUNNETH OVER**
Ed Ames *[I Do! I Do!]*

22 **WIND IT UP**
Gwen Stefani *[The Sound Of Music]*

23 **THEME FROM "THREE PENNY OPERA"**
Richard Hayman & Jan August
[The Threepenny Opera]

24 **I DON'T KNOW HOW TO LOVE HIM**
Helen Reddy *[Jesus Christ, Superstar]*

25 **SUPERSTAR**
Murray Head *[Jesus Christ, Superstar]*

26 **WHAT KIND OF FOOL AM I**
Sammy Davis, Jr. *[Stop The World—I Want To Get Off]*

27 **I LOVES YOU, PORGY**
Nina Simone *[Porgy And Bess]*

28 **TONIGHT**
Ferrante and Teicher *[West Side Story]*

29 **DON'T CRY FOR ME ARGENTINA**
Madonna *[Evita]*

30 **SOME ENCHANTED EVENING**
Jay & the Americans *[South Pacific]*

The Top 100 Songs by
MALE SOLO ARTISTS

Brian McKnight

IT SHOULDN'T be any surprise that in the Eisenhower years of rock and roll, male singers dominated the *Billboard* chart. Twenty-two of the top 100 songs by male solo artists are from the 1950s; in contrast, only four of the top 100 songs by female solo artists are from the same decade.

Elvis Presley dominates the men's top 100 with 10 songs listed, but for the first time he has a close competitor. Usher now has eight songs on the chart, which means he could overtake the King in the next few years. Michael Jackson has four songs on the list, followed by Rod Stewart and Lionel Richie with three each.

Elvis has six songs in the top 30, including the two-sided hit "Don't Be Cruel" and "Hound Dog," ranked No. 2. Seven of his hits in the top 100 are from the '50s; the ballads "It's Now Or Never" and "Are You Lonesome Tonight?" and the more uptempo "Stuck On You" are from the '60s.

After Presley, the most successful single by a male solo artist in the '50s is Pat Boone's "Love Letters In The Sand." Rudy Vallee and Bing Crosby had recorded it in decades gone by; a recording by Ted Black and His Orchestra reached the top 10 in 1931. Boone recorded it because Dot Records founder Randy Wood had been getting numerous requests for the song at the record shop he ran in Galatin, Tennessee. After Boone cut the track, it remained on the shelf until the producers of the film *Bernadine* decided to take advantage of Boone's role in the movie to add two of his songs to the soundtrack. Johnny Mercer wrote the title song and "Love Letters In The Sand" was dusted off as the second choice.

The next highest-ranked male vocal from the '50s is Bobby Darin's "Mack The Knife," a song first heard in its original form in 1928 when Bertold Brecht and Kurt Weill wrote it for *The Threepenny Opera*. Inspired by Louis Armstrong's earlier recording of the song, Darin included it in his *That's All* album to demonstrate his diversity. It was released as a single against his wishes.

Guy Mitchell's recording of "Singing The Blues" was a cover version of a song also released on Columbia by Marty Robbins. Melvin Endsley wrote the song in 1954, but no one recorded it until Robbins cut his version in 1956. Robbins' single spent 13 weeks at No. 1 on the country chart. Columbia's A&R chief Mitch Miller thought his label could have a pop hit with the same song, so he produced Mitchell's remake. That single topped the Best Sellers in Stores chart for nine weeks.

Tennessee Ernie Ford was so busy appearing on NBC five times a week with a daytime show that he fell behind in his recording schedule for Capitol Records. Pressed for time, he cut two songs he had performed on TV: "You Don't Have To Be A Baby To Cry" and a song written by Merle Travis in 1947, "Sixteen Tons." During rehearsal, Ford snapped his fingers to set the tempo. Producer Lee Gillette called out from the booth for Ford to leave the finger snapping in when he recorded the song.

Chubby Checker's "The Twist" is the highest-ranked male vocal from the '60s, thanks to the single having two separate chart runs—and topping the Hot 100 both times. That's because the first time around, in the autumn of 1960, the Twist was a dance craze for teenagers. While Chubby moved on to other dance hits like the Pony and the Fly, and the Twist became passe among teens, the adults started twisting like mad. Society columnist "Cholly Knickerbocker" mentioned that Prince Serge Obolensky was seen dancing the Twist at the Peppermint Lounge in New York City, and suddenly it was a worldwide sensation among the elite who found themselves frequenting trendy discotheques. Chubby was booked to sing his year-old No. 1 hit on Ed Sullivan's show Oct. 22, 1961, prompting Cameo-Parkway execs to re-release the single. A full-page ad in *Billboard* declared, "'The Twist' dance rage explodes into the adult world!" The grown-ups bought enough copies of Chubby's "The Twist" single to return it to the Hot 100 the week of November 13, and by January 1962 it was once again No. 1.

Bobby Lewis' "Tossin' And Turnin'" and Marvin Gaye's "I Heard It Through The Grapevine" had something in common—both had seven week reigns on the Hot 100, the longest for any solo male artist in the '60s. Indianapolis-born Lewis moved to New York at the urging of Jackie Wilson, but despite help from Wilson and his manager, Lewis was turned down by many record labels. Lewis didn't give up, and during a weeklong gig at the Apollo Theater met a nervous group of white singers, the Fireflies, who had a hit in 1959 with "You Were Mine." Three weeks later, Lewis was auditioning at Beltone Records when he saw a familiar face—Ritchie Adams, lead singer of the Fireflies. The group was a Beltone act. Adams and label owner Joe Rene thought Lewis had talent, and asked him to sing a song they had written. When they heard him, they knew they had the right man to sing "Tossin' And Turnin'."

When Marvin Gaye recorded Norman Whitfield and Barrett Strong's "I Heard It Through The Grapevine," Motown founder Berry Gordy passed over it, in favor of a Holland-Dozier-Holland composition, "Your Unchanging Love." Whitfield was so sure he had written a hit song, he kept after Gordy to allow him to record "Grapevine" with another Motown artist. The Miracles had cut it before Gaye, and so had the Isley Brothers. Gordy agreed that Gladys Knight & the Pips could record the song. Their version was the first to see the light of day, and Whitfield was redeemed: their single went to No. 2 in 1967. But Whitfield still wanted Gaye's version released, so he convinced the label's head of quality control to include it in Gaye's album *In The Groove.* But it wasn't scheduled for single release; another track called "Chained" was issued on 45. A Chicago DJ, E. Rodney Jones at WVON, played the track and the station's phones lit up. An order for 100,000 singles from Chicago finally persuaded the label to release the song with the tom-tom beat, and it became the biggest hit of Gaye's career.

By the time Andy Gibb was 10, his three older brothers were already famous as the Bee Gees. Oldest brother Barry Gibb wrote Andy's first single, "I Just Want To Be Your Everything," in a two-day session at Robert Stigwood's Bermuda estate. "Shadow Dancing" was written by Andy, Barry, and twins Maurice and Robin Gibb while they were filming *Sgt. Pepper's Lonely Hearts Club Band* in Los Angeles. They are the two highest-ranked male solo recordings of the '70s.

Kenny Rogers let Lionel Richie's publisher know that he was interested in recording a song written by the Motown star. Two weeks after they first met in Las Vegas, the project was completed. The result: "Lady" topped the Hot 100 for six weeks and was a true crossover success, charting not just pop but country, R&B, and Adult Contemporary. The only solo No. 1 of Rogers' career, it is the highest-ranked male solo recording of the '80s.

The No. 1 male solo single of the rock era is Elton John's two-sided hit, "Candle In The Wind 1997"/"Something About The Way You Look Tonight." The song "Candle In The Wind" first appeared on Elton's 1973 album *Goodbye Yellow Brick Road.* Issued as a single in the U.K., where it peaked at No. 11, it was passed over in the U.S. in favor of the R&B-infused "Bennie And The Jets." A live recording was released as a single in 1988. Nine years later, the world watched Elton sing Bernie Taupin's revised lyrics in Westminster Abbey at the funeral of Diana, Princess of Wales.

The Top 100 Songs by
FEMALE SOLO ARTISTS

Diana Ross

B Y THE end of the 1950s, there were a number of male singers who had established themselves as consistent hitmakers. Elvis Presley led the pack, followed by artists like Pat Boone, Fats Domino, and Ricky Nelson. While female singers like Gale Storm and Teresa Brewer had more than one top 10 hit, there weren't any women who were in the same class as Elvis, Ricky, or Fats.

In the early '60s, Connie Francis and Brenda Lee seriously challenged the men for chart superiority, but it wasn't until the '70s that female singers like Diana Ross, Barbra Streisand, Donna Summer, and Olivia Newton-John could legitimately be called superstars. That trend continued into the '80s, and by the '90s women were equal to and often ahead of the men on the Hot 100.

Four of the top 100 songs by female solo artists are from the '50s. The highest-ranked from this decade is Debbie Reynolds' "Tammy," the first song by an individual woman to reach No. 1 after the men had shut the women out of pole position for 15 months. It would be almost three years before another solo female would top the chart—Connie Francis ended the drought in June 1960 with "Everybody's Somebody's Fool."

The second highest-ranked song by a solo female from the '50s is Gogi Grant's "The Wayward Wind." The single spent six weeks at No. 1 and had the distinction of knocking off Elvis Presley's first No. 1 hit, "Heartbreak Hotel." Ironically, "The Wayward Wind" was written for a man to sing.

Composer Herb Newman, owner of the Era label, had written "The Wayward Wind" with Stan Lebousky when they were students at UCLA. The lyrics were altered so a woman could sing the tune, and with 15 minutes of studio time, Grant recorded the song that would take Elvis down a peg.

The top-rated song from the '60s is Lulu's "To Sir With Love," the title song of the motion picture she starred in with Sidney Poitier. Brenda Lee is in second place for the decade with "I'm Sorry," followed by Bobbie Gentry's "Ode To Billie Joe" and the Singing Nun's "Dominique."

Of the 13 songs in the top 100 from the '70s, Debby Boone comes in first with "You Light Up My Life." The single was No. 1 for 10 weeks, the longest run at the top since Elvis Presley had an 11-week reign with "Don't Be Cruel" and "Hound Dog." Donna Summer is the decade's runner-up with "Hot Stuff," followed by Roberta Flack's interpretation of Ewan MacColl's "The First Time Ever I Saw Your Face." Gloria Gaynor's declaration of independence, "I Will Survive," is next. While this inspiring anthem of defiance is one of the hallmarks of the disco era, it began life as the intended B-side of Gaynor's "Substitute." It was meant to be a comeback song for the original queen of disco. That wasn't just a casual nickname— there was actually a coronation ceremony in March 1975 by the National Association of Discotheque Disc Jockeys in Manhattan, recognizing the artist for blazing the way with dance floor hits like "Never Can Say Goodbye" and "Honey Bee." But when Donna Summer replaced her as the disco queen, Gaynor's career slowed to a crawl and she suffered personal setbacks, including being hospitalized for spinal surgery. When her health returned, she went into the studio with producer Freddie Perren. "Substitute" was supposed to revive her career, but DJs preferred the B-side, and "I Will Survive" made its way onto the Hot 100, going all the way to No. 1.

Female singers remained strong on the chart during the '80s. There are 11 songs from that decade in the top 100, headed by Olivia Newton-John's "Physical," which matched Debby Boone's "You Light Up My Life" from the previous decade with a 10-week reign. Runner-up for the '80s is Kim Carnes' version of the Jackie DeShannon and Donna Weiss composition, "Bette Davis Eyes." It held sway for nine weeks, even though Carnes wasn't crazy about the song the first time she heard it. After producer George Tobin played it for her, she told him it wasn't a hit. When Carnes started working with another producer, Val Garay, songwriter Weiss sent her the song again. This time, synthesizer musician Bill Cuomo changed the chords and gave the song a different feel, and Carnes knew it would be a smash. DeShannon and Weiss received a note from the legendary actress mentioned in the song title, thanking them for making her "a part of modern times." When they won a Grammy for the song, a gracious Davis sent them roses.

In third place among female solo artists of the '80s is Irene Cara with "Flashdance...What A Feeling," from the film starring Jennifer Beals. The next two women on the list were into their third decade of making hit records by the '80s. Barbra Streisand first made an impression on the Hot 100 with "People" in 1964. After recording Laura Nyro's "Stoney End" in 1970 and scoring No. 1 hits with "The Way We Were" and "Love Theme

From *A Star Is Born* (Evergreen)," she began the '80s by recording an album written and produced by Barry Gibb of the Bee Gees. The first single from *Guilty*, "Woman In Love," is the fourth highest-ranked solo female performance of the decade. In fifth place is Diana Ross, who had hits in the top 100s of the '60s and '70s. She also teamed up with a hot production team for her first major hit of the decade. Nile Rodgers and Bernard Edwards produced the *diana* album, and the first single, "Upside Down," was No. 1 for four weeks.

Bonnie Tyler's first chart entry was the 1978 single "It's A Heartache," but it was her second entry that made the most impact. "Total Eclipse Of The Heart" spotlighted the gravelly voice of the Welsh-born artist. Executives at Columbia Records first approached writer/producer Jim Steinman about working with Tyler. He was busy with a film project and declined. So Tyler was surprised when he called her one day out of the blue and asked if she had found a producer yet, because he was very interested in collaborating. She flew to New York to meet with Steinman and he played "Total Eclipse" on his grand piano, practically knocking it through the floor, according to Tyler. The single topped the Hot 100 for four weeks in 1983.

Leading the charge for the '90s is the woman with the No. 1 solo female song of the rock era. Servern, Maryland–born Toni Braxton grew up in a strict household. Her father was a conservative apostolic minister, and Toni had to wait for him to go grocery shopping before she could watch *Soul Train* on television. Even though she ended up singing sultry songs like "You're Makin' Me High," her father supported her and prayed for his daughter's records to race up the *Billboard* charts. Someone was listening, because "Un-Break My Heart" was No. 1 for 11 weeks.

Whitney Houston's version of Dolly Parton's "I Will Always Love You" from *The Bodyguard* soundtrack is in second place for the '90s, followed by two artists who first hit it big on the country charts: LeAnn Rimes (with "How Do I Live") and Shania Twain (with "You're Still The One").

The No. 1 song on the top 100 female solo songs is from the 21st century. After a long stint on Columbia and a short stay at Virgin, Carey signed with the Island label and returned to form with the album *The Emancipation of Mimi*, her biggest album in 10 years. The second single, "We Belong Together," ruled for 14 weeks and outpointed her collaboration with Boyz II Men, "One Sweet Day," to become the second most successful song of the rock era.

In second place for the 21st century is "Foolish'" by Ashanti. Before Ashanti wrote the lyrics, the track, composed by 7 Aurelius, was intended for British R&B singer Craig David. But when the head of the Murder Inc. label, Irv Gotti, heard the track, he asked Ashanti to come up with words. "He gave me the concept to write about a girl dealing with a guy who doesn't do the right thing but she stays with the guy," says Ashanti. Stepping out of the vocal booth after recording her own lyrics, she found Gotti screaming, "I love it!"

70 **SINCE U BEEN GONE**
Kelly Clarkson *RCA* 05

71 **WHAT A GIRL WANTS**
Christina Aguilera *RCA* 00

72 **MAGIC**
Olivia Newton-John *MCA* 80

73 **THE WAY WE WERE**
Barbra Streisand *Columbia* 74

74 **MACARTHUR PARK**
Donna Summer *Casablanca* 78

75 **NOTHING COMPARES 2 U**
Sinead O'Connor *Ensign* 90

76 **WHAT'S LOVE GOT TO DO WITH IT**
Tina Turner *Capitol* 84

77 **CASE OF THE EX (WHATCHA GONNA DO)**
Mya *University* 00

78 **HIT 'EM UP STYLE (OOPS!)**
Blu Cantrell *Arista* 01

79 **DOMINIQUE**
The Singing Nun *Philips* 63

80 **BREATHE AGAIN**
Toni Braxton *LaFace* 94

81 **LOVE THEME FROM "A STAR IS BORN" (EVERGREEN)**
Barbra Streisand *Columbia* 77

82 **MY HEART HAS A MIND OF ITS OWN**
Connie Francis *MGM* 60

83 **I'LL REMEMBER**
Madonna *Maverick* 94

84 **HE WASN'T MAN ENOUGH**
Toni Braxton *LaFace* 00

85 **9 TO 5**
Dolly Parton *RCA* 81

86 **EVERYBODY'S SOMEBODY'S FOOL**
Connie Francis *MGM* 60

87 **I'LL BE THERE**
Mariah Carey *Columbia* 92

88 **HAVE YOU EVER?**
Brandy *Atlantic* 99

89 **COME ON OVER BABY (ALL I WANT IS YOU)**
Christina Aguilera *RCA* 00

90 **BITCH**
Meredith Brooks *Capitol* 97

91 **LOVE TAKES TIME**
Mariah Carey *Columbia* 90

92 **VISION OF LOVE**
Mariah Carey *Columbia* 90

93 **WHATEVER WILL BE, WILL BE (QUE SERA, SERA)**
Doris Day *Columbia* 56

94 **SITTIN' UP IN MY ROOM**
Brandy *Arista* 96

95 **MY ALL**
Mariah Carey *Columbia* 98

96 **IF I AIN'T GOT YOU**
Alicia Keys *J* 04

97 **VOGUE**
Madonna *Sire* 90

98 **PON DE REPLAY**
Rihanna *SRP/Def Jam* 05

99 **LET'S HEAR IT FOR THE BOY**
Deniece Williams *Columbia* 84

100 **WITHOUT YOU / NEVER FORGET YOU**
Mariah Carey *Columbia* 94

The Top 100 Songs by
GIRL GROUPS

Wilson Phillips

I N MODERN vernacular, "girl groups" could be misconstrued as a sexist term, but in the late '50s and early '60s, it was an accurate description of a genre of music that included groups like the Chantels, the Shirelles, the Ronettes, the Crystals, and the Shangri-Las. The best songs by girl groups combined teenage angst and innocence, with a wide appeal to the 15-year-old girls who were buying 45s.

Included in the list of the top 100 songs by girl groups are any group of three or more women who recorded together. Individual singers who personified the girl group sound like Lesley Gore and Diane Renay were not included, nor were any groups that included men, like the Orlons and the Exciters.

There were female singing groups long before there were girl groups. In the '30s, the Boswell Sisters from New Orleans had a number of successful records, including "The Object Of My Affection" and "Rock And Roll," the first song to ever use those words together in a title. After the Boswells came the Andrews Sisters, three siblings from Minneapolis. Patti, Maxene, and LaVerne were the most successful female group before 1955.

There were three prominent female vocal groups at the beginning of the rock era. The Fontane Sisters had hits as early as 1951, and the Chordettes and the McGuire Sisters first hit the charts in 1954. On the R&B chart, Shirley Gunter & the Queens had a top 10 single in 1954 with "Oop Shoop." But the group that really initiated the girl group sound was a quintet of teenagers from the Bronx, all students at Saint Anthony of Padua School. They took their name from their rival school, Saint Francis de Chantelle.

Arlene Smith was the leader of the Chantels, and her inspiration for forming her group was a man—or rather, a teenage boy. "Alan Freed came on the radio and played Frankie Lymon & the Teenagers singing 'Why Do Fools Fall In Love,'" Smith told Charlotte Greig in *Will You Still Love Me Tomorrow?* "It was a lovely high voice and a nice song. Then Freed announces that Frankie is just 13! Well! I had to sit down. It was a big mystery, how to get into this radio stuff. . . . It seemed so far removed, but I made a conscious decision to do the same."

When Frankie Lymon played a theater in the Bronx, Arlene took her group to meet Richard Barrett, Lymon's manager. Backstage, the Chantels sang one of Arlene's songs, "The Plea." Barrett liked them enough to tell record company owner George Goldner that he wanted to sign them. Their first release was "He's Gone" on Goldner's End label; it peaked at No. 71. Their next single, "Maybe," went to No. 15.

The Chantels' success inspired four teenaged girls from Passaic, New Jersey, to sing together. They even thought about calling themselves the Chanels, but that sounded too close. Eventually they settled on the Shirelles. A friend from school, Mary Jane Greenberg, wanted them to audition for her mother. Florence Greenberg signed the Shirelles to her Tiara label and released "I Met Him On A Sunday." The record became so popular that Decca bought the master, but subsequent releases were issued on Florence's Scepter label. In 1960, the Shirelles became the first girl group to have a No. 1 song in the rock era, when "Will You Love Me Tomorrow" moved to the top of the Hot 100.

The girl group sound flourished on both coasts. In New York, writers like Barry Mann and Cynthia Weil, Carole King and Gerry Goffin, and Jeff Barry and Ellie Greenwich wrote hits for the Chiffons, the Cookies, the Crystals, and the Ronettes. On the West Coast, Phil Spector was producing hits for those last two groups at Gold Star Studios. The Crystals recorded "He's A Rebel," "Da Doo Ron Ron," and "Then He Kissed Me." The Ronettes' first single was "Be My Baby," a No. 2 hit in 1963. That same summer, the Angels went to No. 1 with "My Boyfriend's Back."

In 1964, two labels helped boost the surge of popularity for girl groups. George Goldner started the Red Bird label with Jerry Leiber and Mike Stoller. Their first release was "Chapel Of Love" by the Dixie Cups, three young girls from New Orleans. Red Bird also signed the Shangri-Las, two sets of sisters from Queens, New York. Their first single, "Remember (Walking In The Sand)," seemed dramatic enough, but they went over the top with the sound-effects laden "Leader Of The Pack," an updating of the same theme explored in "He's A Rebel."

The other label that fostered the girl group sound in 1964 was based in Detroit. Motown had experienced success with girl groups like the Marvelettes ("Please Mr. Postman") and Martha & the Vandellas ("Heat Wave"), but 1964 was the year the Supremes began their string of five consecutive No. 1 singles. By the end of the decade, the Supremes had established themselves as the most successful girl group of the rock era. They have 13 of the top 100 songs by girl groups.

The first girl group to become successful in the '70s was the Honey Cone. Brian Holland, Lamont Dozier, and Eddie Holland, the trio responsible for writing and producing the first 10 No. 1 hits by the Supremes, left Motown and founded their own labels, Invictus and Hot Wax. Darlene Love's sister, Edna Wright, asked her friend Eddie Holland to watch her sing backing vocals with Carolyn Willis and Shellie Clark on a Burt Bacharach TV special in 1969. Eddie suggested they form a group, and signed them to Hot Wax. "Want Ads" went to No. 1 in 1971.

The female vocal groups that followed the Honey Cone in the '70s were influenced by the times. They were still working with male producers, but their lyrics were more assertive and the image was more aggressive. The most prominent female group of the decade was the Pointer Sisters.

Many of the songs by female groups in the '70s were disco-oriented, like the Emotions' "Best Of My Love." Patti LaBelle and the Blue Belles had been making records since 1963, but they didn't become well known until they changed their name to Labelle, adopted a space-age glitter image, and recorded the disco smash "Lady Marmalade." Silver Convention began as three anonymous studio singers in Germany on "Fly, Robin, Fly." They were replaced by three other women for their next hit, "Get Up And Boogie (That's Right)."

A new breed of girl groups arose in the '80s. Their influences weren't so much the Chiffons or the Ronettes, but the early female rock bands, like Fanny and the Runaways. The Go-Go's and the Bangles played their own instruments and wrote many of their own songs. There were still girl groups who were produced by men, like Bananarama and Exposé. The success of the latter gave rise to a whole slew of girl groups like the Cover Girls, Seduction, and Sweet Sensation.

In the first half of the '90s, the most successful girl group—with three No. 1 hits racked up in a short time—was Wilson Phillips. Wendy and Carnie Wilson were the daughters of Beach Boy Brian Wilson, and Chynna Phillips was the daughter of Mama Michelle Phillips and Papa John Phillips. In the second half of the '90s, the role model was clearly the Supremes. R&B groups like En Vogue, SWV, Jade, and TLC dominated the charts. Britain's biggest export during this time wasn't a male rock group or a boy band, but the five women known as the Spice Girls. And by the time the new century rolled around, the hottest girl group was Destiny's Child. They were so successful that eight of their songs between 1998 and 2004 are included in the top 100 girl group songs, including the one at the top of the list: "Independent Women Part I" from a movie about a "girl group"— Charlie's Angels.

69 TWO TO MAKE IT RIGHT
   Seduction *Vendetta* 90
70 DANCING IN THE STREET
   Martha & the Vandellas *Gordy* 64
71 WHEN WILL I SEE YOU AGAIN
   The Three Degrees *PIR* 74
72 NEVER EVER
   All Saints *London* 98
73 HOLD ON
   En Vogue *Atlantic* 90
74 HE'S SO SHY
   Pointer Sisters *Planet* 80
75 REFLECTIONS
   Diana Ross & the Supremes *Motown* 67
76 G.H.E.T.T.O.U.T.
   Changing Faces *Big Beat* 97
77 STICKWITU
   The Pussycat Dolls *A&M* 05
78 LOLLIPOP
   The Chordettes *Cadence* 58
79 BACK IN MY ARMS AGAIN
   The Supremes *Motown* 65
80 DEDICATED TO THE ONE I LOVE
   The Shirelles *Scepter* 61
81 I'M SO INTO YOU
   SWV *RCA* 93
82 WHAT ABOUT YOUR FRIENDS
   TLC *LaFace* 92
83 JUMP (FOR MY LOVE)
   Pointer Sisters *Planet* 84
84 MANIC MONDAY
   Bangles *Columbia* 86
85 HAZY SHADE OF WINTER
   Bangles *Columbia* 88
86 IF YOU LOVE ME
   Brownstone *MJJ* 95
87 2 BECOME 1
   Spice Girls *Virgin* 97
88 SUGARTIME
   McGuire Sisters *Coral* 58
89 ANGEL IN YOUR ARMS
   Hot *Big Tree* 77
90 I'LL NEVER GET OVER YOU (GETTING OVER ME)
   Exposé *Arista* 93
91 WHAT ABOUT US
   Total *LaFace* 97
92 DIGGIN' ON YOU
   TLC *LaFace* 95
93 SALLY, GO 'ROUND THE ROSES
   The Jaynetts *Tuff* 63
94 AINT 2 PROUD 2 BEG
   TLC *LaFace* 92
95 HEY MR. D.J.
   Zhané *Flavor Unit* 93
96 POPSICLES AND ICICLES
   The Murmaids *Chattahoochee* 64
97 GIVING HIM SOMETHING HE CAN FEEL
   En Vogue *Atco EastWest* 92
98 HE'S MINE
   MoKenStef *OutBurst* 95
99 IMPULSIVE
   Wilson Phillips *SBK* 90
100 TRIPPIN'
   Total (f/Missy Elliott) *Bad Boy* 98

The Top 100 INSTRUMENTALS

Roger Williams

I N THE early years of the rock era, it was easy to have a hit with an instrumental recording. But as the decades have passed, it has become increasingly difficult to succeed without lyrics. The evidence is in the list of the top 100 instrumentals of the rock era. There are 31 titles on the list from the '50s, 40 from the '60s, 22 from the '70s, five from the '80s, and two from the '90s.

Exactly one-quarter of the songs on the list reached No. 1. The first instrumental to achieve pole position in the rock era is also the most successful: "Autumn Leaves" remains the biggest chart instrumental of the entire rock era. The tune was originally a French melody called *"Les Feuilles-Mortes,"* written by Joseph Kosma. French lyrics were added by Jacques Prevert and English lyrics were later written by Johnny Mercer. There were many vocal versions of the song released in America—by artists like Bing Crosby and Jo Stafford—but no one had a hit with "Autumn Leaves" until Roger Williams played it on his piano.

The next instrumental to be No. 1 is the third most successful of the rock era. Nelson Riddle heard about a Portuguese melody called *"Lisbon Antigua"* ("In Old Lisbon") from the sister of Nat King Cole's manager. She was living near Mexico City and heard a local version by a band called Los Churambalis. Riddle was told by executives at Capitol Records to copy that version for his own recording.

Unlike "Autumn Leaves" and *"Lisbon Antigua,"* there was an instrumental in 1956 that was an original composition by the artist who recorded it. Bill Doggett, born in Philadelphia in 1916, formed his own band in 1938. He arranged material for the Ink Spots, Lionel Hampton, Louis Jordan, and many others. He wrote "Honky Tonk" with Billy Butler, Shep Sheppard, and Clifford Scott. Lyrics were added later by Henry Glover.

Other instrumentals that were successful in the '50s include "The Poor People Of Paris" by Les Baxter, "Moonglow And Theme From *Picnic*" by Morris Stoloff, "Tequila" by the Champs, "Sleep Walk" by Santo and Johnny, and "Canadian Sunset" by Hugo Winterhalter with Eddie Heywood.

The most successful instrumental of the '60s is Percy Faith's version of "Theme From *A Summer Place*," composed for the film by Max Steiner. It is the only instrumental to be the No. 1 single of the year, and its popularity remained strong enough for it to be included in the film *Batman* in a scene where the Joker invites Vicki Vale to lunch.

The second most popular instrumental of the '60s is conductor Paul Mauriat's "Love Is Blue." Mauriat was one of the writers of a previous No. 1 hit, "I Will Follow Him" by Little Peggy March, but he didn't write "Love Is Blue." Andre Popp composed the music and Pierre Cour wrote the lyrics for the song, selected to be Luxembourg's entry in the 1967 Eurovision Song Contest. Vicky Leandros performed the song at that year's competition, held in Vienna. The song placed fourth, losing to the British entry, Sandie Shaw's "Puppet On A String." Leandros recorded the song in 19 different languages—but none of the versions, including the French *"L'amour Est Bleu,"* was a hit. Mauriat included it on his *Blooming Hits* album; released as a single in America, "Love Is Blue" became the first instrumental to hit No. 1 in more than five years.

The Surfaris' "Wipe Out" was a hit twice. The five teenagers from Glendora, California, first made the Hot 100 in 1963 when "Wipe Out" spent a week at No. 2. In 1966, the song peaked at No. 16. The combined chart runs helped make the song the No. 35 instrumental of the rock era.

The highest-ranked instrumental of the '70s is from an artist who had scored with several instrumental hits in the '60s—as well as a No. 1 vocal performance. Herb Alpert's "Rise" was one of the last No. 1 hits of the 1970s. The co-founder of A&M Records had been absent from the Hot 100 for over five years when "Rise" debuted. He originally went into the studio to record a disco version of his very first hit, "The Lonely Bull." But 10 minutes into the session, he called a halt to the project, realizing how awful it sounded. Herb's cousin, writing under the name Randy Badazz, supplied his famous relative with a song he had written with Andy Armer. "Rise" was meant to be a dance song, but Alpert slowed down the beat so couples could dance and hug each other at last call. The song's popularity was bolstered by its use as a love theme on ABC-TV's *General Hospital.*

The second most successful instrumental of the '70s is Walter Murphy's "A Fifth Of Beethoven." A Madison Avenue jingle writer, Murphy was fascinated with pop hits that had been adapted from classical music pieces, like "A Lover's Concerto" by the Toys and "Joy" by Apollo 100. Murphy wanted to do the same thing, but with a disco beat. He sent a demo tape of several classical tunes recorded with a contemporary rhythm to every record company in New York City. The response was underwhelming, but Larry Uttal at Private Stock Records liked what Murphy had done to Symphony No. 5 In C Minor, composed by Ludwig van Beethoven in 1807. Although Murphy played almost all of the instruments, his record label thought the song should be credited to a group, so the "Big Apple Band" was created in name only.

Another of the decade's biggest instrumentals was a Barry White composition recorded by his 40-piece Love Unlimited Orchestra. "Love's Theme" was the overture for an album by the female trio Love Unlimited, featuring White's wife, Glodean. The instrumental opening segued into the vocal track "Under The Influence Of Love," and the two tracks combined for eight minutes and 17 seconds of disco heaven.

"Chariots Of Fire" is the biggest instrumental of the '80s. The opening track on the *Chariots Of Fire* soundtrack, it was simply called "Titles" when first released. It wasn't retitled until its eighth week on the Hot 100. Vangelis, born Evangelos Papathanassiou in Athens, Greece, was given his first major film composing assignment by *Chariot*'s producer, David Puttnam. Vangelis' work won an Oscar for Best Original Score.

The second most successful instrumental of the '80s is still the most recent instrumental to go to No. 1. Jan Hammer, born in Czechoslovakia, scored his first film, *A Night In Heaven,* in 1983. A year later, he met producer Michael Mann, who described a new project he was creating for NBC. Hammer scored the pilot of *Miami Vice* and ended up writing 20 minutes of original music for each episode. MCA released a soundtrack for the series, and Hammer's main title theme was issued as a single.

In third place among '80s instrumentals is Harold Faltermeyer's "Axel F" from the soundtrack to *Beverly Hills Cop.* In fourth place is a rarity for its time—an instrumental not from a film or TV series. Saxophonist Kenny G had his first top 10 hit in 1987 with "Songbird." Kenny, whose real last name is Gorelick, also has one of two '90s instrumentals in the top 100. "Forever In Love" came from his *Breathless* album. The other '90s instrumental in the top 100 is a dance track from Italy that began, according to composer Robert Miles, as an "overnight doodle." It was recorded in one evening and released in Italy, where it failed to catch on. A label head from the U.K. heard it in a Miami club and licensed it for Britain. It then spread to the rest of Europe and was licensed for U.S. release by Arista.

66 **NO MATTER WHAT SHAPE (YOUR STOMACH'S IN)**
The T-Bones *Liberty* 66

67 **ON THE REBOUND**
Floyd Cramer *RCA* 61

68 **PIPELINE**
The Chantays *Dot* 63

69 **RED RIVER ROCK**
Johnny & the Hurricanes *Warwick* 59

70 **SONGBIRD**
Kenny G *Arista* 87

71 **TEA FOR TWO CHA CHA**
The Tommy Dorsey Orchestra *Decca* 58

72 **THE HAPPY WHISTLER**
Don Robertson *Capitol* 56

73 **BORN FREE**
Roger Williams *Kapp* 66

74 **JAVA**
Al Hirt *RCA* 64

75 **RAUNCHY**
Ernie Freeman *Imperial* 57

76 **THE "IN" CROWD**
Ramsey Lewis Trio *Argo* 65

77 **A TASTE OF HONEY**
Herb Alpert & the Tijuana Brass *A&M* 65

78 **PETER GUNN**
Ray Anthony *Capitol* 59

79 **HOOKED ON CLASSICS**
Royal Philharmonic Orchestra *RCA* 82

80 **WHITE SILVER SANDS**
Bill Black's Combo *Hi* 60

81 **LET THERE BE DRUMS**
Sandy Nelson *Imperial* 61

82 **MANHATTAN SPIRITUAL**
Reg Owen *Palette* 59

83 **YELLOW BIRD**
Arthur Lyman Group *Hi-Fi* 61

84 **REBEL-'ROUSER**
Duane Eddy *Jamie* 58

85 **MEMPHIS**
Lonnie Mack *Fraternity* 63

86 **THE LONELY BULL**
Herb Alpert & the Tijuana Brass *A&M* 62

87 **MIDNIGHT COWBOY**
Ferrante and Teicher *UA* 70

88 **ONLY YOU**
Frank Pourcel's French Fiddles *Capitol* 59

89 **CHILDREN**
Robert Miles *Arista* 96

90 **ALLEY CAT**
Bent Fabric & His Piano *Atco* 62

91 **NEAR YOU**
Roger Williams *Kapp* 58

92 **JOY** Apollo 100 *Mega* 72

93 **FOREVER IN LOVE** Kenny G *Arista* 93

94 **PETITE FLEUR (LITTLE FLOWER)**
Chris Barber's Jazz Band *Laurie* 59

95 **FORTY MILES OF BAD ROAD**
Duane Eddy *Jamie* 59

96 **JUNGLE FEVER**
Chakachas *Polydor* 72

97 **DON'T BE CRUEL**
Bill Black's Combo *Hi* 60

98 **AROUND THE WORLD**
Victor Young *Decca* 57

99 **WILD WEEKEND**
The Rockin' Rebels *Swan* 63

100 **HOCUS POCUS**
Focus *Sire* 73

The Top 100 Songs by
U.K. ARTISTS

The Bee Gees

POP MUSIC historians didn't pay much attention to the United Kingdom before 1964. America was the birthplace of rock and roll, and anyone who meant anything in the new idiom was from the good old U.S.A. There would be an occasional foray into the American charts by a British artist, but that was rare, and the momentum was usually not sustained.

Only two of the top 100 songs by U.K. artists are from the pre-Beatles era. In 1962, a clarinet player from Somerset, England, became the first British artist to top the Hot 100. Mr. Acker Bilk's instrumental "Stranger On The Shore" was originally titled "Jenny," named for one of his children. The song was retitled when the BBC asked Bilk if he would play the piece as the title tune for a children's TV series. Later in 1962, the Tornadoes became the first British group to top the Hot 100. The group consisted of five musicians recruited by producer Joe Meek. The instrumental "Telstar" was No. 1 on both sides of the Atlantic.

Other British artists crossed the pond before the Beatles, including early arrivals Russ Hamilton ("Rainbow," No. 4 in 1957) and Laurie London ("He's Got The Whole World (In His Hands)," No. 2 in 1958). But like their countrymen Lonnie Donegan, Marty Wilde, Helen Shapiro, Frank Ifield, and Matt Monro, they didn't make a lasting impact.

Then came the Beatles. The impact was sudden and immediate. Within weeks of their arrival, they were followed by Peter & Gordon, Gerry

& the Pacemakers, the Dave Clark Five, the Searchers, the Hollies, the Kinks, Cilla Black, Dusty Springfield, Herman's Hermits, the Zombies, and many others.

The Beatles have more songs on the U.K. top 100 than any other act. Their 14 titles are led by "Hey Jude" at No. 3, the highest-ranked British song from the '60s. After the Fab Four, the most successful U.K. singles from the '60s are "Honky Tonk Women" by the Rolling Stones and "To Sir With Love" by Lulu.

The top two songs from the '70s are by the same act: the Bee Gees. And keeping it in the family, the next two highest-ranked songs from that decade are by Barry, Robin, and Maurice Gibb's youngest brother, Andy Gibb. "Stayin' Alive" is No. 8 on the U.K. list, followed by "Night Fever" at No. 10. Andy is No. 11 with "Shadow Dancing" and No. 14 with "I Just Want To Be Your Everything." The highest-ranked Brit with a '70s song who is not a member of the Gibb family is Rod Stewart, No. 16 with "Tonight's The Night (Gonna Be Alright)."

Some British musical trends from the '70s didn't cross the Atlantic. The glitter rock movement popularized by acts like Gary Glitter, the Sweet, Alvin Stardust, and Slade didn't catch on, with only Glitter and the Sweet having a small impact in the U.S. Some U.K. recordings missed the boat because the songs were covered by others. Stories did their own take of Hot Chocolate's "Brother Louie" and Bo Donaldson & the Heywoods rushed out "Billy, Don't Be A Hero" before Paper Lace could score with it. Other U.K. artists like Mud, the Real Thing, Wizzard, and Showaddywaddy all had No. 1 hits at home but failed to make an impression in America.

The most successful U.K. chart single of the '80s is Olivia Newton-John's "Physical," No. 1 for 10 weeks. Olivia nurtured her career while living in Australia. She played in coffeehouses on weekends and sang in a group with three other women, the Sol Four. Olivia won a Hayley Mills lookalike contest and two years later won a talent contest that offered a trip to England as a prize. She was doing well in Australia and reluctant to return home, but with encouragement from her mother, she traveled back to the U.K. with her friend Pat Carroll. They recorded together, and when Carroll's visa ran out, Livvy became a regular on Cliff Richard's TV series and joined a Don Kirshner group, Toomorrow. She signed with Pye Records, and John Farrar of the Shadows produced a version of Bob Dylan's "If Not For You." Released on Uni in the States, it was her first American chart entry, peaking at No. 25. Newton-John had four No. 1 singles to her credit by the time "Physical" was released. A well-planned video campaign planted the idea that the song was about working out rather than *really* getting "physical," so a possible censorship campaign was averted. "Physical" became the biggest hit of Newton-John's career.

In second place for the '80s is "Every Breath You Take" by the Police. The Anglo-American trio was formed by Stewart Copeland in 1977. Educated in Britain while his father worked for the CIA, Copeland played in a group called Curved Air and met Gordon Sumner (born in Wallsend) while he was playing bass with a jazz group called Last Exit. They teamed with Andy Summers and several other musicians in an outfit called Strontium 90, and in June 1977 Summers was invited to join the Police. In February

34 **(I CAN'T GET NO) SATISFACTION**
The Rolling Stones *London* 65
35 **SHE LOVES YOU**
The Beatles *Swan* 64
36 **DON'T YOU WANT ME**
The Human League *A&M* 82
37 **GET BACK**
The Beatles w/Billy Preston *Apple* 69
38 **AGAINST ALL ODDS (TAKE A LOOK AT ME NOW)**
Phil Collins *Atlantic* 84
39 **ANOTHER DAY IN PARADISE**
Phil Collins *Atlantic* 89
40 **MY LOVE**
Paul McCartney & Wings *Apple* 73
41 **MAGIC**
Olivia Newton-John *MCA* 80
42 **TEARS IN HEAVEN**
Eric Clapton *Reprise* 92
43 **I'M TOO SEXY**
Right Said Fred *Charisma* 92
44 **LET IT BE**
The Beatles *Apple* 70
45 **KARMA CHAMELEON**
Culture Club *Epic/Virgin* 84
46 **TOO MUCH HEAVEN**
Bee Gees *RSO* 79
47 **WINCHESTER CATHEDRAL**
New Vaudeville Band *Fontana* 66
48 **ESCAPE (PINA COLADA SONG)**
Rupert Holmes *Infinity* 79
49 **FAITH**
George Michael *Columbia* 87
50 **CARELESS WHISPER**
Wham! f/George Michael *Columbia* 85
51 **SWEET DREAMS (ARE MADE OF THIS)**
Eurythmics *RCA* 83
52 **HOW CAN YOU MEND A BROKEN HEART**
Bee Gees *Atco* 71
53 **OWNER OF A LONELY HEART**
Yes *Atco* 84
54 **LET'S DANCE**
David Bowie *RCA* 83
55 **(LOVE IS) THICKER THAN WATER**
Andy Gibb *RSO* 78
56 **BAKER STREET**
Gerry Rafferty *UA* 78
57 **STRANGER ON THE SHORE**
Mr. Acker Bilk *Atco* 62
58 **PHILADELPHIA FREEDOM**
The Elton John Band *MCA* 75
59 **CROCODILE ROCK**
Elton John *MCA* 73
60 **WOMAN**
John Lennon *Geffen* 81
61 **CAN'T BUY ME LOVE**
The Beatles *Capitol* 64
62 **MRS. BROWN YOU'VE GOT A LOVELY DAUGHTER**
Herman's Hermits *MGM* 65
63 **YESTERDAY** The Beatles *Capitol* 65
64 **MISSING YOU**
John Waite *EMI America* 84
65 **DOWNTOWN**
Petula Clark *Warner Bros.* 65
66 **MONEY FOR NOTHING**
Dire Straits *Warner Bros.* 85
67 **WE CAN WORK IT OUT**
The Beatles *Capitol* 66

1978 the group made its American debut—in a TV commercial for chewing gum, with their hair dyed blond. The following month they were signed to A&M Records. Their first U.S. chart entry was "Roxanne," which peaked at No. 32 in April 1979. Their first top 10 single was "De Do Do Do, De Da Da Da" in January 1981, followed by another top 10 single, "Don't Stand So Close To Me." Their final new album as a group, *Synchronicity,* was issued in the summer of 1983; the LP was preceded by its first single, "Every Breath You Take," which spent eight weeks at No. 1 and 22 weeks on the Hot 100.

The most successful U.K. single of the '90s—and of the entire rock era—is Elton John's two-sided hit, "Candle In The Wind 1997"/"Something About The Way You Look Tonight." The latter song was scheduled to be Elton's next single as the summer of 1997 drew to a close. It was a taste of his new album, *The Big Picture.* But then an unimaginable tragedy struck. Diana, Princess of Wales, was killed in an automobile crash in a Paris tunnel. The world mourned, and the Princess' family asked Elton to sing at her funeral service in Westminster Abbey. A misunderstanding over the phone led to lyricist Bernie Taupin rewriting the 1973 song "Candle In The Wind" to suit the occasion, and a studio recording of the rewritten song became the biggest-selling single in history.

While Elton's chart span on the Hot 100 stretches over four different decades, all of his other singles on the U.K. top 100 are from the '70s. "Philadelphia Freedom" ranks No. 57, followed by "Crocodile Rock" (No. 58), "Bennie And The Jets" (No. 73), and his duet with Kiki Dee, "Don't Go Breaking My Heart" (No. 76).

The second-highest ranked U.K. song from the '90s is UB40's remake of an Elvis Presley hit, "Can't Help Falling In Love." The eight-man reggae outfit, named for an unemployment benefits form in their country, submitted their Elvis remake for the soundtrack of *Honeymoon In Vegas.* It was rejected in favor of Bono's version of the same song, but then ended up in the film *Sliver* and became a far bigger hit than any song from *Honeymoon In Vegas.*

The highest-ranked U.K. song from the 21st century is "Thank You" by Dido at No. 84. Two months before she charted on the Hot 100 on her own, she was an uncredited guest on Eminem's "Stan," which heavily sampled "Thank You." Dido told *Billboard*'s Larry Flick how she wrote the song: "I was lying there, talking to my boyfriend, and I asked him to tell me about the things that made his day bad. Afterward, he walked out of the room and I was frantically reaching around for the pen. The entire song came to life on a soggy bit of paper. Needless to say, it was a bit hard to decipher later on."

The Top 100 Songs by
CANADIAN ARTISTS

Shania Twain

ALTHOUGH THE United States and Canada announced the border was being tightened between the two countries in the wake of the terrorist attacks of September 11, 2001, the artistic line between the two nations has generally been porous. Canadian entertainers blend in with Hollywood, New York, and Nashville artists with ease, and unless you check a biography, it's easy to forget a person's origin. Who could be more American than the patriarch of the Cartwright clan on *Bonanza?* But the actor who portrayed Ben Cartwright was Lorne Greene, born in Ottawa, Ontario. Greene's deep, powerful baritone served him well in the 1940s, when he replaced Charles Jennings (father of ABC News anchor Peter Jennings) as the chief news broadcaster for the Canadian Broadcasting Company. During World War II, Greene was known as the "Voice of Canada." Acting in television productions and motion pictures brought him to the U.S., and in 1959 he was cast in *Bonanza*. With the series at its peak of popularity in 1964, a producer at RCA Records suggested the cast record an album. It sold well enough that Greene was signed to a recording contract. For a second *Bonanza* cast album, Greene was asked to record a six-stanza poem. A Lubbock, Texas, DJ played "Ringo" and created such a demand for it that a single was issued. It went to No. 1 the week of December 5, 1964.

Greene wasn't the first Canadian to find success on the U.S. singles chart. At the very beginning of the rock era, a quartet from Toronto spent six weeks at No. 2 with a classic vocal group song, "Moments To Remember." The Four Lads met when they were teenagers, at St. Michael's Cathedral Choir School. They sang mass and Gregorian chants, eventually adding spirituals and Barbershop Quartet tunes. When their teachers weren't around, they sang pop songs. A manager showed interest and invited them to New York City. They auditioned for Mitch Miller at Columbia Records. At first, he had them singing backing vocals for Johnnie Ray on hits like "Cry" and "The Little White Cloud That Cried." They backed Doris Day, too, before being allowed to record on their own. After "Moments To Remember," they had follow-up hits with "No Not Much" and "Standing On The Corner," the latter from the Broadway musical *The Most Happy Fella*.

The Crew-Cuts and the Diamonds were also successful Canadian vocal groups in the '50s, the same decade that saw Paul Anka's star rise with hits like "Diana" and "Lonely Boy." Anka continued to chart into the '60s (and beyond), while Toronto-born Percy Faith had the biggest hit by a Canadian artist in the '60s, "Theme From *A Summer Place*." The only Canadian in the top 100 from the latter half of the '60s is Montreal-born Andy Kim. He quit school at 16 to move to New York and pursue a career in music. He met songwriter Jeff Barry, who signed Kim to his Steed label. They hit on a successful formula with Kim remaking Ronettes' songs that Barry had co-written, starting with the 1969 hit "Baby, I Love You." Five years later, Kim had a No. 1 song with "Rock Me Gently."

The highest-ranked Canadian song from the '70s on the top 100 is "Seasons In The Sun" by a musician from Winnipeg, Manitoba. Terry Jacks moved to Vancouver with his family when he was a child. He had a paper route and spent his earnings buying singles by artists like his favorite, Buddy Holly. He thought about being an architect or a professional golfer, but he loved music and formed a group, the Chessmen. During a TV appearance with his group, Jacks met a Vancouver-born singer, Susan Pesklevits. They married, and recorded together as the Poppy Family. In 1970, they went to No. 2 on the Hot 100 with "Which Way You Goin', Billy?" The marriage (and the act) broke up in 1973, and the Beach Boys asked Terry to work with them. He suggested they record a Jacques Brel song, "Seasons In The Sun," and they did—but didn't release their own version. More than a year later, Jacks' version came out on a local label and was picked up by Bell Records for the U.S.

While individuals like Gordon Lightfoot and Dan Hill had hits in the '70s, the most successful group was a Winnipeg outfit that first recorded as Chad Allen & the Expressions. In the days before Canadian content laws, some acts found it difficult to garner radio airplay in their own country. To avoid that problem, the group kept their name off of a single called "Shakin' All Over." Instead, the label read, "Guess Who." The name stuck.

35 **HERO**
Chad Kroeger f/Josey Scott
Columbia/Roadrunner 02

36 **ANGEL**
Sarah McLachlan *Arista* 99

37 **I'M WITH YOU**
Avril Lavigne *Arista* 03

38 **FAR AWAY**
Nickelback *Roadrunner* 06

39 **ROCK ME GENTLY**
Andy Kim *Capitol* 74

40 **WHEN I'M WITH YOU**
Sheriff *Capitol* 89

41 **CAN'T STOP THIS THING WE STARTED**
Bryan Adams *A&M* 91

42 **THE SAFETY DANCE**
Men Without Hats *Backstreet* 83

43 **DON'T WANNA FALL IN LOVE**
Jane Child *Warner Bros.* 90

44 **STANDING ON THE CORNER**
The Four Lads *Columbia* 56

45 **PUT YOUR HAND IN THE HAND**
Ocean *Kama Sutra* 71

46 **YOU AIN'T SEEN NOTHING YET**
Bachman-Turner Overdrive *Mercury* 74

47 **INSENSITIVE**
Jann Arden *A&M* 96

48 **NO, NOT MUCH**
The Four Lads *Columbia* 56

49 **PLEASE FORGIVE ME**
Bryan Adams *A&M* 93

50 **PUPPY LOVE**
Paul Anka *ABC-Paramount* 60

51 **WHICH WAY YOU GOIN', BILLY?**
The Poppy Family *London* 70

52 **SOMETIMES WHEN WE TOUCH**
Dan Hill *20th Century* 78

53 **THAT'S THE WAY IT IS**
Celine Dion *550 Music* 00

54 **HARD TO GET**
Gisele MacKenzie *X* 55

55 **MY TRUE LOVE**
Jack Scott *Carlton* 58

56 **STEAL MY SUNSHINE**
Len *Work* 99

57 **RINGO**
Lorne Greene *RCA* 64

58 **MMM MMM MMM MMM**
Crash Test Dummies *Arista* 94

59 **MORE THAN WORDS CAN SAY**
Alias *EMI* 90

60 **BURNING BRIDGES**
Jack Scott *Top Rank* 60

61 **YOU LEARN / YOU OUGHTA KNOW**
Alanis Morissette *Maverick* 96

62 **NEVER SURRENDER**
Corey Hart *EMI America* 85

63 **IF YOU ASKED ME TO**
Celine Dion *Epic* 92

64 **SAVIN' ME**
Nickelback *Roadrunner* 06

65 **LAST SONG** Edward Bear *Capitol* 73

66 **DON'T FORGET ME (WHEN I'M GONE)**
Glass Tiger *Manhattan* 86

67 **TURN OFF THE LIGHT**
Nelly Furtado *DreamWorks* 01

68 **HEARTBEAT - IT'S A LOVEBEAT**
DeFranco Family f/Tony DeFranco
20th Century 73

Randy Bachman and Burton Cummings wrote their first single for RCA, "These Eyes." After two more 45 releases, the group scored a double-sided No. 1 single in 1970 with "American Woman" / "No Sugar Tonight."

The most successful Canadian female on the Hot 100 during the '70s was a woman from Springhill, Novia Scotia. Anne Murray was so dedicated that when she was 15, she took voice lessons every Saturday from a teacher who lived more than 50 miles away. During her college years, she auditioned for a TV series and though turned down at first, was asked to join a summer edition of the show two years later. The musical director of the program, Brian Ahern, thought she should record on her own, but Murray thought it was a crazy idea. After much persuasion from Ahern, Murray agreed to let him produce an album for a small Canadian label. Then Ahern took her to Toronto to meet with executives at Capitol of Canada. They signed her, and her first album included "Snowbird," which won Murray the first gold record awarded to a Canadian female singer.

Anne Murray isn't the only Canadian female with the initials A.M. to do well in the U.S. In the '90s, Alannah Myles and Alanis Morissette both fared well on the southern side of the border. Myles, a native of Toronto, met MuchMusic VJ Christopher Ward at a party. They became partners both professionally and personally. Working with producer David Tyson, Ward put together a three-song demo tape of Myles and sent it to various record companies. Within 48 hours of its arrival at Atlantic Records in New York, Ward heard back and Myles was signed to the label. Ward and Tyson wrote "Black Velvet," which brought Myles to the top of the chart in March 1990.

Ottawa-born Morissette became a star in a Nickelodeon series when she was only 12 years old. As a teenager, she released two albums of pop-oriented dance music in Canada. Then she teamed up with producer Glen Ballard to work on an album of deeper, more personal songs. She was signed to Madonna's Maverick label, and her album *Jagged Little Pill* spent 12 weeks at No. 1. The track "You Oughta Know" received a lot of airplay, but wasn't released as a commercial single, so Morissette made her Hot 100 debut in March 1996 with "Ironic."

The artists with the most titles on the Canadian top 100 are Bryan Adams and Celine Dion with 10 each. The top song on the list is Nickelback's "How You Remind Me." Chad Kroeger grew up in Hanna, Alberta, and wrote his first song when he was 16. When he finished high school, he joined his brother Mike and friend Ryan Peake in a cover band. When they grew tired of playing other people's music, they broke up but Chad continued to write songs and the band reunited with Ryan Vikedal on drums.

"How You Remind Me" was inspired by a relationship that was going badly for Kroeger. "It does sound like a love ballad," he admits, "but if you finish the sentence, 'This is how you remind me of how I really am,' like you're a jerk, you're insensitive, all the unflattering things you hear throughout a day, that's what the song's about."

69 **I JUST WANNA STOP**
Gino Vannelli *A&M* 78

70 **WASTING MY TIME**
Default *TVT* 02

71 **WHERE DOES MY HEART BEAT NOW**
Celine Dion *Epic* 91

72 **BUILDING A MYSTERY**
Sarah McLachlan *Arista* 97

73 **MY HAPPY ENDING**
Avril Lavigne *Arista* 04

74 **THAT DON'T IMPRESS ME MUCH**
Shania Twain *Mercury* 99

75 **FROM THIS MOMENT ON**
Shania Twain *Mercury* 98

76 **LIVING INSIDE MYSELF**
Gino Vannelli *Arista* 81

77 **SAY IT RIGHT**
Nelly Furtado *Mosley* 07

78 **THE STROLL**
The Diamonds *Mercury* 58

79 **ANGELS IN THE SKY**
The Crew-Cuts *Mercury* 56

80 **I FINALLY FOUND SOMEONE**
Barbra Streisand & Bryan Adams *Columbia* 96

81 **WHAT IN THE WORLD'S COME OVER YOU**
Jack Scott *Top Rank* 60

82 **I'M LIKE A BIRD**
Nelly Furtado *DreamWorks* 01

83 **SUNGLASSES AT NIGHT**
Corey Hart *EMI America* 84

84 **IT'S TIME TO CRY**
Paul Anka *ABC-Paramount* 59

85 **GOODBYE BABY**
Jack Scott *Carlton* 59

86 **SHE'S SO HIGH**
Tal Bachman *Columbia* 99

87 **PINCH ME**
Barenaked Ladies *Reprise* 00

88 **TIMES OF YOUR LIFE**
Paul Anka *UA* 76

89 **RUN TO YOU**
Bryan Adams *A&M* 85

90 **ALMOST PARADISE**
Mike Reno & Ann Wilson *Columbia* 84

91 **BEAUTY AND THE BEAST**
Celine Dion & Peabo Bryson *Epic* 92

92 **SK8ER BOI**
Avril Lavigne *Arista* 02

93 **ALL BY MYSELF**
Celine Dion *550 Music* 97

94 **WILDFLOWER**
Skylark *Capitol* 73

95 **SOMEDAY**
Glass Tiger *Manhattan* 87

96 **STAND TALL**
Burton Cummings *Portrait* 77

97 **DAYDREAM BELIEVER**
Anne Murray *Capitol* 80

98 **I WILL REMEMBER YOU (LIVE)**
Sarah McLachlan *Arista* 99

99 **DO I HAVE TO SAY THE WORDS?**
Bryan Adams *A&M* 92

100 **THOUGHT I'D DIED AND GONE TO HEAVEN**
Bryan Adams *A&M* 92

Rick Springfield

WHILE THE Seekers came close to pole position in the '60s with "Georgy Girl," a No. 2 hit on the Hot 100, the first artist from Australia to top the Hot 100 was a female thrush named Helen Reddy. Born in Melbourne to show business parents, she was only four years old when she first appeared on stage with her comedian father and actress mother. Later, she won an Australian television station's talent contest with first prize of a trip to New York and a record company audition. Arriving in Manhattan, someone from the label took her to lunch and said he hoped she had a lovely visit. End of prize. When her money ran out, she was ready to go home defeated. But friends surprised her with a fund-raising birthday party. An agent named Jeff Wald crashed the party. Four days later he proposed marriage and Reddy said yes. Wald convinced Capitol Records to sign his wife for one single. The label wanted her to record "I Don't Know How to Love Him" from *Jesus Christ Superstar*. Wald hated the song and put it on the B-side, but radio DJs preferred it and Reddy had her first hit.

Rick Springfield (née Richard Lewis Springthorpe) was born in Sydney and settled down in Melbourne. Capitol Records picked up his single "Speak To The Sky" and made it a minor hit in 1972. Relocating to Hollywood, he took acting lessons and studied tae kwon do. He won roles in episodic series like *The Rockford Files* and *The Incredible Hulk,* and joined the cast of *The Young And The Restless.* RCA signed him just two months before he moved over to *General Hospital,* and in August 1981 he topped the Hot 100 with "Jessie's Girl."

Only half of the duo known as Air Supply is Australian by birth. Russell Hitchcock was born in Melbourne, while Graham Russell hails from Sherwood, Nottingham, England. They met each other when they were both cast in a Melbourne production of *Jesus Christ Superstar.* Recording as a duo, they had a top three hit down under, "Love And Other Bruises," and left the show. After opening for Rod Stewart, Graham took six months off in Adelaide and wrote "Lost In Love" and "All Out Of Love," the pair's first two U.S. chart entries. Their fourth single, "The One That You Love," brought them to the top of the chart in 1981.

The following year, while Mel Gibson was doing well at the box office with *Mad Max,* another Australian act dominated the Hot 100. Singer Colin Hay and guitarist Ron Strykert were university students in Melbourne when they met at a band audition. Adding keyboardist Greg Ham, drummer Jerry Speiser, and bassist John Rees, Men at Work spent 18 months playing pubs and clubs before CBS Records matched them up with producer Peter Mclan. He produced their album *Business As Usual,* which yielded two No. 1 hits: "Who Can It Be Now?" and "Down Under."

Darren Hayes grew up in Brisbane, listening to favorite albums like Fleetwood Mac's *Rumours* and Diana Ross & the Supremes' *20 Golden Greats.* "I was listening to Berry Gordy productions when most kids were listening to new wave. Those records became a part of the way I hear music and write music today." Hayes wrote songs, sang in choir, and acted with theater groups. An ad in a trade magazine for a band seeking a vocalist caught his eye. At age 18, Hayes got the job, but then the band broke up. He remained friends with Daniel Jones and they formed a duo, creating cheap demos and sending out hundreds of tapes. Inspired by Anne Rice's *Interview With The Vampire,* they named themselves Savage Garden.

The one person who responded positively to their demo tapes was John Woodruff, manager of Icehouse and the Angels. "He financed the recording of our first album," Hayes explains. "An [American radio] consultant named Guy Zapoleon was in a conference in Australia and heard 'I Want You' and took it back to the U.S. So by the time we started negotiating for a deal, we had an audition set up with Clive Davis [at Arista] and Donnie Ienner [at Columbia]." The latter outbid the former and "I Want You" soared to No. 4 on the Hot 100. "Truly Madly Deeply" and "I Knew I Loved You" were No. 1 hits, and are the top two Australian singles of the rock era.

31 **I TOUCH MYSELF**
Divinyls *Virgin* 91
32 **THE NIGHT OWLS**
Little River Band *Capitol* 81
33 **LONESOME LOSER**
Little River Band *Capitol* 79
34 **WHAT YOU NEED**
INXS *Atlantic* 86
35 **TIE ME KANGAROO DOWN, SPORT**
Rolf Harris *Epic* 63
36 **THE OTHER GUY**
Little River Band *Capitol* 83
37 **I'LL NEVER FIND ANOTHER YOU**
The Seekers *Capitol* 65
38 **AFFAIR OF THE HEART**
Rick Springfield *RCA* 83
39 **TAKE IT EASY ON ME**
Little River Band *Capitol* 82
40 **LADY**
Little River Band *Harvest* 79
41 **LOVE SOMEBODY**
Rick Springfield *RCA* 84
42 **IT'S A MISTAKE**
Men at Work *Columbia* 83
43 **COOL CHANGE**
Little River Band *Capitol* 80
44 **I'VE DONE EVERYTHING FOR YOU**
Rick Springfield *RCA* 81
45 **ELECTRIC BLUE**
Icehouse *Chrysalis* 88
46 **THE LORD'S PRAYER**
Sister Janet Mead *A&M* 74
47 **NEVER TEAR US APART**
INXS *Atlantic* 88
48 **YOU AND ME AGAINST THE WORLD**
Helen Reddy *Capitol* 74
49 **CRAZY**
Icehouse *Chrysalis* 88
50 **YOU'RE MY WORLD**
Helen Reddy *Capitol* 77

Enya

IRELAND HAS a rich heritage of music, with a number of diverse artists who have claimed fame in the U.S., including four Irish acts who have topped the Hot 100. Raymond Edward O'Sullivan, a Waterford-born singer and songwriter, had his first name changed by his manager to Gilbert. Clever by half, it somehow worked for the man who spent six weeks at No. 1 with the oddly charming "Alone Again (Naturally)" and followed it with a No. 2 hit, "Clair."

Sinead O'Connor's antics like tearing up a photograph of the Pope on *Saturday Night Live* often obscured her musical talent. Her second album, *I Do Not Want What I Haven't Got,* was critically acclaimed. It was a commercial success too, thanks to the inclusion of a lesser-known song written by Prince. It was first recorded by the Family, but O'Connor made "Nothing Compares 2 U" her own and took it to No. 1 on the Hot 100.

A rock group with a spiritual base, U2 has been proclaimed by many as the best band of the last two decades of the 20th century. British fans voting for their favorite album of all time in a 2001 poll elected *The Joshua Tree,* which yielded the No. 1 singles "With Or Without You" and "I Still Haven't Found What I'm Looking For."

Roxette

IF YOU look back through the *Billboard* charts, you will find Swedish artists who charted on the Hot 100 before Abba. In 1969, for example, Ola & the Janglers went to No. 92 with "Let's Dance." That may seem insignificant, but it's not: lead singer Ola Hakansson is today head of Stockholm Records (home to the Cardigans and the A*Teens, among others), and one of the most respected figures in the Swedish music business.

There was another pre-Abba Swedish group that did well. On April 6, 1974, the No. 1 song on the Hot 100 was a remake of B.J. Thomas' "Hooked On A Feeling." It was the day everything in the Swedish music industry changed. But not because Blue Swede was on top in America; by some strange coincidence, it was also the day Abba won the Eurovision Song Contest at the Brighton Dome in England with "Waterloo." Benny Andersson and Björn Ulvaeus competed in Eurovision because they knew it was the only way to find success beyond the borders of Sweden. Their plan worked.

Abba's global achievements opened the doors for other Swedish artists. The quartet from Gothenburg known as Ace of Base and the duo of Per Gessle and Marie Fredriksson, better known as Roxette, were the chief beneficiaries.

01 **THE SIGN**
Ace of Base *Arista* 94

02 **ALL THAT SHE WANTS**
Ace of Base *Arista* 93

03 **IT MUST HAVE BEEN LOVE**
Roxette *EMI* 90

04 **DON'T TURN AROUND**
Ace of Base *Arista* 94

05 **HOOKED ON A FEELING**
Blue Swede *EMI* 74

06 **THE LOOK**
Roxette *EMI* 89

07 **DANCING QUEEN**
Abba *Atlantic* 77

08 **JOYRIDE**
Roxette *EMI* 91

09 **LISTEN TO YOUR HEART**
Roxette *EMI* 89

10 **DANGEROUS**
Roxette *EMI* 90

11 **DO YOU KNOW
(WHAT IT TAKES)**
Robyn *RCA* 97

12 **TAKE A CHANCE ON ME**
Abba *Atlantic* 78

13 **SAVE TONIGHT**
Eagle-Eye Cherry *Work* 99

14 **SHOW ME LOVE**
Robyn *RCA* 97

15 **FADING LIKE A FLOWER
(EVERY TIME YOU LEAVE)**
Roxette *EMI* 91

16 **BUFFALO STANCE**
Neneh Cherry *Virgin* 89

17 **CARRIE**
Europe *Epic* 87

18 **THE WINNER TAKES IT ALL**
Abba *Atlantic* 81

19 **BEAUTIFUL LIFE**
Ace of Base *Arista* 95

20 **CRUEL SUMMER**
Ace of Base *Arista* 98

21 **WATERLOO**
Abba *Atlantic* 74

22 **FERNANDO**
Abba *Atlantic* 76

23 **LIVING IN DANGER**
Ace of Base *Arista* 94

24 **THE FINAL COUNTDOWN**
Europe *Epic* 87

25 **DOES YOUR MOTHER KNOW**
Abba *Atlantic* 79

26 **COTTON EYE JOE**
Rednex *Battery* 95

27 **KISSES ON THE WIND**
Neneh Cherry *Virgin* 89

28 **KNOWING ME, KNOWING YOU**
Abba *Atlantic* 77

29 **NEVER MY LOVE**
Blue Swede *EMI* 74

30 **THE NAME OF THE GAME**
Abba *Atlantic* 78

The Top 10 Songs by GERMAN ARTISTS

THE MOST successful Hot 100 entry by a German group is "Another Night," a hook-laden dance hit by a trio dubbed Real McCoy. Berlin-born rapper and songwriter Olaf "O-Jay" Jeglitza loved hip-hop music and spent some time in New York before returning to Germany. He teamed with American singers Patricia Petersen and Vanessa Mason, blending his Euro-rap with their Euro-pop vocals to create "Another Night," the highest-ranked No. 3 song on the Top 5000 Songs of the Rock Era.

Hamburg native Bert Kaempfert was a bandleader, and staff producer for the Polydor label when he recorded the instrumental *Wunderland Bei Nacht*. Under its English title, "Wonderland By Night," it became the first German hit to reach No. 1 on the Hot 100. One act Germany might like to forget is Milli Vanilli, even though the duo is the nation's most successful musical export, with three consecutive No. 1 singles in 1989. It was only later that the world discovered that Rob Pilatus, who grew up in Munich, and Fabrice Morvan, born in the West Indies, did not actually sing the vocals on Milli Vanilli recordings. The act was the brainchild of German producer Frank Farian, the man who made Boney M an internationally successful act.

01 **ANOTHER NIGHT**
Real McCoy *Arista* 94
02 **WONDERLAND BY NIGHT**
Bert Kaempfert *Decca* 61
03 **FLY, ROBIN, FLY**
Silver Convention *Midland* 75
04 **BLAME IT ON THE RAIN**
Milli Vanilli *Arista* 89
05 **GIRL I'M GONNA MISS YOU**
Milli Vanilli *Arista* 89
06 **GET UP AND BOOGIE (THAT'S RIGHT)**
Silver Convention *Midland International* 76
07 **99 LUFTBALLONS**
Nena *Epic* 84
08 **GIRL YOU KNOW IT'S TRUE**
Milli Vanilli *Arista* 89
09 **BABY DON'T FORGET MY NUMBER**
Milli Vanilli *Arista* 89
10 **RETURN TO INNOCENCE**
Enigma *Virgin* 94

The Top 10 Songs by DUTCH ARTISTS

THERE WAS a mini-invasion of music from the Netherlands in 1970 thanks to American record label chief Jerry Ross. After experiencing some success with his Heritage label, he started the Colossus imprint and scored with three Dutch imports by Shocking Blue, Tee Set, and the George Baker Selection. The most successful was "Venus" by Shocking Blue, written by guitarist Robbie van Leeuwen. After recording with '60s beat group the Motions, he formed Shocking Blue in 1967. At a party for well-known Dutch rock band Golden Earring, Shocking Blue's manager was impressed by the performance of the Bumble Bees, especially with the lead vocals of half-German, half-Hungarian singer Mariska Veres. She was invited to join Shocking Blue as their new lead vocalist, and sang on two of their chart hits in Holland before recording "Venus."

Eleven years later, "Venus" was a hit for another Dutch group, though just a fraction of the song was used, and the "group" was a studio assemblage put together by producer Jaap Eggermont. He put together a medley of well-known songs, mostly featuring Beatles tunes, and released it under the name Stars on 45.

01 **MEDLEY: INTRO VENUS...**
Stars on 45 *Radio* 81
02 **VENUS**
Shocking Blue *Colossus* 70
03 **THIS IS YOUR NIGHT**
Amber *Tommy Boy* 97
04 **TWILIGHT ZONE**
Golden Earring *21* 83
05 **HOW DO YOU DO?**
Mouth & Macneal *Philips* 72
06 **MA BELLE AMIE**
Tee Set *Colossus* 70
07 **HOCUS POCUS**
Focus *Sire* 73
08 **RADAR LOVE**
Golden Earring *Track* 74
09 **WE LIKE TO PARTY!**
Vengaboys *Groovilicious* 99
10 **LITTLE GREEN BAG**
George Baker Selection *Colossus* 70

The Top 30 Songs by AMERICAN IDOLS

Diana DeGarmo

FIRST, THERE WAS a TV series in New Zealand called *Popstars*, in which hopeful contestants competed for a spot in a new singing group. The format was duplicated in other countries, including the United Kingdom and the United States. Then ITV in Britain put a new spin on the concept and developed a series called *Pop Idol*, where the goal was not to create a new pop group, but solo stars. The first broadcast was October 5, 2001, and a record-setting 8.7 million phoned in to vote for winner Will Young and runner-up Gareth Gates. Both had No. 1 singles and a number of follow-ups.

Series creator Simon Fuller sold the series to the Fox network in America and the first season began on June 11, 2002. When the finale aired on September 4, 2002, Kelly Clarkson was voted the winner. The song she performed on that season-ending show, "A Moment Like This," took a 52 to 1 jump on the Hot 100, setting a record for the biggest leap to the top in the chart's history.

Clarkson had one more top 10 hit from her first album with "Miss Independent." But it was her second album that yielded a bumper crop of hits and made her a top 40 superstar. "Breakaway," "Since U Been Gone," "Behind These Hazel Eyes," and "Because Of You" all made the top 10.

The *Idol* track record has continued through the first five seasons. Ruben Studdard, Clay Aiken, Kimberley Locke, and Josh Gracin, the second season's top four, all have songs on the *American Idol* top 30. The third season's top two, Fantasia and Diana DeGarmo, are also listed, as are the fourth season's top two, Carrie Underwood and Bo Bice. From the fifth season, the top two finalists, Taylor Hicks and Katharine McPhee, are represented, as is fourth-place Chris Daughtry and top 12 drop-out Mario Vazquez.

T HE FINAL *Billboard* issue of each weekly year is devoted to a wrap-up of the previous 12 months. For chart enthusiasts, the most important section of that annual issue is the part that contains the top 100 singles and albums of the previous year. To be the No. 1 song in any particular week is an achievement, but to be the No. 1 song of the year—that's being a part of history.

The charts on the following pages are not meant to replace the year-end surveys *Billboard* has published over the years. Those charts are a matter of record. Rather, these lists are an opportunity to look at the biggest hits of each year from a different perspective.

One limitation of the annual charts published in *Billboard* is that they are not compiled on a calendar year basis—that is, they do not run from January to December. Because of publishing deadlines, the eligibility period has varied over the years, but generally runs from the beginning of December to the end of November. In the past, this has penalized some records that were hits at the end of the year by leaving them caught in limbo between two particular years, not gaining enough points in either to register on any year-end chart. As a result, songs like "Big Girls Don't Cry" by the Four Seasons, "Come See About Me" by the Supremes, and "I Think I Love You" by the Partridge Family never appeared on a *Billboard* year-end survey because they peaked in November or December.

The charts on the following pages list singles in the year that they peaked. "My Sweet Lord," which went to No. 1 the week of December 26, 1970, is included in the top 100 songs of 1970. In the official *Billboard* charts, it was listed in 1971.

Records were given credit for their entire chart life, even if some weeks of that chart life took place in a different year. "Raindrops Keep Fallin' On My Head" by B.J. Thomas peaked on January 3, 1970; nine weeks of its chart life occurred in 1969. Those nine weeks were included when calculating where the song should be listed in the year-end chart for 1970.

The top 100 songs of each decade were compiled in the same manner. The list for the 1950s includes songs that peaked on or after July 9, 1955. Traditionally, *Billboard* has not published the top singles by decades, so this information is being presented here for the first time in any form.

The Top 100 Songs of 1956

Guy Mitchell

1956 WAS THE year Capitol Records built a round office building in Hollywood that looked like a stack of records; Elvis Presley shook his hips on Milton Berle's television show; and Lerner and Loewe's *My Fair Lady* was the toast of Broadway.

Little Richard and Johnny Cash made their debuts on *Billboard*'s pop singles chart in 1956. Richard Penniman, born in Macon, Georgia, first went into a recording studio in October 1951. Three years later he sent an audition tape to Specialty Records, but held back his wild rock songs in favor of blues material. He had a recording session in New Orleans for the label. "During a break...someone heard me playing 'Tutti Frutti' on the piano and asked me about the song. We ended up recording it and sold 200,000 copies in a week and a half," he told Robert Hilburn of the *Los Angeles Times*. "Long Tall Sally" was the No. 58 song of 1956 and the follow-up, "Tutti Frutti," was No. 95.

J.R. Cash, born in Kingsland, Arkansas, auditioned for Sam Phillips of Sun Records with some gospel songs, but Phillips didn't think there was much of a market for that kind of music. Then he heard a song Cash had written called "Hey Porter" and signed him and the Tennessee Two to the label. Phillips decided to call John R. Cash "Johnny." Soon after marrying his first wife, Vivian, Cash wrote "I Walk The Line" (the title was inspired by Carl Perkins) backstage at a club in Gladewater, Texas. It became his first pop hit and ranked No. 92 for 1956.

Three rock and roll classics were among the top 100 songs of the year. "Blue Suede Shoes" by Carl Perkins ranked No. 21. Perkins was originally signed by Sam Phillips to a Sun subsidiary label, Flip, as a country performer. After Elvis Presley left Sun for RCA, Perkins was moved over to the main label and told to write rock and roll songs. He took Phillips' advice and wrote "Blue Suede Shoes," a song promptly covered by Elvis.

"Why Do Fools Fall In Love" by the Teenagers featuring Frankie Lymon was the No. 33 song of the year. Richard Barrett, lead singer of the Valentines, brought the young group to George Goldner, who owned a couple of record labels. There are differing accounts of how their first hit came to be. One version says that Lymon wrote a composition in school called "Why Do Fools Fall In Love"; another says that he wrote the song after being turned down by a girl. Yet another says that a neighbor had written a poem called "Why Do Birds Sing So Gay" and gave it to the group to adapt as a song. Whatever its origin, Goldner recorded it just after Thanksgiving 1955, and released it on a new subsidiary, Gee.

"Be-Bop-A-Lula" by Gene Vincent was the No. 35 song of 1956. Capitol Records wanted their own version of Elvis Presley, and label producer Ken Nelson thought Vincent would fill the bill. His first recording session for the label took place in Nashville on May 4, 1956. Among the three songs recorded that day were "Woman Love," the track Nelson chose for Vincent's first single. DJs liked the "B" side better and started giving airplay to a song inspired by a comic strip, Little Lulu. "Be-Bop-A-Lula" became a big hit (and the first record that Paul McCartney ever bought).

There were two instrumentals in the year's top 10. "Lisbon Antigua" by Nelson Riddle was No. 7 and "The Poor People Of Paris" by Les Baxter was No. 10.

The No. 1 single of 1956 was a two-sided hit, "Don't Be Cruel" and "Hound Dog" by Elvis Presley. The former was composed by Otis Blackwell, a Brooklyn-born songwriter who sold the rights to "Don't Be Cruel" and five other songs for $25 each on Christmas Eve of 1955. The latter was a Jerry Leiber–Mike Stoller song written for Willie Mae "Big Mama" Thornton, who topped the R&B chart with it in 1953. Elvis had two more songs in the top 10: "Love Me Tender" at No. 3 and "Heartbreak Hotel" at No. 4. The latter was Presley's first pop hit and his first recording for RCA Victor. Mae Axton, who handled public relations in Florida for Elvis' manager, Col. Tom Parker, was inspired to write the song when Tommy Durden showed her a story in the newspaper about someone who had committed suicide. He left a note that read, "I walk a lonely street." Mae suggested to Tommy that they put a "heartbreak hotel" at the end of that lonely street, and in 22 minutes they wrote and recorded a demo of the song. "Love Me Tender" was based on a folk ballad, "Aura Lee." Ken Darby, musical director of Elvis' first movie, wrote the song but gave the credit to his wife, Vera Watson.

"Singing The Blues" by Guy Mitchell was the second most popular chart single of 1956. In pole position for nine weeks, it was originally

35 **BE-BOP-A-LULA**
Gene Vincent & His Blue Caps *Capitol*

36 **SOFT SUMMER BREEZE**
Eddie Heywood *Mercury*

37 **A TEAR FELL / BO WEEVIL**
Teresa Brewer *Coral*

38 **YOU DON'T KNOW ME**
Jerry Vale *Columbia*

39 **MORE / GLENDORA**
Perry Como *RCA*

40 **THE FLYING SAUCER (PARTS 1 & 2)**
Buchanan and Goodman *Luniverse*

41 **SEE YOU LATER, ALLIGATOR**
Bill Haley & His Comets *Decca*

42 **FRIENDLY PERSUASION (THEE I LOVE) / CHAINS OF LOVE**
Pat Boone *Dot*

43 **HEY! JEALOUS LOVER**
Frank Sinatra *Capitol*

44 **CINDY, OH CINDY**
Vince Martin w/the Tarriers *Glory*

45 **A ROSE AND A BABY RUTH**
George Hamilton IV *ABC-Paramount*

46 **(YOU'VE GOT) THE MAGIC TOUCH**
The Platters *Mercury*

47 **THE FOOL**
Sanford Clark *Dot*

48 **MORITAT (A THEME FROM "THE THREE PENNY OPERA")**
The Dick Hyman Trio *MGM*

49 **ANGELS IN THE SKY**
The Crew-Cuts *Mercury*

50 **ROCK-A-BYE YOUR BABY WITH A DIXIE MELODY**
Jerry Lewis *Decca*

51 **CINDY, OH CINDY**
Eddie Fisher *RCA*

52 **BORN TO BE WITH YOU**
The Chordettes *Cadence*

53 **DUNGAREE DOLL**
Eddie Fisher *RCA*

54 **ON THE STREET WHERE YOU LIVE**
Vic Damone *Columbia*

55 **CANADIAN SUNSET**
Andy Williams *Cadence*

56 **THE HAPPY WHISTLER**
Don Robertson *Capitol*

57 **A SWEET OLD-FASHIONED GIRL**
Teresa Brewer *Coral*

58 **LONG TALL SALLY**
Little Richard *Specialty*

59 **SINCE I MET YOU BABY**
Ivory Joe Hunter *Atlantic*

60 **THEME SONG FROM "SONG FOR A SUMMER NIGHT"**
Mitch Miller *Columbia*

61 **GARDEN OF EDEN**
Joe Valino *Vik*

62 **THAT'S ALL THERE IS TO THAT**
Nat King Cole *Capitol*

63 **ROCK ISLAND LINE**
Lonnie Donegan & His Skiffle Group *London*

64 **TRANSFUSION**
Nervous Norvus *Dot*

65 **YOU'LL NEVER KNOW / IT ISN'T RIGHT**
The Platters *Mercury*

66 **TEEN AGE PRAYER / MEMORIES ARE MADE OF THIS**
Gale Storm *Dot*

67 **IVORY TOWER**
Otis Williams & His Charms *DeLuxe*

recorded by Columbia artist Marty Robbins, who took it to No. 1 on the country chart. Mitch Miller of Columbia's A&R department produced a pop version by Mitchell, and came up with two hits on the same song.

The highest-ranked female vocal of 1956 was "The Wayward Wind" by Gogi Grant. The only female vocal performance in the year-end top 10, it ranked No. 5 for the year. After recording for RCA, Gogi moved over to Herb Newman's Era label, where her first single was "Suddenly There's A Valley." While recording the follow-up, "Who Are We," she was shown a manuscript of a song Newman had written as a college student with Stan Lebousky. It was written for a man to sing, so Gogi changed the lyrics to suit a female singer and with 15 minutes of studio time left, recorded "The Wayward Wind." It knocked Elvis' first No. 1 single off the top of the *Billboard* chart and remained there for six weeks.

No. 6 for the year was "The Green Door" by Jim Lowe, a DJ at WNBC radio in New York. The song was released as the "B" side of "A Little Man In Chinatown" on Dot Records, but "The Green Door" proved to be more popular on the radio—that is, everywhere except New York City, where rival stations refused to play Lowe's hit.

Dean Martin had his only year-end top 10 single of the rock era with "Memories Are Made Of This," a song the Capitol A&R department didn't want him to record. But Dean insisted that the song, written by Terry Gilkyson, Richard Dehr, and Frank Miller, had potential. The three song-writers formed a group called the Easyriders and backed Martin on the song, which spent five weeks at No. 1 and ranked No. 8 for the year.

The No. 18 song of the year belonged to a man who turned down an offer to sign with CBS' Okeh label because he thought Capitol was going to sign him. When that Hollywood-based label turned him down, Johnnie Ray said OK to Okeh. His first chart single was a two-sided hit, "Cry" backed with "The Little White Cloud That Cried." The "A" side spent 11 weeks at No. 1 at the beginning of 1952. Ray continued to have hits through the early '50s, but had a down period in 1955. A year later, Joe Johnson, who worked at Columbia Records in Nashville, heard Gene Autry's cover version of "Just Walking In The Rain." The Prisonaires, a group of inmates at Tennessee State Penitentiary, had originally recorded the song in 1953. Ray recorded the song at the tail end of a late-night recording session. Despite being tired and incensed at a rude remark made by Mitch Miller, Ray cut the song in two takes. It reached No. 3 on the Best Sellers chart and was his biggest hit of the rock era.

The Top 100 Songs of 1957

Buddy Holly

1957 WAS THE year Dick Clark convinced ABC to put his local *American Bandstand* show on the network; *Jailhouse Rock* premiered; and calypso music was popularized by Harry Belafonte and the "Banana Boat Song."

Four important artists of the rock era made their chart debuts in 1957. Ricky Nelson, already a familiar face to the 15 million people who watched *The Adventures Of Ozzie And Harriet* on television every week, used his dad's studio orchestra to record a cover version of Fats Domino's "I'm Walkin.'" Ozzie filmed his son recording the song, and took the audio portion to various record companies; 16-year-old Ricky was signed to Verve. The company released the Domino tune backed with "A Teenager's Romance," and the two-sided hit was the No. 28 song of 1957.

Paul Anka was even younger than Ricky when he recorded "Diana" for ABC-Paramount. The teenager from Ottawa, Canada, recorded his composition about his younger siblings' babysitter when he was just 15. The song spent one week on top of the *Billboard* Best Sellers chart, and ranked No. 14 for the year.

The Everly Brothers made their first appearance on the chart with their debut Cadence recording, "Bye Bye Love." The record spent four weeks at No. 2 and ranked No. 9 for the year. The follow-up, "Wake Up Little Susie," spent a week at No. 1 and ranked No. 6 for the year.

Jerry Lee Lewis of Ferriday, Louisiana, made his chart debut with

"Whole Lot Of Shakin' Going On," the No. 27 record of the year. Growing up with his cousins Mickey Gilley and Jimmy Swaggart, Lewis learned to play piano at age nine and made his first public appearance at an auto show in Natchez, Louisiana. With money earned from the sale of 33 dozen eggs, Lewis moved to Memphis in 1956. He auditioned for Jack Clement at Sun Records and was hired by label founder Sam Phillips. He played piano for artists like Carl Perkins and Billy Lee Riley, and had his own single released—a version of Ray Price's "Crazy Arms." While on tour with Sun artists Perkins and Johnny Cash, those two headliners suggested he "make a fuss" on stage. Lewis kicked back his piano stool and became a wild man, cementing his reputation as "The Killer." During his second session he recorded a version of "Whole Lot Of Shakin' Going On," previously cut by both co-writer Roy Hall and Big Maybelle. Jerry Lee's recording was considered "obscene" and was having trouble getting airplay—until he performed the song live on *The Steve Allen Show* on July 28, 1957. The national exposure and Lewis' crazed performance helped send the single up to No. 3 on the *Billboard* chart.

For the second year in a row, Elvis Presley had a trio of singles in the year-end top five: "Jailhouse Rock" backed with "Treat Me Nice" at No. 2, "All Shook Up" at No. 3, and "(Let Me Be Your) Teddy Bear" at No. 4.

Except for the Canadian singers known as the Diamonds, No. 7 for the year with "Little Darlin'," all of the artists in the top 10 were born in the U.S.A. Leading the list was a vocalist born in Jacksonville, Florida. Along with his brother Nick, Pat Boone sang at family gatherings and at church and school functions in Nashville. After appearing on Ted Mack's *The Original Amateur Hour* and *Arthur Godfrey's Talent Scouts* in New York, he was returning home to Denton, Texas, when he stopped to visit his parents in Nashville. His friend Hugh Cherry, a DJ at WMAK, introduced Pat to Dot Records founder Randy Wood, who had seen Boone on Mack and Godfrey's shows. Wood had a record shop in Gallatin, Tennessee, and often got requests for "Love Letters In The Sand," previously recorded by both Rudy Vallee and Bing Crosby. Wood had Boone record the song, but the track remained unreleased until the producers of the film *Bernadine* cast Pat in the lead and included the song in the movie. The single spent five weeks at No. 1, remaining on the Best Sellers chart for 23 weeks.

Debbie Reynolds was the only female vocalist in the year-end top 10 for 1957. She ranked No. 5 with "Tammy," from the film *Tammy and the Bachelor* starring Debbie and Leslie Nielsen. The movie was released by Universal, which also owned Coral Records. Label head Bob Thiele was obligated to release the song, but he didn't think it would sell and decided to issue the track exactly as it was heard in the movie, rather than cut a new version. "Tammy" spent three weeks at No. 1 and helped revive the film at the box office.

Jimmie Rodgers had the No. 11 single of 1957 with "Honeycomb." The singer from Camas, Washington, first heard the song at the Unique Club in Nashville, where he performed while serving at Stewart Air Force Base. Jimmie rearranged the song to match his own style. On a trip to New York, he appeared on *Arthur Godfrey's Talent Scouts,* and auditioned for producers Hugo Peretti and Luigi Creatore at Roulette Records by singing

34 PEGGY SUE
Buddy Holly *Coral*

35 BUTTERFLY
Charlie Gracie *Cameo*

36 SEND FOR ME /
MY PERSONAL POSSESSION
Nat King Cole *Capitol*

37 FASCINATION
Jane Morgan *Kapp*

38 BANANA BOAT (DAY-O)
Harry Belafonte *RCA*

39 THE BANANA BOAT SONG
The Tarriers *Glory*

40 GONE
Ferlin Husky *Capitol*

41 DARK MOON
Gale Storm *Dot*

42 MOONLIGHT GAMBLER
Frankie Laine *Columbia*

43 RAINBOW
Russ Hamilton *Kapp*

44 MY SPECIAL ANGEL
Bobby Helms *Decca*

45 SHORT FAT FANNIE
Larry Williams *Specialty*

46 I'M GONNA SIT RIGHT DOWN
AND WRITE MYSELF A LETTER
Billy Williams *Coral*

47 MR. LEE
The Bobettes *Atlantic*

48 BUTTERFLY
Andy Williams *Cadence*

49 I'M WALKIN'
Fats Domino *Imperial*

50 LOVE ME
Elvis Presley *RCA*

51 MELODIE D'AMOUR
The Ames Brothers *RCA*

52 BONY MARONIE
Larry Williams *Specialty*

53 REMEMBER YOU'RE MINE
Pat Boone *Dot*

54 OLD CAPE COD
Patti Page *Mercury*

55 KISSES SWEETER THAN WINE
Jimmie Rodgers *Roulette*

56 HULA LOVE
Buddy Knox *Roulette*

57 JUST BORN (TO BE YOUR BABY) /
IVY ROSE
Perry Como *RCA*

58 LOVE IS STRANGE
Mickey & Sylvia *Groove*

59 LIECHTENSTEINER POLKA
Will Glahé *London*

60 IN THE MIDDLE OF AN ISLAND
Tony Bennett *Columbia*

61 STARDUST
Billy Ward & His Dominoes *Liberty*

62 START MOVIN' (IN MY DIRECTION)
Sal Mineo *Epic*

63 RAUNCHY
Ernie Freeman *Imperial*

64 MARIANNE
Terry Gilkyson & the Easy Riders *Columbia*

65 WHITE SILVER SANDS
Don Rondo *Jubilee*

66 WHY BABY WHY
Pat Boone *Dot*

"Honeycomb." Back home in Camas, Rodgers was renewing his wedding vows with his wife Colleen when a telegram arrived from Morris Levy, head of Roulette, asking him to return to New York and sign with the label. "Honeycomb" was his first single.

"So Rare," the No. 16 song of the year, was a successful end to a long career for bandleader Jimmy Dorsey. He was a teenager when he formed his first band, Dorsey's Novelty Six, with his younger brother Tommy. The Dorseys formed their own orchestra in 1934. A year later, they were performing at Glen Island Casino when they had a violent argument on stage that led to a long split. Jimmy and Tommy were rivals through the big-band era, and both were successful through the '40s. When Tommy died in 1956, Jimmy continued to lead the orchestra; at the suggestion of Harry Carlson of Fraternity Records, he recorded "So Rare," which had been a No. 1 hit for Guy Lombardo in 1937. "So Rare" entered the chart in February 1957 and was still in the top 10 when Jimmy Dorsey died of cancer on June 12.

The Coasters' second chart single, "Searchin'" backed with "Young Blood," was the No. 21 record of 1957. The group's origin can be traced to the Robins, formed in 1949. They first worked with writer/producers Jerry Leiber and Mike Stoller in 1951, when they recorded "That's What The Good Book Says." The Robins recorded "Riot In Cell Block No. 9" for Leiber and Stoller's Spark label, but when the duo signed with New York–based Atlantic as independent producers, some members of the Robins didn't want to move to the East Coast. Bobby Nunn and Carl Gardner of the Robins recruited new members and followed Leiber and Stoller to New York as the Coasters.

The No. 23 song of 1957 was "Come Go With Me" by the Dell-Vikings, an integrated doo-wop group formed at an Air Force base in Pittsburgh. After winning an Air Force–sponsored talent contest in New York, the members of the group asked DJ Barry Kaye of WJAS in Pittsburgh if they could record some of their material in the studio he had built in the basement of his home. They recorded four songs, including the standard "The White Cliffs Of Dover" and a tune written by their first tenor, Clarence Quick. That song was "Come Go With Me," and when Kaye played it on the air, Fee-Bee label owner Joe Averbach heard the song and signed the Dell-Vikings. He re-recorded the song, speeding up the tempo. After it became a local hit, it was picked up for national release by Dot Records. The follow-up, "Whispering Bells," was No. 71 for the year.

67 **ALL THE WAY**
Frank Sinatra *Capitol*

68 **BLUE MONDAY**
Fats Domino *Imperial*

69 **ROCK & ROLL MUSIC**
Chuck Berry *Chess*

70 **HAPPY, HAPPY BIRTHDAY BABY**
The Tune Weavers *Checker*

71 **WHISPERING BELLS**
The Dell-Vikings *Dot*

72 **OVER THE MOUNTAIN; ACROSS THE SEA**
Johnnie & Joe *Chess*

73 **JENNY, JENNY**
Little Richard *Specialty*

74 **VALLEY OF TEARS / IT'S YOU THAT I LOVE**
Fats Domino *Imperial*

75 **MARIANNE**
The Hilltoppers *Dot*

76 **PARTY DOLL**
Steve Lawrence *Coral*

77 **FOUR WALLS**
Jim Reeves *RCA*

78 **I'M STICKIN' WITH YOU**
Jimmy Bowen w/the Rhythm Orchids *Roulette*

79 **I'M SORRY / HE'S MINE**
The Platters *Mercury*

80 **LITTLE BITTY PRETTY ONE**
Thurston Harris *Aladdin*

81 **DARK MOON**
Bonnie Guitar *Dot*

82 **KEEP A KNOCKIN'**
Little Richard *Specialty*

83 **MAMA LOOK AT BUBU**
Harry Belafonte *RCA*

84 **AROUND THE WORLD**
Victor Young and His Singing Strings *Decca*

85 **WONDERFUL! WONDERFUL!**
Johnny Mathis *Columbia*

86 **LOTTA LOVIN' / WEAR MY RING**
Gene Vincent & His Blue Caps *Capitol*

87 **JAMAICA FAREWELL**
Harry Belafonte *RCA*

88 **I'M AVAILABLE**
Margie Rayburn *Liberty*

89 **ROCK-A-BILLY**
Guy Mitchell *Columbia*

90 **C.C. RIDER**
Chuck Willis *Atlantic*

91 **I LIKE YOUR KIND OF LOVE**
Andy Williams [and Peggy Powers] *Cadence*

92 **YOU DON'T OWE ME A THING**
Johnnie Ray *Columbia*

93 **WHO NEEDS YOU**
The Four Lads *Columbia*

94 **NINETY-NINE WAYS**
Tab Hunter *Dot*

95 **JUST BETWEEN YOU AND ME**
The Chordettes *Cadence*

96 **LOVE ME TO PIECES**
Jill Corey *Columbia*

97 **WALKIN' AFTER MIDNIGHT**
Patsy Cline *Decca*

98 **BLACK SLACKS**
Joe Bennett & the Sparkletones
ABC-Paramount

99 **FABULOUS**
Charlie Gracie *Cameo*

100 **JIM DANDY**
LaVern Baker *Atlantic*

The Top 100 Songs of 1958

Jerry Lee Lewis

1958 WAS THE year Elvis Presley was inducted into the United States Army; RCA became the first major label to issue a wide selection of albums in stereo; and Jerry Lee Lewis admitted he had married his 14-year-old cousin.

It was a very good year for novelty songs—six of them were included in the top 100 songs of the year. The highest-ranked was Sheb Wooley's "The Purple People Eater." It ranked No. 5 for the year. Wooley got the idea for his novelty hit from a friend of his whom repeated a joke his kids had heard in school. Soon after writing the song, Wooley had a meeting with the head of MGM Records. After hearing all of Wooley's ballads, the executive asked what else he had. Wooley said he had one more tune that was "the bottom of the barrel." Within three weeks of its release, it was the No. 1 song in the country.

One rung below "The Purple People Eater" on the year-end recap is "Witch Doctor" by David Seville. Written and produced by Seville under his real name, Ross Bagdasarian, "Witch Doctor" was inspired by a book in his library, *Duel With The Witch Doctor*. The music for the song was recorded two months before the vocals. That's how long it took Bagdasarian to figure out a way to record the voices at different speeds. The voice of the witch doctor was recorded at half-speed and played back at normal speed. That same device was used in Bagdasarian's other novelty No. 1 song of 1958, "The Chipmunk Song" (No. 14 for the year).

After recording "Witch Doctor," Bagdasarian was driving through Yosemite Park in California. He encountered a stubborn chipmunk who refused to budge from the middle of the road. That incident gave birth to the Chipmunks, named after Liberty Records executives Alvin (Al) Bennett, Simon (Sy) Waronker, and Theodore (Ted) Keep. Bagdasarian's youngest son, Adam, was the role model for Alvin. As September rolled around each year, Adam would ask if it were Christmas yet. Ross figured other children were probably pulling the same annoying stunt. The song went through several transformations before it was recorded as "The Chipmunk Song," including something called "In A Village Park."

"Beep Beep" by the Playmates was the No. 42 song of the year. Donny Conn, Morey Cart, and Carl Cicchetti (a.k.a. Chic Hetti) met when they were students at the University of Connecticut. They were signed to Roulette Records as a calypso group and released a song called "Barefoot Girl," but then the calypso craze died and they had to come up with new material. They released a single called "Jo-Ann" that peaked at No. 19 in February 1958. Donny and Carl wrote "Beep Beep," a song about a comedic drag race between a Cadillac and a Nash Rambler. They performed it at a disc jockey convention in Kansas City. Their label didn't want to issue it as a 45 because it changed tempo, named commercial products, and wasn't danceable. When it was included on an album, DJs played it anyway and forced its release as a single.

"Short Shorts" by the Royal Teens was the No. 48 song of 1958. The five members of the New Jersey–based group recorded four songs during a session at Bell Sound Studios in Manhattan. With just a little studio time left, the Teens fooled around by playing one of their old instrumentals. Their manager, Leo Rogers, brought in two teenaged girls he saw in the lobby and asked them to sing something in front of the microphone—a silly phrase he made up, "Who wears short shorts?" The four ballads the group recorded were never heard again, but "Short Shorts" became a regional hit on the small Power label. The master was picked up by ABC-Paramount and went to No. 4 on the Best Sellers chart.

During a Baltimore television appearance, the Royal Teens met another group, the Four Lovers. One of the Teens, Bob Gaudio, struck up a friendship with Frankie Valli of the Four Lovers. Gaudio left the Royal Teens and worked in a printing factory before joining the Four Lovers, who became the Four Seasons.

"Western Movies" by the Olympics was the sixth novelty song on the top 100 of the year, ranked at No. 82. The group was formed by students from two Southern California high schools, Centennial and Jordan. Singer Jesse Belvin introduced them to writer/producers Fred Smith and Cliff Goldsmith, who came up with "Western Movies." The song resembled the novelty hits of the Coasters, and lead singer Walter Ward's voice sounded like the Coasters' lead singer, Carl Gardner. The song made reference to popular TV westerns like *Maverick, Cheyenne,* and *Sugarfoot.* Released on Liberty's Demon subsidiary, it peaked at No. 8 on the Hot 100.

34 **SUGARTIME**
McGuire Sisters *Coral*

35 **RETURN TO ME**
Dean Martin *Capitol*

36 **SPLISH SPLASH**
Bobby Darin *Atco*

37 **PROBLEMS**
Everly Brothers *Cadence*

38 **SECRETLY / MAKE ME A MIRACLE**
Jimmie Rodgers *Roulette*

39 **ONE NIGHT**
Elvis Presley *RCA*

40 **CHANTILLY LACE**
The Big Bopper *Mercury*

41 **LONESOME TOWN**
Ricky Nelson *Imperial*

42 **BEEP BEEP**
The Playmates *Roulette*

43 **TEARS ON MY PILLOW**
Little Anthony & the Imperials *End*

44 **SUSIE DARLIN'**
Robin Luke *Dot*

45 **OH LONESOME ME**
Don Gibson *RCA*

46 **LOOKING BACK**
Nat King Cole *Capitol*

47 **THE STROLL**
The Diamonds *Mercury*

48 **SHORT SHORTS**
The Royal Teens *ABC-Paramount*

49 **WHO'S SORRY NOW**
Connie Francis *MGM*

50 **THE END**
Earl Grant *Decca*

51 **TEA FOR TWO CHA CHA**
The Tommy Dorsey Orchestra *Decca*

52 **DO YOU WANT TO DANCE**
Bobby Freeman *Josie*

53 **OH JULIE**
The Crescendos *Nasco*

54 **BIG MAN**
The Four Preps *Capitol*

55 **QUEEN OF THE HOP**
Bobby Darin *Atco*

56 **WHEN**
Kalin Twins *Decca*

57 **WHAT AM I LIVING FOR /
HANG UP MY ROCK 'N' ROLL SHOES**
Chuck Willis *Atlantic*

58 **BOOK OF LOVE**
The Monotones *Argo*

59 **26 MILES (SANTA CATALINA)**
The Four Preps *Capitol*

60 **I GOT STUNG**
Elvis Presley *RCA*

61 **ARE YOU SINCERE**
Andy Williams *Cadence*

62 **ENDLESS SLEEP**
Jody Reynolds *Demon*

63 **BORN TOO LATE**
The Poni-Tails *ABC-Paramount*

64 **JOHNNY B. GOODE**
Chuck Berry *Chess*

65 **I GOT A FEELING**
Ricky Nelson *Imperial*

66 **REBEL-'ROUSER** Duane Eddy *Jamie*

67 **BELIEVE WHAT YOU SAY /
MY BUCKET'S GOT A HOLE IN IT**
Ricky Nelson *Imperial*

The No. 1 song of 1958 was Danny & the Juniors' "At The Hop," which is also the ABC label's most successful chart single of the rock era. Danny Rapp, Joe Terranova, Frank Maffei, and Dave White started singing in high school as the Juvenairs. When Artie Singer caught their act, he changed their name to Danny & the Juniors and co-wrote a song for them, "Do The Bop." Dick Clark heard a demo of the song and suggested that because the Bop was already passe, they might want to change the lyrics to "At The Hop." Singer released the song on his own label, Singular, and it was picked up by ABC-Paramount.

The No. 2 song of 1958 was Tommy Edwards' "It's All In The Game," originally written as an instrumental in 1912 by Charles Gates Dawes, who would later be vice president of the United States under Calvin Coolidge. Carl Sigman added lyrics in 1951, the year Edwards first recorded the song. It peaked at No. 18 during its original chart run, and seven years later MGM was ready to drop Edwards from its roster. But the label wanted to release singles in stereo, and executive Morty Craft asked Tommy to re-cut the song. The new stereo version had an updated rock and roll ballad arrangement, and MGM had its biggest hit of the rock era. The follow-up, "Love Is All We Need," ranked No. 99 for the year.

Phil Spector had his first year-end top 10 chart single with his first production, "To Know Him Is To Love Him" by the Teddy Bears, ranked No. 10 for the year. Spector wrote the song especially for lead singer Annette Kleinbard.

Billy Vaughn, born in Glasgow, Kentucky, was a member of the Hilltoppers before he was named musical director of Dot Records. As an orchestra leader, he was heard on Dot releases by the Fontane Sisters, Gale Storm, and Pat Boone, among others. Under his own name, Vaughn specialized in covering other artists' recordings. His biggest hit of the rock era was the No. 33 single of 1958, "Sail Along Silvery Moon," backed with "Raunchy." The former was a remake of a Bing Crosby hit from 1937; the latter was a cover of a song by Bill Justis. Vaughn's version hit the chart just two weeks after Justis and competed with it—Justis peaked at No. 2, Vaughn at No. 5. A third version, by Ernie Freeman, went to No. 11 on the Best Sellers chart.

Domenico Modugno of Italy had the first song recorded in a foreign language to be a year-end top 10 single. *Nel Blu Dipinto Di Blu (Volare),"* the No. 4 song of the year, was inspired by the back side of a pack of cigarettes. The song describes a dream in which a man paints his hands blue and flies through the air, the "blue painted in blue."

68 **SUGAR MOON**
Pat Boone *Dot*

69 **WILLIE AND THE HAND JIVE**
The Johnny Otis Show *Capitol*

70 **NEAR YOU**
Roger Williams *Kapp*

71 **OH, BOY!**
The Crickets *Brunswick*

72 **BIMBOMBEY**
Jimmie Rodgers *Roulette*

73 **DEVOTED TO YOU**
Everly Brothers *Cadence*

74 **BUZZ-BUZZ-BUZZ / CRAZY**
Hollywood Flames *Ebb*

75 **ARE YOU REALLY MINE**
Jimmie Rodgers *Roulette*

76 **MAYBE**
The Chantels *End*

77 **WHY DON'T THEY UNDERSTAND**
George Hamilton IV *ABC-Paramount*

78 **FEVER**
Peggy Lee *Capitol*

79 **GINGER BREAD**
Frankie Avalon *Chancellor*

80 **SUMMERTIME BLUES**
Eddie Cochran *Liberty*

81 **CHANSON D'AMOUR**
Art and Dotty Todd *Era*

82 **WESTERN MOVIES**
The Olympics *Demon*

83 **BREATHLESS**
Jerry Lee Lewis *Sun*

84 **KEWPIE DOLL**
Perry Como *RCA*

85 **EVERYBODY LOVES A LOVER**
Doris Day *Columbia*

86 **DON'T YOU JUST KNOW IT**
Huey "Piano" Smith & the Clowns *Ace*

87 **DEDE DINAH**
Frankie Avalon *Chancellor*

88 **GUESS THINGS HAPPEN THAT WAY /**
   COME IN STRANGER
Johnny Cash *Sun*

89 **CRAZY LOVE / LET THE**
   BELLS KEEP RINGING
Paul Anka *ABC-Paramount*

90 **JENNIE LEE**
Jan and Arnie *Arwin*

91 **LA DEE DAH**
Billy and Lillie *Swan*

92 **THE DAY THE RAINS CAME**
Jane Morgan *Kapp*

93 **IF DREAMS CAME TRUE /**
   THAT'S HOW MUCH I LOVE YOU
Pat Boone *Dot*

94 **THE WALK**
Jimmy McCracklin *Checker*

95 **HOW THE TIME FLIES**
Jerry Wallace *Challenge*

96 **LAZY MARY**
Lou Monte *RCA*

97 **FOR YOUR LOVE**
Ed Townsend *Capitol*

98 **DON'T LET GO**
Roy Hamilton *Epic*

99 **LOVE IS ALL WE NEED**
Tommy Edwards *MGM*

100 **I'LL WAIT FOR YOU**
Frankie Avalon *Chancellor*

The Top 100 Songs of 1959

Frankie Avalon

1959 WAS THE year Buddy Holly, Ritchie Valens, and the Big Bopper were killed in a plane crash after a concert at Clear Lake, Iowa; the first Grammys were handed out; and Berry Gordy borrowed $800 to start his own record company.

Elvis Presley was absent from the year-end top 10 for the first time since his chart debut. It wasn't surprising, considering that Elvis spent all of 1959 in the U.S. Army. His only recording session during his military service resulted in five songs, including "A Big Hunk O'Love," his highest-ranked song of the year at No. 20. Also recorded during that session was "(Now And Then There's) A Fool Such As I," the No. 38 song of the year.

Also absent from the top 10 were female lead singers, although the Platters, the Fleetwoods, and the Browns counted women among their members. The only other year in the rock era that saw a shutout of female lead singers from the top 10 was 1976.

The No. 1 song of the year was "Mack The Knife" by Bobby Darin. There had been many renditions of the song, written in 1928 by Kurt Weill and Bertold Brecht for *The Threepenny Opera*. Darin styled his version after Louis Armstrong's recording, and included it in his *That's All* album. He had recorded it to demonstrate his versatility, but didn't plan on having it released as a single. Atco Records overruled him, giving Darin the 33rd most successful single of the rock era.

01 **MACK THE KNIFE**
Bobby Darin *Atco*

02 **THE BATTLE OF NEW ORLEANS**
Johnny Horton *Columbia*

03 **VENUS**
Frankie Avalon *Chancellor*

04 **MR. BLUE**
The Fleetwoods *Dolton*

05 **SMOKE GETS IN YOUR EYES**
The Platters *Mercury*

06 **LONELY BOY**
Paul Anka *ABC-Paramount*

07 **COME SOFTLY TO ME**
The Fleetwoods *Dolphin*

08 **THE THREE BELLS**
The Browns *RCA*

09 **STAGGER LEE**
Lloyd Price *ABC-Paramount*

10 **SLEEP WALK**
Santo and Johnny *Canadian-American*

11 **DONNA**
Ritchie Valens *Del-Fi*

12 **WHY**
Frankie Avalon *Chancellor*

13 **HEARTACHES BY THE NUMBER**
Guy Mitchell *Columbia*

14 **PUT YOUR HEAD ON MY SHOULDER**
Paul Anka *ABC-Paramount*

15 **PERSONALITY**
Lloyd Price *ABC-Paramount*

16 **DREAM LOVER**
Bobby Darin *Atco*

17 **KANSAS CITY**
Wilbert Harrison *Fury*

18 **CHARLIE BROWN**
The Coasters *Atco*

19 **SIXTEEN CANDLES**
The Crests *Coed*

20 **A BIG HUNK O' LOVE**
Elvis Presley *RCA*

21 **DON'T YOU KNOW**
Della Reese *RCA*

22 **THE HAPPY ORGAN**
Dave "Baby" Cortez *Clock*

23 **SEA OF LOVE**
Phil Phillips w/the Twilights *Mercury*

24 **MY HAPPINESS**
Connie Francis *MGM*

25 **SORRY (I RAN ALL THE WAY HOME)**
The Impalas *Cub*

26 **PINK SHOE LACES**
Dodie Stevens *Crystalette*

27 **MY HEART IS AN OPEN BOOK**
Carl Dobkins, Jr. *Decca*

28 **THE BIG HURT**
Miss Toni Fisher *Signet*

29 **IT'S JUST A MATTER OF TIME**
Brook Benton *Mercury*

30 **I'M GONNA GET MARRIED**
Lloyd Price *ABC-Paramount*

31 **LAVENDER-BLUE**
Sammy Turner *Big Top*

32 **('TIL) I KISSED YOU**
Everly Brothers *Cadence*

33 **A LOVER'S QUESTION**
Clyde McPhatter *Atlantic*

34 **THERE GOES MY BABY**
The Drifters *Atlantic*

Runner-up to Darin's single was "The Battle Of New Orleans" by Johnny Horton. The song's origin can be traced back to 1815, the year Andrew Jackson and his troops defeated the British forces of Commander Pakenham at New Orleans. The victory was soon commemorated with an instrumental folk song, "The Eighth Of January." In 1955, Arkansas schoolteacher Jimmy Driftwood wrote lyrics for the tune and retitled it "The Battle Of New Orleans." Horton had been recording country songs since 1951. He was signed to the Cormac, Mercury, and Abbott labels before moving to Columbia, the imprint that gave him his first entry on the country singles chart in 1956. "The Battle Of New Orleans" was his first single to make the pop chart.

The Platters achieved their highest year-end ranking with "Smoke Gets In Your Eyes," the No. 5 song of 1959. The tune was written by Jerome Kern and Otto Harbach for the 1933 stage musical, *Roberta*.

Guy Mitchell, who had the No. 2 song of 1956 with "Singing The Blues," was back in the upper reaches of the year-end chart with "Heartaches By The Number," the No. 13 song of 1959. Like "Singing The Blues," "Heartaches By The Number" was first recorded by another artist on Columbia Records for the country charts. In this case, it was Ray Price who went to No. 1 on the country singles chart with the Harlan Howard song. Mitch Miller produced Mitchell's version, which spent two weeks on top of the Hot 100.

The No. 3 song of 1959 was "Venus" by Frankie Avalon. The Philadelphia native first wanted to be a boxer, but changed ambitions after seeing Kirk Douglas in the film *Young Man With A Horn*. Frankie's dad bought him a used trumpet from a pawn shop for $15. Manager Bob Marcucci persuaded Avalon to become a vocalist and signed him to the Chancellor label. Songwriter Ed Marshall came to Frankie's house and played "Venus" on the piano for him. Avalon asked if anyone else was interested in recording the song. Marshall told him Al Martino liked it very much. Three days later, Frankie was in the studio recording the song. Avalon had four other titles in the top 100 of the year: "Why" (No. 12), "Just Ask Your Heart" (No. 78), "Bobby Sox To Stockings" (No. 86), and "A Boy Without A Girl" (No. 96).

The Fleetwoods, a trio from Olympia, Washington, were in the year-end top 10 with their two No. 1 songs of 1959, "Mr. Blue" at No. 4, and "Come Softly To Me" at No. 7. Gretchen Christopher and Barbara Ellis, born nine days apart in the same hospital, became friends when they were five years old. In their senior year at Olympia High, Gretchen suggested forming a female quartet. When they couldn't find two other women suitable enough to join the group, they performed as a duo called the Saturns. After working up an arrangement of "Stormy Weather," they needed someone who could play blues trumpet and a friend suggested Gary Troxel. "He couldn't play in our key, and we couldn't sing in his," Gretchen remembers. But when he walked her downtown after school, he began humming a phrase that happened to be based on the same chord progression as a song Gretchen was writing, "Come Softly." The song was completed and performed at a couple of high school events. Record promoter Bob Reisdorff liked the song enough to sign the group and release "Come Softly

To Me" on his own label, Dolphin. A conflict with a publishing company led him to change the name to Dolton.

"Mr. Blue" was written for the Fleetwoods by Dewayne Blackwell, who met the group in a hotel room so they could hear his songs. Gretchen loved "Mr. Blue" and couldn't understand why Blackwell didn't record it himself. Blackwell explained that no one knew who he was, but if a group like the Fleetwoods recorded "Mr. Blue," every radio station in the country would play it. He was right.

Paul Anka had his highest year-end ranking with "Lonely Boy," the No. 6 song of the year. He wrote the song and performed it in the movie *Girls Town,* in which he starred with Mamie Van Doren and Mel Torme. It was one of four songs Anka placed in the top 100 of 1959. The others were "Put Your Head On My Shoulder" (No. 14), "It's Time To Cry" (No. 53), and "(All Of A Sudden) My Heart Sings" (No. 93).

New Orleans artist Lloyd Price had three songs in the top 100 of 1959, including "Stagger Lee" at No. 9. Born to a musical family, Price formed a five-piece group in high school. They performed on WBOK radio, and Price wrote jingles for station breaks. One was so popular that Price recorded a full-length version and took it to Specialty Records. The song, "Lawdy Miss Clawdy," topped the R&B chart in 1952. After a military stint, Price formed his own record company, Kent, and leased his masters to ABC-Paramount. With his business partner, Harold Logan, he adapted a folk song called "Stack-O-Lee" that had been a hit for another New Orleans singer, Archibald, in 1950. Price's "Stagger Lee" spent four weeks at No. 1. His other year-end hits in 1959 included "Personality" (No. 15) and "I'm Gonna Get Married" (No. 30).

Ritchie Valens, who perished in the plane crash that also took the lives of Buddy Holly and the Big Bopper, had the number 11 song of the year, "Donna." The song was written for his girlfriend, Donna Ludwig. It was his second release on Del-Fi, following "Come On, Let's Go," which peaked at No. 42 on the Hot 100. "Donna" entered the chart on November 24, 1958. When Valens died on February 3, 1959, "Donna" was No. 3. It held that position for four weeks and then moved to No. 2.

Clyde McPhatter, formerly of the Dominoes and the Drifters, first made the year-end chart on his own in 1956 with "Treasure Of Love," No. 91 for that year. He had his most successful solo chart single in 1959 with "A Lover's Question," the No. 33 song of the year.

69 TURN ME LOOSE
Fabian *Chancellor*

70 ONLY YOU
Franck Pourcel's French Fiddles *Capitol*

71 SEVEN LITTLE GIRLS SITTING IN THE BACK SEAT
Paul Evans *Guaranteed*

72 FRANKIE
Connie Francis *MGM*

73 DANNY BOY
Conway Twitty *MGM*

74 SINCE I DON'T HAVE YOU
The Skyliners *Calico*

75 MAY YOU ALWAYS
McGuire Sisters *Coral*

76 BATTLE HYMN OF THE REPUBLIC
Mormon Tabernacle Choir *Columbia*

77 WHAT'D I SAY (PART 1)
Ray Charles *Atlantic*

78 JUST ASK YOUR HEART
Frankie Avalon *Chancellor*

79 BROKEN-HEARTED MELODY
Sarah Vaughan *Mercury*

80 AMONG MY SOUVENIRS
Connie Francis *MGM*

81 PETITE FLEUR (LITTLE FLOWER)
Chris Barber's Jazz Band *Laurie*

82 FORTY MILES OF BAD ROAD
Duane Eddy *Jamie*

83 TALL PAUL
Annette *Disneyland*

84 I WANT TO WALK YOU HOME
Fats Domino *Imperial*

85 HOUND DOG MAN
Fabian *Chancellor*

86 BOBBY SOX TO STOCKINGS
Frankie Avalon *Chancellor*

87 TELL HIM NO
Travis and Bob *Sandy*

88 ENCHANTED
The Platters *Mercury*

89 BE MY GUEST
Fats Domino *Imperial*

90 I ONLY HAVE EYES FOR YOU
The Flamingos *End*

91 SO FINE
The Fiestas *Old Town*

92 MISTY
Johnny Mathis *Columbia*

93 (ALL OF A SUDDEN) MY HEART SINGS
Paul Anka *ABC-Paramount*

94 IT'S LATE
Ricky Nelson *Imperial*

95 IT WAS I
Skip and Flip *Brent*

96 A BOY WITHOUT A GIRL
Frankie Avalon *Chancellor*

97 BABY TALK
Jan and Dean *Dore*

98 SWEETER THAN YOU
Ricky Nelson *Imperial*

99 MY WISH CAME TRUE
Elvis Presley *RCA*

100 MORGEN
Ivo Robic and the Song-Masters *Laurie*

The Top 100 Songs of 1960

Connie Stevens

1960

1960 WAS THE year Elvis Presley was discharged from the army; Eddie Cochran was killed and Gene Vincent injured in an automobile accident in Chippenham, Wiltshire, England; and *Bye Bye Birdie* was a smash on Broadway.

Percy Faith, whose "Song From *Moulin Rouge*" had been the No. 1 song of 1953, repeated that feat in 1960 with another interpretation of a motion picture tune, "Theme From *A Summer Place*." The music was composed by Max Steiner for the 1959 film, which starred Dorothy McGuire, Richard Egan, Sandra Dee, Troy Donahue, and Arthur Kennedy. "Theme From *A Summer Place*" is the only instrumental No. 1 song of the year in the rock era.

Faith was born in Toronto, Canada. The rest of the artists in the list of top 10 songs of 1960 were Americans. That makes 1960 the last time in the rock era that every song in the year-end top 10 was by an artist from North America until 1991.

Elvis Presley had more than one song in the year-end top 10 for the first time since 1957. All three were in the top five. "Are You Lonesome Tonight?" was written in 1926 and first recorded by Al Jolson. Jaye P. Morgan cut it for MGM in 1959; her version peaked at No. 65 on the Hot 100. Elvis' version was the No. 2 song of the year. "It's Now Or Never," the No. 4 song of the year, was based on an Italian song, *"O Sole Mio,"* written in 1901 and popularized by Mario Lanza. Tony Martin sang an English adaptation in 1949 called "There's No Tomorrow." Aaron Schroeder and Wally Gold wrote new lyrics for Elvis.

The Everly Brothers had the No. 3 song of the year—for the second time. They did it with "All I Have To Do Is Dream" in 1958 and again with "Cathy's Clown" in 1960. The latter was their first single for Warner Bros. after nine consecutive hits on Cadence. One of their last singles for that label, "Let It Be Me," was the No. 65 song of 1960. The Warner Bros. follow-up to "Cathy's Clown" was "So Sad (To Watch Good Love Go Bad)," the No. 74 song of the year.

Brenda Lee made her first appearance on a year-end chart in 1960, with three titles in the top 100. "I'm Sorry" was the No. 6 song of the year. It was recorded at the end of a session, with five minutes of studio time left. Brenda loved the song, but executives at Decca weren't sure that a 15-year-old girl should be singing about unrequited love. The label delayed release for several months, and then issued "I'm Sorry" as the flip side of "That's All You Gotta Do." Both sides charted on the Hot 100, the intended "A" side peaking at No. 6 and "I'm Sorry" spending three weeks at No. 1. Brenda's two other year-end singles were "I Want To Be Wanted" (No. 21) and "Sweet Nothin's" (No. 36). Only two songs performed by women had ranked higher than "I'm Sorry" on a year-end chart in the rock era: "The Wayward Wind" by Gogi Grant and "Tammy" by Debbie Reynolds were the No. 5 songs of 1957 and 1958, respectively. Patti Page, Gale Storm, and Connie Francis had all placed three songs in a year-end top 100, but Brenda was the first to have all three in the top 40 portion of the chart.

Marty Robbins first made the year-end chart in 1957, when "A White Sport Coat (And A Pink Carnation)" was the No. 22 song of the year. He made his debut on the *Billboard* country chart in December 1952, with "I'll Go On Alone," which went to No. 1. Robbins finally made it to the top of the pop chart in 1960 with "El Paso." With a running time of four minutes and 40 seconds, Columbia considered it too long to be a single. It appeared on the album *Gunfighter Ballads And Trail Songs* and proved to be so popular on radio that CBS relented and issued it as a 45 despite its length. It was the No. 7 single of the year.

Chubby Checker made his first appearance on a year-end survey with his cover version of Hank Ballard's "The Twist," the No. 8 song of the year. Ballard had two recordings of his own in the top 100 of 1960: "Finger Poppin' Time" (No. 49) and "Let's Go, Let's Go, Let's Go" (No. 76).

35 **SIXTEEN REASONS**
Connie Stevens *Warner Bros.*

36 **SWEET NOTHIN'S**
Brenda Lee *Decca*

37 **NIGHT**
Jackie Wilson *Brunswick*

38 **BECAUSE THEY'RE YOUNG**
Duane Eddy *Jamie*

39 **WHERE OR WHEN**
Dion & the Belmonts *Laurie*

40 **THEME FROM "THE APARTMENT"**
Ferrante and Teicher *UA*

41 **WAY DOWN YONDER IN NEW ORLEANS**
Freddy Cannon *Swan*

42 **PRETTY BLUE EYES**
Steve Lawrence *ABC-Paramount*

43 **WHAT IN THE WORLD'S COME OVER YOU**
Jack Scott *Top Rank*

44 **MISSION BELL**
Donnie Brooks *Era*

45 **SAILOR (YOUR HOME IS THE SEA)**
Lolita *Kapp*

46 **DEVIL OR ANGEL**
Bobby Vee *Liberty*

47 **PLEASE HELP ME, I'M FALLING**
Hank Locklin *RCA*

48 **HE WILL BREAK YOUR HEART**
Jerry Butler *Vee Jay*

49 **FINGER POPPIN' TIME**
Hank Ballard & the Midnighters *King*

50 **KIDDIO**
Brook Benton *Mercury*

51 **HE'LL HAVE TO STAY**
Jeanne Black *Capitol*

52 **YOU GOT WHAT IT TAKES**
Marv Johnson *UA*

53 **VOLARE**
Bobby Rydell *Cameo*

54 **PAPER ROSES**
Anita Bryant *Carlton*

55 **MULE SKINNER BLUES**
The Fendermen *Soma*

56 **LOVE YOU SO**
Ron Holden *Donna*

57 **LET THE LITTLE GIRL DANCE**
Billy Bland *Old Town*

58 **WHITE SILVER SANDS**
Bill Black's Combo *Hi*

59 **BABY (YOU GOT WHAT IT TAKES)**
Dinah Washington & Brook Benton *Mercury*

60 **YOU TALK TOO MUCH**
Joe Jones *Roulette*

61 **DREAMIN'**
Johnny Burnette *Liberty*

62 **A MILLION TO ONE**
Jimmy Charles *Promo*

63 **CRADLE OF LOVE**
Johnny Preston *Mercury*

64 **BEYOND THE SEA**
Bobby Darin *Atco*

65 **LET IT BE ME**
Everly Brothers *Cadence*

66 **YOU'RE SIXTEEN**
Johnny Burnette *Liberty*

67 **IMAGE OF A GIRL**
Safaris *Eldo*

68 **THE OLD LAMPLIGHTER**
The Browns *RCA*

The No. 9 song of 1960 was by a man who might have been a star baseball pitcher if he hadn't broken both of his ankles while playing for the St. Louis Cardinals in 1947. Jim Reeves became a DJ for KGRI in Henderson, Texas, a station he later bought. Fabor Robinson of Abbott Records heard him singing on the radio and signed him. His first chart single was "Mexico Joe," which topped *Billboard*'s country chart for nine weeks in 1953. Reeves moved over to RCA in 1955 and continued to have success on the country chart. He crossed over to the pop chart in 1957 with "Four Walls." One day in 1959, he heard a song on his car radio written by Joe and Audrey Allison and recorded by Billy Brown. Reeves liked "He'll Have To Go," but didn't want to record it in case Brown's version turned out to be a hit. He waited six months and then recorded the song in Nashville. RCA released it as the "B" side of "In A Mansion Stands My Love." After that song floundered for a month, country radio DJs flipped the record. "He'll Have To Go" spent 14 weeks on top of the country chart and became Reeves' only top 10 pop hit, spending three weeks at No. 2. Jeanne Black, a singer from Pomona, California, recorded an answer record called "He'll Have To Stay," which went to No. 4 on the Hot 100 and ranked No. 51 for the year.

The No. 10 song of 1960 was "Running Bear" by Johnny Preston, a protege of J.P. Richardson—better known as the Big Bopper. When Shelby Singleton signed Richardson to the Mercury label, he also signed Preston. Richardson discovered the teenaged Preston singing in a club in Beaumont, Texas. A recording session was arranged, but Preston was nervous and the results were poor. Still, Richardson believed in his discovery and wrote a song for him inspired by a commercial for Dove soap. Preston didn't think much of "Running Bear," but he recorded it because his mentor believed in it. Mercury was ready to release the song when Richardson was killed on February 3, 1959, in the plane crash that also took the life of Buddy Holly and Ritchie Valens. "Running Bear" was put on hold until the fall of 1959. It entered the Hot 100 on October 12 and five weeks later had only climbed to No. 71—then fell off the chart. After a one-week absence it returned and began its climb to No. 1, where it remained for three weeks.

Connie Francis had her highest-ranked year-end songs in 1960 with "My Heart Has A Mind Of Its Own" at No. 11 and "Everybody's Somebody's Fool" at No. 12. Her first hit, "Who's Sorry Now," was the No. 49 song of 1958. The following year she had four songs on the year-end chart: "My Happiness" (No. 24), "Lipstick On Your Collar" (No. 48), "Frankie" (No. 72), and "Among My Souvenirs" (No. 80). In 1960, Connie had a very good idea of the type of song she wanted to record. Returning from a trip to Europe, she was looking for a country song she could record in different languages. She called Howard Greenfield, who had penned "Stupid Cupid" and "Lipstick On Your Collar" for Connie with his partner, Neil Sedaka. Writing with Jack Keller, Howard had come up with what he described as a LaVern Baker–type blues ballad. Connie told him to change it—"Just take your ballad and play it uptempo like 'Heartaches By The Number,'" she said. The result was "Everybody's Somebody's Fool," Francis' first No. 1 hit.

The Top 100 Songs of 1961

Smokey Robinson & the Miracles

1961 WAS THE year Ricky Nelson grew up and dropped the "y" from his first name; John Hammond signed Bob Dylan to Columbia Records; and Berry Gordy inaugurated a new label, Motown, with "My Beloved" by the Satintones.

Gordy's record company had its first showing on the year-end chart with two singles on the Tamla label. The first was by five high school girls from Inkster, Michigan, who had entered a school talent contest knowing that the winners would be auditioned by Motown. They placed fourth, but their teacher asked the principal if they could join the top three groups for the audition. Motown liked the girls and told them to come up with some original material. Georgia Dobbins asked her songwriting friend, William Garrett, if he had anything they could sing. He suggested a blues song, "Please Mr. Postman." Georgia took the title and wrote a new set of lyrics overnight. Then she told group member Gladys Horton to learn how to sing it, because she was dropping out of the group to take care of her sick mother. With Wanda Young joining the group to replace Dobbins, the girls went back to Motown and sang "Please Mr. Postman" for producers Brian Holland and Robert Bateman. They loved the song and recorded it, with 22-year-old Marvin Gaye on drums. Gordy named the girls the Marvelettes, and they gave the company its first No. 1 single. "Please Mr. Postman" ranked No. 19 for the year.

The other Tamla single on the year-end list was "Shop Around" by the Miracles. Smokey Robinson wrote the song in a few minutes. He wanted to give it to Barrett Strong, who had scored a hit with "Money" in April 1960. But when Smokey played "Shop Around" for Gordy, the Motown chief said he wanted the Miracles to record the song.

The single was in its second week of release, but Smokey wasn't able to promote it. He was bedridden with the flu. His telephone rang at three in the morning. Berry wanted to know what was happening. Not much, a sleepy Robinson told him. Berry told Smokey to come down to the studio right away—the musicians were already on their way in. Berry said he loved "Shop Around" but hated how it had turned out. He wanted to cut a new, faster version. The piano player didn't show up for the session, so Gordy played keyboards himself. The original version was withdrawn and the recut version released in its place. The new "Shop Around" went to No. 2 on the Hot 100, and ranked No. 31 for the year.

The No. 1 song of 1961 was "Tossin' and Turnin'" by Bobby Lewis. Befriended by Jackie Wilson, Lewis accepted the singer's advice and financial support to leave Detroit for New York. During a week's stint at the Apollo Theater, Lewis gave some encouragement to a group of white singers, the Fireflies ("You Were Mine"). Three weeks later, Lewis knocked on the doors of Belltone Records for an audition and was surprised to run into the lead singer of the Fireflies, Ritchie Adams. Signed to Belltone himself, Adams listened to Lewis play his own songs, then suggested he try something Adams had written. The song was called "Tossin' and Turnin'," and it spent seven weeks at No. 1. It is the only single Lewis ever placed on a year-end chart, making him one of four artists who had a No. 1 song of the year and then were never listed again on a year-end survey. The others are Percy Faith, Lulu, and Debby Boone.

Jimmy Dean had the No. 2 hit of 1961 with "Big Bad John," a song he wrote during a flight to Nashville. He was on his way to a recording session and only had three songs ready. "At that time, you recorded four sides a session," he explains. "I had to do something. I had worked with a guy in summer stock named John Mentoe. He was six-foot-five and skinny as a rail, but he was the only guy in the troupe taller than me, and I used to call him Big John. It had a powerful ring to it. So I put him in a mine and killed him...it took me an hour-and-a-half to write."

For the first time since 1956, there were two instrumentals in the year-end top 10. German orchestra leader Bert Kaempfert had the No. 4 song of the year with "Wonderland By Night," originally written as the instrumental title theme for *Wunderland Bei Nacht,* a film that told of the dark side of Germany's "economic miracle." There was a vocal version by Anita Bryant and another instrumental recording by Louis Prima. While all three made the Hot 100, Kaempfert's version fared the best, spending three weeks at No. 1.

The other instrumental in the top 10 was "Calcutta" by Lawrence Welk, at No. 7 Like "Wonderland By Night," "Calcutta" was originally a German song. It was written in 1958 by Heino Gaze as "Tivoli Melody." It went through several other title changes before Randy Wood, founder of Dot Records, brought the song to Welk.

Del Shannon had the biggest hit of his career with his chart debut, "Runaway." The No. 5 song of 1961, it was recorded after DJ Ollie McLaughlin from WGRV in Ann Arbor, Michigan, suggested that Del write some uptempo material. Playing at the Hi-Lo club, Del stopped the show one night when organist Max Crook hit a chord change going from A-minor to G. Del incorporated that chord change into a new song, "Runaway." Shannon had one more hit on the year-end list: "Hats Off To Larry" was No. 62.

Chubby Checker had a top 10 song of the year for the second year in a row. "The Twist" was the No. 8 song of 1960; he came in two notches higher in 1961 with "Pony Time." It was adapted from a 1928 composition called "Boogie Woogie" by Clarence "Pinetop" Smith. Checker was also on the year-end list with "Let's Twist Again" at No. 52 and "The Fly" at No. 59.

The Shirelles had the No. 9 hit of 1961 with the first Gerry Goffin–Carole King song to make a year-end chart. Lead singer Shirley Owens heard Carole's demo of "Will You Love Me Tomorrow" and thought it sounded like a country and western song. She disliked it while rehearsing it, but changed her mind during the recording session when producer Luther Dixon turned it into a pop song. The Shirelles had two other songs on the recap for 1961: "Dedicated To The One I Love" at No. 33 and "Mama Said" at No. 53.

Ricky Nelson had his highest-ranked year-end song with "Travelin' Man," the number 15 single of 1961. His previous year-end high was "Poor Little Fool," the No. 17 song of 1958. Jerry Fuller wrote "Travelin' Man" while waiting in the park for his wife. He had a world atlas with him to help pick out different cities around the world. Fuller took a demo of the song performed by Glen Campbell to Sam Cooke's manager, J.W. Alexander, who didn't think much of it and threw the tape away. Lew Chudd, head of Ricky's label, Imperial, had an office next to Alexander, and bass player Joe Osbourne had heard the demo through the wall. He asked Alexander if he could hear the song again, and Alexander pulled it out of the trash can and gave it to him. The flip side of "Travelin' Man," was "Hello Mary Lou," written by Gene Pitney. It was the No. 47 song of the year.

69 **YOU CAN DEPEND ON ME**
Brenda Lee *Decca*

70 **LET'S GET TOGETHER**
Hayley Mills *Vista*

71 **WALK RIGHT BACK**
Everly Brothers *Warner Bros.*

72 **PORTRAIT OF MY LOVE**
Steve Lawrence *UA*

73 **I UNDERSTAND (JUST HOW YOU FEEL)**
The G-Clefs *Terrace*

74 **GEE WHIZ (LOOK AT HIS EYES)**
Carla Thomas *Atlantic*

75 **SPANISH HARLEM**
Ben E. King *Atco*

76 **THINK TWICE**
Brook Benton *Mercury*

77 **HELLO WALLS**
Faron Young *Capitol*

78 **SAD MOVIES (MAKE ME CRY)**
Sue Thompson *Hickory*

79 **LITTLE SISTER**
Elvis Presley *RCA*

80 **TOGETHER**
Connie Francis *MGM*

81 **DOES YOUR CHEWING GUM LOSE ITS FLAVOR (ON THE BEDPOST OVER NIGHT)**
Lonnie Donegan & His Skiffle Group *Dot*

82 **MEXICO**
Bob Moore *Monument*

83 **BABY SITTIN' BOOGIE**
Buzz Clifford *Columbia*

84 **EMOTIONS**
Brenda Lee *Decca*

85 **YA YA**
Lee Dorsey *Fury*

86 **BREAKIN' IN A BRAND NEW BROKEN HEART**
Connie Francis *MGM*

87 **ONE MINT JULEP**
Ray Charles *Impulse*

88 **SCHOOL IS OUT**
Gary U.S. Bonds *Legrand*

89 **SAN ANTONIO ROSE**
Floyd Cramer *RCA*

90 **PLEASE LOVE ME FOREVER**
Cathy Jean & the Roommates *Valmor*

91 **DON'T BET MONEY HONEY**
Linda Scott *Canadian-American*

92 **YOU'RE THE REASON**
Bobby Edwards *Crest*

93 **MOON RIVER**
Jerry Butler *Vee Jay*

94 **THE WRITING ON THE WALL**
Adam Wade *Coed*

95 **WONDERLAND BY NIGHT**
Louis Prima *Dot*

96 **BABY BLUE**
The Echoes *Seg-way*

97 **YOU MUST HAVE BEEN A BEAUTIFUL BABY**
Bobby Darin *Atco*

98 **EBONY EYES**
Everly Brothers *Warner Bros.*

99 **PRETTY LITTLE ANGEL EYES**
Curtis Lee *Dunos*

100 **THOSE OLDIES BUT GOODIES (REMIND ME OF YOU)**
Little Caesar & the Romans *Del-Fi*

The Top 100 Songs of 1962

Sam Cooke

1962 WAS THE year the Beatles failed their audition with Decca Records in the U.K.; disc jockey Alan Freed went on trial for payola; and the first Motortown Revue played the Howard Theater in Washington, D.C.

"The Twist" by Chubby Checker made pop history when it returned to The Billboard Hot 100, less than a year after its original run. Ranked as the No. 8 song of 1960, it did even better the second time around and was the No. 2 song of 1962. Its two chart runs enabled "The Twist" to become the No. 19 song of the rock era.

In 1960, the Twist was a popular dance with teenagers. They had moved on to other things by the time their parents discovered it at the end of 1961. Society columnist "Cholly Knickerbocker" wrote about the popularity of the Twist at the Peppermint Lounge on West 45th Street in Manhattan, and soon Chubby was invited to perform the song on *The Ed Sullivan Show*. Radio stations were playing "The Twist" as often as brand-new hits, prompting Cameo-Parkway to re-release the single and promote it all over again.

As the Twist craze spread through America, other artists recorded songs about the dance. There were seven Twist songs included in the top 100 of the year. Joey Dee & the Starliters recorded one album for Scepter Records and asked staff producer Luther Dixon for some help in finding live work. He got them a one-night gig at the Peppermint Lounge. It was the morning after their performance that Knickerbocker wrote about Merle Oberon and Prince Serge Oblinski twisting the night away at the club. Joey and his band ended up playing the Peppermint Lounge for 13 months. The group's popularity led to contracts first with Capitol and then with Atlantic, but when nothing was released, Roulette Records stepped in and rushed out the "Peppermint Twist" single (the No. 6 song of 1962) and a live album recorded at the Peppermint Lounge.

Chubby Checker followed his "Twist" revival with one of the only ballads written about the dance. It was recorded with a 16-year-old teenager from Overbrook High School who had been hired to sing backing vocals for Cameo-Parkway. Dee Dee Sharp didn't receive any credit on "Slow Twistin'," the number No. 35 song of 1962, but it did lead to a recording session of her own and the No. 15 song of the year, "Mashed Potato Time."

Gary U.S. Bonds followed "School Is In" with a song called "Havin' So Much Fun," but it wasn't getting any airplay. When Bob Schwartz at Laurie Records suggested promoting the flip side, a song about the Twist called "Dear Lady," writer/producer Frank Guida added the word "Twist" to the title. "Dear Lady Twist" went to No. 9 on the Hot 100 and ranked No. 51 for the year. Bonds' next single, "Twist, Twist Senora," also peaked at No. 9, and ranked No. 98 for the year.

Sam Cooke took "Twistin' The Night Away" to No. 9 on the Hot 100. It was the No. 64 song of the year. The other Twist song on the year-end chart was "Twist And Shout" by the Isley Brothers, No. 90 for the year. When the Beatles covered it, most disc jockeys thought it was a remake of the "original" by the Isley Brothers. But the first group to record the Bert Berns–Phil Medley song was the Top Notes, featuring Derek Martin, on Atlantic. Jerry Wexler told Charlie Gillette about working with Phil Spector on that session: "He and I produced the record and it was horrible. Bert was such a newcomer, he was sitting in the spectator's booth, watching Phil and I butcher his song...we had the wrong tempo, the wrong feel, but we didn't realize that Bert could've produced it himself, and he just sat and watched us ruin it." Bert did produce it himself a year later with the Isley Brothers for Wand Records.

It was a good year for dances. Aside from the seven Twist songs and the Mashed Potato hit on the year-end chart, other dances represented were the Limbo, the Watusi, the Cha-Cha, and a dance made up especially for a song, the Loco-Motion.

Ray Charles had his biggest hit of all time with "I Can't Stop Loving You," the No. 1 song of 1962. Originally recorded by composer Don Gibson, Charles included the song in his landmark *Modern Sounds In Country And Western Music* album. Executives at his label, ABC-Paramount, discouraged Charles from attempting such a project, thinking he would lose his fans. Ray decided to do it anyway. "I didn't want to be a country-western singer," he told Ben Fong-Torres. "I just wanted to take country-western songs. When I sing 'I Can't Stop Loving You,' I'm not singing it *country-western*. I'm singing it like *me*."

The Four Seasons made their chart debut in 1962, after a brush with the Hot 100 in 1956 as the Four Lovers. "Sherry," written by Bob Gaudio

35 **SLOW TWISTIN'**
Chubby Checker *Parkway*

36 **NORMAN**
Sue Thompson *Hickory*

37 **SEALED WITH A KISS**
Brian Hyland *ABC-Paramount*

38 **GREEN ONIONS**
Booker T. & the MG's *Stax*

39 **I KNOW**
Barbara George *AFO*

40 **LET ME IN**
The Sensations *Argo*

41 **BREAK IT TO ME GENTLY**
Brenda Lee *Decca*

42 **LOVERS WHO WANDER**
Dion *Laurie*

43 **PATCHES**
Dickey Lee *Smash*

44 **LET'S DANCE**
Chris Montez *Monogram*

45 **DON'T HANG UP**
The Orlons *Cameo*

46 **THINGS**
Bobby Darin *Atco*

47 **WOLVERTON MOUNTAIN**
Claude King *Columbia*

48 **HAPPY BIRTHDAY, SWEET SIXTEEN**
Neil Sedaka *RCA*

49 **WHEN I FALL IN LOVE**
The Lettermen *Capitol*

50 **THE LONELY BULL**
The Tijuana Brass f/Herb Alpert *A&M*

51 **DEAR LADY TWIST**
Gary U.S. Bonds *Legrand*

52 **A LITTLE BITTY TEAR**
Burl Ives *Decca*

53 **ALLEY CAT**
Bent Fabric & His Piano *Atco*

54 **COTTON FIELDS**
The Highwaymen *UA*

55 **AHAB THE ARAB**
Ray Stevens *Mercury*

56 **CRYING IN THE RAIN**
Everly Brothers *Warner Bros.*

57 **YOU DON'T KNOW ME**
Ray Charles *ABC-Paramount*

58 **SHE CRIED**
Jay & the Americans *UA*

59 **DREAM BABY**
(HOW LONG MUST I DREAM)
Roy Orbison *Monument*

60 **LOVE LETTERS**
Ketty Lester *Era*

61 **BABY IT'S YOU**
The Shirelles *Scepter*

62 **JOHNNY GET ANGRY**
Joanie Sommers *Warner Bros.*

63 **AL DI LA'**
Emilio Pericoli *Warner Bros.*

64 **TWISTIN' THE NIGHT AWAY**
Sam Cooke *RCA*

65 **THEME FROM "DR. KILDARE"**
(THREE STARS WILL SHINE TONIGHT)
Richard Chamberlain *MGM*

66 **(THE MAN WHO SHOT)**
LIBERTY VALANCE
Gene Pitney *Musicor*

67 **YOUNG WORLD**
Rick Nelson *Imperial*

in 15 minutes, was their first No. 1 single. It spent five weeks atop the Hot 100 and came in at No. 5 for the year. The follow-up, "Big Girls Don't Cry," was recorded at the same session and was strongly considered for the debut single. Like its predecessor, it spent five weeks at No. 1. It was the No. 3 song of the year, and the highest-ranked year-end single of the Four Seasons' career.

Bobby Vinton experienced success with his first chart single, "Roses Are Red (My Love)." When Epic Records threatened to drop him, Vinton found the song in a pile of rejected records and told the label's attorneys they owed him two more recordings. "Roses Are Red" became Epic's first No. 1 single and ranked No. 4 for 1962.

Mr. Acker Bilk, a clarinet player from Somerset, England, became the first British artist to have a top 10 song of the year. His instrumental "Stranger On The Shore," originally called "Jenny" after one of his children, ranked No. 7 for the year. The song title was changed when it became the theme song for a BBC children's television series, *Stranger On The Shore*.

David Rose was also in the top 10 with an instrumental, "The Stripper." Born in London, Rose moved to the U.S. when he was seven and later became an American citizen. "The Stripper" began as eight bars of music for a television show called *Burlesque* that Rose scored in 1958. Dan Dailey and Joan Blondell starred in the program, and minutes before they went on the air live, the producer asked Rose for some background music for a scene where the two stars argued behind a closed dressing room door. Soon after the broadcast, Rose was recording a new album and had 10 minutes of studio time remaining. He had the musicians record the song and, as a joke, had copies made for everyone so they could show their families what a "beautiful" string album they had been recording. Friends suggested he release the track, but MGM Records said no. Four years later Rose was rushed into the studio at MGM's request to record a version of "Ebb Tide" to help promote the film *Sweet Bird Of Youth* with Paul Newman and Geraldine Page. There was no time to record something for the "B" side, so someone at MGM went to the master files and pulled the obscure, unreleased song. Los Angeles DJ Robert Q. Lewis liked the "B" side so much, he played it on the air continuously for 45 minutes. That stunt led to "The Stripper" topping the *Billboard* chart and placing No. 18 for the year.

Elvis Presley had four songs included in the top 100 of the year for the first time since 1959. Highest-ranked of the four was "Return To Sender" at No. 10, Presley's final top 10 song on a year-end chart.

68 SHE'S NOT YOU
Elvis Presley *RCA*

69 SPEEDY GONZALES
Pat Boone *Dot*

70 NEXT DOOR TO AN ANGEL
Neil Sedaka *RCA*

71 SURFIN' SAFARI
The Beach Boys *Capitol*

72 LOVER PLEASE
Clyde McPhatter *Mercury*

73 PARTY LIGHTS
Claudine Clark *Chancellor*

74 PLAYBOY
The Marvelettes *Tamla*

75 RELEASE ME
Little Esther Phillips *Lenox*

76 RIDE!
Dee Dee Sharp *Cameo*

77 SHOUT—PART 1
Joey Dee & the Starliters *Roulette*

78 WHAT'S YOUR NAME
Don and Juan *Big Top*

79 THE ONE WHO REALLY LOVES YOU
Mary Wells *Motown*

80 OLD RIVERS
Walter Brennan *Liberty*

81 EVERYBODY LOVES ME BUT YOU
Brenda Lee *Decca*

82 VENUS IN BLUE JEANS
Jimmy Clanton *Ace*

83 UNCHAIN MY HEART
Ray Charles *ABC-Paramount*

84 WHEN THE BOY IN YOUR ARMS (IS THE BOY IN YOUR HEART)
Connie Francis *MGM*

85 THE CHA-CHA-CHA
Bobby Rydell *Cameo*

86 KEEP YOUR HANDS OFF MY BABY
Little Eva *Dimension*

87 FUNNY WAY OF LAUGHIN'
Burl Ives *Decca*

88 GINA
Johnny Mathis *Columbia*

89 TUFF
Ace Cannon *Hi*

90 TWIST AND SHOUT
Isley Brothers *Wand*

91 SMOKY PLACES
The Corsairs *Tuff*

92 WHAT KIND OF FOOL AM I
Sammy Davis, Jr. *Reprise*

93 I REMEMBER YOU
Frank Ifield *Vee Jay*

94 TEEN AGE IDOL
Rick Nelson *Imperial*

95 P.T. 109
Jimmy Dean *Columbia*

96 SHOUT! SHOUT! (KNOCK YOURSELF OUT)
Ernie Maresca *Seville*

97 YOU ARE MY SUNSHINE
Ray Charles *ABC-Paramount*

98 TWIST, TWIST SENORA
Gary U.S. Bonds *Legrand*

99 SNAP YOUR FINGERS
Joe Henderson *Todd*

100 HER ROYAL MAJESTY
James Darren *Colpix*

The Top 100 Songs of 1963

Little Peggy March

1963 WAS THE year Frankie Avalon and Annette Funicello made the first *Beach Party* movie; Patsy Cline was killed in a plane crash in Tennessee; and Phil Spector asked stores to remove his Christmas album after the assassination of President Kennedy.

The No. 1 song of 1963 was "Sugar Shack" by Jimmy Gilmer & the Fireballs. The song was produced by the same man who had worked with Buddy Holly: Norman Petty. "Sugar Shack" was co-written by Keith McCormick, a member of another group Petty produced, the String-a-Longs ("Wheels").

Japan and Belgium were represented on the year-end chart for the first time, both in the top 10. "Dominique," the No. 2 song of the year, was the Belgian entry. Kyu Sakamoto was No. 9 with "Sukiyaki," a song originally titled *"Ue O Muite Aruko,"* which translates "I Look Up When I Walk." Thinking that DJs would have a difficult time with the real title, Pye Records released it under a Japanese name most Westerners would recognize: "Sukiyaki." As *Newsweek* would later point out, it was like releasing "Moon River" in Japan under the title "Beef Stew."

For the first time in the rock era, there were five songs featuring female lead vocalists in the top 10. The Singing Nun was the highest-ranked woman in the top 10. Right below her, Jill Jackson was in the top 10 with the No. 3 song of the year. Jill's aunt ran a boarding house at Howard Payne College in Brownwood, Texas. Ray Hildebrand, a student on a basketball scholarship, was living in the house. Jill asked him to sing with her on a radio benefit for the American Cancer Society. They performed a song Ray had written in the school gym. A local DJ liked it so much, he taped their performance and played "Hey Paula" on his own show. A friend of Ray's suggested they meet with record producer Major Bill Smith in Fort Worth. When an artist failed to show for a session, Smith had Ray and Jill use the studio time he had already paid for to record "Hey Paula." Released on the Major's LeCam label, it sold well in Atlanta and Shelby Singleton of Mercury Records picked it up for the label's Philips subsidiary. Singleton only changed one thing—he thought Ray and Jill wouldn't sell as many records as "Paul and Paula," so he changed their names on the label.

Judy Craig sang lead on the No. 6 song of the year, "He's So Fine" by the Chiffons. Along with her friends in the group—Barbara Lee, Patricia Bennett, and Sylvia Peterson—Judy had recorded for labels like Big Deal, Wildcat, and Reprise, without much success. That all changed when songwriter Ronnie Mack asked them to record some of his songs as demos. Busy with high school graduation, they forgot about the session with Mack. But the writer was busy shopping his tunes around, and he hit paydirt when he walked into the offices of the Tokens ("The Lion Sleeps Tonight"). Phil Margo, Mitch Margo, Hank Medress, and Jay Siegal had signed a production deal with Capitol, although they were still signed to RCA themselves. They produced "He's So Fine" for the Chiffons.

The other females in the top 10 were two teenagers who had No. 1 hits with their first chart entries. Producers Hugo Peretti and Luigi Creatore signed Peggy March to RCA and after misfiring with the title song from the Broadway show Little Me, found a French ditty called "Chariot." Arthur Altman and Norman Gimbel wrote English lyrics and "I Will Follow Him" soared to pole position, making the 15-year-old (and one month) singer the youngest female to ever top the Hot 100. Producer Quincy Jones signed Lesley Gore to Mercury and brought 250 demos to her home to find songs for her to record. The first one they listened to was "It's My Party." Six days after she recorded it, Lesley was driving home from school and heard the song on New York radio station WINS.

Motown had its first top 10 song on a year-end chart in 1963. The company's youngest artist, Little Stevie Wonder, was No. 8 for the year with "Fingertips—Pt. 2." Stevie's first three singles for Motown failed to chart, but he did so well on the Motortown Revues that Berry Gordy decided to record him live. The result was an album called Little Stevie Wonder—The 12-Year-Old Genius. Reaction to the seven-minute track "Fingertips" was so positive that Gordy decided to split it into two parts and release it as a single. DJs preferred side two and Wonder had his first chart single and first No. 1 hit. "Fingertips—Pt. 2" was one of five Motown singles on the top 100 of 1963, a new high for the Detroit record company.

The No. 4 song of 1963 was one of the most controversial of the rock era. Richard Berry, a New Orleans musician who moved to Los Angeles in the early '40s, wrote and recorded "Louie Louie" in 1956 on the Flip label.

It never made the Hot 100, but it was a regional hit in the Pacific Northwest and became a staple of garage bands in the state of Washington. The Frantics, a Seattle group signed to Dolton Records, included it in their shows but never recorded it. Another Seattle group, the Wailers, did commit it to vinyl, but it still wasn't a hit. In 1963, two groups from Portland, Oregon, happened to record "Louie Louie" within 24 hours of each other. Paul Revere and the Raiders cut it for the Sande label and it was picked up by Columbia Records. The Kingsmen recorded it for the Jerden label and six months later a DJ in Boston played their version. It was licensed by Scepter Records for its Wand label. The muffled vocals led many to believe the lyrics were obscene, although this was denied by both the Kingsmen and Richard Berry. "Louie Louie" was a hit at last, spending six weeks at No. 2 on the Hot 100.

Bobby Vinton, who had the No. 4 song of 1962 with "Roses Are Red (My Love)," had another year-end top five hit in 1963 with "Blue Velvet," No. 5 for the year. After recording Burt Bacharach and Hal David's "Blue On Blue" (the No. 46 song of the year), Bobby decided to do a theme album of all "blue" songs. "I picked songs like 'Blue Moon' and 'Blue Hawaii' and everything that was blue in the title," he explains. "Al Gallico, a well-known music publisher, said I ought to do 'Blue Velvet.' He gave his secretary a dollar to run down to the music store and buy the sheet music." An hour later, Bobby was recording the song, but he didn't think it would be the single. His pick was "Am I Blue." When Epic wanted to release "Blue Velvet," he told them he didn't think it was a good idea. The label put it out anyway. Originally a No. 16 song for Tony Bennett in 1951, "Blue Velvet" put Bobby back on top of the Hot 100.

The No. 12 song of the year was not written for the artist who recorded it. After Bobby Vee recorded a number of songs written by Gerry Goffin and Carole King, including "Take Good Care Of My Baby," "How Many Tears," and "Walkin' With My Angel," the husband-and-wife writing team gave Bobby his choice of songs to record next. "It was amazing," Vee told Steve Kolanjian. "I did one session where I recorded 'Sharing You,' 'Go Away Little Girl,' and 'It Might As Well Rain Until September.' They all went on to become top 20 songs and were all written for me, but were not all hits for me. I thought they were all great. I was pleased with all of them. What happened was, when we said, 'We're going to put out "Sharing You," because we think that would be the best single,' they said, 'Well we can't wait for you to decide whether or not you're going to put out "Go Away Little Girl," we'll do it with someone else.' And so Steve Lawrence put it out. Of course it was a No. 1 record, much bigger than 'Sharing You.'"

69 **I CAN'T STAY MAD AT YOU**
Skeeter Davis *RCA*

70 **WALKING THE DOG**
Rufus Thomas *Stax*

71 **OUR WINTER LOVE**
Bill Pursell *Columbia*

72 **DENISE**
Randy & the Rainbows *Rust*

73 **BABY WORKOUT**
Jackie Wilson *Brunswick*

74 **MEAN WOMAN BLUES**
Roy Orbison *Monument*

75 **JUDY'S TURN TO CRY**
Lesley Gore *Mercury*

76 **LOOP DE LOOP**
Johnny Thunder *Diamond*

77 **THEN HE KISSED ME**
The Crystals *Philles*

78 **THOSE LAZY-HAZY-CRAZY DAYS OF SUMMER**
Nat King Cole *Capitol*

79 **LOSING YOU**
Brenda Lee *Decca*

80 **WHAT WILL MARY SAY**
Johnny Mathis *Columbia*

81 **TWO LOVERS**
Mary Wells *Motown*

82 **MARIA ELENA**
Los Indios Tabajaras *RCA*

83 **FROM A JACK TO A KING**
Ned Miller *Fabor*

84 **DRIP DROP**
Dion DiMucci *Columbia*

85 **THE MONKEY TIME**
Major Lance *Okeh*

86 **IT'S UP TO YOU**
Rick Nelson *Imperial*

87 **MORE**
Kai Winding *Verve*

88 **ZIP-A-DEE DOO-DAH**
Bob B. Soxx & the Blue Jeans *Philles*

89 **FOOLS RUSH IN**
Rick Nelson *Decca*

90 **TAKE THESE CHAINS FROM MY HEART**
Ray Charles *ABC-Paramount*

91 **ANOTHER SATURDAY NIGHT**
Sam Cooke *RCA*

92 **DONNA THE PRIMA DONNA**
Dion DiMucci *Columbia*

93 **ONE FINE DAY**
The Chiffons *Laurie*

94 **BE TRUE TO YOUR SCHOOL**
The Beach Boys *Capitol*

95 **DON'T SAY NOTHIN' BAD (ABOUT MY BABY)**
The Cookies *Dimension*

96 **YOUNG LOVERS**
Paul and Paula *Philips*

97 **WIGGLE WOBBLE**
Les Cooper *Everlast*

98 **REVEREND MR. BLACK**
The Kingston Trio *Capitol*

99 **PRIDE AND JOY**
Marvin Gaye *Tamla*

100 **HEY, GIRL**
Freddie Scott *Colpix*

The Top 100 Songs of 1964

Herman's Hermits

<big>1964</big> WAS THE year Jan and Dean hosted the TAMI show; Jim Reeves was killed in a plane crash, Johnny Burnette drowned, and Sam Cooke was shot to death; and 73 million Americans sat down in front of their television sets to watch the Beatles perform live on *The Ed Sullivan Show.*

The Beatles dominated everything musical in 1964, right from the beginning of the year when "I Want To Hold Your Hand" debuted on the Hot 100 for the week ending January 18. It ended up as the No. 1 song of the year, the first British recording to be the highest-ranked song of the year in the rock era. The Beatles were also in the year-end top 10 with "She Loves You" at No. 2, "Can't Buy Me Love" at No. 6, and "I Feel Fine" at No. 10. That made them the first and only act in the rock era to have four songs in a year-end top 10. Other Beatles songs included in the year's top 100 were: "A Hard Day's Night" (No. 14), "Love Me Do" (No. 20), "Twist And Shout" (No. 22), "Please Please Me" (No. 32), "Do You Want To Know A Secret" (No. 34), and "She's A Woman" (No. 58). That gave them a total of 10 songs in the top 100 of the year, another record no one else has ever matched.

Prior to 1964, a total of eight records by artists from the U.K. had made the year-end surveys during the rock era; in 1964 there were 27 U.K. titles included in the top 100 of the year. Joining the Beatles on the chart were: Manfred Mann (No. 11 with "Do Wah Diddy Diddy"); the Animals (No. 16 with "House Of The Rising Sun"); Peter and Gordon (No. 23 with "A

01 I WANT TO HOLD YOUR HAND
  The Beatles *Capitol*

02 SHE LOVES YOU
  The Beatles *Swan*

03 WHERE DID OUR LOVE GO
  The Supremes *Motown*

04 THERE! I'VE SAID IT AGAIN
  Bobby Vinton *Epic*

05 BABY LOVE
  The Supremes *Motown*

06 CAN'T BUY ME LOVE
  The Beatles *Capitol*

07 HELLO, DOLLY!
  Louis Armstrong *Kapp*

08 COME SEE ABOUT ME
  The Supremes *Motown*

09 I GET AROUND
  The Beach Boys *Capitol*

10 I FEEL FINE
  The Beatles *Capitol*

11 DO WAH DIDDY DIDDY
  Manfred Mann *Ascot*

12 CHAPEL OF LOVE
  The Dixie Cups *Red Bird*

13 OH, PRETTY WOMAN
  Roy Orbison *Monument*

14 A HARD DAY'S NIGHT
  The Beatles *Capitol*

15 EVERYBODY LOVES SOMEBODY
  Dean Martin *Reprise*

16 HOUSE OF THE RISING SUN
  The Animals *MGM*

17 MY GUY
  Mary Wells *Motown*

18 MR. LONELY
  Bobby Vinton *Epic*

19 RAG DOLL
  The Four Seasons *Philips*

20 LOVE ME DO
  The Beatles *Tollie*

21 LEADER OF THE PACK
  The Shangri-Las *Red Bird*

22 TWIST AND SHOUT
  The Beatles *Tollie*

23 A WORLD WITHOUT LOVE
  Peter and Gordon *Capitol*

24 LAST KISS
  J. Frank Wilson & the Cavaliers *Josie*

25 BREAD AND BUTTER
  The Newbeats *Hickory*

26 YOU DON'T OWN ME
  Lesley Gore *Mercury*

27 DANCING IN THE STREET
  Martha & the Vandellas *Gordy*

28 MEMPHIS
  Johnny Rivers *Imperial*

29 DAWN (GO AWAY)
  The Four Seasons *Philips*

30 SHE'S NOT THERE
  The Zombies *Parrot*

31 RINGO
  Lorne Greene *RCA*

32 PLEASE PLEASE ME
  The Beatles *Vee Jay*

33 LOVE ME WITH ALL YOUR HEART
  Ray Charles Singers *Command*

34 DO YOU WANT TO KNOW A SECRET
  The Beatles *Vee Jay*

World Without Love"); the Zombies (No. 30 with "She's Not There"); the Dave Clark Five (No. 41 with "Bits And Pieces," No. 44 with "Because," No. 54 with "Glad All Over," and No. 68 with "Can't You See That She's Mine"); Gerry & the Pacemakers (No. 49 with "Don't Let The Sun Catch You Crying"); Billy J. Kramer & the Dakotas (No. 51 with "Little Children" and No. 99 with "Bad To Me"); Dusty Springfield (No. 55 with "Wishin' and Hopin'"); the Rolling Stones (No. 62 with "Time Is On My Side"); the Honeycombs (No. 64 with "Have I The Right?"); Herman's Hermits (No. 69 with "I'm Into Something Good"); the Kinks (No. 72 with "You Really Got Me"); and Chad and Jeremy (No. 78 with "A Summer Song").

While many American artists fell by the wayside in 1964, others maintained their strength despite the onslaught of British artists. One of the most unlikely Americans to have a hit in 1964 was the jazz trumpeter who broke the Beatles' hold on the No. 1 position on the Hot 100. The man known as Satchmo hadn't seen Jerry Herman's Broadway musical starring Carol Channing when he recorded the title song for an album of show tunes. Released as a single, Louis Armstrong's "Hello, Dolly!" became the No. 7 hit of the year and the fourth most successful song from a stage production in the rock era. The song was so popular, most people believed Armstrong was starring in the show. He wasn't, but he did win a role in the film version produced in 1969. Unfortunately, he didn't get to work with Channing—Barbra Streisand played Dolly in the movie.

Roy Orbison made his first year-end chart appearance in 1960, when "Only The Lonely (Know How I Feel)" was the No. 24 song of the year. In 1961 he was No. 23 with "Running Scared" and No. 27 with "Crying." A year later, "Dream Baby (How Long Must I Dream)" was No. 59. In 1963, "In Dreams" was No. 61 for the year and "Mean Woman Blues" was No. 74. Orbison had the biggest hit of his career with "Oh, Pretty Woman," the No. 13 song of 1964. His wife Claudette was the indirect inspiration for the song. She was leaving the house to go shopping one day and Roy asked if she needed any money. Songwriter Bill Dees suggested, "A pretty woman never needs any money," and thought it would make a good song title. By the time Claudette returned, Roy and Bill had written "Oh, Pretty Woman." Another Roy Orbison song, "It's Over," was the No. 80 song of 1964.

The Beach Boys made their first appearance on a year-end chart in 1962, when "Surfin' Safari" was the No. 71 song of the year. They fared better in 1963, when "Surfin' U.S.A." was No. 31 for the year, "Surfer Girl" was No. 55, and "Be True To Your School" was No. 94. In 1964 they reached a new high mark when "I Get Around" placed No. 9 for the year. Two more Beach Boys songs graced the top 100: "Fun, Fun, Fun" at No. 74 and "Dance, Dance, Dance" at No. 90.

After registering its first top 10 song of the year in 1963, Motown landed an impressive three hits in the top 10 of 1964, all by a group that had been called the "no-hit Supremes" until they recorded a song rejected by the Marvelettes, "Where Did Our Love Go." That Holland-Dozier-Holland song landed at No. 3 for the year, the top American song on the list. The Supremes' next two singles were also in the top 10. "Baby Love" ranked No. 5 and "Come See About Me" placed at No. 8. The only other American act to have three songs in a year-end ranking to this date was Elvis Presley.

35 **WE'LL SING IN THE SUNSHINE**
Gale Garnett *RCA*

36 **COME A LITTLE BIT CLOSER**
Jay & the Americans *UA*

37 **SUSPICION**
Terry Stafford *Crusader*

38 **POPSICLES AND ICICLES**
The Murmaids *Chattahoochee*

39 **MY BOY LOLLIPOP**
Millie Small *Smash*

40 **OUT OF LIMITS**
The Marketts *Warner Bros.*

41 **BITS AND PIECES**
Dave Clark Five *Epic*

42 **THE LITTLE OLD LADY (FROM PASADENA)**
Jan and Dean *Liberty*

43 **FORGET HIM**
Bobby Rydell *Cameo*

44 **BECAUSE**
Dave Clark Five *Epic*

45 **HEY LITTLE COBRA**
The Rip Chords *Columbia*

46 **SURFIN' BIRD**
The Trashmen *Garrett*

47 **JAVA**
Al Hirt *RCA*

48 **UNDER THE BOARDWALK**
The Drifters *Atlantic*

49 **DON'T LET THE SUN CATCH YOU CRYING**
Gerry & the Pacemakers *Laurie*

50 **PEOPLE**
Barbra Streisand *Columbia*

51 **LITTLE CHILDREN**
Billy J. Kramer & the Dakotas *Imperial*

52 **G.T.O.**
Ronny & the Daytonas *Mala*

53 **GOIN' OUT OF MY HEAD**
Little Anthony & the Imperials *DCP*

54 **GLAD ALL OVER**
Dave Clark Five *Epic*

55 **WISHIN' AND HOPIN'**
Dusty Springfield *Philips*

56 **IT HURTS TO BE IN LOVE**
Gene Pitney *Musicor*

57 **REMEMBER (WALKIN' IN THE SAND)**
The Shangri-Las *Red Bird*

58 **SHE'S A WOMAN**
The Beatles *Capitol*

59 **DON'T LET THE RAIN COME DOWN (CROOKED LITTLE MAN)**
Serendipity Singers *Philips*

60 **WALK ON BY**
Dionne Warwick *Scepter*

61 **LET IT BE ME**
Jerry Butler and Betty Everett *Vee Jay*

62 **TIME IS ON MY SIDE**
The Rolling Stones *London*

63 **DEAD MAN'S CURVE**
Jan and Dean *Liberty*

64 **HAVE I THE RIGHT?**
The Honeycombs *Interphon*

65 **THE SHOOP SHOOP SONG (IT'S IN HIS KISS)**
Betty Everett *Vee Jay*

66 **BABY I NEED YOUR LOVING**
Four Tops *Motown*

67 **UM, UM, UM, UM, UM, UM**
Major Lance *Okeh*

Motown had another hit in the top 20, thanks to the Smokey Robinson–penned "My Guy," a No. 1 hit for Mary Wells. It was the first chart-topper on the Motown label proper. Wells had come to Berry Gordy's company as a songwriter, but her run of hits didn't begin until she teamed up with Robinson as her writer/producer. Wells had the No. 79 song of 1962 with "The One Who Really Loves You," and the No. 81 song of 1963 with "Two Lovers." After her success with "My Guy," she never appeared on a year-end chart again. At the height of her career she left Motown and signed with 20th Century Fox. Subsequent deals with Atco, Jubilee, and Epic proved equally unsuccessful.

Bobby Vinton had a top five song of the year for the third year in a row, the first artist to accomplish this feat. The song that completed the hat trick for Bobby was "There! I've Said It Again," No. 4 for the year. Like his hit from 1963, "Blue Velvet," this was a recording of a song that was written prior to the rock era. "Blue Velvet" dated back to 1951; "There! I've Said It Again" went back even further. Vaughn Monroe recorded it in 1945 and had a six-week run at No. 1 with the song. Bobby recorded his version after a long-haired DJ in Cincinnati surprised him by screaming at him as he walked on stage that he should record the song. "I still remember that recording session," says Bobby. "It was about 10 after seven and I sang it one time, and it was a quarter after seven. The session was supposed to go to ten o'clock and I said, 'That's it. I could sing this all night, but it's not going to get any better. It's a hit just the way it is, goodnight, everybody.'"

Barbra Streisand made her *Billboard* singles debut in 1964 with "People," a song she performed in the stage musical *Funny Girl.* It was the No. 50 song of the year and Barbra's biggest hit of the decade.

The top-rated television series of the 1964–65 season was *Bonanza,* and during that time the patriarch of the Cartwright clan, actor Lorne Greene, experienced being No. 1 on another chart—The Billboard Hot 100. He did it with "Ringo," not a song about the Beatle, but a spoken word recording about a sheriff who saved the life of gunman Johnny Ringo. Greene's career as a pop star began when a producer at RCA Records suggested that the Cartwrights record an album. A Christmas LP featuring Greene with Michael Landon, Dan Blocker, and Pernell Roberts sold well enough that a second album, *Welcome To The Ponderosa,* was recorded. A DJ in Lubbock, Texas, played "Ringo" from that LP and RCA was inundated with requests to release it as a single. It ended up as the No. 31 song of the year.

The Top 100 Songs of 1965

The Byrds

1965 WAS THE year the Beatles made their second movie, *Help!*, toured America for the second time, and were awarded the MBE by Queen Elizabeth.

The British Invasion continued at full speed. There were five U.K. songs in the year-end top 10, and 32 in the top 100. The Beatles only had four titles on the list, compared to 10 the previous year. Herman's Hermits surpassed them, with five songs in the top 100 of the year. The Manchester group held down the No. 4 spot with "Mrs. Brown You've Got A Lovely Daughter," written in 1963 and originally performed by actor Tom Courtenay in a British television play. Herman's Hermits' version was a track on their *Introducing Herman's Hermits* album, but radio airplay in America forced MGM to release it as a single. That didn't happen in Britain, where the track was never issued on a 45 rpm disc. Other Hermits' singles on the year-end chart included a music hall song from 1911 called "I'm Henry VIII, I Am" (No. 17), "Can't You Hear My Heartbeat" (No. 28), a remake of Sam Cooke's "Wonderful World" (No. 56), and an updating of the Rays' "Silhouettes" (No. 59).

American artists continued to hold their own, especially those signed to Motown. The Supremes were in the top 10 like they were in 1964, but with just one song: "Stop! In The Name Of Love" (No. 8). Their other year-end hits were "I Hear A Symphony" (No. 12) and "Back In My Arms Again" (No. 30). After scoring the No. 92 song of 1964 with "The Way You Do The Things You Do," the Temptations were in the year-end top 30 for the first time thanks to the No. 19 song, "My Girl," featuring a lead vocal by David Ruffin. After recording for Chess and Anna Records, David joined the Motown roster to become a Temptation—but only after brother Jimmy had turned the job down.

Marvin Gaye had three songs on the year-end chart for 1965: "How Sweet It Is To Be Loved By You" (No. 67), "Ain't That Peculiar" (No. 68), and "I'll Be Doggone" (No. 78). Jr. Walker & the All Stars were No. 45 with "Shotgun," and Martha & the Vandellas were No. 90 with "Nowhere To Run." But the highest-ranked Motown song of 1965 was "I Can't Help Myself (Sugar Pie, Honey Bunch)" by the Four Tops. The No. 3 song of the year was written by Brian Holland, Lamont Dozier, and Eddie Holland. It was the first chart-topper for the Tops, who first sang together at a party in 1954. That led to the formation of a group called the Four Aims and a deal with Chess Records in 1956. But their name sounded too much like the Ames Brothers. Their musical conductor asked how they had chosen their name, and Duke Fakir of the group replied they had been "aiming for the top." Their conductor suggested the Four Tops. They had brief tenures with the Red Top and Columbia labels before signing with a lesser-known Motown subsidiary called Workshop. After recording a jazz album, *Breaking Through,* they were assigned to Holland-Dozier-Holland and really broke through with "Baby I Need Your Loving," the No. 66 song of 1964. While recording "I Can't Help Myself," lead singer Levi Stubbs wasn't happy with his vocals and asked to do a third take. Brian Holland insisted it was perfect, but agreed to let Levi try again the next day. There never was another session. "I Can't Help Myself" was released the way Stubbs sang it on take number two.

The No. 1 song of 1965 was of British origin for the second consecutive year. The Rolling Stones' first No. 1 single, "(I Can't Get No) Satisfaction," was the highest-ranked record of the year. The song's origin can be traced to Clearwater, Florida. Keith Richards was having trouble sleeping in a hotel room one night and thought up a chord progression. When he played it back the next morning for Mick Jagger, Keith had some words to go with the riff that was admittedly inspired by Martha & the Vandellas' No. 27 hit from 1964, "Dancing In The Street." Richards considered the lyric "I can't get no satisfaction" to be a working title, not believing it was commercial enough.

The runner-up song of the year was "You've Lost That Lovin' Feelin'" by the Righteous Brothers. Producer Phil Spector asked the husband-and-wife songwriting team of Barry Mann and Cynthia Weil to fly from New York to California to collaborate with him on the duo's debut song for Philles Records. Barry and Cynthia checked into the legendary Chateau Marmont hotel on the Sunset Strip and rented a piano. Their favorite song at the time was the Four Tops' "Baby I Need Your Loving," and that inspired them to come up with "You've Lost That Lovin' Feelin'," although they considered that to be a dummy title. Spector liked the original words enough to keep them.

34 **COUNT ME IN**
Gary Lewis & the Playboys *Liberty*

35 **LOVE POTION NUMBER NINE**
The Searchers *Kapp*

36 **YOU WERE ON MY MIND**
We Five *A&M*

37 **THE BIRDS AND THE BEES**
Jewel Akens *Era*

38 **WHAT'S NEW, PUSSYCAT?**
Tom Jones *Parrot*

39 **CRYING IN THE CHAPEL**
Elvis Presley *RCA*

40 **SAVE YOUR HEART FOR ME**
Gary Lewis & the Playboys *Liberty*

41 **THE NAME GAME**
Shirley Ellis *Congress*

42 **CALIFORNIA GIRLS**
The Beach Boys *Capitol*

43 **I KNOW A PLACE**
Petula Clark *Warner Bros.*

44 **KING OF THE ROAD**
Roger Miller *Smash*

45 **SHOTGUN**
Jr. Walker & the All Stars *Soul*

46 **UNCHAINED MELODY**
Righteous Brothers *Philles*

47 **CARA, MIA**
Jay & the Americans *UA*

48 **THE "IN" CROWD**
Ramsey Lewis Trio *Argo*

49 **A TASTE OF HONEY**
Herb Alpert & the Tijuana Brass *A&M*

50 **I'LL NEVER FIND ANOTHER YOU**
The Seekers *Capitol*

51 **KEEP ON DANCING**
The Gentrys *MGM*

52 **THE JOLLY GREEN GIANT**
The Kingsmen *Wand*

53 **THE JERK**
The Larks *Money*

54 **CATCH US IF YOU CAN**
Dave Clark Five *Epic*

55 **RESCUE ME**
Fontella Bass *Checker*

56 **WONDERFUL WORLD**
Herman's Hermits *MGM*

57 **YOU'RE THE ONE**
The Vogues *Co & Ce*

58 **EVERYBODY LOVES A CLOWN**
Gary Lewis & the Playboys *Liberty*

59 **SILHOUETTES**
Herman's Hermits *MGM*

60 **KEEP SEARCHIN'**
(WE'LL FOLLOW THE SUN)
Del Shannon *Amy*

61 **HOLD ME, THRILL ME, KISS ME**
Mel Carter *Imperial*

62 **SHA LA LA**
Manfred Mann *Ascot*

63 **YES, I'M READY**
Barbara Mason *Arctic*

64 **SEVENTH SON**
Johnny Rivers *Imperial*

65 **FERRY CROSS THE MERSEY**
Gerry & the Pacemakers *Laurie*

66 **WHAT THE WORLD NEEDS NOW IS LOVE**
Jackie DeShannon *Imperial*

67 **HOW SWEET IT IS TO BE LOVED BY YOU**
Marvin Gaye *Tamla*

Petula Clark was the lone solo female vocalist in the top 10. The first British female singer to have a No. 1 song in America during the rock era, she was well-known around the world but was considered a "newcomer" in the U.S. when "Downtown" was released. Living in Paris with husband Claud Wolff, Petula had been recording songs mostly in French, including *"Chariot,"* the original version of "I Will Follow Him." Tony Hatch of Pye Records in Britain told her it was time to record in English again, and she said she would—but only if she could find the right material. Hatch had written some new music and played one of his melodies while Petula went to the kitchen to make tea. She heard the music and came running back to tell Tony that if he could write suitable lyrics to match his title of "Downtown," she would record it. It became the No. 6 song of the year. The follow-up, "I Know A Place," was the No. 43 song of the year.

The Byrds made their chart debut in 1965 and landed two songs on the year-end top 100. A song adapted by Pete Seeger from the Book of Ecclesiastes, "Turn! Turn! Turn!" was No. 7 for the year and an electrified Bob Dylan song, "Mr. Tambourine Man," was No. 18. The Byrds recorded one single for Elektra as the Beefeaters, then were signed to Columbia Records.

Sam the Sham & the Pharaohs were No. 13 for the year with their first chart single, "Wooly Bully." Domingo Samudio played organ for Andy & the Night Riders until two members of the band quit, including Andy. When two new members joined, Samudio became the leader and renamed the band. His friends called him Sam, and the movie *The Ten Commandments* inspired the "Pharaohs." Given the opportunity to record, Sam used his cat's name, "Wooly Bully," to come up with a million-selling single.

The Dunhill label made its first appearance on a year-end chart in 1965, thanks to Barry McGuire's "Eve Of Destruction," No. 15 for the year. A former member of the New Christy Minstrels, McGuire had sung lead on their 1963 singles "Green, Green" and "Saturday Night."

A&M Records had its second year-end entry in 1965 with "You Were On My Mind" by the We Five, a group formed at Mount St. Antonio College in California. Mike Stewart, brother of John Stewart, was a member of the quintet and the song was originally written and recorded by Ian and Sylvia. The We Five version was the No. 36 song of the year and the first A&M single on a year-end chart since "The Lonely Bull" by the Tijuana Brass featuring Herb Alpert was the No. 50 song of 1962. The TJB were also back on the chart with "A Taste Of Honey," which came in at No. 49.

68 **AIN'T THAT PECULIAR**
Marvin Gaye *Tamla*
69 **GOLDFINGER**
Shirley Bassey *UA*
70 **JUST ONCE IN MY LIFE**
Righteous Brothers *Philles*
71 **ALL DAY AND ALL OF THE NIGHT**
The Kinks *Reprise*
72 **CAST YOUR FATE TO THE WIND**
Sounds Orchestral *Parkway*
73 **RED ROSES FOR A BLUE LADY**
Bert Kaempfert *Decca*
74 **PAPA'S GOT A BRAND NEW BAG (PART 1)**
James Brown *King*
75 **DOWN IN THE BOONDOCKS**
Billy Joe Royal *Columbia*
76 **IT'S NOT UNUSUAL**
Tom Jones *Parrot*
77 **DO YOU BELIEVE IN MAGIC**
The Lovin' Spoonful *Kama Sutra*
78 **I'LL BE DOGGONE**
Marvin Gaye *Tamla*
79 **HEART FULL OF SOUL**
The Yardbirds *Epic*
80 **BABY THE RAIN MUST FALL**
Glenn Yarbrough *RCA*
81 **IT'S THE SAME OLD SONG**
Four Tops *Motown*
82 **MAKE THE WORLD GO AWAY**
Eddy Arnold *RCA*
83 **FOR YOUR LOVE**
The Yardbirds *Epic*
84 **HOLD WHAT YOU'VE GOT**
Joe Tex *Dial*
85 **FEVER**
The McCoys *Bang*
86 **MY LOVE, FORGIVE ME**
Robert Goulet *Columbia*
87 **TIRED OF WAITING FOR YOU**
The Kinks *Reprise*
88 **YOU TURN ME ON (TURN ON SONG)**
Ian Whitcomb & Bluesville *Tower*
89 **SHAKE**
Sam Cooke *RCA*
90 **NOWHERE TO RUN**
Martha & the Vandellas *Gordy*
91 **TELL HER NO**
The Zombies *Parrot*
92 **BABY DON'T GO**
Sonny and Cher *Reprise*
93 **ENGLAND SWINGS**
Roger Miller *Smash*
94 **JUST A LITTLE**
Beau Brummels *Autumn*
95 **IT AIN'T ME BABE**
The Turtles *White Whale*
96 **I GO TO PIECES**
Peter and Gordon *Capitol*
97 **AMEN**
The Impressions *ABC-Paramount*
98 **HUSH, HUSH, SWEET CHARLOTTE**
Patti Page *Columbia*
99 **BABY, I'M YOURS**
Barbara Lewis *Atlantic*
100 **I WANT CANDY**
The Strangeloves *Bang*

The Top 100 Songs of 1966

The Monkees

1966 WAS THE year John Lennon said, "The Beatles are probably bigger than Jesus"; NBC premiered *The Monkees* and *Star Trek* in the same week; and Brian Wilson finally completed "Good Vibrations."

There were four singles on the year-end chart by the Sinatra family. Frank had last appeared on a year-end singles chart in 1957, when "All The Way" was the No. 67 song of the year. One year earlier "Hey! Jealous Lover" ranked No. 43. In 1966, Frank was No. 27 with "Strangers In The Night" and No. 57 with "That's Life." Jimmy Bowen, Sinatra's producer and A&R staffer for Reprise, found "Strangers In The Night" when publisher Hal Fine brought him instrumental tracks written for the movie *A Man Could Get Killed* by German orchestra leader Bert Kaempfert ("Wonderland By Night"). Bowen promised Sinatra would record the song if English lyrics were written. Charlie Singleton and Eddie Snyder came up with the words, but by the time Sinatra received the lyrics, Bobby Darin and Jack Jones had cut the song. With three days' notice that Jones' single was about to be released, Bowen asked Ernie Freeman to come up with an arrangement for Sinatra. Three days later a full orchestra was in place and Sinatra arrived at 8 P.M. to record the song. He was finished by 9, and 24 hours later Sinatra's version of "Strangers In The Night" was being played across the land.

The other Sinatra on the year-end chart was Frank's daughter Nancy. She came in 17 places ahead of her father, with "These Boots Are Made For Walkin'," the No. 10 song of the year. Nancy had been recording for Reprise since 1961, when her first single was "Cufflinks And A Tie Clip." By

1965, she knew her time at the label was growing short unless she could come up with a hit record. Producer Lee Hazlewood managed to get her into the lower rungs of the Hot 100 with "So Long Babe." With backing from her father, Nancy insisted on recording "These Boots Are Made For Walkin,'" even though Hazlewood had written it for a man to sing. After it went to No. 1, Nancy continued her association with Lee. A subsequent single, "Sugar Town," was the No. 61 song of 1966.

The Monkees were the first American act to have the top song of the year since Jimmy Gilmer & the Fireballs ruled with "Sugar Shack" in 1963. The TV foursome had the No. 1 song of 1966, "I'm A Believer," as well as the No. 14 song, "Last Train To Clarksville." The former was written by Neil Diamond and the latter by Tommy Boyce and Bobby Hart. The Monkees' TV series was created by producers Bert Schneider and Bob Rafelson, who sold NBC on the idea of crossing the zaniness of the Beatles in *A Hard Day's Night* with the Marx Brothers. The original idea was to build a series around the Lovin' Spoonful, but the producers opted to create their own band. They ran an advertisement in a Hollywood trade paper seeking "four insane boys" to play rock musicians in a new TV series. Michael Nesmith, Micky Dolenz, Peter Tork, and Davy Jones were cast as the Monkees. Don Kirshner was asked to find songs for the quartet to record on the new Colgems label, owned by the studio that produced the Monkees, Columbia Pictures. Hart got the idea for "Last Train To Clarksville" after he heard the Beatles' "Paperback Writer" and mistakenly thought the song was about a "last train." For a follow-up single, Kirshner turned to producer Jeff Barry and asked him to find a song that would sell more copies than "Last Train To Clarksville." Barry had been working with Diamond and thought his "I'm A Believer" would be big for the Monkees. It spent seven weeks in pole position, the longest-running No. 1 since "I Want To Hold Your Hand" in 1964.

The No. 2 song of 1966 was an unlikely hit, "The Ballad Of The Green Berets" by S/Sgt. Barry Sadler. The Green Berets were an elite army combat unit called the Special Forces when President John F. Kennedy created them in 1961. Sadler had spent four years in the Air Force when he enlisted in the Army's airborne school and trained as a combat medic. His service with the Green Berets in Vietnam was cut short when he was injured in a booby trap. While recuperating back in the U.S., a friend suggested he write a song about the Special Forces. Sadler submitted his work to music publisher Chet Gierlach, who showed it to his friend Robin Moore, author of the book *The Green Berets*. Moore thought the song had potential and offered to rewrite it with Sadler. Recorded on a small budget and released just to the military, it became so popular that Moore asked executives at RCA Records if they would be interested in releasing the song commercially. The label financed a new recording session with an orchestra and the new version became RCA's fastest-selling single to date.

The Beatles and the Rolling Stones had the top hits of 1964 and 1965, but the highest-ranked British act in 1966 was the New Vaudeville Band, with "Winchester Cathedral" at No. 3. Composer Geoff Stephens was the man behind the studio group. Working as a staff songwriter at a publishing company in London's Denmark Street, he stared at his calendar one day and was inspired by a picture of Winchester Cathedral. A fan of vaudeville

35 DEVIL WITH A BLUE DRESS ON
& GOOD GOLLY MISS MOLLY
Mitch Ryder & the Detroit Wheels *New Voice*

36 RED RUBBER BALL
The Cyrkle *Columbia*

37 SUNNY
Bobby Hebb *Philips*

38 A GROOVY KIND OF LOVE
The Mindbenders *Fontana*

39 SEE YOU IN SEPTEMBER
The Happenings *B.T. Puppy*

40 BANG BANG (MY BABY SHOT ME DOWN)
Cher *Imperial*

41 BARBARA ANN
The Beach Boys *Capitol*

42 YELLOW SUBMARINE
The Beatles *Capitol*

43 RAINY DAY WOMEN #12 & 35
Bob Dylan *Columbia*

44 I AM A ROCK
Simon and Garfunkel *Columbia*

45 UPTIGHT (EVERYTHING'S ALRIGHT)
Stevie Wonder *Tamla*

46 CALIFORNIA DREAMIN'
The Mamas and the Papas *Dunhill*

47 NO MATTER WHAT SHAPE
(YOUR STOMACH'S IN)
The T-Bones *Liberty*

48 SECRET AGENT MAN
Johnny Rivers *Imperial*

49 FIVE O'CLOCK WORLD
The Vogues *Co & Ce*

50 NOWHERE MAN
The Beatles *Capitol*

51 WHAT BECOMES OF THE
BROKENHEARTED
Jimmy Ruffin *Soul*

52 KICKS
Paul Revere & the Raiders *Columbia*

53 SLOOP JOHN B
The Beach Boys *Capitol*

54 THE PIED PIPER
Crispian St. Peters *Jamie*

55 BORN FREE
Roger Williams *Kapp*

56 YOU DON'T HAVE TO SAY YOU LOVE ME
Dusty Springfield *Philips*

57 THAT'S LIFE
Frank Sinatra *Reprise*

58 LISTEN PEOPLE
Herman's Hermits *MGM*

59 BEAUTY IS ONLY SKIN DEEP
The Temptations *Gordy*

60 BLACK IS BLACK
Los Bravos *Press*

61 SUGAR TOWN
Nancy Sinatra *Reprise*

62 BORN A WOMAN
Sandy Posey *MGM*

63 TIME WON'T LET ME
The Outsiders *Capitol*

64 WALK AWAY RENEE
The Left Banke *Smash*

65 I'M SO LONESOME I COULD CRY
B.J. Thomas & the Triumphs *Scepter*

66 HOORAY FOR HAZEL
Tommy Roe *ABC*

67 LADY GODIVA
Peter and Gordon *Capitol*

music, he recorded the song himself with session musicians and imitated the vocal style of Rudy Vallee, singing through a megaphone. When the song was so popular that he had to tour, Stephens put together a New Vaudeville Band to play live performances.

While they didn't lead the way, the Beatles had the second biggest British hit of the year with "We Can Work It Out" at No. 4, thus becoming the only act aside from Bobby Vinton to make the year-end top 10 three years in a row. There were only two U.K. songs in the top 10, compared to four in 1964 and five in 1965.

The Righteous Brothers had a top 10 single of the year for the second year in a row. "You've Lost That Lovin' Feelin'" was the No. 2 song of 1965, but a year later producer Phil Spector had lost interest in the duo, and sold their contract to MGM for a million dollars. Looking for new material, Bill Medley and Bobby Hatfield turned to the co-writers of "Lovin' Feelin,'" Barry Mann and Cynthia Weill. They had written part of a song as a follow-up to "Lovin' Feelin,'" but stopped because they felt they were copying themselves. When Medley asked them to complete the song, Mann and Weil finished "(You're My) Soul And Inspiration" as a favor to the Righteous Brothers. Medley produced the No. 5 song of the year and Weill says, "He made this terrific record, but it will always be 'Lovin' Feelin'" sideways to me."

The No. 6 song of 1966 was first written as a poem called "Too Many Teardrops" by Rudy Martinez. Born in Mexico and raised in Michigan's Saginaw Valley, he set the tune to music with his band, XYZ. As ? (Question Mark) & the Mysterians, they recorded "96 Tears" and "Midnight Hour" in the living room of their manager, Lilly Gonzalez. She formed a label, Pa-Go-Go, and released the two songs. The band thought "Midnight Hour" would be the hit, but Martinez avidly pushed for "96 Tears."

The Beach Boys equaled their previous year-end high mark with "Good Vibrations," the No. 9 song of 1966. Two years earlier, "I Get Around" had been the No. 9 song of the year.

Motown was out of the top 10 for the first time since 1962, although the Supremes and the Four Tops registered in the top 15, with "You Can't Hurry Love" (No. 12) and "Reach Out I'll Be There" (No. 15), respectively. Another Motown song in the top 100 of 1966 was a cover version. Mitch Ryder & the Detroit Wheels combined Motown artist Shorty Long's "Devil With The Blue Dress" and Little Richard's "Good Golly Miss Molly" in a medley that was the No. 35 song of the year. Jimmy Ruffin, who passed on a chance to join the Temptations in favor of his brother David, gave Motown another year-end entry with "What Becomes Of The Brokenhearted" at No. 51.

68 JUST LIKE ME
Paul Revere & the Raiders Columbia

69 HOMEWARD BOUND
Simon and Garfunkel Columbia

70 I'M YOUR PUPPET
James and Bobby Purify Bell

71 ELUSIVE BUTTERFLY
Bob Lind World Pacific

72 BUS STOP
The Hollies Imperial

73 FLOWERS ON THE WALL
Statler Brothers Columbia

74 COOL JERK
The Capitols Karen

75 IF I WERE A CARPENTER
Bobby Darin Atlantic

76 MY WORLD IS EMPTY WITHOUT YOU
The Supremes Motown

77 SWEET PEA
Tommy Roe ABC-Paramount

78 CRYING TIME
Ray Charles ABC-Paramount

79 LAND OF 1000 DANCES
Wilson Pickett Atlantic

80 OH HOW HAPPY
Shades of Blue Impact

81 AIN'T TOO PROUD TO BEG
The Temptations Gordy

82 YOU DIDN'T HAVE TO BE SO NICE
The Lovin' Spoonful Kama Sutra

83 THE DUCK
Jackie Lee Mirwood

84 WOMAN
Peter and Gordon Capitol

85 EBB TIDE
Righteous Brothers Philles

86 THIS OLD HEART OF MINE
(IS WEAK FOR YOU)
Isley Brothers Tamla

87 DANDY
Herman's Hermits MGM

88 I SAW HER AGAIN
The Mamas and the Papas Dunhill

89 BAREFOOTIN'
Robert Parker Nola

90 PSYCHOTIC REACTION
Count Five Double Shot

91 CHERRY, CHERRY
Neil Diamond Bang

92 HUNGRY
Paul Revere & the Raiders Columbia

93 DAY TRIPPER
The Beatles Capitol

94 A MUST TO AVOID
Herman's Hermits MGM

95 DON'T MESS WITH BILL
The Marvelettes Tamla

96 GLORIA
Shadows of Knight Dunwich

97 WOULDN'T IT BE NICE
The Beach Boys Capitol

98 WORKING IN THE COAL MINE
Lee Dorsey Amy

99 SOMEWHERE, MY LOVE
Ray Conniff & the Singers Columbia

100 GREEN GRASS
Gary Lewis & the Playboys Liberty

The Top 100 Songs of 1967

Sam and Dave

1967 WAS THE year the Beatles released *Sgt. Pepper's Lonely Hearts Club Band;* Cindy Birdsong took Florence Ballard's place in the Supremes; and the Monterey Pop Festival kicked off the Summer of Love.

The focal point for the Summer of Love was San Francisco, the city that spawned the Jefferson Airplane. With lead vocals by Grace Slick, the Airplane landed two hits in the year-end top 100, "Somebody To Love" at No. 85 and "White Rabbit" at No. 90. The city itself was canonized in Scott McKenzie's "San Francisco (Be Sure To Wear Flowers In Your Hair)," the No. 37 song of the year.

There were three different female singers in the top 10, the most since 1963. Two of them were American. Bobbie Gentry, born in Chickasaw County, Mississippi, grew up in the Delta. She was born Roberta Lee Streeter, but changed her name when she was 14 after seeing the movie *Ruby Gentry* with Jennifer Jones. While seeking a publishing deal for her songs, she was signed to Capitol as both songwriter and artist, much to her surprise. Her original recording of "Ode To Billie Joe" ran longer than seven minutes. Capitol edited it down and released it as the "B" side of "Mississippi Delta," but disc jockeys preferred "Ode To Billie Joe," which spent four weeks at No. 1 and became the No. 3 song of the year.

Nancy Sinatra, born in Jersey City, New Jersey, had the No. 10 song of 1966 with "These Boots Are Made For Walkin'." She did even better in

1967, coming in at No. 7 for the year with her father Frank on their duet, "Somethin' Stupid." The song was a remake of a duet between composer C. Carson Parks and his wife, Gaile Foote. They had recorded their own album for Kapp Records and included a couple of Parks' songs to assure them of song royalties. "Cab Driver" was covered by the Mills Brothers and "Somethin' Stupid" was heard by Sinatra associate Sarge Weiss, who suggested Frank record it with Nancy.

The non-American female vocalist in the top 10 was Lulu, born in Glasgow, Scotland. She and Davy Jones of the Monkees, and the Beatles, were the only non-Americans in the top 10. She was born Marie McDonald McLaughlin Lawrie, but manager Marian Massey renamed her because she was a "lulu of a kid." Marian's sister Felice worked for a film agent, and when she read the script for *To Sir With Love* suggested to Marian that Lulu try out for a role. Director James Clavell agreed to attend a Beach Boys concert in London that featured Lulu as a supporting act, and liked her enough to cast her in the film. She was signed to perform the title song, but didn't care for any of the tunes the producers had found. She asked her friend Mark London to write some music, and the next day lyricist Don Black penned the words. Although the song never made the British chart, it was No. 1 in the States for five weeks, good enough to make it the highest-ranking song of the year. That made Lulu the first artist on the Epic label aside from Bobby Vinton to have a year-end top 10 hit, and "To Sir With Love" became the label's biggest hit to date.

The No. 4 song of the year was produced by Dan Penn for $800 at the American Recording Studios in Memphis. Larry Uttal of Bell Records liked the song enough to advance Penn the $800 and released "The Letter" by the Box Tops on the Mala subsidiary. Wayne Carson Thompson, who wrote the song, played guitar on the session and recalls the group didn't have a name yet. Someone suggested they have a contest to find a name, and invite people to send in 50 cents and a box top. Thompson and Penn looked at each other and knew they had found a new moniker for the band. Thompson didn't like the arrangement or 16-year-old Alex Chilton's lead vocals at first, and was bewildered when Penn added in the sound effect of a jet. Only one minute and 58 seconds in duration, "The Letter" shot up the Hot 100 and spent four weeks at No. 1.

The No. 9 song of 1967 was by a Los Angeles quartet formed by two graduates of the film school at UCLA. Jim Morrison and Ray Manzarek started the band and recruited John Densmore and Robbie Krieger during a meditation class. Morrison was inspired to name the band after Aldous Huxley's *The Doors Of Perception,* as well as a passage written by William Blake: "There are things that are known and things that are unknown, in between the doors." The group's first single, "Break On Through (To The Other Side)," did not chart. Elektra Records was reluctant to release "Light My Fire" as a single because of its six-minute, 50-second length. The Doors wanted the complete song released, but agreed to have the label edit it down. Unhappy with the result, the group asked producer Paul Rothchild to make a new edit by deleting a chunk of the instrumental break to bring it down to a time suitable for radio airplay. Ironically, most stations preferred the album-length version and played the full track.

35 **PLEASANT VALLEY SUNDAY**
The Monkees *Colgems*

36 **RELEASE ME (AND LET ME LOVE AGAIN)**
Engelbert Humperdinck *Parrot*

37 **SAN FRANCISCO (BE SURE TO WEAR FLOWERS IN YOUR HAIR)**
Scott McKenzie *Ode*

38 **IT MUST BE HIM**
Vikki Carr *Liberty*

39 **I THINK WE'RE ALONE NOW**
Tommy James & the Shondells *Roulette*

40 **EXPRESSWAY TO YOUR HEART**
Soul Survivors *Crimson*

41 **GOOD THING**
Paul Revere & the Raiders *Columbia*

42 **THIS IS MY SONG**
Petula Clark *Warner Bros.*

43 **THERE'S A KIND OF HUSH**
Herman's Hermits *MGM*

44 **I SAY A LITTLE PRAYER**
Dionne Warwick *Scepter*

45 **SHE'D RATHER BE WITH ME**
The Turtles *White Whale*

46 **APPLES, PEACHES, PUMPKIN PIE**
Jay & the Techniques *Smash*

47 **BOOGALOO DOWN BROADWAY**
The Fantastic Johnny C *Phil-L.A. of Soul*

48 **GEORGY GIRL**
The Seekers *Capitol*

49 **BERNADETTE**
Four Tops *Motown*

50 **HOW CAN I BE SURE**
The Young Rascals *Atlantic*

51 **A WHITER SHADE OF PALE**
Procol Harum *Deram*

52 **PLEASE LOVE ME FOREVER**
Bobby Vinton *Epic*

53 **COME ON DOWN TO MY BOAT**
Every Mother's Son *MGM*

54 **BABY I LOVE YOU**
Aretha Franklin *Atlantic*

55 **FOR WHAT IT'S WORTH (STOP, HEY WHAT'S THAT SOUND)**
Buffalo Springfield *Atco*

56 **UP-UP AND AWAY**
5th Dimension *Soul City*

57 **THEN YOU CAN TELL ME GOODBYE**
The Casinos *Fraternity*

58 **(YOUR LOVE KEEPS LIFTING ME) HIGHER AND HIGHER**
Jackie Wilson *Brunswick*

59 **SOCK IT TO ME-BABY!**
Mitch Ryder & the Detroit Wheels *New Voice*

60 **DON'T YOU CARE**
The Buckinghams *Columbia*

61 **GIMME LITTLE SIGN**
Brenton Wood *Double Shot*

62 **JIMMY MACK**
Martha & the Vandellas *Gordy*

63 **BROWN EYED GIRL**
Van Morrison *Bang*

64 **YOUR PRECIOUS LOVE**
Marvin Gaye & Tammi Terrell *Tamla*

65 **(WE AIN'T GOT) NOTHIN' YET**
Blues Magoos *Mercury*

66 **WORDS OF LOVE**
The Mamas and the Papas *Dunhill*

67 **STANDING IN THE SHADOWS OF LOVE**
Four Tops *Motown*

Another Los Angeles-based group, the Association, was No. 8 for the year with "Windy." Their previous chart-topper, "Cherish," had been the No. 7 song of 1966. Songwriter Ruthann Friedman had submitted a demo tape of 22 songs to producer Bones Howe. His favorite was "Windy," but it was written as a waltz. A new arrangement with four beats to the bar gave the group their second chart-topping single. "Windy" was recorded in a marathon session that began in the afternoon and ended at 6:30 the next morning. Lead vocalists Larry Ramos and Russ Giguere were so burned out by the end of the session, they needed support from everyone present to record the multi-layered vocal chorus finale. Friedman joined in and can be heard singing counter harmony in the fade.

The Monkees had their second top 10 song of the year with "Daydream Believer." Their recording of "I'm A Believer" had been the No. 1 song of 1966. The Turtles, yet another L.A. group in the top 10, were No. 6 for the year with "Happy Together." That was a vast improvement over their ranking in 1965, when they were No. 94 for the year with "It Ain't Me Babe."

The Beatles were in the top 10 for the fourth consecutive year, matching the record set by Bobby Vinton. The Mop Tops' highest-ranking song of 1967 was "Hello Goodbye" at No. 10. "All You Need Is Love" was No. 12 for the year, "Penny Lane" was No. 30, and "Strawberry Fields Forever" was No. 94.

Gladys Knight, born in Atlanta, Georgia, had her first year-end hit since "Every Beat Of My Heart," the No. 63 song of 1961. Her recording of "I Heard It Through The Grapevine" with the Pips was the first version of the song to be released, but not the first recorded. Smokey Robinson & the Miracles, the Isley Brothers, and Marvin Gaye had all cut the Norman Whitfield–Barrett Strong song before Gladys & the Pips, but theirs was the first released. It peaked at No. 2 and ranked No. 16 for the year, making it the biggest Motown release of 1967.

68 **MERCY, MERCY, MERCY**
The Buckinghams *Columbia*
69 **YOU'RE MY EVERYTHING**
The Temptations *Gordy*
70 **98.6**
Keith *Mercury*
71 **YOU BETTER SIT DOWN KIDS**
Cher *Imperial*
72 **MY CUP RUNNETH OVER**
Ed Ames *RCA*
73 **SKINNY LEGS AND ALL**
Joe Tex *Dial*
74 **I NEVER LOVED A MAN (THE WAY I LOVE YOU)**
Aretha Franklin *Atlantic*
75 **I CAN SEE FOR MILES**
The Who *Decca*
76 **ON A CAROUSEL**
The Hollies *Imperial*
77 **FUNKY BROADWAY**
Wilson Pickett *Atlantic*
78 **SILENCE IS GOLDEN**
The Tremeloes *Epic*
79 **CARRIE-ANNE**
The Hollies *Epic*
80 **GET ON UP**
The Esquires *Bunky*
81 **LET IT OUT (LET IT ALL HANG OUT)**
The Hombres *Verve Forecast*
82 **LITTLE OLE MAN (UPTIGHT-EVERYTHING'S ALRIGHT)**
Bill Cosby *Warner Bros.*
83 **FRIDAY ON MY MIND**
The Easybeats *UA*
84 **WESTERN UNION**
The Five Americans *Abnak*
85 **SOMEBODY TO LOVE**
Jefferson Airplane *RCA*
86 **DON'T SLEEP IN THE SUBWAY**
Petula Clark *Warner Bros.*
87 **GIMME SOME LOVIN'**
Spencer Davis Group *UA*
88 **COLD SWEAT (PART 1)**
James Brown *King*
89 **LET'S LIVE FOR TODAY**
The Grass Roots *Dunhill*
90 **WHITE RABBIT**
Jefferson Airplane *RCA*
91 **CLOSE YOUR EYES**
Peaches and Herb *Date*
92 **HONEY CHILE**
Martha Reeves & the Vandellas *Gordy*
93 **ALL I NEED**
The Temptations *Gordy*
94 **STRAWBERRY FIELDS FOREVER**
The Beatles *Capitol*
95 **MIRAGE**
Tommy James & the Shondells *Roulette*
96 **STAND BY ME**
Spyder Turner *MGM*
97 **NASHVILLE CATS**
The Lovin' Spoonful *Kama Sutra*
98 **I HAD TOO MUCH TO DREAM (LAST NIGHT)**
The Electric Prunes *Reprise*
99 **HERE COMES MY BABY**
The Tremeloes *Epic*
100 **THE 59TH STREET BRIDGE SONG (FEELIN' GROOVY)**
Harpers Bizarre *Warner Bros.*

The Top 100 Songs of 1968

The Doors

1968 WAS THE year Elvis Presley revived his career with a one-hour special on NBC; the Beatles launched their Apple label; and Peter Tork quit the Monkees, leaving them a trio.

Paul Mauriat's "Love Is Blue," the No. 3 song of the year, was the first year-end top 10 instrumental since "Stranger On The Shore" by Mr. Acker Bilk, which was the No. 7 title of 1962, and the highest-ranked instrumental hit since "Theme From *A Summer Place*" by Percy Faith topped the recap for 1960.

"I Heard It Through The Grapevine," the No. 17 song of 1967 when it was recorded by Gladys Knight & the Pips, performed even better in 1968, thanks to a version by Marvin Gaye. The Motown artist recorded his version of the Norman Whitfield–Barrett Strong song before Gladys did. The first recording, by Smokey Robinson and the Miracles, remained unreleased as a single. Marvin didn't want to release his version after Gladys had such a big hit with the song, but finally agreed. "I never thought a great deal about the song after recording it," he said in Sharon Davis' *Motown: The History.* "In fact, I wasn't too optimistic about it at all. I had no idea it would sell nearly four million records."

The other Motown song in the top 10 was "Love Child" by Diana Ross & the Supremes, ranked No. 5 for the year. It was the fifth song by the

Detroit trio to make a year-end top 10, following "Where Did Our Love Go," "Baby Love," and "Come See About Me" in 1964, and "Stop! In The Name Of Love" in 1965.

Memphis soul was also represented on the year-end chart. The Stax/Volt label had its biggest hit to date with Otis Redding's "(Sittin' On) The Dock Of The Bay" at No. 7, topping the No. 20 placing of Sam and Dave's Stax single "Soul Man" the year before. "Dock Of The Bay" was the first posthumous No. 1 hit of the rock era. Redding wrote the song (with Steve Cropper) in the summer of 1967 while staying on a houseboat anchored off of Sausalito, California, after performing at the Monterey Pop Festival. He recorded the song in Memphis on December 6 and 7. The following day, he flew to Nashville for a concert. Redding continued on to Cleveland for a TV appearance and another concert. On Sunday, December 10, he was on his way to Madison, Wisconsin, when his private twin-engine Beechcraft plane crashed into Lake Monoma. The 26-year-old singer was killed along with his pilot, valet, and four members of the Bar-Kays.

Although "(Sittin' On) The Dock Of The Bay" would become a No. 1 hit, it had its detractors. Stax founder Jim Stewart wasn't impressed with the recording. "To me, 'Dock Of The Bay,' when I first heard it, was not nearly as strong as 'I've Been Loving You Too Long.' Of course, it was a different kind of record for Otis." Redding's manager, Phil Walden, con-curred. "It was a drastic change. Listening to it in retrospect now, it isn't that much (of a change), but for those times, it sounded like it might have been a little too pop."

Cropper, who also produced the recording, told Edna Gundersen of *USA Today* that Jerry Wexler at Atlantic Records (the distributor for Stax) wanted the track remixed before being released. "Wexler thought the vocal wasn't big enough and that the ocean waves and gulls were too loud. It was hard enough to deal with Otis dying, and it was killing me to change the song. I listened to it one more time, put it in a different box, and sent it back. With all due respect, Atlantic never realized it was the same mix."

Bobby Goldsboro, who had the No. 95 song of 1964 with "See The Funny Little Clown," had his only other year-end hit in 1968 with "Honey," ranked No. 6. The song was written by Bobby Russell, who also penned "Little Green Apples" by O.C. Smith (the No. 19 song of 1968), "The Joker Went Wild" by Brian Hyland, and "The Night The Lights Went Out In Georgia" by Russell's then-wife, Vicki Lawrence. "Honey" was originally recorded by Bob Shane, one of the founding members of the Kingston Trio. After Goldsboro heard the original version, he and producer Bob Montgomery asked Russell if they could also record it. Russell agreed as long as they wouldn't release it as a single to compete with Shane's ver-sion. They agreed to wait four weeks. While Shane's version sold around 100,000 copies, Goldsboro's single sold over five million.

A year after they had the No. 2 song of 1967 with "Groovin'," the Rascals had another top five year-end hit with "People Got To Be Free," No. 4 for 1968. Felix Cavaliere found it difficult to cope with the assassina-tions of Martin Luther King, Jr. and Sen. Robert F. Kennedy in the spring of 1968 and expressed his feelings by writing "People Got To Be Free" with Eddie Brigati. Cavaliere says that Jerry Wexler at Atlantic was reluctant to

35 **MACARTHUR PARK**
Richard Harris *Dunhill*
36 **A BEAUTIFUL MORNING**
The Rascals *Atlantic*
37 **SIMON SAYS**
1910 Fruitgum Co. *Buddah*
38 **I WISH IT WOULD RAIN**
The Temptations *Gordy*
39 **ABRAHAM, MARTIN AND JOHN**
Dion *Laurie*
40 **YUMMY YUMMY YUMMY**
Ohio Express *Buddah*
41 **MONY MONY**
Tommy James & the Shondells *Roulette*
42 **WHO'S MAKING LOVE**
Johnnie Taylor *Stax*
43 **LADY MADONNA**
The Beatles *Capitol*
44 **BEND ME, SHAPE ME**
American Breed *Acta*
45 **MIDNIGHT CONFESSIONS**
The Grass Roots *Dunhill*
46 **VALLERI**
The Monkees *Colgems*
47 **LA-LA—MEANS I LOVE YOU**
The Delfonics *Philly Groove*
48 **THE LOOK OF LOVE**
Sergio Mendes & Brasil '66 *A&M*
49 **COWBOYS TO GIRLS**
The Intruders *Gamble*
50 **THE BALLAD OF BONNIE AND CLYDE**
Georgie Fame *Epic*
51 **I LOVE HOW YOU LOVE ME**
Bobby Vinton *Epic*
52 **I'VE GOTTA GET A MESSAGE TO YOU**
Bee Gees *Atco*
53 **ANGEL OF THE MORNING**
Merrilee Rush & the Turnabouts *Bell*
54 **(SWEET SWEET BABY)**
SINCE YOU'VE BEEN GONE
Aretha Franklin *Atlantic*
55 **SLIP AWAY**
Clarence Carter *Atlantic*
56 **GIRL WATCHER**
O'Kaysions *ABC*
57 **HUSH**
Deep Purple *Tetragrammaton*
58 **HOLD ME TIGHT**
Johnny Nash *JAD*
59 **STORMY**
Classics IV f/Dennis Yost *Imperial*
60 **DIFFERENT DRUM**
Stone Poneys f/Linda Ronstadt *Capitol*
61 **SUNSHINE OF YOUR LOVE**
Cream *Atco*
62 **DANCE TO THE MUSIC**
Sly & The Family Stone *Epic*
63 **TURN AROUND, LOOK AT ME**
The Vogues *Reprise*
64 **OVER YOU**
Gary Puckett & the Union Gap *Columbia*
65 **REACH OUT OF THE DARKNESS**
Friend and Lover *Verve Forecast*
66 **REVOLUTION**
The Beatles *Apple*
67 **BOTTLE OF WINE**
The Fireballs *Atco*
68 **LOVE IS ALL AROUND**
The Troggs *Fontana*

release a political song, as he thought it could hurt the career of the Rascals. Cavaliere believed the song was important and needed to be heard. It was No. 1 for five weeks. Another protest song that was also inspired by assassinations was "Abraham, Martin and John," written by Dick Holler. Dion's recording of the song, No. 39 for the year, gave the Bronx singer his first year-end hit since 1963.

The A&M imprint had its first year-end top 10 single with a vocal recording by one of the label's founders. "This Guy's In Love With You" was written by Burt Bacharach and Hal David and was one of 50 songs submitted to Herb Alpert for use on a CBS-TV special. Alpert sang the song to his (first) wife, Sharon, on the beach at Malibu. When CBS received thousands of calls from viewers asking where they could buy the song, A&M released it as a single the following day. Ranked No. 8 for the year, the song beat A&M's previous best, "You Were On My Mind" by the We Five, the No. 36 song of 1965.

John Fred and His Playboy Band were ranked No. 10 for the year with a song inspired in part by an album released the year before, *Sgt. Pepper's Lonely Hearts Club Band.* When John Fred Gourrier first played that LP, he thought the Beatles were singing about "Lucy in disguise with diamonds." After seeing hundreds of girls wearing sunglasses on the beach in Florida, he came up with lyrics for a song called "Beverly In Disguise (With Glasses)." With writing partner Andrew Bernard, John Fred received another dose of inspiration from a TV commercial for Playtex living bras and finally came up with "Judy In Disguise (With Glasses)."

The original source of John Fred's inspiration, the Beatles, had the No. 1 song of 1968 with "Hey Jude." It was the first time in the rock era that any artist had the number one single of the year for a second time ("I Want To Hold Your Hand" was the top-ranked single of 1964). "Hey Jude" was the first single released on the Beatles' new Apple label. Apple was also represented on the year-end chart with "Those Were The Days" by Mary Hopkin, a music and drama student from Pontardawe, Wales, and with the Beatles' "Revolution."

Gary Puckett & the Union Gap, a group that formed in San Diego, California, had a sensational year in 1968, placing their first four singles on the year-end chart. Their second single, "Young Girl," was the most successful, ranking No. 13. The other three were "Lady Willpower" (No. 29), "Woman, Woman" (No. 33), and "Over You" (No. 64).

The Top 100 Songs of 1969

The Rolling Stones

1969 WAS THE year half a million people attended a three-day festival at Woodstock; Jim Morrison was arrested for indecent exposure at a concert in Miami; and Paul McCartney and John Lennon marched to the altar with Linda Eastman and Yoko Ono—respectively.

One of the bands appearing at Woodstock was Creedence Clearwater Revival. John Fogerty, Stu Cook, and Doug Clifford first played together as the Blue Velvets, a trio formed at El Cerrito Junior High in Northern California in 1959. John's brother Tom joined the group later. Their first recording deal was with the San Francisco Orchestra label in 1961. They were signed to Fantasy Records as the Golliwogs, and a cover version of Van Morrison's "Brown Eyed Girl" sold modestly.

In December 1967, the group became Creedence Clearwater Revival. They had the No. 96 song of 1968 with their first chart single, "Suzie Q. (Part One)." They fared a little better in 1969 –placing four hits on the year-end chart. "Proud Mary" ranked highest at No. 24, followed by "Bad Moon Rising" (No. 26), "Green River" (No. 29), and "Down On The Corner" / "Fortunate Son" (No. 36). "Proud Mary," "Bad Moon Rising," and "Green River" had all peaked at No. 2 on the Hot 100 and "Down On The Corner" peaked at number three. That was as close as they ever came to having a No. 1 single.

The Beatles and the Rolling Stones both had songs in the top 10; it was the first time since 1965 that Britain's two leading exports both registered in the year-end top 10. But the Beatles and the Stones were bested by a band that didn't even exist. The Archies, featuring lead vocals by Ron

Dante, had the No. 2 song of the year with "Sugar, Sugar." The "Archie" comic strip had been created in 1942 by John L. Goldwater, and in 1968 Filmation Studios produced a Saturday morning cartoon show based on the feature. Don Kirshner, hired to supervise the music for the series, asked Jeff Barry to write and produce records for the Archies. Dante, who had been the lead voice of the Laundromats in 1964 for their parody of the Shangri-Las' "Leader Of The Pack" called "Leader Of The Laundromat," multi-tracked his voice and was joined by singer Toni Wine. While "Sugar, Sugar" was in the top five, Dante had another top five single with "Tracy" by the Cuff Links, the No. 84 song of the year.

The No. 1 single of 1969 was a medley of two songs from the Broadway production of *Hair*. The 5th Dimension discovered the songs while appearing at the Americana Hotel in New York City. Billy Davis, Jr. went shopping one afternoon and inadvertently left his wallet in a cab. The next passenger, one of the producers of *Hair,* found it and called him to return it. Billy was grateful and invited him to see their show at the Americana. In return, the producer invited the group to see *Hair.* They were all so taken with Ronnie Dyson's performance of the opening number, "Aquarius," that they wanted to record it. Producer Bones Howe felt it was only half a song and needed something more. When he saw *Hair* in New York, he loved the show's finale, "The Flesh Failures (Let The Sunshine In)." Howe suggested they take the opening and closing numbers and "put them together like two trains."

"Aquarius/Let The Sunshine In" was the second song originally written for the stage to be the No. 1 song of the year. The first was Bobby Darin's 1959 recording of "Mack The Knife" from *The Threepenny Opera.* Three other songs from *Hair* were also listed in the year-end top 100. Oliver had the No. 35 hit with "Good Morning Starshine," Three Dog Night was No. 44 with "Easy To Be Hard," and the Cowsills came in at No. 19 with the title song, "Hair." Bill Cowsill, oldest brother of the Rhode Island family, says it was pure serendipity that the group recorded "Hair." They were signed as guest stars for a Carl Reiner television special. "Carl had this bent idea that it would be really cool to take the squeaky clean Cowsills with no make-up, let the zits show, chains, leather, hair and do the title track from the Broadway play," Bill explains. The four brothers went to a studio in Hollywood to record a track they would lip-synch to in the show. "Then we listened (to it). I looked at Bob—Bob looked at me—two thumbs up!" The Cowsills went to MGM and said they wanted to release "Hair" as a single. "They said, 'You're out of your mind, we're not releasing that! You'll blow your image!'" Bill recalls. While on tour in the Midwest, the Cowsills' father, Bud, convinced an MGM promo rep to take an acetate of the song to radio station WLS in Chicago. The program director agreed to play the song if he couldn't guess who was singing. He lost and the song was added to the playlist, and MGM was forced to release the single.

Psychedelic soul made its mark on the top 100 songs of the year thanks to Sly & the Family Stone. Former San Francisco DJ Sylvester Stewart had the No. 62 song of 1968 with "Dance To The Music." In 1969 he had his highest year-end ranking by placing "Everyday People" at No. 4.

35 **GOOD MORNING STARSHINE**
Oliver *Jubilee*

36 **DOWN ON THE CORNER / FORTUNATE SON**
Creedence Clearwater Revival *Fantasy*

37 **SOULFUL STRUT**
Young-Holt Unlimited *Brunswick*

38 **TRACES**
Classics IV f/Dennis Yost *Imperial*

39 **TIME OF THE SEASON**
The Zombies *Date*

40 **IN THE GHETTO**
Elvis Presley *RCA*

41 **SWEET CAROLINE (GOOD TIMES NEVER SEEMED SO GOOD)**
Neil Diamond *Uni*

42 **LITTLE WOMAN**
Bobby Sherman *Metromedia*

43 **WORST THAT COULD HAPPEN**
Brooklyn Bridge *Buddah*

44 **EASY TO BE HARD**
Three Dog Night *Dunhill*

45 **GRAZING IN THE GRASS**
Friends of Distinction *RCA*

46 **TOO BUSY THINKING ABOUT MY BABY**
Marvin Gaye *Tamla*

47 **MY CHERIE AMOUR**
Stevie Wonder *Tamla*

48 **WHAT DOES IT TAKE (TO WIN YOUR LOVE)**
Jr. Walker & the All Stars *Soul*

49 **ONE**
Three Dog Night *Dunhill*

50 **GET TOGETHER**
The Youngbloods *RCA*

51 **I'LL NEVER FALL IN LOVE AGAIN**
Tom Jones *Parrot*

52 **ELI'S COMING**
Three Dog Night *Dunhill*

53 **ONLY THE STRONG SURVIVE**
Jerry Butler *Mercury*

54 **BABY IT'S YOU**
Smith *Dunhill*

55 **HOOKED ON A FEELING**
B.J. Thomas *Scepter*

56 **SMILE A LITTLE SMILE FOR ME**
Flying Machine *Congress*

57 **HOLLY HOLY**
Neil Diamond *Uni*

58 **CAN I CHANGE MY MIND**
Tyrone Davis *Dakar*

59 **GALVESTON**
Glen Campbell *Capitol*

60 **OH HAPPY DAY**
The Edwin Hawkins Singers *Pavilion*

61 **BACKFIELD IN MOTION**
Mel and Tim *Bamboo*

62 **PUT A LITTLE LOVE IN YOUR HEART**
Jackie DeShannon *Imperial*

63 **BABY, I'M FOR REAL**
The Originals *Soul*

64 **THESE EYES**
The Guess Who *RCA*

65 **RUN AWAY CHILD, RUNNING WILD**
The Temptations *Gordy*

66 **ATLANTIS**
Donovan *Epic*

67 **INDIAN GIVER**
1910 Fruitgum Co. *Buddah*

Another facet of psychedelia was "Crimson And Clover," according to Tommy James, who wrote and produced the song that placed No. 7 for the year. "'Crimson' and 'clover' were two of my favorite words that I put together," James explains. "We had the title before we wrote the song." Tommy and the Shondells placed two songs in the top 20 of 1969, the first time they had made the year-end top 20. "Crystal Blue Persuasion" ranked No. 14 for 1969, a song that Tommy says is his favorite. "The title came right out of the Bible. 'Crystal Blue' meant truth. I said, 'What a title, I only wish it meant something.'"

The Temptations had their best year-end ranking to date with "I Can't Get Next To You" at No. 15. That beat their previous high, when they placed No. 19 for 1965 with "My Girl." Inspired by Sly & the Family Stone, the Temptations turned to psychedelic soul under the aegis of producer Norman Whitfield. Their first effort in that field, "Cloud Nine," was the No. 68 song of 1969. The follow-up, "Run Away Child, Running Wild" was three notches higher at No. 65.

Diana Ross released her final single as lead singer of the Supremes in 1969. "Someday We'll Be Together" was their 12th number one hit, and the first of their chart-topping singles to be a remake of an older song. The original version by songwriters Jackie Beavers and Johnny Bristol had been written and recorded in 1960. Diana's swan song with the Supremes was No. 11 for the year.

Tommy Roe's first No. 1 single, "Sheila," was the No. 23 song of 1962, and in 1963 he placed No. 32 for the year with "Everybody." He surpassed his previous record with "Dizzy," the No. 8 song of 1969. Elvis Presley returned to the top 25 portion of the year-end chart for the first time since 1962, when he was No. 10 with "Return To Sender." His career revitalized by an NBC-TV special in 1968, he scored his 17th and final number one single with "Suspicious Minds," the No. 25 song of 1969. His fellow Sun recording artist, Johnny Cash, had his first year-end placing since "Guess Things Happen That Way" in 1958. "A Boy Named Sue" was his most successful single of the rock era and ranked No. 17 for 1969.

Peter, Paul and Mary's "Leaving On A Jet Plane," No. 9 for the year, marked the folk trio's first appearance on a year-end chart since two of their songs finished in the top 40 of 1963. Ray Stevens' "Gitarzan," No. 78, was his first year-end hit since "Ahab The Arab" was No. 55 for 1962.

68 CLOUD NINE
The Temptations *Gordy*

69 THIS GIRL'S IN LOVE WITH YOU
Dionne Warwick *Scepter*

70 YESTER-ME, YESTER-YOU, YESTERDAY
Stevie Wonder *Tamla*

71 BABY, I LOVE YOU
Andy Kim *Steed*

72 LAY LADY LAY
Bob Dylan *Columbia*

73 BABY, BABY DON'T CRY
Smokey Robinson & the Miracles *Tamla*

74 GOING IN CIRCLES
Friends of Distinction *RCA*

75 THIS MAGIC MOMENT
Jay & the Americans *UA*

76 I'D WAIT A MILLION YEARS
The Grass Roots *Dunhill*

77 THE BOXER
Simon and Garfunkel *Columbia*

78 GITARZAN
Ray Stevens *Monument*

79 COLOR HIM FATHER
The Winstons *Metromedia*

80 MOTHER POPCORN (YOU GOT TO HAVE A MOTHER FOR ME) (PART 1)
James Brown *King*

81 TIME IS TIGHT
Booker T. & the MG's *Stax*

82 TWENTY-FIVE MILES
Edwin Starr *Gordy*

83 CINNAMON
Derek *Bang*

84 TRACY
The Cuff Links *Decca*

85 EVERYBODY'S TALKIN'
Nilsson *RCA*

86 I'VE GOTTA BE ME
Sammy Davis, Jr. *Reprise*

87 HURT SO BAD
The Lettermen *Capitol*

88 HAWAII FIVE-O
The Ventures *Liberty*

89 MORE TODAY THAN YESTERDAY
Spiral Starecase *Columbia*

90 THE CHOKIN' KIND
Joe Simon *Sound Stage 7*

91 THE BALLAD OF JOHN AND YOKO
The Beatles *Apple*

92 RUBY, DON'T TAKE YOUR LOVE TO TOWN
Kenny Rogers & the First Edition *Reprise*

93 GOING UP THE COUNTRY
Canned Heat *Liberty*

94 THIS GIRL IS A WOMAN NOW
Gary Puckett & the Union Gap *Columbia*

95 GAMES PEOPLE PLAY
Joe South *Capitol*

96 POLK SALAD ANNIE
Tony Joe White *Monument*

97 SON-OF-A PREACHER MAN
Dusty Springfield *Atlantic*

98 OH, WHAT A NIGHT
The Dells *Cadet*

99 MY WHOLE WORLD ENDED (THE MOMENT YOU LEFT ME)
David Ruffin *Motown*

100 THAT'S THE WAY LOVE IS
Marvin Gaye *Tamla*

The Top 100 Songs of 1970

The Carpenters

1970 WAS THE year the Beatles movie *Let It Be* premiered; Janis Joplin overdosed in Hollywood; and four students were killed at Kent State University, inspiring Neil Young to write "Ohio."

The Beatles had their final year-end top 10 entry as a group. The single of "Let It Be" ranked No. 6 for the year. The follow-up, "The Long And Winding Road," was No. 24. For the first time, solo recordings by the Beatles were listed on the year-end chart. George Harrison's two-sided hit "My Sweet Lord" and "Isn't It A Pity" bested "Let It Be" by coming in at No. 4 for the year. John Lennon was listed at No. 23 with the Phil Spector produced "Instant Karma (We All Shine On)." Another Apple signing, Badfinger, had two songs on the year-end chart, including the Paul McCartney composition "Come And Get It" at No. 71.

The Motown family of labels had its best year-end showing of the rock era, with 16 titles listed on the top 100 songs of the year. Leading the pack was "I'll Be There," the most successful Jackson Five chart single of all time. It ranked No. 1 for the year and was joined in the top 10 by the group's second Motown single, "ABC." Not far below them at No. 13 was the group's first chart entry, "I Want You Back." That song was originally written as "I Wanna Be Free" and was intended for Gladys Knight & the

Pips, then for Diana Ross. Berry Gordy suggested a rewrite that resulted in "I Want You Back" and gave it to the newly-signed quintet from Gary, Indiana. With "The Love You Save" at No. 15, the Jackson brothers' first four hits all placed in the top 15 of the year.

Another Motown artist in the year-end top 10 was Edwin Starr, with a reworking of "War," a song originally recorded by the Temptations. The label received a flurry of requests to release the Temptations' track as a single, but plans were underway to issue "Ball Of Confusion (That's What The World Is Today)," which became the No. 26 single of the year. Producer Norman Whitfield asked Starr if he'd like to record the song; having been out of the studio for six months he was happy to end his hiatus by recording "War," which placed ninth for the year.

Smokey Robinson & the Miracles had their biggest chart hit to date with a song from their 1967 album *Make It Happen.* When the British arm of Motown issued "The Tears Of A Clown" as a follow-up to a re-release of "The Tracks Of My Tears," it went to No. 1 in the U.K. A month later, Motown had scheduled a new Miracles single for the States when Gordy suggested an American release of "The Tears Of A Clown." It was No. 1 for two weeks and was No. 12 for the year.

In 1970, Motown split its most successful act of the '60s in two. After a final performance at the Frontier Hotel in Las Vegas on January 14, 1970, Diana Ross stepped out of the Supremes for a solo career. Jean Terrell took her place. Diana went into the recording studio with producer Bones Howe and recorded tracks like "Stoney End" (later recorded by Barbra Streisand) and "Love's Lines, Angles and Rhymes" (later recorded by the 5th Dimension), but that material was shelved and she was placed under the supervision of Nickolas Ashford and Valerie Simpson. A remake of their song "Ain't No Mountain High Enough" gave Diana her first solo No. 1 hit and the No. 10 song of 1970. Jean Terrell, Mary Wilson, and Cindy Birdsong made their first public appearance together on *The Ed Sullivan Show* as Jean introduced the first Supremes' single without Diana Ross, "Up The Ladder To The Roof." It became the No. 79 song of 1970. Their third single, "Stoned Love," ranked No. 52 for the year.

Other Motown artists included in the top 100 songs of 1970 were Stevie Wonder at No. 37 with "Signed, Sealed, Delivered I'm Yours," Rare Earth at No. 38 with "Get Ready" and "(I Know) I'm Losing You" at No. 94, R. Dean Taylor at No. 50 with "Indiana Wants Me," and the Four Tops with "Still Water (Love)" at No. 87.

The top 10 of the year included two songs written by Burt Bacharach and Hal David. They had the No. 2 single of the year, "Raindrops Keep Fallin' On My Head" from the film *Butch Cassidy And The Sundance Kid.* Ray Stevens, who turned down the chance to record "Raindrops" after Bacharach screened the film for him, was ranked No. 22 for the year with "Everything Is Beautiful."

The other Bacharach song in the top 10 was "(They Long To Be) Close To You" by the Carpenters. Burt had heard the duo's first single, a remake of the Beatles' "Ticket To Ride," on the radio and liked what he heard. When he found out the Carpenters were signed to A&M like he was, he asked Richard and Karen to open for him at a charity benefit for the Reiss-

33 **GREEN-EYED LADY**
Sugarloaf *Liberty*

34 **CANDIDA**
Dawn *Bell*

35 **LOVE ON A TWO-WAY STREET**
The Moments *Stang*

36 **SPILL THE WINE**
Eric Burdon & War *MGM*

37 **SIGNED, SEALED, DELIVERED I'M YOURS**
Stevie Wonder *Tamla*

38 **GET READY**
Rare Earth *Rare Earth*

39 **VEHICLE**
Ides of March *Warner Bros.*

40 **GYPSY WOMAN**
Brian Hyland *Uni*

41 **HEY THERE LONELY GIRL**
Eddie Holman *ABC*

42 **PATCHES**
Clarence Carter *Atlantic*

43 **IN THE SUMMERTIME**
Mungo Jerry *Janus*

44 **WHOLE LOTTA LOVE**
Led Zeppelin *Atlantic*

45 **ALL RIGHT NOW**
Free *A&M*

46 **GIVE ME JUST A LITTLE MORE TIME**
Chairmen of the Board *Invictus*

47 **RAINY NIGHT IN GEORGIA**
Brook Benton *Cotillion*

48 **TURN BACK THE HANDS OF TIME**
Tyrone Davis *Dakar*

49 **LOVE GROWS (WHERE MY ROSEMARY GOES)**
Edison Lighthouse *Bell*

50 **INDIANA WANTS ME**
R. Dean Taylor *Rare Earth*

51 **HITCHIN' A RIDE**
Vanity Fare *Page One*

52 **STONED LOVE**
The Supremes *Motown*

53 **RIDE CAPTAIN RIDE**
Blues Image *Atco*

54 **CECILIA**
Simon and Garfunkel *Columbia*

55 **UP AROUND THE BEND / RUN THROUGH THE JUNGLE**
Creedence Clearwater Revival *Fantasy*

56 **25 OR 6 TO 4**
Chicago *Columbia*

57 **LAY DOWN (CANDLES IN THE RAIN)**
Melanie w/the Edwin Hawkins Singers *Buddah*

58 **HOUSE OF THE RISING SUN**
Frijid Pink *Parrot*

59 **JULIE, DO YA LOVE ME**
Bobby Sherman *Metromedia*

60 **TIGHTER, TIGHTER**
Alive & Kicking *Roulette*

61 **LOVE OR LET ME BE LONELY**
Friends of Distinction *RCA*

62 **DON'T CRY DADDY** Elvis Presley *RCA*

63 **HE AIN'T HEAVY, HE'S MY BROTHER**
The Hollies *Epic*

64 **REFLECTIONS OF MY LIFE**
Marmalade *London*

65 **MIDNIGHT COWBOY**
Ferrante and Teicher *UA*

66 **EASY COME, EASY GO**
Bobby Sherman *Metromedia*

Davis Clinic at the Century Plaza Hotel in Los Angeles. When Burt asked Richard to arrange a medley of Bacharach songs, Richard searched for some of the composer's more obscure songs. Alpert suggested a song that had already been recorded by Dionne Warwick and Richard Chamberlain. The song didn't fit into the medley, but Richard couldn't get the tune out of his head and decided to record it. "Close To You" ranked No. 5 for the year.

Bacharach and David were also represented in the year-end chart at No. 17 with "One Less Bell To Answer" by the 5th Dimension. After recording for Johnny Rivers' Soul City label, the 5th Dimension wanted to sign with a new company. David Geffen, then an agent with CMA, let Larry Uttal at Bell Records know that the group was available. "We bought them from Johnny Rivers and we paid a big advance," Uttal recalled. "Bones Howe produced the first album. The group wanted a record called 'The Declaration Of Independence' out. It was a real stiff. They had another one they wanted to come out, 'Puppet Man,' and that was a stiff and they were very adamant about it. Bones was siding with the group. There was a song on the album that I felt was going to be a hit record, and that was 'One Less Bell To Answer.' The group didn't want it out, Bones didn't want it out, so we cut about 20 to 30 dubs, gave them out to the radio stations in the New Orleans area, the stations played the record, and within a couple of days they got top 10 requests. So we put the record out. It was against the wishes of the group but we felt it was a hit record."

Uttal had an even bigger hit in 1970 with "I Think I Love You" by the Partridge Family. It was the No. 7 song of the year, and marked the fourth time in a five-year period that a television series–based group had a top 10 hit of the year (the Monkees in 1966 and 1967, the Archies in 1969). Uttal had sold Bell Records to Columbia Pictures, whose Screen Gems TV unit produced *The Partridge Family.* "David Cassidy could really sing," Uttal noted. "So we could maintain legitimacy, we put the Partridge Family in the background. David sang up front and did a terrific job."

Simon and Garfunkel had their second year-end top 10 hit in 1970 with "Bridge Over Troubled Water," their third Hot 100 chart-topper. "The Sounds Of Silence" was the No. 17 song of 1966 and "Mrs. Robinson" was No. 9 for 1968. "Bridge" had been written in the same house in Los Angeles where George Harrison had written "Blue Jay Way." The instrumental track was recorded in Los Angeles and Paul and Art laid down the vocal tracks in New York.

67 **MY BABY LOVES LOVIN'**
White Plains *Deram*

68 **DIDN'T I (BLOW YOUR MIND THIS TIME)**
The Delfonics *Philly Groove*

69 **WITHOUT LOVE (THERE IS NOTHING)**
Tom Jones *Parrot*

70 **MA BELLE AMIE**
Tee Set *Colossus*

71 **COME AND GET IT**
Badfinger *Apple*

72 **OOH CHILD**
Five Stairsteps *Buddah*

73 **PSYCHEDELIC SHACK**
The Temptations *Gordy*

74 **NO TIME**
The Guess Who *RCA*

75 **SNOWBIRD**
Anne Murray *Capitol*

76 **I'LL NEVER FALL IN LOVE AGAIN**
Dionne Warwick *Scepter*

77 **THE WONDER OF YOU**
Elvis Presley *RCA*

78 **ARIZONA**
Mark Lindsay *Columbia*

79 **UP THE LADDER TO THE ROOF**
The Supremes *Motown*

80 **LOLA**
The Kinks *Reprise*

81 **(IF YOU LET ME MAKE LOVE TO YOU THEN) WHY CAN'T I TOUCH YOU**
Ronnie Dyson *Columbia*

82 **I JUST CAN'T HELP BELIEVING**
B.J. Thomas *Scepter*

83 **EVIL WAYS**
Santana *Columbia*

84 **MONTEGO BAY**
Bobby Bloom *L&R*

85 **SOMETHING'S BURNING**
Kenny Rogers & the First Edition *Reprise*

86 **MAKE ME SMILE**
Chicago *Columbia*

87 **STILL WATER (LOVE)**
Four Tops *Motown*

88 **EXPRESS YOURSELF**
Charles Wright & the Watts 103rd Street Rhythm Band *Warner Bros.*

89 **FOR THE LOVE OF HIM**
Bobbi Martin *UA*

90 **UNITED WE STAND**
Brotherhood of Man *Deram*

91 **THE LETTER**
Joe Cocker *A&M*

92 **JAM UP JELLY TIGHT**
Tommy Roe *ABC*

93 **JINGLE JANGLE**
The Archies *Kirshner*

94 **(I KNOW) I'M LOSING YOU**
Rare Earth *Rare Earth*

95 **NO MATTER WHAT**
Badfinger *Apple*

96 **WOODSTOCK**
Crosby, Stills, Nash & Young *Atlantic*

97 **SOMEBODY'S BEEN SLEEPING**
100 Proof Aged in Soul *Hot Wax*

98 **DON'T PLAY THAT SONG**
Aretha Franklin *Atlantic*

99 **5-10-15-20 (25-30 YEARS OF LOVE)**
The Presidents *Sussex*

100 **CALL ME** Aretha Franklin *Atlantic*

The Top 100 Songs of 1971

Three Dog Night

1971 WAS THE year the Rolling Stones launched their own record label; Jim Morrison died in Paris; and Andrew Lloyd Webber and Tim Rice were represented on Broadway with *Jesus Christ Superstar*.

The Osmond family made a strong showing on the year-end chart, with four titles. That was one better than their friendly rivals, the Jackson family. The highest-rated Osmond single at No. 6 was the Osmonds' "One Bad Apple," recorded at Rick Hall's Fame studios in Muscle Shoals, Alabama. Also in the top 10 was Donny Osmond's "Go Away Little Girl," a remake of the Steve Lawrence hit originally recorded by Bobby Vee. It ranked No. 10 and was one of four Carole King songs in the top 20. The Osmonds also scored with "Yo-Yo" (No. 28) and Donny was No. 52 with a remake of a Roy Orbison tune, "Sweet And Innocent."

As for the Jacksons, their highest-ranked single at year-end was "Never Can Say Goodbye" at No. 16. "Mama's Pearl" was No. 35, and the first solo single from Michael, "Got To Be There," was No. 43.

The No. 1 song of the year had been written by Hoyt Axton for a children's animated television special, "The Happy Song." When the show wasn't produced, Axton tried to place the songs from the show with different artists. He had toured as an opening act for Three Dog Night, and dropped by the studio where they were recording one day to play "Joy To The World" for them. Cory Wells didn't think it would be a hit, but the rest

01 JOY TO THE WORLD
Three Dog Night *Dunhill*

02 KNOCK THREE TIMES
Dawn *Bell*

03 MAGGIE MAY / REASON TO BELIEVE
Rod Stewart *Mercury*

04 IT'S TOO LATE / I FEEL THE EARTH MOVE
Carole King *Ode*

05 BRAND NEW KEY
Melanie *Neighborhood*

06 ONE BAD APPLE
The Osmonds *MGM*

07 INDIAN RESERVATION (THE LAMENT OF THE CHEROKEE RESERVATION INDIAN)
The Raiders *Columbia*

08 HOW CAN YOU MEND A BROKEN HEART
Bee Gees *Atco*

09 FAMILY AFFAIR
Sly & the Family Stone *Epic*

10 GO AWAY LITTLE GIRL
Donny Osmond *MGM*

11 THEME FROM "SHAFT"
Isaac Hayes *Enterprise*

12 GYPSYS, TRAMPS & THIEVES
Cher *Kapp*

13 JUST MY IMAGINATION (RUNNING AWAY WITH ME)
The Temptations *Gordy*

14 ME AND BOBBY MCGEE
Janis Joplin *Columbia*

15 BROWN SUGAR
The Rolling Stones *Rolling Stones*

16 NEVER CAN SAY GOODBYE
Jackson 5 *Motown*

17 WANT ADS
The Honey Cone *Hot Wax*

18 YOU'VE GOT A FRIEND
James Taylor *Warner Bros.*

19 SUPERSTAR
Carpenters *A&M*

20 WHAT'S GOING ON
Marvin Gaye *Tamla*

21 RAINY DAYS AND MONDAYS
Carpenters *A&M*

22 PUT YOUR HAND IN THE HAND
Ocean *Kama Sutra*

23 MR. BIG STUFF
Jean Knight *Stax*

24 SHE'S A LADY
Tom Jones *Parrot*

25 TAKE ME HOME, COUNTRY ROADS
John Denver *RCA*

26 HAVE YOU SEEN HER
The Chi-Lites *Brunswick*

27 SPANISH HARLEM
Aretha Franklin *Atlantic*

28 YO-YO
The Osmonds *MGM*

29 THE NIGHT THEY DROVE OLD DIXIE DOWN
Joan Baez *Vanguard*

30 AIN'T NO SUNSHINE
Bill Withers *Sussex*

31 ROSE GARDEN
Lynn Anderson *Columbia*

32 TREAT HER LIKE A LADY
Cornelius Brothers and Sister Rose *UA*

33 UNCLE ALBERT/ADMIRAL HALSEY
Paul and Linda McCartney *Apple*

of the band disagreed and voted to record it. Hoyt was disappointed with their version and was convinced it wouldn't sell. It topped the Hot 100 for six weeks and became the biggest hit of Three Dog Night's career as well as the most successful chart single on the Dunhill label.

Although he had recorded as early as 1961, Tony Orlando hadn't registered on the year-end chart until 1970, when "Candida" by Dawn was the No. 34 song of the year. Orlando's name wasn't listed in the credits because he wanted to keep his day job at a music publishing company, April-Blackwood Music. But after "Knock Three Times" was a hit (and the No. 2 single of 1971), Orlando quit his day job and started a new career with Telma Hopkins and Joyce Vincent Wilson in Dawn.

The No. 3 song of the year was also a two-sided hit, "Maggie May" and "Reason To Believe" by Rod Stewart. "Maggie May" almost wasn't included on the *Every Picture Tells A Story* album. It wasn't intended to be the single—the remake of Tim Hardin's "Reason To Believe" was the original "A" side until DJs flipped it in favor of "Maggie May."

Carole King and James Taylor's appearances on the chart heralded the beginning of the singer/songwriter era, a time of more personal and introspective music. King, who made her debut on the Hot 100 in 1962 with "It Might As Well Rain Until September," had her first year-end chart single in 1971 with a two-sided hit. "It's Too Late" and "I Feel The Earth Move" ranked No. 4 for the year. Both tracks were lifted from her record-breaking *Tapestry* album. Another song on that LP, "You've Got A Friend," was covered and released as a single by Carole's friend, James Taylor. His version was the No. 18 hit of the year.

Aside from Carole, the only other female lead vocalist in the top 10 was Melanie, No. 5 for the year with "Brand New Key." Her previous hit, "Lay Down (Candles In The Rain)," recorded with the Edwin Hawkins Singers on the Buddah label, was the No. 57 song of 1970. Melanie left Buddah and formed her own record label with husband/producer Peter Schekeryk. Her first release on Neighborhood was "Brand New Key," a song written in 15 minutes.

The Bee Gees first made the Hot 100 in 1967. In 1968, they were No. 52 for the year with "I've Gotta Get A Message To You." They made the year-end top 10 for the first time in 1971 with "How Can You Mend A Broken Heart" at No. 8. Barry and Robin Gibb had written the song for Andy Williams, but when he passed on it they decided to record it themselves.

Making the year-end top 10 for the first time was the Raiders. Billed as Paul Revere & the Raiders, they placed three songs in the top 100 of 1966: "Kicks" (No. 52), "Just Like Me" (No. 68), and "Hungry" (No. 92). The following year they had "Good Thing" at No. 41. They set a new high mark for themselves in 1971 with "Indian Reservation (The Lament Of The Cherokee Reservation Indian)." The song had been written and recorded in 1963 by Durham, North Carolina native John D. Loudermilk, whose pop compositions included "Sittin' In The Balcony" by Eddie Cochran, "A Rose And A Baby Ruth" and "Abilene" by George Hamilton IV, "Norman" and "James, Hold The Ladder Steady" by Sue Thompson, and "Tobacco Road" by the Nashville Teens. Loudermilk's version of "Indian Reservation" didn't make the chart—his biggest hit on his own was "The Language Of Love."

In 1968, British singer Don Fardon, lead vocalist for the Sorrows, released a version of "Indian Reservation" in the U.K. It peaked at No. 3 and was released in America, hitting No. 20 on the Hot 100. Jack Gold at Columbia Records suggested to Mark Lindsay that Paul Revere & the Raiders cover the song. It became the Raiders' biggest hit as well as Columbia's best-selling single in history, to that date.

The highest-ranked Motown single of 1971 was "Just My Imagination (Running Away With Me)" by the Temptations, at No. 13. It followed a series of socially relevant songs like "Cloud Nine," "Run Away Child, Running Wild," and "Don't Let The Joneses Get You Down" written for the group by Norman Whitfield and Barrett Strong. After missing the top 30 with *"Ungena Za Ulimwengu* (Unite The World)," Whitfield and Strong returned to the group's earlier sound. "We needed to do something a little different," Barrett recalls. "We had thought of 'Just My Imagination' a year or two before we recorded it, but the timing wasn't right. Norman asked me, 'What was that song we were messing around with a year ago?' I played it on the piano and he said, 'Meet me in the studio because I'm gonna record it today.'" Eddie Kendricks, who sang lead on the Temptations' first national hit, "The Way You Do The Things You Do," performed lead vocals on "Just My Imagination."

Motown didn't turn completely away from "socially relevant" songs. Marvin Gaye had the most critically acclaimed album of his career in 1971, *What's Going On.* The title track was the No. 20 song of the year and the follow-up, "Mercy Mercy Me (The Ecology)" was No. 48.

The second posthumous chart-topping single of the rock era was the No. 14 title of 1971, "Me And Bobby McGee" by Janis Joplin. The song first appeared in *Billboard* in 1969 when Roger Miller's version of the Kris Kristofferson tune peaked at No. 12 on the country singles chart.

Cher bettered the mark set with husband Sonny in 1965 when "I Got You Babe" was the No. 14 song of the year. In 1971, her No. 1 hit "Gypsys, Tramps & Thieves" placed No. 12 for the year.

67 **IF I WERE YOUR WOMAN**
Gladys Knight & the Pips *Soul*

68 **WHATCHA SEE IS WHATCHA GET**
The Dramatics *Volt*

69 **I AM...I SAID**
Neil Diamond *Uni*

70 **IF YOU COULD READ MY MIND**
Gordon Lightfoot *Reprise*

71 **ANOTHER DAY / OH WOMAN OH WHY**
Paul McCartney *Apple*

72 **TEMPTATION EYES**
The Grass Roots *Dunhill*

73 **PEACE TRAIN**
Cat Stevens *A&M*

74 **I'VE FOUND SOMEONE OF MY OWN**
Free Movement *Decca*

75 **ALL I EVER NEED IS YOU**
Sonny and Cher *Kapp*

76 **AMOS MOSES**
Jerry Reed *RCA*

77 **MR. BOJANGLES**
Nitty Gritty Dirt Band *Liberty*

78 **IF YOU REALLY LOVE ME**
Stevie Wonder *Tamla*

79 **STAY AWHILE**
The Bells *Polydor*

80 **I JUST WANT TO CELEBRATE**
Rare Earth *Rare Earth*

81 **SWEET CITY WOMAN**
The Stampeders *Bell*

82 **LIAR**
Three Dog Night *Dunhill*

83 **STICK-UP**
The Honey Cone *Hot Wax*

84 **(WHERE DO I BEGIN) LOVE STORY**
Andy Williams *Columbia*

85 **ONE TOKE OVER THE LINE**
Brewer and Shipley *Kama Sutra*

86 **NEVER ENDING SONG OF LOVE**
Delaney and Bonnie & Friends *Atco*

87 **RESPECT YOURSELF**
The Staple Singers *Stax*

88 **BRING THE BOYS HOME**
Freda Payne *Invictus*

89 **WHEN YOU'RE HOT, YOU'RE HOT**
Jerry Reed *RCA*

90 **HAVE YOU EVER SEEN THE RAIN / HEY TONIGHT**
Creedence Clearwater Revival *Fantasy*

91 **DESIDERATA**
Les Crane *Warner Bros.*

92 **LOVE HER MADLY**
The Doors *Elektra*

93 **SHE'S NOT JUST ANOTHER WOMAN**
The 8th Day *Invictus*

94 **I WOKE UP IN LOVE THIS MORNING**
The Partridge Family *Bell*

95 **WILD WORLD**
Cat Stevens *A&M*

96 **I DON'T KNOW HOW TO LOVE HIM**
Helen Reddy *Capitol*

97 **SUPERSTAR**
Murray Head *Decca*

98 **DOMINO**
Van Morrison *Warner Bros.*

99 **THEME FROM "LOVE STORY"**
Henry Mancini *RCA*

100 **DON'T KNOCK MY LOVE**
Wilson Pickett *Atlantic*

The Top 100 Songs of 1972

The Staple Singers

1972 WAS THE year John Lennon asked for American citizenship to avoid deportation; Diana Ross was nominated for an Oscar for portraying Billie Holiday in *Lady Sings the Blues;* and *Hair* closed on Broadway after 1,729 performances.

Elvis Presley made his first appearance in the top 30 portion of the year-end chart since 1969, when "Suspicious Minds" was No. 25. "Burning Love," the No. 32 song of 1972, marked Elvis' final appearance on a *Billboard* year-end singles chart.

Rick Nelson returned to the top 100 songs of the year after a long absence. He had last appeared in 1964 when "For You" was the No. 77 song of the year. He had the No. 56 song of 1972, "Garden Party," said to have been inspired by a Richard Nader Rock 'n' Roll Revival concert at Madison Square Garden where fans booed him for performing his contemporary material instead of his older songs. "I hate to ruin a legend," guitarist Allen Kemp told Todd Everett, "but after we left the stage, thinking that we had been booed for Dylan songs and long hair, we found out that some guys in the audience had gotten drunk and started a fight, and that the audience was booing them."

Returning after an even longer absence was Chuck Berry, who had the second highest-ranking year-end song of his career with "My Ding-A-Ling," a rude novelty hit recorded live at the 1972 Arts Festival in Lanchester, England. It was the No. 20 song of the year. Berry had two hits on the year-end chart for 1957 ("School Day" at No. 30 and "Rock & Roll Music" at No. 69) and two hits on the year-end chart for 1958 ("Sweet Little Sixteen" at No. 18 and "Johnny B. Goode" at No. 64).

For the second consecutive year, there were no Motown singles in the annual top 10 songs of the year. The highest-ranked Motown single of 1972 was Michael Jackson's remake of Bobby Day's "Rockin' Robin" at No. 26, followed closely by Jackson's title song from the motion picture *Ben* at No. 29. The only other Motown single included in the top 100 was the Temptations' "Papa Was A Rollin' Stone" at No. 30. That is the lowest total of Motown singles on a year-end chart since the pre-Supremes days of 1962.

The No. 1 single of 1972 was "Alone Again (Naturally)" by Gilbert O'Sullivan. The singer, born in Waterford, Ireland, as Raymond Edward O'Sullivan, was given his stage name by manager Gordon Mills, the same man who transformed Tommy Scott into Tom Jones and Arnold George Dorsey into Engelbert Humperdinck. The song sounded autobiographical, but even though O'Sullivan wrote it, he denied that it had anything to do with his own life.

The No. 2 single of the year had first appeared on an album released in 1969. Roberta Flack's *First Take* debut LP for Atlantic included a version of Ewan MacColl's "The First Time Ever I Saw Your Face." The song, written by MacColl for his wife Peggy (sister of Pete Seeger), was performed by Flack on a regular basis when she played piano and sang at a Washington, D.C., restaurant. When Clint Eastwood filmed *Play Misty For Me,* about a disc jockey stalked by a fatally attracted fan, he needed a romantic piece of music to underscore a scene with Donna Mills. He remembered "The First Time Ever I Saw Your Face" and asked Flack for permission to include her song in the movie. The demand for the song to be released as a single was so great that Atlantic edited it down for radio play and issued it. It spent six weeks at No. 1.

In third place was Don McLean's "American Pie." Although the eight-minute and 36-second track was divided into two parts for release as a single, most radio stations played the song in its entirety. McLean was shocked to have a hit record—he was certain "American Pie" was too long to be played on the radio. But his time trip through rock and roll history was too compelling for music directors to ignore.

The No. 4 song of the year was "Without You," Nilsson's second appearance on a year-end chart following "Everybody's Talkin'," the No. 85 song of 1969. Nilsson first heard "Without You" while inebriated. After sobering up he tried to find the song on one of his Beatles' albums. The search proved futile until he realized it was another group on Apple Records—Badfinger. Nilsson took the song to producer Richard Perry and said it ought to be a No. 1 hit. Perry helped make it so.

Joe Tex, who took his name from his home state of Texas, first appeared on a *Billboard* year-end chart in 1965 with "Hold What You've Got," ranked No. 84. In 1967, the former minister was No. 73 for the year with "Skinny Legs And All." He had the biggest hit of his career in 1972 with "I Gotcha," the No. 12 song of the year. Another minister, Al Green, had his most successful single of all time with "Let's Stay Together," the No. 7 song of 1972.

35 BETCHA BY GOLLY, WOW
The Stylistics *Avco*

36 USE ME
Bill Withers *Sussex*

37 YOU OUGHT TO BE WITH ME
Al Green *Hi*

38 I'M STILL IN LOVE WITH YOU
Al Green *Hi*

39 SUNSHINE
Jonathan Edwards *Capricorn*

40 DADDY DON'T YOU WALK SO FAST
Wayne Newton *Chelsea*

41 BACK STABBERS
The O'Jays *PIR*

42 EVERYBODY PLAYS THE FOOL
The Main Ingredient *RCA*

43 SATURDAY IN THE PARK
Chicago *Columbia*

44 IF YOU DON'T KNOW ME BY NOW
Harold Melvin & the Blue Notes *PIR*

45 I'LL BE AROUND
Spinners *Atlantic*

46 SCORPIO
Dennis Coffey & the Detroit Guitar Band *Sussex*

47 PUPPY LOVE
Donny Osmond *MGM*

48 DOWN BY THE LAZY RIVER
The Osmonds *MGM*

49 FREDDIE'S DEAD
Curtis Mayfield *Curtom*

50 DAY AFTER DAY
Badfinger *Apple*

51 YOU ARE EVERYTHING
The Stylistics *Avco*

52 LOOK WHAT YOU DONE FOR ME
Al Green *Hi*

53 NICE TO BE WITH YOU
Gallery *Sussex*

54 IT NEVER RAINS IN SOUTHERN CALIFORNIA
Albert Hammond *Mums*

55 MOTHER AND CHILD REUNION
Paul Simon *Columbia*

56 GARDEN PARTY
Rick Nelson & the Stone Canyon Band *Decca*

57 MORNING HAS BROKEN
Cat Stevens *A&M*

58 CLEAN UP WOMAN
Betty Wright *Alston*

59 EVERYTHING I OWN
Bread *Elektra*

60 NEVER BEEN TO SPAIN
Three Dog Night *Dunhill*

61 THE WAY OF LOVE
Cher *Kapp*

62 (LAST NIGHT) I DIDN'T GET TO SLEEP AT ALL
5th Dimension *Bell*

63 SUMMER BREEZE
Seals and Crofts *Warner Bros.*

64 DAY DREAMING
Aretha Franklin *Atlantic*

65 HOW DO YOU DO?
Mouth and MacNeal *Philips*

66 WHERE IS THE LOVE
Roberta Flack & Donny Hathaway *Atlantic*

67 GO ALL THE WAY
Raspberries *Capitol*

Like Joe Tex, Johnny Nash was also born in Texas. He competed in a local talent show that offered a chance to perform at the Apollo Theater in Harlem, but lost out to Tex. In 1972, he shared a spot in the top 20 songs of the year with Tex. "I Can See Clearly Now" was written and produced by Nash and recorded in Jamaica. Nash had first traveled there in 1957 while filming a part in the Burt Lancaster movie *Take A Giant Step*. Nash returned to Kingston in 1968 to record "Hold Me Tight," the No. 58 song of that year. After a couple of top 10 singles in the U.K., Nash moved to London, signed with CBS Records, and hired a relatively unknown reggae singer named Bob Marley to write for him. Marley wrote "Stir It Up" and "Guava Jelly" for Nash.

America, a trio of Americans who met in London while attending a school for children of military families, had the No. 6 song of 1972. Gerry Beckley, Dewey Bunnell, and Dan Peek opened for well-known groups like Pink Floyd and were popular in London before they signed with the British office of Warner Bros. Records. "A Horse With No Name" was written by Dewey, inspired by his feelings of homesickness for the desert countryside he remembered from when he lived at Vandenberg, an Air Force base near San Luis Obispo, California.

Billy Paul had recorded for Kenny Gamble and Leon Huff's two previous labels, Gamble and Neptune, before signing with their new label, Philadelphia International Records. He gave that label its first No. 1 single with "Me And Mrs. Jones," the No. 9 song of 1972. The PIR label had two other songs included in the top 100 of 1972: "Back Stabbers" by the O'Jays was No. 41 and "If You Don't Know Me By Now" by Harold Melvin & the Blue Notes was No. 44.

Sammy Davis, Jr. appeared on two previous year-end singles charts with songs that had originated in Broadway shows. "What Kind Of Fool Am I," the No. 92 song of 1962, was from *Stop the World—I Want to Get Off*. "I've Gotta Be Me," the No. 86 song of 1969, was from *Golden Rainbow*. Davis had the biggest single of his career when he recorded "The Candy Man," first heard in *Willie Wonka And The Chocolate Factory*. Mike Curb, head of MGM Records, released a version of the song by his own group, the Mike Curb Congregation. When it wasn't a hit, he convinced Davis to overdub his voice, and the recycled track went to No. 1 on the Hot 100 and ranked No. 10 for the year.

The Top 100 Songs of 1973

Eddie Kendricks

1973 WAS THE year Dr. Hook actually made the cover of *Rolling Stone;* Jim Croce was killed in a plane crash and Bobby Darin died after an operation on his heart; and Elvis and Priscilla Presley were divorced.

Paul McCartney, Ringo Starr, and George Harrison were all represented on the year-end chart with No. 1 songs. McCartney ranked No. 5 with "My Love" and was also listed at No. 24 with a song that went to No. 2 on the Hot 100, the James Bond theme "Live And Let Die." Ringo was No. 28 for the year with "Photograph" and George was No. 43 with "Give Me Love (Give Me Peace On Earth)." John Lennon, whose only chart single during 1973 was "Mind Games," was absent from the year-end chart.

Motown rebounded from being shut out of the top 10 the previous two years, thanks to Marvin Gaye. Five years after he had the No. 2 song of the year with his version of "I Heard It Through The Grapevine," Gaye placed fourth for the year with "Let's Get It On." Sitting just outside the top 10 was former Temptation Eddie Kendricks with his first solo hit, "Keep On Truckin' (Part 1)."

For only the second time in the rock era, a solo female artist had the No. 1 song of the year. Matching the achievement of Lulu's "To Sir With Love" in 1967, Carly Simon's "You're So Vain" took top honors for 1973.

Was the song about Warren Beatty or James Taylor or Kris Kristofferson or Carly's backing vocalist on the song, Mick Jagger? She's never said, but she did reveal that when the song was originally written, it was called "Bless You Ben," a name later given to her son. In an interview with her younger brother Peter, she claimed the song wasn't written about a specific individual: "I would say I had about three or four different people in mind when I wrote that song...I actually did think specifically about a couple of people when I wrote it, but the examples of what they did was a fantasy trip."

Roberta Flack was back in the year-end top 10 for the second consecutive year. "Killing Me Softly With His Song," No. 3 for 1973, was coincidentally inspired by a performance of the man who had the No. 3 song of 1972. Singer Lori Lieberman saw Don McLean sing at the Troubadour in Los Angeles and went to writers Norman Gimbel and Charles Fox to put her thoughts into a song. Lieberman recorded the 10-minute epic, which was edited for single release. Flack was on a TWA flight from Los Angeles to New York when she plugged in her headphones and turned the pages of the in-flight magazine. She was intrigued with the title "Killing Me Softly With His Song" and made a point to listen for it. "By the time I got to New York I knew I had to do that song and I knew I'd be able to add something to it," Flack said in *High Fidelity*. She spent three months in the studio perfecting it; she was rewarded with a single that spent five weeks in pole position.

Cher made her first appearance in a year-end top 10 with "Half-Breed," a song that producer Snuff Garrett kept on his desk before telling the artist about it. After producing hits for Cher on her own ("Gypsys, Tramps & Thieves" and "The Way Of Love') as well as for Sonny and Cher ("All I Ever Need Is You"), Garrett had a falling out with Sonny about the kind of material his wife should be recording. When Sonny turned down "The Night The Lights Went Out In Georgia," Garrett ended their association. Songwriter Mary Dean didn't know that when she submitted "Half-Breed" to Garrett. Fortunately for all parties concerned, Garrett reconciled with Cher and "Half-Breed" became her second solo No. 1 single.

The other female vocalist in the top 10 was Gladys Knight, who first made the year-end chart in 1961 with the Pips on the No. 63 song, "Every Beat Of My Heart." In 1967 the group had the No. 16 song of the year with their version of "I Heard It Through The Grapevine," and in 1973 they set a new personal best by placing tenth with "Midnight Train To Georgia." The song had been originally written as "Midnight Plane To Houston" and recorded by its composer, Jim Weatherly. When Cissy Houston recorded it in Atlanta, Weatherly was asked if he minded the song being changed to "Midnight Train To Georgia." "I said, 'No, I don't mind—just don't change the rest of the song,'" he remembers. When Weatherly's publisher sent the song to Gladys Knight & the Pips, they retained the new title and had their first No. 1 hit on the Hot 100.

The No. 2 song of 1973 was "Tie A Yellow Ribbon Round The Ole Oak Tree" by Dawn. Tony Orlando, Telma Hopkins, and Joyce Vincent Wilson were ready to disband the trio after six singles in a row failed to make the top 20. Then producers Hank Medress and Dave Appell called them to a recording session in New York to hear a new song written by Irwin Levine and L. Russell Brown. Tony admitted to Dick Clark that he wasn't that impressed with the material. "I said this was the corniest song I've ever heard in my life, no way am I singing this song. I called up Jimmy Darren and said, 'Listen, have I got a great song for you.' I sent it to him and he turned it down. Then I sent it to Bobby Vinton. Three or four months went by and I couldn't stop singing the chorus." Dawn had been accused of being a bubblegum group, and Tony wanted to shake that image. Telma and Joyce had sung backing vocals on Isaac Hayes' "Theme From *Shaft*'" and Marvin Gaye's "I Heard It Through The Grapevine," and Orlando wanted to show off their talent. He knew the group would be in for more criticism if they recorded a song like "Tie A Yellow Ribbon." "But my publishing instincts came through," he told Clark. "I knew it was a great song . . . I remember standing behind that microphone and saying to myself, 'I'm going to think Bobby Darin. I'm going to think his attitude on this tune, and throughout 'Yellow Ribbon,' there were moments when I was doing Bobby. I was feeling him, I was acting like him on mike." When Tony accepted his American Music Award for the song, he told the audience, "This one's for Bobby Darin."

Elton John had his highest ranked year-end song to date with "Crocodile Rock," the No. 6 hit of 1973. Previously, he had the No. 65 song of 1971 with "Your Song" and the No. 71 song of 1972 with "Rocket Man." Elton admitted that "Crocodile Rock" was an amalgamation of several different songs, including "Little Darlin'" and "Oh! Carol" with some Beach Boys and Eddie Cochran thrown in. Some people felt there was a lot of Pat Boone's "Speedy Gonzales" in there as well.

Charlie Rich scored his first year-end chart single in 1973 with "The Most Beautiful Girl," No. 8 for the year. He first made the Hot 100 in 1960 with "Lonely Weekends," on the Phillips label (as in Sam Phillips).

Jim Croce, who had the No. 87 song of 1972 with his first chart single, "You Don't Mess Around With Jim," had the No. 12 hit of 1973 with "Bad, Bad Leroy Brown." Croce was inspired to write the song by a soldier who went AWOL from Fort Dix, New Jersey, while Croce was there learning how to be a telephone lineman. Croce also had the No. 16 song of 1973 with the third posthumous chart-topper of the rock era, "Time In A Bottle." The song was heard during the telecast of *She Lives*, a TV movie starring Desi Arnaz, Jr. and Season Hubley on ABC-TV September 12, 1973. The night the movie aired, Croce completed his third album, *I Got A Name*. Eight days later, after giving a concert at Northwestern Louisiana University, he boarded his privately chartered plane to take him to his next college engagement, 70 miles away. The plane had an aborted take-off and crashed into a tree, killing Croce and five other people. "I Got A Name" was released as a single and ranked No. 87 for 1973. The week it made the top 10, "Time In A Bottle" was issued.

"Monster Mash" by Bobby "Boris" Pickett & the Crypt Kickers made its second appearance on a year-end chart. It was the no. 17 song of the year during its original release in 1962. It had a brief chart run in 1970, peaking at No. 91 on the Hot 100. Almost three years later it returned to the *Billboard* singles chart for a third time, peaking at No. 10. That was good enough to rank it No. 82 for the year.

67 **DADDY'S HOME**
Jermaine Jackson *Motown*

68 **NATURAL HIGH**
Bloodstone *London*

69 **I BELIEVE IN YOU (YOU BELIEVE IN ME)**
Johnnie Taylor *Stax*

70 **IF YOU WANT ME TO STAY**
Sly & the Family Stone *Epic*

71 **DANNY'S SONG**
Anne Murray *Capitol*

72 **WHY ME**
Kris Kristofferson *Monument*

73 **HELLO IT'S ME**
Todd Rundgren *Bearsville*

74 **SUPERFLY**
Curtis Mayfield *Curtom*

75 **RIGHT PLACE WRONG TIME**
Dr. John *Atco*

76 **GET DOWN**
Gilbert O'Sullivan *MAM*

77 **FEELIN' STRONGER EVERY DAY**
Chicago *Columbia*

78 **LONG TRAIN RUNNIN'**
Doobie Brothers *Warner Bros.*

79 **THE COVER OF ROLLING STONE**
Dr. Hook & the Medicine Show *Columbia*

80 **THE LOVE I LOST (PART 1)**
Harold Melvin & the Blue Notes *PIR*

81 **HERE I AM (COME AND TAKE ME)**
Al Green *Hi*

82 **MONSTER MASH**
Bobby "Boris" Pickett *Parrot*

83 **IF YOU'RE READY (COME GO WITH ME)**
The Staple Singers *Stax*

84 **DANCING IN THE MOONLIGHT**
King Harvest *Perception*

85 **REELING IN THE YEARS**
Steely Dan *ABC*

86 **MY MARIA**
B.W. Stevenson *RCA*

87 **I GOT A NAME**
Jim Croce *ABC*

88 **BREAK UP TO MAKE UP**
The Stylistics *Avco*

89 **DO IT AGAIN**
Steely Dan *ABC*

90 **I'M DOIN' FINE NOW**
New York City *Chelsea*

91 **DON'T EXPECT ME TO BE YOUR FRIEND**
Lobo *Big Tree*

92 **MASTERPIECE**
The Temptations *Gordy*

93 **THE TWELFTH OF NEVER**
Donny Osmond *MGM*

94 **ALL I KNOW**
Art Garfunkel *Columbia*

95 **HOCUS POCUS**
Focus *Sire*

96 **GYPSY MAN**
War *UA*

97 **YES WE CAN CAN**
Pointer Sisters *Blue Thumb*

98 **BOOGIE WOOGIE BUGLE BOY**
Bette Midler *Atlantic*

99 **KNOCKIN' ON HEAVEN'S DOOR**
Bob Dylan *Columbia*

100 **LIVING IN THE PAST**
Jethro Tull *Chrysalis*

The Top 100 Songs of 1974

Barbra Streisand

1974 WAS THE year Cass Elliott died while staying in Harry Nilsson's flat in London; the members of Led Zeppelin launched their Swan Song label; and David Niven was surprised by a streaker at the Academy Awards.

Paul Anka returned to the year-end chart for the first time since 1960, when "Puppy Love" was No. 26 and "My Home Town" was No. 93. He did it with a chart-topping song, "(You're) Having My Baby," written to express his joy at his wife's pregnancy. The single ranked No. 5 for the year, his highest-ranked song on any annual recap, but the National Organization of Women didn't share the joy. They awarded Anka their annual "Keep Her In Her Place Award." "It's the personal statement of a man caught up in the affection and joy of childbirth," Anka responded. Still, Anka changed the lyric in his live performances to "Having Our Baby," a new point of view that quieted his critics. "Baby" was supposed to be a solo effort, but Bob Skaff of United Artists Records suggested that Odia Coates duet with Paul on the track. Coates was a member of the Edwin Hawkins Singers while Paul was producing their album *Oh Happy Day.* After an audition in Las Vegas, Anka agreed to produce Coates for Buddah Records. Eventually she joined him on the UA roster.

Also returning to the year-end chart after an absence were the Righteous Brothers. The last time they showed up in the year-end tally was in 1966, when "(You're My) Soul And Inspiration" was No. 5 and "Ebb Tide" was No. 85. Bill Medley went solo in 1968 while Bobby Hatfield kept the Righteous Brothers going with Jimmy Walker, formerly of the Knickerbockers ("Lies"). In February 1974, Medley and Hatfield got back together and announced their reunion on *The Sonny And Cher Comedy Hour*. They had the No. 51 song of 1974 with "Rock And Roll Heaven," a tune originally recorded by Climax ("Precious And Few").

Ray Stevens had the biggest hit of his career with a song that paid tribute to one of the biggest fads of the day, "The Streak." It was the No. 3 song of the year, besting his previous year-end high in 1970 when "Everything Is Beautiful" was No. 22 for the year. Stevens had read an article about the streaking fad on college campuses while flying from Nashville to Los Angeles. "It was a little bitty article about a college student who took off his clothes and ran through a crowd," Stevens explains. "The article called it 'streaking' and I said it had to be a great idea for a song." Stevens made some notes when he got to his hotel room and intended to finish the song when he returned home. "I didn't know it was going to be such a big fad. One morning I woke up and it was all over the news. Everywhere you turned, people were talking about streakers. So I built a fire under myself and went into the studio and rushed the record out."

Dionne Warwick, with an "e" added to the end of her name for "good luck," was teamed up with the Spinners by producer Thom Bell on "Then Came You." The song took both Warwick and the Spinners into the year-end top 10 for the first time. Dionne had asked the Spinners, a former Motown group that signed with Warner-owned Atlantic, to open for her on a five-week summer tour. That led Bell to suggest Dionne duet with lead singer Phillipe Wynne on "Then Came You." The song, No. 9 for the year, was Dionne's only hit during her long tenure with Warner Bros., the label she joined after leaving Scepter.

There was an instrumental in the year-end top 10 for the first time since 1968, when Paul Mauriat's "Love Is Blue" came in third. "TSOP (The Sound Of Philadelphia)" by MFSB featuring the Three Degrees was No. 8 for the year, the highest annual ranking for any Philadelphia International Records single. MFSB was a collection of almost 40 session musicians. They were the house band at Sigma Sound Studios, the recording facility owned by Kenny Gamble and Leon Huff. Don Cornelius asked MFSB to fashion a theme song for his television series, *Soul Train*. Gamble came up with the title and later used "TSOP" as a name for a new subsidiary label.

There was another instrumental in the top 20. "Love's Theme" by the Love Unlimited Orchestra was No. 19 for the year. The orchestra was a 40-piece studio band led by Barry White. The musicians were used to back White's female singing trio, Love Unlimited. They were originally signed to Uni Records, and when label head Russ Regan moved over to 20th Century he brought the group and Barry White with him. "He's a great talent," Regan says of White. "He had been around quite a while as a writer/producer but had never really done much as an artist." "Love's Theme" was written as an instrumental overture for a vocal album by the trio, *Under The Influence Of Love Unlimited*. "'Love's Theme' was easy to break," according to Regan. "We sent it out to the clubs and to radio. Within a week there was a buzz on it."

36 **TELL ME SOMETHING GOOD**
Rufus *ABC*

37 **DARK LADY**
Cher *MCA*

38 **UNTIL YOU COME BACK TO ME (THAT'S WHAT I'M GONNA DO)**
Aretha Franklin *Atlantic*

39 **DON'T LET THE SUN GO DOWN ON ME**
Elton John *MCA*

40 **THE ENTERTAINER**
Marvin Hamlisch *MCA*

41 **JAZZMAN**
Carole King *Ode*

42 **ROCK THE BOAT**
The Hues Corporation *RCA*

43 **BEST THING THAT EVER HAPPENED TO ME**
Gladys Knight & the Pips *Buddah*

44 **CAT'S IN THE CRADLE**
Harry Chapin *Elektra*

45 **SPIDERS AND SNAKES**
Jim Stafford *MGM*

46 **WHATEVER GETS YOU THRU THE NIGHT**
John Lennon w/the Plastic Ono Band *Apple*

47 **JUNGLE BOOGIE**
Kool & the Gang *De-Lite*

48 **SMOKIN' IN THE BOY'S ROOM**
Brownsville Station *Big Tree*

49 **COME AND GET YOUR LOVE**
Redbone *Epic*

50 **MY MELODY OF LOVE**
Bobby Vinton *ABC*

51 **ROCK AND ROLL HEAVEN**
Righteous Brothers *Haven*

52 **I'VE GOT TO USE MY IMAGINATION**
Gladys Knight & the Pips *Buddah*

53 **CAN'T GET ENOUGH OF YOUR LOVE, BABE**
Barry White *20th Century*

54 **NEVER, NEVER GONNA GIVE YA UP**
Barry White *20th Century*

55 **TIN MAN**
America *Warner Bros.*

56 **LET ME BE THERE**
Olivia Newton-John *MCA*

57 **ROCK ON**
David Essex *Columbia*

58 **MIDNIGHT AT THE OASIS**
Maria Muldaur *Reprise*

59 **SIDESHOW**
Blue Magic *Atco*

60 **LIVING FOR THE CITY**
Stevie Wonder *Tamla*

61 **THE SHOW MUST GO ON**
Three Dog Night *Dunhill*

62 **BEACH BABY**
First Class *UK*

63 **BE THANKFUL FOR WHAT YOU GOT**
William DeVaughn *Roxbury*

64 **MOCKINGBIRD**
Carly Simon & James Taylor *Elektra*

65 **HANG ON IN THERE BABY**
Johnny Bristol *MGM*

66 **JUST DON'T WANT TO BE LONELY**
The Main Ingredient *RCA*

67 **THE BITCH IS BACK**
Elton John *MCA*

The No. 1 song of 1974 was the title song from the movie *The Way We Were*. Barbra Streisand starred in the film as the liberal Katie Morosky, who falls in love with writer Hubbell Gardiner (Robert Redford). Her rendition of the title tune, written by Marvin Hamlisch and Alan and Marilyn Bergman, made her only the third female soloist to have a No. 1 song of the year during the rock era. The first was Lulu, who also did it with the title song from a film that she starred in *(To Sir With Love)*. The second was Carly Simon, who topped the previous annual list with "You're So Vain."

The runner-up song of the year was "Seasons In The Sun" by Canadian singer Terry Jacks. It became the highest ranked year-end single by an artist born in Canada since Percy Faith was No. 1 in 1960 with "Theme From *A Summer Place*." Jacks had made the year-end chart in 1970 as half of the Poppy Family (with his wife Susan Jacks), when "Which Way You Goin' Billy?" was the No. 28 song of the year. Terry had suggested that the Beach Boys record Jacques Brel's *"Le Moribond"* ("The Dying Man"), which had been given English lyrics by Rod McKuen. Jacks was familiar with a Kingston Trio version released in 1964. The Beach Boys took Terry's advice and recorded it, but never released it. Mourning a friend who passed away unexpectedly, Jacks decided to record it for himself. His version sat on a shelf for a year. It was only after a newspaper delivery boy heard it and asked if he could bring his friends over to hear the track that Jacks was convinced it should be released.

Elton John bested his previous record by two notches, when "Bennie And The Jets" placed fourth for 1974. His "Crocodile Rock" had been the No. 6 song of 1973. "Bennie" brought Elton to the *Billboard* R&B singles chart for the first time, an achievement that thrilled him.

Steve Miller, best known for being an album artist, also loved to make singles. "It's like a game, like a crossword puzzle," he said in *Guitar Player*. A song he didn't think would be a hit, "The Joker," ranked No. 10 for the year.

68 **I'M LEAVING IT (ALL) UP TO YOU**
Donny & Marie Osmond *MGM*

69 **RIKKI DON'T LOSE THAT NUMBER**
Steely Dan *ABC*

70 **IF YOU LOVE ME (LET ME KNOW)**
Olivia Newton-John *MCA*

71 **SWEET HOME ALABAMA**
Lynyrd Skynyrd *MCA*

72 **ON AND ON**
Gladys Knight & the Pips *Buddah*

73 **SHA-LA-LA (MAKE ME HAPPY)**
Al Green *Hi*

74 **WATERLOO**
Abba *Atlantic*

75 **THE LORD'S PRAYER**
Sister Janet Mead *A&M*

76 **AMERICANS**
Byron MacGregor *Westbound*

77 **CAN'T GET ENOUGH**
Bad Company *Swan Song*

78 **PLEASE COME TO BOSTON**
Dave Loggins *Epic*

79 **THE AIR THAT I BREATHE**
The Hollies *Epic*

80 **BACK HOME AGAIN**
John Denver *RCA*

81 **OH MY MY**
Ringo Starr *Apple*

82 **CLAP FOR THE WOLFMAN**
The Guess Who *RCA*

83 **JET**
Wings *Apple*

84 **(I'VE BEEN) SEARCHIN' SO LONG**
Chicago *Columbia*

85 **ERES TU (TOUCH THE WIND)**
Mocedades *Tara*

86 **HELP ME**
Joni Mitchell *Reprise*

87 **YOU WON'T SEE ME**
Anne Murray *Capitol*

88 **FOR THE LOVE OF MONEY**
The O'Jays *PIR*

89 **YOU AND ME AGAINST THE WORLD**
Helen Reddy *Capitol*

90 **TUBULAR BELLS**
Mike Oldfield *Virgin*

91 **PUT YOUR HANDS TOGETHER**
The O'Jays *PIR*

92 **LOOKIN' FOR A LOVE**
Bobby Womack *UA*

93 **YOU GOT THE LOVE**
Rufus f/Chaka Khan *ABC*

94 **I'LL HAVE TO SAY I LOVE YOU IN A SONG**
Jim Croce *ABC*

95 **ONE HELL OF A WOMAN**
Mac Davis *Columbia*

96 **OH VERY YOUNG**
Cat Stevens *A&M*

97 **LONGFELLOW SERENADE**
Neil Diamond *Columbia*

98 **WILDWOOD WEED**
Jim Stafford *MGM*

99 **HOLLYWOOD SWINGING**
Kool & the Gang *De-Lite*

100 **ANOTHER SATURDAY NIGHT**
Cat Stevens *A&M*

The Top 100 Songs of 1975

KC & the Sunshine Band

1975 WAS THE year the Who's *Tommy* became a movie; Ron Wood joined the Rolling Stones; and Bruce Springsteen was *Born to Run.*

Several artists made surprise returns to the year-end chart. Simon and Garfunkel, who split up after releasing the *Bridge Over Troubled Water* album in 1970, temporarily reunited in 1975 and released one single, "My Little Town." It was the No. 88 song of the year.

Another unexpected comeback was made by the Four Seasons, absent from the year-end singles chart since 1965, when "Let's Hang On" was the No. 27 song of the year. Signed with Warner/Curb, Frankie Valli and a new set of Four Seasons were No. 43 for the year with "Who Loves You." Valli, signed as a solo artist to Private Stock Records, was on the year-end chart with a song originally recorded during his tenure with Motown. "My Eyes Adored You," which began life as "Blue Eyes In Georgia," was the No. 22 song of 1975.

Neil Sedaka was another '60s artist who proved he could be contemporary in the '70s. He was last seen on the year-end chart in 1962, when he placed three songs in the top 100: "Breaking Up Is Hard To Do" (No. 14), "Happy Birthday, Sweet Sixteen" (No. 48), and "Next Door To An Angel" (No. 70). He was responsible for writing three songs on the top 100 of 1975, two of which he also performed. "Laughter In The Rain" was his big comeback record, No. 19 for the year. "Bad Blood," another chart-topping hit, performed even better, coming in at No. 15. Sedaka's composi-

01 **I'M SORRY / CALYPSO**
John Denver *RCA*

02 **LOVE WILL KEEP US TOGETHER**
Captain and Tennille *A&M*

03 **RHINESTONE COWBOY**
Glen Campbell *Capitol*

04 **PHILADELPHIA FREEDOM**
The Elton John Band *MCA*

05 **THAT'S THE WAY (I LIKE IT)**
KC & the Sunshine Band *TK*

06 **FLY, ROBIN, FLY**
Silver Convention *Midland International*

07 **BEFORE THE NEXT TEARDROP FALLS**
Freddy Fender *ABC/Dot*

08 **ONE OF THESE NIGHTS**
Eagles *Asylum*

09 **LOVIN' YOU**
Minnie Riperton *Epic*

10 **ISLAND GIRL**
Elton John *MCA*

11 **FAME**
David Bowie *RCA*

12 **HE DON'T LOVE YOU (LIKE I LOVE YOU)**
Tony Orlando & Dawn *Elektra*

13 **(HEY WON'T YOU PLAY)**
ANOTHER SOMEBODY DONE
SOMEBODY WRONG SONG
B.J. Thomas *ABC*

14 **FALLIN' IN LOVE**
Hamilton, Joe Frank & Reynolds *Playboy*

15 **BAD BLOOD**
Neil Sedaka *Rocket*

16 **JIVE TALKIN'**
Bee Gees *RSO*

17 **THE HUSTLE**
Van McCoy & the Soul City Symphony *Avco*

18 **BLACK WATER**
Doobie Brothers *Warner Bros.*

19 **LAUGHTER IN THE RAIN**
Neil Sedaka *Rocket*

20 **LADY MARMALADE**
Labelle *Epic*

21 **LET'S DO IT AGAIN**
The Staple Singers *Curtom*

22 **MY EYES ADORED YOU**
Frankie Valli *Private Stock*

23 **I'M NOT IN LOVE**
10cc *Mercury*

24 **LUCY IN THE SKY WITH DIAMONDS**
Elton John *MCA*

25 **BEST OF MY LOVE**
Eagles *Asylum*

26 **PICK UP THE PIECES**
Average White Band *Atlantic*

27 **YOU'RE THE FIRST, THE LAST,**
MY EVERYTHING
Barry White *20th Century*

28 **WHEN WILL I BE LOVED**
Linda Ronstadt *Capitol*

29 **THANK GOD I'M A COUNTRY BOY**
John Denver *RCA*

30 **LISTEN TO WHAT THE MAN SAID**
Wings *Capitol*

31 **FIRE**
Ohio Players *Mercury*

32 **SISTER GOLDEN HAIR**
America *Warner Bros.*

33 **SHINING STAR**
Earth, Wind & Fire *Columbia*

tion of "Love Will Keep Us Together," released as a single by the Captain & Tennille, was the No. 2 song of the year.

John Denver had his second year-end top 10 listing with the two-sided hit "I'm Sorry" and "Calypso." With "I'm Sorry" gaining popularity first and the flip side garnering favor later in the single's chart run, the two sides were able to pin down the No. 1 position for 1975. In 1971 Denver had the No. 25 song of the year, "Take Me Home, Country Roads." In 1973 he was No. 65 with "Rocky Mountain High," and in 1974 he had three songs included in the top 100 of the year: "Annie's Song" (No. 7), "Sunshine On My Shoulders" (No. 25), and "Back Home Again" (No. 80). *Newsweek* called him "the most popular singer in America," and for a time in the '70s, he was. But after "Fly Away," a duet with Olivia Newton-John that was the follow-up to "I'm Sorry" and "Calypso," he never returned to the top 20 portion of the Hot 100.

Toni Tennille was the highest-ranked female voice of 1975. She and her husband Daryl were also in the top 100 with "The Way I Want To Touch You" (No. 56). That song had been recorded on their own Butterscotch Castle label after two disc jockeys saw the couple perform at the Smoke House in Encino, California, and promised to play their songs if they ever recorded anything. After "The Way I Want To Touch You" garnered some local airplay, it was picked up for distribution by Joyce Records. That led to four offers from major labels, including A&M. "A&M was what we wanted, because they were the only ones who would let us produce ourselves, and because Herb Alpert and Jerry Moss had done the kind of thing I always wanted to do," Daryl said in *Billboard*. "But I was afraid because they have the Carpenters, [they didn't] need another female singer/male keyboardist team."

Despite Daryl's misgivings, A&M signed the duo. Kip Cohen of the label's A&R department asked them to listen to a track on the *Sedaka's Back* album, and both Daryl and Toni knew that "Love Will Keep Us Together" was right for them. Two weeks later they had a new arrangement for the song. Released as a single, it spent four weeks in pole position.

The No. 3 song of 1975 was "Rhinestone Cowboy," written by Larry Weiss and recorded by Glen Campbell. Weiss recorded for 20th Century Records and released an album called *Black And Blue Suite* in 1974. "Rhinestone Cowboy" was pulled from the LP as a single, but failed to make the Hot 100. Campbell heard the song on KNX-FM, a Los Angeles adult contemporary station. He asked his secretary to find a copy of the song, although he wasn't sure who the artist was. Meanwhile, he dropped by Al Coury's office at Capitol Records and the label executive asked him to listen to a song—"Rhinestone Cowboy." Weiss was about to drop out of the music business and open a furniture store when he found out Campbell was recording his song. Glen first performed the tune on a telethon, and KHJ Radio program director Paul Drew called Capitol for a copy. The record wasn't pressed yet, but Drew obtained an acetate copy from producer Dennis Lambert and started playing it throughout the RKO radio chain. "In a sense, [Drew] forced everyone, Capitol primarily, to go into an even more accelerated rush release because now the record was on radio," Lambert explains.

34 **HAVE YOU NEVER BEEN MELLOW**
Olivia Newton-John *MCA*

35 **GET DOWN TONIGHT**
KC & the Sunshine Band *TK*

36 **LYIN' EYES**
Eagles *Asylum*

37 **YOU'RE NO GOOD**
Linda Ronstadt *Capitol*

38 **MIRACLES**
Jefferson Starship *Grunt*

39 **PLEASE MR. POSTMAN**
Carpenters *A&M*

40 **WILDFIRE**
Michael Murphy *Epic*

41 **AT SEVENTEEN**
Janis Ian *Columbia*

42 **MANDY**
Barry Manilow *Bell*

43 **WHO LOVES YOU**
The Four Seasons *Warner/Curb*

44 **BOOGIE ON REGGAE WOMAN**
Stevie Wonder *Tamla*

45 **PLEASE MR. PLEASE**
Olivia Newton-John *MCA*

46 **SKY HIGH**
Jigsaw *Chelsea*

47 **JACKIE BLUE**
Ozark Mountain Daredevils *A&M*

48 **FEELINGS**
Morris Albert *RCA*

49 **HOW LONG**
Ace *Anchor*

50 **SOME KIND OF WONDERFUL**
Grand Funk *Capitol*

51 **NO NO SONG / SNOOKEROO**
Ringo Starr *Apple*

52 **JUNIOR'S FARM**
Wings *Apple*

53 **EXPRESS**
B.T. Express *Roadshow*

54 **I'M NOT LISA**
Jessi Colter *Capitol*

55 **FIGHT THE POWER (PART 1)**
Isley Brothers *T-Neck*

56 **THE WAY I WANT TO TOUCH YOU**
Captain & Tennille *A&M*

57 **LOVE WON'T LET ME WAIT**
Major Harris *Atlantic*

58 **BALLROOM BLITZ**
Sweet *Capitol*

59 **WHY CAN'T WE BE FRIENDS?**
War *UA*

60 **BAD TIME**
Grand Funk *Capitol*

61 **THEY JUST CAN'T STOP IT (THE GAMES PEOPLE PLAY)**
Spinners *Atlantic*

62 **NIGHTS ON BROADWAY**
Bee Gees *RSO*

63 **WASTED DAYS AND WASTED NIGHTS**
Freddy Fender *ABC/Dot*

64 **ONLY YESTERDAY**
Carpenters *A&M*

65 **SOMEONE SAVED MY LIFE TONIGHT**
Elton John *MCA*

66 **HOW SWEET IT IS (TO BE LOVED BY YOU)**
James Taylor *Warner Bros.*

67 **CHEVY VAN**
Sammy Johns *GRC*

Elton John was in the annual top 10 for the third consecutive year, but with two titles. In 1973 he had the No. 6 song of the year, "Crocodile Rock." In 1974 he had the No. 4 song of the year, "Bennie And The Jets." In 1975 he matched his previous personal best, with "Philadelphia Freedom" at No. 4. Elton wrote the song for Billie Jean King, coach of the Philadelphia Freedoms tennis team. After he was presented with a custom-made team warm-up suit, the singer told the coach: "Billie, I'm going to write a song for you." She dismissed the idea, but two months later Elton was recording at Caribou Studios in Colorado and showed up at the play-offs in Denver with a tape of "Philadelphia Freedom." His other top 10 hit for 1975 was "Island Girl," ranked tenth.

Morris Albert had the No. 48 song of the year with "Feelings," a chart-topping hit in his native Brazil as well as Venezuela, Chile, and Mexico before being released in the U.S. by RCA. That put "Feelings" into a tie for the second highest-ranking song by a Brazilian artist in the rock era. Los Indios Tabajaras, two brothers from Brazil, had the No. 82 song of 1963 with an instrumental version of "Maria Elena." Astrud Gilberto teamed with Stan Getz on "The Girl From Ipanema," the No. 71 song of 1964. Sergio Mendes, born in Niteroi, Brazil, had two songs on the year-end chart of 1968: "The Look Of Love" (No. 48, matching "Feelings") and "The Fool On The Hill" (No. 81). Deodato, a keyboardist from Rio de Janeiro, took top honors for Brazil with the No. 39 song of 1973, a version of Richard Strauss' "Also Sprach Zarathustra."

Disco music, which was represented on the year-end chart in 1974 with hits by the Love Unlimited Orchestra and MFSB, as well as the Hues Corporation and George McCrae, continued to make an impact in 1975. KC & the Sunshine Band had the No. 5 song of the year with "That's The Way (I Like It)" as well as the No. 35 song with "Get Down Tonight." Silver Convention's made-in-Germany "Fly, Robin, Fly" was right behind KC's hit at No. 6. Other big disco hits on the year-end chart for 1975 included "Jive Talkin'" by the Bee Gees (No. 16), "The Hustle" by Van McCoy (No. 17), "Lady Marmalade" by Labelle (No. 20), "You're The First, The Last, My Everything" by Barry White (No. 27), "Shining Star" by Earth, Wind & Fire (No. 33), "Express" by B.T Express (No. 53), "Walking In Rhythm" by the Blackbyrds (No. 68), "Doctor's Orders" by Carol Douglas (No. 85), "Never Can Say Goodbye" by Gloria Gaynor (No. 86), and "It Only Takes A Minute" by Tavares (No. 100).

The Eagles' first song to make a year-end top 100 was "Witchy Woman," the No. 81 song of 1972. In 1975 the group had its highest-ranked year-end song with "One Of These Nights," No. 8 for the year. Two other Eagles' songs made the year-end chart: "Best Of My Love" was No. 25 and "Lyin' Eyes" was No. 36.

68 **WALKING IN RHYTHM**
Blackbyrds *Fantasy*

69 **POETRY MAN**
Phoebe Snow *Shelter*

70 **MAGIC**
Pilot *EMI*

71 **COULD IT BE MAGIC**
Barry Manilow *Arista*

72 **LOW RIDER**
War *UA*

73 **DANCE WITH ME**
Orleans *Asylum*

74 **ONE MAN WOMAN/
ONE WOMAN MAN**
Paul Anka/Odia Coates *UA*

75 **CUT THE CAKE**
Average White Band *Atlantic*

76 **FEEL LIKE MAKIN' LOVE**
Bad Company *Swan Song*

77 **ONLY WOMEN**
Alice Cooper *Atlantic*

78 **THE WAY WE WERE/
TRY TO REMEMBER**
Gladys Knight & the Pips *Buddah*

79 **MIDNIGHT BLUE**
Melissa Manchester *Arista*

80 **HEAT WAVE / LOVE IS A ROSE**
Linda Ronstadt *Asylum*

81 **LONELY PEOPLE**
America *Warner Bros.*

82 **THIS WILL BE**
Natalie Cole *Capitol*

83 **I DON'T LIKE TO SLEEP ALONE**
Paul Anka *UA*

84 **LADY**
Styx *Wooden Nickel*

85 **DOCTOR'S ORDERS**
Carol Douglas *Midland International*

86 **NEVER CAN SAY GOODBYE**
Gloria Gaynor *MGM*

87 **DYNOMITE—PART 1**
Tony Camillo's Bazuka *A&M*

88 **MY LITTLE TOWN**
Simon and Garfunkel *Columbia*

89 **THAT'S THE WAY OF THE WORLD**
Earth, Wind & Fire *Columbia*

90 **RUN JOEY RUN**
David Geddes *Big Tree*

91 **YOU ARE SO BEAUTIFUL**
Joe Cocker *A&M*

92 **MORNING SIDE OF THE MOUNTAIN**
Donny & Marie Osmond *MGM*

93 **AIN'T NO WAY TO TREAT A LADY**
Helen Reddy *Capitol*

94 **ONLY YOU**
Ringo Starr *Apple*

95 **DON'T CALL US, WE'LL CALL YOU**
Sugarloaf/Jerry Corbetta *Claridge*

96 **I ONLY HAVE EYES FOR YOU**
Art Garfunkel *Columbia*

97 **SUPERNATURAL THING—PART 1**
Ben E. King *Atlantic*

98 **GET DOWN, GET DOWN
(GET ON THE FLOOR)**
Joe Simon *Spring*

99 **EMMA**
Hot Chocolate *Rak*

100 **IT ONLY TAKES A MINUTE**
Tavares *Capitol*

The Top 100 Songs of 1976

Boston

1976 WAS THE year Peter Frampton came alive; Stevie Wonder finally released *Songs In The Key Of Life;* and Paul McCartney flew his *Wings Over America*.

Frampton, the former guitarist for the British band Humble Pie, had two singles on the year-end chart from his *Frampton Comes Alive!* album: "Show Me The Way" was the No. 59 song of the year and "Baby, I Love Your Way" just made the chart at No. 99. It was a good year for U.K. artists—they were responsible for 25 of the year's top 100 songs, the highest mark since the heady British Invasion days of 1965, when there were 32 U.K. songs on the year-end chart.

Britain claimed the No. 1 song of the year in the U.S., thanks to Rod Stewart's "Tonight's The Night (Gonna Be Alright)," which topped the Hot 100 for eight weeks. The only British artist to have a No. 1 song of the year in the '70s, Rod was the first solo male artist from his country to lead an annual recap, and the first British act to do so since the Beatles dominated with "Hey Jude" in 1968.

Right behind Stewart at No. 2 was another British act—Paul McCartney's Wings with "Silly Love Songs." It was McCartney's best showing on a year-end chart as lead vocalist since the aforementioned "Hey Jude," and it was the first time since 1964 that the top two songs of the year were British.

01 TONIGHT'S THE NIGHT (GONNA BE ALRIGHT)
Rod Stewart *Warner Bros.*

02 SILLY LOVE SONGS
Wings *Capitol*

03 PLAY THAT FUNKY MUSIC
Wild Cherry *Epic*

04 DISCO DUCK (PART 1)
Rick Dees & His Cast of Idiots *RSO*

05 I WRITE THE SONGS
Barry Manilow *Arista*

06 A FIFTH OF BEETHOVEN
Walter Murphy & the Big Apple Band *Private Stock*

07 DISCO LADY
Johnnie Taylor *Columbia*

08 DON'T GO BREAKING MY HEART
Elton John & Kiki Dee *Rocket*

09 DECEMBER, 1963 (OH, WHAT A NIGHT)
The Four Seasons *Warner/Curb*

10 KISS AND SAY GOODBYE
Manhattans *Columbia*

11 50 WAYS TO LEAVE YOUR LOVER
Paul Simon *Columbia*

12 AFTERNOON DELIGHT
Starland Vocal Band *Windsong*

13 THE RUBBERBAND MAN
Spinners *Atlantic*

14 IF YOU LEAVE ME NOW
Chicago *Columbia*

15 LOVE HANGOVER
Diana Ross *Motown*

16 YOU SHOULD BE DANCING
Bee Gees *RSO*

17 GET UP AND BOOGIE (THAT'S RIGHT)
Silver Convention *Midland International*

18 LOVE MACHINE (PART 1)
The Miracles *Tamla*

19 I'D REALLY LOVE TO SEE YOU TONIGHT
England Dan and John Ford Coley *Big Tree*

20 RIGHT BACK WHERE WE STARTED FROM
Maxine Nightingale *UA*

21 LET YOUR LOVE FLOW
Bellamy Brothers *Warner/Curb*

22 BOOGIE FEVER
The Sylvers *Capitol*

23 LOVE ROLLERCOASTER
Ohio Players *Mercury*

24 DREAM WEAVER
Gary Wright *Warner Bros.*

25 THE WRECK OF THE EDMUND FITZGERALD
Gordon Lightfoot *Reprise*

26 LOVE TO LOVE YOU BABY
Donna Summer *Oasis*

27 MISTY BLUE
Dorothy Moore *Malaco*

28 (SHAKE, SHAKE, SHAKE) SHAKE YOUR BOOTY
KC & the Sunshine Band *TK*

29 ALL BY MYSELF
Eric Carmen *Arista*

30 THEME FROM "MAHOGANY" (DO YOU KNOW WHERE YOU'RE GOING TO)
Diana Ross *Motown*

31 LOVE IS ALIVE
Gary Wright *Warner Bros.*

32 YOU'LL NEVER FIND ANOTHER LOVE LIKE MINE
Lou Rawls *PIR*

Other U.K. artists performing well in 1976 included:

Elton John and Kiki Dee. Elton was a frequent visitor to the year-end chart, but Kiki Dee made her first appearance when she was invited to duet with Elton on "Don't Go Breaking My Heart," the No. 8 song of the year. Born Pauline Matthews in Bradford, England, Dee was the first British female singer signed to Motown in the U.S. In 1973 Elton signed her to his Rocket label, and in 1974 she went to No. 12 on the Hot 100 with "I've Got The Music In Me."

Maxine Nightingale. Raised in Wembley, she started doing session work at 18 and eventually moved to Los Angeles. Songwriters/producers Pierre Tubbs and Vince Edwards asked her to record their song, "Right Back Where We Started From." It went to No. 8 in the U.K. in 1975, but went even higher in the U.S., where it spent two weeks at No. 2, good enough to make it the No. 20 song of 1976.

Hot Chocolate. Errol Brown, a vocalist from Jamaica, and Tony Wilson, a bass player from Trinidad, got their first break when Mary Hopkin recorded their song "Think About The Children" for Apple. A secretary at Apple suggested they call themselves Hot Chocolate, and they recorded a reggae version of "Give Peace A Chance" for the Beatles' label. They moved to the Rak label and had a No. 1 hit in the U.K. with their song "Brother Louie," covered in the U.S. by Stories. They had their own hit in America in 1975 with "Emma," the No. 99 song of the year, and an even bigger hit in 1976 with "You Sexy Thing," No. 37 for the year.

Bee Gees. After making a comeback in 1975 with "Jive Talkin'," the No. 16 song of the year, the Gibb brothers wanted to work with producer Arif Mardin on their next project. But with the RSO label shifting distribution from Atlantic to Polydor, the Bee Gees lost the services of Mardin, an in-house producer for Atlantic. After an attempt to work with producer Richard Perry failed, the trio produced themselves with the assistance of Albhy Galuten and Karl Richardson, who had worked with Mardin at Criteria Studios during the recording of *Main Course.* The result was the *Children Of The World* album. The first single issued, "You Should Be Dancing," topped the Hot 100 and was the No. 16 song of the year. The follow-up single, "Love So Right," ranked No. 33 for the year.

Other U.K. artists who made the year-end chart in 1976 included Nazareth, a hard-rocking Scottish band that covered Boudleaux Bryant's "Love Hurts," previously recorded by the Everly Brothers and Roy Orbison; Queen, a glam-rock band fronted by Freddie Mercury that had hits in 1976 with "Bohemian Rhapsody" and "You're My Best Friend"; the Bay City Rollers, Scottish teen idols who inspired Rollermania on both sides of the pond, especially in America with their chart-topping "Saturday Night"; David Bowie, who had scored a hit in 1975 with "Fame" and was back again in 1976 with "Golden Years"; Fleetwood Mac, the Anglo-American outfit that had their first year-end chart hits with "Say You Love Me" and "Rhiannon (Will You Ever Win)"; Electric Light Orchestra, the Birmingham band led by Jeff Lynne that melded rock and classical music, resulting in hits like "Evil Woman"; Cliff Richard, who had been charting in England since 1958, but who didn't register on the American year-end chart until "Devil Woman" in 1976; Sweet, the British version of a bubblegum band,

33 **LOVE SO RIGHT**
Bee Gees *RSO*

34 **THEME FROM "S.W.A.T."**
Rhythm Heritage *ABC*

35 **LET 'EM IN**
Wings *Capitol*

36 **LONELY NIGHT (ANGEL FACE)**
Captain & Tennille *A&M*

37 **YOU SEXY THING**
Hot Chocolate *Big Tree*

38 **WELCOME BACK**
John Sebastian *Reprise*

39 **SATURDAY NIGHT**
Bay City Rollers *Arista*

40 **ROCK'N ME**
Steve Miller *Capitol*

41 **MUSKRAT LOVE**
Captain & Tennille *A&M*

42 **CONVOY**
C.W. McCall *MGM*

43 **FOOLED AROUND AND FELL IN LOVE**
Elvin Bishop *Capricorn*

44 **LOWDOWN**
Boz Scaggs *Columbia*

45 **I'LL BE GOOD TO YOU**
Brothers Johnson *A&M*

46 **SARA SMILE**
Daryl Hall and John Oates *RCA*

47 **MOONLIGHT FEELS RIGHT**
Starbuck *Private Stock*

48 **TAKE IT TO THE LIMIT**
Eagles *Asylum*

49 **MORE, MORE, MORE (PT. 1)**
Andrea True Connection *Buddah*

50 **MORE THAN A FEELING**
Boston *Epic*

51 **NADIA'S THEME
(THE YOUNG AND THE RESTLESS)**
Barry DeVorzon & Perry Botkin, Jr. *A&M*

52 **GET CLOSER**
Seals and Crofts *Warner Bros.*

53 **BETH**
Kiss *Casablanca*

54 **LOVE HURTS**
Nazareth *A&M*

55 **BOHEMIAN RHAPSODY**
Queen *Elektra*

56 **YOU ARE THE WOMAN**
Firefall *Atlantic*

57 **I LOVE MUSIC (PART 1)**
The O'Jays *PIR*

58 **SHANNON**
Henry Gross *Lifesong*

59 **SHOW ME THE WAY**
Peter Frampton *A&M*

60 **SHOP AROUND**
Captain & Tennille *A&M*

61 **SHE'S GONE**
Daryl Hall and John Oates *Atlantic*

62 **GOLDEN YEARS**
David Bowie *RCA*

63 **A LITTLE BIT MORE**
Dr. Hook *Capitol*

64 **ROCK AND ROLL MUSIC**
The Beach Boys *Brother*

65 **SWEET THING**
Rufus f/Chaka Khan *ABC*

66 **TIMES OF YOUR LIFE**
Paul Anka *UA*

with "Fox On The Run"; and the Beatles, who returned to the year-end chart for the first time since "Let It Be" and "The Long And Winding Road" in 1970, thanks to Capitol's issue of "Got To Get You Into My Life" as a single.

The No. 3 song of 1976 was "Play That Funky Music" by Wild Cherry, a group that took its name from a box of cough drops. Bob Parissi, leader of the band, was in the hospital and anxious to get out so he could work with the group. They didn't have a name yet, and while the group was visiting him Parissi spied a box of cough drops. He jokingly suggested they name themselves after the flavor of the drops and his visitors took him seriously. The first incarnation of Wild Cherry was signed to the Brown Bag label, owned by Grand Funk manager Terry Knight. When that group broke up, Parissi formed a new Wild Cherry, a rock band frustrated by the popularity of disco music. When they played clubs like the 2001 disco in Pittsburgh, patrons requested that they "play that funky music." Parissi wanted to play rock music and please the people who wanted to hear dance music. Drummer Ron Beitle told him he should do what the customers wanted—"play that funky music, white boy."

The departure of lead singer and charter member Smokey Robinson didn't hurt the Miracles' hit-making status. With new lead vocalist Billy Griffin, the group soared to the top of the Hot 100 with "Love Machine (Part 1)," the No. 18 song of 1976. It was the group's best year-end showing since "The Tears Of A Clown" was the No. 12 song of 1970.

"A Fifth Of Beethoven" by Walter Murphy, the No. 6 song of 1976, became the highest ranking instrumental on a year-end chart since Paul Mauriat's "Love Is Blue" was the No. 3 song of 1968. Murphy, a Madison Avenue jingle writer and former arranger for Doc Severinsen and *The Tonight Show* orchestra, noted how two previous rock hits, "A Lover's Concerto" by the Toys and "Joy" by Apollo 100, had incorporated classical music into pop songs. He wanted to do the same, and made a demo tape of several classical and neo-classical works. Larry Uttal, founder of the Private Stock label, liked Murphy's disco treatment of Beethoven's Symphony No. 5 In C Minor and released the track as a single.

"Mandy" was Barry Manilow's first year-end chart listing, No. 42 for the year 1975. He didn't write it, and vowed it would be the only "outside" song he would ever record. Then Clive Davis sent him "I Write The Songs," composed by Bruce Johnston. Barry went to the Arista office to tell Clive in person of his decision not to record the song. Fortunately, Barry later changed his mind. It ranked No. 5 for the year and was his most successful chart single of all time.

67 **STILL THE ONE**
Orleans *Asylum*

68 **ONLY SIXTEEN**
Dr. Hook *Capitol*

69 **SAY YOU LOVE ME**
Fleetwood Mac *Reprise*

70 **EVIL WOMAN**
Electric Light Orchestra *UA*

71 **FOX ON THE RUN**
Sweet *Capitol*

72 **SING A SONG**
Earth, Wind & Fire *Columbia*

73 **DEVIL WOMAN**
Cliff Richard *Rocket*

74 **SORRY SEEMS TO BE THE HARDEST WORD**
Elton John *MCA/Rocket*

75 **SWEET LOVE**
Commodores *Motown*

76 **GOT TO GET YOU INTO MY LIFE**
The Beatles *Capitol*

77 **DREAM ON**
Aerosmith *Columbia*

78 **SUMMER**
War *UA*

79 **BREAKING UP IS HARD TO DO**
Neil Sedaka *Rocket*

80 **MAGIC MAN**
Heart *Mushroom*

81 **(DON'T FEAR) THE REAPER**
Blue Öyster Cult *Columbia*

82 **LOVE ME**
Yvonne Elliman *RSO*

83 **WAKE UP EVERYBODY (PART 1)**
Harold Melvin & the Blue Notes *PIR*

84 **TURN THE BEAT AROUND**
Vicki Sue Robinson *RCA*

85 **FANNY (BE TENDER WITH MY LOVE)**
Bee Gees *RSO*

86 **DEEP PURPLE**
Donny & Marie Osmond *MGM*

87 **FERNANDO**
Abba *Atlantic*

88 **BABY FACE**
Wing and a Prayer Fife & Drum Corps *Wing and a Prayer*

89 **NIGHTS ARE FOREVER WITHOUT YOU**
England Dan and John Ford Coley *Big Tree*

90 **JUST TO BE CLOSE TO YOU**
Commodores *Motown*

91 **WALK AWAY FROM LOVE**
David Ruffin *Motown*

92 **MONEY HONEY**
Bay City Rollers *Arista*

93 **TRYIN' TO GET THE FEELING AGAIN**
Barry Manilow *Arista*

94 **THIS MASQUERADE**
George Benson *Warner Bros.*

95 **RHIANNON (WILL YOU EVER WIN)**
Fleetwood Mac *Reprise*

96 **THAT'LL BE THE DAY**
Linda Ronstadt *Asylum*

97 **I ONLY WANT TO BE WITH YOU**
Bay City Rollers *Arista*

98 **COUNTRY BOY**
(YOU GOT YOUR FEET IN L.A.)
Glen Campbell *Capitol*

99 **BABY, I LOVE YOUR WAY**
Peter Frampton *A&M*

100 **HAPPY DAYS** Pratt & McClain *Reprise*

The Top 100 Songs of 1977

Abba

1977 WAS THE year the Sex Pistols went through three labels in less than six months; Studio 54 opened in Manhattan; and Elvis Presley was found dead on the floor of his bathroom at Graceland.

The Gibb family nabbed the No. 2 and No. 3 positions on the year-end chart. The Bee Gees were in third place with the first single from *Saturday Night Fever,* "How Deep Is Your Love." Their youngest brother Andy was runner-up for the year with his first American single, "I Just Want To Be Your Everything." It was the only time in the rock era that brothers occupied two out of the top three slots on a year-end chart.

Half of the top 10 songs of the year featured female lead vocalists — the highest total since 1963, when the Singing Nun, Paul and Paula, the Chiffons, Little Peggy March, and Lesley Gore all registered in the top 10. Debby Boone led the list, and became the fourth female soloist of the rock era to have the highest-ranked song of the year, following Lulu in 1967 with "To Sir With Love," Carly Simon in 1973 with "You're So Vain," and Barbra Streisand in 1974 with "The Way We Were." Like Lulu and Barbra, Debby did it with a song from a film. Unlike her predecessors, Debby did not appear in the movie, nor did she perform the song in the film. Didi Conn had the female lead in *You Light Up My Life,* and she lip-synched to vocals

01 **YOU LIGHT UP MY LIFE**
Debby Boone *Warner/Curb*

02 **I JUST WANT TO BE YOUR EVERYTHING**
Andy Gibb *RSO*

03 **HOW DEEP IS YOUR LOVE**
Bee Gees *RSO*

04 **BEST OF MY LOVE**
Emotions *Columbia*

05 **LOVE THEME FROM "A STAR IS BORN" (EVERGREEN)**
Barbra Streisand *Columbia*

06 **SIR DUKE**
Stevie Wonder *Tamla*

07 **YOU DON'T HAVE TO BE A STAR (TO BE IN MY SHOW)**
Marilyn McCoo and Billy Davis, Jr. *ABC*

08 **YOU MAKE ME FEEL LIKE DANCING**
Leo Sayer *Warner Bros.*

09 **DON'T LEAVE ME THIS WAY**
Thelma Houston *Tamla*

10 **NEW KID IN TOWN**
Eagles *Asylum*

11 **DON'T IT MAKE MY BROWN EYES BLUE**
Crystal Gayle *UA*

12 **CAR WASH**
Rose Royce *MCA*

13 **WHEN I NEED YOU**
Leo Sayer *Warner Bros.*

14 **GOT TO GIVE IT UP (PT. 1)**
Marvin Gaye *Tamla*

15 **HOTEL CALIFORNIA**
Eagles *Asylum*

16 **BOOGIE NIGHTS**
Heatwave *Epic*

17 **SOUTHERN NIGHTS**
Glen Campbell *Capitol*

18 **TORN BETWEEN TWO LOVERS**
Mary MacGregor *Ariola America*

19 **UNDERCOVER ANGEL**
Alan O'Day *Pacific*

20 **NOBODY DOES IT BETTER**
Carly Simon *Elektra*

21 **RICH GIRL**
Daryl Hall and John Oates *RCA*

22 **I WISH**
Stevie Wonder *Tamla*

23 **GONNA FLY NOW (THEME FROM "ROCKY")**
Bill Conti *UA*

24 **(YOUR LOVE HAS LIFTED ME) HIGHER AND HIGHER**
Rita Coolidge *A&M*

25 **I'M YOUR BOOGIE MAN**
KC & the Sunshine Band *TK*

26 **KEEP IT COMIN' LOVE**
KC & the Sunshine Band *TK*

27 **DANCING QUEEN**
Abba *Atlantic*

28 **I'M IN YOU**
Peter Frampton *A&M*

29 **LOOKS LIKE WE MADE IT**
Barry Manilow *Arista*

30 **DON'T GIVE UP ON US**
David Soul *Private Stock*

31 **FLY LIKE AN EAGLE**
Steve Miller *Capitol*

32 **BLUE BAYOU**
Linda Ronstadt *Asylum*

33 **DA DOO RON RON**
Shaun Cassidy *Warner/Curb*

by commercial jingle singer Kacey Cisyk. "You Light Up My Life" was the second No. 1 song of the year in the rock era to also be an Oscar winner, following "The Way We Were." Debby's father Pat had the No. 1 song of 1957, "Love Letters In The Sand," making the Boones the only parent and child to both have No. 1 records of the year.

The Emotions had the No. 4 single of 1977 with "Best Of My Love." Sisters Sheila, Wanda, and Jeanette first performed in a gospel group with their father, Joe. Through the Staple Sisters, they were signed to Stax/Volt and recorded secular material. Sister Pam replaced Jeanette, but when Stax folded they were left without a label. They signed a production deal with Maurice White of Earth, Wind & Fire. White co-wrote and produced "Best Of My Love," which spent five weeks atop The Billboard Hot 100.

Barbra Streisand was No. 5 for the year with only the second song she had ever written: the love theme from the third filmed version of *A Star Is Born.* Streisand starred in the production with Kris Kristofferson. The movie garnered only one Oscar nomination: for Best Original Song. The award went to Streisand and her co-writer, Paul Williams. "Evergreen" is Streisand's second-best showing on a year-end chart, topped only by "The Way We Were" in 1974.

Marilyn McCoo and Billy Davis, Jr. made their first appearance on a year-end chart in seven years. As two-fifths of the 5th Dimension, they had the No. 17 song of 1970, "One Less Bell To Answer." They came in ten spots higher in 1977, No. 7 for the year with their duet, "You Don't Have To Be A Star (To Be In My Show)." The husband and wife team departed the 5th Dimension in 1975, attributing their stepping out on their own to having completed est training. Don Davis, producer of Johnnie Taylor's chart-topping hit "Disco Lady," was preparing to record a solo album for Marilyn when Billy decided their first project away from the 5th Dimension should be an album of duets. Davis had a demo by songwriters James Dean and John Glover that wasn't written for two vocalists, but Davis thought it would be perfect for Marilyn and Billy to record together. Released as their second single, "You Don't Have To Be A Star" spent one week atop the Hot 100.

Thelma Houston's remake of Harold Melvin & the Blue Notes' "Don't Leave Me This Way" was the No. 9 song of 1977. The second most successful Kenny Gamble–Leon Huff recording of the rock era, it was a triumph for Houston, who had one minor chart hit on Dunhill before signing with Motown's west coast subsidiary, Mowest, in 1971. Producer Hal Davis admired Teddy Pendergrass' vocal on the original "Don't Leave Me This Way" and decided to have Houston cover it on the Tamla label.

Stevie Wonder had his first year-end top 10 hit since 1963, when he was billed as Little Stevie Wonder. "Fingertips—Pt 2" was No. 8 that year; "Sir Duke" became his highest year-end song to date by coming in sixth place for 1977.

Leo Sayer had three songs included in the top 100 of 1977. "You Make Me Feel Like Dancing" was his biggest hit, ranked No. 8 for the year. Managed by former pop singer Adam Faith, Sayer's name first became known in America as the writer of "The Show Must Go On," a tune covered by Three Dog Night. Linked up with producer Richard Perry, Sayer recorded the *Endless Flight* album and recorded other people's material for the

34 DREAMS
Fleetwood Mac *Warner Bros.*

35 BLINDED BY THE LIGHT
Manfred Mann's Earth Band *Warner Bros.*

36 STAR WARS THEME/CANTINA BAND
Meco *Millennium*

37 I LIKE DREAMIN'
Kenny Nolan *20th Century*

38 THAT'S ROCK 'N' ROLL
Shaun Cassidy *Warner/Curb*

39 DAZZ
Brick *Bang*

40 DON'T STOP
Fleetwood Mac *Warner Bros.*

41 FLOAT ON
The Floaters *ABC*

42 ANGEL IN YOUR ARMS
Hot *Big Tree*

43 FEELS LIKE THE FIRST TIME
Foreigner *Atlantic*

44 (EVERY TIME I TURN AROUND) BACK IN LOVE AGAIN
L.T.D. *A&M*

45 MY HEART BELONGS TO ME
Barbra Streisand *Columbia*

46 DO YOU WANNA MAKE LOVE
Peter McCann *20th Century*

47 COLD AS ICE
Foreigner *Atlantic*

48 EASY
Commodores *Motown*

49 COULDN'T GET IT RIGHT
Climax Blues Band *Sire*

50 HANDY MAN
James Taylor *Columbia*

51 IT'S ECSTASY WHEN YOU LAY DOWN NEXT TO ME
Barry White *20th Century*

52 NIGHT MOVES
Bob Seger *Capitol*

53 SWAYIN' TO THE MUSIC (SLOW DANCIN')
Johnny Rivers *Big Tree*

54 HOT LINE
The Sylvers *Capitol*

55 SO IN TO YOU
Atlanta Rhythm Section *Polydor*

56 HEAVEN ON THE SEVENTH FLOOR
Paul Nicholas *RSO*

57 I FEEL LOVE
Donna Summer *Casablanca*

58 TELEPHONE LINE
Electric Light Orchestra *UA*

59 BABY, WHAT A BIG SURPRISE
Chicago *Columbia*

60 THE THINGS WE DO FOR LOVE
10cc *Mercury*

61 ON AND ON
Stephen Bishop *ABC*

62 LUCILLE
Kenny Rogers *UA*

63 ENJOY YOURSELF
The Jacksons *Epic*

64 MARGARITAVILLE
Jimmy Buffett *ABC*

65 RIGHT TIME OF THE NIGHT
Jennifer Warnes *Arista*

66 AFTER THE LOVIN'
Engelbert Humperdinck *Epic*

first time. He wrote the album's first No. 1 single, "You Make Me Feel Like Dancing," but the next chart-topper, "When I Need You" (No. 13 for the year), was penned by Albert Hammond and Carole Bayer Sager. The follow-up, "How Much Love" (No. 97 for the year), was written by Sayer with Barry Mann.

The Eagles collected their second year-end top 10 hit, as "New Kid In Town" fell into the No. 10 slot. Two years earlier, "One Of These Nights" placed eighth.

"Boogie Nights" by the Anglo-American disco outfit known as Heatwave was the No. 16 single of 1977. Brothers Johnny and Keith Wilder of Dayton, Ohio, served in the army in West Germany and after being discharged decided to remain in Europe. British keyboard player Rod Temperton was working in Germany when he responded to an ad placed by the Wilders in a music paper. After playing clubs in Britain and Air Force bases throughout Europe, they were signed to the GTO label in the U.K. Barry Blue, who had several U.K. hits as a performer in 1973 and 1974, produced their album *Too Hot To Handle* and Temperton wrote their key hits, including "Boogie Nights" and "Always And Forever." He left the group in 1978 but continued to write for Heatwave as well as for some artists produced by Quincy Jones, including George Benson ("Give Me The Night") and Michael Jackson ("Rock With You," "Off The Wall," and "Thriller").

67 **LOST WITHOUT YOUR LOVE**
Bread *Elektra*

68 **I NEVER CRY**
Alice Cooper *Warner Bros.*

69 **I'VE GOT LOVE ON MY MIND**
Natalie Cole *Capitol*

70 **WE'RE ALL ALONE**
Rita Coolidge *A&M*

71 **WHATCHA GONNA DO?**
Pablo Cruise *A&M*

72 **IT'S SO EASY**
Linda Ronstadt *Asylum*

73 **LONELY BOY**
Andrew Gold *Asylum*

74 **JET AIRLINER**
Steve Miller Band *Capitol*

75 **STAND TALL**
Burton Cummings *Portrait*

76 **CARRY ON WAYWARD SON**
Kansas *Kirshner*

77 **BARRACUDA**
Heart *Portrait*

78 **STRAWBERRY LETTER 23**
Brothers Johnson *A&M*

79 **BRICK HOUSE**
Commodores *Motown*

80 **JUST A SONG BEFORE I GO**
Crosby, Stills & Nash *Atlantic*

81 **YOU AND ME**
Alice Cooper *Warner Bros.*

82 **LIVIN' THING**
Electric Light Orchestra *UA*

83 **HEARD IT IN A LOVE SONG**
Marshall Tucker Band *Capricorn*

84 **JEANS ON**
David Dundas *Chrysalis*

85 **LIDO SHUFFLE**
Boz Scaggs *Columbia*

86 **YOU MAKE LOVING FUN**
Fleetwood Mac *Warner Bros.*

87 **MAYBE I'M AMAZED**
Wings *Capitol*

88 **YOU CAN'T TURN ME OFF**
(IN THE MIDDLE OF TURNING ME ON)
High Inergy *Gordy*

89 **SMOKE FROM A DISTANT FIRE**
Sanford/Townsend Band *Warner Bros.*

90 **GO YOUR OWN WAY**
Fleetwood Mac *Warner Bros.*

91 **SOMEBODY TO LOVE**
Queen *Elektra*

92 **WALK THIS WAY**
Aerosmith *Columbia*

93 **ISN'T IT TIME**
The Babys *Chrysalis*

94 **JUST REMEMBER I LOVE YOU**
Firefall *Atlantic*

95 **AIN'T GONNA BUMP NO MORE**
(WITH NO BIG FAT WOMAN)
Joe Tex *Epic*

96 **HIGH SCHOOL DANCE**
The Sylvers *Capitol*

97 **HOW MUCH LOVE**
Leo Sayer *Warner Bros.*

98 **YOU'RE MY WORLD**
Helen Reddy *Capitol*

99 **I WANNA GET NEXT TO YOU**
Rose Royce *MCA*

100 **YEAR OF THE CAT** Al Stewart *Janus*

The Top 100 Songs of 1978

Frankie Valli

1978 WAS THE year the Bee Gees and Peter Frampton starred in *Sgt. Pepper's Lonely Hearts Club Band;* Lucille Ball asked for her photograph to be removed from the cover of the Rolling Stones' *Some Girls* album; and Keith Moon of the Who died.

The films *Saturday Night Fever* and *Grease,* both of which starred John Travolta, were responsible for seven of the songs in the year's top 100. The Bee Gees led the charge with "Stayin' Alive" (No. 2) and "Night Fever" (No. 3), the first time in the rock era that two songs from the same film were in the top five singles of the year. The other song from *Saturday Night Fever* on the chart was "If I Can't Have You," written by the Bee Gees and performed by Yvonne Elliman. It ranked No. 16.

Travolta and his co-star Olivia Newton-John placed two duets from *Grease* on the year-end chart. "You're The One That I Want," the No. 15 song of 1978, was written for the movie while "Summer Nights," No. 60 for the year, had been written for the original Broadway production. Olivia's "Hopelessly Devoted To You," No. 28 for the year, was another song written for the film.

Robert Stigwood's RSO label had five songs in the top 10 and 14 songs in the top 100 of the year. That's the second-highest total of the rock era (Columbia had 15 singles on the year-end charts for 1982 and 1983). In addition to the songs from *Saturday Night Fever* and *Grease,* RSO scored with singles from Player, Eric Clapton, and Andy Gibb.

The group Player was originally signed to Haven, a label owned by producers Dennis Lambert and Brian Potter. When the label folded,

Lambert and Potter signed the group to RSO. Their first album had already been recorded, but not released. Peter Beckett, a guitarist from Liverpool, and John Charles Crowley, a musician from Galveston Bay, Texas, had written "Baby Come Back" after breaking up with their respective girlfriends. The song ranked No. 10 for the year and the follow-up, "This Time I'm In It For Love," was No. 89.

Eric Clapton, a bricklayer's son born in Ripley, England, had the No. 19 song of the year, "Lay Down Sally." He first made the year-end chart in 1968 as part of Cream, when "Sunshine Of Your Love" was the No. 61 song of the year. He bettered that mark in 1974, when "I Shot The Sheriff" came in at No. 29. As a member of Derek & the Dominos, he ranked No. 85 in 1972 with "Layla."

As songwriters, the Gibbs had nine songs included in the year's top 100. Aside from singles by the Bee Gees, Andy Gibb, and their soundtrack material, the Gibbs came up with a tune for Australian vocalist Samantha Sang. She first met Barry Gibb in 1969 when he wrote and produced "Don't Let It Happen Again" for her, but it wasn't a hit. They reunited in Paris in 1977 and Samantha asked for another song. Barry gave her a choice between "Emotion" and "(Our Love) Don't Throw It All Away." She chose the former and the latter was recorded by Andy. Stigwood declined to release Samantha's Bee Gees–sounding single on RSO, and Larry Uttal picked it up for Private Stock. It was the No. 26 song of the year.

The No. 1 song of 1978 was the last song to top the Hot 100 in the calendar year. "Le Freak" by Chic moved into pole position the week ending December 9 and remained there for five weeks. Bernard Edwards and Nile Rodgers thought disco music "was like a gift from heaven." "Discos gave us the perfect opportunity to realize our concept, because it wasn't about being black, white, male, or female. Further, it would give us a chance to get into the mainstream. We wanted millions of dollars, Ferraris and planes—and this seemed like the way to get them," Rodgers said in *Melody Maker*. Edwards confessed that at first, he hated disco. "I got into it, though, and realized that if we did it our way, it'd be pretty good." Despite two rejections by Atlantic Records, they were finally signed to the label. Their first hit, "Dance, Dance, Dance (Yowsah, Yowsah, Yowsah)," was the No. 43 song of 1978. "Le Freak" was their third single. It became the most successful chart single issued on Atlantic to date and firmly established the reputations of Rodgers and Edwards. They went on to produce, as a team and individually, artists as diverse as Diana Ross, David Bowie, Debbie Harry, Duran Duran, Madonna, Carly Simon, and Sister Sledge.

A group named after a song, A Taste of Honey, had the No. 5 record of 1978 with their first chart single, "Boogie Oogie Oogie." The band was fronted by two female guitarists, Janice Marie Johnson and Hazel Payne. Johnson wrote "Boogie Oogie Oogie" with group member Perry Kibble after a frustrating gig at an Air Force club. "We were knocking ourselves out, but getting no reaction from the crowd," Janice recalls. "In fact, they seemed to have contempt for two women who thought they could front a band." Angered at the military chauvinism she felt, Janice went home and started writing the song.

The highest-ranked Motown song of the year was the first chart-topping single by the Commodores. Lionel Richie was inspired to write "Three Times A Lady" at a party celebrating his parents' 37th wedding anniversary. When his father delivered a heartfelt speech thanking his wife, Richie realized he had never really expressed gratitude to his wife, and did so in the form of the song.

Songwriter Jimmy Webb had his first and only top ten song of a year in 1978, thanks to Donna Summer's remake of "MacArthur Park." Ten years earlier, Richard Harris' version of a song intended for the Association went to No. 2 on the Hot 100 and ranked No. 35 for the year. Summer's recording was her first chart-topper, and finished seventh for the year.

Songwriters Mike Chapman and Nicky Chinn had their first American No. 1 with Exile's "Kiss You All Over," the No. 8 song of 1978. "It's a very unusual song and is very much about what music in the U.S. is all about in 1978," Chapman told Jim McCullaugh in *Billboard* at the time.

Paul Davis set a longevity record in 1978 by remaining on the Hot 100 for 40 weeks with "I Go Crazy." The song was originally written as a demo for Lou Rawls. Davis, who first made the Hot 100 with an updating of the Jarmels' "A Little Bit Of Soap," had decided to concentrate on songwriting instead of his recording career. He submitted "I Go Crazy" to Rawls' producer, Kenny Gamble, at Philadelphia International Records. Gamble loved the song and wanted to cut it on Lou, but that response made Davis' label, Bang Records, take notice of the song. Reasoning that if the song was good enough for Lou Rawls, it was certainly good enough for Davis to record, Bang issued Davis' version in the summer of 1977. It began a long climb into the top 10, peaking at No. 7 in its 30th week on the chart.

Nick Gilder's family moved from London, England, to Vancouver in British Columbia, Canada, when he was 10. After college, he formed a group called Sweeney Todd with guitarist Jimmy McCulloch. They signed with London Records, and released a song called "Roxy Roller" in 1976. Group infighting led Gilder and McCulloch to split the band and relocate to Los Angeles. They signed with Chrysalis Records and their former label responded by reissuing "Roxy Roller" with a new lead vocalist. Chrysalis had Gilder record a new version, and a third version was released by a new incarnation of Sweeney Todd. All three singles bombed. Gilder worked with producers George Martin and Stuart Alan Love before Chrysalis teamed him with Mike Chapman. "Hot Child In The City" was one of three tracks recorded in a three-day period. Chapman wanted the label to release "All Because Of Love," but Chrysalis preferred "Hot Child In The City." It topped the Hot 100 and was the No. 14 song of 1978.

68 **YOU BELONG TO ME**
Carly Simon *Elektra*

69 **GET OFF**
Foxy *Dash*

70 **TWO OUT OF THREE AIN'T BAD**
Meat Loaf *Epic*

71 **DISCO INFERNO**
The Trammps *Atlantic*

72 **MY ANGEL BABY**
Toby Beau *RCA*

73 **HOW YOU GONNA SEE ME NOW**
Alice Cooper *Warner Bros.*

74 **SERPENTINE FIRE**
Earth, Wind & Fire *Columbia*

75 **SENTIMENTAL LADY**
Bob Welch *Capitol*

76 **FLASH LIGHT**
Parliament *Casablanca*

77 **GOODBYE GIRL**
David Gates *Elektra*

78 **ON BROADWAY**
George Benson *Warner Bros.*

79 **SWEET TALKIN' WOMAN**
Electric Light Orchestra *Jet*

80 **COPACABANA (AT THE COPA)**
Barry Manilow *Arista*

81 **STRANGE WAY**
Firefall *Atlantic*

82 **FOOL (IF YOU THINK IT'S OVER)**
Chris Rea *UA*

83 **WHAT'S YOUR NAME**
Lynyrd Skynyrd *MCA*

84 **RUNNING ON EMPTY**
Jackson Browne *Asylum*

85 **BLUER THAN BLUE**
Michael Johnson *EMI America*

86 **HOLLYWOOD NIGHTS**
Bob Seger & the Silver Bullet Band *Capitol*

87 **SWEET LIFE**
Paul Davis *Bang*

88 **SHAME**
Evelyn "Champagne" King *RCA*

89 **THIS TIME I'M IN IT FOR LOVE**
Player *RSO*

90 **LIFE'S BEEN GOOD**
Joe Walsh *Asylum*

91 **READY TO TAKE A CHANCE AGAIN**
Barry Manilow *Arista*

92 **BABY HOLD ON**
Eddie Money *Columbia*

93 **RIGHT DOWN THE LINE**
Gerry Rafferty *UA*

94 **WHO ARE YOU**
The Who *MCA*

95 **TURN TO STONE**
Electric Light Orchestra *Jet*

96 **RUNAROUND SUE**
Leif Garrett *Atlantic*

97 **EBONY EYES**
Bob Welch *Capitol*

98 **BACK IN THE U.S.A.**
Linda Ronstadt *Asylum*

99 **ALWAYS AND FOREVER**
Heatwave *Epic*

100 **GOT TO GET YOU INTO MY LIFE**
Earth, Wind & Fire *Columbia*

The Top 100 Songs of 1979

Chic

1979 WAS THE year a Chicago DJ caused a riot at a White Sox game by burning a pile of disco records; Bette Midler starred in *The Rose;* and everybody wanted to *Get The Knack*.

Neil Bogart's Casablanca Records took top honors. There were nine Casablanca singles included in the top 100 songs of the year. That was one better than the previous year's champ, RSO, which had eight songs on the year-end chart for 1979 after a record-setting 14 entries in 1978.

Donna Summer became the first female solo artist in the rock era to have two singles in a year-end top 10. She had the No. 1 record of the year, "Hot Stuff," as well as No. 4, "Bad Girls." She first appeared on a year-end chart in 1976, when "Love To Love You Baby" was the No. 26 song of the year. In 1977, she ranked No. 57 with "I Feel Love," and in 1978 she was No. 7 with "MacArthur Park" and No. 29 with "Last Dance." Her most successful chart single, "Hot Stuff" was written on an old piano in the coffee room of a studio on La Brea Avenue in Hollywood, according to co-writer Keith Forsey. "It was modeled after the tempo of Rod Stewart's 'Da Ya Think I'm Sexy,'" he admits. Critics called it a successful merger of rock with disco. Summer had three other singles included in the top 100 of the year: "No More Tears (Enough Is Enough)" with Barbra Streisand at No. 16, "Dim All The Lights" at No. 24, and "Heaven Knows" with Brooklyn Dreams at No. 34.

After Donna Summer's two top five hits, the next Casablanca song on the annual tally was "Y.M.C.A." by the Village People. Jacques Morali, the French producer of the Ritchie Family's hits ("Brazil" and "The Best Disco In Town"), was inspired by all of the "macho men" he saw at Les Mouches, a gay disco in Greenwich Village. Felipe Rose was there that night, wearing an Indian costume. Morali later told *Rolling Stone:* "I say to myself, 'You

01 HOT STUFF
Donna Summer *Casablanca*

02 MY SHARONA
The Knack *Capitol*

03 I WILL SURVIVE
Gloria Gaynor *Polydor*

04 BAD GIRLS
Donna Summer *Casablanca*

05 DA YA THINK I'M SEXY?
Rod Stewart *Warner Bros.*

06 REUNITED
Peaches and Herb *Polydor*

07 RING MY BELL
Anita Ward *Juana*

08 TOO MUCH HEAVEN
Bee Gees *RSO*

09 GOOD TIMES
Chic *Atlantic*

10 ESCAPE (PINA COLADA SONG)
Rupert Holmes *Infinity*

11 BABE
Styx *A&M*

12 RISE
Herb Alpert *A&M*

13 Y.M.C.A.
Village People *Casablanca*

14 STILL
Commodores *Motown*

15 TRAGEDY
Bee Gees *RSO*

16 NO MORE TEARS (ENOUGH IS ENOUGH)
Barbra Streisand & Donna Summer *Columbia*

17 HEART OF GLASS
Blondie *Chrysalis*

18 WHAT A FOOL BELIEVES
Doobie Brothers *Warner Bros.*

19 SAD EYES
Robert John *EMI America*

20 POP MUZIK
M *Sire*

21 DON'T STOP 'TIL YOU GET ENOUGH
Michael Jackson *Epic*

22 FIRE
Pointer Sisters *Planet*

23 AFTER THE LOVE HAS GONE
Earth, Wind & Fire *ARC*

24 DIM ALL THE LIGHTS
Donna Summer *Casablanca*

25 KNOCK ON WOOD
Amii Stewart *Ariola*

26 A LITTLE MORE LOVE
Olivia Newton-John *MCA*

27 MY LIFE
Billy Joel *Columbia*

28 WE ARE FAMILY
Sister Sledge *Cotillion*

29 THE MAIN EVENT/FIGHT
Barbra Streisand *Columbia*

30 HEARTACHE TONIGHT
Eagles *Asylum*

31 LOVE YOU INSIDE OUT
Bee Gees *RSO*

32 SEND ONE YOUR LOVE
Stevie Wonder *Tamla*

33 IN THE NAVY
Village People *Casablanca*

34 HEAVEN KNOWS
Donna Summer w/Brooklyn Dreams *Casablanca*

know, this is fantastic—to see the cowboy, the Indian, the construction worker with other men around.' And also, I think to myself that the gay people have no group, nobody to personalize the gay people, you know?" Morali put all the stereotypes together and formed the Village People with Victor Willis as lead singer. "San Francisco (You've Got Me)" missed the pop singles chart, but "Macho Man" peaked at No. 25. "Y.M.C.A." was their biggest hit, spending three weeks at No. 2 and remaining on the chart for half a year.

Casablanca was also represented on the year-end chart by Kiss and Cher. The glam-rock band was No. 74 with "I Was Made For Lovin' You," and guitarist Ace Frehley had a solo hit at No. 76 with a cover of Hello's "New York Groove." Cher was No. 82 with "Take Me Home."

There were six singles in the top 10 featuring female lead singers, a new record. In addition to the two titles by Donna Summer, the top 10 included Gloria Gaynor, Peaches (of Peaches and Herb), Anita Ward, and the two female singers in Chic, Luci Martin and Norma Jean Wright.

Gaynor first recorded in 1965 for Johnny Nash's Jocinda label. She had a brief tenure in the Soul Satisfiers group, then released "Honey Bee" on Columbia before signing with MGM. In 1975 she made the year-end chart for the first time with an updating of the Jackson Five's "Never Can Say Goodbye," an early disco record. It was the No. 86 song of the year. Gaynor had been off the chart for three years when "I Will Survive" debuted. It was originally the "B" side of a single featuring a song called "Substitute." But discos and DJs preferred the defiant declaration of independence Gaynor made in "I Will Survive," and that side spent three weeks atop the Hot 100.

Linda Greene was Peaches and Herb Fame was Herb on the duet "Reunited," the No. 6 song of 1979. Greene was the third vocalist to assume the role of "Peaches." Francine Barker was the lead singer of the Sweet Things when she was asked by producer Van McCoy to record a duet with record store clerk Herb Feemster. The original Peaches and Herb were signed to Columbia's Date label and first made the Hot 100 during the last week of 1966 with "Let's Fall In Love." The follow-up, "Close Your Eyes," was the No. 91 song of 1967. Francine took a leave of absence in 1968 and was replaced by Marlene Mack. One day in 1970, Herb took an exam for the Washington, D.C., police department, and when he was given a job on the force he quit Peaches and Herb. Six years later he felt it was time to bring the duo back. McCoy told Herb about Linda Greene, and she became the new Peaches on an MCA album. Then the duo switched to Polydor and teamed with producer Freddie Perren. An upbeat single, "Shake Your Groove Thing," brought them back to the Hot 100 and ranked No. 51 for 1979. "Reunited," a sweet ballad, was released as the follow-up.

Substitute teacher Anita Ward made the year-end top 10 with her very first chart entry. Frederick Knight wrote "Ring My Bell" for 11-year-old Stacy Lattisaw, thinking she was going to sign with his production company, but she went to Atlantic's Cotillion label instead. Knight was recording an album with Ward and needed one more uptempo song to complete the set. Overnight he rewrote the teenybopper "Ring My Bell" for an adult woman

35 **STUMBLIN' IN**
Suzi Quatro & Chris Norman *RSO*

36 **I'LL NEVER LOVE THIS WAY AGAIN**
Dionne Warwick *Arista*

37 **THE DEVIL WENT
DOWN TO GEORGIA**
Charlie Daniels Band *Epic*

38 **MUSIC BOX DANCER**
Frank Mills *Polydor*

39 **SHARING THE NIGHT TOGETHER**
Dr. Hook *Capitol*

40 **SAIL ON**
Commodores *Motown*

41 **JUST WHEN I NEEDED YOU MOST**
Randy Vanwarmer *Bearsville*

42 **SULTANS OF SWING**
Dire Straits *Warner Bros.*

43 **MAKIN' IT**
David Naughton *RSO*

44 **DON'T BRING ME DOWN**
Electric Light Orchestra *Jet*

45 **CHUCK E.'S IN LOVE**
Rickie Lee Jones *Warner Bros.*

46 **WHEN YOU'RE IN LOVE
WITH A BEAUTIFUL WOMAN**
Dr. Hook *Capitol*

47 **LOTTA LOVE**
Nicolette Larson *Warner Bros.*

48 **HEAVEN MUST HAVE SENT YOU**
Bonnie Pointer *Motown*

49 **THE LOGICAL SONG**
Supertramp *A&M*

50 **SHE BELIEVES IN ME**
Kenny Rogers *UA*

51 **SHAKE YOUR GROOVE THING**
Peaches and Herb *Polydor*

52 **LONESOME LOSER**
Little River Band *Capitol*

53 **LEAD ME ON**
Maxine Nightingale *Windsong*

54 **SHAKE YOUR BODY
(DOWN TO THE GROUND)**
The Jacksons *Epic*

55 **MAMA CAN'T BUY YOU LOVE**
Elton John *MCA*

56 **GOODNIGHT TONIGHT**
Wings *Columbia*

57 **HOLD THE LINE**
Toto *Columbia*

58 **DON'T CRY OUT LOUD**
Melissa Manchester *Arista*

59 **BOOGIE WONDERLAND**
Earth, Wind & Fire w/the Emotions *ARC*

60 **GOLD**
John Stewart *RSO*

61 **I WANT YOU TO WANT ME**
Cheap Trick *Epic*

62 **YOU'RE ONLY LONELY**
J.D. Souther *Columbia*

63 **EVERY 1'S A WINNER**
Hot Chocolate *Infinity*

64 **YOU DECORATED MY LIFE**
Kenny Rogers *UA*

65 **OOH BABY BABY**
Linda Ronstadt *Asylum*

66 **LADY**
Little River Band *Harvest*

67 **I WAS MADE FOR DANCIN'**
Leif Garrett *Scotti Bros*

like Ward to sing, keeping the title but changing the lyrics. Ward was reluctant to record the song, but decided to trust Knight's instincts.

After landing the No. 1 single of 1978 with "Le Freak," the members of Chic had to settle for ninth place with their second chart-topper, "Good Times." Ironically, some people later said that the song was a rip-off of Queen's "Another One Bites the Dust," a single that came out a year later.

The Knack had the No. 2 song of the year with their debut single, "My Sharona." Doug Fieger, who said his life was changed when he saw the Beatles on *The Ed Sullivan Show,* was inspired to write the song with Berton Averre after falling deeply in love with a girl named Sharona. The Knack became a hot attraction playing live dates in Southern California—so hot that 13 different labels were bidding for them. Capitol won out and teamed the group with producer Mike Chapman.

Rod Stewart made his third appearance in a year-end top 10 with "Da Ya Think I'm Sexy?" It was the No. 5 song of 1979. His previous top 10 entries were "Maggie May" backed with "Reason To Believe," No. 3 for 1971, and "Tonight's The Night (Gonna Be Alright)," the No. 1 song of 1976.

Rupert Holmes had the No. 10 song of the year with the final Hot 100 chart-topper of the '70s, "Escape (Pina Colada Song)." Holmes, who describes his career as "the *Poseidon Adventure* of pop," was born in England to an American G.I. and a British mother. The family moved to Nyack, New York, and Holmes wrote his first song when he was six years old. He formed a rock band, the Nomads, while in high school. He went to work for a music publisher in Manhattan and scored his first success in 1971 when he wrote "Timothy," a strange song about cannibalism recorded by the Buoys. It peaked at No. 17 on the Hot 100. Three years later, Holmes was signed as an artist to Epic. He didn't have any hits of his own, but Barry Manilow and Dionne Warwick were among those recording his songs. Along with Jeffrey Lesser, he produced Barbra Streisand's *Lazy Afternoon* album and contributed songs to the soundtrack of *A Star Is Born.* Returning to England, Holmes produced albums for Sparks, the Strawbs, Sailor, and John Miles. Back in the States, he signed with Private Stock. His single "Let's Get Crazy Tonight" was moving up the Hot 100 when the label folded. Holmes then signed with Infinity, an MCA-distributed label headed by Ron Alexenburg. "Escape" was moving up the Hot 100 when Infinity folded. This time, momentum was in Holmes' favor. He switched over to MCA and "Escape" kept moving up the chart, not stopping until it reached the summit.

68 SHAKE IT
Ian Matthews *Mushroom*

69 I WANT YOUR LOVE
Chic *Atlantic*

70 SHINE A LITTLE LOVE
Electric Light Orchestra *Jet*

71 HE'S THE GREATEST DANCER
Sister Sledge *Cotillion*

72 YOU CAN'T CHANGE THAT
Raydio *Arista*

73 SHIPS
Barry Manilow *Arista*

74 I WAS MADE FOR LOVIN' YOU
Kiss *Casablanca*

75 I JUST FALL IN LOVE AGAIN
Anne Murray *Capitol*

76 NEW YORK GROOVE
Ace Frehley *Casablanca*

77 DISCO NIGHTS (ROCK-FREAK)
GQ *Arista*

78 ROCK 'N' ROLL FANTASY
Bad Company *Swan Song*

79 LOVIN', TOUCHIN', SQUEEZIN'
Journey *Columbia*

80 SEPTEMBER
Earth, Wind & Fire *ARC*

81 TAKE THE LONG WAY HOME
Supertramp *A&M*

82 TAKE ME HOME
Cher *Casablanca*

83 LOVE IS THE ANSWER
England Dan and John Ford Coley *Big Tree*

84 GOT TO BE REAL
Cheryl Lynn *Columbia*

85 YOU TAKE MY BREATH AWAY
Rex Smith *Columbia*

86 AIN'T NO STOPPIN' US NOW
McFadden and Whitehead *PIR*

87 WHAT YOU WON'T DO FOR LOVE
Bobby Caldwell *Clouds*

88 GOOD GIRLS DON'T
The Knack *Capitol*

89 HEAD GAMES
Foreigner *Atlantic*

90 WE'VE GOT TONITE
Bob Seger & the Silver Bullet Band *Capitol*

91 CRUEL TO BE KIND
Nick Lowe *Columbia*

92 THE GAMBLER
Kenny Rogers *UA*

93 RENEGADE
Styx *A&M*

94 TUSK
Fleetwood Mac *Warner Bros.*

95 PROMISES
Eric Clapton *RSO*

96 BROKEN HEARTED ME
Anne Murray *Capitol*

97 LOVE TAKES TIME
Orleans *Infinity*

98 BAD CASE OF LOVING YOU (DOCTOR, DOCTOR)
Robert Palmer *Island*

99 NO TELL LOVER
Chicago *Columbia*

100 I CAN'T STAND IT NO MORE
Peter Frampton *A&M*

The Top 100 Songs of 1980

The Spinners

1980 WAS THE year of the *Urban Cowboy;* Pink Floyd built *The Wall;* and John Lennon was murdered in front of his apartment building in New York City.

Prince Rogers Nelson made his debut on a year-end chart with "I Wanna Be Your Lover," listed at No. 91. Born in 1958, he became interested in music at the age of five and was proficient in piano by the time he was eight. A James Brown concert in 1968 was a strong influence on him, and in junior high he formed a band, Grand Central, with his cousin Charles Smith and Andre Cymone. In high school the band became Champagne. In 1977 Prince was signed to Warner Bros. after the label agreed he could produce himself. His first chart single, "Soft And Wet," peaked at No. 92 in November 1978. A year later, "I Wanna Be Your Lover" entered the Hot 100 and peaked at No. 11.

Another newcomer was Christopher Cross, with two songs listed in the top 100 of 1980: "Ride Like The Wind" (No. 16) and "Sailing" (No. 19). Born Christopher Geppert in San Antonio, Texas, he formed a local band called Flash and by 1972 had the top group in town. A year later Cross quit the group to focus on his songwriting. As early as 1975, Cross was sending audition tapes to Warner Bros. Records in Burbank, but with no interest from the label. In October of 1978, Michael Ostin of Warner Bros.' A&R staff saw Cross perform in Austin and helped sign him to the company. Producer Michael Omartian was assigned to work with Cross, and his debut album featured stellar guests like Michael McDonald, Don Henley, Nicolette Larson, and J.D. Souther.

Also making a year-end chart debut in 1980 was the Australian duo known as Air Supply. "All Out Of Love" was No. 17 for the year and "Lost In Love" was No. 23. Graham Russell was born in Sherwood, Nottingham, England. His father and new stepmother moved to Australia when he was

13, but Graham ran away from home and didn't join them in Melbourne until three years later. He won a part in the chorus of *Jesus Christ, Superstar* and met fellow cast member Russell Hitchcock. They had a top three hit in Australia with "Love And Other Bruises." They opened for Rod Stewart in tours of Australia and the U.S. before Arista picked up "Lost In Love" for release in America.

Debbie Harry sang lead vocals on the No. 1 song of the year, "Call Me." The Blondie tune was heard in the soundtrack of *American Gigolo,* starring Richard Gere. Producer Giorgio Moroder originally wanted Stevie Nicks of Fleetwood Mac to perform the tune. When she passed, Moroder turned to Harry, who agreed to write the lyrics. She viewed a rough cut of the film on video. "I went home and wrote the song immediately," she recalls. Neither Moroder nor director Paul Schrader restricted her creative freedom. The instrumental track was already recorded, and Harry only took a couple of hours to lay down her vocals, including the harmonies.

The No. 2 song of 1980 was "Another One Bites The Dust" by Queen, who were also in the year-end top 10 with "Crazy Little Thing Called Love" (No. 9). Prior to 1980, Queen's highest year-end ranking was the 1978 double-sided single "We Are The Champions" / "We Will Rock You," which came in at No. 37.

Kenny Rogers, who first made a year-end chart in 1969 with the First Edition's "Ruby, Don't Take Your Love To Town" (No. 92 for that year), had his most successful chart single in 1980. "Lady" ranked No. 3 for the year. The song was written for Rogers by Lionel Richie. "I was about to explode," Rogers explained in *Billboard*. "I needed new input and that's where Lionel came in. I went to who I thought was the very best in the field." Richie flew to Las Vegas to meet with Rogers and played demos of "Lady" and "Goin' Back To Alabama." Both songs were recorded in eight-and-a-half hours. Rogers had two other songs on the year-end chart, both predecessors to "Lady." "Coward Of The County" was No. 22 and "Don't Fall In Love With A Dreamer," a duet with Kim Carnes, was No. 35.

In fifth place for 1980 was "Upside Down" by Diana Ross, her most successful solo chart single. It was also one of her most controversial, as word leaked out about her displeasure with how Bernard Edwards and Nile Rodgers had produced the track. She felt her vocals were not prominent enough and wanted them brought forward. After asking them to remix the album they had produced for her, Diana was still not satisfied and mixed it again with assistance from Motown producer Russ Terrana. Rodgers told of his dismay in *Billboard*. "I was shocked. I was furious and got on the phone right away and called Motown. I was asked to listen to the album and then talk to Diana. I calmed down and listened to the album about 10 times. Then I had to say, 'Hey! I know where they're coming from. I understand what they're doing.' But initially I was not prepared for that kind of shock. I'm not as happy as I would be if it was the way we mixed it, but I'm happy with the album because Diana is happy with it."

The Captain & Tennille returned to the annual top 10 for the first time since 1975, when "Love Will Keep Us Together" was the No. 2 song of the year. "Do That To Me One More Time" was their debut single for Casablanca after a long run on A&M. Daryl Dragon and Toni Tennille first

35 DON'T FALL IN LOVE WITH A DREAMER
Kenny Rogers w/Kim Carnes *UA*

36 DESIRE
Andy Gibb *RSO*

37 MASTER BLASTER (JAMMIN')
Stevie Wonder *Tamla*

38 SEXY EYES
Dr. Hook *Capitol*

39 GIVE ME THE NIGHT
George Benson *Warner Bros.*

40 FAME
Irene Cara *RSO*

41 HUNGRY HEART
Bruce Springsteen *Columbia*

42 SHINING STAR
The Manhattans *Columbia*

43 STEAL AWAY
Robbie Dupree *Elektra*

44 TOO HOT
Kool & the Gang *De-Lite*

45 DRIVIN' MY LIFE AWAY
Eddie Rabbitt *Elektra*

46 HIT ME WITH YOUR BEST SHOT
Pat Benatar *Chrysalis*

47 CARS
Gary Numan *Atco*

48 THIS IS IT
Kenny Loggins *Columbia*

49 YOU'VE LOST THAT LOVIN' FEELING
Daryl Hall and John Oates *RCA*

50 LATE IN THE EVENING
Paul Simon *Warner Bros.*

51 STOMP!
Brothers Johnson *A&M*

52 LADIES NIGHT
Kool & the Gang *De-Lite*

53 NEVER KNEW LOVE LIKE THIS BEFORE
Stephanie Mills *20th Century*

54 MORE LOVE
Kim Carnes *EMI America*

55 AGAINST THE WIND
Bob Seger *Capitol*

56 I'M COMING OUT
Diana Ross *Motown*

57 WHIP IT
Devo *Warner Bros.*

58 SPECIAL LADY
Ray, Goodman & Brown *Polydor*

59 WE DON'T TALK ANYMORE
Cliff Richard *EMI America*

60 THE LONG RUN
Eagles *Asylum*

61 I CAN'T TELL YOU WHY
Eagles *Asylum*

62 HURT SO BAD
Linda Ronstadt *Asylum*

63 LET'S GET SERIOUS
Jermaine Jackson *Motown*

64 HOW DO I MAKE YOU
Linda Ronstadt *Asylum*

65 ON THE RADIO
Donna Summer *Casablanca*

66 DAYDREAM BELIEVER
Anne Murray *Capitol*

67 BRASS IN POCKET (I'M SPECIAL)
The Pretenders *Sire*

68 LOOKIN' FOR LOVE
Johnny Lee *Full Moon*

saw the end of their association with A&M coming at the company Christmas party. Toni was talking with Karen Carpenter, who complained that the label was forgetting "what made most of its money" in favor of a new wave of British artists. "We felt they weren't interested in what we were doing," Tennille explains. Toni and Daryl had met Casablanca founder Nell Bogart about a year before they left A&M at a dinner party arranged by Norman Brokaw, their agent at William Morris. Bogart wanted to expand Casablanca beyond its image as a disco label and thought the Captain & Tennille would bring the company some attention in the adult contemporary market. After signing with Casablanca, Bogart and label vice president Bruce Bird visited the couple in their Pacific Palisades home. "I had finished 'Do That To Me One More Time' and thought it was just a little tune—kind of nice, but it wasn't any big deal," Toni notes. "We played all the other things we had in mind, including some songs that were more powerful." Nell told them that the "little tune" was a smash and should be their first single. It became their second chart-topping hit, and although it only spent one week in pole position, it was on the Hot 100 for 27 weeks, good enough to rank No. 7 for the year.

Pink Floyd had their first and only year-end top 10 single with "Another Brick In The Wall," the No. 10 hit of 1980. Despite a run of successful albums, including the sturdy *Dark Side Of The Moon,* Pink Floyd had only had one chart single prior to "Another Brick In The Wall." That was "Money," a track from *Dark Side* that peaked at No. 13 in 1973.

Michael Jackson gave a hint of his chart dominance to come by placing "Rock With You" in the No. 12 position. The second number one hit from his *Off the Wall* album, it was written by Rod Temperton, formerly of Heatwave ("Boogie Nights"). The first No. 1 single from the LP, "Don't Stop 'Til You Get Enough," had ranked No. 21 for 1979. Two other songs from the album were on the list for 1980: "She's Out Of My Life" was No. 77 and "Off The Wall" was No. 90.

Barbra Streisand had her third year-end top 10 single with "Woman In Love," which finished fourth. The song was written by Barry and Robin Gibb. Streisand got the idea to work with the Gibbs after attending a Bee Gees concert at Dodger Stadium in Los Angeles. Barry was looking for projects outside of his family, and the match-up resulted in the *Guilty* album.

Two former Beatles placed in the year-end top 10. Paul McCartney & Wings ranked No. 8 with the live version of "Coming Up," and John Lennon's posthumous chart-topper, "(Just Like) Starting Over," was two rungs higher at No. 6.

The Top 100 Songs of 1981

Juice Newton

1981 WAS THE year Bill Haley died in Texas; Bob Marley succumbed to cancer in Miami; and Harry Chapin was killed in an automobile accident on the Long Island Expressway.

Some long-absent artists returned to the year-end chart in 1981. Gary U.S. Bonds was listed for the first time since "Dear Lady Twist" and "Twist, Twist Senora" in 1962. The seeds of Bonds' return were sown in 1978 while he was playing the Red Baron club in New Jersey. A local guy who seemed pretty popular was in the audience, and Gary thought he'd give him a break by calling him up on stage. He had no idea who Bruce Springsteen was, but they sang a duet on "Quarter To Three," a song Bruce used as an encore in his own act. They remained in touch and Bruce asked Gary if they could work on an album together. Two years later, after completing *The River*, Springsteen kept his word and with Steve Van Zandt, produced *Dedication*. The first single, "This Little Girl," ranked No. 64 for the year.

The Moody Blues just eked on to the 1981 year-end chart with "Gemini Dream," No. 100 for the year. It was the group's first year-end appearance since "Nights In White Satin" was the No. 21 song of 1972.

For the first time in the rock era, the top three songs of the year featured female vocalists. Olivia Newton-John had the No. 1 song of 1981 with "Physical," Diana Ross earned her highest-placing ever in a duet with

Lionel Richie on the No. 2 song, "Endless Love," and Kim Carnes was No. 3 with "Bette Davis Eyes." Olivia's song was written by Steve Kipner and Terry Shaddick. Kipner recalls how the creative muse struck while he was driving to his manager's office: "I was at the corner of Fairfax and Sunset and it was the first time I sang, 'let's get physical.'" Kipner went running up to his manager's office, thinking he had come up with a good song for Rod Stewart. Instead, Newton-John landed in the year-end top 10 for the first time, after a previous best of ranking No. 13 in 1980 with "Magic."

Lionel Richie was asked to write an instrumental theme for a Brooke Shields movie. Later, director Franco Zeffirelli decided he wanted lyrics. Then the director had one more idea: make the song a duet. Diana Ross' schedule didn't allow time to record in Los Angeles, so Richie met her after a gig in Lake Tahoe, Nevada. By 5 A.M., they had recorded "Endless Love."

"Bette Davis Eyes" was written by Jackie DeShannon and Donna Weiss. DeShannon recorded it on her 1975 album for Columbia, *New Arrangement*. Kim Carnes' producer, George Tobin, gave Kim the song but she thought it wasn't a hit. When Carnes teamed up with a new producer, Val Garay, Weiss sent her the song again. Kim Carnes told Dick Clark who should get the credit for the new arrangement of "Bette Davis Eyes." "It's Bill Cuomo, my synthesizer player, who really came up with the new feel, changing the chords. The minute he came up with that, it fell into place."

"Waiting For A Girl Like You," the song that peaked at No. 2 and remained in that spot longer than any other in the rock era, landed in fourth place for the year. Foreigner spent 10 weeks in the runner-up spot on the Hot 100, most of that time behind "Physical." The Anglo-American outfit was formed by British musician Mick Jones. He heard two albums by a band called Black Sheep and invited their lead singer, Lou Gramm, to join Foreigner. Rick Wills and Dennis Elliott were the other members of the quartet when "Waiting For A Girl Like You" was released.

Rick Springfield made his first appearance on a year-end chart with "Jessie's Girl," his debut for RCA after charting on Capitol, Columbia, and Chelsea. Born in Sydney and raised in Melbourne, he joined a succession of bands, including Rock House, Wackedy Wak, and Zoot. That last group charted in Australia with "Speak To The Sky," and Rick recorded a new, solo version for America. Signed to a contract by Universal Studios, he had guest starring roles in *The Six Million Dollar Man, The Rockford Files,* and *The Incredible Hulk* before joining the cast of *The Young And The Restless.* He was a regular on *General Hospital* when RCA released "Jessie's Girl," and his soap popularity helped the record sail to the top of the Hot 100. It ranked No. 7 for the year.

Kool & the Gang were No. 11 for 1981 with "Celebration," a song used to welcome home the American hostages held in Iran for 444 days. It was also the theme song for the 1981 Superbowl, and the first Hot 100 chart-topper for the group that had been together for 17 years. After a low point in 1978, Robert "Kool" Bell recruited James "J.T" Taylor to become the group's lead singer. A chance meeting with producer Eumir Deodato (*"Also Sprach Zarathustra")* led to the band's resurgence.

Daryl Hall and John Oates just missed the year-end top 10 twice in 1981 with "Private Eyes" at No. 12 and "Kiss On My List" at No. 13. The

34 **ANGEL OF THE MORNING**
Juice Newton *Capitol*
35 **EVERY LITTLE THING SHE DOES IS MAGIC**
The Police *A&M*
36 **FOR YOUR EYES ONLY**
Sheena Easton *Liberty*
37 **WHO'S CRYING NOW**
Journey *Columbia*
38 **A WOMAN NEEDS LOVE (JUST LIKE YOU DO)**
Ray Parker, Jr. & Raydio *Arista*
39 **OH NO**
Commodores *Motown*
40 **EVERY WOMAN IN THE WORLD**
Air Supply *Arista*
41 **YOUNG TURKS**
Rod Stewart *Warner Bros*
42 **TAKE IT ON THE RUN**
REO Speedwagon *Epic*
43 **THE WINNER TAKES IT ALL**
Abba *Atlantic*
44 **(THERE'S) NO GETTIN' OVER ME**
Ronnie Milsap *RCA*
45 **PASSION**
Rod Stewart *Warner Bros*
46 **CRYING**
Don McLean *Millennium*
47 **STEP BY STEP**
Eddie Rabbitt *Elektra*
48 **LIVING INSIDE MYSELF**
Gino Vannelli *Arista*
49 **HERE I AM (JUST WHEN I THOUGHT I WAS OVER YOU)**
Air Supply *Arista*
50 **HEARTS**
Marty Balin *EMI America*
51 **WHY DO FOOLS FALL IN LOVE**
Diana Ross *RCA*
52 **LADY (YOU BRING ME UP)**
Commodores *Motown*
53 **GIVING IT UP FOR YOUR LOVE**
Delbert McClinton *Capitol*
54 **ELVIRA**
Oak Ridge Boys *MCA*
55 **IT'S MY TURN**
Diana Ross *Motown*
56 **THE NIGHT OWLS**
Little River Band *Capitol*
57 **BOY FROM NEW YORK CITY**
Manhattan Transfer *Atlantic*
58 **YOU MAKE MY DREAMS**
Daryl Hall and John Oates *RCA*
59 **HELLO AGAIN**
Neil Diamond *Capitol*
60 **AMERICA**
Neil Diamond *Capitol*
61 **WHILE YOU SEE A CHANCE**
Steve Winwood *Island*
62 **I CAN'T STAND IT**
Eric Clapton *RSO*
63 **HEY NINETEEN**
Steely Dan *MCA*
64 **THIS LITTLE GIRL**
Gary U.S. Bonds *EMI America*
65 **SWEETHEART**
Franke & the Knockouts *Millennium*
66 **DE DO DO DO, DE DA DA DA**
The Police *A&M*

duo first appeared on a year-end chart in 1976, when "Sara Smile" was No. 46 for the year and "She's Gone" was No. 61. The following year, "Rich Girl" was No. 21, and in 1980 they were No. 49 for the year with their remake of "You've Lost That Lovin' Feelin'." "Kiss On My List" was the third single from their breakthrough album, *Voices*. Co-writer Jana Allen, younger sister of Daryl's girlfriend Sara, had never written a song before. She had some lyrics and music and sat down at a borrowed Wurlitzer with Daryl to finish the song. Oates pointed out that most people misunderstood the words, thinking they were singing "Kiss On My Lips." Hall and Oates had one more song on the year-end chart for 1981: "You Make My Dreams" was No. 58.

REO Speedwagon, named for the 1911 fire truck designed by Ransom Eli Olds, made the top 50 portion of the Hot 100 for the first time in 1981. The band was already rolling when Kevin Cronin, lead singer and writer of the year's No. 26 song, "Keep On Loving You," joined. After their first album, guitarist Gary Richrath anonymously called the Musicians Referral Service in Chicago looking for a new lead vocalist. Cronin had started the service to help bands searching for musicians. Cronin told Richrath to come to his apartment to meet a new lead singer, and when he arrived Cronin sang an Elton John song and handed him a demo tape. Within a week, Cronin was the new lead singer of REO Speedwagon.

Virginia-born Judy Cohen became Juice Newton and formed a couple of bands before recording on her own. With Otha Young, she organized Dixie Peach in 1971. The following year they formed Silver Spur. They were signed to RCA in 1975 and made the country singles chart in 1976 with "Love Is A Word." After two albums they moved to Capitol. Newton went solo in 1978 and had her first single on the pop chart, "It's A Heartache." Bonnie Tyler had the hit version while Newton stalled at No. 86. She covered several pop songs and made the country charts with "Lay Back In The Arms Of Someone," "Any Way That You Want Me," and "Sunshine" before returning to the Hot 100 with a remake of Merrilee Rush & the Turnabouts' "Angel Of The Morning," the No. 34 song of 1981. Her next chart single was a cover of "Queen Of Hearts," written by Hank DeVito and first recorded by Dave Edmunds on his *Repeat When Necessary* album. "Queen Of Hearts" spent two weeks at No. 2 and remained on the Hot 100 for 27 weeks. It was No. 28 for the year.

67 **DON'T STOP BELIEVIN'**
Journey *Columbia*

68 **WHAT ARE WE DOIN' IN LOVE**
Dottie West *Liberty*

69 **I'VE DONE EVERYTHING FOR YOU**
Rick Springfield *RCA*

70 **TOGETHER**
Tierra *Boardwalk*

71 **HOLD ON TIGHT**
Electric Light Orchestra *Jet*

72 **I AIN'T GONNA STAND FOR IT**
Stevie Wonder *Tamla*

73 **TOO MUCH TIME ON MY HANDS**
Styx *A&M*

74 **I MADE IT THROUGH THE RAIN**
Barry Manilow *Arista*

75 **I LOVE YOU**
Climax Blues Band *Sire*

76 **TRYIN' TO LIVE MY LIFE WITHOUT YOU**
Bob Seger *Capitol*

77 **SOMEBODY'S KNOCKIN'**
Terri Gibbs *MCA*

78 **A LITTLE IN LOVE**
Cliff Richard *EMI America*

79 **TAKE MY HEART**
(YOU CAN HAVE IT IF YOU WANT IT)
Kool & the Gang *De-Lite*

80 **TELL IT LIKE IT IS**
Heart *Epic*

81 **DON'T STAND SO CLOSE TO ME**
The Police *A&M*

82 **HARD TO SAY**
Dan Fogelberg *Full Moon*

83 **WHEN SHE WAS MY GIRL**
Four Tops *Casablanca*

84 **HER TOWN TOO**
James Taylor & J.D. Souther *Columbia*

85 **HOW 'BOUT US**
Champaign *Columbia*

86 **COOL LOVE**
Pablo Cruise *A&M*

87 **TIME** Alan Parsons Project *Arista*

88 **MISS SUN**
Boz Scaggs *Columbia*

89 **SUPER FREAK (PART 1)**
Rick James *Gordy*

90 **THE BREAKUP SONG**
(THEY DON'T WRITE 'EM)
Greg Kihn Band *Beserkley*

91 **AIN'T EVEN DONE WITH THE NIGHT**
John Cougar *Riva*

92 **TREAT ME RIGHT**
Pat Benatar *Chrysalis*

93 **SAME OLD LANG SYNE**
Dan Fogelberg *Full Moon*

94 **OUR LIPS ARE SEALED**
The Go-Go's *I.R.S.*

95 **WHAT KIND OF FOOL**
Barbra Streisand & Barry Gibb *Columbia*

96 **THEME FROM "HILL STREET BLUES"**
Mike Post *Elektra*

97 **WATCHING THE WHEELS**
John Lennon *Geffen*

98 **THE BEACH BOYS MEDLEY**
The Beach Boys *Capitol*

99 **SHARE YOUR LOVE WITH ME**
Kenny Rogers *Liberty*

100 **GEMINI DREAM**
The Moody Blues *Threshold*

Toni Basil

1982 WAS THE year E.T. phoned home; Trivial Pursuit was introduced; and the American media had a field day with Boy George.

For the first time since 1971, when Three Dog Night led the list with "Joy To The World," the top song of the year was by a male group. Survivor led the pack with "Eye Of The Tiger," from *Rocky III*. It was the fourth No. 1 song of the year to come directly from a soundtrack, following "To Sir With Love," "The Way We Were," and "Call Me."

The theme song from the first *Rocky* film, Bill Conti's "Gonna Fly Now," had ranked No. 23 in 1977. Sylvester Stallone wanted a more rock-oriented theme for his third movie about the heavyweight champ. First he considered Queen's "Another One Bites The Dust," then decided to commission a new song. Tony Scotti, one of the founders of the Scotti Brothers label, had issued a single by Frank Stallone. When he heard that brother Sly was looking for new material, he played Survivor's *Premonition* album for him. "Sylvester liked the beat and the drive of our music so he let us have a shot at writing the theme," Jim Peterik said in the *Los Angeles Times*. Stallone gave Peterik and Frankie Sullivan a video copy of the movie but little guidance as to what kind of song to write, other than insisting on a strong beat and a contemporary theme. Within 90 minutes of seeing the rough cut, the songwriters focused on the phrase "eye of the tiger" and wrote the first draft of the song that would top the Hot 100 for six weeks.

Stevie Wonder collected his third year-end top 10 hit, following "Fingertips—Pt. 2" (No. 8 in 1963) and "Sir Duke" (No. 6 in 1977). He did it by pairing with Paul McCartney on "Ebony And Ivory," a song that "is supposed to say that people of all types could live together," according to McCartney. "It's just an idea that I had heard someone say once, you know the keyboard thing, you can play using just the black notes, or you can play using just the white notes, but combining them gives you great notes. That, I suppose, is a great analogy." Paul got word to Stevie through former Motown staffer Irv Beigel that he wanted them to record together. Stevie suggested a tape be forwarded to his assistant. "I listened to the song and liked it very much," Wonder told Dick Clark. The two superstars met on the island of Montserrat in the West Indies to record "Ebony And Ivory," although the subsequent video found them recording their roles in separate locations.

The No. 3 song of 1982 was "I Love Rock 'n Roll" by Joan Jett & the Blackhearts. It was the debut chart single for Jett, a member of the female rock band the Runaways from 1975–78. While touring England with the Runaways, Joan saw the Anglo-American band the Arrows perform "I Love Rock 'n Roll" on their British TV series. The song was written by Jake Hooker and Alan Merrill of the group as a protest to the Rolling Stones' "It's Only Rock 'n Roll (But I Like It)." Jett asked Hooker if she could cover the song, and he responded that she would do a better job than he did. But she couldn't convince the Runaways to record the tune, and had to wait until she was on her own to cut it. An early version was released as the flip side of a Dutch single, an updating of Lesley Gore's "You Don't Own Me." Jett recorded it a second time with the Blackhearts for release on Neil Bogart's Boardwalk Records. It spent seven weeks atop the Hot 100.

Coming in fourth place for the year was "Centerfold" by the J. Geils Band. The group solidified when former DJ Peter Wolf and drummer Stephen Jo Bladd teamed up with a Boston-based trio led by guitarist Jerome Geils in 1967. Keyboardist Seth Justman joined a year later. They signed with Atlantic in 1969 and turned down a chance to appear at Woodstock. "Three days in the mud, who needs it? That's where we were at," Wolf told Jeff Tamarkin in *Goldmine*. In 1978 the band switched to the new EMI-America label. "Centerfold" was their 12th chart single, and although they had never made the top 10 before, it shot to No. 1 and remained there for six weeks.

Steve Miller topped his previous high mark set in 1974 when "The Joker" was the No. 10 song of the year. "Abracadabra" ranked fifth for 1982. It is Miller's most successful chart single of all time.

John Cougar had his first year-end chart single in 1981 when "Ain't Even Done With The Night" was the No. 91 song of the year. In 1982 he became the first American male solo artist since Elvis Presley to have two songs in the year-end top 10. "Jack And Diane" and "Hurts So Good" occupied adjacent positions at No. 6 and No. 7, respectively. Born John Mellencamp in Seymour, Indiana, he was—much to his surprise—renamed Johnny Cougar by his first manager, Tony DeFries. Dropped from MCA,

35 **LET IT WHIP**
Dazz Band *Motown*

36 **THE SWEETEST THING (I'VE EVER KNOWN)**
Juice Newton *Capitol*

37 **SWEET DREAMS**
Air Supply *Arista*

38 **YOU SHOULD HEAR HOW SHE TALKS ABOUT YOU**
Melissa Manchester *Arista*

39 **YOU CAN DO MAGIC**
America *Capitol*

40 **TROUBLE**
Lindsey Buckingham *Asylum*

41 **KEY LARGO**
Bertie Higgins *Kat Family*

42 **LEATHER AND LACE**
Stevie Nicks w/Don Henley *Modern*

43 **STEPPIN' OUT**
Joe Jackson *A&M*

44 **ONLY THE LONELY**
The Motels *Capitol*

45 **EVEN THE NIGHTS ARE BETTER**
Air Supply *Arista*

46 **TURN YOUR LOVE AROUND**
George Benson *Warner Bros.*

47 **'65 LOVE AFFAIR**
Paul Davis *Arista*

48 **KEEP THE FIRE BURNIN'**
REO Speedwagon *Epic*

49 **LOVE'S BEEN A LITTLE BIT HARD ON ME**
Juice Newton *Capitol*

50 **WASTED ON THE WAY**
Crosby, Stills & Nash *Atlantic*

51 **TAINTED LOVE**
Soft Cell *Sire*

52 **SOMEBODY'S BABY**
Jackson Browne *Asylum*

53 **LEADER OF THE BAND**
Dan Fogelberg *Full Moon*

54 **DID IT IN A MINUTE**
Daryl Hall and John Oates *RCA*

55 **COMIN' IN AND OUT OF YOUR LIFE**
Barbra Streisand *Columbia*

56 **TAKE IT EASY ON ME**
Little River Band *Capitol*

57 **HOOKED ON CLASSICS**
Royal Philharmonic Orchestra *RCA*

58 **COOL NIGHT**
Paul Davis *Arista*

59 **YESTERDAY'S SONGS**
Neil Diamond *Columbia*

60 **HEARTLIGHT**
Neil Diamond *Columbia*

61 **THINK I'M IN LOVE**
Eddie Money *Columbia*

62 **TAKE IT AWAY**
Paul McCartney *Columbia*

63 **ROCK THIS TOWN**
Stray Cats *EMI America*

64 **LOVE IS IN CONTROL (FINGER ON THE TRIGGER)**
Donna Summer *Geffen*

65 **DO YOU BELIEVE IN LOVE**
Huey Lewis and the News *Chrysalis*

66 **PAC MAN FEVER**
Buckner and Garcia *Columbia*

67 **IT'S RAINING AGAIN**
Supertramp *A&M*

Mellencamp signed to Riva, a label formed by his new manager, Billy Gaff. He had only moderate chart success until the 1982 release of his *American Fool* album. The first single, "Hurts So Good," spent four weeks at No. 2 and 28 weeks on the Hot 100. "Jack And Diane" was released so quickly, it was in the top 10 at the same time as "Hurts So Good." "Jack And Diane" spent four weeks at No. 1 and 22 weeks on the Hot 100.

"Don't You Want Me" by the Human League was the second highest-ranked British single of 1982, No. 8 for the year. The first edition of Human League had formed in Sheffield, England, in 1977. Ian Craig Marsh and Martin Ware teamed with vocalist Phil Oakey and took the name Human League from a computer game. In October 1980, Ware and Marsh split to form the British Electric Foundation and an offshoot, Heaven 17. Oakey and Adrian Wright put together a revised version of the Human League. The band is credited with paving the way in America for a new wave British invasion, allowing groups like Culture Club, Dexys Midnight Runners, and Duran Duran to chart.

After narrowly missing the year-end top 10 in 1981 with "Private Eyes" (No. 12) and "Kiss On My List" (No. 13), Daryl Hall and John Oates more than made up for it in 1982 by placing "Maneater" ninth and "I Can't Go For That (No Can Do)" tenth.

Laura Branigan had her first year-end chart single with "Gloria," the No. 14 song of 1982. Educated at the Academy of Dramatic Arts in New York, Branigan, a former back-up singer for Leonard Cohen, was performing at Reno Sweeney's in Manhattan when Atlantic Records founder Ahmet Ertegun caught her act. "I was doing Barry Manilow songs, Edith Piaf numbers, things like that, plus some of my own material," Branigan told Todd Everett. "The other record company people seemed to think that I didn't fit in anywhere. Ahmet, I think, appreciated the fact that I had a real voice and wasn't a gimmick. I remember him saying that I had so much emotion in my voice." Once signed to Atlantic, Branigan was introduced to producer Jack White. He brought her "Gloria." It was originally recorded by Italian star Umberto Tozzi and was a hit throughout Europe. Branigan liked the song but thought it was "too European," so the lyrics were rewritten. "We took basically the same arrangement and just gave it that American kick," Branigan elaborated in *Billboard*. The Italian version is structurally the same but much softer; mine has more guts and a lot more punch." The song debuted on the Hot 100 on July 10 and began a slow climb. It peaked at No. 2 in its 23rd week on the chart, and spent a total of 36 weeks on the survey.

68 CRIMSON AND CLOVER
Joan Jett & the Blackhearts *Boardwalk*

69 LOVE WILL TURN YOU AROUND
Kenny Rogers *Liberty*

70 WAITING ON A FRIEND
The Rolling Stones *Rolling Stones*

71 MAKE A MOVE ON ME
Olivia Newton-John *MCA*

72 MUSCLES
Diana Ross *RCA*

73 CAUGHT UP IN YOU
38 Special *A&M*

74 MIRROR, MIRROR
Diana Ross *RCA*

75 I RAN (SO FAR AWAY)
A Flock of Seagulls *Jive*

76 SHADOWS OF THE NIGHT
Pat Benatar *Chrysalis*

77 BLUE EYES
Elton John *Geffen*

78 DO I DO
Stevie Wonder *Tamla*

79 EMPTY GARDEN (HEY HEY JOHNNY)
Elton John *Geffen*

80 THROUGH THE YEARS
Kenny Rogers *Liberty*

81 HOLD ON
Santana *Columbia*

82 YOU COULD HAVE BEEN WITH ME
Sheena Easton *EMI America*

83 WHAT'S FOREVER FOR
Michael Murphey *Liberty*

84 VACATION
The Go-Go's *I.R.S.*

85 GET DOWN ON IT
Kool & the Gang *De-Lite*

86 BREAK IT TO ME GENTLY
Juice Newton *Capitol*

87 IT'S GONNA TAKE A MIRACLE
Deniece Williams *ARC*

88 EDGE OF SEVENTEEN
(JUST LIKE THE WHITE WINGED DOVE)
Stevie Nicks *Modern*

89 (OH) PRETTY WOMAN
Van Halen *Warner Bros.*

90 MAN ON YOUR MIND
Little River Band *Capitol*

91 MAKING LOVE
Roberta Flack *Atlantic*

92 SHOULD I DO IT
Pointer Sisters *Planet*

93 SOMEONE COULD LOSE
A HEART TONIGHT
Eddie Rabbitt *Elektra*

94 NOBODY
Sylvia *RCA*

95 GOIN' DOWN
Greg Guidry *Columbia*

96 YOU DON'T WANT ME ANYMORE
Steel Breeze *RCA*

97 PERSONALLY
Karla Bonoff *Columbia*

98 I WOULDN'T HAVE MISSED
IT FOR THE WORLD
Ronnie Milsap *RCA*

99 THE BEATLES' MOVIE MEDLEY
The Beatles *Capitol*

100 SPIRITS IN THE MATERIAL WORLD
The Police *A&M*

The Top 100 Songs of 1983

Daryl Hall and John Oates

1983 WAS THE year that compact discs were first sold in record stores; Jennifer Beals inspired women to tear their T-shirts; and Karen Carpenter died of cardiac arrest.

Michael Jackson had six titles on the year-end chart. Only the Beatles had more, when they placed 10 songs in the top 100 of 1964. Three of Michael's 1983 hits were in the year-end top 10, making him the third artist after Elvis Presley and the Beatles to have three songs in the top 10 of a year.

Michael's top-rated single of 1983 was "Say, Say, Say," his duet with Paul McCartney. Jackson contacted McCartney by telephone on Christmas Day, but the former Beatle didn't believe it was really Michael calling. When he finally convinced him, Michael told Paul he was coming to England and wanted to write some songs with Paul. The first record they released together was "The Girl Is Mine," the initial single from Michael's *Thriller* album. It was the No. 18 song of 1983. Two more McCartney-Jackson collaborations appeared on Paul's *Pipes of Peace* album. "The Man" wasn't released as a single, but "Say, Say, Say" was. It was on top of the Hot 100 for six weeks and ranked No. 2 for the year. Just two notches below it was "Billie Jean," the second single from *Thriller.* It was in pole position for seven weeks. The follow-up, "Beat It," was at the summit for three weeks and ranked No. 8 for the year. Michael's other year-end singles were "Wanna Be Startin' Somethin'" at No. 61 and "Human Nature" at No. 77.

The Police had the No. 100 song of 1982, "Spirits In The Material World." In 1983, they appeared at the exact opposite end of the chart. Their single "Every Breath You Take" was the No. 1 record of the year. That

01 **EVERY BREATH YOU TAKE**
The Police *A&M*

02 **SAY, SAY, SAY**
Paul McCartney & Michael Jackson *Columbia*

03 **FLASHDANCE...WHAT A FEELING**
Irene Cara *Casablanca*

04 **BILLIE JEAN**
Michael Jackson *Epic*

05 **ALL NIGHT LONG (ALL NIGHT)**
Lionel Richie *Motown*

06 **TOTAL ECLIPSE OF THE HEART**
Bonnie Tyler *Columbia*

07 **DOWN UNDER**
Men at Work *Columbia*

08 **BEAT IT**
Michael Jackson *Epic*

09 **SWEET DREAMS (ARE MADE OF THIS)**
Eurythmics *RCA*

10 **LET'S DANCE**
David Bowie *EMI America*

11 **ISLANDS IN THE STREAM**
Kenny Rogers & Dolly Parton *RCA*

12 **SHAME ON THE MOON**
Bob Seger & the Silver Bullet Band *Capitol*

13 **ELECTRIC AVENUE**
Eddy Grant *Portrait*

14 **MANIAC**
Michael Sembello *Casablanca*

15 **SAY IT ISN'T SO**
Daryl Hall and John Oates *RCA*

16 **BABY, COME TO ME**
Patti Austin w/James Ingram *Qwest*

17 **DO YOU REALLY WANT TO HURT ME**
Culture Club *Epic/Virgin*

18 **THE GIRL IS MINE**
Michael Jackson & Paul McCartney *Epic*

19 **COME ON EILEEN**
Dexys Midnight Runners *Mercury*

20 **UPTOWN GIRL**
Billy Joel *Columbia*

21 **TELL HER ABOUT IT**
Billy Joel *Columbia*

22 **MAKING LOVE OUT OF NOTHING AT ALL**
Air Supply *Arista*

23 **TIME (CLOCK OF THE HEART)**
Culture Club *Epic/Virgin*

24 **JEOPARDY**
Greg Kihn Band *Beserkley*

25 **SEXUAL HEALING**
Marvin Gaye *Columbia*

26 **DIRTY LAUNDRY**
Don Henley *Asylum*

27 **SHE WORKS HARD FOR THE MONEY**
Donna Summer *Mercury*

28 **AFRICA**
Toto *Columbia*

29 **HUNGRY LIKE THE WOLF**
Duran Duran *Harvest*

30 **THE SAFETY DANCE**
Men Without Hats *Backstreet*

31 **UNION OF THE SNAKE**
Duran Duran *Capitol*

32 **STRAY CAT STRUT**
Stray Cats *EMI America*

33 **OVERKILL**
Men at Work *Columbia*

34 **MR. ROBOTO**
Styx *A&M*

made them the third British group to have the highest-ranked song of the year, following the Beatles and the Rolling Stones. It also made them the first British group to take this honor since 1968. As Sting told Christopher Connelly in *Rolling Stone,* the song was not meant to be a sweet love song. "I consider it a fairly nasty song. It's about surveillance and ownership and jealousy."

The Anglo-American Police were part of the most successful year ever for U.K. artists. There were 33 songs in the year-end top 100 from the British Isles, breaking the record set in 1965. After the Police and Paul McCartney, the highest-ranked U.K. artist for the year was Bonnie Tyler, born in Skewen, South Wales. After winning a local talent contest when she was 17, she quit her job as a candy store clerk to sing in Welsh nightclubs. A year-and-a-half later she developed nodules on her throat. They disappeared, but recurred twice until she had them surgically removed. That left her with a husky voice that reminded some of a female Rod Stewart. In 1978 she broke through in America with "It's A Heartache," which peaked at No. 3 on the Hot 100 and was ranked No. 36 for the year. But she tired of recording material written and produced by her managers and split from them. Under new management and signed to CBS Records, she expressed her wish to work with producer Jim Steinman (*Bat Out Of Hell* for Meatloaf). He was busy with a film project and declined. Later, he surprised Bonnie when he called out of the blue and asked if she was still looking for a producer. She was invited to fly to New York and meet him in his apartment. There he played "Total Eclipse Of The Heart" for her on his grand piano. "When he plays he practically knocks it through the floor, he's incredible!" Bonnie gushed. After "Total Eclipse" went to No. 1 on the U.K. singles chart, Columbia Records waited several months before releasing it in the States. They were rewarded with a song that topped the Hot 100 for four weeks and ranked No. 6 for the year.

The most successful soundtrack single of 1983 was "Flashdance . . . What A Feeling" by Irene Cara. She had the No. 40 song of 1980 with another motion picture theme song, "Fame." The Oscar-winning *Flashdance* theme was written by Cara and Keith Forsey while they were driving to a recording session. Cara hesitated using Giorgio Moroder as a producer because she didn't want "flack" for using Donna Summer's producer. When critics compared Cara to the disco diva, she responded that such criticism was sexist. "There are so many records made by male artists today that sound alike. But nobody makes an issue of that," Cara said in *Songwriter Connection.* "Flashdance . . .What A Feeling," a song that never actually mentioned the word "flashdance" in the lyrics, was the No. 3 record of 1983.

Lionel Richie was back in the year-end top 10 for the first time since "Endless Love" was the No. 2 song of 1981. "All Night Long (All Night)" ranked in fifth place for the year. Richie was worried about getting the right words for the Jamaican chant heard in the song and checked them out with his wife's Jamaican gynecologist.

"Down Under," the third most successful Australian single of the rock era, was the No. 7 song of the year. That bettered the mark set by Men at Work with their first single in 1982, "Who Can It Be Now," which ranked

35 **NEVER GONNA LET YOU GO**
Sergio Mendes *A&M*

36 **TRUE**
Spandau Ballet *Chrysalis*

37 **YOU AND I**
Eddie Rabbitt w/Crystal Gayle *Elektra*

38 **YOU ARE**
Lionel Richie *Motown*

39 **KING OF PAIN**
The Police *A&M*

40 **PUTTIN' ON THE RITZ**
Taco *RCA*

41 **SEPARATE WAYS (WORLDS APART)**
Journey *Columbia*

42 **LOVE IS A BATTLEFIELD**
Pat Benatar *Chrysalis*

43 **ONE THING LEADS TO ANOTHER**
The Fixx *MCA*

44 **YOU CAN'T HURRY LOVE**
Phil Collins *Atlantic*

45 **DER KOMMISSAR**
After The Fire *Epic*

46 **WE'VE GOT TONIGHT**
Kenny Rogers & Sheena Easton *Liberty*

47 **LITTLE RED CORVETTE**
Prince *Warner Bros.*

48 **SHE BLINDED ME WITH SCIENCE**
Thomas Dolby *Capitol*

49 **IS THERE SOMETHING I SHOULD KNOW**
Duran Duran *Capitol*

50 **CUM ON FEEL THE NOIZE**
Quiet Riot *Pasha*

51 **GOODY TWO SHOES**
Adam Ant *Epic*

52 **BACK ON THE CHAIN GANG**
Pretenders *Sire*

53 **STAND BACK**
Stevie Nicks *Modern*

54 **ONE ON ONE**
Daryl Hall and John Oates *RCA*

55 **ROCK THE CASBAH**
The Clash *Epic*

56 **DON'T LET IT END**
Styx *A&M*

57 **(KEEP FEELING) FASCINATION**
Human League *A&M*

58 **THE OTHER GUY**
Little River Band *Capitol*

59 **ALL RIGHT**
Christopher Cross *Warner Bros.*

60 **HEART TO HEART**
Kenny Loggins *Columbia*

61 **WANNA BE STARTIN' SOMETHIN'**
Michael Jackson *Epic*

62 **ALLENTOWN**
Billy Joel *Columbia*

63 **TOO SHY**
Kajagoogoo *EMI America*

64 **AFFAIR OF THE HEART**
Rick Springfield *RCA*

65 **TELEFONE (LONG DISTANCE LOVE AFFAIR)**
Sheena Easton *EMI America*

66 **HEARTBREAKER**
Dionne Warwick *Arista*

67 **CHURCH OF THE POISON MIND**
Culture Club *Epic/Virgin*

68 **SUDDENLY LAST SUMMER**
The Motels *Capitol*

No. 18. When Colin Hay and Ron Strykert first wrote "Down Under," producer Peter McIan felt it wasn't commercial. He took their simple flute and guitar arrangement and added more instruments to give it a reggae sound. Still, the Aussie lyrics left a memorable imprint. Americans even learned what vegemite sandwiches were. Men at Work had two other singles listed on the year-end top 100: "Overkill" was No. 33 and "It's A Mistake" was No. 71.

After making the top 10 of 1981 with "9 to 5" at No. 6, Dolly Parton just missed the top 10 of 1983. "Islands In The Stream," her duet with Kenny Rogers that was co-written and produced by Barry Gibb ranked No. 11. Parton was the fourth female singer to chart in a duet with Kenny Rogers. He had already teamed with Kim Carnes ("Don't Fall In Love With A Dreamer"), Dottie West ("What Are We Doin' In Love"), and Sheena Easton ("We've Got Tonight"). "Islands In The Stream" was Rogers' first single for RCA after a long run of hits on United Artists and Liberty.

Bob Seger, a native of Dearborn, Michigan, first appeared on a year-end chart in 1977 with "Night Moves," the No. 52 song of that year. He almost made the year-end top 10 in 1983 with his remake of Rodney Crowell's "Shame On The Moon," the No. 12 single of the year. He explained how he came to record the song: "Don Henley turned me on to Crowell, who he was listening to a lot, in 1980, but I didn't buy one of his records until '82. When I heard 'Shame On The Moon,' I just stopped and thought, 'Wow, this is a *great* song!' I played it for everyone in the band, and they said, 'Sure, let's do it.' We took it into the studio, and [producer] Jimmy Iovine didn't quite hear it at first, until he heard Glenn Frey and I do the back-up vocals, and then he decided it was a monster. It's more like a western song—a cowboy song—than it is a country and western song. And the track is *flawless,* the best and tightest track on the album. We cut it in like two hours, and everyone decided it was the miracle track. But then we had to decide whether to use it or not because *The Distance* was going to be a real rock album. . . . The next thing we know, the Capitol guys are saying, 'That's the single!'. . . . So thank you, Rodney. It's a great song and I'm beholden to the lad for writing it."

69 TWILIGHT ZONE
Golden Earring *21 Records*
70 (SHE'S) SEXY + 17
Stray Cats *EMI America*
71 IT'S A MISTAKE
Men at Work *Columbia*
72 DELIRIOUS
Prince *Warner Bros.*
73 SOLITAIRE
Laura Branigan *Atlantic*
74 COME DANCING
The Kinks *Arista*
75 OUR HOUSE
Madness *Geffen*
76 FAMILY MAN
Daryl Hall and John Oates *RCA*
77 HUMAN NATURE
Michael Jackson *Epic*
78 I'LL TUMBLE 4 YA
Culture Club *Epic/Virgin*
79 HEART AND SOUL
Huey Lewis & the News *Chrysalis*
80 CRUMBLIN' DOWN
John Cougar Mellencamp *Riva*
81 DON'T CRY
Asia *Geffen*
82 I WON'T HOLD YOU BACK
Toto *Columbia*
83 PROMISES, PROMISES
Naked Eyes *EMI America*
84 SHE'S A BEAUTY
The Tubes *Capitol*
85 TONIGHT, I CELEBRATE MY LOVE
Peabo Bryson/Roberta Flack *Capitol*
86 I'M STILL STANDING
Elton John *Geffen*
87 HOT GIRLS IN LOVE
Loverboy *Columbia*
88 LAWYERS IN LOVE
Jackson Browne *Asylum*
89 HOW AM I SUPPOSED
TO LIVE WITHOUT YOU
Laura Branigan *Atlantic*
90 MY LOVE
Lionel Richie *Motown*
91 THE LOOK OF LOVE (PART ONE)
ABC *Mercury*
92 TAKE ME TO HEART
Quarterflash *Geffen*
93 ALWAYS SOMETHING
THERE TO REMIND ME
Naked Eyes *EMI America*
94 FAITHFULLY
Journey *Columbia*
95 I KNOW THERE'S SOMETHING GOING ON
Frida *Atlantic*
96 FAR FROM OVER
Frank Stallone *RSO*
97 CHINA GIRL
David Bowie *EMI America*
98 BURNING DOWN THE HOUSE
Talking Heads *Sire*
99 WHY ME?
Irene Cara *Geffen*
100 YOUR LOVE IS DRIVING ME CRAZY
Sammy Hagar *Geffen*

The Top 100 Songs of 1984

Cyndi Lauper

1984 WAS THE year Ray Parker Jr. said that he ain't afraid of no ghosts; Pink Floyd's *Dark Side of the Moon* passed the 500-week mark on the *Billboard* album chart; and Marvin Gaye was shot dead by his father on April 1.

Making her first appearance on a year-end chart, Madonna had three titles included in the top 100 songs of the year. "Like A Virgin," the No. 2 song of the year, is her highest ranking on a year-end chart. "Lucky Star" was No. 47 and "Borderline" was No. 57.

Another female singer who made her debut year-end appearance in 1984 was Cyndi Lauper, who was listed with her first four singles. Born in Queens, Cyndi grew up not understanding the creativity burning in her and thought she was crazy or stupid. After a difficult time in high school, she left home and hitchhiked through Canada with her dog Sparkle. She settled down at a Vermont college to study art, but didn't find her creative needs fulfilled. She returned home and sang with a couple of bands until her voice gave out. Doctors told her she would never sing again, but after working with a vocal coach for a year, her voice returned. With musician John Turf, she formed a group called Blue Angel in 1978. After their debut album for Polydor was released, the band broke up. Cyndi was singing in a Japanese piano bar and working in a clothing boutique when she met Dave Wolff, who became her boyfriend and manager. The song that introduced her to the world was "Girls Just Want To Have Fun," No. 23 for the year. The follow-up, "Time After Time," was No. 17. Her next single, "She Bop," ranked No. 30. Her fourth single, "All Through The Night," was No. 60.

The biggest comeback of the year was made by Tina Turner, who triumphed over personal adversity and achieved her greatest chart success. She had first appeared on the Hot 100 in the summer of 1960 coupled with her husband Ike on "A Fool In Love." According to Tina, the marriage started to decay after the first seven years. "I didn't plan to leave, but finally there was one last bit of real violence and I walked," she said in *USA Today*. With 36 cents, a gasoline credit card, and the clothes she was wearing, she checked into a Ramada Inn in Dallas where the manager gave her the best suite in the house. She called her friend Ann-Margret and asked her to buy an airline ticket so Tina could fly to Los Angeles. She stayed with Ann-Margret for six months while Ike searched for her. They were divorced in 1976. Tina's recording career was revived when the British band Heaven 17 asked her to participate in an album project. They produced her version of the Temptations' "Ball Of Confusion." She signed with Capitol Records and Heaven 17 produced her first single, a remake of Al Green's "Let's Stay Together." For her first Capitol album, manager Roger Davies assembled several producers. One of them was British songwriter Terry Britten. Tina heard the demo of a song he had written with Graham Lyle and hated it. Britten said he would arrange it to suit her, and "What's Love Got To Do With It" brought her to the top of the Hot 100 for the first time. It was the No. 7 song of 1984. The follow-up, "Better Be Good To Me," ranked No. 51.

"When Doves Cry" by Prince was the No. 1 single of the year. It was the fifth song from a motion picture to top a year-end chart. It was the initial single from the soundtrack of *Purple Rain*, dubbed "the best rock film ever made" by critic Mikal Gilmore in the *Los Angeles Herald Examiner*. Sneaking in to a preview of the movie in San Diego, Gilmore wrote: "Prince fills the screen like the threat and promise that he is, inspiring the audiences in San Diego to the kind of uncalculated sexual hysteria I haven't heard since the Beatles tore across the opening frames of *A Hard Day's Night*."

The Southern California–based rock group Van Halen made their first year-end appearance in 1982, when they were listed at No. 89 with "(Oh) Pretty Woman," a remake of the Roy Orbison song. In 1984 they had the biggest hit of their career. "Jump" topped the Hot 100 for five weeks and was ranked No. 3 for the year. Eddie Van Halen wrote the music for "Jump" two years before David Lee Roth agreed to write lyrics and record the song. "Eddie wrote this thing on synthesizer," says producer Ted Templeman. "I really hadn't heard it for a long time, then he laid it down one night in the studio. I heard it and it just killed me. It was perfect." Roth wrote the words in the backseat of a 1951 Mercury lowrider while cruising one afternoon through Los Angeles with one of the band's roadies. "Every hour and a half or so, I'd lean over the front seat and say, 'Lar, what do you think of this?' He's probably the most responsible for how it came out," Roth said in *Musician*.

Culture Club, the British band once known as In Praise of Lemmings and then the Sex Gang Children before Boy George renamed them, made their mark in America in 1983 with four singles on the year-end chart: "Do

34 **JUMP (FOR MY LOVE)**
Pointer Sisters *Planet*

35 **STUCK ON YOU**
Lionel Richie *Motown*

36 **OH SHERRIE**
Steve Perry *Columbia*

37 **SELF CONTROL**
Laura Branigan *Atlantic*

38 **HERE COMES THE RAIN AGAIN**
Eurythmics *RCA*

39 **EYES WITHOUT A FACE**
Billy Idol *Chrysalis*

40 **I GUESS THAT'S WHY THEY CALL IT THE BLUES**
Elton John *Geffen*

41 **BREAK MY STRIDE**
Matthew Wilder *Private*

42 **THE GLAMOROUS LIFE**
Sheila E. *Warner Bros.*

43 **RUNNING WITH THE NIGHT**
Lionel Richie *Motown*

44 **PENNY LOVER**
Lionel Richie *Motown*

45 **THAT'S ALL!**
Genesis *Atlantic*

46 **TWIST OF FATE**
Olivia Newton-John *MCA*

47 **LUCKY STAR**
Madonna *Sire*

48 **THE HEART OF ROCK & ROLL**
Huey Lewis & the News *Chrysalis*

49 **AUTOMATIC**
Pointer Sisters *Planet*

50 **NO MORE LONELY NIGHTS**
Paul McCartney *Columbia*

51 **BETTER BE GOOD TO ME**
Tina Turner *Capitol*

52 **THRILLER**
Michael Jackson *Epic*

53 **INFATUATION**
Rod Stewart *Warner Bros.*

54 **SUNGLASSES AT NIGHT**
Corey Hart *EMI America*

55 **SISTER CHRISTIAN**
Night Ranger *MCA/Camel*

56 **I CAN DREAM ABOUT YOU**
Dan Hartman *MCA*

57 **BORDERLINE**
Madonna *Sire*

58 **I'M SO EXCITED**
Pointer Sisters *Planet*

59 **MISS ME BLIND**
Culture Club *Epic/Virgin*

60 **ALL THROUGH THE NIGHT**
Cyndi Lauper *Portrait*

61 **THE WARRIOR**
Scandal f/Patty Smyth *Columbia*

62 **I WANT A NEW DRUG**
Huey Lewis & the News *Chrysalis*

63 **IF THIS IS IT**
Huey Lewis & the News *Chrysalis*

64 **SAD SONGS (SAY SO MUCH)**
Elton John *Geffen*

65 **ALMOST PARADISE**
Mike Reno & Ann Wilson *Columbia*

66 **COVER ME**
Bruce Springsteen *Columbia*

67 **LEGS**
ZZ Top *Warner Bros.*

You Really Want To Hurt Me" (No. 17), "Time (Clock Of The Heart)" (No. 23), "Church Of The Poison Mind" (No. 67), and "I'll Tumble 4 Ya" (No. 78). Their fifth single, "Karma Chameleon," became their biggest hit, and was the No. 9 song of 1984. The follow-up, "Miss Me Blind," ranked No. 59 for the year.

"Hello," a song written for Lionel Richie's first solo album but not included, finally made it onto his second LP and became the No. 5 song of 1984.

In addition to Prince's "When Doves Cry," there were four other soundtrack singles in the top 10. Phil Collins had his first chart-topper with the title song from Taylor Hackford's *Against All Odds.* Hackford had to convince Collins to record a song for his film. He flew to Chicago to meet Phil after a Genesis concert. Hackford screened the movie in a hotel room and the drummer/vocalist agreed to write the title song, which was No. 4 for the year.

Ray Parker Jr. had the No. 6 song of 1984 with the title song from *Ghostbusters.* The most difficult problem in writing the song, Parker said in *USA Today,* was finding a word to rhyme with "ghostbusters." "I figured the best thing to do was to have somebody shout, 'Ghostbusters!' In order for that to work, I had to have something before or after it. That's when I came up with the line, 'Who you gonna call?'"

Stevie Wonder won the Golden Globe and the Oscar for best song with the No. 8 single of 1984, "I Just Called to Say I Love You," from *The Woman In Red.*

Kenny Loggins ranked No. 10 with the title song from *Footloose,* written by Loggins and Dean Pitchford. Pitchford, who wrote the screenplay for the movie, wanted Loggins to perform the main title theme right from the beginning of the project. "It felt to me he was like the voice of the country," Pitchford explains. Three other songs from *Footloose* were included in the top 100 songs of the year: "Let's Hear It For The Boy" by Deniece Williams (No. 12), "Almost Paradise" by Mike Reno and Ann Wilson (No. 65), and "Dancing In The Sheets" by Shalamar (No. 93).

The British progressive rock group Yes made their first year-end chart appearance 13 years after their debut single. The 1984 incarnation of the band started out as a group called Cinema, but by the time they added vocalist Jon Anderson there were so many former members of Yes in the band that they realized they had accidentally formed the group again. "Owner Of A Lonely Heart" returned them to the Hot 100 after a long absence and was the No. 11 single of the year.

68 STRUT
Sheena Easton *EMI America*

69 IF EVER YOU'RE IN MY ARMS AGAIN
Peabo Bryson *Elektra*

70 I CAN'T HOLD BACK
Survivor *Scotti Bros.*

71 TO ALL THE GIRLS I'VE LOVED BEFORE
Julio Iglesias & Willie Nelson *Columbia*

72 LOVE SOMEBODY
Rick Springfield *RCA*

73 YOU MIGHT THINK
The Cars *Elektra*

74 ADULT EDUCATION
Daryl Hall and John Oates *RCA*

75 BREAKDANCE
Irene Cara *Geffen*

76 THEY DON'T KNOW
Tracey Ullman *MCA*

77 GOT A HOLD ON ME
Christine McVie *Warner Bros.*

78 PINK HOUSES
John Cougar Mellencamp *Riva*

79 NOBODY TOLD ME
John Lennon *Polydor*

80 LET THE MUSIC PLAY
Shannon *Mirage*

81 WRAPPED AROUND YOUR FINGER
The Police *A&M*

82 HEAD OVER HEELS
The Go-Go's *I.R.S.*

83 CRUEL SUMMER
Bananarama *London*

84 THINK OF LAURA
Christopher Cross *Warner Bros.*

85 MAGIC
The Cars *Elektra*

86 BREAKIN'... THERE'S NO STOPPING US
Ollie and Jerry *Polydor*

87 NEW MOON ON MONDAY
Duran Duran *Capitol*

88 ROUND AND ROUND
Ratt *Atlantic*

89 LIGHTS OUT
Peter Wolf *EMI America*

90 THE LONGEST TIME
Billy Joel *Columbia*

91 THE LANGUAGE OF LOVE
Dan Fogelberg *Full Moon*

92 I STILL CAN'T GET OVER LOVING YOU
Ray Parker Jr. *Arista*

93 DANCING IN THE SHEETS
Shalamar *Columbia*

94 ON THE DARK SIDE
John Cafferty & the Beaver Brown Band *Scotti Bros.*

95 READ 'EM AND WEEP
Barry Manilow *Arista*

96 BLUE JEAN
David Bowie *EMI America*

97 DESERT MOON
Dennis DeYoung *A&M*

98 DOCTOR! DOCTOR!
Thompson Twins *Arista*

99 AN INNOCENT MAN
Billy Joel *Columbia*

100 SOME GUYS HAVE ALL THE LUCK
Rod Stewart *Warner Bros.*

The Top 100 Songs of 1985

Mr. Mister

1985 WAS THE year Quincy Jones produced "We Are The World" to help feed millions of starving people in Africa and in America; Bob Geldof organized the Live Aid concert to help end the famine in Ethiopia; and Wham! became the first rock group to tour China.

With two singles included in the top 100 songs of the year, Whitney Houston made her first appearance on a year-end chart. Her debut single, "You Give Good Love," was No. 44 for the year and the follow-up, "Saving All My Love For You," ranked No. 25.

There were 33 titles on the top 100 by artists from the United Kingdom, matching the record set in 1983. That included the No. 3 song of the year, "Careless Whisper" by Wham! featuring George Michael. It was written when he was 16 and released in Britain as a solo single by George. Employed as an usher at a cinema in his hometown of Bushey, he was bored with his job and spent his time writing lyrics. He thought up the melody to "Careless Whisper" while riding on a bus.

Phil Collins was responsible for five of the U.K. titles in the top 100 of 1984. Highest-ranked was his duet with Marilyn Martin on Stephen Bishop's song "Separate Lives" at No. 13. The song was composed after Taylor Hackford explained the plot of *White Nights* to Bishop in 1982. When several studios turned down the film project, Bishop grew tired of waiting and never recorded the song he had written. When the film was released in 1985, Collins and Martin sang the tune. Collins was also listed in the year's

01 **SAY YOU, SAY ME**
   Lionel Richie *Motown*
02 **WE ARE THE WORLD**
   USA for Africa *Columbia*
03 **CARELESS WHISPER**
   Wham! f/George Michael *Columbia*
04 **CRAZY FOR YOU**
   Madonna *Geffen*
05 **BROKEN WINGS**
   Mr. Mister *RCA*
06 **CAN'T FIGHT THIS FEELING**
   REO Speedwagon *Epic*
07 **MONEY FOR NOTHING**
   Dire Straits *Warner Bros.*
08 **SHOUT**
   Tears for Fears *Mercury*
09 **I WANT TO KNOW WHAT LOVE IS**
   Foreigner *Atlantic*
10 **EVERYBODY WANTS
   TO RULE THE WORLD**
   Tears for Fears *Mercury*
11 **THE POWER OF LOVE**
   Huey Lewis & the News *Chrysalis*
12 **ST. ELMO'S FIRE (MAN IN MOTION)**
   John Parr *Atlantic*
13 **SEPARATE LIVES**
   Phil Collins & Marilyn Martin *Atlantic*
14 **PARTY ALL THE TIME**
   Eddie Murphy *Columbia*
15 **WE BUILT THIS CITY**
   Starship *Grunt*
16 **A VIEW TO A KILL**
   Duran Duran *Capitol*
17 **ONE MORE NIGHT**
   Phil Collins *Atlantic*
18 **SUSSUDIO**
   Phil Collins *Atlantic*
19 **EVERYTIME YOU GO AWAY**
   Paul Young *Columbia*
20 **HEAVEN**
   Bryan Adams *A&M*
21 **EVERYTHING SHE WANTS**
   Wham! *Columbia*
22 **EASY LOVER**
   Philip Bailey w/Phil Collins *Columbia*
23 **PART-TIME LOVER**
   Stevie Wonder *Tamla*
24 **DON'T YOU (FORGET ABOUT ME)**
   Simple Minds *A&M*
25 **SAVING ALL MY LOVE FOR YOU**
   Whitney Houston *Arista*
26 **TAKE ON ME**
   a-ha *Warner Bros.*
27 **CHERISH**
   Kool & the Gang *De-Lite*
28 **MIAMI VICE THEME**
   Jan Hammer *MCA*
29 **RASPBERRY BERET**
   Prince & the Revolution *Paisley Park*
30 **MATERIAL GIRL**
   Madonna *Sire*
31 **ALIVE AND KICKING**
   Simple Minds *A&M*
32 **OH SHEILA**
   Ready for the World *MCA*
33 **THE HEAT IS ON**
   Glenn Frey *MCA*
34 **YOU BELONG TO THE CITY**
   Glenn Frey *MCA*

top 100 with "One More Night" (No. 17), "Sussudio" (No. 18), "Easy Lover," a duet with Philip Bailey (No. 22), and "Don't Lose My Number" (No. 57).

The Anglo-American group Foreigner had their first year-end entry since "Waiting For A Girl Like You" was the No. 4 song of 1981. "I Want To Know What Love Is" was ranked the No. 9 song for 1985. Mick Jones said in *Billboard* that he was dubious about releasing the song as the first single from *Agent Provocateur* because it was a ballad. "I certainly want to retain the rock image," he explained. "We just put this out because the song was so strong, and because it was coming out at Christmas, and it had the right kind of mood."

Another U.K. band, Dire Straits, caused some controversy with "Money For Nothing," the No. 7 song of the year. Mark Knopfler was inspired to write the song after shopping in an appliance store in the Upper East Side of New York City. There was a wall of television sets tuned to MTV and a sales clerk that Knopfler described as a "blockhead." "I wanted to use a lot of the language that the real guy actually used when I heard him, because it was more real. It just went better with the song, it was more muscular," Knopfler told Bill Flanagan. But the reference to "little faggot" got Knopfler in trouble. "The same thing happened when Randy Newman recorded 'Short People,' a song that was clearly about the stupidity of prejudice," Knopfler said in *The New York Times*. "An editor of *Gay News* in England attacked the song. What surprises me is that an intelligent journalist can misunderstand it."

The other U.K. act in the top 10 was Tears for Fears. Curt Smith and Roland Orzabal met in Bath when they were 13 years old. Six years later they formed a band called Graduate, but they split after releasing one single, "Elvis Should Play Ska." They re-formed as History of Headaches, but renamed themselves after a chapter title in Arthur Janov's *The Primal Scream.* "Everybody Wants To Rule The World" was recorded in three days and was the last song added to their *Songs From The Big Chair* album. It was the No. 10 song of 1985. The follow-up, "Shout," had taken four months to record. It was No. 8 for the year.

The No. 1 song of the year was "Say You, Say Me" by Lionel Richie. It had something in common with the No. 13 song: they were both from the film *White Nights,* although Richie's song didn't appear on the Atlantic Records soundtrack album, at the request of Motown. Lionel was originally asked by Taylor Hackford to write the title theme for the movie, but Lionel's manager Ken Kragen called back to say that his client couldn't seem to write anything called "White Nights." Instead, he had something that he thought was one of his better songs and that it would work in the film. Hackford and Gary LeMel, then head of Columbia Pictures' music department, listened to "Say You, Say Me" and agreed.

For the first time since 1964 when John Lennon and Paul McCartney were the songwriters on the top two singles of the year, the No. 1 and No. 2 songs of the year were written by the same person. Ranked right under "Say You, Say Me" was a song written by Lionel Richie and Michael Jackson. "We Are The World" by USA for Africa was the No. 2 song of 1985. The idea to record the song originated with Harry Belafonte, who suggested the idea of a concert by black artists to raise money for Africa

35 WE DON'T NEED ANOTHER HERO
(THUNDERDOME)
Tina Turner *Capitol*

36 AXEL F
Harold Faltermeyer *MCA*

37 SEA OF LOVE
The Honeydrippers *Es Paranza*

38 ALL I NEED
Jack Wagner *Qwest*

39 IF YOU LOVE SOMEBODY SET THEM FREE
Sting *A&M*

40 YOU'RE THE INSPIRATION
Chicago *Full Moon*

41 RHYTHM OF THE NIGHT
DeBarge *Gordy*

42 LOVERBOY
Billy Ocean *Jive*

43 NEVER SURRENDER
Corey Hart *EMI America*

44 YOU GIVE GOOD LOVE
Whitney Houston *Arista*

45 HEAD OVER HEELS
Tears for Fears *Mercury*

46 NIGHTSHIFT
Commodores *Motown*

47 FREEWAY OF LOVE
Aretha Franklin *Arista*

48 COOL IT NOW
New Edition *MCA*

49 CALIFORNIA GIRLS
David Lee Roth *Warner Bros.*

50 ONE NIGHT IN BANGKOK
Murray Head *RCA*

51 I MISS YOU
Klymaxx *Constellation*

52 SUDDENLY
Billy Ocean *Jive*

53 NEVER
Heart *Capitol*

54 LOVERGIRL
Teena Marie *Epic*

55 FREEDOM
Wham! *Columbia*

56 THE SEARCH IS OVER
Survivor *Scotti Bros.*

57 DON'T LOSE MY NUMBER
Phil Collins *Atlantic*

58 THINGS CAN ONLY GET BETTER
Howard Jones *Elektra*

59 THE BOYS OF SUMMER
Don Henley *Geffen*

60 WE BELONG
Pat Benatar *Chrysalis*

61 SMOOTH OPERATOR
Sade *Portrait*

62 NEUTRON DANCE
Pointer Sisters *Planet*

63 GLORY DAYS
Bruce Springsteen *Columbia*

64 SMALL TOWN
John Cougar Mellencamp *Riva*

65 RUN TO YOU
Bryan Adams *A&M*

66 OBSESSION
Animotion *Mercury*

67 LONELY OL' NIGHT
John Cougar Mellencamp *Riva*

68 SOME LIKE IT HOT
Power Station *Capitol*

to Ken Kragen. Kragen thought a concert wouldn't raise the amount of money needed, and came up with the idea of an American version of Band Aid. That was the name used by the U.K. artists who recorded "Do They Know It's Christmas?," an effort organized by Bob Geldof prior to Live Aid. Kragen called Richie to tell him of Belafonte's idea and enrolled him in the project. Next he asked Quincy Jones to produce, and Quincy brought in Michael Jackson. Lionel and Michael wrote the song and Quincy sent out demo tapes to the artists invited to record the number, requesting they "check their egos at the door." The song was recorded at A&M Studios in Hollywood following the American Music Awards ceremony on January 28, 1985. Less than a year after the release of the "We Are The World" single and album, approximately $44 million had been raised.

"Broken Wings," the No. 5 single of 1985, was written in 20 minutes by Richard Page and Steve George of Mr. Mister with John Lang. "We weren't there to write," says Page. "The drum machine was going. I started with the bass line. Before I knew it, the song was done. It just sort of happened and luckily I had the tape machine on." RCA wanted to release an uptempo track as the first single from the *Welcome To The Real World* album, but the band felt "Broken Wings" was the best track.

Huey Lewis & the News had the No. 11 song with "The Power Of Love" from *Back To The Future*. When Steven Spielberg, director Robert Zemeckis, and producers Bob Gale and Nell Canton asked Lewis to write a song for the movie, he came up with a tune called "In The Nick Of Time." But as negotiations with managers and lawyers dragged on, Huey gave the song away to another movie—*Brewster's Millions,* starring Richard Pryor. "We thought we were going to get that song," laments music supervisor Bones Howe. "Everybody was really upset about it." Lewis told them not to worry, he was writing another song for the film. He came up with "Back In Time." That was used in the film, but it was "The Power Of Love" that was released as a single. Michael J. Fox plays some riffs from it in a scene where Marty McFly is auditioning with his band to play at a high school dance. Lewis played the part of the high school teacher who turned him down. A vocal version by Huey Lewis & the News was heard over a scene where Fox rides his skateboard to school.

The Top 100 Songs of 1986

Peter Gabriel

1986 WAS THE year cassette singles first outsold their 7-inch vinyl counterparts; Aerosmith and Run-D.M.C. combined heavy metal with rap to "Walk This Way;" and the Rock and Roll Hall of Fame inducted its first honorees at a dinner in New York City.

Janet Jackson appeared on the year-end chart for the first time. Working with producers Jimmy Jam and Terry Lewis, she broke out of the teenybopper mold she had been in for her first two albums. She recorded *Control* after her marriage of six months to James DeBarge was annulled. Without the turmoil in her personal life, "The album wouldn't have been the same," she said in *Bam*. "I don't know what it would have been like." She made the album without any help from her father, brother Michael, or any other members of her family. "I wanted the public to like my album because of *me*," she emphasized. Janet had three titles in the top 100 of the year: "When I Think Of You" (No. 15), "Nasty" (No. 50), and "What Have You Done For Me Lately" (No. 52).

Past and present members of Genesis accounted for six of the year's top 100. Peter Gabriel, who left his post as lead vocalist in May 1975, after a concert at St. Etienne, France, was No. 18 for the year with "Sledgehammer." Genesis had two songs listed: "Invisible Touch" at No. 32 and "Throwing It All Away" at No. 53. Mike Rutherford's extracurricular band, Mike + the Mechanics, also had two titles on the chart: "All I Need Is A Miracle" at No. 74 and "Silent Running (On Dangerous Ground)" at No. 77. Phil Collins, the band's drummer and current lead vocalist, was No. 82 with "Take Me Home."

Whitney Houston was in the year-end top 10 for the first time. Her remake of George Benson's "Greatest Love Of All" was No. 4. A song turned down by Janet Jackson, "How Will I Know," was just outside the top 10 at No. 11.

The No. 1 song of 1986 was by Whitney's cousin, Dionne Warwick. Accompanied by Gladys Knight, Stevie Wonder, and Elton John, billed on the label as "and Friends," Dionne triumphed with a Burt Bacharach–Carole Bayer Sager song originally recorded by Rod Stewart in 1982 for the soundtrack of *Night Shift.* The song took on a new meaning when Sager suggested to her friend Elizabeth Taylor that proceeds from the song be donated to the American Foundation for AIDS Research. Dionne, Gladys, and Stevie waited longer than any other artists to have a No. 1 single of the year. Gladys made her *Billboard* Hot 100 debut in 1961 with "Every Beat Of My Heart," Dionne's first chart appearance was in 1962 with "Don't Make Me Over," and Stevie debuted in 1963 with "Fingertips—Pt. 2."

The Bangles had the No. 2 song of 1986 with "Walk Like An Egyptian," a song written by American expatriate Liam Sternberg. The title came to him while crossing the English Channel on a ferry. He recorded a demo of the song in Los Angeles with singer Marti Jones. Sternberg submitted it to Toni Basil ("Mickey"), who turned it down. David Kahne, producer for the Bangles, received a two-song demo tape from a publisher and was asked to consider the first, "Rock And Roll Vertigo," for the Bangles. But the order on the tape was reversed. "So I was listening to 'Walk Like An Egyptian' but thinking it was the other song," laughs Kahne. "I really liked the demo. Marti sang it with an offhand quality I thought was really great."

Patti LaBelle and Michael McDonald were both in the year-end top 10 for the first time. As lead singer for Labelle, Patti had the No. 20 song of 1975, "Lady Marmalade." Michael joined the Doobie Brothers in 1976 and had the No. 18 song of 1979 as lead singer on "What A Fool Believes." Their duet of "On My Own" was the No. 3 song of 1986, giving Burt Bacharach and Carole Bayer Sager two of the year's top three songs. The only other songwriters to accomplish this in the rock era were John Lennon and Paul McCartney; Lionel Richie; and Barry, Robin, and Maurice Gibb, who wrote "Staying Alive" and "Night Fever," the No. 2 and No. 3 songs of 1978, respectively. Barry actually did it twice: in 1977 he was the writer of "I Just Want To Be Your Everything" (No. 2) as well as "How Deep Is Your Love" (No. 3). Although Elvis Presley was listed as one of the songwriters on "Don't Be Cruel" and "Love Me Tender" in 1956, it's commonly acknowledged that he didn't participate in composing either song.

Mr. Mister had a year-end top 10 single for the second consecutive year. *"Kyrie eleison"* means "Lord have mercy" in Greek, and "Kyrie" was the No. 6 song of 1986.

Prince had his first year-end top 10 single since "When Doves Cry" was the No. 1 record of 1984. "Kiss," the first single released from the

35 **THE NEXT TIME I FALL**
Peter Cetera & Amy Grant *Full Moon*

36 **SECRET LOVERS**
Atlantic Starr *A&M*

37 **WHEN THE GOING GETS TOUGH, THE TOUGH GET GOING**
Billy Ocean *Jive*

38 **DANGER ZONE**
Kenny Loggins *Columbia*

39 **MANIC MONDAY**
Bangles *Columbia*

40 **I DIDN'T MEAN TO TURN YOU ON**
Robert Palmer *Island*

41 **MAD ABOUT YOU**
Belinda Carlisle *I.R.S.*

42 **TRUE BLUE**
Madonna *Sire*

43 **R.O.C.K. IN THE U.S.A.**
John Cougar Mellencamp *Riva*

44 **DON'T FORGET ME (WHEN I'M GONE)**
Glass Tiger *Manhattan*

45 **WHY CAN'T THIS BE LOVE**
Van Halen *Warner Bros.*

46 **CRUSH ON YOU**
The Jets *MCA*

47 **HIP TO BE SQUARE**
Huey Lewis & the News *Chrysalis*

48 **I'M YOUR MAN**
Wham! *Columbia*

49 **I CAN'T WAIT**
Nu Shooz *Atlantic*

50 **NASTY**
Janet Jackson *A&M*

51 **TALK TO ME**
Stevie Nicks *Modern*

52 **WHAT HAVE YOU DONE FOR ME LATELY**
Janet Jackson *A&M*

53 **THROWING IT ALL AWAY**
Genesis *Atlantic*

54 **WHO'S JOHNNY**
El DeBarge *Gordy*

55 **CONGA**
Miami Sound Machine *Epic*

56 **TWO OF HEARTS**
Stacey Q *Atlantic*

57 **IF YOU LEAVE**
Orchestral Manoeuvres in the Dark *A&M*

58 **NO ONE IS TO BLAME**
Howard Jones *Elektra*

59 **WHAT YOU NEED**
INXS *Atlantic*

60 **WALK OF LIFE**
Dire Straits *Warner Bros.*

61 **TAKE ME HOME TONIGHT**
Eddie Money *Columbia*

62 **WALK THIS WAY**
Run-D.M.C. *Profile*

63 **WORD UP**
Cameo *Atlanta Artists*

64 **TO BE A LOVER**
Billy Idol *Chrysalis*

65 **YOUR LOVE**
The Outfield *Columbia*

66 **SOMETHING ABOUT YOU**
Level 42 *Polydor*

67 **LET'S GO ALL THE WAY**
Sly Fox *Capitol*

68 **TONIGHT SHE COMES**
The Cars *Elektra*

Parade album, spent two weeks on top of the Hot 100 and ranked in fifth place for the year.

Billy Ocean had his first top 10 song of the year in 1986. Two years earlier, he had the No. 18 song of the year with "Caribbean Queen (No More Love On The Run)." In 1985 he had two songs in the top 100 of the year: "Loverboy" (No. 42) and "Suddenly" (No. 52). Born Leslie Sebastian Charles in Trinidad, he went through several stage names (including Joshua, Big Ben, and Sam Spade) before naming himself Billy Ocean. He left his job installing windshield wipers at a Ford plant after his first chart single, "Love Really Hurts Without You." "There'll Be Sad Songs (To Make You Cry)" was one of the first tunes written for his *Love Zone* album. Co-writer Barry Eastmond recalls, "I had the music in my head for a little while. It seemed perfect for Billy. The lyrics came out of a story my wife told me about a friend of hers. She had just broken up with the fellow she had been going out with for years. There was a particular song that always made her think of her boyfriend. She was at a party given by her new boyfriend and the song came on and reminded her of the old boyfriend. She broke down. We thought that was an interesting story so we wrote the song about it." The song that made her cry was Billy's 1985 hit, "Suddenly."

Brothers Bruce and John Hornsby moved to Los Angeles in 1980 to try their luck at songwriting. As staff writers for 20th Century Fox's music publishing division they were asked to write formula disco songs. "We were terrible at it," Bruce admitted in *Rolling Stone*. Frustrated with trying to adapt to the latest trend, Bruce recorded a four-song demo tape that included "The Way It Is." He sent the tape to Windham Hill Records because he thought the tape sounded too organic to appeal to a major label. Windham Hill offered him a deal, but they weren't interested in his rock material. Paul Atkinson at RCA Records heard the tape and signed Hornsby to the label. Released as his second single, "The Way It Is" topped the Hot 100 and ranked No. 25 for the year.

Derek Schulman of Polygram signed Bon Jovi to Mercury Records. The band had four chart singles beginning in 1984, all of which missed the top 30. Then they enlisted Bruce Fairbairn (Loverboy, Honeymoon Suite) as producer and Desmond Child as a co-writer. With Jon Bon Jovi and Richie Sambora of the group, Child wrote "You Give Love A Bad Name." It was their first chart-topper and the No. 26 record of 1986.

The Top 100 Songs of 1987

Debbie Gibson

1987 WAS THE year the Beatles' albums were first released on compact disc; Billy Joel was back in the U.S.S.R.; and U2 had their American breakthrough with *The Joshua Tree*.

The average age of artists in the year-end top 100 was reduced by the presence of two teenagers: Tiffany and Debbie Gibson.

Michael Jackson was back on the year-end chart with his first singles since *Thriller.* "I Just Can't Stop Loving You," a duet with Siedah Garrett, was No. 24 and "Bad" was No. 33.

After placing third in 1985 with "Careless Whisper," George Michael had the No. 1 hit of the year with "Faith," a song he says described how hopeful and optimistic he felt at the time he wrote it. Michael was the second British solo male artist in the rock era to top an annual recap; Rod Stewart did it first in 1976 with "Tonight's The Night (Gonna Be Alright)."

In the runner-up position for the year was "Alone" by Heart. The group had first scored on a year-end chart with "Magic Man," the No. 80 song of 1976. Nancy Wilson had joined the band just two years earlier, the same year their name was shortened from White Heart. Her sister Ann had joined in 1970. When Ann was offered a solo contract with Mushroom Records, she told them to take the whole band or nothing. After a short tenure with

01 **FAITH**
George Michael *Columbia*
02 **ALONE**
Heart *Capitol*
03 **LIVIN' ON A PRAYER**
Bon Jovi *Mercury*
04 **LA BAMBA**
Los Lobos *Slash*
05 **I WANNA DANCE WITH SOMEBODY (WHO LOVES ME)**
Whitney Houston *Arista*
06 **NOTHING'S GONNA STOP US NOW**
Starship *Grunt*
07 **SHAKEDOWN**
Bob Seger *MCA*
08 **WITH OR WITHOUT YOU**
U2 *Island*
09 **(I'VE HAD) THE TIME OF MY LIFE**
Bill Medley & Jennifer Warnes *RCA*
10 **LEAN ON ME**
Club Nouveau *Warner Bros.*
11 **HERE I GO AGAIN**
Whitesnake *Geffen*
12 **HEAVEN IS A PLACE ON EARTH**
Belinda Carlisle *MCA*
13 **DIDN'T WE ALMOST HAVE IT ALL**
Whitney Houston *Arista*
14 **I STILL HAVEN'T FOUND WHAT I'M LOOKING FOR**
U2 *Island*
15 **LOOKING FOR A NEW LOVE**
Jody Watley *MCA*
16 **I THINK WE'RE ALONE NOW**
Tiffany *MCA*
17 **AT THIS MOMENT**
Billy Vera & the Beaters *Rhino*
18 **HEAD TO TOE**
Lisa Lisa & Cult Jam *Columbia*
19 **MONY MONY**
Billy Idol *Chrysalis*
20 **SHAKE YOU DOWN**
Gregory Abbott *Columbia*
21 **OPEN YOUR HEART**
Madonna *Sire*
22 **ALWAYS**
Atlantic Starr *Warner Bros.*
23 **YOU KEEP ME HANGIN' ON**
Kim Wilde *MCA*
24 **I JUST CAN'T STOP LOVING YOU**
Michael Jackson & Siedah Garrett *Epic*
25 **NOTORIOUS**
Duran Duran *Capitol*
26 **WHO'S THAT GIRL**
Madonna *Sire*
27 **JACOB'S LADDER**
Huey Lewis & the News *Chrysalis*
28 **C'EST LA VIE**
Robbie Nevil *Manhattan*
29 **LOST IN EMOTION**
Lisa Lisa & Cult Jam *Columbia*
30 **(I JUST) DIED IN YOUR ARMS**
Cutting Crew *Virgin*
31 **I KNEW YOU WERE WAITING (FOR ME)**
Aretha Franklin & George Michael *Arista*
32 **IS THIS LOVE**
Survivor *Scotti Bros.*
33 **BAD**
Michael Jackson *Epic*

Mushroom, the group charged breach of contract and signed with Columbia's Portrait label. They reached a new pinnacle of chart success when they signed with Capitol. Billy Steinberg and Tom Kelly wrote "Alone" and had recorded an earlier version under the name i-Ten. Steinberg hated the original track and insisted on recording a new version before submitting it to producer Ron Nevison for Heart.

A year after placing fourth with "Greatest Love Of All," Whitney Houston did almost as well in 1987, ranking fifth with "I Wanna Dance With Somebody (Who Loves Me)." The song was written by the husband-and-wife team of George Merrill and Shannon Rubicam, the same composers who provided Whitney with the No. 11 song of 1986, "How Will I Know." The follow-up, Michael Masser and Will Jennings' "Didn't We Almost Have It All," was No. 13 for the year.

Chart newcomer Robbie Nevil, whose songs had been recorded by the Pointer Sisters, Sheena Easton, Al Jarreau, and El DeBarge, scored with "C'est La Vie," the No. 28 song of 1987. The tune was written in a few hours while Nevil was messing around with his keyboard. He was concerned about releasing it as a single because, as he told Holly Gleason, "It's so light. It doesn't represent the depth there is. It's a dance thing." Then he allowed, "I'd like to think that even if it's just a straight ahead dance song, people will hear an integrity that makes it more than another dance song."

Like Nevil, Gregory Abbott was new to the charts in 1987 when the Marvin Gaye–influenced "Shake You Down" became a hit. The No. 20 song of the year, it was Abbott's first single for Columbia. Born in Harlem, he taught at the University of California at Berkeley before going to work as a researcher for a Wall Street brokerage firm. Some investment bankers financed a recording studio and record label for Abbott. He produced other artists for his label and spent three years writing songs for himself. He recorded 40 songs and chose the best three to submit to Columbia.

"La Bamba," a song that had been on the flip side of Ritchie Valens' "Donna" (the No. 11 single of 1959), was updated by Los Lobos and used as the title song for the film biography of Valens' life starring Lou Diamond Phillips. The East Los Angeles group was signed to Slash Records on the recommendation of the label's leading group, the Blasters. Los Lobos had often performed "La Bamba," a traditional song dating back two centuries, before writer/director Luis Valdez suggested recording new music for the film rather than using Valens' original recordings. Phillips lip-synched to Los Lobos' pre-recorded tracks.

Bon Jovi were in the year-end top 10 for the first time. "Livin' On A Prayer," their second chart-topping single, ranked No. 3 for 1987. The band had recorded more than 35 songs for their third album, and "Livin' On A Prayer" almost didn't make the cut. While writing the song with Richie Sambora and Desmond Child, Jon Bon Jovi told Sambora that they should submit the song for a movie soundtrack because it wasn't right for the band. Producer Bruce Fairbairn disagreed: "I really heard the lyric in that song as being something that spoke to a lot of people, so I liked it for that and I fought for the song. At some point it looked like it might not make the record. I convinced Jon and Richie that it was worth hanging in there, and sure enough, it started to develop. By the time we finished it, everybody had the feeling that it was going to be a single. I thought it could be the biggest single on the record. As it turned out, it was."

The No. 11 song of 1987 had first charted five years earlier in Britain. David Coverdale of Whitesnake wrote "Here I Go Again" when he was in Portugal in 1981. It was recorded for the *Saints And Sinners* album that year, but that LP wasn't released in the U.S. Except for Coverdale, it was a new line-up of musicians in Whitesnake that re-recorded the song at the suggestion of John David Kolodner of Geffen Records. "I wanted to have a more positive backing track," Coverdale explains. "The only thing that stands up on the original version is the emotional security of the vocal performance. There's a very limp performance from some very exceptional musicians."

Belinda Carlisle first appeared on a year-end chart as a member of the Go-Go's. Their debut chart single, "Our Lips Are Sealed," was the No. 94 song of 1981. The following year "We Got The Beat" ranked No. 21. The Go-Go's announced their breakup on May 10, 1985. Belinda's first solo effort, "Mad About You," was the No. 41 song of 1986. She set a new mark in 1987 with "Heaven Is A Place On Earth," No. 12 for the year. Producer Rick Nowels and his songwriting partner Ellen Shipley came up with the song and spent a month recording it with Belinda. Nowels liked the chorus but was uncomfortable with the verse, even after Belinda had finished cutting the track. Nowels asked Shipley to fly from New York to Los Angeles to rewrite the song. It took three days, and then Nowels had to break the news to Carlisle that she would have to record the song again. "I was very nervous about breaking this to her because I put her through a lot of changes to get her to sing the other vocal," the producer admits. But Belinda heard the rewrite and realized it was better. Joined by Michelle Phillips and songwriter Diane Warren on backing vocals, Carlisle re-recorded it and was rewarded with a chart-topping single.

Bill Medley was in the year-end top 10 for the first time in 21 years. "(You're My) Soul And Inspiration" by the Righteous Brothers had been the No. 5 single of 1966. His singing partner back then had been Bobby Hatfield. Now he was teamed with another Orange County, California native, Jennifer Warnes, who had her first year-end chart single in 1977 when "Right Time Of The Night" was No. 65 for the year. With Joe Cocker, she was ranked No. 19 in 1982 with "Up Where We Belong." Medley and Warnes duetted on "(I've Had) The Time Of My Life" from the soundtrack of *Dirty Dancing.*

68 MANDOLIN RAIN
Bruce Hornsby & the Range *RCA*

69 COME GO WITH ME
Exposé *Arista*

70 RHYTHM IS GONNA GET YOU
Gloria Estefan & Miami Sound Machine *Epic*

71 WANTED DEAD OR ALIVE
Bon Jovi *Mercury*

72 CASANOVA
Levert *Atlantic*

73 WHEN SMOKEY SINGS
ABC *Mercury*

74 POINT OF NO RETURN
Exposé *Arista*

75 THE FINER THINGS
Steve Winwood *Island*

76 ROCK STEADY
The Whispers *Solar*

77 BIG TIME
Peter Gabriel *Geffen*

78 WE'LL BE TOGETHER
Sting *A&M*

79 SOMETHING SO STRONG
Crowded House *Capitol*

80 VICTORY
Kool & the Gang *Mercury*

81 THE ONE I LOVE
R.E.M. *I.R.S.*

82 DIAMONDS
Herb Alpert *A&M*

83 CAN'T WE TRY
Dan Hill w/Vonda Sheppard *Columbia*

84 BRILLIANT DISGUISE
Bruce Springsteen *Columbia*

85 HEAT OF THE NIGHT
Bryan Adams *A&M*

86 MIDNIGHT BLUE
Lou Gramm *Atlantic*

87 LET ME BE THE ONE
Exposé *Arista*

88 JUST TO SEE HER
Smokey Robinson *Motown*

89 DOING IT ALL FOR MY BABY
Huey Lewis & the News *Chrysalis*

90 VALERIE
Steve Winwood *Island*

91 CROSS MY BROKEN HEART
The Jets *MCA*

92 BALLERINA GIRL
Lionel Richie *Motown*

93 NOTHING'S GONNA CHANGE MY LOVE FOR YOU
Glenn Medeiros *Amherst*

94 IT'S A SIN
Pet Shop Boys *EMI America*

95 I'VE BEEN IN LOVE BEFORE
Cutting Crew *Virgin*

96 WIPEOUT
Fat Boys & the Beach Boys *Tin Pan Apple*

97 BIG LOVE
Fleetwood Mac *Warner Bros.*

98 RESPECT YOURSELF
Bruce Willis *Motown*

99 WHO WILL YOU RUN TO
Heart *Capitol*

100 RIGHT ON TRACK
Breakfast Club *MCA*

The Top 100 Songs of 1988

Eric Carmen

1988 WAS THE year Cher won an Oscar the day before Sonny was elected Mayor of Palm Springs; the Beatles were inducted into the Rock and Roll Hall of Fame; and Berry Gordy sold Motown to MCA.

It was a transition year for the label that had excelled with the Supremes, the Temptations, the Jackson Five, Lionel Richie, and many other artists. For the first time since 1961, there were no Motown recordings included in the top 100 songs of the year.

George Michael became the first artist in the rock era to have the No.1 song of the year for two years running. "One More Try" led the list for 1988, just as "Faith" had done in 1987. It was a feat not even accomplished by Elvis Presley or the Beatles. Michael was also No. 9 with "Father Figure."

Steve Winwood first appeared on a year-end chart when he was 18 years old as lead singer for the Spencer Davis Group's "Gimme Some Lovin'," the No. 87 song of 1967. His solo single "Higher Love" was the No.

24 song of 1986. He set a new high mark in 1988 when the Stax-influenced "Roll With It" was in second place for the year. It was his first single for the Virgin label after a long association with Island Records. "I didn't say, 'I want to leave Island,'" Winwood told Pete Clark. "I just thought it was time to look at the options and see what other companies might do for me. I suppose changing record companies is a bit like changing insurance companies—there was no lover's tiff involved, it's just a business arrangement."

The No. 3 single of the year was "Every Rose Has Its Thorn" by Poison. The group relocated from Harrisburg, Pennsylvania to Los Angeles in 1983, changed their name from "Paris" and became a sensation on the club circuit. Still, they couldn't get a record company deal until they were signed to the independent Enigma label.

The No. 4 song of 1988 was a Diane Warren song, "Look Away" by Chicago. In 19 years of recording, it was the group's highest-ranked year-end song and their most successful chart single. It was Warren's first song to appear in a year-end top five.

Whitney Houston was in the year-end top five for the third consecutive year. Her recording of Billy Steinberg and Tom Kelly's "So Emotional" was the No. 5 song of 1988. It was the final track recorded for her second album. Clive Davis wanted one more uptempo number and asked the songwriters to submit material. Their demo sounded more like Prince than Whitney, but Davis loved it and passed it on to producer Narada Michael Walden. It took some time for Steinberg and Kelly to appreciate Whitney's recording. "If you fall in love with your version, and you're used to hearing it the way you conceived it, it's always hard to get used to," Kelly explains.

After ranking No. 16 in 1987 with her first hit, a remake of Tommy James & the Shondells' "I Think We're Alone Now," Tiffany had her first year-end top 10 single in 1988 with "Could've Been," the No. 6 song of the year. Her second chart-topping single, it was originally recorded by producer George Tobin as a demo by songwriter Lois Blaisch. Tobin loved the song and submitted it to Crystal Gayle, Dolly Parton, Natalie Cole, and others, with no luck. Finally, he took Blaisch's vocal off the demo and had Tiffany record over the track.

Guns N' Roses' first chart entry and only chart-topping single, "Sweet Child O' Mine," ended up in seventh place for 1988. The song was inspired by Erin Everly, daughter of Don Everly, who last appeared on a year-end recap in 1960, when the Everly Brothers had the No. 3 song of the year with "Cathy's Clown." Erin was the girlfriend of Guns N' Roses' Axl Rose when he wrote the lyrics. Despite their volatile relationship, the couple was married on April 27, 1990, and on May 24 Rose filed for divorce, citing irreconcilable differences. They tried to get back together, but in January 1991 Rose was granted an annulment.

British singer Rick Astley made his chart debut with "Never Gonna Give You Up," the No. 8 song of the year. He was playing drums in a band called FBI and writing original material. The group played at a private club in Warrington, England, and producer Pete Waterman was invited to hear them. "He liked my vocals but wasn't all that interested in the band because we were still very young," Rick recalls. Astley was invited to work at Waterman's company, PWL, as a tape operator and tea boy. At night he

34 **POUR SOME SUGAR ON ME**
Def Leppard *Mercury*
35 **DEVIL INSIDE**
INXS *Atlantic*
36 **THE WAY YOU MAKE ME FEEL**
Michael Jackson *Epic*
37 **DIRTY DIANA**
Michael Jackson *Epic*
38 **GIVING YOU THE BEST THAT I GOT**
Anita Baker *Elektra*
39 **ENDLESS SUMMER NIGHTS**
Richard Marx *EMI Manhattan*
40 **HOW CAN I FALL?**
Breathe *A&M*
41 **SHE'S LIKE THE WIND**
Patrick Swayze f/Wendy Fraser *RCA*
42 **HAZY SHADE OF WINTER**
Bangles *Columbia*
43 **WHAT HAVE I DONE TO DESERVE THIS?**
Pet Shop Boys w/Dusty Springfield
EMI Manhattan
44 **I DON'T WANNA GO ON**
WITH YOU LIKE THAT
Elton John *MCA*
45 **MERCEDES BOY**
Pebbles *MCA*
46 **THE LOCO-MOTION**
Kylie Minogue *Geffen*
47 **I'LL ALWAYS LOVE YOU**
Taylor Dayne *Arista*
48 **ANGEL**
Aerosmith *Geffen*
49 **I GET WEAK**
Belinda Carlisle *MCA*
50 **NAUGHTY GIRLS (NEED LOVE TOO)**
Samantha Fox *Jive*
51 **OUT OF THE BLUE**
Debbie Gibson *Atlantic*
52 **MAKE ME LOSE CONTROL**
Eric Carmen *Arista*
53 **PERFECT WORLD**
Huey Lewis & the News *Chrysalis*
54 **NEW SENSATION**
INXS *Atlantic*
55 **HUNGRY EYES**
Eric Carmen *RCA*
56 **DESIRE**
U2 *Island*
57 **MAKE IT REAL**
The Jets *MCA*
58 **EVERYTHING YOUR HEART DESIRES**
Daryl Hall and John Oates *Arista*
59 **WHAT'S ON YOUR MIND (PURE ENERGY)**
Information Society *Tommy Boy*
60 **I DON'T WANT YOUR LOVE**
Duran Duran *Capitol*
61 **WAITING FOR A STAR TO FALL**
Boy Meets Girl *RCA*
62 **I WANT TO BE YOUR MAN**
Roger *Reprise*
63 **I DON'T WANNA LIVE**
WITHOUT YOUR LOVE
Chicago *Reprise*
64 **1-2-3**
Gloria Estefan & Miami Sound Machine *Epic*
65 **DON'T BE CRUEL**
Cheap Trick *Epic*
66 **TELL IT TO MY HEART**
Taylor Dayne *Arista*

recorded his own demos. He was signed to RCA under the aegis of producers Mike Stock, Matt Aitken, and Waterman, the trio that wrote "Never Gonna Give You Up."

Gloria Estefan & Miami Sound Machine made the year-end top 10 for the first time in 1988, with "Anything For You" ranked No. 10. In 1986, the band was No. 55 with "Conga," No. 73 with "Words Get In The Way," and No. 84 with "Bad Boy." A year later, "Rhythm Is Gonna Get You" ranked No. 70. "Anything For You" was the final song recorded for the album *Let It Loose.* After recording the song with piano and vocals, the group decided it needed a new arrangement. Returning to Miami after a tour, Estefan and company went back into the studio to complete the track.

INXS was only the third Australian group in the rock era to have a No. 1 song on the Hot 100. Air Supply was the first in 1981 and Men at Work reached the summit in 1982 and 1983. INXS lead singer Michael Hutchence was born in Hong Kong of Australian parents. The family moved back home to Sydney when he was 12. After his parents divorced, Hutchence lived with his mother for a year in North Hollywood, California. Then he returned to Sydney and found his childhood friend Andrew Farriss in a band with Garry Beers. Andrew's younger brother Jon and older brother Tim joined the group, as did Kirk Pengilly. With Hutchence handling the vocals, they lived in Perth for 10 months. A roadie suggested they call themselves "In Excess" and they did, but they spelled it "INXS." After experiencing chart success in Australia, they made the American chart with a single titled "The One Thing" in 1983. Their first major success in the U.S. came with "What You Need," the No. 59 song of 1986. While recording their sixth album, they took a short break in Hong Kong where Andrew came up with a riff and Michael added some lyrics. They found a local studio and scheduled time to record "Need You Tonight," which ended up as the No. 13 song of 1988.

George Harrison had the No. 16 song of 1988 with a remake of an obscure song he had first heard in 1963 when he bought an album by James Ray. The LP contained a song the Beatles had been performing live, "If You Gotta Make A Fool Of Somebody." "The album itself was really terrible," George told Timothy White, "but the best three songs were written by this guy who discovered James Ray, a former mailman named Rudy Clark." One of the songs was "Got My Mind Set On You Part One/Part Two," although there was no break between the two parts. Harrison updated the song and changed the chords.

The No. 19 song of 1988 was a medley of Peter Frampton's "Baby, I Love Your Way" and Lynyrd Skynyrd's "Free Bird" put together by Miami disc jockey Bob Rosenberg. With vocalist Suzi Carr and saxophonist Dr. J, he formed a trio called Will to Power, a name inspired by the work of the 19th century German philosopher Friedrich Nietzsche. Rosenberg, a native of Philadelphia, is a second generation Hot 100 artist: his mother, Gloria Mann, charted in 1955 with cover versions of "Earth Angel" and "Teen Age Prayer."

The Top 100 Songs of 1989

Richard Marx

1989 WAS THE year Prince and Danny Elfman both composed soundtracks for *Batman;* the New Kids on the Block were the latest teen idols; and former teen idol Donny Osmond made a surprising comeback.

Osmond had the No. 47 song of the year with "Soldier Of Love," his first year-end chart appearance since "The Twelfth Of Never" was the No. 93 song of 1973. Also making a comeback in 1989 was Donna Summer, ranked No. 88 for the year with a Stock-Aitken-Waterman song, "This Time I Know It's For Real." It was Summer's first year-end chart appearance since 1983, when "She Works Hard For The Money" was No. 27 for the year.

Phil Collins became only the third British male solo artist of the rock era to have a No. 1 song of the year, following Rod Stewart and George Michael. "Another Day In Paradise" was the first single from his . . . *But Seriously* album. A song about homelessness, it inspired critics to question his sincerity. "The way they see it, I'm suddenly coming along and saying I've got a conscience," he complained to Gary Graft. "They don't believe me; they assume I'm doing it for the wrong reason. When I'm driving and I pass 60 or 100 homeless people on the street, I'm not immune to that. I have to write about them the same as Elvis Costello would want to write about them. But because of his track record, no one questions him. But I'm supposed to just go and record another 'Sussudio' or 'Groovy Kind Of Love.'"

After Janet Jackson's multi-platinum success with *Control,* A&M Records suggested a theme for her follow-up album. It would be called *Scandal* and would be a concept album about her family. Janet wrote one song, "You Need Me," about a distant, neglectful father, but turned down the idea of an entire album about the Jackson family. "You Need Me" was released as the "B" side of "Miss You Much," the first single from *Rhythm Nation 1814.* Janet got the idea for the album when she read about the various communities (or "nations") formed in New York City by young people, mostly blacks, seeking a common identity. "I thought it would be great if we could create our own nation...one that would have a positive message and that everyone would be free to join," she told Robert Hilburn in the *Los Angeles Times.* "Miss You Much," No. 2 for 1989, topped the Hot 100 for four weeks and was Janet's biggest chart single until "That's The Way Love Goes."

Paula Abdul was a cheerleader for the Los Angeles Lakers. Then she became a choreographer for Janet Jackson's videos and Tracey Ullman's television series. In 1989 she moved into a more public spotlight. Her third single for Virgin, "Straight Up," was the No. 3 record of the year. Abdul was also No. 12 with "Cold Hearted," No. 21 with "Forever Your Girl," and No. 61 with "(It's Just) The Way That You Love Me."

Debbie Gibson achieved her highest ranking on a year-end chart in 1989 with "Lost In Your Eyes," the No. 4 single of the year. Interested in music from the age of two, Gibson became serious about it at age 12. A year later she wrote "Only In My Dreams," a song that would become her debut single for Atlantic Records three years later. By the time she cut her first album, she had written over 200 songs. "Lost In Your Eyes" was written a year-and-a-half before it was released; it was the lead-off single from her second album, *Electric Youth,* and spent three weeks atop the Hot 100.

Madonna had her third top five hit of a year with "Like A Prayer," the No. 5 song of 1989. She had the No. 2 song of 1984, "Like A Virgin," and the No. 4 song of 1985, "Crazy For You." Written by Madonna with Patrick Leonard, "Like A Prayer" was the first song written for the album that eventually was named after the song. When Pepsi-Cola paid Madonna $5 million to sponsor her tour and feature her in TV commercials, the first spot featured "Like A Prayer." After one airing, fundamentalist groups threatened to boycott the soft drink because they considered the video for the song "blasphemous." The company didn't want to risk confusion between their commercial and the religious imagery of the video.

Richard Marx made the year-end top 10 for the first time, as "Right Here Waiting" placed seventh for 1989. Two years earlier, he was No. 41 with "Should've Known Better" and No. 51 with "Don't Mean Nothing." In 1988, he was No. 27 with "Hold On To The Nights" and No. 39 with "Endless Summer Nights." Marx resisted including "Right Here Waiting" on his *Repeat Offender* album because he considered it too personal. His wife, actress Cynthia Rhodes, was away for three months making a film in Africa, and Marx was on the road touring. Finding the separation difficult, Marx poured his feelings into a song and wrote "Right Here Waiting" in 10 minutes. He sent a demo to his wife but other people heard it and thought it should be released. Marx felt like it was a love letter to his wife that should remain between them, but realized as a songwriter it was his job to communicate and agreed to include the song on his album.

Billy Joel had his first year-end top 10 single in 1989 with "We Didn't Start The Fire," the No. 6 record of the year. His previous highest charted year-end single was "It's Still Rock And Roll To Me," No. 14 for 1980. "We Didn't Start The Fire" compressed 40 years of history into a song that rhymed "Communist bloc" with "Rock Around The Clock" and "Lawrence Of Arabia" with "Beatlemania." Billy Joel talked about the song with Edna Gundersen of *USA Today:* "I'm saying in the chorus that the world's always been a mess, the world's a mess now, it's going to be a mess when we're gone. But we *tried* to fight it. You can't drop out and fall into despair. It's easy to be a cynic."

The name Milli Vanilli will forever be accompanied by an asterisk, as pop historians explain about the two guys who really *weren't* Milli Vanilli. When Diane Warren's song "Blame It On The Rain" (No. 8 for 1989) was on the Hot 100, everyone thought Rob Pilatus of Germany and Fabrice Morvan of France were the exciting dance duo known as Milli Vanilli. It was only when they insisted to producer Frank Farian that they *really* sing the vocals on their second album that Farian blew the whistle. He called a press conference to announce the rumors were true: Rob and Fab weren't the real thing. Charles Shaw, John Davis, and Brad Howe provided the vocals on the album while the dreadlocked duo were the public faces of the group. Rob and Fab returned their Grammy at the request of the National Academy of Recording Arts and Sciences.

Former New Edition member Bobby Brown had five singles included in the top 100 of 1989. "My Prerogative," No. 9 for the year, was his biggest hit, followed by "On Our Own" (No. 27), "Every Little Step" (No. 45), "Roni" (No. 58), and "Rock Wit'cha" (No. 94). Brown, only 14 when the Boston-based New Edition had their first chart single, left the group in 1985 to pursue more mature music. Brown wrote "My Prerogative" with Gene Griffin and says the lyrics are about breaking away from his former managers and New Edition, and a response to false rumors about drug use.

Bette Midler made a dramatic return to the Hot 100 in 1989 with a song from the soundtrack of her film *Beaches.* "Wind Beneath My Wings," a No. 4 song on the country chart by Gary Morris in 1983, was Bette's first No. 1 hit after 17 years of recording. "I made that record against my better judgment, because two people—my hairdresser and my costumer—advised me to do it," she told Tom Green in *USA Today.* The No. 19 single of 1989, it revitalized Bette's recording career and won Grammys for Record of the Year and Song of the Year.

69 **SECRET RENDEZVOUS**
Karyn White *Warner Bros.*
70 **THE WAY YOU LOVE ME**
Karyn White *Warner Bros.*
71 **LAY YOUR HANDS ON ME**
Bon Jovi *Mercury*
72 **ALL THIS TIME**
Tiffany *MCA*
73 **LIVING IN SIN**
Bon Jovi *Mercury*
74 **CLOSE MY EYES (FOREVER)**
Lita Ford w/Ozzy Osbourne *RCA*
75 **PATIENCE**
Guns N' Roses *Geffen*
76 **DON'T CLOSE YOUR EYES**
Kix *Atlantic*
77 **IN YOUR ROOM**
Bangles *Columbia*
78 **SHOWER ME WITH YOUR LOVE**
Surface *Columbia*
79 **JUST LIKE JESSE JAMES**
Cher *Geffen*
80 **ANGEL EYES**
Jeff Healey Band *Arista*
81 **LOVE IN AN ELEVATOR**
Aerosmith *Geffen*
82 **STAND**
R.E.M. *Warner Bros.*
83 **PARADISE CITY**
Guns N' Roses *Geffen*
84 **AFTER ALL**
Cher & Peter Cetera *Geffen*
85 **WHAT I AM**
Edie Brickell & New Bohemians *Geffen*
86 **HEAVEN HELP ME**
Deon Estus *Mika*
87 **SHE WANTS TO DANCE WITH ME**
Rick Astley *RCA*
88 **THIS TIME I KNOW IT'S FOR REAL**
Donna Summer *Atlantic*
89 **WHAT YOU DON'T KNOW**
Exposé *Arista*
90 **IT'S NO CRIME**
Babyface *Solar*
91 **SURRENDER TO ME**
Ann Wilson & Robin Zander *Capitol*
92 **I REMEMBER HOLDING YOU**
Boys Club *MCA*
93 **THE END OF THE INNOCENCE**
Don Henley *Geffen*
94 **ROCK WIT'CHA**
Bobby Brown *MCA*
95 **KEEP ON MOVIN'**
Soul II Soul *Virgin*
96 **THINKING OF YOU**
Sa-Fire *Cutting*
97 **CRAZY ABOUT HER**
Rod Stewart *Warner Bros.*
98 **SMOOTH CRIMINAL**
Michael Jackson *Epic*
99 **DREAMIN'**
Vanessa Williams *Wing*
100 **I DROVE ALL NIGHT**
Cyndi Lauper *Epic*

The Top 100 Songs of 1990

New Kids on the Block

1990 WAS THE year the world found out Milli Vanilli didn't sing, but the Simpsons and the Teenage Mutant Ninja Turtles did; MTV banned Madonna's "Justify My Love"; and obscenity charges were filed against 2 Live Crew and record-store owners who sold their album.

There were eight singles with lead vocals by women in the year-end top 10, a new record for the rock era. The previous high was in 1979, when there were six. Mariah Carey had two titles in the top 10: "Love Takes Time" at No. 3 and "Vision Of Love" at No. 4. Mariah became only the third female soloist in the rock era to have two year-end top 10 hits, after Donna Summer and Whitney Houston. Mariah was the first to accomplish this feat in her debut year.

Carey was raised by her mother, a jazz and classical vocalist who sang with the New York City Opera. At age 18, Mariah was singing backing vocals for Brenda K. Starr ("I Still Believe"). After winding up a four-month tour, Brenda talked Mariah into attending a CBS party with her. Mariah had one of her demo tapes and Brenda tried to hand it to a CBS label executive, who refused to take it. But CBS Records Group president Tommy Mottola observed the transaction and took the tape. On his way home from the party, Mottola listened to the cassette in his limo and liked what he heard so much that he returned to track down the vocalist. Mariah had already left, but he got her phone number and left a message for her.

Carey had been writing songs since high school with her friend Ben Margulies. They wrote Mariah's debut single for Columbia, "Vision Of Love."

After it was recorded, Mottola and Columbia Records president Don Ienner asked Narada Michael Walden to polish the production. Walden's name was absent from the album credits but was later added, sharing producer credit with Rhett Lawrence on the track.

Hoping to defeat the sophomore jinx, Carey and Margulies wrote "Love Takes Time" and planned to save it for Mariah's second album. But after she played it for a Columbia Records executive during an airplane trip, label management insisted that "Love Takes Time" be added to her debut album. The decision was made so late that the song title didn't appear on the packaging for the CD and cassette during the initial press run.

Irish-born Sinead O'Connor made her Hot 100 debut with "Nothing Compares 2 U," the No. 2 record of 1990. The song was written by Prince and originally recorded in 1985 on his Paisley Park label by the Family, a Minneapolis quintet. Although O'Connor was managed by former Prince manager Steve Fargnoli when she recorded the tune, she learned about it from her former manager, Fatchna O'Ceallaigh.

Madonna earned her fifth year-end top 10 hit with "Vogue," a song she intended for release as a "B" side. But Sire Records thought better of the tune and released it as an "A" side. It spent three weeks in pole position on the Hot 100, despite the fact that "vogueing" was an underground club phenomenon already passé when Madonna recorded the song.

"Escapade," the No. 6 single of 1990, was the song Janet Jackson recorded instead of remaking Martha & the Vandellas' "Nowhere To Run," a Motown classic she would hear at Los Angeles Lakers games. Producer Jimmy Jam suggested recording a new song instead, with the feel of the Martha Reeves hit.

Songwriter Oliver Leiber was waiting for his Camaro to be fixed in a suburb of St. Paul, Minnesota, when he wandered into a mini-mall and rummaged through a used bookstore. One of the titles captured his attention, and he turned *Opposites Attract* into the No. 7 song of the year for Paula Abdul and the Wild Pair.

The Swedish duo of Marie Fredriksson and Per Gessle had the No. 8 single of the year, "It Must Have Been Love," from the soundtrack of the Richard Gere/Julia Roberts film, *Pretty Woman.* The song had been a hit in Sweden before the film was produced; the lyrics were rewritten for the movie. Marie was a folk singer and Per was in a band called Gyllene Tider before they formed Roxette in 1986. Their first American chart single, "The Look," was the No. 15 song of 1989. They were also No. 23 for that year with "Listen To Your Heart." "It Must Have Been Love" was one of two songs from the *Pretty Woman* soundtrack on the year-end chart; the other was "King Of Wishful Thinking" by Go West at No. 79.

Wilson Phillips followed their respective parents by placing No. 10 for the year with "Hold On," their debut single. Carnie and Wendy Wilson's father, Brian Wilson, had the number No. 9 song of the year twice. He did it with the Beach Boys in 1964 ("I Get Around") and 1966 ("Good Vibrations"). Chynna Phillips' parents, John and Michelle, never made the year-end top 10 with the Mamas and the Papas; their highest-ranked year-end single was "Monday, Monday," No. 13 for 1966. The three offspring had been friends since they were small children and staged shows for their

34 **(CAN'T LIVE WITHOUT YOUR) LOVE AND AFFECTION**
Nelson *DGC*

35 **RUB YOU THE RIGHT WAY**
Johnny Gill *Motown*

36 **I'LL BE YOUR EVERYTHING**
Tommy Page *Sire*

37 **PRAYING FOR TIME**
George Michael *Columbia*

38 **HOLD ON**
En Vogue *Atlantic*

39 **THE POWER**
Snap *Arista*

40 **RHYTHM NATION**
Janet Jackson *A&M*

41 **DOWNTOWN TRAIN**
Rod Stewart *Warner Bros.*

42 **COME BACK TO ME**
Janet Jackson *A&M*

43 **MORE THAN WORDS CAN SAY**
Alias *EMI*

44 **ROAM**
The B-52's *Reprise*

45 **UNSKINNY BOP**
Poison *Enigma*

46 **PRAY**
M.C. Hammer *Capitol*

47 **GROOVE IS IN THE HEART**
Deee-Lite *Elektra*

48 **EVERYTHING**
Jody Watley *MCA*

49 **IMPULSIVE**
Wilson Phillips *SBK*

50 **SOMETHING TO BELIEVE IN**
Poison *Enigma*

51 **SENDING ALL MY LOVE**
Linear *Atlantic*

52 **GIVING YOU THE BENEFIT**
Pebbles *MCA*

53 **ALRIGHT**
Janet Jackson *A&M*

54 **THE WAY YOU DO THE THINGS YOU DO**
UB40 *Virgin*

55 **I WISH IT WOULD RAIN DOWN**
Phil Collins *Atlantic*

56 **FEELS GOOD**
Tony! Toni! Toné! *Wing*

57 **HOW CAN WE BE LOVERS**
Michael Bolton *Columbia*

58 **HERE AND NOW**
Luther Vandross *Epic*

59 **THE HUMPTY DANCE**
Digital Underground *Tommy Boy*

60 **HAVE YOU SEEN HER**
M.C. Hammer *Capitol*

61 **JANIE'S GOT A GUN**
Aerosmith *Geffen*

62 **U CAN'T TOUCH THIS**
M.C. Hammer *Capitol*

63 **CAN'T STOP**
After 7 *Virgin*

64 **TOM'S DINER**
DNA f/Suzanne Vega *A&M*

65 **LOVE SONG**
Tesla *Geffen*

66 **DO YOU REMEMBER?**
Phil Collins *Atlantic*

67 **I'LL BE YOUR SHELTER**
Taylor Dayne *Arista*

families and friends. But the concept of Wilson Phillips wasn't set into motion until Chynna and Owen Vanessa Elliot, daughter of the late Mama Cass, came up with the idea of recording an anti-drug song. Chynna invited Carnie and Wendy to participate, and although the project fizzled, the four women met with Richard Perry to discuss recording some demos. Elliot was dropped from the group, and Perry's management deal was cut off. The trio then signed with the new SBK label.

The lone male soloist in the top 10 was Stevie B with the No. 1 record of the year, "Because I Love You (The Postman Song)." Born Steven Bernard Hill in Miami, he opened a nightclub in Tallahassee while he was in college. He released "Sending Out For Love" on his own Midtown label in 1980 and had a duo called Friday Friday in 1985. After teaching himself the art of studio engineering, Stevie built his own studio. He concentrated on producing local artists, and in 1987, he decided to record himself once more. He had a local Miami hit that year with "Party Your Body," and was signed by Herb Moelis to his New York–based LMR Records. "Dreamin' Of Love" was Stevie B's first Hot 100 entry, peaking at No. 80 in 1988. "Because I Love You," written in 1986 by Warren Allen Brooks (the other half of Friday Friday), became Stevie's first top 10 single in 1990, spending four weeks at the top of the Hot 100.

The members of the Boston-based boy band New Kids on the Block found themselves in the year-end top 10 for the first time when "Step By Step" became the No. 9 song of 1990. The previous year they placed four titles in the annual recap: "I'll Be Loving You (Forever)" at No. 18, "Hangin' Tough" at No. 34, "Cover Girl" at No. 52, and "You Got It (The Right Stuff)" at No. 57. The group's mentor, Maurice Starr, wrote "Step By Step," but not for the New Kids. The song was composed four years earlier for another Boston group Starr was managing at the time, a Motown act called the Superiors. The label thought the song was a dud, radio apparently agreed, and the single never charted. Under pressure to come up with a new song for the Superiors to record, Starr had written "Step By Step" in 10 minutes. The New Kids were so popular by the time they released their version, the single was the highest-debuting song on the Hot 100 in over five years.

68 SOMETHING HAPPENED ON THE WAY TO HEAVEN
Phil Collins *Atlantic*

69 READY OR NOT
After 7 *Virgin*

70 JUST BETWEEN YOU AND ME
Lou Gramm *Atlantic*

71 GIRLS NITE OUT
Tyler Collins *RCA*

72 GET UP! (BEFORE THE NIGHT IS OVER)
Technotronic *SBK*

73 ALL OR NOTHING
Milli Vanilli *Arista*

74 PRICE OF LOVE
Bad English *Epic*

75 FREE FALLIN'
Tom Petty *MCA*

76 NO MORE LIES
Michel'le *Ruthless*

77 FREEDOM
George Michael *Columbia*

78 ENJOY THE SILENCE
Depeche Mode *Sire*

79 KING OF WISHFUL THINKING
Go West *EMI*

80 EVERYBODY EVERYBODY
Black Box *RCA*

81 EPIC
Faith No More *Slash*

82 I REMEMBER YOU
Skid Row *Atlantic*

83 C'MON AND GET MY LOVE
D-Mob i/Cathy Dennis *FFRR*

84 MAKE YOU SWEAT
Keith Sweat *Vintertainment*

85 I GO TO EXTREMES
Billy Joel *Columbia*

86 WHAT KIND OF MAN WOULD I BE?
Chicago *Reprise*

87 ROMEO
Dino *Island*

88 JERK OUT
The Time *Reprise*

89 HERE WE ARE
Gloria Estefan *Epic*

90 FOREVER
Kiss *Mercury*

91 KNOCKIN' BOOTS
Candyman *Epic*

92 SWING THE MOOD
Jive Bunny & the Mastermixers *Music Factory*

93 MIRACLE
Jon Bon Jovi *Mercury*

94 JUST A FRIEND
Biz Markie *Cold Chillin'*

95 UNCHAINED MELODY
Righteous Brothers *Verve Forecast*

96 NO MYTH
Michael Penn *RCA*

97 STRANDED
Heart *Capitol*

98 WHAT IT TAKES
Aerosmith *Geffen*

99 THIS ONE'S FOR THE CHILDREN
New Kids on the Block *Columbia*

100 THIEVES IN THE TEMPLE
Prince *Paisley Park*

The Top 100 Songs of 1991

Karyn White

1991 WAS THE year that Freddie Mercury of the group Queen announced he had AIDS and then died the very next day; Whitney Houston's "The Star Spangled Banner" was one of several singles that received a chart boost because of the Gulf War; and the methodology used to compute the Hot 100 was changed to include actual sales figures from SoundScan and actual monitored airplay from Broadcast Data Systems.

Bryan Adams became the first Canadian to have a No. 1 single of the year since Percy Faith ruled 1960 with "Theme From *A Summer Place.*" The ballad "(Everything I Do) I Do It For You" was the sixth soundtrack single in the rock era to be the No. 1 song of the year, following "To Sir With Love," "The Way We Were," "Call Me," "Eye Of The Tiger," and "When Doves Cry."

Adams was not first in line to sing the theme from *Robin Hood: Prince Of Thieves.* Kate Bush, Annie Lennox, Lisa Stansfield, and the duo of Peter Cetera and Julia Fordham had all been considered first. Composer Michael Kamen was delighted with the ultimate choice. "He's a genuine rock and roller, so there's no question of it being a soppy ballad. And I love his singing," says Kamen, who disagreed with the vocalist only over the inclusion of a piano in the introduction. "I had kept so-called modern-sounding instruments off the score," Kamen explains. Adams acknowledged that he had trouble convincing Kamen and the film company that his arrangement was going to work. He must have been doing something right, because the single topped the Hot 100 for seven weeks, the longest reign at the top since "Every Breath You Take" by the Police was No. 1 for eight weeks. Coincidentally, those two singles are the only A&M releases to be year-end chart-toppers. Adams appeared twice in the 1991 chart. The follow-up to the year's top-rated single, "Can't Stop This Thing We Started," ranked No. 31 for the year.

Michael Jackson was back in the year-end top 10 for the first time since he was a triple-threat man in 1983. "Black Or White," the initial single from *Dangerous,* was the No. 2 record of 1991. "Billie Jean" and "Beat It," the second and third singles from *Thriller,* were in the year-end top 10 of 1983. The highest posting of a single from *Bad* was the No. 11 ranking of "Man In The Mirror" in 1988.

Paula Abdul had a hot streak in 1989, placing four singles in the annual top 100, including the No. 3 ranking of her first hit, "Straight Up." She tied that mark in 1991, as "Rush Rush" was listed as No. 3 for the year. The follow-up, "The Promise Of A New Day," was No. 36, and the single after that, "Blowing Kisses In The Wind," was No. 56 for the year. While 1991 was the year that Abdul received a star on the Hollywood Walk of Fame, it was also the year that she was a defendant in a class action suit brought against her record label and its distributor by Yvette Marine, who claimed that her lead guide vocals appeared on two tracks on Abdul's first album. It would be another two years before a judge would find in Abdul's favor.

The No. 4 song of 1991 was originally from a motion picture soundtrack, in its original version. "It's So Hard To Say Goodbye To Yesterday" first appeared in the 1975 film *Cooley High* starring Glynn Turman and Lawrence Hilton-Jacobs. G.C. Cameron, formerly of the Spinners, performed the song on the double-disc soundtrack, issued on Motown. The label's hottest act of the '90s, the Philly-based Boyz II Men, remade the song on their debut album, *Cooleyhighharmony.* Its pop success gave Motown its first year-end top 10 single since Lionel Richie's "Say You, Say Me" was the No. 1 song of 1985. Boyz II Men's first single, "Motownphilly," ranked No. 30 for 1991.

Fresno, California, native Timmy Torres, a magician and a puppeteer, had his own local cable TV series by the time he was 14. Three years later, he wrote some music for neighborhood rappers, who called him Timmy Tee. Then he recorded his own song and asked a Fresno station to play it. "Time After Time" was so good, the station added it and turned it into a regional hit. Record labels called the Fresno station to find out how they could sign Torres, who made a deal with Canadian-based Quality Records. For only $200 he produced "One More Try," which gave the newly-christened Timmy T a chart-topping single and the No. 5 hit of 1991.

Legal controversy surrounded the artists with the No. 6 single of the year. Former Weather Girl Martha Wash belted out the refrain "Everybody dance now!" on C + C Music Factory's "Gonna Make You Sweat," but her name didn't appear in the credits and her face and body didn't appear in the video. The C + C in the Music Factory were Robert Clivillés and David Cole. They had met in 1985 in the sound booth of the Times Square underground club Better Days. Clivillés was subbing as the DJ and Cole was a New Jersey teenager who rode the bus to his favorite hangout. After Cole

33 **HIGH ENOUGH**
Damn Yankees *Warner Bros.*

34 **EVERY HEARTBEAT**
Amy Grant *A&M*

35 **IT AIN'T OVER 'TIL IT'S OVER**
Lenny Kravitz *Virgin*

36 **THE PROMISE OF A NEW DAY**
Paula Abdul *Captive*

37 **P.A.S.S.I.O.N.**
Rythm Syndicate *Impact*

38 **TOUCH ME (ALL NIGHT LONG)**
Cathy Dennis *Polydor*

39 **HOLD YOU TIGHT**
Tara Kemp *Giant*

40 **HERE WE GO**
C + C Music Factory Presents Freedom
Williams & Zelma Davis *Columbia*

41 **SENSITIVITY**
Ralph Tresvant *MCA*

42 **FADING LIKE A FLOWER
(EVERY TIME YOU LEAVE)**
Roxette *EMI*

43 **O.P.P.**
Naughty by Nature *Tommy Boy*

44 **SUMMERTIME**
D.J. Jazzy Jeff and the Fresh Prince *Jive*

45 **THIS HOUSE**
Tracie Spencer *Capitol*

46 **THAT'S WHAT LOVE IS FOR**
Amy Grant *A&M*

47 **DON'T CRY**
Guns N' Roses *Geffen*

48 **WHERE DOES MY HEART BEAT NOW**
Celine Dion *Epic*

49 **WIND OF CHANGE**
Scorpions *Mercury*

50 **THINGS THAT MAKE YOU GO HMMMM...**
C + C Music Factory f/Freedom Williams
Columbia

51 **LOSING MY RELIGION**
R.E.M. *Warner Bros.*

52 **LOVE IS A WONDERFUL THING**
Michael Bolton *Columbia*

53 **POWER OF LOVE/LOVE POWER**
Luther Vandross *Epic*

54 **HOLE HEARTED**
Extreme *A&M*

55 **IESHA**
Another Bad Creation *Motown*

56 **BLOWING KISSES IN THE WIND**
Paula Abdul *Captive*

57 **LOVE OF A LIFETIME**
Firehouse *Epic*

58 **I TOUCH MYSELF**
Divinyls *Virgin*

59 **NOW THAT WE FOUND LOVE**
Heavy D. & the Boyz *Uptown*

60 **RHYTHM OF MY HEART**
Rod Stewart *Warner Bros.*

61 **AFTER THE RAIN**
Nelson *DGC*

62 **WILDSIDE**
Marky Mark & the Funky Bunch *Interscope*

63 **PLAY THAT FUNKY MUSIC**
Vanilla Ice *SBK*

64 **LET'S TALK ABOUT SEX**
Salt-N-Pepa *Next Plateau*

65 **SHOW ME THE WAY**
Styx *A&M*

was hired to play keyboards at the club, they decided to work together. They earned a reputation in the industry by remixing hits like Janet Jackson's "The Pleasure Principle," Fleetwood Mac's "Big Love," and Natalie Cole's "Pink Cadillac." Larry Yasgar signed them to produce the girl group Seduction for his A&M-distributed Vendetta Records, and when Yasgar moved to Columbia, he signed Clivillés and Cole as producers. The idea behind C + C Music Factory was that vocalists would come and go, while the two Cs would be the only permanent fixtures. The Music Factory, along with Freedom Williams and Zelma Davis, was No. 40 for the year with "Here We Go." Williams was also included in C + C's No. 50 single of the year, "Things That Make You Go Hmmmm. . ."

Cole and Clivillés became such a hot production team that CBS Records Group president Tommy Mottola suggested they collaborate with Mariah Carey. C + C were asked to produce four songs for Carey's second album. The title track, "Emotions," was the first single, and when it topped the Hot 100, Carey made chart history. She became the first artist to have her first five singles all make No. 1. "Emotions" was the No. 8 song of 1991.

"Justify My Love" was one of two new tracks included on a package of Madonna's hit singles, *The Immaculate Collection.* The video proved too steamy for MTV, which caused Madonna's record label to release the first commercially-available video single. During the course of interviewing Madonna, ABC-TV's *Nightline* aired the video in full. The controversy helped boost the single to the top of the chart, and it ended up as the No. 9 single of the year.

Many people assumed Amy Grant's No. 10 hit of the year, "Baby Baby," was addressed to a lover, but the artist wrote the song for her daughter Millie, just six weeks old at the time. "When Millie's 50 years old, if she happens to drag out one of her fossil mother's albums," Grant says, "it would be nice for her to know that the song was about her."

The Top 100 Songs of 1992

Jon Secada

1992 WAS THE year that digital compact cassettes and the mini-disc were introduced to the public; the New Kids on the Block were accused of lip-synching at their live performances and defended themselves on *The Arsenio Hall Show;* and the British-owned Thorn-EMI acquired the Virgin Music Group for $957 million.

For the first time in the rock era, the top two singles of the year were both from soundtracks. They were also the longest-running No. 1 singles of the rock era, beating the previous record set in 1956 by Elvis Presley, when the two-sided "Don't Be Cruel" and "Hound Dog" reigned for 11 weeks. "End Of The Road" by Boyz II Men briefly held the record when it stayed on top of the Hot 100 for 13 weeks, but it wasn't long before "I Will Always Love You" by Whitney Houston demonstrated unprecedented stamina by remaining in pole position for 14 weeks.

"End Of The Road" gave Boyz II Men (and the Motown label) a top five song on the annual list for the second year in a row. Babyface, who wrote the song with L.A. Reid and Darryl Simmons, recorded the vocals for the demo and started to think about recording the song himself. "But then I thought Boyz II Men would probably take it further. When they heard the song, they loved it. That was probably one of the better feelings I've had in terms of handing a song over to somebody and watching them work it." The song was written specifically for a scene in Eddie Murphy's *Boomerang*, although it wasn't used for the scene Babyface originally intended.

"End Of The Road" isn't the only *Boomerang* track in the year-end top 20. The brothers Cordes, better known as P.M. Dawn, had their second consecutive year-end top 20 hit with "I'd Die Without You," which was also included in the soundtrack.

"Baby Got Back," an ode to large female behinds, became the first rap single to end up as one of the top four titles on a year-end survey. Anthony Ray, dubbed Sir Mix-A-Lot from his disc jockey days, discounted charges of sexism and racism, explaining that the song was meant as a humorous look at standards for beauty established by the worlds of fashion and advertising.

"Baby Got Back" wasn't the only rump-shaking song on the annual list; Wreckx-N-Effect had the No. 11 single of 1992 with "Rump Shaker." And Sir Mix-A-Lot wasn't the only rapper in the top 10. Two rappers from Atlanta joined him. They were kiddie rappers: 13-year-old Chris Smith and 12-year-old Chris Kelly, known as Kris Kross. Smith and Kelly had been buddies for a long time when producer Jermaine Dupri—only 19 himself—spotted them shopping for sneakers in a mall. Dupri noticed their look-alike baggy clothing and asked if they were a group. Over the next two years, he helped develop their image of wearing their oversized clothes backwards and taught them his brand of rapping, minus any hardcore language that would sound odd coming from two youngsters just barely out of puberty. Signed to Columbia's Ruffhouse label, Kris Kross hit paydirt first time out with "Jump," a single that literally jumped up the Hot 100, from 61 to 12 to 3 to No. 1.

The trio known as TLC also made a fashion statement, pinning condoms to their brightly colored clothes. Compared to Kris Kross, they were practically senior citizens: Chilli (Rozonda Thomas) and Tionne "T-Boz" Watkins were 21 and Lisa "Left Eye" Lopes was 20 when they hit the Hot 100 with their first new jill swing single, "Ain't 2 Proud 2 Beg" (the No. 42 song of the year). They gained entry to LaFace when they met Pebbles, the artist married to L.A. Reid. Their second single, "Baby-Baby-Baby," ranked No. 7 for 1992.

Darnell Van Rensalier, Carl "Groove" Martin, Garfield Bright, and Marc Gay were all students at Howard University pursuing different majors when they formed the vocal quartet known as Shai. They worked together for a short time and then took off to New York to audition for various record companies. They were turned down by every one. With $100 left in their budget, they recorded an *a capella* demo of "If I Ever Fall In Love" and sent it to WPGC in Washington, D.C. After winning a "make it or break it" contest on air, the song, still in demo form, was added to the station's regular rotation. The Gasoline Alley label, distributed by MCA, picked up the single for national release, and Shai ended up with the No. 5 song of the year.

Vanessa Williams first showed up on a year-end list in 1989, when she had the No. 99 single of the year with "Dreamin'." Three years later, she ended up on the other side of the list, as "Save The Best For Last" was in

34 **WHAT ABOUT YOUR FRIENDS**
TLC *LaFace*

35 **LIFE IS A HIGHWAY**
Tom Cochrane *Capitol*

36 **LIVE AND LEARN**
Joe Public *Columbia*

37 **FINALLY**
Ce Ce Peniston *A&M*

38 **IF YOU ASKED ME TO**
Celine Dion *Epic*

39 **THE BEST THINGS IN LIFE ARE FREE**
Luther Vandross & Janet Jackson w/BBD & Ralph Tresvant *Perspective*

40 **WOULD I LIE TO YOU?**
Charles & Eddie *Capitol*

41 **COME AND TALK TO ME**
Jodeci *Uptown*

42 **SMELLS LIKE TEEN SPIRIT**
Nirvana *DGC*

43 **AIN'T 2 PROUD 2 BEG**
TLC *LaFace*

44 **2 LEGIT 2 QUIT**
Hammer *Capitol*

45 **GIVING HIM SOMETHING HE CAN FEEL**
En Vogue *Atco EastWest*

46 **WALKING ON BROKEN GLASS**
Annie Lennox *Arista*

47 **THE ONE**
Elton John *MCA*

48 **DAMN I WISH I WAS YOUR LOVER**
Sophie B. Hawkins *Columbia*

49 **TELL ME WHAT YOU WANT ME TO DO**
Tevin Campbell *Qwest*

50 **SHE'S PLAYING HARD TO GET**
Hi-Five *Jive*

51 **MAKE IT HAPPEN**
Mariah Carey *Columbia*

52 **DO YOU BELIEVE IN US**
Jon Secada *SBK*

53 **TENNESSEE**
Arrested Development *Chrysalis*

54 **BREAKIN' MY HEART (PRETTY BROWN EYES)**
Mint Condition *Perspective*

55 **GOOD FOR ME**
Amy Grant *A&M*

56 **PEOPLE EVERYDAY**
Arrested Development *Chrysalis*

57 **PLEASE DON'T GO**
K.W.S. *Next Plateau*

58 **STAY**
Shakespear's Sister *London*

59 **LOVE IS ON THE WAY**
Saigon Kick *Third Stone*

60 **NO SON OF MINE**
Genesis *Atlantic*

61 **MOVE THIS**
Technotronic f/Ya Kid K *SBK*

62 **I CAN'T DANCE**
Genesis *Atlantic*

63 **ONE**
U2 *Island*

64 **LAYLA**
Eric Clapton *Duck*

65 **WISHING ON A STAR**
The Cover Girls *Epic*

66 **ALL I WANT**
Toad the Wet Sprocket *Columbia*

sixth place for 1992. The song was a collaboration by Wendy Waldman, Jon Lind, and Phil Galdston, who wrote the title down in a notebook. Galdston and Lind were struggling to write a song when they composed the music in a 30-minute stream-of-consciousness burst. A month later, Galdston met lyricist Waldman in Nashville and gave her the title he had written in his notebook. Waldman sang lead vocal on the demo and wanted to submit it to all the pop divas of the day, but once Ed Eckstine of Mercury Records heard it, he put a hold on it for the former Miss America who had overcome the disgrace of resigning her title with a successful music career.

The third vocal quartet in the year-end top 10, after Boyz II Men and Shai, was Color Me Badd. In 1991, the group ranked No. 7 for the year with "I Wanna Sex You Up" and No. 12 with "I Adore Mi Amor." Their third single, "All 4 Love," was the No. 8 title of 1992. Bryan Abrams, Kevin Thornton, Mark Calderon, and Sam Watters made their debut at a student talent show at Northwest High School in Oklahoma City. They made a habit of auditioning *a cappella* for artists passing through their hometown, including Ronnie Milsap, Huey Lewis, Sheila E., the O'Jays, and Tony! Toni! Toné! The night they sang for Kool & the Gang proved to be a turning point—Robert "Kool" Bell hooked them up with his manager and they soon had a contract with Giant Records.

Eric Clapton wrote the No. 9 song of 1992, "Tears In Heaven," after the tragic death of his 4-year-old son, Conor. Ironically, the No. 10 song was titled "Heaven" when first written by the members of Right Said Fred. It was a litany of everyday things that bothered someone to a degree that he was looking forward to a peaceful, civilized afterlife. Instead, the song ended up as "I'm Too Sexy," inspired by the attitudes and posings of people working out in a gymnasium.

A long dry spell for country music crossing over to the pop chart ended when Billy Ray Cyrus charted with "Achy Breaky Heart," the No. 28 song of the year. It was the first year-end chart appearance for a country artist since Willie Nelson teamed up with Julio Iglesias on "To All The Girls I've Loved Before," the No. 71 single of 1984.

67 **KEEP ON WALKIN'**
Ce Ce Peniston *A&M*

68 **TO LOVE SOMEBODY**
Michael Bolton *Columbia*

69 **HAZARD**
Richard Marx *Capitol*

70 **FREE YOUR MIND**
En Vogue *Atco EastWest*

71 **MYSTERIOUS WAYS**
U2 *Island*

72 **HAVE YOU EVER NEEDED SOMEONE SO BAD**
Def Leppard *Mercury*

73 **BEAUTY AND THE BEAST**
Celine Dion & Peabo Bryson *Epic*

74 **TOO FUNKY**
George Michael *Columbia*

75 **EROTICA**
Madonna *Maverick*

76 **THE WAY I FEEL ABOUT YOU**
Karyn White *Warner Bros.*

77 **MISSING YOU NOW**
Michael Bolton *Columbia*

78 **DO I HAVE TO SAY THE WORDS?**
Bryan Adams *A&M*

79 **THOUGHT I'D DIED AND GONE TO HEAVEN**
Bryan Adams *A&M*

80 **FRIDAY I'M IN LOVE**
The Cure *Fiction*

81 **IN THE CLOSET**
Michael Jackson *Epic*

82 **UHH AHH**
Boyz II Men *Motown*

83 **WHEN I LOOK INTO YOUR EYES**
Firehouse *Epic*

84 **HOLD ON MY HEART**
Genesis *Atlantic*

85 **WARM IT UP**
Kris Kross *Ruffhouse*

86 **JUSTIFIED AND ANCIENT**
The KLF f/Tammy Wynette *Arista*

87 **EVERYTHING CHANGES**
Kathy Triccoli *Reunion*

88 **LET'S GET ROCKED**
Def Leppard *Mercury*

89 **THINKIN' BACK**
Color Me Badd *Giant*

90 **EVERYTHING ABOUT YOU**
Ugly Kid Joe *Stardog*

91 **TAKE THIS HEART**
Richard Marx *Capitol*

92 **ADDAMS GROOVE**
Hammer *Capitol*

93 **FOREVER LOVE**
Color Me Badd *Giant*

94 **HUMAN TOUCH / BETTER DAYS**
Bruce Springsteen *Columbia*

95 **I WANNA LOVE YOU**
Jade *Giant*

96 **SLOW MOTION**
Color Me Badd *Giant*

97 **BROKEN ARROW**
Rod Stewart *Warner Bros.*

98 **LITTLE MISS CAN'T BE WRONG**
Spin Doctors *Epic Associated*

99 **JUST TAKE MY HEART**
Mr. Big *Atlantic*

100 **WE GOT A LOVE THANG**
Ce Ce Peniston *A&M*

The Top 100 Songs of 1993

Ace of Base

1993 WAS THE year the wasteful 6-by-12-inch CD cardboard longbox was finally banned in the United States; Eric Clapton dominated the Grammy Awards with six honors, including album of the year for *Unplugged;* and the Who's *Tommy* opened on Broadway at the St. James Theatre.

The No. 1 single of the year never made it to the top of the Hot 100. But the ubiquitous "Whoomp! (There It Is)" by Tag Team spent seven weeks at No. 2 and a record 45 weeks on the Hot 100, longer than any other single to this date. "Whoomp! There it is!" was already a catchphrase in the Southeast when Steve (Roll'n) Gibson and Cecil (DC) Glenn recorded their raw, bassline-heavy hip-hop track. Friends since growing up together in Denver, both had relocated to Atlanta. Gibson was attending a music business school and Glenn had a lead on a job with CNN. Their future was set the night they stopped in at a local club, Magic City. Glenn cornered owner Michael Barney and said he wanted to be the club's relief DJ. He got hired to cook in the kitchen. Two orders of chicken wings later, he was filling in for the main DJ. But when he heard another DJ work the expression "Whoomp! There it is!" into his rap, he started using it too. Glenn and Gibson produced a song incorporating the expression and played the tape at Magic City. That created an instant demand for a record. When they couldn't get any major labels interested in "Whoomp!" they borrowed $2,500 from Glenn's parents to have 800 singles manufactured. There was enough local buzz on the song to sell all of those copies in Atlanta, and the track was picked up by Bellmark, a Hollywood-based independent label, and issued on the Life imprint.

"Whoomp!" was Tag Team's first chart entry, making it the first No. 1 single of the year to be a debut single since Debby Boone's "You Light Up My Life" in 1977.

Mariah Carey's chart assault continued unabated in 1993 with the release of the first two singles from her *Music Box* album. "Dreamlover" topped the Hot 100 for eight weeks, while "Hero" ruled for four weeks. The two singles were, respectively, No. 3 and No. 8 for 1993. That makes Carey the only female vocalist of the rock era to have two singles in a year-end top 10 twice. She pulled off the same feat in 1990 with her first two singles, "Vision Of Love" (No. 4 for the year) and "Love Takes Time" (No. 3 for 1990). The only other female solo vocalists to have two singles in a year-end top 10 to this date were Donna Summer and Whitney Houston.

The No. 4 record of 1993 was from the soundtrack of the Sharon Stone film *Sliver,* although the track was originally recorded for another movie. The British reggae outfit UB40, responsible for the No. 24 song of 1988, "Red Red Wine," submitted their updating of Elvis Presley's "Can't Help Falling In Love" (the No. 27 single of 1962) to the producers of the soundtrack for *Honeymoon In Vegas.* All of the songs on the soundtrack were Elvis covers, but the members of UB40 didn't realize how many artists were being asked to submit songs for consideration. Bono of U2 also covered "Can't Help Falling In Love," and his version was chosen for *Honeymoon.* The UB40 track sat on a shelf for two years until executives at Virgin Records in the U.S. asked if it could be included in *Sliver.* It turned out to be the most successful remake of an Elvis song in the rock era.

Janet Jackson had her most successful chart single yet with "That's The Way Love Goes," the first release from her Virgin debut, *janet.* Ranked No. 5, it was Jackson's third year-end top 10 hit, following "Miss You Much," the No. 2 single of 1989 and "Escapade," the No. 6 hit of 1990.

One couldn't help but think of Vanilla Ice in the same breath as Snow, even though the Irish rapper, born in Canada, hated the comparison. Just as Vanilla Ice was a white artist trying his hand at rap, Snow was a white artist who performed the rapid-fire reggae music known as dancehall. Darren O'Brien grew up in a working-class area of Toronto populated by Jamaicans. He was more into fighting, drinking, and stealing than anything else, and dropped out of school during the ninth grade. In 1989, he served a jail sentence for attempted murder but was acquitted. His refusal to "snitch" during his incarceration inspired him to write "Informer." He recorded that, and the balance of his debut album, *12 Inches Of Snow,* before serving a second jail sentence for assault. Snow was the highest-ranking Canadian in 1993, although Bryan Adams was not too far behind, ranking No. 24 with "Please Forgive Me."

The No. 7 track of 1993 was the U.S. chart debut for the Swedish quartet Ace of Base. "All That She Wants" broke Ace of Base globally, after their initial success in Scandinavia with "Wheel Of Fortune." The group is made up of three Berggren siblings—Jonas, Linn, and Jenny—and their friend Ulf Ekberg. Jonas and Ulf produced some reggae groups in their home city of Gothenburg before they decided to found a group of their own with Jonas' sisters. They originally called themselves Tech Noir, for the discotheque in *The Terminator*. Their European record label didn't favor the group's reggae-tinged recordings, but the irresistible blend of Europop synthesizer music and reggae beats proved to be a winning combination for Ace of Base.

Cheryl Gamble, Tamara Johnson, and Leanne Lyons, the three women who made up SWV (Sisters With Voices), had a chart-topping single in 1993 with "Weak," ranked No. 9 for the year. Brian Alexander Morgan wrote the song in the '80s for the Gap Band, but they never recorded it. Morgan cut it himself, and Kenny Ortiz of RCA heard that version and thought it would be perfect for the label's new signing, SWV.

Meat Loaf ended a 15-year dry spell by reuniting with writer/producer Jim Steinman on "I'd Do Anything For Love (But I Won't Do That)," the No. 10 single of 1993. Meat Loaf's only prior appearance on a year-end chart was the No. 70 posting of "Two Out Of Three Ain't Bad" in 1978.

Jade, No. 17 with "Don't Walk Away," was a group literally made to order. Giant Records' president of black music, Cassandra Mills, wanted three women in their mid-20s of the same height who would wear dog tags and boots. If En Vogue aspired to be the Supremes of the '90s, Mills wanted a group that would be a contemporary version of Martha & the Vandellas. She and producer Vassal Benford found three singers experienced in session work: Joi Marshall and Tonya Kelly hailed from Chicago and Di Reed was from Houston. Their first single, "I Wanna Love You" from the soundtrack of *Class Act*, established them on the Hot 100 and paved the way for "Don't Walk Away."

67 **THAT'S WHAT LOVE CAN DO**
Boy Krazy *Next Plateau*

68 **ANGEL**
Jon Secada *SBK*

69 **ANNIVERSARY**
Tony! Toni! Toné! *Wing*

70 **WHEN SHE CRIES**
Restless Heart *RCA*

71 **INSANE IN THE BRAIN**
Cypress Hill *Ruffhouse*

72 **MORE AND MORE**
Captain Hollywood Project *Imago*

73 **REBIRTH OF SLICK (COOL LIKE DAT)**
Digable Planets *Pendulum*

74 **RAIN**
Madonna *Maverick*

75 **IT WAS A GOOD DAY**
Ice Cube *Priority*

76 **COME BABY COME**
K7 *Tommy Boy*

77 **TWO STEPS BEHIND**
Def Leppard *Columbia*

78 **FAITHFUL**
Go West *EMI*

79 **BOOM! SHAKE THE ROOM**
Jazzy Jeff and Fresh Prince *Jive*

80 **BAD BOYS**
Inner Circle *Big Beat*

81 **THE RIGHT KIND OF LOVE**
Jeremy Jordan *Giant*

82 **FOREVER IN LOVE**
Kenny G *Arista*

83 **LIVIN' ON THE EDGE**
Aerosmith *Geffen*

84 **THREE LITTLE PIGS**
Green Jelly *Zoo*

85 **NOTHIN' MY LOVE CAN'T FIX**
Joey Lawrence *Impact*

86 **FLEX**
Mad Cobra *Columbia*

87 **SEX ME (PARTS I & II)**
R. Kelly *Jive*

88 **GET AWAY**
Bobby Brown *MCA*

89 **GIVE IT UP, TURN IT LOOSE**
En Vogue *Atco EastWest*

90 **REASON TO BELIEVE**
Rod Stewart *Warner Bros.*

91 **NO RAIN**
Blind Melon *Capitol*

92 **CONNECTED**
Stereo MC's *Gee Street*

93 **WHO IS IT**
Michael Jackson *Epic*

94 **THE CRYING GAME**
Boy George *SBK*

95 **GIRL, I'VE BEEN HURT**
Snow *EastWest*

96 **IF I EVER LOSE MY FAITH IN YOU**
Sting *A&M*

97 **CAN'T GET ENOUGH OF YOUR LOVE**
Taylor Dayne *Arista*

98 **CHECK YO SELF**
Ice Cube f/Das EFX *Priority*

99 **SOUL TO SQUEEZE**
Red Hot Chili Peppers *Warner Bros.*

100 **SWEET THING**
Mary J. Blige *Uptown*

The Top 100 Songs of 1994

Toni Braxton

1994 WAS THE year Bruce Springsteen won an Oscar for "Streets Of Philadelphia"; the 25th anniversary of Woodstock was celebrated with Woodstock '94; and the Eagles and Barbra Streisand, both long absent from the road, undertook major tours.

After scoring the No. 2 hit of 1992 with "End Of The Road," Boyz II Men went one better and secured the top-ranked single of 1994 with "I'll Make Love To You." Also in the top 10 at No. 4 with the follow-up, "On Bended Knee," Boyz II Men became the first Motown act to have two top five hits on a year-end chart since 1964, when the Supremes were No. 3 with "Where Did Our Love Go" and No. 5 with "Baby Love." According to writer/producer Babyface, "I'll Make Love To You" resulted from him imagining what the follow-up to "End Of The Road" should be—something not exactly the same yet still familiar, so it didn't seem like a total left turn from what had come before. The group members were concerned the new song was too close to their previous hit, but executives at Motown convinced them to record "I'll Make Love To You."

Ace of Base, the Swedish quartet whose debut effort, "All That She Wants," was the No. 7 single of 1993, also did better in 1994. The group's second single, "The Sign," became the most successful song from Sweden in the rock era. Ace of Base also landed at No. 20 with "Don't Turn Around," a song written by Diane Warren and Albert Hammond for Tina Turner. Her rock-ballad version never appeared on an album; it was relegated to the B-side of her "Typical Male" single. Luther Ingram had an R&B hit with it, inspiring reggae group Aswad to record it. Their version topped the British chart. Next, Neil Diamond had an Adult Contemporary hit with the song before it was cut by Ace of Base.

"I Swear," the No. 3 single of 1994, began life as a country song. It was a chart-topper earlier in the year for John Michael Montgomery. Then producer David Foster recorded a smooth doo-wop version with All-4-One as the follow-up to the quartet's initial hit, a remake of the Tymes' "So Much In Love" from 1963. If that sounds like something Foster has done before, there's good reason. In 1992, he turned Dolly Parton's No. 1 country hit "I Will Always Love You" into a huge pop and R&B hit for Whitney Houston. That single from *The Bodyguard* had a 14-week run at the top of the Hot 100. "I Swear" almost duplicated that feat by remaining No. 1 for 11 weeks. It made stardom seem so easy for the four members of All-4-One, who had come together as a group in the fall of 1993 in the Antelope Valley section of California, located just north of Los Angeles County. Tony Borowiak and Alfred Nevarez were high school friends who had sung together. They met Jamie Jones at a talent competition and formed a trio to sing radio station jingles. They wanted to be a quartet, and spotted Delious Kennedy on Arsenio Hall's "Flavor of the Future" show. The Air Force brat thought it was a joke when he was asked to join the group, but soon realized it was a serious offer. All-4-One signed with the Atlantic-affiliated Blitzz label after auditioning with "So Much In Love."

Newcomer Lisa Loeb and her band Nine Stories (named for the J.D. Salinger book) have actor Ethan Hawke to thank for bringing them to the attention of Ben Stiller for his film *Reality Bites*. While "Stay (I Missed You)" wasn't the first single released from the soundtrack, it did become the signature song for the Generation X flick. The single became the biggest non–Elvis Presley hit in the history of RCA to this date, but it was the last the label saw of Loeb. After "Stay" was a hit, she and the band signed with the Geffen label.

There have been a lot of songs called "The Power Of Love," including singles by Joe Simon, Luther Vandross, and Frankie Goes to Hollywood, and the Huey Lewis & the News song from *Back To The Future* that was the No. 11 single of 1985. That same year, Australia's Air Supply recorded a completely different "The Power Of Love." The song originated with a singer from Queens, New York, who was much more popular in Britain than she was at home. Signed to Epic, Jennifer Rush topped the U.K. singles chart for five weeks with a song she co-wrote, "The Power Of Love." After Air Supply failed to make it a hit in America, peaking only at No. 68, the Rush version was released and similarly faltered, only moving up to No. 57. It looked like the biggest American version would belong to Laura Branigan, who reached No. 26 in 1988. Then along came French Canadian singer

34 SHINE
Collective Soul *Atlantic*

35 BACK & FORTH
Aaliyah *Blackground*

36 BECAUSE THE NIGHT
10,000 Maniacs *Elektra*

37 CAN WE TALK
Tevin Campbell *Qwest*

38 STROKE YOU UP
Changing Faces *Big Beat*

39 NOW AND FOREVER
Richard Marx *Capitol*

40 NEVER LIE
Immature *MCA*

41 MMM MMM MMM MMM
Crash Test Dummies *Arista*

42 SAID I LOVED YOU...BUT I LIED
Michael Bolton *Columbia*

43 I'LL STAND BY YOU
The Pretenders *Sire*

44 YOU WANT THIS /
70s LOVE GROOVE
Janet Jackson *Virgin*

45 SO MUCH IN LOVE
All-4-One *Blitzz*

46 FUNKDAFIED
Da Brat *So So Def*

47 LINGER
The Cranberries *Island*

48 I'M READY
Tevin Campbell *Qwest*

49 TURN THE BEAT AROUND
Gloria Estefan *Crescent Moon*

50 CANTALOOP (FLIP FANTASIA)
US3 *Blue Note*

51 CRY FOR YOU
Jodeci *Uptown*

52 BECAUSE OF LOVE
Janet Jackson *Virgin*

53 ANYTIME YOU NEED A FRIEND
Mariah Carey *Columbia*

54 I MISS YOU
Aaron Hall *Silas*

55 AT YOUR BEST (YOU ARE LOVE)
Aaliyah *Blackground*

56 THIS D.J.
Warren G *Violator*

57 GIN AND JUICE
Snoop Doggy Dogg *Death Row*

58 STREETS OF PHILADELPHIA
Bruce Springsteen *Columbia*

59 UNDERSTANDING
Xscape *So So Def*

60 YOUR BODY'S CALLIN'
R. Kelly *Jive*

61 GETTO JAM
Domino *Outburst*

62 COME TO MY WINDOW
Melissa Etheridge *Island*

63 NEVER KEEPING SECRETS
Babyface *Epic*

64 KEEP YA HEAD UP
2Pac *Interscope*

65 WHAT'S THE FREQUENCY, KENNETH?
R.E.M. *Warner Bros.*

66 PRACTICE WHAT YOU PREACH
Barry White *A&M*

67 CRAZY
Aerosmith *Geffen*

Celine Dion, who recorded the song for her *The Colour Of My Love* album.

Dion had already graced the top 10 three times, with "Where Does My Heart Beat Now" (the No. 48 single of 1991), her duet with Peabo Bryson on the title tune from Walt Disney's *Beauty And The Beast* (No. 72 of 1992), and her remake of Patti LaBelle's "If You Asked Me To" (No. 37 of 1992). But it was "The Power Of Love" that brought her superstar status, reigning over the Hot 100 for four weeks and ending up in seventh place for 1994. Even in the U.K., where the Jennifer Rush single had been so huge, Dion's version peaked at No. 4 (and paved the way for "Think Twice," which had a seven-week run at the top of the British singles chart).

Robert Kelly doesn't use his first name on his recordings, but it hasn't been an impediment. After four singles from his debut album *Into The '90s* made the top 60 of the Hot 100, he achieved top 20 status for the first time with "Sex Me (Parts I & II)," the initial single from his *12 Play* release. The real breakthrough came with the pure R&B song "Bump N' Grind." Not only did it top the Hot 100 for three weeks (allowing it to become the No. 8 single of 1994), but it ruled the Hot R&B Singles chart for 12 weeks, the longest run at the top since the chart was reinstated in 1965. Kelly also wrote and produced the No. 35 single of the year, Aaliyah's "Back & Forth."

Toni Braxton's introduction to the public came via the soundtrack to the Eddie Murphy film *Boomerang*. While most of the attention went to Boyz II Men's smash hit "End Of The Road," the singer from Severn, Maryland, impressed with two tracks on the album, "Give U My Heart," a duet with Babyface, and "Love Shoulda Brought You Home," a song originally written for another contralto, Anita Baker. Braxton later thanked Baker for not recording it.

The oldest of six children, Braxton was brought up in a strict home under the supervision of her father, an apostolic minister, and her mother, an amateur opera singer. The young Toni sang in her father's church choir, but wasn't allowed to listen to secular music or view television at home. She watched *Soul Train* when her parents went grocery shopping on Saturdays, but they caught her and she was reprimanded. When she was older and her parents became less rigid, Toni and her four sisters formed a group called the Braxtons. They were signed to Arista in 1989. Even though the single "The Good Life" flopped, it brought them to the attention of producers L.A. Reid and Babyface, who were looking for a female soloist for their fledgling LaFace label. Toni signed a deal and the single "Another Sad Love Song" from her debut album went top 10 and was the No. 50 song of 1993. The follow-up, "Breathe Again," had a healthy enough chart run to rank No. 12 for 1994, while the next single, "You Mean The World To Me," was No. 26 for the year.

68 **LOSER**
Beck *DGC*

69 **ANYTHING**
SWV *RCA*

70 **GROOVE THANG**
Zhané *Illtown*

71 **PRAYER FOR THE DYING**
Seal *ZTT/Sire*

72 **ROCK AND ROLL DREAMS COME THROUGH**
Meat Loaf *MCA*

73 **AMAZING**
Aerosmith *Geffen*

74 **I CAN SEE CLEARLY NOW**
Jimmy Cliff *Chaos*

75 **BEAUTIFUL IN MY EYES**
Joshua Kadison *SBK*

76 **ALWAYS**
Erasure *Mute*

77 **GOT ME WAITING**
Heavy D. & the Boyz *Uptown*

78 **MARY JANE'S LAST DANCE**
Tom Petty & the Heartbreakers *MCA*

79 **MR. VAIN**
Culture Beat *550 Music*

80 **DON'T TAKE THE GIRL**
Tim McGraw *Curb*

81 **STAY**
Eternal *EMI*

82 **LIVING IN DANGER**
Ace of Base *Arista*

83 **ALWAYS IN MY HEART**
Tevin Campbell *Qwest*

84 **BACK IN THE DAY**
Ahmad *Giant*

85 **INDIAN OUTLAW**
Tim McGraw *Curb*

86 **LUCKY ONE**
Amy Grant *A&M*

87 **FAR BEHIND**
Candlebox *Maverick*

88 **WHAT'S MY NAME?**
Snoop Doggy Dogg *Death Row*

89 **THE WAY SHE LOVES ME**
Richard Marx *Capitol*

90 **I'LL TAKE YOU THERE**
General Public *Epic Soundtrax*

91 **THUGGISH RUGGISH BONE**
Bone Thugs-N-Harmony *Ruthless*

92 **CIRCLE OF LIFE**
Elton John *Hollywood*

93 **FOUND OUT ABOUT YOU**
Gin Blossoms *A&M*

94 **LOVE SNEAKIN' UP ON YOU**
Bonnie Raitt *Capitol*

95 **AND OUR FEELINGS**
Babyface *Epic*

96 **BOP GUN (ONE NATION)**
Ice Cube *Priority*

97 **U.N.I.T.Y.**
Queen Latifah *Motown*

98 **DREAMS**
Gabrielle *Go!Discs*

99 **MISLED**
Celine Dion *550 Music*

100 **EVERYDAY**
Phil Collins *Atlantic*

The Top 100 Songs of 1995

Coolio

1995 WAS THE year O.J. Simpson heard a jury deliver a "not guilty" verdict in his trial for the murder of his ex-wife, Nicole Brown, and her friend Ron Goldman; Timothy McVeigh and Terry Nichols were arrested for bombing the Federal Building in Oklahoma City, a terrorist attack that killed 169; and the Canadian liquor distributor Seagram's purchased MCA/Universal.

It would be difficult to find two bigger superstar acts to team up in 1995 than Mariah Carey and Boyz II Men. Their collaboration on "One Sweet Day" lifted Carey to her first No. 1 single of the year, and made Boyz II Men only the second act in the rock era to top the annual recap for two years running, after George Michael did it in 1987 and 1988 with "Faith" and "One More Try." The No. 1 song of 1994, Boyz II Men's "I'll Make Love To You," tied the record for longest No. 1 single by remaining in pole position for 14 weeks. "One Sweet Day" broke that record, managing to stay No. 1 for 16 weeks.

Carey had originally discussed the idea for "One Sweet Day" with producer Walter Afanasieff. Through managers, a meeting was arranged with the four members of Boyz II Men. Nathan Morris of the group was surprised to hear the song, because it coincided with something he had written. Afanaiseff says the two songs were merged and that the recording session was chaotic because there were only two-and-a-half hours in the

Boyz II Men schedule for studio time with Carey. The producer recorded as much of the Boyz as he could, then had Carey record more vocals. The result was one of the top 10 singles of the rock era.

With "Fantasy" in fourth place, Carey became the first female artist in the rock era to have two year-end top 10 hits three different times. "Vision Of Love" and "Love Takes Time" were both in the top five in 1990, and "Dreamlover" and "Hero" both made the top 10 in 1993.

Coolio's remake of Lakeside's "Fantastic Voyage" was the No. 21 song of 1994. A year later, he landed in second place with a song from the soundtrack to a Michelle Pfeiffer movie, *Dangerous Minds*. Music supervisor Kathy Nelson suggested the original, temporary alternative music soundtrack be shelved in favor of an urban sound. She liked Coolio's voice on "Fantastic Voyage" and invited him to view some footage of the film. Soon after, Coolio was in a studio and overheard Larry Sanders, a.k.a. L.V., recording a song based on Stevie Wonder's "Pastime Paradise" from the *Songs In The Key Of Life* album. Coolio asked if he could work on the song with L.V., and three hours later they had finished "Gangsta's Paradise."

TLC was the first "girl group" to place two songs in the year-end top five since the Supremes did it in 1964. Oddly, the songs occupied the same positions: TLC was No. 3 with "Creep" and No. 5 with "Waterfalls," where the Supremes were in third place with "Where Did Our Love Go" and fifth place with "Baby Love." Writer/producer Dallas Austin was afraid his song "Creep" might be too corny but after five months he couldn't get the tune out of his head. T-Boz Watkins of TLC liked what the song had to say about a woman whose man was playing around. Watkins also appreciated the uplifting message of "Waterfalls," a song written for TLC that addressed the issue of AIDS. "Waterfalls" spent seven weeks on top of the Hot 100.

Madonna ended up in the annual top 10 for the seventh time when "Take A Bow" placed sixth for 1995. She wanted an R&B sound for her *Bedtime Stories* album, a quest that led her to Babyface. The two stars met at Madonna's record label office and hit it off. They decided to write songs together, and Madonna drove herself over to Babyface's house for a working session. One of the two songs that resulted was based on a piece of music Babyface had written. "I didn't know where to take it," he confesses. "She immediately heard something in it. She clearly gave the song direction." They agreed that the first line of the song, "Take a bow," should be the title, even though the words weren't repeated in the rest of the song.

Olaf Jeglitza, better known as O-Jay, was the creative force behind the Berlin-based Real McCoy, the fourth German act in the rock era to have a top 10 song of the year. In 1961, Bert Kaempfert was No. 4 with "Wonderland By Night." Silver Convention's disco hit "Fly, Robin, Fly" was the No. 6 song of 1975. And in 1989, the later-to-be-disgraced duo Milli Vanilli had two songs in the annual recap: "Blame It On The Rain" at No. 8 and "Girl I'm Gonna Miss You" at No. 10. Real McCoy's first U.S. chart entry, "Another Night," peaked at No. 3 on the Hot 100 and had a long 45-week chart run, good enough to make it the most successful German single in the rock era.

Whitney Houston was back in the year-end top 10 for the first time since she had the No. 1 single of 1992 with "I Will Always Love You." This time, it was with another soundtrack effort. When she was cast in the film adaptation of Terry McMillan's novel *Waiting To Exhale,* Houston thought she should concentrate on her acting instead of recording a soundtrack, as she did for *The Bodyguard.* Director Forest Whitaker enrolled Babyface in writing songs for the movie. During a set visit, Babyface heard from Houston herself that she was not going to record any songs for the film. But then Babyface let her hear "Count On Me," and she not only reconsidered, she ended up co-writing the song. Still, Houston was determined not to sing the entire soundtrack. She and Babyface made a list of female divas they wanted for the project, including veterans like Aretha Franklin and Chaka Khan. Houston ended up singing three of the 16 songs on the soundtrack, including the title song, "Exhale (Shoop Shoop)," the No. 7 hit of 1995.

Los Angeles–born Montell Jordan sang gospel music in church and by the time he was 17 knew he wanted to pursue a career in music. It didn't happen right away—he was 26 when he auditioned for Russell Simmons by singing *a cappella* in the backseat of a Range Rover and landed a deal. During his college days, Jordan had listened to Slick Rick and considered his "Children's Story" a hip-hop classic. That song provided the sampled loop behind "This Is How We Do It," chosen to be the first single from his debut album. It was a case of best foot forward, as the single topped the Hot 100 for seven weeks, good enough to make it the No. 8 hit of the year.

Born Sealhenry Samuel in the Paddington section of London, the artist known as Seal had written "Kiss From A Rose" even before recording his first album, but didn't consider the song right for that first effort. That debut set did include "Crazy," the No. 78 song of 1991. While assembling the songs for his second album, Seal almost left "Kiss From A Rose" on the cutting room floor again. Seal told producer Trevor Horn, "This song is too different. It doesn't sound like anything else on the album. It doesn't really fit." Horn agreed, until a friend of Seal's heard his new material and said she especially liked the song about the rose. Horn told Seal, "We're silly if we don't put this on it." When Gary LeMel, president of music for Warner Bros.' film division heard "Kiss From A Rose," he thought it was perfect for the soundtrack of *Batman Forever.* Director Joel Schumacher was so enthusiastic about including the song that he directed the music video. "Kiss From A Rose" spent a week on top of the Hot 100 and placed ninth for the year.

Bryan Adams had the No. 10 song of 1994 with the soundtrack hit "All For Love," sung with Rod Stewart and Sting in *The Three Musketeers.* Adams repeated that achievement in 1995 by ranking tenth with another soundtrack tune, "Have You Ever Really Loved A Woman?" from *Don Juan DeMarco.* But Adams' music almost wasn't in the film. Composer Michael Kamen had already talked to Adams about collaborating on a song for the movie when the music supervisor for the film declared, "We don't need Bryan Adams. We have another song." She was determined to use a Tori Amos/Michael Stipe duet. Kamen protested and won, but then director Jeremy Laven favored a Linda Ronstadt song recorded in Spanish. Kamen asked Laven to listen to Adams' demo of "Have You Ever Really Loved A Woman?" and Laven agreed it was perfect for his film.

The Top 100 Songs of 1996

Donna Lewis

1996

1996 WAS THE year Prince Charles and Princess Diana of England ended their marriage; unabomber Ted Kaczynski was finally captured after 17 years; and William Jefferson Clinton defeated Bob Dole and was re-elected president of the United States.

Toni Braxton became the 10th artist to place two records in the top five of an annual recap, when "Un-Break My Heart" was the No. 1 song of 1996 and the two-sided hit "You're Makin' Me High"/"Let It Flow" placed fifth. The only other artists to achieve this before Braxton were Elvis Presley (with three hits in the top fives of 1956, 1957, and 1960), the Four Seasons (1962), the Beatles (1964), the Supremes (1964), the Bee Gees (1978), Donna Summer (1979), Michael Jackson (1983), Mariah Carey (1990), and Boyz II Men (1994).

"Un-Break My Heart" was the first Diane Warren song to be the top hit of the year. Her previous best was "Look Away," the No. 4 title of 1988 for Chicago. When Warren brought the demo to Arista president Clive Davis, she didn't have an artist in mind. She wasn't so much pitching the song as asking Clive's opinion. On first listen, Davis tagged Warren's composition for Braxton and Warren quickly agreed. When producer David Foster played the demo for Babyface, co-founder of Braxton's LaFace label, he told Babyface that the demo was in a low key but he would raise it for Braxton. Babyface protested, but Foster said it was almost in a man's key. "No, it'll be great," Babyface insisted. "It'll be really sexy." The song topped the Hot 100 for 11 weeks.

Just five months earlier, Braxton spent a week in pole position with "You're Makin' Me High," written originally by Bryce Wilson. When Babyface and L.A. Reid heard the song, they didn't care for the lyrics. Dallas Austin rewrote it as "Nothing For You," but it still wasn't there. Babyface brought Wilson back in, and after three days of rewrite the song had provocative new lyrics and a new title. "Toni needed to do something a little more daring," Babyface explains. The B-side was a hit, too. "Let It Flow" was Braxton's contribution to the *Waiting To Exhale* soundtrack.

Anyone who was alive in 1996 couldn't have missed one of the most ubiquitous songs of the rock era. Even Vice President Al Gore was caught attempting the hand-moves to "Macarena." The phenomenon began in the southern Spanish town of Dos Hermanas, where Antonio Romero and Rafael Ruiz were born. They started performing together when they were 14, and by the time "Macarena" washed up on American shores, the pair, known as Los Del Rio, had released 31 albums in their native country, appealing mostly to older audiences in small towns.

The original version of "Macarena," sung in Spanish, was recorded in 1993 for the album *A Mi Me Gusta*. It achieved some popularity overseas before catching on in Miami's South Beach. Local radio station Power 96 was reluctant to give the song airplay because station policy said songs had to be recorded in English. Program director Frank Walsh gave disc jockey John Caride two days to come up with an English remix. Caride turned to a couple of friends who did production work. Carlos De Yarza and Mike Triay structured a new melody and wrote some English lyrics. Jingle singer Patricia Alfaro recorded her vocals at their Bayside Studios and within hours the song was spinning on Power 96.

When the remix of "Macarena" became the most-requested song in the station's history, other stations asked for copies and De Yarza and Triay were deluged with offers from record labels who wanted to issue a single. The original recording was owned by BMG, so a deal was made with one of the corporation's U.S. imprints, RCA. The Bayside Boys remix of "Macarena" topped the Hot 100 for 14 weeks and was the No. 2 single of 1996. It was far and away the biggest American hit to originate in Spain; in 1974, Mocedades had the No. 85 song with "Eres Tu (Touch The Wind)," and in 1984, Julio Iglesias and Willie Nelson were No. 71 with "To All The Girls I've Loved Before."

Diane Warren had two of the year's top three songs, as Celine Dion's "Because You Loved Me" ranked No. 3 for 1996. Warren first contacted Toni Braxton about recording the song, written for the film *Up Close And Personal*. Even after Braxton passed, Warren didn't consider Dion because the Canadian singer had a new album ready for release and the first single

34 ANYTHING
3T *MJJ*

35 WHEN YOU LOVE A WOMAN
Journey *Columbia*

36 WHO WILL SAVE YOUR SOUL
Jewel *Atlantic*

37 DOWN LOW (NOBODY HAS TO KNOW)
R. Kelly f/Ronald Isley *Jive*

38 PONY
Ginuwine *550 Music*

39 ONLY YOU
112 f/the Notorious B.I.G. *Bad Boy*

40 YOU LEARN / YOU OUGHTA KNOW
Alanis Morissette *Maverick*

41 WONDERWALL
Oasis *Epic*

42 I CAN'T SLEEP BABY (IF I)
R. Kelly *Jive*

43 1979
The Smashing Pumpkins *Virgin*

44 YOU'RE THE ONE
SWV *RCA*

45 KISSIN' YOU
Total *Bad Boy*

46 TIME
Hootie & the Blowfish *Atlantic*

47 WHY I LOVE YOU SO MUCH / AIN'T NOBODY
Monica *Rowdy*

48 1, 2, 3, 4 (SUMPIN' NEW)
Coolio *Tommy Boy*

49 ALL THE THINGS (YOUR MAN WON'T DO)
Joe *Island*

50 KEY WEST INTERMEZZO (I SAW YOU FIRST)
John Mellencamp *Mercury*

51 THIS IS FOR THE LOVER IN YOU
Babyface f/LL Cool J, Howard Hewett, Jody Watley & Jeffrey Daniels *Epic*

52 I FINALLY FOUND SOMEONE
Barbra Streisand & Bryan Adams *Columbia*

53 COUNT ON ME
Whitney Houston & CeCe Winans *Arista*

54 WHAT KIND OF MAN WOULD I BE
Mint Condition *Perspective*

55 DOIN' IT
L.L. Cool J *Def Jam*

56 TELL ME
Dru Hill *Island*

57 THE EARTH, THE SUN, THE RAIN
Color Me Badd *Giant*

58 WOO-HAH!! GOT YOU ALL IN CHECK / EVERYTHING REMAINS RAW
Busta Rhymes *Flipmode*

59 IF YOUR GIRL ONLY KNEW
Aaliyah *Blackground*

60 ELEVATORS (ME & YOU)
OutKast *LaFace*

61 TONITE'S THA NIGHT
Kris Kross *So So Def*

62 FASTLOVE
George Michael *DreamWorks*

63 LADY
D'Angelo *EMI*

64 WHO DO U LOVE
Deborah Cox *Arista*

65 CHILDREN
Robert Miles *Arista*

66 YOU MUST LOVE ME
Madonna *Warner Bros.*

had already been chosen. But then Dion, who had already recorded Warren songs like "If You Asked Me To" and "Nothing Broken But My Heart," heard the new song through the head of her label. Dion loved the song and agreed to record it and release it as a single instead of the prior choice. The advertising campaign for the Robert Redford/Michelle Pfeiffer film made heavy use of the song. "It was like Celine Dion had a video on heavy rotation on every network," says Warren. "That's a once-in-a-lifetime exposure for an artist." The single spent six weeks on top of the Hot 100 and helped elevate Dion to superstar status. The follow-up, "It's All Coming Back To Me Now," spent five weeks at No. 2, good enough to make it the No. 10 single of the year. It matched the No. 10 ranking of the last Jim Steinman song to appear in a year-end top 10: Meat Loaf's "I'd Do Anything For Love (But I Won't Do That)" was the No. 10 single of 1993.

One woman who publicly claimed she had never danced the Macarena was Cardiff, Wales-born Donna Lewis, who remained stuck at No. 2 for nine long weeks with her first chart entry, "I Love You Always Forever." And for nine weeks, sitting above her, was Los Del Rio's "Macarena" (Bayside Boys Mix). Lewis wrote her first song when she was 14 and studied classical composition in college. Moving to Birmingham in England, she built a home studio and perfected her craft, ultimately winning a pact with Atlantic Records. The irresistible pop hook of her composition helped make "I Love You Always Forever" one of the top five songs by a U.K. artist in the rock era.

Mariah Carey had been wanting to work with producer Jermaine Dupri since she heard his work on "Jump," the Kris Kross single that was the No. 3 hit of 1992. She got her wish while working on her *Daydream* album. Dupri co-wrote and co-produced "Always Be My Baby," Carey's 11th single to top the Hot 100, and the No. 6 song of 1996.

Five young men from a tough neighborhood in Cleveland boarded a bus out of the ghetto in November 1993 and ended up in Visalia, California, where they knew some friends. A phone call to one of their heroes, Eric (Easy-E) Wright, resulted in a return phone call. They wanted to audition for him but he was heading out on the road with N.W.A. He was going to play Cleveland, so the five members of Bone Thugs-N-Harmony headed home and met with Easy-E. He liked their music and helped them get back to California, signing them to his own Ruthless label. By the time their first album was released, Wright had died from complications of AIDS. The song "Tha Crossroads" had been written as an elegy for a friend who had been gunned down, but it became a tribute to other friends and family members who had passed, including Easy-E. The single spent eight weeks on top of the Hot 100 and ranked No. 7 for the year.

Producer Teddy Riley preferred recording as a member of a group rather than going out on his own. After some success with the trio Guy, Riley helped form another group, BLACKstreet. While working on their second album, a sample of Bill Withers' "Grandma's Hands" turned into "No Diggity." Riley didn't think it should be a single, but Dr. Dre loved it and wanted to add his own rap to it. Female rapper Queenpen was also added, and the folks at Interscope insisted it had to be a single. "No Diggity" spent four weeks on top and ranked No. 8 for 1996.

The Top 100 Songs of 1997

Jewel

1997 WAS THE year Princess Diana and Dodi Fayed were killed in an automobile crash in Paris; Mother Teresa died of heart failure; and the motion picture *Titanic* opened in theaters, on its way to becoming the biggest box office success of all time.

It was the most shocking news you could imagine. Britons woke up the morning of August 31, 1997, to learn the news their American counterparts had been watching all night: Diana, Princess of Wales, and Dodi Fayed were dead. Fayed had been killed when their automobile crashed into a concrete divider in a Paris tunnel, and Diana died shortly after in a hospital. For the next few days, there was a global outpouring of grief. Just a few weeks earlier, Diana had comforted a tearful Elton John at the funeral of fashion designer Gianni Versace. Now, Elton was asked to sing at Diana's funeral in Westminster Abbey.

From England, Elton called Bernie Taupin in Los Angeles and told his lyricist that radio stations all over the U.K. were playing their song "Candle In The Wind" in tribute. Taupin misunderstood and thought Elton wanted him to rewrite the song that had been originally written about Marilyn Monroe. Two hours later, Taupin had rewritten the song in honor of Diana. When he called Elton back, they both realized the mistake, but agreed that the newly-fashioned version would be an appropriate tribute to the late Princess. Two days later, with more than 2.5 billion people watching the proceedings on television, Elton performed the song in public for the first and only time. Tears flowed all over the world.

After the funeral, Elton met producer George Martin at Townhouse Studios in West London and recorded the song. A track from Elton's new album, *The Big Picture,* was already scheduled for release. "Something About The Way You Look Tonight" was moved to the B-side of "Candle In The Wind 1997." The single spent 14 weeks on top of the Hot 100 and sold more than 31 million copies, becoming the best-selling single in history. Proceeds from the single helped raise millions of dollars for Diana's favorite charities.

After capturing the No. 1 and No. 3 positions on the year-end recap of 1996 with Toni Braxton's "Un-Break My Heart" and Celine Dion's "Because You Loved Me," songwriter Diane Warren locked down the No. 2 song of 1997. "How Do I Live" had been written for the film *Con Air* and was intended for rising teen star LeAnn Rimes. The producers of the film thought Rimes was too young to perform the song and went in a different direction: they asked Tricia Yearwood to record Warren's tune for the soundtrack. Yearwood's version went to country radio but a great song is a great song, and Curb Records founder Mike Curb was certain Rimes would have the biggest hit of her career with "How Do I Live." The battle was on. Yearwood triumphed on the country chart, peaking at No. 2. But Rimes tasted sweet victory on the Hot 100. She didn't get to No. 1 but managed a No. 2 peak. More important, her single remained on the Hot 100 for 69 weeks, the longest run of any single in the history of the chart. That allowed her to have the No. 2 song of 1997, as well as one of the top 10 hits of the entire rock era, and the most successful No. 2 song in the history of the Hot 100.

"Candle In The Wind 1997" wasn't the only tribute to a fallen friend in 1997. The No. 3 song of the year was "I'll Be Missing You," a tribute from Sean "Puffy" Combs to his best friend, the rapper known as the Notorious B.I.G. In the days after the rapper's murder in Los Angeles, Combs found himself emotionally shut down, while still focused on funeral arrangements and other responsibilities. Out of the loop on activities at his Bad Boy label during this time, he was surprised when one of his acts, the Lox, recorded a tribute song, "We'll Always Love Big Poppa." Combs realized recording his own tribute would help him move on. Watching a Police video on MTV, Combs was inspired to base his tribute on the No. 1 song of 1983, "Every Breath You Take." He recorded "I'll Be Missing You" with two other acts on his roster—Faith Evans, widow of the Notorious B.I.G., and the group 112.

Sitting right below "I'll Be Missing You" on the annual recap was a song by the man who was the subject of that tribute song. "Mo Money Mo

33 I'M STILL IN LOVE WITH YOU
New Edition *MCA*

34 EVERY TIME I CLOSE MY EYES
Babyface *Epic*

35 IN MY BED
Dru Hill *Island*

36 2 BECOME 1
Spice Girls *Virgin*

37 I BELONG TO YOU
(EVERY TIME I SEE YOUR FACE)
Rome *RCA*

38 SHOW ME LOVE
Robyn *RCA*

39 CUPID
112 *Bad Boy*

40 WHAT ABOUT US
Total *LaFace*

41 FEEL SO GOOD
Mase *Bad Boy*

42 SUNNY CAME HOME
Shawn Colvin *Columbia*

43 THE ONE I GAVE MY HEART TO
Aaliyah *Blackground*

44 BUTTA LOVE
Next *Arista*

45 THIS IS YOUR NIGHT
Amber *Tommy Boy*

46 INVISIBLE MAN
98 Degrees *Motown*

47 I BELIEVE IN YOU AND ME
Whitney Houston *Arista*

48 IT'S YOUR NIGHT
Tim McGraw w/Faith Hill *Curb*

49 WHERE HAVE ALL THE COWBOYS GONE?
Paula Cole *Warner Bros.*

50 BUILDING A MYSTERY
Sarah McLachlan *Arista*

51 NOT TONIGHT
Lil' Kim f/Da Brat, Left Eye, Missy Elliott & Angie Martinez *Undeas*

52 OOH AAH... JUST A LITTLE BIT
Gina G *Eternal/Warner Bros.*

53 LOOK INTO MY EYES
Bone Thugs-N-Harmony *Ruthless*

54 GET IT TOGETHER
702 *Biv 10/Motown*

55 COLD ROCK A PARTY
MC Lyte *EastWest*

56 SOCK IT 2 ME
Missy "Misdemeanor" Elliott f/Da Brat *EastWest*

57 SPICE UP YOUR LIFE
Spice Girls *Virgin*

58 NEVER MAKE A PROMISE
Dru Hill *Island*

59 NO TIME
Lil' Kim f/Puff Daddy *Undeas*

60 ALL BY MYSELF
Celine Dion *550 Music*

61 CRIMINAL
Fiona Apple *Clean Slate*

62 UP JUMPS DA BOOGIE
Magoo & Timbaland *Blackground*

63 I'LL BE
Foxy Brown f/Jay-Z *Violator*

64 I WILL COME TO YOU
Hanson *Mercury*

65 I DON'T WANT TO / I LOVE ME SOME HIM
Toni Braxton *LaFace*

Problems" was the second posthumous chart-topper for the late rapper, following "Hypnotize," No. 13 for the year. Incorporating Diana Ross' "I'm Coming Out," the song was written about the problems Combs and B.I.G. (real name: Christopher Wallace) experienced by having so much money. Combs was featured on the song, and was also in the year-end top 10 at No. 6 with his first chart-topper, "Can't Nobody Hold Me Down." That made Puff Daddy the first artist to occupy three slots in a year-end top 10 since 1983, when Michael Jackson was No. 2 with "Say, Say, Say" (recorded with Paul McCartney), No. 4 with "Billie Jean," and No. 8 with "Beat It." The only other acts to have three records in a year-end top 10 are Elvis Presley and the Beatles (with four in 1964).

Utah-born, Alaska-raised Jewel first made the annual recap of the Hot 100 in 1996 when "Who Will Save Your Soul" was the No. 36 song of the year. In 1997, she ranked seventh with a two-sided hit, "You Were Meant For Me" / "Foolish Games." The single had an extraordinary 65-week run, thanks to timing. "You Were Meant For Me" moved up the chart first, reaching No. 2 and spending two weeks in that spot. The single was moving down and would have disappeared off the chart, save for the song "Foolish Games" being included in remixed form on the *Batman And Robin* soundtrack. "Foolish Games" happened to be the B-side of "You Were Meant For Me," so it became the A-side, then the single reversed course, rebounding to No. 7.

While folks in the music business expected an act like Blur or Oasis to be the next big thing from Britain, the biggest export from Blighty turned out to be a quintet of brash young women with different public personas. Collectively known as the Spice Girls, they weren't just a recording act, but a social phenomenon, influencing fashion and dominating magazine covers and other media. Melanie Chisholm, Geri Halliwell, Melanie Brown, and Victoria Addams attended the first audition after answering a newspaper ad placed by a talent manager. After signing a contract, they were unhappy with him and left. Emma Bunton was added and they came under the aegis of Simon Fuller, manager of acts like the Eurythmics. Labels vied for the Spice Girls, but Fuller ultimately went with a label that had a strong alternative roster, but no major pop act at the time—Virgin. The first single, "Wannabe," topped the charts on both sides of the Atlantic and ranked No. 8 for 1997. The follow-up, "Say You'll Be There," was No. 24 and the third single, "2 Become 1," was No. 36 for the year.

Although they were American, the Orlando, Florida, boy band known as the Backstreet Boys found initial success in Europe. With two hit albums and a slew of hit singles on the Continent, the quintet then took on the U.S. The best tracks from those first two albums were combined into a debut album for America. While the 1995 single "We've Got It Goin' On" stalled at No. 69, "Quit Playing Games (With My Heart)" broke the act in its own country, spending two weeks at No. 2. It was the No. 9 hit of the year.

66 **MY BABY DADDY**
B-Rock & the Bizz *Tony Mercedes*

67 **C U WHEN U GET THERE**
Coolio f/40 Thevz *Tommy Boy*

68 **YOUR WOMAN**
White Town *Chrysalis*

69 **BIG DADDY**
Heavy D *Uptown*

70 **I MISS MY HOMIES**
Master P f/Pimp C & the Shocker *No Limit*

71 **YOU SHOULD BE MINE (DON'T WASTE YOUR TIME)**
Brian McKnight f/Mase *Mercury*

72 **GOTHAM CITY**
R. Kelly *Jive*

73 **FLY LIKE AN EAGLE**
Seal *ZTT/Warner Sunset*

74 **EVERY DAY IS A WINDING ROAD**
Sheryl Crow *A&M*

75 **SMILE**
Scarface f/2Pac & Johnny P *Rap-A-Lot*

76 **ON & ON**
Erykah Badu *Kedar/Universal*

77 **SOMEONE**
SWV f/Puff Daddy *RCA*

78 **SECRET GARDEN**
Bruce Springsteen *Columbia*

79 **DON'T WANNA BE A PLAYER**
Joe *Jive*

80 **EVERYTHING**
Mary J. Blige *MCA*

81 **STREET DREAMS**
NAS *Columbia*

82 **WHAT'S ON TONIGHT**
Montell Jordan *Def Jam*

83 **I SHOT THE SHERIFF**
Warren G *Def Jam*

84 **WHEN YOU'RE GONE / FREE TO DECIDE**
The Cranberries *Island*

85 **BARBIE GIRL**
Aqua *MCA*

86 **DON'T CRY FOR ME ARGENTINA**
Madonna *Warner Bros.*

87 **COCO JAMBOO**
Mr. President *Warner Bros.*

88 **PLEASE DON'T GO**
No Mercy *Arista*

89 **I CARE 'BOUT YOU**
Milestone *LaFace*

90 **I LIKE IT**
The Blackout Allstars *Columbia*

91 **STARING AT THE SUN**
U2 *Island*

92 **STEP BY STEP**
Whitney Houston *Arista*

93 **WHATEVER**
En Vogue *EastWest*

94 **LET IT GO**
Ray J *EastWest*

95 **THINKING OF YOU**
Tony Toni Tone *Mercury*

96 **YOU BRING ME UP**
K-Ci And Jo-Jo *MCA*

97 **GHETTO LOVE**
Da Brat f/T Boz *So So Def*

98 **BUTTERFLY KISSES** Raybon Bros. *MCA*

99 **GO THE DISTANCE**
Michael Bolton *Columbia*

100 **ONE MORE TIME** Real McCoy *Arista*

The Top 100 Songs of 1998

Deborah Cox

1998 WAS THE year President Clinton said he never had sex with that woman; the U.S. House of Representatives impeached the president; and astronaut John Glenn, now 77, paid a return visit to outer space.

The three brothers from Minneapolis known as Next pulled off a surprise by taking home the trophy for the No. 1 song of the year. The only previous chart entry for R.L., Tweety, and T-Low was "Butta Love," the No. 44 song of 1997. "Too Close," which was based on the beat of the early rap hit "X-mas Rappin'" by Kurtis Blow, spent five weeks on top of the Hot 100. It gave Arista the top single of the year for the third time, tying the label with Motown and Warner Bros. in second place among labels with the most No. 1 songs of the year (Columbia was in first place with five). It also made Next only the fourth male R&B duo or group in the rock era to have a No. 1 song of the year, following the Jackson 5 ("I'll Be There" in 1970),

Tag Team ("Whoomp! (There It Is)" in 1993), and Boyz II Men ("I'll Make Love To You" in 1994 and "One Sweet Day" with Mariah Carey in 1995).

The team of Norwood and Arnold had the No. 2 single of 1998. Both teenagers at the time, Brandy and Monica recorded under their first names. "The Boy Is Mine" was a teaming of two of the most successful young R&B divas of the late 1990s, and was the highest-ranked year-end song by two female stars teamed as a duo since Barbra Streisand and Donna Summer had the No. 16 single of 1979 with "No More Tears (Enough Is Enough)." Brandy was the senior member of the duo, born February 11, 1979, in McComb, Mississippi. She was only four when her family moved to California. She signed with Atlantic Records at about the same time she won a role in ABC-TV's comedy series *Thea*. Her first chart entry, "I Wanna Be Down," was the No. 31 song of 1994. A year later, she was No. 36 with "Baby" and No. 71 with "Brokenhearted." In 1996 she had her biggest hit to date when her contribution to the *Waiting To Exhale* soundtrack, "Sittin' Up In My Room," was No. 16 for the year. "The Boy Is Mine," which remained in pole position for 13 weeks, was her first chart-topper on the Hot 100.

It was also the first No. 1 single for duet partner Monica. Born October 24, 1980, in the College Park section of Atlanta, Monica sang gospel music in church and joined a 12-member traveling choir when she was 10, staying with the group for three years. As a fifth-grader she performed in local talent shows, and was introduced to producer Dallas Austin. He was impressed enough to bring her to Clive Davis in New York, and Monica was signed to Austin's Arista-distributed imprint, Rowdy Records. She was only 14 when her first chart entry, "Don't Take It Personal (Just One Of Dem Days)," sped to No. 2 on the Hot 100 and ended up the No. 11 song of 1995. She also had the No. 31 single that year, the two-sided "Before You Walk Out Of My Life" / "Like This And Like That." In 1996, another two-sided hit registered on the annual recap: "Why I Love You So Much" / "Ain't Nobody" was No. 47. In 1997, her song from the *Space Jam* soundtrack, "For You I Will," was No. 18 for the year. The follow-up to "The Boy Is Mine," a solo effort called "The First Night," also topped the Hot 100 and ranked fourth for 1998, giving Monica two hits inside the year-end top five.

Canadian-born Shania Twain (nee Eileen Twain) grew up listening to the country artists her parents loved, like Willie Nelson, Waylon Jennings, and Dolly Parton. But she loved pop music too, and was a big fan of the Supremes, the Carpenters, and the Jackson 5. She performed in musical theater at a resort in her native Canada, and eventually recorded some demos. A lawyer from Nashville caught her act and helped get her tape into the hands of the head of Mercury Records' country division. She recorded two albums for the label that did well, but it was her third release that set the world on fire. Produced by husband Robert John "Mutt" Lange, *Come On Over* helped Twain carve out a piece of chart history when her single "You're Still The One" ended up in third place for 1998. Twain wasn't the only country artist to have a top three hit in the 1990s; LeAnn Rimes had the No. 2 song of 1997 with "How Do I Live." But there was a major difference: Rimes' version of "How Do I Live" was a pop hit, but only managed to get to No. 43 on the country chart, where Trisha Yearwood had the hit

35 BEEN AROUND THE WORLD
Puff Daddy & the Family f/the Notorious B.I.G. & Mase *Bad Boy*

36 I'LL BE
Edwin McCain *Lava*

37 SAY IT
Voices of Theory *H.O.L.A.*

38 I WANT YOU BACK
'N Sync *RCA*

39 MAKE IT HOT
Nicole f/Missy "Misdemeanor" Elliott & Mocha *Gold Mind*

40 MAKE 'EM SAY UHH!
Master P f/Fiend, Silkk the Shocker, Mia X & Mystikal *No Limit*

41 WHAT YOU WANT
Mase f/Total *Bad Boy*

42 I STILL LOVE YOU
Next *Arista*

43 A SONG FOR MAMA
Boyz II Men *Motown*

44 GONE TILL NOVEMBER
Wyclef Jean *Ruffhouse*

45 DAYDREAMIN'
Tatyana Ali *MJJ*

46 TRIPPIN'
Total f/Missy Elliott *Bad Boy*

47 COME WITH ME
Puff Daddy f/Jimmy Page *Epic*

48 DÉJÀ VU (UPTOWN BABY)
Lord Tariq & Peter Gunz *Codeine*

49 TOUCH IT
Monifah *Uptown*

50 I GET LONELY
Janet Jackson f/BLACKstreet *Virgin*

51 FROM THIS MOMENT ON
Shania Twain *Mercury*

52 LOOKING THROUGH YOUR EYES
LeAnn Rimes *Curb*

53 TIME AFTER TIME
INOJ *So So Def*

54 LOVE LIKE THIS
Faith Evans *Bad Boy*

55 GHETTO SUPASTAR (THAT IS WHAT YOU ARE)
Pras Michel f/Ol' Dirty Bastard & Mya *Interscope*

56 LOOKIN' AT ME
Mase f/Puff Daddy *Bad Boy*

57 THEY DON'T KNOW
Jon B. *Yab Yum*

58 THE ARMS OF THE ONE WHO LOVES YOU
Xscape *So So Def*

59 I DO
Lisa Loeb *Geffen*

60 FRIEND OF MINE
Kelly Price *T-Neck*

61 IT'S ALL ABOUT ME
Mya & Sisqo *University*

62 I GOT THE HOOK-UP!
Master P f/Sons of Funk *No Limit*

63 KISS THE RAIN
Billie Myers *Universal*

64 CRUEL SUMMER
Ace of Base *Arista*

65 WE'RE NOT MAKING LOVE NO MORE
Dru Hill *LaFace*

66 LOVE ME
112 f/Mase *Bad Boy*

version. Twain's "You're Still The One" was the first No. 1 song from *Billboard*'s country chart to make it into the top three of the annual Hot 100 recaps since Kenny Rogers' "Lady" was the No. 3 hit of 1980.

The duo known as Savage Garden claimed the highest-ranked Australian hit of the rock era on a year-end chart when "Truly Madly Deeply" became the No. 5 song of 1998. Previously, Rick Springfield had the No. 7 song of 1981 with "Jessie's Girl," and Men at Work tied that mark in 1983 with "Down Under." When Darren Hayes and Daniel Jones first recorded the track, it was called "Magical Kisses." The night before recording his vocal, Hayes went to a café and wrote new lyrics. The song was written about his wife, and was inspired by the 1991 film *Truly Madly Deeply,* starring Juliet Stevenson and Alan Rickman. Hayes wanted the song to be a hidden track on the first Savage Garden album, but producer Charles Fisher convinced him the song would be a smash hit if released as a single. He was right.

Before 1998, the only solo Canadian female singer who had placed a song in the year-end top 10 was Celine Dion; in 1994 she was No. 7 with "The Power Of Love" and in 1996 she was No. 3 with "Because You Loved Me" and No. 10 with "It's All Coming Back To Me Now." Two Canadian females had never occupied the top 10 before, but in 1998 there were three. Shania Twain's No. 3 hit was accompanied by Deborah Cox's "Nobody's Supposed To Be Here" at No. 6 and Celine Dion's duet with R. Kelly on "I'm Your Angel" at No. 9. Cox was born in Toronto of Guayanese parents. Her desire for a career in music was sparked when she was six years old and heard Gladys Knight & the Pips' recording of "Help Me Make It Through The Night." Cox was touring with Celine Dion as a backing singer when she signed her own pact with Clive Davis' Arista Records. In 1996, she had the No. 64 song of the year with "Who Do U Love." Although "Nobody's Supposed To Be Here" didn't make it to No. 1 on the Hot 100, it did spend eight weeks at No. 2.

Teenagers Kia Thornton, Nikki Bratcher, and Tonia Tash didn't mind being compared to two particular girl groups who preceded them into year-end top 10s. Teamed by their managers as Divine, they scored the No. 10 single of 1998 with their first chart entry, "Lately." "We have our own style and our own sound, and we want to be original," Thornton told *Billboard*'s Chuck Taylor. "But we hear a lot of comparisons to En Vogue, and some say the Supremes. We like those best, because they both made their mark in the business."

The Top 100 Songs of 1999

Ricky Martin

1999 WAS THE year *Who Wants To Be A Millionaire* was imported from the U.K. to the U.S.; the first *Star Wars* movie in 16 years opened in theaters; and John F. Kennedy, Jr., along with his wife and sister-in-law, was killed when his private plane crashed.

Two of the acts with songs in the top three of the year set a record for the longest intervals between their first appearances on a year-end chart and earning a spot in the top three. Carlos Santana had the No. 1 single of the year with "Smooth," 29 years after his first appearance on a year-end chart with "Evil Ways," the No. 83 song of 1970.

The rejuvenation of Santana was due in part to Clive Davis, who signed the legendary musician to Arista and helped team him up with contemporary artists like Lauryn Hill, Dave Matthews, and Rob Thomas of matchbox twenty, who co-wrote "Smooth" and sang lead vocals on the track. The first single from the *Supernatural* album, "Smooth" spent 12 weeks on top of the Hot 100 and had a long enough chart run to become the No. 1 single of the rock era. That gave Arista the top tune of the year for the second year running, the first time a label managed that double since 1987 and 1988, when George Michael was No. 1 with "Faith" and "One More Try," both on Columbia.

The other artist in the top three who experienced a long wait was Cher, No. 3 with her British-produced "Believe." Her top three berth came 34 years after she appeared on the 1965 recap at No. 14 with "I Got You Babe" and No. 92 with "Baby Don't Go," both recorded with then-husband Sonny Bono. Until the massive success of "Believe," Cher's highest year-end placement was the No. 7 ranking of "Half-Breed" in 1973.

For the second time in their career, the three women of TLC had two hits in the year-end top 10. "No Scrubs" ranked second and "Unpretty" came in tenth. In 1995, TLC was No. 3 with "Creep" and No. 5 with "Waterfalls." Kevin "She'kspere" Briggs produced "No Scrubs" and wrote it with Kandi Burruss and Tameka Cottle of Xscape, who had their own series of year-end hits, starting with "Just Kickin' It," the No. 18 song of 1993. It was Briggs who wanted Rozonda "Chilli" Thomas to sing lead vocals on "No Scrubs." He explains, "I felt the range would be a little too high for T-Boz, not to mention I thought it would be a change to have Chilli sing lead because I hadn't heard that." The male-bashing lyrics of "No Scrubs" took a bashing of their own in an answer record. "No Pigeons" by Sporty Thievz featuring Mr. Woods ranked No. 98 for 1999.

Buffalo, New York–born Brian McKnight brought the Motown label back to the top five for the first time since Boyz II Men had the No. 1 song of 1994 with "I'll Make Love To You." McKnight's ballad "Back At One" spent eight weeks at No. 2 on the Hot 100, good enough to make it the No. 4 song of the year. McKnight was originally signed to the Mercury label but ended up on Motown when Universal bought PolyGram, bringing the Mercury and Motown labels under Universal's roof.

The resurgence of Santana on the charts coincided with a pop breakthrough for a number of Latin artists. Christina Aguilera, Ricky Martin, and Jennifer Lopez occupied three adjacent spots in the year-end top 10. Aguilera grew up in Pittsburgh, Pennsylvania, daughter of an Irish mother and an Ecuadorian father. She had a stint on *The Mickey Mouse Club,* and sang "Reflection" on the soundtrack of Disney's animated *Mulan* before releasing her first RCA single, "Genie In A Bottle." Writing partners Steve Kipner and David Frank agreed to meet with a songwriter from England, New Zealand–born Pam Sheyne. Their first collaboration was titled "If You Want To Be With Me," and the demo brought immediate reaction. Two different RCA acts wanted the song—a teen girl group called Innocence and an unknown singer named Christina Aguilera. RCA exec Ron Fair guaranteed the song would be Aguilera's first single, and it was Aguilera's manager who suggested the song should be retitled "Genie In A Bottle." Five weeks in pole position helped the song rank No. 5 for the year.

Sometimes one performance becomes the hallmark of an entire career. No one will ever forgot Michael Jackson's bravura moonwalk on the

25th Motown anniversary special, for example. The same can be said of Puerto Rican–born Ricky Martin's sexy, showstopping appearance on the Grammys in February 1999. Swaying his hips, Martin sang "The Cup Of Life," impressing the live audience as well as the millions watching at home on television. Already a superstar in the Latin community, the Grammy spot assured him of crossover pop success, and he earned it immediately with the release of his first English-language album and the premier single, "Livin' La Vida Loca." It had a five-week reign on the Hot 100 and was the No. 6 song of 1999.

Best known for her roles in films like *Selena, U-Turn,* and *Out Of Sight,* Jennifer Lopez also had crossover success in 1999, from an acting career to a musical one. The Bronx-born singer's first chart entry was "If You Had My Love," which ruled the Hot 100 for five weeks and ranked seventh for the year.

After appearing twice in the year-end top 10 of 1998, Monica was back in 1999's top 10 with "Angel Of Mine," a song originally recorded by British femme trio Eternal. Their version peaked at No. 4 in the U.K. in 1997. Monica's remake occupied the top spot on the Hot 100 for four weeks and was No. 8 for the year.

Christina Aguilera wasn't the only former Mouseketeer in the year-end top 10 of 1999. Kentwood, Louisiana–born Britney Spears was No. 9 with her first single, ". . .Baby One More Time." The American teenager was teamed with Swedish writer/producer Max Martin, who had already helmed hits for Ace of Base, Backstreet Boys, and 'N Sync.

68 **I DON'T WANT TO MISS A THING**
Mark Chesnutt *Decca*

69 **TAKE ME THERE**
BLACKstreet & Mya f/Mase & Blinky Blink *Interscope*

70 **BLACK BALLOON**
Goo Goo Dolls *Warner Bros.*

71 **SATISFY YOU**
Puff Daddy f/R. Kelly *Bad Boy*

72 **(YOU DRIVE ME) CRAZY**
Britney Spears *Jive*

73 **GET GONE**
Ideal *Noontime*

74 **SO ANXIOUS**
Ginuwine *550 Music*

75 **ALMOST DOESN'T COUNT**
Brandy *Atlantic*

76 **GIRL ON TV**
LFO *Arista*

77 **WE CAN'T BE FRIENDS**
Deborah Cox w/R.L. *Arista*

78 **SPEND MY LIFE WITH YOU**
Eric Benet f/Tamia *Warner Bros.*

79 **LEARN TO FLY**
Foo Fighters *Roswell*

80 **STAY THE SAME**
Joey McIntyre *C2*

81 **JAMBOREE**
Naughty by Nature f/Zhané *Arista*

82 **YOU**
Jesse Powell *Silas*

83 **BACK 2 GOOD**
matchbox 20 *Lava*

84 **SOMETIMES**
Britney Spears *Jive*

85 **24/7**
Kevon Edmonds *RCA*

86 **ALL NIGHT LONG**
Faith Evans f/Puff Daddy *Bad Boy*

87 **IT AIN'T MY FAULT 1 & 2**
Silkk the Shocker f/Mystikal *No Limit*

88 **GHETTO COWBOY**
Mo Thugs Family f/Bone Thugs-N-Harmony *Mo Thugs*

89 **THESE ARE THE TIMES**
Dru Hill *Def Soul*

90 **TAKING EVERYTHING**
Gerald Levert *EastWest*

91 **C'EST LA VIE**
B*Witched *Epic*

92 **BEAUTIFUL STRANGER**
Madonna *Maverick*

93 **LOST IN YOU**
Garth Brooks as Chris Gaines *Capitol*

94 **I LOVE YOU**
Martina McBride *RCA*

95 **FADED PICTURES**
Case & Joe *Def Jam*

96 **I WANT IT ALL**
Warren G f/Mack 10 *G-Funk*

97 **LARGER THAN LIFE**
Backstreet Boys *Jive*

98 **NO PIGEONS**
Sporty Thievz f/Mr. Woods *Roc-A-Blok*

99 **WRITE THIS DOWN**
George Strait *MCA*

100 **IF I COULD TURN BACK THE HANDS OF TIME**
R. Kelly *Jive*

The Top 100 Songs of 2000

Faith Hill

2000 WAS THE year a six-year-old Cuban boy named Elian Gonzales was rescued from the ocean after his mother died while trying to escape from Cuba; the presidential contest between Vice President Al Gore and Gov. George W. Bush ended in a virtual deadlock on Election Day and wasn't resolved until the Supreme Court stepped in a month later; and the New York Yankees won the World Series for the third consecutive year.

The Arista label had the No. 1 song of the year for an unprecedented third year in a row. Santana, the Carlos Santana–led group that had the top tune of 1999 with "Smooth," became the third act in the rock era to top the year-end recaps twice in a row, after George Michael (1987 and 1988) and Boyz II Men (1994 and 1995). "Maria Maria," which featured the Product G&B, reigned over the Hot 100 for 10 weeks. Arista prexy Clive Davis played some of the tracks for Santana's *Supernatural* album for Wyclef Jean. One of the founders of the Fugees, Jean and his cousin Jerry Duplessis flew to San Francisco to meet with Santana and write a song for the album. "Maria Maria" came to them quickly. "I was at a drum machine creating a beat and Wyclef was on the keys trying to get a groove on," says Duplessis. "Soon we caught the vibe and we said, 'Record it!'" Wyclef was working with a new duo, the Product, and featured them on the track.

Changing personnel didn't hurt the chart fortunes of Destiny's Child. Formerly a quartet, the trio had a higher annual placing each year. In 1998, the group was No. 21 with "No, No, No Part 2." In 1999, the group ended up No. 11 with "Bills, Bills, Bills." And in 2000 their song from the *Charlie's Angels* soundtrack, "Independent Women Part I," was second only to "Maria Maria." Destiny's Child became the third girl group after the Supremes and TLC to have two songs in the year-end top 10, when "Say My Name" ranked ninth for 2000.

Faith Hill was the third country female in four years to have a top three hit on the year-end chart. "Breathe" crossed formats, reaching No. 2 on the Hot 100 and No. 1 for 17 weeks on the Adult Contemporary tally.

Madonna had her first top five hit of a year since 1990, when "Vogue" ranked fifth. At No. 4, "Music" was her highest-charting year-end title since "Crazy For You" also placed fourth in 1985. Her only single to achieve a higher rank was "Like A Virgin," No. 2 for 1984.

Savage Garden matched its No. 5 placing in 1998 with "Truly Madly Deeply" when "I Knew I Loved You" ranked fifth for 2000. The song was written on a dare after producer Walter Afanasieff and the two members of Savage Garden, Darren Hayes and Daniel Jones, played their sophomore album for the heads of their record label. Afanasieff remembers that Columbia president Donnie Ienner took him aside after the listening session and said, "We don't have a 'Truly Madly Deeply.'" The producer explained that the duo didn't want to repeat itself, but Ienner needed a hit single. He told Afansieff to take the guys home and come up with a ballad like "Truly Madly Deeply." Later, the producer broke the news. Hayes got a look in his eye and said, "They want a 'Truly Madly Deeply'? All right, I'll give them one." He and Jones went to the room in Afanasieff's home where they wrote music. Ten minutes later they returned with a song. "Come on, you just left the room," said an astounded Afanasieff. Jones sat down at the piano and played the chords while Hayes sang "I Knew I Loved You." Two days later, the finished track was sent to the folks at Columbia.

Creed, a rock band out of Tallahassee, Florida, didn't get much pop airplay for the songs on their first album, *My Own Prison,* so the four members had to find some other way to build a reputation. They did it by going on the road, giving away a song on the Internet, and working hard on their second album. *Human Clay* yielded two big hits: "Higher" was their breakthrough at top 40 radio. It turned out to be the No. 29 song of 2000, but the follow-up elevated them to another level. "With Arms Wide Open," co-written by lead vocalist Scott Stapp when he learned he was going to be a father, topped the Hot 100 and was the No. 6 song of the year. When producer John Kurzweg heard the songs the band wanted to include on its sophomore set, "With Arms Wide Open" wasn't among them. But when he finally heard it, he liked it immediately, especially the bridge. "I thought the verse and chorus were wonderful but the thing that gave me little chills was the bridge." A radio version remixed to encourage pop airplay included a real string section and re-recorded guitars.

35 **NO MORE**
Ruff Endz *Epic*

36 **(HOT S**T) COUNTRY GRAMMAR**
Nelly *Fo' Reel*

37 **THIS I PROMISE YOU**
'N Sync *Jive*

38 **I TURN TO YOU**
Christina Aguilera *RCA*

39 **I TRY**
Macy Gray *Epic*

40 **HOT BOYZ**
Missy "Misdemeanor" Elliott f/Nas,
Eve & Q-Tip *Gold Mind*

41 **THAT'S THE WAY IT IS**
Celine Dion *550 Music*

42 **GIVE ME JUST ONE NIGHT (UNA NOCHE)**
98 Degrees *Universal*

43 **IT FEELS SO GOOD**
Sonique *Farm Club.com*

44 **BACK HERE**
BBMak *Hollywood*

45 **ABSOLUTELY (STORY OF A GIRL)**
Nine Days *550 Music*

46 **GOTTA TELL YOU**
Samantha Mumba *Wild Card*

47 **SHOW ME THE MEANING
OF BEING LONELY**
Backstreet Boys *Jive*

48 **THEN THE MORNING COMES**
Smash Mouth *Interscope*

49 **I JUST WANNA LOVE U (GIVE IT 2 ME)**
Jay-Z *Roc-a-Fella/Def Jam*

50 **NEVER LET YOU GO**
Third Eye Blind *Elektra*

51 **THE REAL SLIM SHADY**
Eminem *Web/Aftermath*

52 **LET'S GET MARRIED**
Jagged Edge *So So Def*

53 **SHAPE OF MY HEART**
Backstreet Boys *Jive*

54 **WIFEY**
Next *Arista*

55 **BETWEEN ME AND YOU**
Ja Rule f/Christina Milian
Murder Inc./Def Jam

56 **BLUE (DA BA DEE)**
Eiffel 65 *Republic*

57 **SHAKE YA ASS**
Mystikal *Jive*

58 **ALL THE SMALL THINGS**
Blink-182 *MCA*

59 **DESERT ROSE**
Sting f/Cheb Mami *A&M*

60 **OOPS!...I DID IT AGAIN**
Britney Spears *Jive*

61 **PINCH ME**
Barenaked Ladies *Reprise*

62 **I NEED YOU**
LeAnn Rimes *Sparrow*

63 **OTHERSIDE**
Red Hot Chili Peppers *Warner Bros.*

64 **BIG PIMPIN'**
Jay-Z f/UGK *Roc-A-Fella*

65 **SHE BANGS**
Ricky Martin *Columbia*

66 **HE CAN'T LOVE U**
Jagged Edge *So So Def*

67 **BAG LADY**
Erykah Badu *Motown*

One notch below Creed was another Florida rock band. Matchbox twenty, from Orlando, had its biggest hit to date with "Bent," No. 7 for the year. It didn't hurt that lead vocalist Rob Thomas was coming off the No. 1 song of 1999, "Smooth," the Sanata single he co-wrote that featured him as guest singer.

The group with the No. 8 song of 2000 pulled off a pretty amazing stunt—they were the first country group to place a song in the top 10 in an annual recap of the Hot 100. After recording two albums, the members of Lonestar decided to try something fresh and hired a new producer, Dann Huff, for their third set. Huff and the four band members spent every day in the offices of their record label, BNA, listening to songs that had been submitted for them to record. "I remember the day 'Amazed' came in," says the group's lead singer, Richie McDonald. "We all thought it was very passionate and a song people could relate to." They were right. "Amazed" spent eight weeks at the top of the country chart, and then crossed over to pop. A remix for top 40 radio helped garner more airplay, sending "Amazed" to the pinnacle of the Hot 100. That made Lonestar the first country act to top the chart since 1983, when Kenny Rogers and Dolly Parton partnered on "Islands In The Stream," the No. 11 song of that year.

Brooklyn-born Aaliyah was only 15 when she had her first hit. "Back & Forth" was the No. 35 song of 1994. That was her highest-ranked year-end hit until 2000, when "Try Again" was No. 10 for the year. The song, from the soundtrack to *Romeo Must Die* (which starred Jet Li and Aaliyah), made chart history when it became the first album track not available as a commercial single to top the Hot 100. Airplay-only songs not available for sale were unable to chart in previous years, but eligibility rules changed in December 1998. From that point, it was inevitable that someday there would be a No. 1 song that wasn't a single, and that's what happened to "Try Again," although there was a single available after its No. 1 reign.

68 **I WISH**
Carl Thomas *Bad Boy*

69 **TAKE A PICTURE**
Filter *Reprise*

70 **DON'T THINK I'M NOT**
Kandi *Columbia*

71 **WONDERFUL**
Everclear *Capitol*

72 **ONLY GOD KNOWS WHY**
Kid Rock *Top Dog/Lava*

73 **WHAT'S YOUR FANTASY**
Ludacris f/Shawna
Disturbing tha Peace/Def Jam

74 **FADED**
SoulDecision f/Thrust *MCA*

75 **BIG DEAL**
LeAnn Rimes *Curb*

76 **FORGOT ABOUT DRE**
Dr. Dre f/Eminem *Aftermath*

77 **LIAR**
Profyle *Motown*

78 **BOUNCE WITH ME**
Lil Bow Wow f/Xscape *So So Def*

79 **GOODBYE EARL**
Dixie Chicks *Monument*

80 **I THINK I'M IN LOVE WITH YOU**
Jessica Simpson *Columbia*

81 **THAT'S THE WAY**
Jo Dee Messina *Curb*

82 **PARTY UP (UP IN HERE)**
DMX *Ruff Ryders/Def Jam*

83 **SEPARATED**
Avant *Magic Johnson*

84 **SWEAR IT AGAIN**
Westlife *Arista*

85 **THE NEXT EPISODE**
Dr. Dre f/Snoop Dogg *Aftermath*

86 **UNTITLED (HOW DOES IT FEEL)**
D'Angelo *Virgin*

87 **BROADWAY**
Goo Goo Dolls *Warner Bros.*

88 **LUCKY**
Britney Spears *Jive*

89 **BEST OF INTENTIONS**
Travis Tritt *Columbia*

90 **I LIKE IT**
Sammie *Freeworld*

91 **FROM THE BOTTOM OF MY BROKEN HEART**
Britney Spears *Jive*

92 **CRASH AND BURN**
Savage Garden *Columbia*

93 **YES!**
Chad Brock *Warner Bros.*

94 **PUREST OF PAIN (A PURO DOLOR)**
Son by Four *Sony Discos*

95 **WOBBLE WOBBLE**
504 Boyz *No Limit*

96 **THIS TIME AROUND**
Hanson *Moe/Island*

97 **DANCIN'**
Guy *MCA*

98 **MY FIRST LOVE**
Avant f/Ketara Wyatt *Magic Johnson*

99 **COWBOY TAKE ME AWAY**
Dixie Chicks *Monument*

100 **WHAT'CHU LIKE**
Da Brat f/Tyrese *So So Def*

The Top 100 Songs of 2001

Usher

2001 WAS THE YEAR terrorists attacked the United States on September 11; the Taliban were defeated in Afghanistan; and George Harrison died of lung cancer in Los Angeles.

For the first time since Bryan Adams ruled the 1991 recap, a Canadian act had the No. 1 song of the year. Nickelback pulled off this feat with its very first chart entry, "How You Remind Me."

Atlanta-born, New York–raised Mary J. Blige had peaked at No. 2 and No. 3 on the Hot 100, but never had a No. 1 single until 2001, when "Family Affair" ruled for six weeks, helping it to become the No. 2 song of the year. Blige made her debut on the Hot 100 in 1994 with "You Remind Me." "Family Affair" was her fourth song to appear on a year-end recap. In 1995, her collaboration with Method Man on "I'll Be There For You/You're All I Need To Get By" was No. 47 for the year. A year later, her song from the *Waiting To Exhale* soundtrack, "Not Gon' Cry," ranked No. 19 for 1996. And in 1997, "Everything" was No. 80 for the year.

Usher Raymond was the only male artist to have a No. 1 as a solo act in 2001, and he did it twice, with "U Remind Me" and "U Got It Bad." Both ended up in the top 15 for the year, with the latter at No. 3 and the former at No. 11. In 1997 he was No. 7 for the year with "You Make Me Wanna..." and the following year he was No. 8 with "Nice & Slow."

Actress Jennifer Lopez had her most successful song to date with a remix of "I'm Real." The original recording, which appeared on her *J.Lo* album, was a solo effort; the new version sounded so different that some people wondered if it was the same song. Ja Rule, who was also No. 36 for the year with "Livin' It Up," was featured on the remix. "I'm Real" was one of three songs by Lopez on the 2001 recap. "Love Don't Cost A Thing" was No. 29 and "Play" was No. 76. It was the second time that Lopez had a year-end top 10 hit; in 1999, her debut single "If You Had My Love" placed seventh.

Clive Davis' new J Records was immediately successful upon launch— no surprise, given Davis' track record. His biggest success was with R&B newcomer Alicia Keys, who had been signed to Arista in 1998. Davis nurtured her talent and she was one of a handful of artists he took with him when he started J. She had been trained as a classical pianist, and recorded her first album when she was just 19. Keys' first single, "Fallin'," spent six weeks at No. 1 on the Hot 100 and ranked No. 5 for the year.

Of the 14 songs that advanced to No. 1 in 2001, the longest-running chart-topper was Janet Jackson's "All For You," which reigned for seven weeks and ended up in sixth place for the year. During the recording sessions for what would become the *All For You* album, Janet knew she wanted that to be the first single. Producer Jimmy Jam remembers Janet walking into the control room at the studio when they still had five or six more songs to record to complete the album. "She said, 'I don't want to sound crazy, but I think this is the first single. I know we're going to get some more songs and they're going to be really good. I just feel that I want this to be the first thing that people hear from me. When I do my first record after three years, I want this to be the tone of the record.'"

Both of Janet's 2001 hits—"All For You" and the No. 31 song, "Someone To Call My Lover," were based on samples of previous songs. But Jackson wasn't familiar with either one, according to Jimmy Jam. "All For You" is based on Luther Vandross' "The Glow Of Love," released in 1980 when Vandross was lead singer of the group Change. Jimmy Jam recalls, "She didn't know that song and I was really shocked. I was DJ'ing at the time that record was out, so that was a huge record in my life and one that I have always wanted to sample one day and bring it back for people to hear." Jimmy Jam, who grew up listening to pop radio, had the same experience when he played America's "Ventura Highway" for Jackson. "She said, 'I've never heard that.' And I said, 'I'm going to work this one up and I'll send it to you and you tell me what you think.' She loved it and we did it. For me, it's a thrill to hear that on the radio because I imagine people getting the same feeling as if they were hearing it for the first time as I did when I was a kid listening to AM radio."

35	ROCK THE BOAT
	Aaliyah *Blackground*
36	LIVIN' IT UP
	Ja Rule f/Case *Murder Inc./Def Jam*
37	ALL OR NOTHING
	O-Town *J*
38	DRIVE
	Incubus *Immortal*
39	I HOPE YOU DANCE
	Lee Ann Womack *MCA*
40	PUT IT ON ME
	Jay-Z f/Lil' Mo & Vita *Murder Inc./Def Jam*
41	DON'T TELL ME
	Madonna *Maverick*
42	ONLY TIME
	Enya *Reprise*
43	WHEREVER, WHENEVER
	Shakira *Epic*
44	SOUTH SIDE
	Moby f/Gwen Stefani *V2*
45	GET UR FREAK ON
	Missy "Misdemeanor" Elliott *Gold Mind*
46	CRAZY FOR THIS GIRL
	Evan & Jaron *Columbia*
47	CRAZY
	K-Ci & JoJo *MCA*
48	TURN OFF THE LIGHT
	Nelly Furtado *DreamWorks*
49	GONE
	'N Sync *Jive*
50	CARAMEL
	City High f/Eve *Booga Basement*
51	WHEN IT'S OVER
	Sugar Ray *Lava*
52	JADED
	Aerosmith *Columbia*
53	SUPERMAN (IT'S NOT EASY)
	Five for Fighting *Aware*
54	IZZO (H.O.V.A.)
	Jay-Z *Roc-a-Fella/Def Jam*
55	I WISH
	R. Kelly *Jive*
56	FIESTA
	R. Kelly f/Jay-Z *Jive*
57	DANCE WITH ME
	Debelah Morgan *NAS*
58	PROMISE
	Jagged Edge *So So Def*
59	I'M LIKE A BIRD
	Nelly Furtado *DreamWorks*
60	E.I.
	Nelly *Universal*
61	MY BABY
	Lil' Romeo *Soulja/No Limit*
62	MISSING YOU
	Case *Def Soul*
63	SUPERWOMAN PT. II
	Lil' Mo f/Fabolous *EastWest*
64	ONE MINUTE MAN
	Missy "Misdemeanor" Elliott *Gold Mind*
65	LOVERBOY
	Mariah Carey *Virgin*
66	DANGER (BEEN SO LONG)
	Mystikal f/Nivea *Jive*
67	I DO!!
	Toya *Arista*
68	NEVER HAD A DREAM COME TRUE
	S Club 7 *A&M*

The members of Lifehouse first got together in Los Angeles even though they were from different parts of the globe—Arizona, Guatemala, and Camarillo, California. Lead singer Jason Wade had lived in a number of different places, including Hong Kong, Seattle, and Portland, Oregon. The band's debut album, *No Name Face,* received critical raves, and a few weeks after its release, the song "Hanging By A Moment" was sitting on top of the Modern Rock Tracks chart. It crossed over to pop radio, and peaked at No. 2 on the Hot 100. A long chart run helped it to become the No. 7 song of 2001.

Orville Richard Burrell was born in Jamaica, and moved to Flatbush, Brooklyn, in New York when he was 18. In 1991, he was a U.S. Marine serving in Kuwait during the Gulf War. Ten years later, he had the best-selling album of 2001 with *Hotshot,* thanks to two No. 1 singles. "It Wasn't Me," which featured Ricardo "Rikrok" Ducent, was No. 8 for the year, while "Angel," which featured Rayvon, was No. 13. "Angel" was based on "Angel Of The Morning," the No. 53 song of 1968 by Merrilee Rush & the Turnabouts, and the No. 34 song of 1981 by Juice Newton. "Angel" also sampled the Steve Miller Band's "The Joker," the No. 10 hit of 1974. "It Wasn't Me" and "Angel" were Shaggy's highest year-end placings, after ranking No. 23 for 1995 with the two-sided hit, "Boombastic" / "In The Summertime."

Christina Aguilera had reached the top of the Hot 100 three times by the time she teamed up with Lil' Kim, Mya, and Pink on a remake of "Lady Marmalade" for the soundtrack to *Moulin Rouge.* Her three partners all made No. 1 for the first time when the song found itself in pole position for five weeks, beating the one-week reign of the Labelle version. That single was the No. 20 title of 1975, giving the new version another edge, as it finished ninth for 2001.

The events of September 11 resulted in a wave of patriotism that swept the U.S. for the rest of the year. A flood of patriotic songs appeared on the charts, but only one ended up on the year-end list. Aaron Tippin's "Where The Stars And Stripes And The Eagle Fly" ranked No. 77. Other songs not specifically recorded in the wake of the terrorist attacks, like Enya's "Only Time" and Enrique Iglesias' "Hero," became emotional anthems and received increased airplay after September 11.

69 **NOBODY WANTS TO BE LONELY**
Ricky Martin w/Christina Aguilera *Columbia*
70 **EMOTION**
Destiny's Child *Columbia*
71 **IRRESISTIBLE**
Jessica Simpson *Columbia*
72 **HEARD IT ALL BEFORE**
Sunshine Anderson *Soulife*
73 **BEAUTIFUL DAY**
U2 *Island*
74 **EVERYWHERE**
Michelle Branch *Maverick*
75 **#1**
Nelly *Priority*
76 **PLAY**
Jennifer Lopez *Epic*
77 **WHERE THE STARS AND STRIPES AND THE EAGLE FLY**
Aaron Tippin *Lyric Street*
78 **THERE YOU'LL BE**
Faith Hill *Warner Bros.*
79 **NO MORE (BABY I'MA DO RIGHT)**
3LW *Nine Lives*
80 **LIQUID DREAMS**
O-Town *J*
81 **AUSTIN**
Blake Shelton *Giant*
82 **STRONGER**
Britney Spears *Jive*
83 **CONTAGIOUS**
The Isley Brothers f/Ronald Isley aka Mr. Biggs *DreamWorks*
84 **I'M A THUG**
Trick Daddy *Slip-N-Slide*
85 **THE SPACE BETWEEN**
Dave Matthews Band *RCA*
86 **YOU ROCK MY WORLD**
Michael Jackson *Epic*
87 **BE LIKE THAT**
3 Doors Down *Republic*
88 **CAN'T DENY IT**
Fabolous f/Nate Dogg *Desert Storm/Elektra*
89 **UGLY**
Bubba Sparxxx *Beat Club*
90 **PURPLE HILLS**
D12 *Shady*
91 **MUSIC**
Erick Sermon f/Marvin Gaye *NY.LA/Def Jam*
92 **LOVE**
Musiq Soulchild *Def Soul*
93 **GET OVER YOURSELF**
Eden's Crush *143/London/Sire*
94 **I WANNA BE BAD**
Willa Ford *Lava*
95 **RAISE UP**
Petey Pablo *Jive*
96 **BIZOUNCE**
Olivia *J*
97 **POP**
'N Sync *Jive*
98 **SOUTHERN HOSPITALITY**
Ludacris *Disturbing tha Peace/Def Jam*
99 **AIN'T NOTHING 'BOUT YOU**
Brooks & Dunn *Arista*
100 **STRANGER IN MY HOUSE**
Tamia *Elektra*

Missy "Misdemeanor" Elliot

2002 WAS THE YEAR President Bush accused Iraq, Iran, and North Korea of forming an "axis of evil"; the Enron scandal resulted in the resignation of CEO Kenneth Lay; and *American Idol* debuted on television.

It was the year of Nelly. The St. Louis rapper born Cornell Haynes, Jr., had two songs in the top four of the year, the first artist to do so since Monica had a pair of songs in the top four of 1998. "Hot In Herre" and "Dilemma" were successive chart-toppers in the summer of 2002, making Nelly the sixth artist in the rock era to replace himself in pole position, following Elvis Presley, the Beatles, Boyz II Men, Puff Daddy, and Ja Rule.

Nelly first appeared on a year-end list in 2000, when "(Hot S**t) Country Grammar" was No. 36 for the year. In 2001, he had four songs on the annual recap, none higher than No. 17, easily making 2002 the best chart year of his career.

"Hot In Herre" was produced by the Neptunes. Chad Hugo and Pharrell Williams based the groove on a No. 1 R&B hit from 1979, "Bustin' Loose" by Chuck Brown & the Soul Searchers. "We like being inspired by old grooves," says Hugo. "We wanted something simple and everything else was up to Nelly." Once the rapper heard the track, it didn't take him long to write the lyrics. "An idea jumped in my head when I heard it," he recalls. "When I hear the beat, I usually get an idea right away." In this case, the lyrical hook suggesting that you "take off all your clothes" helped send the song to No. 1.

The follow-up, "Dilemma," sampled a Patti LaBelle track, "Love, Need And Want You," written by Kenny Gamble and Bunny Sigler. Producers Bam (Antoine Macon) and Ryan Bowser came up with the idea for "Dilemma" while playing Tetris. They were in the studio one night listening to the track they had written when Bam started humming the Gamble-Sigler song. That's when Nelly decided to incorporate the older song into "Dilemma." "Once I heard it, I wanted to do something special with it," says Nelly. "That was the reason we brought Kelly [Rowland] into the picture. I thought getting her on a solo tip as opposed to getting her in the group [Destiny's Child] would be hot."

The No. 2 single of 2002 was also a rap song. Marshall Mathers topped the box office and the Hot 100 with his film *8 Mile* ending up No. 1 its first week in release and the song from the movie, "Lose Yourself," having a 12-week reign on the Hot 100. Director Curtis Hanson wanted a song written from the point of view of Eminem's character. While on location in Detroit, Eminem worked out of a makeshift recording studio in his trailer so he could work on the music while filming the movie.

While Nelly's two songs in the top four is impressive, another artist went him one better, with three songs in the top 10. Even more amazing, they were her first three chart entries. Ashanti Douglas was 14 when she signed to the Jive label. That didn't work out, nor did a deal with an Epic imprint. But Ashanti didn't give up. She was introduced to Murder Inc. founder Irv Gotti, but his label focused on hip-hop and he wasn't interested in an R&B singer. "I was persistent," says Ashanti. She kept showing up at Gotti's studio and his office and he found ways to employ her, whether it was singing on the hook of someone else's record or writing songs. When writer/producer 7 Aurelius was working on a track for Craig David, Ashanti came up with lyrics and recorded the song herself. "Foolish" spent 10 weeks at No. 1 and finished the year in third place. Ashanti also ranked seventh as the featured artist on Fat Joe's "What's Luv?" and ninth as the featured singer on Ja Rule's "Always On Time."

Only two artists who were in the top 10 of 2001 repeated in 2002. Usher, No. 3 in 2001 with "U Got It Bad," was No. 10 in 2002 by virtue of his featured spot on P. Diddy's "I Need A Girl (Part One)." Jennifer Lopez, No. 4 in 2001 with Ja Rule on "I'm Real," teamed up with Ja Rule again and placed fifth with "Ain't It Funny." It really was a repeat performance. Just as there were two very different versions of "I'm Real," there were two different tracks called "Ain't It Funny." Producer Corey Rooney explains, "It worked so well, we needed to do it again." The first version of "Ain't It Funny" was inspired by a movie Lopez starred in, *The Wedding Planner*, although it wasn't used in the film. The second "Ain't It Funny" was created when Ashanti stopped at Irv Gotti's studio and found Ja Rule playing video games when he was supposed to be working on the Lopez track. Ashanti wrote two verses for the song and recorded a demo version. Lopez recorded that song in Los Angeles; in the middle of the session Ashanti was asked to write one more verse. She wrote it over the phone so the recording session could proceed. Lopez had two other songs on the 2002

34 **I'M GONNA BE ALRIGHT**
Jennifer Lopez f/Nas *Epic*

35 **SHE HATES ME**
Puddle of Mudd *Flawless/Geffen*

36 **DON'T LET ME GET ME**
Pink *Arista*

37 **CLEANIN' OUT MY CLOSET**
Eminem *Web/Aftermath*

38 **GIRLFRIEND**
'N Sync f/Nelly *Jive*

39 **ADDICTIVE**
Truth Hurts *Aftermath*

40 **JUST LIKE A PILL**
Pink *Arista*

41 **NOTHIN'**
N.O.R.E *Def Jam*

42 **WASTING MY TIME**
Default *TVT*

43 **HEY BABY**
No Doubt f/Bounty Killer *Interscope*

44 **SOAK UP THE SUN**
Sheryl Crow *A&M*

45 **GIMME THE LIGHT**
Sean Paul *VP*

46 **OOPS (OH MY)**
Tweet *The Gold Mind*

47 **A WOMAN'S WORTH**
Alicia Keys *J*

48 **HEAVEN**
DJ Sammy & Yanou f/Do *Robbins*

49 **MOVE B***H**
Ludacris f/Mystikal & Infamous 2.0 *DTP/Def Jam South*

50 **DOWN 4 U**
Irv Gotti p/the Inc. f/Ja Rule, Ashanti, Charli Baltimore & Vita *Murder Inc./Def Jam*

51 **NO SUCH THING**
John Mayer *Aware*

52 **HAPPY**
Ashanti *Murder, Inc./Def Jam*

53 **CAN'T GET YOU OUT OF MY HEAD**
Kylie Minogue *Capitol*

54 **HALFCRAZY**
Musiq *Def Soul*

55 **LIKE I LOVE YOU**
Justin Timberlake *Jive*

56 **GOTTA GET THRU THIS**
Daniel Bedingfield *Island*

57 **STILL FLY**
Big Tymers *Cash Money*

58 **7 DAYS**
Craig David *Wildstar*

59 **CAN'T FIGHT THE MOONLIGHT**
LeAnn Rimes *Curb*

60 **RAINY DAYZ**
Mary J. Blige f/Ja Rule *MCA*

61 **HELLA GOOD**
No Doubt *Interscope*

62 **PASS THE COURVOISIER PART II**
Busta Rhymes f/P. Diddy & Pharrell *J*

63 **IF I COULD GO!**
Angie Martinez f/Lil' Mo & Sacario *Elektra*

64 **WHAT ABOUT US?**
Brandy *Atlantic*

65 **BUTTERFLIES**
Michael Jackson *Epic*

66 **WHEN THE LAST TIME**
Clipse *Star Trak*

67 **SK8ER BOI** Avril Lavigne *Arista*

recap: "Jenny From The Block" at No. 19 and "I'm Gonna Be Alright" at No. 34.

Pop music made a resurgence in 2002, led by the No. 8 single of the year, "Complicated" by Avril Lavigne. She was just 17 when her debut effort spent two weeks at No. 2 on the Hot 100. Born in Napanee, Ontario, Canada, she started writing songs early and was in the studio when Arista chief L.A. Reid heard her playing and offered her a contract. Lavigne followed "Complicated" with the upbeat "Sk8er Boi" and had another top 10 single and the No. 67 song of 2002.

America was blissfully unaware of a British phenomenon that began October 5, 2001. *Pop Idol* took that country by storm, and by the series' finale, the top two finalists, Will Young and Gareth Gates, were famous all over the United Kingdom. Young won the competition with 4.6 million votes and Gates finished second with 4.1 million votes. Both were signed to recording contracts and both had mega-selling No. 1 singles. Series creator Simon Fuller tried to sell the concept in America and was turned down everywhere, even by the Fox network, until CEO Rupert Murdoch's daughter Elisabeth told her father about *Pop Idol* and suggested he broadcast an American version.

American Idol debuted on June 11, 2002, retaining many of the elements of its British cousin, including acid-tongued judge Simon Cowell, who was joined by recording artist Paula Abdul and music executive Randy Jackson. The 100-plus contestants were whittled down to 30 and then to a top 10. Week after week, finalists were voted off the show by the public until two remained standing. On the season finale, broadcast September 4, Kelly Clarkson and Justin Guarini stood on the stage of the Kodak Theater in Hollywood, waiting for Ryan Seacrest to pronounce one of them the *American Idol.*

One day after being named the winner, Kelly Clarkson was on the radio airwaves. The song she performed on the finale, "A Moment Like This," was shipped the day after the show, but radio stations were already playing the live version from the TV soundtrack. Foreshadowing the impact *American Idol* would have on the *Billboard* charts, Clarkson's "A Moment Like This" rocketed from 52 to 1 on the Hot 100. It was the biggest jump to the top in the chart's history, besting the 38-year-old record held by the Beatles' "Can't Buy Me Love," which zoomed from 27 to 1 in 1964. "A Moment Like This" ended up as the No. 8 song of 2002.

68 **THE WHOLE WORLD**
OutKast f/Killer Mike *Arista*

69 **ESCAPE**
Enrique Iglesias *Interscope*

70 **I LOVE YOU**
Faith Evans *Bad Boy*

71 **DON'TCHANGE**
Musiq *Def Soul*

72 **WE THUGGIN'**
Fat Joe f/R. Kelly *Terror Squad*

73 **UNDERNEATH YOUR CLOTHES**
Shakira *Epic*

74 **I CARE 4 U**
Aaliyah *Blackground*

75 **BABY**
Ashanti *Murder, Inc./Def Jam*

76 **ROLL OUT (MY BUSINESS)**
Ludacris *DTP/Def Jam South*

77 **DIE ANOTHER DAY**
Madonna *Warner Bros.*

78 **MORE THAN A WOMAN**
Aaliyah *Blackground*

79 **DAYS GO BY**
Dirty Vegas *Credence*

80 **LIGHTS, CAMERA, ACTION!**
Mr. Cheeks *Universal*

81 **HERE IS GONE**
Goo Goo Dolls *Warner Bros.*

82 **THUGZ MANSION**
2Pac *Amaru/Death Row*

83 **THE GOOD STUFF**
Kenny Chesney *BNA*

84 **SOMEBODY LIKE YOU**
Keith Urban *Capitol*

85 **NO MORE DRAMA**
Mary J. Blige *MCA*

86 **FULL MOON**
Brandy *Atlantic*

87 **TRADE IT ALL**
Fabolous f/P. Diddy & Jagged Edge *Epic*

88 **DOWN A** CHICK**
Ja Rule f/Charli "Chuck" Baltimore
Murder Inc./Def Jam

89 **GOOD TIMES**
Styles *Ruff Ryders*

90 **HANDS CLEAN**
Alanis Morissette *Maverick*

91 **THESE DAYS**
Rascal Flatts *Lyric Street*

92 **PO' FOLKS**
Nappy Roots f/Anthony Hamilton *Atlantic*

93 **LONG TIME GONE**
Dixie Chicks *Monument*

94 **A NEW DAY HAS COME**
Celine Dion *Epic*

95 **GOODBYE TO YOU**
Michelle Branch *Maverick*

96 **WHY DON'T WE FALL IN LOVE**
Amerie *Rise/Columbia*

97 **SHE'LL LEAVE YOU WITH A SMILE**
George Strait *MCA*

98 **BREAK YA NECK**
Busta Rhymes *J*

99 **STANDING STILL**
Jewel *Atlantic*

100 **COURTESY OF THE RED, WHITE AND BLUE (THE ANGRY AMERICAN)**
Toby Keith *DreamWorks*

The Top 100 Songs of 2003

Chingy

2003 WAS THE YEAR the United States invaded Iraq; Arnold Schwarzenegger was voted governor of California; and on its 28th mission, the space shuttle Columbia broke apart in a ball of fire while re-entering the Earth's atmosphere, killing the seven astronauts aboard.

Destiny's Child never managed to have the No. 1 song of the year, though the trio came close in 2000, when "Independent Women Part I" finished in second place. The first member of the group to top a year-end recap was Kelly Rowland, who was featured on Nelly's "Dilemma," the No. 1 single of 2002. In 2003, it was Beyoncé's turn. "Baby Boy," featuring Sean Paul, ranked No. 1 for the year. Like Nelly in 2002, Beyoncé had two songs in the top four of 2003. "Crazy In Love," featuring Jay-Z, ended up in fourth place. It was the first single from her *Dangerously In Love* album and it had an eight-week run at No. 1. The follow-up, "Baby Boy," lasted one frame longer, reigning for nine weeks.

While Kelly Rowland was featured on the top song of 2002, Beyoncé was the first lead female artist to have the No. 1 song of the year since 1996, when Toni Braxton led the annual recap with "Un-Break My Heart."

The No. 2 single of 2003 was by Curtis Jackson from South Jamaica, Queens, New York. A drug user and dealer by the time he was 12, he borrowed the name 50 Cent from a local thug. "I'm named after a gangster from the Fort Greene projects," he explains. "There was another 50 Cent ahead of me who was running around the street. Me finding success as a rap artist is a dream that's bigger than anything that guy has ever done in his life, but he'll be remembered because of that name."

50 Cent was originally signed to Columbia Records, but he was dropped from the label after he was shot nine times while on his way to a tattoo parlor. He worked on mix tapes for the independent G-Unit imprint and sent tracks to Eminem's manager. In June 2002, Eminem and Dr. Dre signed 50 Cent to Shady/Aftermath. When 50 Cent heard a track that had been discarded as a D-12 song for the *8 Mile* soundtrack, he grabbed a notepad and within an hour had written the verses and choruses for "In Da Club." He recorded most of his vocals that same night. The single ruled the Hot 100 for nine weeks.

The follow-up, "21 Questions," also went to No. 1 and is the No. 11 song of 2003. It samples a Barry White song, "It's Only Love Doing Its Thing," chopped up and transformed into a different melody. The track found its way to Dino Devaille, senior vice president of A&R for Universal Music, who passed it along to 50 Cent. The rapper declared it was a hit record and wrote the words. "I like to write my lyrics to the music. . . . I start with the chorus because . . . that's what it's about."

Rapper 50 Cent had five songs on the 2003 recap. In addition to "In Da Club" and "21 Questions," he was on the tally with his own "P.I.M.P." at No. 26 and "Wanksta" at No. 63. He was also No. 14 with "Magic Stick," billed to Lil' Kim featuring 50 Cent.

The Atlanta-based duo OutKast had its highest-ranked year-end hit yet with "Hey Ya!" at No. 3, outdistancing the No. 22 position of "Ms. Jackson" in 2001. "Ms. Jackson" topped the Hot 100, but "Hey Ya!" was a runaway smash, sitting at No. 1 for nine weeks, just like "Baby Boy" and "In Da Club." Beyoncé wasn't the only artist with two hits in the top five of the 2003 tally. Her guest artist on "Baby Boy," Sean Paul, was also No. 5 with his own hit, "Get Busy." Paul grew up in Kingston listening to the music that his mother loved—ballads by the Beatles, the Carpenters, and Simon and Garfunkel. He heard reggae music on the radio and started writing his own songs as a teenager. He was the first artist born in Jamaica to have the No. 1 song of the year, but not the first to be in the top 10. In 1974, Carl Douglas ranked No. 6 with "Kung Fu Fighting." Some 20 years later, Ini Kamoze had the No. 9 song of 1994, "Here Comes The Hotstepper." And in 2001, Shaggy and featured artist Ricardo "RikRok" Ducent were No. 8 with "It Wasn't Me."

Nelly, fresh from finishing first and fourth the year before with "Dilemma" and "Hot In Herre," respectively, was back in the annual top 10 with a song from the soundtrack to *Bad Boys II*. "Shake Ya Tailfeather," recorded with P. Diddy and Murphy Lee, was No. 6 for the year. Diddy was also in the top 10 for the second year in a row; he had the No. 10 song of 2002 with "I Need A Girl (Part One)," recorded with Usher and Loon. Diddy was also No. 13 for 2003, thanks to his collaboration with B2K on "Bump, Bump, Bump." "I Need A Girl" and "Bump, Bump, Bump" made 2003 the best chart year for Diddy since 1997, when he was still Puff Daddy. He had the No. 3 song that year, "I'll Be Missing You," with Faith Evans and 112, and the No. 4 song, "Mo Money Mo Problems," with the Notorious B.I.G.

Making an appearance in the year-end top 10 for the third consecutive year was Jennifer Lopez, No. 10 with "All I Have," a song that featured LL Cool J. In 2002, Lopez and Ja Rule were No. 5 with "Ain't It Funny." One year earlier, they were No. 4 with "I'm Real." Teaming with Lopez in 2003 gave LL Cool J his first year-end top 10 hit. He ranked No. 30 in 2002 with "Luv U Better," No. 26 in 1996 with "Loungin," and No. 13 in 1995 with "Hey Lover."

R. Kelly equaled his highest year-end position by placing eighth with "Ignition." He had also been No. 8 in 1994 with "Bump N' Grind." In 1998, his duet with Celine Dion, "I'm Your Angel," ranked ninth. In addition to "Ignition," Kelly was also No. 42 for 2003 with "Step In The Name Of Love," No. 54 with "Thoia Thong," and No. 84 with "Snake," which featured Big Tigger.

Kelly Clarkson had finished the previous year in 18th place with her debut single, "A Moment Like This," the first song by an *American Idol* finalist to appear on a year-end chart. In the second year of the series, the highest-ranked *Idol* song was by that season's runner-up, Clay Aiken. The native of Raleigh, North Carolina, had the No. 39 single of the year with his debut release, "This Is The Night." The song had been written for the first season of the series at a songwriting camp run by Desmond Child. During one session, songwriters Aldo Nova, Gary Burr, and Chris Braide teamed up and wrote the song based on a melody composed by Nova. Clive Davis, head of RCA and J, assigned "This Is The Night" to top four finalists Aiken and Josh Gracin. Gracin was voted off, and Aiken sang "This Is The Night" on the season finale.

At the same time, Davis assigned another song to top four finalists Ruben Studdard and Kimberley Locke. When Locke was voted off, Studdard sang "Flying Without Wings" on the season finale. A remake of a song by Irish boy band Westlife, "Flying Without Wings" finished 2003 as song No. 58. Clarkson was also on the year-end chart with No. 49, "Miss Independent."

66 **IF YOU'RE NOT THE ONE**
Daniel Bedingfield *Island*

67 **IT'S FIVE O'CLOCK SOMEWHERE**
Alan Jackson & Jimmy Buffett *Arista*

68 **HARDER TO BREATHE**
Maroon5 *Octone/J*

69 **ANGEL**
Amanda Perez *Powerhouse*

70 **INTUITION**
Jewel *Atlantic*

71 **LIKE GLUE**
Sean Paul *VP*

72 **STUNT 101**
G-Unit *G-Unit*

73 **WAT DA HOOK GON BE**
Murphy Lee f/Jermaine Dupri *Fo' Reel*

74 **HELL YEAH**
Ginuwine f/Baby *Epic*

75 **DON'T WANNA TRY**
Frankie J *Columbia*

76 **RUNNIN (DYING TO LIVE)**
Tupac f/the Notorious B.I.G. *Amaru*

77 **CHANGE CLOTHES**
Jay-Z *Roc-A-Fella/Def Jam*

78 **19 SOMETHIN'**
Mark Wills *Mercury*

79 **CAN'T STOP, WON'T STOP**
Young Gunz *Roc-A-Fella/Def Jam*

80 **THE REMEDY (I WON'T WORRY)**
Jason Mraz *Elektra*

81 **FAMILY PORTRAIT**
Pink *Arista*

82 **SING FOR THE MOMENT**
Eminem *Web/Aftermath*

83 **SUPERMAN**
Eminem *Web/Aftermath*

84 **SNAKE**
R. Kelly f/Big Tigger *Jive*

85 **LET'S GET DOWN**
Chingy *Capitol*

86 **FIGHTER**
Christina Aguilera *RCA*

87 **FOREVER AND FOR ALWAYS**
Shania Twain *Mercury*

88 **BEER FOR MY HORSES**
Toby Keith w/Willie Nelson *DreamWorks*

89 **WHAT WAS I THINKIN'**
Dirks Bentley *Capitol*

90 **ALL THE THINGS SHE SAID**
t.A.t.U. *Interscope*

91 **HAVE YOU FORGOTTEN?**
Darryl Worley *DreamWorks*

92 **LIFESTYLES OF THE RICH AND FAMOUS**
Good Charlotte *Daylight*

93 **I WANT YOU**
Thalia f/Fat Joe *EMI Televisa*

94 **MY FRONT PORCH LOOKING IN**
Lonestar *BNA*

95 **SICK OF BEING LONELY**
Field Mob *MCA*

96 **PUT THAT WOMAN FIRST**
Jaheim *Divine Mil*

97 **BRIGHT LIGHTS**
matchbox twenty *Atlantic*

98 **SAY YES** Floetry *Soljaz/Dr*

99 **THE BOYS OF SUMMER**
The Ataris *Columbia*

100 **STACY'S MOM**
Fountains of Wayne *S-Curve*

The Top 100 Hits of 2004

Alicia Keys

2004 WAS THE YEAR Martha Stewart was convicted of lying to federal investigators about selling stock in the drug company ImClone; the Olympics returned home to Athens, Greece; and an undersea earthquake near Indonesia triggered a giant tsunami that killed over 125,000 people.

The Hot 100 was all about the House of Usher in 2004. The Atlanta resident dominated the charts with four different No. 1 singles that kept his name on top of the Hot 100 for 28 weeks. On the year-end recap, Usher held down the top two spots, the first artist to do so since the Beatles in 1964. "Yeah!" landed in first place for 2004 and "Burn" was the runner-up.

Usher had never previously scored the top single of the year, or even the second-best single of the year. He had appeared in the year-end top 10s of 2002 (No. 10 with "I Need A Girl (Part One)"), 2001 (No. 3 with "U Got It Bad"), 1998 (No. 8 with "Nice & Slow"), and 1997 (No. 7 with "You Make Me Wanna. . .").

Usher had two more hits in the top 10: "My Boo," a duet with Alicia Keys, was No. 5, and "Confessions Part II" was No. 9. That made Usher the first artist to have three songs in the annual top five since Elvis Presley, who did it in 1956 (No. 1 with "Don't Be Cruel" / "Hound Dog," No. 3 with "Love Me Tender," and No. 4 with "Heartbreak Hotel") and 1957 (No. 2 with "Jailhouse Rock" / "Treat Me Nice," No. 3 with "All Shook Up," and No. 4 with "(Let Me Be Your) Teddy Bear"). Usher was also the first artist to have four songs in the year-end top 10 since the Beatles in 1964 (No. 1 with "I Want To Hold Your Hand," No. 2 with "She Loves You," No. 6 with "Can't Buy Me Love," and No. 10 with "I Feel Fine").

Usher was represented in the year-end top 10 with solo work, a duet, and a song where he was one of three artists. The duet, "My Boo," brought Alicia Keys back into the year-end top five for the first time since her debut single, "Fallin'," was No. 5 for 2001. "My Boo" was the first duet by two stars with equal billing to make the year-end top five since Brandy & Monica had the No. 2 hit of 1998, "The Boy Is Mine."

Billed to Usher featuring Lil Jon & Ludacris, "Yeah!" was the first year-end No. 1 by three people since 2000, when "Maria Maria" by Santana featuring the Product G&B was the top single of the year. "Yeah!" was the first No. 1 song of the year by three individual artists.

"Yeah!" and "Burn" made an unusual pairing by both being one-word titles, making 2004 only the second year in the rock era to have two one-word titles end up in the top two slots of the year. This wordplay at the top of the annual recap first happened in 1987, when George Michael was No. 1 with "Faith" and "Heart" was No. 2 with "Alone."

By teaming with Usher, the featured artists on "Yeah!" both had their highest rankings on a year-end tally. Ludacris had earned a slot in the top 10 of 2003 with "Stand Up." Lil Jon just missed the 2003 top 10; he had the No. 11 song of the year with "Get Low." On the 2004 recap, Ludacris appeared again at No. 47 with "Splash Waterfalls." Lil Jon was also featured on Trick Daddy's "Let's Go" at No. 44 and on the Ying Yang Twins' "Salt Shaker" at No. 61. Lil Jon was also No. 86 with his own hit, "What U Gon' Do."

Aside from Ludacris, two other artists from the top 10 of 2003 encored in the top 10 of 2004. OutKast, No. 3 in 2003 with "Hey Ya!" was No. 3 again with the B-side, "The Way You Move." P. Diddy, No. 6 in 2003, was No. 8 in 2004 with "I Don't Wanna Know." Diddy was the only artist in the 2004 top 10 who had a top 10 listing three years in a row. In 2002, he was No. 10 with "I Need A Girl (Part One)." On "I Don't Wanna Know," Diddy was supporting lead artist Mario Winans, as was Irish singer/composer Enya. She was billed because one of her songs was sampled, but that was good enough to place her in the year-end top 10 for the first time. In 2001, she was No. 42 for the year with "Only Time," her only other single to appear on a year-end chart.

35 **WALKED OUTTA HEAVEN**
Jagged Edge *Columbia*

36 **WHITE FLAG**
Dido *Arista*

37 **IT'S MY LIFE**
No Doubt *Interscope*

38 **DIP IT LOW**
Christina Milian *Island*

39 **NUMB**
Linkin Park *Warner Bros.*

40 **HOTEL**
Cassidy f/R. Kelly *Full Surface/J*

41 **PIECES OF ME**
Ashlee Simpson *Geffen*

42 **OVERNIGHT CELEBRITY**
Twista *Atlantic*

43 **JESUS WALKS**
Kanye West *Roc-A-Fella/Def Jam*

44 **LET'S GO**
Trick Daddy f/Lil Jon & T *Slip-N-Slide*

45 **LEAVE (GET OUT)**
JoJo *Da Family/Blackground*

46 **LOCKED UP**
Akon f/Styles P. *SRC/Universal*

47 **SPLASH WATERFALLS**
Ludacris *DTP/Def Jam*

48 **READ YOUR MIND**
Avant *Magic Johnson*

49 **WONDERFUL**
Ja Rule f/R. Kelly & Ashanti *The Inc./Def Jam*

50 **WITH YOU**
Jessica Simpson *Columbia*

51 **MY HAPPY ENDING**
Avril Lavigne *RCA*

52 **TOXIC**
Britney Spears *Jive*

53 **ON FIRE**
Lloyd Banks *G-Unit*

54 **I LIKE THAT**
Houston f/Chingy, Nate Dogg *Capitol*

55 **ONE THING**
Finger Eleven *Wind-up*

56 **OYE MI CANTO**
N.O.R.E. f/Daddy Yankee, Nina Sky, Big Mato & Gem Star *Roc-A-Fella/Def Jam*

57 **ALL FALLS DOWN**
Kanye West f/Syleena Johnson
Roc-A-Fella/Def Jam

58 **MEANT TO LIVE**
Switchfoot *Red Ink*

59 **ON THE WAY DOWN**
Ryan Cabrera *E.V.L.A.*

60 **SORRY 2004**
Ruben Studdard *J*

61 **SALT SHAKER**
Ying Yang Twins f/Lil Jon *ColliPark*

62 **I'M STILL IN LOVE WITH YOU**
Sean Paul f/Sasha *VP*

63 **MY BAND**
D12 *Shady*

64 **JUST LOSE IT**
Eminem *Shady/Aftermath*

65 **CHARLENE**
Anthony Hamilton *So So Def*

66 **DARE YOU TO MOVE**
Switchfoot *Columbia*

67 **ROSES**
OutKast *LaFace*

Making his first appearance in a year-end top 10 was Snoop Dogg, No. 7 with "Drop It Like It's Hot." The Long Beach, California–born rapper first showed up in a year-end recap in 1994, when he was No. 57 with "Gin And Juice" and No. 88 with "What's My Name." Prior to "Drop It Like It's Hot," he had his two highest-ranked year-end singles in 2003, when he was featured on Chingy's "Holidae Inn" at No. 28 and had his own "Beautiful" at No. 50.

Finishing the year at No. 12 was "The Reason" by Hoobastank on the Island label. This was the first time the imprint had been in the top 30 portion of the year-end chart since 1994, when "I'm The Only One" by Melissa Etheridge was No. 27. Hoobastank gave Island its best year-end placement since U2 was No. 8 in 1987 with "With Or Without You."

Members of Destiny's Child had the No. 1 songs of 2002 and 2003 ("Dilemma" by Nelly featuring Kelly Rowland and "Baby Boy" by Beyoncé featuring Sean Paul), but the group itself hadn't made a year-end appearance since 2001, when "Survivor" was No. 12. After doing some solo work, the trio reunited in 2004 and came in at No. 17 with "Lose My Breath." Beyoncé was back, too, at No. 21 with "Naughty Girl" and No. 34 with "Me, Myself And I." Sean Paul was also back, without Beyoncé. With Sasha as featured artist, Paul was No. 62 with "I'm Still In Love With You."

The highest-ranked remake of 2004 was Sheryl Crow's "The First Cut Is The Deepest," at No. 29, which had originally been recorded by its songwriter, Cat Stevens. Rod Stewart released a single version in 1977, but it didn't rank on that year's top 100. The last time Crow was on a year-end chart was 2002, when she had the No. 44 song of the year, "Soak Up The Sun." Her highest placing was in 1994, when "All I Wanna Do" finished at No. 11.

A sister act occupied three spots on the 2004 chart. Jessica Simpson had already racked up three year-end hits: She was No. 24 in 1999 with "I Wanna Love You Forever," No. 80 in 2000 with "I Think I'm In Love With You," and No. 71 in 2001 with "Irresistible." In 2004, she ranked No. 50 with "With You" and No. 92 with "Take My Breath Away." But she was trumped by younger sister Ashlee Simpson, who landed at No. 41 with "Pieces Of Me."

American Idol was responsible for three hits on the 2004 summary. Kelly Clarkson, who was No. 18 in 2002 with "A Moment Like This," just missed equaling that mark by coming in at No. 19 with "Breakaway," from the soundtrack to *The Princess Diaries 2*. Ruben Studdard was No. 60 with "Sorry 2004," and newly-crowned Fantasia, winner of the series' third season, was No. 78 with her debut single, "I Believe."

68 **WHY?**
Jadakiss f/Anthony Hamilton *Ruff Ryders*
69 **GAME OVER (FLIP)**
Lil' Flip *Sucka Free*
70 **GIGOLO**
Nick Cannon f/R. Kelly *Nick/Jive*
71 **F**K IT (I DON'T WANT YOU BACK)**
Eamon *Jive*
72 **HEADSPRUNG**
LL Cool J *Def Jam*
73 **GO D.J.**
Lil Wayne *Cash Money*
74 **THROUGH THE WIRE**
Kanye West *Roc-A-Fella/Def Jam*
75 **EVERYTIME**
Britney Spears *Jive*
76 **BREATHE**
Fabolous *Desert Storm*
77 **U SHOULD'VE KNOWN BETTER**
Monica *J*
78 **I BELIEVE**
Fantasia *J*
79 **BROKEN**
Seether f/Amy Lee *Wind-up*
80 **HAPPY PEOPLE**
R. Kelly *Jive*
81 **WANNA GET TO KNOW YOU**
G-Unit f/Joe *G-Unit*
82 **BREAKING THE HABIT**
Linkin Park *Warner Bros.*
83 **LET'S GET IT STARTED**
The Black Eyed Peas *A&M*
84 **SOUTHSIDE**
Lloyd f/Ashanti *The Inc./Def Jam*
85 **BALLA BABY**
Chingy *Capitol*
86 **WHAT U GON' DO**
Lil Jon & the East Side Boyz *BME*
87 **HUSH**
LL Cool J f/7 Aurelius *Def Jam*
88 **BREATHE, STRETCH, SHAKE**
Mase f/P. Diddy *Bad Boy*
89 **DON'T TELL ME**
Avril Lavigne *Arista*
90 **SO SEXY**
Twista f/R. Kelly *Atlantic*
91 **SHORTY WANNA RIDE**
Young Buck *G-Unit*
92 **TAKE MY BREATH AWAY**
Jessica Simpson *Columbia*
93 **REDNECK WOMAN**
Gretchen Wilson *Epic*
94 **HEY MAMA**
The Black Eyed Peas *A&M*
95 **BABY IT'S YOU**
JoJo f/Bow Wow *Da Family/Blackground*
96 **1985**
Bowling for Soup *Silvertone*
97 **REMEMBER WHEN**
Alan Jackson *Arista*
98 **U MAKE ME WANNA**
Jadakiss f/Mariah Carey *Ruff Ryders*
99 **LETTERS FROM HOME**
John Michael Montgomery *Warner Bros.*
100 **WHEN THE SUN GOES DOWN**
Kenny Chesney & Uncle Kracker *BNA*

The Top 100 Hits of 2005

Lifehouse

2005 WAS THE YEAR Hurricane Katrina devastated New Orleans and the federal government was criticized for its slow response to the disaster; Pope John Paul II died and a cloud of white smoke signaled the election of Cardinal Joseph Ratzinger as the 265th Pope; and Prince Charles married Camilla Parker Bowles in a civil ceremony.

The biggest chart story of the year was the triumphant return of Mariah Carey. After a long successful run on Columbia Records, Carey's chart fortunes had flagged and she left the label for a new home at Virgin Records. After recording one hit single, "Loverboy," and the soundtrack to the film *Glitter*, Carey was once again shopping for a new label. She signed with Island in 2002 and was given her own imprint, MonarC. Her album *The Emancipation Of Mimi* was released on Island. The first single, "It's Like That," performed well enough to rank No. 66 on the year-end recap. But the follow-up sent Carey back into the stratosphere. "We Belong Together" was No. 1 for 14 weeks on the Hot 100 and finished the year in first place. It was Carey's second time on top of the year-end survey; she had the No. 1 song of 1995, "One Sweet Day," recorded with Boyz II Men. Carey was also No. 11 for 2005 with "Shake It Off" and No. 19 with "Don't Forget About Us." It was the first time in her career that Carey had three songs in the year-end top 20.

Carey's first single, "Vision Of Love," was the No. 4 song of 1990, and the follow-up, "Love Takes Time," finished one place higher. Carey went on to score at least one song in the year-end top 20 for every year of the decade. In 1991 she was No. 8 with "Emotions"; in 1992 she was No. 15 with her remake of the Jackson 5's "I'll Be There"; in 1993 she was No. 3 with "Dreamlover" and No. 8 with "Hero"; in 1994 she was No. 14 with the double-sided hit "Without You" / "Never Forget You"; in 1995 she was No. 4 with "Fantasy" (in addition to being No. 1 with "One Sweet Day"); in 1996 she was No. 6 with "Always Be My Baby"; in 1997 she was No. 17 with "Honey"; in 1998 she was No. 15 with "My All"; and in 1999 she was No. 18 with "Heartbreaker." After that, she didn't return to the year-end top 20 until 2003, when her duet with Busta Rhymes, "I Know What You Like," was No. 20.

Maybe the folks at Virgin weren't happy with Carey's short tenure on their label, but the Island people had to be thrilled. "We Belong Together" gave the imprint its first No. 1 single of the year. In 2004, Island had its second-best showing to that date when Hoobastank had the No. 12 song with "The Reason." Island's only previous top 10 finish before Carey was in 1987 when U2 had the No. 8 song, "With Or Without You."

In 2004, Kanye West and Jamie Foxx just missed being in the year-end top 10. As featured artists on Twista's "Slow Jamz," they ranked No. 11. West was also No. 43 with "Jesus Walks," No. 57 with "All Falls Down," and No. 74 with "Through The Wire." So being No. 2 for the year with "Gold Digger" was a new high point for both West and Foxx. Oscar winner Foxx was the first actor ever to finish in the top two on a year-end summary. Many singers who also acted had done so, including Elvis Presley, Pat Boone, Lulu, Diana Ross, and Whitney Houston, but Foxx was the first actor who also sang to accomplish this.

Gwen Stefani stepped out of her role as lead singer of No Doubt to record a solo album that was laden with hits. "Hollaback Girl" was the No. 5 song of the year, the highest placing to date for either Stefani or No Doubt. In 2001, Stefani showed up twice on the annual recap, both times under her own name. She was featured on Eve's "Let Me Blow Your Mind" at No. 15 and Moby's "South Side" at No. 44. No Doubt first appeared on a year-end survey in 1996, when "Just A Girl" was No. 84. The group scored three hits in 2002: "Underneath It All" was No. 17, "Hey Baby" was No. 43, and "Hella Good" was No. 61. In 2004, No Doubt's remake of Talk Talk's "It's My Life" was No. 37. "Hollaback Girl" was just one of four Stefani songs on the 2005 report. "Rich Girl," recorded with Eve, was No. 43. "Cool" was No. 75, and "Luxurious" was No. 90.

Although they released their first album on Reprise in 1994, Green Day had never appeared on a year-end recap of the Hot 100 until 2005, because the label didn't release any singles by the band until the title track

34 FEEL GOOD INC
Gorillaz *Parlophone*
35 MR. BRIGHTSIDE
The Killers *Island*
36 LET ME HOLD YOU
Bow Wow f/Omarion *Columbia*
37 SWITCH
Will Smith *Overbrook*
38 STICKWITU
The Pussycat Dolls *A&M*
39 WAKE ME UP WHEN SEPTEMBER ENDS
Green Day *Reprise*
40 LONELY
Akon *SRC*
41 LISTEN TO YOUR HEART
D.H.T. *Robbins*
42 WE BE BURNIN'
Sean Paul *VP*
43 RICH GIRL
Gwen Stefani f/Eve *Interscope*
44 I DON'T WANT TO BE
Gavin DeGraw *J*
45 I'M SPRUNG
T-Pain *Konvict Muzik/Jive*
46 HOLIDAY
Green Day *Reprise*
47 STAY FLY
Three 6 Mafia f/Young Buck & Eightball & MJG *Hypnotize Minds*
48 CAUGHT UP
Usher *LaFace*
49 INSIDE YOUR HEAVEN
Carrie Underwood *RCA*
50 GRIND WITH ME
Pretty Ricky *Atlantic*
51 SPEED OF SOUND
Coldplay *Capitol*
52 GET BACK
Ludacris *DTP/Def Jam*
53 I THINK THEY LIKE ME
Dem Franchize Boyz f/Jermaine Dupri, Da Brat & Bow Wow *So So Def*
54 BRING EM OUT
T.I. *Grand Hustle*
55 SCARS
Papa Roach *El Tonal*
56 SOME CUT
Trillville f/Cutty *BME*
57 SUGAR (GIMME SOME)
Trick Daddy f/Ludacris, Lil' Kim & Cee-Lo *Slip-N-Slide*
58 PLAY
David Banner *SRC*
59 PIMPIN' ALL OVER THE WORLD
Ludacris f/Bobby Valentino *DTP/Def Jam*
60 SLOW DOWN
Bobby Valentino *DTP/Def Jam*
61 GET IT POPPIN'
Fat Joe f/Nelly *Terror Squad*
62 MOCKINGBIRD
Eminem *Shady/Aftermath*
63 HUNG UP
Madonna *Warner Bros.*
64 LET ME GO
3 Doors Down *Universal*
65 YOUR BODY
Pretty Ricky *Atlantic*
66 IT'S LIKE THAT
Mariah Carey *Island*

of the *American Idiot* album was issued in 2004. That song stalled at No. 61, but the follow-up gave Green Day its first bona fide Hot 100 hit. "Boulevard Of Broken Dreams" soared to No. 2 on the weekly chart and ranked No. 8 for the year. Green Day repeated at No. 39 with "Wake Me Up When September Ends" and No. 46 with "Holiday."

The A&M label scored its first year-end hit in 1962 when "The Lonely Bull" by The Tijuana Brass featuring Herb Alpert was No. 50. A&M had a top 10 single of the year for the first time in 1968, with Alpert's "This Guy's In Love With You," which sat at No. 8. The first year-end top five hit was "(They Long To Be) Close To You," No. 5 for the Carpenters in 1970. Captain and Tennille had the No. 2 song of 1975, "Love Will Keep Us Together." In 1983, the Police gave A&M the No. 1 single of the year with "Every Breath You Take." But the label didn't place two songs in the year-end top 10 until 1991, when Bryan Adams was No. 1 with "(Everything I Do) I Do It For You" and Amy Grant was No. 10 with "Baby Baby." A&M didn't pull off that double again until 2005, when the label's two best-selling groups of the year ended up in ninth and tenth place. The Black Eyed Peas scored their highest year-end posting yet, with "My Humps" at No. 9. The Pussycat Dolls and featured guest Busta Rhymes were No. 10 with "Don't Cha."

After an absence of two years, Madonna was back on the year-end recap. Based on a sample of Abba's "Gimme! Gimme! Gimme! (A Man After Midnight)," "Hung Up" was No. 63 for 2005. It was Madonna's first appearance on the year-end chart since she had the No. 77 song of 2002, the James Bond theme "Die Another Day."

For the fourth year in a row, *American Idol* had an impact on the annual accounting of hits. This time, the *Idol* franchise had its highest-ranked song to date, as Kelly Clarkson's "Since U Been Gone" came in at No. 12. That beat the previous record, also set by Clarkson. Her debut single, "A Moment Like This," ranked No. 18 for 2002.

Clarkson had two more hits on the year-end chart, both in the top 30. "Because Of You" was No. 21, while "Behind These Hazel Eyes" was No. 26. Clarkson's three entries were just half of the *Idol* story for 2005, the fourth season for the hit series. Carrie Underwood was No. 49 with "Inside Your Heaven." Her closest competitor, runner-up Bo Bice, was No. 86 with the same song. And third-season winner Fantasia returned, settling in at No. 79 with "Truth Is." That was just one rank lower than her No. 78 hit of 2004, "I Believe."

67 **HERE WE GO**
Trina f/Kelly Rowland *Slip-N-Slide*

68 **DAUGHTERS**
John Mayer *Aware*

69 **KARMA**
Alicia Keys *J*

70 **ONLY U**
Ashanti *The Inc./Def Jam*

71 **GOIN' CRAZY**
Natalie *Latium/Universal*

72 **GIRL TONITE**
Twista f/Trey Songz *Atlantic*

73 **BEAUTIFUL SOUL**
Jesse McCartney *Hollywood*

74 **CATER 2 U**
Destiny's Child *Columbia*

75 **COOL**
Gwen Stefani *Interscope*

76 **WAIT (THE WHISPER SONG)**
Ying Yang Twins *ColliPark*

77 **NUMB/ENCORE**
Jay-Z/Linkin Park *Roc-A-Fella/Def Jam*

78 **1 THING**
Amerie *Columbia*

79 **TRUTH IS**
Fantasia *J*

80 **TRUE**
Ryan Cabrera *E.V.L.A.*

81 **INCOMPLETE**
Backstreet Boys *Jive*

82 **WHEN I'M GONE**
Eminem *Shady/Aftermath*

83 **BEST OF YOU**
Foo Fighters *Roswell/RCA*

84 **THESE WORDS**
Natasha Bedingfield *Epic*

85 **GET RIGHT**
Jennifer Lopez *Epic*

86 **INSIDE YOUR HEAVEN**
Bo Bice *RCA*

87 **DON'T LIE**
The Black Eyed Peas *A&M*

88 **KARMA**
Lloyd Banks f/Avant *G-Unit*

89 **COLLIDE**
Howie Day *Epic*

90 **LUXURIOUS**
Gwen Stefani *Interscope*

91 **OUTTA CONTROL (REMIX)**
50 Cent f/Mobb Deep *Shady/Aftermath*

92 **U DON'T KNOW ME**
T.I. *Grand Hustle*

93 **GIRLFIGHT**
Brooke Valentine f/Lil Jon & Big Boi *Subliminal*

94 **JUST THE GIRL**
The Click Five *Lava*

95 **NUMBER ONE SPOT**
Ludacris *DTP/Def Jam*

96 **BABY I'M BACK**
Baby Bash f/Akon *Latium/Universal*

97 **BOYFRIEND**
Ashlee Simpson *Geffen*

98 **WINDOW SHOPPER**
50 Cent *G-Unit*

99 **BACK THEN**
Mike Jones *Swishahouse*

100 **LA TORTURA**
Shakira f/Alejandro Sanz *Epic*

Justin Timberlake

2006 WAS THE YEAR the Democrats recaptured the House and the Senate in the midterm elections; "Crocodile Hunter" Steve Irwin was killed while shooting a TV special off the Great Barrier Reef in Australia; and North Korea conducted an underground test of a nuclear weapon.

For only the fourth time in the rock era, a Canadian artist had the No. 1 song of the year (after Percy Faith in 1960 with "Theme From 'A Summer Place'," Bryan Adams in 1991 with "(Everything I Do) I Do It For You," and Nickelback in 2001 with "How You Remind Me"). Born in Victoria, British Columbia, Nelly Furtado took a very different turn with her music in 2006 by teaming up with writer/producer Timbaland. Their collaboration on "Promiscuous" took Furtado higher on the Hot 100 than she had ever traveled before: She went all the way to No. 1 on the weekly chart and finished in first place for the year. Furtado's previous efforts had registered on the year-end list; her "I'm Like A Bird" was No. 59 for 2001 and the follow-up, "Turn Off The Light," ranked even higher that year, at No. 48.

Furtado was not the only Canadian in the year-end top 10. Right below her, at No. 2, was another British Columbian, newcomer Daniel Powter, with a song that struggled to become a hit in America. "Bad Day" had been an international success after it was heard in a Coca-Cola commercial, but the spot hadn't played in the United States. "Bad Day" needed some media exposure to help it along. Kris Lythgoe, son of *American*

Idol executive producer Nigel Lythgoe, suggested the song as exit music for contestants on the popular Fox TV series. When Powter's music publisher asked him for permission, he said no—at first. Wisely, he changed his mind and that sent "Bad Day" soaring up the Hot 100, all the way to the penthouse, where it stayed for five weeks.

The Furtado-Powter combination marked the first time that Canadians held down the top two slots on a year-end chart. And with Kingston, Jamaica, native Sean Paul in third place with "Temperature," it was the first time in the rock era that the top three positions were all held by international artists (granted, Nelly Furtado's guest artist, Timbaland, was born in Norfolk, Virginia).

Timbaland was also involved with another artist in the top 10 of 2006, Justin Timberlake. The former Mouseketeer first showed up in an annual tally in 1998, when 'N Sync's "I Want You Back" was the No. 38 song of the year. In 1999, 'N Sync was on the recap twice: at No. 53 with "God Must Have Spent A Little More Time On You" and No. 63 with "Music Of My Heart," recorded with Gloria Estefan. Then, 2000 was a banner year for the quintet, with three songs in the year-end top 40: "It's Gonna Be Me" at No. 22, "Bye Bye Bye" at No. 31, and "This I Promise You" at No. 37. In 2001, 'N Sync was No. 49 with "Gone" and No. 97 with "Pop." In 2002, 'N Sync had its final year-end entry, "Girlfriend," recorded with Nelly, at No. 38. And Timberlake had his first year-end listing on his own, coming in at No. 55 with "Like I Love You." In 2003, Timberlake had two songs on the year-end report: "Cry Me A River" at No. 37 and "Rock Your Body" at No. 46. So, no top 10 year-end listings for Timberlake —yet. In 2006, Justin finished the year in fourth place with his biggest hit to date, "SexyBack." He was also No. 16 with "My Love," recorded with T.I.

None of the artists who were in the year-end top 10 for 2005 repeated in 2006. There were also no repeats from the year-end top 10 of 2004. One would have to go back to the top 10 of 2003 to find artists who also showed up in the top 10 of 2006. Beyoncé was back, once again with two titles in the top 10. Her solo effort, "Irreplaceable," was No. 5 and her single featuring Slim Thug, "Check On It," was right behind at No. 6.

The artist sitting in eighth place is almost an anomaly. James Blunt was the first British male solo performer to have a year-end top 10 hit since 1997, when Elton John was No. 1 with "Candle In The Wind 1997" / "Something About The Way You Look Tonight." Blunt, born in Tidworth, Wiltshire, England, served in Kosovo as a member of the British Army before he turned to a recording career. "You're Beautiful" topped the U.K. singles chart and spread to Europe before finally becoming a hit in the United States, where it also flew to No. 1.

After making several year-end appearances with the Black Eyed Peas, Fergie appeared on the 2006 survey on her own. Her "London Bridge" ranked 13th, not quite as high as the Black Eyed Peas' 2005 hit, "My Humps," which placed ninth.

Two artists on the 2006 tally made their first year-end appearances with virtually the same song. Rapper Chamillionaire, from Houston, Texas, with featured artist Krayzie Bone, was No. 15 with "Ridin'." And "Weird Al" Yankovic, who had been making parody recordings for years, had his

35	LEAN WIT IT, ROCK WIT IT
	Dem Franchize Boyz f/Lil *So So Def*
36	SNAP YO FINGERS
	Lil Jon f/E-40 & Sean Paul *BME*
37	ONE WISH
	Ray J *Knockout*
38	(WHEN YOU GONNA) GIVE IT UP TO ME
	Sean Paul f/Keyshia Cole *VP*
39	DIRTY LITTLE SECRET
	The All-American Rejects *Doghouse*
40	MS. NEW BOOTY
	Bubba Sparxxx f/Ying Yang Twins *New South*
41	THERE IT GO! (THE WHISTLE SONG)
	Juelz Santana *Diplomats*
42	UNFAITHFUL
	Rihanna *SRP/Def Jam*
43	AIN'T NO OTHER MAN
	Christina Aguilera *RCA*
44	CALL ME WHEN YOU'RE SOBER
	Evanescence *Wind-up*
45	SAVIN' ME
	Nickelback *Roadrunner*
46	TOO LITTLE TOO LATE
	JoJo *Da Family/Blackground*
47	EVERYTIME WE TOUCH
	Cascada *Robbins*
48	YO (EXCUSE ME MISS)
	Chris Brown *Jive*
49	SAY GOODBYE
	Chris Brown *Jive*
50	SEXY LOVE
	Ne-Yo *Def Jam*
51	WHERE'D YOU GO
	Fort Minor f/Holly Brook *Machine*
52	SHOW STOPPER
	Danity Kane *Bad Boy*
53	SHORTIE LIKE MINE
	Bow Wow f/Chris Brown & Johnta Austin *Columbia*
54	WALK AWAY
	Kelly Clarkson *RCA*
55	GET UP
	Ciara f/Chamillionaire *LaFace/Jive*
56	I'M N LUV (WIT A STRIPPER)
	T-Pain f/Mike Jones *Konvict M*
57	UNPREDICTABLE
	Jamie Foxx f/Ludacris *J*
58	DO IT TO IT
	Cherish f/Sean Paul of the Youngbloodz *Sho'Nuff*
59	BEFORE HE CHEATS
	Carrie Underwood *Arista*
60	BOSSY
	Kelis f/Too $hort *Jive*
61	WALK IT OUT
	Unk *Big Oomp*
62	PULLIN' ME BACK
	Chingy f/Tyrese *Slot-A-Lot*
63	BLACK HORSE & THE CHERRY TREE
	KT Tunstall *Relentless*
64	I KNOW YOU SEE IT
	Yung Joc f/Brandy "Ms. B." *Block/Bad Boy*
65	SO WHAT
	Field Mob f/Ciara *DTP/Def Jam*
66	SHOULDER LEAN
	Young Dro f/T.I. *Grand Hustle*
67	DO I MAKE YOU PROUD
	Taylor Hicks *Arista*

biggest hit ever with his take on "Ridin'" called "White And Nerdy," which came in at No. 85. Chamillionaire and "Weird Al" didn't meet in person until long after both songs were hits—when they were teamed up as presenters at the 2006 American Music Awards.

Aside from "Bad Day," another song by a new artist benefited from *American Idol*. Finalist Katharine McPhee sang KT Tunstall's "Black Horse & The Cherry Tree" during a week the contestants could choose a song from any *Billboard* top 10. "Black Horse" was No. 9 on the Adult Top 40 chart that week, but hadn't become a mainstream hit yet. McPhee's memorable performance, where she sat on the stage in front of two musicians, helped boost Tunstall's original up the Hot 100, and it finished the year at No. 63.

There were only four songs by actual *American Idol* contestants on the 2006 recap, two fewer than the show placed on the 2005 chart. The original "Idol" from season one, Kelly Clarkson, was No. 54 with "Walk Away," the final hit from her multi-platinum album *Breakaway*. Fifth season winner Taylor Hicks was No. 67 with his first single, "Do I Make You Proud." Fourth season victor Carrie Underwood had two songs on the list. "Jesus, Take The Wheel" was No. 77 and "Before He Cheats" was No. 59. This is a good place to note that, because of editorial deadlines for this edition, the year-end chart for 2006 was compiled before all of the songs from 2006 had completed their chart run. "Before He Cheats" had apparently peaked in 2006 by editorial deadline, but in 2007, after it crossed over from country radio to pop, adult contemporary, and adult top 40, it rose to an even higher position. Next time around, "Before He Cheats" will be listed with the top hits of 2007.

Another reality talent TV series was responsible for an entry on the 2006 report. *Making The Band* started out as an ABC-TV series in 2000. O-Town was the first group created by the show. In 2001, that male quintet had the No. 37 song, "All Or Nothing," and the No. 80 song, "Liquid Dreams." One member of O-Town returned to the year-end chart in 2006: Ashley Parker Angel anchored the list as a solo act with "Let U Go." Meanwhile, the newest group to be assembled on *Making The Band*, the five women known as Danity Kane, had the No. 52 song of the year with their debut single, "Show Stopper."

The DECADES

THERE IS NO logical reason for each decade to have its own distinct flavor, and yet there is something unique about each one that sets it apart from the other 10-year frames of the rock era.

The '50s ushered in rock and roll and saw the first chart ink for Elvis Presley as well as founding fathers Chuck Berry, Little Richard, and Fats Domino. By the time the '60s began, rock and roll had smoothed out a little, and the early part of that decade was dominated by teen idols like Ricky Nelson, Bobby Vee, Johnny Tillotson, and Neil Sedaka, and pop princesses like Lesley Gore, Peggy March, Connie Francis, and Brenda Lee.

Halfway through the '60s, everything changed with the introduction of the Beatles and all of the British groups that followed. The '60s also saw the transformation of a small Detroit label called Motown into an independent powerhouse that could score No. 1 hit after No. 1 hit. By the time the decade was coming to a close, we had lived through the Summer of Love and were just entering the age of psychedelic soul. Elvis Presley had his last No. 1 single and so did Diana Ross and the Supremes. In the closing months of 1969, Motown released the first single by its biggest act of the '70s, five brothers from Gary, Indiana, known as the Jackson 5.

The '70s began with the rise of the singer/songwriter, as exemplified by Carole King and James Taylor. The Jackson 5 started off the decade with four consecutive No. 1 songs, and Diana Ross and the Supremes gave their final performance on January 14, 1970, before splitting into two acts. Marvin Gaye and Stevie Wonder produced their signature works (*What's Going On* and *Songs In The Key Of Life*, respectively). Toward the end of the decade, the disco era was in full swing, and its theme song was "Stayin' Alive."

The '80s saw a new British invasion. It wasn't mop tops this time, it was the contemporary sounds of Eurythmics, Culture Club, Human League, ABC, and the Police. Michael Jackson was crowned the king of pop, and music fans had plenty of opportunities to be charitable, through Band Aid, Live Aid, and We Are The World.

The '90s began with Mariah Carey's first No. 1 single, quickly followed by four more. Hip-hop came into its own and became the music of mainstream top 40 radio, with acts like Bone Thugs-N-Harmony, Puff Daddy, the Notorious B.I.G., and 2Pac all rising to pole position.

It's too early to capture the spirit of this decade (let alone figure out what to call it—the '00s just doesn't look right), but strong sales of digital downloads and the influence of *American Idol* helped bring pop music back to the upper ranks of the Hot 100 during the first years of the 21st century. It's also not possible to compile a list of the top 100 songs of the years 2000 to 2010, so that will have to wait for next time.

The list of the top 100 songs of each decade includes songs that peaked in that decade. The list for the 1950s includes only songs that peaked on or after July 9, 1955, the starting date of the rock era.

The Top 100 Songs of THE FIFTIES

Tennessee Ernie Ford

THE ROCK and roll era was officially ushered in on July 9, 1955, when "(Were Gonna) Rock Around The Clock" by Bill Haley & His Comets went to No. 1 on the *Billboard* Best Sellers in Stores chart. The king of this music—music that was unlike any that had been heard before—was crowned in April 1956, when Elvis Presley's "Heartbreak Hotel" became his first No. 1 song. But there were detractors, too. Rev. John Carroll said, "Rock and roll inflames and excites youth, like jungle tom-toms readying warriors for battle. . . . The suggestive lyrics are, of course, a matter for law enforcement agencies."

The top 100 songs of the '50s include many titles that had nothing to do with rock and roll. While Elvis appears 12 times, the list also includes Roger Williams, Jimmy Dorsey, Nelson Riddle, Perez Prado, Doris Day, Nat King Cole, Frank Sinatra, and even the man who spoke out against rock, Mitch Miller.

Many of the songs were composed before the advent of rock and roll. Seven titles in the top 10 were recorded by other artists prior to 1955.

The Top 100 Songs of
THE SIXTIES

The Beatles

ONLY THREE artists who were listed on the top 100 songs of the '50s were also included in the top 100 songs of the '60s: Elvis Presley, the Everly Brothers, and Frank Sinatra.

Still, the early part of the '60s didn't sound that different from the '50s. Hits like "Tossin' and Turnin'" and even "The Twist" could have been popular in either decade. One difference was the rising influence of women—Connie Francis and Brenda Lee were major artists, and the Shirelles were the first "girl group" to make an impact.

Then came January 1964, and everything changed. The Beatles arrived from England, ushering in the British Invasion. Few American artists survived this period, though Bobby Vinton, the Four Seasons, and the Beach Boys remained popular.

The '60s also saw the rise of Motown, beginning with the staggering hit streak of the Supremes in 1964. The label's success continued with the Four Tops, the Temptations, Marvin Gaye, and Martha & the Vandellas.

The Top 100 Songs of
THE SEVENTIES

Roberta Flack

TO MANY baby-boomers who grew up in the '50s and '60s, the '70s paled by comparison. Contrasted to decades that gave birth to Elvis Presley and the Beatles, the '70s might suffer. But during the years 1970 and 1971, singer/songwriters like Carole King and James Taylor became successful with their personal, introspective music, and 1972 saw "American Pie" top the chart. The decade couldn't have been all that bad.

The Beatles may have broken up, but Paul McCartney, John Lennon, George Harrison, and Ringo Starr continued to chart on their own. Motown's hottest act of the '60s split in two, with Diana Ross going solo and Jean Terrell taking her place as lead singer of the Supremes.

The latter part of the decade is hailed by some and condemned by others for the rise of disco music. The top songs of the decade include hits by Chic, Donna Summer, the Village People, and Gloria Gaynor. Dominating the years 1977 through 1979 were the Bee Gees (thanks to the *Saturday Night Fever* soundtrack) and their youngest brother Andy.

The Top 100 Songs of
THE EIGHTIES

Kim Carnes

HALF OF the top 10 singles of the '80s featured women singing lead vocals, including the top three songs of the decade, "Physical" by Olivia Newton-John, "Endless Love" by Diana Ross & Lionel Richie, and "Bette Davis Eyes" by Kim Carnes. That's an improvement from the '50s when there were no females in the top 10, the '60s where there was only one female lead vocal, and the '70s, where there were three.

There were three singles taken directly from motion picture soundtracks in the top 10, equaling the number of movie songs in the top 10 of the '70s. The '80s movie hits: "Endless Love," "Eye Of The Tiger," and "Flashdance...What A Feeling."

The decade's top 100 includes music of all genres, including disco or dance music like "Celebration" by Kool & the Gang; some classic British rock like "Owner Of A Lonely Heart" by Yes; Motown singles from Diana Ross, Stevie Wonder, and Smokey Robinson; adult contemporary hits like "Lady" by Kenny Rogers; country music from Eddie Rabbitt and Dolly Parton; and classic rock and roll from Van Halen and the J. Geils Band.

The Top 100 Songs of
THE NINETIES

LeAnn Rimes

THE NO. 1 single of the decade was by a group that first charted in the '60s, but Santana was a rarity. There were only three other acts in the top 100 of the 1990s that had first recorded in the 1960s: Cher, Michael Jackson, and Eric Clapton. The dominant genres in the '90s were R&B and rap. Motown's harmonic quartet Boyz II Men had three songs in the decade's top 10; something accomplished previously only by Elvis Presley and the Bee Gees. Rap artists like the Notorious B.I.G., Coolio, Tag Team, Mase, Kris Kross, Bone Thugs-N-Harmony, and Dr. Dre had hits in the top 100. Mariah Carey, the first artist in the rock era to have a No. 1 song in every year of a decade, placed five hits in the decade's top 100.

Country artists were represented, with LeAnn Rimes and Shania Twain on board. The highest-ranked Brit was Elton John, who was joined by the U.K.'s biggest new export of the decade, the Spice Girls.

The SUBJECTS

ONE OF MY FAVORITE writing projects in the '80s and '90s was when I was asked to fill in for a vacationing Pam Miller as the writer of the nationally syndicated weekly radio series *Dick Clark's Rock, Roll and Remember.* At the top of each hour, I would have to come up with a set of songs that were related to each other in some fashion. One segment might feature three songs about food; another could spotlight songs that have articles of clothing in the title. This section is dedicated to anyone in radio who has had to find three songs by artists born in Philadelphia on a Tuesday (when it was raining).

Strangely, this part of the book was one of the more difficult ones to compile. Strict rules were set up to determine which songs belonged in a category. It wasn't so hard to decide if a song had a day of the week in the title; that was clear-cut. What constituted a song about a place was a trickier matter. Did "Chantilly Lace" qualify, even though the French town was being used as an adjective? Yes. Did fictional locations like Harper Valley count? Yes. What about "Margaritaville," which was a state of mind more than an actual location? In this case, no.

The list of top 100 songs about animals includes many songs that aren't actually about animals. "Cat's In The Cradle" refers to a children's game, not a feline, and "Hungry Like The Wolf" isn't about an actual wolf. Still, any song with an animal in its title—even a metaphoric animal—is on the list.

For those who are curious about some subjects not included in this book, the top three fashion-statement songs are "Blue Suede Shoes" by Carl Perkins, "A White Sport Coat (And A Pink Carnation)" by Marty Robbins, and "The Ballad Of The Green Berets" by S/Sgt. Barry Sadler. And the top three songs with land vehicles in the title are "Midnight Train To Georgia" by Gladys Knight & the Pips, "Morning Train (Nine To Five)" by Sheena Easton, and "Chariots Of Fire" by Vangelis.

The Top 100 Songs About PLACES

Mitch Miller

CALIFORNIA IS the place that shows up most frequently in the top 100 geographic songs. Considered for the list were any songs that mentioned a specific place in the title or were clearly about a specific geographic location. Continents, countries, states, and cities qualified, and so did locales in a city, such as Baker Street and the West End in London, or Washington Square and Broadway in Manhattan. Locations used as adjectives, such as "Chantilly Lace" or "China Girl," were also included.

Seven California songs are in the top 100, starting with "California Love" by 2Pac featuring Dr. Dre & Roger Troutman, at No. 8. The city with the most mentions is New Orleans, showing up in songs by Johnny Horton, Freddy Cannon, Gary U.S. Bonds, and Fats Domino. Countries? The U.S.A. gets three mentions and America gets two; other countries in the top 100 with one song each are Australia ("Down Under"), China, and Spain.

The Top 100 Songs with
BOYS' NAMES IN THE TITLE

Jim Croce

THE BIG bad name of John is the most popular on the list of the top 100 songs with boys' names in the title, with six mentions for John and Johnny, headed by Jimmy Dean's "Big Bad John." Jack, which can be a nickname for John, is tied for second place with four showings on the list, starting with John Cougar's "Jack And Diane." Tied for third place is Bobby, led by Janis Joplin's recording of "Me And Bobby McGee," and a name that graced the title of a Shakespeare play, Romeo. There may not be a lot of men sporting the name today, but Romeo shows up three times on the top 100, led by Henry Mancini's instrumental "Love Theme From *Romeo And Juliet.*"

"Hey Jude" is the top song inspired by a real person, John Lennon's son Julian. Other names of real people on the top 100 include Duke (Ellington), Smokey (Robinson), Amadeus (Mozart), and (Ludwig van) Beethoven.

The Top 100 Songs with
GIRLS' NAMES IN THE TITLE

Laura Branigan

THE NAME mentioned most often in the top 100 songs with girls' names in the title is Sue and Susie, with five songs on the list. Leading the way is "Runaround Sue" by Dion, but there's also "A Boy Named Sue" by Johnny Cash and "Peggy Sue" by Buddy Holly, as well as "Wake Up Little Susie" by the Everly Brothers and "Susie Darlin'" by Robin Luke. In second place is a more mythological figure, Venus. She's the subject of Frankie Avalon's No. 1 hit from 1959, Shocking Blue's top 10 single from 1970, Bananarama's remake of that hit, and the medley by Stars on 45 that includes a few bars of the same song.

The most popular real woman on the list is Macarena, a revered historical figure in Spain (as well as the name of a neighborhood in Seville named after her). In third place is legendary film actress Bette Davis, whose eyes were immortalized in a hit by Kim Carnes. Fictional women on the list include matchmaker Dolly Gallagher Levi in Louis Armstrong's "Hello, Dolly!" and Shakespeare's star-crossed lover Juliet in Henry Mancini's instrumental "Love Theme From *Romeo And Juliet*."

34 **SARA**
Starship *Grunt* 86

35 **LAY DOWN SALLY**
Eric Clapton *RSO* 78

36 **ANGIE**
The Rolling Stones *Rolling Stones* 73

37 **CRACKLIN' ROSIE**
Neil Diamond *Uni* 70

38 **SHEILA**
Tommy Roe *ABC-Paramount* 62

39 **LITTLE JEANNIE**
Elton John *MCA* 80

40 **PATRICIA**
Perez Prado *RCA* 58

41 **JENNY FROM THE BLOCK**
Jennifer Lopez f/Styles *Epic* 02

42 **MONY MONY**
Billy Idol *Chrysalis* 87

43 **LIL' RED RIDING HOOD**
Sam the Sham & the Pharaohs *MGM* 66

44 **A BOY NAMED SUE**
Johnny Cash *Columbia* 69

45 **AMANDA** Boston *MCA* 86

46 **HANG ON SLOOPY**
The McCoys *Bang* 65

47 **DELTA DAWN**
Helen Reddy *Capitol* 73

48 **RUBY TUESDAY**
The Rolling Stones *London* 67

49 **'03 BONNIE & CLYDE**
Jay-Z f/Beyoncé *Roc-a-Fella/Def Jam* 02

50 **PROUD MARY**
Creedence Clearwater Revival *Fantasy* 69

51 **CLAIR**
Gilbert O'Sullivan *MAM* 72

52 **LUCY IN THE SKY WITH DIAMONDS**
Elton John *MCA* 75

53 **VENUS**
Bananarama *London* 86

54 **HELP ME, RHONDA**
The Beach Boys *Capitol* 65

55 **BREAKFAST AT TIFFANY'S**
Deep Blue Something *Interscope* 96

56 **RUBY BABY**
Dion *Columbia* 63

57 **OH SHEILA**
Ready for the World *MCA* 85

58 **JOANNA**
Kool & the Gang *De-Lite* 84

59 **DIRTY DIANA**
Michael Jackson *Epic* 88

60 **DAWN (GO AWAY)**
The Four Seasons *Philips* 64

61 **JEAN**
Oliver *Crewe* 69

62 **DANI CALIFORNIA**
Red Hot Chili Peppers *Warner Bros.* 06

63 **PEGGY SUE**
Buddy Holly *Coral* 57

64 **ANGIE BABY**
Helen Reddy *Capitol* 74

65 **DEVIL WITH A BLUE DRESS ON & GOOD GOLLY MISS MOLLY**
Mitch Ryder & the Detroit Wheels
New Voice 66

66 **TAKE A LETTER MARIA**
R. B. Greaves *Atco* 69

67 **MANDY**
Barry Manilow *Bell* 75

68 **SUNNY**
Bobby Hebb *Philips* 66

69 **OH SHERRIE**
Steve Perry *Columbia* 84

70 **CANDIDA** Dawn *Bell* 70

71 **867-5309/JENNY**
Tommy Tutone *Columbia* 82

72 **GEORGIA ON MY MIND**
Ray Charles *ABC-Paramount* 60

73 **SARA SMILE**
Daryl Hall & John Oates *RCA* 76

74 **JACKIE BLUE**
Ozark Mountain Daredevils *A&M* 75

75 **BARBARA ANN**
The Beach Boys *Capitol* 66

76 **SALLY, GO 'ROUND THE ROSES**
The Jaynetts *Tuff* 63

77 **SAY, HAS ANYBODY SEEN MY SWEET GYPSY ROSE**
Dawn f/Tony Orlando *Bell* 70

78 **GLENDORA**
Perry Como *RCA* 56

79 **SWEET CAROLINE (GOOD TIMES NEVER SEEMED SO GOOD)**
Neil Diamond *Uni* 69

80 **TINA MARIE**
Perry Como *RCA* 55

81 **CARRIE**
Europe *Epic* 87

82 **SHORT FAT FANNIE**
Larry Williams *Specialty* 57

83 **SUSIE DARLIN'**
Robin Luke *Dot* 58

84 **CINDY, OH CINDY**
Vince Martin & w/the Tarriers *Glory* 56

85 **NADIA'S THEME (THE YOUNG AND THE RESTLESS)**
Barry DeVorzon & Perry Botkin, Jr. *A&M* 76

86 **MONY MONY**
Tommy James & the Shondells *Roulette* 68

87 **A ROSE AND A BABY RUTH**
George Hamilton IV *ABC-Paramount* 56

88 **I'M NOT LISA**
Jessi Colter *Capitol* 75

89 **IESHA**
Another Bad Creation *Motown* 91

90 **BONY MARONIE**
Larry Williams *Specialty* 57

91 **CINDY, OH CINDY**
Eddie Fisher *RCA* 56

92 **BETH**
Kiss *Casablanca* 76

93 **ELVIRA**
Oak Ridge Boys *MCA* 81

94 **JACK AND JILL**
Raydio *Arista* 78

95 **LOVE GROWS (WHERE MY ROSEMARY GOES)**
Edison Lighthouse *Bell* 70

96 **LAYLA**
Eric Clapton *Duck* 92

97 **LUCILLE**
Kenny Rogers *UA* 77

98 **IVY ROSE**
Perry Como *RCA* 57

99 **ANGELIA**
Richard Marx *EMI* 80

100 **VALLERI**
The Monkees *Colgems* 68

The Top 100 Songs About ANIMALS

Culture Club

DOGS MAY BE man's best friend, but more songs have been written about birds. Perhaps it's because birds are considered to be more musical, although anyone who has heard the Singing Dogs warble "Jingle Bells" might disagree. To compute the top 100 songs about animals, all living creatures (except for humans, of course) were considered, even insects—such as the butterfly and the ladybug. Metaphoric references were included, and so were mythical creatures,   such as the unicorn and the dragon.

Birds of one type or another account for 24 of the top 100 songs. Doves, robins, eagles and mockingbirds have three mentions each, while ducks have two. The highest-ranked bird song is Prince's "When Doves Cry," from the soundtrack of *Purple Rain*.

Dogs placed a respectable second, with 11 songs included in the top 100; cats are right behind dogs with nine songs in the top 100.

The Top 100 Songs About COLORS

Tony Orlando & Dawn

T HE DICTIONARY DEFINES "blue" as the color of the clear sky and the deep sea, or feeling melancholy or low. The latter definitions have helped make blue the color of choice for most songwriters; 32 of the top 100 songs with colors in the title mention blue or the blues in the title, starting with the No. 1 song on the list, Guy Mitchell's "Singing The Blues." The second-highest ranked "blue" tune is Domenico Modugno's Italian-language "Nel Blu Dipinto Di Blu (Volare)," from 1958.

The runner-up color is black, with 13 mentions. Michael Jackson's "Black Or White" is the top-ranked black song, as well as the top song with white in the title. Next in line is red, with 11 titles on the list. The highest-ranked red song is Bobby Vinton's "Roses Are Red (My Love)," from 1962. Next is TLC's "Red Light Special" from 1995. Green gets mentioned nine times in the top 100, starting with Jim Lowe's classic "The Green Door," from 1956.

The Top 100 LOVE SONGS

Celine Dion

S ONGS HAVE BEEN written about almost every subject imaginable, but one thing has remained constant through the years: love songs are always in style. The top 100 songs with the word *love* in the title come from all six decades of the rock era.

Topping the list is "I'll Make Love To You," written and produced by Babyface for Boyz II Men. The single equaled the 14-week run at No. 1 enjoyed by the No. 2 song on the list, Whitney Houston's remake of Dolly Parton's "I Will Always Love You." Houston has four songs on the top 100, while the Beatles only have three—ironic, since Cirque de Soleil built a whole Beatles show around the theme of "love."

But the lead vocalist with the most love songs on the top 100 is the woman who headed the "Return to Love" tour in 2000: Diana Ross. Five of the Supremes' songs are on the tally, along with two of Diana's post-Supremes hits, headed by her "Endless Love" duet with Lionel Richie at No. 6.

The Top 100 Songs About
THE BODY

Billy Ray Cyrus

I T SHOULD BE no surprise—considering the popularity of love songs—that the part of the body most composers prefer to write about is the heart. Thirty-eight of the top 100 songs about the body mention the heart in the title, starting with the No. 1 song on the list, Toni Braxton's "Un-Break My Heart."

In second place is the part of the body considered to be the "windows to the soul." That could explain why eyes are mentioned in the titles of 20 of the top 100 body songs, starting with the entry at No. 3, "Bette Davis Eyes" by Kim Carnes.

Hands are in third place, with eight titles out of 100, starting with "I Want To Hold Your Hand" by the Beatles. The head (six) and the face (five) are close behind, led by B.J. Thomas' "Raindrops Keep Fallin' On My Head" and Roberta Flack's "The First Time Ever I Saw Your Face."

Rupert Holmes

I F FOOD BE the love of music, play on. If that's not exactly the Shakespeare quote, it will do in this case. Food and drink can supply sensual pleasures and you don't have to have seen the film *Tom Jones* to understand the link between food and sex. The top 30 songs that mention foor and/or drink in their titles include metaphorical references as well as literal ones.

You won't find any substitute sweeteners on the list, but there are six references to sugar, led by the Archies' chart-topper from 1969, "Sugar, Sugar." Jimmy Gilmer & the Fireballs sang an ode to a "Sugar Shack," the Guess Who complained about "No Sugar Tonight," the Rolling Stones praised their "Brown Sugar," Fall Out Boy warned, "Sugar, We're Goin' Down," and the Four Tops managed to work in three sweet references in "I Can't Help Myself (Sugar Pie, Honey Bunch)."

The list does lean to the sweet side. There's the "Peppermint Twist" as well as "Incense And Peppermints," Labelle's first hit version of "Lady Marmalade" as well as the remake by Christina Aguilera, Lil' Kim, Mya, and Pink, Don McLean's serving of "American Pie," plus "Candy Shop" by 50 Cent featuring Olivia, "Candy Rain" by Soul for Real, and "The Candy Man" by Sammy Davis, Jr.

Vegetables are in short supply—no one has recorded "One Bad Asparagus"—but there is enough fruit, including a "Blueberry" and a couple of "Apples."

Main courses are also rare, although there is a helping of "Mashed Potato Time." British record label executives are responsible for sticking the inappropriate title of "Sukiyaki" on a cover version of Kyu Sakamoto's Japanese hit in 1963 and the name stuck when Sakamoto's original recording was released in America.

Bill Haley & His Comets

T HE UNCERTAINTY of who recorded the first song to be considered "rock and roll" is so great that an entire book has been written on the subject—*What Was The First Rock 'N' Roll Record* by Jim Dawson and Steve Propes. The authors suggest 50 credible candidates, while noting that the original connotation of "rock and roll" had nothing to do with music, but was strictly sexual in nature.

In case you weren't already certain, that should leave no doubt as to the true meaning of "My Man Rocks Me (With One Steady Roll)," recorded in the '20s by Trixie Smith on Black Swan. Long before Bill Haley, Elvis Presley, or any of their R&B predecessors committed their vocals to wax, the Boswell Sisters recorded a song called "Rock And Roll" in the '30s. It was disc jockey Alan Freed, host of the syndicated radio program *The Rock And Roll Show* in 1954, who helped popularize the phrase even before "(We're Gonna) Rock Around The Clock" ascended to the top of the *Billboard* chart.

The first No. 1 hit of the rock era to use "rock and roll" in the title wasn't by Haley or Presley, but popular female vocalist Kay Starr. Switching from Capitol to RCA, the first song her new label wanted her to record was "Rock And Roll Waltz." Some 24 years later, Billy Joel went to No. 1 with "It's Still Rock And Roll To Me," written in response to the Rolling Stones' "It's Only Rock 'N Roll." Another two years passed before Joan Jett recorded "I Love Rock 'N Roll," a cover of an obscure British single by the Anglo-American group the Arrows.

The Mamas and the Papas

I F FRIDAY'S Child is full of woe, it may be because she hasn't had very many songs written about her. There are only four Friday titles on the list of the top 30 songs about days of the week, but that's better than Tuesday (with two) and poor Wednesday and Thursday (with none).

The weekend is the most popular part of the week to write songs about. There are 11 Saturday songs, led by the Bay City Rollers' "Saturday Night" at No. 4. Also in the top 10 is "Saturday In The Park" by Chicago, with "Another Saturday Night" by Cat Stevens and the original by Sam Cooke sitting just outside the top 10.

Sunday is not far behind, with eight songs in the top 30. The top Sunday song is "Pleasant Valley Sunday" by the Monkees. Spanky & Our Gang loved the day, and the group scored its first chart entry with "Sunday Will Never Be The Same."

Monday is a day of dread for many people, whether it's blue or manic. There are five Monday songs in the top 30, starting with the Mamas and the Papas' No. 1 hit, "Monday, Monday." Oddly, five of the six Monday songs are in the top 10, including the Carpenters' "Rainy Days And Mondays." The Friday songs are led by the Cure's "Friday I'm In Love." Tuesday is represented by the Rolling Stones' "Ruby Tuesday" and the Moody Blues' "Tuesday Afternoon."

Only one Wednesday song has made the *Billboard* chart during the entire rock era. The Royal Guardsmen's fourth single was titled "Wednesday," and it peaked at No. 97.

The Top 5000 Songs of the ROCK ERA

THE TOP 5000 Songs of the Rock Era are ranked in order of their chart performance on The Billboard Hot 100—the weekly survey of the most popular songs in the U.S.—and the Hot 100's prior incarnation, the Best Sellers in Stores chart.

Singles eligible for inclusion in the Top 5000 appeared on *Billboard*'s pop singles charts between July 9, 1955, and February 3, 2007. Pop historians generally agree that the "rock era" began in July 1955, when Bill Haley and His Comets' "(We're Gonna) Rock Around the Clock" went to No. 1.

Beginning with the chart dated July 9, 1955, songs received 500 points for every week they were in the No. 1 position, 400 points for every week at No. 2, 300 points for every week at No. 3, 200 points for every week at No. 4, and 100 points for every week at No. 5. Songs at No. 6 received 95 points, No. 7 received 94 points, and so on down to 71 points for No. 30. Fifty bonus points were added to a song's total for every week it was No. 1.

When all of the points were added, there were multiple ties. Those were broken by considering each song's peak position and the number of weeks spent in peak position. Further ties were broken by determining the number of weeks spent in the top 10, the top 40, and on the entire Hot 100. The few remaining ties were broken by entry position.

Billboard listed both sides of a single in the same chart position prior to the creation of the Hot 100 in August 1958. After that date, "A" and "B" sides were ranked separately. That policy changed on November 29, 1969, and two-sided hits such as "Come Together" and "Something" by the Beatles were once again listed in the same position. This practice was later discontinued, and then reinstated the week of November 30, 1991, when *Billboard* started using Nielsen SoundScan sales data and Nielsen Broadcast Data Systems airplay information to compile the Hot 100. Chart methodology changed again the week of December 5, 1998, when airplay-only tracks were allowed to chart without a commercial single available in stores. That effectively changed the Hot 100 from a singles chart to a tally of the most popular songs in the country, which meant "B" sides (still called that, despite there being no "B" side of a CD single) charted separately again.

Since both peak position and length of time on the Hot 100 determine where a song is ranked on the Top 5000, a No. 1 hit that had a short chart life is likely to have a lower placing on the chart than a No. 3 song that had a very long chart run. "Can't Buy Me Love" by the Beatles was No. 1 for five weeks, but was only on the Hot 100 for a total of 10 weeks. That's why the song is ranked No. 535, while a No. 3 hit like Real McCoy's "Another Night," which was on the Hot 100 for 45 weeks, finishes at No. 78.

While the final ranking of the 5000 songs was totally objective, it's understandable if some hits seem manipulated into place. What are the odds that "Silent Lucidity" by Queensrÿche would land one rung higher than "Silent Running (On Dangerous Ground)" by Mike + the Mechanics? Or that Rare Earth's "Get Ready" would be immediately under Tevin Campbell's "I'm Ready"? Some of the adjacent rankings are good for a laugh, like Terri Gibbs' "Somebody's Knockin'" and Pat Boone's "At My Front Door," or Jerry Lee Lewis' "Breathless" and Rex Smith's "You Take My Breath Away." There are many more, but they are best discovered on your own. The Chart Muse would like it that way.

0001 SMOOTH
Santana f/Rob Thomas *Arista* 99

0002 WE BELONG TOGETHER
Mariah Carey *Island* 05

0003 UN-BREAK MY HEART
Toni Braxton *LaFace* 96

0004 MACARENA (BAYSIDE BOYS MIX)
Los Del Rio *RCA* 96

0005 YEAH!
Usher f/Lil Jon & Ludacris *LaFace* 04

0006 ONE SWEET DAY
Mariah Carey & Boyz II Men *Columbia* 95

0007 I'LL MAKE LOVE TO YOU
Boyz II Men *Motown* 94

0008 I WILL ALWAYS LOVE YOU
Whitney Houston *Arista* 92

**0009 CANDLE IN THE WIND 1997 /
SOMETHING ABOUT THE WAY
YOU LOOK TONIGHT**
Elton John *Rocket* 97

0010 HOW DO I LIVE
LeAnn Rimes *Curb* 97

0011 END OF THE ROAD
Boyz II Men *Biv 10* 92

0012 DILEMMA
Nelly f/Kelly Rowland *Fo' Reel* 02

0013 GOLD DIGGER
Kanye West f/Jamie Foxx *Roc-A-Fella/
Def Jam* 05

0014 TOO CLOSE
Next *Arista* 98

0015 THE BOY IS MINE
Brandy & Monica *Atlantic* 98

0016 THE SIGN
Ace of Base *Arista* 94

0017 HOW YOU REMIND ME
Nickelback *Roadrunner* 01

0018 DON'T BE CRUEL / HOUND DOG
Elvis Presley *RCA* 56

0019 LET ME LOVE YOU
Mario *3rd Street/J* 05

0020 MARIA MARIA
Santana f/the Product G&B *Arista* 00

0021 I'LL BE MISSING YOU
Puff Daddy & Faith Evans f/112
Bad Boy 97

0022 I SWEAR
All-4-One *Blitzz* 94

0023 MO MONEY MO PROBLEMS
The Notorious B.I.G. f/Puff Daddy & Mase
Bad Boy 97

0024 THE TWIST
Chubby Checker *Parkway* 60

0025 YOU'RE STILL THE ONE
Shania Twain *Mercury* 98

0026 INDEPENDENT WOMEN PART I
Destiny's Child *Columbia* 00

0027 BABY BOY
Beyoncé f/Sean Paul *Columbia* 03

0028 LOSE YOURSELF
Eminem *Shady* 02

0029 FOOLISH
Ashanti *Murder Inc./Def Jam* 02

0030 GANGSTA'S PARADISE
Coolio f/L.V. *MCA Soundtracks* 95

0031 FAMILY AFFAIR
Mary J. Blige *MCA* 01

0032 U GOT IT BAD
Usher *Arista* 01

0033 IN DA CLUB
50 Cent *Shady/Aftermath* 03

0034 RUN IT!
Chris Brown *Jive* 05

0035 I'M REAL
Jennifer Lopez f/Ja Rule *Epic* 01

0036 BURN
Usher *LaFace* 04

0037 FALLIN'
Alicia Keys *J* 01

0038 ON BENDED KNEE
Boyz II Men *Motown* 94

0039 YOU LIGHT UP MY LIFE
Debby Boone *Warner/Curb* 77

**0040 YOU WERE MEANT FOR ME /
FOOLISH GAMES**
Jewel *Atlantic* 97

0041 HEY YA!
OutKast *Arista* 03

0042 HOT IN HERRE
Nelly *Fo' Reel* 02

0043 WHOOMP! (THERE IT IS)
Tag Team *Life* 93

**0044 (WE'RE GONNA) ROCK
AROUND THE CLOCK**
Bill Haley & His Comets *Decca* 55

0045 THE WAY YOU MOVE
OutKast f/Sleepy Brown *Arista* 04

0046 GOODIES
Ciara f/Petey Pablo *Sho'nuff/LaFace* 04

0001 Santana

0060 Gwen Stefani

0170 Avril Lavigne

0230 Sheryl Crow

0252 **BRIDGE OVER TROUBLED WATER**
Simon and Garfunkel *Columbia* 70

0253 **LONDON BRIDGE**
Fergie *will.i.am/A&M* 06

0254 **SLOW MOTION**
Juvenile f/Soulja Slim *Cash Money* 04

0255 **HONKY TONK WOMEN**
The Rolling Stones *London* 69

0256 **LIKE A VIRGIN**
Madonna *Sire* 84

0257 **DON'T CHA**
The Pussycat Dolls f/Busta Rhymes
A&M 05

0258 **BIG BAD JOHN**
Jimmy Dean *Columbia* 61

0259 **CRAZY LITTLE THING CALLED LOVE**
Queen *Elektra* 80

0260 **JACK AND DIANE**
John Cougar *Riva* 82

0261 **SMACK THAT**
Akon f/Eminem *SRC/Up Front/Konvict* 06

0262 **UNPRETTY**
TLC *LaFace* 99

0263 **TO SIR WITH LOVE**
Lulu *Epic* 67

0264 **DA YA THINK I'M SEXY?**
Rod Stewart *Warner Bros.* 79

0265 **ANOTHER BRICK IN THE WALL**
Pink Floyd *Columbia* 80

0266 **JUMP**
Van Halen *Warner Bros.* 84

0267 **IT'S TOO LATE /**
I FEEL THE EARTH MOVE
Carole King *Ode* 71

0268 **EVERYTHING YOU WANT**
Vertical Horizon *RCA* 00

0269 **DOWN UNDER**
Men at Work *Columbia* 83

0270 **MY SWEET LORD / ISN'T IT A PITY**
George Harrison *Apple* 70

0271 **BYE BYE LOVE**
Everly Brothers *Cadence* 57

0272 **GIVE ME ONE REASON**
Tracy Chapman *Elektra* 96

0273 **THE PURPLE PEOPLE EATER**
Sheb Wooley *MGM* 58

0274 **AIN'T THAT A SHAME**
Pat Boone *Dot* 55

0275 **WITCH DOCTOR**
David Seville *Liberty* 58

0276 **THREE TIMES A LADY**
Commodores *Motown* 78

0277 **FUNKYTOWN**
Lipps, Inc. *Casablanca* 80

0278 **YOU'RE SO VAIN**
Carly Simon *Elektra* 73

0279 **DOESN'T REALLY MATTER**
Janet Jackson *Def Jam/Def Soul* 00

0280 **BRAND NEW KEY**
Melanie *Neighborhood* 71

0281 **RUSH RUSH**
Paula Abdul *Captive* 91

0282 **ROCK AND ROLL WALTZ**
Kay Starr *RCA* 56

0283 **TIE A YELLOW RIBBON ROUND**
THE OLE OAK TREE
Dawn *Bell* 73

0284 **MISSING**
Everything But The Girl *Atlantic* 96

0285 **DON'T / I BEG OF YOU**
Elvis Presley *RCA* 58

0286 **LONELY BOY**
Paul Anka *ABC-Paramount* 59

0287 **I WANNA LOVE YOU**
Akon f/Snoop Dogg *SRC/Up Front/
Konvict* 06

0288 **HIPS DON'T LIE**
Shakira f/Wyclef Jean *Epic* 06

0289 **GET LOW**
Lil Jon & the East Side Boyz *BME* 03

0290 **BECAUSE I LOVE YOU**
(THE POSTMAN SONG)
Stevie B *LMR* 90

0291 **KILLING ME SOFTLY WITH HIS SONG**
Roberta Flack *Atlantic* 73

0292 **PEOPLE GOT TO BE FREE**
The Rascals *Atlantic* 68

0293 **EVERYDAY PEOPLE**
Sly & the Family Stone *Epic* 69

0294 **BIG GIRLS DON'T CRY**
The Four Seasons *Vee Jay* 62

0295 **SHAKE IT OFF**
Mariah Carey *Island* 05

0296 **HURTS SO GOOD**
John Cougar *Riva* 82

0297 **I DON'T WANT TO MISS A THING**
Aerosmith *Columbia* 98

0298 **(I CAN'T GET NO) SATISFACTION**
The Rolling Stones *London* 65

0299 **LET'S GET IT ON**
Marvin Gaye *Tamla* 73

0300 **SHE LOVES YOU**
The Beatles *Swan* 64

0301 **ROCK WITH YOU**
Michael Jackson *Epic* 80

0302 **CANDY RAIN**
Soul for Real *Uptown* 95

0303 **STUCK ON YOU**
Elvis Presley *RCA* 60

0304 **SAY YOU, SAY ME**
Lionel Richie *Motown* 85

0305 **REUNITED**
Peaches and Herb *Polydor* 79

0306 **HOT DIGGITY (DOG ZIGGITY BOOM) /**
JUKE BOX BABY
Perry Como *RCA* 56

0307 **RIDIN'**
Chamillionaire f/Krayzie Bone *Universal
Motown* 06

0308 **LOVE CHILD**
Diana Ross & the Supremes *Motown* 68

0309 **DON'T YOU WANT ME**
Human League *A&M* 82

0310 **GET BACK**
The Beatles w/Billy Preston *Apple* 69

0311 **AGAINST ALL ODDS**
(TAKE A LOOK AT ME NOW)
Phil Collins *Atlantic* 84

0312 **GROOVIN'**
The Young Rascals *Atlantic* 67

0313 **TEQUILA**
The Champs *Challenge* 58

0314 **ROSES ARE RED (MY LOVE)**
Bobby Vinton *Epic* 62

0315 **(THEY LONG TO BE) CLOSE TO YOU**
Carpenters *A&M* 70

0316 **NUTHIN' BUT A "G" THANG**
Dr. Dre *Death Row* 93

0317 **RUNAROUND SUE**
Dion *Laurie* 61

0318 **U REMIND ME**
Usher *Arista* 01

0319 **SURVIVOR**
Destiny's Child *Columbia* 01

0320 **I'M SORRY**
Brenda Lee *Decca* 60

0321 **ANOTHER DAY IN PARADISE**
Phil Collins *Atlantic* 89

0322 **ODE TO BILLIE JOE**
Bobbie Gentry *Capitol* 67

0323 **SLOW JAMZ**
Twista f/Kanye West & Jamie Foxx
Atlantic 04

0324 **MY LOVE**
Paul McCartney & Wings *Apple* 73

0325 **RING MY BELL**
Anita Ward *Juana* 79

0326 **BEAT IT**
Michael Jackson *Epic* 83

0327 **THE GREAT PRETENDER**
The Platters *Mercury* 56

0328 **HOW DO U WANT IT /**
CALIFORNIA LOVE
2Pac f/KC & JoJo - f/Dr. Dre & Roger
Troutman *Death Row* 96

0329 **SINCE U BEEN GONE**
Kelly Clarkson *RCA* 05

0330 **WHAT A GIRL WANTS**
Christina Aguilera *RCA* 00

0331 **HELLO**
Lionel Richie *Motown* 84

0332 **ALL 4 LOVE**
Color Me Badd *Giant* 92

0333 **ANGEL**
Shaggy f/Rayvon *MCA* 01

0334 **HONEY**
Bobby Goldsboro *UA* 68

0335 **THE REASON**
Hoobastank *Island* 04

0377 Linkin Park

0444 The Kingsmen

0461 Marc Anthony

0503 Jagged Edge

0684 Dido

0739 Train

0814 Duncan Sheik

0876 Kelis

0883 Pearl Jam

0961 Dionne Farris

1020 The Gin Blossoms

1022 Paula Cole

1039 TOO MUCH, TOO LITTLE, TOO LATE
Johnny Mathis & Deniece Williams
Columbia 78

1040 DON'T STOP 'TIL YOU GET ENOUGH
Michael Jackson *Epic* 79

1041 MOUTH
Merril Bainbridge *Universal* 96

1042 MAKING LOVE OUT
OF NOTHING AT ALL
Air Supply *Arista* 83

1043 LOVE ME DO
The Beatles *Tollie* 64

1044 (YOUR LOVE HAS LIFTED ME)
HIGHER AND HIGHER
Rita Coolidge *A&M* 77

1045 I'D REALLY LOVE TO
SEE YOU TONIGHT
England Dan and John Ford Coley
Big Tree 76

1046 INCENSE AND PEPPERMINTS
Strawberry Alarm Clock *Uni* 67

1047 DAMN!
Youngbloodz f/Lil Jon *So So Def* 03

1048 I'M YOUR BOOGIE MAN
KC & the Sunshine Band *TK* 77

1049 EVERYTHING IS BEAUTIFUL
Ray Stevens *Barnaby* 70

1050 RIGHT BACK WHERE
WE STARTED FROM
Maxine Nightingale *UA* 76

1051 GREEN TAMBOURINE
The Lemon Pipers *Buddah* 68

1052 PATRICIA
Perez Prado *RCA* 58

1053 AT THIS MOMENT
Billy Vera & the Beaters *Rhino* 87

1054 THERE YOU GO
Pink *LaFace* 00

1055 OUR DAY WILL COME
Ruby & the Romantics *Kapp* 63

1056 KEEP IT COMIN' LOVE
KC & the Sunshine Band *TK* 77

1057 LEADER OF THE PACK
The Shangri-Las *Red Bird* 64

1058 POISON
Bell Biv Devoe *MCA* 90

1059 I GOT YOU BABE
Sonny and Cher *Atco* 65

1060 JENNY FROM THE BLOCK
Jennifer Lopez f/Jadakiss & Styles *Epic* 02

1061 KIND OF A DRAG
The Buckinghams *U.S.A.* 67

1062 CAN'T LET GO
Mariah Carey *Columbia* 92

1063 THE GAME OF LOVE
Santana f/Michelle Branch *Arista* 02

1064 HOW TO SAVE A LIFE
The Fray *Epic* 06

1065 WHEN I SEE YOU SMILE
Bad English *Epic* 89

1066 ADDICTED TO LOVE
Robert Palmer *Island* 86

1067 HEAD TO TOE
Lisa Lisa & Cult Jam *Columbia* 87

1068 I WANT TO BE WANTED
Brenda Lee *Decca* 60

1069 MONY MONY
Billy Idol *Chrysalis* 87

1070 THE LOOK
Roxette *EMI* 89

1071 LET YOUR LOVE FLOW
Bellamy Brothers *Warner/Curb* 76

1072 IF YOU WANNA BE HAPPY
Jimmy Soul *SPQR* 63

1073 GOOD LOVIN'
The Young Rascals *Atlantic* 66

1074 JUST ANOTHER DAY
Jon Secada *SBK* 92

1075 SHAKE YOU DOWN
Gregory Abbott *Columbia* 87

1076 BOOGIE FEVER
The Sylvers *Capitol* 76

1077 DON'T WALK AWAY
Jade *Giant* 93

1078 GOT MY MIND SET ON YOU
George Harrison *Dark Horse* 88

1079 LIL' RED RIDING HOOD
Sam the Sham & the Pharaohs *MGM* 66

1080 DUELING BANJOS
Eric Weissberg & Steve Mandell
Warner Bros. 73

1081 PEACHES & CREAM
112 *Bad Boy* 01

1082 YAKETY YAK
The Coasters *Atco* 58

1083 HUMAN
Human League *A&M* 86

1084 EASIER SAID THAN DONE
The Essex *Roulette* 63

1085 SLEDGEHAMMER
Peter Gabriel *Geffen* 86

1086 NEVER MY LOVE
The Association *Warner Bros.* 67

1087 SHOW AND TELL
Al Wilson *Rocky Road* 74

1088 A BIG HUNK O'LOVE
Elvis Presley *RCA* 59

1089 ICE ICE BABY
Vanilla Ice *SBK* 90

1090 I CAN HELP
Billy Swan *Monument* 74

1091 LOVE WILL LEAD YOU BACK
Taylor Dayne *Arista* 90

1092 LOVE WILL NEVER DO (WITHOUT YOU)
Janet Jackson *A&M* 91

1093 A BOY NAMED SUE
Johnny Cash *Columbia* 69

1094 YOU'RE IN LOVE
Wilson Phillips *SBK* 91

1095 BOBBY'S GIRL
Marcie Blane *Seville* 62

1096 GIRLS JUST WANT TO HAVE FUN
Cyndi Lauper *Portrait* 84

1093 Johnny Cash

1117 Puddle of Mudd

1150 Des'ree

1120 Peter Frampton

1261 98 Degrees

1304 LFO

1311 Uncle Kracker

1474 Brandy

1507 Craig David

1523 The O'Jays

1580 Macy Gray

1609 Kevin Lyttle

1631 Eagle-Eye Cherry

1650 Collective Soul

1707 Clay Aiken

1836 Crash Test Dummies

1903 The Pretenders

2029 Nirvana

2053 The Cranberries

2073 Shawn Colvin

2078 Nelly Furtado

2189 Sugar Ray

2204 En Vogue

2354 Harold Melvin & the Blue Notes

2410 Jamie Walters

2430 **SHAKE YOUR LOVE**
Debbie Gibson *Atlantic* 87

2431 **WHOLE LOTTA LOVE**
Led Zeppelin *Atlantic* 70

2432 **I LOVE YOU BECAUSE**
Al Martino *Capitol* 63

2433 **I'VE GOT TO USE MY IMAGINATION**
Gladys Knight & the Pips *Buddah* 74

2434 **BUTTERFLY**
Andy Williams *Cadence* 57

2435 **JUST WHEN I NEEDED YOU MOST**
Randy Vanwarmer *Bearsville* 79

2436 **COULDN'T GET IT RIGHT**
Climax Blues Band *Sire* 77

2437 **SULTANS OF SWING**
Dire Straits *Warner Bros.* 79

2438 **COULD IT BE I'M FALLING IN LOVE**
Spinners *Atlantic* 73

2439 **HUNGRY HEART**
Bruce Springsteen *Columbia* 80

2440 **NOT TONIGHT**
Lil' Kim f/Da Brat, Left Eye, Missy Elliott &
Angie Martinez *Undeas/Big Beat* 97

2441 **DON'T MEAN NOTHING**
Richard Marx *Manhattan* 87

2442 **PASSION**
Rod Stewart *Warner Bros.* 81

2443 **PEOPLE EVERYDAY**
Arrested Development *Chrysalis* 92

2444 **PLEASE DON'T GO**
K.W.S. *Next Plateau* 92

2445 **THINGS THAT MAKE YOU GO HMMM...**
C + C Music Factory f/Freedom Williams
Columbia 91

2446 **HANDY MAN**
James Taylor *Columbia* 77

2447 **LOSING MY RELIGION**
R.E.M. *Warner Bros.* 91

2448 **ALL RIGHT NOW**
Free *A&M* 70

2449 **ON FIRE**
Lloyd Banks *G-Unit* 04

2450 **I LIKE THAT**
Houston f/Chingy, Nate Dogg & I-20
Capitol 04

2451 **GIVING YOU THE BENEFIT**
Pebbles *MCA* 90

2452 **LOVE IS A WONDERFUL THING**
Michael Bolton *Columbia* 91

2453 **CHANGE OF HEART**
Cyndi Lauper *Portrait* 87

2454 **WILL YOU STILL LOVE ME?**
Chicago *Full Moon* 87

2455 **I MISS YOU**
Klymaxx *Constellation* 85

2456 **MAKE IT REAL**
The Jets *MCA* 88

2457 **MOVE B***H**
Ludacris f/Mystikal & Infamous 2.0
DTP/Def Jam South 02

2458 **EVERYTHING YOUR
HEART DESIRES**
Daryl Hall and John Oates *Arista* 88

2459 **UNPREDICTABLE**
Jamie Foxx f/Ludacris *J* 06

2460 **POWER OF LOVE/LOVE POWER**
Luther Vandross *Epic* 91

2461 **IT'S ECSTASY WHEN YOU
LAY DOWN NEXT TO ME**
Barry White *20th Century* 77

2462 **I DON'T WANNA FIGHT**
Tina Turner *Virgin* 93

2463 **OH LONESOME ME**
Don Gibson *RCA* 58

2464 **NIGHT MOVES**
Bob Seger *Capitol* 77

2465 **SUDDENLY**
Billy Ocean *Jive* 85

2466 **CALIFORNIA DREAMIN'**
The Mamas and the Papas *Dunhill* 66

2467 **CRYING**
Don McLean *Millennium* 81

2468 **WHOOT, THERE IT IS**
95 South *Wrap* 93

2469 **LOVE IS A BATTLEFIELD**
Pat Benatar *Chrysalis* 83

2470 **SHAPE OF MY HEART**
Backstreet Boys *Jive* 00

2471 **BRING EM OUT**
T.I. *Grand Hustle* 05

2472 **WHAT'S ON YOUR MIND
(PURE ENERGY)**
Information Society *Tommy Boy* 88

2473 **I GUESS THAT'S WHY THEY
CALL IT THE BLUES**
Elton John *Geffen* 84

2474 **ONE THING**
Finger Eleven *Wind-up* 04

2475 **ONE THING LEADS TO ANOTHER**
The Fixx *MCA* 83

2476 **OYE MI CANTO**
N.O.R.E. f/Daddy Yankee, Nina Sky, Gem
Star & Big Mato *Roc-A-Fella/Def Jam* 04

2477 **CAN'T GET ENOUGH
OF YOUR LOVE, BABE**
Barry White *20th Century* 74

2478 **HOLE HEARTED**
Extreme *A&M* 91

2479 **I DON'T WANT YOUR LOVE**
Duran Duran *Capitol* 88

2480 **STAY**
Shakespear's Sister *London* 92

2481 **1, 2, 3, 4 (SUMPIN' NEW)**
Coolio *Tommy Boy* 96

2482 **LOVE IS ON THE WAY**
Saigon Kick *Third Stone* 92

2483 **YOU CAN'T HURRY LOVE**
Phil Collins *Atlantic* 83

2484 **LITTLE LIES**
Fleetwood Mac *Warner Bros.* 87

2485 **A ROSE AND A BABY RUTH**
George Hamilton IV *ABC-Paramount* 56

2486 **STEP BY STEP**
Eddie Rabbitt *Elektra* 81

2487 **(YOU'VE GOT) THE MAGIC TOUCH**
The Platters *Mercury* 56

2488 **NO SON OF MINE**
Genesis *Atlantic* 92

2489 **SCARS**
Papa Roach *El Tonal* 05

2490 **LOOKING THROUGH YOUR EYES**
LeAnn Rimes *Curb* 98

2491 **SIGNS**
Five Man Electrical Band *Lionel* 71

2492 **I'M NOT LISA**
Jessi Colter *Capitol* 75

2493 **ONLY IN MY DREAMS**
Debbie Gibson *Atlantic* 87

2494 **NEVER**
Heart *Capitol* 85

2495 **LEATHER AND LACE**
Stevie Nicks w/Don Henley *Modern* 82

2496 **OOH AAH . . . JUST A LITTLE BIT**
Gina G *Eternal/Warner Bros.* 97

2497 **SHINING STAR**
The Manhattans *Columbia* 80

2498 **WIFEY**
Next *Arista* 00

2499 **IESHA**
Another Bad Creation *Motown* 91

2500 **WHAT HAVE YOU DONE
FOR ME LATELY**
Janet Jackson *A&M* 86

2501 **WAITING FOR A STAR TO FALL**
Boy Meets Girl *RCA* 88

2502 **STEAL AWAY**
Robbie Dupree *Elektra* 80

2503 **GRAZING IN THE GRASS**
Friends of Distinction *RCA* 69

2504 **BREAK MY STRIDE**
Matthew Wilder *Private I* 84

2505 **SHORTIE LIKE MINE**
Bow Wow f/Chris Brown & Johnta Austin
Columbia 06

2506 **SWAYIN' TO THE MUSIC
(SLOW DANCIN')**
Johnny Rivers *Big Tree* 77

2507 **BELIEVE**
Elton John *Rocket* 95

2508 **YOUR MAMA DON'T DANCE**
Loggins and Messina *Columbia* 73

2509 **I'M WALKIN'**
Fats Domino *Imperial* 57

2510 **DOWN 4 U**
Irv Gotti p/the Inc. f/Ja Rule, Ashanti, Charli
Baltimore & Vita *Murder Inc./Def Jam* 02

2511 **ALRIGHT**
Janet Jackson *A&M* 90

2512 **I MISS YOU**
Aaron Hall *Silas* 94

2590 Eiffel 65

2603 Kylie Minogue

2646 PENNY LOVER
Lionel Richie *Motown* 84

2647 SORRY 2004
Ruben Studdard *J* 04

2648 BEFORE HE CHEATS
Carrie Underwood *Arista* 06

2649 KOOKIE, KOOKIE
(LEND ME YOUR COMB)
Edward Byrnes & Connie Stevens
Warner Bros. 59

2650 ELVIRA
Oak Ridge Boys *MCA* 81

2651 KING OF THE ROAD
Roger Miller *Smash* 65

2652 SHE BLINDED ME WITH SCIENCE
Thomas Dolby *Capitol* 83

2653 COME SAIL AWAY
Styx *A&M* 78

2654 BOSSY
Kelis f/Too $hort *Jive* 06

2655 THAT'S ALL!
Genesis *Atlantic* 84

2656 LOOKIN' AT ME
Mase f/Puff Daddy *Bad Boy* 98

2657 IT'S MY TURN
Diana Ross *Motown* 81

2658 LOVE OF A LIFETIME
Firehouse *Epic* 91

2659 TIN MAN
America *Warner Bros.* 74

2660 SHOTGUN
Jr. Walker & the All Stars *Soul* 65

2661 THE HAWAIIAN WEDDING SONG
Andy Williams *Cadence* 59

2662 MY CHERIE AMOUR
Stevie Wonder *Tamla* 69

2663 WHAT IN THE WORLD'S
COME OVER YOU
Jack Scott *Top Rank* 60

2664 LOVE HURTS
Nazareth *A&M* 76

2665 I DON'T WANNA LIVE
WITHOUT YOUR LOVE
Chicago *Reprise* 88

2666 I THINK WE'RE ALONE NOW
Tommy James & the Shondells *Roulette* 67

2667 JACK AND JILL
Raydio *Arista* 78

2668 STILL THE SAME
Bob Seger & the Silver Bullet Band
Capitol 78

2669 FEELS GOOD
Tony! Toni! Toné! *Wing* 90

2670 BABY, WHAT A BIG SURPRISE
Chicago *Columbia* 77

2671 UNDERSTANDING
Xscape *So So Def* 94

2672 SALT SHAKER
Ying Yang Twins f/Lil Jon & the East Side
Boyz *ColliPark* 04

2673 MISSION BELL
Donnie Brooks *Era* 60

2674 HOW CAN WE BE LOVERS
Michael Bolton *Columbia* 90

2675 ON THE REBOUND
Floyd Cramer *RCA* 61

2676 WHAT BECOMES OF THE
BROKENHEARTED
Jimmy Ruffin *Soul* 66

2677 HE
McGuire Sisters *Coral* 55

2678 WHAT DOES IT TAKE
(TO WIN YOUR LOVE)
Jr. Walker & the All Stars *Soul* 69

2679 EVEN THE NIGHTS ARE BETTER
Air Supply *Arista* 82

2680 WHO'S JOHNNY
El DeBarge *Gordy* 86

2681 HERE AND NOW
Luther Vandross *Epic* 90

2682 PULLIN' ME BACK
Chingy f/Tyrese *Slot-A-Lot* 06

2683 RONI
Bobby Brown *MCA* 89

2684 GOTTA GET THRU THIS
Daniel Bedingfield *Island* 02

2685 LET ME IN
The Sensations *Argo* 62

2686 YOU ARE THE WOMAN
Firefall *Atlantic* 76

2687 TURN BACK THE HANDS OF TIME
Tyrone Davis *Dakar* 70

2688 PIPELINE
The Chantays *Dot* 63

2689 PROMISE
Jagged Edge *So So Def* 01

2690 HERE WE GO AGAIN!
Portrait *Capitol* 93

2691 STILL FLY
Big Tymers *Cash Money* 02

2692 YOUR BODY'S CALLIN'
R. Kelly *Jive* 94

2693 YOU GOT IT ALL
The Jets *MCA* 87

2694 FREDDIE'S DEAD
Curtis Mayfield *Curtom* 72

2695 IS THERE SOMETHING
I SHOULD KNOW
Duran Duran *Capitol* 83

2696 1-2-3
Gloria Estefan & Miami Sound Machine
Epic 88

2697 KICKS
Paul Revere & the Raiders *Columbia* 66

2698 THIS IS IT
Kenny Loggins *Columbia* 80

2699 LOVERGIRL
Teena Marie *Epic* 85

2700 BEND ME, SHAPE ME
American Breed *Acta* 68

2701 I GET AROUND
2Pac *Interscope* 93

2702 7 DAYS
Craig David *Wildstar* 02

2703 ONE
U2 *Island* 92

2704 WHEN THE CHILDREN CRY
White Lion *Atlantic* 89

2705 ONE
Three Dog Night *Dunhill* 69

2706 CUM ON FEEL THE NOIZE
Quiet Riot *Pasha* 83

2707 IT'S A SIN TO TELL A LIE
Somethin' Smith & the Redheads *Epic* 55

2708 THEY DON'T KNOW
Jon B. *Yab Yum* 98

2709 CRYIN'
Aerosmith *Geffen* 93

2710 SHAKE YA ASS
Mystikal *Jive* 00

2711 CONGA
Miami Sound Machine *Epic* 86

2712 FREEDOM
Wham! *Columbia* 85

2713 HIGHER GROUND
Stevie Wonder *Tamla* 73

2714 DON'T BE CRUEL
Cheap Trick *Epic* 88

2715 TWO OF HEARTS
Stacey Q *Atlantic* 86

2716 CAN'T FIGHT THE MOONLIGHT
LeAnn Rimes *Curb* 02

2717 BREAK IT TO ME GENTLY
Brenda Lee *Decca* 62

2718 THE WAY I WANT TO TOUCH YOU
Captain & Tennille *A&M* 75

2719 LOVE GROWS (WHERE MY
ROSEMARY GOES)
Edison Lighthouse *Bell* 70

2720 EXPRESSWAY TO YOUR HEART
Soul Survivors *Crimson* 67

2721 THE SEARCH IS OVER
Survivor *Scotti Bros.* 85

2722 WHO CAN I RUN TO
Xscape *So So Def* 95

2723 I'M LIKE A BIRD
Nelly Furtado *DreamWorks* 01

2724 HEAVEN MUST HAVE SENT YOU
Bonnie Pointer *Motown* 79

2725 WHO'S SORRY NOW
Connie Francis *MGM* 58

2726 DON'T LOSE MY NUMBER
Phil Collins *Atlantic* 85

2727 LAYLA
Eric Clapton *Duck* 92

2728 IF YOU LEAVE
Orchestral Manoeuvres in the Dark
A&M 86

2729 FORGET HIM
Bobby Rydell *Cameo* 64

2744 Divinyls

2770 Vic Damone

2909 Taylor Hicks

2943 Gerry & the Pacemakers

3035 Sade

3092 Cameo

3094 (OUR LOVE) DON'T THROW IT
ALL AWAY
Andy Gibb *RSO* 78

3095 HAPPILY EVER AFTER
Case *Def Soul* 99

3096 IT'S SO EASY
Linda Ronstadt *Asylum* 77

3097 ARE YOU SINCERE
Andy Williams *Cadence* 58

3098 ENDLESS SLEEP
Jody Reynolds *Demon* 58

3099 COWBOYS TO GIRLS
The Intruders *Gamble* 68

3100 STUCK IN THE MIDDLE WITH YOU
Stealers Wheel *A&M* 73

3101 LONELY BOY
Andrew Gold *Asylum* 77

3102 I WANT YOU TO WANT ME
Cheap Trick *Epic* 79

3103 I LOVE HOW YOU LOVE ME
Bobby Vinton *Epic* 68

3104 TIMES OF YOUR LIFE
Paul Anka *UA* 76

3105 AMERICA
Neil Diamond *Capitol* 81

3106 LEADER OF THE BAND
Dan Fogelberg *Full Moon* 82

3107 ARE YOU HAPPY NOW?
Michelle Branch *Maverick* 03

3108 LONG TALL SALLY
Little Richard *Specialty* 56

3109 THE BALLAD OF BONNIE AND CLYDE
Georgie Fame *Epic* 68

3110 WHILE YOU SEE A CHANCE
Steve Winwood *Island* 81

3111 SHORT DICK MAN
20 Fingers *SOS* 95

3112 IF I WANTED TO /
LIKE THE WAY I DO
Melissa Etheridge *Island* 95

3113 SPICE UP YOUR LIFE
Spice Girls *Virgin* 97

3114 BORN TOO LATE
The Poni-Tails *ABC-Paramount* 58

3115 I'VE GOTTA GET A MESSAGE TO YOU
Bee Gees *Atco* 68

3116 ROCK & ROLL MUSIC
Chuck Berry *Chess* 57

3117 MUSIC OF MY HEART
'N Sync & Gloria Estefan *Miramax* 99

3118 RUN TO YOU
Bryan Adams *A&M* 85

3119 TO BE A LOVER
Billy Idol *Chrysalis* 86

3120 THE LONG RUN
Eagles *Asylum* 80

3121 I CAN'T WAIT ANOTHER MINUTE
Hi-Five *Jive* 91

3122 OBSESSION
Animotion *Mercury* 85

3123 ALMOST PARADISE
Mike Reno & Ann Wilson *Columbia* 84

3124 LITTLE CHILDREN
Billy J. Kramer & the Dakotas *Imperial* 64

3125 I GOT THE HOOK-UP!
Master P f/Sons of Funk *No Limit* 98

3126 GARDEN PARTY
Rick Nelson & the Stone Canyon Band
Decca 72

3127 HAPPY, HAPPY BIRTHDAY BABY
The Tune Weavers *Chess* 57

3128 SOMETHING TO TALK ABOUT
Bonnie Raitt *Capitol* 91

3129 LONELY OL' NIGHT
John Cougar Mellencamp *Riva* 85

3130 A TASTE OF HONEY
Herb Alpert & the Tijuana Brass *A&M* 65

3131 NEVER MAKE A PROMISE
Dru Hill *Island* 97

3132 I CAN'T TELL YOU WHY
Eagles *Asylum* 80

3133 THAT'S WHAT LOVE CAN DO
Boy Krazy *Next Plateau* 93

3134 JET AIRLINER
Steve Miller Band *Capitol* 77

3135 NO TIME
Lil' Kim f/Puff Daddy *Undeas* 97

3136 SOME LIKE IT HOT
Power Station *Capitol* 85

3137 BLACK DENIM TROUSERS
The Cheers *Capitol* 55

3138 YOU'RE ONLY LONELY
J.D. Souther *Columbia* 79

3139 COVER ME
Bruce Springsteen *Columbia* 84

3140 KISS THE RAIN
Billie Myers *Universal* 98

3141 PRACTICE WHAT YOU PREACH
Barry White *A&M* 94

3142 I'LL NEVER FIND ANOTHER YOU
The Seekers *Capitol* 65

3143 EVERY 1'S A WINNER
Hot Chocolate *Infinity* 79

3144 SHAKE THAT
Eminem f/Nate Dogg *Shady/
Aftermath* 06

3145 NIGHTS ON BROADWAY
Bee Gees *RSO* 75

3146 RAIN ON ME
Ashanti *Murder Inc./Def Jam* 03

3147 HURT SO BAD
Linda Ronstadt *Asylum* 80

3148 3 A.M. ETERNAL
The KLF *Arista* 91

3149 READY OR NOT
After 7 *Virgin* 90

3150 IF IT ISN'T LOVE
New Edition *MCA* 88

3151 LOVE IS LIKE OXYGEN
Sweet *Capitol* 78

3152 I NEED YOU
LeAnn Rimes *Sparrow* 00

3153 CRAZY
Aerosmith *Geffen* 94

3154 COME TO ME
Diddy f/Nicole Scherzinger *Bad Boy* 06

3155 STILL THE ONE
Orleans *Asylum* 76

3156 MORNING HAS BROKEN
Cat Stevens *A&M* 72

3157 ONLY SIXTEEN
Dr. Hook *Capitol* 76

3158 STONEY END
Barbra Streisand *Columbia* 71

3159 I LIKE IT
Dino *4th & B'way* 89

3160 BOOGALOO DOWN BROADWAY
The Fantastic Johnny C
Phil-L.A. of Soul 67

3161 LEGS
ZZ Top *Warner Bros.* 84

3162 TOO SHY
Kajagoogoo *EMI America* 83

3163 YOU DECORATED MY LIFE
Kenny Rogers *UA* 79

3164 STRUT
Sheena Easton *EMI America* 84

3165 AFFAIR OF THE HEART
Rick Springfield *RCA* 83

3166 I CAN'T STAND IT
Eric Clapton *RSO* 81

3167 WOO-HAH!! GOT YOU ALL IN CHECK /
EVERYTHING REMAINS RAW
Busta Rhymes *Flipmode* 96

3168 WHISPERING BELLS
The Dell-Vikings *Dot* 57

3169 BROKENHEARTED
Brandy *Atlantic* 95

3170 JUST BETWEEN YOU AND ME
Lou Gramm *Atlantic* 90

3171 ANGEL OF THE MORNING
Merrilee Rush & the Turnabouts *Bell* 68

3172 SURFER GIRL
The Beach Boys *Capitol* 63

3173 BEAUTY AND THE BEAST
Celine Dion & Peabo Bryson *Epic* 92

3174 THAT'S LIFE
Frank Sinatra *Reprise* 66

3175 TEMPTATION
Corina *Cutting* 91

3176 YOUR LOVE
The Outfield *Columbia* 86

3177 HOLLY HOLY
Neil Diamond *Uni* 69

3178 WASTED DAYS AND WASTED NIGHTS
Freddy Fender *ABC/Dot* 75

3179 CRUEL SUMMER
Ace of Base *Arista* 98

3180 SK8ER BOI
Avril Lavigne *Arista* 02

3217 The Cars

3240 Nas

3295 **THE WAY I FEEL ABOUT YOU**
Karyn White *Warner Bros.* 92

3296 **BUT I DO**
Clarence "Frogman" Henry *Argo* 61

3297 **ON THE RADIO**
Donna Summer *Casablanca* 80

3298 **GIRL WATCHER**
The O'Kaysions *ABC* 68

3299 **OUR LOVE**
Natalie Cole *Capitol* 78

3300 **ESCAPE**
Enrique Iglesias *Interscope* 02

3301 **HUSH**
Deep Purple *Tetragrammaton* 68

3302 **JUST DON'T WANT TO BE LONELY**
The Main Ingredient *RCA* 74

3303 **YOUR BODY**
Pretty Ricky *Atlantic* 05

3304 **MANDOLIN RAIN**
Bruce Hornsby & the Range *RCA* 87

3305 **YELLOW BIRD**
Arthur Lyman Group *Hi-Fi* 61

3306 **MAYBELLENE**
Chuck Berry *Chess* 55

3307 **NATURAL HIGH**
Bloodstone *London* 73

3308 **BABY (YOU GOT WHAT IT TAKES)**
Dinah Washington & Brook Benton
Mercury 60

3309 **WINGS OF A DOVE**
Ferlin Husky *Capitol* 61

3310 **YOU TALK TOO MUCH**
Joe Jones *Roulette* 60

3311 **KEEP ON DANCING**
The Gentrys *MGM* 65

3312 **A WHITER SHADE OF PALE**
Procol Harum *Deram* 67

3313 **I BELIEVE IN YOU**
(YOU BELIEVE IN ME)
Johnnie Taylor *Stax* 73

3314 **THE JOLLY GREEN GIANT**
The Kingsmen *Wand* 65

3315 **SUMMER NIGHTS**
John Travolta & Olivia Newton-John
RSO 78

3316 **DAYDREAM BELIEVER**
Anne Murray *Capitol* 80

3317 **IF YOU WANT ME TO STAY**
Sly & the Family Stone *Epic* 73

3318 **MISSING YOU NOW**
Michael Bolton *Columbia* 92

3319 **PUT A LITTLE LOVE IN YOUR HEART**
Jackie DeShannon *Imperial* 69

3320 **I WAS MADE FOR DANCIN'**
Leif Garrett *Scotti Bros.* 79

3321 **BARRACUDA**
Heart *Portrait* 77

3322 **WE'RE NOT MAKING LOVE NO MORE**
Dru Hill *LaFace* 98

3323 **LIVING IN AMERICA**
James Brown *Scotti Bros.* 86

3324 **PERFECT WAY**
Scritti Politti *Warner Bros.* 85

3325 **WANKSTA**
50 Cent *G-Unit/Shady* 03

3326 **THE BITCH IS BACK**
Elton John *MCA* 74

3327 **REBEL-'ROUSER**
Duane Eddy *Jamie* 58

3328 **I CAN'T HOLD BACK**
Survivor *Scotti Bros.* 84

3329 **I WILL REMEMBER YOU (LIVE)**
Sarah McLachlan *Arista* 99

3330 **I LOVE YOU**
Faith Evans *Bad Boy* 02

3331 **DREAMIN'**
Johnny Burnette *Liberty* 60

3332 **BRASS IN POCKET (I'M SPECIAL)**
The Pretenders *Sire* 80

3333 **I'M LEAVING IT (ALL) UP TO YOU**
Donny & Marie Osmond *MGM* 74

3334 **SHE BANGS**
Ricky Martin *Columbia* 00

3335 **DONTCHANGE**
Musiq *Def Soul* 02

3336 **EX-FACTOR**
Lauryn Hill *Ruffhouse* 99

3337 **BELIEVE WHAT YOU SAY /**
MY BUCKET'S GOT A HOLE IN IT
Ricky Nelson *Imperial* 58

3338 **BRIDGE OVER TROUBLED WATER**
Aretha Franklin *Atlantic* 71

3339 **DO I HAVE TO SAY THE WORDS?**
Bryan Adams *A&M* 92

3340 **I NEED YOUR LOVE TONIGHT**
Elvis Presley *RCA* 59

3341 **DOESN'T SOMEBODY WANT**
TO BE WANTED
The Partridge Family *Bell* 71

3342 **WHAT ARE WE DOIN' IN LOVE**
Dottie West *Liberty* 81

3343 **HOLD ME TIGHT**
Johnny Nash *JAD* 68

3344 **STORMY**
Classics IV *Imperial* 68

3345 **WOLVERTON MOUNTAIN**
Claude King *Columbia* 62

3346 **THINK I'M IN LOVE**
Eddie Money *Columbia* 82

3347 **BLACK IS BLACK**
Los Bravos *Press* 66

3348 **TO ALL THE GIRLS I'VE**
LOVED BEFORE
Julio Iglesias & Willie Nelson *Columbia* 84

3349 **DECK OF CARDS**
Wink Martindale *Dot* 59

3350 **THOUGHT I'D DIED AND**
GONE TO HEAVEN
Bryan Adams *A&M* 92

3351 **BABY I'M FOR REAL**
The Originals *Soul* 69

3352 **EVERYTHING I OWN**
Bread *Elektra* 72

3353 **A MILLION TO ONE**
Jimmy Charles *Promo* 60

3354 **NEVER BE ANYONE ELSE BUT YOU**
Ricky Nelson *Imperial* 59

3355 **GOIN' OUT OF MY HEAD**
Little Anthony & the Imperials *DCP* 64

3356 **HE CAN'T LOVE U**
Jagged Edge *So So Def* 00

3357 **GAME OVER (FLIP)**
Lil' Flip *Sucka Free* 04

3358 **GIMME THAT**
Chris Brown f/Lil' Wayne *Jive* 06

3359 **SHAKE IT**
Ian Matthews *Mushroom* 79

3360 **DIFFERENT DRUM**
Stone Poneys f/Linda Ronstadt *Capitol* 68

3361 **LOVE ME**
112 f/Mase *Bad Boy* 98

3362 **GIGOLO**
Nick Cannon f/R. Kelly *Nick/Jive* 04

3363 **RIKKI DON'T LOSE THAT NUMBER**
Steely Dan *ABC* 74

3364 **FOOLISH LITTLE GIRL**
The Shirelles *Scepter* 63

3365 **LOOKIN' FOR LOVE**
Johnny Lee *Full Moon* 80

3366 **SHE'S A FOOL**
Lesley Gore *Mercury* 63

3367 **ELECTION DAY**
Arcadia *Capitol* 85

3368 **POISON IVY**
The Coasters *Atco* 59

3369 **I DO!!**
Toya *Arista* 01

3370 **SO FAR AWAY**
Staind *Flip/Elektra* 03

3371 **HOW SWEET IT IS**
(TO BE LOVED BY YOU)
James Taylor *Warner Bros.* 75

3372 **SUNSHINE OF YOUR LOVE**
Cream *Atco* 68

3373 **HAPPY BIRTHDAY, SWEET SIXTEEN**
Neil Sedaka *RCA* 62

3374 **FOR THE GOOD TIMES**
Ray Price *Columbia* 71

3375 **NEVER BEEN TO SPAIN**
Three Dog Night *Dunhill* 72

3376 **FOX ON THE RUN**
Sweet *Capitol* 76

3377 **CRADLE OF LOVE**
Johnny Preston *Mercury* 60

3378 **LOVE SOMEBODY**
Rick Springfield *RCA* 84

3379 **REAL LOVE**
Doobie Brothers *Warner Bros.* 80

3420 The Cure

3432 **I'M ALRIGHT**
Kenny Loggins *Columbia* 80

3433 **ROCK THIS TOWN**
Stray Cats *EMI America* 82

3434 **RIGHT PLACE WRONG TIME**
Dr. John *Atco* 73

3435 **REAL REAL REAL**
Jesus Jones *SBK* 91

3436 **IT'S A MISTAKE**
Men at Work *Columbia* 83

3437 **THE JERK**
The Larks *Money* 65

3438 **DANCE WITH ME**
Peter Brown *Drive* 78

3439 **RHYTHM IS GONNA GET YOU**
Gloria Estefan & Miami Sound Machine
Epic 87

3440 **ANGEL**
Madonna *Sire* 85

3441 **HIM**
Rupert Holmes *MCA* 80

3442 **WANTED DEAD OR ALIVE**
Bon Jovi *Mercury* 87

3443 **I WANT YOUR LOVE**
Chic *Atlantic* 79

3444 **WELCOME TO THE JUNGLE**
Guns N' Roses *Geffen* 88

3445 **LET IT BE ME**
Everly Brothers *Cadence* 60

3446 **TIGHTER, TIGHTER**
Alive & Kicking *Roulette* 70

3447 **THEME SONG FROM "SONG FOR A SUMMER NIGHT"**
Mitch Miller *Columbia* 56

3448 **TAKE ME THERE**
BLACKstreet & Mya f/Mase & Blinky Blink
Interscope 99

3449 **IT'S FIVE O'CLOCK SOMEWHERE**
Alan Jackson & Jimmy Buffett *Arista* 03

3450 **CASANOVA**
Levert *Atlantic* 87

3451 **WISHIN' AND HOPIN'**
Dusty Springfield *Philips* 64

3452 **TIME, LOVE AND TENDERNESS**
Michael Bolton *Columbia* 91

3453 **WHEN I FALL IN LOVE**
The Lettermen *Capitol* 62

3454 **HUMMINGBIRD**
Les Paul & Mary Ford *Capitol* 55

3455 **REBIRTH OF SLICK (COOL LIKE DAT)**
Digable Planets *Pendulum* 93

3456 **THE LONELY BULL**
The Tijuana Brass f/Herb Alpert *A&M* 62

3457 **GOT TO GET YOU INTO MY LIFE**
The Beatles *Capitol* 76

3458 **DANCE TO THE MUSIC**
Sly & the Family Stone *Epic* 68

3459 **RAIN**
Madonna *Maverick* 93

3460 **UHH AHH**
Boyz II Men *Motown* 92

3461 **WHEN SMOKEY SINGS**
ABC *Mercury* 87

3462 **WALKING IN RHYTHM**
Blackbyrds *Fantasy* 75

3463 **TAKE GOOD CARE OF HER**
Adam Wade *Coed* 61

3464 **SLEEPING BAG**
ZZ Top *Warner Bros.* 85

3465 **POETRY MAN**
Phoebe Snow *Shelter* 75

3466 **ROMEO AND JULIET**
Sylk-E. Fyne f/Chill *Grand Jury* 98

3467 **COME ON DOWN TO MY BOAT**
Every Mother's Son *MGM* 67

3468 **SWEET FREEDOM**
Michael McDonald *MCA* 86

3469 **DELIRIOUS**
Prince *Warner Bros.* 83

3470 **YOU'RE SIXTEEN**
Johnny Burnette *Liberty* 60

3471 **FASTLOVE**
George Michael *DreamWorks* 96

3472 **I'VE HAD IT**
The Bell-Notes *Time* 59

3473 **SOLITAIRE**
Laura Branigan *Atlantic* 83

3474 **I WILL COME TO YOU**
Hanson *Mercury* 97

3475 **IT WAS A GOOD DAY**
Ice Cube *Priority* 93

3476 **BLACK BALLOON**
Goo Goo Dolls *Warner Bros.* 99

3477 **GROOVE THANG**
Zhané *Illtown* 94

3478 **HERE WE GO**
Trina f/Kelly Rowland *Slip-N-Slide* 05

3479 **I WANT HER**
Keith Sweat *Vintertainment* 88

3480 **MAGIC**
Pilot *EMI* 75

3481 **THE OLD LAMPLIGHTER**
The Browns *RCA* 60

3482 **IMAGE OF A GIRL**
Safaris *Eldo* 60

3483 **YOU MAY BE RIGHT**
Billy Joel *Columbia* 80

3484 **DEAR LADY TWIST**
Gary U.S. Bonds *Legrand* 62

3485 **COULD IT BE MAGIC**
Barry Manilow *Arista* 75

3486 **COME DANCING**
The Kinks *Arista* 83

3487 **ATLANTIS**
Donovan *Epic* 69

3488 **GET DOWN**
Gilbert O'Sullivan *MAM* 73

3489 **HARBOR LIGHTS**
The Platters *Mercury* 60

3490 **COOL CHANGE**
Little River Band *Capitol* 80

3491 **WOULD I LIE TO YOU?**
Eurythmics *RCA* 85

3492 **ROCKET 2 U**
The Jets *MCA* 88

3493 **FAST CAR**
Tracy Chapman *Elektra* 88

3494 **LOW RIDER**
War *UA* 75

3495 **TURN AROUND, LOOK AT ME**
The Vogues *Reprise* 68

3496 **I'VE DONE EVERYTHING FOR YOU**
Rick Springfield *RCA* 81

3497 **COUNT ON ME**
Jefferson Starship *Grunt* 78

3498 **SHINE A LITTLE LOVE**
Electric Light Orchestra *Jet* 79

3499 **ADULT EDUCATION**
Daryl Hall and John Oates *RCA* 84

3500 **FEELIN' STRONGER EVERY DAY**
Chicago *Columbia* 73

3501 **INDIAN GIVER**
1910 Fruitgum Co. *Buddah* 69

3502 **CLOUD NINE**
The Temptations *Gordy* 69

3503 **THIS GIRL'S IN LOVE WITH YOU**
Dionne Warwick *Scepter* 69

3504 **YESTER-ME, YESTER-YOU, YESTERDAY**
Stevie Wonder *Tamla* 69

3505 **OUR HOUSE**
Madness *Geffen* 83

3506 **PRICE OF LOVE**
Bad English *Epic* 90

3507 **WORDS GET IN THE WAY**
Miami Sound Machine *Epic* 86

3508 **OVER YOU**
Gary Puckett & the Union Gap
Columbia 68

3509 **FREE FALLIN'**
Tom Petty *MCA* 90

3510 **IMAGINARY LOVER**
Atlanta Rhythm Section *Polydor* 78

3511 **BREAKDANCE**
Irene Cara *Geffen* 84

3512 **CHERISH**
David Cassidy *Bell* 71

3513 **IS THIS LOVE**
Survivor *Scotti Bros.* 87

3514 **LOVE IS IN CONTROL (FINGER ON THE TRIGGER)**
Donna Summer *Geffen* 82

3515 **UP ON THE ROOF**
The Drifters *Atlantic* 63

3516 **LAY YOUR HANDS ON ME**
Thompson Twins *Arista* 85

3557 D'Angelo

3579 Burl Ives

3622 **TOO MUCH TIME ON MY HANDS**
Styx *A&M* 81

3623 **SEVEN LITTLE GIRLS**
SITTING IN THE BACK SEAT
Paul Evans *Guaranteed* 59

3624 **NEAR YOU**
Roger Williams *Kapp* 58

3625 **DON'T GET ME WRONG**
Pretenders *Sire* 86

3626 **HOLD ON MY HEART**
Genesis *Atlantic* 92

3627 **MARIANNE**
The Hilltoppers *Dot* 57

3628 **ANGEL**
Amanda Perez *Powerhouse* 03

3629 **NITE AND DAY**
Al B. Sure! *Warner Bros.* 88

3630 **STILL**
Bill Anderson *Decca* 63

3631 **KING OF WISHFUL THINKING**
Go West *EMI* 90

3632 **LIVING IN SIN**
Bon Jovi *Mercury* 89

3633 **FRANKIE**
Connie Francis *MGM* 59

3634 **SAY IT RIGHT**
Nelly Furtado *Mosley* 07

3635 **HEART AND SOUL**
Huey Lewis & the News *Chrysalis* 83

3636 **EVERYBODY EVERYBODY**
Black Box *RCA* 90

3637 **CATCH US IF YOU CAN**
Dave Clark Five *Epic* 65

3638 **SUMMER BREEZE**
Seals and Crofts *Warner Bros.* 72

3639 **PARTY DOLL**
Steve Lawrence *Coral* 57

3640 **CRUMBLIN' DOWN**
John Cougar Mellencamp *Riva* 83

3641 **EPIC**
Faith No More *Slash* 90

3642 **GET OFF**
Foxy *Dash* 78

3643 **IF I WERE YOUR WOMAN**
Gladys Knight & the Pips *Soul* 71

3644 **CUT THE CAKE**
Average White Band *Atlantic* 75

3645 **EMOTION**
Destiny's Child *Columbia* 01

3646 **WARM IT UP**
Kris Kross *Ruffhouse* 92

3647 **PRAYER FOR THE DYING**
Seal *ZTT/Sire* 94

3648 **CRIMSON AND CLOVER**
Joan Jett & the Blackhearts *Boardwalk* 82

3649 **DON'T CRY**
Asia *Geffen* 83

3650 **YOU DON'T KNOW WHAT YOU'VE GOT**
(UNTIL YOU LOSE IT)
Ral Donner *Gone* 61

3651 **PRIVATE DANCER**
Tina Turner *Capitol* 85

3652 **IF YOU'RE READY**
(COME GO WITH ME)
The Staple Singers *Stax* 73

3653 **BABY LOVE**
Regina *Atlantic* 86

3654 **SHE'S OUT OF MY LIFE**
Michael Jackson *Epic* 80

3655 **REVOLUTION**
The Beatles *Apple* 68

3656 **BETTER LOVE NEXT TIME**
Dr. Hook *Capitol* 80

3657 **SUDDENLY THERE'S A VALLEY**
Gogi Grant *Era* 55

3658 **RESCUE ME**
Fontella Bass *Checker* 65

3659 **I'LL GIVE ALL MY LOVE TO YOU**
Keith Sweat *Vintertainment* 91

3660 **MAGIC MAN**
Heart *Mushroom* 76

3661 **WHATCHA SEE IS WHATCHA GET**
The Dramatics *Volt* 71

3662 **VICTORY**
Kool & the Gang *Mercury* 87

3663 **RING THE ALARM**
Beyoncé *Columbia* 06

3664 **DANCING IN THE MOONLIGHT**
King Harvest *Perception* 73

3665 **KARMA**
Alicia Keys *J* 05

3666 **I REMEMBER YOU**
Skid Row *Atlantic* 90

3667 **CLOSE MY EYES (FOREVER)**
Lita Ford w/Ozzy Osbourne *RCA* 89

3668 **FEEL LIKE MAKIN' LOVE**
Bad Company *Swan Song* 75

3669 **LOVE WILL TURN YOU AROUND**
Kenny Rogers *Liberty* 82

3670 **INTUITION**
Jewel *Atlantic* 03

3671 **FRESH**
Kool & the Gang *De-Lite* 85

3672 **I WON'T HOLD YOU BACK**
Toto *Columbia* 83

3673 **TWO OUT OF THREE AIN'T BAD**
Meat Loaf *Cleveland Intl/Epic* 78

3674 **SUGAR TOWN**
Nancy Sinatra *Reprise* 66

3675 **SPIES LIKE US**
Paul McCartney *Capitol* 86

3676 **SENTIMENTAL STREET**
Night Ranger *MCA/Camel* 85

3677 **C'MON AND GET MY LOVE**
D-Mob i/Cathy Dennis *FFRR* 90

3678 **MY BABY DADDY**
B-Rock & the Bizz *Tony Mercedes* 97

3679 **REELING IN THE YEARS**
Steely Dan *ABC* 73

3680 **OH, BOY!**
The Crickets *Brunswick* 58

3681 **C U WHEN U GET THERE**
Coolio f/40 Thevz *Tommy Boy* 97

3682 **ONLY U**
Ashanti *The Inc./Def Jam* 05

3683 **I'M NOT IN LOVE**
Will to Power *Epic* 91

3684 **BIMBOMBEY**
Jimmie Rodgers *Roulette* 58

3685 **PATIENCE**
Guns N' Roses *Geffen* 89

3686 **GO D.J.**
Lil Wayne *Cash Money* 04

3687 **YOUR WOMAN**
White Town *Chrysalis* 97

3688 **MY MARIA**
B.W. Stevenson *RCA* 73

3689 **DON'T DO ME LIKE THAT**
Tom Petty & the Heartbreakers
Backstreet 80

3690 **JESSE**
Carly Simon *Warner Bros.* 80

3691 **BORN A WOMAN**
Sandy Posey *MGM* 66

3692 **ROCK AND ROLL DREAMS COME**
THROUGH
Meat Loaf *MCA* 94

3693 **GARDEN OF EDEN**
Joe Valino *Vik* 56

3694 **WONDERFUL WORLD**
Herman's Hermits *MGM* 65

3695 **MAKE YOU SWEAT**
Keith Sweat *Vintertainment* 90

3696 **BOTTLE OF WINE**
The Fireballs *Atco* 68

3697 **I GOT A NAME**
Jim Croce *ABC* 73

3698 **DISCO INFERNO**
The Trammps *Atlantic* 78

3699 **PROMISES, PROMISES**
Naked Eyes *EMI America* 83

3700 **TWO STEPS BEHIND**
Def Leppard *Columbia* 93

3701 **THROUGH THE WIRE**
Kanye West *Roc-A-Fella/Def Jam* 04

3702 **REMEMBER (WALKIN' IN THE SAND)**
The Shangri-Las *Red Bird* 64

3703 **GOT A HOLD ON ME**
Christine McVie *Warner Bros.* 84

3704 **(DON'T FEAR) THE REAPER**
Blue Öyster Cult *Columbia* 76

3705 **JUST ANOTHER DREAM**
Cathy Dennis *Polydor* 91

3706 **THE ONE I LOVE**
R.E.M. *I.R.S.* 87

3707 **DANNY BOY**
Conway Twitty *MGM* 59

3708 **DEVOTED TO YOU**
Everly Brothers *Cadence* 58

3705 Cathy Dennis

3765 **YOU'RE THE ONE**
The Vogues *Co & Ce* 65

3766 **EVERYBODY LOVES A CLOWN**
Gary Lewis & the Playboys *Liberty* 65

3767 **TRYIN' TO LIVE MY LIFE WITHOUT YOU**
Bob Seger *Capitol* 81

3768 **ROCK 'N' ROLL FANTASY**
Bad Company *Swan Song* 79

3769 **I'M SORRY / HE'S MINE**
The Platters *Mercury* 57

3770 **SADENESS PART 1**
Enigma *Charisma* 91

3771 **ANOTHER DAY / OH WOMAN OH WHY**
Paul McCartney *Apple* 71

3772 **LAWYERS IN LOVE**
Jackson Browne *Asylum* 83

3773 **EVERYTIME**
Britney Spears *Jive* 04

3774 **IRRESISTIBLE**
Jessica Simpson *Columbia* 01

3775 **AN AMERICAN DREAM**
The Dirt Band *UA* 80

3776 **EVERYTHING CHANGES**
Kathy Triccoli *Reunion* 92

3777 **THE LORD'S PRAYER**
Sister Janet Mead *A&M* 74

3778 **ROUND AND ROUND**
Tevin Campbell *Paisley Park* 91

3779 **DEEP PURPLE**
Donny & Marie Osmond *MGM* 76

3780 **FAITHFUL**
Go West *EMI* 93

3781 **AMERICANS**
Byron MacGregor *Westbound* 74

3782 **WHERE IS THE LOVE**
Roberta Flack & Donny Hathaway *Atlantic* 72

3783 **DON'T LET THE RAIN COME DOWN (CROOKED LITTLE MAN)**
Serendipity Singers *Philips* 64

3784 **SERPENTINE FIRE**
Earth, Wind & Fire *Columbia* 78

3785 **LIKE GLUE**
Sean Paul *VP* 03

3786 **GO, JIMMY, GO**
Jimmy Clanton *Ace* 60

3787 **SILHOUETTES**
Herman's Hermits *MGM* 65

3788 **EVERY BEAT OF MY HEART**
The Pips *Vee Jay* 61

3789 **MAY YOU ALWAYS**
McGuire Sisters *Coral* 59

3790 **HOW AM I SUPPOSED TO LIVE WITHOUT YOU**
Laura Branigan *Atlantic* 83

3791 **STUNT 101**
G-Unit *G-Unit* 03

3792 **STILL NOT A PLAYER**
Big Punisher f/Joe *Loud* 98

3793 **AHAB THE ARAB**
Ray Stevens *Mercury* 62

3794 **TOWER OF STRENGTH**
Gene McDaniels *Liberty* 61

3795 **HURDY GURDY MAN**
Donovan *Epic* 68

3796 **HEARD IT IN A LOVE SONG**
Marshall Tucker Band *Capricorn* 77

3797 **GO ALL THE WAY**
Raspberries *Capitol* 72

3798 **MY LOVE**
Lionel Richie *Motown* 83

3799 **MANY TEARS AGO**
Connie Francis *MGM* 60

3800 **WAT DA HOOK GON BE**
Murphy Lee f/Jermaine Dupri *Fo' Reel* 03

3801 **HELL YEAH**
Ginuwine f/Baby *Epic* 03

3802 **THE LOOK OF LOVE (PART ONE)**
ABC *Mercury* 83

3803 **GIRL TONITE**
Twista f/Trey Songz *Atlantic* 05

3804 **HOT ROD HEARTS**
Robbie Dupree *Elektra* 80

3805 **TAKE TIME TO KNOW HER**
Percy Sledge *Atlantic* 68

3806 **HURT**
Timi Yuro *Liberty* 61

3807 **IN THE RAIN**
The Dramatics *Volt* 72

3808 **BLAME IT ON THE BOSSA NOVA**
Eydie Gorme *Columbia* 63

3809 **BATTLE HYMN OF THE REPUBLIC**
Mormon Tabernacle Choir *Columbia* 59

3810 **BEAUTIFUL SOUL**
Jesse McCartney *Hollywood* 05

3811 **I CARE 4 U**
Aaliyah *Blackground* 02

3812 **THE VALLEY ROAD**
Bruce Hornsby & the Range *RCA* 88

3813 **LITTLE BITTY PRETTY ONE**
Thurston Harris *Aladdin* 57

3814 **MIDNIGHT BLUE**
Melissa Manchester *Arista* 75

3815 **GOING IN CIRCLES**
Friends of Distinction *RCA* 69

3816 **SO ANXIOUS**
Ginuwine *550 Music* 99

3817 **TIME WON'T LET ME**
The Outsiders *Capitol* 66

3818 **CRYING IN THE RAIN**
Everly Brothers *Warner Bros.* 62

3819 **AT MY FRONT DOOR (CRAZY LITTLE MAMA)**
Pat Boone *Dot* 55

3820 **SOMEBODY'S KNOCKIN'**
Terri Gibbs *MCA* 81

3821 **FERNANDO**
Abba *Atlantic* 76

3822 **THE MAN IN THE RAINCOAT**
Priscilla Wright *Unique* 55

3823 **I LOVE HOW YOU LOVE ME**
The Paris Sisters *Gregmark* 61

3824 **SO SAD (TO WATCH GOOD LOVE GO BAD)**
Everly Brothers *Warner Bros.* 60

3825 **LOVIN', TOUCHIN', SQUEEZIN'**
Journey *Columbia* 79

3826 **BIG DADDY**
Heavy D *Uptown* 97

3827 **1, 2, 3, RED LIGHT**
1910 Fruitgum Co. *Buddah* 68

3828 **CATER 2 U**
Destiny's Child *Columbia* 05

3829 **YOU DON'T KNOW ME**
Ray Charles *ABC-Paramount* 62

3830 **SYLVIA'S MOTHER**
Dr. Hook & the Medicine Show *Columbia* 72

3831 **WHAT'D I SAY (PART 1)**
Ray Charles *Atlantic* 59

3832 **WALK ON BY**
Dionne Warwick *Scepter* 64

3833 **TEMPTATION EYES**
The Grass Roots *Dunhill* 71

3834 **A LITTLE IN LOVE**
Cliff Richard *EMI America* 81

3835 **SHE CRIED**
Jay & the Americans *UA* 62

3836 **JUST ASK YOUR HEART**
Frankie Avalon *Chancellor* 59

3837 **ALMOST DOESN'T COUNT**
Brandy *Atlantic* 99

3838 **DREAM BABY (HOW LONG MUST I DREAM)**
Roy Orbison *Monument* 62

3839 **PEACE TRAIN**
Cat Stevens *A&M* 71

3840 **BOOM! SHAKE THE ROOM**
Jazzy Jeff & Fresh Prince *Jive* 93

3841 **THIS AIN'T A LOVE SONG**
Bon Jovi *Mercury* 95

3842 **BABY FACE**
Wing and a Prayer Fife & Drum Corps *Wing and a Prayer* 76

3843 **THAT'S ALL THERE IS TO THAT**
Nat King Cole *Capitol* 56

3844 **LET IT BE ME**
Jerry Butler and Betty Everett *Vee Jay* 64

3845 **CAN'T GET ENOUGH**
Bad Company *Swan Song* 74

3846 **BREAK UP TO MAKE UP**
The Stylistics *Avco* 73

3847 **HEAT WAVE / LOVE IS A ROSE**
Linda Ronstadt *Asylum* 75

3848 **TIME IS ON MY SIDE**
The Rolling Stones *London* 64

3849 **BAD BOYS**
Inner Circle *Big Beat* 93

3894 Metallica

3968 Hayley Mills

4031 David Ruffin

4099 Fantasia

4125 Chris Isaak

4162 SWEET LOVE
Anita Baker *Elektra* 86

4163 BE MY GUEST
Fats Domino *Imperial* 59

4164 YOUR WILDEST DREAMS
The Moody Blues *Threshold* 86

4165 THINK OF LAURA
Christopher Cross *Warner Bros.* 84

4166 EVIL WAYS
Santana *Columbia* 70

4167 EVERYBODY'S TALKIN'
Nilsson *RCA* 69

4168 MONTEGO BAY
Bobby Bloom *L&R* 70

4169 KNOCKIN' BOOTS
Candyman *Epic* 90

4170 LOVIN' EVERY MINUTE OF IT
Loverboy *Columbia* 85

4171 (WHERE DO I BEGIN) LOVE STORY
Andy Williams *Columbia* 71

4172 BREATHLESS
Jerry Lee Lewis *Sun* 58

4173 YOU TAKE MY BREATH AWAY
Rex Smith *Columbia* 79

4174 SUSAN
The Buckinghams *Columbia* 68

4175 THAT'LL BE THE DAY
Linda Ronstadt *Asylum* 76

4176 I ONLY HAVE EYES FOR YOU
The Flamingos *End* 59

4177 YOU CAN'T TURN ME OFF (IN THE
MIDDLE OF TURNING ME ON)
High Inergy *Gordy* 77

4178 WALKING THE DOG
Rufus Thomas *Stax* 63

4179 SOMETHING'S BURNING
Kenny Rogers & the First Edition
Reprise 70

4180 SWING THE MOOD
Jive Bunny & the Mastermixers *Music
Factory* 90

4181 LOTTA LOVIN' / WEAR MY RING
Gene Vincent & His Blue Caps *Capitol* 57

4182 ALONE AT LAST
Jackie Wilson *Brunswick* 60

4183 GET IT ON (BANG A GONG)
Power Station *Capitol* 85

4184 MAKE ME SMILE
Chicago *Columbia* 70

4185 PORTRAIT OF MY LOVE
Steve Lawrence *UA* 61

4186 ONE TOKE OVER THE LINE
Brewer and Shipley *Kama Sutra* 71

4187 YOU
Jesse Powell *Silas* 99

4188 TIME HAS COME TODAY
Chambers Brothers *Columbia* 68

4189 MAGIC
The Cars *Elektra* 84

4190 INCOMPLETE
Backstreet Boys *Jive* 05

4191 WHO SAYS YOU CAN'T GO HOME
Bon Jovi *Island* 06

4192 GYPSY MAN
War *UA* 73

4193 SMOKE FROM A DISTANT FIRE
Sanford/Townsend Band *Warner Bros.* 77

4194 IT'S A SIN
Pet Shop Boys *EMI America* 87

4195 BREAKIN'... THERE'S NO
STOPPING US
Ollie and Jerry *Polydor* 84

4196 OFF THE WALL
Michael Jackson *Epic* 80

4197 YES WE CAN CAN
Pointer Sisters *Blue Thumb* 73

4198 DARE ME
Pointer Sisters *RCA* 85

4199 BOOGIE WOOGIE BUGLE BOY
Bette Midler *Atlantic* 73

4200 OUR WINTER LOVE
Bill Pursell *Columbia* 63

4201 GO YOUR OWN WAY
Fleetwood Mac *Warner Bros.* 77

4202 KEEP ON MOVIN'
Soul II Soul *Virgin* 89

4203 KEWPIE DOLL
Perry Como *RCA* 58

4204 EVERYBODY LOVES A LOVER
Doris Day *Columbia* 58

4205 I UNDERSTAND (JUST HOW YOU FEEL)
The G-Clefs *Terrace* 61

4206 DYNOMITE-PART 1
Tony Camillo's Bazuka *A&M* 75

4207 CHINA GIRL
David Bowie *EMI America* 83

4208 PUT YOUR HANDS TOGETHER
The O'Jays *PIR* 74

4209 I SAY A LITTLE PRAYER
Aretha Franklin *Atlantic* 68

4210 SOMEBODY TO LOVE
Queen *Elektra* 77

4211 AIN'T NO STOPPIN' US NOW
McFadden & Whitehead *PIR* 79

4212 BULLET WITH BUTTERFLY WINGS
The Smashing Pumpkins *Virgin* 96

4213 WHEN I'M GONE
Eminem *Shady/Aftermath* 05

4214 RUSH HOUR
Jane Wiedlin *EMI-Manhattan* 88

4215 MY LITTLE TOWN
Simon and Garfunkel *Columbia* 75

4216 NEW MOON ON MONDAY
Duran Duran *Capitol* 84

4217 BROWN EYED GIRL
Van Morrison *Bang* 67

4218 THEME FROM "DR. KILDARE" (THREE
STARS WILL SHINE TONIGHT)
Richard Chamberlain *MGM* 62

4219 I WANNA BE YOUR LOVER
Prince *Warner Bros.* 80

4220 STILL WATER (LOVE)
Four Tops *Motown* 70

4221 HER TOWN TOO
James Taylor & J.D. Souther *Columbia* 81

4222 THAT'S THE WAY OF THE WORLD
Earth, Wind & Fire *Columbia* 75

4223 EXPRESS YOURSELF
Charles Wright & the Watts 103rd Street
Rhythm Band *Warner Bros.* 70

4224 NEVER ENDING SONG OF LOVE
Delaney and Bonnie & Friends *Atco* 71

4225 EVERYBODY PLAYS THE FOOL
Aaron Neville *A&M* 91

4226 SO FINE
The Fiestas *Old Town* 59

4227 BABY I NEED YOUR LOVING
Four Tops *Motown* 64

4228 SANDY
Larry Hall *Strand* 60

4229 LET'S MAKE A NIGHT TO REMEMBER
Bryan Adams *A&M* 96

4230 ANTICIPATION
Carly Simon *Elektra* 72

4231 IS IT LOVE
Mr. Mister *RCA* 86

4232 WHAT YOU WON'T DO FOR LOVE
Bobby Caldwell *Clouds* 79

4233 I'VE BEEN IN LOVE BEFORE
Cutting Crew *Virgin* 87

4234 BURNING DOWN THE HOUSE
Talking Heads *Sire* 83

4235 DENISE
Randy & the Rainbows *Rust* 63

4236 TWO OCCASIONS
The Deele *Solar* 88

4237 I COULD NEVER TAKE THE
PLACE OF YOUR MAN
Prince *Paisley Park* 88

4238 I'VE GOTTA BE ME
Sammy Davis, Jr. *Reprise* 69

4239 DROWNING IN THE SEA OF LOVE
Joe Simon *Spring* 72

4240 I ONLY WANT TO BE WITH YOU
Bay City Rollers *Arista* 76

4241 IVORY TOWER
Otis Williams & His Charms *DeLuxe* 56

4242 UM, UM, UM, UM, UM, UM
Major Lance *Okeh* 64

4243 LOOKIN' FOR A LOVE
Bobby Womack *UA* 74

4244 IT WOULD TAKE A STRONG
STRONG MAN
Rick Astley *RCA* 88

4245 GEE WHIZ (LOOK AT HIS EYES)
Carla Thomas *Atlantic* 61

4246 YOU GOT THE LOVE
Rufus f/Chaka Khan *ABC* 74

4463 Eternal

4497: Kid Rock

4510 CRYING TIME
Ray Charles *ABC-Paramount* 66

4511 WHIP APPEAL
Babyface *Solar* 90

4512 PIECE OF MY HEART
Tara Kemp *Giant* 91

4513 JAM UP JELLY TIGHT
Tommy Roe *ABC* 70

4514 GET DOWN ON IT
Kool & the Gang *De-Lite* 82

4515 DEJA VU
Beyoncé f/Jay-Z *Columbia* 06

4516 FOR YOU
Rick Nelson *Decca* 64

4517 LET'S THINK ABOUT LIVING
Bob Luman *Warner Bros.* 60

4518 AIN'T NO WAY TO TREAT A LADY
Helen Reddy *Capitol* 75

4519 ONE MINT JULEP
Ray Charles *Impulse* 61

4520 MY CUP RUNNETH OVER
Ed Ames *RCA* 67

4521 SCHOOL IS OUT
Gary U.S. Bonds *Legrand* 61

4522 RIGHT ON TRACK
Breakfast Club *MCA* 87

4523 SHAME
Evelyn "Champagne" King *RCA* 78

4524 LAYLA
Derek & the Dominos *Atco* 72

4525 JINGLE JANGLE
The Archies *Kirshner* 70

4526 GOING UP THE COUNTRY
Canned Heat *Liberty* 69

4527 BROKEN ARROW
Rod Stewart *Warner Bros.* 92

4528 ONLY YOU
Ringo Starr *Apple* 75

4529 A SUMMER SONG
Chad and Jeremy *World Artists* 64

4530 JENNIE LEE
Jan and Arnie *Arwin* 58

4531 DREAMIN'
Vanessa Williams *Wing* 89

4532 DON'T CALL US, WE'LL CALL YOU
Sugarloaf/Jerry Corbetta *Claridge* 75

4533 SKINNY LEGS AND ALL
Joe Tex *Dial* 67

4534 STAY IN MY CORNER
The Dells *Cadet* 68

4535 ROCK-A-BILLY
Guy Mitchell *Columbia* 57

4536 FLEX
Mad Cobra *Columbia* 93

4537 JUNGLE LOVE
The Time *Warner Bros.* 85

4538 SOMETIMES
Britney Spears *Jive* 99

4539 HOLLYWOOD SWINGING
Kool & the Gang *De-Lite* 74

4540 OH GIRL
Paul Young *Columbia* 90

4541 BOTH SIDES NOW
Judy Collins *Elektra* 68

4542 I NEVER LOVED A MAN
(THE WAY I LOVE YOU)
Aretha Franklin *Atlantic* 67

4543 THIS GIRL IS A WOMAN NOW
Gary Puckett & the Union Gap
Columbia 69

4544 THE GOOD STUFF
Kenny Chesney *BNA* 02

4545 FUNKY TOWN
Pseudo Echo *RCA* 87

4546 I DROVE ALL NIGHT
Cyndi Lauper *Epic* 89

4547 HOT ROD LINCOLN
Commander Cody & His Lost Planet Airmen
Paramount 72

4548 THIS TIME I'M IN IT FOR LOVE
Player *RSO* 78

4549 OUR LIPS ARE SEALED
The Go-Go's *I.R.S.* 81

4550 ALWAYS IN MY HEART
Tevin Campbell *Qwest* 94

4551 I WANT TO COME OVER
Melissa Etheridge *Island* 96

4552 THE HOUSE THAT JACK BUILT
Aretha Franklin *Atlantic* 68

4553 DRIP DROP
Dion DiMucci *Columbia* 63

4554 DANCING IN THE STREET
Mick Jagger/David Bowie *EMI America* 85

4555 TROUBLE MAN
Marvin Gaye *Tamla* 73

4556 VENUS IN BLUE JEANS
Jimmy Clanton *Ace* 62

4557 WHEN YOU'RE HOT, YOU'RE HOT
Jerry Reed *RCA* 71

4558 WHAT KIND OF FOOL
Barbra Streisand & Barry Gibb
Columbia 81

4559 I WANNA GET NEXT TO YOU
Rose Royce *MCA* 77

4560 I ONLY HAVE EYES FOR YOU
Art Garfunkel *Columbia* 75

4561 WHAT'S YOUR FANTASY
Ludacris f/Shawnna *Disturbing tha
Peace/Def Jam South* 00

4562 YOU'RE ALL I NEED TO GET BY
Marvin Gaye & Tammi Terrell *Tamla* 68

4563 THE WORLD IS A GHETTO
War *UA* 73

4564 I SAW HIM STANDING THERE
Tiffany *MCA* 80

4565 I CAN SEE FOR MILES
The Who *Decca* 67

4566 GAMES PEOPLE PLAY
Joe South *Capitol* 69

4567 BROKEN
Seether f/Amy Lee *Wind-up* 04

4568 DO YOU WANT ME
Salt-n-Pepa *Next Plateau* 91

4569 ALL DAY AND ALL OF THE NIGHT
The Kinks *Reprise* 65

4570 WHEN I'M BACK ON MY FEET AGAIN
Michael Bolton *Columbia* 90

4571 (I KNOW) I'M LOSING YOU
Rare Earth *Rare Earth* 70

4572 (YOU GOTTA) FIGHT FOR YOUR RIGHT
(TO PARTY!)
Beastie Boys *Def Jam* 87

4573 YOU DON'T MESS AROUND WITH JIM
Jim Croce *ABC* 72

4574 THE MONKEY TIME
Major Lance *Okeh* 63

4575 DOCTOR MY EYES
Jackson Browne *Asylum* 72

4576 PAPER IN FIRE
John Cougar Mellencamp *Mercury* 87

4577 LOVE ZONE
Billy Ocean *Jive* 86

4578 LA DEE DAH
Billy and Lillie *Swan* 58

4579 ON A CAROUSEL
The Hollies *Imperial* 67

4580 POISON
Alice Cooper *Epic* 89

4581 NO MATTER WHAT
Badfinger *Apple* 70

4582 COCONUT
Nilsson *RCA* 72

4583 SAN ANTONIO ROSE
Floyd Cramer *RCA* 61

4584 PROMISES
Eric Clapton *RSO* 79

4585 UNCHAIN MY HEART
Ray Charles *ABC-Paramount* 62

4586 SOMEBODY LIKE YOU
Keith Urban *Capitol* 02

4587 CAN'T STAY AWAY FROM YOU
Gloria Estefan & Miami Sound Machine
Epic 88

4588 IT'S UP TO YOU
Rick Nelson *Imperial* 63

4589 TALK BACK TREMBLING LIPS
Johnny Tillotson *MGM* 64

4590 YEAR OF THE CAT
Al Stewart *Janus* 77

4591 WE CAN'T GO WRONG
Cover Girls *Capitol* 90

4592 MAMA
Connie Francis *MGM* 60

4593 WITHOUT YOU
Mötley Crüe *Elektra* 90

4594 YOU MADE ME BELIEVE IN MAGIC
Bay City Rollers *Arista* 77

4629 Wilson Pickett

4654 THE FINAL COUNTDOWN
Europe *Epic* 87

4655 ZIP-A-DEE DOO-DAH
Bob B. Soxx & the Blue Jeans *Philles* 63

4656 HANG 'EM HIGH
Booker T. & the MG's *Stax* 69

4657 IT'S GONNA TAKE A MIRACLE
Deniece Williams *ARC* 82

4658 I SAW RED
Warrant *Columbia* 91

4659 SHE'S NOT JUST ANOTHER WOMAN
The 8th Day *Invictus* 71

4660 EMMA
Hot Chocolate *Rak* 75

4661 ALPHABET ST.
Prince *Paisley Park* 88

4662 TOUCH OF GREY
Grateful Dead *Arista* 87

4663 IT ONLY TAKES A MINUTE
Tavares *Capitol* 75

4664 SOME KIND OF LOVER
Jody Watley *MCA* 88

4665 5-10-15-20 (25-30 YEARS OF LOVE)
The Presidents *Sussex* 70

4666 WALK THE DINOSAUR
Was (Not Was) *Chrysalis* 89

4667 WALKING AWAY
Information Society *Tommy Boy* 89

4668 CAN'T GET IT OUT OF MY HEAD
Electric Light Orchestra *UA* 75

4669 THE RAIN
Oran "Juice" Jones *Def Jam* 86

4670 IT'S NOT UNUSUAL
Tom Jones *Parrot* 65

**4671 IN MY LITTLE CORNER
OF THE WORLD**
Anita Bryant *Carlton* 60

4672 OH HOW HAPPY
Shades of Blue *Impact* 66

4673 THE ROCKFORD FILES
Mike Post *MGM* 75

4674 EVERY DAY IS A WINDING ROAD
Sheryl Crow *A&M* 97

4675 WITH YOUR LOVE
Jefferson Starship *Grunt* 76

4676 FOOLS RUSH IN
Rick Nelson *Decca* 63

4677 LONG TALL GLASSES (I CAN DANCE)
Leo Sayer *Warner Bros.* 75

4678 TENDER LOVE
Force M.D.'s *Warner Bros.* 86

4679 SHINY HAPPY PEOPLE
R.E.M. *Warner Bros.* 91

**4680 THE MIGHTY QUINN (QUINN THE
ESKIMO)**
Manfred Mann *Mercury* 68

4681 THE OLD MAN DOWN THE ROAD
John Fogerty *Warner Bros.* 85

4682 MEET ME HALF WAY
Kenny Loggins *Columbia* 87

4683 (SITTIN' ON) THE DOCK OF THE BAY
Michael Bolton *Columbia* 88

**4684 EDGE OF SEVENTEEN (JUST LIKE
THE WHITE WINGED DOVE)**
Stevie Nicks *Modern* 82

4685 IF YOU KNOW WHAT I MEAN
Neil Diamond *Columbia* 76

4686 GIRLS, GIRLS, GIRLS
Mötley Crüe *Elektra* 87

**4687 TAKE THESE CHAINS
FROM MY HEART**
Ray Charles *ABC-Paramount* 63

4688 DO YOU BELIEVE IN MAGIC
The Lovin' Spoonful *Kama Sutra* 65

4689 LITTLE HONDA
The Hondells *Mercury* 64

4690 STRAIGHT FROM THE HEART
Bryan Adams *A&M* 83

4691 CRY
Waterfront *Polydor* 89

**4692 WHEN THE BOY IN YOUR ARMS
(IS THE BOY IN YOUR HEART)**
Connie Francis *MGM* 62

4693 THE CHA-CHA-CHA
Bobby Rydell *Cameo* 62

4694 1999
Prince *Warner Bros.* 83

4695 LONELY TEENAGER
Dion *Laurie* 60

4696 I WOKE UP IN LOVE THIS MORNING
The Partridge Family *Bell* 71

4697 LET'S GO!
Wang Chung *Geffen* 87

4698 PUT A LITTLE LOVE IN YOUR HEART
Annie Lennox & Al Green *A&M* 89

4699 THIS COULD BE THE NIGHT
Loverboy *Columbia* 86

4700 WALKING DOWN YOUR STREET
Bangles *Columbia* 87

**4701 THE HAPPIEST GIRL IN
THE WHOLE U.S.A.**
Donna Fargo *Dot* 72

4702 SUZIE Q. (PART ONE)
Creedence Clearwater Revival *Fantasy* 68

4703 I'LL BE DOGGONE
Marvin Gaye *Tamla* 65

**4704 GOOD TIME CHARLIE'S GOT THE
BLUES**
Danny O'Keefe *Signpost* 72

4705 LOVE YOU DOWN
Ready for the World *MCA* 87

**4706 DO YOU KNOW THE WAY
TO SAN JOSE**
Dionne Warwick *Scepter* 68

4707 KEEP ON PUSHING
The Impressions *ABC-Paramount* 64

**4708 OPPORTUNITIES
(LET'S MAKE LOTS OF MONEY)**
Pet Shop Boys *EMI America* 86

4709 READY TO TAKE A CHANCE AGAIN
Barry Manilow *Arista* 78

4710 SILENCE IS GOLDEN
The Tremeloes *Epic* 67

**4711 IF DREAMS CAME TRUE /
THAT'S HOW MUCH I LOVE YOU**
Pat Boone *Dot* 58

4712 BOOGIE CHILD
Bee Gees *RSO* 77

4713 ONE
Bee Gees *Warner Bros.* 89

4714 CARRIE-ANNE
The Hollies *Epic* 67

4715 WHEN I LOOKED AT HIM
Exposé *Arista* 89

4716 THE WALK
Jimmy McCracklin *Checker* 58

4717 SOMEBODY
Bryan Adams *A&M* 85

4718 CHERRY PIE
Skip and Flip *Brent* 60

4719 YOUNG EMOTIONS
Ricky Nelson *Imperial* 60

4720 HIGH ON YOU
Survivor *Scotti Bros.* 85

4721 UNEASY RIDER
Charlie Daniels Band *Kama Sutra* 73

4722 MISLED
Kool & the Gang *De-Lite* 85

4723 JUST GOT PAID
Johnny Kemp *Columbia* 88

4724 PLAYGROUND
Another Bad Creation *Motown* 91

4725 MY, MY, MY
Johnny Gill *Motown* 90

**4726 THIS OLD HEART OF MINE
(IS WEAK FOR YOU)**
Rod Stewart w/Ronald Isley
Warner Bros. 90

4727 HYSTERIA
Def Leppard *Mercury* 88

4728 HI, HI, HI
Wings *Apple* 73

4729 IF YOU CAN WANT
Smokey Robinson & the Miracles
Tamla 68

4730 VOICES THAT CARE
Voices That Care *Giant* 91

4731 WILD WORLD
Cat Stevens *A&M* 71

4732 TAKE THE MONEY AND RUN
Steve Miller *Capitol* 76

4733 IT WAS I
Skip and Flip *Brent* 59

4734 SOLID
Ashford and Simpson *Capitol* 85

4735 BROKEN HEARTED ME
Anne Murray *Capitol* 79

4736 (OH) PRETTY WOMAN
Van Halen *Warner Bros.* 82

4737 **SATURDAY NIGHT'S ALRIGHT FOR FIGHTING**
Elton John *MCA* 73

4738 **PLEASE LOVE ME FOREVER**
Cathy Jean & the Roommates *Valmor* 61

4739 **DUDE (LOOKS LIKE A LADY)**
Aerosmith *Geffen* 87

4740 **YOU GOT IT**
Roy Orbison *Virgin* 89

4741 **I KNOW WHAT I LIKE**
Huey Lewis & the News *Chrysalis* 87

4742 **A BOY WITHOUT A GIRL**
Frankie Avalon *Chancellor* 59

4743 **LAUGHING**
The Guess Who *RCA* 69

4744 **GET ON UP**
The Esquires *Bunky* 67

4745 **LIFE IN THE FAST LANE**
Eagles *Asylum* 77

4746 **I'LL BE OVER YOU**
Toto *Columbia* 86

4747 **THE BEACH BOYS MEDLEY**
The Beach Boys *Capitol* 81

4748 **VINCENT / CASTLES IN THE AIR**
Don McLean *UA* 72

4749 **LOVE CHILD**
Sweet Sensation *Atco* 90

4750 **I WANT YOU TO BE MY GIRL**
Frankie Lymon & the Teenagers *Gee* 56

4751 **ROOM TO MOVE**
Animotion *Polydor* 89

4752 **NOTHIN' AT ALL**
Heart *Capitol* 86

4753 **SAY IT LOUD—I'M BLACK AND I'M PROUD (PART ONE)**
James Brown *King* 68

4754 **GET DANCIN'**
Disco Tex & His Sex-O-Lettes *Chelsea* 75

4755 **ONE OF A KIND (LOVE AFFAIR)**
Spinners *Atlantic* 73

4756 **SMUGGLER'S BLUES**
Glenn Frey *MCA* 85

4757 **A THEME FROM "THE THREE PENNY OPERA"**
Richard Hayman and Jan August *Mercury* 56

4758 **SHARE YOUR LOVE WITH ME**
Kenny Rogers *Liberty* 81

4759 **DON'T BET MONEY HONEY**
Linda Scott *Canadian-American* 61

4760 **THE DOCTOR**
Doobie Brothers *Capitol* 89

4761 **BABY TALK**
Jan & Dean *Dore* 59

4762 **ANOTHER SATURDAY NIGHT**
Sam Cooke *RCA* 63

4763 **LET IT OUT (LET IT ALL HANG OUT)**
The Hombres *Verve Forecast* 67

4764 **GEMINI DREAM**
The Moody Blues *Threshold* 81

4765 **GET RIGHT**
Jennifer Lopez *Epic* 05

4766 **I LOVE YOU**
People *Capitol* 68

4767 **JUNK FOOD JUNKIE**
Larry Groce *Warner Bros.* 76

4768 **SWEETER THAN YOU**
Ricky Nelson *Imperial* 59

4769 **TUFF ENUFF**
Fabulous Thunderbirds *CBS Associated* 86

4770 **SOME GUYS HAVE ALL THE LUCK**
Rod Stewart *Warner Bros.* 84

4771 **DON'T TELL ME LIES**
Breathe *A&M* 89

4772 **WHEN THE NIGHT COMES**
Joe Cocker *Capitol* 90

4773 **ROCK AND ROLL ALL NITE**
Kiss *Casablanca* 76

4774 **GIMME GIMME GOOD LOVIN'**
Crazy Elephant *Bell* 69

4775 **PILOT OF THE AIRWAVES**
Charlie Dore *Island* 80

4776 **ARE YOU JIMMY RAY?**
Jimmy Ray *Epic* 98

4777 **BLACK PEARL**
Sonny Charles & the Checkmates *A&M* 69

4778 **PICNIC**
McGuire Sisters *Coral* 56

4779 **I NEED YOU**
America *Warner Bros.* 72

4780 **DON'T WANT TO BE A FOOL**
Luther Vandross *Epic* 91

4781 **I'M GONNA MAKE YOU MINE**
Lou Christie *Buddah* 69

4782 **HAPPY-GO-LUCKY ME**
Paul Evans *Guarantee* 60

4783 **IF I CAN DREAM**
Elvis Presley *RCA* 69

4784 **SMILE**
Scarface f/2Pac & Johnny P *Rap-A-Lot* 97

4785 **THINKIN' BOUT IT**
Gerald Levert *EastWest* 98

4786 **ALL OVER THE WORLD**
Electric Light Orchestra *MCA* 80

4787 **MAN ON YOUR MIND**
Little River Band *Capitol* 82

4788 **SING FOR THE MOMENT**
Eminem *Web/Aftermath* 03

4789 **BACK IN THE DAY**
Ahmad *Giant* 94

4790 **HEART FULL OF SOUL**
The Yardbirds *Epic* 65

4791 **BABY HOLD ON**
Eddie Money *Columbia* 78

4792 **DO YOUR THING**
Watts 103rd Street Rhythm Band *Warner Bros.* 69

4793 **BABY THE RAIN MUST FALL**
Glenn Yarbrough *RCA* 65

4794 **THERE'S THE GIRL**
Heart *Capitol* 88

4795 **RIGHT DOWN THE LINE**
Gerry Rafferty *UA* 78

4796 **PHOTOGRAPH**
Def Leppard *Mercury* 83

4797 **EVEN NOW**
Bob Seger & the Silver Bullet Band *Capitol* 83

4798 **MAKING LOVE**
Roberta Flack *Atlantic* 82

4799 **I DON'T KNOW HOW TO LOVE HIM**
Helen Reddy *Capitol* 71

4800 **WHITE AND NERDY**
"Weird Al" Yankovic *Way Moby/Volcano* 06

4801 **YOU'RE THE REASON**
Bobby Edwards *Crest* 61

4802 **DON'T KNOW WHAT YOU GOT (TILL IT'S GONE)**
Cinderella *Mercury* 88

4803 **ON & ON**
Erykah Badu *Kedar/Universal* 97

4804 **MY WISH CAME TRUE**
Elvis Presley *RCA* 59

4805 **I'D LIKE TO TEACH THE WORLD TO SING**
Hillside Singers *Metromedia* 72

4806 **MORGEN**
Ivo Robic *Laurie* 59

4807 **MAJOR TOM (COMING HOME)**
Peter Schilling *Elektra* 83

4808 **UNFORGETTABLE**
Natalie Cole with Nat King Cole *Elektra* 91

4809 **SUPERSTAR**
Murray Head *Decca* 71

4810 **INSIDE YOUR HEAVEN**
Bo Bice *RCA* 05

4811 **KEEP IT TOGETHER**
Madonna *Sire* 90

4812 **TALK DIRTY TO ME**
Poison *Capitol* 87

4813 **DO YOU FEEL LIKE WE DO**
Peter Frampton *A&M* 76

4814 **MIDNIGHT MARY**
Joey Powers *Amy* 64

4815 **THE GOONIES 'R' GOOD ENOUGH**
Cyndi Lauper *Portrait* 85

4816 **YOU SPIN ME ROUND (LIKE A RECORD)**
Dead or Alive *Epic* 85

4817 **DO IT ANY WAY YOU WANNA**
People's Choice *TSOP* 75

4818 **JUST ANOTHER NIGHT**
Mick Jagger *Columbia* 85

4819 **KEEP YOUR HANDS OFF MY BABY**
Little Eva *Dimension* 62

4820 **THE TIJUANA JAIL**
The Kingston Trio *Capitol* 59

4785 Gerald Levert

4948 Natalie Cole

4997 Bow Wow

Back In The Day
  Ahmad, **4789**
Back In The U.S.A.
  Linda Ronstadt, **4998**
Back On The Chain Gang
  Pretenders, **2751**
Back Stabbers
  The O'Jays, **2304**
Back That Thang Up
  Juvenile f/Mannie Fresh & Lil' Wayne, **1928**
Back To Life
  Soul II Soul (f/Caron Wheeler), **2050**
Back To The Hotel
  N2Deep, **1985**
Back 2 Good
  matchbox 20, **4339**
Backfield In Motion
  Mel and Tim, **3245**
Bad
  Michael Jackson, **1525**
Bad, Bad Leroy Brown
  Jim Croce, **763**
Bad Blood
  Neil Sedaka, **1099**
Bad Boy
  Miami Sound Machine, **3940**
Bad Boys
  Inner Circle, **3849**
Bad Case Of Loving You (Doctor, Doctor)
  Robert Palmer, **4880**
Bad Day
  Daniel Powter, **68**
Bad Girls
  Donna Summer, **242**
Bad Medicine
  Bon Jovi, **1328**
Bad Moon Rising
  Creedence Clearwater Revival, **1527**
Bad Time
  Grand Funk, **2960**
Bag Lady
  Erykah Badu, **3581**
Bailamos
  Enrique Iglesias, **595**
Baker Street
  Gerry Rafferty, **483**
Ballad Of Bonnie And Clyde, The
  Georgie Fame, **3109**
Ball Of Confusion (That's What The World Is
  Today)
  The Temptations, **1560**
Ballad Of John And Yoko, The
  The Beatles, **4475**
Ballad Of The Green Berets, The
  S/Sgt. Barry Sadler, **386**
Ballerina Girl
  Lionel Richie, **4092**
Ballroom Blitz
  Sweet, **2781**
Banana Boat (Day-O)
  Harry Belafonte, **2094**
Banana Boat Song, The
  The Tarriers, **2116**
Band Of Gold
  Don Cherry, **1825**
Band Of Gold
  Freda Payne, **1759**
Band On The Run
  Paul McCartney & Wings, **1489**
Bang A Gong (Get It On)
  Power Station, **4183***
  T. Rex, **4606**
  *Get It On (Bang A Gong)
Bang Bang (My Baby Shot Me Down)
  Cher, **2123**
Barbara Ann
  The Beach Boys, **2126**
Barely Breathing
  Duncan Sheik, **814**

Barracuda
  Heart, **3321**
Batdance
  Prince, **1354**
Battle Hymn Of The Republic
  Mormon Tabernacle Choir, **3809**
Battle Of New Orleans, The
  Johnny Horton, **109**
Be My Baby
  The Ronettes, **1097**
Be My Guest
  Fats Domino, **4163**
Be My Lover
  La Bouche, **1561**
Be Near Me
  ABC, **3618**
Be Thankful For What You Got
  William DeVaughn, **3081**
Be With You
  Enrique Iglesias, **490**
Be Without You
  Mary J. Blige, **547**
Beach Baby
  First Class, **3013**
Beach Boys Medley, The
  The Beach Boys, **4747**
Beat It
  Michael Jackson, **326**
Beatnik Fly
  Johnny & the Hurricanes, **4374**
Beautiful
  Christina Aguilera, **825**
Beautiful
  Snoop Dogg f/Pharrell & Uncle Charlie Wilson,
  2327
Beautiful Day
  U2, **4047**
Beautiful In My Eyes
  Joshua Kadison, **4000**
Beautiful Life
  Ace of Base, **3041**
Beautiful Morning, A
  The Rascals, **2178**
Beautiful Soul
  Jesse McCartney, **3810**
Beautiful Sunday
  Daniel Boone, **4899**
Beauty And The Beast
  Celine Dion & Peabo Bryson, **3173**
Beauty Is Only Skin Deep
  The Temptations, **3293**
Be-Bop-A-Lula
  Gene Vincent & His Blue Caps, **2117**
Be-Bop Baby
  Ricky Nelson, **1611**
Because
  Dave Clark Five, **2840**
Because I Love You (The Postman Song)
  Stevie B, **290**
Because Of Love
  Janet Jackson, **2264**
Because Of You
  Kelly Clarkson, **881**
Because Of You
  98 Degrees, **1261**
Because The Night
  10,000 Maniacs, **1662**
Because They're Young
  Duane Eddy, **2276**
Because You Loved Me
  Celine Dion, **52**
Bed Of Roses
  Bon Jovi, **2807**
Been Around The World
  *Puff Daddy & the Family f/the Notorious B.I.G.
  & Mase,* **1762**
Beep
  The Pussycat Dolls f/will.i.am, **4646**

Beep Beep
  The Playmates, **2231**
Before He Cheats
  Carrie Underwood, **2648**
Before I Let You Go
  BLACKstreet, **1818**
Before The Next Teardrop Falls
  Freddy Fender, **726**
Before You Walk Out Of My Life
  Monica, **1516**
Beginnings
  Chicago, **3531**
Behind These Hazel Eyes
  Kelly Clarkson, **1101**
Being With You
  Smokey Robinson, **495**
Believe
  Cher, **86**
Believe
  Elton John, **2507**
Believe What You Say
  Ricky Nelson, **3337**
Ben
  Michael Jackson, **1687**
Bend Me, Shape Me
  American Breed, **2700**
Bennie And The Jets
  Elton John, **604**
Bent
  matchbox twenty, **166**
Bernadette
  Four Tops, **3255**
Best Disco In Town, The
  Ritchie Family, **4400**
Best Of My Love
  Eagles, **1369**
Best Of My Love
  The Emotions, **201**
Best Of Times, The
  Styx, **1197**
Best Of You
  Foo Fighters, **4356**
Best Thing That Ever Happened To Me
  Gladys Knight & the Pips, **1962**
Best Things In Life Are Free, The
  *Luther Vandross & Janet Jackson w/BBD &
  Ralph Tresvant,* **2012**
Betcha By Golly, Wow
  The Stylistics, **1973**
Beth
  Kiss, **2636**
Bette Davis Eyes
  Kim Carnes, **61**
Better Be Good To Me
  Tina Turner, **2846**
Better Days
  Bruce Springsteen, **4351**
Better Love Next Time
  Dr. Hook, **3656**
Between Me And You
  Ja Rule f/Christina Milian, **2539**
Beverly Hills
  Weezer, **646**
Beyond The Sea
  Bobby Darin, **3413**
Bible Tells Me So, The
  Don Cornell, **2577**
Big Bad John
  Jimmy Dean, **258**
Big Daddy
  Heavy D, **3826**
Big Girls Don't Cry
  The Four Seasons, **294**
Big Hunk O' Love, A
  Elvis Presley, **1088**
Big Hurt, The
  Miss Toni Fisher, **1630**
Big Love
  Fleetwood Mac, **4382**

Chain Hang Low
Jibbs, **3034**
Chain Of Fools
Aretha Franklin, **1543**
Chains Of Love
Pat Boone, **2065**
Chains Of Love
Erasure, **4902**
Chances Are
Johnny Mathis, **1316**
Change Clothes
Jay-Z, **4096**
Change Of Heart
Cyndi Lauper, **2453**
Change The World
Eric Clapton, **850**
Chanson D'Amour
Art and Dotty Todd, **4120**
Chanté's Got A Man
Chanté Moore, **3233**
Chantilly Lace
The Big Bopper, **2087**
Chapel Of Love
The Dixie Cups, **636**
Chariots Of Fire
Vangelis, **607**
Charlene
Anthony Hamilton, **3201**
Charlie Brown
The Coasters, **951**
Chasing Cars
Snow Patrol, **1355**
Check On It
Beyoncé f/Slim Thug, **155**
Cherish
The Association, **700**
David Cassidy, **3512**
Cherish
Kool & the Gang, **1226**
Cherish
Madonna, **1752**
Cherry Bomb
John Cougar Mellencamp, **4007**
Cherry Hill Park
Billy Joe Royal, **4839**
Cherry Pie
Skip and Flip, **4718**
Chevy Van
Sammy Johns, **3424**
Chick-A-Boom (Don't Ya Jes' Love It)
Daddy Dewdrop, **3528**
Childhood
Michael Jackson, **4253**
Children
Robert Miles, **3594**
Children Of The Night
Richard Marx, **4921**
Children's Marching Song, The
Mitch Miller, **494**
Children's Marching Song, The
Cyril Stapleton, **4986***
*The Children's Marching Song (Nick Nack Paddy Whack)
China Girl
David Bowie, **4207**
Chipmunk Song, The
The Chipmunks w/David Seville, **669**
Chokin' Kind, The
Joe Simon, **4342**
Chuck E.'s In Love
Rickie Lee Jones, **2587**
Church Of The Poison Mind
Culture Club, **3205**
Cindy, Oh Cindy
Eddie Fisher, **2622**
Vince Martin w/the Tarriers, **2402**
Cinnamon
Derek, **4085**

Circle In The Sand
Belinda Carlisle, **4101**
Cisco Kid, The
War, **1644**
Clair
Gilbert O'Sullivan, **1356**
Clap For The Wolfman
The Guess Who, **3964**
Classical Gas
Mason Williams, **1563**
Clean Up Woman
Betty Wright, **3202**
Cleanin' Out My Closet
Eminem, **2111**
Close My Eyes (Forever)
Lita Ford w/Ozzy Osbourne, **3667**
Close To You
Maxi Priest, **1026**
Closer I Get To You, The
Roberta Flack w/Donny Hathaway, **1317**
Closer To Free
BoDeans, **3861**
Cloud Nine
The Temptations, **3502**
C'mon And Get My Love
D-Mob i/Cathy Dennis, **3677**
C'mon And Swim
Bobby Freeman, **4348**
C'mon N' Ride It (The Train)
Quad City DJ's, **806**
Coconut
Nilsson, **4582**
Cold As Ice
Foreigner, **2367**
Cold Hearted
Paula Abdul, **985**
Cold Rock A Party
MC Lyte, **2950**
Color Him Father
The Winstons, **3981**
Colors Of The Wind
Vanessa Williams, **1880**
Come A Little Bit Closer
Jay & the Americans, **2171**
Come And Get It
Badfinger, **3885**
Come And Get Your Love
Real McCoy, **4509**
Redbone, **2357**
Come And Talk To Me
Jodeci, **2022**
Come Baby Come
K7, **3599**
Come Back To Me
Janet Jackson, **1814**
Come Back When You Grow Up
Bobby Vee, **1529**
Come Dancing
The Kinks, **3486**
Come Go With Me
The Dell-Vikings, **1263**
Come Go With Me
Exposé, **3409**
Come In Stranger
Johnny Cash, **4303**
Come On Down To My Boat
Every Mother's Son, **3467**
Come On Eileen
Dexys Midnight Runners, **919**
Come On Over Baby (All I Want Is You)
Christina Aguilera, **433**
Come Sail Away
Styx, **2653**
Come See About Me
The Supremes, **554**
Come Softly To Me
The Fleetwoods, **348**
Come To Me
Diddy f/Nicole Scherzinger, **3154**

Come To My Window
Melissa Etheridge, **2845**
Come Together
The Beatles, **757**
Come Undone
Duran Duran, **2566**
Come With Me
Puff Daddy f/Jimmy Page, **2283**
Comforter
Shai, **2120**
Comin' In And Out Of Your Life
Barbra Streisand, **3184**
Coming Out Of The Dark
Gloria Estefan, **1137**
Coming Up (Live At Glasgow)
Paul McCartney & Wings, **249**
Complicated
Avril Lavigne, **170**
Confessions Part II
Usher, **206**
Conga
Miami Sound Machine, **2711**
Constantly
Immature, **3407**
Control
Janet Jackson, **2999**
Convoy
Gwen Stefani, **1718**
Cool
Gwen Stefani, **3867**
Cool Change
Little River Band, **3490**
Cool It Now
New Edition, **2282**
Cool Jerk
The Capitols, **4403**
Cool Love
Pablo Cruise, **4312**
Cool Night
Paul Davis, **3216**
Copacabana (At The Copa)
Barry Manilow, **3986**
Corinna, Corinna
Ray Peterson, **3924**
Cotton Fields
The Highwaymen, **3755**
Could It Be I'm Falling In Love
Spinners, **2438**
Could It Be Magic
Barry Manilow, **3485**
Could This Be Love
Seduction, **4901**
Couldn't Get It Right
Climax Blues Band, **2436**
Could've Been
Tiffany, **748**
Count Me In
Gary Lewis & the Playboys, **1848**
Count On Me
Whitney Houston & CeCe Winans, **2763**
Count On Me
Jefferson Starship, **3497**
Counting Blue Cars
Dishwalla, **1342**
Country Boy (You Got Your Feet In L.A.)
Glen Campbell, **4262**
Cover Girl
New Kids on the Block, **2151**
Cover Me
Bruce Springsteen, **3139**
Cover Of "Rolling Stone," The
Dr. Hook & the Medicine Show, **3553**
Coward Of The County
Kenny Rogers, **1183**
Cowboys To Girls
The Intruders, **3099**
Cowboy's Work Is Never Done, A
Sonny and Cher, **3987**

Cracklin' Rosie
  Neil Diamond, **986**
Cradle Of Love
  Billy Idol, **1257**
Cradle Of Love
  Johnny Preston, **3377**
Crazy
  Aerosmith, **3153**
Crazy
  Gnarls Barkley, **181**
Crazy
  Hollywood Flames, **3872**
Crazy
  Icehouse, **4397**
Crazy
  K-Ci & JoJo, **1998**
Crazy
  Seal, **3525**
Crazy About Her
  Rod Stewart, **4304**
Crazy For This Girl
  Evan & Jaron, **1983**
Crazy For You
  Madonna, **513**
Crazy In Love
  Beyoncé f/Jay-Z, **58**
Crazy Little Thing Called Love
  Queen, **259**
Crazy Love
  Paul Anka, **4396**
Cream
  Prince & the New Power Generation, **776**
Creep
  TLC, **50**
Criminal
  Fiona Apple, **3254**
Crimson And Clover
  Tommy James & the Shondells, **379**
  Joan Jett & the Blackhearts, **3648**
Crocodile Rock
  Elton John, **518**
Cross My Broken Heart
  The Jets, **4090**
Cruel Summer
  Ace of Base, **3179**
  Bananarama, **4134**
Cruel To Be Kind
  Nick Lowe, **4338**
Cruisin'
  Smokey Robinson, **1584**
Crumblin' Down
  John Cougar Mellencamp, **3640**
Crush
  Jennifer Paige, **505**
Crush On You
  The Jets, **2075**
Cry
  Godley + Creme, **4993**
Cry
  Waterfront, **4691**
Cry Baby
  Garnett Mimms & the Enchanters, **3272**
Cry For Help
  Rick Astley, **3253**
Cry For You
  Jodeci, **2253**
Cry Like A Baby
  The Box Tops, **1335**
Cry Me A River
  Justin Timberlake, **1626**
Cryin'
  Aerosmith, **2709**
Crying
  Roy Orbison, **1557**
  Don McLean, **2467**
Crying In The Chapel
  Elvis Presley, **2161**
Crying In The Rain
  Everly Brothers, **3818**

Crying Time
  Ray Charles, **4510**
Crystal Blue Persuasion
  Tommy James & the Shondells, **859**
Cum On Feel The Noize
  Quiet Riot, **2706**
Cupid
  112, **1959**
Cupid/I've Loved You For A Long Time
  Spinners, **1909**
Cut The Cake
  Average White Band, **3644**
Da' Dip
  FreakNasty, **1582**
Da Doo Ron Ron (When He Walked Me Home)
  Shaun Cassidy, **1250***
  The Crystals, **2602**
  *Da Doo Ron Ron
Da Ya Think I'm Sexy?
  Rod Stewart, **264**
Daddy Cool
The Rays, **1323**
Daddy Don't You Walk So Fast
  Wayne Newton, **2226**
Daddy's Home
  Jermaine Jackson, **3289**
  Shep & the Limelites, **1768**
Damn!
  Youngbloodz f/Lil Jon, **1047**
Damn I Wish I Was Your Lover
  Sophie B. Hawkins, **2300**
Dance, Dance
  Fall Out Boy, **1450**
Dance, Dance, Dance (Yowsah, Yowsah, Yowsah)
  Chic, **2382**
Dance To The Music
  Sly & the Family Stone, **3458**
Dance With Me
  Peter Brown, **3438**
Dance With Me
  Debelah Morgan, **2609**
Dance With Me
  Orleans, **3567**
Dancing In The Dark
  Bruce Springsteen, **631**
Dancing In The Moonlight
  King Harvest, **3664**
Dancing In The Sheets
  Shalamar, **4418**
Dancing In The Street
  Mick Jagger/David Bowie, **4554**
  Martha & the Vandellas, **1513**
Dancing Machine
  Jackson 5, **1017**
Dancing On The Ceiling
  Lionel Richie, **1393**
Dancing Queen
  Abba, **1110**
Danger (Been So Long)
  Mystikal f/Nivea, **3079**
Danger Zone
  Kenny Loggins, **1790**
Dangerous
  Roxette, **1457**
Dani California
  Red Hot Chili Peppers, **1627**
Daniel
  Elton John, **1743**
Danny Boy
  Conway Twitty, **3707**
Danny's Song
  Anne Murray, **3394**
Dare Me
  Pointer Sisters, **4198**
Dare You To Move
  Switchfoot, **3209**
Dark Lady
  Cher, **1819**

Dark Moon
  Bonnie Guitar, **3947**
  Gale Storm, **2141**
Daughters
  John Mayer, **3600**
Dawn (Go Away)
  The Four Seasons, **1607**
Day After Day
  Badfinger, **2733**
Day Dreaming
  Aretha Franklin, **3737**
Day The Rains Came, The
  Jane Morgan, **4627**
Daydream
  The Lovin' Spoonful, **1635**
Daydream Believer
  The Monkees, **367**
  Anne Murray, **3316**
Daydreamin'
  Tatyana Ali, **2232**
Days Go By
  Dirty Vegas, **4313**
Dazz
  Brick, **1587**
Dazzey Duks
  Duice, **1940**
De Do Do Do, De Da Da Da
  The Police, **3238**
Dead Man's Curve
  Jan and Dean, **3898**
Dear Lady Twist
  Gary U.S. Bonds, **3484**
Dear Mama
  2Pac, **2246**
December
  Collective Soul, **2081**
December, 1963 (Oh, What A Night)
  The Four Seasons, **247**
Deck Of Cards
  Wink Martindale, **3349**
Dede Dinah
  Frankie Avalon, **4299**
Dedicated To The One I Love
  The Mamas and the Papas, **1620**
  The Shirelles, **1769**
Deep Purple
  Donny & Marie Osmond, **3779**
  Nino Tempo and April Stevens, **953**
Deeper And Deeper
  Madonna, **3077**
Déjà Vu
  Beyoncé f/Jay-Z, **4515**
Déjà Vu (Uptown Baby)
  Lord Tariq & Peter Gunz, **2291**
Delirious
  Prince, **3469**
Delta Dawn
  Helen Reddy, **1167**
Denise
  Randy & the Rainbows, **4235**
Der Kommissar
  After The Fire, **2535**
Desert Moon
  Dennis DeYoung, **4621**
Desert Rose
  Sting f/Cheb Mami, **2827**
Desiderata
  Les Crane, **4615**
Desire
  Andy Gibb, **2003**
Desire
  U2, **2388**
Devil Inside
  INXS, **1554**
Devil Or Angel
  Bobby Vee, **2812**
Devil Went Down To Georgia, The
  Charlie Daniels Band, **2177**

Don't Mean Nothing
  Richard Marx, **2441**
Don't Mess With My Man
  Nivea f/Brian & Brandon Casey, **1714**
Don't Phunk With My Heart
  The Black Eyed Peas, **897**
Don't Play That Song
  Aretha Franklin, **4651**
Don't Pull Your Love
  Hamilton, Joe Frank & Reynolds, **2628**
Don't Rush Me
  Taylor Dayne, **1809**
Don't Say You Don't Remember
  Beverly Bremers, **4930**
Don't Shed A Tear
  Paul Carrack, **4114**
Don't Stand So Close To Me
  The Police, **3976**
Don't Stop
  Fleetwood Mac, **1908**
Don't Stop Believin'
  Journey, **3277**
Don't Stop 'Til You Get Enough
  Michael Jackson, **1040**
Don't Take It Personal (Just One Of Dem Days)
  Monica, **243**
Don't Take The Girl
  Tim McGraw, **4406**
Don't Talk To Strangers
  Rick Springfield, **619**
Don't Tell Me
  Madonna, **1753**
Don't Tell Me Lies
  Breathe, **4771**
Don't Think I'm Not
  Kandi, **3757**
Don't Turn Around
  Ace of Base, **812**
Don't Walk Away
  Jade, **1077**
Don't Wanna Fall In Love
  Jane Child, **1345**
Don't Wanna Lose You
  Gloria Estefan, **1349**
Don't Wanna Try
  Frankie J, **3934**
Don't Want To Be A Fool
  Luther Vandross, **4780**
Don't Worry
  Marty Robbins, **1887**
Don't Worry Be Happy
  Bobby McFerrin, **1146**
Don't You Care
  The Buckinghams, **3994**
Don't You (Forget About Me)
  Simple Minds, **995**
Don't You Just Know It
  Huey "Piano" Smith & the Clowns, **4288**
Don't You Know
  Della Reese, **1116**
Don't You Know What The Night Can Do?
  Steve Winwood, **3974**
Don't You Want Me
  Human League, **309**
Don't You Want Me
  Jody Watley, **3082**
Dontchange
  Musiq, **3335**
Doo Wop (That Thing)
  Lauryn Hill, **701**
Double Vision
  Foreigner, **1442**
Down By The Lazy River
  The Osmonds, **2588**
Down By The Station
  The Four Preps, **4158**
Down 4 U
  Irv Gotti p/the Inc. f/Ja Rule, Ashanti, Charli Baltimore & Vita, **2510**

Down In The Boondocks
  Billy Joe Royal, **4640**
Down Low (Nobody Has To Know)
  R. Kelly f/Ronald Isley, **1783**
Down On The Corner
  Creedence Clearwater Revival, **1917**
Down Under
  Men at Work, **269**
Downtown
  Petula Clark, **555**
Downtown
  SWV, **743**
Downtown Train
  Rod Stewart, **1779**
Draggin' The Line
  Tommy James, **2946**
Dre Day
  Dr. Dre, **2831**
Dream Baby (How Long Must I Dream)
  Roy Orbison, **3838**
Dream Is Still Alive, The
  Wilson Phillips, **4857**
Dream Lover
  Bobby Darin, **871**
Dream On
  Aerosmith, **3539**
Dream Weaver
  Gary Wright, **1125**
Dreamin'
  Johnny Burnette, **3331**
Dreamin'
  Vanessa Williams, **4531**
Dreaming
  Cliff Richard, **3542**
Dreamlover
  Mariah Carey, **70**
Dreams
  Fleetwood Mac, **1253**
Dreamtime
  Daryl Hall, **3918**
Dress You Up
  Madonna, **4401**
Drift Away
  Dobie Gray, **2574**
  Uncle Kracker f/Dobie Gray, **1311**
Drip Drop
  Dion DiMucci, **4553**
Drive
  The Cars, **1665**
Drive
  Incubus, **1691**
Drivin' My Life Away
  Eddie Rabbitt, **2549**
Drop It Like It's Hot
  Snoop Dogg f/Pharrell, **87**
Drops Of Jupiter (Tell Me)
  Train, **739**
Drowning In The Sea Of Love
  Joe Simon, **4239**
Duck, The
  Jackie Lee, **4865**
Dude (Looks Like A Lady)
  Aerosmith, **4739**
Dueling Banjos
  Eric Weissberg & Steve Mandell, **1080**
Duke Of Earl
  Gene Chandler, **578**
Dum Dum
  Brenda Lee, **2567**
Dungaree Doll
  Eddie Fisher, **2766**
Dust In The Wind
  Kansas, **2589**
Dynamite
  Jermaine Jackson, **4962**
Dynomite—Part 1
  Tony Camillo's Bazuka, **4206**
Earth, The Sun, The Rain, The
  Color Me Badd, **2993**

Easier Said Than Done
  The Essex, **1084**
Easy
  Commodores, **2420**
Easy Come, Easy Go
  Bobby Sherman, **3596**
Easy Lover
  Philip Bailey w/Phil Collins, **978**
Easy Loving
  Freddie Hart, **4970**
Easy To Be Hard
  Three Dog Night, **2381**
Ebb Tide
  Righteous Brothers, **4940**
Ebony And Ivory
  Paul McCartney & Stevie Wonder, **132**
Ebony Eyes
  Bob Welch, **4904**
Edge Of Seventeen (Just Like The White Winged Dove)
  Stevie Nicks, **4684**
E.I.
  Nelly, **2754**
Eight Days A Week
  The Beatles, **1589**
808
  Blaque, **2621**
867-5309/Jenny
  Tommy Tutone, **1930**
18 And Life
  Skid Row, **2779**
El Paso
  Marty Robbins, **387**
Election Day
  Arcadia, **3367**
Electric Avenue
  Eddy Grant, **566**
Electric Blue
  Icehouse, **3569**
Elenore
  The Turtles, **4411**
Elevators (Me & You)
  OutKast, **3246**
Eli's Coming
  Three Dog Night, **2888**
Elusive Butterfly
  Bob Lind, **4381**
Elvira
  Oak Ridge Boys, **2650**
Emma
  Hot Chocolate, **4660**
Emotion
  Destiny's Child, **3645**
  Samantha Sang, **1429**
Emotional Rescue
  The Rolling Stones, **1458**
Emotions
  Mariah Carey, **589**
Emotions
  Brenda Lee, **4470**
Empty Garden (Hey Hey Johnny)
  Elton John, **4300**
Enchanted
  The Platters, **4119**
Encore
  Jay-Z/Linkin Park, **4014***
  **Numb/Encore*
End, The
  Earl Grant, **2759**
End Of The Innocence, The
  Don Henley, **4130**
End Of The Road
  Boyz II Men, **11**
End Of The World, The
  Skeeter Davis, **1412**
Endless Love
  Diana Ross & Lionel Richie, **53**
  Luther Vandross & Mariah Carey, **1004**

Good, The Bad And The Ugly, The
Hugo Montenegro, **1552**
Good Thing
Fine Young Cannibals, **1388**
Good Thing
Paul Revere & the Raiders, **2919**
Good Time Charlie's Got The Blues
Danny O'Keefe, **4704**
Good Times
Chic, **396**
Good Timin'
Jimmy Jones, **1699**
Good Vibrations
The Beach Boys, **773**
Good Vibrations
*Marky Mark & the Funky Bunch f/Loleatta
Holloway,* **915**
Goodbye Baby
Jack Scott, **2958**
Goodbye Cruel World
James Darren, **1623**
Goodbye Girl
David Gates, **3889**
Goodbye To Love
Carpenters, **4652**
Goodbye Yellow Brick Road
Elton John, **1143**
Goodies
Ciara f/Petey Pablo, **46**
Goodnight Tonight
Wings, **2899**
Goody Two Shoes
Adam Ant, **2750**
Goonies 'R' Good Enough, The
Cyndi Lauper, **4815**
Gossip Folks
Missy "Misdemeanor" Elliott f/Ludacris, **2551**
Got A Hold On Me
Christine McVie, **3703**
Got Me Waiting
Heavy D. & the Boyz, **4074**
Got My Mind Set On You
George Harrison, **1078**
Got To Be Real
Cheryl Lynn, **4071**
Got To Be There
Michael Jackson, **2526**
Got To Get You Into My Life
The Beatles, **3457**
Got To Give It Up (Pt. 1)
Marvin Gaye, **856**
Gotham City
R. Kelly, **4631**
Gotta Get Thru This
Daniel Bedingfield, **2684**
Gotta Tell You
Samantha Mumba, **1861**
Gotta Travel On
Billy Grammer, **2137**
Grazing In The Grass
Friends of Distinction, **2503**
Hugh Masekela, **1357**
Grease
Frankie Valli, **629**
Great Balls Of Fire
Jerry Lee Lewis, **1130**
Great Pretender, The
The Platters, **327**
Greatest Love Of All
Whitney Houston, **663**
Green Door, The
Jim Lowe, **120**
Green-Eyed Lady
Sugarloaf, **1864**
Green Onions
Booker T. & the MG's, **2359**
Green River
Creedence Clearwater Revival, **1625**

Green Tambourine
The Lemon Pipers, **1051**
Greenfields
Brothers Four, **681**
Grillz
Nelly f/Paul Wall, Ali & Gipp, **197**
Grind With Me
Pretty Ricky, **2209**
Groove Is In The Heart
Deee-Lite, **2086**
Groove Line, The
Heatwave, **3388**
Groove Me
King Floyd, **2580**
Groove Thang
Zhané, **3477**
Groovin'
The Young Rascals, **312**
Groovy Kind Of Love, A
Phil Collins, **1032***
The Mindbenders, **1871**
*Groovy Kind of Love
Groovy Situation
Gene Chandler, **4895**
G.T.O.
Ronny & the Daytonas, **3287**
Guess Things Happen That Way
Johnny Cash, **4303**
Guilty
Barbra Streisand & Barry Gibb, **1602**
Gum Drop
The Crew-Cuts, **4607**
Gypsy Man
War, **4192**
Gypsy Woman
Brian Hyland, **2173**
Gypsys, Tramps & Thieves
Cher, **530**
Hair
The Cowsills, **1202**
Halfcrazy
Musiq, **2619**
Half-Breed
Cher, **673**
Hands
Jewel, **2405**
Hands To Heaven
Breathe, **1378**
Handy Man
Jimmy Jones, **1015**
James Taylor, **2446**
Hang 'Em High
Booker T. & the MG's, **4656**
Hang On In There Baby
Johnny Bristol, **3237**
Hang On Sloopy
The McCoys, **1147**
Hang Up My Rock And Roll Shoes
Chuck Willis, **2997**
Hangin' Tough
New Kids on the Block, **1471**
Hanging By A Moment
Lifehouse, **106**
Hanky Panky
Tommy James & the Shondells, **1184**
Happening, The
The Supremes, **1451**
Happiest Girl In The Whole U.S.A., The
Donna Fargo, **4701**
Happily Ever After
Case, **3095**
Happy
Ashanti, **2531**
Happy Birthday, Sweet Sixteen
Neil Sedaka, **3373**
Happy Days
Pratt & McClain, **4341**
Happy-Go-Lucky Me
Paul Evans, **4782**

Happy, Happy Birthday Baby
The Tune Weavers, **3127**
Happy Organ, The
Dave "Baby" Cortez, **1276**
Happy People
R. Kelly, **4626**
Happy Together
The Turtles, **383**
Happy Whistler, The
Don Robertson, **2854**
Harbor Lights
The Platters, **3489**
Hard Day's Night, A
The Beatles, **677**
Hard Habit To Break
Chicago, **1494**
Hard Headed Woman
Elvis Presley, **928**
Hard To Get
Gisele MacKenzie, **1682**
Hard To Say
Dan Fogelberg, **3996**
Hard To Say I'm Sorry
Az Yet f/Peter Cetera, **1024**
Chicago, **437**
Harden My Heart
Quarterflash, **1178**
Harder To Breathe
Maroon5, **3529**
Hardest Thing, The
98 Degrees, **2122**
Harlem Shuffle
The Rolling Stones, **4366**
Harper Valley P.T.A.
Jeannie C. Riley, **625**
Hate It Or Love It
The Game f/50 Cent, **417**
Hats Off To Larry
Del Shannon, **3736**
Have I The Right?
The Honeycombs, **3903**
Have I Told You Lately
Rod Stewart, **2021**
Have I Told You Lately That I Love You?
Ricky Nelson, **1611**
Have You Ever?
Brandy, **432**
Have You Ever Needed Someone So Bad
Def Leppard, **2942**
Have You Ever Really Loved A Woman?
Bryan Adams, **193**
Have You Ever Seen The Rain
Creedence Clearwater Revival, **4603**
Have You Never Been Mellow
Olivia Newton-John, **1654**
Have You Seen Her
The Chi-Lites, **1639**
M.C. Hammer, **2741**
Hawaii Five-O
The Ventures, **4307**
Hawaiian Wedding Song, The
Andy Williams, **2661**
Hazard
Richard Marx, **2893**
Hazy Shade Of Winter
Bangles, **1810**
He
Al Hibbler, **1258**
McGuire Sisters, **2677**
He Ain't Heavy, He's My Brother
The Hollies, **3562**
He Can't Love U
Jagged Edge, **3356**
He Don't Love You (Like I Love You)
Tony Orlando & Dawn, **966**
He Loves U Not
Dream, **622**
He Wasn't Man Enough
Toni Braxton, **415**

I Ain't Gonna Stand For It
  Stevie Wonder, **3620**
I Ain't Got Nobody
  David Lee Roth, **4946***
  **Just A Gigolo/I Ain't Got Nobody*
I Almost Lost My Mind
  Pat Boone, **572**
I Am A Rock
  Simon and Garfunkel, **2313**
I Am . . . I Said
  Neil Diamond, **3743**
I Am Woman
  Helen Reddy, **778**
I Beg Of You
  Elvis Presley, **285**
I Believe
  Blessid Union of Souls, **1728**
I Believe
  Fantasia, **4340**
I Believe I Can Fly
  R. Kelly, **177**
I Believe In You And Me
  Whitney Houston, **2164**
I Believe In You (You Believe In Me)
  Johnnie Taylor, **3313**
I Belong To You (Every Time I See Your Face)
  Rome, **1881**
I Can
  Nas, **3240**
I Can Do That
  Montell Jordan, **4951**
I Can Dream About You
  Dan Hartman, **2896**
I Can Help
  Billy Swan, **1090**
I Can Love You Like That
  All-4-One, **1103**
I Can See Clearly Now
  Jimmy Cliff, **3949**
  Johnny Nash, **487**
I Can See For Miles
  The Who, **4565**
I Can't Dance
  Genesis, **2638**
(I Can't Get No) Satisfaction
  The Rolling Stones, **298**
I Can't Get Next To You
  The Temptations, **873**
I Can't Go For That (No Can Do)
  Daryl Hall and John Oates, **366**
I Can't Help Myself (Sugar Pie, Honey Bunch)
  Four Tops, **507**
I Can't Hold Back
  Survivor, **3328**
I Can't Sleep Baby (If I)
  R. Kelly, **1996**
I Can't Stand It
  Eric Clapton, **3166**
I Can't Stand It No More
  Peter Frampton, **4892**
I Can't Stay Mad At You
  Skeeter Davis, **4109**
I Can't Stop Loving You
  Ray Charles, **223**
I Can't Tell You Why
  Eagles, **3132**
I Can't Wait
  Nu Shooz, **2099**
I Can't Wait Another Minute
  Hi-Five, **3121**
I Care 4 U
  Aaliyah, **3811**
I Could Never Take The Place Of Your Man
  Prince, **4237**
I Cried A Tear
  LaVerne Baker, **2901**
I Didn't Mean To Turn You On
  Robert Palmer, **1884**

I Do
  Lisa Loeb, **2865**
I Do!!
  Toya, **3369**
I Do (Cherish You)
  98 Degrees, **2329**
I Don't Ever Want to See You Again
  Uncle Sam, **1744**
I Don't Have The Heart
  James Ingram, **1265**
I Don't Know How To Love Him
  Helen Reddy, **4799**
I Don't Like To Sleep Alone
  Paul Anka, **3952**
I Don't Need You
  Kenny Rogers, **1628**
I Don't Wanna Cry
  Mariah Carey, **1230**
I Don't Wanna Fight
  Tina Turner, **2462**
I Don't Wanna Go On With You Like That
  Elton John, **1904**
I Don't Wanna Know
  Mario Winans f/Enya & P. Diddy, **147**
I Don't Wanna Live Without Your Love
  Chicago, **2665**
I Don't Want To
  Toni Braxton, **3593**
I Don't Want To Be
  Gavin DeGraw, **1990**
I Don't Want To Live Without You
  Foreigner, **3917**
I Don't Want To Miss A Thing
  Aerosmith, **297**
  Mark Chesnutt, **3419**
I Don't Want To Wait
  Paula Cole, **1022**
I Don't Want Your Love
  Duran Duran, **2479**
I Drove All Night
  Cyndi Lauper, **4546**
I Feel Fine
  The Beatles, **575**
I Feel For You
  Chaka Khan, **1169**
I Feel Love
  Donna Summer, **2581**
I Feel The Earth Move
  Carole King, **267**
I Finally Found Someone
  Barbra Streisand & Bryan Adams, **2629**
I Found Someone
  Cher, **4272**
I Get Around
  The Beach Boys, **569**
I Get Around
  2Pac, **2701**
I Get Lonely
  Janet Jackson f/BLACKstreet, **2332**
I Get Weak
  Belinda Carlisle, **2051**
I Go Crazy
  Paul Davis, **1596**
I Go To Extremes
  Billy Joel, **3992**
I Got A Feeling
  Ricky Nelson, **3192**
I Got A Man
  Positive K, **3015**
I Got A Name
  Jim Croce, **3697**
I Got 5 On It
  Luniz, **2222**
I Got Rhythm
  The Happenings, **2025**
I Got Stung
  Elvis Presley, **3064**
I Got The Feelin'
  James Brown, **3854**

I Got The Hook-Up!
  Master P f/Sons of Funk, **3125**
I Got You Babe
  Sonny and Cher, **1059**
I Got You (I Feel Good)
  James Brown, **1724**
I Gotcha
  Joe Tex, **696**
I Guess That's Why They Call It The Blues
  Elton John, **2473**
I Hate Myself For Loving You
  Joan Jett & the Blackhearts, **4022**
I Have Nothing
  Whitney Houston, **1431**
I Hear A Symphony
  The Supremes, **992**
I Hear You Knocking
  Dave Edmunds, **3247**
  Gale Storm, **967**
I Heard A Rumour
  Bananarama, **2269**
I Heard It Through The Grapevine
  Marvin Gaye, **198**
  Gladys Knight & the Pips, **1127**
I Honestly Love You
  Olivia Newton-John, **1009**
I Hope You Dance
  Lee Ann Womack, **1692**
I Just Called To Say I Love You
  Stevie Wonder, **370**
I Just Can't Help Believing
  B.J. Thomas, **4145**
I Just Can't Stop Loving You
  Michael Jackson & Siedah Garrett, **1229**
(I Just) Died In Your Arms
  Cutting Crew, **1297**
I Just Fall In Love Again
  Anne Murray, **3740**
I Just Wanna Love U (Give It 2 Me)
  Jay-Z, **2046**
I Just Wanna Stop
  Gino Vannelli, **2108**
I Just Want To Be Your Everything
  Andy Gibb, **133**
I Just Want To Celebrate
  Rare Earth, **4065**
I Keep Forgettin' (Every Time You're Near)
  Michael McDonald, **2103**
I Knew I Loved You
  Savage Garden, **118**
I Knew You Were Waiting (For Me)
  Aretha Franklin & George Michael, **1305**
I Knew You When
  Donny Osmond, **4495**
I Know
  Dionne Farris, **961**
I Know
  Barbara George, **2600**
I Know A Place
  Petula Clark, **2541**
(I Know) I'm Losing You
  Rare Earth, **4571**
I Know There's Something Going On
  Frida, **4142**
I Know What I Like
  Huey Lewis & the News, **4741**
I Know What You Want
  *Busta Rhymes & Mariah Carey f/the Flipmode
  Squad*, **845**
I Know You See It
  Yung Joc f/Brandy "Ms. B" Hambrick, **2839**
I Like Dreamin'
  Kenny Nolan, **1558**
I Like It
  Dino, **3159**
I Like It Like That, Part 1
  Chris Kenner, **1509**
I Like That
  Houston f/Chingy, Nate Dogg & I-20, **2450**

I Like The Way (The Kissing Game)
Hi-Five, **998**
I Love
Tom T. Hall, **4877**
I Love A Rainy Night
Eddie Rabbitt, **508**
I Love How You Love Me
The Paris Sisters, **3823**
Bobby Vinton, **3103**
I Love Me Some Him
Toni Braxton, **3593**
I Love Music (Part 1)
The O'Jays, **2743**
I Love Rock 'N Roll
Joan Jett & the Blackhearts, **136**
I Love The Nightlife (Disco 'Round)
Alicia Bridges, **1915**
I Love The Way You Love
Marv Johnson, **4454**
I Love You
Climax Blues Band, **3754**
I Love You
Faith Evans, **3330**
I Love You
People, **4766**
I Love You Always Forever
Donna Lewis, **79**
I Love You Because
Al Martino, **2432**
I Love Your Smile
Shanice, **500**
I Made It Through The Rain
Barry Manilow, **3718**
I Miss My Homies
Master P f/Pimp C & the Shocker, **4352**
I Miss You
Aaron Hall, **2512**
I Miss You
Klymaxx, **2455**
I Need A Girl (Part One)
P. Diddy f/Usher & Loon, **411**
I Need A Girl (Part Two)
P. Diddy & Ginuwine f/Loon, **1100**
I Need To Know
Marc Anthony, **461**
I Need You
America, **4779**
I Need You
LeAnn Rimes, **3152**
I Need Your Love Tonight
Elvis Presley, **3340**
I Never Cry
Alice Cooper, **2984**
I Never Loved A Man (The Way I Love You)
Aretha Franklin, **4542**
I Only Have Eyes For You
The Flamingos, **4176**
Art Garfunkel, **4560**
I Only Want To Be With You
Bay City Rollers, **4240**
I Ran (So Far Away)
A Flock Of Seagulls, **4094**
I Remember Holding You
Boys Club, **4113**
I Remember You
Skid Row, **3666**
I Saw Him Standing There
Tiffany, **4564**
I Saw Red
Warrant, **4658**
I Say A Little Prayer
Aretha Franklin, **4209**
Dionne Warwick, **2969**
I Second That Emotion
Smokey Robinson & the Miracles, **2194**
I Shot The Sheriff
Eric Clapton, **1456**
I Still Believe
Mariah Carey, **2250**
Brenda K. Starr, **3763**

I Still Can't Get Over Loving You
Ray Parker Jr., **4358**
I Still Haven't Found What I'm Looking For
U2, **947**
I Still Love You
Next, **2155**
I Swear
All-4-One, **22**
I Thank You
Sam and Dave, **4270**
I Think I Love You
The Partridge Family, **428**
I Think They Like Me
Dem Franchize Boyz f/Jermaine Dupri, Da Brat
& Bow Wow, **2344**
I Think We're Alone Now
Tommy James & the Shondells, **2666**
Tiffany, **1035**
I Touch Myself
Divinyls, **2744**
I Try
Macy Gray, **1580**
I Turn To You
Christina Aguilera, **1530**
I Understand (Just How You Feel)
The G-Clefs, **4205**
I Wanna Be A Cowboy
Boys Don't Cry, **4845**
I Wanna Be Down
Brandy, **1474**
I Wanna Be Rich
Calloway, **1443**
I Wanna Be Your Lover
Prince, **4219**
I Wanna Dance With Somebody (Who Loves Me)
Whitney Houston, **633**
I Wanna Get Next To You
Rose Royce, **4559**
I Wanna Have Some Fun
Samantha Fox, **4639**
I Wanna Know
Joe, **446**
I Wanna Love You
Akon f/Snoop Dogg, **287**
I Wanna Love You
Jade, **4431**
I Wanna Love You Forever
Jessica Simpson, **1018**
I Wanna Sex You Up
Color Me Badd, **567**
I Want A New Drug
Huey Lewis & the News, **3070**
I Want Her
Keith Sweat, **3479**
I Want It That Way
Backstreet Boys, **1121**
I Want To Be Wanted
Brenda Lee, **1068**
I Want To Be Your Man
Roger, **2524**
I Want To Come Over
Melissa Etheridge, **4551**
I Want To Hold Your Hand
The Beatles, **124**
I Want To Know What Love Is
Foreigner, **641**
I Want To Walk You Home
Fats Domino, **3958**
I Want You
Robert Palmer, **4992***
*Mercy Mercy Me (The Ecology)/I Want You
I Want You
Savage Garden, **1377**
I Want You Back
Jackson 5, **559**
I Want You Back
'N Sync, **1883**
I Want You, I Need You, I Love You
Elvis Presley, **612**

I Want You To Be My Girl
Frankie Lymon & the Teenagers, **4750**
I Want You To Want Me
Cheap Trick, **3102**
I Want Your Love
Chic, **3443**
I Want Your Sex
George Michael, **1681**
I Was Made For Dancin'
Leif Garrett, **3320**
I Was Made For Lovin' You
Kiss, **3720**
I Was Made To Love Her
Stevie Wonder, **1422**
I Will Always Love You
Whitney Houston, **8**
I Will Come To You
Hanson, **3474**
I Will Follow Him
Little Peggy March, **506**
I Will Remember You (Live)
Sarah McLachlan, **3329**
I Will Survive
Gloria Gaynor, **221**
I Wish
R. Kelly, **2523**
I Wish
Skee-Lo, **3762**
I Wish
Carl Thomas, **3608**
I Wish
Stevie Wonder, **993**
I Wish It Would Rain
The Temptations, **2325**
I Wish It Would Rain Down
Phil Collins, **2615**
I Woke Up In Love This Morning
The Partridge Family, **4696**
I Wonder What She's Doing Tonite
Tommy Boyce and Bobby Hart, **4501**
I Wonder Why
Curtis Stigers, **4871**
I Won't Hold You Back
Toto, **3672**
I Write Sins Not Tragedies
Panic! at the Disco, **1698**
I Write The Songs
Barry Manilow, **521**
Ice Ice Baby
Vanilla Ice, **1089**
I'd Die Without You
P.M. Dawn, **608**
I'd Do Anything For Love (But I Won't Do That)
Meat Loaf, **165**
I'd Lie For You (And That's The Truth)
Meat Loaf, **4149**
I'd Like To Teach The World To Sing
Hillside Singers, **4805**
New Seekers, **4473**
I'd Love You To Want Me
Lobo, **1638**
I'd Really Love To See You Tonight
England Dan and John Ford Coley, **1045**
I'd Wait A Million Years
The Grass Roots, **3931**
Iesha
Another Bad Creation, **2499**
If
Bread, **3003**
If
Janet Jackson, **1510**
If Dreams Came True
Pat Boone, **4711**
If Ever You're In My Arms Again
Peabo Bryson, **3258**
If I Ain't Got You
Alicia Keys, **466**
If I Can Dream
Elvis Presley, **4783**

Right Place Wrong Time
Dr. John, **3434**
Right Thurr
Chingy, **152**
Right Time Of The Night
Jennifer Warnes, **2847**
Rikki Don't Lose That Number
Steely Dan, **3363**
Ring My Bell
Anita Ward, **325**
Ring The Alarm
Beyoncé, **3663**
Ringo
Lorne Greene, **1797**
Rise
Herb Alpert, **520**
River Of Dreams, The
Billy Joel, **1308**
Roam
The B-52's, **1860**
Rock-A-Billy
Guy Mitchell, **4535**
Rock-A-Beatin' Boogie
Bill Haley & His Comets, **3400**
Rock-A-Bye Your Baby With A Dixie Melody
Jerry Lewis, **2620**
Rock And Roll All Nite
Kiss, **4773**
Rock And Roll Dreams Come Through
Meat Loaf, **3692**
Rock And Roll Heaven
Righteous Brothers, **2411**
Rock & Roll Music
The Beach Boys, **3036***
Chuck Berry, **3116**
*Rock And Roll Music
Rock And Roll Part 2
Gary Glitter, **4600**
Rock And Roll Waltz
Kay Starr, **282**
R.O.C.K. In The U.S.A.
John Cougar Mellencamp, **2023**
Rock Island Line
Lonnie Donegan & His Skiffle Group, **3877**
Rock Me Amadeus
Falco, **836**
Rock Me Gently
Andy Kim, **1273**
Rock Me Tonite
Billy Squier, **4882**
Rock 'N' Roll Fantasy
Bad Company, **3768**
Rock On
Michael Damian, **1610**
David Essex, **2787**
Rock Steady
The Whispers, **3563**
Rock The Boat
Aaliyah, **1643**
Rock The Boat
The Hues Corporation, **1949**
Rock The Casbah
The Clash, **2830**
Rock This Town
Stray Cats, **3433**
Rock Wit'cha
Bobby Brown, **4160**
Rock Wit U (Awww Baby)
Ashanti, **899**
Rock With You
Michael Jackson, **301**
Rock Your Baby
George McCrae, **1493**
Rock Your Body
Justin Timberlake, **2149**
Rocket Man
Elton John, **3084**
Rocket 2 U
The Jets, **3492**

Rockford Files, The
Mike Post, **4673**
Rockin' Good Way (To Mess Around And Fall In Love), A
Dinah Washington & Brook Benton, **4021**
Rockin' Pneumonia–Boogie Woogie Flu
Johnny Rivers, **3038**
Rockin' Robin
Bobby Day, **1113**
Michael Jackson, **1591**
Rockin' Roll Baby
The Stylistics, **4944**
Rock'n Me
Steve Miller, **1548**
Rocky Mountain High
John Denver, **3229**
Roll Out (My Business)
Ludacris, **3925**
Roll To Me
Del Amitri, **1808**
Roll With It
Steve Winwood, **581**
Romantic
Karyn White, **796**
Romeo
Dino, **4027**
Romeo And Juliet
Sylk-E. Fyne f/Chill, **3466**
Romeo's Tune
Steve Forbert, **4274**
Rompe
Daddy Yankee, **4335**
Roni
Bobby Brown, **2683**
Ronnie
The Four Seasons, **4499**
Room To Move
Animotion, **4751**
Rosanna
Toto, **403**
Rose, The
Bette Midler, **1243**
Rose And A Baby Ruth, A
George Hamilton IV, **2485**
Rose Garden
Lynn Anderson, **1789**
Roses
OutKast, **3257**
Roses Are Red (My Love)
Bobby Vinton, **314**
Round And Round
Tevin Campbell, **3778**
Round And Round
Perry Como, **454**
Round And Round
Ratt, **4263**
Rub You The Right Way
Johnny Gill, **1500**
Rubber Ball
Bobby Vee, **3383**
Rubberband Man, The
Spinners, **788**
Ruby Baby
Dion, **1484**
Ruby, Don't Take Your Love To Town
Kenny Rogers & the First Edition, **4489**
Ruby Tuesday
The Rolling Stones, **1211**
Rumors
Timex Social Club, **3556**
Rump Shaker
Wreckx-N-Effect, **361**
Run Away
Real McCoy, **1632**
Run Away Child, Running Wild
The Temptations, **3412**
Run It!
Chris Brown, **34**

Run Joey Run
David Geddes, **4329**
Run Through The Jungle
Creedence Clearwater Revival, **2988**
Run To Him
Bobby Vee, **1472**
Run To You
Bryan Adams, **3118**
Run-Around
Blues Traveler, **844**
Runaround Sue
Dion, **317**
Leif Garrett, **4890**
Runaway
Janet Jackson, **585**
Runaway
Del Shannon, **353**
Runaway Train
Soul Asylum, **2008**
Runnin (Dying To Live)
Tupac f/the Notorious B.I.G., **3935**
Running Bear
Johnny Preston, **402**
Running On Empty
Jackson Browne, **4290**
Running Scared
Roy Orbison, **1341**
Running With The Night
Lionel Richie, **2635**
Rush Hour
Jane Wiedlin, **4214**
Rush Rush
Paula Abdul, **281**
Sad Eyes
Robert John, **1014**
Sad Movies (Make Me Cry)
Sue Thompson, **4378**
Sad Songs (Say So Much)
Elton John, **3090**
Sadeness Part 1
Enigma, **3770**
Safety Dance, The
Men Without Hats, **1337**
Said I Loved You . . . But I Lied
Michael Bolton, **1891**
Sail Along Silvery Moon
Billy Vaughn, **1745**
Sail On
Commodores, **2370**
Sailing
Christopher Cross, **914**
Sailor (Your Home Is The Sea)
Lolita, **2805**
Sally, Go 'Round The Roses
The Jaynetts, **2125**
Salt Shaker
Ying Yang Twins f/Lil Jon & the East Side Boyz, **2672**
Same Old Lang Syne
Dan Fogelberg, **4506**
San Antonio Rose
Floyd Cramer, **4583**
San Francisco (Be Sure To Wear Flowers In Your Hair)
Scott McKenzie, **2337**
Sandy
Larry Hall, **4228**
Sara
Fleetwood Mac, **3913**
Sara
Starship, **920**
Sara Smile
Daryl Hall and John Oates, **1981**
Satisfied
Richard Marx, **1708**
Satisfy You
Puff Daddy f/R.Kelly, **1604**
Saturday In The Park
Chicago, **2336**

Saturday Night
  Bay City Rollers, **1481**
Saturday Night's Alright For Fighting
  Elton John, **4737**
Save The Best For Last
  Vanessa Williams, **149**
Save The Last Dance For Me
  The Drifters, **598**
Save Tonight
  Eagle-Eye Cherry, **1631**
Save Your Heart For Me
  Gary Lewis & the Playboys, **2284**
Savin' Me
  Nickelback, **2027**
Saving All My Love For You
  Whitney Houston, **1177**
Saving Forever For You
  Shanice, **1593**
Say Goodbye
  Chris Brown, **2182**
Say, Has Anybody Seen My Sweet Gypsy Rose
  Dawn f/Tony Orlando, **2211**
Say It
  Voices of Theory, **1873**
Say It Isn't So
  Daryl Hall and John Oates, **649**
Say It Loud—I'm Black And I'm Proud (Part One)
  James Brown, **4753**
Say It Right
  Nelly Furtado, **3634**
Say My Name
  Destiny's Child, **228**
Say, Say, Say
  Paul McCartney & Michael Jackson, **94**
Say You Love Me
  Fleetwood Mac, **3212**
Say You, Say Me
  Lionel Richie, **304**
Say You Will
  Foreigner, **3546**
Say You'll Be There
  Spice Girls, **1348**
Scar Tissue
  Red Hot Chili Peppers, **1843**
Scarlet Ribbons (For Her Hair)
  The Browns, **4832**
Scars
  Papa Roach, **2489**
School Day
  Chuck Berry, **1550**
School Is Out
  Gary U.S. Bonds, **4521**
School's Out
  Alice Cooper, **3892**
Scorpio
  Dennis Coffey & the Detroit Guitar Band, **2538**
Scream
  Michael Jackson & Janet Jackson, **4253**
Sea Of Love
  The Honeydrippers, **1690**
  Phil Phillips w/the Twilights, **1324**
Sealed With A Kiss
  Brian Hyland, **2183**
Search Is Over, The
  Survivor, **2721**
Searchin'
  The Coasters, **904**
Seasons Change
  Exposé, **1302**
Seasons In The Sun
  Terry Jacks, **406**
Second Chance
  .38 Special, **3199**
Second Time Around, The
  Shalamar, **3866**
Secret
  Madonna, **1375**
Secret Agent Man
  Johnny Rivers, **2605**

Secret Lovers
  Atlantic Starr, **1666**
Secret Rendezvous
  Karyn White, **3519**
Secretly
  Jimmie Rodgers, **2041**
See You In September
  The Happenings, **2040**
See You Later, Alligator
  Bill Haley & His Comets, **2267**
Self Control
  Laura Branigan, **2001**
Semi-Charmed Life
  Third Eye Blind, **526**
Send For Me
  Nat King Cole, **1832**
Send One Your Love
  Stevie Wonder, **1725**
Sending All My Love
  Linear, **2386**
Sensitivity
  Ralph Tresvant, **1971**
Sentimental Lady
  Bob Welch, **3859**
Sentimental Street
  Night Ranger, **3676**
Separate Lives
  Phil Collins & Marilyn Martin, **810**
Separate Ways (Worlds Apart)
  Journey, **2364**
September
  Earth, Wind & Fire, **3860**
Serpentine Fire
  Earth, Wind & Fire, **3784**
Set Adrift On Memory Bliss
  P.M. Dawn, **794**
Set The Night To Music
  Roberta Flack w/Maxi Priest, **3213**
Set U Free
  Planet Soul, **4870**
7
  Prince & the New Power Generation, **2239**
7 Days
  Craig David, **2702**
Seven Little Girls Sitting In The Back Seat
  Paul Evans, **3623**
Seventeen
  Boyd Bennett & His Rockets, **1910**
  Fontane Sisters, **2739**
Seventh Son
  Johnny Rivers, **4363**
70s Love Groove
  Janet Jackson, **1916**
Sex And Candy
  Marcy Playground, **1716**
Sex Me (Parts I & II)
  R. Kelly, **4608**
Sexual Healing
  Marvin Gaye, **1235**
SexyBack
  Justin Timberlake, **111**
Sexy Eyes
  Dr. Hook, **2326**
Sexy Love
  Ne-Yo, **2248**
Sha La La
  Manfred Mann, **4156**
Shadow Dancing
  Andy Gibb, **117**
Shadows Of The Night
  Pat Benatar, **4157**
Shake It
  Ian Matthews, **3359**
Shake It Off
  Mariah Carey, **295**
Shake It Up
  The Cars, **1643**
(Shake, Shake, Shake) Shake Your Booty
  KC & the Sunshine Band, **1176**

Shake That
  Eminem f/Nate Dogg, **3144**
Shake Ya Ass
  Mystikal, **2710**
Shake Ya Tailfeather
  Nelly, P. Diddy, & Murphy Lee, **140**
Shake You Down
  Gregory Abbott, **1075**
Shake Your Body (Down To The Ground)
  The Jacksons, **2795**
Shake Your Groove Thing
  Peaches and Herb, **2774**
Shake Your Love
  Debbie Gibson, **2430**
Shakedown
  Bob Seger, **770**
Sha-La-La (Make Me Happy)
  Al Green, **3576**
Shambala
  Three Dog Night, **1923**
Shame
  Evelyn "Champagne" King, **4523**
Shame On The Moon
  Bob Seger & the Silver Bullet Band, **533**
Shannon
  Henry Gross, **2782**
Shape Of My Heart
  Backstreet Boys, **2470**
Share Your Love With Me
  Kenny Rogers, **4758**
Sharing The Night Together
  Dr. Hook, **2342**
Shattered Dreams
  Johnny Hates Jazz, **1131**
She Ain't Worth It
  Glenn Medeiros f/Bobby Brown, **880**
She Bangs
  Ricky Martin, **3334**
She Believes In Me
  Kenny Rogers, **2748**
She Blinded Me With Science
  Thomas Dolby, **2652**
She Bop
  Cyndi Lauper, **1536**
She Cried
  Jay & the Americans, **3835**
She Drives Me Crazy
  Fine Young Cannibals, **1289**
She Hates Me
  Puddle of Mudd, **2054**
She Loves You
  The Beatles, **300**
She Wants To Dance With Me
  Rick Astley, **4042**
She Will Be Loved
  Maroon5, **1005**
She Works Hard For The Money
  Donna Summer, **1269**
She'd Rather Be With Me
  The Turtles, **3049**
Sheila
  Tommy Roe, **991**
Sherry
  The Four Seasons, **360**
She's A Beauty
  The Tubes, **3717**
She's A Fool
  Lesley Gore, **3366**
She's A Lady
  Tom Jones, **1420**
She's A Woman
  The Beatles, **3709**
She's All I Ever Had
  Ricky Martin, **1680**
She's Gone
  Daryl Hall and John Oates, **2849**
She's Just My Style
  Gary Lewis & the Playboys, **1736**

She's Like The Wind
  Patrick Swayze f/Wendy Fraser, **1781**
She's Not Just Another Woman
  The 8th Day, **4659**
She's Not There
  The Zombies, **1652**
She's Not You
  Elvis Presley, **4367**
She's Out Of My Life
  Michael Jackson, **3654**
She's Playing Hard To Get
  Hi-Five, **2333**
(She's) Sexy + 17
  Stray Cats, **3390**
She's So High
  Tal Bachman, **2968**
Shifting, Whispering Sands, The
  Rusty Draper, **2014**
  Billy Vaughn, **2140***
  *Shifting, Whispering Sands (Parts 1 & 2), The
Shine
  Collective Soul, **1650**
Shine A Little Love
  Electric Light Orchestra, **3498**
Shining Star
  Earth, Wind & Fire, **1649**
Shining Star
  The Manhattans, **2497**
Shiny Happy People
  R.E.M., **4679**
Ships
  Barry Manilow, **3606**
Shoop
  Salt-N-Pepa, **1445**
Shoop Shoop Song (It's In His Kiss), The
  Betty Everett, **3921**
Shop Around
  Captain & Tennille, **2841**
  The Miracles, **1754**
Short Dick Man
  20 Fingers, **3111**
Short Fat Fannie
  Larry Williams, **2365**
Short People
  Randy Newman, **1352**
Short Shorts
  The Royal Teens, **2633**
Shortie Like Mine
  Bow Wow f/Chris Brown & Johnta Austin,
    2505
Shotgun
  Jr. Walker & the All Stars, **2660**
Should I Do It
  Pointer Sisters, **4831**
Shoulder Lean
  Young Dro f/T.I., **2871**
Should've Known Better
  Richard Marx, **1989**
Shout
  Tears for Fears, **592**
Shout—Part 1
  Joey Dee & the Starliters, **4445**
Show And Tell
  Al Wilson, **1087**
Show Me Love
  Robin S., **1766**
Show Me Love
  Robyn, **1888**
Show Me The Meaning Of Being Lonely
  Backstreet Boys, **1894**
Show Me The Way
  Peter Frampton, **2794**
Show Me The Way
  Styx, **2985**
Show Must Go On, The
  Three Dog Night, **2994**
Show Stopper
  Danity Kane, **2299**

Shower Me With Your Love
  Surface, **3890**
Shy Guy
  Diana King, **2343**
Sideshow
  Blue Magic, **2844**
Sign, The
  Ace of Base, **16**
Sign 'O' The Times
  Prince, **2576**
Sign Your Name
  Terence Trent D'Arby, **2981**
Signed, Sealed, Delivered I'm Yours
  Stevie Wonder, **2047**
Signs
  Five Man Electrical Band, **2491**
  Tesla, **3571**
Silence Is Golden
  The Tremeloes, **4710**
Silent Lucidity
  Queensrÿche, **3559**
Silent Running (On Dangerous Ground)
  Mike + the Mechanics, **3560**
Silhouette
  Kenny G, **4851**
Silhouettes
  Herman's Hermits, **3787**
  The Rays, **1323**
Silly Love Songs
  Wings, **231**
Simon Says
  1910 Fruitgum Co., **2288**
Simply Irresistible
  Robert Palmer, **1347**
Since I Don't Have You
  The Skyliners, **3722**
Since I Fell For You
  Lenny Welch, **2427**
Since I Met You Baby
  Ivory Joe Hunter, **3286**
Since U Been Gone
  Kelly Clarkson, **329**
Sing
  Carpenters, **2180**
Sing A Song
  Earth, Wind & Fire, **3381**
Sing For The Moment
  Eminem, **4788**
Singing The Blues
  Guy Mitchell, **54**
Sink The Bismarck
  Johnny Horton, **1969**
Sir Duke
  Stevie Wonder, **715**
Sister Christian
  Night Ranger, **2895**
Sister Golden Hair
  America, **1629**
(Sittin' On) The Dock Of The Bay
  Michael Bolton, **4683**
  Otis Redding, **349**
Sittin' Up In My Room
  Brandy, **457**
Sixteen Candles
  The Crests, **1025**
Sixteen Reasons
  Connie Stevens, **1978**
Sixteen Tons
  Tennessee Ernie Ford, **83**
'65 Love Affair
  Paul Davis, **2735**
Sk8er Boi
  Avril Lavigne, **3180**
Skinny Legs And All
  Joe Tex, **4533**
Sky High
  Jigsaw, **1968**
Slam
  Onyx, **2277**

Sledgehammer
  Peter Gabriel, **1085**
Sleep
  Little Willie John, **4350**
Sleep Walk
  Santo & Johnny, **523**
Sleeping Bag
  ZZ Top, **3464**
Slide
  Goo Goo Dolls, **674**
Slip Away
  Clarence Carter, **3285**
Slip Slidin' Away
  Paul Simon, **2556**
Sloop John B
  The Beach Boys, **2835**
Slow Down
  Bobby Valentino, **2639**
Slow Hand
  Pointer Sisters, **971**
Slow Jamz
  Twista f/Kanye West & Jamie Foxx, **323**
Slow Motion
  Color Me Badd, **4457**
Slow Motion
  Juvenile f/Soulja Slim, **254**
Slow Twistin'
  Chubby Checker, **2134**
Smack That
  Akon f/Eminem, **261**
Small Town
  John Cougar Mellencamp, **3065**
Smells Like Teen Spirit
  Nirvana, **2029**
Smile
  Scarface f/2Pac & Johnny P, **4784**
Smile A Little Smile For Me
  Flying Machine, **3091**
Smiling Faces Sometimes
  The Undisputed Truth, **2084**
Smoke From A Distant Fire
  Sanford/Townsend Band, **4193**
Smoke Gets In Your Eyes
  The Platters, **248**
Smoke On The Water
  Deep Purple, **2642**
Smokin' In The Boy's Room
  Brownsville Station, **2237**
Smoky Places
  The Corsairs, **4994**
Smooth
  Santana f/Rob Thomas, **1**
Smooth Criminal
  Michael Jackson, **4482**
Smooth Operator
  Sade, **3035**
Smuggler's Blues
  Glenn Frey, **4756**
Snake
  R. Kelly f/Big Tigger, **4953**
Snap Yo Fingers
  Lil Jon f/E-40 & Sean Paul of the YoungbloodZ,
    1802
Snookeroo
  Ringo Starr, **2324**
Snoopy Vs. The Red Baron
  Royal Guardsmen, **804**
Snowbird
  Anne Murray, **3985**
So Alive
  Love and Rockets, **2071**
So Anxious
  Ginuwine, **3816**
So Emotional
  Whitney Houston, **737**
So Far Away
  Staind, **3370**
So Fine
  The Fiestas, **4226**

Step In The Name Of Love
  R. Kelly, **1853**
Steppin' Out
  Joe Jackson, **2516**
StickWitU
  The Pussycat Dolls, **1642**
Stick-Up
  The Honey Cone, **4117**
Still
  Bill Anderson, **3630**
Still
  Commodores, **628**
Still Fly
  Big Tymers, **2691**
Still Not A Player
  Big Punisher f/Joe, **3792**
Still The One
  Orleans, **3155**
Still The Same
  Bob Seger & the Silver Bullet Band, **2668**
Still Water (Love)
  Four Tops, **4220**
Stir It Up
  Johnny Nash, **4325**
Stomp!
  Brothers Johnson, **2769**
Stoned Love
  The Supremes, **2820**
Stoned Soul Picnic
  5th Dimension, **1755**
Stoney End
  Barbra Streisand, **3158**
Stood Up
  Ricky Nelson, **960**
Stop Draggin' My Heart Around
  Stevie Nicks w/Tom Petty & the Heartbreakers,
  863
Stop! In The Name Of Love
  The Supremes, **601**
Stormy
  Classics IV, **3344**
Straight From The Heart
  Bryan Adams, **4690**
Straight Up
  Paula Abdul, **609**
Stranded
  Heart, **4391**
Strange Magic
  Electric Light Orchestra, **4881**
Strange Way
  Firefall, **4026**
Stranger On The Shore
  Mr. Acker Bilk, **494**
Strangers In The Night
  Frank Sinatra, **1373**
Strawberry Letter 23
  Brothers Johnson, **3386**
Stray Cat Strut
  Stray Cats, **1573**
Streak, The
  Ray Stevens, **462**
Streets Of Philadelphia
  Bruce Springsteen, **2640**
Strike It Up
  Black Box, **4111**
Stripper, The
  David Rose, **792**
Stroke You Up
  Changing Faces, **1734**
Stroll, The
  The Diamonds, **2608**
Strong Enough
  Sheryl Crow, **1727**
Strut
  Sheena Easton, **3164**
Stuck In The Middle With You
  Stealers Wheel, **3100**
Stuck On You
  Elvis Presley, **303**

Stuck On You
  Lionel Richie, **1867**
Stuck With You
  Huey Lewis & the News, **832**
Stumblin' In
  Suzi Quatro & Chris Norman, **1993**
Stunt 101
  G-Unit, **3791**
Stupid Girls
  Pink, **4359**
Stutter
  Joe f/Mystikal, **207**
Suddenly
  Billy Ocean, **2465**
Suddenly Last Summer
  The Motels, **3230**
Suddenly There's A Valley
  Gogi Grant, **3657**
Suga Suga
  Baby Bash f/Frankie J, **1163**
Sugar (Gimme Some)
  Trick Daddy f/Ludacris, Lil' Kim & Cee-Lo,
  2554
Sugar Moon
  Pat Boone, **3574**
Sugar Shack
  Jimmy Gilmer & the Fireballs, **373**
Sugar, Sugar
  The Archies, **194**
Sugar Town
  Nancy Sinatra, **3674**
Sugar, We're Goin' Down
  Fall Out Boy, **975**
Sugartime
  McGuire Sisters, **1911**
Sukiyaki
  4 P.M., **1555**
  Kyu Sakamoto, **586**
  A Taste of Honey, **1331**
Sultans Of Swing
  Dire Straits, **2437**
Summer
  War, **3561**
Summer Breeze
  Seals and Crofts, **3638**
Summer Girls
  LFO, **1304**
Summer In The City
  The Lovin' Spoonful, **745**
Summer Nights
  John Travolta & Olivia Newton-John, **3315**
Summer Of '69
  Bryan Adams, **3389**
Summer Song, A
  Chad and Jeremy, **4529**
Summertime
  D.J. Jazzy Jeff and the Fresh Prince, **2072**
Summertime Blues
  Eddie Cochran, **4069**
Sundown
  Gordon Lightfoot, **1124**
Sunglasses At Night
  Corey Hart, **2892**
Sunny
  Bobby Hebb, **1870**
Sunny Came Home
  Shawn Colvin, **2073**
Sunshine
  Jonathan Edwards, **2216**
Sunshine
  Lil' Flip f/Lea, **510**
Sunshine Of Your Love
  Cream, **3372**
Sunshine On My Shoulders
  John Denver, **1279**
Sunshine Superman
  Donovan, **1241**
Super Freak (Part 1)
  Rick James, **4386**

Superfly
  Curtis Mayfield, **3430**
Superman
  Eminem, **4840**
Superman (It's Not Easy)
  Five for Fighting, **2339**
Supernatural Thing—Part 1
  Ben E. King, **4634**
Superstar
  Carpenters, **1200**
Superstar
  Murray Head, **4809**
Superstition
  Stevie Wonder, **918**
Superwoman Pt. II
  Lil' Mo f/Fabolous, **2949**
Surf City
  Jan and Dean, **941**
Surfer Girl
  The Beach Boys, **3172**
Surfin' Bird
  The Trashmen, **2883**
Surfin' Safari
  The Beach Boys, **4417**
Surfin' U.S.A.
  The Beach Boys, **2038**
Surrender
  Elvis Presley, **675**
Surrender To Me
  Ann Wilson & Robin Zander, **4100**
Survivor
  Destiny's Child, **319**
Susan
  The Buckinghams, **4174**
Susie Darlin'
  Robin Luke, **2366**
Suspicion
  Terry Stafford, **2175**
Suspicions
  Eddie Rabbitt, **4941**
Suspicious Minds
  Elvis Presley, **1505**
Sussudio
  Phil Collins, **917**
Suzie Q. (Part One)
  Creedence Clearwater Revival, **4702**
Sway
  Bobby Rydell, **4823**
Swayin' To The Music (Slow Dancin')
  Johnny Rivers, **2506**
Sweat (A La La La La Long)
  Inner Circle, **3068**
Sweet And Innocent
  Donny Osmond, **3066**
Sweet Caroline (Good Times Never Seemed So
Good)
  Neil Diamond, **2262**
Sweet Child O' Mine
  Guns N' Roses, **758**
Sweet City Woman
  The Stampeders, **4068**
Sweet Dreams
  Air Supply, **2305**
Sweet Dreams
  La Bouche, **1541**
Sweet Dreams (Are Made Of This)
  Eurythmics, **434**
Sweet Freedom
  Michael McDonald, **3468**
Sweet Home Alabama
  Lynyrd Skynyrd, **3534**
Sweet Lady
  Tyrese, **2000**
Sweet Life
  Paul Davis, **4432**
Sweet Little Sixteen
  Chuck Berry, **913**
Sweet Love
  Anita Baker, **4162**

I READ A LOT OF science fiction when I was young, so I don't remember where I read this, but I do recall someone predicting that one day we wouldn't purchase records in a store. Instead, our music would be beamed into a cube in our homes. Well, iPods may be rectangular, but there are some MP3 devices that are cube-shaped, so even though the prediction seemed as far out as the idea that one day we would transport ourselves *Star Trek*–style, I have to give credit to that unknown prognosticator.

The availability of legally purchased digital downloads has changed the music industry forever. Compact discs, introduced in the 1980s, are becoming irrelevant, though many music lovers still prefer to have a tangible product. To the newest generation of music fans, recordings are simply digital signals that are beamed into their personal "cubes." The good news is that the singles market, which had all but disappeared in the United States, is healthier than ever. Sales had diminished to the point where the Hot 100, a chart compiled by adding sales and airplay together, was completely dominated by airplay. Since the first Hot Digital Songs chart was published on February 12, 2005, and since the sales of digital downloads have been fully integrated into the Hot 100, that pop singles chart has become more balanced between the two elements. The instant availability of digital downloads has affected the chart, with songs making huge leaps and high debuts.

This chart appears as a bonus section because it is the only one in the book not based on the Hot 100. It is based on the Hot Digital Songs chart and reflects the most successful titles in that chart's short history.

01 HOLLABACK GIRL
Gwen Stefani *Interscope* 05

02 GOLD DIGGER
Kanye West f/Jamie Foxx
Roc-a-Fella/Def Jam 05

03 BAD DAY
Daniel Powter *Warner Bros.* 06

04 MY HUMPS
The Black Eyed Peas *A&M* 05

05 YOU'RE BEAUTIFUL
James Blunt *Custard/Atlantic* 06

06 CRAZY
Gnarls Barkley *Downtown/Lava* 06

07 PROMISCUOUS
Nelly Furtado f/Timbaland *Mosley* 06

08 SINCE U BEEN GONE
Kelly Clarkson *RCA* 05

09 CANDY SHOP
50 Cent f/Olivia *Shady/Aftermath* 05

10 DON'T PHUNK WITH MY HEART
The Black Eyed Peas *A&M* 05

11 FERGALICIOUS
Fergie *will.i.am/A&M* 06

12 BOULEVARD OF BROKEN DREAMS
Green Day *Reprise* 06

13 SMACK THAT
Akon f/Eminem *SRC/Up Front/Konvict* 06

14 SEXYBACK
Justin Timberlake *Jive* 06

15 IRREPLACEABLE
Beyoncé *Columbia* 06

16 TEMPERATURE
Sean Paul *VP* 06

17 PHOTOGRAPH
Nickelback *Roadrunner* 05

18 DON'T CHA
The Pussycat Dolls f/Busta Rhymes *A&M* 05

19 SUGAR, WE'RE GOIN' DOWN
Fall Out Boy *Fueled by Ramen/Island* 05

20 LONDON BRIDGE
Fergie *will.i.am/A&M* 06

21 PON DE REPLAY
Rihanna *SRP/Def Jam* 05

22 BEVERLY HILLS
Weezer *Geffen* 05

23 LIPS OF AN ANGEL
Hinder *Universal Republic* 06

24 LAFFY TAFFY
D4L *Geffen* 06

25 GRILLZ
Nelly f/Paul Wall, Ali & Gipp
Derrty/Fo' Reel 06

26 HIPS DON'T LIE
Shakira f/Wyclef Jean *Epic* 06

27 SWITCH
Will Smith *Overbrook* 05

28 FEEL GOOD INC
Gorillaz *Parlophone* 05

29 WE BELONG TOGETHER
Mariah Carey *Island* 05

30 HOW TO SAVE A LIFE
The Fray *Epic* 06

31 YOU AND ME *Lifehouse Geffen* 05

32 CHECK ON IT
Beyoncé f/Slim Thug *Columbia* 06

33 RICH GIRL
Gwen Stefani f/Eve *Interscope* 05

34 MR. BRIGHTSIDE
The Killers *Island* 05

35 LOSE CONTROL
Missy Elliott f/Ciara and Fat Man Scoop
The Gold Mind 05

36 UNWRITTEN
Natasha Bedingfield *Epic* 06

37 RIDIN'
Chamillionaire f/Krayzie Bone
Universal Motown 06

38 I WANNA LOVE YOU
Akon f/Snoop Dogg *SRC/Up Front/Konvict* 06

39 1, 2 STEP
Ciara f/Missy Elliott
Sho'Nuff/MusicLine/LaFace 05

40 OVER MY HEAD (CABLE CAR)
The Fray *Epic* 06

41 MY LOVE
Justin Timberlake f/T.I. *Jive* 06

42 RUN IT! Chris Brown *Jive* 05

43 MOVE ALONG
The All-American Rejects *Doghouse* 06

44 DANI CALIFORNIA
Red Hot Chili Peppers *Warner Bros.* 06

45 BUTTONS
The Pussycat Dolls f/Snoop Dogg *A&M* 06

46 JUST THE GIRL
The Click Five *Lava* 05

47 HUNG UP
Madonna *Warner Bros.* 05

48 I WRITE SINS NOT TRAGEDIES
Panic! At the Disco *Decaydance* 06

49 BEHIND THESE HAZEL EYES
Kelly Clarkson *RCA* 05

50 WAKE ME UP WHEN SEPTEMBER ENDS
Green Day *Reprise* 05

51 DANCE, DANCE
Fall Out Boy *Fueled by Ramen/Island* 06

52 ALL I WANT FOR CHRISTMAS IS YOU
Mariah Carey *Columbia* 05

53 MONEY MAKER
Ludacris f/Pharrell *DTP/Def Jam* 06

54 LONELY
Akon *SRC* 05

55 HOLIDAY
Green Day *Reprise* 05

56 WAITING ON THE WORLD TO CHANGE
John Mayer *Aware* 06

57 AIN'T NO OTHER MAN
Christina Aguilera *RCA* 06

58 I'M N LUV (WIT A STRIPPER)
T-Pain f/Mike Jones *Konvict/Jive* 06

59 WHEN I'M GONE
Eminem *Shady/Aftermath* 05

60 FAR AWAY
Nickelback *Roadrunner* 06

61 SO SICK Ne-Yo *Def Jam* 06

62 DISCO INFERNO
50 Cent *Shady/Aftermath* 05

63 BECAUSE OF YOU
Kelly Clarkson *RCA* 05

64 EVERYTIME WE TOUCH
Cascada *Robbins* 06

65 HOW WE DO
The Game f/50 Cent *Aftermath* 05

66 MS. NEW BOOTY
Bubba Sparxxx f/Ying Yang Twins
New South 06

67 SAVIN' ME
Nickelback *Roadrunner* 06

68 LIFE IS A HIGHWAY
Rascal Flatts *Lyric Street* 06

69 LISTEN TO YOUR HEART
D.H.T. *Robbins* 05

70 ME & U
Cassie *NextSelection/Bad Boy* 06

71 HATE IT OR LOVE IT
The Game f/50 Cent *Aftermath* ??

72 UNFAITHFUL
Rihanna *SRP/Def Jam* 06

73 SOUL SURVIVOR
Young Jeezy f/Akon *Corporate/Def Jam* 05

74 SHOW STOPPER
Danity Kane *Bad Boy* 06

75 STICKWITU
The Pussycat Dolls *A&M* 05

76 THESE BOOTS ARE MADE FOR WALKIN'
Jessica Simpson *Columbia* 05

77 CHAIN HANG LOW
Jibbs *Geffen* 06

78 SAY IT RIGHT
Nelly Furtado *Mosley* 07

79 JUST A LIL BIT
50 Cent *Shady/Aftermath* 05

80 TOO LITTLE TOO LATE
JoJo *Da Family/Blackground* 06

81 WE BE BURNIN'
Sean Paul *VP* 05

82 SCARS
Papa Roach *El Tonal* 05

83 IT ENDS TONIGHT
The All-American Rejects *Doghouse* 06

84 BEFORE HE CHEATS
Carrie Underwood *Arista* 07

85 IT'S GOIN' DOWN
Yung Joc *Block/Bad Boy* 06

86 BEST OF YOU
Foo Fighters *Roswell/RCA* 05

87 WHAT YOU KNOW
T.I. *Grand Hustle* 06

88 SPEED OF SOUND
Coldplay *Capitol* 05

89 THERE IT GO! (THE WHISTLE SONG)
Juelz Santana *Diplomats* 05

90 COLLIDE
Howie Day *Epic* 05

91 SOMEBODY TOLD ME
The Killers *Island* 05

92 SUGAR (GIMME SOME)
Trick Daddy f/Ludacris, Lil' Kim & Cee-Lo
Slip-N-Slide 05

93 DROP IT LIKE IT'S HOT
Snoop Dogg f/Pharrell *Doggystyle* 05

94 WHITE & NERDY
'Weird Al' Yankovic *Way Moby/Volcano* 06

95 WELCOME TO THE BLACK PARADE
My Chemical Romance *Reprise* 06

96 SNAP YO FINGERS
Lil Jon f/E-40 & Sean Paul of the
YoungbloodZ *BME* 06

97 WHERE'D YOU GO
Fort Minor f/Holly Brook *Machine Shop* 06

98 PUMP IT
The Black Eyed Peas *A&M* 06

99 SHAKE THAT
Eminem f/Nate Dogg *Shady/Aftermath* 06

100 OH
Ciara f/Ludacris
Sho'Nuff/MusicLine/LaFace 05

Photo Credits

Photo by Lorenzo Agius: page 515. • Photo by Mert Alas & Marcus Piggott: 558. • Photo by Pablo Alfaro: 459. • Photo by Kwaku Alston: 514. • Photo by Brian Arias: 89. • Photos by Sherry Rayn Barnett: 135, 187. • Photos by Chapman Baehler: 246, 532. • Photo by Marc Baptiste: 540. • Photo by Gilles Bensimon: 29. • Photo by Robert Blakeman: 83. • Photo by Dan Borris: 125. • Photo by Marina Chavez: 249. • Photos by Danny Clinch: 57, 528, 535, 638. • Photo by Anton Corbijn: 540. • Photo by Anthony Cutajar: 103. • Photo by Roberto D'Este: 266. • Photos by Patrick DeMarchelier, 46, 254 • Photo by Patrick DeMervelec: 58. • Photo by James Dimmock: 538. • Photo by Sante D'Orazio: 34. • Photo by Philip Dixon: 508. • Photos by Frank Driggs: 138, 155, 268, 288. • Photo by Yuri Elizondo: 276. • Photo by Gavin Evans, 545. • Photo by Davis Factor: 517. • Photo by Chess Files: 281. • Photos by Simon Fowler: 324, 585. • Photo by David Gahr: 531. • Photo by Donald Graham: 575. • Photo by Ellie Greenwich: 140. • Photo by Georg Grieshaber: 441. • Photo by Per Gustafsson: 572. • Photo by Ross Halfin: 577. • Photo by John Halpern: 38. • Photo by Michael Halsband: 531. • Photo by Kevin Scott Hees, 542. • Photo by Olaf Heine: 88. • Photo by Colm Henry: 92. • Photo by George Holz: 567. • Photo courtesy of Home Box Office: 50. • Photo by Eric Johnson: 549. • Photo by Dennis Keeley, 530. • Photo by Markus Klinko & Indroni, 527. • Photo by Nick Knight: 78. • Photo by Fritz Kok: 468. • Photo by James J. Kreigman: 53. • Photo by Christian Lantry: 591. • Photo by Rocco Laspata: 462. • Photo by Ed Lee: 539. • Photo by Andrew Macpherson: 77. • Photo by Jonathan Mannion: 76, 471. • Photo by Wayne Maser: 75. • Photo by Robert Matheu: 52. • Photo by Clay McBride: 519. • Photo by Phillipe McClelland: 526. • Photo by David McClister: 536. • Photos by James R. Minchin: 304, 516. • Photo by Tom Munro: 556. • Photo by Michael Muller: 541. • Photo by Peter Nash: 492. • Photo by Melanie Nissen: 581. • Photos courtesy of the Michael Ochs Archive/ Venice, California: 137, 145, 170. • Photo by Frank W. Ockenfels: 547. • Photo by Stephanie Pfriender: 521. • Photos courtesy of Photofeatures International: 54, 63, 80, 85, 147, 168—David Wainwright: 205. 294 • Photo by Ross Pilton: 178. • Photos by Neal Preston: 39, 525. • Photo by Aaron Rapoport: 551. • Photo by Reisig & Taylor: 48. • Photo by Terry Richardson: 480. • Photo by Herb Ritts: 91. • Photo courtesy Ebet Roberts: 188. • Photo by David Roth: 529. • Photo by Douglas Rowell: 79. • Photo by Albert Sanchez: 319. • Photos by Norman Seeff: 149, 438. • Photo by Alan Silfen: 181. • Photo by Piotr Sikora: 540. • Photo by Rocky Schneck: 592. • Photo by Matthew Jordan Smith: 176. • Photo by Isabel Snyder: 580. • Photo by Andrew Southam: 201. • Photo by Rod Spicer: 32. • Photos by Randee St. Nicholas: 270, 444, 450. • Photo by Lance Staedler, 534. • Photo by Stephen Stickler: 447, 550. • Photo courtesy of Sundazed Music. 520 • Photo by Alberto Tolot: 66. • Photo by Trinifold: 95. • Photo by David Vance: 50. • Photos courtesy of Universal Music Archives: 33, 41, 74, 233, 240. • Photo by Ellen Von Unwerth: 98. • Photos by Sacha Waldman: 522, 568. • Photos by Albert Watson: 45, 189, 564. • Photo by Ben Watt: 474. • Photo by Cliff Watts: 161. • Photo by Matthew Welch: 477. • Photo by Katherine Wessel: 549. • Photo by Timothy White: 544. • Photo by Andy Wilson: 154. • Photo by Laura Wilson: 546. • Photo by Kevin Winter: 586. • Photo by Jim Wright: 562.